Tourism in Developing Countries

Economics and Management of Tourism

Series Editors: Larry Dwyer
Qantas Professor of Travel and Tourism Economics
University of New South Wales, Australia
Peter Forsyth
Professor of Economics
Monash University, Australia

1.   Managing Tourism Destinations
Andreas Papatheodorou

2.   Tourism in Developing Countries
Twan Huybers

Future titles will include:

Managing Tourism Firms
Clive L. Morley

Wherever possible, the articles in these volumes have been reproduced as originally published using facsimile reproduction, inclusive of footnotes and pagination to facilitate ease of reference.

For a list of all Edward Elgar published titles visit our site on the World Wide Web at
www.e-elgar.com

Tourism in Developing Countries

Edited by

Twan Huybers

Senior Lecturer
University of New South Wales, Australia

ECONOMICS AND MANAGEMENT OF TOURISM

An Elgar Reference Collection
Cheltenham, UK • Northampton, MA, USA

Published by
Edward Elgar Publishing Limited
Glensanda House
Montpellier Parade
Cheltenham
Glos GL50 1UA
UK

Edward Elgar Publishing, Inc.
William Pratt House
9 Dewey Court
Northampton
Massachusetts 01060
USA

A catalogue record for this book is available from the British Library

Library of Congress Control Number: 2006937363

ISBN: 978 1 84376 998 9

Printed and bound in Great Britain by MPG Books Ltd, Bodmin, Cornwall

Contents

Acknowledgements

The editors and publishers wish to thank the authors and the following publishers who have kindly given permission for the use of copyright material.

Blackwell Publishing Ltd for article: J. Diamond (1976), 'Tourism and Development Policy: A Quantitative Appraisal', *Bulletin of Economic Research*, **28** (1), May, 36–50.

Elsevier for articles: Jafar Jafari (1974), 'The Socio-Economic Costs of Tourism to Developing Countries', *Annals of Tourism Research*, **1**, May, 227–62, reset; P.G. Sadler and B.H. Archer (1975), 'The Economic Impact of Tourism in Developing Countries', *Annals of Tourism Research*, **III** (1), September/October, 15–32, reset; Eric E. Rodenburg (1980), 'The Effects of Scale in Economic Development: Tourism in Bali', *Annals of Tourism Research*, **VII** (2), 177–96; C.L. Jenkins (1982), 'The Effects of Scale in Tourism Projects in Developing Countries', *Annals of Tourism Research*, **9** (2), 229–49; C.L. Jenkins and B.M. Henry (1982), 'Government Involvement in Tourism in Developing Countries', *Annals of Tourism Research*, **9** (4), 499–521; Matthew McQueen (1983), 'Appropriate Policies Towards Multinational Hotel Corporations in Developing Countries', *World Development*, **11** (2), 141–52; Ronald A. Francisco (1983), 'The Political Impact of Tourism Dependence in Latin America', *Annals of Tourism Research*, Special Issue, **10** (3), 363–76; François J. Bélisle (1983), 'Tourism and Food Production in the Caribbean', *Annals of Tourism Research*, **10** (4), 497–513; Hugh Latimer (1985), 'Developing-Island Economies: Tourism v Agriculture', *Tourism Management*, **6** (1), March, 32–42; Auliana Poon (1990), 'Flexible Specialization and Small Size: The Case of Caribbean Tourism', *World Development*, **18** (1), 109–23; Martin Oppermann (1993), 'Tourism Space in Developing Countries', *Annals of Tourism Research*, **20** (3), 535–56; John P. Lea (1993), 'Tourism Development Ethics in the Third World', *Annals of Tourism Research*, **20** (4), 701–15; Brian Archer and John Fletcher (1996), 'The Economic Impact of Tourism in the Seychelles', *Annals of Tourism Research*, **23** (1), 32–47; John Brohman (1996), 'New Directions in Tourism for Third World Development', *Annals of Tourism Research*, **23** (1), 48–70; David J. Telfer and Geoffrey Wall (1996), 'Linkages Between Tourism and Food Production', *Annals of Tourism Research*, **23** (3), July, 635–53; Dallen J. Timothy and Geoffrey Wall (1997), 'Selling to Tourists: Indonesian Street Vendors', *Annals of Tourism Research*, **24** (2), April, 322–40; Pablo Martin de Holan and Nelson Phillips (1997), 'Sun, Sand, and Hard Currency: Tourism in Cuba', *Annals of Tourism Research*, **24** (4), October, 777–95; Michael J. Clancy (1999), 'Tourism and Development: Evidence from Mexico', *Annals of Tourism Research*, **26** (1), January, 1–20; D. Omotayo Brown and Francis A. Kwansa (1999), 'Using IRR and NPV Models to Evaluate Societal Costs of Tourism Projects in Developing Countries', *International Journal of Hospitality Management*, **18**, 31–43; Cevat Tosun (2000), 'Limits to Community Participation in the Tourism Development Process in Developing Countries', *Tourism Management*, **21**, 613–33; Vinod Sasidharan, Ercan Sirakaya and Deborah Kerstetter (2002),

'Developing Countries and Tourism Ecolabels', *Tourism Management*, **23**, 161–74; Guntur Sugiyarto, Adam Blake and M. Thea Sinclair (2003), 'Tourism and Globalization: Economic Impact in Indonesia', *Annals of Tourism Research*, **30** (3), 683–701; David Fisher (2004), 'The Demonstration Effect Revisited', *Annals of Tourism Research*, **31** (2), 428–46.

IP Publishing Ltd for article: Michelle Catherine Baddeley (2004), 'Are Tourists Willing to Pay for Aesthetic Quality? An Empirical Assessment from Krabi Province, Thailand', *Tourism Economics*, **10** (1), March, 45–61.

Multilingual Matters Ltd for article: Robert G. Healy (1994), '"Tourist Merchandise" as a Means of Generating Local Benefits from Ecotourism', *Journal of Sustainable Tourism*, **2** (3), 137–51.

Oxford University Press for article: Lein Lein Chen and John Devereux (1999), 'Tourism and Welfare in Sub-Saharan Africa: A Theoretical Analysis', *Journal of African Economies*, **8** (2), 209–27.

Taylor and Francis Ltd (http://www.tandf.co.uk/journals) for articles: M. Thea Sinclair and Asrat Tsegaye (1990), 'International Tourism and Export Instability', *Journal of Development Studies*, **26** (3), April, 487–504; M. Thea Sinclair (1998), 'Tourism and Economic Development: A Survey', *Journal of Development Studies*, **34** (5), June, 1–51.

Tourism Program, School of Business, James Cook University of North Queensland for article: Irmgard Bauer (1999), 'The Impact of Tourism in Developing Countries on the Health of the Local Host Communities: The Need for More Research', *Journal of Tourism Studies*, **10** (1), May, 2–17.

University of Chicago Press for article: Robert E. Wood (1980), 'International Tourism and Cultural Change in Southeast Asia', *Economic Development and Cultural Change*, **28** (3), 561–81.

John Wiley and Sons Ltd for articles: Cevat Tosun and Carson L. Jenkins (1998), 'The Evolution of Tourism Planning in Third-World Countries: A Critique', *Progress in Tourism and Hospitality Research*, **4** (2), June, 101–14; Robert Cleverdon and Angela Kalisch (2000), 'Fair Trade in Tourism', *International Journal of Tourism Research*, **2**, 171–87; Salih Kusluvan and Kurtulus Karamustafa (2001), 'Multinational Hotel Development in Developing Countries: An Exploratory Analysis of Critical Policy Issues', *International Journal of Tourism Research*, **3**, 179–97.

In addition the publishers wish to thank the Marshall Library of Economics, University of Cambridge, UK, the Library at the University of Warwick, UK, and the Library of Indiana University at Bloomington, USA, for their assistance in obtaining these articles.

Introduction

Twan Huybers

The travel and tourism industry can be a vital contributor to socio-economic progress in developing countries. The potential for the industry to be a driving force for the development process by way of increased income, employment, foreign exchange earnings and industry structure diversification is widely discussed and reported in the literature. At the same time, serious questions are asked about the development risks associated with economies that rely to a large extent on tourism activity. There is little need to demonstrate the vulnerability of the travel and tourism industry (in developing countries) to natural disasters such as the 2004 Boxing Day tsunamis in the Indian ocean, to health scares like the 2003 SARS outbreaks in East Asia and to the on-going safety and security concerns of terrorism activity. In a wry sense, crises like these highlight the importance of the tourism industry to many developing countries. They also serve to remind the many and varied business sectors that they are, to various extents, part of the tourism industry. That this is not always so apparent is directly related to the difficulty of the supply-side definition of the tourism industry and the ensuing low level of identification of many sectors with the industry. However, as the Maldives' Finance Minister Mr Mohamed Jaleel expressed it following the tsunami disaster: 'We all have shirts on our back because of tourism' (WTO 2005a).

There are obvious risks to the long-term benefits of the tourism industry in developing countries in relation to natural disasters and health and security concerns. There are, however, many other issues – irrespective of major, catastrophic events – that are important with a view to the effects of tourism on socio-economic development. These include the philosophical notion of developing nations' dependence on international tourism and associated travel and tourism systems; the potential negative socio-cultural effects (including demonstration effects) and environmental impacts; the significance of international economic leakages detracting from economic benefits; and the appropriate scale of development. They are among the aspects covered in the contributions to this volume. While many of these issues apply to both developed and developing countries (see, for instance, Sinclair 1998; Chapter 3, this volume), the significance of the issues in the context of the less developed countries is highlighted in this book.

The Importance of Tourism

The travel and tourism industry makes a significant contribution to the world economy. The latest figures from the World Tourism Organization show that international tourism receipts made up some 6 per cent of global exports of goods and services and 30 per cent of global services exports in 2003 (WTO 2005b). It consistently ranks highly in the list of global exports of goods and services along with chemicals, automotive products and fuels. While estimated relative export earnings figures and rankings change from year to year, it is clear that tourism is an important global export industry. It certainly appears to be the largest global services export industry. Further, using tourism satellite accounting methods, travel and tourism's expected contribution – both direct and indirect – to global GDP in 2005 is 10.6 per cent, generating 8.3 per cent of total employment (WTTC 2005). While these figures are only estimates and have to be viewed in the context of the estimation methods, they confirm tourism's global importance as an industry.

It is worth noting that behind these aggregate figures lies a distribution that is generally biased against developing countries. With respect to the labour market, for example, the estimated share of people employed in the tourism industry in 2005 in South Asia, Southeast Asia and Latin America is below the average at 5.2 per cent, 7.9 per cent and 7.3 per cent, respectively (WTTC 2005). Similarly, in terms of the share of GDP, the respective estimates are 5.5 per cent, 7.5 per cent and 7.6 per cent.[1] Also, developing countries' share of total international tourist arrivals and tourism receipts is disproportionately low with a strong bias towards Europe and North America (WTO 2004a).

Nevertheless, tourism remains important to many developing countries including the least developed countries. For instance, in a report prepared for the UK Department for International Development it is estimated that the contribution of international tourism to most of its aid recipients is significant, the latter defined as either at least 2 per cent of GDP or 5 per cent of export earnings (DFID 1999). This includes eleven out of twelve countries that account for 80 per cent of the world's poor with incomes of below one US dollar per day. In addition, the growth rates of international tourism (total arrivals, total expenditure and expenditure per arrival) in the decade between 1990 and 2000 were substantially higher in developing countries compared with those in developed countries (WTO 2002). In that same period, developing countries' (in particular least developed countries') growth rates of international tourism receipts as a proportion of receipts from all goods and services exceeded that of developed countries.

These figures in themselves do not demonstrate that tourism is a preferred vehicle for economic development. Yet they provide the context to the oft expressed favourable prospects for tourism's contribution to improving living standards in developing countries. To illustrate, at a recent WTO sponsored gathering, Dr Dawid de Villiers, Deputy Secretary-General of the WTO, referred to tourism as 'one of the world's pace setting activities, with a very positive future and a tendency to bounce back with vigour after a crisis' implying that tourism 'can, and should, be managed in such a way that it addresses the most challenging problems of our time, foremost of which is the reduction of poverty' (WTO 2004b). Tourism's role in alleviating global poverty is also reflected in the 'Sustainable Tourism – Eradication of Poverty' programme (jointly by the World Tourism Organization and the United Nations Conference on Trade and Development) in which tourism is highlighted as an industry whose activities can be of direct benefit to the world's poorest.

Some Economic Aspects of Tourism-led Development

The tourism industry possesses certain characteristics that allow it a special position in the development process. These characteristics give rise to international comparative advantages of the tourism industry compared with other industries. While the production of tourism services requires financial and human capital assets, the key resources for many developing countries are their natural assets such as beaches, national parks and general beauty and scenery. In accordance with international trade theory, the relative abundance of those kinds of natural assets in developing countries provide the international comparative advantage of those countries in natural asset-related tourism. The identification of comparative advantage extends to the relative abundance of cultural/heritage attractions in many developing countries (man-made attractions such as the rich cultures of ancient civilisations and archaeological sites of importance). Additionally, it is often suggested that the tourism industry is characterised by a relatively high degree of labour intensity. To the extent that that is the case, developing countries' relative labour abundance also provides a strong basis for the international comparative advantage in tourism. Overall, by exchanging tourism services for imports of goods and services from other countries, international trade has the potential to yield benefits to the countries involved.

Whether these potential benefits actually come to fruition depends on various factors. One crucial factor is the extent to which trade is allowed to occur in the first place. This is where tourism has had an advantage over other potential export industries: the barriers to international trade in tourism are low compared with the cases of agricultural and textile products (whose labour intensities may be higher than those in tourism). While there are issues to be resolved within the World Trade Organization with respect to developing countries' request for trade liberalisation regarding tourism (including access to distribution channels and air transport regulation), the freedom of global travel and tourism flows is relatively high. The dim prospect of achieving economic development through the genuine opening of developed countries' export markets to agricultural products renders tourism to be a key export industry for developing countries in the foreseeable future.

Other positive effects may flow from the potential of tourism-led economic development. For instance, since tourism consumption requires the movement of the consumer to the product – in an international context, it is a non-traded export – its diversity as an industry offers potential for a wide scope of participation and benefit for various linked sectors at the local level. However, attaining this potential depends on the extent to which local sectors are actually linked and the associated extent of international 'leakages' away from the local sectors. The extent of leakages is one of the economic factors that detracts from the gross economic benefits from tourism in the form of the generation of income, employment and foreign exchange. If the linkages between tourism activity and domestic sectors are weak, increased tourism expenditure leads to higher imports depending on the associated propensity to import.

A number of points related to high levels of international leakages – in essence, a country's low ability to retain domestic value added – are worth making. Firstly, large leakages can be the result of high levels of foreign ownership, possibly due to vertical integration within multinational companies. A number of papers in this volume draw the parallel between this aspect of market structure and the neo-colonial dependence of developing nations on Western countries. Secondly, the focus in terms of the leakage issue is often on primary industries (food, agriculture). However, with a view to infrastructural investment in the tourism industry, the lack of adequate linkages between tourism and secondary, manufacturing industries is equally important. The change in the industrial base in developing countries has often occurred by moving from primary industries to tertiary, service industries. This has resulted in insufficient local capacity to provide manufacturing goods and services which will then have to be secured internationally (Walpole and Goodwin 2000). Thirdly, the development of partnerships and cooperation between (small) businesses in local tourism clusters has been suggested as a way of promoting economic development (Gollub, Hosier and Woo 2002). This involves enhancing local links within tourism but also with non-tourism sectors such as agriculture and construction. The resulting local, integrated tourism product would reduce the level of import leakages and, in the process, provide an alternative to enclave tourism projects. Finally, while the issue of import leakage resulting from tourism expenditure is relevant, an important consideration is the relative extent of leakage effects in tourism compared to other potential export industries for developing countries.

In addition to the potential for leakages (whether through imports or additionally via salaries to foreign expatriates or repatriated profits) there are other implications of tourism activity that may moderate its positive economic effects. Dwyer and Forsyth (1993) provide a comprehensive discussion of these implications in the context of international tourism, but they apply to tourism activity more generally. The economy-wide, general equilibrium effects of an expansion of tourism expenditure cannot be ignored in an analysis of the net impacts. This includes the possible increase in input costs which affects economic activity in other sectors. The extent of these economic costs is negatively related to the existence of spare capacity in the economy and the scope for efficiency-enhancing redistributions of production factors among sectors. The latter aspect, resulting in more productive use of resources, has been shown to have the potential to increase economic growth in developing countries (Skerritt and Huybers 2005). Nevertheless, the opportunity costs of tourism output generation, supply side constraints and possible adverse effects on exchange rates need to be considered to assess the net economic impacts of tourism on income, employment and the balance of payments.

Computable general equilibrium (CGE) models can be used to assess such comprehensive, economy-wide implications of tourism development. As discussed in Dwyer, Forsyth and Spurr (2004), CGE models were developed to deal with the main disadvantages of input–output models. In particular, CGE models allow the implementation of varying degrees of inter-sectoral factor substitution, as well as price and wage flexibility. In the context of tourism, the application of CGE models has virtually been limited to developed economies (see, for instance, Blake, Sinclair and Sugiyarto 2003). Yet, CGE modelling can offer important insights to researchers into the effects of tourism on economic development. CGE models reveal to what extent the economic benefits of tourism expansion are offset by losses of output in other sectors and provide estimates of the associated implications for employment (in aggregate and across sectors), wages, foreign exchange earnings, (the regional distribution of) tax revenues, and other relevant policy issues. The development and application of CGE models to developing countries is one item that should feature prominently on the future research agenda of those interested in the economic aspects of tourism and development.

Two further issues offer ample scope for future research as they are also under-researched in the literature. The first of these is the measurement of tourism's effect on long-term economic growth and development. Empirical evidence of tourism's longitudinal impact on economic development is scant; Modeste (1995), Durbarry (2004) and Skerritt and Huybers (2005) are relatively recent contributions that have sought to fill that gap in the literature. The findings from those studies suggest that tourism has long-term beneficial effects on economic growth in developing countries.

The other issue that, to date, has not received sufficient attention in the literature pertains to studies that emanate from institutional economics and focus on property rights. The issue of property rights is crucial to the assessment of the potential economic benefits of tourism to developing countries. As argued earlier, natural and cultural assets often provide the basis for developing countries' comparative advantage as a tourism destination. However, the distribution of the associated economic benefits depends on the ownership of these resources. Given the right circumstances, the benefits could set in motion a virtuous endogenous growth cycle by way of increased development across the population (higher incomes and enhanced health and education levels) and the protection of natural and cultural assets. The challenge is to find the adequate institutional structure to provide the right incentives framework. This requires policy decisions on (a mix of) the private and common property rights of the key assets.

The Wider Perspective

Tourism development does not simply equate to economic growth let alone to development in a broad sense. While the term 'sustainable tourism' is controversial and has been defined in many different ways, it nevertheless appears that the focus on economic impacts and growth needs to be broadened by including social, environmental and cultural effects. If tourism is to be a long-term basis for improving living standards in developing countries, those additional effects are part of the overall picture of development. Advances in living standards are reflected in measures that go beyond GDP per capita figures and include, for example, social indicators on health and education, and environmental indicators. While the relationship between economic measures and such indicators is debated in the economic development literature, it is clear that those indicators are an integral part of the overall assessment of advances in living standards. Also, given that the key tourist attractions of many developing countries are natural or cultural resources, maintaining their quality is essential in the long run.

The wider focus on tourism impacts is manifest in the UN-accepted 2001 'Global Code of Ethics for Tourism'. This code is intended to 'help minimise the negative impacts of tourism on the environment and on cultural heritage while maximising the benefits for residents of tourism destinations' to 'safeguard the future of the tourism industry and expand the sector's contribution to economic prosperity, peace and understanding among all the nations of the world'. This collection of principles, like many of its kind, is voluntary but seeks to provide guidance to the industry, government, local communities and tourists with a view to the process of development.

Increased tourism industry output has the potential to result in social, cultural and environmental disruption. While this is not unique to tourism-led development, the big test is whether policy makers in developing countries are able to find the balance between the different implications of tourism expansion. Economic, socio-cultural and environmental benefits are not mutually exclusive. What is needed is a debate which involves insights from the various perspectives. This wider view is adopted in the current volume whose contributions are now discussed in more detail.

Selection and Scope of Papers

The selection process for this volume occurred by way of a number of filtering stages resulting in the final selection of papers. One general quality standard criterion applied to the contributions to this volume was that they be articles published in peer-reviewed scholarly journals. The journals covered in the literature review on tourism in developing countries were in the field of tourism as well as journals in the area of development studies. These included, among others, *Annals of Tourism Research*; *Tourism Management*; *International Journal of Tourism Research*; *Progress in Tourism and Hospitality Research*; *Journal of Sustainable Tourism*; *Tourism Economics*; *Journal of Development Studies*; and *World Development*.

The review produced numerous case studies at country or regional levels. Most of these were not considered for inclusion in this volume because they were mainly descriptive in nature. Further, many case studies were excluded as candidates because they did not constitute a new empirical application of a known methodology or conceptual framework. However, papers in which conceptual issues are combined with case study evidence were deemed suitable.

No specific time criterion was applied in the selection process. In some instances, it was felt that some longitudinal overview was warranted from a scholarly perspective. For instance in the case of economic impact analysis, providing a flavour of the development in research techniques and methodologies as applied to developing countries was considered to be appropriate. Also, some of the early contributions to the tourism and economic development debate contain issues that are as relevant now as they were at the time of their publication. Nevertheless, the vast majority of the selected articles were published after 1990.

The articles contained in this volume reflect the attempt to find a suitable balance along two dimensions in particular. Firstly, it consists of papers that provide insights at a conceptual and theoretical level as well as articles that include the empirical findings of applied studies. Secondly, the volume reflects the literature in terms of 'pros and cons' of tourism as an agent for development; that is, the positive effects and opportunities as well as the potential for adverse effects are covered. Along a third dimension, papers that employ quantitative techniques complement the majority of papers that contain qualitative research.

The 34 articles selected for this volume are divided into three parts. The broad themes in these three parts are further structured into smaller groups. Part I covers the issue of tourism and development in a general sense. It also approaches the issue from the political economy and government involvement perspectives. Part II is the core of the volume and focuses on the economic perspectives on the nexus between tourism and development. It includes the sub-themes of economic cost and benefit analysis, local economic linkages, international aspects and the issue of scale in tourism development. Part III is an acknowledgement that the study of development requires multidisciplinary insights. It, therefore, provides the wider perspectives on the implications of tourism in developing countries comprising papers dealing with spatial, socio-cultural, environmental and ethical issues.

While the selection process for a volume like this is necessarily subjective, hopefully the papers included provide a balanced set of viewpoints that aid in our understanding of the complex role of tourism in the development process.

Discussion of Papers

Part I   General Perspectives

THE GENERAL ISSUE
Brohman (1996; Chapter 1, this volume) builds on Britton's (1982) analysis of the organisation of the international tourism system in a historical and political context. The author provides a critical evaluation of tourism-led development as part of the outward-oriented development strategies adopted by Third World countries. The common pitfalls of tourism development that are highlighted include foreign control of the local industry, international leakages, socio-economic and spatial inequality of the distribution of tourism benefits, environmental degradation, and loss of cultural identify. To address these problems, the author recommends that tourism planning be subject to a democratic process of local community participation, and that governmental authorities be actively engaged in coordinated planning activities to ensure the benefits of tourism in the long run. While acknowledging the difficulties surrounding the concept of alternative tourism, the author puts forward its associated general features (small scale development, local ownership, community participation and sensitivity to socio-cultural and environmental implications) to argue that this type of tourism is the preferred vehicle for suitable development.

The critical tone is continued in Cleverdon and Kalisch (2000; Chapter 2, this volume) who focus on the dependence of peripheral developing countries on the metropolitan centres in the industrialised countries. The authors highlight the barriers and opportunities of extending the notion of 'fair trade' in commodities to trade in tourism. While a definition of fair trade in tourism is not provided, the inherent characteristics are articulated – combating poverty, bringing consumer and producer closer together, emphasising small scale, and enhancing the bargaining power of local tourism operators in developing countries.

Sinclair (1998; Chapter 3, this volume) is a balanced overview of the relationship between tourism and development from an economic perspective. The survey includes the well documented economic benefits of tourism while also highlighting the economic costs (such as the need for infrastructure expenditure, the loss of potential benefits through leakages and inadequate local networks of primary and secondary producers, and volatility in tourism earnings). According to the author, increased imperfect competition in various tourism supply sectors has reduced the benefits of tourism to developing countries. For instance, the high levels of vertical integration and concentration in the case of intermediaries has affected the bargaining position of businesses in developing countries. However, despite some of the negative aspects of tourism, it is argued that 'there are no superior alternatives in the short run' (p. 40).

POLITICAL ECONOMY
Clancy (1999; Chapter 4, this volume) draws attention to modern theories of the political economy of development to study tourism in developing countries. The author warns against the debate between modernisation and dependency views and proposes to investigate tourism development through the prism of three political economy frameworks: neoliberalism, statism and the post-dependency approach. This is illustrated with a case study of Mexico.

An innovative quantitative empirical analysis of the relationship between tourism and dependence between Latin America and the US is reported in Francisco (1983; Chapter 5, this volume). Three hypotheses, drawn from the dependency concept, relate political compliance to US tourist arrivals; political compliance to US foreign investment, and US (military) aid to US tourist arrivals. Based on an analysis of correlations, the author rejects all three hypotheses. A fourth hypothesis, in which US tourist arrivals are linked with overall trade with the US, is not rejected, which is possibly evidence of economic dependence in the form of import leakages.

GOVERNMENT POLICIES AND PLANNING

Jenkins and Henry (1982; Chapter 6, this volume) put forward a rationale for government involvement in the growth of the tourism sector in developing countries. A distinction is made between active, operational involvement and a passive, enabling government role. The authors argue that the level of government involvement is determined importantly by the stage of development. Analogous to the infant industry notion regarding trade protectionism, initial active government influence on tourism development is intended to change gradually into private sector involvement due to enhanced entrepreneurial expertise.

Tourism development, regardless of the mix of government and private sector participation, requires planning. A critical evaluation of the way in which tourism has been planned in developing countries is the topic in Tosun and Jenkins (1998; Chapter 7, this volume). The authors caution against third world countries' adoption of tourism planning approaches that are designed for the situation in developed countries. Part of the blame for the implementation of these approaches in developing countries is directed at international funding agencies. The authors argue for the development of more local tourism planning expertise to enable a better tailoring of the planning process to local social, cultural, political and economic conditions.

Part II   Economic Perspectives

ANALYSIS OF COSTS AND BENEFITS

Sadler and Archer (1975; Chapter 8, this volume) is one of the first contributions to the literature to address the economic impacts of tourism in developing countries. It provides an elegant and succinct overview of the likely benefits and costs that, to this day, is found in discussions of tourism's economic effects. The authors also propose a model to evaluate alternative development projects by way of measuring the net value added generated per unit of the scarce resource of capital. Recognising the constraint of data availability and, hence, the difficulties in constructing a full input–output model for developing countries, the authors develop a method that allows the calculation of cost–benefit ratios for each sector as a measure for the social return on capital.

Brown and Kwansa (1999; Chapter 9, this volume) extend this notion in their approach to introduce social, cultural and environmental costs into the cost–benefit analysis of tourism capital investments in developing countries. Drawing from finance theory, they argue for the inclusion of proper valuations of benefits and costs in the calculations of net present values and internal rates of return. Acknowledging the problems involved in establishing shadow prices, the authors propose non-market valuation surveys as one way to provide estimates.

As pointed out in Diamond (1976; Chapter 10, this volume), cost–benefit analysis is suited for comparative evaluations of capital allocation decisions. While recognising the strict assumptions underlying multiplier analysis (including fixed factor proportions and constant relative prices), the author argues that multiplier analysis provides insights into overall economic impacts of tourism that are relevant to policy makers in developing countries. The author presents two models (one with the general Keynesian 'spare capacity' assumption, the other incorporating a foreign exchange induced supply constraint) that yield output multipliers for each sector. The author incorporates final demand into the models, thereby dealing with one of the earlier major shortcomings of multiplier analysis based on input–output tables. Applied to the case of Turkey, the author estimates the effects of tourism expenditure on income, employment, foreign exchange and capital requirements. Importantly, the author introduces sensitivity analysis which has become commonplace in contemporary economic impact studies, for instance those employing computable general equilibrium models.

Archer and Fletcher (1996; Chapter 11, this volume) is one of the many contributions of these authors on the use of input–output analysis to estimate tourism's economic impacts. This study presents empirical results for the Seychelles, in particular with respect to the differential impacts by visitors' countries of origin. Depending on the particular policy objective (including per tourist income and employment) the most effective countries of origin are identified. From a practical point of view, it is noteworthy that, while the reported data collection process appears by no means straightforward, there is a marked difference in the quality and availability of input–output tables and other required data for a developing country in the early 1990s compared with studies of some fifteen years earlier (such as Sadler and Archer 1975).

As stated earlier, computable general equilibrium (CGE) models have been developed as a response to the main disadvantages of input–output models. One of the few applications of CGE modelling to developing countries is reported in Sugiyarto, Blake and Sinclair (2003; Chapter 12, this volume). The authors use a CGE model to examine the effects of globalisation policies (falls in import tariffs and indirect taxation rates) in the context of growth in the tourism sector in Indonesia (an increase in expenditure by foreign tourists). This is a pertinent issue for developing countries for which tourism is a significant sector at a time when domestic policies are increasingly framed by international competitiveness concerns in a globalised business environment. Encouragingly, the findings of the simulated scenarios suggest that tourism growth enhances the positive effects of the globalisation polices on GDP, employment and welfare while moderating their negative impact on the balance of payments.

LINKAGES WITH LOCAL INDUSTRY

The poor backward linkages between tourism and local sectors – and the associated import leakage – are frequently used as an argument against the adoption of tourism-led economic development. In the context of a study of the Caribbean islands, Belisle (1983; Chapter 13, this volume) identifies four areas of required research into the relationship between tourism and local food production: the extent of the reliance on food imports; the competition between tourism and agriculture for labour and land; the reasons for the extent of food imports; and – in the context of the latter – a special emphasis on the effect of the particular features of the tourism sector such as hotel ownership structures and location.

After providing a review of the case against tourism-led economic development, Latimer (1985; Chapter 14, this volume) questions the aspect of the alleged competition between tourism and agriculture in developing island countries. The author argues that the transfer of land and labour from agriculture to tourism in these countries has been minor. Regarding land, the author argues, for instance, that climatic conditions (areas with little rain and beaches versus those with plenty of rain and good soil) actually helped the allocation of land towards its best use. Findings from other studies are also used to cast doubt on the extent to which labour is drawn from agriculture. While concluding that the 'anti-tourism lobby among developmentalists can be regarded as positively mischievous' (p. 42), the author concedes that the local links between tourism and primary industries warrant further attention.

This issue is addressed in Telfer and Wall (1996; Chapter 15, this volume) who provide a conceptual overview of the relationship between tourism and local food production which ranges from conflict to symbiosis. This is complemented by a case study of an Indonesian resort that adopted a programme to encourage backward economic linkages by using more local food supplies. The programme was successful in generating enhanced employment and income to the local farming and fishing sector while providing high-quality food to the resort. However, not all business relationships are stable enough to survive and the authors attribute this to the challenges of institutionalising the business relationships away from reliance on particular individuals. Importantly, the findings show that there is not necessarily a conflict between enclave types of tourism and the reduction of foreign exchange leakage through backward linkages.

Healy (1994; Chapter 16, this volume) reinforces this positive sentiment in his focus on the potential of tourist merchandise products to yield economic benefits to developing countries. The innovative aspect of the paper is its focus on the people who live in or close to developing countries' protected areas used for ecotourism, the benefits of which often do not accrue to the local residents. The author argues that, apart from providing opportunities for income and employment for the poorest people, there is ample scope for the development of products, particularly if that involves the proper use of local materials. In addition, there are opportunities to extend local art production to tourist education programmes. These encouraging findings are in stark contrast to the plight of the artisans portrayed in Britton (1982).

The extent of economic linkages is one of the theoretical constructs applied in Timothy and Wall (1997; Chapter 17, this volume) with respect to the informal tourism sector. The findings of a case study of street vendors in a popular Indonesian town destination show a high level of backward linkages with most products made locally from local materials. In addition, much of the employment generated in this informal sector is full time. Importantly, the empirical evidence suggests a blurring between formal and informal sectors due to increasing government recognition and regulation of the informal activities.

INTERNATIONAL ISSUES
Martin de Holan and Phillips (1997; Chapter 18, this volume) assess the international competitiveness of the tourism industry in the context of the Cuban case of a less developed, centrally planned economy. In particular, they use Porter's (1990) framework for analysing the international competitive advantage of domestic industries. Essentially, this framework postulates that international industry competitiveness depends on the degree of dynamics and competitive challenges in the industries' domestic business environment as characterised by the 'national diamond'. The authors evaluate the determinants in the diamond for Cuba's tourism industry. They find that, while Cuba possesses high-quality natural resources, the other conditions for international competitiveness are lacking. Importantly, high levels of monopolisation and scale prevent the required competition and innovation, and there is a lack of local support industries. One recommendation is to abandon the focus on volume and to attract

high-yield segments of visitors, in the process reducing potentially adverse social and environmental effects.

Sinclair and Tsegaye (1990; Chapter 19, this volume) is a seminal paper that addresses the issue of the volatility of foreign exchange earnings. While international tourism is often seen as an important avenue towards the diversification of developing countries' production and export bases, the stability of export earnings is a concern. The authors find, on the basis of an analysis of different export stability measures, that tourism exports reinforce the export earnings instability of commodity exports.

Based on Copeland (1991), Chen and Devereux (1999; Chapter 20, this volume) apply a theoretical, general equilibrium international trade model to tourism to assess the welfare effects of tourism in developing countries. They find that tourism is welfare enhancing depending on the trade policies in place. In the case of a regime of import tariffs and export subsidies, as generally adopted by developing countries, tourism has a positive effect on welfare. However, in the case of export taxes and/or import subsidies, which applies to many sub-Saharan economies, the welfare effects are ambiguous. In addition, the authors show that the presence of foreign direct investment in tourism does not alter the above welfare effects.

One of the earliest contributions to the study of the involvement of multinational companies (MNCs) in the accommodation sector in developing countries is provided in McQueen (1983; Chapter 21, this volume). Drawing from the theories of MNCs in manufacturing, the author poses three main propositions. Firstly, MNCs' competitive advantage is based on the product being an experienced good and, hence, brand-related quality assurances offer transaction cost economies to potential clients. Secondly, the type of involvement of MNCs, evidenced by high degrees of control mainly through management contracts, is due to the companies' internalisation of their key resources: knowledge of the market and (tacit) knowledge of hotel operations. Thirdly, since this knowledge will eventually be shared with local hotels, there is a role for governments in the host developing countries to become involved in the negotiations of the management contracts. The degree of expertise on the part of the government affects the bargaining power of the parties involved.

The choice of the type of MNCs' involvement in the hotel sector in developing countries, and the monitoring of business contracts and operations are among the seven host government policy aspects highlighted in Kusluvan and Karamustafa (2001; Chapter 22, this volume). These aspects are derived from a synthesis of the literature on the potential costs (such as overdependence and perceptions of foreign dominance) and benefits (including knowledge transfer and enhanced destination image) of multinational hotel involvement. Other policy aspects include the need to justify foreign involvement, effecting economic linkages with local sectors, facilitating and providing the development of local employees, and the provision of appropriate incentives to attract MNCs.

SCALE OF DEVELOPMENT
The scale of hotel development is one of the policy features emphasised in Kusluvan and Karamustafa (2001). The debate about the scale of tourism development in developing countries was very much initiated by Rodenburg (1980; Chapter 23, this volume). The key argument against large scale tourism projects, and in favour of small and craft scale levels, is derived from data on three levels of accommodation scale in Bali. The author bases his argument on the varying relationships between scale and the objectives of economic development

(including income, employment, entrepreneurship and minimisation of social and cultural effects).

Jenkins (1982; Chapter 24, this volume) is a direct critique on Rodenburg (1980). The author argues that, in the context of developing countries' overall objective to develop an international tourism sector, economic considerations are likely to be paramount. Governments' ranking of the various development objectives would imply an important role for large scale projects. The importance of external economies of scale and the interrelationships between large scale and smaller scale projects are highlighted. A dynamic perspective is introduced by arguing that initial large scale projects can be complemented more and more by smaller scale ventures once the destination has established its attractiveness to tourists. Most importantly, the author argues for adequate government involvement by planning and managing the co-existence of enterprises of different scale, including the active encouragement of links between large hotels and local food suppliers and the development of local human resources through education and training.

In an innovative paper, Poon (1990; Chapter 25, this volume) approaches the issue of tourism scale from a different angle by relating it to the concept of flexible specialisation. Flexibility is a 'systems concept' comprising mutually reinforcing dimensions including entrepreneurship/innovation, design, sourcing, organisation, (information) technology, marketing and strategy. In a comparison of flexible specialisation in the Superclub chain of hotels in the Caribbean and the Italian Benetton textile company, the author demonstrates how both were highly innovative in both product and process terms. The Superclub hotels pioneered the idea of all-inclusive holidays with a view to carefully targeted demand segments. The medium sized Superclub hotels have benefited from the synergy effects as part of the chain network. The author cautions against the seemingly promising and obvious implications for small scale tourism in developing countries. Scale is not a necessary condition and certainly not a sufficient condition for successful flexible specialisation and the ability to be innovative in adapting to the dynamic changes in target markets.

Part III   Broader Perspectives

The first of the papers on the wider perspectives of tourism in developing countries is Oppermann (1993; Chapter 26, this volume) who provides a spatial perspective. A review of theories reveals a lack of spatial focus and a biased analysis towards the formal or 'upper circuit' tourism sector. This sector is typified by high standard accommodation and largely Western tastes as opposed to the informal or 'lower circuit' sector. The author develops a model that shows the inter temporal implications of tourism space for a hypothetical non-island developing country. One of the important insights is that the dual formal–informal tourism structure, initially concentrated around the capital, gradually spreads across the country. The other is that, throughout the developmental stages, informal tourism destinations are far more connected spatially and the associated informal tourists far more mobile compared with the high levels of concentration and isolation of the formal, resort-style sector. These spatial-temporal insights have obvious implications for regional benefits of tourism.

Despite the potential benefits of small scale, informal tourism to developing countries, a possible negative impact of this type of tourism is discussed in Bauer (1999; Chapter 27, this volume). The author highlights the lack of research on tourism's impact on the health of host communities with the literature on the tourism–health nexus focusing on the health of tourists. In particular, the activities of adventure tourism involve close contact between tourists and locals which has the potential of spreading infectious diseases. Additional, indirect effects include those that operate through environmental and socio-cultural effects (for instance, water pollution, mosquito plagues after land clearance, prostitution and crime). The author puts forward a framework on which future research in the tourism–health nexus can be built.

Jafari (1974; Chapter 28, this volume) is a seminal contribution to the critical analysis of the socio-economic impacts of tourism in developing countries. The author focuses on what were at the time 'less known and relatively ignored' (p. 228) socio-economic costs of tourism development. While the tone of the article is necessarily negative since it provides a critical perspective, some of the issues raised in the article are as current today as ever. One of the less conventional aspects in the discussion on economic costs is the linking of the demonstration effect and the 'contagious disease' (p. 235) of citizens of developing countries travelling to developed countries thereby adding to the import leakages. The social costs discussed include the potential for xenophobia through the perceived commoditisation of local culture and traditions. One noteworthy policy option discussed – particularly in the context of contemporary notions of open economies and globalisation – is that of halting inbound tourism and isolating the country from the influence of tourists of developed countries thereby following the isolation experiences of Japan and the USSR.

The implementation of the concept of community involvement in the development of tourism in developing countries has been advocated strongly by, among others, Brohman (1996). Arguing that this is not straightforward in the historically shaped socio-political, economic and cultural context of many developing countries, Tosun (2000; Chapter 29, this volume) discusses the nature and extent of the implementation limits. These include structural barriers like highly centralised bureaucratic decision-making processes; the wealth and power distribution biased towards foreign interests and local elite groups; the lack of local communities' economic ownership of tourism development; and the low degree of local expertise in tourism planning. Hence, to make participatory tourism development work in developing countries, major structural barriers like these have to be overcome.

Fisher (2004; Chapter 30, this volume) provides a critical analysis of the notion of the demonstration effect which is often seen as one of the adverse tourism effects on developing countries. This paper is a relatively recent contribution to the tourism literature which is surprising since the idea of the demonstration effect has been around for quite a while and, as argued by the author, has been largely unquestioned and inadequately supported by empirical evidence. The paper provides a theoretical analysis of the underlying decision-making processes and derives four different imitation decisions. Importantly, the author emphasises that it is crucial that the analysis of the demonstration effect allows the separation of the impact of the physical presence of tourists as one possible vehicle of influence from other sources of influence including information and communication technologies which are increasingly available in developing countries.

The need to look beyond direct interactions between tourists and the local population is also one of the three points of criticism of the conceptual treatment of the cultural effects of tourism in the tourism literature highlighted in Wood (1980; Chapter 31, this volume). The other two are the dominance of normative, Western values about the need to preserve local cultures, and the misguided assumption of culture as a passive, undifferentiated and static concept. In addition, the author emphasises the lack of empirical evidence on the effects of tourism on culture. An agenda for research is set out which includes the need to investigate the growing role of the state with respect to cultural tourism.

While Baddeley (2004; Chapter 32, this volume) provides an economic perspective, it is included in the third part of this volume since it addresses the issue of environmental protection in tourism development. The author argues that price (and profit) premiums are required to provide the incentives for tourism projects of high environmental quality. By charging relatively high prices, tourism establishments can signal the quality level in the face of adverse selection problems. The ensuing question of whether tourists are willing to pay for an experience of higher environmental quality is explored with an econometric analysis – of a main tourism region in Thailand – of the relationship between the level of room rents and a number of factors including environmental quality. The latter is reflected in the degrees of noise pollution, traffic congestion and aesthetic pollution. The results indicate a negative relationship between aesthetic environmental quality and room rents which the author interprets as possibly leading to a 'vicious circle of environmental degradation and economic decline' (p. 57).

One of the possible reasons for the above empirical finding, as suggested in Baddeley (2004), is the lack of reliable environmental information available to tourists for their holiday choice decision. The related issue of the relevance of tourism ecolabels for developing countries is investigated in Sasidharan, Sirakaya and Kerstetter (2002; Chapter 33, this volume). The paper comprises a set of propositions that question various aspects of the ecolabelling process which compromise ecolabelling's ability to educate tourists. The authors argue that the scientific environmental impact assessment methods are ambiguous and that the resulting criteria, negotiated by various stakeholders, do not provide reliable and comprehensive information to tourists about the true environmental impacts. Also, due to the lack of financial resources, small scale tourism businesses in developing countries are unlikely to be able to participate in ecolabelling programmes. Overall, the authors are not optimistic about the potential of ecolabelling to further the cause of environmentally sensitive tourism in developing countries.

Lea (1983; Chapter 34, this volume) addresses the issue of tourism ethics with a view to social, cultural and environmental impacts on developing countries. From the previous discussions, it appears obvious that ethics – one definition of which is provided as 'the reflective study of what is good and bad in that part of human conduct for which men have some responsibility' (p. 703) – is an aspect that is relevant with respect to tourism's role in economic development. The article is insightful in that it identifies three spheres of ethical concern that are relevant to tourism in developing countries. At the general level, to the extent that tourism is important to many developing countries, it forms part of the overall development ethics paradigm as discussed in the sociology of development literature. At the industry level, ethics concerns are linked with the notion of a capitalist system controlled by rich, Western countries and the ensuing dependence of developing countries. Finally, at the individual level, ethics is associated with the growing notion of 'responsible travel' based on a tourist's understanding of the host culture, respect for the host community and sensitivity to the local environment. The article provides interesting insights into the varied origins of the idea of tourism ethics. The article then goes on to discuss the emergence of local anti-tourism activism and protest movements (and a case study of Goa, India) with the observation that it is not obvious whether 'local people in the developing world faced with the impacts of mass tourism are at all convinced that the new ideas [of ethical concern in responsible travel] will be adopted in time to reverse present trends' (p. 708).

A Final Word

As the contributions to this volume show, there is more to tourism in developing countries than economic growth. The various economic, social, cultural and environmental ramifications of tourism provide multi-disciplinary inputs into the debate about tourism as a catalyst for economic development. In particular, the extent to which people in the local host communities benefit from tourism is a contentious issue in the literature. Academic debate about such issues is imperative. However, the importance of tourism as the provider of livelihoods to large parts of local populations in developing countries becomes – unfortunately – most evident when disaster strikes in the form of natural or man-made disasters. It is to be hoped that tourism can provide a positive contribution to putting 'shirts on backs' of people in developing countries.

Note

1. Naturally, the distribution of output and employment shares within the group of developing countries is not uniform either.

References

Blake, A., T. Sinclair and G. Sugiyarto (2003), 'Quantifying the Impact of Foot and Mouth Disease on Tourism and the UK Economy', *Tourism Economics*, **9** (4), 449–465.

Britton, S. (1982), 'The Political Economy of Tourism in the Third World', *Annals of Tourism Research*, **9** (3), 331–358.

Copeland, B. (1991), 'Tourism, Welfare and De-industrialisation in a Small Open Economy', *Economica*, **58** (232), 515–529.

DFID (1999), 'Sustainable Tourism and Poverty Elimination Study', London: Department for International Development.

Dwyer, L. and P. Forsyth (1993), 'Assessing The Benefits and Costs of Inbound Tourism', *Annals of Tourism Research*, **20** (4), 751–768.

Dwyer, L., P. Forsyth and R. Spurr (2004), 'Evaluating Tourism's Economic Effects: New and Old Approaches', *Tourism Management*, **25** (3), 307–317.

Durbarry, R. (2004), 'Tourism and Economic Growth: the Case of Mauritius', *Tourism Economics* **10**, (4), 389–401.

Gollub, J., A. Hosier and G. Woo (2002), 'Using Cluster-based Economic Strategy to Minimise Tourism Leakages', Madrid: World Tourism Organization.

Modeste, N.C. (1995), 'The Impact of Growth in the Tourism Sector on Economic Development: The Experience of Selected Caribbean Countries', *Economia Internazionale*, **48** (3), 375–384.

Porter, M. (1990), *The Competitive Advantage of Nations*, New York: The Free Press.

Sinclair, M.T. (1998), 'Tourism and Economic Development: A Survey', *Journal of Development Studies*, **34** (5), 1–51.

Skerritt, D. and T. Huybers (2005), 'The Effect of International Tourism on Economic Development: An Empirical Analysis', *Asia-Pacific Journal of Tourism Research*, **10** (1), 23–43.

Walpole, M. and H. Goodwin (2000), 'Local Economic Impacts of Dragon Tourism in Indonesia', *Annals of Towns in Research*, 27 (3), 559–576.

WTO (2002), 'Tourism and Poverty Alleviation', Madrid: World Tourism Organization.

WTO (2004a), 'Tourism Highlights – Edition 2004', Madrid: World Tourism Organization.

WTO (2004b), 'Final Report, Seminar on Sustainable Tourism Development and Poverty Alleviation –

Special Programme of Activities to Promote Tourism Development in Sub-Saharan Africa', Arusha, Tanzania, 7–9 September 2004, Madrid: World Tourism Organization.

WTO (2005a), 'Serial Report Number 2 of Tsunami Recovery in Maldives', Madrid: World Tourism Organization.

WTO (2005b), 'Facts and Figures – Information, Analysis and Know-how', http://www.world-tourism. org/facts/menu.html, Madrid: World Tourism Organization.

WTTC (2005), 'Sowing the Seeds of Growth – The 2005 Travel and Tourism Economic Research', London: World Travel and Tourism Council.

Part I
General Perspectives

A
The General Issue

[1]

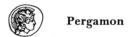 **Pergamon**

Annals of Tourism Research, Vol. 23, No. 1, pp. 48–70, 1996
Copyright © 1996 Elsevier Science Ltd
Printed in Great Britain. All rights reserved
0160-7383/96 $15.00+0.00

0160-7383(95)00043-7

NEW DIRECTIONS IN TOURISM FOR THIRD WORLD DEVELOPMENT

John Brohman
Simon Fraser University, Canada

Abstract: The Third World tourism industry has grown rapidly, but has also encountered many problems common to other outward-oriented development strategies, including: excessive foreign dependency, the creation of separate enclaves, the reinforcement of socioeconomic and spatial inequalities, environmental destruction, and rising cultural alienation. To avoid such problems, institutional mechanisms need to be created to encourage active state and community participation in tourism planning. Appropriateness of tourism strategies ought to be measured according to the changing conditions and interests of each host community; and tourism-led development should always conform to the long-term interests of the popular majority instead of the short-term goals of an elite minority. **Keywords:** outward-oriented growth, tourism problems, alternative strategies, community participation, state intervention.

Résumé: Nouvelles directions pour le tourisme dans le développement du Tiers-Monde. L'industrie du tourisme des pays en voie de développement est en plein essor, mais fait face à de nombreux problèmes communs à d'autres stratégies de développement tournées vers l'extérieur: une trop grande dépendance de l'étranger, la destruction de l'environnement et une aliénation culturelle grandissante. Pour éviter ces problèmes, on doit créer des mécanismes pour encourager une participation active de l'état et de la communauté dans la planification du tourisme. Toute stratégie pour le tourisme doit correspondre aux besoins toujours changeants et aux intérêts de chaque communauté hôte; le développement du tourisme doit toujours se conformer aux intérêts à long terme de la majorité plutôt qu'aux intérêts à court terme de l'élite minoritaire. **Mot-clés:** croissance orientée vers l'extérieur, problèmes du tourisme, stratégies alternatives, participation de la communauté, intervention de l'état.

INTRODUCTION

With the renewed emphasis on outward-oriented growth which has accompanied the rise of neoliberal development strategies in the South, increasing attention has been focused on international tourism as an important potential growth sector for many countries. The international tourism sector has indeed enjoyed prolonged, rapid growth in many areas of the South during the postwar period. However, there are also a number of common problems that have been linked to Third World tourism which call into question its usefulness as a component of development strategies. These include foreign domination and dependency, socioeconomic and spatial polarization, environmental destruction, cultural alienation, and the loss of social control and identity among host communities.

John Brohman is Assistant Professor of Geography and Associate Member of Spanish and Latin American Studies at Simon Fraser University (Burnaby, British Columbia, Canada V5A 1S6; email john_brohman@sfu.ca). His research interests focus on theories and strategies of Third World development.

JOHN BROHMAN   49

This paper analyzes these problems and explores ways in which they may be overcome by introducing changes in tourism development. Particular emphasis is placed on the design of alternative tourism strategies that call for increased community participation and more coordinated state involvement in tourism planning to serve broadly based development goals.

TOURISM IN THIRD WORLD COUNTRIES

During the early postwar period, a strong current of "export pessimism" pervaded mainstream development theories. Many influential development theorists and policymakers contended that global trade, especially for primary commodities, was too erratic to form the principal "engine of growth" for Third World economies. Instead, it was believed that more inward-oriented strategies (e.g., import-substitution industrialization) would offer a more secure and orderly basis for the generation of sustained growth. Since the late 60s, however, support for inward-oriented development models among mainstream theorists has gradually been replaced by a renewed emphasis on outward-oriented growth. This shift in development thinking has paralleled the resurgence of neoclassical economics as the centerpiece of the neoliberal counterrevolution in development studies. Among the first to criticize inward-oriented development models was a group of neoclassical theorists (e.g., Bauer and Yamer 1968; Haberler 1950; Viner 1953) who argued that these approaches interfere with the "natural process" of development based on "comparative advantage". Their view, which has remained popular among neoliberals, was that Third World countries, at least during their initial stages of development, should uniformly specialize in primary exports rather than attempt to develop more sophisticated industrial sectors through state intervention that would not conform to comparative advantages based on factor proportions.

The rise of outward-oriented neoliberal development strategies has also been accompanied by increasing interventionism by the International Monetary Fund (IMF) and World Bank into Third World policymaking via mechanisms such as structural adjustment lending. Generally, this means that continued access to such lending, as well as most other external sources of financing, has been made conditional on the adoption of policy reforms designed to reduce state economic intervention and generate market-oriented growth. In many countries such pressures have contributed to a decisive shift in development strategy away from an inward- toward an outward-orientation, including an emphasis on the expansion of hitherto ignored sectors such as international tourism. With increasing frequency, international tourism is being grouped together in the development literature with other major new "growth sectors" (e.g., export-oriented industries, nontraditional agricultural exports) that are believed to show much promise for stimulting rapid growth based on the "comparative advantages" of Third World countries.

Rising support for outward-oriented growth within mainstream development theory is based on seven interrelated arguments based in neoclassical theory. First, given low levels of domestic demand in many developing countries, growth in a range of economic sectors is believed to be largely dependent on gaining access to global markets via outward-oriented strategies. Second, outward-oriented policies are regarded as normally the least damaging in terms of microeconomic efficiency, in that they benefit total factor productivity more than any other popular policy option. Third, multiplier effects associated with foreign trade and tourism may facilitate long-term growth by expanding overall production and employment. Fourth, earnings from trade and tourism may foster macroeconomic stability by contributing to a more favorable balance of trade and external accounts, which is important for attaining better ratings in international financial markets (and thus easier access to foreign loans and other investment capital). Fifth, such earnings may also provide foreign exchange for imported goods, particularly capital goods needed to increase the production potential of an economy. Sixth, rising volume in the external sector and increased competition within global markets are believed to create economic efficiencies associated with increasing scale economies and technological diffusion. Seventh, given these theoretical arguments, rapid economic growth among (especially East Asian) export-oriented NICs (New Industrializing Countries), as well as a series of country studies showing strong correlations between an outward-orientation and economic performance, is interpreted as empirical evidence supporting the externally-led growth hypothesis.

Taken together, these arguments present a powerful case for the adoption by most countries of an outward economic orientation. However, a review of the development literature also underscores the need to proceed cautiously if growth in trade and tourism is not to be accompanied by many problems historically linked with outward-oriented development strategies. In particular, if stress is not placed on the creation of local linkages to spread the benefits of growth in social, sectoral, and regional terms, neoliberal outward-oriented strategies risk replicating the vicious cycles of polarization and repression so commonly associated with past export-oriented development models. What is missing from strategies that focus only on increasing international trade or tourism is a concern for the broader development goals of raising living standards of the popular majority and promoting more balanced growth among different economic sectors and geographic regions. In the absence of well-developed linkages between the external sectors and the rest of the economy, a limited and polarized form of development takes place that cannot act as a stimulus for broadly based development.

A set of criteria may be developed to evaluate the effects of outward-oriented growth on overall development. These might include the following: the extent of linkages to the domestic economy; the creation of employment and value-added; the effect on external accounts and balance of payments; the fostering of genuine and appropriate technology transfer rather than merely technology relocation; the generation of jobs for skilled labor as well as local managers, technicians, and other highly trained personnel; the establishment of favorable wages and working conditions relative to those prevailing in the country; and the rise of a relatively equitable social, sectoral, and regional distribution of the costs and benefits of growth. This would mean that maldevelopment accompanying outward-oriented growth might be associated with some combination of the destruction of internal linkages in the domestic economy; the failure to create satisfactory levels of local employment, income, and value-added; the worsening of balance-of-payments problems and foreign indebtedness; the transfer of inappropriate (often capital-intensive) technologies developed for factor intensities in the North rather than South; the loss of local skills and the failure to create skilled jobs for the local population; the intensification of labor exploitation; and the inequitable distribution of the costs and benefits of growth.

Reports of many of these problems appear with disturbing frequency in the development literature. At a general level, Black, for example, notes "the failure of the [outward-oriented growth] strategy to promote balanced and equitable growth in most Third World countries" (1991:85). Similarly, Frobel, Heinricks and Kreye (1980) argue that externally-led growth, especially that associated with foreign-controlled enclaves, has produced only a truncated, severely circumscribed type of development that has excluded the majority from participating in the benefits of growth. In a study of outward-oriented development models, Sklair concludes that "open-door strategies seem to offer a way out of the awful dilemma between dependency without development and capitalist development without social justice but. . .there is little evidence to suggest that this is anything more than a false promise in the interests of transnational capitals and its partners, capitalist or otherwise, in the Third World" (1990:124). Indeed, an extensive perusal of the contemporary development literature indicates that the relatively successful experience of a few (especially East Asian) NICs with outward-oriented development is the exception rather than the rule. The reality for the rest of the South is much more problematic.

Tourism as a New Outward-Oriented Growth Sector

Serving as a centerpiece for the neoliberal strategy of outward-oriented development in many countries is the promotion of new growth sectors such as tourism or nontraditional exports (NTEs). Until now, in the development literature, most of the attention on new growth sectors has focused on NTEs. However, for many of the same reasons, tourism is also increasingly being promoted as an important source of outward-oriented growth. Development theorists contend that increased tourism may contribute to economic diversification away from an excessive dependency on a few traditional exports, especially in many low-income countries that lack possibilities for rapid industrialization. Moreover, tropical and Southern Hemisphere countries may attract tourists from developed Northern countries by utilizing their comparative advantage of warm weather during the Northern winter season combined with other local attractions (e.g., beaches, mountains, ecotourism, cultural heritage sites). Lower transportation costs, improved public health standards, infrastructure development, and hospitable environments for tourists in many destinations have combined with higher discretionary incomes, smaller family size, and changing demographics in many Northern countries to make many distant areas in the South more accessible and affordable for Northerners. In addition, many tourists are also originating from the South itself, particularly from some of the more affluent NICs.

In terms of both volume and expenditures, international tourism has risen dramatically over the past four decades and the trend toward further rapid growth seems to be continuing. International tourist arrivals jumped from 25.3 million in 1950 to 443.5 million in 1990, while expenditures climbed from $2.1 billion to $254.8 billion over the same period (World Tourism Organization, 1989, 1993). Although tourism growth has slowed somewhat in comparison to the initial "take-off" period in the early postwar era, average annual growth rates remained strong in the 80s for both international tourist arrivals (5.6%) and expenditures (14.9%). Forecasts now call for some 600 million tourists to cross international boundaries by the year 2000.

It should be noted, however, that although there has generally been an upward trend in international tourism in recent years, not all global regions and countries have shared equally in that growth. Overwhelmingly, the countries of the North continue to dominate international tourism, although the South's share has been rising slowly: from 19.6% of international tourist arrivals in 1980 to 23.1% in 1990 (Table 1). Within the South itself, tourism growth has also been quite uneven: in the 80s strong annual growth rates in tourist arrivals were experienced by Asia and the Pacific (14.2%) and Africa (11.2%), but the growth rates in Latin America and the Caribbean (5.5%) and the Middle East (3.7%) hovered only around the global average. Furthermore, within most Third World regions, tourism has been monopolized by a few countries to the exclusion of the rest. For example, in Africa, three countries (Egypt, Morocco, and Tunisia) accounted for 52.6% of the continent's international tourists in 1991, while seven countries (the above three countries and Algeria, Kenya, South Africa, and Zimbabwe) represented 76.9% of this total. Similarly, in Southeast Asia, three countries (Malaysia, Singapore, and Thailand) had 79.8% and, in Oceania, three countries (Australia, Guam, and New Zealand) had 78.1% of their respective region's international tourists in 1991 (World Tourism Organization 1993).

It is argued that tourism has become the world's third largest industry, after oil and vehicle production, contributing about 12% of global GNP (World Tourism Organization 1987). Although the majority of tourism receipts go to developed countries, the developing countries' share is estimated to be 25.3% and has been rising steadily since the late 60s (World Tourism Organization 1993). Alongside non-traditional exports, tourism represents a high-growth sector in much of the South, making a signficiant contribution to the

Table 1. International Tourism by Region (1980–1990)

Region	Volume (000s arrivals)		
	1980	1985	1990
North	228,942	252,787	341,203
South	55,879	68,453	102,274
North America	35,376	38,588	55,030
Europe	194,884	211,444	281,378
Latin America & Caribbean	18,327	20,212	28,407
Africa	7070	9805	15,235
Middle East	6937	9243	9501
Asia & Pacific	22,247	31,948	53,926

Region	Average Annual Growth (%)			World Share (%)		
	1980–1985	1985–1990	1980–1990	1980	1985	1990
North	2.1	7.0	4.9	80.4	78.7	76.9
South	4.5	9.9	8.3	19.6	21.3	23.1
North America	1.8	8.5	5.6	12.4	12.0	12.4
Europe	1.7	6.6	4.4	86.4	65.8	63.4
Latin America & Caribbean	2.1	8.1	5.5	6.4	6.3	6.4
Africa	7.7	11.1	11.6	2.5	3.1	3.4
Middle East	6.6	0.6	3.7	2.4	2.9	2.1
Asia & Pacific	8.7	13.8	14.2	7.8	9.9	12.2

Source: World Tourism Organization (1991).

balance of payments of many countries. For example, in 1990 developing countries as diverse as the Bahamas, Jamaica, Egypt, Kenya, and Thailand achieved a positive trade balance (Table 2).

Common Problems of Third World Tourism Sectors

Like NTEs, tourism holds out the promise of becoming a substantial new growth sector for many Third World economies. However, again similar to NTEs, reliance on tourism to generate growth is not without its own potential contradictions. Some of the shortcomings commonly associated with the Third World tourism industry include high rates of foreign ownership contributing to a loss of control over local resources; substantial overseas leakage of tourism earnings; lack of articulation with other domestic economic sectors; low multiplier and spread effects outside of tourism enclaves; reinforcement of patterns of socioeconomic inequality and spatial unevenness; widely fluctuating earnings due to factors such as global recessions and the seasonality of tourism in some places; environmental destruction, often involving the irretrievable loss of nonrenewable resources and foundation assets; and rising alienation among the local population because of problems such as increasing crime, overcrowding and overloaded infrastructures, pollution and other environmental

Table 2. Tourism Balance in Selected Countries (1990)[a]

Country	Tourism Receipts (millions)	Tourism Expenditure (millions)	Balance	Tourism Exports[b]	as % of GDP	Receipts per Capita
Bahamas	$1333	$196	$1137	$73.2	NA	$5332
Barbados	494	47	447	59.0	NA	1900
Brazil	1444	1559	−115	4.6	0.3	10
Costa Rica	275	156	119	13.1	4.8	92
Ecuador	188	175	13	5.7	1.7	17
Egypt	1994	129	1865	22.0	6.0	38
Fiji	227	41	186	24.8	NA	310
India	1437	394	1043	6.3	0.6	2
Indonesia	2105	967	1138	7.1	2.0	12
Israel	1382	1485	−103	7.4	2.6	297
Jamaica	740	54	686	31.8	18.6	306
Kenya	443	38	405	19.8	5.9	18
Mexico	3934	2171	1763	9.5	1.7	46
Morocco	1259	184	1075	19.9	5.0	50
Peru	398	770	−372	9.6	1.1	18
Singapore	4719	1821	2898	6.5	1.4	1573
Sri Lanka	132	79	53	5.5	1.8	8
Thailand	4326	854	3472	13.8	5.4	76

[a] In US dollars.
[b] Exports of all goods and services; NA = Not available.
Sources: International Monetary Fund (1993), World Bank (1993a, 1993b), and World Tourism Organization (1993).

damage, conflicts over access to scarce resources, and the perceived loss of cultural identity and social control to outsiders.

Because of the monopolistic controls exerted by transnational corporations (TNCs) over the ownership and organizational structure of most countries' mass-tourism sectors, many analysts contend that the Third World tourism industry often replicates problems of dependency, internal disarticulation, and foreign exchange leakages usually associated with underdeveloped economies dominated by foreign-owned export enclaves (Britton 1982; Hills and Lundgren 1977; Matthews 1977; Nash 1989). The technical, economic, and commercial characteristics of many mass-tourism sectors tend to favor the development of large-scale, integrated, multinational enterprises. If provisions are not made to increase local economic participation, this greatly increases the likelihood of the domination of Third World tourism sectors by transnational capitals from the metropolitan core. For this reason, tourism has sometimes been called "a neo-colonial extension of economic forms of underdevelopment" that reproduces historical patterns of structural inequalities between developed and developing countries (Britton 1980:149). Foreign domination and external dependency often seriously reduce tourism's potential for generating broadly based growth, as well as the net financial advantages that the industry brings to developing

JOHN BROHMAN   55

economies. The three most lucrative components of Third World tourism (i.e., marketing and the procurement of customers, international transportation, and food and lodging) are normally handled by vertically integrated global networks, with airlines and other transnationals occupying dominant positions (Erisman 1983:347).

A further negative impact of foreign domination of the Third World tourism industry has been the loss of control over local resources, which may adversely effect the social, economic, and ecological well-being of the host communities. Local people commonly find themselves enmeshed in a globally integrated system of resource use over which they cannot exercise control. They and the resources upon which they depend become the targets of top-down decision-making by elitist bodies exogenous to the community. Decisions governing their lives, even those that address local matters, are normally made elsewhere according to the narrow interests of those that control the tourism industry. This has led many authors to assert that the struggle for control over local resources is an element of tourism that generally has not been properly recognized by local governments:

> It would appear that the struggle for control over resources between internal and external interests is a dynamic and continuing aspect of tourist development. It is a struggle which local governments in general have been slow to recognize, but one they can ill afford to ignore. The need for local governments to adopt political economic policies which effect a balance between local and external resources and control over those resources as well as between tourism and other sectors of the local economy is increasingly crucial as more and more regions are developed for mass tourism. . .(Oliver-Smith, Arrones and Lisón Arcal 1989: 350).

Foreign domination of the tourism industry often also contributes to the overseas leakage of a substantial portion of the earnings. In many tourism sectors, especially of the enclave variety, foreign capitals construct and own the major part of hotel accommodations, restaurants, and other services, as well as the principal transportation links and travel agencies. Profit repatriations and payments for imported goods and services widen the leakage of foreign exchange earnings from tourism and frequently put a heavy burden on the host country's balance of payments. Data collected by a number of authors show that such leakages are often substantial, especially in smaller countries with tourism sectors dominated by foreign-controlled resort enclaves (e.g., 56% in Fiji, 50% in the Cook Islands, 45% for St. Lucia, 43% for the Bahamas, 41% for Antigua, Aruba, and Hong Kong, and 29% for Singapore) (Britton 1987; English 1986; Khan, Chase and Wong 1990; Richards 1983; Seward and Spinard 1982).

One should note that these figures measure the foreign exchange leakage ratio only of the "first round" of firms directly linked to the tourism industry in each country. The cumulative effect of the multiplier from a sector such as tourism may take several rounds to calculate, so that these figures probably tend to understate total foreign exchange leakages. When factors such as changing consumption habits resulting from mass tourism are also taken into consideration, these leakages may be even higher. In Fiji, for example, Britton (1980:148–149) demonstrates that some 70% of the foreign exchange generated by tourism in 1975 was lost in the form of payments for imports, foreign staff salaries, profit repatriation by tourism companies, and rising consumption by locals of imported goods made available through this industry. Given this problem of excessive leakages, many analysts contend that the apparent advantage of higher revenues offered by concentrated, foreign-controlled mass tourism over more dispersed, smaller-scale, and locally owned tourism alternatives may be illusory (Rodenburg 1980; Weaver 1991).

In many developing countries, problems of excessive foreign exchange leakage within tourism have been aggravated by the sector's lack of articulation with other parts of the local economy, especially agriculture (Oliver-Smith et al 1989:345). By contrast, most tourism sectors in the developed world are much better linked to their local economies and consequently have significantly lower foreign exchange leakage ratios (Harrison 1992; Weaver 1988). These linkages allow the revenues to circulate through the domestic economy, producing larger multiplier effects in terms of both employment and income for the local population.

Tourism studies in both the North and South have correlated multiplier values with different forms of tourism (Pearce 1989:210–211). Generally, lower multipliers have been associated with highly concentrated, large-scale, foreign-owned tourism complexes, while higher multipliers have been connected to more dispersed, smaller-scale, locally owned operations that tend to be better linked to the local economy. Studies of the Cook Islands by Milne (1987) and of Thailand by Meyer (1988), for instance, report that small, locally owned firms have been more successful in generating income, employment, and government revenue than larger, internationally-owned establishments.

Some countries have recently initiated efforts to increase local multipliers by strengthening links between the tourism industry and the domestic economy, and by encouraging alternative, smaller-scale forms of tourism. Within the Caribbean, for example, Jamaica, Montserrat, and St. Lucia have tried to increase multipliers and decrease foreign exchange leakages for food imports by strengthening linkages between tourism and local agriculture (Momsen 1986), while Dominica has encouraged the development of small-scale, dispersed ecotourism operations as a deliberate alternative to conventional resort enclaves (Weaver 1991).

Not only is Third World tourism often associated with high foreign exchange leakages and weak local multiplier effects, but earnings generated by tourism are also subject to dramatic fluctuations resulting from factors such as global recessions or climatic variations. Because tourism is a discretionary consumption expenditure, global economic downturns result in an especially steep decline in revenues. The effects of such declines are further magnified for many distant destinations in the South, as Northern tourists switch their vacations to closer, less expensive destinations during periods of financial hardship. It has been argued that tourism offers possibilities for diversifying many Third World economies away from increasingly unstable traditional export sectors. However, a recent study found that tourism did not significantly decrease the instability of export earnings in either developing or developed countries. In fact, tourism contributed to increased instability in the export sectors of a number of the countries studied, particularly those with small, open economies (Sinclair and Tsegaye 1990:487).

Parallel to a tendency to aggravate export instabilities, dependent tourism development has also tended to reinforce existing spatial disparities, in the South. As in the case of multiplier effects and foreign exchange leakages, however, various forms of tourism appear to produce differential effects on spatial patterns of development. As might be expected, concentrated enclave-type tourism resorts have commonly been linked to widening spatial inequalities (Britton 1980, 1982; Jenkins 1982; Pearce 1987). By contrast, alternative, smaller-scale, more dispersed operations that encourage tourist mobility are believed to contribute to a more uniform distribution of tourism expenditure which may foster a more spatially equitable pattern of regional development (Oppermann 1992). Despite these apparent linkages, many tourism impact studies fail to adequately consider the differential impact of various types of tourism and tend to divorce its impacts from the broader context of development. In fact, much enclavic development that has exacerbated spatial inequities in Third World countries has been promoted not only by transnational capitals, but also by international aid agencies and central governments (Pearce 1989:95–98, 183).

In many Third World countries, tourism enclaves have acted to reinforce longstanding (neo)colonial patterns of socioeconomic and spatial polarization. Within the Caribbean, for example, tourism studies have noted a structural tendency toward spatial polarization within both the modern tourism industry, based on resort enclaves in the most desirable coastal locations, and the older plantation-based economy, rooted in concentrated landholdings within the most desirable agricultural locations. The result has been the construction of a "plantation tourism landscape. . .[which] is characterized by the juxtapostion of an elite resort-based coast with an impoverished labor-supplying interior, thereby attesting to the tendency of tourism to perpetuate the structural and spatial inequalities (i.e., underdevelopment) of the plantation system" (Weaver 1988:319). Essentially, tourism has reinforced the core-periphery structure of the traditional plantation economy; this reflects both the inherent characteristics of the tourism industry itself and its adaptability to preexisting sociospatial structures. A pronounced spatial dichotomy has evolved in much of the Caribbean between a privileged (tourist and elite) space along choice spots of coastline and a underprivileged space in the interior of many countries. Similarly, a study of the spatial organization of tourism in Fiji found that traditional patterns of development rooted in the colonial past have been reinforced by the tourism industry:

There seems to be little doubt that the spatial organization of tourism activity is directly related to pre-existing fixed capital originally developed to serve colonial interests...tourism plant located in areas that were historically a part of Fiji's colonial export economy accounted for $69.536 million, or 94.7% of tourist industry turnover. The portion of turnover generated outside these regions by tourism plant located in areas historically dominated by the subsistence economy amounted to only 5.3% (Britton 1980:159–60).

Tourism has also often been linked with environmental destruction, a declining quality of life, and rising feelings of loss of control and cultural alienation among the local population of Third World countries. Large-scale, foreign-owned, enclave-type resorts have been particularly associated with these problems. In some cases, the natural "foundation assets" (e.g., sandy beaches, tropical forests, coral reefs, clear seas) upon which tourism is based are being irreparably damaged by overuse and unsound environmental practices (Wilkinson 1989). Substantial ecological damage can often result from the cumulative effect of many small increases in environmental degradation, none of which appears to be serious in itself (Pigram 1992). Conversely, one of the main goals of more ecologically sustainable forms of tourism would be to avoid such cumulative negative threshold effects. A definition of sustainable development in the context of tourism has recently been offered by Butler:

> ... tourism which is developed and maintained in an area (community, environment) in such a manner and at such a scale that it remains viable over an indefinite period and does not degrade or alter the environment (human and physical) in which it exists to such a degree that it prohibits the successful development and well-being of other activities and processes (1993:29).

As more areas of the South are being subjected to ecologically destructive and unsustainable forms of tourism development, conflicts have begun to emerge among various operations and other economic sectors and social groups (Dieke 1991; Poirier and Wright 1993). In some cases, organized protest movements have arisen, such as the Federation of Ecological Societies of the Dominican Republic (FEDOMASEC), which has recently called for international support to combat massive damage from tourism-related development to Caribbean forests, mangroves, and marine life (de Kadt 1992). As the following statement indicates, ecological destruction from international tourism may provoke considerable resentment as people in the popular destinations of the South see their environments being "consumed" by Northern tourists:

> Having ruined their own environment, having either used up or destroyed all that is natural, people from the advanced consumer societies are compelled to look for natural wildlife, cleaner air, lush greenery and golden beaches elsewhere. In other words, they look for other environments to consume. Thus armed with their bags,

tourists proceed to consume the environment in countries of the
Third World — the last "unspoiled corner of earth" (Hong 1985:12).

In addition to environmental destruction, other problems that
often accompany tourism (e.g., overcrowding and conflicts over
resource use, rising prostitution and other crime, the collapse of
social control, and the loss of cultural identity) have contributed to
a perception among the local population in many popular destinations of a declining quality of life (Tsartas 1992). Tourism development creates "winners" and "losers" among local residents, often
without any common acceptance as to the equity of such redistribution. Moreover, many of the "winners" in Third World resort communities are outsiders who then may be viewed "as exploiters of the
native population and rapists of the land" (Smith and Eadington
1992:9). Locals may feel that the economic benefits of tourism
(which themselves may be questionable) are outweighed by its social
and cultural costs.

Indeed, many case studies have demonstrated the adverse social
and cultural effects of the Third World tourism industry, particularly
if dominated by resort enclaves (Erisman 1983; Poirier and Wright
1993; Smith 1989; Mansfield 1992). Typically, resort enclaves in the
South are constructed as "parks" within which outside (Northern)
values and activities reign supreme. Sights which may be common
in Northern countries (e.g., scantily clad visitors on beaches, open
affection between men and women, public alcohol drinking) may
offend the local population by violating cultural mores or religious
taboos. Contact with the indigenous culture tends to be packaged
rather than spontaneous, contrived rather than original, whether in
terms of organized exhibitions or mass-produced artifacts.
Increasingly, local people may feel a sense of alienation rooted in
feelings of a loss of social control and cultural identity. As the
pressures of mass tourism intensify, strong feelings of resentment
may arise toward foreign tourists–as are expressed in the following
statement by a native Hawaiian at a church-sponsored conference
on Third World tourism:

> We don't want tourism. We don't want you. We don't want to be
> degraded as servants and dancers. This is cultural prostitution. I
> don't want to see a single one of you in Hawaii. There are no
> innocent tourists (quoted in Pfafflin 1987:577).

Community Participation in Tourism Planning

In many Third World countries, a more appropriately planned
tourism development process is needed which would both spread its
costs and benefits more equitably and which would be more sensitive to its social and cultural impacts. This would not only reduce
the need for local residents to trade off quality of life and social costs
for economic growth, but would also contribute to a more broadly
based positive attitude toward tourism (Mansfield 1992). A large
proportion of the local population should benefit from tourism,

rather than merely bearing the burden of its costs. Moreover, the industry ought not to forget that destinations are essentially communities (Blank 1989). Accordingly, a community-based approach to tourism development which considers the needs and interests of the popular majority alongside the benefits of economic growth ought to be adopted. Community-based tourism development would seek to strengthen institutions designed to enhance local participation and promote the economic, social, and cultural well-being of the popular majority. It would also seek to strike a balanced and harmonious approach to development that would stress considerations such as the compatibility of various forms of tourism with other components of the local economy; the quality of development, both culturally and environmentally; and the divergent needs, interests, and potentials of the community and its inhabitants.

The success of a strategy of tourism development ought not to be measured just in terms of increasing tourist numbers or revenues. Tourism should also be assessed according to how it has been integrated into the broader development goals of existing local communities, as well as the ways in which tourism-related investments and revenues have been used to benefit those communities. Tourism development can indeed be positive for local communities if their needs and interests are given priority over the goals of the industry *per se*. The view that its planning should, above all, respect the desires of local residents is gaining support in the literature. Clark, for example, reports that the findings of the Pacific Area Travel Association, based on research in several countries, assert "that for long-term stability of the [tourism] industry, residential input and positive residential attitudes are essential [and that] local attractions [should] only be promoted when endorsed by residents" (1988:3).

Tourism should be seen as a local resource. Its management according to the needs and interests of local communities ought to be the principal criterion upon which its development is evaluated. Given the polarization that characterizes numerous Third World tourism industries, many analysts call for greater local participation in the sector to permit a more equitable distribution of its costs and benefits (Blank 1989; Wilkinson 1989). However, calls for greater community participation often ignore the well-known tendency of local elites to "appropriate" the organs of community participation for their own benefit. Studies, for example, of Provence, France (Bromberger and Ravis-Giordani 1977), and the Costa Brava, Spain (Morris and Dickinson 1987), show how uncontrolled tourism expansion can result from the skilful manipulation of community organizations by a few dominant local developers. Unless specific measures are taken to encourage meaningful participation in community decision making by members of the popular sectors, including traditionally disadvantaged groups, increased local participation may simply transfer control over development from one elite group to another.

Institutional mechanisms to facilitate popular participation in tourism development may, of course, vary significantly among communities according to local conditions, needs, and interests. Generally, however, tourism planning should be designed to transcend the sterile state-versus-market dichotomy that currently characterizes much development debate. The problem is to find the correct mixture of market orientation and state intervention, given divergent development conditions in individual countries, and then to devise a set of institutional and organizational arrangements that are compatible with this particular mixture. Neither the state nor markets are neutral institutions; both can work for good or ill. The question for tourism strategies should be under what conditions states and markets can work to serve broad development objectives and how to bring about these conditions. Solutions will necessarily be particular to individual countries and will involve more than just economic considerations.

In most countries, increased popular participation in tourism requires institutional reform to provide possibilities for various groups to organize, represent themselves, and exert influence over decision-making. Hierarchical institutional structures and elite-imposed development projects should be replaced by more democratic, two-way planning processes that empower people to design policies in their own interests and build on their own resources to overcome the problems that they will inevitably confront. Institutional mechanisms should create conditions under which strong social partners can participate in decision-making to enable a local consensus or "social contract" to be constructed over how tourism and related development should proceed. Popular organizations and associational groups (e.g., community, indigenous, and environmental groups) should be given an opportunity to take an active and responsible part in the decision-making process, alongside representatives of the tourism industry itself. Since its planning necessarily involves difficult choices over how the costs and benefits of development are to be distributed, tourism strategies must obviously be based on a fair degree of social consensus if they are to be sustained without resort to authoritarianism. This means that tourism planning should be made accountable to local, democratically elected bodies (e.g., municipal, regional, and aboriginal councils). Moreover, the institutional design of tourism planning should facilitate the participation of various social groups that represent the diverse interests of the broader community. This would not only discourage undemocratic, top-down decision making, but also provide opportunities for communities to use their own resources and popular creativity to find locally appropriate methods of tourism development. As Levitt remarks, "development cannot be imposed from without" in a top-down manner, and "is not [simply] about financial flows" and other economic considerations, but fundamentally "concerns the capacity of a society to tap the root of popular creativity, to free up and empower people to exercise their intelligence and collective wisdom" (1990:1592).

State Intervention in Tourism Planning

Tendencies toward socioeconomic polarization in many developing countries underscore the need for more active state involvement if the process of tourism planning is to be more participatory. Market forces by themselves, especially within highly polarized communities, are incapable of resolving issues related to either long-term sustainability or the distribution of costs and benefits generated by tourism. Without state intervention, tourism development will likely lack the cohesion and direction necessary to sustain itself over the long term. Unregulated short-term initiatives which serve the narrow interests of powerful forces in the industry may well jeopardize the sustainability and longer-term tourism potential of many communities upon which majority interests are based. Recently an "action strategy for sustainable tourism development" has been formulated by Nelson (1993:17) which contains a long list of areas in which active state involvement is necessary. This includes undertaking area and sector specific research on overall tourism effects; assisting and supporting lower levels of government to develop their own tourism development strategies in conjunction with conservation strategies; developing standards and regulations for environmental and cultural impact assessments, and monitoring and auditing existing and proposed tourism developments; designing and implementing public consultation techniques and processes in order to involve all stakeholders in making tourism-related decisions; designing and implementing educational and awareness programs which will sensitize people to the issues of sustainable tourism development; developing design and construction standards which will ensure that tourism development projects are sympathetic with local culture and natural environments; ensuring that carrying capacities of tourism destinations reflect sustainable levels of development and are monitored and adjusted appropriately; regulating and controlling tourism in environmentally and culturally sensitive areas, and incorporating tourism in land-use and spatial planning.

In many developing countries, more active involvement by higher levels of the state is needed to coordinate tourism with other economic sectors and national planning objectives. In some cases, coordination may be necessary to ensure that valuable tourism assets are not irreparably damaged by other economic activities (e.g., forestry, mining, oil exploration, and refining). Development of major infrastructure to serve resorts (e.g., roads, airports, electrical grids, and water supply) should also be coordinated to meet not only the demands of the industry, but also broader economic and social needs. In addition, tourism planning should be integrated with national cultural projects such as the promotion of traditional arts and culture or the preservation of cultural heritage sites.

Tourism planning may also be used by the central state to pursue regional development objectives through the encouragement of growth in certain areas rather than others. In some instances, the geographical spread of tourism might be restricted so as to limit some of its socially disruptive impacts; or, depressed areas with high tourism potential might be designated for state support. In Mexico, for example, the state has encouraged a more geographically dispersed pattern of regional growth by planning tourism complexes (e.g., Cancún, Huatulco, Ixtapa-Zihuatanejo, and Los Cabos) in

JOHN BROHMAN   63

outlying and economically depressed areas. According to Collins, the Mexican state has established a number of specific criteria to assist in the planning of these new tourism complexes to meet national development objectives:

> New tourist centers should develop new sources of employment in areas with tourist potential. These areas should be located near important rural centers with low incomes and few alternatives to develop other productive activities in the near future. New resorts should spur regional development with new agricultural, industrial, and handicraft activities in the zones (1979:354).

State promotion of tourism-related development is neither necessarily beneficial nor harmful. There is nothing inherently wrong with increasing state support for new outward-oriented growth sectors such as nontraditional exports or tourism. As with NTEs, though, much depends on the way that tourism meets the needs and interests of the local population and how it fits together with broader social goals of development. Moreover, if tendencies toward polarization are to be avoided, mechanisms will need to be created to ensure a more equitable distribution of the costs and benefits of tourism. In many countries, this may require targeting state intervention (e.g., through credit provisions, technical and marketing assistance) to allow local residents to take better advantage of tourism opportunities. It will also require the integration of tourism with other elements of development planning, especially through the creation of participatory institutions at the local/regional level. Many aspects of local/regional development may be effectively controlled by democratic institutions and planning mechanisms to influence the nature and degree of local participation in the tourism sector; these include the scale and form of tourist development, the speed with which this development takes place, and the manner by which tourism is introduced into a locale.

Alternative Tourism Strategies

Several authors have suggested that, under some circumstances, alternative tourism strategies might be promoted, either by themselves or in concert with mainstream tourism, to encourage more community participation in tourism planning, a more equitable distribution of the costs and benefits of tourism, and more culturally appropriate and environmentally sustainable forms of tourism (e.g., Britton and Clarke 1987; Butler 1990; Dernoi 1981; Jenkins 1982; Smith and Eadington 1992; Weaver 1991). Disillusionment with mass tourism and the many problems it has triggered has led many analysts to turn away from past methods of tourism development in favor of "alternative tourism". Over the past decade, the concept of alternative tourism has emerged as one of the most widely used (and abused) phrases in the tourism literature. In fact, alternative tourism has been used to mean almost anything that can be juxtaposed to conventional mass tourism; travelers who do not take "normal" types of vacations are often lumped together under the general heading of alternative tourism. As Butler notes:

> Like sustainable development [alternative tourism] sounds attractive, it suggests concern and thought, a new approach and philosophy toward an old problem, and it is hard to disagree with... As with sustainable development, [however,] the phrase can mean almost anything to anyone (1992:31).

Nevertheless, there are a number of recurring themes in the alternative tourism literature that may be used to define the concept. First, alternative tourism is thought to consist of smaller-scale, dispersed, low-density developments. Often these developments are located in and organized by villages or communities, where it is hoped they will foster more meaningful interaction between tourists and local residents, as well as be less socially and culturally disruptive than enclave-type resorts. Second, ownership patterns in alternative tourism are weighted in favor of local, often family-owned, relatively small-scale businesses rather than foreign-owned transnationals and other outside capitals. By stressing smaller-scale, local ownership, it is anticipated that alternative tourism will increase multiplier and spread effects within the host community and avoid problems of excessive foreign exchange leakages. Third, alternative tourism encourages community participation in local/regional planning concerning tourism and related development. By creating democratic institutions to allow local residents to participate in decision making, it is expected that more appropriate forms of tourism development will be established that will be viewed positively by local residents. Fourth, alternative tourism emphasizes sustainability, in both an environmental and cultural sense. Alternative tourism ought to be ecologically sound and should avoid the types of environmental damage and conflicts over resource use that have often marred mass tourism developments. Finally, alternative tourism should not denigrate or damage the host culture; instead, it should try to encourage sensitivity and respect for cultural traditions by creating opportunities for education and cultural exchange through interpersonal dialogue and organized encounters.

Most of the attention that has been given to alternative tourism has come in the form of normative statements in the tourism literature rather than from practical examples in the real world. However, there have also been a few developing countries that have initiated new forms of tourism that might be termed alternative. Perhaps the most widely cited of the officially sponsored alternative tourism programs is that of the Lower Casamance region of Senegal, described as an example of "integrated rural tourism" (Bilsen 1987), which has focused on accommodating tourists in traditional Diola dwellings in small villages. Many of the Caribbean islands have also experimented with alternative tourism programs, including the "indigenous and integrated" tourism of St. Vincent (Britton 1977), the "meet-the-people" program of Jamaica (Dernoi 1981), ecotourism in the mountainous interior of Dominica (Weaver 1991), and attempts by Puerto Rico and Guadeloupe to diversify tourism into small-scale accommodations away from resort concentrations (Pearce 1987). A number of Pacific Rim countries have also initiated similar types of alternative tourism programs, including bungalow-type and family-run accommodations located outside the major resort enclave of Bali (Rodenburg 1980) and in some of the outlying islands in French Polynesia (Blanchet 1981), as well as clan-run Tufi guest houses in some isolated areas of Papua New Guinea (Ranck 1980). Ecotourism programs have also been established in a growing number of countries, particularly in Latin America. Most notable is Ecuador's creation of a preservation zone in the Galapagos Islands (Getino 1990), but ecotourism is also growing quickly in countries such as Brazil, Peru, and Costa Rica (Place 1991). Some countries have encouraged small-scale, dispersed tourism based on their cultural and ethno-historical attractions. Latin American countries such as Ecuador, Guatemala, Mexico, and Peru have been particularly successful in promoting such tourism, which has drawn on a mixture of pre-Columbian archaeological sites, colonial Spanish architecture, and contemporary handicraft industries and markets in indigenous areas (Pearce 1989). This type of tourism also tends to appeal to longer-term, younger "adventure travelers" seeking more meaningful cross-cultural relationships than mass tourism can provide. Such adventure tourism may be particularly useful in fostering positive development impacts based on the converging interests of developing economies, indigenous populations, cultural and environmental sustainability, and the tourists themselves (Cutler 1988; Zurick 1992).

Proponents of alternative tourism argue that it provides scope for less negative impacts, yet retains, and in some cases enhances, the positive economic benefits of tourism, and contributes to a more appropriate form of development. As was indicated above, alternative tourism strategies have a number of broadly similar elements, including their stress on small-scale, locally-owned developments, community participation, and cultural and environmental sustainability. However, it should also be remembered that, beyond these broad similarities, the appropriateness of particular strategies should be defined according to the changing conditions and interests of individual countries. What may be appropriate for specific communities, regions, or countries may not be for others. For example, some countries may want alternative tourism strategies to extend development opportunities into remote regions, while others may want to restrict tourism in certain areas for cultural or environmental reasons.

Whatever alternative tourism strategy a country chooses, it should focus on the individuality, uniqueness, and particular strengths of its communities and regions — which may vary from place to place. In virtually all cases, it must also be recognized that a variety of different forms of tourism is needed. At least in the short term, alternative tourism cannot realistically be expected to replace mass tourism in most Third World countries. Nevertheless, it can complement mass tourism in various ways, as well as provide ideas and methods by which mass tourism might be reformed to more resemble an alternative strategy. Making simplistic and idealized comparisons between mass and alternative tourism, by saying that one is necessarily undesirable and the other close to perfection, is empirically inaccurate and grossly misleading (Butler 1992). Moreover, it offers little of practical relevance for most developing countries that need to devise multifaceted, realistic tourism strategies to meet changing conditions and diverse interests.

Even mass tourism need not be foreign controlled, enclavic, unplanned, short-term, culturally destructive, and environmentally unsustainable. With more selective and deliberate planning, community participation, and local control over development, tourism in general can be made to conform more to the objectives of an alternative strategy. Developing countries may avoid many of the problems that have plagued past tourism by stressing a number of interrelated considerations: by contemplating a broader range of tourism options and development paths, by relating special conditions of supply more closely to changing patterns of demand, by linking particular impacts with various elements of different tourism processes, and by involving diverse social groups from the popular sectors of local communities in decision making. This will require a proactive rather than reactive approach toward tourism which stresses a series of balances linking tourism with broader development goals (e.g., economic growth and distributional equity, environmental sustainability, promotion of indigenous cultures, community participation and local control, capital investment and technology transfer). As with nontraditional exports, import substitution, or any other development strategy that has become popularized in recent years, tourism-led development needs to be planned according to such goals if it is to meet the long-term interests of the popular majority rather than the immediate objectives of an elite minority.

CONCLUSIONS

If new directions are not taken, the Third World tourism industry will be threatened by many of the problems that have plagued other outward-oriented development strategies in the South during the postwar era. These problems include excessive foreign dependency contributing to a loss of local control over resources and substantial overseas leakage of tourism earnings; the lack of articulation between tourism enclaves and domestic economic sectors, producing low multiplier and spread effects; the reinforcement of neocolonial patterns of socioeconmomic and spatial polarization; environmental destruction, often involving nonrenewable resources and foundation assets; and rising alienation among the local population of host communities due to the unequal distribution of the costs and benefits of tourism and the perceived loss of cultural identity and social control to outsiders.

Such problems underscore the point that tourism strategies ought to be assessed not just in terms of increasing tourist numbers or revenues, but according to how well tourism has been integrated into the broader development goals of local communities, regions, and countries. For tourism to begin contributing to the broader social, political, and economic goals of development, institutional mechanisms need to be put in place to facilitate the participation of local residents in tourism planning. These institutional mechanisms may vary significantly among communities according to local conditions, needs, and interests. In general, however, tourism planning should be made accountable to local, democratically elected bodies. The institutional design of tourism planning should also facilitate the participation of various social groups that represent the diverse interests of the broader community. Moreover, more active state involvement at various scales is needed to guide tourism according to national planning objectives, coordinate tourism with other economic sectors and provisions of infrastructure, and resolve issues related to overall sustainability and the distribution of costs and benefits generated by tourism.

In many cases, alternative tourism strategies ought to be designed, either by themselves or in concert with mainstream tourism, to provide more appropriate forms of development that reduce the negative impacts and increase the positive effects of tourism. Although the concept of alternative tourism has been used to mean many things by different authors, there are also a number of core elements of the concept that can be used to define a more appropriate development strategy to meet Third World needs. These include a stress on small-scale, locally owned developments that increase local multiplier and spread effects, greater community participation in tourism planning, and more attention for the cultural and environmental sustainability of tourism projects. Beyond these general elements of alternative tourism, however, the appropriateness of particular strategies should be defined according to the changing conditions and interests of individual communities and countries. As with any other development strategy, tourism-led development in the South should be planned to meet the diverse, long-term interests of the popular majority rather than the narrow, immediate goals of an elite minority. □ □

REFERENCES

Bauer, P., and B. Yamey
    1968 Markets, Market Control and Marketing Reform. London: Weidenfeld and
        Nicolson.
Bilsen, F.
    1987 Integrated Tourism in Senegal: An Alternative. Tourism Recreation
        Research 13:19–23.
Black, J.
    1991 Development in Theory and Practice: Bridging the Gap. Boulder: Westview.
Blanchet, G.
    1981 Les Petites et Moyennes Enterprises Polynesiennes. Travaux et Documents
        de L'ORSTOM 136. Paris: ORSTOM.
Blank, U.
    1989 The Community Tourism Industry Imperative: Its Necessity, Opportunities,
        and Potentials. State College: Venture Publishing.
Britton, R. A.
    1977 Making Tourism More Supportive of Small State Development: The Case
        of St. Vincent. Annals of Tourism Research 6:269–278.

Britton, S. G.
   1980 The Spatial Organisation of Tourism in a Neo-Colonial Economy: A Fiji
      Case Study. Pacific Viewpoint 21:144–165.
   1982 The Political Economy of Tourism in the Third World. Annals of Tourism
      Research 9:331–358.
Britton, S. and W. Clarke, editors
   1987 Ambiguous Alternative: Tourism in Small Developing Countries. Suva: The
      University of the South Pacific.
Bromberger, C., and G. Ravis-Giordani
   1977 La Deuxieme Phylloxera? Facteurs, Modalités et Conséquences de
      Migrations de Loisirs dans la Région Provence-Côte d'Azur. Étude Comparée
      de Quelques Cas. Aix-en-Provence: Service Régional de l'Equipement/CETE.
Butler, R.
   1990 Alternative Tourism: Pious Hope or Trojan Horse? Journal of Travel
      Research 28:40–45.
   1992 Alternative Tourism: The Thin Edge of the Wedge. *In* Tourism Alternatives:
      Potentials and Problems in the Development of Tourism, V. Smith and W.
      Eadington, editors, pp. 31–46. Philadelphia: University of Pennsylvania Press.
Butler, R.
   1993 Tourism–An Evolutionary Perspective. *In* Tourism and Sustainable
      Development: Monitoring, Planning, Managing, J. G. Nelson, R. Butler, and
      G. Wall, editors, pp. 27–44. Waterloo: Heritage Resources Centre and
      Department of Geography, University of Waterloo.
Clark, L.
   1988 Planning for Tourism in Far North Queensland. Unpublished paper
      presented at Conference on Frontiers in Australian Tourism, Canberra.
Collins, C. O.
   1979 Site and Situation Strategy in Tourism Planning: A Mexican Case Study.
      Annals of Tourism Research 6:351–366.
Cutler, B.
   1988 Anything for a Thrill. American Demographics 10:38–41.
Dernoi, L.
   1981 Alternative Tourism: Towards a New Style in North-South Relations.
      International Journal of Tourism Management 2:253–264.
Dieke, P.
   1991 Policies for Tourism Development in Kenya. Annals of Tourism Research
      18:269–294.
English, E.
   1986 The Great Escape? An Examination of North–South Tourism. Ottawa: The
      North–South Institute.
Erisman, H.
   1983 Tourism and Cultural Dependency in the West Indies. Annals of Tourism
      Research 10:337–361.
Frobel, H., J. Heinricks, and O. Kreye.
   1980 The New International Division of Labour. Cambridge: Cambridge
      University Press.
Getino, O.
   1990 Turismo y Desarrollo en América Latina. Mexico: Editorial Limusa.
Haberler, G.
   1950 Some Problems in the Pure Theory of International Trade. Economic
      Journal 60:223–240.
Harrison, D., editor
   1992 Tourism and the Less Developed Countries. London: Belhaven Press.
Hills, T., and J. Lundgren
   1977 The impact of Tourism in the Caribbean: A Methodological Study. Annals
      of Tourism Research 4:248–267.
Hong, E.
   1985 The Third World While it Lasts: The Social and Environmental Impact of
      Tourism with Special Reference to Malaysia. Penang: Consumers' Association
      of Penang.
International Monetary Fund

1993 International Financial Statistics Yearbook (annual). Washington DC: International Monetary Fund.

Jenkins, C.
1982 The Effects of Scale in Tourism Projects in Developing Countries. Annals of Tourism Research 9:229–249.

de Kadt, E.
1992 Making the Alternative Sustainable: Lessons from Development for Tourism. *In* Tourism Alternatives: Potentials and Problems in the Development of Tourism, V. Smith and W. Eadington, editors, pp. 47–75. Philadelphia: University of Pennsylvania Press.

Khan, H., F. Chou and E. Wong
1990 Tourism Multiplier Effects on Singapore. Annals of Tourism Research 17:408–418.

Levitt, K.
1990 Debt, Adjustment, and Development: Looking to the 1990s. Economic and Political Weekly 25:1585–1584.

Mansfeld, Y.
1992 Group Differentiated Perceptions of Social Impacts Related to Tourism Development. Professional Geographer 44:377–392.

Matthews, H.
1977 Radicals and Third World Tourism: A Caribbean Focus. Annals of Tourism Research 5:20–29.

Milne, S.
1987 Differential multipliers. Annals of Tourism Research 14:499–515.

Momsen, J.
1986 Linkages Between Tourism and Agriculture: Problems for the Smaller Caribbean   Economies. Seminar Paper No. 45, University of Newcastle upon Tyne, Dept. of Geography.

Morris, A., and G. Dickinson
1987 Tourist Development in Spain: Growth Versus Conservation on the Costa Brava. Geography 72:16–25.

Nash, D.
1989 Tourism as a Form of Imperialism. *In* Hosts and Guests: The Anthropology of Tourism, V. Smith , editor, pp. 37–52. Philadelphia: University of Pennsylvania Press.

Nelson, J.
1993 An Intoduction to Tourism and Sustainable Development with Special Reference to Monitoring. *In* Tourism and Sustainable Development: Monitoring, Planning, Managing, J. G. Nelson, R. Butler, G. Wall, editors, pp. 3–23. Waterloo: Heritage Resources Centre and Department of Geography, University of Waterloo.

Oliver-Smith, A., F. Arrones, and J. Lisón Arcal
1989 Tourist Development and the Struggle for Local Resource Control. Human Organization 48:345–351.

Oppermann, M.
1992 International Tourism and Regional Development in Malaysia. Tijdschrift voor Economische en Sociale Geografie 83:226–233.

Pearce, D.
1987 Tourism Today: a Geographical Analysis. New York: Wiley.
1989 Tourist Development (2nd ed). New York: Wiley.

Pfafflin, G.
1987 Concern for Tourism: European Perspective and Response. Annals of Tourism Research 14:576–579.

Pigram, J.
1992 Alternative Tourism: Tourism and Sustainable Resource Management. *In* Tourism Alternatives: Potentials and Problems in the Development of Tourism, V. Smith and W. Eadington, editors, Philadelphia: University of Pennsylvania Press.

Place, S.
1991 Nature Tourism and Rural Development in Tortuguero. Annals of Tourism Research 18:186–201.

Poirier, R., and S. Wright
1993 The Political Economy of Tourism in Tunisia. Journal of Modern African Studies 31:149–162.

70 THIRD WORLD COUNTRIES

Ranck, S.
1980 The Socio-Economic Impact of Recreational Tourism on Papua New Guinea. *In* Tourism in the South Pacific, D. Pearce, editor, pp. 55–68. UNESCO Man and the Biosphere Report No. 6. Christchurch NZ: National Commission for UNESCO/Department of Geography, University of Canterbury.

Richards, V.
1983 Decolonization in Antigua: Its Impact on Agriculture and Tourism. *In* The New Caribbean: Decolonization, Democracy, and Development, P. Henry and C. Stone, editors, pp. 15–35. Philadelphia: Institute for the Study of Human Issues.

Rodenberg, E.
1980 The Effects of Scale in Economic Development: Tourism in Bali. Annals of Tourism Research 7:177–196.

Seward, A. and B. Spinard, editors
1982 Tourism in the Caribbean: The Economic Impact. Ottawa: International Development Research Centre.

Sinclair, M., and A. Tsegaye
1991 International Tourism and Export Instability. Journal of Development Studies 26:487–504.

Sklair, L.
1990 Regional Consequences of Open-Door Development Strategies: Export Zones in Mexico and China. *In* Third World Regional Development: A Reappraisal, D. Simon, editor, pp. 109–126. London: Paul Chapman.

Smith, V. and W. Eadington, editors
1992 Tourism Alternatives: Potentials and Problems in the Development of Tourism. Philadelphia: University of Pennsylvania Press.

Smith, V., editor
1989 Hosts and Guests: The Anthropology of Tourism. (2nd ed). Philadelphia: University of Pennsylvania Press.

Tsartas, P.
1992 Socioeconomic Impacts of Tourism on Two Greek Isles. Annals of Tourism Research 19:516–533.

Viner, J.
1953 International Trade and Economic Development. Oxford: Clarendon Press.

Weaver, D.
1988 The Evolution of a "Plantation" Tourism Landscape on the Caribbean Island of Antigua. Tijdschrift voor Economische en Sociale Geografie 79:319–331.

Weaver, D.
1991 Alternatives to Mass Tourism in Dominica. Annals of Tourism Research 18:414–432.

Wilkinson, P.
1989 Strategies for Tourism in Island Microstates. Annals of Tourism Research 16:153–177.

World Bank
1993a World Development Report (annual). New York: Oxford University Press.
1993b World Tables (annual). New York: Oxford University Press.

World Tourism Organization
1987 Report of the Secretary-General on the Activities of the Organization. Madrid: World Tourism Organization.
1989 Current Travel and Tourism Indicators. Madrid: World Tourism Organization.
1991 Travel and Tourism Barometer. Madrid: World Tourism Organization.
1993 Yearbook of Tourism Statistics. Madrid: World Tourism Organization.

Zurick, D.
1992 Adventure Travel and Sustainable Tourism in the Peripheral Economy of Nepal. Annals of Association of American Geographers 82:608–28.

Submitted 26 July 1994
Resubmitted 30 November 1994
Accepted 21 December 1994
Refereed anonymously
Coordinating Editor: Paul F. Wilkinson

[2]

INTERNATIONAL JOURNAL OF TOURISM RESEARCH
Int. J. Tourism Res. **2**, 171–187 (2000)

Fair Trade In Tourism

Robert Cleverdon[1]* and Angela Kalisch[2]

[1]*Business School, University of North London, Stapleton House, 277–281 Holloway Road, London N7 8HN, UK*

[2]*Policy Co-ordinator 'Fair Trade in Tourism', Tourism Concern, London, UK*

ABSTRACT

Tourism as an industry is increasing rapidly in developing countries. Due to historical inequality in global trading relationships on the basis of 'core–periphery' dependency, globalisation and liberalised free trade, mainstream mass tourism reinforces the social and economic disadvantages of southern destinations. The 'Fair Trade Movement' has sought to redress unequal trading by promoting fair trade in commodities with small producers in the South, enabling them to take control over the production and marketing process and challenging the power of transnational corporations. This paper examines the feasibility of fair trade in tourism. It explores the obstacles and opportunities that might lead to establishing a definition of fair trade in tourism, incorporating criteria that would be workable and practical for both partners in the South and North. Copyright © 2000 John Wiley & Sons, Ltd.

Received 18 October 1997· Revised 16 July 1998; Accepted 10 September 1998

Keywords: unequal trading relations; social and economic inequality; fair trade in services; control; capital and land ownership; distribution of benefits.

* Correspondence to: R. Cleverdon, University of North London, Stapleton House, 277–281 Holloway Road, London N7 8HN

INTRODUCTION

Increase of tourism in developing countries

Tourism in developing countries is on the increase, with growth rates exceeding those of developed countries. Between 1980 and 1992, tourism receipts in developing countries increased from 3.0% to 12.5%, which makes an average of 8.4%. World Tourism Organization (WTO) in Burns and Holden, 1995). Although the developed countries still dominate the main world share of tourism receipts at 60%, arrivals and receipts are decreasing, particularly in Europe. Europe's share of international tourist arrivals has dropped from 65.56% in 1980 to 60.13% in 1993, North America's share of arrivals in the same period has dropped from 16.65% to 15.11%. The sharpest rise has been recorded in the Asia–Pacific region, from 7.37% in 1980 to 13.58% in 1993 (WTO, 1995 in Tourism Concern, 1996). As short-haul destinations in the Mediterranean have begun the process of saturation, western Europeans are attracted by cheap long-haul package tours to destinations in tropical, exotic locations, frequently marketed by the industry in the North as paradise. Africa, Asia and the Pacific have become fashionable, affordable and easily accessible to the average middle-income European citizen. The hedonistic sun, sea and sand mentality of those cheap short-haul charters with the emphasis on lowest price rather than quality threatens to infiltrate the developing South. Recent reports indicate that beaches in Goa, Thailand (already under considerable environmental threat) and South Africa are beginning to be appropriated by fun-seeking all-night ravers, high on drugs such as hashish and ecstasy. Although environmental groups are trying to fight against this trend to retain some ecological balance and cultural integrity, ra-

172   R. Cleverdon and A. Kalisch

vers and 'clubbers' (the majority from Britain) state that 'the world is our oyster'. There are a million beautiful beaches. It's a free world and it's our money to spend where we like' (Williamson, 1997).

Tourism reinforces social and economic inequality

Tourism has become the most important earner of foreign currency in most developing countries. For those who have no other competitive export commodity base it has become the only export, the mono-crop (Tourism Concern, 1996). The arguments condoning mass tourism in developing countries emphasise that any money spent by tourists there is benefiting the economy and bringing some wealth to the people there. However, there is ample evidence that although some of the more fortunate sections of the society, ruling elites, landowners, government officials or private businesses might benefit, the poor, landless, rural societies are getting poorer, not just materially but also in terms of their culture and resources. Eviction and displacement for construction of tourism resorts, rising land, food and fuel prices, and commoditisation of cultural assets are just some examples (de Kadt, 1979; Kent, 1983; O'Grady, 1990; Patterson, 1992; Monbiot, 1994; Equations, 1995). Far from bringing economic prosperity to the developing world, tourism has great potential to reinforce social inequality and economic dependency. Contemporary mainstream tourism has to be seen as a part of the existing trade system built on classic liberal economic theories of 'comparative advantage', the 'trickle down effect' and modernisation (Bauer, 1983; Rostow, 1991). Opposing theories of dependency and underdevelopment elaborate the historical relationships of the core to the periphery—the industrialised metropoles to the agricultural economies of the developing countries (Hall, 1994). 'Centres or metropoles exploit peripheries or satellites through the mechanism of unequal exchange' (Harrison, 1992 p. 9). This unequal exchange is fostered by the co-operation between wealthy and powerful elites in developing countries and the metropolitan centres and economic benefits being either repatriated to metropolitan

centres or directed into channels controlled by the elites (Lea, 1988; Barrat-Brown, 1993. Peet (1991 p. 48) highlights the unfavourable terms of trade for developing countries as a result of 'classical economic theory of trade' whereby products of the centre have higher costs attached, 'while devaluing the exports of the periphery'. He concludes that 'unequal exchange is 'a hidden mechanism of surplus extraction and economic stagnation in the periphery'. Barratt-Brown (1993 p. 43) states that unequal trading relations 'have become incorporated in the operations of the large transnational company' throughout the Third World, who 'with their control over both buying and selling of the goods entering international trade, provide the final explanation for the weakness of the millions of small Third World producers in the world market'.

FAIR TRADE

Within the current climate of free trade and globalisation, where transnationals from the 'metropoles' dominate the tourism industry as any other industry in the developing countries, concepts of ethical trading and investment practices, human rights issues, social and environmental accountability of corporations are slowly appearing on the agenda of boardroom discussions. Consumer and media pressure, spurred by the initiatives of nongovernmental organisations (NGOs) such as the Global Supermarkets Campaign by Christian Aid (Bellos, 1997) and the possibility of competitive advantage, not to forget a basis of social consciousness on the part of some of the companies, represent the driving forces of a change in trading relationships with producers in the South.

The concept

The concept of fair trade as a mark of distinction for a particular trading process and product, and distinguished from free trade, is beginning to make inroads into the mainstream business world. In the UK, the Fair Trade Foundation (FTF) assists companies in implementing fair trade practices in the development of their products in order to grant them a licence for the use of the Fair Trade

Mark.

Products such as coffee, tea, chocolate, nuts and handicrafts have developed from a niche market in the early 1990s to a place on the supermarket shelf. Cafedirect, a fair trade coffee brand commands 3% of the market. It worked its way into supermarkets just 2 years after its inception in 1989, when Safeways in Scotland began to stock it as a result of consumer pressure. The British Supermarket Companies, Sainsbury's and the Co-op (CWS — Co-operative Wholesale Society) are in close negotiation with the FTF to develop ethical trading practices with their suppliers in the South (FTF, personal communication, 24 June 1997). Tesco, albeit after pressure from NGOs and the media, have set up an ethical trading monitoring group. B&Q, the do-it-yourself store, 'have introduced independent monitoring of foreign labour conditions and from 1999 will only buy timber from sustainable sources approved by an independent certifier' (Bellos, 1997). The Bodyshop, a multinational corporation set up in Britain in the 1970s, selling hair and skin care products, has long prided itself on being established along socially and environmentally responsible policy guidelines incorporating fair trade (The Bodyshop, 1996).

Consumer Response

Market research indicates that consumers are beginning to demand more responsibility and ethical standards in business. A Gallup poll in 1996 established that 74% and 92% of consumers believe that standards of honesty and of behaviour, respectively, are getting worse. Sixty-seven per cent of adults claim to consider a company's ethical stance when buying products and 57% of adults believe corporate ethics have declined over the past 5 years. An NOP survey, commissioned by Christian Aid in 1993 found that 68% claimed that they 'would pay more for fair trade products' and 85% agreed that 'workers in the Third World are exploited and do not get enough for their produce' (Ogilvy and Mather, 1996). Whether such statements made at a particular point in time would translate into action and result in a boom in fair trade products would have to be seen.

Further research into attitudes and behaviour patterns of tourism consumers in relation to ethical issues needs to identify whether good intentions and ethical awareness would be translated into actual purchasing decisions. Price, performance and convenience are deemed to be the prime criteria for consumers' decisions. Existing research in psychological studies recognises a discrepancy between attitudes and behaviour amongst so-called green consumers (Balooni, 1997). This means that a consumer, concerned about poverty in the Third World might support fair trade in a questionnaire survey, but when it comes to booking a holiday, old habits and considerations of finance and convenience could well determine their purchasing decision.

Nevertheless, the figures above reveal a general mistrust in business and corporate behaviour among consumers that needs to be built on by fair trade in tourism supporters.

Definition of Fair Trade

The Fair Trade Movement is represented by organisations at European and international level: International Federation for Alternative Trade (IFTA)/and the European Fair Trade Association (EFTA).

According to EFTA, the definition of fair trade is:

(1) to support efforts of partners in the South who by means of co-operation, production and trade strive for a better standard of living and fairness in the distribution of income and influence;
(2) to take initiatives and participate in activities aimed at establishing fair production and trade structures in the South and on the global market (EFTA, 1996).

The Max Havelaar Organisation, the Fair Trade Mark Organisation in countries such as The Netherlands, Switzerland and France and the Fair Trade Foundation in the UK, set up by a number of NGOs, including Christian Aid, Traidcraft Exchange and Oxfam conclude that: 'Fair trade aims to ensure a fairer deal for Third World Producers in international trade … by influencing mainstream commercial practices and consumer attitudes, so that consumer demand in the UK for a greater availability of more equitably traded products

174   *R. Cleverdon and A. Kalisch*

can be both stimulated and met. It is hoped that resources may be available to ... encourage discussion and action on fair trade issues among manufacturers, retailers and the public' (Tourism Concern, 1996).

Fair Trade criteria

The Fair Trade Foundation in its Third World Supplies Charter lays down the criteria used for assessing suppliers and trading relationships. Apart from minimum standards that should be met relating to international labour standards on working conditions, health and safety, equality of treatment and forced labour, more precise criteria have been developed that might be adapted to different product groups.

The following are based on the Cafedirect criteria.

(1) *Fair Price*: should be fixed by producers (service providers) in consultation with purchasing partners, allow a decent standard of living, 'internalise' any social, cultural and environmental degradation and reflect a long-term trading relationship.
(2) *Premium*: added to basic price to consumer, which providers can use to develop community infrastructure, such as schools, hospitals or training programmes to improve skills.
(3) *Advance payments*: deposits or payments of 50% of the price in advance are a crucial component to enable local small-scale businesses with no access to capital to invest in their 'product'. Present practices among tour operators of paying too late or not at all in the case of cancellations cause serious debts and degradation of the product.
(4) *Long-term relationship*: contracts incorporating future commitment provide security and enhance credibility of partners in the South for obtaining credit from conventional lending institutions. It allows for a gradual improvement of product, skills, experience and business acumen for local people.
(5) *Direct trading relationship*: fair trade partnerships cut out the middle men' ('coyotes' in the coffee trade). In tourism an analysis of

the operations would have to reveal to what extent this aspect affects the trading relationship.

Factors of distinction from free trade

Although the term 'fair' used in the free trade context is semantically similar to that used by the Fair Trade Movement it is essential to highlight the features that make it distinct from a free trade approach.

(1) The main aim of fair trade is to *fight against poverty in the Third World*. The intention is to redress historical trade imbalances created by colonial practices and by the politics of dependency, which have produced a comparative disadvantage to developing countries in relation to the industrialised metropoles, rather than a 'comparative advantage'. This disadvantage embodied by the low level of prices and demand of their primary export commodities and the high prices of imported manufactured goods from the metropoles has actually been caused by the free trade ideology. It is considered to be the root of the extreme levels of poverty in those countries.

'Famines do not occur, they are organised by the grain trade' (Berthold Brecht, quoted in George, 1986).

(2) *It brings the consumer in touch with the producer* (especially so in tourism). Normally, the consumer knows little about the people behind the production process. Most products are made by large impersonal multinationals, with the labour of hundreds of people in standardised conditions, people who usually have no say in the production process. The only information consumers have of those companies is through highly sophisticated advertising. Fair trade products attempt to provide the consumer with honest information about the producers and the details of the production process. It gives consumers a chance to be actively involved in fighting against poverty, not through charity or donations but by means of a just exchange of goods.
(3) Fair trade *targets small-scale producers*. They

are people at the bottom of the economic scale of productivity who would otherwise be waiting in vain for the 'trickle down effect'. They have few or no assets but enough skills to sell a product or their labour to earn a living. Fair trade offers them fair wages and working conditions, credit and loans at affordable interest rates, as well as advance payments and professional assistance with product and skills development. As such it not only brings the consumer and producer closer into contact but also creates a symbiotic relationship between the purchasing partner and producer. It creates a framework for collaboration and improvement rather than exploitation. Without fair trade these small-scale businesses would have little chance of gaining access to a world market, dominated by transnational corporations.

(4) The components of the trading method are intended *to strengthen the partner's position* in a proactive way, to increase their bargaining position. This includes assistance from northern partners with product development, access to marketing techniques and control over image and representation.

Fair trade in services/tourism — characteristics of difference to commodities

So far, all the products that carry the Fair Trade Mark are primary commodities. Little or nothing is known about fair trade in services, let alone fair trade in the hospitality sector. Ethical investment policies have been developed in the banking and investment sector, such as the Co-operative and Triodos Banks, and Shared Interest which is organised along the lines of a building society, providing credit for producer groups in the South. Considering that the service sector has been outgrowing the manufacturing sector and that tourism, a 'multi-sectoral service activity' (Jenkins, 1994) is claimed to be the largest industry and the leading job creator in the 21st century (WTTC, 1995, 1997) it may be high time to examine how fair trade could become an integral part of the tourism industry's partnerships with southern host destinations.

The initial experience of fair trade in commodities helps to determine to what extent it could be adapted in tourism. On a broad level, the fair trade criteria that have been developed for commodities are also relevant to tourism. However, the economic implications and the feasibility of issues such as the fixing of price levels or long-term relationships in an economic climate where the success of the industry is determined by price wars and short-term, flexible investments in fashionable destinations, will require careful research.

Fair trading organisations are non-profit making. With the exception of the Bodyshop, most of the trading organisations based in the North are non-profit making, mostly NGOs, many with a religious mission. They have been motivated by social and moral responsibility and are committed to the principle of using trade as a means of relieving poverty by increasing self-reliance in grassroots communities in the South. Cafedirect operates as a company and the trading arm of NGOs such as Traidcraft and Oxfam. Although Traidcraft and Oxfam, with a strong tradition in fair trade in commodities, have run holidays for their members to the projects they operate abroad none of them have as yet been active in the professional promotion of holidays to the broader public along fair trade criteria.

Small and medium independent tour operators who practice some of the fair trade policies, such as direct trading relationships, equitable partnerships and community benefits, currently exist in the UK. The issue for them, however, in contrast to grant receiving NGOs is one of economic viability and survival rather than of altruism or a moral commitment to equality and poverty alleviation. They could, on the other hand, represent a starting point for a more intensive development process of an economically viable fair trade operation in tourism, which could eventually influence mainstream tour operators.

Tourism's 'product' is intangible and invisible. Commodities such as tea and coffee are easily definable and tangible. Tourism, however, is a multisectoral service activity, incorporating many diverse service functions and overlapping with many different sectors, such as transport and agriculture. As a 'product' it is

R. Cleverdon and A. Kalisch

intangible. It is an invisible export trade item, the raw material of which is the living organism and dynamic of people (generally called 'hosts'), cultures and natural resources (Tourism Concern, 1996). The product that is being traded on the world market therefore is different from any other product within the world trading system. In fact, the people who are part of this living organism might question whether they would want to be regarded as a product. Nevertheless, it is packaged as such for profit maximisation.

Burns and Holden (1995) list a number of definitions that have evolved in the past 20 years in tourism studies. It is a seen as a 'system' (Mill and Morrison, 1985), a 'study of man away from his usual habitat, the industry and impacts' (Jafari, 1977) a 'pan-humanistic process' (Nash and Smith, 1991) or an industry. Burns and Holden (1995) come to the conclusion that in view of its complexity it should be regarded as a 'traded commodity, displaying some of the characteristics of the trade in commodities (prices set in metropoles, being subject to market manipulation, and the tenuous links between cost of production and selling price)'. As such it has been transformed from pilgrimage and education into a standardised global consumer mass product.

Under normal circumstances a product for sale would be processed from raw materials. The raw materials and the processing know-how constitute the asset and the capital of the producers, which gives them the competitive edge on the market. In tourism it could be argued that the capital itself is for sale, it is then processed by the purchasers, the tour operators, into a packaged commodity and sold to their customers, who consume the product on the producers' soil, the raw material of the product. Selling the capital makes little business sense (Schumacher, 1974; Goodland *et al.*, 1992). Surrendering the components of the process that make it competitive to the purchaser is economically unviable for the producer and deprives them of any bargaining power. The capital is used up gradually, because the producers are not gaining enough from the sale to replenish it, if indeed it is replenishable. Some natural resources, such as ground water and topsoil, sometimes cannot be replaced (ECOMOST, 1994).

The success of the tourism industry depends on low, flexible prices. Coffee has a *world price,* which can be used as a means of setting a fair price. Cafedirect have pledged to pitch their price at a certain percentage above the world price whatever it might be. In tourism no such ceiling exists. The implications of standardising prices on a global level would need serious attention. Indeed, the question might arise whether price is actually the most important issue in the discussion on fair trade in tourism or whether other issues, such as the distribution of benefits and democratic control at local level, are of greater relevance.

The quality of the product is of utmost importance for its commercial viability, both in commodities as in tourism. Consumers will not buy a product purely for ethical reasons. It has to correspond with their taste, with 'trends and fashions' (EFTA, 1995). The price difference to conventional products (or premium) needs to be carefully evaluated. If the price is too high it will not sell.

Commercialisation of hospitality − a new concept in developing countries. All the fair trade commodities, such as bananas, coffee, tea and handicrafts, have historically been export products by the countries involved. The tradition of agricultural and craft production in developing countries has thus created a wealth of experience and skills among local communities that assists them in managing and controlling their own production processes.

Tourism is not a traditional industrial activity in most developing countries. The concept of hospitality as a free gift to a travelling guest or friend is centuries old in many cultures and a particular aspect of rural and remote societies. Commercialising such a gift in monetary forms, commercialising the relationship between host and guest is a new process to which most people who do not belong to local elites are initially unaccustomed (Zarkia, 1996). Analysing the socio-cultural and psychological effects of this process is not the purpose of this paper. Suffice to say, however, that the difference between trading a traditional commodity such as sugar or tea and trading tourism is substantial. If fair trade targets grass-roots communities that have little experience of using tourism as an export trade item, this needs to be addressed. It involves a profound learning and development process not just on an economic level but also in terms of psychological adjustment.

No history of collective organisation. Producer communities in the South are usually organised as collectives in the form of co-operatives, many of which have been in existence when fair trade purchasers from the North approached them. Oxfam deals with many groups who are linked to the development work they do. Some of the fair trade coffee producers also deal with conventional partners, in some cases transnationals. Approximately 25% of their business might be with fair trade partners (Cafedirect, personal communication, 30 September 1996).

In structural terms, the collective organisation of tourism operations for small-scale tourism providers and producers is a new and unaccustomed concept. Tourism is normally based on competitive entrepreneurship. Collective co-ordination of and decision-making over the diversity of tourism activities in any location, the promotion and marketing process, product development and financial planning would need to be approached differently from a co-operative selling coffee. Creating a professional high quality leisure and pleasure product which is acceptable to western taste and western expectations within the context of Third World underdevelopment is a difficult and sometimes impossible task. Satisfying the conflicting needs of the western tourist for a certain level of familiarity, comfort and security combined with the need for the exotic, strange, mysterious and adventurous is a sophisticated skill. Any fair trade in tourism policy needs to address that, either in the context of how western expectations are shaped or how communities are going to respond to the demand. Whatever the definition of fair trade in tourism, the 'product' or the tourist 'experience' that is for sale has to be attractive to the consumer and commercially viable so that it can bring the desired benefits for all stakeholders involved.

Social and cultural intrusion. Commodities are transported out of the producer community. Producers will not usually come into contact with the consumer or the culture where their product is sold. The fact that tourism is consumed in the place of origin puts it into a substantially different realm from any other commodity. Exporting coffee or tea might have environmental implications. The effects of certain planting methods and the 'carrying capacity' of a plantation can be measured and addressed with some degree of scientific planning. However, the 'demonstration effect' and the social implications of encountering the consumer face to face is not something that needs to be taken into account in coffee production. The effects of this encounter have been analysed in detail by sociologists and anthropologists (de Kadt, 1979; Smith, 1989; Cohen, 1993; Hitchcock *et al.*, 1993; Crick, 1994; Boissevain, 1996; Selwyn, 1996). Although their analysis as to the changes that can be directly attributed to tourism and those which might be exacerbated by tourism varies, they all come to the conclusion that the presence of the tourist in a developing country is an important factor in changing cultures and social structures.

A positive consequence of this encounter in fair trade terms could be the fact that the consumer is able to see the benefits of his/her particular contribution in buying a fair trade holiday, while also monitoring whether fair trade criteria are being implemented.

Definition of fair trade in tourism

As yet a definition of fair trade in tourism does not exist. At present, research is being undertaken in a joint initiative by the University of North London, Volunteer Service Overseas (VSO) and Tourism Concern (TC), an NGO campaigning for just and responsible tourism, to achieve a definition of fair trade in tourism for the industry that reflects a North–South collaboration, is realistic and workable in practice. It is intended that it should not just be conceived as a theoretical statement merely to be used as a public relations exercise and a marketing ploy to provide a competitive edge.

The term 'fair' in the classic economic free trade and modernisation context, is used to ensure fairness in competition among businesses in the North. In the UK, the Fair Trading Office has been charged with overseeing that process. On a global scale, the General Agreement on Trade in Services (GATS) is intended as 'a negotiated freedom of fair trade in services' in the context of 'obstacle-free competition' for the countries involved. 'Level playing fields' should thus be created to enable foreign companies 'equal access' to natural resources and investment nationally and internationally (WTO, 1995).

'Fair Trade' as examined in this paper is about providing a better deal for producers or, in the case of tourism, service providers in the South. This approach could be seen as emanating from theories of underdevelopment and dependency in the 1970s, which were based in the premise that the 'existing economic structures had been strongly stacked against the economic interests of developing countries' (Cho, 1995). Thus, in formulating a definition for fair trade in tourism, the South needs to play a determinant role. Industry practices in the North need to be examined as to whether and how they might create or reinforce unequal trading patterns. Company policies and codes of conduct can be expected to refer to principles of responsibility and accountability not just to shareholders but also to the public and to trading partners in the southern destinations. Developing and implementing fair trade policies, however, has to be done in collaboration with stakeholders in the South to ensure a southern perspective in all aspects of the trading operation. At present, the concept of fair trade is largely infused by a northern perspective.

Preliminary consultation with representatives from southern organisations involved in tourism has resulted in a more concise awareness as to the prerequisites for fair trade in tourism. It needs to address the root causes of inequality in tourism as perceived by grass-roots communities in the South: i.e. *access to capital, ownership of resources, distribution of benefits and control over representation of the destination in tourist-generating countries, and it needs to ensure transparency of tourism operations, including price and working conditions.* Research into 'fair trade tourism' needs to establish who benefits by how much and in what way. This needs to be examined against a background of historic structures of benefit distribution and of the political and social dynamics in a

particular location. (Richter 1993, p. 192)

Access to capital. As outlined earlier, developing economies as a whole have been submitted on a global level to an 'unequal exchange' through the concept of comparative advantage. Any benefits that do flow into countries, in the form of foreign investment, aid or loans generally do not reach communities at grass-roots level that are involved in a daily struggle to overcome often extreme levels of poverty. They are too poor to qualify for credit or loan and are unable to make any investments enabling them to escape from the poverty trap. Barratt-Brown (1993, p. 43) considers the 'real inequality' in trade to be based on the fact that

> the machinery and the new technology together with the capital available for investment to increase productivity, are in the hands of the capitalists in the developed First World economies. Third World industrialists must find their capital and equipment mainly from outside their frontiers and pay for both at First World prices or borrow at First World interest rates.

By making credit available at favourable interest rates or in return for goods or services, fair trade can break the 'vicious circle of poverty'.

Burns and Holden (1995, p. 92) create a 'virtuous circle of economic development' as opposed to the 'vicious circle of poverty'. In the virtuous circle the escape route from the poverty trap is marked by an injection of capital as a pump-priming initiative. The result is an increase in capital and higher productivity. The ideas inherent in fair trade of advance payments and microcredit or credit directly paid to producer organisations by ethical investment companies in the North, such as Shared Interest, could provide an answer to this issue.

Ownership. Land ownership, land use and rising land prices as a result of tourism development are among the most contentious issues in tourism in the South. Land is the most precious and sought after resource by rich capitalists seeking to invest and by governments seeking to gain from the investment. In this process of land acquisition the beaches occupied for centuries by fisherfolk, the forests nurtured by tribals and the savannahs and deserts guarded by nomads who traditionally have had unquestioned land rights as part of their livelihood have been taken away without consultation or compensation. Such compensation as has been granted has often been inappropriate. Groups such as the Maasai in Kenya have been excluded from National Parks and fertile land to make room for tourism developments and conservation projects (Monbiot, 1994). Fair trade would need to ensure that people's livelihoods are enhanced rather than destroyed. 'Land must ... serve all people rather than simply those who control it. Development must become the tool of those who need development most — the homeless and the dispossessed — rather than benefiting only the developers' (Monbiot, 1997).

Distribution of benefits. Hoogvelt (1982) argues that economic growth and development depend on who owns the 'productive activities'. If they are owned by foreigners income will be remitted abroad rather than invested in the country of production. Even if they are owned by the state, it will depend on the political and social development policies of national and local governments whether the poorest section of society or the people involved (either actively or passively) in the tourism process will reap the benefits of the trading process. Research indicates that all too often it serves to 'deepen social inequalities' and widen the gap between those with access to capital and those who are landless and on the threshold of subsistence (Hoogvelt, 1982; Richter, 1993).

In tourism, distribution of benefits and the control over the distribution process is largely in the hands of northern business, in particular the transnationals. The way in which most package, charter and 'all-inclusive' tours are organised, none of the money ever paid by the consumer in the North even touches the host destination. The tour operators have the power to determine where they send their customers and how they portray the destination in their brochures without being obliged to consult with any stakeholders in the destination (Jenkins, 1994).

Stakeholders. Fair trade targets small-scale producers, without the means to gain access to the world market. In order to ensure that benefits do reach the people who need them most these producers or providers need to be identified. Owing to the complexity and diversity of tourism operations in the destinations, owned privately or publicly, locally or foreign, often incorporating a substantial informal sector such as ungraded family-run hotels, guest houses, paying guest accommodation or taxis and rickshaws, it is often hard to establish who to make business with. In many developing countries tourism has developed on the basis of private sector initiative, often in an unplanned, fragmented and uncoordinated manner by a government lacking the professional experience and understanding of modern tourism development (Pattullo, 1996). Even if tourism has begun to be incorporated into national economic development plans, lack of funding and experience has placed tourism development largely into the realm of private sector initiative and investment. If issues of distribution and ownership are to be addressed, an analysis of who is involved or affected and how any benefits are distributed in any given location needs to take place.

The terms 'local' or 'community' are often used in the context of people who are living in a tourist resort. For the purpose of Fair Trade, they need to be clearly identified as 'interest groups' or 'stakeholders' involved in or affected by tourism.

Transparency of trading operations. One of the strongest criticisms levelled at transnational corporations is the fact that they have a great deal of power over the economic resources and the stability of a country, yet they are in no way accountable to either the government or the people (Korten, 1996; Vidal, 1997; Clarke, 1995). Most companies consider the responsibility to their shareholders, their dividends and profit levels, but not to the public or their trading partners.

Fair trade in tourism could introduce a process of opening up trading operations to an independent monitoring and verification process against a set of bench marks covering minimum labour standards, fair trade criteria and the development of an ethical code of conduct (NEF/CIIR, 1997).

The idea of environmental accounting has begun to capture the imagination of innovative and concerned businesses, added to this a system of social accounting would introduce a method of examining the validity of a people-centred approach by way of a stakeholder consultation (Traidcraft Exchange, 1996; The Bodyshop, 1996).

Representation of southern tourist destinations in tourist-generating countries. In order to sell conventional mass tourism, or in many cases even specialised ecotourism to long-haul destinations in the South, the industry in the North uses images and descriptions of destinations that tend to mystify and romanticise by playing on the consumers' dreams and fantasies. This representation often provides a distorted and unrealistic impression of the country. In many cases, stereotypes, racism, sexism and colonial behaviour structures are reinforced (Dann, 1996; Hutt, 1996; Crick, 1996). It is usually developed for the purpose of profit-maximisation for the company to influence customer choice without consultation of stakeholders in tourist resorts. Such marketing also substantially tends to influence tourist attitudes to people and cultures in the destinations.

Equality in the trading partnership would mean that stakeholders in the South, including 'small-scale' stakeholders, have a voice and control over the way they are represented to potential visitors from the North. In this context, the issue of intellectual property rights would need to be more closely examined (Aotearoa Maori Tourism Federation, 1994).

OBSTACLES TO THE IMPLEMENTATION OF FAIR TRADE IN TOURISM

International trade agreements

Discussion on fair trade in tourism must take into account the global economic context, which, it could be argued, is moving in the opposite direction. Although the GATS is hailed as introducing fairer trading practices between nations, which should give developing countries free market access to developed

countries, the practical reality does not always bear this out. The negotiations of the Uruguay Round were permeated with criticisms from developing countries with respect to the advantageous position of the rich industrial nations, which they claimed would be maintained with the implementation of the GATS. According to these criticisms, the GATS was designed to make it easier for foreign companies, particularly transnationals, to gain access to developing countries, encouraged by favourable incentives, whereas developing economies could be denied similar advantages in developed countries because most transnationals are based in the North and restrictive trade and immigration policies, expensive set-up costs and uncompetitive business practices would impede southern nations from gaining mutual advantages (Equations, 1995; Tourism Concern, 1996). The Multilateral Agreement on Investment (MAI), currently under negotiation, within the Organisation for Economic Co-operation and Development (OECD), will in effect give investors a free hand to create a business climate that will essentially obliterate any regulations that could hamper the capital accumulation of a company investing in any foreign country. The agreement gives legal authority to investors to repatriate profits, acquire ownership over resources and capital assets in the host country, ban performance requirements in exchange for market access, such as investment in the local economy and responsible behaviour, and to lower wages, working conditions, environmental and consumer-safety standards. Governments of nation states will have little control over such trading practices. They will, in fact find themselves having to repeal and modify their own national laws to fit in with the requirements of this agreement (Monbiot, 1997; WWF, 1997.

Competition within the tourism industry

Competition in the UK tourism industry is fierce. The three largest companies, dominating the mass market, Thomson, Airtours and First Choice command 80% of all package tours (Madeley, 1995). Vertical integration has enabled them to gain a stronghold over the cheapest possible prices, including increasingly holidays to long-haul destinations, such as Goa, Kenya and Thailand. Their success relies on keeping the price low and keeping ahead of the price war game with their competitors. Small and medium-sized tour operators complain about the stranglehold these companies exert over them through, for example, ownership of the travel agents which demand high commissions for displaying their brochures and discriminate in favour of the owners in the sale of their holidays (Farrell *et al.*, 1996). As fair trade requires raising the price in favour of the producers and implementing an environmental and social code of conduct, thus raising the quality of the product, it might seem difficult to convince mainstream tour operators of the commercial advantage of such an initiative. Critical voices from within the industry state that the conventional tour operator pays little attention to ethical principles and believes in shifting the responsibility and accountability for the company's trading practices on to host destinations and governments (Focus Group FTinT, 1997[1]). This is borne out by research, which indicates that tour operators and other components of the industry are aware of the need for sustainable practices but would only be encouraged to implement them if they were cost-saving devices (Forsyth, 1996). 'Profit-maximisation remains paramount in the decision-making of tourism enterprises' (Cater, 1991), and Rees, in an argument supported by Mehmet (1995), states that 'historic levels of profit are not compatible with sustainable development' (Rees, 1990, in Cater, 1991).

The Niche Product

Fair trade products currently comprise around 3% of the commodity market. Small and medium-sized tour operators comprise about 12% of the tourism market. Considering this small market position and the competitive

pressures of those operators, the question arises whether the development of fair trade tourism as a niche product could be viable, both in commercial terms but also in terms of making an impact on the world trading system. Should the priority be for large-scale companies to adopt a code of conduct incorporating fair trade, and implementing it with the help of publicly approved independent monitoring procedures? Or would it be more efficient to develop exemplary fair trade holidays, which could be used to act as catalysts and be adopted by mainstream tour operators in the same way that supermarkets are beginning to stock fair trade products?

Experience in primary commodities demonstrates that creating competitive and public pressure by the introduction of a fair trade product on the market does move mainstream companies to review their practices and implement change. It also creates a choice and an alternative for the consumer, who can actively evaluate the different trading processes through personal experience. However, if one argues that in mass tourism the product currently traded on the world market is inherently inequitable, it would follow that not only the trading relationship and the method would have to be changed, but *the nature of the 'product' itself* and the way it is promoted by the industry. Less emphasis should be placed on the one hand on cheapness relying on low price and low wage economies in the South, and on the other on expensive, capital intensive investments inappropriate to the local ecosystem and culture but attractive to high-spending, high-quality tourists. More emphasis needs to be placed on quality and equality, with lower levels of western consumption patterns. This will require a more complex and thorough development and public education process. One of the determinant factors in the quality of the tourism product should be the economic well-being of the host community.

Any fair trade tourism operation would currently have to survive in a free-market context. In order to be economically viable, it would have to be promoted as professionally as mainstream holidays but according to a different set of quality criteria. Mass tourism has made travel accessible to a wide section of

---

[1] This was a meeting hosted by Tourism Concern, University of North London and Voluntary Service Overseas. Representatives from developing countries were brought together with European Travel Industry Representatives to find common links and mutual interest in developing Fair Trade. 'FTinT' means Fair Trade in Tourism.

low and middle income people who would otherwise never have been able to afford to travel abroad. Ethics in tourism should not be confined to an expensive niche market for sophisticated 'ego-tourists' (Wheeller, 1993; Munt, 1994). It has to permeate all operations not as an option but as a matter of principle.

OPPORTUNITIES

The climate is right

Over the past 20 years, a commitment to environmental responsibility has become an integral part of many companies' policies. Environmental pressure groups have raised the level of public awareness and mobilised public opinion to exert an influence on economic and political decision-makers. European and national government legislation has proved an important motivating force for businesses to make the necessary resources available to affect change. The media can exert an important influence over a company's public image. Recent publicity of the environmental and human rights practices of large transnationals such as BP and Shell in developing countries have caused enough concern amongst corporate directors to consider policy changes not just to improve their environmental performance but also their human rights record (Beavis and Brown, 1996). The libel case in the UK against McDonalds has demonstrated that it is possible to challenge the power of transnationals and to compel them to make themselves more accountable to the public. These examples also show that in addition to environmental policy, social policy is beginning to become a considered entity in corporate decision-making. The political climate in the UK is beginning to change in such a way that ethics in business are becoming an integral part of discussions on trade.

Sustainable tourism and the industry

In tourism, the World Travel and Tourism Environmental Research Council (WTTERC) has published a comprehensive policy document on 'Environment and Development' (1993), incorporating 'consideration of the local community in development decisions'

and the 'development of forms of tourism appropriate to the local area' (p. 36). The successful implementation of such mission statements would depend on a detailed definition of those concepts.

The World Tourism Organisation has recently published indicators designed to measure social impact and levels of satisfaction among both visitors and local people (Croall, 1996). British Airways (1994) and British Airways Holidays (1997) are addressing environmental issues through impact assessments and guidelines in their brochures to encourage their clients' environmental responsibility and a commitment to support the local economy. These are all initiatives that could be confirmed by an independent monitoring process and built upon to include fair trade criteria.

As with all policy statements, however, there is generally a tendency to pay lip-service and make token gestures, primarily for marketing and promotion purposes (Cater, 1991 p. 19; Forsyth 1996). In relation to fair trade in tourism, concern for the environmental sphere needs to be extended to include issues of human rights, distribution of economic benefits control and ownership, as outlined earlier in this paper. Terms such as 'community participation' and 'consultation' sound politically correct from a northern perspective, but overall little understanding and experience exists (even among the Fair Trade Movement) about the successful implementation of such concepts particularly in tourism. Knowledge of a community-centred approach in tourism, initiated by communities of tourism resorts in the South, particularly in undemocratic political structures, is scant. A superficial approach can lead to confusion, token gestures and disappointment among those communities (Wahab and Pigram, 1997; Betz, 1998). Until such terms are backed up by an integrated action plan, genuine political and financial commitment, necessary resources and practical evidence on the ground it will be difficult to give credence to any such statements on paper.

Open Trading

Amongst alternative trading circles there is now a movement emerging to encourage mainstream businesses to add social account-

Int. J. Tourism Res. **2**, 171–187 (2000)

ing and auditing procedures to their existing financial and environmental accounting processes. Any policy statements relating to social objectives would have to be measured against the company's actual track record, by means of independent monitoring and verification procedures currently under discussion among NGOs (Traidcraft, 1996; NEF/CIIR, 1997). Such a transparent and open trading process would have to determine *measurable targets* that would reflect equitable trading criteria. Organisations such as The Fair Trade Foundation (although resources are limited) and relevant consultancies would be assisting companies in the development process to achieve this, as is currently happening with supermarkets. The aim would not necessarily need to be a Fair Trade Mark as such but a more general seal of approval on the basis of achievable targets. The Fair Trade Foundation believe that the effect that such accreditation would have on business performance and the company's public image with the support of consumer pressure would be sufficient encouragement for companies to become involved in this process (FTF, personal communication, 24 June 1997). Increasingly, a synergy between the business community and NGOs will have to take place recognising their interdependence in creating more responsible and publicly accountable trading patterns.

In tourism, 'measurable' targets for fair trade as yet do not exist. For this to happen, stakeholders in the South at public, private and local community level might have to create a collective consultation and planning process determining fair trade criteria in tourism acceptable to all stakeholders in a particular resort and then become actively involved in specifying the terms of the trading relationship with tourism organisers in the North. Targets would have to embrace a general global dimension, a minimum set of criteria followed by the whole of the industry as well as a set of location-specific criteria, taking into consideration that the organisation and structure of tourism varies considerably in different destinations. They could also allow for a specific alternative fair trade operation to be developed.

Minimum fair trade policies would address

a commitment to the following:

(1) creating *social, cultural and economic benefits* for host destinations, in particular economically stressed communities, and minimising leakage;
(2) being aware of and *respecting national laws* addressing environmental and sociocultural sustainability (the GATS needs to be reviewed with regard to making this possible, without contravening 'free market access' rules);
(3) developing *strong structures of consultation* both between northern tourism organisers and 'host communities' and among key stakeholders in the 'host community', including local people affected but not involved in tourism;
(4) *transparent and open trading operations*, including social and environmental audits independently verified;
(5) *ecological sustainability* on the basis of scientific advice to governments and local people;
(6) *respect for human rights*, including decent working conditions, equality between men and women, avoidance of forced labour, child labour and prostitution.

The possibility for appropriate legislation and regulation of the tourism industry to underpin these objectives might need to be considered.

Fair trade eliminates poverty

One of the main goals of sustainable development discussed at the recent Earth Summit in New York is to relieve (if possible eradicate) poverty in the developing world. There is evidence that fair trade achieves this goal in some areas. Co-operatives in Nicaragua producing fair trade coffee for Cafedirect claim that although unemployment in their country is as high as 60%, their members have employment and have been able to pay off all their debts (Tourism Concern, 1996).

The elements of advance payments, credit and long-term relationship have provided small-scale producer groups with the credibility to obtain loans from conventional lending institutions at favourable interest rates in their locality. They have thus been able to raise their business viability (Cafedirect, personal communication, 1996). Whether similar successes can be achieved by fair trade in tourism has to be seen.

Community-based tourism

Evidence suggests that there are many small-scale initiatives around the world where people in villages or small communities are trying to join the tourism business and make a modest living with scarce resources, sometimes not only out of economic need but also to counter discrimination and abuse of their cultures.

The Maori in New Zealand set up the Aotearoa Maori Tourism Federation in 1988 to 'support the aspirations and needs' of Maori involved in tourism as operators, as investors and as employees' and to research and promote a 'Maori Tourism Product' that reflects Maori culture authentically, interpreted by Maori who have a direct relationship with that culture (Aotearoa Maori Tourism Federation, 1997).

In Venezuela the number of micro-enterprises in tourism is growing. An important sector of grass-roots tourism are the so-called posadas, guest houses 'run by a family or as a small business and providing rooms and food' (Pattullo, 1996).

The Inuit in the Canadian Arctic have taken control over the management of their visitor industry after their land rights were restored by the Canadian Government (Smith, 1996).

The major challenge of such enterprises is the competition and the threat posed by large-scale tourism resorts in their vicinity, who with their rich resources and their sophisticated marketing techniques often not only take away the business but also copy any new ideas that might be developed by those small entrepreneurs (Ascher, 1985; Afrikan Heritage, personal communication 1996). The challenge for the tourism industry and policy makers is to find a way in which large mass tourism and small-scale grass-roots tourism projects can co-exist, feeding into each other and assisting each other in a positive way as part of an integrated local economic development policy, in the knowledge that the market needs not

just one but a diversity of tourism provision that is of a high quality and can reflect changing consumer demand.

CONCLUSION

Poon (1993) and Urry (1995) both argue that the age of mass tourism is coming to an end. Poon (1993) believes that modern tourists are by now experienced travellers, well educated, world wise and informed and ready for a change from the traditional sun, sand and sea mentality. She thinks that there will be a need for more natural, more authentic and 'down-to-earth' vacations (p. 120). Urry (1995) points out that 'there seems to be a move away from the organised tourism characteristic of the modern period to a much more differentiated and fragmented pattern of mobility which one could almost describe as the end of tourism per se'. These views seem to be echoed by the industry, who have to either resort to ever cheaper prices to attract customers or become much more 'sophisticated in the way the market is segmented' Poon (1993). If this analysis is right then these are signs of a social transformation that augurs well for the proponents of fair trade in tourism as a more sophisticated and more 'authentic' tourism experience. As yet the process of determining what exactly fair trade in tourism means in practice and whether it can be implemented successfully has only recently started. Initially, it will be a question of challenging the priorities of the existing trade system and making the case for a different kind of tourism experience in countries where the poverty levels of the population are high and ecosystems are fragile. This might also mean challenging the western view that as long as one has money to spend, one has the right to use the world as a playground and an amusement centre. Although the Earth Summit in June 1997 has brought few concrete commitments, the fair trade concept offers a concrete and practical opportunity for business operations in the North and South to make sustainability in tourism a reality and a way of life. It is recognised that control, ownership and land use are not likely to be relinquished with ease by power wielding forces in North or South. Historically, the concept of fair trade as providing a better deal for producers in the South has emerged from development theories directly opposed to the existing dominant economic theory. However, the economic dynamics of the world are changing rapidly. Globalisation and technological advances are increasing the ability of the South to match the North. These modern tools need to be used in a positive way to enhance communication and information procedures that could create 'level playing fields' for grass-roots communities in remote societies. It is those communities that will have to take the lead in determining how fair trade in tourism could provide them with a better chance in life. '… it is grassroots activism and not lobbying that provides the muscle' (Athanasiou, 1997). One could argue that it is a combination of both and that responsible sources in the North have to collaborate with responsible sources in the South to effect change.

REFERENCES

Aotearoa Maori Tourism Federation. (1994), The Protection of Maori Cultural and Intellectual Property within the Tourism Industry. Rotorua, Aotearoa New Zealand: Aotearoa Maori Tourism Federation.

Aotearoa Maori Tourism Federation (1997), Report on the Current Market Position of Maori Tourism Product, Rotorua, Aotearoa New Zealand: Aotearoa Maori Tourism Federation.

Ascher, F. (1985), *Transnational Corporations and Cultural Identities*. Paris: United Nations Education and Scientific Organisation (UNESCO).

Athanasiou, T. (1997), Wising up to the new world order, *The Guardian*, **19 February**.

Balooni, K. (1997), Green consumerism – the new challenge. *Indian Management*, **October**.

Barratt-Brown, M. (1993), *Fair Trade*. London: ZED Books.

Bauer, P. (1983), *Equality, The Third World and Economic Delusion*. Cambridge, Massachusetts, USA: Harvard University Press.

Beavis, S., and Brown, P. (1996), Shell has human rights rethink. *The Guardian*. **8 November**.

Bellos, A. (1997), Tout little, too late. *The Guardian*, **26 February**.

Betz, K. (1998), Nichts geht ohne die Hardliner. *Die Zeit*, **28 May**.

Boissevain, J. (Editor) (1996), *Coping with Tourists*. Oxford: Berghahn.

British Airways (1994), A Life-cycle Analysis of a Holiday Destination: Seychelles. UK Centre for Economic and Environmental Developments (CEED), Environment Report. No. 41. London.

British Airways Holidays (1997), Worldwide Holiday Brochure, British Airways. Crawley.

Britton, S. (1982), The political economy of tourism in the third world. *Annals of Tourism Research*, **9**, 3, 331–358.

Burns, P., and Holden, A. (1995), *Tourism: a New Perspective*. Englewood Cliffs. NJ: Prentice Hall.

Cater, E. (1991), Sustainable Tourism in the Third World: Problems and Prospects. Reading: University of Reading, Department of Geography, Discussion Paper No. 3.

Cho, G. (1995), *Trade, Aid and Global Interdependence*. London: Routledge.

Clarke, T. (1995), *Dismantling Corporate Rule*. San Francisco: International Forum on Globalisation.

Cohen, E. (1993), The study of touristic images of native people: mitigating the stereotype of a stereotype in Pearce, D. and Butler, R. (Editors), *Tourism Research: Critiques and Challenges*. London: Routledge, 36–69

Crick, M. (1994), *Resplendent Sites, Discordant Voices*. Reading, Harwood.

Crick, M. (1996), Representations of tourism in the social sciences: sun, sex, sights, savings and servility, in Apostolopoulos, Y. (Editor), *The Sociology of Tourism*. London: Routledge, 15–50.

Croall, J. (1996), On the road to disaster. *The Guardian*, **14 August**.

Dann, G. (1996), The people of tourist brochures, in Selwyn, T. (Editor), *The Tourist Image*. Chichester, Wiley, 61–81.

De Kadt, E. (1979), *Tourism: Passport to Development*. Oxford: Oxford University Press.

ECOMOST Project (1994), *Planning for Sustainable Tourism*. Lewes: International Federation of Tour Operators (IFTO).

Equations (1995), Draft Statement on the General Agreement on Trade in Services. Bangalore: Equations.

EFTA (1995), *Fair Trade Yearbook*. Maastricht: European Fair Trade Association.

EFTA (1996), EFTA Fair Trade Guidelines–25 July 1996. Maastricht: European Fair Trade Association.

Forsyth, T. (1996), *Sustainable Tourism–Moving from Theory to Practice*. Godalming: World Wild Fund for Nature.

George, S. (1986), *How the Other Half Dies*. London: Penguin.

Goodland, R., Daly, H., and El Serafy, S. (1992), The urgent needs for environmental assessment and environmental accounting for sustainability, in *Industrial and Third World Environmental Assess-*

                          Int. J. Tourism Res. **2**, 171–187 (2000)

ment: *The Urgent Transition to Sustainability.* Washington, DC: World Bank, Annual Meeting of International Association for Impact Assessment.

Hall, C. M. (1994), *Tourism and Politics – Policy, Power and Place.* Chichester: Wiley.

Harrison D. (1992), *Tourism and the Less Developed Countries.* London: Belhaven Press.

Hitchcock, M., King, V. T., and Parnwell, M. J. G. (1993), *Tourism in South-East Africa.* London: Routledge.

Hoogvelt, A. (1982), *The Third World in Global Development.* Basingstoke, MacMillan.

Hutt, M. (1996), Looking for Shangri-La: from Hilton to Lamichane, in Selwyn, T. (Editor), *The Tourist Image.* Chichester: Wiley, 49–60.

Jenkins, C. (1994), Tourism in developing countries: the privatisation issue, in Seaton, A. V., Jenkins, C. L., Wood, R. C., Deke, P. V. C., Bennett, M. M., MacLellan, R., and Smith, R. (Editors), *Tourism: State of the Art.* Chichester: Wiley, 3–9.

Jafari, J. (1977), Editorial. *Annals of Tourism Research.* 1.

Kent, N. (1983), *Hawaii: Islands Under the Influence.* New York: Monthly Review Press.

Korten, D. (1996), Development is a sham. *New Internationalist.* 278, 12–13.

Lea, J. (1988), *Tourism and Development in the Third World.* London: Routledge.

Madeley, J. (1995), *Foreign Exploits: Transnationals and Tourism.* London: Catholic Institute for International Relations (CIIR).

Mehmet, O. (1995), *Westernizing the Third World.* London: Routledge.

Mill, R., and Morrison, A. (1985), *The Tourism System: an Introductory Text.* Englewood Cliffs, NJ: Prentice Hall.

Monbiot, G. (1994), *No Man's Land.* London, Macmillan.

Monbiot, G. (1997), A charter to let loose the multinationals. *The Guardian,* 15 April.

Munt, I. (1994), Ecotourism or ego-tourism? *Race and Class,* 36, 1, 49–60.

Nash, D., and Smith, V. (1991), Anthropology and tourism. *Annals of Tourism Research.* 18, 1, 12–25.

NEF/CIIR (1997), Open Trading –Options for Effective Monitoring of Corporate Codes of Conduct (Executive Summary). New Economics Foundation/Catholic Institute for International Relations.

Ogilvy and Mather (1996), Ethical Marketing Research –Gallup 1995, NOP for Christian Aid (1993), Presentation for Sainsbury and Cafedirect.

O'Grady, A. (Editor) (1990), *The Challenge of Tourism.* Bangkok: Ecumenical Coalition on Third World Tourism.

Patterson, K. (1992), Aloha for sale. *In Focus,* 4, 4–5.

Pattullo, P. (1996), *Last Resorts.* London:Cassell.

Peet, R. (1991), *Global Capitalism – Theories of Societal Development.* London: Routledge.

Poon, A. (1993), *Tourism, Technology and Competitive Strategies.* Wallingford: CAB International.

Richter, L. (1991), Political issues in tourism policy: a forecast, in World Travel and Tourism Review. Vol. 1. Wallingford: CAB International, 189–194.

Richter, L. (1993), Tourism policy-making in South-East Asia, in Hitchcock, M. (et al.) *Tourism in South-East Asia.* London: Routledge. 179–199.

Rostow, W. (1991), *The Stages of Economic Growth.* Cambridge: Cambridge University Press.

Schumacher, E. F. (1974), *Small is Beautiful.* London: Abacus.

Selwyn, T. (Editor) (1996), *The Tourist Image.* Chichester: Wiley.

Smith, V. (1996), The Inuit as hosts: heritage and wilderness tourism in Nunavbut, in Price, M. (Editor), *People and Tourism in Fragile Environments.* Chichester: Wiley. 33–50.

Smith, V. (1989), *Hosts and Guests.* USA: University of Pennsylvania.

The Body Shop (1996), *Our Agenda – Social, Environmental and Animal Protection Statements.* Watersmead, Littlehampton: The Body Shop International.

Tourism Concern (1996), *Trading Places: Tourism as Trade.* London: Tourism Concern.

Traidcraft Exchange (1996), *Social Accounts 1995/ 1996.* Gateshead: Traidcraft Exchange.

Urry, J. (1995), *Consuming Places.* London: Routledge.

Vidal, J. (1997), *The real politics of power. The Guardian,* 30 April.

Wahab, S. and Pigram, J. (Editors) (1997), *Tourism Development and Growth – the Challenge of Sustainability.* Routledge: London.

Wheeller, B. (1993), Sustaining the ego. *Journal of Sustainable Tourism,* 1, 2.

Williamson, N. (1997), They came in search of paradise. *The Observer,* 25 May.

WTO (1995), *GATS and Tourism – Agreeing on Trade and Tourism.* Madrid: World Tourism Organization.

WTTC (1995), *Agenda 21 for the Travel and Tourism Industry.* London: World Travel and Tourism Council.

WTTC (1997), World travel and tourism leaders in job-creation. London: World Travel and Tourism Council, News Release, 17 April.

WTTERC (1993), *World Travel and Tourism Environmental Review.* Oxford: World Travel and Tourism Environmental Research Council.

WWF (1997), The OECD Multilateral Agreement on

Investment — WWF Briefing. Godalming: World Wildlife Fund.

Zarkia, C. (1996), Philoxenia: receiving tourists — but not guests — on a Greek Island, in Boissevain, J. (Editor), *Coping with Tourists*. Oxford: Berghahn, 143–173.

[3]

Tourism and Economic Development:
A Survey

M. THEA SINCLAIR

This article surveys the literature on tourism and economic development, identifying the contribution that tourism can make to development, including foreign currency, income and employment, and the costs that it entails. Single equation and system of equations models for estimating tourism demand are provided, indicating developing countries' potential to benefit from increasing expenditure on tourism but their susceptibility to deterioration in price competitiveness. The main sectors of tourism supply – transportation, tour operators, travel agents and accommodation – are examined and the importance of cross-country integration between firms is highlighted. The article argues that many of the problems associated with the use of environmental resources for tourism stem from market failure, and it considers methods for increasing, sustainably, the returns from them.

I. INTRODUCTION

Faced with the problems of declining terms of trade for agricultural products and high levels of protection against manufactures, many developing countries have turned to tourism as a possible alternative source of growth. Resources have been devoted to the provision of airports, local transport infrastructure and hotels, mainly aimed towards the international tourism market. Such supply-side improvements have been fuelled by the increasing demand for "long haul" tourism as air transport technology has improved and accessibility to developing country destinations has increased. Thus, tourism has become a major economic activity within developing countries, often contributing more foreign currency than traditional primary commodity exports.

M. Thea Sinclair, Department of Economics, University of Kent. The author is indebted to Mike Stabler for providing the basis for the environmental section of this survey and to Alan Pack, Tony Thirlwall, Peter Sanfey and two anonymous referees for constructive comments.

The Journal of Development Studies, Vol.34, No.5, June 1998, pp.1–51
PUBLISHED BY FRANK CASS, LONDON

Despite its increasing importance, tourism has attracted relatively little attention in the literature on economic development. Analysis has tended to focus on the contributions of the agricultural and manufacturing sectors, rather than those of service activities. There are, however, a considerable number of studies which, while not expressly directed towards the topic of tourism's role in developing countries, are indirectly relevant to it. In addition, a smaller number have focused explicitly on tourism's economic contribution in developing countries. The main emphasis has been on estimating tourism demand and income generation via the multiplier process.

The purpose here is to provide a comprehensive survey of the literature on the economics of tourism which is relevant to development. The article will take account of both the benefits that tourism can bring and the costs that it entails. The positive contributions that tourism can make to development include the provision of hard currency to alleviate a foreign exchange gap and to finance imports of capital goods; increases in the numbers of full-time and part-time jobs, in gross national product and personal incomes; and the provision of tax revenue for the government.

Tourism expansion also involves considerable costs, including expenditure on the provision and maintenance of infrastructure in the form of additional roads, airports, water, sanitation and energy, much of which is specific to tourism rather than of more general use. In addition to being intensive in physical capital, the tourism sector requires various types of skilled labour and, hence, investment in human capital. Expenditure by foreign tourists may alter domestic consumption patterns via the demonstration effect and can be inflationary. Land acquisition for tourism construction has repercussions on the domestic distribution of wealth, while tourism expansion may deplete the country's natural resource base. Many of the economic costs and benefits associated with tourism will be considered in the course of the survey. Non-economic costs and benefits, such as the social and cultural effects of tourism, will not be considered as, although extremely important, they are the subject of an additional huge literature.

The discussion of tourism and economic development will commence with an analysis of the demand for tourism. This will provide a context for the rest of the paper by indicating the scale and growth of international tourism in developing countries. As in the following sections of the survey, the discussion will include the relevant economic theory, its application to tourism and the implications of the empirical evidence for development. The section is divided into two parts. The first reviews and critically evaluates the studies of tourism demand which have been undertaken using single equation models, and the second examines system of equations models of demand. The implications for development of the elasticity values estimated from the models are considered.

The third section of the article focuses on key non-environmental components of tourism supply: transportation, travel agents, tour operators and accommodation. Particular attention is paid to identifying the economic features of tourism supply, which almost invariably occurs within an imperfectly competitive context. It is posited that vertical integration between international tour operators and travel agencies in industrialised countries, airlines, and accommodation in tourist destinations, constitutes not only a characteristic of market structure but also a competitive strategy which can affect firms' performance. The nature of the different types of integration which occur between firms in industrialised and developing countries is considered.

The foreign currency, income and employment generation effects of tourism are examined in the fourth section of the article. The section starts by considering tourism within the balance of payments accounts and identifies both its direct contribution to foreign currency earnings, and the imports, salary and profits remittance leakages which it entails. Attention is then paid to multiplier studies of income generation from tourism, which have been a major focus of attention in the literature. Keynesian multiplier models are examined initially, followed by input-output models which consider the inter-sectoral effects of tourist expenditure. Multiplier values which have been estimated for developing countries are provided and examined. The discussion also alludes to the possible role for computable general equilibrium models in identifying and estimating the effects of tourism, including its repercussions for exchange rates and the distribution of income. The effects of international tourism on the level and structure of employment in developing countries are then considered. The final part of the section discusses the issue of instability in foreign currency receipts from tourism and methods of measuring the instability of tourism earnings are provided. The possible effects of instability and their implications for growth in developing countries are considered.

The environment is of key importance to tourism, and many developing countries have a comparative advantage in supplying natural resources such as wildlife or coral reefs. In some cases, tourist demand for natural resources has provided revenue which has been used to further development. In others, environmental resources have been subject to market failure owing to externalities and their public good nature, resulting in non-optimal utilisation and limited returns to the local population. The penultimate section of the article will discuss some of the problems associated with the use of developing countries' environments for tourism, the methods which have been used to value environmental assets and associated policy implications. The final section will provide an overview and conclusions.

4   THE JOURNAL OF DEVELOPMENT STUDIES

II. TOURISM DEMAND AND DEVELOPING COUNTRIES

The United Nations Conference on International Travel and Tourism of 1963 provided the generally accepted definition of tourists as temporary visitors who spend more than 24 hours in destinations other than their normal place of residence, whose journey is for the purpose of holiday-making, recreation, health, study, religion, sport, visiting family or friends, business or meetings. Those who spend less than 24 hours in their destinations are defined as excursionists. Tourism revenues obtained by host countries include direct and indirect foreign currency payments made by tourists for goods and services, although international fares to and from the destination are usually specified separately. By 1996, receipts from international tourism totalled $404 billion, approximating 1.5 per cent of world GDP, and having increased at a mean rate of 7 per cent since 1992 [*Euromonitor, 1997*]. Tourism was, thus, the third largest economic activity in the world, surpassed only by oil and motor vehicles.

Although many developing countries have experienced high rates of growth of tourist arrivals and foreign currency receipts, they have minor shares of global arrivals and receipts. In contrast, Europe accounted for 59 per cent of world arrivals and 51 per cent of world receipts in 1996, and the USA and Canada for a further 10.5 per cent of arrivals and 17 per cent of receipts, as is shown in Table 1. Central and Latin American countries obtained nine per cent of world tourist arrivals and eight per cent of receipts; African countries had the relatively small shares of 3.5 per cent of arrivals and two per cent of receipts, while South Asian countries accounted for less than one per cent of the global totals. East Asia and the Pacific, excluding Australia, Japan and New Zealand, attained the higher shares of 13 per cent of world arrivals and 16 per cent of receipts.

TABLE 1

INTERNATIONAL TOURIST ARRIVALS AND RECEIPTS, 1996

	Arrivals (thousands)	Arrivals as % of total	Receipts ($US millions)	Receipts as % of total
Africa	20562	3.5	8031	1.9
Central & Latin America	52529	8.8	33005	7.8
USA & Canada	62177	10.5	73186	17.3
Europe	351612	59.2	215743	51.0
Middle East	15256	2.6	8037	1.9
East Asia & Pacific	87025	14.7	80780	19.1
South Asia	4477	0.7	3963	0.9
World	593638	100.00	422745	100.0

Source: World Tourism Organisation, primary data

TOURISM AND ECONOMIC DEVELOPMENT: A SURVEY 5

While small relative to world totals, developing countries' receipts from tourism make an important contribution to their economies in terms of their income and employment-generating effects and the provision of currency which can be used to finance essential imports. It is, therefore, useful to review and evaluate the studies which have attempted to investigate the determinants of tourism demand, and the estimated elasticity values, which have interesting implications for policy-making. The two main approaches which have been used to estimate tourism demand, single equation models and system of equations models, will now be discussed.

Single Equation Models of Tourism Demand

Most of the studies which have estimated tourism demand have used single equation models and have attempted to explain demand, measured by tourism receipts (expenditure) or arrivals (departures), at the aggregate, cross-country level [*Archer, 1976; Johnson and Ashworth, 1990; Sheldon, 1990; Sinclair, 1991a*]. Equation (1) exemplifies the approach, regressing tourism demand, D_{ij}, on income per capita, Y_i, relative prices, $P_{ij/k}$, exchange rates, $E_{ij/k}$, transport costs, $T_{ij/k}$ and dummy variables for one-off events, DV.

$$D_{ij} = f(Y_i, P_{ij/k}, E_{ij/k}, T_{ij/k}, DV) \qquad (1)$$

where i refers to the tourist origin country, j refers to the destination and k to competing destinations.

Studies which have estimated single equation models of tourism demand have generally been somewhat *ad hoc*. Different studies have used different specifications of the tourism demand equation. In some cases, for example, relative prices and exchange rates have been combined as real effective exchange rates and in others no account has been taken of demand for competing destinations or of transport costs. The time periods for which the demand equations have been estimated are equally disparate. Attention has focused on a limited number of developing countries, some of which are now classified as newly industrialising, and demand by US tourists has commonly been the dependent variable.

The elasticity values which have been estimated for a range of destinations are included in Table 2. One of the interesting features is the variation in the estimated values, including some particularly high values for the income elasticities. An early study by Gray [*1966*], for example, provided per capita income elasticities of 5.13 for US demand for tourism in the rest of the world and 6.6 for Canadian demand. Jud and Joseph [*1974*] estimated a per capita income elasticity of 1.74 for US expenditure on tourism in 17 Latin American countries, and of 2.58 for total international demand. Stronge and Redman [*1982*] estimated an income elasticity of 2.99 for US expenditure on Mexican tourism. The per capita income elasticities

TABLE 2

ELASTICITY VALUES FOR TOURISM DEMAND

Author	Destination – origin	Tourism demand	Income	Relative prices	Exchange rates	Travel cost	Dummy variables
Gray (1966)	Rest of World - USA	Expenditure	5.13* (per capita) 2.86* (aggregate)			-0.49 -0.10	
	Rest of World - Canada		6.60*(per capita) 3.33* (aggregate)		-2.40* -2.57*	-0.21 -0.25	
Bechdolt (1973)	Hawaii - USA	Arrivals	3.15* (per capita)			-2.68*	
Jud and Joseph (1974)	17 Latin American countries – rest of World	Receipts	0.71-9.17*(per capita) 2.58* (pooled regression)	-0.37 - -4.24 -1.12 (pooled regression)		-0.66* (pooled regression)	
	17 Latin American countries – USA	Expenditure	1.74* (per capita) 2.49 (pooled regression)	-0.92* -1.53 *(pooled regression)		-2.02 (pooled regression)	
Diamond (1977)	Turkey - international tourism	Arrivals	1.27 - 1.60*			-0.90 - -1.75*	
Stronge and Redman (1982)	Mexico - USA Mexican border - USA	Expenditure	0.45 2.99*	0.36 (Mex - USA) -1.20* (Mex-overseas)			
	Mexican interior - USA		0.96*	-0.12 (Mex - USA) -0.63* (Mex - overseas)			
Uysal and Crompton (1984)	Turkey - 11 countries	Expenditure Arrivals	0.92 - 5.95* (per capita) 1.59 - 6.07 * (per capita)	-0.23 - -2.06* -0.03 - -2.38*	0.18 - 4.22* 1.09 - 6.63*		
Papadopoulos and Witt (1985)	Greece - 8 countries	Arrivals	0.13 - 8.22* (aggregate)	-0.51 - -1.66*		-0.04 - -0.51	
Gunadhi and Boey (1986)	Singapore - Australia, Indonesia, Japan, UK, USA, World	Arrivals	0.81 - 7.30* (per capita)	-1.11 - -2.99* (shop prices) -0.91 - -1.12* (hotel prices)	-1.62*		

TABLE 2 (cont.)

Author	Destination – origin	Tourism demand	Income	Relative prices	Exchange rates	Travel cost	Dummy variables
Summary (1987)	Kenya - UK, USA, Italy, Germany, Switzerland	Arrivals	0.08 - 4.17 (per capita)	0.04 - 5.66	-0.08 - 3.88	-0.01 - -0.43	
Broomfield (1991)	Fiji - Australia Japan USA	Arrivals	0.18* (per capita lagged) 8.1* (per capita lagged) 1.08* (per capita)		Effective -0.16 -1.9* 1.5*	-0.31 -1.10 -1.80*	
Seeberger (1992)	Reunion - rest of World	Arrivals	0.21* (per capita)		Effective -0.60*	-0.08	
Shamsuddin (1995)	Malaysia - Australia Japan UK USA Singapore Thailand	Arrivals	(per capita) 2.53* 2.34* 3.44* 1.57 0.94* -0.73	0.81 -1.80 2.62* 0.51 0.20 -2.77	0.35 0.08 -0.78* 0.35 1.27* -1.39	-0.38 (lagged) -0.10 (lagged) -0.94* (lagged)	Visit Malaysia year 0.37* 0.94* 0.34* 0.85* 0.36

Note: * denotes significance at the 0.05 level.

for expenditure in Turkey by 11 industrialised countries ranged between 0.92 and 5.95 [*Uysal and Crompton, 1984*]. A set of income elasticities has also been estimated for tourist arrivals and includes values of 3.15 for US arrivals in Hawaii [*Bechdolt, 1973*], 1.59 to 6.07 for arrivals in Turkey from a range of origins [*Uysal and Crompton, 1984*], 0.81 to 7.3 for Singapore [*Gunadhi and Boey, 1986*], 0.18 to 8.1 for Fiji [*Broomfield, 1991*], 0.21 for Reunion [*Seeberger, 1992*] and 0.94 to 3.44 for Malaysia [*Shamsuddin, 1995*].

The elasticity values for relative prices and exchange rates show less variation. Turkey demonstrated the lowest and highest estimates for the price elasticities for both expenditure (-0.23 and -2.06) and arrivals (-0.03 and -2.38) [*Uysal and Crompton, 1984*]. The exchange rate elasticities ranged between 0.18 and 4.22 for expenditure and 1.09 and 6.63 for arrivals in Turkey [*Uysal and Crompton, 1984*] but varied between only -0.78 and 1.27 in Malaysia [*Shamsuddin, 1995*]. Gunadhi and Boey [*1986*] estimated an effective exchange rate elasticity of -1.62 for Singapore. Broomfield [*1991*] found the corresponding value for Japanese arrivals in Fiji to be -1.9 and Seeberger [*1992*] estimated a value of -0.6 for total arrivals in Reunion.

Transport costs have either been excluded from most of the single equation models or proved to be insignificant. Exceptions included Bechdolt's [*1973*] study of Hawaii which provided a transport cost elasticity value of -2.68, and Jud and Joseph's [*1974*] estimates of -0.66 for international tourism and -2.02 for US tourism in Latin American countries. Dummy variables for exceptional events such as the oil crisis were generally insignificant. However, the Visit Malaysia Year of 1990 demonstrated significant but less than unitary values for most of the origin countries considered [*Shamsuddin, 1995*], and its absolute impact appeared to be substantial.

The implications of the estimated elasticity values are that developing countries can benefit from the rising real income associated with the growth of tourism, indicated by the high values of the income elasticities of demand for many destinations. The effect of changes in relative prices and exchange rates varies between countries, so that deteriorating price competitiveness is a greater cause for concern in some countries than others. Changes in transport costs do not appear as a significant determinant of demand in most cases, but one-off publicity campaigns may be effective. However, these conclusions must be qualified on a variety of counts.

First, the single equation approach to tourism demand modelling lacks an explicit theoretical basis and takes no account of the microfoundations of demand [*Sinclair and Stabler, 1997*]. The nature of consumer decision-making concerning expenditure on tourism relative to other goods and services, and the allocation of time to tourism relative to paid work or unpaid activities, are not examined. Second, virtually all of the studies have

TOURISM AND ECONOMIC DEVELOPMENT: A SURVEY   9

TABLE 3

LONG RUN INCOME, EFFECTIVE OWN-PRICE AND EFFECTIVE
SUBSTITUTE-PRICE ELASTICITIES FOR TOURISM DEMAND

	Italy	Greece	Portugal	Spain	Turkey
Income Elasticities					
France	2.30	2.72	1.84	1.00	1.00
W. Germany	1.00	1.00	2.85	1.79	2.80
Sweden	2.20	2.10	1.79	1.96	1.57
UK	2.40	2.13	2.80	1.00	2.77
USA	1.93	1.00	3.32	1.96	1.00
Effective Own-Price Elasticities					
France	–	–	–	–	–
W. Germany	1.61	1.56	2.23	1.61	1.44
Sweden	1.50	2.20	1.75	1.50	–
UK	1.20	0.78	1.84	1.20	–
USA	0.38	2.78	1.61	0.38	1.80
Effective Substitute-Price Elasticities					
France	2.39	2.72	3.63	0.80	1.94
W. Germany	2.22	2.40	–	–	–
Sweden	3.30	–	–	–	1.00
UK	1.80	2.81	2.56	–	2.80
USA	0.32	1.58	1.03	1.25	3.60

Note: – denotes statistically insignificant result.

Source: Syriopoulos [*1995*].

ignored possible intertemporal relationships between tourism expenditure
and income or relative prices/exchange rates, in contrast, for example, to the
huge literature on intertemporal choice in aggregate consumption [*Deaton,
1992*]. Third, little attention has been paid to the issue of whether it is
appropriate to include relative prices and exchange rates as separate
determinants of demand or whether real effective exchange rates are the
relevant explanatory variable. Fourth, the theoretical case for including or
excluding the cost of transport between the origin and destination has not
been examined rigorously and the measures of transport costs which have
been used in empirical work may be inappropriate proxies for the true data.
Fifth, most studies fail to include the full range of test statistics so that the
results cannot be assessed by normal econometric criteria. As Johnson and
Ashworth [*1990*] note, in some cases estimates, which the test statistic
indicates to be insignificant, have been presented as of equal validity to
those which appear significant. The majority of studies fail to consider

lagged explanatory variables and may be subject to omitted variables bias and problems of identification and simultaneity. Sixth, the issue of the appropriate level of aggregation at which to examine tourism demand – by the individual or group, for components of tourism such as accommodation or for tourism as a bundle of goods and services – is rarely discussed.

The econometric model of tourism expenditure in the south Mediterranean destinations of Greece, Italy, Portugal, Spain and Turkey estimated by Syriopoulos [*1995*] tackles the second, third and fifth problems by estimating a dynamic model of demand, including relative prices adjusted for nominal relative exchange rates, using the general to specific error correction approach [*Davidson et al., 1978; Hendry and Mizon, 1978; Hendry, 1983*]. This approach has the advantage of separating short-run dynamics from the long-run relationship and provides estimates of short-run and long-run elasticities. The values of the long-run income, effective own-price, and effective substitute-price, elasticities for the Mediterranean destinations are given in Table 3. The estimated income-elasticity values are generally greater than unity and attain a maximum of 3.32 for US demand for Portuguese tourism, followed by 2.85 for German demand. Hence, they are lower than the very high values estimated in studies of other developing or newly industrialising countries and are, perhaps, more plausible. The long-run effective price elasticities are more similar to those estimated in other studies (Table 2) and show price competitiveness to be a significant determinant of tourism demand. The generally elastic values of the substitute-price variables indicate the importance of price competition between tourism destinations and the possibility that tourism demand can switch between established destinations with relative ease. Further evidence is provided by the system of equations models which have been developed in more recent literature.

System of Equations Models

System of equations models attempt to provide a rigorous theoretical basis for tourism demand modelling using microeconomic theories of demand. The objective has been to build a model which allows for generalisation on the basis of a representative individual who behaves according to the axioms of consumer choice: negativity, involving an inverse relationship between demand and price; the adding-up condition, whereby total expenditure is equal to the sum of individual expenditures; homogeneity, according to which a proportional change in expenditure and all prices has no effect on quantities purchased; and symmetry, ensuring consistency of consumer choice.

System of equations models of tourism expenditure allocation posit that consumers make decisions according to a stage budgeting process. The

TOURISM AND ECONOMIC DEVELOPMENT: A SURVEY 11

consumer's decision-making initially involves allocating the expenditure budget among broad groups of goods and services, for example, food, housing and tourism, and subsequently among sub-groups such as holidays in Africa, Asia, Europe, North America and other regions of the world. Expenditure is then allocated to countries within the chosen regions and to types of tourism expenditure within the chosen countries. The approach has been used to explain the allocation of the tourism expenditure budget among different countries [*White, 1982; O'Hagan and Harrison, 1984; Smeral, 1988; Syriopoulos and Sinclair, 1994*] and among types of tourism expenditure [*Fujii et al., 1987; Sakai, 1988; Pyo et al., 1991*].

The almost ideal demand system (AIDS) model formulated by Deaton and Muellbauer [*1980a, 1980b*] provides an attractive specification for tourism demand estimation, incorporating both the axioms of consumer choice and the stage budgeting process. Its main concern is to explain changes in the budget shares of tourism expenditure attributed to destinations or goods and services, rather than changes in the levels of tourism demand which are the focus of single equation models. The model incorporates PIGLOG (price-independent generalised linearity) consumer preferences which allow for perfect aggregation over consumers and uses the cost (expenditure) function $c(u,p)$ that defines the minimum expenditure necessary for a level of utility, u, given prices, p. This may be written as

$$\log c(u,p) = (1-u) \log \{a(p)\} + u \log \{b(p)\}$$

Linear, homogeneous, concave functions of prices, $a(p)$ and $b(p)$, apply to the price vector, p, and the functional forms used are:

$$\log a(p) = a_o + \sum_{t=1}^{n} a_i \log p_i + \frac{1}{2} \sum_{i=1}^{n} \sum_{j=1}^{n} \gamma_{ij}^* \log p_i \log p_j$$

and

$$\log b(p) = \log a(p) + b_o \prod_{i=1}^{n} p_1^{bi}$$

The AIDS cost (expenditure) function is given by

$$\log c(u,p) = a_o + \sum_{t=1}^{n} a_i \log p_i + \frac{1}{2} \sum_{i=1}^{n} \sum_{j=1}^{n}$$

$$\gamma_{ij}^* \log p_i \log p_j + ub_o \prod_{i=1}^{n} p_1^{bi} \tag{2}$$

where a_i, b_i and γ_{ij}^* are parameters.

Since the price derivatives of the cost function are the quantities demanded

$$\frac{\partial c(u,p)}{\partial p_i} = qi \qquad (3)$$

If both sides of equation (3) are multiplied by $p_i/c(u,p)$ we obtain, in log form

$$\frac{\partial \log c(u,p)}{\partial \log p_i} = \frac{p_i q_i}{c(u,p)} = w_i \qquad (4)$$

where w_i is the budget share of the ith good. Using equation (2) and differentiating with respect to $\log p_i$, using equations (3) and (4), and letting $\gamma_{ij} = \frac{1}{2}(\gamma_{ij}{}^* + \gamma_{ij}{}^*)$, the AIDS model is obtained

$$w_i = a_i + \sum_{j=1}^{n} \gamma_{ij} \log p_j + b_i \log\left(\frac{x}{P}\right) + u_i, \quad i = 1,\ldots,n \qquad (5)$$

Equation (5) defines a system of budget equations for each of n goods, where w_i is the budget share of the ith good, p_i is the price of the ith good, x is total expenditure on all goods in the group (system), P is the aggregate price index for the group and u_i is the normal disturbance term with zero mean and constant variance. In the case of the allocation of tourism expenditure among a range of destinations, for example, w_i is the share of the budget that residents of origin j allocate to tourism in destination i, p_j is the effective price level (adjusted by exchange rates) in origin j, x is the budget for tourism expenditure by residents of origin j and P is an index of effective prices in the destinations. Thus, the model takes account of the role of the expenditure budget and relative prices in explaining tourism demand, in accordance with consumer demand theory.

The system of equations approach provides a considerable amount of information about tourism demand, including uncompensated and compensated own-price and cross-price elasticities as well as expenditure elasticities for the range of origins and destinations or types of tourism expenditure under consideration. The assumptions of homogeneity and symmetry can also be tested. The order of magnitude of the elasticities estimated is illustrated in Table 4, which provides the expenditure and effective uncompensated own-price elasticities for tourism demand in south Mediterranean countries.

It is interesting to note that the estimated expenditure elasticity values are particularly high for the relatively low income tourism destinations of Turkey, Greece and Portugal, indicating the possible advantages of tourism expansion for these countries. It is also apparent that the elasticity values for

TOURISM AND ECONOMIC DEVELOPMENT: A SURVEY 13

TABLE 4

EXPENDITURE AND EFFECTIVE UNCOMPENSATED OWN-PRICE ELASTICITIES
FOR TOURISM DEMAND

	Italy	Greece	Portugal	Spain	Turkey
	Expenditure Elasticities				
France	0.85	1.26	1.45	1.08	2.40
W. Germany	1.02	1.07	1.01	0.81	1.73
Sweden	0.91	2.08	1.32	1.06	2.09
UK	0.88	1.05	1.58	0.90	2.65
USA	0.83	1.43	1.61	0.72	1.75
	Effective Uncompensated Own-Price Elasticities				
France	-0.95	-0.27	-1.90	-1.17	-0.51
W. Germany	-0.80	-2.03	-1.35	-1.82	-1.67
Sweden	-1.82	-2.44	-3.17	-1.53	-1.89
UK	-1.59	-2.61	-2.81	-1.11	-0.60
USA	-0.63	-0.87	-3.33	-0.44	-1.66

Source: Syriopoulos and Sinclair [*1993*].

particular destinations vary between origin countries, implying differences in the market potential of the different origins. Relative effective price competitiveness is also important for destinations as the price elasticities are significant and notably in excess of unity for most of the destinations and origins. Portugal appeared to be a particularly price-elastic destination and the UK and Sweden were relatively price-elastic origins. The model has not been estimated for other developing or newly industrialising countries. However, Fujii *et al.* [*1987*] applied the model to different types of expenditure, such as expenditure on food and drinks, in Hawaii and found the uncompensated own-price elasticities to be insignificant, while the expenditure elasticity values approximated unity. Thus, the application of the model to different types of tourism expenditure provides information which may be useful for pricing and marketing strategies, and research on a wider range of countries would be useful.

The system of equations approach overcomes a number of the problems which characterise many single equation studies of tourism demand. In particular, it has an explicit theoretical basis which permits aggregation from the individual to all tourism consumers. Progress has also been made towards incorporating intertemporal relationships in demand modelling [*Blundell, 1991*]. However, it is less flexible than the single equation approach in that it requires a common specification and lag structure for the system of equations to be estimated so that atypical events in particular destinations cannot be taken into account. Empirical work has cast doubt on the validity of the homogeneity and symmetry conditions underlying the model [*Syriopoulos and Sinclair, 1993*]. Moreover, modelling on the basis of a representative tourism consumer fails to reveal many of the interactions within and between social groups, such as those within the household, which affect preference formation and the decision-making process. Thus, further studies of tourism demand at the individual and group level, as well as research on the demand for particular tourism components, such as transport and accommodation, would be useful.

III. TOURISM SUPPLY AND MARKET STRUCTURE

Tourism is a composite product, involving transport, accommodation, catering, entertainments, natural resources and other facilities and services such as shops and currency exchange. It differs from other products in that it cannot be examined prior to purchase, cannot be stored and involves an element of travel. It is useful to examine it not as an industry *per se* but as a collection of interrelated industries and markets located in both industrialised and developing countries. The following discussion will focus on three of the main components in tourism supply: air transport, tour operators and travel agents, and accommodation. Consideration of the environment is left to the penultimate section of the article, since the use of, and returns from, environmental resources in developing countries raise issues of market failure which require specific attention.

Air Transport

Expenditure on air transport is usually the largest component of international tourism spending. Most developing countries have the potential to benefit from it owing to their total or partial ownership of their national airline. However, whereas some airlines are profitable, others have proved an expensive drain on the public purse and the opportunity cost of the funds diverted to them has been high. One of the key determinants of an airline's performance is the market structure and regulatory environment within which it operates, which has varied both over time and between different international routes. The Bermuda Agreement of 1946 provided the basis for regulation of scheduled international air transport via bilateral agreements between governments. These cover such issues as entry to designated routes and landing points, the nature of the traffic to be carried, the number of airlines using the route, flight frequency and capacity [*O'Connor, 1995; Doganis, 1985*]. Agreements between the airlines which used specific routes also determined frequency, capacity, and traffic and revenue-sharing between the national and foreign airlines. In this way, the governments and airlines of developing countries had some control over their operating conditions.

The International Air Transport Association (IATA) was responsible for setting the prices of scheduled flights. Foreign participation in domestic air transport markets and control of national airlines was usually prohibited by governments [*Stockfish, 1992*], and non-scheduled charter flights were regulated by government bodies of destination countries [*National Consumer Council, 1986*]. Agreements concerning the numbers, frequency and capacity of non-scheduled flights were often determined by the relative bargaining skills of the government bodies and the airlines concerned, and developing countries with little negotiating ability failed to extract their maximum advantage from the process [*Sinclair et al., 1992*]. Others have imposed restrictive regimes, as in the case of Mauritius where the government prohibited charter flights, enabling the national airline to charge a relatively high price for its seats [*Burns and Cleverdon, 1995*].

The growth of charter traffic, promoted by tour operators and travel agents, undermined the price regulation of many scheduled services as national airlines sold blocks of seats to tour operators at discounted prices. The case against regulation was also promoted on the grounds that regulation results in higher fares and lower services than would occur under competitive conditions [*Douglas and Miller, 1974; Panzar, 1979; Levine, 1987*], as well as over-capacity [*O'Connor, 1995; Vietor, 1990*]. The advent of deregulation by the USA in 1978 significantly altered the operating environment for airlines as bilateral agreements between the US and foreign governments became more liberal with respect to pricing and capacity, resulting in increasing competition on the corresponding routes. There was also some liberalisation at the multilateral level, such as the EU–Andean Pact agreement [*Mason and Gray, 1991*]. Deregulation was accompanied by moves towards airline privatisation, including foreign direct investment, not only within industrial countries but also in developing and newly industrialising economies, for example, Jamaica, Trinidad and Tobago, Brazil and Mexico. It was argued that privatisation could provide smaller airlines with a source of scarce capital, a larger route network and access to computer reservation systems, resulting in increasing efficiency.

Deregulation did not prove to be the panacea anticipated by its advocates, as liberalisation was quickly followed by greater market concentration. The US market was dominated by three airlines and it was argued that in the context of liberalised bilateral agreements, their market power could be prejudicial to developing countries [*Jönsson, 1981*]. Nuutinen [*1992, 1993*], for example, has provided evidence of some of the adverse effects resulting from US airlines' growing participation in the Latin American market. Doganis [*1993*] posits that liberalisation could be beneficial to non-industrialised countries if undertaken within a context of bilateral agreements which take account of their needs.

Deregulation has led to considerable re-configuration of airline route networks and to the emergence of the hub and spoke system. Large airlines have gained market power from network configuration and network economies [*Caves et al., 1984; Hurdle et al., 1989; Leigh, 1990*], route and airport dominance [*Borenstein, 1989*], the imposition of entry barriers [*Strassman, 1990*], industrial experience [*Baker and Pratt, 1989*], computer reservation systems and frequent flyer programmes involving pre-commitment by clients, notably business tourists [*Bharadwaj et al., 1993*]. The larger charter airlines have integrated vertically with travel agents and tour operators so that the market is now divided into a first tier of a few dominant airlines, and a second tier of non-aligned carriers with poor growth prospects [*French, 1995*]. Increasing numbers of tourists are transported to long haul destinations, although they remain a small proportion of total traffic, for example, around six per cent of all European charter traffic in 1994.

Developing countries' airlines can compete within this context as, despite the existence of economies of scope, there are constant returns to scale within most segments of the markets which airlines serve. Smaller airlines use smaller planes with lower load factors and shorter route stage length and serve less dense markets [*Caves et al, 1984; Gillen et al., 1990*]. Their total factor productivity is relatively high and unit costs are low; for example, three Asian airlines have achieved the lowest unit costs in the world owing, in particular, to their low labour costs [*Windle, 1991*].

Although the airlines of many developing and newly industrialising countries are highly cost competitive, their overall performance is determined largely by the regulatory regime within which they operate. This varies between different routes. Melville [*1995*] has undertaken one of the few in-depth studies of a developing country airline, BWIA (British West Indies Airline) of Trinidad and Tobago, and has shown that the airline's market share was determined by capacity restrictions on the regulated London route and by routing and market growth on the more competitive New York route. Its performance in terms of market share and yield tended to be superior on the New York route, although there was a negative relationship between its market share and the growth of the market. The degree of market concentration was particularly important on the London route, where market share was limited by capacity restrictions. BWIA's unit operating costs were equivalent to those of the major US airlines, American, Delta and United, but it failed to attract high yield business and holiday traffic. The London route attracted a high share of low yield clients provided by tour operators and demand was only elastic with respect to changes in scheduled air fares on the New York route.

TOURISM AND ECONOMIC DEVELOPMENT: A SURVEY 17

It appears that improvements in price competitiveness by BWIA, even if unmatched by rivals, would only produce a limited gain in its overall performance. The provision of a higher quality service would entail prohibitively higher costs. On the other hand, it may be possible for the airline to maintain a competitive position in the Caribbean, as large airlines are ceasing to provide flights on some short stage routes for which there may be a natural monopoly. Co-operation with other regional airlines in relation to route network configuration could lower the costs associated with low average stage length and multiple stops, while alliances with major international airlines could raise demand by providing access to wider route networks, frequent flyer programmes and computer reservation systems. In practice, collaborative alliances between airlines take such forms as equity holdings or equity exchanges, code-sharing, joint services, block seat or block booking arrangements, marketing agreements, joint fare-setting, franchise agreements, and flight schedule co-ordination [*French, 1997*]. An example is the strategic alliance between Singapore Airlines and Lufthansa, which enables each airline to sell seats on the other's flights and to co-ordinate ticketing and frequent-flyer schemes. This may be a prelude to Singapore Airline's membership of the Star Alliance between Lufthansa, Air Canada, Scandinavian Airlines System, United Airlines, Thai Airways and Varig. International alliances are of growing importance in the airline sector and, by using these types of strategies, airlines of developing countries may be able to fill niche positions in the market.

Tour Operators and Travel Agents

Much of the demand for international airline seats, as well as for accommodation in developing countries, is channelled through tour operators and travel agents in industrial countries. These intermediaries alleviate market inefficiency in such forms as imperfect information and transactions costs [*Coase, 1960; Williamson, 1985, 1986; North, 1990*], providing knowledge about unseen purchases and means of avoiding the high per unit costs of negotiating individual tourism contracts across borders. Tour operators and travel agents also operate in developing countries but are mainly concerned with catering for travel by local residents and for some internal transport of foreign tourists. As foreign intermediaries play the major role in channelling tourism demand to developing countries, it is pertinent to examine the structure of the markets in which they operate, their changing nature and the associated implications for destinations.

One of the most striking features of tour operations is the considerable market share which is held by a small number of operators. In the USA, for example, 40 operators (three per cent of the total) controlled approximately one-third of the market for package holidays in the early 1990s [*Sheldon, 1994*]. The degree of concentration was even higher in the UK in the same period, when 62.5 per cent of package holidays were sold by only five companies, approximating 0.05 per cent of the total. This figure may be compared with the lower share of 49.5 per cent of sales in 1983, demonstrating a notable increase in the level of concentration in the sector. Concentration is also high in France and Germany, where the top four tour operators sold around 55 per cent of holidays at the end of the 1980s [*Morandy, 1988; Cazes, 1989a; Leguevaques, 1989*] and is significant in Italy where four operators accounted for 25 per cent of sales [*EIU, 1990*].

A further feature of tour operations is the high level of entry to and exit from the sector. In both the USA and Europe, only one-third of the operators in existence in the late 1970s were in business in the late 1980s [*Sheldon, 1994*]. In the UK, 44 operators went out of business between 1992 and 1994, although the total number increased. It appears that despite concentration ratios which are suggestive of oligopoly, the tour operator sector is highly contestable. Large firms have competed on the basis of high volume, low margin sales and economies of scale and scope. Competition has often been intense and large operators have commonly engaged in price discounting as a strategy for increasing their market share. The corresponding pressure on tour operators to lower the cost of their package holiday inputs is reflected in the generally low prices which they pay for accommodation in developing countries. These may be attained via monopolistic purchasing arrangements which operators negotiate with particular hoteliers,' who accept low returns in return for higher occupancy rates. It is the large operators with high volume sales that are in a position to negotiate particularly preferential rates.

The travel agent sector has also experienced increasing concentration over time. By the 1990s, the top five travel agents in the UK were responsible for approximately half of all sales, compared with around one-third in 1986 [*Saltmarsh, 1986*] although the degree of concentration is somewhat lower in countries in which tour operators are permitted to engage in direct sales to the public [*Bote Gómez and Sinclair, 1991*]. The structure of the travel agent sector resembles that of tour operations in being divided into small firms and larger, integrated companies [*Liston, 1986*].

The degree of vertical integration between tour operators and travel agents in Europe has increased markedly over time, via take-overs, mergers or cross-shareholding, resulting in higher market concentration [*Smith and Jenner, 1994; Sinclair and Stabler, 1997*]. Some of the major travel agents and tour operators from industrialised countries also have equity holdings in hotels in developing countries and, although the degree of vertical integration is continuing to increase, there is no uniformity in the type of

integration which occurs either within or between countries [*Bywater,
1994*]. Whereas some groups are characterised by complex mutual
shareholdings, others have a simpler form of direct investment. In some
cases, airlines and/or hotels are included in the group and in others, they are
not. There is a debate as to whether such integration promotes greater
efficiency or restrictive practices in the form of preferential sales of the tour
operators' holidays, in jointly owned or controlled airlines and hotels. What
is clear from the point of view of developing countries is that the larger size
resulting from integration is correlated, *ceteris paribus*, with greater
concentration and market power in the origin country, higher volume sales
and increased bargaining power *vis-à-vis* hoteliers in developing country
destinations who, as a result, tend to receive relatively low receipts per room
occupied by tour operators' clients.

Hotel Accommodation and International Integration

Hotel accommodation is characterised by fixed capacity, associated fixed
costs and economies of scale at the level of both individual establishments
and hotel chains [*Horwath Consulting, 1994*]. The existence of economies
of scale at the group level provides a rationale for horizontal integration in
the form of common ownership or management control of hotels, while
franchising arrangements provide a means of transferring specialist
knowledge across the group of franchisees. Cross-border integration
between hotels in developing and industrial countries is not unusual and
many major hotel chains own or manage hotels in capital cities or coastal
tourism areas of developing country destinations [*Dunning and McQueen,
1982; Go, 1988; Cazes. 1989b; Dieke, 1993*]. Hotel chains based in
developing and newly industrialising countries have also increased their
international operations. Thailand's Dusit Thani Group, for example, has
management contracts with hotels in Indonesia and tourism development
and hotel projects in Vietnam and Laos, in addition to its domestic franchise
agreements [*Sinclair and Vokes, 1993*]. The trend of cross-border
integration appears to be continuing and the higher expenditure segment of
the hotel market is dominated by major international groups, whose
expansion is concentrated in the emerging economies [*Wise, 1993*]. While
host countries benefit in terms of a higher level of receipts from such
tourism, they also incur the wider economic and social costs associated with
increasing tourist numbers.

The scale of foreign ownership and control of hotels in developing
countries can be very high. In Kenya, for instance, 66 per cent of hotels in
Nairobi, National Parks and Reserves, and 78 per cent of major hotels on
the coast, have some foreign ownership, although less than 20 per cent are
totally foreign-owned [*Sinclair et al., 1992*]. Moreover, particular

destinations are often characterised by a multiplicity of types of integration. There are examples of hotels with minority or majority investment by one foreign multinational corporation (MNC) but management by another, or of hotel leasing in association with investment, marketing or management agreements [*Dunning and McQueen, 1982*]. Integration in forms other than ownership characterised many US, French and Japanese MNCs' involvement in hotels in developing countries in the early 1980s, in contrast to the more predominant form of ownership by MNCs based in other west European countries. Franchising and marketing agreements were common in such destinations as Mexico and Brazil, which have expertise in hotel operation. Hotels in many Caribbean countries were leased or partially owned by foreign firms and foreign ownership and franchising were common in Asia. Conglomerate integration occurs between hotels in developing countries and firms in sectors other than tourism, Thomson's printing and publishing as well as tourism activities being a case in point.

Hotels in many developing countries are also vertically integrated with airlines, tour operators and/or travel agents in industrial countries. For example, Kenyan hotels have received equity investment by British Airways and Lufthansa, as well as by French, German, Italian, Swiss and UK tour operators. Foreign direct investment may be disadvantageous to the destination country if foreign firms provide little training or expertise to local participants and external remittances are high, as in the case of hotels in the British Virgin Islands and Grand Cayman, where it was estimated that 43 per cent of wages and salaries were paid to expatriates during the 1970s [*Bryden, 1973*]. Many governments of Caribbean countries have also spent large amounts on tourism infrastructure provision and provided very favourable fiscal incentives for development, including sizeable tax concessions and credit provision. In other regions, for instance, the South Pacific, inadequate infrastructure, along with limited frequency and reliability of air transport, constitutes a constraint on foreign direct investment in tourist accommodation [*King and McVey, 1997*]. The provision of infrastructure is often very costly, and Bird [*1992*] argued that the case for additional investment incentives is weak and that most developing countries would benefit from introducing tourist 'charging' policies and taxes on hotel accommodation.

Tax concessions and government investment in infrastructure can, however, result in considerable private investment in tourism. In Egypt, for example, government and World Bank-financed provision of infrastructure, ten year tax holidays and liberal provisions for the repatriation of profits and initial capital investment have underpinned large-scale foreign and domestic private investment and tourism receipts approximating $3 billion in the mid-1990s. The initial investment by the government may be partially recouped by the imposition of hotel accommodation taxes [*Mak and Nishimura, 1979; Hughes, 1981; Fish, 1982; Weston, 1983; Fujii et al., 1985*]. Moreover, foreign participation in hotels transfers some of the risks associated with the enterprise to foreign firms, which have an incentive to increase tourism demand for the destination, as well as to supply the knowledge which is necessary for the efficient operation of the business [*Dwyer and Forsyth, 1994*].

The nature and effects of integration in forms other than equity investment also differ between destinations, as in the case of the contractual arrangements negotiated between hoteliers in developing countries and foreign hotel groups and tour operators [*Dunning and McQueen, 1982*]. For example, contracts between tour operators and hoteliers in Kenya were often denominated in terms of domestic currency, whereas the same tour operators negotiated room rates in sterling or dollars in other countries [*Sinclair et al., 1992*]. Management operating contracts for similar hotels in alternative destinations have often involved notable differences in the level of remuneration for the foreign hotel group as well as disparities in the degree of local training provision [*Dunning and McQueen, 1982*]. In general, firms from industrial countries have first mover and informational advantages in negotiations [*Alam, 1995*] while firms in developing countries have little knowledge of the terms which are negotiated for similar contracts in alternative destinations. Even in cases where local agents obtain more information about comparative contractual terms and seek to improve their own conditions, foreign intermediaries can use their market power to substitute alternative tourist destinations, as occurred when hoteliers in the Caribbean attempted to increase the returns they obtained from foreign tour operators. Contrary examples of reductions in foreign intermediaries' market power are hard to find owing, in large part, to the nature of the tourism product.

Foreign participants can also take advantage of domestic sources of capital and can acquire supply expertise as well. Hence, as in other sectors of the economy, the effect of foreign participation in the host country may be immiserising rather than growth-enhancing, particularly if local firms are forced out of business, as took place in the Tahitian hotel sector [*Robineau, 1975*]. The overall outcome depends, in part, on the degree to which the foreign participants transfer their specialist knowledge to domestic firms. International organisations could consider providing developing countries with support for training in negotiating skills, which might assist them in negotiating contracts which incorporate such knowledge transfers. This type of human capital is likely to be as important to developing countries as the training in hotel and catering management which is more normally supported.

22   THE JOURNAL OF DEVELOPMENT STUDIES

IV. EFFECTS OF INTERNATIONAL TOURISM

Tourism and the Balance of Payments

Tourism's appeal to developing countries is based, in large part, on its provision of foreign currency earnings and corresponding alleviation of the balance of payments constraint [*Thirlwall, 1979; Thirlwall and Nureldin-Hussein, 1982*]. The values of tourism receipts and their contribution to total export earnings from goods and services in a range of developing, newly industrialising and oil exporting countries are shown in Table 5. International tourism has been and remains one of the most important sources of foreign currency, in terms of both absolute value and growth, in many developing countries [*UNCTAD, 1973; English, 1986; Lee, 1987; Lea, 1988; Euromonitor, 1997*]. In Kenya, tourism has overtaken the traditional primary commodity sectors of coffee and tea to become the country's main foreign currency earner [*Sinclair, 1991b*]. It is the second most important 'export' in The Gambia [*Dieke, 1993*] and, in Egypt, foreign currency earnings from tourism have only been exceeded by remittances from abroad [*Huband, 1997*]. Asian countries such as Thailand and Indonesia are renowned for their high levels of tourism receipts and many small-island economies, for instance Fiji [*Varley, 1978*], Jamaica [*Curry, 1992*], Bermuda [*Mudambi, 1994; Archer, 1995*], the Maldives [*Sathiendrakumar and Tisdell, 1989*] and the Seychelles [*Archer and Fletcher, 1996*], are highly dependent upon tourism activities [*Conlin and Baum, 1995*].

Foreign currency receipts from tourism have provided an important means of economic development by financing imports of capital goods necessary for the growth of the manufacturing sector. Spain is a prime example of a country whose transition to the ranks of the newly industrialising nations followed the path of a decline in agriculture and rise in tourism and construction activities, which financed the expansion of manufacturing [*Sinclair and Bote Gómez, 1996*]. The emerging Asian economies also found tourism to be an important source of finance for capital-goods imports during their industrialisation process [*Delos Santos et al., 1983; Lin and Sung, 1983; Song and Ahn, 1983*].

Tourism's direct contribution to foreign currency receipts is not, however, a reliable indicator of the sector's overall role in the economy. This is only partly due to the problems of inaccuracies in the published balance of payments statistics for tourism receipts [*Grünthal, 1960; Archer, 1976:37; White and Walker, 1982*], as studies demonstrating methods for providing more accurate estimates have been undertaken [e.g., *Baretje, 1982, 1987; Instituto Español de Turismo, 1980, 1983*]. The main reason lies in cross-country differences in the degree of linkages between tourism and other economic sectors [*Cazes, 1992*]. In contrast to large economies

TOURISM AND ECONOMIC DEVELOPMENT: A SURVEY 23

TABLE 5

TOURISM AND TOTAL EXPORT RECEIPTS IN DEVELOPING,
NEWLY INDUSTRIALISING AND OIL EXPORTING COUNTRIES, 1995

Low Income Countries

	Tourism Receipts ($m)	Total Exports ($m)	Tourism as % of total exports		Tourism Receipts ($m)	Total Exports ($m)	Tourism as % of total exports
Angola	10	2750	0.4	Ivory Coast	72	4170	1.7
Bangladesh	23	4130	0.6	Kenya	454	2970	15.3
Benin*	27	410	6.6	Lesotho	18	214	8.4
Bhutan*	4	88	4.5	Madagascar	60	746	8.0
Burkina Faso*	21	266	7.9	Malawi	6	422	1.4
Burundi	1	132	0.8	Mali	17	541	3.1
Central African				Mauritania	11	538	2.0
Republic	5	208	2.4	Nepal	117	1030	11.4
China	8733	146000	6.0	Nicaragua*	40	451	8.9
Comoros	9	43	20.9	Pakistan	114	9950	1.1
Congo	4	1340	0.3	Rwanda	1	68	1.5
Djibouti	4	206	1.9	Sao Tomé and			
Egypt	2800	10100	27.7	Principe*	2	12	16.7
El Salvador	75	1990	3.8	Senegal	130	1540	8.4
Equatorial				Sierra Leone	6	105	5.7
Guinea*	2	68	2.9	Sri Lanka	224	4640	4.8
Ethiopia	36	778	4.6	Tanzania	259	1070	24.2
Gambia	23	205	11.2	Togo	8	389	2.1
Ghana	233	1580	14.7	Uganda	79	677	11.7
Guinea	1	773	0.1	Vietnam	86	7310	1.2
Haiti*	46	66	69.7	Yemen*	19	1960	1.0
Honduras	80	1400	5.7	Zambia	47	1280	3.7
India	2754	39700	6.9				

Middle Income Countries

	Tourism Receipts ($m)	Total Exports ($m)	Tourism as % of total exports		Tourism Receipts ($m)	Total Exports ($m)	Tourism as % of total exports
Barbados*	598	850	70.4	Malaysia	3910	81500	48.0
Bolivia*	131	1100	11.9	Mauritius	430	2290	18.8
Botswana	162	2130	7.6	Morocco	1163	8840	13.2
Chile	900	19700	4.6	Panama	310	2860	10.8
Colombia	851	11700	7.3	Papua New			
Cook Islands	45	3770	11.9	Guinea	60	2970	2.0
Cyprus*	1700	3550	47.9	Paraguay*	197	2850	6.9
Dominican				Peru	520	6850	0.8
Republic	1604	2920	54.9	Philippines	2450	26900	9.1
Fiji	312	1060	29.4	Swaziland	35	893	3.9
Guatemala*	258	2500	10.3	Thailand	7664	69300	11.1
Guyana	47	434	10.8	Trinidad and			
Israel	2784	21700	12.8	Tobago	73	2100	3.5
Jamaica	1069	3040	35.2	Tunisia	1325	8090	16.4
Jordan*	582	2990	19.5	Turkey	4957	33400	14.8
Lebanon*	672	4580	14.7	Uruguay	611	3410	17.9

24   THE JOURNAL OF DEVELOPMENT STUDIES

TABLE 5 (cont.)

	Tourism Receipts ($m)	Total Exports ($m)	Tourism as % of total exports		Tourism Receipts ($m)	Total Exports ($m)	Tourism as % of total exports
Newly Industrialising Countries							
Argentina	4306	23900	18.0	Hong Kong	9604	211000	4.6
Brazil	2097	47900	4.4	Mexico	6164	63700	9.7
Greece	4106	20300	20.2	South Korea	5587	151000	3.7

	Tourism Receipts ($m)	Total Exports ($m)	Tourism as % of total exports		Tourism Receipts ($m)	Total Exports ($m)	Tourism as % of total exports
Oil Exporting Countries							
Algeria	27	11100	0.2	Nigeria	54	6630	0.8
Ecuador	255	5160	4.9	Oman*	88	4590	1.9
Gabon	4	2870	0.1	Saudi Arabia*	1140	48100	2.4
Indonesia	5228	50400	10.4	Venezuela	811	20100	4.0

Note: * refers to 1994 data. Tourism receipts exclude international transport.

Source: World Tourism Organisation, primary data; World Bank, *World Development Indicators*.

such as Spain which supply a high proportion of the goods and services which tourists consume, many developing countries are characterised by relatively weak linkages between tourism and other sectors of the economy, including primary products in which many developing countries are supposed to have a comparative advantage. Small-island economies and micro-states, which are often dependent on tourism for high proportions of their foreign currency earnings, are particularly vulnerable in this respect. Typical examples include Fiji [*Varley, 1978*] and islands in the Caribbean [*Cazes, 1972; Bryden, 1973; Belisle, 1983*]. In the case of Fiji, the import content of tourist expenditure on food was around 56 per cent and of beverages 45 per cent [*Varley, 1978*] while the corresponding figures for food and beverage consumption by tourists in the Caribbean were over 60 per cent [*Cazes, 1972*].

It is clear that much closer links between the tourism sector and the local economy would raise the former's income and employment generating capacity and, in this context, increased purchasing from local producers of the agricultural and marine products which tourists consume would be particularly useful. The promotion of domestic tourism is necessary, not only as an important objective in its own right, but also owing to the relatively high local content of the products which domestic tourists consume. International tourism has the advantage of providing considerable amounts of foreign currency to support the growth of manufacturing activities, and appropriately planned spatial expansion can ensure that the development of the two sectors is complementary. The danger is, of course, that short-term gains associated with inadequately-zoned construction will predominate, prejudicing the foreign currency and associated benefits which tourism can provide over the long run.

The development of a network of local producers of primary and manufactured tourism inputs results in a considerable increase in the proportion of foreign currency earnings which are directly retained by the tourist host country. A pertinent comparison is that of Kenya and The Gambia, where the percentages of gross foreign currency earnings retained in 1992 were 65 per cent for the former in contrast to 20 per cent for the latter, owing to The Gambia's underdeveloped productive base [*Dieke, 1995*]. The expansion of the productive base is particularly problematic in some countries, notably small economies, and greater reliance on intra-regional specialisation and trade is an option which could be considered in this context.

One approach for modelling the trade effects of tourism which is attracting increasing attention is computable general equilibrium (CGE) modelling, reviewed, in the context of trade policy in developing countries, by de Mello [*1988*]. The theoretical effects of tourism on economic structure, income distribution and welfare in a small open economy were examined by Copeland [*1991*], who concluded that destination country welfare rises if tourism demand has the effect of increasing the prices of non-traded goods and services consumed by tourists, thereby improving the 'terms of trade', or if tourists are taxed. The effects of tourism on economic structure and income distribution were ambiguous.

The CGE model was applied to tourism in Hawaii by Zhou *et al.* [*1997*], who compared the model's findings with those obtained by input–output analysis. CGE modelling is more flexible than the latter in that it is not restricted by linearity constraints and incorporates endogenous price determination. It is based on the assumptions of utility maximisation, cost minimisation, zero supernormal profit, market clearing, imperfect substitution between imported and domestic goods, and full factor mobility over the long run. Assuming the small country case, Zhou *et al.* found the effects of a ten per cent decrease in tourist expenditure on trade, domestic output, factor demands and prices on different sectors of the economy to be lower than those predicted by input-output analysis, owing to the fact that the CGE approach takes account of domestic resource reallocation. Adams and Parmenter [*1995*] argue that further empirical applications of the CGE model to tourism are necessary.

Income Multiplier Effects

Tourist expenditure and associated investment results in significant induced income generation in the host economy in addition to its direct and indirect effects on the tourism sector and its input suppliers. The multiplier effects of tourist spending constitute one of the better researched areas within the tourism economics literature [*Archer, 1977; Sheldon, 1990; Fletcher and Archer, 1991*]. Two main approaches have been used to estimate tourism multiplier values: the Keynesian multiplier model and the input-output technique. Both approaches can be used to estimate the multiplier values associated with different types of tourist expenditure or tourism-related investment or government spending. The Keynesian model requires less data but provides less information about the interrelationships within the economy than the input-output approach.

A basic equation which can be used to estimate multiplier values using the Keynesian model is given as

$$k = \frac{1-l}{1-c(1-t_i)(1-t_d-u)+m} \qquad (6)$$

where l are first round leakages, c is the marginal propensity to consume, t_i is the marginal rate of indirect tax, t_d is the marginal rate of direct tax, u is the marginal rate of transfer payments and m is the marginal propensity to import. The formula can be modified to allow for the effects of induced increases in investment and of feedback from the rest of the world, and the first-round leakages can be tailored to the specific nature of the initial injection and the definition of income to be measured [*Sinclair and Sutcliffe, 1978, 1988*]. Further refinements include the incorporation of first-round propensities which apply at the disaggregated firm level [*Archer and Owen, 1971*] and propensity values which are appropriate for different time periods, permitting the estimation of short- and long-run multiplier values [*Sinclair and Sutcliffe, 1989*]. Firm-specific propensities were used in Milne's [*1987*] study of differential multiplier values for tourist accommodation and handicraft firms and tour operators in the Cook Islands, the relevant model being

$$Y_a = \frac{W(1-h-t_w)+P(1-t_p)+F(1-t_w)\sum_{j=1}^{l}S_{ai}Y_i}{D_a} \qquad (7)$$

where Y_a is the local income creation coefficient by establishment, W is gross wages and salaries of residents, h is national insurance and other deductions from wages and salaries, t_w is direct taxes, P is local profits, t_p is taxes on profits, F is rent paid to residents, S_{ai} is business purchases from the ith business, Y_i is destination income generation coefficient for the ith business and D_a is total turnover of the business. The results showed that smaller firms were associated with higher multiplier values than larger establishments owing largely to their relatively low propensities to import and to repatriate profits overseas.

The input–output technique requires more detailed information about inter-sectoral transactions in order to estimate the impact of tourist spending on different sectors within the economy. Using the matrix of technical coefficients for the economy, $\mathbf{A}$, and the vector of gross output, $\mathbf{X}$, the vector of final demand, $\mathbf{Y}$, can be written as

$$\mathbf{Y} = \mathbf{X}(\mathbf{I} - \mathbf{A}) \tag{8}$$

where $\mathbf{I}$ is the identity matrix. Equation (8) can be rearranged to give

$$\mathbf{X} = (\mathbf{I} - \mathbf{A})^{-1}\, \mathbf{Y} \tag{9}$$

so that
$$\Delta\mathbf{X} = (\mathbf{I} - \mathbf{A})^{-1}\, \Delta\mathbf{Y} \tag{10}$$

This basic model can be used to obtain different categories of multiplier. Type I income multipliers are the ratio of direct and indirect income generated by the initial injection to the direct income generated. Type II multipliers are the ratio of total direct, indirect and induced income generated to the direct income and are obtained by considering household income and expenditure as endogenous within the transactions matrix. Type III multipliers are similar to type I and type II multipliers but also take account of alterations in consumption as income increases [*Fletcher and Archer, 1991*]. Comparability with 'normal' multiplier definitions can be achieved by calculating the total income generated within each sector of the economy per unit increase in the exogenous final demand for the output of the sector. Output and employment multipliers giving, respectively, the total output and full-time job equivalents as ratios of the initial change in tourist expenditure can also be calculated.

The input-output technique assumes proportionality in inter-sectoral relationships and constant returns to scale but has been refined to incorporate the effects of the changes in consumption patterns that occur as income rises, as in the model formulated by Sadler *et al.* [*1973*] which was based on the equation

$$(\mathbf{I}\text{-}\mathbf{A})^{-1} \left[\mathbf{I} - \sum_{h=n+1}^{p} \mathbf{C}_h(\mathbf{I} - \mathbf{A})\mathbf{B}_h\, (\mathbf{I} - \mathbf{A})^{-1}\right]^{-1} \mathbf{Y} = \mathbf{X} \tag{11}$$

28   THE JOURNAL OF DEVELOPMENT STUDIES

where X is a vector of output by sector, C_h is one of p matrices giving household consumption patterns, B_h is one of p diagonal matrices giving household earning categories and Y is the vector of final demand.

Further improvements were made in Wanhill's [*1988*] model of tourist expenditure in Mauritius, which introduced capacity constraints into the basic model of equation (10) so that

$$\Delta X = (I - RA)^{-1} \, R\Delta T \qquad (12)$$

where R is a matrix of capacity constraints ranging from 0 to 1 and ΔT is a matrix of the change in tourist spending. If labour market constraints are also incorporated into the model, the change in employment generated by the change in tourist spending, ΔL, can be written as

$$\Delta L = NE^*(I - RA)^{-1} \, R\Delta T \qquad (13)$$

where E^* is a partitioned matrix of employment coefficients and N is an employment restrictions matrix which takes account of job creation in the destination area. The application of the model demonstrated the importance of allowing for capacity constraints as the calculated income multiplier values were up to 28 per cent lower than those resulting from the unconstrained model and the employment multiplier values were up to 34 per cent lower [*Wanhill, 1988; Fletcher and Archer, 1991*].

It is not surprising that the income multiplier values which have been estimated for a range of developing countries vary in magnitude, as is indicated by Table 6. The estimated values are not directly comparable owing to differences in time periods and the definitions of income measured. None the less, as Archer [*1989*] points out, the multiplier values are not directly correlated with the size of the direct and indirect import coefficients, indicating cross-country differences in the initial degree of value added. As is expected, the tourism multiplier values in Table 6 are generally lower than those estimated for higher income economies, such as the estimates of 1.7 for the United Kingdom and 1.8 for Ireland [*Richards, 1972*]. They also vary between some relatively similar economies, for instance the Cayman Islands (0.7), Antigua (0.9) and Dominica (1.2), as shown by Bryden [*1973*]. Pollard [*1976*] argued that it is perhaps less important to consider the differences in the extent of inter-sectoral linkages within each of the countries, indicated by the differing multiplier values, than to examine the degree to which inter-sectoral linkages extend across the Caribbean as a whole, so that the maximum possible value added occurs within developing regions.

Before leaving the topic of multiplier models, it is worth paying some attention to the issue of the total value of tourist spending directly received by the destination country. This is important because even if the multiplier

TABLE 6

INCOME MULTIPLIER VALUES FOR TOURISM

Country	Multiplier Value	Direct and indirect import coefficient
Bahamas	0.78	0.45
Bermuda	1.09	0.44
Hong Kong	0.87	0.41
Mauritius	0.96	0.43
Philippines	0.82	0.11
Seychelles	1.03	0.30
Sri Lanka	1.59	0.27
West Samoa	0.66	0.55

Source: Archer [*1989*].

values are high, total income is low if the direct injection of tourist expenditure in the developing country (the multiplicand) is low. It is in this context that international integration between tourism firms is relevant. As has been seen, much tourist spending is channelled to developing countries via tour operators, located and owned in industrialised countries, who frequently use airlines and hotels which are jointly owned or controlled. A large proportion of tourists' total spending remains with the origin country to cover tour operator, travel agent and airline costs and profits, and to obviate remittances of profits by jointly owned hotels, so that even if total expenditure by tourists is high, the amount received by the destination is often relatively low, even before first-round leakages occur. For example, only 42 per cent of the price of a package holiday was received by Spain when tourists travelled to and from the country on a non-Spanish airline [*Instituto Español de Turismo, 1987*].

The case of a package holiday in a Kenyan beach location in 1990 is similar, as approximately 38 per cent of a UK tourist's spending on the package in 1990 was received by Kenya if the tourist travelled on a non-Kenyan airline [*Sinclair, 1991b*]. The use of the local airline can considerably increase this figure as packages incorporating beach and safari holidays which used Kenya Airways for internal transport provided Kenya with around 66 per cent of the holiday price, while the use of Kenya Airways for the international travel component of the holiday raised the corresponding figure to around 80 per cent. The policy implications are complicated by the fact that many developing country airlines have been loss-making and are forming alliances with larger airlines from industrialised countries, so that the issue of the form of integration which is most appropriate to the needs of developing countries once again reappears.

It is evident that policy-makers in developing countries need to pay more attention to the issue of the segments of the tourism market that they wish to attract; for example, the costs and benefits of low price, high volume, mass tourism relative to high price, low volume, special interest tourism. The example of Kenya illustrates the notably higher expenditure per capita but somewhat smaller multiplier which is associated with safari relative to beach tourism The policy of encouraging the growth of beach tourism resulted in considerably lower average foreign currency receipts per capita for the country as a whole by the late 1980s [*Sinclair, 1992*] and beach tourism has also been subject to instability in the face of political problems. On the other hand, safari tourism requires considerable expenditure on the maintenance of transportation and related infrastructure in relatively remote areas. The use of such techniques as portfolio models and cost-benefit analysis, discussed below, can provide policy-makers with some guidance concerning the ways in which developing countries can select a mix of tourism types, which provides them with their desired trade-off between income (or foreign currency) receipts and the instability associated with them.

Employment Effects of Tourism

Tourism's ability to generate employment, not only in the formal sector but also in informal sector activities [*Elkan, 1975*], has been cited as one of its key advantages for developing countries [*de Kadt, 1979*]. Empirical studies have confirmed that the level of employment in tourism activities is high, for instance, accounting for 0.5 million jobs in Spain [*Sinclair and Bote Gómez, 1996*] and around five million in India [*ESCAP, 1991*]. However, it is also useful to consider direct employment in tourism as a share of total employment. In Spain the relevant share was relatively high at around 6.2 per cent at the beginning of the 1990s [*Bote Gómez, 1993*], compared with 2.1 per cent of formal sector employment in India. Shares for many other developing countries are of a similar order, for instance, 0.9 per cent for the Philippines [*Delos Santos et al., 1983*], 1.4 per cent for Sri Lanka [*Attanayake et al., 1983*] and 1.3 per cent for Zimbabwe [*EXA International, 1993*].

One of the more unexpected results to have emerged from empirical studies is the relatively skill-intensive nature of tourism employment. This was pointed out at an early stage by Diamond [*1974*] in his research on international tourism demand in Turkey and has been confirmed by studies of other countries. For example, Delos Santos *et al.* [*1983*] found the tourism labour force in the Philippines to consist of 38 per cent semi-skilled workers, 32 per cent skilled and 14 per cent supervisors, compared with only 16 per cent unskilled. The capital intensity of tourism during its early expansion phase can also be relatively high. Incremental capital–output (ICOR) ratios were estimated as 4.0 for Turkey in 1967 [*Diamond, 1974, 1977*], 2.4–3.0 for Kenya in 1964–67 [*Mitchell, 1970*], 2.5 for Mauritius in 1980 [*Wanhill, 1982*] and 4.0 for hotels and catering in the former Yugoslavia in 1962–67 [*UNCTAD, 1971*]. Comparable ICOR values for agriculture and manufacturing were 2.3 and 2.1 for Turkey, 2.7 and 4.4 for Kenya, 3.3 and 3.9 for Mauritius and 3.4 and 3.4 for Yugoslavia, indicating that tourism in Turkey and hotel and catering production in Yugoslavia have been more capital-intensive than other sectors in those countries.

Much of the labour force in the accommodation and catering sector is employed on a seasonal and/or part-time basis or are unwaged participants in a family establishment. In Spain, just under ten per cent of full-time and around four per cent of part-time workers in hotels and guesthouses were unwaged in 1990 [*Sinclair and Bote Gómez, 1996*]. The number of full-time waged workers was 23 per cent greater in the high season than in the low season and 34 per cent greater for unwaged workers, while the corresponding figures for part-time workers were 117 per cent and 77 per cent respectively. Employment in hotels in The Gambia was at least 100 per cent greater in the high season than in the low season and the larger hotels have frequently employed hotel management companies and expatriates to run them [*Farver, 1984*]. Similarly, expatriates have filled the highest managerial posts in other developing countries, such as Fiji [*Samy, 1975*]. However, employment of expatriates has decreased over time, as developing countries have followed policies of indigenisation. In Kenya, for example, local residents now fill almost all of the top positions in tourism activities [*Sinclair, 1990*].

Tourism employment in both developing and industrialised countries is structured by gender in that most of the top jobs are undertaken by men while the lower paid, part-time and seasonal jobs are predominantly filled by women [*Sinclair, 1997*]. However, it is interesting to note that the growth of tourism has created new opportunities for women. In the case of Turkish Cyprus, Cypriot women have usually carried out cleaning, bed-making and cooking in small guesthouses while men have been responsible for financial and social interactions with tourists and women from Eastern Europe have worked as croupiers in casinos [*Scott, 1997*]. Large hotels which cater mainly for foreign tourists have provided employment opportunities for young and relatively well educated Cypriot women. Women in Barbados [*Levy and Lerch, 1991*] and Sri Lanka [*Samarasuriya, 1982*] have been employed in tourist guesthouses, in jobs related to their domestic responsibilities. In Bali, women have established small-scale, tourism-related businesses such as homestays or souvenir shops, although it is generally unacceptable for married women to be employed in tourism activities which are less closely related to their traditional domestic roles

[*Cukier et al., 1996; Long and Kindon, 1997*]. The growth of international tourism has also been accompanied by considerable increases in employment in prostitution in developing countries owing, particularly, to the vastly superior earnings which can be obtained by people who previously resided in poor rural and urban areas and to the shortage of alternative opportunities for them [*Lee, 1991; Chant, 1997*].

It is clear that research on the distributional effects of tourism has usually centred on particular case studies [*e.g, Forsyth, 1995b; Cukier et al., 1996*]. Governments and international organisations have provided some aid for tourism development in relatively poor but environmentally well-endowed rural areas, with the aim of increasing local income and employment. Long's [*1991*] study of a tourism development project in Las Bahias de Huatulco, Mexico, has shown how many local residents failed to share the income and employment gains from tourism but were, instead, adversely affected by rising inflation and the expropriation of their property for tourism construction. A contrasting example of an internationally-supported tourism and wildlife programme which has a high level of local community participation is Zimbabwe's CAMPFIRE (Communal Area Management Programme for Indigenous Resources) programme [*Barbier, 1992*]. The programme is based on the allocation of wildlife hunting quotas, via a system of licences, to tourism safari operators. A considerable proportion of the revenue obtained from the sale of the licences, meat, hide and skins is channelled to the local community, who determine its allocation between cash for individuals and households and expenditure on community services and infrastructure, such as footbridges, clinics and creches. In addition, the meat sales raise local nutritional input. The fact that much of the revenue from tourism has been received by the community has contributed to the ongoing popularity of the programme in the areas where it was initiated, although it has been less successful in the more densely populated areas where it was subsequently implemented, owing to the lower returns per capita received by local people.

Tourism Earnings Instability and Economic Growth

Tourism is sometimes perceived as a high risk option for developing countries as the earnings which it provides may be unstable over time. For example, relatively high elasticities of demand with respect to changes in inflation, exchange rates or political instability are often associated with considerable changes in earnings. In Kenya, real dollar earnings from tourism, both total and per tourist, were higher during the 1970s than during much of the 1980s, owing partly to the fact that contracts between tour operators and hoteliers were often negotiated in terms of the depreciating Kenyan shilling [*Sinclair, 1990, 1992*]. Instability of tourism earnings can bring about various adverse effects in the host economy [*Rao, 1986*]. Decreases in earnings not only cause falls in income and employment but may also induce decreases in investment. Instability, *per se*, can cause rising uncertainty which acts as a further deterrent to investment and constrains imports of capital goods. The fiscal yield is less predictable, which may deter spending on infrastructure and human capital formation and lower the rate of growth.

An alternative set of theories, based on Friedman's [*1957*] permanent income hypothesis of consumption, proposes the contrary view that export earnings instability is beneficial to growth. It is argued that unstable export earnings are likely to be perceived as transitory rather than permanent income, bringing about increases in savings, rises in investment and higher growth [*Knudsen and Parnes, 1975*]. The implication is that instability in tourism earnings is not a problem.

There is little evidence on the scale or effects of instability in tourism earnings. However, research on a sample of developing and newly industrialising countries with relatively large tourism sectors was undertaken by Sinclair and Tsegaye [*1990*] using the following definitions of instability:

$$I_1 = 100/n \sum_{t=1}^{n} | (X_t - X_t^*) | /X_t^* \qquad (14)$$

and

$$I_2 = 100[1/n \sum_{t=1}^{n} \{(X_t - X_t^*)/X_t^*\}^2]^{1/2} \qquad (15)$$

where X_t is the actual value of export earnings in time period t, X_t^* is the trend value of earnings estimated from a regression of earnings against time and n is the number of observations. Additional instability measures were calculated on the basis of deviations from a five year moving log average. Positive correlation coefficients between the instability measures for tourism and merchandise export earnings for the period 1960 to 1985 indicated that tourism had a net destabilising effect on the earnings of Fiji, Jamaica, Cyprus, Greece and Turkey. Coefficients which were insignificant or positively signed for one measure but negatively signed for another indicated an insignificant or ambiguous effect for India, Mexico, Morocco, Singapore, Thailand and Tunisia. Buckley's [*1993*] study of the later 1978–89 period found a net stabilising effect for Cyprus, Greece and Turkey. Further research indicating the level and trends in dependence of specific developing countries on particular tourist origin countries, and on the associated degree of earnings instability, would be useful.

The possibility of using portfolio analysis to determine the optimal mix of tourism and other exports, or of different nationalities or types of tourist, has been suggested by Board *et al.* [*1987*] and Buckley [*1993*]. Portfolio analysis is based on Markowitz's [*1959*] model for risk reduction in financial asset holdings and its application to tourism and other exports involves treating export earnings analogously to the returns on assets and the instability of earnings as a measure of risk. The model can be used to assist countries to select their desired trade-off between the level of earnings and their degree of instability. Thus, developing countries which are prone to adverse effects of instability may aim to attain a portfolio of tourism and other exports which involves a lower risk-return trade-off than industrialised countries whose larger reserves of foreign currency enable them to cope more effectively with any problems arising from instability.

V. TOURISM AND THE ENVIRONMENT

Increasing specialisation in tourism would, at first sight, appear to be beneficial to developing countries which are well endowed with environmental resources 'demanded' by tourists from high income nations. However, they rarely achieve the optimal use of and returns from their assets owing to problems of market failure. Natural resources are frequently unpriced public goods which are subject to degradation through over-use, as in the case of the loss of flora and fauna due to climbing [*Pawson et al., 1984*], hunting [*Smith and Jenner, 1989*] and other forms of tourist activity [*Andronikou, 1987*]. Problems also arise from off-road use of vehicles [*Sindiyo and Pertet, 1984*] as in the case of African game reserves, and from excess demand for scarce resources such as water and energy [*Romeril, 1989*].

Attention has been paid to the relationship between tourism and the environment and to the problems associated with tourism expansion [*Pearce, 1985; Romeril, 1989; Farrell and Runyan, 1991; Cater and Goodall, 1992; Eber, 1992; Jenner and Smith, 1992*]. It is also recognised that tourism can benefit poor countries by providing a return from their environmental resources [*Boo, 1990*]. One methodology which would seem to be appropriate for taking account of the complete set of costs and benefits associated with tourism is cost-benefit analysis [*Bryden, 1973*]. However, applications of the technique have generally failed to take account of environmental resources, owing to the difficulties of valuing them and of quantifying the inter- and intra-generational effects of alternative rates and types of utilisation.

The issue of inter-generational inequity in resource use is of particular relevance to developing countries which risk depleting their stocks of natural assets and foregoing the long-run returns from them. The concept of sustainable development (SD) has arisen in the context of concerns about short time horizons in resource use and requires the maintenance of a constant value or constant stock of natural resources, thereby avoiding inter-generational inequity. Pearce *et al.* [*1989*] argue that it is more appropriate to use the stock of resources than the value since a constant value might imply a smaller quantity of higher-priced resources. The weak definition of SD requires the maintenance of the total stock of natural and human-made capital but permits the substitution of one type of capital for another, implying that natural resources may be degraded. The strong definition precludes such substitution.

The term 'sustainable tourism' (ST) has been introduced in the context of the wider debate about environmental sustainability and logically implies a form and level of tourism which maintains the total stock of capital. However, in general, the use of the term by the commercial sector has either implicitly assumed that the weak definition of SD holds [*Cook et al., 1992; Beioley, 1995*] or has involved an alternative definition of ongoing tourism business profitability [*Wight, 1993, 1994; Forsyth, 1995a; Stabler and Goodall, 1996*]. The consequence is that the numbers of tourists which are consistent with the maintenance of a constant stock of natural resources, such as plants, fish, coral or game, may be exceeded [*Bell, 1991; Hawkins and Roberts, 1994*].

The root causes of tourism development which is unsustainable in terms of the stock of resources are to be found in market failure. Many natural resources are public goods and free access to them often results in over-use. Negative externalities occur as, for example, hotel construction creates additional pollution. Tourism expansion can also magnify intra-generational inequity as local residents are displaced from their homes, as has occurred in, for example, Egypt, The Gambia, Mexico, Morocco, Myanmar and the Philippines [*Long, 1991; Tourism Concern, 1995*] and agricultural and fishing areas are polluted, as in Hawaii [*Helu Thaman, 1992*].

Responses to the problems of market failure vary. One school of thought suggests that market imperfections in such forms as externalities and public goods can be resolved by means of internalisation and the allocation of property rights [*Coase, 1960; Demsetz, 1969; Randall, 1993*] so that further intervention is inefficient and unnecessary. An alternative school views many imperfections as inherent within markets [*Stiglitz, 1989*], and the theory of the second best has been used to argue that if one of the standard efficiency conditions cannot be met, the others may no longer be desirable [*Lipsey and Lancaster, 1956–57*]; thus, there is scope for policy intervention. It is clear that tourist destinations in many developing countries are characterised by ambiguous or non-existent access and property rights and that government regulations and legislation are ill-defined or unenforced. Hence in the short run, at least, there is a case for examining some of the measures which may be taken to counter market failure.

Since one of the main obstacles to achieving the sustainable use of environmental resources is that they are freely available or under-priced, it is necessary to attribute a social value to them. The total economic value of the resources consists of use value (which is likely to exceed the price owing to the existence of consumers' surplus), option value which takes account of consumers' willingness to pay for the option of using the resources in the future and existence value, which is consumers' willingness to pay to ensure the continued existence of the resources, irrespective of whether they will use them.

A number of techniques have been developed for the purpose of valuing environmental resources, those most usually applied being the hedonic pricing model (HPM), the travel cost model (TCM) and the contingent valuation model (CVM). The HPM [*Rosen, 1974*] conceptualises goods as bundles of characteristics and is concerned to estimate the implicit price of each. In the case of tourism, it may be used to estimate the implicit price of environmental resources as well as of other components of tourism, such as accommodation and travel. It has mainly been used to estimate the effect of natural resources such as forestry or waterway proximity on residential property prices [e.g. *Garrod and Willis, 1991; Willis and Garrod, 1993a*] but has also been used to evaluate the location component of package holidays in southern Spain [*Sinclair et al., 1990*].

The travel-cost model [*Clawson and Knetsch, 1966*] assumes that the cost of travel to recreational or tourism locations is a measure of consumers' willingness to pay and, hence, of their valuation of the locations and the resources within them. The model has been applied to fishing [*Smith et al., 1991*] and deer-hunting sites [*Loomis et al., 1991*]. Brown and Henry [*1989*] applied both the TCM and the contingent valuation model to elephant viewing in Kenya and estimated that it contributed between $23 and $30 million in 1989. The CVM involves asking consumers about their willingness to pay for the resource in question and has also been applied to canals [*Willis and Garrod, 1993a*], forestry [*Hanley and Ruffel, 1992, 1993*], wildlife [*Willis and Garrod, 1993b*] and national parks [*Lockwood et al., 1993*].

The above approaches constitute useful steps towards correcting the under-valuation of environmental resources but are subject to a variety of limitations. The HPM, for example, only takes account of the characteristics that are incorporated in market prices and is based on such assumptions as the full availability to consumers of information about products and their features, as well as market-clearing. The TCM poses the problem of which transport costs are relevant when tourists engage in international travel to and from a country as well as travel within it. The CVM is subject to the obvious issue of whether tourists provide accurate estimates of their willingness to pay when they do not actually have to do so. A further approach to the valuation of environmental resources, known as the Delphi technique, acknowledges that subjectivity is inherent in some valuation models and uses a panel of 'experts' to estimate the value of environmental resources, via an iterative process [*Dalkey and Helmer, 1963; Green et al., 1990*]. Korca [*1991*] included local residents in a panel questioned about the impact of tourism expansion in the Mediterranean, and Hunter and Green [*1995*] have also argued that the local community should be involved in decision-making.

Models for valuing resources form the basis of price-based policies for environmental resources. Taxes and subsidies can correct for under- or over-pricing [*Mourmouras, 1993*]. For example, subsidies have been used to support the conservation of environmental resources including traditional architecture, as in the case of the conversion of historic buildings into hotels (paradors) during Spain's early development of tourist accommodation. Admission charges can be levied where the existing level of tourist demand causes environmental damage [*Wanhill, 1980*]. In Macquarie Island, as well as the Annapurna conservation area, tourists are charged on arrival and the revenue is channelled towards environmental protection. Cross-subsidisation may occur; for instance, foreign tourists have paid higher charges for admission to wildlife parks and reserves in Kenya than local residents [*Sinclair, 1992*].

Regulation has also been used as a means of limiting access to and controlling the quality of environmental resources [*Inskeep, 1991*]. The relative merits of regulation and the price mechanism have been the subject of some debate [*Turner, 1988*]. Favoro's [*1983*] study of tourism and fishing in Uruguay argued that a policy of both limitations on tourist numbers and taxation to alter prices should be considered. The Galapagos Islands is an example of a location where quotas have been placed on the number of tourist visitors [*Marsh, 1987*]. However, the implementation of quotas and other forms of regulation is subject to pressure group activity [*Favoro, 1983*] and regulations are sometimes unenforced [*George, 1987; Ecoforum, 1993*]. Control over environmental resources is problematic if ownership or control resides in the hands of non-nationals who do not have a long-term interest in the future of the country [*Britton, 1982*] or with local elites who wish to maximise short term profitability [*Richter, 1989*].

International organisations are becoming increasingly favourable towards the goal of sustainable development and have provided assistance for environmental conservation as well as for the more usual objectives of physical and human capital formation [*Davis and Simmons, 1982; Asian Development Bank, 1995; Pack and Sinclair, 1995a, 1995b*]. The European Union, for instance, provided financial aid for the Pacific Regional Tourism Development Programme, which included environmental guidelines for tourism development and specified criteria for environmental impact assessments, environmental monitoring and tourist behaviour management [*Arndell, 1990*]. However, the issue of whether the strong or weak definition of sustainable tourism development should be supported has rarely been discussed.

VI. CONCLUSIONS

At first sight, tourism appears an attractive option for developing countries with few immediate alternatives. It is characterised by high growth and, with the exception of the airline sector, low protectionism. It provides increasing per capita income, foreign currency and government revenue which can be used to promote the growth of manufacturing. Tourism also generates employment and enables some members of the population to move from the domestic or informal sector to higher-paid jobs in the formal sector. Although expenditure on training and infrastructure per job created may be considerable and the stock of natural assets may decrease, such effects also result from other forms of economic expansion. Thus, in an early study of tourism and developing countries, Erbes [*1973: 4*] concluded that 'the development of the tourism sector is, a priori, a no less rational choice, economically speaking, than any other'.

None the less, the question remains as to whether developing countries are obtaining an optimal return from tourism. Examination of this issue is complicated by the fact that tourism is a composite product whose components are supplied by firms operating in a variety of generally imperfectly competitive market structures in different countries. Not only is there enormous variation between developing countries in the degree and types of integration between firms in tourism and other sectors of the domestic economy but also between tourism firms across borders. Hence, developing countries need to consider the extent and forms of integration which are likely to be most beneficial to them.

The issue of integration between tourism firms from developing countries and foreign firms is exemplified by the air transport sector, which generally accounts for the major share of total holiday or business tourist expenditure. Most developing countries have their own national airline which operates in markets which are competitive, oligopolistic and/or monopolistic, according to the inter-governmental agreements for the particular origin-destination routes. The ability of their airlines to compete on highly regulated routes is curtailed by market share restrictions, while competitive long-haul routes are characterised by price and quality competition between relatively large airlines from industrialised countries. Thus, the overall context within which airlines formulate their strategies is one in which inter-governmental negotiations determine the regulatory regime and affect the market structure, so that strategic policies by governments have an important influence on firm performance. As Krugman [*1989*] and Alam [*1995*] indicate, the governments of small developing countries are relatively disadvantaged in their ability to formulate and implement the strategic policies which would be most beneficial to domestic firms. However, developing countries may have a comparative advantage in particular market niches. In the case of airlines, this might involve supplying short-haul feeder services to long-haul routes, as well as internal flights. A number of airlines are also joining alliances which pool frequent flyer programmes, airline booking, ticketing and related facilities. Privatisation, including foreign direct investment, is a further option whose effects remain to be seen.

A variety of forms of integration between domestic and foreign firms also occur in the hotel accommodation sector in developing countries, including foreign direct investment, management or franchising agreements with international hotel chains and contractual arrangements with foreign tour operators and travel agents. It is not surprising to find that destinations which are relatively well endowed with workers skilled in hotel and catering activities tend to engage in franchising rather than management agreements and are also recipients of foreign direct investment. What are more surprising are the notable cross-country differences in the contractual terms for similar service provision. These are, in part, due to market failure in the form of informational deficiencies, for example, hoteliers' lack of knowledge of prevailing terms for contracts with international hotel management companies or tour operators from industrialised countries. The effect is that contractual terms are significantly worse for countries with less human capital in the form of negotiating skills, contributing to relatively low and sometimes decreasing foreign currency returns per incoming tourist.

Even those countries with significant information and bargaining abilities are not immune to problems, owing to the high and increasing level of market power exercised by large, vertically-integrated tour operators *vis-à-vis* the generally fragmented accommodation sectors of host countries. It is difficult for individual hoteliers, and even hotel groups, to negotiate favourable rates with tour operators in the context of the high level of competition which exists between accommodation suppliers, not only within the country but also at the international level. If hoteliers demand significantly higher prices, tour operators can divert tourists to alternative destinations with relative ease. Attempts to improve the quality of accommodation as a means of extracting higher returns from tour operators are usually impeded by local financial constraints. Hence, hoteliers in developing regions such as the South Pacific are caught in a vicious circle of low quality accommodation, low returns from tour operators and inadequate revenue to fund quality improvements [*King and McVey, 1997*]. Within this context, foreign direct investment may appear an attractive option but can result in enclave resort development and excessive concentration of tourists by nationality. Those countries which are able to limit access to particularly desirable areas, for instance, the Galapagos Islands, are sometimes able to challenge tour operators' market power and obtain higher revenue per capita from a smaller number of tourists.

A further problem is associated with the expansion of tourist accommodation and transportation and concerns the high level of expenditure on associated infrastructure such as water and energy provision, roads and airports. Much of the additional infrastructure is specific to the tourism sector so that tourism is neither a cheap nor a generally beneficial option for residents of developing countries. On the other hand, some developing countries have received aid from such international organisations as the World Bank or Asian Development Bank for the purpose of physical or human capital formation in tourism and 'new' growth theory indicates that this may have positive external effects on overall growth [*Lucas, 1988; Barro, 1990; Barro and Sala-i-Martin, 1992*]. Moreover, there are no obviously superior alternatives in the short run since the expansion of manufacturing is neither cheaper in terms of capital provision nor rapidly attainable. It would, however, be useful to examine the possible means of developing the tourism sector in conjunction with other sectors of the economy along the lines of Kaldor's model of agricultural and manufacturing development [*Thirlwall, 1986*].

Tourism demand also merits further attention as developing countries rely, to a considerable extent, on demand from industrialised countries and low levels of demand result in unemployment and unutilised tourism capacity during particular months or years. Developing countries are often ill-equipped to deal with variations in demand and the associated instability of earnings. They have little control over the international demand for their resources, which is mediated by travel agents and tour operators in industrialised countries. However, these intermediaries are also beneficial since they have informational advantages about tourism markets which are not immediately accessible to agents from developing countries and can generate increasing demand while bearing the associated costs. Moreover, developing countries could obtain greater control over tourism demand by gearing their marketing efforts towards agents, operators and individual tourists in the range of origin countries which would provide the mix of tourist nationalities and types consistent with their desired risk-return trade-off. This would require prior investigation of the determinants of demand by different nationalities and types of tourist, including the degree of complementarity or substitutability between them.

Environmental resources are key attractions of tourist demand and constitute the most obvious area in which developing countries do not achieve an optimal return. In some countries, under-utilisation of available resources means that returns which might otherwise be available are foregone. In others, excessive use resulting from the public good and under-priced nature of the assets gives rise to a level of degradation which threatens tourism's resource base and the long-run returns from it. Debates within environmental economics concerning appropriate definitions of sustainability, methods for valuing resources and price or regulation-based techniques for achieving sustainable resource use have indicated possible means of attaining ongoing returns from environmental assets. However, in practice, lack of consensus over the appropriateness of the weak or strong definition of sustainability is reflected in disagreements concerning the type and extent of policy formulation and implementation. Moreover, many developing countries are understandably reluctant to engage in a level of environmental protection which was not observed by industrialised countries during a similar stage of development.

The issue of the sustainability of tourism and its ongoing contribution to the wider development process is related to both the intra- and inter-generational distribution of the returns from tourism. There is some evidence that environmental resources are more likely to be conserved when local residents participate in decision-making, obtain a return from them and perceive the duration of the return to be linked to resource conservation [*Cater, 1994*], as in the case of wildlife in African game reserves [*Barbier, 1992; Curry and Morvaridi, 1992*]. It is clear that the operation of the market, *per se*, will not ensure an outcome of sustainability and an equitable intra- or inter-generational distribution of returns owing to the notable market failures which occur in the context of environmental resource valuation and utilisation. However, the market mechanism, via pricing and fiscal policy measures, can be used to assist the conservation of tourism's resource base.

It may be concluded that although market failures have limited the returns which developing countries obtain from tourism, they could gain greater and more sustainable returns from it. Clearly, more detailed research on the costs, benefits and policy implications of different forms of tourism

42   THE JOURNAL OF DEVELOPMENT STUDIES

in specific developing-countries is necessary. Although the scope for developing country firms and governments to exercise effective strategic policy is limited, it is by no means non-existent and game theory analyses might indicate a range of feasible strategies and outcomes. By implementing strategies of market regulation and cross-border integration, developing countries could alter both market structure and firm performance. They could also increase the returns which they gain from tourism by mitigating market failures in such forms as information deficiencies, thereby obtaining more favourable production and contractual conditions. Perhaps most obviously, they could obtain notably greater returns from the environmental resources in which they have a comparative advantage.

final version received January 1998

REFERENCES

Adams, P.D. and B.R. Parmenter, 1995, 'An Applied General Equilibrium Analysis of the Economic Effects of Tourism in a Quite Small, Quite Open Economy *Applied Economics*, Vol.27, No.10, pp.985–94.
Alam, A., 1995, 'The New Trade Theory and its Relevance to the Trade Policies of Developing Countries', *The World Economy*, Vol.23, No.8, pp.367–85.
Andronikou, A., 1987, 'Cyprus: Management of the Tourist Sector', *Tourism Management*, Vol.7, No.2, pp.127–9.
Archer, B.H., 1976, *Demand Forecasting in Tourism*, Occasional Papers in Economics, No.9, Bangor: University of Wales Press.
Archer, B.H., 1977, *Tourism Multipliers: The State of the Art*, Occasional Papers in Economics, No.11, Bangor: University of Wales Press.
Archer, B.H., 1989, 'Tourism and Island Economies: Impact Analyses', in C.P. Cooper, (ed.), *Progress in Tourism, Recreation and Hospitality Management*, Vol.1, London: Belhaven.
Archer, B.H., 1995, 'Importance of Tourism for the Economy of Bermuda', *Annals of Tourism Research*, Vol.22, No.4, pp.918–30.
Archer, B.H. and J. Fletcher, 1996, 'The Economic Impact of Tourism in the Seychelles', *Annals of Tourism Research*, Vol.23, No.1, pp.32–47.
Archer, B.H. and C. Owen, 1971, 'Towards a Tourist Regional Multiplier', *Regional Studies*, Vol.5, No.4, pp.289–94.
Arndell, R., 1990, 'Tourism as a Development Concept in the South Pacific', *The Courier*, 122, pp.83–6.
Asian Development Bank, 1995, *Indonesia–Malaysia–Thailand Growth Triangle Development Project*, Regional Technical Assistance 5550, Vol.VI Tourism, Manila: Asian Development Bank.
Attanayake, A., Samaranayake, H.M.S. and N. Ratnapala, 1983, 'Sri Lanka', in E.A. Pye and T-B. Lin (eds.), *Tourism in Asia: The Economic Impact*, Singapore: Singapore University Press.
Bachmann, P., 1988, *Tourism in Kenya: Basic Need for Whom?* Berne: Peter Lang.
Baker, S. and J. Pratt, 1989, 'Experience as a barrier to contestability in airline markets', *Review of Economics and Statistics*, Vol.71, No.2, pp.352–6.
Barbier, E.B., 1992, 'Community-Based Development in Africa', in T.M. Swanson and E.B. Barbier (eds.) *Economics for the Wilds*, London: Earthscan.

TOURISM AND ECONOMIC DEVELOPMENT: A SURVEY 43

Baretje, R., 1982, 'Tourism's External Account and the Balance of Payments', *Annals of Tourism Research*, Vol.9, No.1, pp.57–67.

Baretje, R., 1987, 'La contribution nette du tourisme international a la balance des paiements', *Problems of Tourism*, Vol.10, No.4, pp.51–88.

Barro, R.J., 1990, 'Government Spending in a Simple Model of Endogenous Growth', *Journal of Political Economy*, Vol.98, pp.S103–25.

Barro, R.J. and X. Sala-i-Martin., 1992, 'Public Finance in Models of Economic Growth', *Review of Economic Studies*, Vol.54, pp.646–61.

Bechdolt Jr., B.V., 1973, 'Cross-Sectional Travel Demand Functions: US Visitors to Hawaii, 1961–70, *Quarterly Review of Economics and Business*, Vol.13, pp.37–47.

Beioley, S., 1995, 'Green Tourism – Soft or Sustainable?' *Insights*, May, pp.B75–89.

Belisle, F.J., 1983, 'Tourism and Food Production in the Caribbean', *Annals of Tourism Research*, Vol.10, No.4, pp.497–513.

Bell, P.R.F., 1991, 'Impact of Wastewater Discharges from Tourist Resorts on Eutrophication in Coral Reef Regions and Recommended Methods of Treatment', in M.L. Miller and J. Auyong (eds.), *Proceedings of the 1990 Congress on Coastal and Marine Tourism, Honolulu, Hawaii*, Newport: National Coastal Resources Research and Development Institute.

Bharadwaj, S.G., Varadarajan, P.R. and J. Fahy, 1993, 'Sustainable Competitive Advantage in Service Industries', *Journal of Marketing*, Vol.57, No.4, pp.83–99.

Bird, R.M., 1992, 'Taxing Tourism in Developing Countries', *World Development*, Vol.20, pp.1145–58.

Blundell, R., 1991, 'Consumer Behaviour: Theory and Empirical Evidence – A Survey', in A.J. Oswald (ed.), *Surveys in Economics*, Vol.2, Oxford: Basil Blackwell.

Board, J., Sinclair, M.T. and C.M.S. Sutcliffe, 1987, 'A Portfolio Approach to Regional Tourism', *Built Environment*, Vol.13, No.2, pp.124–37.

Boo, E., 1990, *Ecotourism: The Potential and Pitfalls*, Washington: World Wildlife Fund.

Borenstein, S., 1989, 'Hubs and High Fares: Dominance and Market Power in the United States Airline Industry', *Rand Journal of Economics*, Vol.20, No.3, pp.344–65.

Bote Gómez, V., 1993, 'La necesaria revalorización de la actividad turística española en una economía terciarizada e integrada en la CEE', *Estudios Turísticos*, No.118, pp.5–26.

Bote Gómez, V. and M.T. Sinclair, 1991, 'Integration in the Tourism Industry', in M.T. Sinclair and M.J. Stabler (eds.), *The Tourism Industry: An International Analysis*, Wallingford: CAB International.

Britton, S.G., 1982, 'The Political Economy of Tourism in the Third World', *Annals of Tourism Research*, Vol.9, No.3, pp.331–58.

Broomfield, J.G., 1991, Demand for Tourism in Fiji, MA Dissertation in Development Economics, University of Kent at Canterbury.

Brown, G. Jr. and W. Henry, 1989, *The Economic Value of Elephants*, London Environmental Economics Centre Paper 89–12, University College London.

Bryden, J.M., 1973, *Tourism and Development: A Case Study of the Commonwealth Caribbean*, Cambridge: Cambridge University Press.

Buckley, P.J., 1993, 'Tourism and Foreign Currency Receipts', *Annals of Tourism Research*, Vol.20, No.2, pp.361–7.

Burns, P. and R. Cleverdon, 1995, 'Destination on the Edge? The Case of the Cook Islands', in M.V. Conlin and T. Baum (eds.), *Island Tourism*, Chichester: John Wiley.

Bywater, M., 1994, 'Who Owns Whom in the European Travel Trade', *Travel and Tourism Analyst*, No.3, pp.73–92.

Cater, E. and Goodall, B., 1992, 'Must Tourism Destroy its Resource Base? in A.M. Mannion and S.R. Bowlby (eds.), *Environmental Issues in the 1990s*, Chichester: Wiley.

Cater, E., 1994, 'Ecotourism in the Third World', in E. Cater and G. Lowman (eds.), *Ecotourism. A Sustainable Option?* Chichester: John Wiley.

Caves, D.W., Christensen, L.R. and M.W. Tretheway, 1984, 'Economies of Density versus Economies of Scale: .Why Trunk and Local Service Airline Costs Differ', *Rand Journal of Economics*, Vol.15, No.4, pp.471–89.

Cazes, G., 1972, 'Le rôle du tourisme dans la croissance économique: reflexions a partir de trois examples antillais', *The Tourist Review*, Vol.27, No.3, pp.93–98 and 144–8.

Cazes, G., 1989a, *Le tourisme international: Mirage ou strategie d'avenir*, Paris: Hatier.

Cazes, G., 1989b, *Les nouvelles colonies de vacances? Le tourisme international à la conquête du tiers-monde*, Paris: L'Harmattan.

Cazes, G., 1992, *Tourisme et tiers-monde: Un bilan controversé*, Paris: L'Harmattan.

Chant, S., 1997, 'Gender and Tourism Employment in Mexico and the Philippines', in M.T. Sinclair (ed.), *Gender, Work and Tourism*, London and New York: Routledge.

Clawson, M. and J.L. Knetsch, 1966, *Economics of Outdoor Recreation*, Baltimore, MD: John Hopkins University Press.

Coase, R., 1960, 'The Problem of Social Cost', *Journal of Law and Economics*, Vol.3, pp.1–44.

Conlin, M.V. and T. Baum, 1995, *Island Tourism*, Chichester: John Wiley.

Cook, S.D., Stewart, E. and K. Repass, 1992, *Discover America: Tourism and the Environment*, Washington: Travel Industry Association of America/London: Belhaven.

Copeland, B.R., 1991, 'Tourism, Welfare and De-industrialization in a Small Open Economy', *Economica*, Vol.58, No.4, pp.515–29.

Cukier, J., Norris, J. and G. Wall, 1996, 'The Involvement of Women in the Tourism Industry of Bali, Indonesia', *Journal of Development Studies*, Vol.33, No.2, pp.248–70.

Curry, S., 1992, 'Economic Adjustment Policies and the Hotel Sector in Jamaica', in P. Johnson and B. Thomas (eds.), *Perspectives on Tourism Policy*, London: Mansell.

Curry, S. and B. Morvaridi, 1992, 'Sustainable Tourism: Illustrations from Kenya, Nepal and Jamaica', in C.P. Cooper and A. Lockwood (eds.), *Progress in Tourism, Recreation and Hospitality Management*, Vol.4, London: Belhaven.

Dalkey, N. and O. Helmer, 1963, 'An Experimental Application of the Delphi Method of the Use of Experts', *Management Science*, Vol.9, No.3, pp.458–67.

Davidson, J.E., Hendry, D.F., Srba, F. and S. Yeo, 1978, 'Econometric Modelling of the Aggregate Time-Series Relationship Between Consumers' Expenditure and Income in the United Kingdom', *Economic Journal*, No.88, pp.661–92.

Davis, H.D. and J.A. Simmons, 1982, 'World Bank Experience with Tourism Projects', *Tourism Management*, Vol.3, No.4, pp.212–7.

de Kadt, E., 1979, *Tourism – Passport to Development*, Oxford: Oxford University Press.

de Mello, J., 1988, 'Computable General Equilibrium Models for Trade Ppolicy Analysis in Developing Countries: A Survey, *Journal of Policy Modelling*, No.10, pp.469–503.

Deaton, A.S., 1992, *Understanding Consumption*, Oxford: Clarendon Press.

Deaton, A.S. and J. Muellbauer, 1980a, 'An Almost Ideal Demand System', *American Economic Review*, Vol.70, No.3, pp.312–26.

Deaton, A.S. and J. Muellbauer, 1980b, *Economics and Consumer Behaviour*, Cambridge: Cambridge University Press.

Delos Santos, J.S., Ortiz, E.M., Huang, E. and F. Secretario, 1983, 'Philippines', in E.A. Pye and T.-B. Lin (eds.), *Tourism in Asia: The Economic Impact*, Singapore: Singapore University Press.

Demsetz, H., 1969, 'Information and Efficiency: Another Viewpoint', *Journal of Law and Economics*, Vol.12, No.1, pp.1–22.

Diamond, J., 1974, 'International Tourism and the Developing Countries: A Case Study in Failure', *Economica Internazionale*, Vol.27, Nos.3–4, pp.601–15.

Diamond, J., 1977, 'Tourism's Role in Economic Development: The Case Reexamined', *Economic Development and Cultural Change*, Vol.25, No.3, pp.539–53.

Dieke, P.U.C., 1993, 'Tourism in The Gambia: Some Issues in Development Policy', *World Development*, Vol.21, No.2, pp.277–89.

Dieke, P.U.C., 1995, 'Tourism and Structural Adjustment Programmes in the African Economy', *Tourism Economics*, No.1, pp.71–93.

Doganis, R., 1985, *Flying Off Course*, London: George Allen & Unwin.

Doganis, R., 1993, 'The Bilateral Regime for Air Transport: Current Position and Future Challenges', in *International Air Transport: The Challenges Ahead*, Paris: Organisation for Economic Cooperation and Development.

Douglas, G.W. and J.C. Miller, 1974, *Economic Regulation of Domestic Air Transport: Theory and Policy*, Washington, DC: The Brookings Institution.

TOURISM AND ECONOMIC DEVELOPMENT: A SURVEY   45

Dunning, J.H. and M. McQueen, 1982, *Transnational Corporations in International Tourism*, New York: United Nations Centre for Transnational Corporations.

Dwyer, L. and P. Forsyth, 1994, 'Foreign Tourism Investment: Motivation and Impact', *Annals of Tourism Research*, Vol.21, No.3, pp.512–37.

Eber, S. (ed.), 1992, *Beyond the Green Horizon. Principles for Sustainable Tourism*, Godalming: World Wide Fund for Nature.

Ecoforum, 1993, *Fish, Curry and Rice. A Citizens' Report on the State of the Goan Environment*, Goa: Other India Press.

Economic and Social Commission for Asia and the Pacific (ESCAP), 1991, *Investment and Economic Cooperation in the Tourism Sector in Developing Asian Countries*, ESCAP Tourism Review No.8, Bangkok.

Economist Intelligence Unit (EIU), 1990, 'The Travel and Tourism Industry in Italy', *Travel and Tourism Analyst*, No.4, pp.74–8.

Elkan, W., 1975, 'The Relation Between Tourism and Employment in Kenya and Tanzania', *Journal of Development Studies*, Vol.11, No.2, pp.123–30.

English, E.P., 1986, *The Great Escape? An Examination of North-South Tourism*, Ottawa: North-South Institute.

Erbes, R., 1973, *International Tourism and the Economy of Developing Countries*, Paris: Organisation for Economic Cooperation and Development.

Euromonitor, 1997, *World Tourism 1997*, London: Euromonitor.

EXA International/CHL Consulting Group, 1993, *The Economic Significance of Tourism in Zimbabwe*, EXA International.

Farrell, B.H. and D. Runyan, 1991, 'Ecology and Tourism', *Annals of Tourism Research*, Vol.18, No.1, pp.26–40.

Farver, J.A.M., 1984, 'Tourism and Employment in the Gambia', *Annals of Tourism Research*, Vol.11, No.2, pp.249–65.

Favoro, E., 1983, 'Dos enfoques para el analisis de externalidades: examen de la interaccion pesca vs. turismo en La Paloma', in M. Arana *et al.*, *Medio ambiente y turismo*, Buenos Aires: Consejo Latinoamericano de Ciencias Sociales.

Fish, M., 1982, 'Taxing International Tourism in West Africa', *Annals of Tourism Research*, Vol.9, No.1, pp.91–103.

Fletcher, J.E. and B.H. Archer, 1991, 'The Development and Application of Multiplier Analysis', in C.P. Cooper (ed.), *Progress in Tourism, Recreation and Hospitality Management*, Vol.1, London: Belhaven.

Forsyth, T., 1995a, 'Business Attitudes to Sustainable Tourism: Responsibility and Self Regulation in the UK. Outgoing Tourism Industry', Paper presented at the Sustainable Tourism World Conference, Lanzarote.

Forsyth, T., 1995b, 'Tourism and Agricultural Development in Thailand', *Annals of Tourism Research*, Vol.22, No.4, pp.877–900.

French, T., 1995, 'Charter Airlines in Europe', *Travel and Tourism Analyst*, No.4, pp.4–19.

French, T., 1997, 'Global Trends in Airline Alliances', *Travel and Tourism Analyst*, No.4, pp.81–101.

Friedman, M., 1957, *A Theory of the Consumption Function*, Princeton, NJ: Princeton University Press.

Fujii, E., Khaled, M. and J. Mak, 1985, 'The Exportability of Hotel Occupancy and Other Tourist Taxes', *National Tax Journal*, Vol.38, No.2, pp.169–77.

Fujii, E., Khaled, M. and J. Mak, 1987, 'An Empirical Comparison of Systems of Demand Equations: An Application to Visitor Expenditure in Resort Destinations', *Philippine Review of Business and Economics*, Vol.24, Nos.1–2, pp.79–102.

Garrod, G. and K. Willis, 1991, 'The Environmental Economic Impact of Woodland: A Two-Stage Hedonic Price Model of the Amenity Value of Forestry in Britain', *Applied Economics*, No..24, pp.715–28.

George, V., 1987, 'Tourism on Jamaica's North Coast', in S. Britton and W.C. Clarke (eds.), *Ambiguous Alternative. Tourism in Small Developing Countries*, Suva, Fiji: University of the South Pacific.

Gillen, D.W., Oum, T.H. and M.W. Tretheway, 1990, 'Airline Cost Structure and Policy

Implications', *Journal of Transport Economics and Policy*, Vol.24, No.1, pp.9–34.

Go, F., 1988, 'Key Problems and Prospects in the International Hotel Industry', *Travel and Tourism Analyst*, No.1, pp.27–49.

Gray, H.P., 1966, 'The Demand for International Travel by the United States and Canada', *International Economic Review*, Vol.7, No.1, pp.83–92.

Green, H., Hunter, C. and B. Moore, 1990, 'Assessing the Environmental Impact of Tourism Development: Use of the Delphi Technique', *Tourism Management*, Vol.11, No.2, pp.111–20.

Grünthal, A., 1960, 'Foreign Travel in the Balance of Payments', *The Tourist Review*, No.1, pp.14–20.

Gunadhi, H. and C.K. Boey, 1986, 'Demand Elasticities of Tourism in Singapore', *Tourism Management*, Vol.7, No.4, pp.239–53.

Hanley, N. and R. Ruffell, 1993, 'The Valuation of Forest Characteristics', *Queen's Discussion Paper* 849.

Hawkins, J.P. and C.M. Roberts, 1994, 'The Growth of Coastal Tourism in the Red Sea: Present and Future Effects on Coral Reefs', *Ambio*, No.23, pp.503–8.

Helu Thaman, K., 1992, 'Beyond Hula, Hotels and Handicrafts', *In Focus*, Vol.4, Summer, pp.8–9.

Hendry, D.F., 1983, 'Econometric Modelling: The 'Consumption Function' in Retrospect', *Scottish Journal of Political Economy*, No.30, pp.193–220.

Hendry, D.F. and G.E. Mizon, 1978, 'Serial Correlation as a Convenient Simplification, Not a Nuisance', *Economic Journal*, No.88, pp.549–63.

Heng, T.M. and L. Low, 1990, 'The Economic Impact of Tourism in Singapore', *Annals of Tourism Research*, Vol.17, No.2, pp.246–69.

Horwath Consulting, 1994, *United Kingdom Hotel Industry 1994*, London: Horwath International.

Huband, M., 1997, 'Something Big to Sing About', *Financial Times*, 13 May.

Hughes, H.L., 1981, 'A Tourism Tax – The Cases For and Against', *International Journal of Tourism Management*, Vol.2, No.3, pp.196–206.

Hunter, C. and H. Green, 1995, 'Tourism and the Environment: A Sustainable Relationship?', Londo: Routledge.

Hurdle, G.J., Johnson, R.L., Joskow, A.S., Werden, G.J. and M.A. Williams, 1989, 'Concentration, Potential Entry and Performance in the Airline Industry', *Journal of Industrial Economics*, Vol.38, No.2, pp.119–39.

Inskeep, E., 1991, *Tourism Planning: An Integrated and Sustainable Approach*, The Hague: Van Nostrand Reinhold.

Instituto Español de Turismo, 1980, 'La balanza de pagos turística de España en 1977', *Estudios Turísticos*, No.65, pp.91–15.

Instituto Español de Turismo, 1983, 'Balanza de pagos turística de España: Años 1979 y 1980', *Estudios Turísticos*, Nos.77–8, pp.133–57.

Instituto Español de Turismo, 1987, 'El gasto turístico: Analisis del escandalo de los paquetes turísticos. *Estudios Turísticos*, No.93, pp.3–26.

Jenner, P. and C. Smith, 1992, 'The Tourism Industry and the Environment', Special Report 2453, London: Economist Intelligence Unit.

Johnson, P. and J. Ashworth, 1990, 'Modelling Tourism Demand: A Summary Review', *Leisure Studies*, Vol.9, No.2, pp.145–60.

Jönsson, C., 1981, 'Sphere of Flying: The Politics of International Aviation', *International Organisation*, Vol.35, No.2, pp.273–302.

Jud, G.D. and H. Joseph, 1974, 'International Demand for Latin American Tourism', *Growth and Change*, No.5, pp.25–31.

King, B. and M. McVey, 1997, 'Hotel Investment in the South Pacific', *Travel and Tourism Analyst*, No.5, pp.63–87.

Knudsen, O. and A. Parnes, 1975, *Trade Instability and Economic Development*, Lexington, MA: D.C. Heath.

Korca, P., 1991, 'Assessment of the Environmental Impacts of Tourism', proceedings of an *International Symposium on the Architecture of Tourism in the Mediterranean*, Istanbul, Turkey: Yildiz University Press.

TOURISM AND ECONOMIC DEVELOPMENT: A SURVEY 47

Krugman, P.R., 1989, 'New Trade Theory and the Less Developed Countries', in G. Calvo *et al.*, (eds.), *Debt, Stabilization and Development*, Oxford: Basil Blackwell.

Lea, J., 1988, *Tourism and Development in the Third World*, London and New York: Routledge.

Lee, G., 1987, 'Tourism as a Factor in Development Cooperation', *Tourism Management*, Vol.8, No.1, pp.2–19.

Lee, W., 1991, 'Prostitution and Tourism in South-East Asia', in N. Redclift and M.T. Sinclair (eds.), *Working Women: International Perspectives on Labour and Gender Ideology*, London and New York: Routledge.

Leguevaques, M., 1989, 'Les tour operators européens et la destination à France', in *Collection Hôtellerie et Tourisme*, Paris: Assemblée Permanente des Chambres de Commerce et de'Industrie, Centre d'Etude de la Commercialisation et de la Distribution.

Leigh, L.E., 1990, 'Contestability in Deregulated Airline Markets: Some Empirical Tests', *Transportation Journal*, Vol.30, No.2, pp.49–57.

Levine, M.E., 1987, 'Airline Competition in Deregulated Markets: Theory, Firm Strategy and Public Policy', *Yale Journal of Regulation*, No.4, pp.393–494.

Levy, D.E. and P.B. Lerch, 1991, 'Tourism as a Factor in Development: Implications for Gender and Work in Barbados', *Gender and Society*, Vol.5, No.1, pp.67–85.

Lin, T-b. and Y.-W. Sung, 1983, 'Hong Kong', in E.A. Pye and T.-B. Lin (eds.), *Tourism in Asia: The Economic Impact*, Singapore: Singapore University Press.

Lipsey, R.G. and K.J. Lancaster, 1956–7, 'The General Theory of the Second Best', *Review of Economic Studies*, 24, pp.11–32.

Liston, K., 1986, 'David and Goliath', *The Courier*, Nov./Dec., pp.19–21.

Lockwood, M., Loomis, J. and T. DeLacy, 1993, 'A Contingent Valuation Survey and Benefit-Cost Analysis of Forest Preservation in East Gippsland, Australia', *Journal of Environmental Managment*, No.38, pp.233–43.

Long, V.H., 1991, 'Government–Industry–Community Interaction in Tourism Development in Mexico', in M.T. Sinclair and M.J. Stabler (eds.), *The Tourism Industry: An International Analysis*, Wallingford: CAB International.

Long, V.H. and S.L. Kindon, 1997, 'Gender and Tourism Development in Balinese Villages', in M.T. Sinclair (ed.), *Gender, Work and Tourism*, London and New York: Routledge.

Loomis, J.B., Creel, M. and T. Park, 1991, 'Comparing Benefit Estimates from Travel Cost and Contingent Valuation Using Confidence Intervals from Hicksian Welfare Measures', *Applied Economics*, No.23, pp.1725–31.

Lucas, R.E. Jr., 1988, 'On the Mechanics of Economic Growth', *Journal of Monetary Economics*, No.22, pp.3–42.

Mak, J. and E. Nishimura, 1979, 'The Economics of a Hotel Room Tax', *Journal of Travel Research*, Spring, pp.2–6.

Markowitz, H., 1959, *Portfolio Selection: Efficient Diversification of Investments*, New York: John Wiley.

Marsh, J.S., 1987, 'National Parks and Tourism in Small Developing Countries', in S. Britton and W.C. Clarke (eds.), *Ambiguous Alternatives: Tourism in Small Developing Countries*, Suva, Fiji: University of the South Pacific.

Mason, K. and R. Gray, 1991, 'The Liberation of Civil Aviation in the European Community – An Overview', *European Research*, July, pp.11–15.

Melville, J.A., 1995, 'Some Empirical Results for the Airline and Air Transport Markets of a Small Developing Country', Ph.D. thesis, University of Kent at Canterbury.

Milne, S.S., 1987, 'Differential Multipliers', *Annals of Tourism Research*, Vol.14, No.4, pp.499–515.

Mitchell, F., 1970, 'The Value of Tourism in East Africa', *East Africa Economic Review*, Vol.2, No.1, pp.1–21.

Morandy, G., 1988, 'Les tour operators en Europe', in *Collection analyses de secteurs*, Paris: Eurostaf Dafsa.

Mourmouras, A., 1993, 'Conservationist Government Policies and Intergenerational Equity in an Overlapping Generations Model with Renewable Resources', *Journal of Public Economics*, No.51, pp.249–68.

Mudambi, R., 1994, 'A Ricardian Excursion to Bermuda: An Estimation of Mixed Strategy Equilibrium', *Applied Economics*, No.26, pp.927–36.

National Consumer Council, 1986, *Air Transport and the Consumer: A Need for Change*, London: H.M.S.O.

North, D.C., 1990, *Institutional Change and Economic Performance*, Cambridge: Cambridge University Press.

Nuutinen, H., 1992, 'Rules of Engagement in the Battle of the Atlantic', *The Avmark Aviation Economist*, Sept., pp.4–10.

Nuutinen, H., 1993, 'Fighting to Beat Back the US Majors', *The Avmark Aviation Economist*, Dec., pp.11–18.

O'Connor, W.E., 1995, *An Introduction to Airline Economics*, London: Praeger.

O'Hagan, J.W. and M.J. Harrison, 1984, 'Market shares of US Tourist Expenditure in Europe: An Econometric Analysis', *Applied Economics*, Vol.16, No.6, pp.919–31.

Pack, A. and M.T. Sinclair, 1995a, 'Tourism, Conservation and Sustainable Development, Indonesia', Report for the Overseas Development Administration, London.

Pack, A. and M.T. Sinclair, 1995b, 'Tourism, Conservation and Sustainable Development, India', Report for the Overseas Development Administration, London.

Panzar. J., 1979, 'Equilibrium and Welfare in Unregulated Airline Markets', *American Economic Review*, Vol.69, No.2, pp.92–5.

Papadopoulos, S.I and S.F. Witt, 1985, 'A Marketing Analysis of Foreign Tourism in Greece', in S. Shaw, L. Sparks and E. Kaynak (eds), *Proceedings of the Second World Marketing Congress*, University of Stirling.

Pawson, I.G., Stanford, D.D., Adams, V.A. and M. Nurbu, 1984, 'Growth of tourism in Nepal's Everest Region: Impact on the Physical Environment and Structure of Human Settlements', *Mountain Research and Development*, Vol.4, No.3, pp.237–46.

Pearce, D., 1985, 'Tourism and Environmental Research: A Review', *International Journal of Environmental Studies*, Vol.25, No.4, pp.247–55.

Pearce, D.W., Markandya, A. and E.B. Barbier, 1989, *Blueprint for a Green Economy*, London: Earthscan Publications.

Pollard, H.J., 1976, 'Antigua, West Indies: An Example of the Operation of the Multiplier Process Arising from Tourism', *Revue de Tourisme*, No.3, pp.30–34.

Pyo, S.S., Uysal, M. and R.W. McLellan, 1991, 'A Linear Expenditure Model for Tourism Demand', *Annals of Tourism Research*, No.18, pp.443–54.

Rao, A., 1986, *Tourism and Export Instability in Fiji*, Occasional Papers in Economic Development No.2, Faculty of Economic Studies, University of New England, Australia.

Randall, A., 1993, 'The Problem of Market Failure', in R. Dorfman and N.S. Dorfman (eds.), *Economics of the Environment*, New York: Norton.

Richards, G., 1972, 'Tourism and the Economy: An Examination of Methods for Evaluating the Contribution and Effects of Tourism in the Economy', Summary Report based on a Ph.D. thesis, University of Surrey.

Richter, L.K., 1989, *The Politics of Tourism in Asia*, Honolulu, HI: University of Hawaii Press.

Robineau, C., 1975, 'The Tahitian Economy and Tourism', in B.R. Finney and K.A. Watson (eds.), *A New Kind of Sugar: Tourism in the Pacific*, Honolulu, HI: East–West Center.

Romeril, M., 1989, 'Tourism and the Environment: Accord or Discord' *Tourism Management*, Vol.10, No.3, pp.204–08.

Rosen, S., 1974, 'Hedonic Prices and Implicit Markets: Production Differentiation in Pure Competition', *Journal of Political Economy*, Vol.82, No.1, pp.34–55.

Sadler, P., Archer, B.H. and C. Owen, 1973, *Regional Income Multipliers*, Occasional Papers in Economics, No.1, Bangor: University of Wales Press.

Sakai, M.Y., 1988, 'A Micro-Analysis of Business Travel Demand', *Applied Economics*, No.20, pp.1481–96.

Saltmarsh, G., 1986, 'Travel Retailing in the UK: Survey of the Agents, Their Costs, Markets and Mergers', *Travel and Tourism Analyst*, Sept., pp.49–62.

Samarasuriya, S., 1982, 'Who Needs Tourism? Employment for Women in the Holiday Industry of Sudugama, Sri Lanka', Colombo: Research Project for Women and Development.

Samy, J., 1975, 'Crumbs from the Worker's Table? The Worker's Share in Tourism', in B.R. Finney and K.A. Watson (eds.), *A New Kind of Sugar: Tourism in the Pacific*, Honolulu, HI: East–West Center.

Sathiendrakumar, R. and C. Tisdell, 1989, 'Tourism and the Economic Development of the Maldives', *Annals of Tourism Research*, Vol.16, No.2, pp.254–9.

Scott, J., 1997, 'Chances and Choice: Women and Tourism in Northern Cyprus', in M.T. Sinclair (ed.), *Gender, Work and Tourism*, London and New York: Routledge.

Seeberger, V.M., 1992, 'Potential European Demand for Tourism in Reunion Island (France)', MA dissertation in Development Economics, University of Kent at Canterbury.

Shamsuddin, S., 1995, 'Tourism Demand in Peninsular Malaysia', MA dissertation in Development Economics, University of Kent at Canterbury.

Sheldon, P.J., 1990, 'A Review of Tourism Expenditure Research', in C.P. Cooper (ed.), *Progress in Tourism, Recreation and Hospitality Management*, Volume Two, London: Belhaven.

Sheldon, P.J., 1994, 'Tour Operators', in S.F. Witt and L. Moutinho (eds.), *Tourism Management and Marketing Handbook*, Hemel Hempstead: Prentice Hall.

Sinclair, M.T., 1990, *Tourism Development in Kenya*, Washington, DC: World Bank.

Sinclair, M.T., 1991a, 'The Economics of Tourism', in C.P. Cooper (ed.), *Progress in Tourism, Recreation and Hospitality Management*, Vol.3, London: Belhaven.

Sinclair, M.T., 1991b, 'The Tourism Industry and Foreign Exchange Leakages in a Developing Country', in M.T. Sinclair and M.J. Stabler (eds.), *The Tourism Industry: An International Analysis*, Wallingford: CAB International.

Sinclair, M.T., 1992, 'Tour Operators and Tourism Development Policies in Kenya', *Annals of Tourism Research*, Vol.19, No.3, pp.555–8.

Sinclair, M.T., 1997, 'Issues and Theories of Gender and Work in Tourism', in M.T. Sinclair (ed.), *Gender, Work and Tourism*, London and New York: Routledge.

Sinclair, M.T., Alizadeh, P. and E. Atieno Adero Onunga, 1992, 'The Structure of International Tourism and Tourism Development in Kenya', in D. Harrison (ed.), *Tourism and the Less Developed Countries*, London: Belhaven.

Sinclair, M.T. and Bote Gómez, V., 1996, 'Tourism, the Spanish Economy and the Balance of Payments', in M. Barke, M. Newton and J. Towner (eds.), *Tourism in Spain: Critical Perspectives*, Wallingford: C.A.B. International.

Sinclair, M.T., Clewer, A. and A. Pack, 1990, 'Hedonic Prices and the Marketing of Package Holidays', in G. Ashworth and B. Goodall (eds.), *Marketing Tourism Places*, London and New York: Routledge.

Sinclair, M.T. and M.J. Stabler, 1997, *The Economics of Tourism*, London and New York: Routledge.

Sinclair, M.T. and C.M.S. Sutcliffe, 1978, 'The First Round of the Keynesian Income Multiplier', *Scottish Journal of Political Economy*, Vol.25, No.2, pp.177–86.

Sinclair, M.T. and C.M.S. Sutcliffe, 1988, 'The Estimation of Keynesian Income Multipliers at the Sub-National Level', *Applied Economics*, Vol.20, No.11, pp.1435–44.

Sinclair, M.T. and C.M.S. Sutcliffe, 1989, 'Truncated Income Multipliers and Local Income Generation Over Time', *Applied Economics*, Vol.21, No.12, pp.1621–30.

Sinclair, M.T. and A. Tsegaye, 1990, 'International Tourism and Export Instability', *Journal of Development Studies*, Vol.26, No.3, pp.487–504.

Sinclair, M.T. and R. Vokes, 1993, 'The Economics of Tourism in Asia and the Pacific', in M. Hitchcock, V.T. King and M. Parnwell (eds.), *Tourism in South-East Asia: Theory and Practice*, London and New York: Routledge.

Sindiyo, D.M. and F.N. Pertet, 1984, 'Tourism and its Impact on Wildlife in Kenya', *Industry and Environment*, Vol.7, No.1, pp.14–19.

Smeral, E., 1988, 'Tourism Demand, Economic Theory and Econometrics: An Integrated Approach', *Journal of Travel Research*, Vol.26, No.4, pp.38–43.

Smith, C. and P. Jenner, 1989, 'Tourism and the Environment', *Travel and Tourism Analyst*, No.5, pp.68–86.

Smith, C. and P. Jenner, 1994, 'Travel Agents in Europe', *Travel and Tourism Analyst*, No.3, pp.56–72.

Smith, V.K., Palmquist, R.B. and P. Jakus, 1991, 'Combining Farrel Frontier and Hedonic Travel Cost Models for Valuing Estuarine Quality', *Review of Economics and Statistics*, Vol.63, No.4, pp.694–9.

Song, B.-N. and C.-Y. Ahn, 1983, 'Korea', in E.A. Pye and T.-B. Lin (eds.), *Tourism in Asia: The Economic Impact*, Singapore: Singapore University Press.

Stabler, M.J. and B. Goodall, 1996, 'Environmental Auditing in Planning for Sustainable Island Tourism', in L. Briguglio, B. Archer, J. Jafari and G. Wall, *Sustainable Tourism in Islands and Small States: Issues and Policies*, London: Pinter (Cassell).

Stiglitz, J.E., 1989, 'Imperfect Information in the Product Market', in R. Schmalensee and R.D. Willig (eds.), *Handbook of Industrial Organisation*, Vol.1, Amsterdam: North Holland.

Stockfish, B., 1992, 'Opening Closed Skies: The Prospect for Further Liberalisation of Trade in International Transport Services', *Journal of Air Law and Commerce*, Vol.57, pp.569–77.

Strassman, D., 1990, 'Potential Competition in the Deregulated Airlines', *Review of Economics and Statistics*, Vol.27, No.4, pp.696–702.

Stronge, W.B. and M. Redman, 1982, 'US Tourism in Mexico: An Empirical Analysis', *Annals of Tourism Research*, Vol.9, No.1, pp.21–35.

Summary, R., 1987, 'Multivariable Regression Analysis: Evidence from Kenya', *Tourism Management*, No.8, pp.317–22.

Syriopoulos, T., 1995, 'A Dynamic Model of Demand for Mediterranean Tourism', *International Review of Applied Economics*, Vol.9, No.3, pp.318–36.

Syriopoulos, T. and M.T. Sinclair, 1993, 'An Econometric Study of Tourism Demand: The AIDS Model of US and European Tourism in Mediterranean Countries, *Applied Economics*, Vol.25, No.12, pp.1541–52.

Telfer, D.J. and G. Wall, 1996, 'Linkages Between Tourism and Food Production', *Annals of Tourism Research*, Vol.23, No.3, pp.635–53.

Thirlwall, A.P., 1979, 'The Balance of Payments Constraint as an Explanation of International Growth Rate Differences', *Banca Nazionale del Lavoro Quarterly Review*, No.128, pp.45–53.

Thirlwall, A.P., 1986, 'A General Model of Growth and Development on Kaldorian Lines' *Oxford Economic Papers*, No.38, pp.199–219.

Thirlwall, A.P. and M. Nureldin-Hussein, 1982, 'The Balance of Payments Constraint, Capital Flows and Growth Rate Differences Between Developing Countries', *Oxford Economic Papers*, No.34, pp.498–510.

Tourism Concern, 1995, 'Our Holidays, Their Homes' (special issue on people displaced by tourism), *In Focus*, Vol.15, Spring, pp.3–13.

Turner, R.K. (ed.), 1988, *Sustainable Environmental Management: Principles and Practice*, London: Belhaven Press.

United Nations Conference on Trade and Development (UNCTAD), 1971, *The Development of Tourism in Yugoslavia*, TD/ B/C.3/89, Add.3.

United Nations Conference on Trade and Development (UNCTAD), 1973, *Elements of Tourism Policy in Developing Countries*, Report by the Secretariat of UNCTAD, TD/B/C.3/89, Add.3, Geneva: UNCTAD.

Uysal, M. and J.L. Crompton, 1984, 'Determinants of Demand for International Tourist Flows in Turkey', *Tourism Management*, Vol.5, No.4, pp.288–97.

Varley, R.C.G., 1978, *Tourism in Fiji: Some Economic and Social Problems*, Occasional Papers in Economics, No.12, University of Wales Press, Bangor.

Vietor, R.H.K., 1990, 'Contrived Competition: Airline Regulation and Deregulation, 1925–78', *Business History Review*, No.64, pp.61–108.

Wanhill, S.R.C., 1980, 'Charging for Congestion at Tourist Attractions', *International Journal of Tourism Management*, Vol.1, No.3, pp.168–74.

Wanhill, S.R.C., 1982, 'Evaluating the Resource Costs of Tourism', *Tourism Management*, Vol.3, No.4, pp.208–11.

Wanhill, S.R.C., 1986, 'Which Investment Incentives for Tourism?' *Tourism Management*, Vol.7, No.1, pp.2–7.

Wanhill, S.R.C., 1988, 'Tourism Multipliers Under Capacity Constraints', *Service Industries Journal*, 8, pp.136–42.

Weston, R., 1983, 'The Ubiquity of Room Taxes', *Tourism Management*, Vol.4, No.3, pp.194–8.

White, K.J., 1982, 'The Demand for International Travel: A System-wide Analysis for US Travel to Western Europe', Discussion Paper No.82–28, University of British Columbia, Canada.

White, K.J. and M.B. Walker, 1982, 'Trouble in the Travel Account', *Annals of Tourism Research*, Vol.9, No.1, pp.37–56.

TOURISM AND ECONOMIC DEVELOPMENT: A SURVEY   51

Wight, P. (1993, 'Ecotourism: Ethics or Eco-sell?', *Journal of Travel Research*, No.31, pp.3–9.

Wight, P. (1994, 'The Greening of the Hospitality Industry: Economic and Environmental Good Sense', in A.V. Seaton (ed.), *Tourism: The State of the Art*, Chichester: Wiley.

Williamson, O.E., 1985, *The Economic Institutions of Capitalism*, New York: Free Press.

Williamson, O.E., 1986, *Economic Organisation: Firms, Markets and Policy Control*, Brighton: Wheatsheaf.

Willis, K. and G. Garrod, 1993a, 'The Value of Waterside Properties: Estimating the Impact of Waterways and Canals on Property Values Through Hedonic Price Models and Contingent Valuation Methods', *Countryside Change Unit Working Paper 44*, Newcastle: University of Newcastle.

Willis, K. and G. Garrod, 1993b, 'Valuing Wildlife: The Benefits of Wildlife Trusts', *Countryside Change Unit Working Paper 46*, Newcastle: University of Newcastle.

Windle, R.J., 1991, 'The World's Airline: A Cost and Productivity Comparison', *Journal of Transport Economics and Policy*, Jan., pp.31–49.

Wise, B., 1993, 'Hotel Chains in the Asia Pacific Region', *Travel and Tourism Analyst*, No.4, pp.57–73.

WTO (World Tourism Organisation), 1992, *Tourism Trends Worldwide and in Europe*, Madrid: World Tourism Organisation.

Zhou, D., Yanagida, J.F., Chakravorty, U. and P. Leung, 1997, 'Estimating Economic Impacts from Tourism', *Annals of Tourism Research*, Vol.24, No.1, pp.76–89.

B
Political Economy

[4]

Pergamon

Annals of Tourism Research, Vol. 26, No. 1, pp. 1–20, 1999
© 1998 Elsevier Science Ltd. All rights reserved
Printed in Great Britain
0160-7383/98 $19.00+0.00

PII: S0160-7383(98)00046-2

TOURISM AND DEVELOPMENT
Evidence from Mexico

Michael J. Clancy
University of Hartford, USA

Abstract: Few recent studies of tourism in the third world have explicitly adopted approaches drawing from contemporary theories of the political economy of development. Instead they have either turned away from political economy to alternative approaches or are mainly empirical in nature. This paper contends that some recent strands of development theory hold particular promise in this field and illustrates their use by examining tourism in Mexico over the past 30 years. Specifically, findings suggest that a statist approach, augmented by considerations of the structure of the international tourism industry, help explain both growth and distributional effects in Mexico over that period. **Keywords:** development, political economy, export-led growth, statism, neoliberalism, post-dependency, hotels. © 1999 Elsevier Science Ltd. All rights reserved.

Résumé: Tourisme et développement: l'exemple du Mexique. Peu d'études récentes du tourisme au tiers monde se sont inspirées de manière explicite des théories contemporaines de l'economie politique de développement. Elles se sont plutôt éloignées de l'économie politique pour s'orienter vers d'autres champs de recherche, ou elles sont essentiellement empiriques. Cette analyse tente de démontrer que certaines hypothèses de la théorie de développement sont particulièrement utiles pour les études touristiques. Cette analyse se sert de ces hypothèses, prenant comme exemple le tourisme au Mexique pendant les trente dernières années. Des recherches suggèrent qu'une telle approche étatiste, renforcée par des considérations sur la structure de l'industrie touristique internationale, facilite la compréhension des effects du tourisme sur la croissance et la distribution au Mexique. **Mots-clés:** développement, économie politique, croissance menée par l'exportation, étatisme, néo-libéralisme, postdépendance, hôtels. © 1999 Elsevier Science Ltd. All rights reserved.

INTRODUCTION

The effects of international tourism on developing societies have long been of interest to both scholars and policymakers. Today more than 27% of global tourism expenditures—excluding transportation—are destined for these countries, up from about 20% in the late 80s (WTO 1996:9). As tourism becomes increasingly important to the larger process of economic development, it will continue to draw widespread attention—as well as controversy. Unfortunately, while this economic sector and the question of development appear to be more intertwined than ever, tourism and development studies have drifted apart in recent years. In other words, the industry was

Michael Clancy recently received his Ph.D. in political science from the University of Wisconsin-Madison. His primary interest is in international political economy and third world development, and his doctoral dissertation examines the intersection of international and domestic variables affecting tourism development in Mexico from 1967–92. He is currently assistant professor at the University of Hartford (Department of Politics and Government, College of Arts and Sciences, West Hartford, CT 06117-1599, USA. Email ⟨clancy@mail.hartford.edu⟩).

2   TOURISM AND DEVELOPMENT

immersed in key debates relating to the political economy of development during the 60s and 70s. More recently, however, while broader
development debates have progressed and become more refined,
studies of tourism in developing countries have either turned away
from political economy or have become less theoretical altogether.
This is not to suggest that alternative approaches are not promising,
but instead to ask whether the paucity of political economy studies
indicates a common belief that they are likely to lead to a dead end.

The purpose of this article is twofold: first is to reintegrate tourism
studies with more current theoretical strands of development literature, especially the most prevalent debates relating to states and
markets. By no means are *all* different directions in which development theory has moved to be covered here. That task is simply too
demanding in today's environment of theoretical eclecticism. Instead
emphasis is placed on three political economy approaches, specifically
neoliberalism, statist or instutional approaches, and what might be
called post-dependency frameworks in asking whether these models
aid one in gaining a better understanding of tourism development.
The second purpose is to turn to tourism in Mexico over the past 30
years in order to examine an important case of its development from
a theoretically informed standpoint. Mexico is an ideal case because
although it possesses a large and diversified economy, the country is
a primary global destination, ranking 10th in international arrivals
and 12th in earnings in 1994 (WTO 1996:12–3). Tourism constitutes
one of the leading sources of foreign exchange for the country and
has consistently served as the second largest source of employment
after agriculture.

TOURISM AND DEVELOPMENT

The growth of tourism to developing societies has not come without
controversy, and much of the literature on the subject reflects this.
When developing countries promote this trade—the provision of tourism-related goods and services to foreign visitors—they are, in effect,
embracing greater integration into the world economy. It is the terms
of this integration, and the direct economic and political effects stemming from them, that invite this controversy. As a result, such studies
quickly became immersed in larger debates over the political economy
of development, especially during the 70s and early 80s. This was most
evident within the most important development debate of that period,
that of modernization versus dependency approaches. Briefly, the
modernization school viewed development as a linear process, with
many poor countries simply "behind" their wealthier counterparts.
Developing societies were seen as being "undeveloped" in the sense
of lacking development. They were viewed, however, as being in the
midst of transforming themselves from traditional to modern; and
although modernizing was viewed largely as an endogenous and often
cultural process, economic ties between North (or West) and South
were considered beneficial, or at the very least benign (Almond and

MICHAEL CLANCY 3

Closeman 1960; Rostow 1962; Weiner 1966; Valenzuela and Valenzuela 1978).

Modernization approaches, which encompassed a broad range of social science disciplines, were thus consistent with ideas of economic liberalism. In addition, at least in earlier forms, there existed a broad optimism that economic growth would coincide with political democracy, a view sometimes summarized by supporters and critics alike that "all good things go together." Later a more sober view of the process of development emerged (Huntington 1968) where modernization was seen as accompanied by a significant period of societal transition and the potential for unrest if crucial social and political institutions were absent. Key assumptions remained, however, most important of which was that the primary obstacle to development was endogenous and found within the traditional nature of society. Optimism over the long term remained and development continued to be viewed as inevitable and along Western lines.

In contrast, dependency theory distinguished between "undeveloped" and "underdeveloped", arguing that poor societies generally conformed to the latter, where they had experienced negative consequences associated with colonialism and other ties to advanced Western societies. Inspired by theories of imperialism, colonialism and Marxism, dependency writers generally argued that development was not a linear process but instead more holistic, where wealth and poverty were intimately linked on a global scale. In its more vulgar form, underdevelopment in the South and development in the North were argued to constitute "two sides of the same coin" (dos Santo 1970; Frank 1967, 1969). Development in the metropole, in other words, came at the expense of the periphery. As such, greater economic integration would only lead to greater poverty and misery.

A more sophisticated dependency approach (often ignored in North American social sciences) viewed development as less zero sum in nature, but also argued that among poor societies it took place in a fundamentally different atmosphere than earlier capitalist development. By utilizing the historical structural method and emphasizing class rather than nationality or region, this body of work argued that the development process was significantly influenced by the historic terms of insertion into the world economy. Moreover, while wealth creation or development was viewed as possible under certain conditions, it was commonly referred to as associated dependent development, where growth was often distorted, experiencing "stop–go" cycles and benefitting only small portions of society (Cardoso and Faletto 1979; Evans 1979; Gereffi 1983; Valenzuela and Valenzuela 1978). From a more overtly political economy standpoint, the terms of international trade and the power of foreign investors were identified as structures and agents of dependency, and both were viewed as inhibiting national development or at least threatening national control over the development process.

Tourism studies were quickly immersed into this larger debate between modernization and dependency. Most early calls for encouraging tourism exports were explicitly or implicity made from modernization assumptions. Tourism meant greater integration into the

4   TOURISM AND DEVELOPMENT

world economy and created opportunities for movement by the population into the "modern" sector from the "traditional" subsistence
agricultural sector. The economic benefits associated with this trade
were especially emphasized, not only by policymakers encouraging its
development, but also by academic treatments seeking to understand
its broader political economy. These benefits include employment
creation, foreign exchange earnings, government revenues, the establishment of forward and backward linkages, and income and employment multipliers (Gray 1970; Lea 1988; Matthews 1978; Pearce 1981;
Pye and Lin 1983). Moreover, tourism was frequently cited as a growth
industry, having expanded more rapidly than overall international
output and trade over the past several decades, and it was claimed
that it also tends to escape traditional barriers to trade.
    These rosy treatments were countered by dependency theory-
inspired critical studies of tourism within developing countries.
Although Bryden (1973) and Turner and Ash (1976) were among the
pioneers in highlighting costs associated with the industry, Britton
was among the first to specifically link tourism to dependency, arguing
that it had to be integrated into larger "historical and political processes that determine development" (1982:332). Britton and others
argued that its economic benefits were often overstated. They also
suggested that understanding the political economy of tourism
required study of the international political economy of the industry
itself and attention to boarder historical economic and political
relations among regions, countries, and classes. Thus, Britton (1981,
1982) contended that small Pacific island destinations are frequently
dependent on multinational corporations (MNCs), which control
much of transport, accommodation, and packaged tourism products.
In a classic dependency situation, local groups—mainly élite classes—
also share some benefits, while subordinated classes enjoy the smallest
proportion. Countless other studies have also questioned the supposed
benefits of tourism exports, frequently finding that multiplier effects
are overstated, leakages are excessively high, and job creation is
seasonal and more capital intensive than once believed (Crick 1989;
Lea 1988; Nash 1977; Perez 1974; Turner 1976; Wood 1979).
    In essence little has changed theoretically within political economy
treatments of tourism and third world development since these earlier
works. Today few studies explicitly invoke either modernization or
dependency perspectives, which is understandable as each has fallen
from academic favour. By emphasizing the balance sheet of positives
and negatives deriving from tourism, however, many subsequent studies continue to be influenced by the two approaches. As Wood argues,
lively debate continues on the extent of tourism's role in the development process, but most contributions continue to be value laden,
failing to move beyond the "simplistic normative categories" of adding
up the good and the bad of the activity (1993:48–49). The most
common alternative has been to adopt more descriptive approaches.
    As a result much of the recent literature, while adding significant
contributions to the understanding of tourism in individual developing
countries or regions (Harrison 1992; Richter 1989; Schlüter 1994),
has done less to advance the field theoretically. Still other approaches

MICHAEL CLANCY   5

emphasize "sustainable" or alternative tourism as a means to development (Broman 1996; Smith and Eadington 1992), but these works are largely prescriptive rather than explanatory in nature. These are by no means to be devalued, but the reality is that much of third world tourism today is not small-scale, ecologically oriented, or even broadly participatory. Finally, some have moved away from political economy, adopting ambitious theoretical approaches including gender or post-modernism (Kinnaird and Hall 1994; MacCannell 1992; Swain 1995; Urry 1990, 1995) that promote seeing tourism from alternative sets of lenses that frequently view theorizing itself as intimately tied to power. The larger point, however, is that while important exceptions exist (Leheny 1995; Sinclair, Alizadeh, Antieno and Aononga 1992; Sinclair and Stabler 1991) few contemporary studies of tourism and development explicitly utilize empirical political economy approaches that are theoretically informed.

This is especially unfortunate because considerable progress has been made in the larger discipline of political economy and development studies. While criticisms of modernization and dependency approaches became something of a cottage industry during the 80s, less value-laden and mid-level theoretical inroads have subsequently been made and lively debate flourishes. Again, the intent here is to focus on those strands of more recent development theory most closely tied to political economy. Aside from obvious practical issues, in large part this is because these strands represent the most dominant approaches of development theory in academic and policy circles today. Simultaneously they constitute the most glaring absence in contemporary tourism studies. Most relevant for purposes here have been overlapping policy and theoretical debates that center on the role of the state in affecting developmental outcomes. In terms of policy, the relevant question is the package of policies that make up the development strategies of import substitution industrialization versus export-led growth strategies as a means for achieving development. At the theoretical level two debates predominate: between statist and neoliberal approaches and statists and post-dependency writers.

The policy debate, which heated up during the 80s, stemmed from variation in development performance within the third world and facilitated the demise of dependency theory. In large part, it emerged from the East Asian success stories of countries such as Taiwan, South Korea, Hong Kong, and Singapore. Rather than being condemned to underdevelopment, these countries achieved remarkable, consistent economic growth and fairly equitable income distribution through export-oriented industrialization. In contrast, many countries in Latin America pursued inward-oriented strategies, which contributed to inefficient and uncompetitive industries, exacerbated external indebtedness and heightened inequality. Although this opposition between import substitution ISI and export promotion EOI is frequently oversimplified (Gereffi 1990), the lesson taken by policymakers was, and continues to be, fairly clear: outward-oriented development strategies appear to be more promising in achieving basic development goals such as growth, industrialization, and equity. The East Asia experience revolutionized development studies in that it reintroduced policy choice and domestic politics to the agenda. It led many to chastise dependency theory as denying both as well as mistaking symptoms identified with dependency—unemployment, economic stagnation, and income inequality—with poor policy choices (Amsden 1979; Haggard 1990). Modernization theory was open to similar charges due to its focus on culture and values and failure to pay serious attention to development strategies and policy choice.

The lessons of export promotion, however, produced new empirical and theoretical challenges. Was it in fact exports which served as the engines of development and if so, what was the nature of these export strategies? If export promotion was so clearly superior, why did policymakers elsewhere fail to adopt similar strategies? The short answer to these questions is that the jury is still out. While certainly export growth coincided with rapid economic expansion in most cases, some (Taylor 1986) have argued that there is little evidence to suggest the former caused the latter. In fact, the reverse could be true. The question of the nature of these programs is even more interesting and pits neoliberal explanations against those of statists. Many neoliberal explanations focus on the magic of market mechanisms in the East Asian miracle economies (Page 1994; World Bank 1993, 1995). A significant amount of evidence, however, suggests that there was considerable variation in market friendliness among East Asian countries, and that in many cases an interventionist state played a key role in shaping development outcomes.

Such statist arguments take different forms. At one extreme are those who contend that strong states were necessary to overcome collective action problems among societal groups by imposing and enforcing costs associated with development (Haggard 1990; Haggard and Moon 1990). Others go further, suggesting that interventionist states shaped markets by targeting industries, creating financial incentives and punishments for private actors, and frequently undertaking production itself. In short, such states "got the prices wrong" in order to tap into future-oriented comparative advantage (Amsden 1989; Wade 1990). Despite these differences, what statist explanations hold in common are two requirements. First, state actors must initiate farsighted and dynamic economic strategies that vary from simply letting the market operate freely or serving the needs of particular societal interests. Second, they must have the power to put their plan into action. In other words, the state must possess the technical capacity to undertake an autonomous development project as well as the autonomy or power to put it into place.

Those arguing from a neoliberal standpoint have responded by downplaying the importance of statist interventions in East Asia, on one hand, and by suggesting that even if they did matter, only a particular species of state was capable of formulating and implementing such policies. Thus, the World Bank, perhaps the leading beacon of neoliberal explanations and policy prescriptions, finally acknowledged an institutional basis to developmental dynamism in the region in 1993, although Page, a chief architect of the study was still quick to point out in a summary:

> In parts of Africa and Latin America, and elsewhere in Asia, activist govern-
> ment involvement in the economy has too often gone awry. The fact that
> interventions were an element of some East Asian economies' success does
> not mean that they should be attempted everywhere, nor should they be
> used as an excuse to resist needed market-oriented reform (1994:624).

Page's comments are also consistent with neoclassical approaches
to the state, which view policymakers as rational actors and thus
susceptible to incentives which may benefit them individually but
inhibit or retard the larger development process (Findlay 1991; Krueger 1974, 1990; Lal 1985). If statists, in other words, have identified
developmental states in East Asia that frequently serve as the *solution*
to development challenges, neoclassical writers have found predatory
states where public officials frequently act as the primary *problem* to
such challenges and can explain that behavior using microeconomic
theory (Evans 1992, 1995).

As a result of this more recent research, the fundamental development debate has now come to center on domestic politics and
especially the key role played by the state in affecting development
patterns. It may be argued, in fact, that state actors and policies have
become the primary, if not solitary set of independent variables that
explain successes and failures to the exclusion of other factors. Indeed
representatives from both modernization (Almond 1988) and dependency (Evans 1987) camps have granted the central importance of the
state in the development process, while arguing that they never truly
neglected it but rather treated it as *one of several* important variables.
Therefore, they also contend that the current movement toward
returning to the state goes too far in ignoring key theoretical findings
made by these and other schools.

This last issue has recently been taken up by an eclectic group of
writers who argue that attention to the role of the state in affecting
a wide range of development outcomes must also be augmented by
additional explanatory factors. The state, in order words, cannot
explain all. Here these writers are referred to as post-dependency in
part, because some earlier wrote from a dependency perspective, but
more importantly because all tend to emphasize additional international influences. Thus, Gereffi (1990) and Stallings (1990) point
to the varying effect that transitional economic linkages had on East
Asia and Latin America. Stallings, for instance, demonstrates that
foreign capital flows to the former primarily took the form of aid,
which directly strengthened states with respect to their own economies and societies. In contrast, most capital flows to Latin America
before the 70s came through multinational corporations (MNCs), a
key agent for dependency writers. Rather than strengthening states
through concessional aid, this form for foreign capital sometimes
threatened state control over its own economy.

In an alternative but consistent approach, Cumings (1984) contends
that modernization theory, which he suggests lives in the form of both
statist and neoliberal explanations, fundamentally misunderstands
the success of East Asian states due to the fallacy of disaggregation.
In contrast, he argues from a world systems standpoint that dynamism
within individual East Asian countries can *only* be understood within

8   TOURISM AND DEVELOPMENT

the context of the broader evolution of the global and especially
regional economy. Thus, the rise of Korea and Taiwan—rather than
simply the product of strong states—cannot be separated from
Japanese imperialism, the regional product cycle and the power vacuum created by Japan's demise in World War II. A third "post-
dependency" approach also acknowledges international influences
on development but does so at the industry level. In other words,
development patterns are investigated at the level of individual economic activities. The role of state policy in industrial development is
viewed as integral, but does not supersede questions of the domestic
and international organization of the industry, geography, and firm
strategies. While placing more (Evans 1995) or less (Appelbaum and
Gereffi 1994; Gereffi 1994; Gereffi and Korzeniewicz 1990) weight on
state policy, these works all call into question the idea that domestic
politics in general, and the state in particular, primarily account for
development outcomes.

   To summarize, these three political economy approaches have
driven development studies into new directions in recent years. To be
sure, consensus has not emerged and attempts at theory building take
place at a more middle level than either modernization or dependency.
This, however, is also the advantage of these new avenues. One may
proceed more inductively, and at a more micro-level, both factors
that are ideal for considering tourism within the broader context of
development and within the larger political economy of individual
countries.

   If Wood's (1993) critique of the overly normative nature of tourism
and development studies is correct, an alternative approach is to ask
not whether tourism helps or hinders development, but rather to
evaluate tourism as a particular *form* of development and ask what
determines its status at any given place and time. In this manner,
tourism moves from independent to dependent variable. The advantage is that much of the ideological baggage of both dependency and
modernization, as well as "development", is left behind. Choices
are still made in terms of which aspects of tourism are elevated to
importance and which are left out, but no claim is being made that
one is escaping all forms of value judgement with this approach. Yet
it does allow for proceeding in a more inductive—and inclusive—
manner that fosters continued theoretical debate. It is also consistent
with more contemporary works in political economy, which have
attempted to proceed in a less value-laden manner through investigating what various authors refer to as "development patterns" (Gereffi 1990; Gereffi and Wyman 1989), "structural change" (Evans
1992), "industrial transformation" (Evans 1995), or "industrial change" (Haggard 1989).

   One useful strategy is to proceed through a variation of Gereffi's
(1990:17–22) questions surrounding what he calls "development patterns". He simply asks, what are the most prominent economic activities within a country, are they inwardly or outwardly oriented, and
who are the primary economic agents relied upon to carry them out?
These amount to that which is to be explained. In the case of tourism,
the industry in question (in most cases, export-oriented), can be

MICHAEL CLANCY 9

investigated as to how it came to prominence within a country and as to who owns and controls it. Again, to its advantage, this approach largely bypasses the more ideological debates found between modernization and dependency theorists, while still focusing on key actors and issues. For example, modernization theorists generally view MNCs as a positive influence, but dependency theorists view them negatively. Here it is worth noting the extent to which MNC activity exists without attempting to settle a decades-old controversy.

Finally, this opens the door to addressing more interesting questions, the most central of which is why. In other words, one can ask what determines development patterns in tourism just as others have attempted to account for the rise of steel and automobile industries in various third world countries, explain change in agricultural patterns or the rise of in-bond assembly plants. One need not expect identical factors to operate in the exact same manner but proceeding in this way both aids the analyst in pointing to common candidates affecting change and constitutes approach that contributes to theory building across economic sectors.

The Political Economy of Mexican Tourism

As the third world country that has attracted the largest number of foreign tourists and hard currency over the past 25 years, Mexico presents itself as ideal for analysis. Tourism has become increasingly important during this time, but the country, with a large and diversified economy, is by no means dependent on tourism. The record of tourism growth, however, is impressive, and until recently no third world country drew as many tourists or tourism dollars. As Table 1 demonstrates, arrivals grew from two to 17 million between 1970 and 1994, while receipts increased from $415 million to $6.4 billion. As is noted above, the industry is the second largest employer in Mexico, behind agriculture, and has traditionally ranked as the second or third largest export. Tourism growth—measured by export earnings—has outpaced overall growth consistently during this period as well. At the same time, the activity represents less than 3% of GDP and hardly constitutes a mono-export as it does in many countries in the Caribbean and South Pacific. Further, Mexico's share of international tourists, about 4.2% in 1980, has declined to 3.15% in 1994 (WTO 1996), but this is consistent with the region and is largely traceable to the remarkable growth of the Asian region over that period.

Two questions, stemming from the earlier discussion on the determinants of development patterns, deserve particular attention here: how has tourism become a leading industry in the country and what determines ownership and control of the activity? The more recent literature relating to the political economy of development suggests the place to begin is with the state. What, if any, role did it play? Was it activist or did it allow the market to operate freely? How, if at all, did it affect both growth and distribution of ownership? The method utilized in answering these questions is eclectic, based upon historical documents, limited secondary services, and the use of what Evans refers to as "key informant interviews" (1995:19).

10   TOURISM AND DEVELOPMENT

Table 1. Mexican Tourism Arrivals and Receipts (1970–1995)

Year	Arrivals (millions)		Variation (%)	Receipts (billions)		Variation (%)
1970	2.25			0.415		
1971	2.51		11.5	0.461		11.1
1972	2.92		16.2	0.563		22.0
1973	3.23		10.7	0.724		28.7
1974	3.36		4.2	0.842		16.3
1975	3.22		−4.3	0.800		−5.0
1976	3.11		−3.4	0.836		4.4
1977	3.25		4.5	0.867		3.7
1978	3.75		15.6	1.121		29.4
1979	4.13		10.1	1.443		28.8
1980	4.14		0.2	1.671		15.8
1981	4.04		−2.6	1.759		5.3
1982	3.77		−6.7	1.405		−20.1
1983	4.75		26.1	1.625		15.5
1984	4.66		−2.0	1.953		20.2
1985	4.21		−9.6	1.720		−11.9
1986	4.63		9.9	1.792		4.2
1987	5.41		16.9	2.274		26.9
1988	5.69	(14.14)	5.3	2.544	(4.0)	11.9
1989	6.19	(14.96)	8.7	2.954	(4.7)	16.1
1990	6.39	(17.18)	3.3	3.401	(5.5)	15.1
1991	6.37	(16.28)	−0.3	3.783	(5.9)	11.3
1991	6.37	(16.28)	−0.3	3.783	(5.9)	11.3
1992		(17.15)	(6.8)		(6.1)	(2.1)
1993		(16.44)	(−3.1)		(6.2)	(1.4)
1994		(17.18)	(4.5)		(6.4)	(3.2)

Note: Figures in parentheses reflect a revised methodology for counting tourist arrivals and receipts in order to conform to WTO methodology.
Source: SECTUR (1992); WTO (1996).

In fact the evidence suggests that a statist interpretation is more accurate than a neoliberal one. Beginning in the late 60s, the state, through the tourism ministry (SECTUR) and especially through a national tourism development trust fund (INFRATUR and later FON-ATUR), took the lead in planning and implementing a multi-year master plan for the country. Until that point tourism to Mexico had largely been market driven. The country clearly benefited from its proximity to the United States and as a result the industry grew rapidly, but most foreign tourism was confined to Mexico City and border regions. This would change due to the actions of SECTUR and FONATUR. Together, the agencies spearheaded the planning and construction of five new resorts—Cancún, Ixtapa, Los Cabos, Loreto, and Huatulco—essentially building them from the ground up. FON-ATUR took the lead in planning, construction of infrastructure and several hotels, providing financing for private investors, and taking on ownership of tourism enterprises.

MICHAEL CLANCY   11

The argument pursued here is not that state action was good, but only that it mattered in shaping development patterns in tourism. State behavior did resemble that of "developmental states" so often cited in East Asia, in that public agencies first embarked on an autonomous project, and second altered market incentives for private sector actors in order to channel resources in a manner that fostered development of the activity. There is little evidence that demonstrates state tourism plans in the 60s and 70s came in response to demands from societal groups. Tourism, while growing, remained a nascent economic activity, and organization by mainly small producers (hotel owners) was hindered by geographical dispersion. In fact, state actors have demonstrated a willingness to pursue their tourism plans despite opposition from societal groups, most commonly residents in the targeted zones (Long 1991; Reynosa y Valle and De Regt 1979).

Instead, state action toward tourism is better understood in the context of the larger development strategies pursued by the state itself. By the late 60s, Mexico had experimented with import substitution for 30 years. Although producing the "Mexican Miracle" of enviable growth rates and significant industrialization, this model was falling under growing economic and social pressures. Tourism was aimed primarily at addressing two of these pressures: deficits in the balance of payments and uncontrolled growth of urban areas. Mexico had run a current account deficit every year between 1955 and 1981. By the 60s, the annual deficit approached 3% of gross domestic product (NAFIN: various issues; Looney 1978). Meanwhile the industrialization push resulted in a neglect of agriculture, especially for small producers. The resulting internal migration put pressure on already overcrowded cities. Tourism was viewed as a means of overcoming bottlenecks in secondary import substitution through enhancing export earnings and promoting regional development. Initial loan applications to the World Bank and Inter-American Development Banks, as well as summaries of plans, frequently cited both these rationales in support of the projects (Bosselman 1978:37–57; FONATUR nd; INFRATUR nd)

State action during the early years of the tourism push was crucial not only for the growth of the five planned tourism "poles", but also for the overall growth of arrivals and receipts to Mexico. Within the planned resorts, which were all beach sites and geared toward international class mass tourists, state agencies took on a series of roles ranging from planning, buying and selling land, and provision of infrastructure, to local governance. Most significant—and the strongest argument for a statist explanation of the Mexican case—is the roles the state took in overcoming collective action problems in the new resorts. Despite providing tens of millions of dollars worth of infrastructure, the state initially found few private sector actors willing to invest in the poles. As one public sector official put it, "not one hotel chain wanted to operate a hotel in a place where there was nothing" (author interview). State managers responded with a two-track strategy. The first one was to build, own, and operate their own hotels, mainly through the Nacional Hotelera chain, a domestic firm that had recently been acquired by the state while on the verge of

12   TOURISM AND DEVELOPMENT

bankruptcy. The second strategy was to alter price incentives for the
private sector by offering preferential loans for hotels. FONATUR
both guaranteed and subsidized the loans in order to hasten hotel
construction. Between 1974 and 1992, Mexico added more than
100,000 rooms, to total more than 300,000.

The early success of tourism promotion in effect helped make
continued import substitution viable. More important, however, was
the discovery of huge amounts of oil reserves in the early 70s. Mexico
became a net oil exporter in 1976 and by 1981 was among the largest
exporters in the world. Despite the relief this provided for the overall
export sector, promotion of tourism exports continued. In part this is
best explained by momentum. Cancún began attracting foreign visitors in 1974, but original plans called for three stages of construction
over more than 10 years. Construction had also begun on Loreto and
Los Cabos by the late 70s even though the resorts would not come on
line until 1980 and 1981, respectively. In addition to momentum,
the second initial rationale for the resorts, regional development,
continued to drive their development. Further, the resorts themselves
were in line with the overall preferences for "big" development projects that prevailed under the presidential administrations of Luis
Echeverría (1970–76) and José López Portillo (1976–82).

Mexico's political economy changed drastically with the onset of
the debt crisis in 1982. Since then state development strategy has
alternated between austerity and structural adjustment before
embarking on a new long-term emphasis on integration with the world
economy. Perhaps ironically little has changed with respect to tourism.
To be sure, the privatization of state-owned enterprises during the
80s and early 90s included many tourism firms, including Nacional
Hotelera, but by then the private sector had become quite eager to
invest in the sector. Instead, today tourism is best seen as a leading
sector within Mexico's larger development strategy of export-led
growth. The industry is clearly market based, in that it is mainly in
the hands of the private sector, and export-oriented, with centers such
as Cancún attracting roughly three-fourths of its visitors from abroad
(SECTUR 1992).

Despite this, a statist interpretation is still warranted. It is because
today tourism in Mexico is largely the product of the original statist
vision of the 60s and subsequent actions over the next three decades.
The alternative is a weak counterfactual. Certainly growth rates
achieved over the past 25 years would have been difficult to match if
the industry had been left to the market alone. Yet even if growth
had occurred without the heavy hand of the state, the primary *form* of
tourism to Mexico has also changed to concentrate on the sun and
sea segment and attracting the masses. Previously, outside of Acap-
ulco, most tourists confined themselves to the major cities or the
borderlands. By 1989 Cancún passed the Federal District, which
encompasses Mexico City, to become the single largest destination in
the country (Hiernaux 1989; SECTUR 1992), and Huatulco is slated
to be even bigger and draw larger numbers when it is completed. All
of this is directly attributable to state planners. The more intriguing
question is whether a statist explanation of tourism development in

Mexico is by itself sufficient. Evidence suggests it is not. While it was the case that state tourism officials had few domestic constraints during the 60s, they were confronted with a clearly structured international industry, one that ultimately shaped distributional patterns. In other words, while state behavior accounts for much of the record of tourism growth during this period, it is the international industry that influenced ownership and control patterns. This was most evident in the hotel industry, which is detailed below.

To the extent that Mexico wanted to tap into the global mass tourism market, it is also needed to attract global firms, especially in the hotel sector. This decision was made evident under the Echeverría administration. An outspoken nationalist, Echeverría oversaw the implementation of one of the most strict direct foreign investment laws in Mexico in 1973. It prohibited foreign firms from many areas of the Mexican economy and placed tight limits on all others. Interestingly, however, under this administration foreign holding of land near coasts was made easier through the implementation of a trust mechanism (Tancer 1972; Truett and Truett 1982). This apparent contradiction is best explained by considering the nature of hotels and the hospitality product. Foreign hotel chains had already been entering the Mexican market, but because most entered through management contracts or franchising, they would easily fit under any equity ceilings set by the 1973 foreign investment law. The choice for policymakers was clear. If foreign hotel chains were needed to foster exports, and were in fact establishing a significant presence in the market anyway, they may as well inject some of their own capital. The alternative would be a local hotel industry that was marked by significant foreign control with little or no foreign equity. Alternatively, public officials should have also further limited foreign hotel participation but the risk was too great. They needed the well-known brand names in order to attract foreign tourists to new resorts.

In fact Dunning and McQueen (1982) found that Mexico became the developing country with the highest number of foreign affiliated hotel and rooms by 1978, and by 1987 one estimate held that 71% of the top two classes of hotels in Mexico were tied to foreign chains (Schédler 1988). More recent evidence, however, contradicts more crude dependency expectations that the hotel industry would fall completely into foreign hands. Instead, a more complex pattern has emerged. For instance, the largest chain operating in Mexico, Grupo Posadas (formerly Posadas de México), bought out its foreign partner Holiday Inn in the early 90s and has since become the biggest hotel chain in Latin America and 62nd largest (by rooms) in the world (*Hotels* 1995). Grupo Situr, another local conglomerate, has also been among the largest chains in the country, even after running into financial difficulties associated with the 1994–95 peso crisis. Both Posadas and Situr began largely as passive real estate investors before moving into the more lucrative operating side of the hospitality sector, and eventually each developed its own brand name. As Table 2 demonstrates, a third domestically owned chain, Camino Real Hotels (Real Turismo), has also become one of the top five chains in Mexico by size despite the fact that it also has undergone a recent crisis.

14   TOURISM AND DEVELOPMENT

Table 2. Largest Hotel Chains in Mexico

Firm	Rooms	Hotels
Grupo Posadas	8,493	34
Holiday Inn Worldwide	6,159	35
Grupo Situr	6,135	25
Hoteles Camino Real	3,556	15
Best Western International	3,281	36

Source: *Hotels* (1996).

Rather than denationalization, the past 15 years in particular have been marked by heavy foreign participation by chains as well as the entry of several large Mexican business groups moving into the hospitality sector, first as real estate investors but increasingly also as operators and franchisers. Among Mexican investors entering the hotel industry are the nation's leading industrial conglomerates, many headed by Mexico's new billionaires, such as grupos ICA, Cemex, Carso, Gutsa, and Sidek (through subsidiary Situr), along with the large domestic banks Banamex and Bancomer. All have done so, however, through forming strategic alliances with major international hotel chains. In addition, others (DESC and Situr) have invested in tourism real estate through a series of new state-planned mini resorts, called Megaprojects. Table 3 summarizes the alliances as they existed in the early 90s. Several have since broken up and realigned, and most notably the newly privatized Mexican banks have moved out of the tourism business.

In short, the Mexican hotel industry has become more structured over the past 15 years. Most significant, ownership *and* control of the tourist class hotels is largely confined to international and internationally-oriented domestic capital. TNC presence has certainly increased over time and some evidence suggests that management contracts and franchise agreements have been augmented by growing levels of equity investment. Since the 80s, however, the more significant change has been the increased participation of what were formerly domestic steel, cement, telecommunications, and construction firms. In other words, as tourism has become big business in Mexico it has been Mexican big business—frequently allied with international capital—that has primarily benefited from the boom.

CONCLUSION

The Mexican case does not conform neatly to either modernization or dependency interpretations, but few cases of tourism in the third world do. More modest but still useful observations relating to the political economy of Mexican tourism over the past 25 years, however, may be made in the context of more recent work on the political economy of development. In particular, special attention is given to the state *and* to the nature of the industry itself in explaining growth

MICHAEL CLANCY   15

Table 3. Strategic Alliances in the Mexican Hotel Sector (1992)

Firms	Flag	Hotels	Rooms
Posadas/Holiday Corp.	Fiesta Americana	13	4,975
	Holiday Inn	9	2,487
	Holiday Inn Crowne Plaza	3	1,309
	Fiesta Inn	4	457
	(Various Others)[a]	7	1,431
Situr/Posadas/Sheraton	Continental Plaza	13	3,902
	Plaza las Glorias		
	Fiesta Americana		
	Sheraton		
Carso/Choice	Calinda Quality Inn	18	3,002
ICA/Banamex/Radisson	Paraíso Radisson	4	1,176
Banamex/Inter-Continental	Sierra	3	847
ICA/Sheraton	Sheraton Pirámides del Rey	6	1,741
Xabre/Westin	Camino Real	8	1,108
Bancomer/Hilton	Conrad Hotels	3	n/d
Presidente/Stouffer	Stouffer Presidente	7	2,170
Cemex/Marriott	Marriott	2	883
	Marriott Courtyard		

[a] Others refer to management and ownership interest in seven hotels in the United States operating under the brands Holiday Inn, Sheraton Fiesta, Border Inn, and Hampton Inn.
Note: n/d=no data
Source: Compiled from company reports, internal private sector market study, March, 1992, undated; untitled overview of lodging companies in Mexico produced by Morgan Stanley; newspaper reports, author interviews, Mexico City, 1992.

and distribution. In this manner, the analysis here sides with a statist rather than neoliberal account of tourism dynamism. Certainly most neoliberals would term tourism in Mexico a success. It is an export-oriented industry that possesses few if any protectionist barriers. Growth has been extremely rapid and the sector is largely in private hands. The problem is that it is difficult to imagine this transformation having taken place without the presence of an activist Mexican state. Again the alternative is an unlikely counterfactual suggesting the market alone could have produced identical or better results.

This is not to suggest that in this case the Mexican state was solely the "solution" to development problems where elsewhere it is frequently portrayed as the problem. Rumours and stories of corruption and other inefficiencies surrounding tourism development are fairly common. Politicians and those with political ties certainly benefited from the growth of the industry, although it should be noted that such stories have proliferated since the move toward privatization and market orientation. State tourism agencies were not above politics and in fact political ties may have enhanced their effectiveness. This is not uncommon, however, even among developmentalist states (Evans

1995). The larger point also remains that today in Mexico the tourism industry is largely a product of state action.

The last question relating to the case is accounting for the distribution of benefits associated with the industry. The evidence above indicates that within the hotel industry ownership and control is confined mainly to foreign chains and large-scale Mexian business. Here one could continue with a statist interpretation and argue that public officials intended such an outcome. A somewhat more complex scenario, however, is more compelling and points to the limits of statist explanation. State officials faced few domestic constraints, especially early on, in implementing their own vision of tourism promotion. Because they targeted the export market, however, certain choices were in effect closed off. Simply put, in order to attract large numbers of foreign tourists to new and remote resorts Mexico first needed to attract foreign hotel chains. Name recognition, trust, and ties with tourism generating markets made the chains all but indispensable. Over time these chains formed local partnerships with large-scale Mexian business groups to largely control the most upscale and lucrative segment of the local hotel market. As such, the structure of international tourism did not close off the possibility of Mexican private sector participation. Yet firm specific advantages, the ability to separate control from ownership, and the nature of the hospitality product itself pointed to a narrow distribution of benefits. They all but ensured that only MNCs *and* large-scale Mexican capital would reap most of benefits associated with the industry.

State officials may have favored such an outcome. But, already noted, state behavior toward hotel MNCs was strikingly different than it was to foreign capital operating elsewhere in the Mexican economy, suggesting other factors were at work. The more appropriate question in whether another outcome was possible. Certainly, but state actors' choice of promoting beach tourism to masses of foreigners made it highly unlikely. They could have closed off the sector to foreign firms, but only at great risk. Instead the nature of demand and of the international tourism industry all but dictated their inclusion, and ultimately significantly structured future development patterns in Mexico.

Moving from the case back to the theoretical level, two other significant conclusion may be drawn. Tourism studies can benefit from contemporary mid-level theories of political economy and development. Certainly the costs and benefits of tourism in the former third world still matter, and controversy will undoubtedly continue. By stepping back from the "good" and "bad" of tourism, to the "why" of particular tourism development, analysts can overcome the often frustrating dead end that frequently accompanies cost-benefit analysis, and ultimately ask and answer more interesting questions. Such an approach lends itself to easy sectoral comparison. State policies in tourism may be contrasted with those in other industries, and similar comparisons may be made at the level of international industrial organization. Commonly tourism researchers view their subject as fundamentally different from other economic activities and yet simultaneously lament the isolation of their studies within the broader

MICHAEL CLANCY   17

social sciences. By no means it is argued that the exact framework adopted here should be applied to all studies of tourism and development. However, what is contended is that approaches such as this one not only allow for a useful dialogue between theory and data, but also invite dialogue with political economists and other social scientists outside of tourism studies. ■

Acknowledgments—The author wishes to thank Mary Geske and Greg White for their useful comments on various drafts of this article. Thanks also to Mike Barnett and Leigh Payne for guidance on the larger project from which this piece is drawn.

REFERENCES

Almond, Gabriel A.
  1988 The Return to the State. American Political Science Review 82:853–874.
Almond, Gabriel A., and James S. Coleman
  1960 The Politics of Developing Areas. Princeton: Princeton University Press.
Amsden, Alice
  1979 Taiwan's Economic History: A Case of Etatisme and a Challenge to Dependency Theory. Modern China 5(3):341–80.
  1989 Asia's Next Giant: South Korea and Late Industrialization. New York: Oxford.
Appelbaum, Richard P., and Gary Gereffi
  1994 Power and Profits in the Apparel Commodity Chain. *In* Global Production: The Apparel Industry in the Pacific Rim, Edna Bonacich, Lucie Cheng Norma Chinchilla, Nora Hamilton, and Paul Ong, eds., pp.42–62. Philadelphia: Temple University Press.
Bosselman, Fred P.
  1978 In the Wake of the Tourist: Managing Special Places in Eight Countries. Washington DC: The Conservation Foundation.
Britton, Stephen G.
  1981 Tourism, Dependency and Development: A Mode of Analysis. Development Studies Center Occasional Paper No. 23. Canberra: The Australian National University.
  1982 The Political Economy of Tourism in the Third World. Annals of Tourism Research 9:331–358.
Brohman, John
  1996 New Directions in Tourism for Third World Development. Annals of Tourism Research 23:48–70.
Bryden, John
  1973 Tourism and Development: A Case Study of the Commonwealth Caribbean. Cambridge: Cambridge University Press.
Cardoso, Fernando Henrique, and Enzo Faletto
  1979 Dependency and Development in Latin America. Berkeley: University of California Press.
Crick, Malcolm
  1989 Representations of International Tourism in the Social Sciences: Sun, Sex, Sights, Savings, and Servility. Annual Review of Anthropology 18:307–344.
Cumings, Bruce
  1984 The Origins and Development of the Northeast Asian Political Economy: Industrial Sectors, Product Cycles, and Political Consequences. International Organization 38(1):1–40.
dos Santos, Theotonio
  1970 The Structure of Dependence, American Economic Review 60:231–236.
Dunning, John H., and Matthew McQueen
  1982 Multinational Corporations in the International Hotel Industry. Annals of Tourism Research 9:69–90.
Evans, Peter B.

18   TOURISM AND DEVELOPMENT

1979 Dependent Development: The Alliance of Multinational, State, and Local Capital in Brazil. Princeton: Princeton University Press.
1987 Class, State and Dependence in East Asia: Lessons for Latin Americanists. *In* The Political Economy of the New Asian Industrialism, Frederic C. Deyo, ed., Ithaca NY: Cornell University Press.
1992 The State as Problem and Solution: Predation, Embedded Autonomy, and Structural Change. *In* The Politics of Economic Adjustment: International Constraints, Distributive Conflicts and the State, Stephan Haggard and Robert R. Kaufman, eds., pp. 139–81. Princeton NJ: Princeton University Press.
1995 Embedded Autonomy: States and Industrial Transformation. Princeton NJ: Princeton University Press.

Findlay, Ronald
1991 The New Political Economy: Its Explanatory Power for LDCs. *In* Politics and Policy Making in Developing Countries: Perspectives on the New Political Economy, Gerald M. Meier, ed., pp. 13–40. San Francisco: ICS Press.

FONATUR
nd Resumen de la Propuesta de Préstamo a Nacional Financiera, S.A., Proyecto de Desarrollo Turístico Cancún. Undated internal document.

Frank, Andre Gunder
1967 Capitalism and Underdevelopment in Latin America. New York: Monthly Review Press.
1969 Latin America: Underdevelopment or Revolution. New York: Monthly Review Press.

Gereffi, Gary
1983 The Pharmaceutical Industry and Dependency in the Third World. Princeton NJ: Princeton University Press.
1990 Paths of Industrialization: An overview. *In* Manufacturing Miracles: Paths of Industrialization in Latin America and East Asia, Gereffi and Donald L. Wyman, eds., pp. 3–31. Princeton NJ: Princeton University Press.
1994 Contending Perspectives on Regional Integration: Development Strategies and Commodity Chains in Latin America and East Asia. Paper presented at the 18th International Congress of Latin American Studies, Atlanta.

Gereffi, Gary, and Donald L. Wyman
1989 Determinants of Development Strategies in Latin America and East Asia. *In* Pacific Dynamics: The International Politics of Industrial Change, Stephan Haggard and Chung-in Moon, eds., pp. 23–52. Boulder CO: Westview.

Gereffi, Gary, and Miguel Korzeniewicz
1990 Commodity Chains and Footwear Exports in the Semiperiphery. *In* Semiperipheral States in the World-Economy, William G. Martin, Ed., pp. 45–68. Westport CT: Greenwood Press.

Gray, H. Peter
1970 International Tourism: International Trade. Lexington MA: Heath Lexington Books.

Haggard, Stephan
1989 Introduction: The International Politics of Industrial Change. *In* Pacific Dynamics: The International Politics of Industrial Change, Haggard and Chung-in Moon, eds., pp. 1–21. Boulder CO: Westview.
1990 Pathways from The Periphery: The Politics of Growth in the Newly Industrializing Countries. Ithaca NY: Cornell University Press.

Haggard, Stephan, and Chung-in Moon
1990 Institutions and Economic Policy: Theory and a Korean Case Study. World Politics 42:210–37.

Harrison, David, ed.
1992 Tourism and the Less Developed Countries. London: Belhaven.

Hiernaux, Daniel
1989 Mitos y Realidades del Milagro Turístico. *In* Teoría y Praxis del Espacio Turístico, Hiernaux, ed., pp. 109–20. Mexico City: UAM-Xochimilco.

Hotels
1995 Volume 29(7):38–40.
1996 Volume 30(9):44–6.

Huntinton, Samuel P.
1968 Political Order in Changing Societies. New Haven: Yale University Press.

MICHAEL CLANCY 19

INFRATUR
 nd Basic Facts of the Tourist Project of Cancún. Mexico City: INFRATUR.
Kinnaird, Vivian, and Derek Hall, eds.
 1994 Tourism: A Gender Analysis. New York: Wiley.
Krueger, Anne
 1974 The Political Economy of the Rent Seeking Society. American Economic
   Review 64:291–303.
 1990 Government Failures in Development. Journal of Economic Perspectives
   4(2):9–23.
Lal, Deepak
 1985 The Poverty of Developmental Economics. Cambridge: Harvard.
Lea, John
 1988
 1992 Tourism and Development in the Third World, London: Routledge.
Leheny, David
 1995 The Political Economy of Asian Sex Tourism. Annals of Tourism Research
   22:367–384.
Long, Veronica
 1991 Government–Industry–Community Interaction in Tourism Development in
   Mexico. In The Tourism Industry: An International Analysis, M. Thea Sinclair
   and M.J. Stabler, eds., 205–22. Oxford: CAB International.
Looney, Robert E.
 1978 Mexico's Economy: A Policy Analysis with Forecasts to 1990. Boulder CO:
   Westview.
MacCannell, Dean
 1992 Empty Meeting Grounds: The Tourist Papers. London: Routledge.
Matthews, Harry
 1978 International Tourism: A Political and Social Analysis. Cambridge: Schenk-
   man.
Nash, Dennison
 1977 Tourism as a Form of Imperialism. In Hosts and Guests: The Anthropology
   of Tourism, Valene Smith, ed., Pittsburgh PA: University of Pittsburgh Press.
NAFIN
 Various Years La Economía Mexicana en Cifras. Mexico City: NAFIN.
Page, John M.
 1994 The East Asian Miracle: An Introduction. World Development 22:615–625.
Pearce, Douglas
 1981 Tourist Development. Harlow: Longman Group.
Perez, L.A.
 1974 Aspects of Underdevelopment: Tourism in the West Indies. Science and
   Society 37:473–80.
Pye, Elwood A., and Tzong-biau Lin, eds.
 1983 Tourism in Asia: The Economic Impact. Singapore: National University of
   Singapore
Reynosa y Valle Augustín, and Jacomina P. De Regt
 1979 Growing Pains: Planned Tourism Development in Ixtapa-Zihuatanejo. In
   Tourism: Passport to Development? Emanuel de Kadt, ed., pp. 111–34. New
   York: Oxford.
Richter, Linda K.
 1989 The Politics of Tourism in Asia. Honolulu: University of Hawaii Press.
 1993 Tourism Policy Making in South-East Asia. In Tourism in South-east Asia,
   Michael Hitchcock, Victor T. King and Michael J.G. Parnwell, eds., pp. 179–199.
   London: Routledge.
Rostow, W.W.
 1960 The Stages of Economic Growth: A Non-Communist Manifesto. London:
   Cambridge University Press.
Schédler, Andreas
 1988 El Capital Extranjero en México: El Caso de la Hotelería. Investigación
   Económica 184:137–175.
Schlüter
 1994?
SECTUR

20   TOURISM AND DEVELOPMENT

1991 Mexico's Tourism Sector: The Year in Review, 1990 mimeo, December.
1992 Estadísticas Básicas de la Actividad Turística. Mexico City: SECTUR.
Sinclair, M. Thea, and M.J. Stabler, eds.
  1991 The Tourism Industry: An International Analysis. Wallingford: CAB International.
Sinclair, M. Thea, Parvin Alizadeh, Elizabeth Atieno, and Adero Aonunga
  1992 The Structure of International Tourism and Tourism Development in Kenya. *In* Tourism and the Less Developed Countries, David Harrison, ed., pp. 47–63. London: Belhaven.
Smith, Valene, and W. Eadington, eds.
  1992 Tourism Alternatives: Potentials and Problems in the Development of Tourism. Philadelphia: University of Pennsylvania Press.
Stallings, Barbara
  1990 The Role of Foreign Capital in Economic Development. *In* Manufacturing Miracles: Paths of Industrialization in Latin America and East Asia, Gary Gereffi and Donald L. Wyman, eds., pp. 55–89. Princeton NJ: Princeton University Press.
Swain, Margaret Byrne, ed.
  1995 Gender in Tourism. Annals of Tourism Research (Special Issue) 22:2.
Tancer, Robert S.
  1972 Tourist Promotion in Mexico. Law and the Social Order, 4:559–79.
Taylor, Lance
  1986 Trade and Growth. The Review of Black Political Economy, 4(4):17–36.
Truett, Lila J., and Dale B. Turett
  1982 Public Policy and the Growth of the Mexican Tourism Industry, 1970–1979. Journal of Travel Research 20(4):11–19.
Turner, Louis
  1976 The International Division of Leisure and Tourism in the Third World. World Development 4:253–260.
Turner, Louis, and John Ash
  1975 The Golden Hordes: International Tourism and the Pleasure Periphery. London: Constable.
Urry, John
  1990 The Tourist Gaze: Leisure and Travel in Contemporary Societies. London: Sage.
  1995 Consuming Places. London: Routledge.
Valenzuela, J. Samuel, and Arturo Valenzuela
  1978 Modernization and Dependency: Alternative Perspectives in the Study of Latin American Underdevelopment. Comparative Politics 10:543 557.
Wade, Robert
  1990 Governing the Market: Economic Theory and the Role of Government in East Asian Dynamism. Princeton NJ: Princeton University Press.
Weiner, Myron, ed.
  1966 Modernization: The Dynamics of Growth, New York: Basic Books.
Wood, Robert E.
  1979 Tourism and Underdevelopment in Southeast Asia. Journal of Contemporary Asia 9:274–287.
  1993 Tourism, Culture and the Sociology of Development. *In* Tourism in South-East Asia, Michael Hitchcock, Victor T. King and Michael J.G. Parnwell, eds., pp. 49–70. London: Routledge.
World Bank
  1993 The East Asian Miracle: Economic Growth and Public Policy. New York: Oxford University Press.
  1995 World Development Report. New York: World Bank.
World Tourism Organization
  1996 Yearbook of Tourism Statistics (46th ed.). Madrid: WTO.

Submitted 14 May 1997
Resubmitted 29 October 1997
Accepted 6 February 1998
Refereed anonymously
Coordinating Editor: Douglas G. Pearce

[5]

THE POLITICAL IMPACT OF TOURISM DEPENDENCE IN LATIN AMERICA

Ronald A. Francisco
Department of Political Science
University of Kansas, USA

ABSTRACT

This research seeks to test empirically the validity of hypotheses drawn from dependency theory that suggest that economic reliance on tourism creates political dependence. Specifically, it seeks to determine whether the Caribbean region, strongly dependent on U.S. tourism, is demonstrably more compliant politically with the United States than other, less dependent, Latin American nations. In addition, the paper examines the relation between political compliance and other indicators of dependence, e.g., investment, aid, and trade. Compliance is measured basically by correlating each nation's voting behavior in the UN General Assembly with that of the United States. A series of tests on a number of relevant economic and political variables yields no confirmation of the dependency argument in the political realm. **Keywords:** tourism, dependence, Latin America, Caribbean.

Ronald Francisco is an associate professor of political science (University of Kansas, Lawrence, KS 66045, USA). His primary teaching and research interests are in international relations and the interdependence of foreign policy and domestic and international political forces. His publications focus mostly on domestic and international public policies in Europe.

Annals of Tourism Research, Vol. 10, pp. 363-376, 1983
Printed in the USA. All rights reserved.

0160-7383/83 83.00 + .00
© 1983 J. Jafari and Pergamon Press Ltd

TOURISM DEPENDENCE IN LATIN AMERICA

RÉSUMÉ

L'Impact politique de la dépendance à l'égard du tourisme en Amérique Latine. Cet article cherche à mettre à l'épreuve empiriquement des hypothèses qui dérivent de la théorie de la dépendance qui suggèrent que la dépendance économique du tourisme entraîne forcément la dépendance politique. En particulier, il cherche à déterminer si la région caraïbe, qui dépend fortement du tourisme américain, fait preuve de plus d'acquiescement politique aux Etats-Unis que d'autres nations latino-américaines qui en dépendent moins. En plus, l'article examine le rapport entre l'acquiescement politique et d'autres indicateurs de la dépendance, tels que l'investissement, l'aide et le commerce. L'acquiescement est mésurée concrètement en comparant les votes de chaque nation dans l'Assemblée Générale des Nations Unies avec ceux des Etats-Unis. Une série de tests ayant à faire avec plusieurs variables économiques et politiques pertinentes ne donne aucune confirmation de la théorie de la dépendance dans le domaine politique. **Mots Clef:** tourisme, dépendance, Amérique Latine, Caraïbe.

INTRODUCTION

Does economic reliance on tourism create political dependence and international political compliance? Suggestions for this view have become more numerous and more emphatic in very recent years. This paper attempts to provide an empirical assessment of this perspective. Specifically, it seeks to determine whether the Caribbean region, so strongly dependent on U.S. tourism, is demonstrably more compliant politically with U.S. wishes than are other, less dependent, Latin American nations. In addition, the paper examines the relation of political compliance with other indicators of dependence, e.g., investment, aid, and trade.

The paper is a response to two trends within the academic treatment of tourism. First, international tourism is increasingly recognized by dependency theorists as a powerful vehicle for metropolitan manipulation of the periphery (e.g., Matthews 1978:79; Bryden 1973:79, 90). Second, the growing attention to political and sociological aspects of international tourism (e.g., Matthews 1978; Young 1973) has not yet been extended to the level of the international system. While economists have probed the international

RONALD A. FRANCISCO

network of capital exchange and trade, political scientists have concentrated on the domestic effects of international dependence.

TOURISM AND DEPENDENCY THEORY

Dependency theory emerged in Latin America in the early and mid-1960s and recently has made great strides among North American scholars as well. This adoption (more accurately, transfer) has not been without its inherent frustration. Latin American *dependencia* theory derives itself largely from neo-Marxist and Leninist theory and is heavily normative. It contains few readily testable propositions; few clear, operationalized concepts; and little more than illustrative evidence.

These shortcomings have been overcome in the past few years by much clearer reformulations of the dependency argument in North America. These reduce dependency to a series of reasonably testable propositions. They contend basically that the international system of capital and trade results in a center-periphery relationship that perpetuates (even creates) underdevelopment, authoritarianism, military government, and international political servitude. As Chilcote and Edelstein argue:

> The political result of economic dependence...ha(s) not changed. Just as landed elites and merchants who exported Latin America's wealth pursued their interest in maintaining dependent economic patterns, modern industrial managers and military elites favor foreign interests. They also fear the demands of the masses within their own nations, preferring military dictatorship to nationalistic reform or revolution (1974:27).

James Caporaso, in one of the most lucid reformulations of the dependency argument, cites three sets of factors that are important conditions for dependency. Two of these are international factors:

Magnitude of reliance
1. large share of needs supplied externally
2. large share of markets is foreign
3. large ratio of foreign to domestic capital, technology, production facilities, etc.

Choice-based measures
1. heavy reliance on one partner
2. high opportunity cost (reliance not easily shifted)

TOURISM DEPENDENCE IN LATIN AMERICA

3. few opportunities for diversification, for allies, etc. (for "natu-ral" and political reasons)
4. commodity concentration of exports and commodity concen-tration of total domestic production (1978:25-26).

When these conditions exist, there is supposed to be a high proba-bility of the kinds of political effects that Chilcote and Edelstein note, as well as what Richard Fagen has called decreased "decisional latitute" (dependence, diminished autonomy) in international deal-ings and activities (1977:17).

Although these hypotheses are drawn largely from work based on the effects of the traditional international trade and investment sectors, recently they have been applied directly to international tourism as well. Gray has pointed out that international travel is simply a special form of international trade (1970). He calls it "invisible trade" and calls attention to its magnitude and critical importance to developing nations.

Bryden underscores the special character of tourism that renders this sector even more liable to dependence effects than others. It is vulnerable to changes in fashion, national disasters and political disturbances, the economic health of developed nations, and the uncertainty of foreign capital. The latter uncertainty arises for several reasons. First, economic decisions are taken by non-nationals and may conflict with national goals. Second, the inflow of foreign capital is sensitive to national policies; dependence upon this inflow reduces the range of freedom a national government enjoys in the determination of its own economic policies (Bryden 1973:90).

Matthews summarizes the dependency argument for the tourist sector in similar terms:

> The intermingled foreign policies of metropolitan governments and their own corporations lead to suspicions within developing countries that corporate tourism has hidden motives. Profit is the apparent goal of the corporation. Political influence exercized through those companies by parent governments causes fears that tourism has become a means of political and economic domination of host countries. This influence often is interpreted as direct. That is, metropolitan diplomacy in host countries is highly focused upon the welfare of the metropolitan business in those states (1978:79).

Hence, developing countries may not only need to satisfy the eco-nomic desires of patron states, but political ones as well (Richter 1980:145).

RONALD A. FRANCISCO

Circumstantial evidence of this relationship can be cited in a number of cases. The political upheaval in Cuba in 1958 effectively terminated the Caribbean's most thriving travel industry (Ohiorhenuan 1979:6). Mexico's decision to support a UN General Assembly resolution equating Zionism with racism resulted in a flood of angry cancellations in resort areas. The Mexican government sought with difficulty to soften its position and restore good-will among American Jews (Kaiser and Helber 1978:11-12). Similarly, failure of host governments to constrain extreme nationalist elements, Black Power gangs, and other violent elements has led to a severe decline in tourist business in several Caribbean nations (cf. Goodsell 1980). Yet such instances are memorable precisely because they are rare. They provide no substitute for general, empirical investigation of the relationship between economic dependence on tourism and political compliance.

POLITICAL COMPLIANCE HYPOTHESES

The dependency argument predicts that there should be relationships among a network of economic and political factors in international tourism. Because tourism involves not just the small business groups that normally dominate international trade and investment but also huge numbers of middle- and upper middle-class North Americans as well, the political effects of tourism dependence should be very strong. For example, while United States bankers may have seen the true motive behind Mexico's vote on the Zionism resolution in the United Nations (for more influence within the Third World), the rather less sophisticated horde of American vacationers reacted quite differently. Similarly, random shootings on the golf course may not forestall investment in most industries, but they quickly poison both tourism and tourist investments.

Hence, one can expect the following relationships to exist, based largely upon the argument of dependency theory:

1. A positive relationship exists between the level of U.S. tourists in total tourist arrivals and host nation political compliance with the United States.

1a. The larger the share of tourism in the host nation's economy, the stronger this compliance should be.

2. The larger U.S. foreign investment in the host nation, the larger the degree of political compliance with the U.S.

3. The larger the number of U.S. tourists, the more U.S. foreign assistance flows to the host nation.

TOURISM DEPENDENCE IN LATIN AMERICA

4. The larger the size of the U.S. tourist sector, the larger the level of U.S. trade with the host nation.

Concepts and Data

Political compliance is difficult to gauge empirically. It is operationalized here as an index of agreement between U.S. and Latin American votes in the United Nations General Assembly. Other, nonquantitative and more general evidence, is considered as a check on the reliability of the UN evidence.

Of course, there is no question that votes on specific UN resolutions are less important to the U.S. than many other kinds of foreign policy behavior of western hemisphere nations. Yet one considers here the aggregate effect of 150 randomly chosen votes in the 33rd General Assembly (1978). Hence, one gains a general impression of the level of agreement many Latin American nations share with the U.S. on a wide range of issues.

That such agreement is important to the United States is currently apparent in its dispute with Iran. National votes are monitored and measured at all times by the Department of State and considered an important measure of compliance with the United States (Richardson 1976:1101). Nor is it always ignored by the American public, as Mexico's Zionism vote demonstrated. Hence, 19 Latin American nations were selected and their (dichotomously coded) votes, with the United States, were correlated. Part of the sample relies heavily upon U.S. tourism for economic welfare, especially the Caribbean (Ohiorhenuan 1979:7), while many South American nations are largely free from U.S. economic influence in the tourist, aid, and investment spheres (Robinson 1976:378-379).

Dependence is measured both as a function of the relative proportion of U.S. tourists in the annual tourist population of each nation and the relative importance of the tourism sector as a percentage of the annual Gross Domestic Product. Again, there is a wide disparity among Latin American nations on these dimensions. Once more, the Caribbean emerges as strongly dependent on both measures.

Data for other variables are drawn from traditional government sources. Foreign assistance is measured separately in its economic and military guises. Investment is operationalized as total U.S. foreign investment for 1976, two years before the period of UN voting to allow for the long-term nature of the investment and sufficient lag-time for political effects.

RONALD A. FRANCISCO

Table 1
Pearson Correlations of 150 National Votes at 33rd UN General Assembly

Countries	Argentina	Bahamas	Barbados	Bolivia	Brazil	Chile	Colombia	Costa Rica	Dom. Rep.	Ecuador	Guatemala	Jamaica	Mexico	Nicaragua	Panama	Paraguay	Peru	Trinidad & Tobago	USA	Venezuela
Argentina	1.00	.656	.693	.833	.816	.641	.600	.616	.392	.533	.443	.664	.734	.624	.748	.643	.574	.639	-.533	.633
Bahamas	.656	1.00	.761	.718	.586	.433	.480	.601	.494	.603	.439	.634	.574	.645	.533	.592	.523	.674	-.478	.534
Barbados	.693	.761	1.00	.713	.682	.512	.612	.623	.575	.664	.403	.776	.716	.622	.655	.570	.574	.829	-.520	.603
Bolivia	.833	.718	.713	1.00	.851	.650	.655	.712	.591	.657	.527	.654	.748	.774	.733	.775	.570	.640	-.423	.651
Brazil	.816	.586	.682	.851	1.00	.750	.595	.629	.448	.561	.483	.631	.725	.606	.724	.706	.535	.713	-.451	.602
Chile	.641	.433	.512	.650	.750	1.00	.750	.792	.684	.750	.621	.655	.666	.757	.799	.781	.402	.591	-.201	.785
Colombia	.600	.480	.612	.655	.595	.750	1.00	.792	.684	.750	.621	.655	.666	.757	.799	.781	.402	.563	-.201	.785
Costa Rica	.616	.601	.623	.712	.629	.792	.792	1.00	.696	.799	.627	.715	.702	.809	.807	.797	.425	.531	-.260	.853
Dominican Republic	.392	.494	.575	.591	.448	.684	.684	.696	1.00	.879	.591	.674	.531	.764	.604	.696	.329	.553	-.133	.708
Ecuador	.533	.603	.664	.657	.561	.750	.750	.799	.879	1.00	.566	.765	.669	.782	.689	.730	.362	.645	-.293	.775
Guatemala	.443	.439	.403	.527	.483	.621	.621	.627	.591	.566	1.00	.505	.500	.713	.599	.661	.359	.455	-.153	.629
Jamaica	.664	.634	.776	.654	.631	.655	.655	.715	.674	.765	.505	1.00	.798	.658	.730	.630	.486	.824	-.462	.829
Mexico	.734	.574	.716	.748	.725	.666	.666	.702	.531	.669	.500	.798	1.00	.618	.797	.718	.575	.740	-.410	.791
Nicaragua	.624	.645	.622	.774	.606	.757	.757	.809	.764	.782	.713	.658	.618	1.00	.756	.797	.444	.582	-.191	.740
Panama	.748	.533	.655	.733	.724	.799	.799	.807	.604	.689	.599	.730	.797	.756	1.00	.824	.533	.618	-.341	.836
Paraguay	.643	.592	.570	.775	.706	.781	.781	.797	.696	.730	.661	.630	.718	.797	.824	1.00	.419	.563	-.181	.769
Peru	.574	.523	.574	.570	.535	.402	.402	.425	.329	.362	.359	.486	.575	.444	.533	.419	1.00	.489	-.267	.463
Trinidad & Tobago	.639	.674	.829	.640	.713	.591	.563	.531	.553	.645	.455	.824	.740	.582	.618	.563	.489	1.00	-.508	.675
United States	-.533	-.478	-.520	-.423	-.451	-.201	-.201	-.260	-.133	-.293	-.153	-.462	-.410	-.191	-.341	-.181	-.267	-.508	1.00	-.289
Venezuela	.633	.534	.603	.651	.602	.785	.785	.853	.708	.775	.629	.829	.791	.740	.836	.769	.463	.675	-.289	1.00

Note: Data were coded dichotomously and correlated in a product-moment model. All correlations are significant at the .05 level, two-tailed, and all except the USA correlations are significant at the .001 level. The votes were cast at the 33rd General Assembly session, from 19 September 1978 to 29 January 1979. 150 separate votes were analyzed, although the N is lower for some correlations because of absences for specific votes.

Source: U.S. Department of State (1980).

TOURISM DEPENDENCE IN LATIN AMERICA

Tests

Political Compliance: UN Agreement. The results of the correlation of U.S. and Latin American votes in the 33rd UN General Assembly are summarized in Table 1 and are striking. Note that no Latin American nation correlates negatively with any other, and that no Latin American nation correlates positively with the United States. This is in spite of the tremendous variety not only in dependence, but in political outlook among Latin American nations. Naturally, one can explain this partially by acknowledging that many General Assembly resolutions are nothing more than lip service to superficially shared Third World views. Nonetheless, there were many votes among the 150 surveyed that loomed very important for the U.S., e.g., Cold War and Middle East issues, and even some that affected Latin America itself (e.g., condemnation of Chile).

In view of the concerns of this paper, it is particularly interesting that more tourism-dependent Caribbean nations exhibit even less political compliance with the United States than with their more autonomous southern neighbors. Indeed, correlations with Barbados ($r = -.520$), Trinidad and Tobago ($r = -.508$), Bahamas ($r = -.478$), and Jamaica ($r = -.462$) demonstrate more disagreement with the United States than that of any Latin American nation except Argentina ($r = -.533$). All of these correlations are highly significant statistically and cluster closely together. This is a most unexpected outcome in view of the dependency perspective. But is it valid?

In fact, it does seem quite valid in view of other evidence. Jamaica had declared the United States ambassador *persona non grata* as early as 1973. In 1978, it lurched suddenly leftward once more, and Prime Minister Manley went so far as to support Castro's incursion in Angola. While Barbados maintains cordial relations with the United States, it exhibits no signs of servility in international affairs. For example, it decided to recognize Cuba as early as 1973. Trinidad and Tobago has been steadfastly anti-colonial since its own independence, even though it steers a largely pro-Western course. This often puts it at odds with the United States. Indeed, the entire Caribbean region has displayed signs of independence in recent years that have dismayed U.S. policymakers. Cuba's influence seems to be growing, and there is apparently little that the United States can do to stem this tide (Christian Science Monitor 1980). Once certainly does not emerge from this first test with a confirmation of the *dependencia* perspective.

RONALD A. FRANCISCO

Table 2
Correlations of Political and Economic Dependence in Latin America

	UN Agreement	% Trade U.S.	% Tourists U.S.	Import of Tourism	U.S. Grants	Military Aid	U.S. Invest.
UN Agreement	1.00	.006[a]	.043	.357	—.082	—.109	—.285
	19	19[b]	13	19	18	18	11
		.490[c]	.444	.067	.373	.334	.198
% Trade U.S.	.006	1.00	.882	.403	—.125	—.468	—.008
	19	19	13	19	18	18	11
	.490		.000	.044	.304	.025	.491
% Tourists U.S.	.043	.882	1.00	.418	—.172	—.601	—.034
	13	13	13	13	13	12	8
	.444	.000		.077	.287	.019	.468
Import of Tour	—.357	.403	.418	1.00	—.211	—.289	—.108
	19	19	13	19	18	18	11
	.067	.044	.077		.201	.122	.376
U.S. Grants	—.082	—.129	—.172	—.211	1.00	.522	.655
	18	18	13	18	18	17	11
	.373	.304	.287	.201		.016	.014
Military Aid	—.109	—.468	—.601	—.289	.522	1.00	.540
	18	18	12	18	17	18	11
	.334	.025	.019	.122	.016		.043
U.S. Investment	—.285	—.008	—.304	—.108	.655	.540	1.00
	11	11	8	11	11	11	11
	.198	.491	.468	.376	.014	.043	

a. Pearson product-moment correlation
b. Number of cases (nations)
c. Level of significance, two-tailed test

Note: UN Agreement is the correlation of U.S. with Latin American UN Votes.
% Trade U.S. is the proportion of U.S. trade in total trade.
% Tourists U.S. is the proportion of U.S. tourists in total tourist arrivals.
Import of Tourism is the receipts from tourism as a percent of GDP.
U.S. Grants are the net total from 1975 to 1978.
Military Aid is the total from 1970 to 1978.
U.S. Investment is the total for 1976.

Sources: U.S. Bureau of the Census 1979:854-859, 861-863; U.S. Department of Commerce 1978:27-28; U.S. Travel Service 1978: 22-23; *The World Almanac 1980:* 514-595.

Economic Factors and the Dependence Network

Selection of the prominent tourist centers of the Caribbean may amount to having jumped a bit too far ahead of this analysis. The

TOURISM DEPENDENCE IN LATIN AMERICA

hypotheses, after all, are expressed in aggregate terms and integrate economic measures with a basic index of political compliance. Table 2 displays the results of correlation analysis of these variables.

Once again, the outcome seems unambiguous and widely at variance with the dependency hypotheses. In the sample of 19 Latin American nations, there seems to be no relationship in the predicted direction. Indeed, there are stronger indications that the United States finds great difficulty in wielding political influence in the western hemisphere.

No significant correlations exist between the measures of economic dependence and political compliance. In fact, the strongest tendencies are toward a *negative* relationship between political compliance and the importance of tourism, development grants, military aid, and investment. American tourists do tend to travel to areas that are heavily dependent upon U.S. trade, but this has absolutely no measurable effect on host nations' "decisional latitude." It is also apparent that the dependency theorists are correct when they suggest that U.S. economic and military aid correlates highly with levels of U.S. investment. Yet what is not apparent is the direction of causal flow in this relationship. It is certainly possible that investment follows, rather than precedes, economic and military aid since investors quite naturally seek security for their funds (Kaufman et al. 1975:321-2).

Hence, there is no support for hypothesis 1, above. There is no relationship between the level of U.S. tourists in total tourist arrivals and host nation political compliance with the United States. Hypothesis 1a reflects an axiom of dependency theory—that stronger economic dependence ought to result in greater compliance. Yet even if one calculates partial correlations, controlling in every instance for the percentage contribution of tourism to the GDP, there are no significant relationships with political compliance (Table 3).

Hypothesis 2 is also disconfirmed. There is no positive relationship between U.S. foreign investment in the late 1970s and political compliance with the U.S. in the United Nations. Indeed, the tendency, although not statistically significant, is toward lower levels of compliance among recipients of U.S. foreign investment.

Nor is there any support for hypothesis 3. Nations that enjoy larger economic benefits from U.S. tourist spending tend not to get economic grants from the U.S. and do not get military aid in significant amounts ($r = -.601$, $p = .019$). The only hypothesis that is confirmed is hypothesis 4. The larger the size of the U.S. tourist sector, the larger the level of U.S. trade with the host nation ($r = .882$, $p = .001$). This squares with traditional economic analyses that stress the

RONALD A. FRANCISCO

Table 3
Partial Correlations, Controlling for
Economic Importance of Tourism

	UN Agreement	% Trade U.S.	% Tourists U.S.	U.S. Grants	Military Aid	U.S. Investment
UN Agreement	1.00	.176	.227	—.172	—.237	—.348
	19	16	10	15	15	8
		.243	.239	.254	.179	.162
% Trade U.S.	.176	1.00	.858	—.050	—.402	.039
	16	19	10	15	15	8
	.243		.000	.425	.055	.457
% Tourists U.S.	.227	.858	1.00	—.095	—.552	.012
	10	10	13	10	9	5
	.239	.000		.385	.039	.489
U.S. Grants	—.172	—.050	—.095	1.00	.493	.650
	15	15	10	18	14	8
	.254	.425	.385		.026	.021
Military Aid	—.237	—.402	—.552	.493	1.00	.534
	15	15	9	14	18	8
	.179	.055	.039	.026		.056
U.S. Investment	—.348	.039	.012	.650	.534	1.00
	8	8	5	8	8	11
	.162	.457	.489	.021	.056	

Note: Format, variables, and sources are the same as in Table 2.

import dependence that luxury tourism creates and the export leakage that occurs (e.g., Ohiorhenuan 1979:22).

ANALYSIS

It is striking that only the strictly *economic* hypothesis derived from dependency theory is confirmed for the tourism sector. There appears to be no measurable decline in *political* maneuverability (decisional latitude). Was it realistic to expect any? Certainly the *dependencia* theorists believe it is. If one looks at clearly dependent relationships around the globe, for example, among Cuba, Eastern Europe, and the Soviet Union, there is no question that decisional latitude is severely constrained.

But does the same expectation apply to the U.S. and Latin America? There is reason to believe so. First, Keohane has argued that "the more dependent a state is on a great power for trade, aid, or protection, the more responsive it is likely to be to pressure" in the

TOURISM DEPENDENCE IN LATIN AMERICA

General Assembly (1966:19). Second, Richardson analyzed the relationship of U.S. trade dominance and UN voting in the 1960s. His findings were consistent with Keohane's view in the western hemisphere, but only in the western hemisphere (1976:1110). Third, recently the United States has exhibited increasing concern that radicalism in the Caribbean is being transferred and expressed in the General Assembly (Wiznitzer 1980).

Yet even Richardson is unwilling to conclude that there is an international political component to economic dependence. Although he found a positive correlation between U.S. dependency and Latin American UN votes, he was unable to attribute this to U.S. pressure.

Fagan offers two suggestions to resolve this puzzle. First, it is fairly clear that times have changed. "Today's Latin America is not the easily manipulable and obedient Latin America of the 1960s." Moreover, "the models of unequal international exchange and theories of transnational capitalist accumulation so central to dependency thinking do not have direct analogs...in the political realm" (1977:17).

Hirschman explains the lack of U.S. leverage quite simply as Washington's inability to focus attention on the western hemisphere while it deals with more salient problems in other parts of the globe (1978). Yet the real explanation probably lies in the complexity of international political and economic interaction, and the costs over time from the application of leverage of any time (Knorr 1977).

The results of this study are consistent with a growing number of others that probe empirically the impact of various kinds of economic dependence. While there is no question that levels of economic dependence are high in Latin America, there is no direct evidence of decreased decisional latitude or internal political consequences (see, for example, Kaufman et al. 1975). Economic reliance on tourism, then, may result in distorted economic development, foreign economic leakage, domestic social dissatisfaction, and resentment, but it does not result in political compliance at the international level. □ □

REFERENCES

Bryden, John M.
    1973 Tourism and Development: A Case Study of the Commonwealth Caribbean. Cambridge: Cambridge University Press.
Caporaso, James A.
    1978 Dependence, Dependency, and Power in the Global System: A Structural and Behavioral Analysis. International Organization 32(1):13-44.

RONALD A. FRANCISCO

Chilcote, Ronald H. and Joel C. Edelstein, eds.
   1974   Latin America: The Struggle with Dependency and Beyond. Cambridge, MA:
   Schenkman Publishing Co.
Christian Science Monitor
   1980   Keeping Castrosim at Bay in the Caribbean. Christian Science Monitor
   (March 27:24.
Fagen, Richard R.
   1977   Studying Latin American Politics: Some Implications of the Dependencia
   Approach. Latin American Research Review 12(2):3-26.
Goodsell, James Nelson
   1980   Tropical St. Croix Stung by Wave of Killings. Christian Science Monitor
   (February 4):8.
Gray, Peter H.
   1970   International Travel—International Trade. Lexington: Heath Lexington
   Books.
Hirschman, Albert O.
   1978   Beyond Asymmetry: Critical Notes on Myself as a Young Man and on Some
   Other Old Friends. International Organization 32(1):45-40.
Kaufman, Robert R., Harry I. Chernotsky, and Daniel S. Geller
   1975   A Preliminary Test of the Theory of Dependency. Comparative Politics
   7(3):303-330.
Keohane,Robert O.
   1966   Political Influence in the General Assembly. International Conciliation No.
   557 (March).
Knorr, Klaus
   1977   International Economic Leverage and its Uses. In Economic Issues and
   National Security, K. Knorr and F. Trager, eds. pp. 99-126. Lawrence: Regents
   Press of Kansas.
Matthews, Harry G.
   1978   International Tourism: A Political and Social Analysis. Cambridge, MA:
   Schenkman Publishing Company.
Ohiorhenuan, John F. E.
   1979   The Social and Economic Implications of Technology Transfer in Jamaican
   Tourism. United Nations: UN Conference on Trade and Development.
Richardson, Neil R.
   1976   Political Compliance and U.S. Trade Dominance. American Political Science
   Review 70(4):1098-1109.
Richter, Linda
   1980   Land Reform and Tourism Development: Policy-Making in Martial Law
   Philippines. Ph.D. dissertation, University of Kansas.
Robinson, Harry
   1976   A Geography of Tourism. London: Macdonald and Evans.
U.S. Bureau of the Census
   1979   Department of Commerce. Statistical Abstract of the United States.
U.S. Department of Commerce
   1978   Survey of Current Business (August).
U.S. Department of State
   1980   Office of Multilateral Affairs. Votes at the Thirty-third Regular Session of the
   General Assembly.
U.S. Travel Service
   1978   Department of Commerce. Summary and Analysis of International Travel
   To/From the U.S.

TOURISM DEPENDENCE IN LATIN AMERICA

Wiznitzer, Louis
    1980   Controversy Brews Over Role of Micro-States in UN. Christian Science
      Monitor (March 27):7.
Young, George
    1973   Tourism, Blessing or Blight? London: Pelican.

Submitted 25 October 1982
Accepted 8 December 1982
Refereed anonymously

C
Government Policies and Planning

[6]

GOVERNMENT INVOLVEMENT IN TOURISM IN DEVELOPING COUNTRIES

C.L. Jenkins
B.M. Henry
University of Strathcylde, UK

ABSTRACT

The article examines the case for involvement of government in the tourism sector in developing countries and makes definitional distinctions between passive and active involvement. It is argued that in most developing countries government involvement in tourism is required not only to attain long-term objectives but to compensate for the absence of a strong and tourism-experienced private sector. Five areas of concern for government involvement are discussed, and conclusions relate to the need for government-private sector cooperation for development purposes. **Keywords:** tourism policies, developing countries, government involvement.

Carson L. Jenkins is a Senior Lecturer in Tourism at the Scottish Hotel School, University of Strathclyde, Glasgow. He has a special teaching and research interest in the formulation of tourism policies in developing countries. **B.M. Henry** is a Jamaican postgraduate student completing his Ph.D. thesis on "The Impact of Tourism on the Development of Jamaica."

Annals of Tourism Research, Vol. 9, pp. 499-521, 1982
Printed in the USA. All rights reserved.

0160-7383/82/040499-23$3.00/0
© 1982 J. Jafari and Pergamon Press Ltd

GOVERNMENT INVOLVEMENT IN TOURISM IN DEVELOPING COUNTRIES

RÉSUMÉ

L'intervention governementale dans développement du tourisme des pay en voi de développement. Cet article a pour but d'apprécier les raisons pour la participation de l'état dans le développement du secteur touristique des pays en voi de developpement, et établit la differénce qui existe sur le plan de la définition entre la participation active et la participation passive. On peut soutenir que dans la plupart des pays en voie de développement la participation governementale est nécessaire pour réaliser les objectifs a long terme et pour compenser l'absence d'un secteur privé bien assis et riche en expérience touristique. Les auteurs de cet article examinent cinq points d'intéret et les conclusions touchent à la nécessité d'une coopération entre le governement et le secteur privé pour les besoins de développement. **Mots clef:** les politiques touristiques, pays en voie développement, participation governementale.

INTRODUCTION

The increasing amount of literature on tourism reflects the growing involvement by academics, professionals, and specialist agencies in what might be loosely described as the "tourism industry." Within the general literature can be discerned contributions from specialist sub-groups of the social sciences—economics, sociology, anthropology, geography, etc.—which all help to create a wide, multidisciplinary perspective for tourism. Despite this wide perspective, a recent bibliography by Jafari (1979) suggests that an area of relative neglect in the literature concerns the role of government in the process of developing a tourism industry. This statement does not overlook the fact that some writers such as Eden (1974) and Wahab (1973) have made some examination of this role, while other studies (UNCTAD 1971; Green 1979) have done so by implication rather than by specific analysis.

The aim of this article is to consider and present the case for active government involvement in the development of tourism and, in particular, to examine the need for this action by government in developing countries. Social scientists have long held interests in the role of government in the economic, social, and political life of countries. While there is considerable and continuing debate surrounding the nature and extent of this role, most observers would

C.L. JENKINS AND B.M. HENRY

accept that some degree of government intervention is essential. In developing countries, it will be argued that a greater degree of intervention by government is required to achieve material objectives because of the absence of a developed and innovative private sector. In many if not all developing countries, government has to undertake an entrepreneurial role to ensure that "pioneer" activities are initiated. This type of government intervention is common both to developed and developing countries, and it is suggested that this action is no less appropriate for tourism than other sectors of an economy. It will be further argued that because of the characteristics of tourism activity, there is a requirement for active rather than passive intervention by government.

An increasing number of studies have been made on the non-economic impact of tourism on host communities (de Kadt 1979; Smith 1978). It will be suggested in the context of this article that the impact of tourism on a host country is primarily a concern and responsibility of government. Government responsibility is much wider than that of the private sector *per se*. Private sector involvement in tourism is likely to be initiated by opportunities for profitable investment, and priorities are likely to be related to financial and economic considerations. There are many conflicts and problems relating to the development of tourism which can only be resolved by government, particularly when private sector interests have to be evaluated against the interests of the community and country as a whole.

Many of these conflicts and problems emerge long after the initial tourism investment has been made. The growing awareness of long-term problems associated with often uncontrolled tourism development has made governments more conscious of the need for careful monitoring and selective action to curb potential problems, as Bounds (1978) noted in the Bahamas.

THE NATURE OF GOVERNMENT INVOLVEMENT: SOME DEFINITIONS

In the context of this article, *active involvement* is seen as a deliberate action by government, introduced to favor the tourism sector. Conversely, *passive involvement* occurs where government undertakes an action which may have implications for tourism, but is not specifically intended to favor or influence tourism.

1. Passive Involvement

The characteristics of passive involvement by government in

GOVERNMENT INVOLVEMENT IN TOURISM IN DEVELOPING COUNTRIES

tourism might be usefully categorized into *mandatory* and *supportive* actions:

a. Mandatory: Passive mandatory involvement will usually be linked with legislative provision. Three examples will illustrate this concept. First, a government enacts legislation relating to the employment of foreign nationals within the country. Second, a government introduces legislation offering investment incentives. Third, government negotiates a bilateral air services agreement. In these three examples, government is using mandatory authority to introduce legislation which relates to the country as a whole and is not intended to discriminate in favor of the tourism sector, although these measures may have implications for tourism.

b. Supportive: This situation could arise where government does not deliberately inhibit the development of tourism, but neither does it actively encourage it. An example would be where a group of hoteliers and travel businesses establish a "national" tourist board with the approval of government but lacking any specific governmental input, such as finance. Another example would be where government provides some general, e.g., clerical and vocational courses which may or may not have relevance to the needs of the tourist sector. In an alternative phrase, the World Bank (1972) had described the situation as one of "benign neglect."

2. Active Involvement

Active involvement implies not only a recognition by government of the specific needs of the tourism sector, but also of the necessity for its operational participation to attain stated objectives. It is this specific action which distinguishes active from passive involvement, and it might be categorized as below:

a. Managerial: In this case, government not only sets tourism objectives (possibly in a tourism development plan), but also introduces necessary organizational and legislative support to attain the objectives. In terms of the three examples cited previously, government can discriminate in favor of foreign nationals seeking employment in tourism; second, government could introduce specific tourism investment incentives legislation (and might establish a tourism development bank); and third, it could negotiate bilateral air agreements with the specific interests of tourist traffic in mind. In these circumstances, involvement is essentially selective and specific.

C.L. JENKINS AND B.M. HENRY

b. Developmental: Developmental involvement is seen when government or its agencies undertake an operational role in the tourist sector. This role might be taken because of ideological reasons, as in many centrally-planned economies. However, in developing countries, government usually undertakes this role because of the inability or unwillingness of the private sector to become involved in tourism. In many developing countries, e.g., India and Ghana, government has both financed and operated hotels. Another example would be in Kenya where government has introduced specific training facilities for the tourism industry. In this latter example, it may be argued that it is a function of government to provide training facilities, but to do so specifically for an industry is an example of active government intervention.

The essence of active involvement by government in tourism is an action or series of actions which discriminate in favor of the tourism sector. It is pertinent to note that the nature and extent of this involvement will reflect not only the stage of development of a country, but also the political philosophy of its government.
In socialist, centrally-planned economies, the private sector is small or non-existent (e.g., Yugoslavia, Bulgaria), and government assumes the dominant entrepreneurial role. In developed, mixed-economy countries, most of the entrepreneurial investment has been generated by the private sector with government providing infrastructure and other selective help. Whatever the political ethos of government, its involvement is likely to reflect the importance of tourism within the economy.

Most developing countries are characterized by a scarcity of resources for development, with private sectors which often have little experience of tourism as an industry. Not all developing countries fit this generalization, but in many cases government has to become the main dynamo for economic growth by adopting an entrepreneurial role. In most developing countries, government is the largest employer of labor, the only source of investment funds, and the guarantor for foreign loans. One recognizes Bauer's (1972) critique that the centralization of development initiative does not make it necessarily more efficient or effective—"comprehensive planning does not augment resources, it only concentrates power." However, for many developing countries with few export options available to earn hard currency, the attractions of tourism are often very real to many governments, as Jenkins (1981a) has noted.

GOVERNMENT INVOLVEMENT IN TOURISM IN DEVELOPING COUNTRIES

GOVERNMENT INVOLVEMENT IN TOURISM

Many of the problems inhibiting economic progress in the developing countries are intensifying. As the World Development Report (World Bank 1981:1) summarizes: "The external pressures on developing countries have shown little sign of easing over the last 12 months. The combined current account deficit of the oil-importing developing countries rose from $26 billion in 1978 to $70 billion in 1980 and may rise even higher this year. Slow growth in the industrial countries is curbing demand for developing countries' exports while the price of petroleum (a product that now constitutes some 25% of developing countries import bills) increased by over 80% in real terms between 1978 and 1980. While many of the better-off developing countries have been able to expand exports and borrow extensively in commercial markets, for most of the poorer countries these new pressures come at the end of a decade in which they have made little progress."

To this gloomy analysis might be added the twin specter of increasing populations and labor forces which also constitute major problems for most poor countries. The population pressure exacerbates existing problems of unemployment and under-employment. The introduction by most developed countries of strict immigration policies has closed what was once thought of as a channel for "exporting" unemployed labor. Given the extent and variety of problems facing most developing countries, it is perhaps not surprising that many of them regard tourism, with its relatively unhindered trade flow, as an opportunity to relieve some of the constraints on the development process.

The data on international tourism in developing countries are unreliable. In some cases these countries do not file data with the World Tourism Organization. Other countries do not use standard methods of measuring tourism activity and thereby make reliable international comparisons very difficult, if not impossible. However, given these limitations, it is still possible to discern the general trends of international tourism activity in the developing countries.

Cleverdon (1979:13) has produced estimates of tourism performance based on data from 30 developing countries which together "account for approximately two-thirds of internatinal tourism activity in less developed countries." His analysis shows that between 1973-77 the share of these developing countries of international tourism arrivals increased from 13.7% to 15%, but there was virtually no increase in their share of international tourism expenditure—from 17.6% in 1973 to 18.5% in 1977. The reasons for this

C.L. JENKINS AND B.M. HENRY

stagnation of earning are varied and complex. Cleverdon (1979:13) suggests that "this is due, in part, to the locus of control of distribution, and in some cases, to the ownership of less developed countries." Tourist products being with corporations or individuals based outside the country. He also notes the important problem of the high degree of leakage of gross tourism expenditure from these countries to pay for imports of goods and services.

Although Cleverdon's data are representative, the experiences of individual countries might differ considerably from the general trend. It is well to acknowledge that the categorization "less developed country" covers a wide range of levels of development, socioeconomic structures, and political administrations. In the following table, 10 developing countries, all with established tourism sectors, have been selected to illustrate how general economic pressures will have different levels of impact in each country. Table 1 provides some general economic indicators for the 10 countries and shows the range of five economic indicators for the selected countries. In each country the rate of growth indicator should be related

Table 1
Economic Indicators for Selected Tourist-Receiving Developing Countries

Countries	G.N.P Per Capita U.S.$ 1979[a]	Population (millions) mid-1979[a]	% Average Annual Growth of Population 1970-79[a]	% Average Annual Growth of Labor Force 1970-80[a]	% Contribution of Earnings from International Tourism to GDP 1977[b]
Asia					
India	190	659.2	2.1	1.7	N.A.
Thailand	590	45.5	2.4	2.7	1.2
Sri Lanka	230	14.5	1.7	2.0	2.1[c]
Philippines	600	46.7	2.6	2.4	1.5
Caribbean					
Jamaica	1.260	2.2	1.6	2.2	N.A.
Haiti	260	4.9	1.7	1.2	2.8
Costa Rica	1.820	2.2	2.5	3.6	1.8
Africa					
Egypt	480	38.9	2.0	2.0	3.5
Kenya	380	15.3	3.4	2.8	2.6
Morocco	740	19.5	2.9	3.0	3.2

Sources:
a. Compiled from World Develpment Report (1981), Tables 1, 17, 19.
b. Economic Review of World Tourism (1980: 62-68).
c. Contribution to National Income.

GOVERNMENT INVOLVEMENT IN TOURISM IN DEVELOPING COUNTRIES

to the base population statistic. In India for example, any percentage increase in population growth would have a proportionately greater impact than a similar rate of increase would have in Thailand.

For each developing country, the degree of active involvement by government in the tourism sector will reflect the importance of tourism in the economy. This economic importance is usually measured in four broad ways: contribution to Gross Domestic Product and National Income, earnings from foreign exchange, employment and income generated, and contribution to government revenues. Using these four indicators, one would expect government to intervene actively in the tourist sector when either tourism is of major economic significance or where government follows a system of centrally-planned economic activity.

In the discussion which follows, five general "areas of concern" in the formulation of tourism policy have been identified. It is probable that most governments would be involved in policy-making in each area, if only in a passive role. Even a necessarily brief consideration of each area will indicate the need for active government involvement. Without such involvement, many developing countries will likely confront the progression of problems noted by UNESCO (1980): "It is essential that the developing countries take all the necessary precautions to avoid killing the goose that lays the golden egg." The progression which has become all too familiar in many developing countries, according to the same source, could have been avoided (had there been active involvement by government). It goes as follows: "Unspoiled place with unique character attracts tourists; new buildings and amenities necessary to house tourists bring about change; more tourists produce more change; loss of initial attractive character becomes element responsible for departure of tourists; and final result is economic, social and financial disaster."

Such a progression suggests that potential conflicts between short-term benefits and longer-term objectives have not been recognized or anticipated. To achieve tourism objectives, it will be necessary to monitor and control the nature and pace of tourism development in a country. It is not a simple process to control tourism development, depending, as it often does, on the availability of foreign investment. Any government can ultimately reject foreign investment. But where there is strong competition for investment funds, then government might be tempted to permit some types of investment (e.g., casinos rather than have no investment at all). As in most government decisions, evaluation should be seen in terms of political economy rather than mere economic rationale. However, if the above progression is to be avoided, then government must

C.L. JENKINS AND B.M. HENRY

establish objectives for the tourism sector and use these objectives as the rationale for policy decisions. An example of this process can be given in relation to five areas of concern noted below.

Foreign Exchange Earnings

A strong economic argument for government support for the tourism industry is related to foreign exchange earnings. A shortage of foreign exchange is one of the continuing constraints on the development effort in most non-oil exporting developing countries. Early studies by Mitchell in Kenya (1968) and UNCTAD (1971) have shown that tourism can be an effective and efficient earner of foreign exchange. Government will want to maximize foreign exchange derived from tourism, and one means to this end would be to reduce "leakages" from tourist expenditures. In some very "open" economies, leakages have severely reduced the multiplier effect of tourism expenditure (Checci 1969; Bryden 1973).

In order to minimize these leakages, government should carefully review the nature and level of tourism-related imports and explore the possibility of introducing and encouraging an import-substitution strategy. As Demas (1965) has noted, this strategy can embrace two broad themes. In the first case, an import replacement strategy would seek to replace a foreign manufactured product with a domestically manufactured one. In circumstances where the foreign product is not protected by a patent, a high level of technology, or particular brand loyalty, then this type of import replacement not only has a direct impact on balance of payments, but also encourages the "linkage effect" which has wider stimuli on the economy. It may be that the private sector manufacturers recognize the potential for import replacement but require specific government assistance to protect initial ventures into the field. As an example, one can cite the case of Barbados where much of the decorative/security ironwork in hotels and private residences is now manufactured within the island, with manufacturers receiving "pioneer" status for tax purposes.

A second category is import-displacement substitution, an area usually related to consumable products. An example from the Caribbean would be an attempt to persuade tourists to drink Trinidad orange juice rather than imported frozen Florida juice, or to replace apple juice with guava juice. It is probable that this type of displacement will be limited in scope by the quality, availability, and acceptability to the tourist of the alternative product. In many countries, the scope for substitution-displacement is an apparent

GOVERNMENT INVOLVEMENT IN TOURISM IN DEVELOPING COUNTRIES

rather than a realistic option. Most tour operators in generating countries agree on "acceptable" menus with hoteliers in the receiving countries. It is usual for these menus to reflect the tastes and preferences of the tourists usual home-style. In these circumstances, the "invariant menus" noted by Rodenburg (1980) become very difficult to change by substituting local foodstuffs for more internationally recognized offerings. Hoteliers can and do make available a range of local dishes and products, but there is no reported evidence of any developing country being able to achieve a significant level of menu substitution.

This inability to generate a linkage effect through substitution is a cause for concern in many developing countries, as the Prime Minister of Grenada-recently observed: "In tourism the pattern has been that the tourist economy has been entirely separate from the rest of the economy. They [the tourists] are not eating our food. They are not buying our handicrafts but buying goods made in Taiwan and Hong Kong. We want to fully integrate the tourist economy as regards foods and handicrafts" (Bishop 1979).

This situation is not merely a consequence of tourism. In relation to Barbados, an early study by Gooding (1971) observed that "where it is perfectly true to say that any dollar the tourist spends on food, about two-thirds is spent on imported items, this is not so very different from the situation for the average Barbadian." The tourism sector then and now reflects the very open nature of most Caribbean economies, a fact on which Holder (1980) has also commented.

It will usually require strong government action to devise and implement policies to secure the most benefits from potential intersectoral linkages. In a developing country with no tradition of tourism, many of the inputs to the primary stage of tourism development will have to be imported. When this initial development is undertaken by foreign investors, it is likely that they will import not only capital, but also senior management and its existing market connections. In this situation, and particularly where the initial investment is made by a multinational company, many of the decisions relating to purchasing policy are made outside the country of location. As existing supply arrangements are presumably based on a reputation for quality of product and/or service, there is no reason to assume that there are any inherent reasons to induce management to alter the arrangements.

When a destination is developed to a secondary or "mature" level, the existing supply patterns will probably have been consolidated. It will have become progressively more difficult for local suppliers to break into the market. Barriers to entry can relate to the inability of

C.L. JENKINS AND B.M. HENRY

the local suppliers to meet the scale and quality of product or service demanded, and the absence of commercial "know-how" to overcome the barriers. Without the active support and encouragement of government, it is difficult to see how individual local producers or even cooperative producers can enter this supply market. It might be suggested that if local competitors are not price and quality effective, then they should not be encouraged. In the context of developing countries, this is a weak argument, as most businesses in developing countries require support and, usually, some form of protection. However, as tourism is an internationally competitive industry, government cannot merely legislate to protect domestic suppliers from more efficient foreign suppliers. To promote and stimulate potential local suppliers will require active government intervention, often over a long period of time.

It may require that government undertake a survey of food purchasing patterns in the tourism sector to determine whether import substitution possibilities exist. To turn any possibilities into realities will require specific policy decisions. An example might be where local suppliers can meet the demand from the tourism industry for poultry meat, but that cold storage facilities need to be available to meet seasonal demand fluctuations. There may also be problems associated with quality standards. It is often overlooked that most foodstuffs producers in developing countries are essentially small-scale or peasant agriculturalists. Any transition from this level of production will usually be beyond the means—and experience—of the individual producer. Without active intervention by government, many of the potential supply opportunities will remain unrealized.

There is no doubt that import leakages are a continuing problem for most developing countries. For some products with a "brand-loyalty" (e.g., Scotch whisky and French wines), there may be no acceptable substitutes, but it is likely that there will be a range of substitutes for other products used in the tourism sector such as local fabrics, furniture, and handicrafts. In the early 60's, for example, the government of Barbados established a handicrafts village near the Deep-Water Harbour (Pelican Village). This was an active intervention by the government to encourage local craftsmen to produce for visiting tourists and industry generally. Government supported this development by providing simple but adequate premises at very low rents.

In the tourism literature, most emphasis in examining import-substitution possibilities is given to foodstuffs. However, one should not ignore the availability and the need to support local services. The

GOVERNMENT INVOLVEMENT IN TOURISM IN DEVELOPING COUNTRIES

range of services available in any country will vary. Most foreign investors will use some locally available professional services such as lawyers, architects, and possibly planners. However, there is a need to encourage other services and trades such as electrical, plumbing, heating and air-conditioning, etc., which are likely to be required for maintenance work in the tourism industry. Such linkage development not only increases the employment impact of international tourism, but where local employees are substituted for foreign, this will also have some savings effect on the amount of foreign exchange needed to pay for foreign workers.

It will require strong government action to obtain linkage effects, particularly in developing countries where many foreign-owned tourist enterprises have traditional lines of supply, established tourist preferences, and probably a local sector not immediately geared to meet the needs of tourist demand. Without active government intervention, it is difficult to see how these linkage effects can be generated with a consequent impact on the proportion of tourist expenditure retained within the economy.

Foreign investment

It is generally recognized that most developing countries need to attract foreign investment to support their development efforts. Scarcity of domestic capital or a reluctance to use what is available for investment in tourism often results in government having to specifically encourage foreign investors by making investment incentives available. The nature and extent of these incentives is central to tourism policy-making. Without some level of investment incentives, available funds might be "competed away" by other countries. It is the international competition for funds which has resulted in many developing countries offering investors a competitive level of incentives without basing this offer on a careful analysis of the development needs of the tourist sector. Too many pieces of incentive legislation are monuments to competitive forces rather than to domestic need. Government has an overriding responsibility to decide whether or not to introduce investment incentives, and, if introduced, to apply them selectively and monitor the ensuing consequences.

Foreign investment in a country is an emotive as well as an economic consideration. When there is a large proportion of foreign investment in a country or industry, it can give rise to political pressure on governments to control foreign investors. It is possible to cite cases in tourism where foreign investors are given incentives

C.L. JENKINS AND B.M. HENRY

to provide facilities, yet local entrepreneurs do not have the same privileges. In the longer term, local initiative might be suppressed. As Demas (1965) commented, "Where a country is dominated by foreign private investment over a long period of time, the effect is to distort development, to fail to produce linkages between economic activities and sectors, to cripple and discourage the development of local initiative, local entrepreneurship, and local institutions for mobilizing savings, and to remove from national control powers of effective decision-making in economic matters."

Demas' stricture refers to the continuing use of foreign private investment. However, it is well recognized that this type of investment is mostly made in revenue-generating projects such as hotels, casinos, restaurants, etc. To attract this risk capital, government will need to provide suitable infrastructure. The provision of infrastructure is often a great financial strain for government, requiring, as it often does, substantial capital outlays which usually have to be borrowed from abroad. In order to make the best use of this type of long-term investment, government should ensure that the type of incentives offered to foreign (and domestic) investors are geared to attract the type of facility which best meets the objectives of the tourism development plan. A basic need is for government to harmonize public and private sector investment objectives.

There are a number of broad objectives which might be noted. First, the levels of incentives offered should be sufficient to attract foreign investment. Second, the incentive legislation should include incentives to encourage the reinvestment of profits earned from operations in the country. Third, the incentive legislation should specifically include the participation of domestic investors. Fourth, the incentives offered should be reviewed within a five year period at least. This, of course, does not mean that the original level of incentives given to an investor be reviewed (for this would endanger investor confidence), but that the levels of incentives offered to subsequent investors be evaluated. Fifth, the granting of incentive assistance should be given selectively. Sixth, any incentive legislation should be promulgated against the background of a carefully considered tourism development plan.

A detailed discussion of the use of investment incentives in the development of tourism is outside the scope of this article. However, it can be appreciated that it is a very important aspect of tourism investment in most developing and developed countries. What is indisputable is that it is an area where only government can legislate; it is also an area where government can be active or passive. Active intervention would suggest a carefully balanced set of incen-

GOVERNMENT INVOLVEMENT IN TOURISM IN DEVELOPING COUNTRIES

tives drawn up against a careful analysis of the tourism sector, with the aim of meeting specific objectives.

Unfortunately, in many developing countries, although objectives are noted in many tourism development plans, they are either ignored or not implemented. In these circumstances, legislation is introduced to meet competition for investment funds from other countries rather than designed to stimulate particular types of investment. It is not therefore unusual to find many countries with incentive legislation which has remained undisturbed on the statute books for many years.

Employment in Tourism

Few developing countries can expand and sustain a tourism industry without using foreign expertise. The use of foreign expertise is often the only means of jumping the development gap between the level of indigenously available management and technical skills and the level of experience and competence needed to organize and sustain an international industry. In the short term, the use of foreign nationals in the tourist sector must be regarded as one of the costs of development, although terms of contract might well create an identifiable elite which can cause social and political pressures. In the long term, an integral part of development strategy will be, wherever and whenever possible, to replace foreign employees by local people. To accomplish this objective, government must adopt an interventionist role.

Most countries control the employment of foreign nationals by a system of work permits. In itself, such a system is essentially a passive intervention by government because it does nothing to encourage the development of indigenous skills or training. To contribute active intervention, government must ensure that not only is the employment of foreign nationals controlled, but that this is allied to a policy for training of needed skills. Counterpart training by foreign experts for local people may be difficult for jobs beyond relatively non-professional, middle-skill levels. Above this level, barriers to training might include such factors as inadequate education, absence of special training facilities, instructors, etc. Most tourist-receiving countries undertake basic training for employees in the tourism sector, especially the hotel industry (waiters, cooks, housekeepers, etc.). For more senior positions, training usually has to be carried out overseas, as they are on the tourism training courses run by the International Labor Organization in Turin, and by the World Tourism Organization in Mexico City. In relation to the

C.L. JENKINS AND B.M. HENRY

need to train public sector employees to plan and manage the tourism sector, Jenkins (1980b) has suggested that this specialist training must be sought abroad because of the lack of advanced training facilities in most developing countries.

Given the scarcity of resources in most developing countries and therefore the attendant priorities of resource allocation, government should take an overview of employment problems and possibilities by commissioning a manpower development plan. Without such an analysis, most decisions relating to the employment of foreign nationals are likely to be taken on the basis of ad hoc judgements and will not contribute to the longer term aim of training and employing indigenous labor. In Kenya, the government, aided by Swiss technical assistance, established the Hotel and Tourism Training College which now provides a substantial number of trained people for employment in tourism.

Not every country will extensively use foreign labor as Chib (1980) has observed in the case of India, where very few foreign nationals are employed in the hotel sector. It may be that a too rapid attempt to indigenize management will have serious and adverse effects on tourism as Bound (1978) noted in the case of the Bahamas. In an earlier article, Elkan (1975) observed (in relation to Kenya and Tanzania) that the employment impact of tourism is often over-stated.

It is unlikely that the potential opportunities for local employment will be fully realized without active government intervention. Although one of the main attractions of tourism development is said to be the relatively labor-intensive nature of the activity, it is also noted that in the short term, much of the employment offered will be of a low-skills, low-paid type. In the longer term, to make certain that nationals are able to take advantage of career opportunities in tourism, government must ensure that there are suitably educated and trained people available. It does not necessarily follow that government has the sole responsibility for education or vocational training. The private sector, particularly by on-the-job training, often plays a very important part in developing local skills. However, at senior management levels, the process of indigenization of management can only take place if government takes steps to train and encourage nationals. In some Caribbean countries, Jamaica and Barbados, for example, scholarships for study overseas are awarded to students who are training for employment in trades and professions which government has deemed to be of national priority. This is another example of active government intervention.

It should also be noted that employment policies will have an effect

GOVERNMENT INVOLVEMENT IN TOURISM IN DEVELOPING COUNTRIES

on the amount of foreign exchange "leaked" from the country to buy foreign expertise. As the local-for-foreign labor substitution takes place, one would expect to see a reduction in the foreign exchange used to employ foreigners. The position is complicated because the foreign exchange saved by labor substitution will not be without cost; it is probable that much of the training for local people will have to be done by foreigners and this should be offset against the savings made. In the long term, probably more significant than the savings of foreign exchange will be the nonquantifiable effect of having an indigenous management cadre.

Land Use Policies

In most developing countries, land use will be identified with agriculture, and in a few cases, with mining. The allocation and use of land for tourism development will require that government anticipate future problems and conflicts related to site allocation and ownership. A land use policy for tourism involves allocating zones for development, probably after examining a whole range of competing demands.

Most developing countries recognize the need for land use planning and the requirements of planning for tourism development. In Egypt, Indonesia, Ghana, and many more developing countries, there are master plans for the development of tourism. These plans attempt to harmonize the needs of the tourism sector with the often conflicting needs of other sectors. A critical concern is to balance tourism development with the problems of conserving and protecting the natural environment (Dasman 1973; WTO 1980).

Tourism development poses particular problems in relation to land use policies. In most developing countries where the natural environment and habitat comprise the main tourism attractions, uncontrolled development can result in serious environmental problems. Many tourist developments are based in areas of outstanding natural attractiveness, and without careful management, overuse by tourists can result in a diminution of the scenic value and, sometimes physical erosion of the site. Government has the responsibility to consider the impact of any proposed development on the environment and society. Often the conflicts arising between development and conservation lobbyists can only be resolved by the use of value judgements. In many instances, the value judgements can only be exercised by government. A common example would be a situation where a development application is made for a site which has historical or ecological significance, or a situation where a develop-

C.L. JENKINS AND B.M. HENRY

ment would interfere with the traditional cultural pattern of a location. This is a very important area of tourism policymaking, and one where active government intervention is needed.

In some countries (e.g., Kenya, Tanzania, and Zimbabwe) where wild-life is a major tourist attraction, governments have had to devise and implement strict conservation policies. There are, of course, strong arguments in support of wild-life conservation even where tourism is not a consideration. The conservation of wild-life often conflicts with the traditional hunting rights of native people and is another example of the need for government intervention in evaluating competing claims and needs.

Although land use planning implies a rational evaluation for competing demands, the ownership of land is a more emotive consideration. In many developing countries, a high proportion of tourism-developed land is owned by foreigners. As the amount of land owned by foreigners increases, this may give rise to political concern. In the Seychelles, it was only after one quarter of the land was owned by foreigners that government intervened to prevent further sales (de Kadt 1980).

Tourism investment and land use are closely related. Successful (i.e. profitable) tourist investment tends to attract further investment. On the west coast of Barbados (the so-called "Platinum Coast"), the heavy concentration of tourist development has had the effect of not only rapidly increasing the price of land, but also pricing it beyond the reach of most locals. Resentment was caused by this price spiral, particularly because it is an area dominated by foreign investment. It is not an unusual situation, as Jackson (1973) noted in the comments of the then Minister of Power and Communications in Kenya—"the privilege of free seller, free buyer is being greatly abused... this racket in land prices is having a serious effect on poor African farmers." This effect, of course, is not limited to developing countries. In the United Kingdom, as a current example, one could suggest that much of the wrath of the nationalist political movements stems from purchases of land by foreigners, particularly in Wales and Scotland.

In attracting foreign investment and offering required guarantees relating to the repatriation of profits and capital, government must consider the long-term effects of foreign ownership of land. It may be that to avoid future problems, a system of long-term leases on land should be used as is done in Cyprus. In this way, investors are given a continuity of ownership without totally alienating national sovereignty.

There are many problems associated with the use of land for

GOVERNMENT INVOLVEMENT IN TOURISM IN DEVELOPING COUNTRIES

tourism purposes. In many countries, the pattern of land use and ownership had been determined in the period before the granting of political independence. In these countries, the role of government is to establish policies for future land use and to try and protect the rights and interests of local people against the need to increase development options. Without active government intervention, it would not be unusual to find that small, local grievances can escalate into major social and political problems. If the outcome of this escalation is violence, as, for example, in the so-called "black power" disturbances in Trinidad in 1970, then it may have the effect of dissuading tourists from visiting not only a country but also a region.

Air Transport and Tourism

Many developing countries rely on air transport to bring tourists to their countries, particularly those routes which are long hauls from the main tourist-generating countries. In the immediate post-war period, few developing countries had international airlines, but in the 1960's and 1970's an increasing number of these countries created and expanded their airlines. In most cases, the impetus to establish an airline coincided with the need to develop communication and commercial links with other countries, with the need to help promote a national identity abroad, and with the need to foster tourist traffic. Where the promotion of tourism traffic was important, the existence of a national carrier provided government with some control over traffic development through the negotiation of bilateral air service agreements or via International Air Transport Association traffic conferences (if the airline was a member). Without a designated national carrier, government would have to rely on the whims and vagaries of foreign carriers to transport tourists. In the latter case, although government might operate an "open skies" policy to encourage a proliferation of services, it would have very limited influence on capacity offered, prices, and nature of services, i.e., non-stop or indirect flights, an important consideration in the marketing of a destination.

Many of these countries have limited control over the development of air transport services. As a recent United Nations (1980:87) study commented, "the problem of developing countries is both one of a lack of bargaining power and of inability (because of insufficient economies of scale) to compete effectively for the main international air routes. This inevitably leads to a degree of dependence (for instance the Caribbean islands) on foreign airlines for transportation

C.L. JENKINS AND B.M. HENRY

of tourists there. Should the routes involving these countries become less profitable than alternative routes, foreign airlines might cease to supply them, thus causing the host countries economic difficulties." This was the case in the Caribbean countries before the establishment of national flag carriers in Trinidad-Tobago, Jamaica, and Barbados. The existence of national carriers has allowed these countries to penetrate markets in, for example, Europe and North America which otherwise would have required the goodwill of foreign airlines to develop. As Chernick (1978) noted, these three countries probably suffered less than other regional countries in stimulating tourism markets because of the existence of their own carriers, which through bilateral negotiations gave them access to destinations which otherwise might not have been serviced.

The decision as to whether a country should establish its own national airline or designate a "national" carrier is complex. There will be no general set of circumstances which apply to every country, and in many cases the decision to establish a national airline may have nothing to do with economics at all, but may merely reflect political judgements. However, given these limitations, it is possible to identify some of the reasons why a country might decide to introduce its own airline.

First, a country with its own airline—however small its fleet—will have some control over air services to and from the country. This allows it to reduce its dependency on foreign airlines. Second, the existence of a national airline gives the government the opportunity to negotiate and develop through bilateral agreements new air services. It can establish market links which, particularly in the field of tourism, allow it to "tap" markets which it would not otherwise be able to do without the agreement of foreign carriers. Third, it can share in the foreign exchange earnings accruing from air fares, particularly on routes with a high density of tourist traffic. Fourth, in addition to reasons of an economic nature, a national airline is often regarded as a source of pride and a means of supplementing the creation of an international image. Although these reasons are not meant to be exhaustive, they are often important considerations in the decision to establish a national airline.

There are also persuasive reasons to suggest that establishing a national airline is likely to be an expensive and difficult undertaking. First, a developing country will usually have limited capital available to invest in modern aircraft and related facilities. This initial outlay can be reduced by the use of lease-buy arrangements or by purchasing used aircraft. The type of aircraft bought will obviously affect the nature and quality of services offered, which might cause problems

GOVERNMENT INVOLVEMENT IN TOURISM IN DEVELOPING COUNTRIES

in marketing the service. Second, the necessary support services for airline operation such as maintenance facilities, reservation and ground support systems, etc., will usually have to be brought-in with a consequent drain on foreign exchange earnings. Third, because of the small scale of initial operations, unit operating costs relative to bigger airlines will be higher, thus putting pressure on operating margins, particularly where the fare structure is internationally agreed. Fourth, most developing countries' airlines would require time to establish a reputation for quality of service and for safety. They may find it difficult to attain a viable share of traffic on specific routes. Where governments insist on an equal share of traffic, a market with a strong demand may not be properly serviced because of the inability of the national carrier to acquire aircraft to meet rising demand. Fifth, major increases in fuel and other costs have caused serious problems for all airlines, but particularly for the smaller airlines of developing countries. These pressures have resulted in intensified price competition, major changes in route networks, and demands for government protection against "unfair" competition. The impact of this increased competition and government subsidization of carriers has been described by Tye (1980).

From the short summary given above, it is clear that a government would have to evaluate carefully the advantages and disadvantages of establishing a national airline. It may be that the government can achieve some, if not all, of its civil aviation policy objectives by allowing an "open skies" approach to air route development. It can also decide to designate an airline as a "national carrier" without having to take the risk of making a heavy financial commitment to the airline. When the government of Barbados designated International Caribbean Airways as its national carrier in 1969, it had a small financial participation in the airline's equity. Despite the perils of launching a national airline, some developing countries such as Singapore, Hong Kong, Thailand, and Pakistan have all been able to establish viable, efficient, and reputable national carriers. Whatever decision is reached, air transport developments require the active interest and involvement of government. The existence of the International Civil Aviation Organization's convention ensures that any country's airline has a "free and equal opportunity" to participate in international air commerce. Without active and powerful government support, many of the smaller airlines from the developing countries will find that these opportunities to participate in route development are neither particularly free of restrictions nor equitably granted.

C.L. JENKINS AND B.M. HENRY

CONCLUSION

This paper has presented the case for active intervention by government in the tourism industry in developing countries. Although the detailed management of, and response to, changing tourism demand factors are patently best met by the flexibility and entrepreneurial flair of the private sector, the government must be involved to attain macro-objectives. As Wood (1980) noted:

> Tourism represents a new relationship with both the national and world economy and, because of this, nearly always involves a greatly expanded role of the state. At the minimum, the state must cooperate with tourism development, for example, in visa policy, foreign exchange requirements, and import regulations. But usually the state plays an active role in opening up new areas to mass tourism because either government expenditure or resources from international agencies are required for the provision of infrastructure...and often for tourist facilities themselves.

In developing countries, limitations inherent in the private sector require government to take an operational role in the tourism industry. As private sector experience and confidence develop, it may be possible for government to move away from this operational role and merely create an ambiance conducive to the growth of a successful tourism industry. Active involvement by government should not be a manifestation of political rhetoric, but rather an organized, sustained, and flexible approach to tourism planning with the aim of optimizing the social and economic returns from tourism. □ □

REFERENCES

Bauer, P.T.
1972   Dissent on Development: Studies and Debates in Development Economics. Boston: Harvard University Press.
Bishop, M.
1979   The Revolution Begins. Caribbean Chronicle (August-September):25.
Bounds, J.H.
1978   The Bahamas Tourism Industry: Past Present and Future. Revista Geografica 88(3):167–211.
Bryden, J.M.
1973   Tourism and Development: A Case Study of the Commonwealth Caribbean. Boston: Cambridge University Press.
Checci and Company
1969   A Plan for Managing the Growth of Tourism in the Commonwealth of the Bahamas Islands. Nassau:

GOVERNMENT INVOLVEMENT IN TOURISM IN DEVELOPING COUNTRIES

Chernick, S.
  1978 The Commonwealth Caribbean: The Integration Experience. World Bank Country Economic Report.
Chib, S.N.
  1980 Financing Tourism Development: A Recipient's View. International Journal of Tourism Management 1(4).
Cleverdon, R.
  1979 Economic and Social Impact of International Tourism on Developing Countries. Economist Intelligence Unit Special Report 60 (May):11–14.
Dasman, R.F., J.P. Miller, P.H. Freeman
  1973 Ecological Principles for Economic Development. London: John Wiley & Sons.
Demas, W.G.
  1965 The Economics of Development in Small Countries with Special Reference to the Caribbean. Montreal: McGill University.
Eden, J.
  1974 Tourism and Government. *In* Management of Tourism, Burkart and Medlik, eds., pp. 177–181. London: Heinemann Educational Books.
Elkan, W.
  1975 The Relation between Tourism and Employment in Kenya and Tanzania. Journal of Development Studies 11(2):123–130.
Gooding, E.C.B.
  1971 Food Production in Barbados with Particular Reference to Tourism. Produced as Appendix 1. *In* The Tourism Industry in Barbados, G.V. Doxey, ed. Ontario: Disco Graphics Ltd.
Green, R.H.
  1979 Towrds Planning Tourism in African Countries. *In* Tourism: Passport to Development? E. de Kadt., ed. London: Oxford University Press.
Holder, J.S.
  1980 Buying Time and Tourism in the Caribbean. International Journal of Tourism Management 1(2):76–83.
Jackson, R.J.
  1973 Problems of the Tourist Industry Development on the Kenyan Coast Geography 58(1):62–65.
Jafari, J.
  1979 Tourism and the Social Sciences: A Bibliography 1970–78. Annals of Tourism Research 6(2):149–194.
Jenkins, C.L.
  1980a Tourism Policies in Developing Countries: A Critique. International Journal of Tourism Management 1(1):22–29.
  1980b Education for Tourism Policy-Makers in Developing Countries. International Journal of Tourism Management 1(4):238–242.
de Kadt, E., ed.
  1979 Tourism: Passport to Development? London: Oxford University Press.
Mitchell, F.
  1971 The Economic Value of Tourism in Kenya, Ph.D. Thesis, University of California.
Rodenburg, E.
  1980 The Effects of Scale on Economic Development: Tourism in Bali. Annals of Tourism Research 7(2):177–196.
Smith, V., ed.
  1978 Hosts and Guests: The Anthropology of Tourism. Philadelphia: University of Pennsylvania Press.

C.L. JENKINS AND B.M. HENRY

Tye, W.B.
   1980   Competition and Subsidies in International Air Transport. International
      Journal of Tourism Management 1(4):199–206.
United Nations Center on Transnational Corporations
   1980   Transnational Corporations in International Tourism. New York: UN.
United Nations Conference on Trade and Development
   1971   Elements of Tourism Policy in Developing Countries. Geneva: UN.
United Nations Educational, Scientific and Cultural Organization
   1975   The Effects of Tourism on Socio-Cultural Values. Paris: UNESCO.
Wahab, S.E.
   1974   Elements of State Policy on Tourism with Special Emphasis on Developing
      Countries. Turin: Italigraphica.
Wood, R.E.
   1980   International Tourism and Cultural Tourism in South East Asia. Economic
      Development and Cultural Change 28(3):561–581.
World Bank
   1972   Tourism Sector Working Paper. London: The John Hopkins University Press.
   1981   World Development Report, Washington, DC: World Bank.
World Tourism Organisation
   1980   Regional Seminar on Integrated Planning for Tourism Development. Co-
      lombo, Sri Lanka. Washington, DC: World Bank.

Submitted 24 March 1981
Revised version submitted 2 October 1981
Accepted 3 December 1981
Final revisions submitted 15 April 1982
Refereed anonymously

[7]

PROGRESS IN TOURISM AND HOSPITALITY RESEARCH
Prog. Tourism Hospit. Res. 4, 101–114 (1998)

The Evolution of Tourism Planning in Third-World Countries: A Critique

Cevat Tosun and Carson L. Jenkins*

The Scottish Hotel School, University of Strathclyde, 94 Cathedral Street, Glasgow G4 0LG, UK

ABSTRACT

The trend in tourism development has been to use comprehensive, flexible, community driven and systematic planning approaches. These approaches seek to sustain tourism as an agent for socio-cultural and economic development. Contemporary planning approaches were developed by taking into account the socio-economic, political and human resources conditions in developed rather than in developing countries. Therefore, these planning approaches may not be transferable to and implementable in developing countries without considerable adaptations. © 1998 by John Wiley & Sons, Ltd.

*Received 11 March 1996; Revised 24 February 1997;
Accepted 13 March 1997
Progr. Tourism Hospit. Res.*

Keywords: tourism; planning; Third World; critique

INTRODUCTION

Planning is complex and extremely ambiguous (Waterson, 1974; Rose, 1984). It is a many sided phenomenon, including consideration of social, economic, political, psychological, anthropological and technological factors. It is, therefore, difficult to define (Hall, 1974). Some people consider plan-

* Correspondence to: C. L. Jenkins.
Contract grant sponsor: Mustafa Kamel University.

CCC 1077–3509/98/020101–14 $17.50

ning as 'not much more than applied common sense' (Waterston, 1974, p. 8, quoting Morris, 1947) while some others contend that 'it is a complex clustering of problems to be explored, not defined' (Elliott, 1958, p. 55). Moreover, it is suggested to be a 'separate language with its own vocabulary and grammar' (Kornai, 1979, p. 718). In fact, planning is a field with a common process and set of tools that can be used for many different purposes (Alterman and Macrae, 1983). It is not an obvious and definite subject with a fixed set of rules through which only one right solution can be found; it depends upon what one wants to achieve (Greed, 1993). Hence, the question of what planning means may never be answered to everybody's satisfaction.

EVOLUTION OF TOURISM PLANNING

Since the definition and scope of planning is ambiguous, its implications are also ambiguous. During the post World War II period, tourism demand has rapidly increased. This post-war tourism boom has enticed many entrepreneurs and governments to invest in the tourism industry without considering either the viability of tourism, or the spillover affects of tourism development (Murphy, 1985). Most scholars of tourism planning have contended that tourism was developed during the last four or five decades in most areas of the world as an unplanned activity (Seth, 1985; Pearce, 1989; Inskeep, 1991).

Indeed, tourism development was guided by many types and different scales of plans at various levels in different parts of the world, but,

102

as Murphy (1985) emphasised, the planning approach to tourism development was entirely myopic. Historically, tourism development planning has been concentrated either on the physical requirements or on the economic considerations relevant to an area. Tourism development planning was not prepared systematically until the 1960s. Therefore, most studies for tourism planning contained serious shortcomings (Baud-Bovy and Lawson, 1977; Murphy, 1983). Apparently, *ad hoc* planning for tourism development was undertaken in a number of tourist destinations (Getz, 1984).

The review of the literature indicates that the evolution of tourism development planning may be broken down into five stages. These are:

(1) *Unplanned tourism development era:* in this period, 'the planning of tourism was uncommon, unpopular and even an unwanted idea' (Gunn, 1988, p. ix). Consequently, tourism development took place in most areas of the world as an unplanned activity. Moreover, many countries in the Third World did not know the importance of the tourism industry and the impacts that it can have (Bhatia, 1986), and many governments have deemed the industry to be the business of the private sectors (the Working Group of the National Tourist Organisations of the EEC, 1983).

(2) *Beginning of partly supply oriented tourism planning period:* the main concern was to build physical amentiies such as hotels, restaurants, telecommunication systems, etc. As Inskeep (1991) contended, tourism planning was seen as a simple process of building hotel and transportation links to tourism destination areas.

(3) *Entirely supply oriented tourism planning period:* to meet rapidly increased tourism demand and to capture an increased share from the market were the main objectives of tourism planning. As Gunn (1988) stated, the facilities of the tourism industry have developed haphazardly: environment, host community, tourists satisfaction, etc., were not considered in the planning process of tourism development.

(4) *Market or demand oriented tourism development planning period:* to lure a larger number of tourists was the focal point of tourism plans. As Archer and Cooper (1994) stated, the needs of tourists and the provision of interesting experiences have directed planning and marketing efforts in the industry.

(5) *Contemporary planning approach period:* after noting the social and environmental consequences of careless and myopic tourism development planning approaches, many scholars, governments and development agencies have commenced considering environmental, social and cultural issues along side economic consideration in tourism development. This new approach may help sustain tourism as an agent for socio-cultural and economic development.

It is accepted that these five stages are not separate and distinctive, but are continuous and have evolved over time. As tourism planning may be carried out by governments, on behalf of governments and by the private sector, there is no single model of 'best planning practice'. What is noticeable, however, is with the disintegration of the former Soviet Union rigid central-planning used in part as a resource-allocation mechanism, has fallen into disfavour. What has emerged is a more comprehensive approach to planning taking into account the many variable factors which influence the successful implementation of the plan. Recent prominence given to the social, cultural, environmental and community aspects of tourism development are indicative of this change of emphasis.

CONTEMPORARY PLANNING APPROACHES

Before forming a critique of the contemporary planning approaches in developing countries, it is necessary to describe some of the main concepts used in this article.

Definition of the Third World

The terms 'the Third World', 'underdeveloped countries', 'developing countries', 'poor countries', 'the South' and 'less-developed countries' (LDC's) are mostly used interchangeably. However, it is not an easy task to define precisely what is meant by these terms (McQueen, 1977). However, Buchanan (1971, p. 20, quoting New Left Review, 1963, p. 4) describes 'the Third World is a universe of radical scarcity. Defining and determining every dimension of men's relationship to each other ... the inadequacy of means of livelihood is the first and distinguishing truth of this area'. In order to give a more clear meaning of the term, it is worth quoting Todaro at some length:

> 'The 143 African, Asian and Latin American member countries of the United Nations often collectively refer to themselves as the 'Third World'. They do this primarily to distinguish themselves from the economically advanced 'Capitalist' ('First World') and 'Socialist' ('Second World') countries. Although the precise origin of the term 'Third World' is obscure, it has become widely accepted and utilised by economically poor nations themselves ... While it is unfortunate that numbers such as 'First', 'Second' and 'Third' occasionally bear the regrettable connotation of superiority and inferiority when used in reference to different groups of nations, the fact remains that the term 'Third World' is widely used among developing nations in a concerted effort to generate and represent a new sense of common identity and growing unity of purpose.' (Todaro, 1982, p. xxi)

For the purpose of this article, the Third World includes all those countries who are not members of the Organisation for European Co-operation and Development (OECD). This broad-brush defintion is still imprecise because it does not take into account relative development levels in countries in the Middle East, and South Africa, etc.

For the purposes of elaboration, six approaches to planning for tourism development are discussed below.

(1) Sustainable Development Approach
The focus of development in the 1970s emphasised the provision of facilities to meet the basic needs of poor people (Stewart, 1985). Generally, development implies a process that makes an effort to improve the living conditions of people (Bartelmus, 1986). It involves broader concerns with the quality of life such as life expectancy, infant mortality, educational attainment, access to basic freedoms, nutritional status and spiritual welfare (Pearce *et al.*, 1990). The main objective of development is to meet human needs and wants (WCED, 1987). Additionally, the sustainable development approach proposes to carry devel-

opmental achievements into the future in such a way that future generations are not left worse off (WECD, 1987; Pearce *et al.*, 1990). One of the pioneer definitions and statement of principles were developed by the Globe 90 Conference For Sustainable Tourism Development, held at Vancouver, B.C., Canada (1991). This conference defined it as follows:

> Sustainable tourism development can be thought of as meeting the needs of present tourists and host regions while protecting and enhancing opportunity for the future ... Sustainable tourism development is envisaged as leading to management of all resources in such a way that can fulfil economic, social, and aesthetic needs while maintaining cultural integrity, essential ecological processes, biological diversity and life support systems. (Globe '90 Conference, 1991)

This definition is one of many that seeks to define sustainability. As a concept, sustainability has become perhaps one of the most used words relative to tourism planning. It features prominently in international conference discussions and in lending and donor-agency prognoses. Yet little evidence exists to determine how effective the concept has been in practice. In the Third World whose immediate and short-term needs are pressing, the concept rests uneasily with the need for long-term planning for the tourism sector. The forces of pragmatism may be stronger than those of idealism.

(2) System Approach
'System' has many meanings based upon the context in which it is used (Wilson, 1990). In general, system is defined as a set of elements standing in interrelationship (Bertalanffy, 1968; Chadwick, 1978). Mill and Morrison (1985, p. xix) contended that 'system is like a spider's web—touch one part of it and reverberation will be felt throughout'. To them, 'The Tourism System consists of four parts — Market; Travel; Destination and Marketing'. The elements of a tourism system have such a relationship that a change in one element of the system will induce and affect the rest of the system. To Harssel (1994), the tourism system consists of demand and supply components. Transportation and promotion as elements of the system link the

supply and demand components with each other. In order to recognise the significance of planning for tourism development, it is necessary to comprehend the system and its various impacts.

Leiper (1990) saw tourism as a system that has three basic components; these are tourists, geographical elements and the tourism industry. The tourist is the actor in this system' (Cooper, 1993, p. 2). Traveller-generating regions, tourist destination regions and transit route regions are three components of the geographical elements of Leiper's tourism system. The traveller generating region is the origin of tourism demand and provides the 'push' factor for travel (Cooper, 1993). 'Part of the tourist industry functions in the generating region' (Travis, 1994, p. 29). The tourist destination region is 'the sharp end of tourism'. It is 'the *raison d'être* for tourism. The pull to visit destinations energises the whole tourism system and creates demand for travel in the generating region'. Therefore, 'the most noticeable and dramatic consequences of the system occur at the destination' (Leiper, 1990, p. 23). The tourism industry is another component of Leiper's model. Various businesses and organisations exist in this element to deliver the tourist product (Cooper, 1993). Leiper's basic tourism system is a component of the whole environment. It operates in human, socio-cultural, economical, technological, physical, political and legal spheres.

Since 'tourism is viewed as an interrelated system, it should be planned as such, utilising systems analysis techniques' (Inskeep, 1991, p. 29). It was argued that the system approach to tourism planning has two advantages. First, since the system approach is flexible, it can be applied at various levels with a different emphasis at each level (Murphy, 1985). Second, 'in system planning there is a programmed learning and continuous improvement' (Gravel, 1979, p. 123). 'Continuous monitoring ties together the twin objectives of planning and management' (Murphy, 1985, p. 173). The behaviour of the whole tourism system is usually something very much more than the sum of the individual elements. Therefore, Jenkins has suggested that 'as a wide-ranging activity tourism must be approached through multidisciplinary analytical studies' (Jenkins, 1980, p. 28. Since tourism is an amalgam of various industries, 'A system

approach is invaluable' for tourism development planning (Murphy, 1985, p. 174). In general, the system approach has the advantage of taking a broader view instead of being myopic and isolated. It leads to examine, define and synthesise different angles from an overall perspective. The system approach contains holistic, process-oriented, interdisciplinary, analytic, and pragmatic kinds of thinking, which creates the advantages of a systems approach. It may be said that it is useful for grasping 'real life' issues (Kaspar and Laesser, 1994).

(3) Community Approach

Community is a word of ancient usage in sociology (Halsey, 1978). It consists of people in different life cycles who are the members of various ethnic groups (Sanders, 1966). The members of communities live in a common territorial area in which daily activities of the members take place. Moreover, community is a framework for actions and as a territorial unit has political and socio-economic functions. Hence, it is attractive (Halsey, 1978) for various interest groups. In this article the word community is used as a group of local people (Wilson and Kolb, 1949) sharing a common area, environment (Bannon, 1976), 'facilities and services distributed within a settlement' (Sanders, 1966, p. 26). The group of people 'represent a bonding of people and place' (Murphy, 1988, p. 96). Closeness, common feelings and mutual concern among community members (Bannon, 1976) create 'its own unique features and power for survival in an 'increasingly impersonal and big business world' (Murphy, 1988, p. 96). It is possible to obtain political power through which the community has its needs and desires satisfied. In a democratic society, community support may be the only factor to determine conditions of success for any type of plans and actions. Therefore, 'appropriate policy in a democracy is determined through a process of political debate' (Davidoff, 1965, p. 332). Community involvement in the policy planning process and decision making is an important component of the political debate.

It has been observed that there is a trend from centralisation to decentralisation. Some political power has moved away from central government to states, cities, towns and neighbourhoods. This trend has given opportunity to local people to deal with their own problems (Naisbitt, 1994). It can be argued that the community approach to planning is ushered in by the decentralisation trend that is the result of a democratisation process and that community involvement encourages democratic government. Davidoff (1965) stated that if democratic urban government is encouraged by the planning process then citizens' participation must be guided and supported in the planning process.

It is proposed by some authors (Murphy, 1985; Haywood, 1988; Keogh, 1990) that the community approach to tourism planning and management must be advocated as one way to create harmonious host–guest relationships within destination communities. Murphy (1992) argued that the community-oriented tourism development planning requires to find a way of creating 'more workable partnerships between the tourism industry and local communities' and develop facilities both for host and guest. Since the destination community is seen as an important component of the tourism product (D'Amore, 1983; Murphy, 1983; Simmons, 1994), involvement of residents in the decision-making process is essential for sustainable tourism development. It has been seen as one of the basic rights that 'the people who must live with planning decisions should be involved in their formulation' (Rosenow and Pulsipher, 1979, p. 81).

Community participation in planning exercises is not an innovative practice. It has been used extensively in developed countries and in sectors such as agriculture, health and infrastructure provision in some Third World countries. However, it is a recent innovation in tourism planning, particularly in the Third World where the concept of the community is less formalised than in the developed world, and where democratic participation is less visible in decision-making. Community participation may be a desirable goal to contribute to achieving a long-term sustainable tourism sector, but it is not a panacea for poor planning.

(4) Integrated Planning Approach to Tourism Development
Integrated planning recognises that planning of a specific project requires inputs from different sectors, agencies or disciplines. This implies that integrated planning is an approach to planning

which 'cuts across' sectoral planning (Conyers and Hills, 1986). In tourism, integrated planning refers to an approach to facilitate integration of tourism into overall sub-national, national and international tourism markets. In the system approach, integrated tourism planning is more than adding tourism planning to other sectoral plans; it requires a harmony within its own components. A balance between tourism demand and supply should also be one of the main concerns of the integrated planning approach. As Baud-Bovy (1982, p. 308) stated:

> Any tourism development plan has to be integrated into the nation's socio-economic and political policies, into the natural and man-made environment, into the socio-cultural traditions, into the related sectors of the economy and its financial schemes, and into the international tourism market.

The above discussion indicates that the integrated planning approach to tourism development has two implications. One is internal integration which refers to integration of the various components of the tourism sector. Second is external integration that implies the integration of the tourism sector into the macro system which includes socio-cultural, economic, political, environmental factors and the international tourism distribution system itself.

(5) Comprehensive Planning
The comprehensive approach was not created as a special concept by planners. It is created by 'a mind trained to a holistic view' (Friedmann, 1965). It is thought that the most important functions of comprehensive planners are: to create a master plan that will be able to guide specialist planners; to review suggestions of specialist planners in the light of the master plan; and to organise the planning of specialist agencies (Altshuler, 1965). In order to maximise the specialised contributions of technical experts to a solution of tourism's problems, comprehensive planning for tourism development must be achieved by a process that will involve all components of the tourism sectors.

The purpose of comprehensive planning is to succeed in improving coherence among all relevant elements (Bannon, 1976). It seems to be difficult to achieve sustainable tourism development   without   taking   into   account   a

C. Tosun and C. L. Jenkins

comprehensive approach. As Jenkins contended, a comprehensive planning approach to tourism development and management is imperative. Without considering this approach environmental problems will come out and 'sustaining tourism resources in the long term may not be possible' (Jenkins, 1992, p. 14).

(6) Continuous and Flexible Approach

In the past, planning referred to preparation of 'the end state master plan' which often were too rigid to cope with rapidly changing socio-cultural, economic and technological and other conditions such plans were therefore not possible to implement (Inskeep, 1991). The shortcomings and failure of many previous master plans gave a lesson to planners that planning is an ongoing process (Baud-Bovy, 1982) and should be flexible in order to cope with rapidly changing conditions. This is more valid for the tourism industry 'sensitive to the slightest changes in politics, economy or fashion' (Baud-Bovy, 1982, p. 313).

Continuity and flexibility are common characteristics of the contemporary planning approach to tourism development. Continuity may refer to planning processes which are developed based on continuous research and feedback. Flexibility does not mean *laissez-faire*. It implies that planning should be adaptable and able to respond to rapidly changing environments. It is a recent trend in planning theory to recognise planning as a continuous process that has great value (Gunn, 1994). Tourism as a multi-sectoral activity and the tourism product as an amalgam of inputs, requires a flexible and continuous planning approach to its development. An advocate of tourism development planning explains the concept as follows:

> Although still based on an adopted policy and plan, tourism planning is seen as a continuous process with adjustments made as needed based on monitoring and feedback, but within the framework of maintaining the basic objectives and policies of tourism development. (Inskeep, 1991, p. 29)

Socio-cultural, economic and technological evolution has created new forms of tourism that are very different from old tourism. 'New tour-

ism is the tourism of the future. It is characterised by flexibility, segmentation and more authentic tourism experiences' (Poon, 1994, p. 91). 'Constant evaluation and reassessment of directions will make the planning process more adaptable to changes in the tourism system, and will lead to greater ability to predict such changes' (Getz, 1986, p. 32).

> ... the new planning-approach to tourism development must combine planning (the initial goal and development strategy) with management (day-to-day, season-to-season operational decisions), because the ability to adjust to changing markets or seasonal conditions is of paramount importance in such a competitive business. (Murphy, 1985, p. 153).

As a result, it may be said that 'the need for flexibility' is one of the basic elements for 'the success of tourism in developing countries' (Dieke, 1988, p. ii).

These six approaches to tourism planning are presented for illustrative purposes; no one approach is claimed to be superior to another. In practice, a tourism planner will incorporate elements of each or some of the approaches depending very much on the circumstances of the planning exercise. In the field of tourism planning and particularly in developing countries, the approach adopted will usually be determined by pragmatic rather than by conceptual reasoning. Little research has been done on why planners use particular approaches or methodologies; it is an area of mystery which would support research investigation. Much has been written on planning techniques, but little on the choice of appropriate methodology.

CONTEMPORARY TOURISM PLANNING APPROACHES: A CRITIQUE

Most of the described approaches to tourism planning have emerged and been refined in the context of the developed countries. It is therefore perhaps not surprising that most of the tourism development planning done in Third-World countries is undertaken by consultants from developed countries. These consultants have had to develop an awareness of the different socio-cultural, environmental and political conditions prevailing in the developing world. It is these conditions which determine the choice of planning approach to use.

Very little is known about how consultants choose a methodology to undertake and eventually implement a tourism planning exercise. The experience of one of the authors in such planning exercises suggests that methodologies emerge from the cumulative experience of the consulting team. There is usually no great debate or reference to the published literature. The process is *ad hoc* and essentially pragmatic. Some evidence to support this contention can be gleaned from the World Tourism Organisation's (1994) *National and Regional Tourism Planning* which briefly describes some 25 planning case studies which are noticeably similar in format, although undoubtedly sensitised to reflect local conditions. However interesting and informative these studies are, they tend to be examples of the *nature* and *scope* of tourism planning rather than offering information on *how* the methodologies were selected and *which* alternative approaches were considered. This is a neglected area of tourism research. Further investigation would not only inform our understanding of methodological issues, but also give some information on the extent to which academic publications influence practitioners.

The choice of methodology used in tourism planning in the absence of conflicting evidence is much influenced by the international agencies who mainly fund these exercises, and by the multi-national companies who carry them out.

Some of the earlier exercises in tourism planning and development were carried out in the Caribbean region. Studies by Shankland Cox (1974), Checci *et al.* (1969) Zinder *et al.* (1969) and basically used standard marketing and planning approaches which had been adapted from practices in the developed countries. The studies were biased towards marketing and economic impact considerations, and were remarkably optimistic of the future benefits to accrue from tourism development. This optimism was not shared by Bryden (1975) in his analysis of Caribbean tourism. The Zinder study in particular through its miscalculation of the income multiplier was to gain a certain notoriety (Levitt and Gulati, 1970). However, many of these companies still operate today and have developed recognised expertise and reputations in the field of tourism development planning.

These multinational companies hold very powerful market positions. They are not only tourism consulting companies, but are often part of wider organisational structures. Some examples would include a Danish company, Carl Bro Management, a consulting company specialising in engineering and infrastructure projects employing over 2500 professional staff, but with a small Tourism and Aviation department, and W.S. Atkins, a British engineering and technology consulting group with over 7500 professional staff and who have interests in the field of recreation and tourism. Some consulting groups such as K.P.M.G. and Touche Ross are other examples of very large international companies who are active in the tourism planning and development field. Inevitably, the more tourism planning exercises these companies do the more expertise they accumulate and the more they will tend towards a tried and trusted methodology. This accumulated experience becomes, in effect, a form of intellectual overhead capital, very useful in bidding for future projects.

Despite this expertise there are still *problems of fit* in transferring tourism planning practices from developed to developing countries. Some of these problems are briefly discussed below.

Due to a lack of financial resources and often, tourism planning expertise, many developing countries' governments approach the international funding agencies and other organisations to seek assistance with tourism development. The World Bank and its associated regional affiliates, e.g. African Development Bank have played a relatively small but increasingly significant role in supporting tourism plannig and development. The major support has come from the United Nations Development Programme working in conjunction with specialist agencies such as the International Labour Organisation and the World Tourism Organisation acting as Executing Agencies for tourism projects. In the 1990s the European Union through its Lome Convention for the ACP countries and its PHARE programme for Eastern European countries has probably become the major source of funding for tourism and tourism-related planning and investment programmes. These international organisations are concerned to ensure that the commissioned studies are pro-

108

fessionally executed and therefore there is a tendency to select the established multinational companies to undertake these major studies. This does not imply that smaller tourism planning companies are less able or professionally competent, but rather they can suffer from a deficiency in professional economies of scale.

The power of the multi-national companies in tourism has been noted amongst others by Erbes (1972), Dunning and McQueen (1982) and Britton (1989). Noticeably, little attention has been given to the role of the international consulting companies in the development of tourism. This neglect is curious as the link between international funding for tourism development planning and available international expertise in this area is very difficult to weaken. It is a good example of continuing dependency by the developing countries on the developed world. Perhaps an increasing sensitivity to the charge that in the developing countries tourism is an industry for foreigners run by foreigners has caused the international funding agencies to seek to encourage a more active participation in tourism development planning by indigenous organisations and local consulting companies. As noted below, some agencies such as the United Nations Development Programme encourages indigenous bodies such as National Tourism Organisations to act as Executing Agencies for some projects. This institutional co-operation is another aspect of the aim to *transfer knowledge*.

Even where goodwill between parties exists, the knowledge transference process is often frustrated at the human level by personality clashes, cultural barriers, or perhaps by the inability of the tourism expert to 'teach' the counterpart. At the institutional level bureaucracy is sometimes a formidable barrier to attaining the transference objective.

A further problem in the developing countries is that little attention has been given to training tourism planners. These countries will therfore remain dependent on foreign expertise. Other countries in this group such as India, Indonesia and Egypt are already developing indigenous expertise through a combination of overseas training and the introduction of tourism planning courses in indigenous institutions. As an encouraging feature it should be noted that as many developing countries have had to train

macro planners to contribute to the formulation of Five Year Development Plans, there seems to be no apparent reason why specialist tourism planners cannot also be trained.

It should be noted that although much emphasis has been given to institutions building and transference of knowledge in development, limited evaluation has been done on this aspect of the development process in the tourism sector. The three major approaches to tourism development planning are considered below.

Sustainable Tourism Development Approach

In general, sustainable development is criticised as being a rhetorical, not practical catch-all phrase (Adams, 1990; Shiva, 1992). Indeed, it seems to be a more ambiguous, complex and multi-faceted phenomena since it embraces consideration of equity for present and future generations. Mannion (1992) strongly contends that

'What may be sustainable, i.e. supported or maintained at a local level, may not be sustainable regionally, etc. The spatial scale is thus all-important. The terms is even more difficult to define if inter-generation equity is considered, which introduces a temporal scale; what may be sustainable over a decade may not be sustainable over a century, etc. Moreover, the longer the time-span is, the more difficult it will be to determine whether a practice will be sustainable. And what is sustainable is sustainable only for one time. And only for one place. (Mannion, 1992, p. 297).

Mannion's critique raises many questions about sustainable development. Is it implementable? Can it be applied to all countries and tourism destinations in developing countries? What are the yardsticks to measure risks for the present and future generations? Is it possible to determine these criteria in an objective way? In which time period will it be achieved? If it cannot be achieved in the average life span of the people in a destination area, it will not provide any benefits for the present generation. As the President of Turkey, Demirel (1992), said: 'People live daily and consider their current needs'. There must be a time limit. Some part of public expectation must also be satisifed in the short term. The approach to sustainable development may leave current generations with poorer prospects and greater risks than future generations may face. On the other hand, to practise the concept in developing countries may be very difficult, if not impossible, since the community often lives on the margin of basic needs. It is unrealistic to expect communities to consider future generations' welfare without some contribution to satisfying their current basic needs. Rees (1989) argued that successful implementation of sustainable development 'requires integrated policy, planning, and social learning processes; its political viability depends on the full support of the people it affects through their governments, their social institutions, and their private activities' (Rees, 1989, p. 13).

Rees's suggestions about the implementation of sustainable development contain complex conditions which may not be met by many developing countries. What does 'full support of the people' imply? How can it be achieved? Particularly in tourist destinations in underdeveloped regions of a developing country, 'full support of the people' may mean the desire and willingness of the elite class in the region to support tourism, which may not help arrive at the aims of sustainable development. Although Gunn (1994) accepts Rees's argument as most applicable to planning for sustainable tourism development, it is not clear what the 'social learning process' is and how it can be achieved. How the full support of the people will be gained is also problematic. On the other hand, sometimes it may not be necessary to get the support of all the people who are affected by tourism development, because only groups of people represent and direct the community in the destination area. Without this group's support, implementation of plans may not be possible even though more general popular support is evinced.

The sustainable tourism development concept has been considerably censured by some authors (Owen *et al.*, 1993). Although sustainable tourism development involves desirable principles, it has many goals which are often conflicting. To keep some balance between present and future, amongst economic development and socio-cultural and environmental issues is very difficult. In developing countries this difficulty become larger since they do not have sufficient experts

with adequate training to guide proposals, and do not have adequate social and political administration systems to support development. (Archer, 1996)

The principles of sustainable tourism development seem to be good, but it requires hard political choices and logical decisions based upon cumbersome social, economic and environmental trade-offs (McIntyre *et al.*, 1993). It was argued that tourist movements are moving towards megamass tourism and the problems of these ever-increasing tourist numbers are also increasing (Wheeller, 1992). Sustainable tourism as a concept may have successful implementation at the indivdual project level, 'but at the macro level because of the enormity and complexity of the task, it becomes cumbersome, uncontrollable and unplannable' (Wheeller, 1991). Example of positive management of tourist destinations can be found, but these 'examples of positive management of tourist influx are the exception, not the rule' (Wheeller, 1991, p. 95). The principles and experience of sustainable tourism development are not universally applicable and directly transferable to other destinations (D'Amore, 1992) 'It just does not follow that success at the localised level guarantees similar success on the wider, more complicated plane. Moving from the specific to the general is problematic' (Wheeller, 1991, p. 94).

Another criticism is that the concept of sustainable development has been brought about largely by developed countries whose unsustainable uses of resources have accelerated their high quality of life. Poor countries need economic growth and have to rely on many natural and environmental resources which are already under stress (de Kadt, 1992). The struggle to overcome extreme conditions of poverty are the main source of many environmental problems in developing countries (Bartelmus, 1986). Poor people often have no choice. Hence, they obtain immediate economic benefits at the expense of the long-term sustainability of development (Barbier, 1987). For example, some countries or regions have no choice but to opt to develop tourism for immediate economic benefits at the expense of socio-cultural and environmental impacts.

Sustainable development requires projects to be adjusted to the needs, skills and qualification of people who are assumed to benefit from them (Uphoff, 1985). Since a developing country does not have sufficient skilled and qualified human resources (Nafziger, 1990), implementing this may be very difficult for a developing country. Particularly, small developing countries have difficulties in planning, since they have limited capacity in this area. Besides, they have not developed their own planning techniques and approaches. They have tried to adapt the techniques and approaches developed by others; usually by developed countries, which do not meet their planning needs (de Kadt, 1979a).

Community Participation Approach

The community-based approach to tourism development planning has been formulated by advocates writing on developed countries. Thus, their claims can be valid in developed countries, but it may not necessarily be applicable to, and beneficial in developing countries since the community there may be imprisoned by the basic need to merely survive.

Community participation requires decentralisation which it is suggested will give an opportunity to local people to become involved in the decision-making process. Community participation is defined so as to encourage democratic government, but it is not possible for all countries. The level of education and consciousness of the community may determine the form and way of democratisation. If decentralisation gives authority and responsibility to local people, the local people may not use this power efficiently and effectively; particularly people who have no experience of tourism. These people can be exploited by various interest groups. As de Kadt (1979b) pointed out, the ability of local authorities to impose laws and regulations are limited and directed by important interest groups outside the community.

'The public's right to participate in the planning of activities that affect their daily lives is now a widely accepted principle throughout the democratic world' (Simmons, 1994, p. 99). In many developing countries it is difficult to find well-established political and public administration institutions to operate this principle in a democratic way. Thus, in many developing countries community involvement in tourism planning may be impossible at this time without

improvements to democratise institutions.

In most developing countries there is not available the technical manpower to sustain a 'continuous' approach to planning. Once the planning exercise has been completed, most available expertise is diverted to implementing plans, often with very low levels of success. It is now becoming more usual in developing countries for governments to involve the private sector in planning (often at the insistence of donor agencies) and to place major emphasis on the private sector to implement the plans.

The United Nations Development Programme (UNDP) has increasingly sought to involve national agencies in tourism development planning wherever this is possible. For example, in Indonesia the preparation of the Indonesian Tourism Development Strategy was managed as Executing Agency by the Directorate General of Tourism with technical assistance being provided by the World Tourism Organisation. This type of involvement in projects provides both a managerial and training opportunity for local participants which transcends project participation based on counterpart training. It is more likely in the longer term to contribute to one of the basic development objectives — institution building. Laudable though this change in emphasis by UNDP may be, its achievement is often fraught with difficulties. In some developing countries there is no institution of sufficient stature and/or experience to undertake the role of an Executing Agency. In other situations the available planning expertise may be of a general nature and of limited relevance to the needs of the tourism sector.

In addition to encouraging greater indigenisation of tourism project management, institutional lenders are now insisting on greater involvement of the private sector in the formulation of tourism policies, planning and the implementation phases of tourism investment. This is part of the trend to decentralise much of government's role in tourism (and other sectors) and where possible, to couple decentralisation with more privatisation (Jenkins, 1994). However, in many developing countries, there may not be a representative tourism sector body. As part of the preparation of the Medium Term National Strategy and Action Plan for Zambia (European Union, 1995) it was necessary to persuade the various private sector companies and organisations to form themselves into a representative tourism sector body — the Tourism Council of Zambia. Without such representative organisations democratically formed and legally constituted, vested and singular interests are often mistaken as being representative and no genuine consensus views can emerge. The trend towards more decentralisation of government powers and increasing privatisation is continuing. In a planning scenario what is important is to evaluate the current capacity of the country and its institutions to undertake the changing roles and what measures are required to support these changes.

This change in approach has put considerable pressure on governments to open and to improve channels of communications with the private sector and between government departments. In many countries this co-operation is embryonic and tenuous. However, without commitment from governments to decentralise and privatise, they are unlikely to receive the support of the international funding agencies.

System, Comprehensive and Integrated Planning Approaches

These three planning approaches require large numbers of experts and large financial resources, both of which are very scarce in developing countries. Thus, it may be difficult to use these planning approaches for tourism.

Contemporary planning approaches involve a list of desired objectives which are established by taking into account the socio-economic and political conditions in the countries. Therefore, to move from the list for outcomes to a realistic agenda for action is a major problem (Lea, 1988). Implementability is the most important feature of every type and scale of plans for developing countries. If a plan is unimplementable, it is not important how worthy the plan is.

In order to implement contemporary planning approaches to tourism development

There needs to be a co-ordination among national, regional, metropolitan, and local levels of government on policy and planning and in developing infrastructure, among the several different government agencies involved in aspects of tourism at

each level, and between the public and private sectors at each level. (Inskeep, 1991, p. 431).

These are very difficult things to achieve in a developing country due to the inadequate public administration system.

The choice of approach to planning assignments will be conditioned by many factors. Perhaps the predominant factors will be related to the stage of political and economic development in the particular country. The approach adopted will usually reflect past experience and current conditions, with budgetary considerations being a major issue. Compromise will have to be found to balance the aims of the exercise with the reality of local conditions and resources.

CONCLUSION

A review of approaches to tourism development planning indicates that they have moved from a historical, narrow consideration of demand, supply and physical requirements to more comprehensive, and integrated approaches. Unfortunately, this evolution has limited applicability in Third World countries. As de Kadt (1979a) stated, adapting the techniques and approaches developed by others do not meet developing countries' needs. Hence, it is necessary for developing countries to approach tourism development planning by considering their own socio-cultural and political conditions, economic and human resources.

Perhaps the most appropriate way to address these needs is to train and develop indigenous planning expertise. This is already happening in a number of developing countries where tourism is an important sector in the economy. More effort and resources should be given to this training — not only to develop expertise with more sensitivity to local conditions, needs and aspirations, but also to reduce dependency on foreign experts. This process is inevitably long term, but it has to start sometime. The changes now being demanded by the international lending agencies for more indigenous participation by both public and private sectors in tourism development are clear signals of the expectations from future development planning exercises. To

112

meet these expectations governments, where appropriate and possible, should seek to encourage the introduction of tourism planning courses in selected academic institutions.

The reality of the present situation is that in most developing countries tourism development planning often proceeds in an *ad hoc* way. Until a country reaches a certain stage of development, and depending on the importance of tourism in the economy, substantive tourism planning is usually donor-assistance driven. It is unusual for a lengthy debate to take place on the methodological approach to the planning exercise. The planning team is based on foreign expertise (being paid for by foreign donors) with some counterpart training. The 'steering committee' to oversee the planning exercise, is usually more concerned with outputs rather than objectives. In these circumstances, notions of 'sustainability' and 'community participation' are icons to current development jargon rather than realistic implementable parameters.

Although the development of tourism is essentially built on long-term investment, there is usually a priority for short-term benefits. Sustainability as a long-term objective can only have relevance if it can gather the support of present day beneficiaries. If development is about the need to improve the everyday lives of people, the methodological approach to planning may be irrelevant; what is important is the output from this planning.

REFERENCES

Adams, W. M. (1990), *Green Development*, London: Routledge.

Alterman, R., and Macrae, D. (1983), Planning and policy analysis, *Journal of The American Planning Association*, **49**, 2, 200–215.

Altshuler, A. (1965), The goals of comprehensive planning, *Journal of The American Institute of Planners*, **30**, 1, 186–94.

Archer, B. H. (1996), Sustainable tourism — do economists really care?, *Progress in Tourism and Hospitality Research*, **2**, 3/4.

Archer, B., and Cooper, C. (1994), The positive and negative impacts of tourism, in Theobald, W. F. (Editor), *Global Tourism*, Oxford: Butterworth-Heinemann, pp. 73–91.

Bannon, J. J. (1976), *Leisure Resources. Its Comprehensive Planning*, Englewood Cliffs, NJ: Prentice-Hall.

Barbier, E. B. (1987), The concept of sustainable economic development, *Environmental Conservation*, **14**, 2, 101–10.

Bartelmus, P. (1986), *Environment and Development*. Boston, MA: Allen and Unwin.

Baud-Bovy, M., and Lawson, F. (1982), New concepts in planning for tourism and recreation, *Tourism Management*, **3**, 4, 308–313.

Baud-Bovy, M., and Lawson, F. (1977), *Tourism and Recreation Development*. London: The Architectural Press.

Bertalanffy, L. (1968), *General System Theory*, New York: George Braziller.

Bhatia, A. K. (1986), Tourism Development Principle and Practice, New Delhi, Sterling Publisher Private Ltd.

Britton, S. (1989), Tourism dependency and development: a mode of analysis, in Singh. T. J., Theuns, H. L., and Go, F. M. (Editors), *Towards Appropriate Tourism: The Case of Developing Countries*, Geneva: Lang.

Buchanan, K. (1971), Profiles of the Third World and the Third World — and beyond, in Mountjoy, B. A. (Editor), *Developing the Underdeveloped Countries*. Bristol: Macmillan, pp. 17–51.

Bryden, J. M. (1975), *Tourism and Development: A Case Study of the Commonwealth Caribbean*. Cambridge, MA: Cambridge University Press.

Chadwick, G. (1978), *A System View of Planning Towards a Theory of the Urban and Regional Planning Process*. Oxford: Pergamon.

Checci et al. (1969), A Plan for Managing Tourism in the Bahama Islands, Washington, DC.

Conyers, D., and Hills, P. (1986), *An Introduction to Development Planning in the Third World*. New York: John Wiley and Sons.

Cooper, C. (1993), An introduction to tourism, in Cooper, C., Fletcher, J., Gilbert, D., and Wanhill, S. (Editors), *Tourism Principles and Practice*. London: Pitman, pp. 7–12.

D'Amore, L. J. (1983), 'Guidelines to planning in harmony with the host community', in Murphy, P. E. (Editor), *Tourism in Canada: Selected Issues and Options*. Western Geographical Series, Vol. 21, pp. 135–160.

D'Amore, L. J. (1992), Promoting sustainable tourism — the Canadian approach, *Tourism Management*, **13**, 3, 258–262.

Davidoff, P. (1965), Advocacy and pluralism in planning, *Journal of the American Institute of Planners*, **31**, 4, 331–338.

de Kadt, E. (1979a), Social planning for tourism in the developing countries, *Annals of Tourism Research*, **6**, 1, 36–48.

de Kadt, E. (1979b), Politics, planning, and control, in de Kadt (Editor), *Tourism Passport to Development?*

Published for The World Bank and UNESCO. Oxford: Oxford University Press, pp. 18–33.

de Kadt, E. (1992), Making the alternative sustainable: lessons from development for tourism, in Smith, V. L., and Eadington, W. R. (Editors), *Tourism Alternatives: Potentials and Problems in the Development of Tourism*. Philadelphia, PA: University of Pennsylvania Press, pp. 47–75.

Dieke, P. U. C. (1988), *The Development of Tourism in Kenya and the Gambia: A Comparative Analysis*, Doctoral Thesis, The Scottish Hotel School, University of Strathclyde, UK.

Dunning, J. J., and McQueen, M. (1982), Multinational corporations in the international hotel industry, *Annals of Tourism Research*, 9, 1.

Elliott, J. E. (1958), Economic planning reconsidered, *Quarterly Journal of Economics*, 76, 1, 55–76.

Erbes, R. International Tourism and the Economy of Developing Countries, OECD, Paris, 1993.

European Union (1995), Medium Term National Tourism Strategy and Action Plan for Zambia, Brussels.

Friedmann, J. (1965), A conceptual model for analysis of the planning behaviour, *Administrative Science Quarterly*, 12, 225–252.

Getz, D. (1984), Regional and local tourism planning in Ontario, *Environments*, 17, 1, 68–70.

Getz, D. (1986), Models in tourism planning: towards integration of theory and practice, *Tourism Management*, 7, 1, 21–32.

Globe '90 (1991), *Tourism Stream Conference, Action Strategy for Sustainable Tourism Development*. Ottawa: Tourism Canada.

Gravel, J. P. (1979), Tourism and recreational planning: a methodological approach to the valuation and calibration of tourism activities, in Perks, W. T. and Robinson, I. M. (Editors), *Urban and Regional Planning in a Federal State: The Canadian Experience*. Stoudsburg: Penn, Dowden, Hutchinson and Ross, pp. 122–134.

Greed, C. (1993), *Introducing Town Planning*. London: Longman.

Gunn, C. A. (1988), *Tourism Planning* (2nd edition), New York: Taylor and Francis.

Gunn, C. A. (1994), *Tourism Planning* (3rd edition), London: Taylor and Francis.

Hall, P. (1974), *Urban and Regional Planning*, Harmondsworth: Penguin.

Halsey, A. H. (1978), Government against poverty in school and community, in Bulmer, M. (Editor), *Social Policy Research*. London: Macmillan, pp. 139–159.

Harssel, J. V. (1994), *Tourism: An Exploration*. Englewood Cliffs, NJ: Prentice Hall.

Haywood, K. M. (1988), Responsible and responsive tourism planning in the community, *Tourism Management*, 9, 2, 105–118.

Inskeep, E. (1991), *Tourism Planning. An Integrated and Sustainable Development Approach*. New York: Von Nostrand Reinhold.

Jenkins, C. L. (1980), Tourism policies in developing countries: a critique, *International Journal of Tourism Management*, 1, 1, 36–48.

Jenkins, C. L. (1992), *Tourism in Third World Development, Fact or Fiction?* The Inaugural Lecture. Glasgow: The Scottish Hotel School, University of Strathclyde.

Jenkins, C. L. (1994), Tourism in developing countries: the privatisation issue, in Seaton, A. V. (Editor), *Tourism the State of the Art*. Chichester: John Wiley and Sons.

Kapsar, C., and Laesser, C. (1994), System approach, in Witt, S. F. and Mountinho, L. (Editors), *Tourism Marketing and Management Handbook*, (2nd edition). Hertfordshire: Prentice-Hall, pp. 170–177.

Keogh, B. (1990), Public participation in community tourism planning, *Annals of Tourism Research*, 17, 449–465.

Kornai, J. (1979), Appraisal of project appraisal, in Boskin, M. J. (Editor), *Economic and Human Welfare: Essay in Honour of Tibor Scitousky*. New York: Academic Press, pp. 91–96.

Lea, J. (1988), *Tourism and Development in the Third World*. London: Routledge.

Leiper, N. (1990), *Tourism System. Occasional Paper 2*. Auckland, New Zealand: Massey University.

Levitt, K. and Gulati, I. (1970), Income effects of tourism spending: mystification multiplied; a critical comment on the Zinder Report, *Social and Economic Studies*, 19, 3.

Mannion, A. M. (1992), Sustainable development and biotechnology, *Environmental Conservation*, 19, 4, 297–306.

McIntyre, G., Hetherington, A., and Inskeep, E. (1993), *Sustainable Tourism Development Guide for Local Planner*. Madrid: World Tourism Organisation.

McQueen, M. (1977), *Britain, the EEC and the Developing World*. London: Heinemann Educational Books.

Mill, R. C., and Morrison, A. M. (1985), *The Tourism System*. Englewood Cliffs,: Prentice-Hall.

Morrison (1947)

Murphy, P. E. (1983), Tourism as a community industry, *Tourism Management*, 4, 180–193.

Murphy, P. E. (1985), *Tourism: A Community Approach*. New York: Methuen.

Murphy, P. E. (1988), Community driven tourism planning, *Tourism Management*, 9, 2, 96–104.

Murphy, P. E. (1992), Data gathering for community oriented tourism planning: case study of Vancouver Island, British Columbia, *Leisure Studies*, 11, 65–79.

Nafziger, E. W. (1990), *The Economics of Developing Countries*, (2nd edition). Englewood Cliffs, Prentice-Hall.

114

Naisbitt, J. (1994), *Megatrends*, New York: Warner Books.

Owen, R. E., Witt, W. F., and Susan, G. (1993), Sustainable tourism development in Wales, *Tourism Management*, 14, 6, 463–474.

Pearce, D. G. (1989), *Tourism Development* (2nd edition). Harlow: Longman Scientific.

Pearce, D., Barbier, E., and Markandya, A. (1990), *Sustainable Development, Economics and Environment in the Third World*. Aldershot: Edward Elgar.

Poon, A. (1994), The new tourism revolution, *Tourism Management*, 15, 2, 91–92.

Rees, W. E. (1989), *Defining Sustainable Development*. CHS Research Bulletin, University of British Columbia, May 3.

Rose, E. A. (1984), Philosophy and purpose in planning, in Bruton, M. J. (Editor), *The Spirit and Purpose of Planning*. London: Hutchinson, pp. 31–66.

Rosenow, J., and Pulsipher, G. L. (1979), *Tourism. The Good, Bad and Ugly*. Nebraska: Media Productions and Marketing.

Sanders, I. T. (1966), *The Community: An Introduction to A Social System* (2nd edition). New York: Ronald Press.

Seth, P. N. (1985), *Successful Tourism Management*. New Delhi: Sterling.

Shankland Cox *et al.* (1974), *Tourism Supply in the Caribbean Region*. Washington, DC: World Bank.

Shiva, V. (1992), Recovering the real meaning of sustainability, in Cooper, D. E., and Palmer, J. A. (Editors), *The Environment in Question*. London: Routledge, pp. 187–193.

Simmons, D. G. (1994), Community participation in tourism planning, *Tourism Management*, 15, 2, 98–108.

Stewart, F. (1985), *Planning to Meet Basic Needs*. London: Macmillan.

Todaro, M. P. (1982), *Economics for a Development World*. New York: Longman.

Travis, A. S. (1994), Tourism destination area development (from theory into practice), in Witt, S. F. and Mountinho, L. (Editors), *Tourism Marketing and Management Handbook* (2nd edition). London: Prentice-Hall, pp. 29–40.

Uphoff, N. (1985), Fitting projects to people, in Cernea, M. M. (Editor), *Putting People First: Sociological Variables in Rural Development*. Published for the World Bank. Oxford: Oxford University Press, pp. 359–395.

Waterston, A. (1974), *Development Planning Lessons of Experience*. London: The Johns Hopkins University Press.

Wheeller, B. (1991), Tourism's troubled times, *Tourism Management*, 12, 2, 91–97.

Wheeller, B. (1992), Is progressive tourism appropriate?, *Tourism Management*, 13, 1, 104–105.

Wilson, B. (1990), *Systems, Concepts, Methodologies and Applications*. Chichester: John Wiley and Sons.

Wilson, L., and Kolb, W. L. (1949), *Sociological Analysis*. New York: Harcourt Brace and World, Inc.

Working Group of the National Tourist Organisations of the EEC (1983), *The Economic Significance of Tourism Within the European Community*. London: British Tourist Authority.

World Commission on Environment and Development (WLED) (1987), *Our Common Future*. Oxford: Oxford University Press.

World Tourism Organisation (1994), National and Regional Tourism Planning: Methodologies and Case Studies, Routledge, London.

Zinder, H. S. and Associates (1969), The Future of Tourism in the Eastern Caribbean, Washington, D.C.

Part II
Economic Perspectives

A
Analysis of Costs and Benefits

[8]

The Economic Impact of Tourism in Developing Countries

P.G. Sadler and *B.H. Archer**

Abstract

Sadler, P.G. and B.H. Archer, 'The Impact of Tourism in Developing Countries',** *Annals of Tourism Research*, Vol. III, No. 1, September/October, pp. 15–33 The paper examines the costs and benefits brought by tourism to the economies of developing countries. The criteria for decision making are discussed and the main policy implications are mentioned. The paper concludes with a suggested model for evaluating the effects of specific projects within the framework of a sectoral analysis of an economy. [15]

Introduction

The economies of developing countries differ in a number of ways from those of more developed nations. In the first place, property ownership and incomes are very unevenly distributed with, in many cases, quite large sectors of the population living at subsistence level. The primary base of most of these economies is agricultural – some cash cropping, but largely subsistence farming. Many of the manufacturing industries established in recent years are partially foreign owned or controlled and, in consequence, there is a substantial 'leakage' of profits and expatriate earnings out of the developing economies. Furthermore in some countries development, especially when financed from outside sources, has been concentrated into particular regions and the resultant relatively prosperous enclaves have created little, if any, secondary benefits to other sectors of the economy or to other parts of the country. The main problem here, that of backward linkages, is discussed in a later part of this paper. Industrial growth is also hampered by the small size of the domestic market (small because of the low incomes of the indigenous population) and by the increasing difficulties experienced by most developing countries in marketing their manufactured products abroad in the face of severe competition from other countries.

In brief, developing countries are characterized by low levels of domestic income, very uneven distributions of both income and wealth, high levels of unemployment or under-employment, a heavy dependence upon the export of a small range of cash crops and products and, partly in consequence, a general shortage of foreign exchange.

The main aim of this paper is to propose a model which can be used by economists and others to provide some guidelines for a development strategy. The model can be used firstly to examine the various sectors of a developing country's economy in order to select those sectors which create the highest levels of domestic income and employment. The model can be used to choose various projects from within the selected sectors on the basis of their contribution [16] to the social and economic welfare of the indigenous population.

Before examining this model in detail, however, attention should be paid to the sector with which this paper is primarily concerned – namely, tourism.

Tourism

Only a small number of developing countries are heavily dependent upon tourism, Of these, the most notable is Lebanon (where tourist revenue accounts for over 10% of national income) and some Caribbean states. To the countries of North Africa, tourism is a more modest source of income, and to most West African countries it is of minor importance. Table 1 provides an indication of the volume of tourist traffic to each of the African countries in 1970 and 1971.

Table 1: The volume of international tourism in Africa

Sub-region and country	Foreign visitors		Increase
	1970	1971	%
North Africa	1,842,988	2,264,609	23
Algeria	236,000	250,000[a]	6
Morocco	746,957[b]	823,259[b]	11
Tunisia	410,749	610,000	49
Libya	76,621[c]	133,297	74
Egypt	357,661	428,053	20
Sudan	(15,000)	(20,000)	
Central Africa	71,756	99,207	38
Cameroon	(20,000)	(20,000)	
Central African Republic	(1,800)	(2,000)	
Chad	(5,000)	(2,000)	
Congo	(1,500)	(1,500)	
Gabon	(5,108)	(6,400)	
Zaire	38,348	63,307	65
East Africa	881,533	1,108,485	26 [17]
Ethiopia	53,187	64,000[a]	
Somalia	(1,000)	1,037	

Table 1 (continued)

Sub-region and country	Foreign visitors		Increase
	1970	1971	%
Kenya	343,500	414,200	20
Uganda	80,400	88,400	10
Rwanda	(5,000)	(5,400)	
Burundi	(20,000)	23,898	
Tanzania	79,020	(92,000)	16
Malawi	19,806	19,203	
Zambia	46,970	70,352	50
Botawana	(10,000)	(10,000)	
Swaziland	(150,000)	216,000	
Lesotho	(25,000)	45,000	
Madagascar	(20,000)	(24,000)	
Mauritius	27,650	(35,000)	
West Africa	228,439	276,589	21
Nigeria	(25,000)	(40,000)	
Togo	(15,000)	(16,000)	
Dahomey	(11,000)	(11,000)	
Ghana	35,084	(35,000)	
Ivory Coast	44,826[d]	48,820[d]	
Guinea	n.a.	n.a.	
Liberia	n.a.	n.a.	
Sierra Leone	(12,000)	(12,000)	
Upper Volta	4,331	6,369	
Niger	(1,500)	(1,500)	
Mali	6,698	(7,000)	
Senegal	(51,000)	(75,000)	47
Gambia	2,300[e]	7,000[e]	200
Equatorial Guinea	n.a.	n.a.	
Mauritania	19,700	16,900	
Other African Countries	1,245,979	1,530,098	23
South Africa	385,896	458,059	19
Angola	81,013	95,129	17
Mozambique	415,000	583,000	40
Rhodesia	364,070	393,910	8
Namibia	n.a.	n.a.	
			[18]
African Total	4,270,695	5,278,985	24

Notes: The figures in brackets are estimates not recorded figures.
a, Provisional figure; b, with cruise passengers these figures are 852,475 in 1970 and 915,000 in 1971; c, arrivals at hotel; d, arrivals at hotels in Abidjan; e, holiday visitors arriving on group package tours.

Source: United Nations Economic and Social Council, *Le Tourisme en Afrique en 1972* (Bulletin Annuel), U.N.E.C.A., Addis Ababa, April 1973.

In economic terms tourism is an invisible export which differs from other forms of international trade transactions in several ways:

> The consumer 'collects' the service himself from the 'exporting' country and, in consequence, the 'exporting country' incurs no direct freight charges or service costs outside its boundaries, except in cases where the airlines owned by the developing countries themselves are used.

> Demand for long-distance pleasure travel is in the 'luxury' category and local inconveniences or political troubles cause much of this traffic to divert to other destinations. At the same time, international tourism is in general both price and income elastic (the evidence to support this claim is somewhat conflicting (1)) and changes in either of these two variables cause a more than proportional change in pleasure travel.

> By means of import duties and export taxes the 'exporting' country can operate exchange rates for tourists completely different from the price at which other foreign trade takes place whilst permitting tourists to buy in the domestic market at the prices prevailing for the indigenous consumers (there are, of course, exceptions to this, e.g. duty-free tourist shops, tourist tax rebates, etc.).

> Unlike other export industries, tourism is a highly differentiated product which directly affects several sectors of a national economy: tourist expenditure is injected into hotels and other accomodation units, local shops and restaurants, local transport facilities and many [19] other outlets, including the purchase of locally made souvenirs.

> Tourism brings with it many non-pecuniary benefits and costs. This aspect of tourism has received considerable attention in recent years from researchers such as Mitchell (8, pp. 1–21) and Bryden (2), and has to be taken into account, as far as is practicable, in any form of cost–benefit analysis.

The Costs and Benefits of Tourism

Among the economic and social advantages and disadvantages brought by tourism, the following appear to be the most significant.

1. The effect on foreign exchange earnings.
2. Income effects.
3. Employment effects.
4. Infrastructural changes.
5. The effect on domestic price levels.
6. Economic dependence upon tourism.
7. Environmental and ecological effects.
8. Social and psychological results.

1. The Effects on Foreign Exchange Earnings

Data on foreign exchange earnings from tourism are very incomplete. Countries with foreign exchange controls record such information, but these figures are smaller than the amount which it can reasonably be expected that foreign tourists would spend in the country. The government agencies responsible for the preparation of balance of payments figures therefore base their calculations on other data. International tourism data are derived from the numbers of the various categories of foreign visitors, their length of stay in the country and their typical daily expenditure. Table 2 provides information on the gross foreign exchange receipts from international tourism in 1971 for selected African countries.

Table 2   Gross foreign exchange earnings from tourism

Country	Year	Earnings (US$ millions)
Morocco	1971	162
Tunisia	1971	108
(Tunisia	1972	147)
Libya	1971	6.6
Tanzania	1971	13.7
Kenya	1971	67.4
Uganda	1971	16.5
Mauritius	1971	6.8
Senegal	1972 (6 months)	1.7

Note: These figures exclude the foreign exchange earning of national airlines.

Source: United Nations Economic and Social Council, Le Tourisme en Afrique en 1972 (Bulletin Annuel), U.N.E.C.A., Addis Ababa, April 1973.

Foreign exchange is required by developing countries to purchase the capital goods and other imports essential for development. Tourist receipts form one important source of foreign exchange. In 1968, for example, tourist receipts of £18.9 million ($45 million) accounted for approximately 11% of the total foreign exchange earnings of Kenya (3, p. 42). Mitchell (8, pp. 3–6), disagreeing with the magnitude of this tourist expenditure figure, showed that at least 78% of Kenya's tourist receipts represented net foreign exchange [20] earnings on current account (the remaining 22% is accounted for by the direct import content of tourist receipts and the direct payments made to non-resident owners of factors of production).

In common with the export earnings of other sectors, however, much of this tourist-derived foreign currency 'leaks out' of the economy at subsequent stages of transaction. Tourism, for example, creates an increased demand for imports to satisfy the higher living standards demanded by visitors. At the same time further foreign currency is lost to the economy as expatriate labor remits some of its earnings overseas. In Mauritius, for example, it has been calculated that only 10% of the total tourist receipts from inclusive tours represent foreign exchange earnings to the island's economy (4, p. 43). The remaining 90% includes the takings of overseas airlines and foreign tour operators, imports of provisions for tourists and the repatriation of profits and labor earnings.

The problem, not peculiar to tourism, is one of insufficient backward linkages to the traditional sectors of the developing country's economy, i.e. the economies of such countries are not yet geared to supplying the quality of goods and services or the requisite factors of production in sufficient [21] quantity to satisfy the demand created by modern forms of development, of which international tourism is but one.

2. *Income Effects*

The income effects created by tourism are perhaps the most controversial and least understood aspect of tourist research. Apart from the general inadequacy of the available data and the multiplicity of methodologies used to measure tourist receipts, few serious attempts have been made to assess the level of personal incomes which accrues to the indigenous populations of the developing countries or the net value of such income to the economy. Several misleading studies have been published and have received public (though not expert) acceptance, but for rigorous and serious research one must turn to the work of Bryden in the West Indies (2) and Mitchell in East Africa (8).

Bryden showed by means of income multiplier analysis the effect of tourist expenditure on the level of incomes in Antigua. For each $1 of tourist spending injected into the economy of this country about 86 cents of personal income was created. His findings were largely supported by an independent analysis carried out the same year by Levitt and Gulati (6, pp. 326–343). Perhaps the most accurate method of assessing the primary and secondary income generated by injections of foreign spending, i.e. the income multiplier effect, is by input–output analysis. This forms part of the model described in the second section of this paper.

Bryden, however, was less than wholly convinced about the value of using multiplier analysis as a partial measure of the benefits or potential benefits to be gained by an expansion of tourism in the long run. Perhaps his most telling argument was that, even assuming that sufficient capacity exists (in terms of resources and factors of production) to support a growth in tourism, many of the required factors, including labor, are likely to have alternative uses, i.e. their opportunity cost is likely to be greater than zero. Thus any attempt to use the level of income generated by tourism as a partial measure of the benefits gained would considerably overstate these benefits. A more correct measurement of the benefits would be to offset the income obtained from tourism against the possible income which could have been derived from an alternative employment of the same resources and factors. Such accounting, of course, forms an intrinsic part of cost–benefit analysis.

The argument was advanced still further by Mitchell who, at one point, claimed that if all resources were valued at their opportunity cost, then in the extreme case the net value of tourism would consist of only indirect taxes paid on goods purchased by tourists plus receipts to the government for [22] services provided minus the cost to the government of providing the services used by tourists and in promoting tourism. Under this restricted definition, he calculated that the net value of tourism to Kenya by non-East African residents would amount to only 4% of their expenditures in 1966–67. He later relaxed this restricted definition of net value to take account of several factors such as some intramarginal rental earnings, pure profit accruing to local residents, the possible over-valuation of local currency in terms of foreign currency, the fact that some labor will be paid more than its alternative earnings, together with various secondary beneficial effects. He concluded that the value to East Africa of non-resident tourism probably amounted to between Ł0.8 and Ł2.1 million ($1.9 and $5 million), i.e. only 5 to 10% of total tourist receipts.

Perhaps one of the most important aspects of tourist expenditure is not its income generation effect but the income re-distribution which it brings about. Tourism affects income distribution through the combination of inputs which it requires: some goods and factors of production are required in greater quantity than before, whilst the demand for other inputs may even decline. At the same time tourist demand creates changes in the relative prices of the goods consumed by local residents and these changes affect various groups of people differentially: some gain, others lose. It is possible that such changes could, under certain circumstances, retard future growth, particularly if resources are diverted away from sectors or projects which create higher net values to the economy.

Income creating in the personal sector is not even necessarily an entirely desirable aspect of development, particularly in the short run. The primary object should be to create the opportunity for investment (particularly through the obtaining of foreign exchange) in order to create greater income and wealth in the future. To this extent, increases in present levels of consumption can only be achieved at the expense of a lower rate of economic growth in the future.

3. Employment Effects

Much of what has already been discussed above applies equally to employment creation. Tourism is labor intensive and can absorb a large number of semi-skilled and unskilled workers which, in a developing country, is largely drawn from the traditional sectors. Even in the more advanced economies, the semi-skilled and unskilled workers recruited by the tourist industry make up almost three-quarters of their total requirements. In Mexico, for example, an investment of $80,000 in tourism in 1969 created 41 jobs, compared with only 16 in the petroleum industry, 15 in metal trades and 8 in the electricity industry (9). In Morocco, the addition of an extra 100 bedroom hotel creates direct employment for 40 workers plus some additional secondary employment (5). Mitchell calculated that if the present rate of expansion of tourism [23] to Kenya is maintained, an additonal 12,000 direct jobs will be created and a further 9,000 workers will be required in the secondary activities which supply the tourist establishments. (8, p. 10).

The deployment of a large number of workers into the tourism industry might in some cases create conditions suitable for the production of a marketable surplus in the more traditional sectors of the economy, but it is likely in the majority of cases to do little more than partially relieve some of the general condition of under-employment.

4. Infrastructural Changes

The growth of tourism creates a need for an improved infrastructure in developing economies. Transportation systems require a degree of modernization; water supplies and sanitation arrangements may need improvement; access roads, airports, telephone systems and other public utilities may have to be extended. In economic terms many of these services are indivisible in the sense that if the government provides them for tourists they are at the same time making them available to local residents. Improved roads benefit farmers in outlying areas, whilst airstrips constructed primarily to aid tourism may open up the economies of remote regions.

In addition, through the operation of the multiplier effect, the monetary benefits of tourist spending spill over into various sectors of the economy including the coffers of the government itself. The government derives tax and excise revenue directly from tourist expenditure and indirectly by taxing the higher incomes and profits of local residents and tourist establishments. Some of these government funds can, of course, be used to finance further infrastructural development.

As welfare economists, however, the authors of this paper are concerned not with these infrastructural changes per se, but with whether similar or better net benefits could be achieved by the development of sectors other than tourism. Indeed the model described in the second half of this paper is designed to test just such a hypothesis.

5. *The Effect on Domestic Price Levels*

The expansion of international tourism in a developing economy creates an increased demand both for imported goods and for local products and factors of production. Shop prices rise and the cost of factors of production, particularly land, is likely to be bid up. To the extent that the domestic population is adversely affected by some resultant inflation, this can be considered an additional cost of tourist development. [24]

6. *Economic Dependence on Tourism*

Many writers have drawn attention to the dangers inherent in overdependence upon tourism as a source of revenue. Tourism, as it has already been pointed out, above, is income and price elastic and so responds more than proportionally to changes in these variables. At the same time, tourism is subject not only to regular seasonal fluctuations but also to irregular swings as (a) world political and economic conditions alter and (b) consumer tastes change, e.g. in Monaco during 1939 there were 70 hotels with 3,580 beds, but by 1969, as a result of a fall in demand, the supply of hotels had dwindled to 31 with a total of 1,650 beds (11).

On the other hand, it can be argued that tourism as an export industry complements other exporting sectors and so adds a greater stability to foreign exchange earnings. Receipts from tourism are expected in the long run to rise. The recent increases in world fuel prices and the relative price elasticity of tourism are not likely to be sufficient in the medium run to offset favorable variables such as the increasing incomes of people in developed countries, more leisure-time and longer vacations, increasing population and higher levels of education. Tourist receipts should tend to cycle around a more pronounced upward trend than those for most primary products.

7. *Environmental and Ecological Effects*

Uncontrolled tourist development can damage environmental conditions, spoil the aesthetic appearance of the affected parts of a developing country and prejudice the future of rare wildlife. Such factors are taken into account in cost–benefit analysis to the extent that they adversely affect the welfare of the indigenous population.

It can, however, be argued that with careful planning tourism can be a major positive factor in helping to preserve particular environmental and ecological heritages. Certainly the growth of 'educational tourism' has aided the development of the national park system in many developing countries, although tourist demand has increased in recent years to such an extent that the environmental character of many of these parks is now threatened.

8.   Social and Psychological Results

The impact of international tourism on the social and psychological values of the indigenous populations of developing countries has been analyzed by specialists in fields more relevant than this, but no account of tourism can be complete without at least a list of the possible effects.

In the first place, it has been maintained that the so-called 'demonstration effect' of the tourists' way of life may stimulate the native population into working harder to improve its own living standards. Against this it can [25] reasonably be argued that a display of prosperity in the midst of poverty is more likely to create resentment than approbation. In extreme cases, resentment has turned to violence and it is not uncommon in many developing countries for tourist hotels to be patrolled by armed guards. Secondly, the merit of social intercourse between tourists and the indigenous population as a means towards fostering better understanding and goodwill between nations has been extolled as a major social benefit obtained from tourism. Whilst this may be true in some cases, particularly in developing countries where tourist are still comparatively rare, it is certainly not true in many countries where tourists' tastes and habits have proved offensive to particular sectors of the local population. Indeed in some countries, e.g. Tanzania, tourist development is largely concentrated away from major population centres and contacts with the local people are minimal.

Lastly, whilst tourist development may help to preserve historic sites and national parks, the governments of several developing countries fear that too much tourist development may impair their national identity. The infusion of groups of tourists into outlying areas disrupts the traditional cultures of the local people, whilst in the cities the construction of large 'soulless' modern hotels and shops produces a general uniformity of development which obscures the local architectural heritage.

9.   Some Conclusions

Tourism is often justified by reference to several criteria. Many of these are complementary to each other, while some are actively conflicting. It is tempting, therefore, for supporters of varying projects in different sectors to attempt to justify them in the most favorable light. The adoption of a series of projects, chosen according to differing criteria, may well be self defeating if each is only outweighing others' disadvantages. Thus, one could well find agricultural projects being supported because of their contribution to the level of employment, and tourism supported because of their contribution to the level of employment, and tourism supported because of its contribution to foreign exchange. Yet, an increase in employment and, with it, incomes in the agricultural sector can mean both a reduction in exports as the peasantry consume more, and an increase in imports as they demand more manufactured goods. Further, this is not nearly so far-fetched an example as it seems.

This piecemeal approach tends to bag the whole question of resource allocation in developing countries, for if some machinery of allocation is necessary it must imply that at least one resource is scarce relative to the demand for it. For consistent choice to be made between alternatives, therefore, it is first of all necessary to find some common measurement by which projects may be compared one with another. [26]

Usually, while different criteria are used in comparing sectors and projects, there is some vague underlying assumption that the criteria are, in turn, measuring contributions made to the development of the country concerned, albeit sometimes in a wider sense. Thus, when we justify one project on the grounds of its high exchange earnings, and another on its contribution to the level of employment, in both instances assumptions are made that the country will benefit by being able to bring more resources into play, and that development will be facilitated. In the second instance, of course, some would argue that increased employment is by itself good, but in a developing country unemployment as such is often different from unemployment in developed countries. There is often much concealed unemployment on the land where the removal of labor may have little effect on output, and where the allocation of such labor to industrial activity will increase total output by much more than it is reduced. There may also be a pool of completely unemployed in the urban centres, but as fast as this is reduced by increased industrial activity it is usually replenished from the underemployed on the land who come to the town in search of work. Consequently, the mere provision of wage work on the grounds that it is a good thing cannot often be justified under conditions of development, except perhaps by its effect on the social structure when it breaks traditional attitudes and reduces reliance on the land. What is needed, therefore, is some way in which the contribution to employment, foreign exchange earnings and other attributes deemed desirable of each project can be recast in the terms of the overall contribution of each of these to the ultimate aim. This requires the determination of a maximand to which the relative contribution to each to the two concepts distinct for, even though there must inevitably be a close relationship between them, they are not the same thing and much confusion has been caused in the literature by failing to maintain this important distinction.

The method devised by Professors Little and Mirrlees of Nuffleld College, Oxford, is an excellent example of one whereby as many variables as possible are integrated via a single numeraire into a consistent relationship with a maximand. It is presumed that growth, in its widest sense, is the aim of the country concerned; this growth is not merely physical output but may include health, education or infrastructural improvements. Thus, any investable funds in the hands of the government can be devoted to the promotion of that growth, so, whereas profit in the hands of private industry may be ploughed back into productive capacity, government has the alternative of increasing productive capacity or improving infrastructure or education as well. Investable funds in the hands of the government are consequently a convenient numeraire quantity, and all other allocations of output from a project can be given a comparative evaluation in terms of this numeraire. So, if private profit were to be seen as being worth only 50% of government investment, all profit generated would be valued at 50% of its monetary value when re-casting the accounts of a project on a social basis. On the other hand, the cost of imported goods may include a large tariff. This must be removed in the [27] social accounts as, of course, this accrues to the government and will increase the funds available. Again a large amount of cost is incurred, maybe in wages for unskilled labor. As shown above, the cost to the economy will usually be less than the wage. Also it may be desirable that the lowly-paid should be able to increase their consumption as part of the development process. Not all the money-wages, therefore, should be shown as costs in the accounts and they should be reduced by a factor which allows for this. (Naturally, the Manual of Cost Benefit Analysis of Industrial Projects in Developing Countries, printed by O.E.C.D. and written by I.M.D. Little and J.A. Mirrlees (7), deals with these topics far more deeply and theoretically, and readers are referred to that volume for further details.) A further point is in order, however, which is of especial importance to tourism. The Little and Mirrlees method values everything at world prices or their equivalent so, where the maintenance of a currency at artificially high level is being practiced, this is allowed for by valuing all goods produced and the resources used at the prices they would bring on the world market. This reduces all costs to a common 'opportunity cost' basis in that it indicates clearly what the economy forgoes in using or consuming individual resources and what it can earn in potential output. As most development requires an initial quantity, at least, of purchased foreign capital goods, and as any departure from an exchange rate which does not represent 'purchasing power parity' cannot be maintained over a long period, this is both reasonable and realistic. An international tourism almost by definition implies the inflow of foreign exchange it should, of course, be amenable to this particular form of analysis.

A Suggested Model

The following model is based on 'The integration of project and sector analysis', by P.G. Sadler (10).

A common method of evaluating projects is by testing the total amount of value added which is generated – in this way a project which requires an initial input of foreign capital and then, during operation, requires an inflow in the form of raw materials, will also generate private income in the form of wages and profits and social income in the form of taxes and levies. In general, the value added will be the net amount of both accruing to the economy. Projects which generate the greatest amount of value added per unit of capital used will be deemed the best to adopt. (This presupposes, of course, that the scarce resource being allocated is capital.) However, as shown above, various forms of value added can have different valuation in the social context. First of all, shadow prices or social accounting prices must be assessed. This will show the relative value for the components of the value added by projects in terms of a numeraire before any valid comparisons can be made. Also, there is another problem touched on earlier in the paper which is rarely, if ever, considered in value added computations, but which can be of vital importance [28] when evaluating tourist projects. That is, the effect of changes in income and also the impact of the project itself on the patterns of individual consumption. Thus the net amount of value added of a project may be measured by deducting all imports of capital and raw materials from total output. However, if the increased incomes or changes in the way of life cause workers to switch their consumption to imported goods, the results of the analysis will be invalid. In fact, this seems to be a prevalent occurrence in many developing countries.

What is suggested below is a model which will take account of these problems. Ideally it would be necessary to build a complete input–output model of the country to provide full information necessary. However, as this is rarely available in a developing economy, it may often be more appropriate to rely on the concepts used rather than to attempt to construct a model with spurious accuracy.

Suppose a system as follows:

$$
\begin{matrix}
x_1 \\
x_2 \\
\vdots \\
x_n
\end{matrix}
\qquad = X = \text{Changes in level of activity in each of } n \text{ sectors}
$$

$$
\begin{matrix}
y_1 \\
y_2 \\
\vdots \\
y_n
\end{matrix}
\qquad = Y = \text{Changes in created surplus in each of } n \text{ sectors}
$$

$$
\begin{matrix}
a_{11} & a_{12} & \cdots & a_{1n} \\
a_{21} & a_{22} & \cdots & a_{2n} \\
\vdots & \vdots & & \vdots \\
a_{n1} & a_{n2} & \cdots & a_{nn}
\end{matrix}
\qquad = A = \text{Matrix of input/output coefficients}
$$

[29]

$$
\begin{matrix}
b_{1h} & 0 & \cdots & 0 \\
0 & b_{2h} & \cdots & 0 \\
\vdots & \vdots & & \vdots \\
0 & \cdots 0 & \cdots & b_{nh}
\end{matrix}
\qquad = B_h \quad \text{Income creation coefficients for each of the } h \text{ receiving sectors } \quad (h = n+1, \ldots, p)
$$

$$
\begin{matrix}
C_{1h} & C_{1h} & \cdots & C_{1h} \\
C_{2h} & C_{2h} & \cdots & C_{2h} \\
\vdots & \vdots & & \vdots \\
C_{ah} & C_{nh} & \cdots & C_{nh}
\end{matrix}
\qquad = C_h = \text{Marginal propensities to consume of each of the } h \text{ sectors}
$$

which yields:

$$
X - AX - C_{n+1}(I-A)\,B_{n+1}\,X - \ldots - C_P(I-A)\,B_P\,X = Y
$$

Factorising:

$$
X = (I-A)^{-1}\left| I - \sum_{n+1}^{p} C_h(I-A)\,B_h(I-A)^{-1} \right|^{-1} Y
$$

The changes in output levels, X, are quite straightforward but the changes in created surplus need amplification. In fact, they represent that part of an increase in total output which is not consumed, i.e. it includes balance of payments surplus, increases in taxation and in saving, and so on. Also, while some sectors are international in that their outputs are exportable, others are domestic, in that their output cannot be imported or exported, e.g. electricity or construction. If one now postulates an increase in created surplus in one international sector (*i*) but hold the output of all other international sectors (*j*) constant, the result will be (a) a reduction in exports (or increase in imports) in the international sectors *j* as the ith sector requires more inputs, (b) an increase in output of domestic sectors (*d*) for the same reason, and (c) a further reduction in exports (increase in imports) in the *j* sectors, an increase in outputs in sector *i*, and the domestic sectors (*d*) created by increases in incomes in sector *i* and sector *d*. The net change in created surplus would thus be the increase postulated in *i* minus the reductions in the surpluses in sector *j*, i.e.

$$\sum_{1}^{n} y_i$$

[30]

The social benefit, however, will be the re-investable surplus plus an allowance for extra consumption which is deemed equivalent to re-investment. (In the Little and Mirrlees terminology, the excess of the actual wage over the shadow edge.) So, if we add $W - SW / W$ times the extra income accruing to the peasantry (where W = actual wage, SW = shadow wage), we have the total net benefit. On the assumption the peasant worker consumes all his income, the extra consumption $C^{\circ} W - SW / W$ will give us this total (where C° = increase in present income). The peasant consumption will be one of the C_h matrices in the model, and the proportion of extra consumption generated and accruing to the peasantry can be obtained from the computer by a slight manipulation.

Total benefits will now be $\qquad \sum_{1}^{n} y_i + C^{\circ} \left(\dfrac{W - SW}{W} \right)$

But, as these benefits accrue over time, it will be necessary to treat them by an appropriate discount factor (*r*) and the total benefits over time will be shown below:

$$\sum_{1}^{t} \left[\frac{\sum_{1}^{n} y_i + C^{\circ} \left(\dfrac{W - SW}{W} \right)}{(1 + r)^t} \right] = \frac{(1 + r)^{t-1}}{r(1 + r)^t} \left[\sum_{1}^{n} y_i + C^{\circ} \left(\frac{W - SW}{W} \right) \right]$$

where *t* is the life of capital invested in the sector *i*.

The costs are the costs of capital incurred in creating the net benefits mentioned in the previous paragraph. Thus, by multiplying the changes in output in section *i* and the consequent changes in output in the domestic sector *j* by their appropriate capital output ratios (*k*) one arrives at the cost in terms of the amount of investable surplus, which will need to be devoted to the creation of the required capital

$$x_i k_i + \Sigma x_j k_j.$$

With the costs and benefits, a cost–benefit ratio for each sector can now be established

$$\sum_{1}^{t} \left[\frac{\sum_{1}^{n} y_i + C° \left(\frac{W - SW}{W} \right)}{(1 + r)^t} \right]$$

$$x_i k_i + \sum_{1}^{n} x_j k_j$$

and the sector which exhibits the highest ratio will, of course, be the one which promises the highest social return to the use of the scarce resource of capital. [31]

Notes

* P.G. Sadler, Director, Institute for the Study of Sparsely Populated Areas, University of Aberdeen, Aberdeen, Scotland; B.H. Archer, Director, Institute of Economic Research, University College of North Wales, Bangor, Wales.

** This article was first printed, in its original form, in *Tourism in Africa and the Management of Related Resources*, Center for African Studies, University of Edinburgh, 1974. The article has been revised by the authors for publication in *Annals*.

Bibliography

1. Bond, M.E. and Ladman, Jerry R., 'International Tourism and Economic Development: A Special Case for Latin America', *Mississippi Valley Journal of Business and Economics*, Vol. III, Number 1, 1972.
2. Bryden, John M., *Tourism and Development*, Cambridge University Press, 1973.
3. *International Tourism Quarterly*, The Economist Intelligence Unit, Number 1, 1971, p. 42.
4. *International Tourism Quarterly*, The Economist Intelligence Unit, Number 1, 1972.
5. Lasry, J., *Le Tourisme en Morac*, Institut Superieur de Commerce, Paris, 1965.
6. Levitt, Kari and Gulati, Igbal, 'Income Effect of Tourist Spending, Mystification Multiplied: A Critical Comment on the Zinder Report', *Social and Economic Studies*, Vol. 19, Number 3, September 1970, pp. 326–343.
7. Little, I.M.D. and Mirrlees, J., *Manual of Industrial Project, Analysis in Developing Countries*, Organization for Economic Cooperation and Development, 1968.
8. Mitchell, Frank, 'The Value of Tourism in East Africa', *East African Economic Review*, Vol. 2, Number 1, June 1970.
9. Ruiz, Abel Garrido, 'Effects del turismo en la economia nacional', Reunion Nacional de Chapala, Diciembre 2, 1969, Departmento de Turismo, Mexico.
10. Sadler, P.G., 'Integration of Sector and Project Analysis', *New Essays in Economics*, ed. Parkin, Longmans, 1973.
11. Young, George, *Tourism: Blessing or Blight?* Pelican Books, 1973.

Please note folios in square brackets throughout text represent original page numbers.

[9]

PERGAMON

Hospitality Management 18 (1999) 31–43

International Journal of
Hospitality
Management

Using IRR and NPV models to evaluate societal costs of tourism projects in developing countries

D. Omotayo Brown[a],*, Francis A. Kwansa[b]

[a]*Hospitality and Tourism Program, University of Kentucky, 210a Erikson Hall, Lexington, KY 40506-0050, USA*
[b]*University of Delaware, Newark, DE 19716, USA*

Abstract

This paper examines some societal costs involved in tourism development in developing countries, and argues – using the theory of developmental economics – that although the social value of an act of tourism investment should exceed its social cost, the valuation techniques used to estimate these costs during the investment decision process are not fully developed. It provides modified internal rate of return (*IRR*) and net present value (*NPV*) models, as possible measurement tools to be considered in the investment criteria to help solve this problem. Policy makers can incorporate these models into studies of tourism's overall desirability. © 1999 Elsevier Science Ltd. All rights reserved.

Keywords: Developing countries; Tourism; Societal costs; Project evaluation; Internal rate of return (*IRR*); Net present value (*NPV*)

1. Introduction and background

In the majority of developing countries the private sector is so underdeveloped that the various governments have no choice but to assume responsibility for economic development – a role which automatically qualifies them as the direct recipients of foreign aid (Chib, 1980). Since capital is not unlimited, government investment in one sector of the economy leads to a re-distribution of capital away the other sectors (opportunity costs). This means that governments in developing countries that embark on massive investments in tourism infrastructure, must postpone or ignore other projects such as irrigation, small scale manufacturing, diversification of agriculture and education among others. Rodenburg (1980) argues that these might be more worthwhile investments in terms of the economic rate of return and in long-term benefits to the people of the countries.

---

*Corresponding author. E-mail: omotayo@pop.uky.edu

0278-4319/99/$ – See front matter © 1999 Elsevier Science Ltd. All rights reserved.
PII: S0278-4319(98)00043-7

32   *D.O. Brown, F.A. Kwansa/Hospitality Management 18 (1999) 31–43*

2. The problem

Associated with the economic benefits of tourism are the adverse economic, socio cultural and environmental impacts that have been extensively reported by Liu and Var (1986), Long et al. (1990) and Milne (1990). The present methods used by developing countries to evaluate tourism projects (especially on a large scale) are not quite clear. Some are embarked upon because they are "white elephants" of politicians, others because of lack of knowledge and information on the part of planners. Whatever the reasons, the cost/benefit ratios of large scale tourism projects in majority of developing countries are underestimated in the majority of circumstances. With few exceptions, no systematic attempts have been made to apply valuation of societal cost techniques in estimating tourism capital investment in developing countries. Yet it is important to know the expected marginal social costs of pollution, destruction of culture, crime and all other societal ills that have been identified in the tourism sociological literature. Since most developing countries lack strong capital markets, their sources of financing for tourism development are mainly from funds available within the country, from international funding agencies, bilateral or multilateral aid, and by lending agencies established by governments (Chib, 1980).

3. Purpose of study

The purpose of this paper is to examine some societal costs that are usually involved in the development of large scale tourism and to propose methods of estimating and incorporating them in investment decision criteria for tourism development in developing countries. This estimation will highlight the problem of incomplete recognition of all costs associated with an investment project, and provide help in alleviating some of the financial costs of poor investment decisions in these countries.

4. Theoretical framework

The theoretical underpinning of this paper is guided by the theory of development economics, which helps to explain the poverty of nations. During the last three decades or so, explanations of the persistence of poverty were fairly unanimous: poverty set ups – associated with various conditions which retarded economic progress. This resulted in a body of literature which established developmental economics as a distinct specialization. Essentially, most developmental economic theory centers around the view that the level of investment in a country is strongly influenced by individual investors' expectations of the future rate of growth of the economy. By the same logic, an investment will tend to produce a stream of benefits in excess of the private returns to the investor by expanding the size of the market and thus tending to induce further capital formation by others. Hence the social value of an act of investment should exceed its social cost (Killick, 1978). Thus, the prevailing

D.O. Brown, F.A. Kwansa/Hospitality Management 18 (1999) 31–43   33

question that this paper addresses is: How are these social costs estimated in developing countries?

5. The need to estimate social cost

The current literature seems to suggest that the discount rate in international tourism development has neither been appropriately accounted for because of the social cost factor, nor do they provide suitable concepts for calculating the non-monetary aspects of tourism development. A number of studies in the environmental literature have addressed this issue (for example, Dixon and Hufschmidt, 1986; Dixon and Sherman, 1990; Dixon et al., 1988; Hufschmidt et al., 1983). However, although similar studies have been conducted in the field of tourism, few have suggested ways to quantify costs. For example: Lindberg et al., (1997) suggested the contingent-valuation (CV) method as a technique for measuring the economic value of selected actual social impacts associated with tourism; Dwyer et al., (1997) have measured the yield from foreign tourism by going beyond visitor expenditure. They propose taking into account a wide range of economic, environmental and social costs of tourism development; Sinclair (1998) has suggested both a single and a system of equation models for estimating tourism's costs. Since one of the basic facts about international tourism is that it deals with populations of developing countries who face large groups of tourists (mass tourism), the objective of a social cost estimation is to guide the decision makers in the choice of capital projects and expenditures which will maximize the gains to the citizens.

Economic theory suggests that resources are limited. Therefore, undertaking of a public investment will divert resources from an alternative use – perhaps another public investment, or an investment in the private sector. In other words, there is an opportunity cost to carrying out the tourism project. Thus, tourism planners in developing countries should be interested in the benefits to be derived from the expenditure on a tourism project compared to the benefits that would be obtained if the capital had been used elsewhere. It follows therefore that there should be a ranking system which should reflect the difference between benefits that would have been obtained from a given project, say a resort development, and the benefits that would be obtained from the project which is foregone, say an irrigation project. Thus, tourism planners in developing countries must come to terms with finding ways to measure (a) the physical benefits and costs and (b) societal costs, once the physical costs are found. Furthermore, if societal costs are estimated and included in financial cost/benefit decision criteria models, the discount factor might be adjusted in an upward manner which might reduce the net present values of the expected cash flows.

Finally, new developments always take place in a geographical setting. They draw upon resources and people from other locations. These actions affect not only the development location itself, but also others. As May (1991) suggests, environmental impact assessment has not taken sufficient notice of the wider implications of development. Thus there is the need to provide appropriate information for specialists and non-specialists, so that decision makers are made aware of potential conditions that may stand in the way of the social welfare of the citizens.

6. Defining an international tourism project

For the purposes of this paper, international tourism projects are those consisting of a set of facilities at a fixed location in which income is derived principally from expenditures of foreign visitors. A number of "facilities" make up such projects, but for convenience, they can be grouped into two investment categories:
1. Superstructure.
" Hotels and other forms of lodging.
" Tour services.
" Restaurants and other forms of entertainment.
" Shops.
2. Basic infrastructure
" Attraction restoration and/or site development.
" Basic utilities: water, sewage and solid waste disposal, electricity, telecommunications etc.
" Transport: access roads, airports, harbors.
" Employee training facilities.
" Special services to the permanent community: education, health care etc.

7. Economic motives for tourism investment

The literature highlighting the potential economic benefits to developing countries are numerous. For example, Mathieson and Wall (1982); Seward et al. (1982); Duffield (1982). The majority agree that developing countries tend to adopt tourism as an export industry because it has the following *economic* implications on their economies:
- The creation of new local requirements for equipment, food and other supplies, thereby fostering new industries and commercial activities and opening up new markets.
- The creation of a favorable impact upon employment in the country e.g. new jobs in hotels, travel agencies, government, handicraft industries etc.
- An increase in urbanization through the continuous growth of construction and renovation of tourist facilities.
- Helps increase the governments' earnings of foreign currency which developing countries badly need for bridging or reducing their deficits in balance of payments, thus fostering the development of their national economies.
- Acts as a channel for redistribution of wealth by redistributing capital between developed and developing countries.
- Accelerating the multiplier effect within the economy of a country.

D.O. Brown, F.A. Kwansa/Hospitality Management 18 (1999) 31–43 35

8. Defining costs

Costs measure the extent to which activities of a program are displaced elsewhere in a society to the extent to which they would have contributed to the objective of the program. Thus, in a perfectly functioning competitive economy, financial outlays measure the cost of a given project. However, market prices do *not* always measure what the economy forgoes. The social costs of increased prostitution, crime, environmental destruction, bastardization of culture for example, do not equal zero. Thus costs, with respect to societal decay are sacrifices that particular groups or regions bear as a result of the implementation of mass tourism in developing countries.

9. Some societal costs associated with tourism development

Tourism is concerned with the movement of, and contact between people in different geographical locations (Mill et al., 1985). Sociologically, this involves the behavior of the host population, which has to reconcile economic gain and benefits with the costs of living with strangers amongst others. In developing countries, it is unclear whether the social costs that are frequently the by-products of such relationships are estimated and factored into the monetary variables when investment decisions are made. The existing literature on the social costs of tourism does not seem to emphasize the exorbitant costs incurred by governments in developing countries and hence to the citizens who make up the social unit. Familiar examples of societal costs or spillover effects of tourism development are effects on flora, fauna, rainfall, soil the creation of artificial lakes, prostitution and crime and other ecological and sociological effects that ultimately touch the welfare of the citizens. Also included are congestion suffered by all the traffic from additional vehicles coming onto the roads, the noise pollution arising from additional operation of airports, etc. Although it can be argued that these effects are not deliberately produced, it is also true to say that they also *cannot* be deliberately absorbed by others in the society – at least without incurring expenses (Mishan, 1973). What follows is a brief discussion of some societal costs or spillover effects of tourism in developing countries. In terms of estimation, some of them can already be assigned monetary costs, e.g., the costs of policing increased crime, the amount of welfare payments to citizens unemployed, the costs of imports due to demonstration effects. The issues in question here, however are: (a) What are the financial costs of ecological spillover as a result of tourism development and growth? (b) Do developing countries' tourism planners include these costs in the investment outlay or reflect them in the discount rate during the present value computations?

9.1. Demonstration effects

In some developing countries one of the consequences of mass tourism has been the adoption of the life-styles of the tourists by some sections of the local population. This has caused a new social stratum that demand the supply of the various consumption needs of tourists from developed countries. In this regard, two kinds of costs are incurred by developing countries: (a) the cost of services to the foreign tourists and (b) the cost of the imported goods for the local population. In terms of the latter, these costs relate to additional imports of consumer goods, which constitute a drain or leakage effect to the society as a whole because the earnings or potential earnings from the tourism sector is spent on purchasing consumer goods which for the most part are imported or have very large import contents. Furthermore, a more serious sign of this demonstration effect takes place when residents of developing countries imitate the spending patterns of residents of developing countries. The fact that tourists demand such goods allows the local residents concerned to justify their importation for both the use of tourists and theirs. Thus, a tourism development project brings about a social cost because it allows an excess amount of goods to be imported which otherwise would not have been, or would have been subject to certain quotas.

9.2. Prostitution

Although prostitution existed long before the age of mass tourism, Mathieson and Wall (1982) suggest that it is exceedingly difficult to measure how much, if at all, tourism has been responsible for its upsurge in developing countries. They propose that in order to explain the increase, one or more of the following hypotheses must be put forward (p. 149):
(1) Tourism development has created locations and environments which attract prostitutes and their clients; (2) By its very nature, tourism means that people are away from the puritanical bonds of normal living and that since they are away from home and have discretionary incomes, anonymity is assured. These circumstances are conducive to the survival and expansion of prostitution; (3) Tourism may be used as a scapegoat for the general loosening of morals; (4) As tourism affords employment for women, it may upgrade their economic status. This in turn may lead to their liberalization and, eventually to their involvement in prostitution to maintain or acquire new economic levels. In most developing countries there is some evidence to confirm some of these assertions, although no formal study has been done to that effect. However, as Mathieson et al. put it, "advertising, which exploits the four Ss of tourism [to developing countries] – sea, sun, sand and sex ....has created images of havens of sexual enjoyment". These attitudes, in addition to the desire of local women for "western economic status" are genuine grounds for the escalation of prostitution in developing countries. The consequence of this rise in prostitution invariably is cost-effective law enforcement. It is doubtful whether spending on prostitution control buys anything of a positive nature. Furthermore, some studies have concluded that this spending is a "waste", and the "revolving-door" arrest and prosecution of prostitutes results in "hardening the individuals, burdening the court system, ... and adversely affecting police morale" (Weitzer, 1991). Therefore, there is the need to estimate the

D.O. Brown, F.A. Kwansa/Hospitality Management 18 (1999) 31–43 37

expected incremental cost in law enforcement and to incorporate it in the capital budgeting process.

9.3. Crime

In their research on tourism and crime in Mexico, Lin and Loeb (1977) cited three factors as being critical in influencing relationships between tourism and crime (p. 165):
1. The population density during the tourist season;
2. The location of the resort in relation to an international border;
3. The per capita incomes of hosts and tourists, large differences between them tending to encourage tourism.

Many developing countries meet at least one of these criteria. Furthermore, some studies have linked the tourist season to higher crime rates (see for example McPheters and Stronge, 1974). These crimes are mainly economic ones such as robbery, larceny and burglary. In addition, Lehman (1980) suggests that the development of black markets has been encouraged by the increase in international tourism in developing countries. These facts suggest that police protection, prison guards, administrative staff and the like must be greatly increased during such periods. Thus, the social and monetary costs to developing countries as summarized by Mathieson and Wall (p. 151) are:
1. Increased expenditures on law enforcement during the tourist season
2. Monetary losses from burglary and larceny, property damage from vandalism, commercial embezzlement, tax dodging and growth of black markets.
3. Heightened tension.

10. Estimation of societal costs

In general, estimation of societal costs involves using monetary units of measure to transform all values into a single dimension (Abelson, 1996). This creates two main technical problems. Firstly, domestic prices often differ from international prices. Secondly, the value of monetary units varies over time with changes in price levels. This issue becomes particularly problematic in tourism projects since estimation of societal costs essentially involves computation of the present value of the total costs, discounted at some appropriate interest rate. However, the use of market prices for estimation purposes will be improper if:
(a) market prices are not equal to marginal costs;
(b) marginal cost does not reflect the true social cost of resources.

While the results of any societal cost estimation may be approximate, it is important to remember that the 'correct' degree of approximation of any result depends on the purpose for which the results are desired. Hence the question of accuracy of estimation methods of societal costs in developing countries must be seen in the context of what this paper proposes, namely, evaluation of investment decisions subject to the constraints of scarce economic resources.

11. The use of shadow prices

Shadow prices can be defined as the marginal rate of substitution between the 'alternatives' in question. For instance, an increase in tourism capacity by one hundred may mean one hundred units more of environmental pollution, prostitution, rape, burglary, cultural degradation and the like. Although there are no observable prices, there are 'shadow' prices, since each must have an opportunity cost in terms of some foregone alternative. The use of shadow pricing is a difficult process, one of the drawbacks being its arbitrariness. However, several strategies can be employed.

Firstly, consumer questionnaires can be used in which suitably phrased questions could probe citizens' willingness to pay for x. If x is a nuisance for example, would they be prepared to say "I/we would collectively pay $100, $200, $300 or some other amount a year rather than have an additional 100 tourist"? If they are prepared to put a figure on the social cost of receiving the extra tourist capacity, and perhaps serve some of them in what they may feel to be a subordinate capacity, then these amounts can be averaged out and added to the investment outlay (Bottomley et al., 1976). For example, the survey can be based on a benefit–cost approach in which any ith person made better off on balance by the spillover, would be asked to offer a maximum positive sum, V_i, rather than go without it, such sum being prefixed by a positive sign. On the other hand, any ith person made worse off on balance could be offered a minimum sum V_i to induce him to put up with the spillover – such sum to be received being prefixed by a negative sign. Mishan (1973) calls these sums compensating variations, for if paid by the former, or if received by the latter, his welfare will remain unchanged. Assuming n persons are affected, if the condition $\sum_{i=1}^{n} V_i > 0$ is met and the algebraic sum of the individual compensating variation is positive, we can conclude that gainers can more than compensate losers, and the value of the excess gain over loss is the value to be attributed to the spillover effect in question. However, if $\sum_{i=1}^{n} V_i < 0$ then an excess of loss over gain can be attributed to the spillover.

Secondly, the cost of providing the service could be used to represent its societal cost. In the case of developing countries, the extra cost of police services, prison services, judicial administrators, etc. that follow due to the influx of tourists can be incorporated into the investment outlay.

Thirdly, tourism planners may decide that the effort is not worth it because the degree of arbitrariness is too high, or there may be no precise way of estimating the costs. In this case, the costs should at least be listed as 'contingencies'. In this regard, if benefits exceed costs by $10 million, and an estimate of the number of additional criminals, prostitutes, environmental damage etc. are available over the period in question, at the very least, the decision-maker's problem is reduced to asking if those estimates are 'worth' the $10 million net benefit.

On the other hand, it can be argued that some societal costs have infinite value. Some examples would be destruction to the community, the loss of flora and fauna. However, if this argument is recognized as being true, then there would be no change or improvement in their status as societal ills. Hence the real danger

D.O. Brown, F.A. Kwansa/Hospitality Management 18 (1999) 31–43   39

to avoid in developing countries is ignoring losses simply because they cannot be valued.

12. Applying the investment decision criteria

The types of choices facing the decision-maker in tourism development can be classified as follows:

(i) Accept–reject
Here, the decision-maker is faced with a set of independent projects, and no constraint on the number which can be undertaken.

There may also be mutually exclusive projects where the acceptance of one project depends on the rejection of another. However, there must be a decision as to which (if any) is worthwhile.

(ii) Ranking
If some input, such as capital is limited in supply, it may well be that all 'acceptable' projects cannot be undertaken. Therefore, projects must be rank ordered subject to a given budget constraint.

The most commonly used measures of investment desirability are net present values (*NPV*) and internal rate of return (*IRR*). Gapenski (1989) defines net present value as the sum of the present values of a project's cash flow, with the present values found by discounting all flows – both costs or outflows, and inflows – at the project's cost of capital. The internal rate of return, on the other hand, is the discount rate at which the net present value of discounted cash flows is equal to zero.

The generic formulas from finance theory for these investment decision tools are as follows:

Net present value:

$$NPV = \sum_{t=0}^{n} \frac{Ct}{(1 = K)^t},$$

where C_t is the cash inflows and outflows and K the cost of capital or discount rate. Internal rate of return:

$$IRR: \sum_{t=0}^{n} \frac{Ct}{(1 + IRR)^t} = 0,$$

where C_t is the cash inflows and outflows and IRR the Internal rate of return.

These formulas are applicable to any economic investment that is expected to generate future benefits. The proper application of these formulas will lead to investment decisions that maximize the wealth of the constituent shareholders and stakeholders. It is important to note, however, that the effectiveness of the formulas depends significantly on the inclusion of all pertinent benefits and costs to a proposed investment project and it is only when this is done that one can be assured that stakeholders' wealth can be maximized.

40   *D.O. Brown, F.A. Kwansa/Hospitality Management 18 (1999) 31–43*

For the purpose of evaluating tourism projects in developing countries, the generic investment decision tools discussed above have been modified to incorporate societal benefits and costs. The proposed modified formulas for evaluating tourism investment projects are as follows:

Net present value:

$$NPV: \sum_{t=1}^{n} \frac{(B_t + P_t) - (K_t + S_t)}{(1 + i)^t} - IO.$$

Internal rate of return:

$$IRR: \sum_{t=1}^{n} \frac{(B_t + P_t) - (K_t + S_t)}{(1 + IRR)^t} - IO = 0,$$

where i is the cost of capital or discount rate, B_t the total benefits in year t, P_t the total societal/spillover benefits in year t, K_t the other project costs in year t, S_t the project's societal/spillover costs in year t, IO the initial outlay and , IRR the internal rate of return.

13. Discussion

In the case of tourism projects in developing countries, the discount rate (i) would be the cost of capital, for example, the World Bank's interest rate (where relevant), or the general market interest rate for that country. Additionally, an applicable discount rate, especially where a market interest rate is meaningless or unavailable, would be the opportunity cost of capital. That is, the potential return that could be accrued from using the same funds for another desirable project would serve as the discount rate used in this formula. Total benefits (B_t) refers to the direct sales of revenues accruing from the tourism project. This could be the sale of tickets, passes or user fees. Total societal/spillover benefits refer to the indirect benefits that result from the tourism project. These could be cash flows from derivative commercial businesses and services that are developed as a consequence of the tourism project. These will constitute the multiplier effect of the project to the region or city. Both B_t and P_t represent cash inflows adjusted for their corresponding operating costs.

Examples of other project costs, (K_t) may include cost over-runs for the project, additional capital costs that may be anticipated in the future if capital cost is not constant over the project's life. This variable may also be used to capture legitimate bribes that are paid during the negotiation, bidding and implementation of a tourism project – which constitute costs of doing business (a phenomenon peculiar in many developing countries). The project's societal or spillover costs (S_t), which are typically ignored in such analyses, will include additional law enforcement costs, environmental costs, welfare costs etc. These are unplanned indirect costs that result from the introduction of tourists into a community's environment. Shadow pricing represents

D.O. Brown, F.A. Kwansa/Hospitality Management 18 (1999) 31–43 41

one way of estimating its various components. The project's initial outlay (IO) represents the associated development and construction costs involved.

The decision rule in the application of the NPV is that a project is acceptable if its NPV is greater than zero. That is, taking into consideration the development and construction costs, any additional capital costs and estimates of societal costs. If, after discounting the cash flows at the country's cost of capital there is a residual, then the country as a whole will be gaining wealth that did not exist previously. With regard to IRR, a tourism project will be acceptable if the IRR that is calculated is greater than a country's cost of capital.

14. Limitations

In applying the proposed models suggested in this paper, it is important to note the following. First, estimating all of the relevant societal benefits and costs in many developing countries will be challenging. This is because the markets in many of these countries are not well developed and monetized. This presents problems in valuing some goods and services that may indirectly arise from a planned tourism project. Second, political risk is a key variable that may affect tourist flows into a developing country and must be considered in evaluating a tourist project. This variable can be accommodated in both the NPV and IRR decision tools through the risk-adjustment of the discount upwards if political risk is present.

15. Conclusions and implications

In assessing whether or not a tourism project should be undertaken, tourism planners in developing countries can properly make decisions by taking into account all the effects arising from the construction and operation of the project; all costs and all benefits, and therefore all societal or spillover costs also. For example, building a resort may have the following incidental consequences: (1) creation of a more than normal amount of congestion; (2) destruction of the flora and fauna in the immediate location; (3) creation of increased noise levels at the airport. These could be regarded as *negative* spillovers. Furthermore, if the resort is to be constructed on an eroding shoreline, how will clearance of land for the resort affect local streams and soil erosion, and how will this affect the beach? Each aspect is to be evaluated in the manner suggested above, and added together algebraically to the positive and negative benefits of the project, and included in the NPV and IRR calculations. This process will ensure a more comprehensive and effective method of tourism project evaluation for developing countries. Since these countries are the most vulnerable and least able to protect themselves against poorly evaluated tourism projects, the approaches suggested in this paper should help eliminate some projects which would otherwise be considered feasible and appropriate.

42   *D.O. Brown, F.A. Kwansa/Hospitality Management 18 (1999) 31–43*

References

Abelson Peter, 1996. Project Appraisal and Valuation of the Environment: General Principles and Six Case-Studies in Developing Countries. Macmillan, New York.

Bottomley Anthony, et al., 1976. Is tourist residential development worthwhile? – the anegada project. Social Development Studies, 25(1), 1–33.

Chib, S.N., 1980. Financing tourism development: A recipient's view. Tourism Management 1(4), 231–37.

Dasgupta, Ajit, K., Pearce, D.W., 1972. Cost–Benefit Analysis: Theory and Practice. Macmillan, London.

Dixon, J.A., Carpenter, R.A., Fallon, L.A., Sherman, P.B., Manopimoke, S., 1988. Economic Analysis of the Environmental Impacts of Development Projects. Earthscan Publications, London.

Dixon, J.A., Hufschmidt, M.A., (Eds.), 1986. Economic Valuation Techniques for the Environment: A Case Study Workbook. Johns Hopkins University Press, Baltimore.

Dixon, J.A., Sherman, J., 1990. Economics of Protected Areas: A New Look at the Costs and Benefits. Earthscan Publications, London.

Duffield, Brian S., 1982. Tourism: the measurement of economic and social impact. Tourism Management 3(4), 8–37.

Dwyer, Larry, Peter Forsyth, 1997. Measuring benefits and yield from foreign tourism. International Journal of Social Economics 24(1), 223–36.

Erbes, R., 1973. International Tourism and the Economy of Developing Countries. Organization for Economic Coorperation and Development, Paris.

Gapenski Louis, C., 1989. A better approach to internal rate of return. Healthcare Financial Management, 43, 93–4.

Hufschmidt, H.M., James, D.E., Meister, A.D., Bower, B.T., Dixon, J.A., 1983. Environment, Natural Systems and Development: An Economic Valuation Guide. Baltimore: Johns Hopkins University Press.

Killick Tony, 1978. Development Economics in Action: A Study of Economic Policies in Ghana. St. Martin's Press, New York.

Lehmann, A.C., 1980. Tourists, black markets and regional development in West Africa. Annals of Tourism Research 7, 103.

Lin, V.L., Loes, P.D., 1977. Tourism and Crime in Mexico: Some comments. Social Science Quarterly 58, 146–7.

Lindberg, Kreg, Rebecca L. Johnson, 1997. The economic values of tourism's social impacts. Annals of Tourism Research 24, 90–116.

Liu, J.C., Var, T., 1986. Resident attitudes toward tourism's impacts in Hawaii. Annals of Tourism Research 13(2), 193–214

Long, P.T., Perdue, R.R., Allen, L., 1990. Rural resident tourism perceptions and attitudes by community level of tourism. Journal of Travel Research 28, 3–9.

Marglin Stephen, A., 1967. Public Investment Criteria: Benefit-Cost Analysis for Planned Economic Growth. M.I.T. Press, Cambridge.

Mathieson, Alister, Geoffrey Wall., 1982. Tourism: Economic, Physical and Social Impacts. Longman: London/New York.

May Vincent, 1991. Tourism, environment, and development. Tourism Management 12(2), 112.

McPheters, L.R., Stronge, W.B., 1974. Crime as an environmental externality of tourism: Florida. Land Economics, 50, 288–92.

Mill, Robert, Morrison, Alastair, M., 1985. The Tourism System: an Introductory Text. Prentice Hall, New Jersey.

Milne, S., 1990. The Impact of Tourism Development in Small Pacific Island States: An Overview. New Zealand Journal of Geography 89, 16–21.

Misham, E.J., 1973. Economics for Social Decisions: Elements of Cost Benefit Analysis. Praeger Publishers: New York.

Rodenburg, E.E., 1980. The Effects of Scale in Economic Development: Tourism in Bali. Annals of Tourism Research, 7, 21–37.

D.O. Brown, F.A. Kwansa/Hospitality Management 18 (1999) 31–43 43

Rothenberg, J., 1965. Urban renewal programs In: Dorfman, R. (Ed.), Measuring Benefits of Government Investments. Brookings Institution, Washington.

Sargent, J.R., 1967. The limits of tourism as a growth generator. Development Digest 5(2).

Seward, Shirly B., Bernard K. Spinrad. (Eds.), 1982. Tourism in the Caribbean: Ottawa: International Development Research Center.

Sinclair M. Thea, 1998. Tourism and economic development: a survey. Journal of Development Studies 34(5), 1–51.

Weitzer, Ronald., 1991. Prostitutes' rights in the united States: the failure of a movement. The Sociological Quarterly 32(1), 23–41.

[10]

TOURISM AND DEVELOPMENT POLICY: A QUANTITATIVE APPRAISAL*

ABSTRACT

Within the last decade the promotion of tourism has gained a prominent place in many development plans. Recently, however, doubts have been cast on previous attempts to analyse its contribution to development. This paper describes a quantitative technique which remedies some of their more obvious defects. The method is then applied to the Turkish situation, and the implications of the results are examined in the light of an explicit policy preference function.

1. The Quantitative Analysis of Tourism

In the past decade international tourism has been promoted in developing countries as a solution to some of their more pressing problems. Although for a number of these countries tourism has indeed proved a means of relieving growing unemployment and foreign exchange shortage, unfortunately, for other developing countries the returns from tourism have been rather disappointing. As a result doubts have been raised about the wisdom of tourism promotion and criticism directed at techniques used to analyse its impact on developing economies. Specifically, the use of tourism's 'foreign trade' multiplier as a measure of tourism's impact on the domestic economy has been singled out for attack. The conventional approach has been to quantify the tourism multiplier in broad aggregate terms (Craig, 1963; Gorra, 1967; Checchi, 1969; Peters, 1969; IUOTO, 1970). Unfortunately, the lack of integration which characterizes these economies suggests the macro approach involves important errors in aggregation. Recognition of the need to divide the economy into more homogeneous categories has resulted in the adoption of a disaggregative approach to the problem, based on input-output tables (Clement, 1961; Pakistan State Planning Centre, 1965; Turkish State Planning Organization, 1968). However, such attempts have suffered from defects common to the input-output approach. Typically output rather than the more policy-relevant income multipliers have been estimated, and all final demand repercussions are ignored. While the method does offer the advantages of a disaggregative approach to the problem, there is more than a suspicion that the gains in disaggregation are outweighed by the neglect of final demand effects. More generally, the use of the multiplier as the conceptual scheme of analysis has been criticized on two other grounds. Firstly, its relevance to policy has been questioned because it concentrates on short-run adjustments while the principal problems of developing countries are typically viewed as long-run. Secondly, its dependence on unrealistic assumptions, particularly that of supply elasticity in all sectors of the economy, has been

* This paper is derived from a thesis recently submitted for the degree of D.Phil., at the University of York (Diamond, 1973). I would like to acknowledge the debt to my thesis supervisor, Professor A. T. Peacock, with the usual absolution. The author, a member of the Public Sector Studies Research Programme at York, acknowledges the financial assistance received from the Social Science Research Council.

criticized as restricting its usefulness for developing economies. As a result, it has recently been claimed that one should abandon this approach in favour of cost-benefit analysis (Bryden, 1973).

However, when selecting a theoretical framework with which to analyse the policy implications of tourism in developing economies, it must be recognized that no single approach can hope to meet all the demands policy analysts are likely to make on it. Because of this, the cost benefit approach is likely to provide only some of the answers. Nor can one agree with the claim that the multiplier approach should be rejected 'as yielding no useful guidelines to policy makers as regards the merits of tourism as compared with alternatives' (Bryden, 1973, p. 217). On the contrary, it will be demonstrated how, with suitable modifications, this approach can make a useful contribution to policy-making, especially in the short-run. It should be appreciated that both approaches are addressed to different policy questions, and because of this there is no antithesis between them. The cost-benefit approach stresses the need to make sensible investment decisions. Thus the typical policy question it seeks to answer is of the form: what are the long-run gains from increasing capacity in the tourism industry and how do these compare with equivalent investments in other industries? However, apart from this planning problem, the policy analyst may also care to examine the present performance of the tourism industry in the light of some preference function. Here the question posed by the multiplier approach takes the form: what is the impact of an extra unit of tourism expenditure, and given a certain policy objective function, how does this compare with an equivalent increment in the demand for the output of other sectors?

It must be recognized that all measuring devices, like cost-benefit analysis, not only are designed for a particular purpose, but also for use in a particular economic and institutional environment.[1] In so far as the real world diverges from the required norm then the greater are the inaccuracies in measurement and the more frequent are unmeasurable quantities encountered. Certainly, it is by no means clear that the underlying assumptions of the multiplier approach are less realistic than those of cost-benefit analysis. Indeed the stereotype of under-developed economies experiencing full utilization of their productive capacity is under review. Several recent studies suggest that low capacity utilization, particularly in industry, is endemic to these economies (Little, Scitovsky, Scott, 1970; Winston, 1971). Certainly recent Turkish experience seems to confirm this (IBRD, 1971). In the following section two different specifications of a short-run model of income determination for the Turkish economy are described, each is based on different assumptions as to the cause of economic 'slack' in the economy. While the simplifying assumptions on which both versions are based — rigid factor proportions, linearity in behavioural functions, constancy in relative prices — are undoubtedly limiting, it can be fairly claimed that they are not disabling and still permit a fruitful assessment of tourism's impact on the Turkish economy. Further, it will be shown how this framework is sufficiently flexible to incorporate variables deemed important for the purposes of policy making.

---

[1] Perhaps one of the most thorough attempts to gear cost-benefit analysis to the particular circumstances of UDCs is the method suggested by Little and Mirrlees (1969).

2. *Two Analytical Models*

MODEL A

This may be described by a set of balance equations, analogous to an input-output system, but admitting some components of final demand. The fundamental balance equation for each sector, i, is expressed in equation (1):

$$X_i = \sum_{j=1}^{N} a_{ij} X_j - m^*_i X_i + \sum_{j=1}^{N} c_{ij} Y_j - m_i Y_i + (E_i + I_i) \qquad (1)$$

$$\underbrace{\hphantom{X_i = \sum a_{ij} X_j - m^*_i X_i}}_{\substack{\text{intermediary} \\ \text{demands}}} \quad \underbrace{\hphantom{\sum c_{ij} Y_j - m_i Y_i}}_{\substack{\text{endogenous} \\ \text{final demands} \\ (=d)}} \quad \underbrace{\hphantom{(E_i + I_i)}}_{\substack{\text{exogenous} \\ \text{final demands} \\ (=f)}}$$

Where: a_{ij} = intermediary demand of goods from sector i for the output of sector j, a function of the output of j;

X_i = output of sector i;

m^*_i = import coefficient of sector i, expressing the quantity of imported input required per unit of output;

m_i = sector i's import propensity, dependent on income;

Y_i = income of sector i;

c_{ij} = final demand deliveries from sector i to sector j, a function of sector j's income level;

E_i = export deliveries by sector i;

I_i = investment deliveries by sector i.

Re-writing (1) in matrix notation:

$$(I - A + M^*) \, x = d + f \qquad (2)$$

This represents a partially closed Leontief input-output system, where:

I = unit matrix of order n;

A = square matrix of input-output coefficients, a_{ij};

M^* = diagonal matrix of import coefficients, m^*_i;

x = column vector of sector output levels;

d = column vector of consumption demand (including imports);

f = column vector of exogenous final demands.

Treating final consumption and import demand, d, as an endogenous variable, it is possible to transfer the household sector to the processing sectors, in such a way that $d = D.v$, where:

D_{ii} = $(c_{ii} - m_i)$, sector consumption coefficients minus import propensities;

D_{ij} = c_{ij} when $i \neq j$;

and v = vector of value-added coefficients, v_i.

By definition, income in the Leontief system equals total output (X) minus intermediary inputs (R): $Y = X - R$

and $R = A.x$

then $y = (I - A).x$, when y, vector of income levels,

but $y = v$, vector of value-added coefficients,

thus $d = D. (I - A).x$.

It is now possible to re-write (2) assuming an increment of exogenous demand, Δf:

$$(I - A + M^*) \, \Delta x = D(I - A) \, \Delta x + \Delta f \tag{3}$$

which may be written in the form:

$$[(I - D) \, (I - A) + M^*] \, \Delta x = \Delta f . \tag{4}$$

Solving for the increase in output:

$$\Delta x = [(I - D) \, (I - A) + M^*]^{-1} . \, \Delta f . \tag{5}$$

This inverse matrix represents the output multiplier matrix. The multipliers for each sector, derived by summing along columns, include both supply *and* demand repercussions between sectors as well as induced leakages abroad caused by the production process. In previous studies the latter have been ignored, or inconsistently treated in an analogous manner to consumption imports.

MODEL B

Although the above model has some obvious drawbacks, it represents a considerable improvement over previous methods and yields results in a form more amenable for policy decisions. Yet its relevance may be questioned because of the adoption of the standard Keynesian assumption that overall deficiency in effective demand is the cause of economic 'slack' in the economy. Turkish experience, like that of many industrializing countries, has been one of recurring supply bottlenecks, particularly those caused by shortages of foreign exchange needed to purchase essential inputs (cf. Pearson, 1969, Annex I). To depict the Turkish situation with greater realism and hence gain a more meaningful estimate of tourism's multiplier, an attempt must be made to incorporate such supply constraints into the Keynesian income generating process.

This may be accomplished by re-writing the balance equations (1) in their inequality form:

$$X_i \geqslant \sum_{j=1}^{N} a_{ij} X_j - m^*_i X_i + \sum_{j=1}^{N} c_{ij} Y_j - m_i Y_i + (E_i + I_i) \tag{6}$$

The following capacity constraint may be introduced to augment the above set of inequalities:

$$\left[B + \sum_{i=1}^{N} b_i X_i \right] \leqslant 0 \tag{7}$$

where B = balance of payments, a constant such that the trade balance must not fall below an exogenously given limit. For expository convenience this was assumed zero, implying the desirability of an overall trade balance.

b_i = balance on foreign account for each sector, given by the difference in export and import coefficients (see Appendix I).

Combining equations (6) with equation (7), and specifying a unit exogenous injection in each sector, then by maximizing output subject to these constraints, we describe the following programming problem:

$$\text{Maximize} \quad \sum_{i=1}^{N} x_i$$

$$\text{Subject to} \quad [I - \mathcal{Z}] \, x \geqslant \varDelta f$$

$$\sum_{i=1}^{N} b_i \, x_i \leqslant B$$

$$\text{and all} \quad x_i \geqslant 0$$

where I = the unit matrix;

$\mathcal{Z}$ = matrix of endogenous demands $[= D\,(I - A) + A - M^*]$, as defined in equation (3).

The equations are solved by reducing the above system to its normal form by introducing artificial variables and employing the revised simplex algorithm (Danzig and Orchard-Hays, 1953). The constrained multiplier matrix is derived from the simplex tableau for the optimal basis in the following manner.

Given the standard linear programming problem, Maximize $z = cx$, subject to $Ax = b$, and all $x \geqslant 0$. For the above problem matrix A represents the n equations of (6) plus the foreign balance constraint (7). Vector b equals a unit vector of final demand, $\varDelta f$, augmented by the foreign balance target. In the revised simplex technique the objective function is included as a new constraint, so we may write the problem in partitioned form:

$$\begin{pmatrix} \mathrm{I} & -c \\ \mathrm{o} & A \end{pmatrix} \begin{pmatrix} z \\ x \end{pmatrix} = \begin{pmatrix} \mathrm{o} \\ b \end{pmatrix} \tag{8}$$

or

$$\begin{pmatrix} z \\ x \end{pmatrix} = \begin{pmatrix} \mathrm{I} & -c \\ \mathrm{o} & A \end{pmatrix}^{-1} \begin{pmatrix} \mathrm{o} \\ b \end{pmatrix} \tag{9}$$

By choosing an optimal basis, $\hat{B}$, of inter-industry activities to maximize the objective function, $z = \bar{z}$, at output levels, $\bar{x}$, then:

$$\begin{pmatrix} \bar{z} \\ \bar{x} \end{pmatrix} = \begin{pmatrix} \mathrm{I} & -c \\ \mathrm{o} & \hat{B} \end{pmatrix}^{-1} \begin{pmatrix} \mathrm{o} \\ b \end{pmatrix} \tag{10}$$

or

$$\begin{pmatrix} \bar{z} \\ \bar{x} \end{pmatrix} = \begin{pmatrix} \mathrm{I} & c\hat{B}^{-1} \\ \mathrm{o} & \hat{B}^{-1} \end{pmatrix} \begin{pmatrix} \mathrm{o} \\ b \end{pmatrix} \tag{11}$$

Since the partitioned matrix represents the revised simplex tableau for the optimal basis, solving for optimal output levels gives:

$$\bar{x} = \hat{B}^{-1} \cdot b \tag{12}$$

With b equal to the unit vector, the matrix $\hat{B}^{-1}$ is equivalent to the constrained multiplier matrix. Summing by columns, estimates of the constrained output multipliers are derived for comparison with the unconstrained multipliers of equation (5).

The 1967 Turkish input-output table was used to identify matrices A and M^*, and matrix D was derived from surveys of the size and pattern of consumption

TOURISM AND DEVELOPMENT POLICY 41

TABLE 1

ESTIMATES OF INDUSTRY OUTPUT MULTIPLIERS

Industry		Estimated Multipliers		
No.	Description	MODEL A (1)	MODEL B (2)	Percentage Difference (1) — (2)
1	Agriculture	2.766	2.440	−11.8
2	Forestry	2.565	2.261	−11.8
3	Animal Husbandry, fishing	2.820	2.488	−11.7
4	Coal Mining	2.882	2.534	−12.1
5	Iron-ore Mining	2.317	2.013	−13.1
6	Other mining, quarrying	3.181	2.877	− 9.6
7	Sugar	2.700	2.389	−11.5
8	Tobacco	2.455	2.159	−12.1
9	Alcoholic Beverages	2.587	2.282	−11.8
10	Other food products	2.800	2.472	−11.7
11	Textiles, apparels	2.697	2.369	−12.2
12	Wood Products	2.634	2.309	−12.4
13	Paper and Printing	1.777	1.478	−16.8
14	Leather	2.268	1.968	−13.2
15	Rubber, plastics	1.612	0.768	−52.4
16	Chemicals, pharmaceuticals	2.059	1.167	−43.3
17	Fertilizers	2.822	1.960	−30.5
18	Petroleum Refining	1.893	1.244	−34.3
19	Non-metallic Products	2.395	1.697	−29.2
20	Cement	2.610	1.694	−35.1
21	Iron and Steel	2.502	1.784	−28.7
22	Non-ferrous metals	2.709	2.124	−21.6
23	Metal Products	2.231	1.247	−44.1
24	Non-electrical machinery	1.915	1.173	−38.7
25	Electrical Machinery	2.080	1.237	−40.6
26	Transport equipment	2.204	1.650	−25.1
27	Electricity	2.713	1.899	−30.0
28	Railway Transportation	2.807	1.792	−36.2
29	Other Transportation	3.258	1.777	−45.5
30	Trade, distribution	3.498	2.365	−32.4
31	Communications	2.927	1.609	−45.0
32	Banking, insurance, co-ops	2.983	1.921	−35.6
33	Professions, personal services	3.091	2.455	−20.6
34	Non-building Construction	2.660	1.968	−26.2
35	Building Construction	2.916	2.161	−25.9
36	Public Services	4.862	4.463	− 8.2

carried out by the State Institute of Statistics.[1] Other data and their sources are described in Appendix I. The results obtained from equation (5) and equation (12) are shown in Table 1 (columns 1 and 2 respectively), as is the percentage difference between them (column 3).

3. *Tourism's Relative Impact*

Having quantified multipliers for each of the industrial categories of the input-output table, we are still faced with the problem that the tourist industry is not specifically identified. Narrowly defined, tourism consists of the accommodation industry (e.g. hotels, pensions, guesthouses, etc); broadly defined, one could conceivably include external transportation such as airlines, shipping lines, as well as all domestic subsidiary activities such as catering, entertainment, local transportation, etc. Ambiguity is increased by the fact that international tourism is only a minor part of the tourism industry in Turkey.[2] International tourists use much of the 'plant' and facilities available to domestic tourists so that it is difficult to impute an exact fraction to the income generated by international tourism. Difficulties are further increased by the industry's multi-product character and the nature of the activities making up the 'mix' of tourism services. In less developed economies suffering from population pressure, like Turkey, one can expect activities like personal services, local transportation, small-scale distribution, etc., to conceal under-employment and over-capacity. This makes the measurement of the extra inputs required to meet extra tourist demand extremely difficult to measure.

With such qualifications in mind it is proposed to use average expenditure patterns for foreign tourists as the best indication of the industry's composition. Thus the pattern adopted in the State Planning Officer's attempt to measure tourism's multiplier (S.P.O., 1968), is allocated to the relevant industrial categories in the input-output table to derive a 'composite' multiplier for international tourism. This is shown in the final row of Table 2.

Model A thus yielded a 'tourism multiplier' of 3.2 in terms of output. From an examination of Table 1 it is apparent that this is higher than the average for the economy as a whole, supporting tourism's favourable image. However, the estimated tourism multiplier in Model B is 2.3, which represents a notable relative decline from its position in Model A. The foreign exchange constraint thus restricts attainable output for tourism industries on average by over a quarter (27%). It is also noticeable from column 3 of Table 1 that there is a wide disparity between sectors in their sensitivity to the foreign exchange constraint. The agricultural complex (industry nos. 1–14) shows an average cutback in output of 12 per cent as compared to 30–40 per cent in the industrial sector. The latter result is caused by the heavy import requirements of industries which include assembly plants. What is perhaps more surprising is the sensitivity of the service sector to the foreign exchange gap. This is not merely an indication of its poor export performance and its relatively high import intensity, but also the structural characteristics of the economy. Since services display a high

---

[1] The actual data sources and the method of computation are contained in Diamond (1973, Appendices 2A and 2B).
[2] In 1968 equal to 30 per cent by numbers of tourists, according to the State Planning Organization (1968, p. 6).

TOURISM AND DEVELOPMENT POLICY 43

degree of inter-dependence with the rest of the economy, especially the modern industrial sector (industry nos. 21–26), they are particularly sensitive to the constraints operating on other sectors'[1] Or course, the importance of inter-industry linkages also implies sensitivity to any other constraints (e.g. in agricultural output, energy supplies, skilled manpower, etc.), which we may care to include in our analysis. Rather than pursuing this possibility, it is sufficient to note the degree to which this move to realism in initial assumptions causes a relative decline in tourism's multiplier effects.[2]

TABLE 2

ESTIMATES OF THE TOURISM MULTIPLIER, 1967

Type of Tourist Demand	Percentage of Total Expenditure(a)	Industry Code No.(b)	Output Multipliers(c)	
			Model A	Model B
Overnight Stay	27	33	3.091	2.455
Food and Drink	32	30, 33(d)	3.294	2.411
Shopping	15	30	3.498	2.365
Tours and Entertainment	13	33	3.091	2.455
Local Transport	13	29	2.258	1.777
Weighted estimate of the tourism multiplier	=		3.198	2.339

Notes: (a) source (S.P.O., 1968, p. 17.); these percentages are used as weights for the industry multipliers.
(b) see Table 1 for descriptions of these code numbers.
(c) source Table 1.
(d) allocated equally between the two sectors.

A difficulty with these comparative statics results is the possibility of their sensitivity to different assumptions about transactions velocity. For example, Clement found considerable discrepancy between multipliers derived from different estimates of how fast money would turn over in the economy (Clement, 1961). To investigate this possibility the above comparative statics multiplier must be formulated in dynamic terms. Suppose the process of adjustment from an old equilibrium output level, vector x', to a new equilibrium consequent on an exogenous increase in the final demand vector, Δf, takes m time periods, however defined. Then time period one's vector of output levels, x_1, can be described by $x_1 = x' + \Delta f$. In the next period output will increase not only by the exogenous increase Δf, but also by a fraction of the first period's output that is respent within the sectoral system. This fraction can be shown to represent a matrix of spending coefficients defined in equation (2) equal to

---

[1] For a demonstration of this and a detailed examination of the structure of inter-industry transactions in the Turkish economy, see (Diamond, 1974).
[2] Certainly both Models A and B cast doubts on previous estimates of the Turkish tourism multiplier which have tended to be rather optimistic. For example, the State Planning Organization estimated the tourism multiplier as 3.89 (S.P.O., 1968).

44   TOURISM AND DEVELOPMENT POLICY

$(D (I - A) + A - M^*)$, henceforth called matrix Z. If spending is assumed to die out over m time periods then at a new equilibrium output, x_t, the increase in output which can be expected is given by:

$$x_t - x' = [(I - Z^n) / (I - Z)] \cdot \Delta f \qquad (13)$$

This equation represents the dynamic matrix multiplier from which the output change $(x_t - x')$ for any time period, $t = 1, 2, \ldots m$, can be derived.[1] By experiment it was found that the dynamic process approximated the comparative statics solution within 1 per cent difference when the series was truncated at $t = 9$ time periods. Thus employing Clement's assumptions and truncating the dynamic multiplier process at $t = 5$ and $t = 6$ resulted in approximations no more than 5–10 per cent below those obtained for the tourism multiplier using the comparative statics specification. Only in the case of $t < 5$ were multipliers substantially changed.

Apart from sensitivity to assumptions about transactions velocity and supply constraints, it is important to analyse the sensitivity of the results to the values of critical coefficients. In particular, it should be apparent that our estimates of the tourism multiplier were derived from the assumption that international tourism requires the same level of imported inputs as activity generally associated with the supplying sectors, and at the same time, displays the same average return in foreign exchange. Two features of international tourism seem to contradict this easy assumption: firstly, tourism may require a much higher import content; and secondly, it may have a higher export coefficient. An official estimate of the tourism import coefficient of 8.4 per cent,[2] much in line with estimates for other countries,[3] was allocated to the different supplying sectors. A sensitivity analysis was performed on both models A and B which revealed that tourism's multiplier effects were not radically altered by the value assumed for the import coefficient. For example, an increase in the import coefficient of 10 per cent only reduced the tourism multiplier by 2–4 per cent in both models. However, a different picture emerged when a more realistic value for the export coefficient was taken. This was based on official Turkish estimates of the international tourism industry having a value added of 30 m. U.S. dollars and earning 21 m. U.S. dollars of foreign exchange in 1968 at current rates of exchange (Ministry of Tourism, 1969). The effect of the new export coefficient when allocated to sectors in proportion to the expenditure pattern of Table 3 is to considerably alter the foreign balance constraint described by equation (7) in Model B. As a consequence the tourism multiplier estimated from Model B increased from 2.3 to 2.7 — a 18 per cent increase. The reason why an increase in the export coefficient of almost 40 per cent only yielded a 18 per cent increase in output is apparent from the argument presented above: namely, the high degree of inter-industry dependence of these service sectors causes them to be highly sensitive to the foreign exchange constraint operating in other sectors.

---

[1] At the limit, $t \to \infty$, then: $x_t - x' = \Delta f / (I - Z) = (I - Z)^{-1} \cdot \Delta f$, which corresponds exactly to the comparative static multiplier described above. The power series method is, of course, an established method for approximating the inverse of a square matrix having all principal minors positive.

[2] Imputed imported inputs for tourist spending patterns are given in Ministry of Tourism (1969).

[3] See, for example, various estimates quoted in Peters (1968, Chapter 6).

5. *Some Policy Implications*

The above multipliers are measured in terms of unweighted increases in output which are obviously not the most relevant indices for policy formulation. Rather, for policy purposes the multipliers must be related to an objective function reflecting Turkish planning priorities. The way in which long-term development aims have generated acute short-term problems suggests some likely policy weightings. For example, the single-minded pursuit of rapid industrialization resulted in a rather capital-intensive form of development throughout the 1960s, to the detriment of employment. Unfortunately the employment position also suffered from an extremely rapid population increase and in urban areas was further aggravated by a substantial rural influx. Distinct from unemployment, poverty also remains a crucial problem. With 60 per cent of the population still dependent on agricultural production, the emphasis on industrial expansion has inevitably resulted in the benefits from development by-passing the majority of workers. Further, industrialization by a strategy of import substitution has implied a continual dependence for foreign exchange on the earnings of a few staple exports facing stagnating international demand. Unfortunately there has been a minimal increase in industrial exports. As a result, despite the considerable contribution of workers' remittances, there is evidence that shortage of foreign exchange is jeopardizing Turkey's industrialization effort. Recent Turkish experience thus suggests that the long-run priority of industrialization must be reconciled with pressing short-run needs to increase income, employment and foreign exchange earnings while economizing in the use of capital.

By adopting simple linear functions, these four objectives may be incorporated into the above short-run analysis. For example, if the concern is with income creation, by multiplying the industry output multipliers with coefficients of value-added per unit of output, the relevant income multipliers are derived. In a similar fashion it is possible to use as policy weights ratios of employment per unit of output, incremental capital-output ratios, and net foreign exchange used per unit of output[1] (see Appendix I for data and sources). The results give estimates of the income and employment created, and the capital and foreign exchange used, per unit of final demand in each industry. The correlations between them indicate the degree of compatability between different policy objectives. These are shown in Table 3 for both Models A and B.

From Table 3 it is evident that there are important inter-industry policy conflicts. Most noticeable is the degree to which industries minimizing the negative effect on the balance of payments perform poorly when judged by other criteria. This results in a negative relationship between the objective of minimizing the use of foreign exchange and the objectives of maximizing income and employment (e.g. for Model A the correlations are -0.65 and -0.49 respectively). In a similar fashion, industries which allow a maximum return in employment and income after all multiplier repercussions have been accounted for, tend to be heavy users of capital. Thus while there appears some degree of

---

[1] Defined as the difference between exports delivered per unit of output and imported inputs required per unit of output. (The export and import coefficients, and their sources, are shown in Appendix I.)

46   TOURISM AND DEVELOPMENT POLICY

policy compatibility between maximizing employment and income (correlation
= 0.51), these objectives are inconsistent with the aims of minimizing capital
used and minimizing the negative effect on the foreign balance. At the same
time, capital intensive industries also tend to be heavy net users of foreign
exchange. These tend to be the newer metal-based and energy industries which
either do not directly export and require imported inputs, or even when they do
export they have a large proportion of assembly plants heavily dependent on
imported inputs. The results for Model B present a similar picture. If anything,
inter-industry policy conflicts are increased under the assumption that expansion
in the economy is constrained by the shortage of foreign exchange. In particular,
our results reveal the dangers of maximizing the employment or income per unit
of final demand while neglecting required inputs of scarce resources such as
capital and foreign exchange.

TABLE 3

CORRELATIONS BETWEEN INDUSTRIES BY POLICY OBJECTIVE

MODEL A

Objective:	Maximize Income	Maximize Employment	Minimize Capital	Minimize Foreign Exchange
Max. Income	1.0			
Max. Employment	0.51	1.0		
Min. Capital	−0.50	−0.21	1.0	
Min. F. Exchange	−0.65	−0.49	0.39	1.0

MODEL B

Objective:	Maximize Income	Maximize Employment	Minimize Capital	Minimize Foreign Exchange
Max. Income	1.0			
Max. Employment	0.78	1.0		
Min. Capital	−0.53	−0.40	1.0	
Min. F. Exchange	−0.79	−0.60	0.49	1.0

Of course, tourism, characterized as a labour-intensive foreign exchange
earner, appears particularly attractive in a situation characterized by foreign
balance and capital constraints. Our results permit a quantitative assessment of
the policy implications of tourism compared with other industries. In order to
gauge their relative impact on the Turkish economy, industries were ranked by
each policy weighting. The top six rankings are displayed for Models A and B in
Table 4. For comparison the tourism multiplier is measured under the most
favourable assumptions that its import coefficient is no higher than the average
for its supply sectors, and that its export coefficient is almost 40 per cent higher
than the average. Thus tourism is compared with the other sectors of the
Turkish economy on the basis of an output multiplier of 3.2 for Model A and 2.7
for Model B. The results for Model A suggests tourism performs best when the

objective is minimizing foreign exchange used and maximizing income, but performs rather poorly when the objective is minimizing the use of capital. Tourism's relative impact on employment is also rather disappointing (i.e. ranked only 9th by this objective). It should be noted that the effect of including the foreign exchange constraint (Model B) alters tourism's relative position. The industry becomes an even more attractive policy option when the objective is to minimize foreign exchange used or maximize income, but its relative position with respect to maximizing employment and minimizing capital is not noticeably improved.

TABLE 4

INDUSTRIES WITHIN THE FIRST SIX RANKINGS BY POLICY OBJECTIVE

Rank	Maximize Income	Maximize Employment	Minimize Capital	Minimize Foreign Exchange
	MODEL A			
1	No. 36	No. 1	No. 34	No. 6
2	No. 30	No. 3	No. 35	No. 1
3	No. 6	No. 36	No. 15	Tourism
4	No. 31	No. 30	No. 25	No. 22
5	No. 32	No. 28	No. 3	No. 30
6	No. 29	No. 31	No. 23	No. 36
	Tourism's rank = 7	Tourism's rank = 9	Tourism's rank = 20	
	MODEL B			
1	No. 36	No. 1	No. 15	No. 6
2	No. 6	No. 3	No. 34	Tourism
3	No. 30	No. 36	No. 35	No. 1
4	Tourism	No. 2	No. 25	No. 22
5	No. 1	No. 30	No. 23	No. 30
6	No. 4	No. 4	No. 24	No. 36
		Tourism's rank = 10	Tourism's rank = 15	

The typical picture of tourism as a labour-intensive sector facing a bouyant international demand, hence a good income and foreign exchange earner, is not entirely borne out by the above results. When all inter-industry repercussions are accounted for, tourism is not as labour-intensive as is sometimes suggested, and the maintenance and expansion of this productive capacity is rather capital intensive. Moreover, although the direct effect on the foreign balance is more favourable than most sectors, due to its high degree of integration with those sectors which are constrained by foreign exchange availability, the indirect impact of tourism as a foreign exchange earner is less than might be expected. Our findings thus suggest that the usual arguments for tourism promotion in an overall development strategy should only be accepted in the Turkish case with certain reservations. In so far as the Turkish situation typifies the experience of this industry in other developing economies facing similar problems, our analysis suggests the need for greater circumspection in assessing the potentialities of tourism promotion as a means of solving the economic problems of developing countries.

J. DIAMOND

INSTITUTE OF ECONOMIC AND SOCIAL RESEARCH, YORK

REFERENCES

1. J. M. BRYDEN, *Tourism and Development: A Case Study of the Commonwealth Caribbean* (Cambridge, 1973).
2. BRYDEN, J. and FABER, M., 'Multiplying the Tourism Multiplier', *Social and Economic Studies*, Vol 20 (March 1971), pp. 61–82.
3. CHECCHI and Co., *A Plan for Managing the Growth of Tourism in the Commonwealth of the Bahama Islands* (Washington, D.C., 1969).
4. CLEMENT, H. G., *The Future of Tourism in the Pacific and Far East* (U.S. Department of Commerce, Washington, 1961).
5. CRAIG, P. G., *The Future Growth of Hawaiian Tourism and its Impact on the State and Neighbouring Islands* (Economic Research Centre, Hawaii, 1962).
6. DANTZIG, G. B., and ORCHARD-HAYS, W., 'Notes on linear programming: part V — alternative algorithm for the revised simplex method using product form for the inverse', *RAND Corporation Research Memorandum*, 1953, RM — 1268.
7. DIAMOND, J., 'The Economic Impact of International Tourism on Developing Countries: The Case of Turkey in the 1960s' (unpublished D.Phil thesis, University of York, 1973).
8. DIAMOND, J., 'The Analysis of Structural Constraints in Developing Economies: A Case Study', *Oxford Bulletin of Economics and Statistics*, Vol. 36 (May 1974), pp. 95–108.
9. International Bank for Reconstruction and Development, *The Development Prospects of Turkey* (Report No. EMA — 30a, New York, 1971).
10. International Union of Official Tour Operators, *Economic Review of World Tourism, 1970* (Geneva, 1970).
11. GORRA, P., *Nouvelle Etude Prospective sur L'Apport du Tourisme au developpement economique du Liban* (Department Recherches et Documentation, Lebanon, 1967).
12. LITTLE, I. M. D., and MIRRLEES, J. A., *Manual of Industrial Project Analysis, Vol. II* (O.E.C.D. Development Centre, Paris, 1969).
13. LITTLE, I. M. D., SCITOVSKY, T., and SCOTT, M., *Industry and Trade in Some Developing Countries* (Oxford University Press, 1970).
14. Ministry of Tourism, *Development of Tourism in Turkey* (Ankara, 1969).
15. Pakistan State Planning Centre, *The Master Plan for Development of Tourism in Pakistan* (Karachi, 1965).
16. PEARSON, L. B., *Partners in Development: Report of the Commission on International Development* (New York, 1969).
17. PETERS, M., *International Tourism* (London, 1968).
18. State Planning Organization, *Report on the Tourism Sector* (Ankara, 1968).
19. WINSTON, G. C., 'Capacity Utilization in Economic Development', *Economic Journal*, Vol. 81 (March 1971), pp. 36–60.

TOURISM AND DEVELOPMENT POLICY 49

Appendix I

The Data and Sources

	Industry	Labour-Output Ratio(a)	Value-added Ratio(b)	Import Coefficient (c)	Export Coefficient (d)	I.C.O.R. (e)
No.	Description					
1	Agriculture	119.1	0.7714	0.0148	0.1075	2.300
2	Forestry	49.6	0.6808	0.0059	0.0153	3.049
3	Animal Husbandry	105.8	0.5588	0.0011	0.0145	0.430
4	Coal Mining	35.2	0.7407	0.0039	0.0000	3.171
5	Iron-ore Mining	36.1	0.5555	0.0634	0.0000	3.171
6	Other mining, quarrying	37.1	0.8355	0.0048	0.1442	3.171
7	Sugar	8.5	0.5287	0.0013	0.0303	0.600
8	Tobacco	11.4	0.5487	0.0040	0.0000	0.943
9	Alcoholic beverages	6.8	0.5927	0.1090	0.0063	1.149
10	Other food products	8.5	0.2513	0.0092	0.0261	0.443
11	Textiles, apparels	20.3	0.5261	0.0692	0.0031	0.800
12	Wood products	21.5	0.3509	0.0206	0.0005	0.632
13	Paper and printing	15.8	0.3365	0.2769	0.0024	0.987
14	Leather	10.6	0.3368	0.1235	0.0524	0.641
15	Rubber, plastics	9.8	0.3673	0.4406	0.0029	0.534
16	Chemicals, pharmaceuticals	10.5	0.3859	0.3074	0.0107	0.902
17	Fertilizers	22.9	0.5384	0.0897	0.0000	0.999
18	Petroleum refining	1.0	0.5428	0.1513	0.0010	1.042
19	Non-metallic products	22.9	0.5429	0.0718	0.0044	0.677
20	Cement	17.6	0.4642	0.0013	0.0000	1.425
21	Iron and steel	22.9	0.3814	0.0639	0.0038	2.090
22	Non-ferrous metals	17.6	0.5428	0.1066	0.1618	2.066
23	Metal products	6.1	0.3357	0.1578	0.0010	0.552
24	Non-electrical machinery	11.4	0.3646	0.3089	0.0006	0.699
25	Electrical machinery	12.5	0.4482	0.2236	0.0010	0.500
26	Transport equipment	19.6	0.3483	0.2523	0.0004	0.562
27	Electricity	2.5	0.5438	0.0020	0.0000	7.500
28	Railway transportation	48.1	0.5890	0.0174	0.0328	4.875
29	Other transportation	24.6	0.6848	0.0075	0.0339	1.250
30	Trade, distribution	38.9	0.8651	0.0001	0.0424	0.400
31	Communications	45.1	0.8162	0.0000	0.0000	3.800
32	Banking, insurance, co-ops	30.4	0.7918	0.0005	0.0053	0.500
33	Professions, personal services	25.1	0.5889	0.0153	0.0458	0.632
34	Non-building construction	30.8	0.3778	0.0149	0.0000	0.234
35	Building construction	30.8	0.5918	0.0330	0.0000	0.234
36	Public services	30.4	0.9426	0.0037	0.0238	3.200

4

50   TOURISM AND DEVELOPMENT POLICY

NOTES TO APPENDIX I

(a) Numbers employed per m.TL. output, 1967 current prices. Source: N. Ozfirat and
     V. Dincerler, *Türk Imalat Sanayiinin Yapisi ve Etkenligi* (State Planning Organiza-
     tion, Ankara, 1969).

(b) Value added divided by total output at factor cost (1967 prices). Source: State
     Planning Organization, *Inter-industry Transactions Matrix for Turkey, 1967* (Ankara,
     1971).

(c) Intermediate imports (c.i.f.) m.TL. at official exchange rates, divided by total
     output at factor cost (1967 prices). Source: as (b).

(d) Exports in m.TL. valued at ex factory prices net of internal distribution and
     transport margins (at official exchange rates) divided by total output at factor cost
     (1967 prices). Source: as (b).

(e) Incremental capital-output ratios are estimated in m.TL. at base year prices, 1967,
     by S. Yanin and N. Uras, *Uçuncu Beşilylik Kalkinna Plani Doneminin Sermaye —
     Uretim Illskileri* (State Planning Organization, Ankara, 1971).

[11]

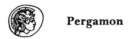
Pergamon

Annals of Tourism Research, Vol. 23, No. 1, pp. 32–47, 1996
Copyright © 1996 Elsevier Science Ltd
Printed in Great Britain. All rights reserved
0160-7383/96 $15.00+0.00

0160-7383(95)00041-0

THE ECONOMIC IMPACT OF TOURISM IN THE SEYCHELLES

Brian Archer
John Fletcher
University of Surrey, UK

Abstract: The paper describes the results of a detailed study to analyze the impact made by 1991 tourism expenditure on incomes, employment, public sector revenue and the balance of payments in the Seychelles. Details of the methodology and data sources are provided and the results and policy implications are analyzed. These tourism impacts, found to vary by visitors' countries of origin, provide useful policy and marketing implications, although this variation was found to be related almost entirely to the different magnitudes of expenditure than to variations in the size of the multiplier by country of residence. **Keywords:** The Seychelles, tourism expenditure, multipliers, input–output analysis, employment, impact, government.

Résumé: L'impact économique du tourisme aux Seychelles. Cet article décrit les résultats d'une étude sur l'impact des dépenses touristiques sur les salaires, l'emploi, le revenu du secteur publique et la balance des paiements aux Seychelles en 1991. L'auteur explique la méthodologie utilisée dans la recherche, révèle ses sources d'informations et analyse en profondeur les résultats obtenus ainsi que leurs implications politiques. Il est apparent que les impacts des visiteurs sont différents par pays d'origine, ce qui a des implications politiques et commerciales intéressantes. Toutefois, ces variations sont presque entièrement dues à la différence dans le chiffre de leurs dépenses plutôt qu'à la différence dans la valeur des multiplicateurs dans chaque pays de résidence. **Mot-clés:** Seychelles, dépense touristique, multiplicateurs, analyse input–output, emploi, impact, gouvernement.

INTRODUCTION

The Republic of Seychelles situated in the Indian Ocean, consists of two distinct groups of islands: the Mahé group of 45 granitic islands, three of which contain almost all of the population of 70,438 (mid-1991) and the outlying coralline group of 49 islands. The total land area is 171.4 square miles and its capital, Victoria (population 25,000), is situated on the largest island, Mahé, which is 17 miles long and 7 miles at its widest point. The Republic of Seychelles is one of the most isolated and scenically attractive groups of islands in the world, offering high quality beach holidays, based on year-round sunshine and coral beaches fringed with tropical vegetation backed by attractive, accessible mountain ranges.

The beginning of modern tourism in the Seychelles dates from the opening of the international airport on Mahé in 1971. From 3175 visitor arrivals in the same year the number increased to a peak of

Brian Archer is Professor of Tourism Management at the University of Surrey (Guildford GU2 5XH, United Kingdom; email msp1db@surrey.ac.uk). From 1987 to 1994, he was Pro-Vice Chancellor of the University; earlier he was Head of the Department of Management Studies for Tourism and Hotel Industries. **John Fletcher** is Managing Director of Surrey Research Group and is also Reader in Tourism at the University of Surrey.

78,852 in 1979. During the 80s, visitor arrivals fluctuated widely from a low of 47,280 in 1982 to a new peak of 86,093 in 1989. 1990 was a record year with 103,770 arrivals, after which the total dropped to 90,050 in 1991, followed by a recovery to 98,547 in 1992. From 1971 to 1979, visitor arrivals increased by an annual average rate of over 26%, compared with an equivalent increase of about 6% in world visitor arrivals over the same period. Average length of stay increased from 10.5 days in 1973 to 11.0 in 1977, after which it declined to 9.1 days in 1979, partly due to a shift from two-week to one-week holidays.

In common with many other long-haul destinations, the world recession of the early 80s affected tourism to the Seychelles. Visitor arrivals declined in 1980 (by about 9%) and again in 1981 (by a further 15.8%). During the early 80s, tourism to the Seychelles was slow to recover. An abortive coup caused some uncertainty among tour operators about the future, but by the second half of the 80s, these fears had been dispelled. Arrivals rose by over 7% in 1987, a further 8% in 1988, 11% in 1989, and over 20% to a peak of 103,770 in 1990.

Europe is the predominant market area for the Seychelles, providing 63% of all visitors in 1981 and over 71% in 1991. Within Europe, the principal generating countries are France,Italy, the United Kingdom, and Germany. Table 1 shows the actual number of visitors from each country and region from 1986 to 1991.

Seasonality is much less of a problem in the Seychelles than most other long-haul destinations, largely because of its equatorial climate. In consequence, the pattern of visitor arrivals is related principally to the main holiday periods (spring, summer and late December/early January) of the principal generating countries in Europe.

As is consistent with the tourism product, most of the accommodation establishments are situated near beaches and the majority are dispersed around the principal island of Mahé. Hotels account for approx. 80% of all visitor-nights. The remainder are in self-catering apartments, private homes, and the houses of friends and relatives.

The principal aim of this paper is to measure the economic impact of tourism on the Republic of Seychelles in total and by visitors' countries of residence and, on the basis of the results, to indicate those productive sectors in which tourism expenditure yields the greatest economic returns. The research methodology involves the use of an input–output model constructed for this specific study.

It is not the purpose of this paper to provide a detailed literature survey and readers are referred to the principal sources mentioned here. A major literature survey and critique of existing approaches up to 1977 was provided by Archer (1977) and this was partially updated by a later paper (Archer and Fletcher 1990). Between those dates, a considerable number of input–output and multiplier studies was undertaken, the majority of which, however, were principally applications of existing techniques to particular countries and regions. A small number of studies contained advances in method-

34   ECONOMIC IMPACT OF TOURISM

Table 1. Visitor Arrivals in Seychelles (1986–91)

Country of Residence	Year					
	1986	1987	1988	1989	1990	1991
Europe						
UK and Eire	13,955	16,856	19,935	19,346	19,207	14,877
France	14,133	13,906	14,304	16,278	21,900	15,193
Germany	5886	5276	5501	7371	9018	9321
Italy	11,517	14,358	14,604	15,175	19,281	15,238
Switzerland	4353	3346	3126	2882	2771	2520
Other countries	5234	5879	6714	7561	9059	7406
Subtotal	55,078	59,621	64,184	68,613	81,236	64,555
Africa						
Réunion	1789	1670	1348	2091	2131	3543
Mauritius	571	388	606	885	1072	968
East Africa	1267	1311	1432	1309	1287	1135
South Africa	939	949	2947	5056	9897	11,774
Other countries	1490	1322	1624	1832	1484	1405
Subtotal	6056	5640	7957	11,173	15,871	18,825
Asia						
Middle East	2293	1916	1779	1870	1873	1806
Indian Subcontinent	260	202	262	419	339	479
Hong Kong	48	47	36	71	250	237
Japan	371	344	268	371	481	463
Other countries	246	381	388	542	602	775
Subtotal	3218	2890	2733	3273	3545	3760
Oceania	366	1102	330	443	504	504
America	2064	2473	2197	2591	2614	2406
Total overnight visitors	66,782	71,626	77,401	86,093	103,770	90,050
Cruiseship visitors	2855	4573	2876	1549	7564	7618
Total visitors	69,637	76,199	80,277	87,642	111,334	97,668

Source: Adapted from Statistics Division, Migration and Tourism Statistics (annual).

ology and/or critical insights into the technique. Among these are papers by Sinclair and Sutcliffe (1978, 1982), Milne (1987), and Wanhill (1988).

THE ECONOMIC IMPACT OF TOURISM

The model used for the study described in this paper was a basic input–output one with a consumption feedback mechanism included in some runs of the model and excluded in others in order to measure separately the effects of consumer spending induced by the increased direct and indirect economic activity. Models of similar type have been used widely for studies of this nature under a variety of circumstances. Justification for this approach and examples of applications are provided in the literature (Archer 1977; Archer and Fletcher 1990).

The model is in essence a Leontief inversion with several adaptations which owe much to the work of Wanhill (Archer and Wanhill 1980) Later adaptations were made by Fletcher (1989):

$$X = AX + Y \qquad (1)$$
$$P = BX \qquad (2)$$

where X is a vector of gross output, A is a matrix of production coefficients, Y is a vector of final demand, P is a vector of primary factors, and B is a matrix of factor coefficients.

From equations (1) and (2), it is possible to predict the change in gross output and the employment of primary factors for a given change in final demand. For example, let the change in final demand be ΔF, then

$$\Delta X = A\Delta X + \Delta F \qquad (3)$$
$$\Delta P = B\Delta X \qquad (4)$$

then

$$(I - A)\, \Delta X = \Delta F$$

and

$$B\Delta X = \Delta P$$

then

$$\Delta X = (I - A)^{-1}\, \Delta F \qquad (5)$$

and

$$B\,(I - A)^{-1}\Delta F = \Delta P \qquad (6)$$

The direct and indirect impact of additional income, imports, government revenue, etc., can be found by the use of equation (5). An $n \times n$ matrix ΔT is substituted for ΔF and the diagonals of this matrix record the given changes in export earnings with the off-diagonals zeros. This gives

$$B_m\,(I - A)^{-1}\, \Delta P_m \qquad (7)$$

where ΔP_m is an $n \times n$ matrix in which each row now contains the effects of the items of export earnings on a particular primary factor.

For the M_{th} row

$$B_m\,(I - A)^{-1}\, \Delta T = \Delta P_m \qquad (8)$$

so that the multipliers for each category of export earnings are:

$$\frac{\Delta P_{ms}}{i \Delta t_{ss}} \ s = 1, \dots n \tag{9}$$

and the overall multiplier is:

$$\frac{\Delta P_m i}{i \ \Delta T_i} \tag{10}$$

where i is the unit vector.

The direct, indirect, and induced multipliers are calculated by including an additional column and row within the A matrix. This column is that part of final demand which constitutes consumer expenditure; the row is income payments to the personal sector. Let A^* be the new $(n + 1) \times (n + 1)$ augmented matrix with the $n + 1$th row the household sector. The system can then be written as:

$$(I - A^*) \ \Delta X^* = \Delta F^* \tag{11}$$
$$B \ \Delta X^* = \Delta P^* \tag{12}$$

Substituting ΔT^* for ΔF^* gives

$$(I - A^*)^{-1} \Delta T = \Delta X^* \tag{13}$$

and the impact on incomes merges in the $n + 1$th row of ΔX^*. The individual income multiplier is:

$$\frac{\Delta x^*_{n + 1}{}^s}{\Delta t_{ss}} \ s = 1 \dots n + 1. \tag{14}$$

There is also, however, an element of national income which does not accrue to the personal sector. This consists of the retained earnings of the corporate sector plus any surplus in the public sector. These are exogenous to the $I - A^*$ matrix, but can be found in the primary factor matrix in a defined row or rows, say row m. Thus, in addition to equation (1), it is necessary to calculate the effects of export earnings on retained earnings from:

$$B^*_m \ (I - A)^{-1} \ \Delta T = \Delta p^*_m \tag{15}$$

In consequence equation (12) now becomes:

$$\frac{\Delta x^*_{n + 1}{}^s + \Delta P^*_{ms}}{\Delta t_{ss}} \tag{16}$$

and the overall multiplier

$$\frac{\Delta X^*_{n + 1} + \Delta p^*_m \ i}{i \ \Delta T_i} \tag{17}$$

The same formulae are then used to calculate the employment effects by substituting employment coefficients for income in the household row. This assumes linear employment functions, an assumption which is consistent with the linear technology of input–output models

Sources and Methods

The input–output table was constructed specifically for this study in conjunction with the Management Information Services Division (MISD) of the government of Seychelles for the base year 1991. The sources of data used by MISD for the construction of the *I/O* table were the national accounts, government accounts, the MISD's own annual national accounts inquiry questionnaire, the 1991 household expenditure survey, the external trade statistics, and others. Details of the procedures used are described in an Annex to MISD's annual national income and expenditure reports. The national accounts questionnaires were sent to 256 private sector establishment of which a total of 167 responded (a response rate of 64%), which included all the larger establishments. A large quantity of additional data relating to imports by establishments had to be obtained from the records and files of several public and private sector organizations in order to obtain a detailed break-down of intermediate consumption into its local and imported components. Again this work was carried out in cooperation with MISD.

Originally, it was been intended to attempt very substantial disaggregation of the principal tourism sectors. Unfortunately, the data obtained for some of the intended subsectors were too sparse to permit the separation of some of these categories and the eventual version of the model contained only 18 sectors. It did prove possible, however, to include separate rows and columns for distributive trade, large hotels; other tourism accommodation; restaurants; car hire; other land transportation, especially taxis and buses; air transportation and sea transportation (Table 2). This permitted the tourism expenditure pattern to mesh directly into the relevant sectors of the economy and so avoided the need to use heavily aggregated sectors as is so often the case when pre-existing input–output tables are used for tourism impact analysis.

Information about tourism expenditure patterns was obtained from the results of airport exit surveys undertaken by MISD during 1991, together with additional data provided by the Central Bank of the Seychelles. Each departing individual or family group was issued with a questionnaire to complete in the departure lounge at the airport during three selected one-week periods in January, April, and August. The processed tourism expenditure data were weighted to conform with the actual number of arrivals by country of residence (derived from the immigration cards). Whereas the survey periods can be criticized as being too short and not extending over the whole year, the results were generally compatible with the findings of previous visitor surveys in the Seychelles.

38   ECONOMIC IMPACT OF TOURISM

Table 2. Backward and Forward Linkages

| | Backward Linkage | | Forward Linkage | |
Sector	Value	Rank	Value	Rank
Agriculture and forestry	0.97	12=	0.97	8=
Fishing	0.81	17=	0.81	10=
Food/beverage manufacture	1.14	9=	1.22	6=
Petroleum products	0.89	16	0.81	10=
Other manufacturing	0.81	17=	0.65	12=
Electricity and water	0.97	12=	1.22	6=
Construction	0.97	12=	0.49	16=
Distributive trade	0.97	12=	1.70	3=
Hotels (large)	1.22	6=	0.65	12=
Other tourist accommodation	1.14	9=	0.49	16=
Restaurants	1.22	6=	0.65	12=
Car rental	1.06	11	0.49	16=
Land transport	1.30	4=	0.65	12=
Air transport	1.54	1=	2.03	1
Sea transport	1.30	4=	0.97	8=
Communications	1.54	1=	1.46	5
Other services	1.46	3	1.70	3=
Government	1.22	6=	1.95	2

The extent of inter-linkage among the various sectors of the Seychelles' economy is shown in Table 2 where the backward linkages shows the amount of purchases made by each sector in order to produce a unit of output and the forward linkages indicate the amount of sales made within the Seychelles per unit of purchases. It is interesting to note that the principal tourism sectors have strong backward linkages within the economy and most have strong forward linkages as well.

The Results

During 1991, visitors spent approximately SEYRs528 million (about US$98 million) in the Seychelles and, with the addition of cruise passengers, tourism expenditure was over SEYRs532 million (about US$99 million). Table 3 shows the amount spent in 1991 by visitors on each of eleven categories of goods and services from eight different countries and regions. Perhaps not surprisingly, accommodation (including in-house meals and beverages) accounted for almost two-thirds of visitor spending, followed by local transportation (18%), restaurants (8%) and handicrafts (5%).

The highest 1991 spenders, in terms of total volume, were visitors from Italy, followed by the UK and Eire, Africa, France, and Germany. In terms of expenditure per capita and per capita per day, however, the highest spenders were visitors from Germany with SEYRs7,567, followed by those from Switzerland (SEYRs6,891), Italy (SEYRs6,414), "Other" European countries (SEYRs6,205) and the UK and Eire (SEYRs6.093). Visitors from Africa and other non-listed

Table 3. Expenditure by Category and by Country of Residence (1991)ᵃ

Category of Expenditure	Country of Residence								
	UK/Eire	France	Germany	Italy	Switzer	Europe (other)	Africa	Other Countries	Total
Accommodation	61,232	49,686	43,710	60,210	11,140	27,313	54,734	22,938	330,963
Restaurants	5598	7909	6312	7425	1749	4406	6150	2594	42,143
Car rental	4737	5763	4464	7468	919	2987	4570	1870	32,778
Land transport —other	1713	1639	1337	1740	374	914	1651	934	10,302
Excursions	6601	5679	4399	7523	906	3531	7454	1368	37,461
Air tickets	1385	1894	1621	1642	605	844	1782	529	10,302
Boat tickets	641	877	1169	1522	160	391	1445	351	6556
Handicrafts	3466	5192	2706	6123	536	2479	5524	1133	27,159
Sports	1863	2548	2425	1893	466	1041	2198	677	13,111
Other shopping	1701	697	1991	1152	319	1425	2323	694	10,302
Other items	1712	1262	400	1042	192	625	1155	168	6556
Total	90,649	83,146	70,534	97,740	17,366	45,956	88,986	33,256	527,633

ᵃRs (thousands).
Source: Seychelles Visitor Surveys (1991); Migration and Tourism Statistics (1991).

40 ECONOMIC IMPACT OF TOURISM

Table 4. The Impact of Tourism Expenditure on Income and Government Revenue (1991)

Country of Residence	Tourism Expenditure	Income	Government Revenue
UK/Eire	90,649	80,485	25,870
France	83,146	73,164	23,841
Germany	70,534	62,613	20,049
Italy	97,740	86,150	26,883
Switzerland	17,366	15,361	4991
Europe (other)	45,956	40,470	12,845
Africa	88,986	78,579	24,777
Other countries	33,256	29,416	9274
Total	527,633	466,238	148,530

Note: Government revenue excludes airport landing fees, port and marina fees and sales, and some excise duties attributable to tourism.

countries spent well below average, as did those from France. With length of stay taken into account, however, the situation changes and visitors from Africa are the highest spenders.

The amount of income generated by tourism expenditure in 1991 is shown in Table 4. The first column of figures shows the volume of expenditure by tourists from each country of residence; the second column shows the amount of income generated in the Seychelles by these expenditures, and the third column shows the amount of government revenue created. Overall it can be seen that in 1991 SEYRs527,633,000 of tourist expenditure generated SEYRs466,238,000 of income and SEYRs148,530,000 of government revenue. Due to the magnitude of their expenditure, the most substantial contributions were made by visitors from Italy (19.9% of the total income created), and UK and Eire together (18.6%). The contribution of tourism in 1991 to Gross Domestic Product (GDP) *as conventionally measured* was 18.4%. With the secondary effects resulting from the multiplier action, however, tourism contributes approx. 23.5% to GDP.

The government receives revenue *directly* from tourists in the form of departure taxes, tourism taxes, etc., and *indirectly* in the form of other taxes and licenses (paid by those establishments which trade directly or indirectly with tourists). To this must be added the personal taxes, customs duties, and excise duties on goods and services paid for either to service tourists or to satisfy the secondary increase in economic activity created by tourism expenditure. The figure of SEYRs148.53 million shown in Table 4, however, excludes items such as airport landing fees and port and marine fees.

In 1991, tourism made a net contribution to the balance of payments of SEYRs359.3 million (i.e. SEYRs527.6 million minus the SEYRs168.3 million of direct and indirect imports) (Table 5). In addition, a further SEYRs149.9 million of imports were required to provide goods and services to households in Seychelles as a result of

Table 5. The Impact of Tourism on the Balance of Payments (1991)[a]

Tourism Expenditure (+) (excluding cruise visitors)		527,633
Imports (–) Direct and indirect		(168,314)
Net effect on balance of payments		+359,319
Imports: induced (–)	(149,864)	

Notes: *Direct* imports are those goods and services imported directly by the establishments which receive tourist spending. *Indirect* imports are the additional goods and services imported by other establishments as a result of the initial tourist spending. *Induced* imports are the additional imports required to provide goods and services to Seychellois households as a result of their increased incomes from the direct and indirect effects of tourism.

[a] This is *not* the normal method of presenting balance of payments data, but it is formulated in this manner to illustrate more clearly the impact made by tourism.

the additional income which they received from the direct and secondary effects of tourism.

As mentioned earlier, the amount of income generated in a country by a unit of tourism spending is known as the tourism income multiplier. Although it can be defined in various ways, in this paper it is taken to be the contribution made by a unit of tourism spending to all incomes except the government. The total revenue accruing to the government is measured separately, although the household income generated by the respending of government revenue is included within the multiplier.

The direct, indirect, induced and total (direct + indirect + induced) value-added by an average rupee of tourism spending is shown in Table 6. Thus, for example, an average 62.73 cents of each

Table 6. The Local Value-Added by an Average Rupee Spent by Tourists (1991)

Category of Expenditure	Pattern of Expenditure	Direct Value-Added (weighted)	Total Value-Added (weighted)
Accommodation	0.6273	0.2169	0.5573
Restaurants	0.0799	0.0164	0.0616
Car rental	0.0621	0.0331	0.0597
Transportation	0.1225	0.0390	0.0972
Sports	0.0248	0.0056	0.0356
Shopping (other)	0.0195	0.0119	0.0109
Handicrafts	0.0515	0.0214	0.0434
Other items	0.0124	0.0028	0.0179
Totals	1.0000	0.3471	0.8836

Note: Total value-added includes the induced effects of consumer re-spending.

42   ECONOMIC IMPACT OF TOURISM

Table 7. The Amount of Employment Generated in the Seychelles by
Country of Residence (1991)

Country of Residence	Tourist Income Multipliers	Amount of Employment Generated		
		Direct	Total	Per 100 Tourists
UK/Eire	0.8879	665	1447	9.7
France	0.8799	596	1312	8.6
Germany	0.8877	498	1106	11.9
Italy	0.8814	681	1529	10.3
Switzerland	0.8856	121	273	10.8
Europe (other)	0.8806	328	721	9.7
Africa	0.8830	642	1397	7.4
Other countries	0.8845	241	527	7.9
Average (weighted)	0.8836	—	—	9.2
Total	—	3772	8312	—

Note: In this and subsequent tables, the number of jobs is expressed in full-time
job equivalents.

rupee is spent at the place of accommodation and the total direct
and secondary effects of this expenditure creates 55.7 cents of
income in the Seychelles. The "Total" row shows that the expenditure of an average rupee creates 88.36 cents of income in the
Seychelles. Thus, 0.8836 is an approximation of the average tourism
income multiplier.

Due to these different expenditure patterns, not all visitors create
the same impact per rupee on incomes. The tourism income multipliers by country of residence are shown in Table 7. Largely because
expenditure at the place of accommodation accounts for such a
substantial element of total expenditure, the differences between
the highest and lowest countries is less than 1%.

Employment generation is another major consequence of tourism
expenditure. Of the almost 24,000 workers in employment in 1991,
over 21% were employed in social and community services, almost
11% in public administration, over 11% in manufacturing, and 9%
in agriculture, forestry and fishing. Hotels and restaurants together
employed 3362 people (13% of total employment) and tourism
related transport a further 1056 people (4.4% of total employment).

The direct employment in hotel, restaurant, and tourism related
transport business compared with other industries in each of the
years 1981 and 1990 to 1992 is shown in Table 8. The bottom row
of the table reveals that, whereas such employment comprised 16%
of the total in 1981, in the years 1990–1992 these sectors together
accounted for over 22% of total employment.

The amount of direct employment attributable to tourism in 1991
was 3772. The total (direct and secondary) employment generated
by tourism in Seychelles the same year, however, was 8312 (Table 7).
The same table shows the contributions made to this employment
by tourist by country of residence. The second column of figures

Table 8. Formal Employment Compared with Other Industries (1981, 1990–92)

Industry	1981	1990	1991	1992
Hotels	1872	2846	2847	2872
Restaurants	211	479	515	498
Transport-tourism	618	1018	1056	1109
Subtotal	2701	4343	4418	4479
Other industries	14,216	19,169	19,540	19,977
Tourism subtotal as % of total	16.0	22.7	22.6	22.4

Source: Adapted from MIS Division, Statistical Abstract (annual).

shows the direct impact on employment created by the flow of the tourism generated rupees through the economy. The third column shows the total impact. Thus, in 1991, tourism expenditure was responsible for approximately 3772 full-time equivalent jobs and an additional 4540 secondary jobs. The ratio, therefore, between the total employment generated and the direct employment created by tourism was 2.20 — i.e., an average direct job supported an additional 1.2 secondary jobs. It should not be assumed, however, that in the absence of tourism all of the 4540 secondary jobs would be lost. In reality some would be maintained, especially the 1766 jobs which catered primarily for household demand, but at a very much reduced real level of remuneration.

A measurement of the amount of employment created by an average 100 tourists in 1991 by country of residence is shown in the final column of the same table. Per 100 tourists, the greatest impact was made by visitors from Germany (29% above average), Switzerland (17% above average) and Italy (12% above). The smallest impact was made per 100 visitors by those from Africa (20% below average) and "Other Countries" (14% below).

The number of tourists needed to create one job by country of residence is shown in Table 9. The "average" row at the bottom of

Table 9. The Number of Tourists Needed to Create One Job (1991)

	Number of Tourists Needed to Create One Job	
Country of Residence	Direct	Direct and Secondary
UK/Eire	22.37	10.28
France	25.49	11.58
Germany	18.72	8.43
Italy	22.38	9.96
Switzerland	20.83	9.23
Europe (other)	22.58	10.27
Africa	29.32	13.48
Other countries	27.68	12.66
Average weighted	23.87	10.83

44   ECONOMIC IMPACT OF TOURISM

Table 10. The Partial (or Sectoral) Multiplier Coefficients for the Tourism Related Sectors of the Seychelles Economy

Sector	Sectoral Multiplier Coefficients		
	Income	Employment	Government Revenue
Large hotels	0.866	0.014	0.268
Small hotels	0.962	0.020	0.306
Restaurants	0.771	0.015	0.321
Car rental	0.962	0.012	0.210
Taxis/buses	0.940	0.029	0.243
Shopping	0.929	0.008	0.134
Other services	1.068	0.023	0.850
Air transport	0.911	0.013	0.243
Sea transport	1.045	0.018	0.217

the table shows that, overall, 23.87 tourists created one direct job but, with secondary jobs taken into account as well, only 10.8 tourists were needed to support one job. The table stresses again the relative importance of tourists from Germany. The impact made on employment by each of these tourists is over 20% greater than average and 26% greater than by tourists from Africa.

Not surprisingly these tables indicate that the greatest overall impact on employment is made by tourists with the highest spending. Tourists from Germany, for example, accounted for only 10.35% of the total, but their expenditure contributed over 13% of the tourism-related employment, whereas Africa, which yielded 20.9% of all tourists accounted for only 16.8% of tourism-generated jobs.

The analysis of the "complete" multiplier values demonstrates that certain types of visitors to the Seychelles are economically more beneficial than others. It is clear that higher spending tourists are likely to have a greater economic impact per visitor than others. However, it need not simply be the volume of expenditure per visitor that is important in determining impact. The pattern of visitor expenditure is also important and, because the multiplier values are calculated per Rupee of tourism expenditure, explains the variation in multiplier coefficients between visitors from different countries.

Visitor expenditure is distributed over a variety of productive sectors and each of these sectors has a different set of multiplier values associated with its output. For example, a Rupee of expenditure on each of the tourism-related sectors will, on average, generate between 0.771 and 1.068 rupees of income depending upon which sector receives that expenditure (Table 10). The multiplier values shown in Table 10 show the partial (or sectoral) multiplier values for each of the tourism-related sectors. Such detailed information allows the government to determine not only which tourist groups should be targeted in order to maximize the economic benefits, but also in which sectors they should encourage visitor spend. For instance, if the government wishes to maximize income generation from tourism expenditure, it should encourage tourists to spend more on other services (1.068) and local sea transport (1.045); encourage car rental (0.968) rather than the use of taxis and buses (0.940); and to stay in small hotels (0.962) rather than their larger counterparts (0.866).

On the other hand, if employment creation is the primary objective it can be seen that the taxi and bus services sector (0.029) performs much better than the car rental sector (0.012); the other services (0.023) and small hotels (0.020) are also relatively strong generators of job opportunities. If the primary objective is to maximize government revenue then, again, the other services (0.850), restaurants (0.321), and small hotels (0.306) are the stronger sectors.

This type of analysis can assist the government in deciding which sectors should be promoted and encouraged given the priority of policy objectives. It should not be forgotten, however, that multiplier analysis is only one part of the issue and that the demand and market factors must also be taken into account when determining policy actions on the basis of impact results.

CONCLUSIONS

Although the principal purpose of this study was to analyze in detail the impacts made by visitors from different countries, the results do suggest that certain markets are more effective than others in terms of their contributions to the economy of the Seychelles.

Largely because of its physical isolation and the absence of nearby large markets, the Seychelles is not dominated to the same extent as the Caribbean countries by any single market. Even so, in 1991 almost 72% of the tourists (over 77% of the tourist-nights) were accounted for by Europe. Indeed five countries together (Italy, UK and Eire, France, and Germany) provided 60.7% of all tourists and 65.7% of tourist-nights. The expenditure of European tourists contributed almost 77% of total tourism receipts and almost the same percentage of the amount of income and employment generated by tourists in the economy of the Seychelles.

The contributions made by visitors from each of eight origin countries and regions are summarized in Table 11. From this table it can be seen that the highest spending visitors per capita are those from Germany, Switzerland, Italy, "Other European", and UK and Eire. Perhaps not surprisingly, visitors from these countries are also the most efficient in generating income and employment.

In order to maximize the impact of tourism on incomes, employment and public sector revenue, the Seychelles should concentrate upon increasing the number of high spending visitors from long-haul countries such as Germany, Switzerland, Italy, UK and Eire, which the analysis has shown generate the largest impact on employment per visitor. The extent to which it is financially feasible to woo relatively small markets such as Switzerland and the Nordic countries needs to be investigated as a separate study.

Whereas Europe will remain the principal market area for the Seychelles in the foreseeable future, the South African market offers

Table 11. The Impact of Tourism by Country of Residence (1991)

Category of Expenditure	Country of Residence							
	UK/Eire	France	Germany	Italy	Switzer	Europe (other)	Africa	Other Countries
Tourists (number)	14,877	15,193	9321	15,238	2520	7406	18,825	6670
Tourist nights (number)	168,110	145,245	131,426	170,666	31,500	77,022	156,835	56,538
Expenditure (Rs 000s)	90,649	83,146	70,534	97,740	17,366	45,956	88,986	33,256
Expenditure per tourist (Rs)	6093	5473	7567	6414	6891	6205	4727	4986
Expenditure per tourist-night (Rs)	539	572	537	573	551	597	606	604
Income generated (Rs 000s)	80,485	73,164	62,613	86,150	15,361	40,470	78,579	29,416
Income generated per tourist (Rs)	5410	4816	6717	5654	6096	5464	4174	4260
Direct employment generated	665	596	498	681	121	328	642	241
Total employment generated	1447	1312	1106	1529	273	721	1397	527
Number of tourists needed to create one direct job	22.4	25.5	18.7	22.4	20.8	22.6	29.3	27.7

considerable potential for growth and yields high spending tourists who make an above average impact on incomes and employment. Unfortunately insufficient data were available to isolate these visitors from the category "Africa" and so it did not prove possible to quantify their impact accurately.

The study shows that input–output analysis can do more than merely quantify impacts. It can produce data which is of importance to policymakers and provide guidance to marketing experts. It also provides a strong indication to government which sectors of the economy should be promoted and encouraged to meet particular policy objects — increased income and/or employment and/or public sector revenue. Multiplier analysis, however, is only one element in policymaking and demand and market forces must be taken into account before decisions are made on the basis of impact analysis. □ □

REFERENCES

Archer, B. H
  1977 Tourism Multipliers: The State-of-the-Art. Cardiff: University of Wales Press.
Archer, B. H., and J. E. Fletcher
  1990 Multiplier Analysis in Tourism, Cahiers du Tourism c.103. Aix-Marseille: Centre des Hautes Etudes Touristiques.
Archer, B. H., and S. R. C. Wanhill
  1980 Tourism in Bermuda: An Economic Evaluation. Bermuda: Bermuda Department of Tourism, Hamilton.
Fletcher, J. E.
  1989 Input–Output Analysis and Tourism Impact Studies. Annals of Tourism Research 16:541–556.
Fletcher, J. E., and B. H. Archer
  1991 The Development and Application of Multiplier Analysis. Progress in Tourism, Recreation and Hospitality Management: pp.28–47.
Government of Seychelles
  Annual National Income and Expenditure Accounts. Victoria: MISD, Government of Seychelles.
Milne, S. S.
  1987 Differential Multipliers. Annals of Tourism Research 14:495–515.
Sinclair, M. T., and C. M. S. Sutcliffe
  1978 The First Round of the Keynesian Income Multiplier. Scottish Journal of Political Economy 25:177–186.
  1982 Keynesian Income Multipliers with First and Second Round Effects: An application to Tourism Expenditure. Oxford Bulletin of Economics and Statistics 44:321–323.
Wanhill, S. R. C.
  1988 Tourism Multipliers and Capacity Constraints. Service Industries Journal 8:136–142.

Submitted 18 August 1994
Resubmitted 24 October 1994
Accepted 21 December 1994
Refereed anonymously
Coordinating Editor: Linda Low

[12]

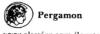

Pergamon

www.elsevier.com/locate/atoures

Annals of Tourism Research, Vol. 30, No. 3, pp. 683–701, 2003
© 2003 Elsevier Science Ltd. All rights reserved.
Printed in Great Britain
0160-7383/03/$30.00

doi:10.1016/S0160-7383(03)00048-3

TOURISM AND GLOBALIZATION
Economic Impact in Indonesia

Guntur Sugiyarto
Adam Blake
M. Thea Sinclair
University of Nottingham, UK

Abstract: The issue of whether globalization is beneficial remains controversial, particularly because globalization policies are often examined without consideration of their interactions with key sectors of the economy, notably tourism. This paper uses a computable general equilibrium model of the Indonesian economy to examine the effects of globalization via tariff reductions, as a stand-alone policy and in conjunction with tourism growth. The results show that tourism growth amplifies the positive effects of globalization and lessens its adverse effects. Production increases, while welfare improves, while adverse effects on government deficits and the trade balance are reduced. **Keywords:** globalization, taxation, economic impact, computable general equilibrium. © 2003 Elsevier Science Ltd. All rights reserved.

Résumé: Tourisme et mondialisation : impact économique en Indonésie. La question des avantages de la mondialisation reste controversée, surtout parce que les politiques de la mondialisation sont souvent étudiées sans égard à leurs interactions avec les secteurs clé de l'économie, en particulier le tourisme. Cet article utilise un modèle d'équilibre général calculable de l'économie indonésienne pour étudier les effets de la mondialisation par des réductions de tarifs douaniers, comme politique indépendante et conjointement avec la croissance du tourisme. Les résultats montrent que la croissance du tourisme amplifie les effets positifs de la mondialisation et en réduit ses effets négatifs. La production augmente et le bien-être s'améliore, tandis que les effets négatifs sur les déficits gouvernemental et extérieur sont réduits. **Mots-clés:** mondialisation, taxation, impact économique, équilibre général calculable. © 2003 Elsevier Science Ltd. All rights reserved.

INTRODUCTION

In recent years, tourism and its associated economic repercussions have taken place within a wider context of globalization of the world economy. Macroeconomic policymakers have been concerned to decrease barriers which impede international flows of goods, services and financial capital and to ensure flexibility of exchange rates, interest rates, and wages, with the aim of inducing markets to operate more efficiently. The introduction of such macroeconomic policies has been

The authors are respectively Research Associate, Research Fellow, and Professor at the Christel DeHaan Tourism and Travel Research Institute (Nottingham University Business School, Nottingham NG8 1BB, UK. Email <guntur.sugiyarto@nottingham.ac.uk>). The authors' research interests cover a wide range of topics including tourism economics and policies, modeling the economic effects of tourism, demand analysis, taxation, competitiveness, and other development economics and tourism related issues.

683

a source of some controversy because of the implications for income and employment, as well as income distribution and the welfare of local populations. Policies to promote trade liberalization are a case in point. Trade liberalization is occurring in conjunction with World Trade Organization, International Monetary Fund, and World Bank pressures for lower tariffs and the elimination of import quotas, and also as part of the process of integration within regional trading blocs.

Although trade liberalization is supposed to bring about long-term benefits by allowing countries to reap gains from specialization in production on the basis of their comparative advantage (for example, Begg, Fischer and Dornbusch, 2000:553–71; Krugman and Obstfeld 1997:13–37), a number of problems may occur. The first can take the form of a balance of trade deficit, as consumers purchase increasing quantities of the cheaper imports. The second involves a government budget deficit, as the government receives less revenue from the lower tariffs, especially if exports are not stimulated by reciprocal liberalization by trade partners. The third concerns the effects of trade liberalization on the distribution of income and levels of welfare of the local population, and particularly on the income levels of the poorest households in the economy. Thus, the issue addressed here is whether the growth of tourism can help to resolve the problems inherent in trade liberalization by decreasing the trade deficit, increasing government revenues, and improving income distribution.

This issue has received little attention from macroeconomic policy-makers, who have tended to formulate and implement policies without taking account of their predicted effects in the context of tourism growth, even in countries whose economies are highly dependent on this industry. Nor has the issue received much attention in the literature, which has tended to concentrate on the income and employment impacts of tourism *per se*, rather than on its wider range of economic impacts, including those on distribution and welfare, in alternative macroeconomic contexts. Therefore, the aim of this paper is to develop existing research in the area by examining the economic impacts of tourism within the macroeconomic context of globalization in the form of increasing trade liberalization, as well as in the context of lower domestic taxation. The issue will be examined for the case of Indonesia, the fourth largest country in the world in terms of its population of over 210 million. As one of the former "Asian tigers", Indonesia is an important emerging economy which has experienced both growth in tourism and a push towards increasing trade liberalization in recent years. It has a wide range of attractions and natural resources. The growing international demand for these assets, in the context of decreasing levels of trade protection, has significant implications for domestic income and employment generation, income distribution, and welfare. This paper will examine these effects in the cases of tourism, trade, and tax policies in Indonesia.

The paper will build on previous contributions to research in the area of tourism impact analysis, which has been undertaken using direct and indirect income changes (Gartner and Holecek 1983; Gartner 1987), input–output models (Archer 1995; Archer and

Fletcher 1996; Fletcher 1989; Johnson and Moore 1993) and, subsequently, by using a social accounting matrix (Wagner 1997) and computable general equilibrium (CGE) models (Adams and Parmenter 1995 for the Australian economy; Zhou, Yanagida, Chakravorty and Leung 1997 for Hawaii; Alavalapati and Adamowicz 2000 for the environmental impacts of tourism in Canada; Blake 2000 for Spain; and Dwyer, Forsyth, Madden and Spurr 2000 for the Australian economy). All of these approaches have the advantage of taking account of the interrelationships between tourism and other sectors of the economy. This paper will use a CGE model, which has the advantages of incorporating the full range of feedback between the different sectors of the economy, along with flexibility of prices and factor substitutability. It is well suited for examining the effects of tariff reductions and of domestic taxation, which are a topic of growing concern in the tourism literature (Jensen and Wanhill 2002).

The CGE model developed in this study is used to undertake the analysis, enabling the full range of economic impacts to be quantified within a multisectoral framework. The model is particularly useful for understanding the characteristics of the economy and for quantifying the effects of alternative policies in relation to tourism, trade liberalization, and taxation. The results from using the model to measure the effects of trade liberalization *per se* and of trade liberalization combined with decreases in domestic taxation will be compared with the results obtained from implementing these policies in a context of tourism growth.

TOURISM AND TRADE LIBERALIZATION

Indonesia is the largest archipelago in the world, stretching 5,110 km along the equator from east to west and 1,888 km from north to south. It consists of five major islands (Java and Bali, Sumatra, Kalimantan, Sulawesi, and Irian Jaya) and about 30 smaller groups, with more than 17,000 islands in total. The chain of islands divides the Indian and Pacific Oceans and is enriched with natural resources and diverse cultures, offering a vast range of tourism activities. It has long been a popular destination.

Foreign tourism is an integral part of the Indonesian economy. For the decade prior to the 1997 crisis, the industry experienced strong growth, with large increases in foreign arrivals (Figure 1), tourist spending, and investment. The growth of the former was more than 15% per year, contributing to an increase in foreign currency receipts as both foreign tourists' expenditure and their length of stay increased. The number of arrivals in 1997 was 5.2 million, contributing around $6.6 billion to export income, or about 3% of GDP (World Bank 2002). In 2005, the number of arrivals from abroad is expected to be around 11 million, generating foreign currency receipts of over $15 billion. Tourism contributed 16% of total job creation in 1995, and in 2007 it is estimated that 1 of every 11 new jobs will originate from tourism (Kompas 1999a). Despite short-term disruptions of tourism and criticisms of its adverse effects (Copeland 1991; Pleumarom 1999a, 1999b),

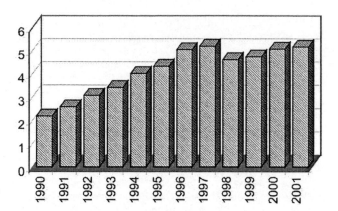

Figure 1. Tourist Arrivals (in Millions) to Indonesia

tourism in Indonesia is expected to play a more important role in the longer-term future. The increasing reliance on tourism is also demonstrated by the government's efforts to attract more international investment in the industry by allowing 100% foreign ownership, introducing a tax holiday, and welcoming non-national professional workers in this field (Kompas 1999b).

Other policies pursued by the Indonesian government have been concerned with trade liberalization. Decreases in the world prices of oil and other primary products, along with the international debt crisis of 1982, resulted in deterioration of the current account of the balance of payments and encouraged the government to introduce remedial measures. These included cuts in the number of tariffs from 25 to 11 and a reduction in the top tariff rate from 225% to 60%. Following the fall in the price of oil in 1986, many import licenses were converted to tariffs and the licensing procedures for hotels and other tourism facilities were simplified.

During the 90s, there were further reductions in tariffs in line with Indonesia's membership in the ASEAN Free Trade Agreement and the Asia-Pacific Economic Cooperation agreement. After the Asian crisis of 1997, import tariffs on over 150 goods were decreased, import subsidies on some goods were eliminated and import quotas were replaced by tariffs. Thus, the policy is one of moving away from an import substitution strategy towards an outward-oriented economy. However, various problems remain. The trade balance remains highly vulnerable to changes in world prices of oil and other natural resources and the government has also incurred budget deficits. Employment levels, poverty, and income distribution worsened considerably following the crisis (Asian Development Bank 2000a, 2000b). The question of whether a policy of further trade liberalization combined with tourism growth can contribute to alleviating these difficulties presents itself as an important research topic.

The CGE Model for Tourism in Indonesia

Despite the important role of foreign tourism in the Indonesian economy, there has been a lack of comprehensive studies of its economic impacts, especially in the form of economy-wide modeling using the CGE approach. Its previous applications to the Indonesian economy were not concerned with tourism (Behrman, Lewis and Lofti 1989; Devarajan, Ghanem and Theirfelder 1997; Robinson, El-Said and San 1997; Roland-Holst 1992; Thorbecke 1992). Therefore, this is the first attempt at developing such a model, in line with similar research on different economies (for instance Adams and Parmenter 1995, Blake 2000 and Zhou et al 1997). In addition to these "flexible price" CGE models, there have been some economic impact studies using "fixed-price" input–output or SAM-based multiplier models (for instance Bergstrom Cordell, Ashley and Watson 1990; Fletcher 1989; Heng and Low 1990; Huse, Gustavsen and Almedal 1998; Khan, Seng and Cheong 1990; Loomis 1995; Wagner 1997; West 1993).

The tourism-CGE model of Indonesia presented in this paper permits a range of analysis relating to ongoing economic issues related to this industry (see Sugiyarto, Blake and Sinclair 2002 for more details about the construction of the model). Its use for policy analysis (comparing simulation results with benchmark conditions) is directed towards, first, encapsulating the main characteristics of the Indonesian economy, especially with regard to the current level of foreign tourism and the globalization process. Second the model will facilitate analysis of the economy-wide effects and distributional implications of globalization and the growth in foreign tourism. Third, the results that are obtained from the model should provide useful implications for future economic policymaking, compatible with the growth of foreign tourism and the overall development of the economy. An early version of the model was developed for analyzing the economic effects and distributional implications of economic reform policies on the Indonesian economy (Sugiyarto 2001)

In the model, foreign tourists are treated as economic actors, who consume a range of exported commodities, particularly services. This assumption is in line with the United Nations and World Tourism Organization recommendations on Tourism Satellite Accounts that some parts of exports should be attributed to the foreign tourism. Given the way that the industry is modeled, it is important to note that this study does not aim to measure the "actual-definitive" magnitude of the tourism impacts (as commonly estimated in fixed-price input–output and models based on Social Accounting Matrix, for instance Alavalapati and Adamowicz 2000; Archer 1995; Archer and Fletcher 1996), but rather to measure the "overall-indicative" directions of the effects, especially on production activities, factor markets, foreign trade, the welfare of domestic residents and income distribution (that is, the general equilibrium economy-wide effects).

The globalization process is represented by changes in government policies towards more open international trade, while maintaining an open capital account. The move towards greater trade liberalization seems inevitable, given the Indonesian government's commitments to the World Trade Organization, Asia-Pacific Economic Cooperation, and Association of South East Asian Nations agreements to liberalize international trade. In addition, the lowering of tariffs, in conjunction with other measures such as domestic tax reform and the replacement of quantitative restrictions by tariffs, has been part of the policy package of the International Monetary Fund/World Bank conditional loans, in which the Indonesian government is currently involved.

The Social Accounting Matrix

A Social Accounting Matrix (SAM) is a system of representing the economic and social structure of a country (region) at a particular time, by defining its representative economic agents and recording their transactions. It is an accounting record for a whole economy. The disaggregation level and choice of representative actors depend on the motivation underlying its development and the availability of data, so that there is no "standard SAM". In a statistical system, it provides complementary economic indicators, which concern not only the macroeconomic aggregates of the System of National Accounts but also the socioeconomic structure and distributional aspects of the economy. Accordingly, it can be thought of as a further development of input–output accounts, which concentrate only on the production side of the economy. Entries in a SAM can be categorized into two groups, one that reflects flows across markets (represented in the sales of goods and services, employment of labor, and use of capital markets) and the other that reflects nominal flows or transfer payments such as income allocations from different categories of labor to different categories of households and transfer payments among the latter, firms, and the government. The transactions are presented in a square matrix, with rows representing receipts and columns recording expenditures. It then follows that every income has its corresponding expenditure, and the inflows and outflows of any account always balance.

The SAM captures the circular flows of income from activities to factors and then to institutions, which create demand for goods and services. The factor accounts receive factor incomes from both domestic activities and the rest of the world, while current transfers are recorded in the intersection of rows and columns of institutions (households, firms, government, and the rest of the world). These transfers constitute the non-factor incomes, which augment the factor incomes to yield the income of institutions.

In the disaggregated version of the Indonesian SAM 1993 adopted in the model, production activities are classified into 18 categories. Each production activity employs different kinds of labor and capital. Labor is categorized into eight groups based on a combination of sector, type of workers, and job status (namely, wage and non-wage). The former refers to employees while the non-wage category includes employers, self-employed, and family workers. In the Indonesian economy context, the former tends to be associated with higher income groups as most of the latter consists of self-employed and unpaid family workers. On the capital side, it is disaggregated into five categories based on its ownership and nature. Land and other agricultural capital, for instance, are combined into one category, while private domestic capital is an aggregation of corporate and non-corporate private sources. The other two categories are government and foreign capital.

Households are classified into 10 groups, based on a combination of income sources, area of residence, and job status of the head of household or the highest income earner. First, households are divided into agricultural and non-agricultural households. The former is then divided into employee landless farmers, small farmers (land size <0.5 hectare), medium farmers (between 0.5–1.0 hectare), and large farmers (>1.0 hectare). For the non-farmers, the disaggregation is based on area of residence (urban and rural), level of income, and a combination of occupation and job status. Based on these variables, the non-farmers in each area are then classified into low, dependent, and high-income groups. The dependent term refers to the households whose highest income earner (head of the household) is not in the labor-force, relying instead on transfer incomes from relatives, friends, and the government. The household classification has been developed based on "real" variables, which can easily be identified for policy targeting, as commonly suggested in the development of a SAM. The main source of information is the Indonesian Central Bureau of Statistics (1994, 1996). The development of SAMs in Indonesia has been conducted continuously since 1975 as an integral part of its national statistical system, based on initial collaboration between the Central Bureau of Statistics and the Institute of Social Studies, the Netherlands. The method of updating the 1993 SAM is explained in Sugiyarto (2001).

Supply and Demand Sides of the Model

The schematic representation of the production system adopted in the model is shown in Figure 2 (the main equations used in the model are provided in Sugiyarto et al 2002). As depicted in the figure, output is specified as an input-output function of intermediate inputs and

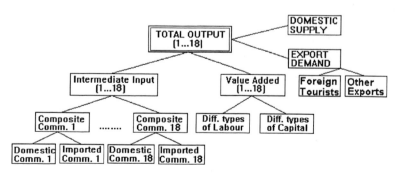

Figure 2. Schematic Representation of Production System

value added. Intermediate input consumption is a constant elasticity of substitution aggregation of domestically produced and imported commodities allowing imperfect substitution between the two commodities, with a different degree of substitution for each type of commodity, as reflected by the value of elasticity used. Value added is a Cobb Douglas function of eight different types of labour (wage earning and self-employed farmers, production workers, clerical workers, and professional workers) and five different types of capital (land and agricultural, non-corporate private domestic, corporate private domestic, foreign and government capital). The "wages" term refers to employees while the "self employed" category includes employers, self-employed, and family workers. In the context of the Indonesian economy, the former tends to be associated with higher earnings as most non-wage employment consists of self employed and unpaid family workers. Moreover, the wage rates of farmers and production workers are fixed to reflect the excess supply and various government interventions to control the wage rates of these types of workers. For other types of labour and capital, wages and rents are flexible to clear the market. These market-clearing levels reflect the marginal productivity of the factor.

Total production is allocated to domestic demand and exports, which are then disaggregated into two product categories: services, and agriculture and manufacturing. Most of the former is assumed to be consumed by foreign tourists, while the latter is other exports. This treatment of tourism is reasonable, as fluctuations in consumption by foreign tourists should be reflected in the fluctuations of service exports, as most exports of services are consumed by them. With regard to the CGE model, policy analysis should place more emphasis on the general equilibrium effects or direction of the impacts rather than on the magnitude of the change. For the latter, a more refined method for estimating foreign tourist consumption should, ideally, be used prior to the development of the CGE model. This may be possible in the future if a Tourism Satellite Account is calibrated for Indonesia.

Total final demand in the domestic market consists of demand for consumption and for investment purposes. Consumption is the sum of household and government consumption, while the demand for investment is generated by the aggregated saving-investment (capital) account. A schematic representation of the demand system of the model (Figure 3) depicts that households have a fixed consumption pattern and the government is assumed to have planned consumption, which is not affected by commodity prices or the government's income. In addition, the government has access to foreign borrowing for balancing its budget deficit. Since 1967, the Indonesian government has continuously adopted a budget deficit, which is financed by foreign funds. The same applies to domestic firms, so that the two deficits have been contributing to Indonesia's total foreign commitments. Aggregate investment is fixed (in quantity), reflecting the "investment-driven" nature of the economy.

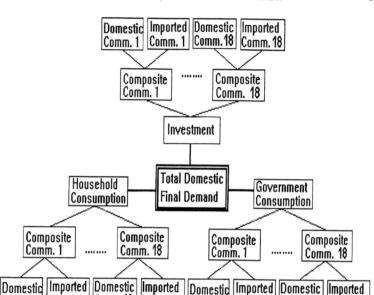

Figure 3. Schematic Representation of Demand System

Price, Incomes, Expenditure, Savings-Investments, Wages and Foreign Trade

The domestic price of each composite commodity is a constant elasticity of substitution function of the domestic prices of imported and domestically produced goods. On the import side, the adoption of the small country assumption implies that the domestic economy is a price taker and there is unlimited supply from the rest of the world at the given world price. Assuming that domestic products sold in the international market face a downward sloping demand curve, the export price depends on domestic prices, the export subsidy rate, and the exchange rate.

Household incomes consist of factor incomes (wages and rent payments for capital used domestically and abroad) and transfer incomes from the government, domestic firms, other households and the rest of the world. Firms' incomes include payments for capital used in production, transfers from other firms and transfers from from the rest of the world. Government income can be categorized into payments for capital used in production activities, income taxes from domestic institutions (households, domestic firms, and government-owned companies), income from indirect taxes levied on commodities, and transfers from the rest of the world. The transfer payments consist of foreign loans, grants, and other transfers.

Household expenditure consists of consumption of composite commodities, direct tax payments to the government, transfers to other household groups, and savings. The expenditures of firms consist of transfers to households, direct tax payments to the government, transfers to other firms (retained profit), transfers to the rest of the world and savings. Government expenditure consists of consumption of composite commodities, as well as transfers to households, to the government, and to the rest of the world and savings.

Total savings in the domestic economy consist of household, firms', and government savings, and capital injections from the rest of the world. In equilibrium, total saving equals total investment, which is distributed to each sector based on fixed shares. Aggregate final demand consists of consumption by households, the government, and private investment. For non-agricultural and non-production workers in Indonesia, wages are set in competitive markets and reflect the marginal product of labor. However, for labor in the agricultural sector and production workers, wages are fixed. The balance of payments equilibrium consists of the sum of imports, transfers from government and firms, and capital payments from foreign capital used in domestic production to the rest of the world (remittances), which are equal to exports, capital payments and transfers to domestic households, firms, and government. The model was used to quantify the effects of trade liberalization, changes in taxation, and foreign tourism growth in the Indonesian economy.

Study Results

Two main macroeconomic policy scenarios were considered, first in isolation and subsequently in conjunction with foreign tourism growth. The first is termed "partial globalization" and is modeled by a reduction of 20% in the tariffs on imported commodities. This reflects external pressure on the government to implement tariff reductions in conjunction with Indonesia's membership of the ASEAN Free Trade Agreement and the Asia-Pacific Economic Cooperation group. It occurs in the context of the government's reluctant attitude towards globalization, stemming from its increasing reliance on revenue from import tariffs. Despite its trade liberalization efforts, especially after 1982, revenue from import tariffs contributed 4% of total government income in 1985. This amount more than doubled to 10% in 1993 (Sugiyarto et al 2001). In this scenario, the government is assumed to reduce tariffs on imports and to maintain other taxes at their original level.

In the second scenario, "far-reaching globalization", the government is more pro-business and balances the "involuntary" (externally determined) import tariff cuts with a "voluntary" removal of distortions in the domestic market. The latter is represented by the same reduction (20%) in indirect taxation levied on domestic commodities. Another reason for considering a combination of the two policies is that reductions in the level of indirect taxation on domestic commodities are a common feature of tax reform policies, especially in developing countries (Ahmad and Stern 1991; Bird 1992; Bird and Oldman 1990; Gillis 1989; Newbery and Stern 1988; Rao 1993).

The two scenarios are analyzed by using the CGE model to estimate the effects of partial and far-reaching globalization on key economic variables: GDP, employment, a range of measures of inflation, external performance, welfare, household, and foreign tourist consumption. The results are given in Table 1 and are calculated as percentage changes from the benchmark data, where the benchmark refers to the equilibrium values of the variables prior to the simulations. In most cases, a positive number reflects an improvement and vice versa. Percentage changes in balance of payments deficits and trade balances should be interpreted carefully since the absolute numbers can switch from negative to positive.

Table 1a. Effects of Globalization and Foreign Tourism Growth (%)

Variables (1)	Main Scenarios				
	PG[a] (2)	FG[a] (3)	DI[a] (4)	PG & DI (5)	FG & DI (6)
A. Macroeconomic Aggregates					
1. GDP	0.05	0.64	0.06	0.11	0.70
a. Agriculture	−0.06	1.54	0.17	0.11	1.71
b. Mining	0.00	−0.74	−0.14	−0.14	−0.88
c. Manufacturing	−0.04	0.33	−0.05	−0.09	0.28
d. Services	0.04	0.46	0.14	0.18	0.60
Hotels	0.04	0.87	2.81	2.90	3.60
Restaurants	0.00	1.47	0.53	0.54	1.98
2. Employment	−0.01	1.34	0.16	0.15	1.49
B. External Conditions					
1. Foreign Trade					
a. Real Exports	0.64	−0.18	0.24	0.88	0.05
b. Real Imports	0.91	1.86	0.20	1.11	2.06
c. Trade Balance	−2.43	−23.49	0.70	−1.75	−22.90
2. Balance of Payments Deficits					
a. Government	349.15	1195.34	30.41	380.35	1227.58
b. Firms	−14.65	−42.91	−3.58	−18.28	−46.47
c. Total	0.53	8.76	−2.16	−1.64	6.70
C. Welfare and Distribution					
1. Domestic Absorption	0.09	1.06	0.05	0.14	1.11
2. Household Real Consumption	0.16	1.97	0.15	0.32	2.12
a. Farmers	0.15	2.15	0.13	0.28	2.28
b. Rural Households	0.14	1.92	0.14	0.28	2.05
c. Urban Households	0.19	1.83	0.18	0.38	2.01
3. Foreign Tourist Consumption					
a. Hotels and Restaurants	0.10	0.92	9.37	9.65	10.08
b. All other Services	0.13	−0.28	9.37	9.67	8.80

[a] PG and FG are Partial and Far-reaching Globalization, while DI is Foreign Tourist Demand Increase.

Partial Globalization

The effect of decreases in tariffs is to reduce government revenue and also to lower the price of imported commodities in the domestic market. As the domestic economy is a price taker, this will increase the demand for imported products, contributing to an increase in the availability of products in the domestic economy. Producers export more as some of the lower price imported commodities are also used as intermediate inputs. The stronger price effects on imports result in a worsening of the trade balance as imports increase by more than exports. The decrease in the price of imported intermediate inputs

Table 1b. Effects of Globalization and Foreign Tourism Growth (%)

	Sensitivity Analysis				
Variables (1)	PG[a] (7)	FG[a] (8)	DI[a] (9)	PC&DI (10)	FG&DI (11)
A. Macroeconomic Aggregates					
1. GDP	0.11	0.69	0.03	0.14	0.72
a. Agriculture	0.02	1.65	0.12	0.14	1.77
b. Mining	−0.06	−0.81	−0.11	−0.17	−0.91
c. Manufacturing	0.08	0.41	−0.09	0.00	0.33
d. Services	0.05	0.45	0.12	0.17	0.56
Miles:Hotels	−0.02	1.21	2.73	2.70	3.74
Restaurants	0.04	1.58	0.50	0.53	2.04
2. Employment	0.11	1.42	0.10	0.21	1.51
B. External Conditions					
1. Foreign Trade					
a. Real Exports	0.88	−0.10	0.14	1.02	0.03
b. Real Imports	1.09	1.87	0.12	1.21	1.99
c. Trade Balance	−1.56	−22.60	0.36	−1.23	−22.33
2. Balance of Payments Deficits					
a. Government	357.45	1189.06	24.74	382.20	1213.55
b. Firms	−16.48	−43.32	−2.63	−19.10	−45.79
c. Total	−0.88	8.10	−1.49	−2.36	6.76
C. Welfare and Distribution					
1. Domestic Absorption	0.14	1.09	0.03	0.17	1.12
2. Household Real Consumption	0.25	2.01	0.11	0.36	2.11
a. Farmers	0.22	2.24	0.09	0.31	2.32
b. Rural Households	0.23	1.97	0.09	0.32	2.06
c. Urban Households	0.29	1.83	0.13	0.43	1.95
3. Foreign Tourist Consumption					
a. Hotels and Restaurants	−0.04	2.20	9.09	9.03	10.67
b. All other Services	0.00	−0.26	9.09	9.09	8.08

[a] PG and FG are Partial and Far-reaching Globalization, while DI is Foreign Tourist Demand Increase.

and accompanying fall in the price of goods in the domestic market result in a rise in real income and rise in demand for domestically produced goods. The net effect is a rise in GDP.

Column 2 in Table 1 summarizes the effects of introducing import tariff reductions on the key variables concerned, measured by the percentage changes from the benchmark. It can be seen that the tariff reductions increase imports and foreign trade, thus increasing the availability of products in the domestic economy (by 0.09%). This, in turn, creates additional demand and stimulates production activities so that GDP increases by 0.05%. Adverse effects of the policy take the form of a worsening of the trade balance (imports increase by more than exports) and the government current account deficit. The deficit deteriorates significantly due to the government's loss of revenue from tariffs and low reliance on direct tax revenue, combined with adherence to its planned expenditure. Welfare improves, as indicated by the increases in total domestic absorption (0.09%) and household real consumption (0.16%).

Foreign tourists are also better off as they can consume more with their benchmark level of spending. Their expenditure on hotels and restaurants (the main items of expenditure for them) increases by 0.10%. The modeling procedure assumed that there is no change in the total income (equals total spending) of foreign tourists. The increase in their consumption may be higher, as the lower prices of domestic commodities may encourage them to consume more or even attract more of them to visit Indonesia (see Sinclair and Stabler 1997, for discussion of the microeconomic foundations of tourism demand, and Smith 1994 and Watson and Kopachevsky 1994 for analyses of tourism as a commodity). Moreover, a wide range of studies, reviewed by Crouch (1994a, 1994b), indicates that price is a crucial factor for most tourists when choosing a destination. Note that while total GDP increases, some (import competing) sectors experience a decline in output and GDP contribution. These losses are concentrated in agriculture (−0.06%) and manufacturing (−0.04%). Therefore, there may be additional adjustment costs as the economy reacts to tariff liberalization by reducing employment in these sectors.

Far-reaching Globalization

The positive effects of partial globalization discussed above are amplified in the far-reaching globalization scenario, when import tariff reductions are combined with reductions in indirect taxation on domestic commodities. The reason for this can be traced from the effects of introducing the indirect tax reductions. On the production side, this policy will reduce the domestic prices of domestic products, making them more competitive. This, in turn, stimulates domestic production, creates more employment, and increases GDP. The greatest expansions are in the trade, food processing, and hotel and restaurant sectors. The increases in domestic production and employment raise household incomes, which creates more demand for goods in the domestic market. Imports increase to meet the higher domestic demand but exports decrease as producers find it more profitable to switch their production to meet the higher level of domestic demand for the more competitively priced goods sold internally. This way, the trade balance deteriorates. The policy will reduce the government's income from indirect taxation and worsen its deficit, as the loss of tax revenue has made the government less able to finance its planned expenditure (the revenue loss from the indirect tax cuts is higher than the increases in the government incomes as a result of higher household incomes and hence direct tax revenue). The policy has positive impacts on welfare, as domestic absorption (including household and government consumption as well as investment) and household consumption increase.

Column 3 in Table 1 summarizes the effects of the far-reaching globalization. The direct effect of the combined cuts is a decrease in the domestic prices of imported and domestic commodities. The demand coming from higher household incomes (as a result of the cuts in indirect taxation) magnifies the increase in import demand due to lower import prices (resulting from the first policy). Therefore, the trade balance deteriorates further as imports increase, while the positive impact of import tariff reductions on exports is offset by the negative effects of indirect tax reductions on exports. The end results show that imports increase by 1.86% while exports decrease by 0.18% and the trade balance deteriorates by 23.49%. The increasing availability of products in the domestic economy creates additional demand and stimulates production activities, which results in higher GDP (0.64% increase) and employment (1.34% increase). The government continues to experience adverse effects on its current account deficit. Welfare improves, as can be seen from the increases in total domestic absorption (1.06%), and household real consumption (1.97% increase). Foreign tourists are better off by paying lower prices for the products and services they consume. Their real consumption in hotels and restaurants increases by 0.92%.

Indonesia achieved high growth rates for tourism during the past decade. Events, such as the travel warnings given to tourists after the Bali bombings, may cause arrivals to fall in the short run. However, tourism is likely to grow over the long run and the purpose of this paper is to show the effects of trade liberalization in the presence of tourism growth occurring after a short term disruption. Therefore, a 10% increase in foreign tourist expenditures is simulated and is then combined with the previous globalization simulations. Columns 4–6 in Table 1 summarize the results.

As shown in column 3, the increase in foreign tourism demand will create more production and employment (with market-determined supply responses, GDP increases by 0.06%, and employment increases by 0.16%); however, at the same time, this puts pressure on domestic prices. This is clearly shown in the real consumption by foreign tourists which increases by 9.37% (less than the 10% increase introduced in the initial simulation). Welfare improves, as domestic absorption and household real consumption increase. Domestic absorption increases by 0.05%, while household real consumption increases by 0.15%.

Exports increase by more than imports, resulting in an improvement in the trade balance (increases by 0.70%). The improvement also applies to the balance of payments deficits (reduced by 2.16%).

The next two simulations consider the globalization scenarios in the context of foreign tourism growth. The results, given in columns 5 and 6, show that growth of foreign tourism demand amplifies the positive effects of globalization and, at the same time, reduces its adverse effects. The levels of GDP and employment are higher, particularly in the case of the combination of tourism growth, trade, and tax liberalization (column 6). The trade balance is in deficit, but to a lesser extent than in case of trade and tax liberalization without growth in this industry. The balance of payments deficit is reduced, owing to the increased income from foreign tourism.

Therefore, an obvious policy that the government can undertake is to embark on globalization by reducing its reliance on import tariffs and indirect taxation at a rate that enables the revenue lost by tariff and tax reductions to equal the additional income due to the growth of foreign arrivals. The income from tourism will enable the government's income to be maintained at the benchmark level, so that involvement in globalization will not disrupt its expenditure program. This is a means by which governments, including Indonesia's, can maintain their credibility and avoid fiscal problems. The ability to maintain the expenditure level is also important within a context of overall deflation, as expenditure by the government can help to offset reductions in other components of aggregate demand, such as exports of primary products.

The results obtained from different policy scenarios were subjected to sensitivity analysis, in order to examine their robustness to changes in the export demand elasticity value. This parameter value quantifies the responsiveness of the demand for Indonesia's exports to changes in their price and is particularly important for an economy which is increasingly open to international trade and a depreciating exchange rate. Columns 7–11 in Table 1 summarize the results of the sensitivity analysis, which is conducted by doubling the export demand elasticity values used in the five simulations. The increase in the elasticity values will make the demand from the rest of the world more elastic, so that domestic market prices will be determined, to a greater extent, by the export market. The results confirm that the elasticity values are important in determining the overall results, including the magnitude and, in some cases, the direction of the changes. For any policy changes introduced in the model, higher export demand elasticity values will produce bigger impacts on the real/quantity variables, as clearly shown in the case of globalization (columns 7 and 8). On the other hand, the increase in foreign tourism demand will result in lower price effects for the domestic economy, as shown by the results of the third simulation (column 9). The outcomes of these offsetting effects are shown by the last two simulations (columns 10 and 11). In general, the sensitivity analysis shows the robustness of the results and functional specifications employed in the models, as the results conform to the theoretical predictions.

CONCLUSION

This study has shown that globalization combined with tourism does not necessarily have adverse effects on the domestic economy, in contrast to the past portrayal of the combination as "a deadly mix" (Chavez 1999). Globalization and foreign tourism growth can, in fact, reduce the domestic price level and increase the amount of foreign trade and availability of products in the national economy, thereby stimulating further production. The end result in the Indonesian case is improved macroeconomic performance and welfare, as domestic absorption and household consumption increase. Foreign tourists are also better off, for they can consume more, given their spending level, and also benefit from the greater availability of products. The trade balance and current account deficits are of concern, indicating the need for appropriate accompanying policies, such as the promotion of investment in manufacturing, underpinned by the booming service sector. Moreover, the positive findings from this study do not take account of effects that foreign tourism may have on the environment and culture.

The combined effects of the growth of foreign tourism and globalization are beneficial, overall, as the foreign tourism growth amplifies the positive effects of globalization and at the same time reduces its adverse effects. The trade balance and government accounts are in a better position, owing to the additional receipts from tourism. The ongoing growth of foreign tourism also reduces the government's burdens as a result of embarking on globalization, by enabling it to reduce its reliance on import tariffs and indirect taxation while, at the same time, maintaining the level of income necessary to finance its expenditure. In essence, tourism growth would enable the government to follow a fiscal policy of revenue neutral globalization, allowing it to finance its expenditure without imposing higher taxes on the Indonesian population. ∎

REFERENCES

Adams, P., and B. Parmenter
  1995   An Applied General Equilibrium Analysis of the Economic Effects of Tourism in a Quite Small, Quite Open Economy. Applied Economics 27:985–994.
Ahmad, E., and N. Stern
  1991   The Theory and Practice of Tax Reform in Developing Countries. Cambridge: Oxford University Press.
Alavalapati, J., and W. Adamowicz
  2000   Tourism Impact Modeling for Resource Extraction Regions. Annals of Tourism Research 27:188–202.
Archer, B.
  1995   Importance of Tourism for the Economy of Bermuda. Annals of Tourism Research 22:918–930.
Archer, B., and J. Fletcher
  1996   The Economic Impact of Tourism in the Seychelles. Annals of Tourism Research 23:32–47.
Asian Development Bank
  2000a   Asian Development Outlook 2000. New York: Oxford University.
  2000b   Country Economic Review. Manila: Asian Development Bank.
Begg, D., S. Fischer, and R. Dornbusch

2000 Economics. Maidenhead: McGraw-Hill.
Behrman, J., J. Lewis, and S. Lofti
1989 The Impact of Commodity Price Instability: Experiments with A General Equilibrium Model for Indonesia. *In* Economics in Theory and Practice: An Eclectic Approach, L. Klein and J. Marquez, eds., pp. 59–100. Dordrecht: Kluwer Academic Publisher.
Bergstrom, J., H. Cordell, G. Ashley, and A. Watson
1990 Economic Impacts of Recreational Spending on Rural Areas: A Case Study. Economic Development Quarterly 4:29–39.
Bird R., ed.
1992 Tax Policy and Economic Development. London: John Hopkins University Press.
Bird R., and O. Oldman, eds.
1990 Taxation in Developing Countries. London: John Hopkins University Press.
Blake, A.
2000 A Computable General Equilibrium Model of Tourism in Spain. Mimeo, Christel DeHaan Tourism and Travel Research Institute, University of Nottingham Business School, UK.
Central Bureau of Statistics
1994 The Indonesian Social Economic Accounting System (Sistem Neraca Sosial Ekonomi Indonesia) 1990, Volumes I and II. Jakarta: Central Bureau of Statistics.
1996 The Indonesian Social Economic Accounting System (Sistem Neraca Sosial Ekonomi Indonesia) 1993, Volumes I and II. Jakarta: Central Bureau of Statistics.
Chavez, R.
1999 Globalization and Tourism: Deadly Mix for Indigenous Peoples. Third World Network. <http://www.twnside.org.sg>
Copeland, B.
1991 Tourism, Welfare and De-Industrialization in a Small Open Economy. Economica 58:515–530.
Crouch, G.
1994a The Study of International Tourism Demand: A Survey of Practice. Journal of Travel Research 32(4):41–55.
1994b The Study of International Tourism Demand: A Review of Findings. Journal of Travel Research 33(1):12–23.
Devarajan, S., H. Ghanem, and K. Thierfelder
1997 Economic Reform and Labor Unions: A General Equilibrium Analysis Applied to Bangladesh and Indonesia. The World Bank Economic Review 11. Washington DC: The World Bank.
Dwyer, L., P. Forsyth, J. Madden, and R. Spurr
2000 Economic Impacts of Inbound Tourism under Different Assumptions Regarding the Macroeconomy. Current Issues in Tourism 3:325–363.
Fletcher, J.
1989 Input-Output Analysis and Tourism Impact Studies. Annals of Tourism Research 16:514–529.
Gartner, W.
1987 Environmental Impacts of Recreational Home Developments. Annals of Tourism Research 14:38–57.
Gartner, W., and D. Holecek
1983 Economic Impact of Annual Tourism Industry Exposition. Annals of Tourism Research 10:199–212.
Gillis M., ed.
1989 Tax Reform in Developing Countries London: Duke University Press.
Heng, T., and L. Low
1990 Economic Impact of Tourism in Singapore. Annals of Tourism Research 17:246–269.
Huse, M., T. Gustavsen, and S. Almedal
1998 Tourism Impact Comparisons among Norwegian Towns. Annals of Tourism Research 25:721–738.

700   TOURISM AND GLOBALIZATION

Jensen, T., and S. Wanhill
    2002 Tourism's Taxing Times: Value Added Tax in Europe and Denmark.
        Tourism Management 23:67–79.
Johnson, R., and E. Moore
    1993 Tourism Impact Estimation. Annals of Tourism Research 20:279–283.
Khan, H., C. Seng, and W. Cheong
    1990 Tourism Multiplier Effects on Singapore. Annals of Tourism Research
        17:408–418.
Kompas
    1999a Citra Pariwisata 1998, terburuk dalam satu decade (Tourism profile in
        1998: the worst in a decade). <http://www.kompas.com/ kompas%2Dcetak/
        9902/06/ ekonomi/citr03.htm>
    1999b Menteri Pariwisata se ASEAN: Investasi di pariwisata diberi "tax holiday"
        (Tourism Ministers of the ASEAN countries: "tax holiday" for investments in
        the tourism industry). <http://www.kompas.com/kompas%2Dcetak/9901/
        30/ekonomi/ inve02.htm>
Krugman, P., and M. Obstfeld
    1997 International Economics Theory and Policy. New York: Addison Wesley.
Loomis, J.
    1995 Four Models for Determining Environmental Quality Effects on Rec-
        reation Demand and Regional Economics. Ecological Economics 12:55–66.
Newbery D., and N. Stern, eds.
    1988 The Theory of Taxation for Developing Countries New York: Oxford Uni-
        versity Press.
Pleumarom, A.
    1999a Eco-Tourism: An Ecological and Economic Trap for Third World Coun-
        tries. Third World Network. <http://www.twnside.org.sg>
    1999b The Rise and Fall of South-East Asian Tourism. Third World Network.
        <http://www.twnside.org.sg)>
Rao, M.
    1993 Reform of Indirect Taxes in Developing Countries: Selected Issues. Asian
        Development Review 10:145–158.
Robinson, S., M. El-Said, and N. San
    1998 Rice Policy, Trade and Exchange Rate changes in Indonesia: A General
        Equilibrium Analysis. Journal of Asian Economics 9:393–423.
Roland-Holst, D.
    1992 Stabilization and Structural Adjustment in Indonesia: An Intertemporal
        General Equilibrium Analysis. Paris: OECD.
Sinclair, M., and M. Stabler
    1997 The Economics of Tourism. London: Routledge.
Smith, S.
    1994 The Tourism Product. Annals of Tourism Research 21:582–595.
Sugiyarto, G.
    2001 The Economic Effects and Distributional Implications of Economic
        Reform Policies on the Indonesian Economy: A CGE Approach. Ph.D. thesis
        submitted for the School of Economics, University of Nottingham.
Sugiyarto, G, A., Blake, and M. Sinclair
    2001 The Economic Effects and Distributional Implications of Globalization
        and Foreign Tourism Boom in the Indonesian Economy: A CGE Assessment.
        Paper presented at the Far Eastern Meeting of the Econometric Society,
        Kobe, Japan.
    2002 Economic Impact of Tourism and Globalization in Indonesia, Christel
        DeHaan Tourism and Travel Research Institute Discussion Paper 2002/2.
        <http://www.nottingham.ac.uk/ttri/>
Thorbecke, E.
    1992 Adjustment and Equity in Indonesia. Paris: OECD.
United Nations and World Tourism Organization
    2000 Recommendations on Tourism Statistics. New York: UN.
Wagner, J.
    1997 Estimating the Economic Impacts of Tourism. Annals of Tourism
        Research 24:592–608.

Watson, G., and J. Kopachevsky
  1994   Interpretation of Tourism as Commodity. Annals of Tourism Research
    21:643–660.
West, G.
  1993   Economic Significance of Tourism in Queensland. Annals of Tourism
    Research 20:490–504.
World Bank
  2002   World Development Indicator Data Base. <http://www.worldbank.org>
Zhou, D., J. Yanagida, U. Chakravorty, and P. Leung
  1997   Estimating Economic Impacts of Tourism. Annals of Tourism Research
    24:6–89.

Submitted 11 April 2002. Resubmitted 20 November 2002. Accepted 1 December 2002. Final version 7 February 2003. Refereed anonymously. **Coordinating Editor: Stephen L.J. Smith**

B
Linkages with Local Industry

[13]

TOURISM AND FOOD PRODUCTION IN THE CARIBBEAN

François J. Bélisle
International Development Research Centre
Ottawa, Canada

ABSTRACT

Foreign-exchange leakage through food imports for tourist consumption reduces the net economic impact of tourism in the Caribbean. Yet little is known on the interface between tourism and local food production. Tourism's competition for agricultural labor and land, and its impact on land values, land use and food prices, are disputed by researchers and are poorly understood. Thorough studies are needed on the nature and extent of tourism food imports and associated foreign-exchange leakages; the reasons a large proportion of the food for tourist consumption is imported; and the variation in food supply patterns according to quality, size, ownership, and location of tourist establishment. Further research will help formulate policies designed to increase the net economic impact of tourism. **Keywords:** agriculture, Caribbean, development, food, hotel, import substitution, leakage, tourism.

François Bélisle (Ph.D., University of Georgia) is Program Officer in the Social Sciences Division, International Development Research Centre (P.O. Box 8500, Ottawa, K1G 3H9, Canada). His main research interests include the economic and social impact of tourism in developing countries, particularly in the Caribbean.

Annals of Tourism Research, Vol. 10, pp. 497-513, 1983
Printed in the USA. All rights reserved.

0160-7383/83 $3.00 + .00
© 1983 J. Jafari and Pergamon Press Ltd

TOURISM AND FOOD PRODUCTION

RÉSUMÉ

Tourisme et production alimentaire dans les Antilles. Les fuites de devises étrangères par le biais des importations alimentaires pour consommation touristique, diminuent les retombées économiques du tourisme dans les Antilles. On connaît peu, cependant, les relations entre tourisme et production alimentaire locale. La concurrence du tourisme pour la main d'oeuvre et les terres agricoles, ainsi que son effet sur la valeur et l'utilisation du sol et sur les prix alimentaires, font l'objet de controverses. Des études détaillées font défaut sur la nature et l'ampleur des importations alimentaires pour touristes et des pertes afférentes en devises étrangères; les raisons pour lesquelles les aliments pour touristes sont importés en grande partie; et la variation dans les patrons d'approvisionnement alimentaire en fonction de la qualité, taille, propriété et localisation des établissements touristiques. De plus amples recherches seront utiles pour la formulation de politiques visant à accroître les retombées économiques du tourisme. **Mots Clef:** agriculture, aliments, Antilles, développement, hotel, substitution d'importations, tourisme.

INTRODUCTION

Many Caribbean islands have limited resources for agricultural or industrial development and are turning to tourism to generate income and employment. Caribbean tourism literature shows, however, that there is no consensus on the net economic impact of tourist spending for the islands. This impact is reduced by several foreign-exchange leakages, including the high import content of the food (including beverages) used in hotels. The purpose of this article is to discuss the various facets of the relationship between tourism and food production in the Caribbean and to identify critical areas for further research.

As food accounts for approximately one-third of tourist expenditure, the proportion of food imports for tourist consumption can affect significantly the economic and social impact of tourism. First, if food is imported for tourist consumption, there is a commensurate loss of foreign exchange. Second, there is a loss of opportunity to expand, diversify and, possibly modernize the local food production and processing sectors. Third, there is a corresponding loss of potential employment and income in local food production, process-

FRANÇOIS J. BÉLISLE

ing, distribution, and preparation. Fourth, if certain groups, such as farmers, fail to partake of the economic benefits of tourism while other groups derive considerable profits, increased maldistribution of wealth—a major cause of social unrest in the area—may result. Fifth, the spatial distribution of tourism benefits may be affected if food-producing areas do not supply hotels. Such areas would not benefit from tourist spending, therefore increasing variability in the regional multiplier effect and making the national multiplier reflect inadequately the spatial dimension of tourism impact. Sixth, negative attitudes toward tourists may result among the local population from the social or spatial concentration of tourism benefits. Such attitudes would likely decrease the satisfaction of tourists and reduce their inflow, curtailing further the economic benefits of tourism in the host country.

Leakages of tourism foreign exchange are varied and extensive in the Caribbean, though estimates of their magnitude differ considerably from one study to another. Bryden (1973:218) noted that several leakages reduce the net economic impact of tourism in the Caribbean, including the degree of foreign ownership in the industry, the employment of non-nationals in skilled and professional positions in the industry, and the extent of government involvement through the provision of infrastructure and incentives. Pérez (1973-1974: 474-475) goes further and contends that travel receipts "failed singularly to generate economic development... imported materials, foods prepared abroad, and expatriate staff make up the 'invisible' support system accompanying the traveler to the region." He concludes (p. 480) that "in converting former agricultural monoculture economies to travel monoculture, tourism renews and reinforces the historical process of underdevelopment."

The study prepared for the World Bank (Shankland Cox Partnership 1974:58-59) evaluated for selected islands the proportion of first-round leakage (defined as "the extent to which the recipients lose revenue from tourism in the first round of expenditure"). The overall percentage of first-round leakage was found to be 21 in Puerto Rico, 30 in Bermuda and the Cayman Islands, 34 in Jamaica, 35 to 50 in St. Vincent (depending on class of tourist facilities), and 42 in Barbados.

The Zinder Report prepared for the Agency for International Development gave a multiplier effect of 2.23 for food and miscellaneous purchases, and 2.46 for lodging, sightseeing, and local transportation (Zinder 1969:44-45). These values implied an unrealistically low degree of leakage and were severely criticized by Levitt and Gulati (1970) and Bryden and Faber (1971). The former found,

TOURISM AND FOOD PRODUCTION

after recalculation, that the income multiplier was approximately 1.0. They concluded that an increase in Caribbean tourism and a reduction of the import content of the industry are desirable economic and social objectives.

TOURISM AND FOOD PRODUCTION

Research on the impact of tourism on food production in the Caribbean and in other developing areas has been almost totally neglected. In Cullinan's (1969) assessment of tourism impact on the Latin American economy the food production sector was not mentioned. In 1975 the Organization for Economic Cooperation and Development sponsored an international seminar on tourism research in developing countries; of 20 topics then being researched in the participating countries, none related to food production (Organisation pour la Coopération et le Développement Economiques 1975:21). The Caribbean Tourism Research and Development Centre, based in Barbados and created in the early 1970s, has produced to date numerous studies on tourism impact but none dealing specifically with the relationships between tourism and food production.

Mings (1971:318) noted that little is known about the impact of tourism on agricultural production in the Caribbean, and pointed to the need for further research on ways to maximize use of local food (Mings 1981:340). As Jefferson (n.d.) observed, the potential for linkages is perhaps greatest with agriculture. Tourism can influence agriculture in four interrelated ways: It can modify agricultural employment by attracting labor out of agriculture (competition for labor); reduce availability of agricultural land through an increase in use of land for recreational purposes (competition for land); modify land values and land use in areas surrounding tourism developments; and create incentives for local farmers to expand and diversify their production (and possibly improve production techniques) to meet tourism food demand.

Tourism and Competition for Labor

The impact of tourism on agricultural employment is disputed. Bryden's (1974) view is that tourism is in direct competition for resources with other sectors of the economy, particularly agriculture. He claims tourism attracts workers from, and to the detriment of, agriculture. Jefferson (1972:183) wrote that tourism "raises the reserve price of labor. Some people prefer to remain idle rather than

FRANÇOIS J. BÉLISLE

work for lower wages offered elsewhere—notably in agriculture" O'Loughlin (1968:147) observed in Antigua that "tourism has tended to make the sugar industry even less economic by forcing up wage rates..." Archibald (1970:35) estimated that in the St. Kitts-Nevis-Anguilla area "Tourism at the level anticipated is likely to need about five thousand additional labour units in the next two to three years. This figure is almost the total labour force presently employed in the sugar industry." Similarly, Alleyne (1974:146) believes in detrimental competition for labor between tourism and agriculture: "Under the present structure where tourism in Barbados attracts labour from agriculture, and raises the reserve price of labour in agriculture, the prospects are that expanding tourism in the present circumstances will generate a dying farm sector." Glover's (1976:41) criticism of tourism in the Bahamas is that it led the nation away from farming and fishing which would provide a more stable economy if combined with tourism.

Others, however, have argued that outmigration from the rural areas started before tourism became an attractive employment alternative. Marshall (n.d.:17-18), for example, wrote that in the Bahamas:

> Workers were moving away from agriculture even when there were no alternatives in the islands themselves...Those concerned about agriculture must look at the argument about competition of resources more carefully so that they can be certain that they are not accepting an available and superficially convincing argument as a substitute for a real commitment to agriculture.

Tourism and Competition for Land

There is no consensus regarding competition for land between tourism and agriculture in the Caribbean. Bryden (1973:47, 1974: 154) contends that in the Leewards and the Northern Group, particularly Antigua and Montserrat, agricultural decline has been a direct result of the competition for land by tourism real estate development. Tourism, however, has grown rapidly in these small islands and is of greater relative significance than in the larger islands such as Jamaica, Puerto Rico, the Dominican Republic, and Haiti.

Wibberly (1972:2), on the other hand, maintains that "Although hotels appear to have been lavish in their demands for land, much of this land is not of particularly good agricultural quality." Similarly, Brown (1974:140) examined the decline of Jamaican agriculture

TOURISM AND FOOD PRODUCTION

·and concluded that it "cannot be explained in terms of the fact that the development of the tourist industry deprived agriculture of critical resources (land and capital) to any significant extent."

Tourism, Land Values, and Land Use

Reliable studies concerning the impact of tourism on land values, land use, and land ownership are lacking. Jefferson (1972:183) noted the following paradox:

> while tourism increases the demand for food it may also reduce the supply through its effect on land prices and the availability of the labour force. If food production is adversely affected the import content of tourism, as well as of domestic consumption, may actually rise as the industry expands.

Bryden (1973:218) stated that, although he did not thoroughly examine the issue, "the most likely group of losers are the small peasant farmers, whether they own or rent their land." Birla and McIntosh (1974:215) reported that a discussion group agreed that "Although the expansion of tourism may have aggravated many of its problems, agriculture is plagued with some difficulties which would persist even if the tourist sector did not exist..."

Other Tourism Impacts

O'Loughlin (1968:147) noted in Antigua that tourism tends to create seasonal inflation of food prices. The tourist season increases demand for food, especially certain items of which tourists are fond. If the local production does not expand to satisfy tourist food demand and if food is not imported, price inflation generally occurs (Bélisle and Hoy 1980:93).

TOURISM AS AN INCENTIVE FOR INCREASED LOCAL FOOD PRODUCTION

Although in theory tourism creates an incentive for increased local food production, most of the food for tourist consumption in the Caribbean is imported. Cazes (1972:145) reported that in 1968 Jamaican hotels imported 69.4% of their food supplies and 62.3% of their beverage and cigarettes. Similarly, Gooding (1971: 91) estimated that in Barbados two-thirds of the food consumed by tourists is imported.

FRANÇOIS J. BÉLISLE

It should be noted, however, that tourist expenditure on food benefits more than the agricultural, fishing, and food processing sectors of the host economy. Only between one-third and one-half of all tourist expenditure for food reaches the producer, wholesaler, and retailer. The rest is a value-added cost for food preparation and service. Therefore, even if all the food is locally produced, sold by local middlemen, prepared by local cooks, and served by local waiters, a substantial leakage of food-related tourism foreign exchange may occur if profits are invested outside the host country.

Reasons for Lack of Linkages

The obvious question that comes to mind is: why do the potential linkages between tourism and agriculture largely fail to emerge during the course of tourism development in the Caribbean? There may be several reasons hotels do not use a greater proportion of local food: (a) tourists prefer the type and taste of food consumed in their home countries; (b) imported food is cheaper than local food; (c) hotels accept an opportunity cost to ensure superior quality and/or regularity of food supply; (d) deficient quality of local food (particularly hygienic quality); (e) hotel entrepreneurs are not fully aware of the type and quantity of locally available food; (f) local farmers do not want to change their traditional crop production; (g) farmers cannot increase their production; (h) farmers lack information on the types and quantities of food needed by hotels; (i) farmers are inhibited from dealing with hotels or vice-versa; and (j) farmers or intermediaries are unreliable in terms of regularity of supply or fulfilling other contract agreements. However, available information on the nature and extent of, and reasons for, food imports for tourist consumption is generally both superficial and inconclusive. Hills and Lundgren (1974:6) write:

> At your first meal, a menu, probably designed in Toronto, Chicago or Miami will provide you with a selection of food, imported for the greater part from North America—good familiar, homogenized, taste free food, dressed up with a touch of local colour.

And Floyd (1974:429) observes:

> Particularly sad is the fact that vast quantities of foodstuffs are flown or shipped into Jamaica from the American mainland to meet the discriminating palates of the visitors. The hoped-for stimulus to Jamaican peasants and livestock farmers to produce

TOURISM AND FOOD PRODUCTION

high-quality foodstuff has, as yet, failed to materialise. Hotel managers speak of erratic supplies and inferior domestic produce.

Almost 90% of all tourists in the Caribbean are North American,
and the vast majority of them are notorious for their established and
conservative food preferences. In general, they may be willing to try
local products and dishes, but as Krause, Jud and Joseph (1973:57)
noted, "United States travelers, it is sometimes said, 'want to see the
world, but really don't want to go very far out of their way in the
process'." Gooding (1971:93) reported the general belief among
Barbados hotel and guest-house managers is that "for the general
run of his meals the tourist wants and demands foods he is
accustomed to. Most want to try local dishes, but not to be fed
continuously on them." Doxey's (1973:15) impression was that in
Barbados "many visitors wanted at least an opportunity to try
traditional local foods—an important factor when one considers
ways and means of localizing the industry." But in practice, local
dishes generally account for only a small proportion of menu
offerings, and often do not sell well. The idea of "indigenizing" hotel
food offerings in order to increase linkages with domestic agriculture and reduce food imports has often been expressed (cf. Goffe
1975:31). As Lundberg (1974:84) observed, however, "The argument
in favor of serving locally produced foods makes good economic
sense if the produce can be sold; if not, the argument is wasted."

If preferences and attitudes discussed above are correct, and
assuming it is unrealistic to expect the majority of North American
tourists to change radically their food preferences during their short
stay, then it would appear that local supply should adapt in order to
satisfy tourist demand. It would be useful to compare the Caribbean
with other Third World tourism destinations to determine whether
in some cases tourists consume a greater proportion of local food
and, if so, the reasons they do. One possible reason may be cultural.
Caribbean hoteliers often point out that European, as opposed to
North American, tourists are generally more adventurous in their
eating behavior. De Farcy and De Gunzbourg (1969:72), however,
noted in Europe that tourists visiting rural areas do not modify
substantially their food preferences.

An important and frequently neglected reason that local food is
not used to a greater extent in Caribbean tourism relates to the
historical evolution and current status of food production in the
area. For centuries the development of export crops, especially sugar
cane, has been given priority over the production of food crops for
domestic consumption. The major export crops continue to occupy

FRANÇOIS J. BÉLISLE

the best level land, usually in the form of modern plantations. Small-scale food crop production, on the other hand, is largely relegated to lower-quality land. During the past few decades the agricultural sector in most islands has experienced continued decline (Hope 1981) and the area as a whole has gone from net exporter to net importer of food. There are also physical, behavioral, economic, technological, and marketing obstacles to increasing local food supplies. Much of the land is mountainous with variable precipitation and uneven soil quality. Slavery has deeply affected attitudes toward agricultural work. Small farmers tend to resist innovations and change. The population often lacks confidence in the quality of local food. Maldistribution of land is a serious impediment to increasing the region's food supplies, production costs are relatively high, praedial larceny is common, and private and public investment is insufficient. Technological obstacles include the rudimentary level of farming techniques, the lack of farm equipment and machinery, the limited use of fertilizers and pesticides, and the lack of agricultural research and its proper diffusion. Marketing and storage inadequacies hinder food distribution from producer to consumer; supply is poorly adjusted to demand, with frequent periods of shortage or oversupply and commensurate wide price fluctuations. Food processing in the region is limited by the lack of low-priced regular food supplies, the high cost of imported processing equipment and materials, and insufficient technical expertise. Against this background it is clear that the inability of local food production to supply a greater share of tourist food needs in the Caribbean is the reflection of a much larger problem. Interestingly, Wilson (1979: 222) found similarities in the Seychelles.

Other reasons that may account for some of the reliance of Caribbean hotels on imported food include the links between foreign-owned and managed establishments (particularly those pertaining to transnational hotel chains) and overseas food suppliers, and the type of training received by hotel food and beverage decision-makers. While foreign hotel ownership remains important in the Caribbean, it has decreased in many islands since the 1960s. In Jamaica, for example, most of the existing hotel capacity is now owned by Jamaican public and private interests. Large hotels belonging to foreign chains do not account for a large proportion of hotels although their share of the total number of hotel rooms, and consequently their total food demand, is usually much more considerable. In other cases, however, large hotels may be locally owned, but their management is leased to specialized foreign firms for a set fee and often a profit share. This arrangement appears in fact to be

TOURISM AND FOOD PRODUCTION

increasingly popular; it reduces the threat posed to foreign investors by changing local regulations affecting foreign ownership, including possible nationalization, and it increases local control and pride in the industry. It is probable that the links between foreign-owned and operated hotels and overseas food suppliers account for part of the food imports for tourist consumption; how much, however, remains to be determined through further research. Similarly, whereas 10 or 20 years ago the proportion of expatriates in food and beverage decision-making positions was quite large, it has decreased considerably. Now only some of the higher-category hotels boast a foreign chef or food and beverage manager. Many locals have been trained and have replaced expatriates in these positions. Some, however, have been trained in North America and have probably become accustomed to using frozen, canned, dried, or otherwise processed foods, as well as portion-controlled foods, because these are more convenient and sometimes cheaper than their fresh counterpart. In the Caribbean, however, most of these foods are imported. The origin and training of the personnel making decisions on menus and food purchases hence may account for some of the food imports, but their effect, difficult to measure, can be better understood only through further study.

THE DEMONSTRATION EFFECT

The demonstration effect is the phenomenon whereby tourist consumption patterns influence those of the residents. If tourists consume local food, the demonstration effect can be a positive force for local production and import substitution. Doxey (n.d.:82) writes that:

> If the tourist can be persuaded that the local product is part of the tourist experience, the inhabitants of the destination will likewise tend to reflect the preferences of the tourists. Thus, for instance, instead of moving up to whiskey, the tourist and locals should be persuaded to roll along with rum!

Moreover, tourists can be favorably impressed by local products such as tropical fruit or vegetables. When they return to their home country they may become occasional or regular buyers of such products, thus stimulating exports of countries they visited.

At present, however, the demonstration effect would appear to be generally detrimental to local production. Pérez (1975:31) states that "insofar as tourists serve as a reference group, they necessarily

FRANÇOIS J. BELISLE

influence consumption patterns of the island populations. This may, inevitably, augur an increasing preference for imported commodities over goods produced locally." Bryden (1973:214) also believes that the demonstration effect is partly responsible for increased food imports and declining agricultural production in those islands which have experienced rapid tourism growth.

HOTEL FOOD SUPPLY

Hotel food supply in the Caribbean has been examined, among others, by Lundgren, Gooding, and Momsen. Lundgren (1971, 1974, 1975a, 1975b) described how six Jamaican hotels purchase selected local products, and identified the geographical patterns of supply of these products according to perishability. Lundgren's (1975b:64) research addresses "the composition, structure, and range of the agricultural food supply response to hotel-generated demands, in general." Despite the small sample size, Lundgren shed some light on hotel food supply. He found hotel food hinterlands to be wider than suspected, although two-thirds of the supply of several commodities come from within 10 miles. Hotels deal with farmers, fixed retailers, and "higglers" (itinerant intermediaries). The majority of transactions are concluded with nearby producers. Such transactions are characterized by a relatively high frequency but low volume of sales. Lundgren also examined the spatial supply structure for tomatoes, cucumbers, and Irish potatoes, and showed that different supply patterns emerge as a function of perishability.

In the book on *The Tourist Industry in Barbados* by Doxey and Associates, Gooding (1974) discussed tourism and food. A questionnaire was completed by three hotels, one guest house, and one supermarket (serving mostly tourist apartments). It was found that about one-half of the food by weight, but only one-third by value, is of local origin. Gooding (1971:91) hypothesized, however, that it "seems highly probable that the cheaper guest houses use a greater proportion of locally produced foods." The supermarket only used about 20% of local food by value. The hotel owners surveyed thought Barbadian food prices were high, quality of local food was low (except for pork and fish) and not graded, but availability was irregular. It was also calculated that the daily value of food consumed by a tourist is more than five times that of the average Barbadian, and it was suggested that Barbadian food producers would find it beneficial to supply the tourist industry to the extent possible.

Momsen (1972, 1973) wrote two reports on food production and tourism, one on St. Lucia, and the other on Montserrat. The emphasis

TOURISM AND FOOD PRODUCTION

of both reports is on agriculture, and their format and methodology are similar for comparison purposes. Despite statistical presentation that limits interpretation, Momsen's findings are of interest. In St. Lucia, hotel representatives stated that seafood and milk were the local foods least urgently needed. Most hotels obtain their local food from several sources (the producer, hawker, market, marketing board, agent, supermarket, and own estate). Most hotel representatives complained of the uncertainty of supply. The results of the Montserrat study (Momsen 1973) revealed little difference with those of the St. Lucia study.

IS FOOD IMPORT SUBSTITUTION POSSIBLE?

In 1966 the British Ministry of Overseas Development published the *Report of the Tripartite Economic Survey of the Eastern Caribbean*, still considered a valid statement on the Caribbean economy. With respect to tourism and food, the report (Great Britain 1966:ix and xi) concludes:

> Though tourism can be the prime generator of economic development, growth cannot be based on expanding tourism alone. Tourism must be supplemented by a major effort in the direction of import substitution, particularly of food items...The agricultural sector must grow in order to provide increased exports and import substitutes. While there are real possibilities for growth for some of the existing export crops, taken as a whole these will not generate the necessary rate of growth in the economy. There is, however, considerable scope for increasing output in the rest of the agricultural sector.

In addition, it was stated that "the long-term potential for a fishing industry seems good."

Many authorities believe that stronger linkages could exist in the Caribbean between the tourist industry and food production and that food import substitution is practicable. For example, Alleyne (1974:144) contends that "the case that the imports could not be replaced by domestic production cannot be substantiated." He calculated for Barbados that, assuming reasonable yields, approximately 15 square miles or less than 10% of the total area of Barbados would be needed to substitute for imports (for both tourists and locals) of vegetables, fresh fruit, and nuts. However, he considers the land ownership structure and inadequate marketing facilities major obstacles to food import substitution. The Caribbean Ecumenical Consultation for Development (1972:37) also argues that "much of

FRANÇOIS J. BÉLISLE

the future economic development in the region, through industrialization and the diversification of agriculture, can be directed at an import substitution policy in support of tourism." Ramsaran (1979: 87) pointed out that in the Bahamas the food sector could be substantially expanded and provide more food for tourists. Based on a recent study of tourism impact in selected Caribbean islands, however, Bélisle, Seward, and Spinrad (1982:159) noted that some islands have potential for expanding agricultural production to serve tourist demand but others have very limited possibilities, and that improvements in quality control, storage, and distribution would have to accompany agricultural expansion. They concluded that "it does not seem reasonable to expect major changes that will increase linkages between tourism and other sectors of the economy rapidly," although fruit, vegetable and seafood production could be stimulated.

Several Caribbean nations have attempted over the past two decades to pursue food import substitution in order to save on foreign exchange. Generally import substitution policies and programs have aimed at increasing domestic production through improved support to small farmers and guaranteed prices for selected commodities, and they have focused on the internal market as opposed to the tourist market. Although detailed studies on the success or failure of such policies and programs are lacking, on the whole results do not appear to have been very successful as attested by the continued decline of food production in many parts of the Caribbean basin. More research is needed on the type and degree of success or failure of institutional factors seeking to prevent hotels buying and local food producers supplying more of the food consumed by tourists.

CONCLUSION

Food imports for tourist consumption in the Caribbean are a source of foreign-exchange leakage and reduce the net economic impact of tourist spending. Yet, the paucity of research into the relationships between tourism and food production makes it difficult to draw conclusions that could support new policy initiatives. This article suggests four major critical gaps for research. First, the nature and extent of food imports and associated foreign-exchange leakages need thorough examination to provide a basis for formulating, improving, and monitoring food import substitution policies and programs. Second, competition of tourism for agricultural labor and land, and tourism impact on land values, land use, and food

TOURISM AND FOOD PRODUCTION

prices, require further study for more reliable conclusions. Third, the reasons a large proportion of the food for the tourist industry is imported instead of produced locally should be analyzed. Fourth, it should be shown whether the consumption of local or imported food varies with structural characteristics of tourism such as hotel quality, size, ownership, or location. Further research into these critical areas will improve understanding of the interaction between tourism and food production in the Caribbean, with potential relevance to other developing regions, and will help formulate policies and programs designed to increase the net economic impact of tourism. □ □

ACKNOWLEDGEMENT

The author gratefully acknowledges the Inter-American Foundation which supported the research on which this article is based.

REFERENCES

Alleyne, F.
 1974 The Expansion of Tourism and Its Concomitant Unrealised Potential for Agriculture Development in the Barbadian Economy. Proceedings, West Indies Agricultural Economics Conference 9: 143-152.
Archibald, M.A.
 1970 Some Aspects of the Possible Effects of Tourism on Agricultural Development in the State of St. Kitts-Nevis-Anguilla. Proceedings. West Indies Agricultural Economics Conference 5:34-40.
Bélisle, F.J. and D.R. Hoy
 1980 The Perceived Impact of Tourism by Residents: A Case Study in Santa Marta, Colombia. Annals of Tourism Research 7(1):83-101.
Bélisle, F.J., S.B. Seward, and B.K. Spinrad
 1982 Summary and Conclusions. *In* Tourism in the Caribbean: The Economic Impact, S.B. Seward and B.K. Spinrad, eds. pp. 151-163. Ottawa, Canada: International Development Research Centre.
Birla, S.C. and C.E. McIntosh
 1974 The Relationship Between Tourism and Agriculture. Proceedings, West Indies Agricultural Economics Conference 9: 215-220.
Brown, H.
 1974 Impact of the Tourist Industries on the Agricultural Sectors: The Competition for Resources and the Market for Food Provided by Tourism; The Case of Jamaica. Proceedings, West Indies Agricultural Economics Conference 9:129-142.
Bryden, J.M.
 1973 Tourism and Development: A Case Study of the Commonwealth Caribbean. Cambridge, England: Cambridge University Press.
 1974 Impact of the Tourist Industries on the Agricultural Sectors: The Competition for Resources and Food Demand Aspects (With Special Reference to the Smaller Economies of the Region). Proceedings, West Indies Agricultural Economics Conference 9: 153-161.

FRANÇOIS J. BÉLISLE

Bryden, J.M. and M. Faber
   1971 Multiplying the Tourist Multiplier. Social and Economic Studies 18(1) 61-82.
Caribbean Ecumenical Consultation for Development
   1972 The Role of Tourism in Caribbean Development. Report of the Ecumenical
         Consultation, Study Paper No. 3. Bridgetown, Barbados: Cadec Publications.
Cazes, G.
   1972 Le Rôle du Tourisme dans la Croissance Economique: Réflexions à Partir de
         Trois Exemples Antillais. The Tourist Review 27(3): 93-98 and 144-148.
Cullinan, T.
   1969 Tourism in Latin America. A Research Report by the Long Range Planning
         Service, Stanford Research Institute. Report No. 380.
Doxey, G.V.
   n.d. Tourism as a Tool of Development. *In* Caribbean Tourism: The Economic
         Impact of Tourism, pp.70-79. Christ Church, Barbados: Caribbean Tourism
         Research Centre.
   1973 Ensuring a Lasting Tourist Industry: The Barbados Experience. Paper Pre-
         sented at the Pacific Area Travel Association Research Seminar, Suva, Fiji,
         October 15-19.
De Farcy, H. and P. De Gunzbourg
   1967 Tourisme et Milieu Rural: Un Débouché Rentable pour l'Agriculture. Paris:
         Flammarion.
Floyd, B.
   1974 The Two Faces of Jamaica. Geographical Magazine 46(8):424-431.
Glover, W.G.
   1976 Tourism as an Impetus to Economic Change and Development: A Case from
         the Bahamas. Florida Journal of Anthropology 1(2):33-43.
Goffe, P.W.
   1975 How Developing Nations View Tourism: Development Potential of Interna-
         tional Tourism in Jamaica. The Cornell Hotel and Restaurant Administration
         Quarterly 16(3):24-31.
Gooding, E.G.B.
   1971 Food Production in Barbados with Particular Reference to Tourism (Ap-
         pendix One). *In* G.V. Doxey and Associates, The Tourist Industry in Barbados: A
         Socio-Economic Assessment, pp. 73-116. Kitchener, Canada: Dusco Graphics.
Great Britain, Ministry of Overseas Development
   1966 Report of the Tripartite Economic Survey of the Eastern Caribbean. London,
         England: Her Majesty's Stationery Office.
Hills, L. and J. Lundgren
   1974 The Impact of Tourism: A Methodological Study with Examples from the
         Caribbean and Possible Lessons for the South Pacific. Montreal, Canada: McGill
         University, Department of Geography (Mimeographed).
Hope, K.R.
   1981 Agriculture and Economic Development in the Caribbean. Food Policy
         6(4):253-265.
Jefferson, O.
   n.d. Some Economic Aspects of Tourism. *In* Caribbean Tourism: The Economic
         Impact of Tourism, pp. 53-69. Christ Church, Barbados: Caribbean Tourism
         Research Centre.
   1972 The Post-War Economic Development of Jamaica. Kingston: University of the
         West Indies, Institute of Social and Economic Research.

TOURISM AND FOOD PRODUCTION

Krause, W., G.D. Jud, and H. Joseph
    1973   International Tourism and Latin American Development. Austin, Texas:
            University of Texas at Austin, Graduate School of Business.
Levitt, K. and I. Gulati
    1970   Income Effect of Tourist Spending: Mystification Multiplied: A Critical Com-
            ment on the Zinder Report. Social and Economic Studies 19(3):326-343.
Lundberg, D.E.
    1974   Caribbean Tourism: Social and Racial Tensions. The Cornell Hotel and
            Restaurant Administration Quarterly 15(1):82-87.
Lundgren, J.O.J.
    1971   Agricultural Marketing and Distribution Arrangements with Respect to the
            Resort Hotel in the Caribbean. The Tourist Review 26:(3)86-93.
    1974   The Entrepreneurial Structure in the Caribbean Hotel Food Supply System.
            Paper presented at the Ninth West Indies Agricultural Economics Conference,
            Kingston, Jamaica.
    1975a   Tourist Impact/Island Entrepreneurship in the Caribbean. In Geographical
            Analysis for Development in Latin America and the Caribbean, R.P. Momsen, ed.,
            pp. 12-19. Chapel Hill: CLAG Publications.
    1975b   Tourist Penetration/The Tourist Product/Entrepreneurial Response. In
            Tourism as a Factor in National and Regional Development, Occasional Paper No.
            4, pp. 60-70. Peterborough, Canada: Trent University Department of Geography.
Marshall, D.
    n.d.   Agriculture and Tourism in the Barbados: The Competition for Resources.
            Kingston, Jamaica: University of the West Indies, Institute of Social and Eco-
            nomic Research (Mimeographed).
Mings, R.C.
    1971   Research on the Tourist Industry in Latin America: Its Present Status and
            Future Needs. In Geographic Research on Latin America: Benchmark 1970, B.
            Lentnek, R.L. Carmin, and T.L. Martinson, eds., pp. 315-323. Muncie, Indiana:
            Ball State University, CLAG Publications.
    1981   Tourism Development in Latin America and Related Needs. In Geographic
            Research on Latin America: Benchmark 1980, T.L. Martinson and G.S. Elbow,
            eds. pp. 336-346. Proceedings of the Conference of Latin Americanist Geo-
            graphers 8.
Momsen, J.D.
    1972   Report on Vegetable Production and the Tourist Industry in St. Lucia.
            Calgary, Canada: University of Calgary.
    1973   Report on Food Production and the Tourist Industry in Montserrat. Calgary,
            Canada: University of Calgary.
O'Loughlin, C.
    1968   Economic and Political Change in the Leeward and Windward Islands. New
            Haven: Yale University Press.
Organisation de Coopération et de Développement Economiques
    1975   Séminaire sur la Recherche Concernant le Tourisme dans les Pays en
            Développement. Paris: Organisation de Coopération et de Développement
            Economiques, Centre de Développement.
Pérez, L.A. Jr.
    1973-1974 Aspects of Underdevelopment: Tourism in the West Indies. Science and
            Society 37:473-480.
    1975   Underdevelopment and Dependency: Tourism in the West Indies. El Paso,
            Texas: University of Texas at El Paso, Center for Inter-American Studies.

FRANÇOIS J. BÉLISLE

Ramsaran, R.
  1979 Tourism in the Economy of the Bahamas. Caribbean Studies 19(1-2):75-91.
Shankland Cox Partnership
  1974 Tourism Supply in the Caribbean Region. A Study for the World Bank.
Wibberly, G.
  1972 Tourist Development in the Caribbean and its Effects on Land Use and
    Agricultural Policy. London: University of London, Countryside Planning De-
    partment (Mimeographed).
Wilson, D.
  1979 The Early Effects of Tourism in the Seychelles. *In* Tourism: Passport to
    Development? E. de Kadt, ed., pp. 205-236. New York: Oxford University Press.
Zinder, H. and Associates
  1969 The Future of Tourism in the Eastern Caribbean. A report prepared under
    contract with the Agency for International Development. Washington, DC: H.
    Zinder and Associates, Inc.

Submitted 15 April 1982
Revised version submitted 23 July 1982
Accepted 10 November 1982
Final version submitted 31 December 1982
Refereed anonymously

[14]

Developing–island economies — tourism v agriculture

Hugh Latimer

During the peak years of international tourism in developing countries, 1960–1974, the anti-tourism literature claimed that tourism was destroying other sectors, particularly agriculture, by competing for labour and land resources, and by increasing their reserve prices. Evidence is derived mainly from islands where movement of food, and labour supplies, were restricted, and many were suffering from the long-term decline in the sugar and copra trades. The article casts doubt on Bryden's proof by cost–benefit analysis that tourism had a poor social return, and even questions whether agriculture *did* decline in the critical period. Labour and land competition are shown to be inherently implausible, although the reserve price of labour may have been raised by the construction industry.

Keywords: developing countries; tourism; agriculture

The 1960s and early 1970s (up to the oil price increases of 1973 to 1974) were the golden age of tourism earnings growth for developing countries, with annual rates of increase in gross receipts rising by 15% in the Caribbean and Asia compared to 9% or 10% in Europe and North America. The earlier trend of a gradually falling share of developing countries in world receipts was thus reversed.[1] By 1975 lower- and middle-income countries ($2 500 per annum per capita or less) earned $10 000 million from tourism against $5 600 million from sugar and $3 900 million from coffee, the next highest earners.[2] Not included in this group are the Hawaiian Islands whose arrivals grew from 300 000 to 3 million per annum in 10 years after becoming one of the States of the USA in 1959.[3]

A tourism project which is attractive commercially is likely to have an even better social return. This is because its gains are in foreign exchange and most of its costs in domestic resources; it employs some labour whose opportunity cost elsewhere would be very small; and above all, because of indirect benefits. Investment in a tourist attraction, for instance, benefits not only its promoters but also those in the accommodation, food and drink, internal transportation, entertainments and shopping industries, as well as government.

Hugh Latimer is visiting lecturer at the Project Planning Centre for Developing Countries, University of Bradford, Bradford, UK.

When any new industry is established, or an existing industry grows, it will compete with other economic pursuits for available resources, change social hierarchies and cause envy. The literature of tourism impact, in the early 1970s, was almost universally hostile, concentrating on the negative impact of effects. For example in a work that was highly influential because of its detailed data and careful phrasing, Bryden advanced the hypothesis that tourism grew in the Commonwealth Caribbean in competition with other sectors, principally export and domestic agriculture, bidding directly for labour and sometimes land, and also "for particular resources which would serve to change the production functions in agriculture — in particular scarce skilled manpower and domestic capital, especially government's." He also hypothesized, without evidence however, that the advance of tourism would be "immiserating", ie make the poor poorer, and that this "can explain why hostility towards tourists arises".[4]

For Barbados, Frank Alleyne warned that "under the present structure, where tourism in Barbados attracts labour from agriculture, the prospects are that expanding tourism will generate a dying farm sector", (1974).[5] In the pointedly named collection "A New Kind of Sugar", Kent alleges that even beyond the normal tendency of capitalist industry to overproduction, the tourist industry has proved particularly vulnerable to economic trends and business recessions.[6] The flow of anti-tourism literature has abated since 1977.

The 1974 oil price hike showed, not that tourists would be discouraged (they began to flood back again as early as 1976) but that hotel investors, except in the Far East, had become shy. After 1975 90.6% of new associations with trans-national companies in developing countries were by management contract or franchising, not partnerships nor leasing.[7] But the reactions of the mid 1970s have not been challenged and have become the accepted wisdom of today. To quote

0261-5177/85/010032-12$03.00 © 1985 Butterworth & Co (Publishers) Ltd a recent statement by an influential economist with the British Overseas Development Administration:

> The experience of many small countries is that tourism displaces existing sectors of the economy and makes it more difficult for new ones to develop . . . In this respect a tourism boom is not unlike the discovery and exploitation of oil. The effect of tourism works through via (*sic*) its demand for labour, its pressure on wage levels, its boost to local inflation, and its effect in keeping the exchange rate for the local currency higher than otherwise. In most countries, traditional agriculture simply cannot compete, since most producers and farm workers are very happy to abandon the hard and poorly regarded work in farming for what they perceive as the easier life in the various tourist sectors. The same is true of export agriculture, which in the West Indies is redolent of slavery.[8]

Though this section of Winpenny's paper specified small countries, it was headed "Should a country opt for a major expansion of tourism?" against which it advised the governments of Jamaica, Barbados and Mauritius after previously commending the alleged policy of Egypt and Turkey in limiting tourism development.

The message is repeated to development economists generally in a reference book by Bridges and Winpenny published the following year: "Many countries have seen a decline in other sectors of the economy as resources have been drawn into an expanding tourist sector." Here the better paid work into which agricultural labourers are said to be attracted is specified as "hotels, restaurants, taxis, etc".[9]

These and similar assumptions are overdue for questioning. The ambivalent wording makes it impossible to quarrel entirely with Winpenny. It will be argued in this paper that export agriculture has indeed declined in tropical islands, but not because of tourism; that traditional agriculture has also declined where national income has risen, whether through tourism or any other cause, but that it remains to be proved that agriculture as a whole has suffered or will suffer. Correlation is not causation.

What differentiates tropical islands?

The experience of all these writers derives mainly from the small island economies of the Caribbean and the Pacific. It is misleading without further evidence to generalize from the experience of Caribbean islanders, and the fears of Pacific islanders to the developing world as a whole, even in relation to social impact. The experience of these small island economies in relation to economic impact cannot be extrapolated to countries like Egypt and Turkey, both with splendid tourism potential inadequately exploited, and with agricultural sectors so extensive that they could never seriously be considered in danger from any much needed increase in tourism earnings. Egypt's hotel

sector, 91% privately owned, is arguably the most efficient in the economy. Egypt is the one country which could possibly give colour to the oil analogy, for oil, tourism and Suez Canal dues together currently maintain the currency at a higher level than would otherwise be possible. Egypt's tourist attractions are unique so that only war and disturbance, not high cost, will keep tourists away. But most countries are not in such a happy position; they have competitors. Generally (and Egypt is not immune from this rule) an overrated currency is a self-regulating tap turning off the flow of earnings so that tourism and high currency values cannot happily coexist.[10]

What features differentiate larger tourism economies? Kenya and Tunisia, whose domestic net earnings have been estimated as 60% and 70% of gross earnings,[11] may suggest an answer. Kenya enjoys a variety of climates and soil conditions; labour and commodities can be freely transferred within its territory; it has an adaptable farm sector, mixed farming rather than plantation-orientated, and a developed marketing system. Thus the sunbathing tourist on the Coast may have excellent lamb and pork from the Aberdares, vegetables from the Kikuyu Highlands, and pineapples and tropical fruit from the vicinity, while his vehicle is serviced and his curios produced by Kamba tribesmen, themselves rarely visited by tourists in their own territory. Certainly tourism in a larger country like Colombia can raise local prices[12] but buyers have an opportunity of buying further afield and entrepreneurs of locating elsewhere.

By contrast, populations of the mini-economies of the Caribbean, range from 238 000 (Barbados: 1970) to the still colonial territories of Montserrat (12 000 in 1960), Cayman Islands (9 000 in 1970), British Virgin Islands (10 500 in 1970), and Turks and Caicos (8 000). Each of these jealously cultivates job opportunities for its own nationals or 'belongers' and restricts immigration, though seasonal migration is allowed.

Although attempts have been made through Caricom and other trading treaties to establish a free trade area, the aim of agricultural self-sufficiency pursued by governments generally relates to small ecologically restricted terrains, Barbados for instance is low-lying and 85% coral limestone. The larger islands, like Jamaica, Hispaniola, Cuba and Puerto Rico, have wider production possibilities.[13]

Bryden's analysis. Bryden was concerned to correct the inflated accounts of the benefits to be gained from tourism by studies such as the Zinder Report.[14] He quoted corrections of the multiplier used, but showed quite conclusively that the tourism multiplier is no guide to decision-making because it does not take into

account opportunity costs.[15] Social cost–benefit analysis was recommended instead, and for this purpose he
constructed an imaginary project from a feasibility
study. The main 'social' effect was to apply a shadow
wage rate of 74% or 80% to the local labour
employed, which would improve the social internal
rate of return (IRR) of the project; and to include net
benefits from the tourists' spending outside the hotel.
Both these would serve to make the social IRR of the
project higher than the private one. However other
assumptions were less defensible:

● First, he took the data for a feasibility study on a
  marginal new 100-bed hotel in Antigua and
  applied to it the average occupancy levels in
  small islands (not then benefitting from the
  reduction of seasonality which has since occurred); these were 31.8% bed occupancy per
  annum in the first year of operation, rising to
  45% in the 4th, 55% in the 9th and 65% in the
  15th. Such projected occupancy rates would have
  scared any investor. The project ceased in year
  20: Bryden omitted to include the residual value.

● Average profit take-off from the Antiguan hotel
  sector in 1965 was a mere 1.4% of turnover, but
  Bryden took the gross profit from the feasibility
  study of 22.8% and assumed that it was all
  repatriated, thus a loss to the economy, leaving
  nothing for replacements or even tax.[16]

● Of the payroll no less than 40% was assumed to
  go to expatriates (including West Indians from
  other islands); this datum was taken from the
  Cayman Islands, which with a total population of
  9 000 in 1970 naturally employs a high proportion of non-belongers in its hotels. All this
  'expatriate' income was accounted a loss to the
  economy, even the proportion respent (which is
  not normal practice).

● Bryden then adds to the project cost the
  government infrastructure cost, estimated at
  69% of the cost of the hotel, but omits to subtract
  the return to government from the telephone,
  electricity and water charges.

● On top of that, he adds promotional costs to the
  tourist office of $3 000 per room per year, though
  this was not an inescapable consequence of
  building a new hotel.

As a result of these corrections, which must be
regarded as illicit, Bryden reduces the social return
from a preliminary 15.5% to 8.63% per annum.[17]
    Among the more challenging assumptions which
Bryden made was that no contribution to the new
hotel's inputs or to those of ancillary industry could be
expected at all from domestic agriculture in the 20

years of project life. This might indeed have seemed
reasonable for Antigua, for that island, always dry and
with a correspondingly chequered history of crises for
its sugar and cotton industries, was suffering in
1960–1969 from a nine-year drought.[18] But the
assumption that other Caribbean islands can meet no
extra demands at all for food and drink from their
agricultural and fishing sectors was common at the
time and based on a pessimistic political theory and an
'optical illusion'. For just at the time when food
self-sufficiency had become a public objective in the
Caribbean, under the influence of the then rising
dependency school of development economics and the
related Black Power movement, the arrival of tourism
with extra demands meant that total food imports rose.
    Bryden himself justified his conclusion by a dubious
table which showed that GDP in domestic agriculture
fell in three out of six islands of the Commonwealth
Caribbean between the years 1962 and 1966, a period
in which hotels and services rose in five out of six of
these islands. (Here Antigua has been omitted from
Bryden's table because of the drought.) A close look at
the table shows however that *total* agricultural output
rose in five out of the six, because of a temporary
upturn in export agriculture (eg if a farmer grows
beans that is domestic: if next year he turns to bananas
that is export).[19]

Impact of tourism on agriculture

In 1974 (ironically after the tourism growth boom in
the Caribbean was over) the Ninth West Indian
Agricultural Economics Conference addressed the
whole subject of the relationship of agriculture to other
sectors, with particular reference to the competition for
resources. Apart from two papers on bauxite and
petroleum, tourism was the main alternative industry
discussed. Of the data which are summarized in
Table 1, Headley Brown, Director of Social Planning,
Jamaica, commented "This trend is one of the most
important indicators of the failure of domestic agriculture during the last seven years".[20]
    In relative terms, imports provided a higher propor-
tion of the total, 69% against 66%, in 1972 than in 1965
giving rise to pessimism. On the other hand, an
increase in domestic supplies from $3.6 million to $9.3
million ($6.36 million in 1965 prices), hardly represents
failure. Import supplies are almost always infinitely
elastic; the elasticity of domestic supply must always be
less, at least in the short run of seven years. Johnson
and Strachan showed that in constant prices of 1960,
domestic agriculture in Jamaica rose from $15.5 million
in 1962 to $21.9 million in 1971 (or 5.4% per annum)
and livestock and hunting from $9.6 million to $15.8

Table 1. Total expenditure on food and drink by the tourist industry, Jamaica 1965 (EC $ million).

	Total	Estimated imports	Domestic supply	Cost of living index	Domestic supply (1965 $)
1965	11.8	8.2	3.6	100	3.6
1970	20.3	15.06	5.24	129.6	4.04
1972	27.6	18.3	9.3	146.1	6.36

Source: Op cit, text reference 20, p 137, table 3.

million (or 5.7% per annum).[21]

Similarly, for the period 1969–1973, during which Barbados tourism arrivals rose by 60%, production of poultry meat and cucumbers trebled, that of onions, cabbage and pumpkins increased fourfold, while beet production increased sixfold and carrots ninefold. Though islands vary in their adaptability, the thesis that Caribbean agriculture did not respond at all to the tourist boom must be rejected. However the responses did raise problems, as outlined below.[22]

Hotel imports. It seems to be a common statistic of this period that two thirds of hotel supplies were imported. Gooding estimates that in Barbados two thirds of food eaten by tourists was imported, Cazes gives 69.4% food and 62.3% beverage and cigarette imports for Jamaican hotels in 1968.[23]

The reasons, briefly discussed by Belisle, may be:

● most tourists are Americans and/or conservative in their tastes;
● imported food may be cheaper;
● hotels will pay more to be sure of quality and supply;
● local food may be unhygienic;
● hotel supply managers are unaware of local possibilities; and
● producers do not know how to contact the hotel trade.[24]

The response of island agriculturalists as entrepreneurs to the new opportunities in Seychelles where the author had the good fortune to work for four months of the winter of 1975–76, was positive but patchy. They were quick to meet the demand for broiler chicken meat, as also seems to have been the pattern in the Caribbean. One Seychelles entrepreneur started an avocado orchard; in Jamaica Lundgren found that a single large pineapple plantation was supplying most hotels on the North Coast. In tracing food sources for a hotel sample, he found that while most produce came from nearby, a minority of farmers were supplying specialities from the most distant parts of Jamaica. He concluded that agricultural enterprise was certainly alive.[25] In Seychelles the most remarkable response came from the fishermen (traditionally all Seychellois

are fishermen) who trebled their supplies to the Victoria market over the worst years of the imported inflation, with the result that year-round average fish prices remained steady during these years.[26] Wilson's report to the contrary, dates from an earlier period, suggesting that time must be allowed before judgment is made on entrepreneurial response in islands.[27] As an example of non-response, however, a hotel supply manager in Seychelles told the author that he had tried without success to obtain supplies of mangoes, which grow freely in every back yard, and had never been marketed before. The price he was offered would, he said, have made a breakfast mango as expensive as in Paris, and so he gave up trying.

From the pioneering work of Lundgren and from other experience, a summary can be made of some ways in which food agricultural inputs into a tourist industry can be improved:[28]

Island food production

● Most management input is expended on the most quickly degradable materials which need to be delivered to hotels most frequently.
● More planning is required for supplies from local sources, which receive rhetorical rather than practical help in most small islands. Improvement of road systems (in Jamaica) may be less important than help with contracts, insurance for non-delivery, and back-up supply arrangements for the hotel manager if the supplier cannot deliver.
● The hotel supply manager, whose rank is relatively junior in the hotel hierarchy, is operating on a very tight working capital budget and his efficiency will be judged by worldwide industrial criteria, eg how many times a year the inventory is turned over. Therefore it is not enough to rely on cold storage at the hotels; there must also be cold storage for the producer, cooperative or wholesaler who can recoup their costs by buying during a surplus and selling during a scarcity. Hotels will not perform this function.
● Official advice is needed about shading, night temperatures, fertilizer, etc suitable for grow-

ing temperate vegetables in tropical climates.
- If possible, as in Bali, the government should set up an experimental farm to pass on information to local farmers.[29]
- Local specialities and cuisine add to the quality of a tourist venue and they should be promoted by the tourism office. But only by financial pressure can the industry dissuade the North American holiday-maker away from his preference for crisp lettuce, 'Irish' potatoes, and prime cuts of beef. The levy of differential duties is influential in guiding hotel buyers into domestic sourcing. Unfortunately the way chosen by most Caribbean governments has been rhetoric followed by outright prohibition, which simply makes the prohibited article more desirable. Regular meetings between the domestic authorities and supply managers should be instituted, but if quotas are imposed, this at once makes the managers advocates of imports rather than of domestic sourcing.

Agriculture today. A decade has now elapsed since the end of the golden age of tourism. International tourist arrivals in the Caribbean have continued to grow and the time interval should have helped domestic production to raise its share of tourist supplies. To decide whether or not it has will demand more physical data from a number of islands, taking into account the various restrictions imposed by governments, which have not always been successful. A recently published survey on food and drink supplies in the Caribbean yields disappointingly little post-1974 information. But Belisle does show that the conditions of which Bryden complained are no longer operative.[30] Only a minority of hotels are now foreign-owned; managers taking decisions about food and drink are now much more likely to be Caribbean nationals.

A recent study showed that some Caribbean islands have potential for expanding production to serve tourist demand but others have very limited possibilities, and improvements in quality control, storage and distribution are important.[31] Government attempts to increase self-sufficiency have mostly concentrated on 'peasant' production for domestic demand. The irony is that for years experts

have been lamenting the division in the Caribbean between an extensive plantation export sector in control of the best land, and a backward so-called 'peasant' hill-farming. Now that the demand has at last arrived for a modern industrial-type domestic agriculture, to serve not only the hotels and restaurants but also the supermarkets, in which locals as well as condominium-dwellers buy their food, the opportunity is hardly being seized with eager hands.

Decline in export agriculture

That tourism 'exports' gained while agricultural exports lost ground can not be disputed, as evinced by Table 2. The tropical paradises which became prime tourist islands were mostly either sugar producers or copra producers. The decline of the sugar export trade since 1963, when the world market price reached one of its peaks, has been a feature of tropical development. Basically it has been caused by many new entrants to the market; the increase in irrigation and use of chemicals, leading to increased productivity; the similar advance of beet sugar; and a change in the flows of the market. Sugar is a commodity with inelastic demand at high incomes but elastic demand at low incomes, which means that the demand growth comes from developing countries themselves. Hence import substitution, not only in protectionist Europe, but also throughout the world. Though there will always be some trade, the historic function of the 'sugar' islands may have ended.

It has been possible for sugar economies to protect themselves by trade supply agreements at price levels above the world price, which thus acts only as a market for residual output after quotas have been filled. Cuba, the world's largest exporter/producer, made a historic marketing decision when in 1959 it opted for the Soviet trading bloc. Hawaii and Puerto Rico, tied to the US Sugar Act which was not renewed after 1974, saw their sugar economy quickly dissolving as marginal fields went out of production and companies moved to the Philippines, where labour was cheaper.[32] Was the US legislature less willing to protect Hawaii because of the contemporary rise in tourism arrivals from 300000 in 1960 to 3 million in 1974? Possibly, but not for long. Fiji,

Table 2. Agricultural exports and tourist arrivals, Caricom, 1965–1974.

	1965	1966	1967	1968	1969	1970	1971	1972	1973	1974
Sugar (long tons ×10³)	1190	1100	1080	1130	1051	970	1020	950	840	940
Bananas (long tons ×10³)	358	342	338	319	305	253	249	246	200	269
Tourist arrivals (×10³)	–	–	–	610	670	733	852	946	978	992

Source: op cit, text reference 34, tables 5.2 and 6.1.

using quotas under the Lomé agreement, tied to the intervention price for beet sugar, was able to double its output between 1975 and 1980, but at declining prices.[33] The Commonwealth Caribbean, with an export price based on the Commonwealth Sugar Agreement, which remained almost static in Barbados dollars from 1960 to 1970, and subsequently at the Lomé Agreement price, has been less fortunate. With sugar yields per acre of only about 2.5 tons against Belgium's 4 tons and Hawaii's 9 tons, and costs generally 30% higher than Fiji's, the sugar industry, which is still favoured by Caribbean governments for the foreign exchange it earns, needs the best land available to keep in production at all.[34] Production is still falling.

The Jamaica banana industry (marketed by Fyffes and others in the UK) had been declining for some time, and much of the trade was captured by new developments in the Windward Islands (marketed by Geest). Exports of bananas fell steadily from 180 000 long tons in 1965 to 72 000 long tons in 1974 (Jamaica) and from 178 000 tons to 96 000 tons (Windward Islands). Yields per acre were believed to be very low compared to those obtained in Central America, Africa or the French Antilles. Poor cultivation practices, insufficient or inefficient use of inputs, and unsuitable land were among the causes. There was approximately 25% wastage of harvested fruit, due partly to poor roads. Bananas are grown on smallholdings as a rule and only rarely on plantations. Exports were dependent on the UK market, which was inclined to switch to cheaper alternative suppliers.[35]

The productivity of Seychelles coconut plantations reached a peak in 1952 and entered a gradual decline in 1955 (reported by Cooke in 1958 and quoted in Wilson).[36] In the mid-1970s most plantations were run-down. Tourism only began after the completion of the airport in 1971. In 1975 the Seychelles government permitted a French company to take over the lease of the island of Silhouette in return for reconstituting a traditional plantation there, combined with a limited tourism development, an interesting way of combining the two industries. Wilson discusses whether the pre-1960 traditional economy could have been maintained without tourism, and without deciding the issue, comments that it certainly could not have offered the same income per head.[37]

Competition and economic impact

It is necessary to deal briefly with Bryden's charges that tourism took resources of land, labour and

capital away from other industries, and with the more subtle case of Winpenny that it affected other industries by raising the reserve price of labour and introduced inflation.

Land

The direct competition for land between tourism and agriculture would seem to be a minor issue in most islands. Headley Brown admitted that tourism had taken only marginal land in Jamaica.[38] In many island groups, of which the Master Plans for St Vincent and the Grenadines, for Tonga, and for Bali are witnesses, islands enjoy ecological contrasts which facilitate the allocation problem. Areas with little rainfall have dependable sunshine, sandy beaches or rocky coasts, while good agricultural areas have good rainfall, alluvial soil and protection from sea-winds. Nusa Dua in Bali and Cancun in Mexico were chosen for their poor agricultural potential, among other reasons. Bryden's claim, repeated several times, refers to one event only, the loss of 1 200 acres in Montserrat, of which 500 seems to have been good agricultural land, to retiree settlements schemes.[39] Now this is a different sort of tourism, and in any case may sometimes provide more horticultural produce than without the settlement. It affected Hawaii too, but the proportion of resort to agricultural acreage in the state is 100 000 acres in agriculture to 1 000 acres in resorts.[40]

More serious issues arise, not in tropical islands, but in the game parks of Africa. Unquestionably the designation of parks reduces the economic opportunities of the tribes whose herds formerly grazed them.[41] Most such tribesmen already possess enough land however; in other cases, attempts should be made to provide alternative occupation as rangers, if only to protect the game from poaching.[42]

Fishermen, unlike agriculturalists, do have to compete for shore space with tourism, and if only on tourism grounds, need to have their harbours and houses protected by land planning. The economic criterion in case of a dispute between different users of scarce resources should not be the finances of the different industries, but the social cost to each claimant industry of moving elsewhere, probably weighted by income distribution criteria. This is only necessary where each industry must be accommodated in the overall strategy of the country concerned.

Labour

It is difficult to disprove the thesis that agricultural labourers are drawn to the hotel, restaurant and taxi trades, but if it were so, surely their presence as waiters or barmen would be more evident? Entrants to the hotel trade are normally recruited either direct from school or come from the *urban* unemployed. Bryden himself carried out a survey of hotel staff in the Cayman Islands; of 100 employees 48 came from a previous job in the same sector and 24 had no previous job. He mentions none from agriculture.[43] The largest hotel in Seychelles opened in 1976; it drew no labour from nearby villages.

Samy however found that of 466 employees of a hotel in a rural part of Fiji, 23% had previously been cane farmers. Of these half were Fijian and half Fijian Indian. Most Indians said they had left their land because their farms had been returned to Fijians; the Fijians alone said that they preferred hotel work, in which, Samy shows, they have better prospects than the Indians. Thus there was little evidence that hotel employment was responsible for the fall in sugar production locally.[44]

Hotel and restaurant work often has a special appeal to women who tend to have a second job as housekeepers even when 'unemployed'. But if tourism taking labour from agriculture simply means that women in rural communities are offered a chance of employment, it is hard to take it seriously.

Headley Brown is the authority who made the most serious attempt to prove the draw from agriculture into tourism.[45] He cites the fall in the numbers of agricultural workers in Jamaica between 1960 and 1972 (7%) together with the doubling over the same period of numbers employed in the hotel and restaurant trade. As additional evidence, he points out the decline in the population of sugar parishes combined with the rise in that of St James parish, which has the largest tourist sector in the island. Instead of going to the overcrowded capital, Kingston, they went to the North Coast. But the rise in employment in one industry combined with the fall in another does not itself prove that one takes workers from another.

In Jamaica, particularly, numbers are against the Headley Brown thesis. The Jamaican hotel industry's labour force rose from 4 350 in 1960 to 9 000 in 1972. During the same period those in agriculture fell from 229 719 to 214 700. Thus in 1960 there was one job in the hotels for every 50 in agriculture, and by 1972 there were two jobs in hotels to every 50. The increase in hotel employment, though welcome, was equal to just one year's net addition to the Jamaican labour force from the schools.

Indirect competition. Headley Brown, Bryden and others also refer to the pull of the indirect tourism sector. Indirect employment is in sectors catering to

the hotels or, outside the hotels, directly to the tourists, as in transport, mechanical repair work, boats, crafts, entertainment and shops. It can be considerable in countries like Kenya or Tunisia, where it can constitute four or six times direct employment in hotels.[46] But in newly developing tourist economies like Seychelles and the Gambia, Holm-Petersen has estimated that for every job in a hotel only 0.24 of a job is created in Seychelles and 0.18 in the Gambia.[47] Small islands in the Caribbean probably approximate more to the Seychelles pattern than to that of Kenya, while Jamaica is somewhere between. So it can be concluded that only in a developed tourism economy is there a significant pull from agriculture to the indirect sector, but not in an undeveloped tourism economy. Development will include upgrading the agricultural input. In Kenya for every direct job created, 0.56 of a job is thought to be created in agriculture; in Tunisia 0.72 to 0.9 of a job.[48]

There is serious misconception created by the use of the phrase 'population employed in agriculture' and of the even more loaded phrase 'peasant agriculture' for islands like those in the Caribbean, the Pacific and Seychelles. There are indeed true peasants in Mauritius and Fiji, Bali and even the Channel Isles. The term implies a dogged attachment to the land as a way of life. In Seychelles there was no such attachment — people are much attached to their own plot of land (which once would have been a grace and favour of some plantation owner) but the land is seen as a form of social security, a place from which family members go out to earn money at sea or for a spell of paid employment elsewhere and to which they return after emigration. In the West Indies the pattern seems to have been similar. There, in order to obtain adequate labour supplies for the sugar factory, plantation owners would accept outlyer production. The 'peasants' would supplement an inadequate income by seasonal work cane-cutting on the plantation. But perhaps only one member of the family could be accounted a serious and full-time farmer — the father, which explains why so many 'peasant' agriculturalists in the West Indies are found to be 50 years old and more.[49] It is a convenience of the census takers to call them agriculturalists. As soon as some full time employment makes its appearance, those enumerated in the agricultural sector become fewer. They are a residual of the population counts.

Reserve price for labour

Hotel work, like agricultural work, is notoriously

underpaid so it seems unlikely that tourism can raise the reserve price for labour. But closer inspection inclines one to believe that, historically, at least, in the period 1960–1974, the rise of tourism did raise the reserve price of labour for agriculture in the Caribbean, as also in Hawaii and the Pacific, though the prime factor was not so much tourism itself as the construction boom which preceded it. In some islands (Seychelles for instance) this was directly connected with the tourism boom itself (the airport), but in others it was due to the general and successful impulse for economic development which obtained in the 1950s and 1960s.

Table 3 shows that in Barbados, until 1975, the average weekly wage in hotels had indeed been allowed to rise above that in sugar-cane growing and other agriculture. In the Caribbean where traditionally any other occupation (except perhaps domestic service) is preferred because of the historical connection of agriculture with slavery, this would certainly explain the upward pull on agricultural wages. In 1975 this anomaly was corrected by a 40% jump in agricultural wages, and hotel work became, as in other islands, a sector with pay only just above that of domestic service. Significantly in Hawaii the tourist industry was criticized for the *low* wages it offered and its pull on *immigrant* labour.[50]

Payroll costs. It was not a case of the hotel industry being able to afford to pay higher wages than the sugar plantations. Both were caught up in a wage–price spiral in the 1970s which threatened the viability of export industries. The fastest growing

activity in this period was not tourism-related, but government service. First class hotels in the Caribbean area, for the whole period from 1975 to 1981 inclusive, were combining third-world standards of employment (generally one employee per bedroom, against American and Hawaiian standards of about 0.6) with high payroll and payroll-related costs of about 35% of total annual sales — comparable to those of Western Europe. Payroll costs in Mexico, emerging as the Caribbean's chief local rival for American tourists, were about 26% of total sales in comparable hotels; and for new luxury hotels in the Far East, payroll costs are only about 18% of sales, although employment there may be between 1.5 and 2 per bedroom. Thus the Caribbean group of first-class hotels has been debited every year until 1982 with the worst productivity record — total sales per dollar spent on payroll costs (see Table 4).

Food costs. At the same time, food costs as a proportion of food sales are also among the highest in the world; because of the inadequate attention paid to reducing the cost of local sourcing already referred to. Combined with some over-capitalization in the first place, this has made the returns on fixed assets and on sales in the region, notoriously the lowest in the whole world (see Table 5).

Increased competitiveness. The tourist for his part was paying more per day in the hotel sector than in comparable destinations, eg in Mexico and Central America. Barbados, with the US Virgin Islands, Puerto Rico and other tourist destinations with similar high cost problems, found an economic answer — the development of the condominium. This enables the now more down-market US tourist to avoid high hotel and food costs. A major element which followed 1974 was, of course, the decline in absolute predominance of US citizens among total visitors. Other areas responded in different ways:

- by seeking new markets;
- by reducing the cost of food and drink as a proportion of sales of food and drink; and
- in resort locations especially, by reducing the capital cost of hotels to conform with the

Table 3. Average weekly wage in selected activities in Barbados. (Barbados dollars; = 50 cents US).

	1972	1973	1974	1975	1976
Hotels	17.20	26.47	27.00	27.00	27.00
Domestic service	14.75	15.18	17.85	19.82	22.32
Sugarcane growing[a]	15.70	15.70	22.50	31.30	31.30
Other agriculture	14.50	16.00	23.00	32.00	32.00
Construction	25.66	29.00	30.40	31.80	41.45

Note: [a]Out-of-season wage rates; wages are higher during the harvest.
Source: Department of Labour, Barbados, quoted in L.M. Bayro, 'Barbados', in T.A. Powers, ed, *Estimating Accounting Prices for Projects Appraisal*, Inter-American Development Bank, Washington DC, USA, 1981.

Table 4. Total payroll and related costs as a percentage of total sales, luxury and first-class hotels 1975–1982.

	1975	1976	1977	1978	1980	1981	1982
Caribbean	38.7	37.3	36.9	36.9	33.4	39.4	25.8
Mexico	26.7	28.2	26.2	26.5	26.5	n.a.	33.7
Hawaii and Pacific	36.2	32.7	33.8	30.1	32.9	30.9	31.3
USA	37.9	36.4	35.1	35.8	33.7	33.6	36.2
Far East	27.4	23.8	18.6	17.7	19.1	16.5	29.2

Table 5. Income before fixed charges as a percentage of total sales, luxury and first class hotels, 1979–1982.

	1979	1980	1981	1982
Caribbean	1.1	7.5	2.2	8.3
Mexico	27.5	31.1	—ᵃ	26.4
Hawaii and Pacific	25.1	27.9	24.3	20.7
USA	26.4	26.5	25.6	21.7
Far East	37.4	38.5	39.0	27.2

Note: ᵃnot available.
Source: Horwath and Horwath International, *Worldwide Lodging Industry,* 1976 to 1983, New York, USA.

tourist's providential desire for a simpler (if still luxurious) vacation-style.

Hawaii and the Pacific also reduced the labour force sharply towards US standards; and in the Caribbean, there was a trend away from the hotel model altogether.

Construction industry impact. From Table 3 it is clear that the industry which really did draw agricultural workers away from the land was the construction industry, whose wages (and this is true of all islands) far surpassed the others. This is for four reasons:

- construction contracts do not last forever;
- the contracts have to be finished within a time schedule and unskilled labour pay is generally not the major element in costs;
- construction companies were in competition with one another; and
- labour, even though unskilled, needs to be physically able and male.

Unlike tourism, construction normally draws labour direct from the land.

Common pattern

Every island's experience of the golden age of tourism differs. But it is possible, from three island groups, Tahiti–Moorea, Antigua and Seychelles, to discern a common pattern of how wage and wage expectation inflation arose. Though all three had previously a significant tourist image (otherwise the boom could not have occurred) the major development of the tourist industry followed rather than preceded the inflationary boom in each.

Agricultural decay. The first stage was the decay of the traditional agricultural export industry. In Seychelles, by 1955 most of the coconut palms were 80 years old. Vanilla exports reached their peak in Tahiti about 1961, copra in 1966.[51] Antigua is generally a semi-arid island, (annual rainfall less

than 45 inches) and has inadequate irrigation. The drought which lasted from 1960 to 1969 put an end to 300 years of admittedly patchy sugar production. From an average of 26 000 tons in the years 1956 to 1960 production fell to 14 000 tons in 1965, and the following year the company gave up production. The Antigua government took over with subsidies but itself gave up production in 1972.[52] The sugar industry was restarted later, but for local consumption.

Alternative employment. The Antiguans emigrated mainly to the UK. The rate of population growth was zero for the years 1961 to 1966, compared with an average of 2.5% per annum for similar islands in the group.[53] Seychellois took service in the Pioneer Corps or in the merchant navy, and Seychelloises as nannies in the Middle East — giving many of them excellent training for their later careers in the hotel industry.

The economic event which rescued Tahiti and Moorea from its export decline was the establishment in 1963–1964 of the Centre d'Experimentation du Pacifique, the French nuclear testing base. Construction workers were being paid four times the average wage. Although tourist arrivals grew steadily from 1960 they were still only 16 000 in 1966. Tourism really took off in 1967–1968. This continued the building boom which had started with the base. The result gave the islands one of the highest living costs in the Pacific.

Antigua's inflationary boom was caused by the completion of the petroleum refinery in 1966 when a formidable 41.5% of GDP was accounted for by the construction industry. It fell back to 27.5% in 1967 when the refinery came on stream, and later to a more normal 9%, but wage levels rose. The cost of labour was already high. It was 40.6% of total sales in hotels and boarding houses in 1963, which must be one of the highest in the world.[54]

Tourist composition. US tourist arrivals stopped growing. Antigua gained more fellow West Indians, but the average length of stay fell to between two and three days, showing that many were using Antigua only as a stop-over. Blume commented in 1974 that there were little other than expensive hotels.[55] The 1974 oil-price rise caused the US tourists to seek nearer shores like those of Bermuda and Bahamas; when they returned they were more price-conscious and the Caribbean holiday concept had changed.

Economic revival. The final stage is of economic revival, which may or may not take an agricultural form and may have no overt connection with tourism. Barbados was industrial. Seychelles had the fishing industry — some enterprising yachtsmen in 1975 were exporting fish to Italy, and it is probable that marine-based activities would have developed if these had been encouraged. In Moorea a dynamic market-gardening sector made its appearance. The Antigua government took the initiative and managed to push back the contribution of agriculture to GDP up from 0.9% in 1967 to 4% in 1971.

Despite Antigua's temporary misfortunes tourism may be considered as a second commodity crop to support the fluctuations in the established crop. Even the North American depression in the three years from 1980 to 1982 only reduced Caribbean tourist arrivals by 3.4%. Island export agriculture is never secure. Guernsey tomatoes were originally a substitute for hospital grapes; now that the seasonal pre-eminence of the tomato is in its turn being threatened by the Dutch, tourism (and banking) provides a cushion while islanders experiment with freesias and other crops. Singapore lost its agriculture and fishing but now exports orchids, while Jamaica is doing well with rum. Only in one respect is international tourism more sensitive than other commodity exports — it is highly susceptible to war and civil disturbance.

Inflation

Inflation and exchange variations do not themselves inhibit earning, provided that the economic controllers are aware of the need to take account of the interests of the tourism trade in international competition, eg as in Spain. But in a small island it can do a great deal of damage to land-hungry investment through speculation. Prices in Seychelles began to rise as early as 1971, because of the intention to build an airport. The colonial Seychelles government, which showed itself quick to nip wage inflation in the bud, was too slow to prevent good tourism sites from falling into speculative hands. Zonal planning was introduced too late. As a result when Seychelles badly needed new hotels in 1976 to keep up the planned rate of economic growth, landowners were asking uneconomic prices. This example suggests that it is not enough for agricultural and fishing areas to be protected by physical planning; an island government must actually designate the best tourism areas and allocate them itself in the public interest. Inflation also damaged tourism and agriculture in Puerto Rico and Hawaii, but in some other islands there is still surplus plantation land seeking economic use.

Prosperity

Not all wage- and land-price increases are detrimental to growth. On the contrary, they can reflect the rising real incomes which result from successful export based growth. In tourism islands this process is obvious, eg Bermuda has a higher GNP than the UK and the Bahamas are approaching that level. In other island groups, such as Singapore and Hong Kong, the achievement of visitor levels of over two million annually is merely another indication of the economic opportunism which brings the inhabitants economic success in trade and manufacture. This change can be traumatic. Medium family income in North Kohala rose from $4 363 to $8 380 in one year, 1969–1970.[56]

When people rise from poverty, they change their living standards, and with them some agricultural pursuits which derive from poverty. They give up hunting and gathering and take to serious production. Some forms of agriculture, export-orientated as well as subsistence, become obsolete. At a certain wage per hour the cost of sending someone shinning up a coconut tree becomes greater than the value of the coconuts. Sentimentalists deplore the loss of the 'breadfruit way of life'. This may be justified culturally but tropical islanders themselves do not prefer breadfruit and poverty in paradise, and they have good reason for resenting the attempts to keep them in 'paradise' by academics and civil servants who themselves are among the classes who compete with tourists and do not gain from the industry.[57]

Conclusion

This paper has reviewed the more serious developmental arguments against international tourism as a vehicle of economic growth, especially its effects on agriculture. It is suggested that these effects are particular to small tropical island groups with limited growing potential and restrictive import policies. Even in these, it is questionable whether tourism took sizeable resources of land and labour away from agriculture and even whether there was any net decline in agriculture at all, though more facts are needed on this issue. It has been claimed that better use for public money could have been found in agriculture than in supporting the infrastructure of tourism but this seems unlikely. It is agreed that more could have been done to aid the development of agricultural and fishing inputs into tourism and other growth-related demand.

Developmentally, a recent survey by the Fund and Bank has distinguished the disadvantages suffered by small island economies. They have to move into dynamic sectors where economies of scale play little part or where they have resource advantages; the main avenues are tourism, fisheries, and light manufactures for export, in that order.[58] In larger islands, such as Mauritius, (over dependent on sugar) the Bank is currently pursuing structural adjustment programmes which include the development of tourism. The anti-tourism lobby among developmentalists can be regarded as positively mischievous. Of course a society has a right and a government a duty, to avoid tourism where it is feared that the social and cultural consequences will be disastrous. But from a strictly economic view, where the analysis is entirely quantitative, if projected benefits outweigh costs, tourism ranks with any other export choice.

Notes and references

[1] J.M. Bryden, *Tourism and Development*, Cambridge University Press, Cambridge, UK, 1973.
[2] E. de Kadt, ed, *Tourism, Passport to Development*, Oxford University Press, Oxford, UK, 1976, p 3.
[3] L. Fukunaga, 'A new sun in North Kohala', in B.R. Finney and K.A. Watson, eds, *A New Kind of Sugar*, University Center for South Pacific Studies, Santa Cruz, CA, USA, 1977.
[4] J.M. Bryden, 'The impact of the tourist industries on the agricultural sectors; the competition for resources and food demand aspects', in *Proceedings of the 9th West Indies Agricultural Economics Conference*, UWI, 1974.
[5] F.A. Alleyne, 'The expansion of tourism and its concomitant unrealised potential for agricultural development in the Barbadian economy', *Proceedings of the 9th West Indies Agricultural Economics Conference*, UWI, 1974.
[6] N. Kent, 'A new kind of sugar', in Finney and Watson, eds, *Op cit*, Ref 3, p 181.
[7] J.H. Dunning and M. MacQueen, *Transnational Corporations in International Tourism*, United Nations Centre on Transnational Corporations, United Nations, 1982.
[8] J.T. Winpenny, 'Some issues in the identification and appraisal of tourism projects in developing countries', paper presented at the Surrey International Tourism Conference, September 1982, in *Tourism Management*, Vol 3, No 4, December 1982, pp 218–221.
[9] G.A. Bridger and J.T. Winpenny, *Planning Development Projects*, Overseas Development Association, London, UK, 1983, p 190.
[10] As has been shown by the fluctuating fortunes of US and UK tourism in the 1980s.
[11] R.H. Green, 'Towards planning tourism in African countries', in *op cit*, Ref 2, p 82.
[12] F.J. Belisle and D.R. Hoy, 'The perceived impact of tourism by residents; a case study in Santa Maria, Colombia', *Annals of Tourism Research*, Vol 7, No 1, 1980.
[13] Helmut Blume, *The Caribbean Islands*, Longman, London, 1974.
[14] J.M. Bryden and M.L.O. Faber, 'Multiplying the tourist multiplier', *Social and Economic Studies*, March 1971.
[15] Bryden, *op cit*, Ref 1, chapter 5.
[16] *Ibid*, p 166.
[17] *Ibid*, chapter 10.
[18] Blume, *op cit*, Ref 13, p 326.
[19] Bryden, *op cit*, Ref 1, Table 3.9.
[20] Headley Brown, 'The impact of the tourist industries on the agricultural sectors', in 'The competition for resources and the market for food provided by Jamaica', *Proceedings of the 9th West Indies Agricultural Economics Conference*, UWI, 1974, p 136.
[21] I.E. Johnson and M.O. Strachan, 'Agricultural development in Jamaica', *Proceedings of the 9th West Indies Agricultural Economics Conference*, UWI, 1974, p 19.
[22] Alleyne, *op cit*, Ref 5.
[23] E.G.B. Gooding, 'Food production in Barbados with particular reference to tourism', in G.V. Doxey *et al*, eds, *The Tourist Industry in Barbados*, Kitchener, Canada, 1971, pp 73–116, p 91; and G. Cazes, 'Le rôle du tourisme dans la croissance économique: reflexions à partir de trois examplaires Antillais', *The Tourist Review*, Vol 27, No 3, 1972, p 43.
[24] J. Francois Belisle, 'Tourism and food production in the Caribbean', *Annals of Tourism Research*, Vol 10, No 4, 1983, p 502.
[25] J.O. Lundgren, 'Agricultural marketing and distribution arrangements with respect to the Resort Hotel in the Caribbean', *Proceedings of the 6th West Indies Agricultural Economics Conference*, UWI, 1971, p 176.
[26] Government of Seychelles, 1975, p 60, Table 60.
[27] D. Wilson, 'The early effects of tourism in the Seychelles', in *op cit*, Ref 2, p 205.
[28] Lundgren, *op cit*, Ref 25.
[29] IBRD Nusa Dua Project, 1973.
[30] Belisle, *op cit*, Ref 24, p 509.
[31] J.O. Belisle, S.B. Seward, and B.K. Spinrad, 'Summary and conclusions', in S.B. Seward and B.K. Spinrad, eds, *Tourism in the Caribbean: the Economic Impact*, International Development Research Centre, 1982, p 169.
[32] Fukunaga, *op cit*, Ref 3.
[33] Fiji Government, *Eighth Development Plan 1981–1985*, Vol 1, Central Planning Office, Suva, Fiji, 1980.
[34] S. Chernick, ed, *The Commonwealth Caribbean*, IBRD, 1978, p 420.
[35] *Ibid*, p 142.
[36] Wilson, *op cit*, Ref 27, p 209.
[37] *Ibid*, p 233.
[38] Headley Brown, *op cit*, Ref 20, p 131.
[39] Bryden, *op cit*, Ref 4, p 41.
[40] Donald Tong, 'Planning for tourism on the island of Hawaii', in Finney and Watson, eds, *op cit*, Ref 3.
[41] S.C. Curry, 'Tourism circuit planning; carrying capacity at Ngorongoro Crater, Tanzania', Bradford University, forthcoming.
[42] IBRD: Kenya Wildlife Study, 1976.
[43] Bryden, *op cit*, Ref 1, p 131.
[44] J. Samy, 'Crumbs from the table? The workers' share in tourism', in Finney and Watson, eds, *op cit*, Ref 3.
[45] Headley Brown, *op cit*, Ref 20, p 129.
[46] de Kadt, *op cit*, Ref 2, p 38.
[47] Erik Holm-Petersen, *Consequences of Mass Tourism in Developing Countries: Case Studies of Seychelles and the Gambia*, Hoff and Overgaard, Copenhagen, Denmark, 1978.
[48] de Kadt, *op cit*, Ref 2, p 38.
[49] Headley Brown, *op cit*, Ref 20.
[50] Kent, *op cit*, Ref 6; Fukunaga, *op cit*, Ref 3.
[51] Claude Robineau, 'The Tahitian economy and tourism', in Finney and Watson, eds, *op cit*, Ref 3.
[52] Blume, *op cit*, Ref 13.
[53] Bryden, *op cit*, Ref 1, p 12.
[54] *Ibid*, Table 7.9.
[55] Blume, *op cit*, Ref 13.
[56] Fukunaga, *op cit*, Ref 3, p 217.
[57] H. Latimer, 'Consumer and producer surpluses in tourism', *Tourism Management*, Vol 2, No 3, September 1981.
[58] B. Legarda, 'Small island economies', *Finance and Development*, June, 1984, p 43.

[15]

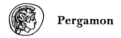
Pergamon

Annals of Tourism Research, Vol. 23, No. 3, pp. 635–653, 1996
Copyright © 1996 Elsevier Science Ltd
Printed in Great Britain. All rights reserved
0160-7383/96 $15.00+0.00

0160-7383 (95) 00087-9

LINKAGES BETWEEN TOURISM AND FOOD PRODUCTION

David J. Telfer
Geoffrey Wall
University of Waterloo, Canada

Abstract: The relationships between food production and tourism range from conflict over competition for land, labor and capital to symbiosis where both sectors mutually benefit from each other. This paper reviews the literature on relationships between food production, particularly agriculture and tourism. It then examines the efforts of a resort on the island of Lombok, Indonesia, to increase the amount of local food products used in its restaurants through the establishment of two projects involving local food producers. It is argued that there is potential to increase backward linkages between tourism and local food production but that there are substantial challenges to be overcome in doing so. **Keywords:** agriculture, fishing, backward linkages, Lombok, Indonesia. Copyright © 1996 Elsevier Science Ltd

Résumé: Liens entre le tourisme et la production alimentaire. Les rapports entre le tourisme et la production alimentaire varient entre des conflits pour la terre, la main-d'oeuvre et le capital et une symbiose où les deux secteurs se portent des bénéfices mutuels. On passe en revue la littérature sur le tourisme et la production alimentaire, en particulier l'agriculture. Puis on examine les efforts d'une station balnéaire à l'île de Lombok (Indonésie) pour augmenter l'utilisation des produits alimentaires locaux dans ses restaurants dans l'établissement de deux projets avec des producteurs locaux de comestibles. On soutient qu'il serait possible d'augmenter les liens en sens inverse entre le tourisme et la production alimentaire locale, mais qu'il y a des difficultés importantes à surmonter. **Mots-clés:** agriculture, pêche, liens en sens inverse, Lombok, Indonésie.

INTRODUCTION

International tourism receipts totaled over US$297 billion in 1992 with developing countries accounting for 25.2% of the total (WTO 1994). Developing countries use tourism to generate foreign exchange, to increase employment, to attract development capital, and to promote economic independence (Britton 1982:336). Through employment, tourism provides the opportunity for direct and indirect linkages with the local community. Efforts to maximize the economic benefits derived from tourism in destination areas have centered on increasing the number of tourists, increasing the tourists' length of stay, and increasing tourists' overall expenditures. A complementary way to enhance the benefits of tourism is to expand the backward economic linkages by increasing the amount of local food used in the tourism industry. There is a need to investigate and strengthen the economic linkages between tourism areas and their hinterlands.

David Telfer is Doctoral Candidate and **Geoffrey Wall** is Professor in the Department of Geography, University of Waterloo (Waterloo Ontario N2L 3G1, Canada. Email gwall@watserv1.uwaterloo.ca). The first author's research is on linkages between tourism and agriculture. The second author has undertaken various tourism studies in Indonesia.

Considering that food represents approximately one-third of all tourist expenditures, the level of imports used can greatly affect the economic and social impacts of tourism (Belisle 1983). Despite the importance of food as an input in the tourism sector, it continues to receive very little attention in the literature. Belisle noted that "research on the impact of tourism on food production in the Caribbean and in other developing areas has almost been totally neglected" (1983:500). Again in 1991, Bowen, Cox and Fox reinforced this comment by stating that "little is known about the proportions of products purchased directly and indirectly by tourists. Even less information is available for tourism-linked agricultural services" (1991:53). Theoretically, domestic agriculture and fishing and those associated with them, provided that surplus production is available for sale, have the potential to benefit from increased tourist demand. According to Wilkinson tourism has the potential to be a "focus for local economic and social development tied into the maintenance and enhancement of the biophysical environment' (1992:24). However, a series of natural and human barriers exist which often prevent this potentially symbiotic relationship from evolving.

A lack of communication and understanding often exists between the tourism industry and local food-producing sectors in developing countries. If the local food producers are to participate fully in tourism, ways must be found to institutionalize working relationships. This paper will focus on the Sheraton Senggigi Beach Resort in Lombok, Indonesia, as a case where a major resort has worked closely with local food producers. The resort initiated two projects (farming and fishing) in order to take advantage of local resources and to integrate itself into the local economy and community. This paper documents these projects, which constitute examples of a large tourism development attempting to increase the linkages with local food producers for their mutual benefit. Such linkages have the potential to benefit local residents by keeping the tourist expenditures in the host economy.

FOOD PRODUCTION AND TOURISM

Conflicting opinions in the literature on the linkages between tourism and agriculture reveal the complexity of the relationship between them. There is a general recognition that there should be an increased reliance on local resources. Many studies warn of the large leakages which can occur when the tourism industry relies on imported foods (Belisle 1983; Taylor, Morison and Fleming 1991; Wilkinson 1987). Milne's (1992) study on tourism development in the South Pacific microstates recommends increased dependence on local resources and integrating tourism development with service and facility provision, such as roads, housing, and education for the local population. Government development policies, such as those in the Gambia, also explicitly state the need to increase the links between tourism and agriculture (Dieke 1993). Relationships between tourism and food production can be placed on a continuum from conflict through coexistence to symbiosis, similar to Budowski's (1976) classification of relationships between tourism and environmental conservation. Within this continuum, agriculture and fishing can be seen as being more than sources of food, for they may contribute positively to tourism experiences through the landscapes and rural activities which visitors can observe.

Conflict Between Tourism and Food Production

Several studies stress competition for the resources of land and labor between food production and tourism. Bryden, writing on the Caribbean, found that tourism grows in competition with other economic sectors, "principally export and domestic agriculture" (1973:214). This takes the form of competition for land, labor, and other resources related to the production of food, including skilled manpower and domestic capital. He also suggested that there is a demonstration effect that influences locals in contact with the tourist industry to demand similar products to those which are being consumed by tourists. According to Bryden, this demonstration effect, along with tourists' demands, increases the amount of food which is imported.

Latimer (1985) questioned Bryden's (1973) findings that tourism takes land, labor, and capital away from other industries, including agriculture. Latimer refers to several examples to illustrate his point, but these are not taken from the Caribbean. With respect to competition for land, Latimer cites Nusa Dua in Bali and the Cancun in Mexico as major resorts whose locations were selected partly due to the poor agricultural potential of the land (Latimer 1985:37). Concerning fishing, Latimer (1985:37) points out that fishermen do not compete for shore space with tourists. However, they do need to have their harbors and houses protected by land-use planning and there are numerous examples from many parts of the world where fishermen have been displaced by resort development (Long 1992).

In reference to labor, Latimer states that it is difficult to disprove that agricultural laborers are drawn into the tourism sector: "the rise in employment in one industry combined with the fall in another does not itself prove that one takes workers from another" (1985:38). Hermans stated that, while tourism has caused an increase in wages and has drawn labor from other sectors including agriculture, the fact that younger generations do not want to work in agriculture cannot be totally blamed on tourism. Rather, according to Hermans, it is part of a more general phenomenon of a "decline of the prestige of agricultural work" (1981:477).

Similar findings to those of Bryden (1973) were also found in the Caribbean by Weaver (1988) leading him to develop a "plantation model" of tourism development. Weaver noted that in many parts of the Caribbean tourism has replaced agriculture as the dominant economic activity. However, he suggests that the development of tourism itself did not cause the decline of agriculture. Rather, the demise of agriculture can be "attributed largely to the emergence of tourism as a viable alternative to a chronically unstable agricultural sector, prompting the lateral transfer of investment capital by local and expatriate plantation interests from agriculture to tourism" (Weaver 1988:324).

Other authors state that there is a trade-off between the two sectors (Bowen, Cox and Fox 1991; Cox, Fox and Bowen 1995). Tourism may increase the cost of production, but laborers and landowners benefit from increased wages and resource values and infrastructure improvements. Tourism-induced improvements in the marketing system may encourage the production of high-value, non-traditional agricultural products and tourism may stimulate landscaping and other services based in agriculture which offset decreases in traditional agricultural activities (Bowen, Cox and Fox 1991:43). The regional impact depends on the availability of resources and how they are managed by governments (Bowen, Cox and Fox 1991:45).

Tourism is at the center of land utilization conflicts on the Spanish Mediterranean coast. Tyrakowski (1986) found that there was a loss of high-yielding agricultural land due to tourism development. Agricultural laborers were leaving the land in search of jobs in construction and services. Only in a small number of cases did tourism lead to more intensive tillage (Tyrakowski 1986). Conversely, Hermans (1981) had earlier found a more positive relationship between tourism and agriculture on the Spanish coast. According to Hermans, "Indirectly tourism has been the motor of the develop-ment of agriculture in Cambrils" (1981:471). Although agriculture in Cambrils was already profitable, tourism caused the commercial-ization of agriculture by providing a nearby market for close to half of the summer fruit and vegetable production which could be sold at high prices.

One of the more recent issues in the debate concerning the alloca-tion of resources between tourism and agriculture is the rise in the number of golf courses which have been appearing throughout the developing world. In Indonesia alone, more than 90 courses have been developed and 20 more are in the planning stage. After protests, the government placed a ban on development permits for new courses (Toronto Star 1993). Golf course construction can result in displacement of residents from the land and often is associated with competition for agricultural resources, including labor, land and water.

The importance of water as a resource for agriculture and tourism has been identified by McTaggart (1988) for Bali, Indonesia. This island has a large population and limited resources with agriculture and tourism being the most promising economic activities. Careful hydrological management is important to both sectors so develop-ment and investment must proceed with care. McTaggart (1988) identified the importance of the *subak* (traditional irrigation associ-ation covering an area of rice cultivation that draws its irrigation water from one conduit and is responsible for irrigation infrastruc-ture), modern forms of irrigation management, and the provincial government as playing important roles in water management. Large tourism resort developments use a great deal of water and the requirements of the agricultural community need to be considered.

Agriculture and Imported Foods

A useful conceptual model of market linkages between tourism and agriculture has been developed by Bowen, Cox and Fox (1991). The model outlines the market linkages between the following sectors: the external economy, visitors, the visitor industry, agricultural production and agriculturally-based services, and resources (natural resources, labor, capital and entrepreneurship). The authors note that non-market linkages, including the aesthetic value of agricultural land as a commodity for tourism, are not included in their model.

Belisle (1984) examined the structure of the hotel food supply in Jamaica and found that the three major sources of food are wholesalers (69% by value), small local suppliers (27.9%), and markets and supermarkets (3.1%). Wholesalers supply imported and bulk goods, including canned, dry, and frozen foods, while avoiding perishable items. Hotels buy little, or as much as 80% of their food, from four dominating wholesalers. A small number of local suppliers act as middlemen making frequent deliveries of a wide range of foods (fresh fruit and vegetables, seafood, eggs, honey) from local producers. A typical large hotel also uses a large number of small suppliers who make a small number of deliveries of a more limited product line. Small local suppliers were found to account for up to 63% of individual hotel purchases. Moreover, markets and supermarkets are often used in an emergency when there are delays in delivery. While Belisle (1984a) found that hotel food demand is small compared to total annual demand in Jamaica and, therefore, it does not provide a major stimulus to local food production, hotel food supply is very important to the tourism industry which, in turn, is crucial to the economies of many areas in the Caribbean.

Belisle (1983:498–499) also found that food represents approximately one-third of tourist expenditures and the degree to which the industry relies on imported food can significantly affect the social and economic impacts of tourism. Importing food results in a loss of foreign exchange earnings. With greater reliance on imports, there is a reduced opportunity to expand and modernize local food production and processing. This results in a potential loss of local income and employment. Farmers and fishermen may feel alienated from the industry and social unrest may develop if there is an uneven distribution of wealth from tourism. If local food-producing areas are not supplying the industry, there will be regional variations in incomes and economic multipliers which will cause the national multiplier to reflect inadequately the spatial distribution of tourism impacts. Furthermore, the local population may develop negative attitudes towards tourists if there are social or spatial concentrations of tourism benefits. These negative attitudes may eventually result in a decrease in the number of tourists coming to the destination, thereby further decreasing the economic benefits of tourism.

640   TOURISM AND FOOD PRODUCTION

The tourism industry imports agricultural products for a variety of reasons including variations in the availability, consistency, and quality of products (Bowen, Cox and Fox 1991:45). Belisle (1983, 1984b) developed a comprehensive list of factors which discourage hotels from using more local agricultural products. The reasons include tourists' preference for similar foods to those found in their own countries; imported food may be cheaper; hotels are willing to pay more for imports to ensure quality and/or a reliable supply; the quality of local food is not as good as imports (especially hygienic quality); hotel entrepreneurs may not be aware of the types and qualities of local foods available; farmers want to maintain their traditional crops and are not able to increase their production; farmers lack information food requirements of hotels; hotels and farmers are inhibited from dealing with each other; and farmers or intermediaries are unreliable in maintaining a regular supply of local products or fulfilling contract agreements.

Barriers and Economic Impacts

There may be many barriers to increasing local food production for the tourism industry as Belisle found in the Caribbean. These include "physical, behavioral, economic, technological, and marketing obstacles" (1983:505). The historical evolution and present status of agriculture can place restrictions on its expansion. Export crops may be given the best land while small-scale farming may be regulated to lower-quality land. Physical attributes, such as topography, soil types, and amount of precipitation may individually or collectively prevent agricultural expansion. The distribution of land ownership and the technologies available to farmers are also possible barriers. Lack of marketing and storage facilities may hinder food distribution and prevent the food from getting to the consumer. Other authors, including Bryden (1973, 1982) and Britton (1982, 1991) argue that the organizational structure of the international tourism industry itself acts as a barrier to domestic suppliers. Hotels which are foreign-owned, or operated, may have strong links to overseas food suppliers and, as a result, may have a tendency to rely on them rather than on local suppliers (Belisle 1983). To a considerable extent, the situation can be generalized as a concern with the scales of enterprises, the interrelationships between entrepreneurs with differing access to resources, and the sizes of enterprises and their associated linkages which are most conducive to the successful development of international tourism and the involvement of local people. These topics have been discussed for Bali, Indonesia, by Rodenburg (1980) and Jenkins (1982).

A theoretical study on the Bahamas used input–output tables to investigate the effects of a 25% reduction of food imports and a corresponding 25% increase in food supplied by local farmers (Taylor, Morison and Fleming 1991). Changes in tourism multipliers were presented to reflect the change in the origins of agricultural inputs. The study found that, with import substitution, a one Bahamian dollar increase in sales in the tourism sector resulted in an increase in output of 43.1 cents in the rest of the economy compared to 39.5 cents using the existing level of foreign inputs. The crop, fruit, and vegetable sector would also experience an expansion of 650 jobs. There would be some job losses in the wholesale, retail and trade sectors. However some jobs may be replaced by the increase in trade between local agricultural producers and hotels.

The study also found weak linkages between the local agricultural and industrial sectors. For example, an expansion of the agricultural sector may result in increased purchases of imported inputs such as fertilizers. The authors note that if there is sufficient demand, there may be justification for providing incentives to expand industries supplying inputs to local agriculture. This, in turn, would strengthen the linkages between agriculture and the rest of the economy (Taylor, Morison and Fleming 1991). The authors emphasize that several assumptions were used in their analyses: that local production would be competitive, that production and consumption functions are linear, and that suppliers are able to produce more and that adjustments in production take place immediately. They state that no definite conclusions can be made on the net benefits of food import substitution, but they do raise some interesting possibilities.

Increasing the Use of Local Foodstuffs

Based on the work of Lundgren and others, Latimer (1985:35–36) developed suggestions of ways to increase the amount of local foods used in the tourism industry. More planning and assistance is required to enhance the supply of local agricultural products and this has received "rhetorical rather than practical help in most small islands" (Latimer 1985:35). Official information dissemination is needed on growing vegetables in tropical climates. One way in which this can be done is through the establishment of experimental farms as was done in Bali (Latimer 1985:35).

Referring to Jamaica, Latimer (1985) suggests that improvements in infrastructure, such as roads, may be less important than help with contracts, insurance against non-delivery, and back-up supply arrangements in case the supplier is unable to deliver the products. Cold storage should be developed for the producer, cooperative, or wholesaler. The hotel supplies manager is often operating under a tight capital budget and, as a result, cannot afford to keep a large inventory in cold storage. Moreover, the availability of local cuisine in hotels and restaurants should be promoted by the tourism office. In an effort to increase the use of local products, regular meetings should be held between domestic authorities and supply managers. Latimer suggests that duties can be used to guide the purchases of hotel buyers, but warns that the imposition of quotas or prohibition of use of imported products, as was done in the Caribbean, can lead to an increased desire for the restricted goods.

One of the ways in which food imports can be reduced is through the development of import substitution. Several Caribbean nations attempted such policies through improving support to small farmers as well as guaranteeing prices for their commodities (Belisle

1983:509). These measures were focused only on the internal market and, while they have not received a great deal of study, it appears that they have not been very successful. There has been continued decline in food production throughout the Caribbean basin (Belisle 1983:509). As Belisle (1983:509) points out, more research is needed on the successes and failures of institutional arrangements and policy options which influence the use of local food by the tourist industry.

In the case of the Bahamas, where there is widespread unemployment and rural–urban drift and, with the effects of import substitution falling mainly on rural areas, Taylor, Morison and Fleming (1991:58–59) suggested that the government should assist the agricultural sector in meeting the increased demands of the tourism sector. This assistance could take the form of servicing new lands with roads and electricity, providing credit to new farmers, expanding extension services especially with more information dissemination on new techniques and providing assistance for the purchase of material inputs. Taylor, Morison and Fleming (1991:58) note, however, that these types of policy decisions must be made in a wider context. Gomes (1993) recommends that hotels be sampled during a representative week to determine information on food purchases and sources of supply. When high import items are identified, they should be targeted for import substitution. He also suggests that pilot projects should be established involving private growers or landowners and that they should be supported with government assistance.

In 1990, the State of Hawaii developed an innovative economic diversification policy based on the concept of "one job/one room" (Mak 1993). This policy dictates that hotel developers create one non-tourism job in the economy in order to obtain state permission to build one hotel room in resort developments that involve the reclassification of land from agricultural, rural, or conservation categories to urban land. The developer is also allowed to make a payment of $25,000 per proposed hotel room for the financing of job training, business loans, or other incentive programs to promote economic diversification. This policy is seen as a method of extracting rents from "largely non-resident hotel developers" to finance other projects which the state desires (Mak 1993:259). While there are acknowledged flaws in the policy, it does present interesting possibilities which could be used in the developing world in relation to agriculture. Funds generated from such a policy could be used to develop local agriculture by improving storage facilities and transportation networks; providing training and technical assistance; and purchasing needed equipment.

Symbiotic Relationship of Agriculture and Tourism

Tourism and agriculture have the potential to work together in a symbiotic relationship. Improvements in the transportation system for tourism can benefit agriculture through increased ease of access to potential markets (Bowen, Cox and Fox 1991). This improved infrastructure not only helps agriculture but also allows the tourists to travel and view the agricultural landscapes. Tourism promotion can focus on agricultural products which may stimulate export demand, while agricultural promotion may focus on the regional landscape and lead to a growth in tourism (Bowen, Cox and Fox 1991:49). Dilley (1986) found that the promotion of landscapes in international tourism brochures accounted for just under one third of the total messages portrayed. With the recent growth of interest in ecotourism, the proportion now may be even higher. While coastal and mountain landscapes dominated, a number of brochures presented "pleasant farmscapes and pastures" to attract potential tourists (Dilley 1986:60). Tourism can also help to stimulate agricultural services such as landscaping, tours of farms, and processing sites, as well as farm holidays (Bowen, Cox and Fox 1991). A classification scheme developed by Cox and Fox (1991) for agriculturally-based leisure attractions establishes three main components: retail sales, tours, and other leisure activities. While their article goes beyond the scope of this paper, which concentrates on the food inputs from agriculture to tourism, it highlights the complexity of the relationship between tourism and agriculture.

Socher and Tschurtschenthaler (1994) categorize agriculture as having two separate but linked supply values for the tourism industry. The first is direct supply, which involves the sale of agricultural products to the industry. The second is indirect supply, which involves preservation and cultivation of the landscape which acts as a backdrop or tourism resource. Farmers produce positive externalities (attractive landscapes) which cost but do not necessarily produce revenues. Alpine agriculture is facing economic difficulties as a result of increased competition and changing agricultural policies. These pressures may lead to a reduction in alpine agriculture which would have negative consequences for alpine tourism. Socher and Tschurtschenthaler (1994) present options concerning compensation for farmers for the positive externalities of their activities. These suggestions include increased prices to tourists to include the costs of preservation if tourism facilities are owned by the farmers; voluntary payments by tourism organizations to agriculture; transfer of taxes from tourism organizations to agriculture; and subsidies and transfers from general tax receipts to agriculture. The authors advocate a direct form of compensation along with indirect compensation from general tax receipts when needed. The authors also noted that the government of Tyrol recently decided to increase the tariff on the tourism tax and that the additional funds raised should be paid by the central tourism organization to farmers for preservation. This recent decision, however, was more political than financial in its implications.

The relationship between tourism and agriculture can also be incorporated under the concept of sustainable tourism development which has received greater attention in the literature recently (Eber 1992; McKercher 1993; Nelson, Butler and Wall 1993). If the hotels are using local products produced in the community, this may imply a more sustainable path for development. Successful examples of establishments using this green, environmentally friendly, tourism philosophy are difficult to find (Lane 1993). One successful example is in the village of Waltensburg in southeastern Switzerland where a local cooperative has built and operates the 72-bed Hotel Ucliva according to sustainable tourism principles. With respect to food, as much as possible is obtained locally. Organic, semi-organic, or free-range food is preferred over factory-produced food. Traditional and regional recipes are used in the restaurant. Fruits and vegetables in season are preferred to preserved foods. Menus using organic foods have been introduced slowly so that local farmers and suppliers can adapt their techniques to respond to the demand. Assistance in new growing methods has been provided by the hotels to the local farmers. By 1989, all eggs, butter, milk, and meat were purchased locally, as well as 70% of the vegetables (Lane 1993). As this study will identify, the Sheraton Senggigi Beach Resort has started down a similar path by interacting with the local agricultural and fishing communities so that it can benefit from the use of local resources.

Agriculture and Tourism Cycles

Butler's tourism area cycle of evolution traces a hypothetical path taken by a tourism area through the stages of exploration, involvement, development, consolidation, and stagnation. From this point, the tourism area can either decline or be rejuvenated (Butler 1980). As Butler points out, perhaps "the later stages of the cycle are more significant, then, because of the implications which they hold for tourism in general and for the planning and arrangement of tourist areas in particular" (1980:10). Such a cycle has great implications for the local agricultural sector. As Hermans points out, if tourism were to decline, it would affect the farmers' economic position as they would receive "lower prices for their fruit and vegetables in the summer, and also their earnings from tourism-related activities would decline" (1981:477).

The concept of cycles can also be further examined in relation to seasonality. From this perspective, there are two factors which affect agriculture and its relationship to tourism. The first has to do with fluctuations in occupancy rates throughout the year. As the peak tourism season arrives, restaurants and hotels will have greater demand for food inputs. Food producers should be made aware of the timing of these fluctuations and be prepared to accommodate these demands.

The second aspect of seasonality relates to growing seasons. Different locations have varying seasons and different crops are ready for harvest at different times of the year. If the cycles of peak tourism season and harvest time are not synchronous, then this will have implications for the potential inputs local agriculture can have to the tourism industry. The hotels and restaurants may be forced to import food to meet the increase in demand in the peak season. In The Gambia, when the peak tourism season ends in April, hotel staffs are reduced to half. When the season resumes six months later, it coincides with the harvest of the annual groundnut crop.

With respect to employment, the relationship between tourism and farming is competitive with limited trade-off possibilities (Farver 1984).

AN INDONESIAN CASE STUDY

Lombok is located in the province of Nusa Tenggara Barat (NTB) and is the island immediately to the east of Bali. The island is in the initial stages of tourism development. An analysis of tourist spending in NTB in 1993 found that, on average, international tourists spend US$61 a day and, of that, 28.25% or US$17.23 is spent on food. Domestic tourists spend Rp 68,500 (approximately US$40) per day and 24.87% of that is spent on food (Dinas Pariwisata Daerah Tingkat I Nusa Tenggara Barat 1993). These results are similar to Belisle's findings that food expenditures constitute approximately one third of all tourist expenditures.

The Sheraton Senggigi Beach Resort is the only four-star hotel on the island of Lombok. There are no five-star hotels. The Sheraton has 156 rooms. It was opened in 1991, and is located on four hectares of landscaped gardens on the north-west corner of Senggigi beach, 20 minutes from Selaparang airport by taxi. The hotel has many recreational facilities including swimming pool, tennis courts, and health club. The Sheraton also offers a departure lounge at the airport. Restaurant and beverage services include Kebun Anggrek (200+ seats), Bawang Puthi poolside pizzeria and BBQ restaurant, Gilligan's restaurant and disco, Putri Duyung poolside snack bar, and 24-hour room service and special theme buffets. In an effort to purchase more food locally, the Sheraton established two specific programs with close ties to local food producers. One project was organized with a local fisherman to provide fresh seafood and the second with a farmer to supply fresh herbs and vegetables. These two programs were initiated by the Executive Chef.

Sheraton Fish Program

Recognizing that the island of Lombok is surrounded by excellent fishing grounds, the Sheraton wanted to take advantage of this and provide their guests with fresh seafood. The main concern of the hotel, however, is with the quality of the food offered in their establishment. Being a four-star hotel and a member of the Sheraton chain, the hotel has very strict standards to follow. The hotel wanted to provide fresh seafood yet it had to be of top quality and well-stored for transport to the hotel. As a result, a fish project was established by the Executive Chef between the hotel and a local fisherman. In order to ensure safe transport of the seafood to the hotel, the fisherman was provided with three coolers (2 large, 1 small) and, in return, he agreed to supply all of the seafood required by the Sheraton.

These coolers have excellent insulation and are filled with ice to keep the seafood fresh. The fisherman travels Lombok to the various fish markets and purchases fresh seafood for the Sheraton which is delivered every two or three days. On delivery, the seafood is carefully inspected by one of the receivers or one of the chefs. All seafood items are checked for color, size, smell and touch; and a few of the fish are opened as a further test of their quality. Orders for the next shipment are either given at the time of delivery or, alternatively, the fisherman comes to the hotel to pick up the next order. The key to the project is the provision of a steady supply of fresh seafood. To ensure this, the Sheraton places small orders on a frequent basis. The first author accompanied the fisherman on one of his purchasing trips to obtain fresh fish for the hotel. The trip left on Saturday, 26 February 1994 at 6:00 a.m. to Tanjung Luar which is a fishing village on the east coast of Lombok. The fisherman makes this trip to Tanjung Luar three times each week. He had an order which was to be delivered on Monday as no deliveries are made on Sunday to the Sheraton.

Local fishermen from the Tanjung Luar area generally fish all night and bring their catch to the market early in the morning. Lights from the small fishing craft attract the fish. Interestingly, at full moon, the catches are smaller as the night sky is much lighter. Between the east coast of Lombok and the west coast of the neighboring island of Sumbawa, there are very good fishing grounds for lobster and fish. Cempi Bay, also off the coast of Sumbawa, is a good area for prawns. When they arrive back on shore, they sell their catch to the people who work in the Tanjung Luar fish market. The Sheraton fisherman then buys seafood from the people in the market. Keeping the order in mind, he circulates through the market looking for the best quality fish at the best price. Negotiations are often carried out away from the crowd so that only the fisherman and the seller know the agreed price. As he purchases the various seafood items, they are placed in one of the large cold boxes which are filled with ice. When he has finished purchasing, the cold box is loaded onto his truck and his driver brings the order to the Sheraton or to his home if it is to be delivered on a Monday.

The fish project has had significant impacts on both the Sheraton and the fisherman who has become a middleman. The hotel now has a reliable source of fresh seafood at an excellent price. The product arrived packaged in ice in the Sheraton's cold boxes and, as a result, the high quality standards of the hotel are met. Ordering small quantities on a frequent basis ensures that high quality is maintained. The hotel does not have to purchase large quantities of seafood and keep it in storage but, instead, can rely on a constant fresh supply. The hotel has reduced the amount it had to pay for importing fish and associated transportation costs. The Sheraton is also able to use the expertise of a former local fisherman to help them get the best quality seafood. This is in sharp contrast to the findings of Belisle (1984b) in Jamaica where hotels imported three-quarters of the shrimp and over 40% of the fish consumed.

The project has had profound implications for the fisherman. The agreement with the Sheraton changed his employment. He has gone from being a fisherman to being a fish supplier. His status has grown in the industry and his income has risen. At the fish market, it was apparent that he was an important customer. He owns his own truck and motorcycle which he uses in his business. His brother and a driver both have the opportunity to work for him during some of his purchasing trips. Thus, it is apparent that the fish project has benefited the Sheraton resort in that it has ensured the provision of high quality seafood at a reasonable price and it has also increased the income and status of one member of the local community.

Sheraton Vegetable and Herb Program

The second program of interest involved the production of herbs and vegetables. This program was also started by the Executive Chef at the Sheraton who spent some time touring Lombok looking for an area in which herbs and vegetables, which were then imported, could be grown locally. The chief made an agreement with a local farmer from the village of Pajeruk in Ampenan. The chef supplied the farmer with seeds every three months from different countries. In return, the farmer grew the various seeds and, when they were ready to be harvested, he would contact the Sheraton. The chef could then plan the menu around the special crops which were ready. The agreement stipulated that the herbs and vegetables could only be sold to the Sheraton.

The farmer grew the crops in two locations in Pajeruk — beside his home and on his uncle's land a short distance away on higher ground. Two sites were chosen because different crops have varied soil and drainage requirements and the performance of different crops was evaluated according to their productivity in both dry and wet seasons. For example, celery and head lettuce grew best in the dry season, carrots and chives in the wet season, and strawberries, broccoli and cauliflower did not grow well at all. The farmer also became a general suppliers to the Sheraton for other fruits and vegetables. If the hotel needed other produce not grown by him, he would travel to one of the local markets in Lombok to purchase what the hotel ordered. All deliveries to the hotel by the farmer were made by public *bemo* (small local bus). The three main people who received employment from this program were the farmer, his uncle, and one other casual worker.

Unfortunately, this program is no longer in operation. When the two production sites were visited later, one was already in the process of being converted back to rice and the second field was on its last harvest from the seeds provided by the Sheraton chef. The project failed for a combination of reasons. The chef who initiated the project left the Sheraton Senggigi Beach Resort to work at another Sheraton in Thailand. The project itself required constant supervision and a large commitment from the Sheraton whose primary business is running a hotel. The occupancy rates fluctuated seasonally and the hotel did not always need the quantity of the products that the farmer grew. Sheraton is the only four-star hotel on the island and is a large business operation. On the other hand, the farmer is a very traditional, small-scale producer and not used to serving the needs of a large establishment. It is also generally a Sheraton policy to have at least two suppliers.

648   TOURISM AND FOOD PRODUCTION

Seasonality of the Food Production Programs

Figure 1 displays the Sheraton monthly occupancy rates for 1993 along with the monthly invoice totals for the fish and farming programs. The first three months of the year are the low season for the resort. In April 1993, Ramadan (the fasting period for Moslems) ended and was followed by the Islamic celebration known as Lebaron. During this time, the occupancy rates increased rapidly in the resort. The majority of those staying at this time at the Sheraton were domestic tourists celebrating Lebaron. The high tourism season for the Sheraton occurs during the months of July, August, and September. These months correspond to the summer holidays for Europeans and North Americans and, as a result, foreign tourists constitute a large proportion of those staying at the hotel at this time. The occupancy rates decrease over the last quarter of the year but remain higher than the first quarter as Christmas approaches. It is important to note that the occupancy rates are given on a monthly basis which may disguise short periods when the resort is actually at full occupancy. Also, these figures are reported based on the Sheraton's calendar which, in turn, is based on the ITT Corporation's fiscal calendar year. As a result, the last few days of a month may be added on to the beginning of the next month.

As illustrated in Figure 1, both the farming and the fish projects responded to the increases and decreases in the occupancy rates of the hotel. The data for these two projects constitute the monthly invoice totals submitted to the Sheraton. Invoices accompanied each delivery. The monthly totals are based on a standard calendar year which differs from the hotel's calendar as outlined above. Despite possible minor errors involved in comparing across two different calendars, the matching trends can still be identified.

The invoice data starts in February 1993 for both programs and runs to February 1994 for the fish program and to January 11 for the agricultural program. The monthly invoice totals start off in the low tourism season of February and then climb to meet the demands of the hotel as Lebaron arrives in April. Both programs reduced their level of supply in May and started to increase again in June as the foreign tourists arrived. The agricultural project maintained a

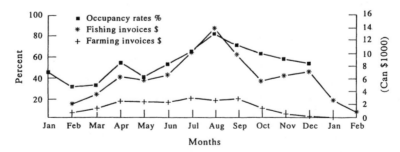

Figure 1. Sheraton Occupancy Rates 1993 and Food Invoices Based on ITT Financial Year, Farming Project Ended 11 January 1994

fairly consistent level of supply throughout the peak season, while the fishing project tended to respond more dramatically to an increase in visitors. Both experienced a drop in demand for their goods from September through October. The fish project responded again by increasing deliveries to cover the Christmas season, while the agricultural program continued to decline until its demise in January of 1994. The fish project experienced another decline in the low season of January and February 1994.

A closer examination of the monthly farming invoices reveals that farmers must deal with both a fluctuation in the number of tourists and with agricultural seasonality. Lombok has two seasons: a wet and a dry season. The wet season goes from October to April and the dry season goes from May to September. More crops grew favorably in the dry season compared to the wet season. This suggests that, for the crops grown by the farmer, the peak season (July–September) coincides with the best growing season (dry). The drop off of tourists from September to October also marks the beginning of the wet season. As mentioned above, the level of supply from the agricultural project gradually dropped until it ended in January 1994. The relationship of the decline in supply and the commencement of the wet season must also be viewed in the context of the demise of the project itself. It was also during this time that the originator of the project left and was replaced by a new Executive Chef who did not rely on the agricultural project to the same extent as his predecessor.

The Importance of Institutionalization

In the two projects described above, initial contact with local producers was made by the Executive Chef. Ultimately, if the projects are to succeed, traditional, small-scale producers must be able to meet the requirements of the modern, large-scale, tourism sector. Institutionalizing and maintaining agreements with local producers and suppliers is difficult. However, when this is done successfully, both parties can benefit.

As illustrated by these two projects, strong business relationships can be made with local food producers. The Sheraton Resort overcame some of the many obstacles suggested in the literature (Belisle 1983) to establish these links with a local farmer and a fisherman. On the initiative of the Executive Chef, who took time to investigate the potential use of locally-produced products, supply and purchase agreements were established. Through ongoing communication with the local suppliers, quality standards were established and maintained. Over time, the Sheraton rejected progressively fewer local products as the suppliers adapted to the high quality standards imposed by the hotel. New crops were introduced to the farmer and he responded by growing high-quality herbs and vegetables. The fish project established by the Executive Chef continued to operate after his departure and a supply of high-quality seafood continued to be provided to the Sheraton.

However, with the ending of the agricultural project comes the realization that the forces which must be overcome to promote the

650   TOURISM AND FOOD PRODUCTION

use of local inputs are formidable. Not least of the challenges is the establishment of institutional commitments which transcend the interests and involvement of specific individuals. While this specific project has ended, the Sheraton continues to use two other local suppliers who make daily deliveries of fruits and vegetables to the Sheraton. These two suppliers go to a number of local markets including the two major markets in nearby Mataram (Sweta and Ampenan) to make their purchases from local sellers. The Sheraton also purchases rice, chicken, eggs, lamb, and some meat from local suppliers.

As a result of these projects and other efforts to become integrated into the local economy, such as training and employing local people, the Sheraton Resort has a very positive image in the community. One of the important factors in ensuring the continuance of these relationships is their institutionalization so that they do not depend solely upon the interest and commitment of one person. The type of initiative taken by the Sheraton and its Executive Chef constitutes a possible blueprint for other hotel operators to follow to develop linkages with local food producers. Increased communication between hotel operators and suppliers is needed so that expectations on both sides are understood and high quality products are delivered on time. The Sheraton's strict adherence to quality has, over time, influenced their local suppliers to raise their standards.

CONCLUSIONS

Indonesian development policies have placed increased emphasis on tourism in successive five-year plans. International tourist arrivals in Indonesia are expected to increase from just over 4 million in 1994 to more than 7 million by the year 2000, the latter figure constituting an annual growth rate of 11.1% from a 1992 base year (Cleverdon 1993). In recognition of this, The National Tourism Strategy recommends that the government select tourism as a "national development component of a higher economic priority" (1992:2). The National Strategy stresses that tourism developments should conform to the highest environmental standards and that consideration be given to the social and cultural norms of the host community.

However, if tourism is to contribute to the well-being of destination residents, it is important that careful consideration be given to enhancing backward economic linkages. Agritourism and ecotourism are encouraged in the National Tourism Strategy where there is a potential demand and there are appropriate resources but, whatever the form of tourism development, it is important that local economic linkages are forged and enhanced if local people are to benefit economically. It is insufficient to set goals simply in terms of numbers of visitors or their gross expenditures for, unless employment opportunities and expenditures reach local residents, they may lose more than they gain from tourism development.

Conflicts continue to circulate in the literature over the merits of tourism as an agent of development and the nature of its linkages to agriculture (Bowen, Cox and Fox 1991; Latimer 1985). Some authors state that development through tourism reinforces dependency of third world nations (Britton 1982, 1991), while others explore the more recent paradigm of sustainable development and how tourism organizations can work towards that end (Haywood 1993). Provided that a surplus for sale can be produced, encouragement of the greater use of local foodstuffs by the tourism industry can move the relationship away from one of conflict in the direction of symbiosis. □ □

Acknowledgments — The authors are most grateful to the Sheraton Senggigi Beach Resort for providing access to facilities and information. The research was undertaken with the support of a scholarship from the Asian Institute of Technology, Thailand, and a research award from the Social Sciences and Humanities Research Council of Canada, and was facilitated through linkages with the Bali Sustainable Development Project funded by the Canadian International Development Agency. A research permit was provided by Lembaga Ilum Pengetahuan Indonesia (LIPI), the Indonesian Institute of Science.

REFERENCES

Belisle, Francois J.
   1983 Tourism and Food Production in the Caribbean. Annals of Tourism Research 10:497–513.
Belisle, Francois J.
   1984a The Significance and Structure of Hotel Food Supply in Jamaica. Caribbean Geography 1(4):219–233.
Belisle, Francois J.
   1984b Tourism and Food Imports: The Case of Jamaica. Economic Development and Cultural Change 32:819–841.
Bowen, Richard L., Linda J. Cox, and Morton Fox
   1991 The Interface between Tourism and Agriculture. Journal of Tourism Studies 2:43–54.
Britton, Stephen
   1982 The Political Economy of Tourism in the Third World. Annals of Tourism Research 9:331–358.
Britton, Stephen
   1991 Tourism, Capital and Place: Towards a Critical Geography of Tourism. Environment and Planning D. Society and Space 9:451–478.
Bryden, John M.
   1973 Tourism and Development: A Case Study of the Commonwealth Caribbean. London: Cambridge University Press.
Bryden, John M.
   1982 Tourism Development: An Alternative Strategy. The Traveller 12:50–53.
Budowski, Gerardo
   1976 Tourism and Environmental Conservation: Conflict, Coexistence, or Symbiosis? Environmental Conservation 3:27–31.
Butler, Richard W.
   1980 The Concept of a Tourist Area Cycle of Evolution: Implications For Management of Resources. Canadian Geographer 24:5–12.
Cleverdon, R.
   1993 Tourism Forecast: Indonesia. Jakarta: Directorate General of Tourism, Government of Indonesia.
Cox, Linda J., and Morton Fox.
   1991 Agriculturally Based Leisure Attractions. The Journal of Tourism Studies 12:18–27.
Cox, Linda J., Morton Fox, and Richard L. Bowen.
   1995 Does Tourism Destroy Agriculture? Annals of Tourism Research 22:210–213.
Dieke, Peter U. C.
   1993 Tourism in The Gambia: Some Issues in Development Policy. World Development 21:277–289.

Dilley, Robert S.
  1986 Tourist Brochures and Tourist Images. The Canadian Geographer 30:59–65.
Dinas Pariwisata Daerah Tingkat I Nusa Tenggara Barat
  1993 Analisis Pasar Wisata Nusa Tenggara Barat. Mataram: Dinas Pariwisata.
Directorate General of Tourism, UNDP
  1992 Tourism Sector Programming and Policy Development Final Report: Output
    1 National Tourism Strategy. Jakarta: Government of Indonesia.
Eber, Shirley, ed.
  1992 Beyond The Green Horizon: Principles for Sustainable Tourism. Surrey:
    World Wide Fund For Nature.
Farver, Jo Ann M.
  1984 Tourism and Employment in The Gambia. Annals of Tourism Research
    11:249–265.
Gomes, Albert
  1993 Integrating Tourism and Agricultural Development. *In* Tourism Marketing
    and Management in the Caribbean, Dennis J. Gayle and Jonathan N. Goodrich,
    eds., pp. 155–156. New York: Routledge.
Haywood, K. Michael
  1993 Sustainable Development for Tourism: A Commentary with an
    Organizational Perspective. *In* Tourism and Sustainable Development:
    Monitoring, Planning, Managing. Department of Geography Publications
    Series Number 37, J. Gordon Nelson, Richard W. Butler and Geoffrey Wall,
    eds., pp. 233–241. Waterloo: University of Waterloo.
Hermans, Dymphna
  1981 The Encounter of Agriculture and Tourism: A Catalan Case. Annals of
    Tourism Research 8:462–479.
Jenkins, Carson
  1982 The Effects of Scale in Tourism Projects in Developing Countries. Annals
    of Tourism Research 9:499–521.
Lane, Bernard
  1993 The Hotel Ucliva: A Rural Hotel Built and Operated on Ecological Principles.
    In The Greening of Tourism From Principles to Practice: A Casebook of Best
    Environmental Practice in Tourism, Suzanne Hawkes and Peter Williams, eds., pp.
    21–26. Burnaby: Centre For Tourism Policy Research, Simon Fraser University.
Latimer, Hugh
  1985 Developing Island Economies: Tourism v. Agriculture. Tourism
    Management 6:32–42.
Long, Veronica
  1992 Social Mitigation of Tourism Development Impacts: Bahias de Huatalco,
    Oaxaca, Mexico. *In* Spatial Implications of Tourism, Conny A. M. Fleischer-
    van Rooijen, ed., pp. 185–201. Groningen: Geo Pers.
Mak, James
  1993 Exacting Resort Developers to Create Non-Tourism Jobs. Annals of Tourism
    Research 20:50–261.
McKercher, Bob
  1993 The Unrecognized Threat to Tourism: Can Tourism Survive 'Sustainability'?
    Tourism Management 14:131–136.
McTaggart, W. Donald
  1988 Hydrologic Management in Bali. Singapore Journal of Tropical Geography
    9:96–111.
Milne, Simon
  1992 Tourism and Development in South Pacific Microstates. Annals of Tourism
    Research 19:191–212.
Nelson, J. Gordon., Richard W. Butler, and Geoffrey Wall, eds.
  1993 Tourism and Sustainable Development: Monitoring, Planning, Managing.
    Department of Geography Publication Series No. 37. Waterloo: University of
    Waterloo.
Rodenburg, Eric
  1980 The Effects of Scale in Economic Development: Tourism in Bali. Annals of
    Tourism Research 7:177–196.
Socher, Karl, and Paul Tschurtschenthaler
  1994 Tourism and Agriculture in Alpine Regions. The Tourist Review 50:35–41.

Taylor, B. E., J. B. Morison, and E. M. Fleming
    1991 The Economic Impact of Food Import Substitution in The Bahamas. Social and Economic Studies 40:45–62.
The Toronto Star
    1993 "Golf War" Sweeps Indonesia. The Toronto Star (Saturday June 12): E10.
Tyrakowski, Konrad
    1986 The Role of Tourism in Land Utilization Conflicts on the Spanish Mediterranean Coast. GeoJournal 13:19–26.
Weaver, David
    1988 The Evolution of a "Plantation" Tourism Landscape on the Caribbean Island of Antigua. Tijdschrift voor Economische en Sociale Geographie 79:319–331.
Wilkinson, Paul F.
    1987 Tourism in Small Island Nations: A Fragile Dependence. Leisure Studies 6:128–146.
Wilkinson, Paul F.
    1992 Tourism: Development Imperatives and Environmental Problem. *In* Discussion Forum II on the Graduate Program in Development Studies at the Bandung Institute of Technology, Development Imperatives and Emerging Environmental Problems, Fred Carden, ed., pp. 24–32. Waterloo: The University Consortium on the Environment, University of Waterloo.
World Tourism Organization
    1994 Yearbook of Tourism Statistics. Madrid: WTO.

Submitted 27 January 1995
Resubmitted 28 April 1995
Accepted 22 June 1995
Refereed anonymously
Coordinating Editor: John Bryden

[16]

'Tourist Merchandise' as a Means of Generating Local Benefits from Ecotourism

Robert G. Healy
School of the Environment, Duke University, Durham, NC 27707, USA

Long term protection of national parks and nature reserves is very difficult unless economic benefits can be secured for local people. Ecotourism offers a possible income source, provided that there is a means of local revenue capture from the visitors. This article examines the sale of handicrafts and other 'tourist merchandise' as a possible means of generating local benefits. The article considers issues of supply and demand, new product development, marketing, and the sustainability of supply of materials used as inputs. It concludes that strong possibilities exist for market development and creation of new, sustainable, culturally acceptable products. Of particular interest are active linking of tourist merchandise production to agricultural or forestry projects that provide a sustainable supply of inputs, use of 'craft as performance' to promote product sale, and development of products that educate tourists about park resources and local cultures.

Introduction

As more national parks, nature reserves, and other protected natural areas are established around the world, both new and existing areas have come under increasing pressure from the growth of human population and economic activities. The International Union for the Conservation of Nature estimated that in 1990 there were 6,931 fully or partially protected natural areas worldwide, aggregating some 651 million hectares (World Resources Institute, 1992).

In many developing countries, large numbers of rural people live around or even inside park boundaries. A key consideration in reserve management, therefore, is how to give local residents an economic incentive to help maintain the resources which the parks protect. In many cases, the creation of parks and reserves initially hurts local people by cutting them off from opportunities to hunt, gather forest products, or clear new agricultural land (for a well-documented case study, see Shyamsundar, 1993). A recent study, based on more than twenty case examples worldwide, observes that 'An emerging view among conservationists is that the successful management of protected areas (PAs) must include the cooperation and support of local people. Excluding people who live adjacent to PAs from use of these resources, without providing them with alternatives, is increasingly viewed as politically infeasible and ethically unjustifiable' (Brandon & Wells, 1992).

Many parks and reserves are experiencing substantial increases in tourism, much of which comes from high-income countries or from affluent domestic urban populations. Often this sort of tourism is called 'ecotourism', a word that describes both the motivation of tourists (to visit natural ecosystems) and the expected conservation benefits to be had from it (Boo, 1990; Whelan, 1991). Yet there is growing concern that little of the revenue from ecotourism reaches local people. The report from the World Parks Congress, a major international meeting

0966-9582/94/03 0137-15 $1.80/0
JOURNAL OF SUSTAINABLE TOURISM
©1994 R.G. Healy
Vol. 2, No. 3, 1994

of environmentalists and park managers held in Caracas in 1992, noted that 'In order to compensate local people for the loss of use of nearby resources, and to obtain their collaboration in protecting parks, a larger proportion of tourism revenues should be recycled locally' (Munasinghe, 1992). Participants at a 1993 symposium on ecotourism and local communities, sponsored by the Rockefeller Foundation in Bellagio, Italy, found it almost impossible to cite specific parks or reserves where tourism had produced local economic benefits.

In practice, the options for local capture of tourist revenue are relatively few: entrance fees or tourist taxes can be distributed to local governments or community organisations; local people can operate or be employed in establishments providing lodging, food, or services to the tourists; or local people can sell the tourists souvenirs, crafts, or other merchandise. To date, none of these revenue-capture options has been adequately documented. Lindberg (1990) and Western (1982) have undertaken some analysis of fee-sharing systems. There is a large literature on tourism and employment creation in the lodging and tourist service sector, but only a few studies involving Third World rural areas impacted by nature tourism (e.g. Place, 1991; Healy, 1988; Boo, 1990.) Wells & Brandon (1992) offer a number of case studies of park-related communities, but little data on how they have benefited economically (or failed to benefit) from tourism.

The least-explored option for revenue-capture is through sale of what might be termed 'tourist merchandise', that is, tangible products sold directly to tourists. This article is an investigation of the possibilities for using sales of tourist merchandise as a means of supporting local economic development, particularly in areas adjoining parks and nature reserves in developing countries.

The Demand for Handicrafts and Other Tourist Merchandise

Tourist interest in on-site purchases of goods can too easily be dismissed as 'souvenir hunting'. In one view, tourist purchases are associated with mass produced, low-quality articles that borrow (and sometimes even mock) cultural themes and which are purchased by the tourist with the intent of providing a personal memento of the visit. However, closer examination of tourist purchases reveals a much more complex picture, both in types of goods purchased and in the tourist's motivation for buying them. (For general background, and typologies of products and buyer motivations, with an emphasis on artistic items sold to tourists, see *inter alia* Graburn, 1976; Cohen, 1993.)

Tourist merchandise is defined here as 'any tangible item purchased by tourists at a destination and intended to be transported subsequently off-site'. This definition does not include on-site food and lodging, or intangible services, such as guide and transportation services. Tourist merchandise does include: (1) Natural products, including nuts, shells, rocks, and unprocessed foodstuffs (fruit, raw coconuts); (2) Handicrafts, defined as goods that are hand-made or made with the use of simple tools or equipment and that incorporate a substantial element of craft skill; (3) Other hand-made items, including artisanal processed foodstuffs (coffee beans, honey, sugar cane juice, vanilla); (4) Local manufactures, such as beer, furniture and other factory-made items; or (5) Non-local goods retailed at tourist sites, including film, postcards, guidebooks, T-shirts, and sporting equipment.

In addition to on-site sales to tourists, merchandise produced at tourist destinations may have substantial sales potential elsewhere. For example, handicrafts
produced in rural areas are often sold in urban markets, at capital city hotels
frequented by tourists, at cruise ship docks and in airports. They may also be
exported.

Looking at motivation for tourist purchases, it is obvious that some tourist
merchandise is bought as a souvenirs. However, remembrance is only one of
several possible functions of goods purchased by tourists. Littrell (1990) identified five clusters of motivations. Some purchasers' motivations were associated
with only a single cluster; others were multidimensional. The clusters included:
shopping oriented tourists (for whom the *process* of acquisition is important);
authenticity seeking tourists; special trip tourists; apparel oriented tourists; and
tourists who simply valued the 'intrinsic beauty' of the item.

Research by Keown (1989) on purchases by Japanese tourists in Hawaii found
another motivation for tourist purchases — their cost relative to the cost of similar
merchandise available in the tourist's home country. Although tourist merchandise offered in rural areas of developing countries may be quite different in
materials and appearance from goods available to the tourist at home, there may
be many parallels in terms of *function* (e.g. articles of clothing; tableware; deco-
rative items). The lower cost and/or higher quality of the developing country
item may induce a sale even where souvenir or authenticity value is minimal.
Tourist buying preferences are likely to vary with such characteristics of the
individual tourist as income, age, education, sex, past travel experience and
nationality, as well as with the reason for visiting the destination area (e.g.
cultural tourism vs. outdoor recreation). Littrell, Anderson & Brown (1993) found
evidence suggesting that tourists interested in active outdoor recreation were
more likely than other tourists to attribute authenticity to crafts that were usable
items not available in their home communities. Other groups of tourists were
more likely to attribute authenticity to items exhibiting traditional colours and
natural materials. They also found that 'while younger tourists associate authenticity with unique and original items, these qualities declined in importance
among tourists over age 60'. Older tourists were more likely to associate authenticity with 'the cultural or historic integrity and the genuineness of a craft'.

Even though the value of individual transactions is small, total sales of tourist
merchandise are sometimes quite significant, even at the national level. Waters
(1991) observed, for example, that between 1979 and 1988, sales of tourist commodities brought China $4 billion, making up 35% of the country's tourist
income. In Guatemala, a survey taken by the National Tourism Institute
(INGUAT) indicated that the average tourist arriving by air purchased $82 in
handicrafts (Rose, 1988). There are even a few tours organised specifically for the
appreciation and purchase of Third World crafts, and some of them include visits
to national parks for wildlife viewing.

Some interesting evidence on the tastes and motivations of tourists is provided
by consumer research surveys conducted in several countries which are major
sources of international travellers (US Travel and Tourism Administration, 1988–
90). 'Shopping' was among the tourist activities most frequently engaged in by
long-distance, international tourists, being reported by more than 85% of travel-

lers in the countries surveyed. An interest in 'local crafts' and in 'unique cultural groups' was reported with some frequency, although it was by no means top-ranked.

Sophisticated analytic techniques were used in these market research studies to group tourists according to desired 'product segments'. Among them were 'culture and nature travellers', who accounted for between 16% (France) and 23% (Japan) of potential tourists. The identified product segments differed among countries, but there was frequently a mixture of interest in natural features and cultural features, and both were generally associated with an interest in local crafts and unique cultural groups. These data suggest that ecotourists are potential handicraft consumers, and that people interested in cultural heritage (and presumably in cultural artifacts) are potential visitors to natural areas.

Supply of Tourist Merchandise

It is very difficult to generalise about the origins of merchandise sold to tourists (see Connelly-Kirch, 1982 and Wagner, 1982). Handicrafts, for example, may be made under conditions ranging from individual producers working in their own homes, to cooperative village workshops, to large urban factories such as are found in parts of India's hand-knotted rug industry. Some products, particularly those requiring high degrees of skill or those best made in large batches, are produced only by specialists. Others, such as simple jewellery and woven bracelets, can be made by almost anyone, even small children. Some products are made almost casually, in spare moments between other activities or while sitting in the marketplace awaiting a customer. Although craft production and food processing are very often done by women, there are many tourist items where production is exclusively a male occupation (much African wood carving, for example).

In general, inexpensive items requiring large amounts of hand labour input are necessarily made by the poor. Because entry into the business is usually easy and products are standardised, severe price competition tends to hold returns down to the lowest possible level (see Wagner, 1982 for an excellent case study of market competition). But a few producers of tourist merchandise — recognised artists, for example, or those who have particularly good marketing outlets — make quite a good living from it, at least by local standards. One can also point to entire communities, such as Taxco, Mexico; Monimbo, Nicaragua; Sarchi, Costa Rica; and Otavalo, Ecuador, whose overall prosperity clearly rests on the sale of tourist merchandise.

Perhaps the best generalisation is simply to state that there is enormous potential variation in tourist merchandise production, depending on the nature of the product and, in some cases, on local custom and tradition. But unlike many types of livelihood, there is ample opportunity for participation by the poor, the rural, the landless, and those lacking formal education. The challenge is to find products, production systems, and marketing strategies that allow producers operating in or near a national park or nature reserve to make an income from sales to tourists that is both adequate and sustainable.

Home- and village-based production systems

Most handicrafts are products of home- and village-based production systems, an arrangement that offers several potential advantages to the producer. First, the worker can obtain cash income while remaining in the rural setting. This is an important consideration, given that many alternative cash-producing occupations (e.g. hiring out for field harvest) require that the worker temporarily move or commute to another area. It also may help alleviate pressure for permanent migration to overcrowded urban areas, a nearly worldwide phenomenon.

Second, many handicrafts lend themselves to episodic work — the producer can work on the item during slack periods between other tasks. This may involve work episodes during the day (e.g. work at the loom whenever time is available) or work episodes during seasonal slack times. The ability to work episodically helps explain why craft producers find it worthwhile to produce even when returns seem too low to justify the effort. In the Peruvian town of Taquile, for example, weaving output has increased dramatically in recent years even though returns are usually less than US$1 per day (Healy & Zorn, 1983: 7).

A third advantage of handicraft production is that it can provide a cash return to work by women, children, the handicapped and the elderly.[1] These sometimes work as part of a production system that involves the entire family. For example a study of 375 (male) handloom weavers in India found that they had 722 dependents assisting them with their work (Rao, 1990). In many places, moreover, handicrafts offer an independent source of income for persons who would otherwise find it difficult to find work for cash. This may be especially significant for young people, who may spend their earnings on education. 'A survey of 54 households with school-age children in three neighbourhoods of Peliatan, Indonesia, a major tourist destination, showed that 43 of them had high-school-age children paying their own school fees from work in carving or painting' (Sutton, 1989: 14).

Handicrafts also provide income for the elderly. Annis (1987) has analysed the economics of producing *petates*, a type of mat produced in Guatemala by interweaving marsh reeds. He found that 22 of 74 families studied obtained income from *petate* production, but none subsisted solely on this enterprise. Though mean annual production was only $47, it would provide the equivalent of 500 person-days of tortillas, a significant contribution for elderly members of a poor family.

It is difficult to generalise across diverse societies, but there are frequently gender distinctions in handicraft production. In many cases, these distinctions reserve the higher-paying jobs for males. Handicrafts, however, can in some cases raise the economic status of women within the family by affording them the opportunity for independent cash-income production. In Coqueiral, a small fishing village in Brazil that has become a summer destination for Brazilian tourists, tourism has stimulated a local handicraft industry. 'Women and teen-aged girls plait straw into hand bags, wallets, hats, shopping baskets, and carry-cots for babies and the revenues, however small, are important during bad fishing seasons... These new work opportunities have modified male–female relationships. Thanks to handicrafts and tourism, women can be financially independent. Several widows and divorced women said that they would never remarry because they were better off than before' (Robben, 1982).

How tourist merchandise is sold

Merchandise is sold to tourists in several ways. Perhaps the most common is the official or unofficial marketplace, where multiple sellers gather to place their wares before the tourist. These are often located near the entrance to attractions, in the nearest village, along roads, or at transportation foci such as bus stations or cruise ship docks. Tourist merchandise is also sold in shops, including general merchandise stores, cooperatives, hotel or museum gift shops and privately owned shops selling a full line of tourist goods or specialising in selected items (e.g. jewellery, art objects). Tourist merchandise is sometimes sold at the workshop where it is manufactured, as in the metalworkers' bazaars of the Middle East.

Marketing may consume as much time and effort as does the actual manufacture of the tourist merchandise. Indeed, Wagner's (1982) study of dyed-cloth sellers in The Gambia found that selling a piece of cloth required on average *fifteen times* as many hours as did its preparation. The method by which tourist merchandise is marketed helps determine both how much employment is generated and how the revenues are distributed within the community. A situation in which there are many sellers, each with an equal chance to 'catch' a tourist, means a large number of jobs and a relatively low return to each seller. Domination by a few shops means fewer jobs and higher returns, enjoyed mainly by a small number of shop owners and, perhaps, their employees. Domination of sales by park management or concessionaries offers the possibility of higher net revenues (by extracting monopoly profits from the tourists) and direction of those revenues to purposes chosen by the park.

Intra-community relations

Not all members of a given community have the skill or inclination to make handicrafts or other tourist merchandise; some community members may already have more lucrative opportunities. However, creation of a new tourist-based industry can change economic relationships. For example, persons with unusual skills may earn disproportionately high returns. Persons with the requisite management skills (and language ability) may become traders and middlemen, selling crafts made by others. Where cooperatives or craft promotion projects are created, one or more salaried managers may be employed.

Although this inequality can have negative effects, it also has positive aspects. Even in traditional, non-tourist areas, there frequently is a history of inequality of income, assets and opportunities (see Hill, 1986). Revenue from producing tourist merchandise, along with other tourist-based income, can greatly modify the traditional local hierarchy. In one Brazilian community, for example, growth of tourism overturned the dominance of local palm grove planters, and 'the children of traditional powerholders are migrating to cities' (Robben, 1982). Furthermore, development of tourist merchandise enterprises can contribute to changes in social position for the craftsperson, even aside from income changes. Frankowski-Braganza (1983) reports that in two west Mexican towns, potters had a poor self image, had low status in the community, and were ignored or criticised by local youth. As foreign tourists come to purchase their wares, they 'receive a welcome change in self image from the tourists, who regard them as "primitive" artists and not as manual laborers'.

Issues in Production of Tourist Merchandise

Innovation and 'authenticity'

'Belief in their authenticity', writes Ichaporia (1980: 47) 'lends tremendous weight and value to objects'. Knowledge that an object is handmade is an important ingredient in establishing its authenticity — 'things made by hand are "genuine"; mass-produced commodities are in the realm of the "plastic", a word connoting flimsiness, superficiality, flashiness, artificiality, whether in concept or material' (Ichaporia, 1980: 45).

Cohen (1988) observes that cultural products, such as handicrafts, which are at first considered contrived or unauthentic, may over time become recognised as authentic. He refers to this process as 'emergent authenticity', and notes that such products may eventually be accepted as authentic even by experts. Among the products cited by Cohen are Eskimo soapstone carvings, Haida argillite carvings, and figurative embroideries made by Hmong refugees from Laos. Graburn (1976) provides a useful typology of types of tourist arts, ranging from those originally produced for local consumption to arts incorporating (and often transforming) non-indigenous artistic traditions and intended to be sold to visitors.

In general, product innovation can take three forms. First, products indigenous to a society can be adapted to better suit tourist needs and preferences; second, a community can adopt products made in other regions or even in other countries and produce them locally as 'native' arts; and third, craftspeople may create entirely new products. All three of these methods have been used successfully by handicraft makers in developing and developed nations (Institute of Social Studies Trust, 1987; Ryerson, 1976; and E. Graham, 1991).

Marketing tourist merchandise

The marketing function includes identification of what potential customers might want, product development, pricing, promotion and distribution. Marketing specialists assert that marketing works best when it is regarded not merely as the selling of a product but as the integration of all of these elements, driven by an understanding of how products satisfy consumers' wants. In many cases, traditional handicrafts are not ideal for the tourist market. For example, textiles may be too large or too brightly coloured. There also may be significant differences in merchandise demand among tourists of different nationalities.

The typical way in which makers and sellers of tourists goods determine what tourists want is through the market — some goods sell and others don't. Some rudimentary market research, however, might make this trial-and-error process much more effective. For example, simple survey instruments and checklists could be devised through which makers and promoters of tourist merchandise can obtain information from tourists about their preferences.

Although it is important to determine what tourists might like to buy, it is also useful to educate the tourist about local products and design traditions. This is particularly important in a national park or nature reserve setting, where marketing efforts can educate tourists about the relationship that particular crafts have to park protection and sustainable development. 'Alternative Trading

Organisations' such as SERRV, Pueblo to People, and SelfHelp Crafts (a project of the Mennonite Central Committee) have found that retail customers in the US are attracted by the belief that their Third World imports are produced under circumstances that benefit the producer and the environment, and they empha-sise that aspect in mail order catalogues and other sales literature. A staff member at SERRV, which markets Third World crafts through churches, observes that '[our customers] buy because of why we buy and who we buy from. They know that the profits go back to the producer'.(Fogle, 1992). Although ecotourists are unlikely to buy a product that does not attract them in other ways, the knowledge that a given craft or souvenir benefits a park or a neighbouring community may make them more likely to buy from a park-approved outlet or to pay somewhat more than the prevailing price.

Consumer education can also help reduce consumer demand for souvenirs made from endangered species. TRAFFIC (USA) an affiliate of World Wildlife Fund, produces attractive educational brochures giving general guidance to tourists regarding such merchandise. Where wildlife souvenirs are a problem, park visitor centres should provide targeted displays and consumer literature. Ideally, tourists should be shown that there are alternatives to environmentally destructive purchases (e.g. substitution of other tropical hardwoods for those in short supply). Tour operators should also be encouraged to distribute pamphlets and educate travellers. A recent book (S. Graham, 1991) on 'responsible tourism' not only warns about endangered species souvenirs but gives some useful advice on how tourists can orient their purchases to maximise the positive local impacts.

A final aspect of marketing might be termed 'non-tourist/post-tourist' sales. Although the emphasis in this article has been on development and marketing of merchandise that is sold on site to tourists, many such items also have possibilities in the national tourist market (e.g. sales in urban public markets and hotel gift stores) and as export products. Promoters of tourist merchandise should be alert to possibilities for placing merchandise in alternative outlets and, where demand warrants it, letting tourists know where they can buy items after their visit.

Non-craft tourist merchandise

Although handicrafts are undoubtedly the most obvious type of merchandise purchased by tourists, they are by no means the only potential products. Food items also offer possibilities. In Costa Rica, tourists visiting the Monteverde Cloud Forest Reserve buy significant quantities of cheese from the local coopera-tively owned factory. At the same site, a farm family supplements its income by selling 'trail mix' to tourists. The product combines nuts and raisins purchased in San Jose with bananas produced and dried in Monteverde (Healy, 1988). Honey and 'natural' chewing gum made from chicle (a tropical sap) might also be popular.

Food items can be sold to tourists for on-site consumption, as well as serving as low-cost souvenirs. They can also be distributed in tourist-originating coun-tries as promotional materials by tour operators and NGOs. In some cases, commercial export markets can be created, with the sale to tourists serving both to bolster sales and to create future export customers. Customer loyalty may be particularly strong where the product is understood by the tourist-consumer to be part of a sustainable development project.

Another potential product is educational materials concerning the site. These include books, pamphlets, maps, videos, recordings, bird lists, posters, postcards, and wildlife photographs. These articles are generally produced off-site, so there is little profit for local people except for the retail margin. In a few cases, production of such items offers a source of income to one or two highly skilled persons — for example a biologist may write a guide to the site's fauna or a photographer may sell high quality prints. Sale of these products is clearly worthwhile from an educational and promotional standpoint, and they often contribute greatly to the tourist's enjoyment of the experience. Books, trail maps and bird lists may also have the advantage of inducing tourists to remain longer at a given site, by increasing their awareness of possible things to see and do.

Nature tourists are also likely to be interested in educational materials that deal with the culture of the areas they visit. Elder (1983) offers a long list of tourism products that might be developed from the rich folklore of the Caribbean. They include 'anthologies of folk poetry, cassettes of recorded speech, broadsheets of folk tales, photographs and slides of tale-tellers, video-tapes of tale-telling sessions, costumes and "tools" of folk dramatists, painting(s) of folklore...figures'. He also finds possibilities for product development in folk medicine and folk music.

T-shirts — A special case

Among the most ubiquitous of souvenir items are T-shirts. Many parks and reserves have logo-adorned T-shirts; so do nearly all organised environmental groups. T-shirts and related decorated clothing items have several purposes. They create a sense of organisational identification for employees and volunteers. Furthermore, because they are almost standard garb for tourists, they can serve as a very effective advertising medium. It is very common to see members of a tour group wearing clothing items embossed with designs or logos of tour operators or previously visited destinations.

Inexpensive and easily packed, T-shirts make excellent items for tourists to purchase. The head of a souvenir industry trade group says that T-shirts are 'by far the Number 1 tourist souvenir item' (Borowsky, 1992). From the seller's standpoint, however, T-shirts are less than ideal merchandise. The major problem is their relatively low local labour content. T-shirts are typically made in mass quantities in automated knitting mills. When purchased in bulk, a good quality unadorned shirt has a wholesale cost of US$3–4. Even at that price, it is economically infeasible for most local retailers to buy blank shirts and print their own logos or designs on them, since the necessary machinery is very expensive. Unless the anticipated quantity to be sold is quite high (more than several hundred yearly) it may be best to contract for high quality printed shirts, preferably from a domestic supplier.

Even though they may not be produced locally, however, T-shirts can bring in significant tourist revenues, especially if park and reserve managers are able to take advantage of T-shirt popularity to charge higher prices, incorporating an explicit 'donation for support of the reserve'.

Sustainability

Because tourist goods are generally made, in whole or in part, from locally obtained materials, it is necessary to consider the sustainability of material supplies.

Among the least sustainable are products whose manufacture involves use of endangered species of fauna or flora (see Mathieson & Wall, 1982). These include turtle products, skins and pelts, stuffed animals, feathers, and ivory. They also include fossils and antiquities sold in contravention of local laws, and endangered animals sold live as pets (e.g. psittacine birds). Although local laws may prohibit trade in endangered species, and the Convention on International Trade in Endangered Species prohibits or regulates their importation into other countries, they are still offered for sale to tourists in many places. In Mexico, for example, it is reported that available tourist goods include tortoise shell jewellery, jaguar and ocelot skin products, stuffed caimans, iguanas, birds, and turtles, and live parrots — all illegal for US tourists to import (TRAFFIC, 1989).

Other products might be termed 'potentially unsustainable'— products whose inputs are now relatively abundant but which cannot sustain significant expansion. Many tropical wood products are in this category, at least under current forest management practices. In some cases the shortage of a particular raw material can be directly traced to increased production of a specific tourist product. For example, in the Mexican state of Guerrero, local people began around 1959 to paint designs formerly used on pottery onto paper made from the bark of the amate (wild fig) tree (Stromberg, 1976). The product became wildly successful and soon threatened extermination of the trees from which the bark was stripped.

Producers can be rather innovative in finding substitute materials when supplies of traditional ones begin to dry up. In Thailand, for example, where teak has become difficult to procure, makers of jewellery boxes, picture frames and carved products have substituted other, cheaper, types of rain forest wood, although they are often still sold by dealers as 'teak'. Now even the substitute species are becoming limited in supply and are brought from great distances. In similar fashion, scarcity of rattan in the Philippines and Thailand has increased use of bamboo for some craft items.

A third category of products are those utilising abundant materials that can sustain significant expansion, for example gourds, bamboo, and cotton cloth. Pottery products are a staple of Third World tourist crafts and are almost always based on abundant local clays (although sometimes the wood or charcoal used for firing them has become scarce). Salable products can also be made from waste materials, such as corn stalks and coconut husks. In Feni, Bangladesh, for example, a project initiated by SelfHelp Crafts employs over 60 persons in making writing and wrapping paper from jute residues.

At the most positive end of the sustainability spectrum are products that might be termed 'actively sustainable' — products that use materials produced as part of independent sustainable use projects. For example, an existing Honduran cashew project and a proposed Belize chicle-based chewing gum project not only result in income for processors and retailers but can also create a profitable enterprise for farmers who supply the raw materials. These products would also have the ecologically beneficial side-effect of keeping tree cover on the land.

Another important issue of sustainability is the geographic source of the material. Park managers must decide whether certain materials should be harvested within the entire park or only in designated areas or buffer zones. In some cases, materials for tourist merchandise can be cultivated under monocultural plantation conditions or through agroforestry or polyculture. In this case, production might best take place in village areas, whether inside or outside formal park boundaries. However, it may be difficult to identify materials that are thus cultivated from similar 'wild' materials extracted illegally from the park proper.

Production activities as a tourist attraction

The production of tourist merchandise can itself be of great interest to tourists. Many tourists like the idea of being permitted to look 'backstage' in the society they visit, seeing how people live their daily lives and perform their economic activities. This intimate glimpse of another culture may be authentic or may be carefully controlled — a sort of false backstage carefully designed for the tourist's benefit (see MacCannell, 1973). In either case, the pleasure gained by the tourist in seeing an object produced can add significantly to its perceived value and hence to the price the tourist is willing to pay.

It is not uncommon for crafts producers to make their goods in view of potential customers. Where the product can be made in a marketplace (weaving, basketry) sellers often try to utilise productively the time spent waiting for the next customer. Because tourists are often fascinated by how unfamiliar things are made, public production can also be a marketing tool. In North America and Europe, public demonstration of craft production is formally incorporated into open air museums, living historical farms, and 'ecomuseums', many of which sell craft products in addition to charging admission fees. However, this type of facility is much less common in developing countries (see Stanton, 1977).

The process of food production is often of great interest to tourists. The growing of rice, for example, is a novelty for many tourists, who would be eager to learn more about both how the plants are cultivated and how the harvest is processed. Such tropical crops as coffee and cacao lend themselves well to tourist observation and the product is well suited for sale to tourists as a reminder of what they have seen.

In the tropics, there appear to be significant possibilities for combining tourism with the management of 'extractive reserves' — that is, with the sustainable harvest of non-timber forest products, such as rubber and natural chewing gum. One form of extractive activity that is likely to have particular appeal to visitors to tropical forests is the harvesting of medicinal plants. Nature walks that emphasise local uses of plants are frequently offered at jungle lodges in many tropical parks. In western Belize, the Panti Trail is a privately operated tourist destination, where visitors can take a guided forest walk on a trail laid out with advice from an 86 year old Mayan 'bush doctor'. In addition to charging for admission and guided tours, the enterprise sells one-ounce packages of Belizean elixirs made from local plants, ranging from Bellyache Tea to Party Punch (Mahler, 1992).

Although many tourists are content to be spectators, there are some who crave more active participation in local cultures and the chance to learn new skills. This presents an interesting opportunity for local artisans to earn money by providing instruction, which would simultaneously educate the tourist, provide the crafts-person with a significant profit opportunity, and radically change the interaction between tourist and local resident from a seller–customer relationship to a teacher–student relationship.

Conclusion

There are strong arguments for considering opportunities for sale of tourist merchandise in planning Third World parks and reserves in areas where local residents need a sustainable livelihood and where tourist visitation is expected to be fairly high. The first argument is sheer necessity — experience around the world has shown that where there are large numbers of people living in and near a park, there is often great danger to the protected resources unless local people feel that they derive economic benefits. Making money from tourist visitation is among a relatively short list of potential economic enterprises that can coexist with resource protection. There appears to be a substantial market, actual and potential, for tourist merchandise. Given that the tourists will continue to come only if park resources remain intact, and that tourist merchandise can be sold only if the tourists continue to come, a clear link might be forged between local economic prosperity and resource protection.

The second argument is that production and sale of tourist merchandise offer an opportunity to even the poorest participant in the local economy. Other forms of participation in the tourist industry, such as entrepreneurship in lodging, transportation and guide service, frequently require capital, command of foreign languages and other prerequisites not easily available to the poor.

Third, there is enormous scope for product development. Although the stereotype of tourist merchandise is the tawdry mass-produced souvenir, rural societies have been successful in selling traditional products, modified products, and entirely new products. Many of these products have actually revitalised local craft traditions and even, in some cases, created new ones that have reinforced local identity.

Fourth, tourist merchandise offers the possibility of using local materials sustainably and even of providing a new market for the output of local agriculture and forestry enterprises specifically targeted toward resource protection. Creating a local market for these materials can substantially increase revenues to producers and can create markets for entirely new materials and for byproducts formerly discarded.

Finally, tourist merchandise can be a useful tool for publicising the park and for educating tourists about the relation between the park and local people. Non-governmental organisations involved in park protection can use sale of tourist merchandise as part of campaigns to generate donations and continuing support from past park visitors.

However, there are several pitfalls to be avoided. These include possible reductions in product quality to meet the volume of tourist demand, depletion of natural resources used as inputs for tourist merchandise, crowding of tourist sites by vendors, and social tensions brought on when some members of the community benefit more than others from tourist merchandise sales. Park and reserve managers can avoid or mitigate at least some of these problems by explicitly incorporating tourist merchandise in site management plans, providing appropriate vending sites (including park-operated shops), encouraging training and other incentives for tourist merchandise producers, and encouraging local development projects that provide sustainable supplies of the materials used in making tourist merchandise.

Acknowledgements

The author gratefully acknowledges the research assistance of Dorothy Zbicz, the helpful comments of Gustavo Arcia (Research Triangle Institute), William Ascher (Duke University), Robertson Collins (Tourism Development/Heritage Conservation Ltd., Singapore), Julie Johnson (Duke University), Jan Laarman (North Carolina State University), Toddi Steelman (Duke University), and anonymous reviewers for this journal and the comments and editorial assistance of Erika Nystrom. This work was supported by the US Agency for International Development through the Duke University Center for Tropical Conservation.

Note

1. One must of course look closely at any production opportunity that involves child labour. For poor families, it seems likely that the potential for exploitation or for school absence or drop-out because of handicraft work will be more than offset by the improvement in child nutrition and health afforded by handicraft income and the greater potential for paying cash expenses (tuition, uniforms) associated with school attendance.

References

Annis, Sheldon (1987) *God and Production in a Guatemalan Town.* Austin: University of Texas Press.

Boo, Elizabeth (1990) *Ecotourism: The Potentials and Pitfalls.* Washington, DC: World Wildlife Fund.

Borowsky, Scott (1992) President of Souvenir and Novelty Trade Association, Upper Darby, Pennsylvania. Telephone interview with Robert Healy, August 5.

Brandon, Katrina Eadie and Wells, Michael (1992) Planning for people and parks: Design dilemmas. *World Development* 20 (4), 557–70.

Cohen, Erik (1988) Authenticity and commoditization in tourism. *Annals of Tourism Research* 15, 371–86.

— (1993) Introduction: Investigating tourist arts. *Annals of Tourism Research* (Special Issue on Tourist Arts) 20 (1), 1–8.

Connelly-Kirch, Debra (1982) Economic and social correlates of handicraft selling in Tonga. *Annals of Tourism Research* 9, 383–402.

Elder, J.D (1983) Folklore, folk art and craft in the Caribbean: Their role in tourism product development. In *Organization of American States, Cultural Patrimony and the Tourism Product: Towards a Mutually Beneficial Relationship* (pp. 53–68). Report of an OAS/CTRC Regional Seminar. Washington, DC: OAS.

Fogle, Barbara (1992) Manager of Purchasing and Producer Development, SERRV Handicrafts. New Windsor, Maryland. Telephone interview, August 7.

Frankowski-Braganza, Ann Christine (1983) Host/guest interaction and its impact on social identity (Mexico). Doctoral Dissertation, Department of Cultural Anthropology, Indiana University.

Graburn, Nelson H.H. (ed.) (1976) *Ethnic and Tourist Arts*. Berkeley: University of California Press.

Graham, Ellen (1991) The discreet charm of Nantucket is now being patented. *Wall Street Journal*, October 7.

Graham, Scott (1991) *Handle With Care: A Guide to Responsible Travel in Developing Countries*. Chicago: The Noble Press.

Healy, Kevin and Zorn, Elayne (1983) Lake Titicaca's campesino-controlled tourism. *Grassroots Development* 6 (2)/7 (1), 5–10.

Healy, Robert G. (1988) *Economic Considerations in Nature-Oriented Tourism: The Case of Tropical Forest Tourism* (FPEI Working Paper No. 39). Research Triangle Park, NC: US Forest Service.

Hill, Polly (1986) *Development Economics on Trial*. Cambridge: Cambridge University Press.

Ichaporia, Niloufer (1980) Crazy for foreign: The exchange of goods and values on the international ethnic arts market. PhD Dissertation, Department of Anthropology, University of California, Berkeley.

Institute of Social Studies Trust (1987) *Small Scale Forest Based Enterprises With Special Reference to the Roles of Women: Karnataka State Overview Paper*. Bangalore: Institute of Social Studies Trust.

Keown, Charles F. (1989) A model of tourists' propensity to buy: The case of Japanese visitors to Hawaii. *Journal of Travel Research* 27 (3), 31–4.

Lindberg, Kreg (1991) *Policies for Maximizing Nature Tourism's Ecological and Economic Benefits*. Washington, DC: World Resources Institute.

Littrell, Mary Ann (1990) Symbolic significance of textile crafts for tourists. *Annals of Tourism Research* 17, 228–45.

Littrell, Mary Ann, Anderson, Luella F. and Brown, Pamela J. (1993) What makes a craft souvenir authentic? *Annals of Tourism Research* 20 (1), 197–208.

MacCannell, Dean (1973) Staged authenticity: Arrangements of social space in tourist settings. *American Journal of Sociology* 79 (3), 589–603.

Mahler, Richard (1992) The ancient art of Mayan healing thrives along Belize's Panti trail. *Great Expeditions* 71, 10–3.

Mathieson, Alister and Wall, Geoffrey (1982) *Tourism: Economic, Physical and Social Impacts*. London: Longman.

Munasinghe, Mohan (1992) Summary of proceedings of workshop on economics of protected areas. World Parks Congress. To be published by International Union for the Conservation of Nature.

Place, Susan (1991) Nature tourism and rural development in Tortuguero. *Annals of Tourism Research* 18, 186–201.

Rao, K. Rama Mohana (1990) *Development of Handloom Industry: A Study of Andhra Pradesh*. New Delhi: Discovery Publishing House.

Robben, Antonius C.G.M (1982) Tourism and change in a Brazilian fishing village. *Cultural Survival Quarterly* 6 (3), 18–19.

Rose, Dietmar (1988) Report submitted to USAID/ROCAP Guatemala: Guatemala Biodiversity and Tropical Forest Assessment. Guatemala City.

Ryerson, Scott H. (1976) Seri ironwood carving: An economic view. In Nelson H.H. Graburn (ed.) *Ethnic and Tourist Arts* (pp. 118–36). Berkeley: University of California Press.

Shyamsundar, Priya (1993) Economic implications of tropical forest protection for local residents: The case of the Mantadia National Park in Madagascar. PhD dissertation, School of the Environment, Duke University.

Stanton, Max (1977) The Polynesian Cultural Center. In Ben R. Finney and Karen Ann Watson (eds) *A New Kind of Sugar: Tourism in the Pacific* (pp. 229–36). Santa Cruz, CA: Center for South Pacific Studies.

Stromberg, Gobi (1976) The Amate bark-paper paintings of Xalitla. In Nelson H.H.

Tourist Merchandise   *151*

Graburn (ed.) *Ethnic and Tourist Arts* (pp. 149–62). Berkeley: University of California Press.

Sutton, Margaret (1989) Bali: From five star hotels to intimate homestays. *World Development* 2 (6), 13–14.

TRAFFIC (USA) (1989) *Watch Out for Wildlife Products — Mexico*. Washington, DC: TRAFFIC/World Wildlife Fund.

United States Travel and Tourism Administration (1988–90) *Pleasure Travel Markets to North America*. Series of country reports. Washington, DC: US Government Printing Office.

Wagner, Ulla (1982) *Catching the Tourist: Women Handicraft Traders in the Gambia*. Stockholm: Department of Social Anthropology, University of Stockholm.

Waters, Somerset (1991) *The Big Picture: Travel Industry World Yearbook, 1991*. New York: Child and Waters.

Whelan, Tensie (1991) *Nature Tourism: Managing for the Environment*. Washington, DC: Island Press.

Wells, Michael and Brandon, Katrina with Lee Hannah (1992) *People and Parks: Linking Protected Area Management With Local Communities*. Washington, DC: World Bank.

Western, David (1982) Amboseli National Park: Enlisting land owners to conserve migratory wildlife. *Ambio* 11 (5), 302–8.

World Resources Institute (1992) *World Resources, 1992–93*. New York: Oxford University Press.

[17]

Pergamon

Annals of Tourism Research, Vol. 24, No. 2, pp. 322–340, 1997
© 1997 Elsevier Science Ltd
Printed in Great Britain. All rights reserved
0160-7383/97 $17.00+0.00

PII: S0160-7383(96)00057-6

SELLING TO TOURISTS
Indonesian Street Vendors

Dallen J. Timothy
Central Connecticut State University, USA
Geoffrey Wall
University of Waterloo, Canada

Abstract: If it is considered at all, the informal sector is often viewed as a problem by tourism planners. This paper examines street vendors in Yogyakarta, Indonesia, a center for cultural tourism, using the concepts of heterogeneity and differentiation, economic linkages, and government involvement. It is shown that the distinction between the informal and formal sectors is becoming increasingly blurred. The Yogyakarta vendors exhibit many of the characteristics commonly ascribed to participants in the informal sector but differ in others, particularly in legal status and government regulation. The latter can be viewed, in part, as a means of influencing the nature of resident–visitor encounters and influencing the quality of tourists' experiences. **Keywords:** economic linkages, government regulation, Indonesia, informal sector, vendors. © 1997 Elsevier Science Ltd. All rights reserved

Résumé: Vendre aux touristes: les vendeurs ambulants en Indonésie. Le secteur informel, pour peu qu'on le considère, se voit le plus souvent comme problème par les planificateurs touristiques. L'article étudie les vendeurs ambulants à Yogyakarta, en Indonésie, un centre de tourisme culturel, en utilisant les concepts de l'hétérogénéité et la différenciation, les liens économiques et l'engagement gouvernemental. On voit que la distinction entre les secteurs formel et informel devient de plus en plus floue. Les vendeurs de Yogyakarta démontrent beaucoup de caractéristiques du secteur informel, mais ils diffèrent dans d'autres, comme le statut légal et les règlements du gouvernement. Ces derniers peuvent être un moyen d'influencer la nature des rencontres entre habitants et visiteurs et la qualité des expériences touristiques. **Mots-clés:** liens économiques, règlements gouvernementaux, Indonésie, secteur informel, vendeurs. © 1997 Elsevier Science Ltd. All rights reserved

INTRODUCTION

The informal sector is of great significance in many developing economies, especially in large cities and tourism destination areas. The term "informal sector" was initially used by Hart (1973) and the International Labor Office (ILO 1972) in the context of dual economic systems in Africa, which were viewed as being polarized into formal and informal sectors. Simply stated, the informal economy is a process of income generation which is "unregulated by the institutions of society, in a legal and social environment in which similar activities are regulated" (Castells and Portes 1989:12). Informal ventures generally

Dallen Timothy is Assistant Professor in the Department of Geography, Central Connecticut State University (New Britain CT 06050, USA. Email timothy@ccsua.ctstateu.edu). He is interested in tourism planning in developing countries and borders and international travel. **Geoffrey Wall** is Professor in the Department of Geography, University of Waterloo (Waterloo, Ontario, Canada N2L 3G1. Email gwall@watserv1.uwaterloo.ca). He is researching the impacts of different types of tourism, particularly as revealed in Indonesia.

operate without legal recognition and are neither registered and
enumerated nor officially taxed (Michaud 1991; Wahnschafft 1982).
In contrast, the formal sector includes enterprises which are licensed,
taxed, and eligible for state funding.

In addition to legal status, formal and informal activities differ in
many other ways. Formal-sector characteristics include difficult entry,
frequent reliance on imported resources, corporate ownership, large
scale of operation, capital-intensiveness, and often imported technology, formally-acquired skills (often expatriate), and protected markets through tariffs, quotas, and licenses (ILO 1972:6). In contrast,
informal activities generally exhibit ease of entry, reliance on indigenous resources, family ownership, small scale of operation, labor inten-
siveness, skills acquired outside the formal school system, part-time
labor, locally-based ventures, and unregulated and competitive markets (Henry 1982; ILO 1985). Within the formal sector, the means of
production are usually privately-owned by a small class, and are operated by workers for the profit of that owning class. In contrast, in the
informal sector, the means of production are usually owned by those
who operate them (Davies 1979:89).

Growth of the informal sector in urban and, by extension, resort
areas in the developing world is most commonly attributed to rural to
urban migration which puts increased pressures on scarce employment opportunities (ILO 1985; Sethuraman 1981a). McGee (1979)
suggests that the existence of much of the informal sector is directly
linked to the need of the urban poor to augment their income. Hart
echoes this perspective in stating that "petty capitalism, often as a
supplement to wage-employment, offers itself as a means of salvation"
(1973:66). Petty capitalism, or informal employment, is one response
to the unavailability of formal employment opportunities and low
wages, and it has been suggested that informal enterprises can
advance economic development through their ability to absorb large
quantities of labor (Griffith 1987; Thomas 1992; Tokman 1978).

Although it is useful for heuristic purposes, it is an oversimplification to dichotomize the economy into two distinct sectors.
For example, Bromley and Gerry (1979) depict employment categories along a continuum from "stable wage work" to "true self-
employment" and Gerry and Birkbeck (1981) suggest a classification
which includes: direct wage workers who either rent or are "given"
capital and are paid on commission; disguised wage workers who may
only rent part of their capital; and self-employed workers who provide
their own capital through savings. According to ILO (1972), the informal sector can be further broken down into skilled, semi-skilled, and
unskilled categories.

Trager (1987:239) suggests three issues that merit attention in
investigations of the informal sector: heterogeneity and differentiation; linkages with other economic sectors; and the effect of
government regulatory policies on the informal sector. The first issue
refers to the considerable variation in products, producers, markets,
and sellers in an area. Even within a subsector, such as services, a
diversity of undertakings may be found, including hawkers, shoe
shiners, rooms for minimal rent, unofficial tourism guides, and pros-

titutes. Furthermore, hawkers sell a multiplicity of products, ranging from hot food to used car parts to souvenirs of many kinds.

As to the second issue, many researchers of informal employment are interested in the linkages which may exist with other sectors of the economy, especially formal-sector activities (Sethuraman 1981b; Thomas 1992; Trager 1987; Wahnschafft 1982). Both backward and forward linkages may exist. The former refers to the purchase of products and services from the formal sector by informal enterprises. Forward linkages exist when informal-sector entrepreneurs supply goods or services to the formal sector (ILO 1985).

One of the most important distinctions between the formal and informal sectors is the third issue: that governments officially recognize the former but not the latter. One consequence of this is that governmental assistance, such as the allocation of favorable locations, loans, subsidies, tariff protection, and management training may be available to the formal but not the informal sector (ILO 1985). Informal-sector workers have been viewed as being unemployed or sporadically employed, contributing little to urban income, while adding to health, fire, and political hazards. Informal-sector operations have often been viewed by officialdom as being temporary and employing migrants, many of whom might be pressured to return to rural areas. Governments have often been reluctant to make improvements to conditions in the informal sector for fear of drawing more migrants into the field (ILO 1972). In fact, governments have often taken a negative position towards the informal sector (Tokman 1978), even to the extent that many officials view informal activities as ones to be eliminated (Trager 1987). However, some authorities are more tolerant of informal workers if they agree to be licensed and to relocate to uncrowded areas predetermined by the government (IDRC 1975; McGee and Yeung 1977).

In developing countries, the tourism industry can be roughly divided into formal and informal activities (Davis 1978) which together form a dualistic "whole economy" (Harris and Nelson 1993). The formal-sector tourism economy is based on legally-recognized ventures, such as hotels, airlines, and restaurants which are licensed, enumerated, and taxed by the government. On the other hand, the informal tourism sector is comprised of tourism-related activities which are generally beyond the effective control of the tourism authorities (Crick 1992).

Although many developing countries have tourism plans, they tend to concentrate on the development and distribution of facilities and infrastructure and very few such plans address the needs of the informal sector or even acknowledge its existence (Wall 1996). This is an important oversight because, as indicated above, the informal sector is a very important component of most developing country economies. According to Michaud (1991), there are three categories of informal activities related to tourism: lodging; services and craft-related activities; and other businesses, including, souvenir vendors, pedicab drivers, prostitutes, unlicensed guest houses, unofficial guides, and small food stalls (Crick 1992; Cukier-Snow and Wall 1993; Griffith 1987; Wahnschafft 1982). Long and Wall (1995) and Farver (1984) note that small-scale, informal-sector employment offers opportunities for indigenous, grassroots participation in the tourism industry. Similarly, in terms of government regulations, Kermath and Thomas (1992) conclude that the informal sector responds predictably to the growth of tourism, and that a less-stringent attitude by planners towards informal activities can help to decrease the likelihood of friction developing between the industry and local people.

Shopping is a popular activity among tourists, and one of the most common encounters Western tourists have while traveling in developing countries is with stationary or roaming vendors. These peddlers bombard tourists with T-shirts, jewelry, leather products, food, postcards, handicrafts and other items, and play on tourists' propensity to spend discretionary income on inessential goods and services (Griffith 1987). Such peddlers may operate illegally, in that they are not licensed by local government agencies, and much of what they sell may be of dubious quality and legality. Souvenir and craft vendors are one of the most ubiquitous segments of the informal sector in developing countries, and one which has widespread tourist appeal (Griffith 1987; IDRC 1975). While a number of researchers have addressed aspects of informal-sector employment in tourism (Crick 1992; Dahles 1994; Farver 1984; Harris and Nelson 1993; Kermath and Thomas 1992; Michaud 1991; Wahnschafft 1982), with the notable exception of prostitution, the informal sector, including informal vendors, has not received attention in the tourism literature commensurate with its importance. In fact, there are few studies of informal vendors and their role in the tourism industry (Cukier and Wall 1994; Griffith 1987).

In an attempt to remedy this deficiency, this paper examines the operations of street vendors in Yogyakarta, Indonesia. This will be done through consideration of heterogeneity and differentiation, economic linkages, and government treatment of street vendors in Yogyakarta. The paper is especially concerned with the extent to which stationary street vendors in Yogyakarta conform to the characteristics of informal-sector employees as described in the economic development literature.

STREET VENDORS IN YOGYAKARTA

Yogyakarta (Figure 1) is the third most visited destination for international travelers to Indonesia after Jakarta (many of whose visitors are on business) and Bali. Tourism in Yogyakarta was negligible until the early 70s, owing to a lack of promotion, inadequate tourism accommodation, and unreliable transportation services. As these problems began to be addressed by government agencies, the numbers of arrivals grew rapidly. It was estimated that 21% of all foreign tourists to Indonesia visited Yogyakarta in 1970. By 1975, however, estimates placed this figure at over 35% (Hill and Mubyarto 1978). In 1967, only 46,600 foreign and domestic tourists were recorded as staying in the largest hotels in Yogyakarta. By 1970, the total number of tourists had increased to 103,400. In 1980, 280,619 tourists were reported to have stayed in Yogyakarta, while in 1990 the city hosted 587,185 foreign and domestic tourists. The steady expansion

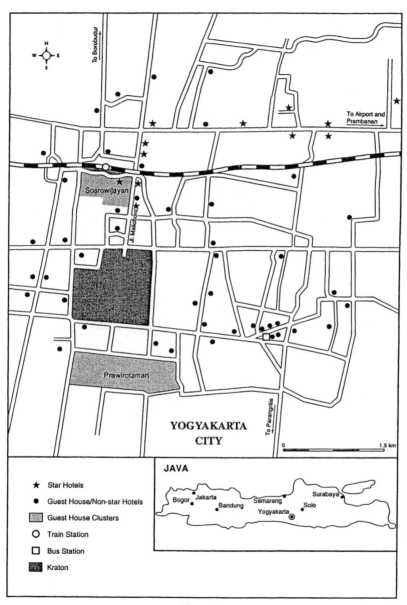

Figure 1

during the 70s and 80s can be attributed to improvements in road and railway transportation as well as increased numbers of domestic flights, and additional domestic mobility associated with economic growth. In 1994 the total reached 963,995 foreign and domestic tourists, excluding those staying with friends and relatives. While the majority were domestic travelers, approximately 150,000 were international visitors. Total tourist spending in Yogyakarta was estimated to be US$176 million in 1994 (Deparpostel 1984, 1995). This constitutes little more than US$18 per head; this may appear to be quite small but lengths of stay are short, many foreign tourists are backpackers and the main temple sites are in the neighboring Central Java Province and attract visitors away from the city.

Yogyakarta is often referred to as the "cultural capital" of Java. It has played a particularly important role in the political history of Indonesia and is also home to one of the most prominent and influential royal courts (sultanates) in Java. Most of the city's tourism resources are directly linked to its cultural and political heritage and the province's official tourism policy is one of cultural tourism (Dinas Pariwisata 1988). The most prominent attractions are the temple complexes of Borobudur and Prambanan, which are UNESCO world heritage sites. They are both located to the north of the city in Central Java Province and draw visitors away from the city center. These ancient structures are the most significant attractions for international tourists. The city itself functions as the base for sightseeing at the temples and it provides many additional cultural and historical attractions, including rich traditions of dance, music, festivals, and crafts of many kinds—including batik, leather work, silver, wood-carving, and puppetry (Timothy and Wall 1995).

Although Yogyakarta receives a large number of visitors, length of stay is quite short (averaging approximately 1.6 days for foreigners and 1.7 days for domestic visitors) and has declined further in recent years (Dinas Pariwisata 1994). It appears that foreign visitors, in particular, are not generally aware of the wealth of cultural attractions in Yogyakarta and vicinity and many plan only to visit Borobudur and Prambanan before moving on. Yogakarta is not serviced by international flights which, in essence, makes it a secondary destination for international visitors. Furthermore, while an increase in the frequency of domestic flights connecting with Bali and Java have improved communications, it has made Yogyakarta a day-trip destination for some Japanese tour packages based in Bali. The lack of a strong image outside of Indonesia and the lack of direct international flights have contributed in large part to the perception among international travelers that Yogyakarta is a supporting rather than a main destination (Wall 1993).

The city is oriented around a cosmic line between the *Kraton* (the sultan's palace) and volcanic Mount Merapi to the north. Malioboro Street (Figure 1) follows this line and tourism activity within the city is largely concentrated in its vicinity (Deparpostel 1992; Timothy and Wall 1995). The city's largest concentration of budget accommodation lies immediately to the west of Malioboro Street, and a number of star and non-star hotels have been built nearby. The majority of the city's attractions are located in the historic core in close proximity to Malioboro. The street itself is lined with a variety of stores and restaurants, including a number of fast-food outlets, which cater to locals and foreign and domestic tourists. Furthermore, many of the city's Western-style fast-food restaurants are found along or within walking distance of Malioboro Street.

During the day and into the evening, Malioboro, the main shopping street for both tourists and residents, particularly on the colonnaded, shaded, western side, is lined with *kakilima* (vendors) of various goods and services ranging from brooms and radios to snack foods and souvenirs. For tourists in Yogyakarta, these street peddlers, with their colorful products (which include many locally-made items) and their affinities for bargaining, are a major attraction (Antara 1995; Cahyono 1991; Yogya Post 1991). At night, the same street, particularly on the eastern side, is lined with *lesehan* (sit-on-the-ground, temporary cafes). These cater largely to an Indonesian clientele, but foreign tourists also sometimes eat with the locals in this traditional Javanese manner. However, it is the daytime activities and, in particular, the vendors of Malioboro Street, which are the focus of this paper.

Research Methods

Fieldwork for this study was undertaken in May and June 1995. As is usually the case in informal-sector situations, there was no listing of vendors from which a sample could be taken. Therefore, Malioboro Street was initially walked and a thorough daytime inventory between the railroad tracks and the *Kraton* (Sultan's palace) (Figure 1) revealed a total of 967 vendor stalls. At the same time, a record was also made of the gender of the vendors and the products being sold.

Subsequently, interviews were conducted with a sample of vendors. Surveyors were instructed to interview every fifth vendor and refusals were not replaced. Given the number of stalls, this meant that a potential of approximately 193 interviews could have been undertaken. In all, 78 interviews were completed for a response rate of just over 40%. The system worked satisfactorily although some people were not interviewed because they were not at their stall and there was also a substantial number of refusals. Some vendors were reluctant to participate for two main reasons: they were tired of being interviewed for other vendor studies had recently been carried out by the municipal government and the university, and they were afraid that the surveyors were employed by the taxation department to find out additional information about their business affairs. However, there is no indication of systematic biases in non-response. Surveys were administered in Javanese or Indonesian by hired research assistants who were students at a local university. Vendors were asked about their businesses, items sold, legal issues, their impressions of tourism, their role in Yogyakarta's tourism industry, and forward and backward economic linkages.

In addition to the random surveys, 20 additional open-ended interviews were conducted with street vendors to permit more detailed probing of their activities and concerns and a further 20 key-informant interviews were conducted with a mix of tourism planning officials, academic planners, private tourism planning consultants, interest-group representatives, and business managers as part of a broader investigation of tourism planning in Yogyakarta. These interviews provided additional information on economic linkages, business associations, and issues of legality.

Study Results

Following Trager (1987), the survey results are presented under three major headings: heterogeneity and differentiation; economic linkages; and government involvement.

1. Heterogeneity and Differentiation

Demographic Characteristics. While it was not possible to observe the sex of 19% of vendors during the undertaking of the daytime inventory (because they were not present at their stalls), of those that were recorded, 69% were male, 30% were female, and 1% were a male/ female team. This is consistent with the sex of informal vendors in Bali who were also predominantly male (Cukier and Wall 1994). While women are involved in entrepreneurial activities in developing countries, in Yogyakarta, women were involved in the sale of foodstuffs both on Malioboro Street and in adjacent markets; whereas in Bali, women worked in tourism-oriented small shops or kiosks in designated "art markets", resulting in tourism-oriented informal-sector vending being predominantly a male activity (Cukier and Wall 1995).

As determined by the subsequent survey, the majority (67%) of vendors were between 20 and 40 years old, with 30% older than 40 and 3% younger than 20. These results are similar to those of Dharoko (1994a, 1994b), who has also investigated the characteristics of the permanent vendors on Malioboro Street. However, they differ some-what from the itinerant vendors in Bali interviewed by Cukier and Wall (1994) in that, although mostly male in both cases, the Bali vendors tended to be somewhat younger.

Unlike Michaud's (1991) findings from northern India, which suggested that most street vendors were not from the local vicinity, and Cukier and Wall's (1994) study which showed that most itinerant vendors in Bali came from Java, almost half (42.5%) of Malioboro vendors were from Yogyakarta originally or from nearby villages (28.5%). Only 29% originally came from outside the Special Province of Yogyakarta.

Work Attributes. Farver found it difficult to estimate the number of handicraft sellers in relation to the number of producers, because many were unlicensed, part-time sellers, who were supplementing an income gained from other sources (1984:258). In contrast to this and to Henry's (1982) assertion that informal activities are overwhelmingly part-time, 92% of the Yogyakarta vendors worked at their job full-time. For some of the small proportion of part-time workers, vending was a seasonal activity, since several worked as farmers during the wet season. As with most informal-sector activities, hawking in Yogyakarta is labor-intensive. Almost all (97%) of respondents worked at their stalls every day and, according to Dharoko's (1994a) survey, approximately 72% of Malioboro's peddlers worked between 8–16 hours per day.

Selling on the streets of Yogyakarta can be quite profitable. One of the leather sellers interviewed stated that, on a good day, he could make as much as Rp.200,000 (US$1 is about Rp.2,000). However, this happens only on occasion, especially when domestic tourist numbers are at their highest during school holidays, and it is definitely not the norm for most vendors. According to Dharoko's (1994a) study, only approximately 30% of the vendors earned more than Rp.200,000 per month. This is a very acceptable return when one considers that the average minimum-wage worker in the formal tourism industry earned between Rp.80,000–90,000 per month. However, 11% of the vendors earned less than Rp.50,000 per month, but 18% earned over Rp.300,000. Thus, there were considerable variations in income.

Some of the stalls were family-run businesses. It was often the case that one family member operated the business in the morning while a different member tended the stall in the afternoon and evening. However, many of the single, younger, male vendors tended their business all day. Furthermore, respondents had been street vendors for an average of 10.8 years. However, the range spanned from 1 week to 55 years. Hawking and other market-type economic endeavors have long been an important aspect of Javanese community life (Geertz 1963), and many of the older vendors had been doing this work for many years, since even before the onset of tourism. Two women who had worked as vendors for over 50 years continued to sell their original products: fruits and prepared foods. Of the remaining 10 who had been selling since the mid-50s, all but two now sold non-food items, including puppets, leather purses, woodcrafts, batik art, and silver-works, largely for a foreign tourism market. Several interviewees agreed that tourism had caused a shift in the types of products sold by peddlers on Malioboro Street.

Product Diversity. Of all the products sold by hawkers in the historic core of Yogyakarta, clothing was the most common, being sold by 262 vendors. The clothes ranged from outrageous styles, which only foreign tourists would be likely to buy, to traditional Indonesian dress which would probably be purchased by local shoppers and domestic tourists. Table 1 shows the kinds of goods sold by the vendors in Yogyakarta and the number of occurrences of each product. In addition to clothing, leather and wood products were common items, together with food and refreshments. However, overall, a diversity of products was available for sale.

A number of small, informal, cooperative ventures had been formed, often based on similar products. For example, many of the batik sellers had formed an unofficial group for the purpose of reducing the costs of supplies through high-volume purchasing. Such unofficial groups of vendors should not be mistaken for the official cooperative associations which will be discussed later. This finding differs from that of Michaud (1991), who did not observe cooperation among vendors of similar products based on common interests in Ladakh.

Tourism in Developing Countries

Table 1. Frequencies of Goods for Sale on Malioboro Street

Product	Frequency	Product	Frequency
Clothing	262	Books/Magazines	8
Leather Jewelry	131	Rubber Stamps	8
Leather Belts	94	Bolts of Cloth	7
Canvas Bags/Backpacks	90	Brooms	7
Keychains	87	Painted Goat Skins	7
Leather Purses	74	Ceramic Trinkets	6
Designer Jewelry	72	Islamic Emblems	6
Leather Bags/Backpacks	60	Picture Frames	6
Shoes/Sandals	50	Plastic Temples	6
Wood Carvings/Toys	50	Cigarettes	5
Candy/Snacks	45	Place mats	5
Fans	43	Posters	5
Silverworks	42	Scarves	5
Hot Food	40	Nationalist Emblems	4
Hats	36	Handkerchiefs	3
Fresh Fruits	33	Watchbands	3
Sunglasses	31	Gems	2
Watches	31	Hangers	2
Wicker Products	29	Radios	2
Javanese Headwear	27	Taxidermy	2
Net Bags	25	Bumper Stickers	1
Wayang Puppets	21	Calculators	1
Batik Card/Paintings	20	Cigarette Holders	1
Drinks	19	Combs	1
Masks	15	Flashlights	1
Oil Paintings	15	Glass Blowing	1
Cigarette Lighters	14	Letter Openers	1
Toys	14	Luggage	1
Imitation Name-Brand Purses	13	Napkin Holders	1
Make-Up Bags	11	Old Coins	1
Wooden Whistles	11	Portrait Painting	1
Painted Tiles/Plates	10	Scales for Weighing Customers	1
Swords	10	Shoe Horns	1
Socks	9	Spears	1
Brassworks	8	Trophies	1

Spatial Variations. There are two principal strips of vendors on Malioboro Street: on the west (A) and the east (B) sides of the street (Figure 2). Both strips front the shops and, rarely, the office buildings that line the street. Each strip is further divided into two sections. These are directly in front of the shops (sections 1 and 4) and on the outer edge of the sidewalks (sections 2 and 3) next to the street. Vendor stalls come in two sizes. The ones on the inside of the sidewalks (sections 1 and 4), nearest the stores, are approximately 0.75 × 1 meter. The stalls along the edge of the road average 1.5 × 3 meter. Generally speaking, there is one vendor per stall, but it is not uncommon for one person to run two or more adjacent spaces.

In Chichicastenango, a Guatemalan market town, Hudman (1978) found a distinct spatial pattern of tourism and local products. Simi-

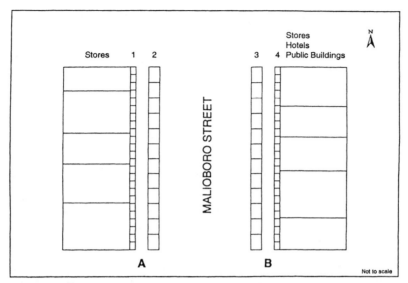

Figure 2. Patterns of Vendor Stalls on Malioboro Street

larly, there was a distinct spatial pattern of key product types along different sections of Malioboro Street in Yogyakarta. The highest concentration of souvenir sellers was located on the west side of the street between the railroad tracks and Pajeksan Street (Figure 3). However, this area was also popular with locals for such things as sunglasses, watches, and leather products. This zone was highly con-

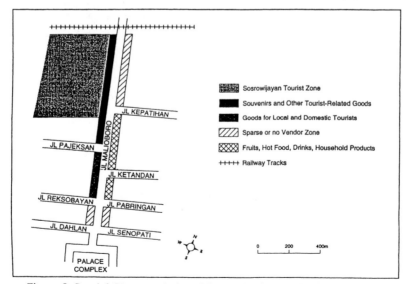

Figure 3. Spatial Characteristics of Street Vendors on Malioboro Street

centrated with tourism-related goods reflecting close proximity to Sosrowijayan, the area of relatively cheap accommodation, restaurants, and other tourist services, just to the west of Malioboro. Clothing, electronics, leather products, jewelry, and snacks dominated the west side between Pajeksan and Reksobayan Streets. This area appeared to be most popular with domestic tourists and local shoppers. Further south, between Reksobayan and A. Dahlan Streets, there were no vendors because of a ban on hawkers in front of government buildings.

The east side of Malioboro Street, between the railroad tracks and Kepatihan Street, had few vendors—only one or two sold cold drinks—because of the ban on hawkers in front of the Garuda Hotel, the Legislative Building, and the new Malioboro Mall, which are all located in that area. Between Kepatihan and Ketandan Streets, household goods, snack foods, and fruits were sold. The area between Ketandan and Pabringan Streets was dominated by hot foods and drinks. The east side was generally less tourism-oriented, even though there are a number of hotels on that side of the street, as well as a McDonalds restaurant and a newly-constructed major shopping mall. There were also few vendors in front of the museum and monument located between Pabringan and Senopati Streets. Of course there were exceptions to these generalizations and, due to a high degree of product overlap among vendors, the spatial divisions are only approximate, based on the dominant product types found in each area.

2. Economic Linkages

Dharoko (1994a) found that local residents are the largest market for Yogyakarta's vendors, followed by domestic tourists, then foreign tourists. Foreign tourists, because of health concerns, purchase goods least often from food vendors, who estimated that only 3% of their customers are foreign tourists. For other types of vendors, foreign tourists comprise approximately a quarter of all customers.

Backward Linkages. In many third-world cities few linkages exist between the formal and informal sectors. Instead, most raw materials and products used in the informal sector are purchased from other small-scale, informal ventures (Aryee 1981; Sethuraman 1981b; Trager 1987). Leather and some cotton fabrics are finished in Yogyakarta by small-scale, informal producers. However, raw materials for the production of souvenirs and household products are often purchased from formal-sector suppliers. For example, dyes and waxes for making batik are usually purchased from local formal-sector suppliers.

Although souvenirs are available which are produced in Bali and even Thailand, the majority of products sold by informal vendors in Yogyakarta are made locally, by one of the city's estimated 13,441 informal, home-based, enterprises (Marsoyo 1992). Wahnschafft (1982) found that home production of souvenirs in Pattaya, Thailand, is one of the most important informal sources of income for many people in squatter settlements. Similarly, in Yogyakarta, the locally-produced merchandise is usually made by craftsmen in various *kampungs* (urban squatter settlements), mostly located very near Malioboro Street. Many vendors prefer these nearby suppliers since their close proximity cuts down on expenditures of time and transport costs.

Masks and leather products are made in Yogyakarta. These are very important home-made products, and the majority of them are sold to tourists on Malioboro Street (Ag 1991). In addition to leather goods, all canvas bags and food products are produced in Yogyakarta. Nearly all the clothes are manufactured locally, with nearby Surakarta as a secondary source. Many of the wood carvings are locally produced, though several vendors sell Balinese painted woodcrafts and some wooden boxes come from nearby Magelang in Central Java Province. Silverworks are almost all made in Kotagede on the southern edge of the city. A favorite with tourists, batik cloth, and *wayang kulit* and *wayang goleg* puppets are from both Yogyakarta and nearby Sentolo. Products which are not produced in Yogyakarta are sunglasses, watches, cigarette lighters, imitation name-brand purses, books, watchbands, calculators, combs, and flashlights. The origin of these products was always given as Jakarta or "foreign country".

As indicated, most of the products are made or assembled locally in small-scale informal ventures. Several interviewees claimed to have a full-time employee, the business owners in these cases tending the stall while their workers produced merchandise in the owner's home. This is believed to be a common pattern. Some vendors produce their own goods at their stalls, which adds to the ambiance for tourists. Many vendors purchase goods from local informal-sector suppliers who buy directly from the producers. Despite the overwhelming proportion of locally-made products, 73% of the vendors surveyed claimed to have a supplier different from the producer. Two types of supplier are common: hired hands, who work specifically for the vendor or supply only them with goods; and suppliers, who purchase large volumes from local artisans and who sell to a number of different vendors.

Forward Linkages. In his study, Aryee (1981) found that there were virtually no product sales to the formal sector by informal ventures. In the context of Yogyakarta, it is difficult to say what percentage of informally-produced goods and services are consumed by the formal sector, but it is likely to be small. Most products sold on Malioboro Street are finished products which are unlikely to constitute the raw materials of other producers and souvenirs leave the local economy with the tourists.

3. Government Involvement

Although informal-sector workers, by definition, operate outside of the governmental system, the latter may be interested in controlling the activities of informal entrepreneurs and, as will be demonstrated, this may blur the distinction between the formal and informal sectors.

Licensing and Legal Status. As mentioned above, Trager (1987) noted the negative attitude taken by many governments towards informal activities. In many parts of the world, informal workers have been forced to move and they have sometimes been viewed as having little role to play in a modernizing economy. In fact, very few tourism plans address the needs of the informal sector or the roles which it might play in development and integrated resorts often attempt to eliminate informal vendors from their premises (Wall 1996).

In Yogyakarta, however, the local government has recently taken a more positive stance towards street vendors. Until the mid-80s, the vendors along Malioboro Street functioned illegally, albeit without a great deal of disturbance from government officials. Today, however, most of the vendors are legally recognized by the local authorities. Of the vendors polled, 90% indicated that they had acquired a vending license. In other parts of Indonesia, municipal governments have issued permits to street vendors for some time and have attempted to relocate them into uncrowded areas of town (IDRC 1975).

Despite their long history in Yogyakarta, only relatively recently have the vendors recognized themselves as a group with common interests. In 1984, the hawkers (in section 2 of Figure 2) formed a cooperative known as *Tri Dharma*. The purposes of this cooperative were to make the vendors legal under the auspices of a formally-recognized organization, as well as to provide a savings and loan service to its members. The cooperative offers members low-interest loans, and pays interest on funds deposited. In 1993 and 1994, the vendors (in sections 3 and 4) joined the *Tri Dharma* organization. In 1993, the smaller vendors (in section 1) formed an association by the name of *Pemalni*. The purpose of this alliance was solely to act as a legal liaison between the sellers and the municipal government and it does not provide the services offered by *Tri Dharma*. Almost all vendors along Malioboro Street, with the exception of food vendors, belong to one of these two organizations. Members must pay obligatory dues of Rp.200 per day. Yogyakarta is not unique in such arrangements for, during the same time period and for the same reasons, similar associations were established in other developing countries (Griffith 1987).

Taxes. As part of the legal status of the vendors, they are required to pay taxes to the municipal taxation office. Taxes are collected by roving collectors three times each day. The *Pemalni* vendors reported different tax amounts ranging between Rp.200–500 per day. One interviewee indicated that variation in taxes is grounded on a vendor's ability to pay, based on products, size of enterprise, and income. The daily tax for *Tri Dharma* vendors ranged from Rp.400 to 600. However, certain irregularities in this system exist. One drink vendor admitted not having a license, nor does he belong to either of the cooperatives. However, if he pays the tax collectors every day, the officials do not bother him. Receipts are given for each payment.

The vendors in Yogyakarta are now legally recognized by the government, and this is facilitated by the fact that they are stationary. In many other developing areas, however, mobile vendors, who are more difficult to control by government, are either not required to be licensed or fail to acquire a license (Wahnschafft 1982).

Involvement in Tourism Planning. Of the vendors surveyed, when asked specifically, only 9% indicated that local people should be consulted in tourism planning and development. Most felt that planning is the sole responsibility of the government, and that the system should inform the people of its decisions once they have been made. This probably reflects the marked heirarchical structure and deference to authority which is a characteristic of Javanese culture (Anderson 1972; Moedjanto 1986). However, when asked if they have ever been involved in tourism planning, 23% answered that they had been. Upon further inquiry, it was revealed that their involvement in local tourism planning merely reflected exhortations by local government officials in recent years to keep the sidewalks clean and uncrowded, not to be too aggressive to tourists, and to maintain a safe environment around their stalls.

Local governments in several developing countries are attempting to educate street hawkers in foreign language acquisition, hygiene, accounting, and marketing (IDRC 1975). This has been viewed as being very important for tourism since many of the vendors are in constant contact with domestic and foreign tourists. In Yogyakarta, the provincial government is about to take steps to educate the vendors in a similar fashion. English courses have been offered to taxi and *becak* (pedicab) drivers, as well as courses on understanding foreign cultures. According to provincial tourism planning officials, the street vendors will soon be offered the same kind of training as long as funds remain available.

CONCLUSION

It has been argued that the informal sector is involved in serving tourists in many developing area destinations but it has received very little scrutiny in the academic literature and is often overlooked in tourism planning exercises. Yet research suggests that the informal sector is a substantial proportion of the tourism economy and, although outside the scope of this paper, it would be of considerable interest to know more about the economic and social importance of vendors and other informal sector workers who interact with tourists.

This paper has examined street vendors in Yogyakarta, a cultural tourism destination in Indonesia, using the constructs of heterogeneity and differentiation, economic linkages, and governmental involvement which have been employed previously in the studies of the informal sector in cities but not, hitherto, considered in the context of tourism. It was found that the street vendors of Yogyakarta, many of whom served predominantly tourists, were a heterogeneous group and exhibited many of the characteristics commonly ascribed to the informal sector: small scale of operation, individual or family ownership and operation, high labor intensity, and reliance on indigenous resources and skills acquired outside the formal sector. However, in contrast to the attributes described in the literature, most worked at their jobs full-time and, in contrast to Bali where many in the informal sector are migrants from Java (Cukier and Wall 1993), few Yogyakarta vendors were outsiders.

With respect to economic linkages, since they sell mainly finished products to tourists, there are few forward economic linkages. However, much of their stock is produced locally, reflecting the strong craft traditions of the city and the surrounding area and, in consequence, much of their money is spent in the local economy. Furthermore, Yogyakarta differs from many other situations with respect to the extent of government involvement with the informal sector. The importance of the vendors on Malioboro Street is officially acknowledged and most Yogyakarta street vendors are legally recognized, licensed, enumerated, taxed and have their own business organizations. Furthermore, the claim that informal-sector activities are easy to enter should be qualified for Yogyakarta, at least in the tourism section of town. The spaces are already crowded and there are now legal and association mechanisms for controlling small-scale entrepreneurs, which must be considered and muddled through in order to be legal on the street. In fact, in these circumstances, as the general employment literature is beginning to indicate, the distinction between the informal and formal sectors is becoming increasingly blurred.

In some areas of the developing world, street vendors, at least stationary ones, do not completely fit the informal-sector stereotype. In the case of Yogyakarta, the vendors exhibit many of the characteristics on which the definition of the informal sector is usually based. Nevertheless, they can at best be considered only semi-informal owing to the considerable official recognition and the regulation of their activities. Governmental involvement in regulating the vendors can be viewed, in part, as a means of controlling the nature of resident–visitor encounters in shopping activities and thus influencing the nature of tourists' experiences.

When it is considered at all, the informal sector is often viewed as a problem by tourism planners. In Bali, in an attempt to prevent vendors from worrying tourists, they have been grouped into "art markets" and prevented by hotel guards from approaching tourists above the break of slope on beaches. In spite of these actions, a recent UNDP planning study suggested that control of itinerant vendors is a priority area for action in the pursuit of quality tourism (Hassall and Associates 1992). While many visitors are undoubtedly frustrated by the persistence of vendors, they also appreciate the opportunity to talk to, bargain with, and buy goods from local people. Furthermore, involvement in the formal sector provides many local residents (who might otherwise be disadvantaged through the development of the industry) with access to the tourism economy.

The informal sector is not a set of aberrant activities which will disappear with modernization: it is a fundamental component of developing economies. It appears that this has been recognized in Yogyakarta and that the activities of informal vendors have been accepted and legitimized as a valued aspect of the guest experience and the tourism economy. This is a lesson which can be learned by

338   STREET VENDORS

other destinations in the interests of providing greater local access to
the economic benefits of tourism and colorful shopping experiences
for visitors. However, organization and regulation of vendors reduces
the degree of informality in host–guest interaction and makes the
distinction between the informal and formal sectors a false dichotomy.
□ □

Acknowledgments—The authors are grateful for partial financial support from the
Environmental Management and Development in Indonesia project, funded by the
Canadian International Development Agency, and the Social Sciences and Humani-
ties Research Council of Canada.

REFERENCES

Ag, L. S.
    1991 Tas Kulit Dan Topeng DIY Sebagai Komoditas Turisme. Kedaulatan Rakyat
        (March 10):3.
Anderson, B. R. O.
    1972 The Idea of Power in Javanese Culture. *In* Culture and Politics in Indonesia,
        C. Holt, ed., pp. 1–70. Ithaca NY: Cornell University Press.
Antara
    1995 Souvenirs. The Jakarta Post (May 22):11.
Aryee, G.
    1981 The Informal Manufacturing Sector in Kumasi. *In* The Urban Informal
        Sector in Developing Countries: Employment, Poverty and Environment, S. V.
        Sethuraman, ed., pp. 90–100. Geneva: International Labor Office.
Bromley, R., and C. Gerry
    1979 Who Are the Casual Poor? *In* Casual Work and Poverty in Third World Cities,
        R. Bromley and C. Gerry, eds., pp. 3–23. Chichester: Wiley.
Cahyono, B. T.
    1991 Malioboro Sebagai Obyek Wisata. Kedaulatan Rakyat (January 17):4–7.
Castells, M., and A. Portes
    1989 World Underneath: The Origins, Dynamics, and Effects of the Informal
        Economy. *In* The Informal Economy: Studies in Advanced and Less Developed
        Countries, A. Portes, M. Castells, and L. A. Benton, eds., pp. 11–37. Baltimore
        MD: Johns Hopkins University Press.
Crick, M.
    1992 Life in the Informal Sector: Street Guides in Kandy, Sri Lanka. *In* Tourism
        and the Less Developed Countries, D. Harrison, ed., pp. 135–147. London:
        Belhaven.
Cukier, J., and G. Wall
    1994 Informal Tourism Employment: Vendors in Bali, Indonesia. Tourism Man-
        agement 15:464–467.
    1995 Tourism Employment in Bali: A Gender Analysis. Tourism Economics 1:389–
        401.
Cukier-Snow, J., and G. Wall
    1993 Tourism Employment: Perspectives from Bali. Tourism Management 14:195–
        201.
Dahles, H.
    1994 Ticket To a Better Life: The Unlicensed Guides of Yogyakarta. *In* Proceedings:
        Expert Meeting on Sustainability in Tourism and Leisure, pp. 69–89. Katholieke
        Universiteit Brabant: Tilburg.
Davies, R.
    1979 Informal Sector or Subordinate Mode of Production? *In* Casual Work and
        Poverty in Third World Cities, R. Bromley and C. Gerry, eds., pp. 87–104.
        Chichester: Wiley.
Davis, D.
    1978 Development and the Tourist Industry in Third World Countries. Society and
        Leisure 1:301–322.

Deparpostel
    1984 Data Statistik Pariwisata DIY. Yogyakarta: Departemen Pariwisata, Pos dan
    Telekomunikasi.
    1992 Yogyakarta: Malioboro. Yogyakarta: Departemen Pariwisata, Pos dan Tele-
    komunikasi.
    1995 Statistik Pariwisata, Pos dan Telekomunikasi, Daerah Istimewa Yogyakarta,
    Tahun 1994. Yogyakarta: Departemen Pariwisata, Pos dan Telekomunikasi.
Dharoko, A.
    1994a Karakteristik Perdagangan Kakilima Tugu—Kraton Yogyakarta. Yogyak-
    arta: The Gadjah Mada University, Department of Architecture.
    1994b Studi Karakteristik dan Pola Kerja Pedagang Kakilima Di Kawasan
    Malioboro Yogyakarta. Manusia dan Lingkungan 2:50–63.
Dinas Pariwisata
    1988 Rencana Induk Pengembangan Pariwisata, Daerah Istimewa Yogyakarta,
    Buku I. Yogyakarta: Pusat Penelitian Perencanaan Pembangunan Nasional,
    Universitas Gadjah Mada, Dinas Pariwisata.
    1994 Statistik Pariwisata, Daerah Istimewa Yogyakarta, Tahun 1993. Yogyakarta.
Farver, J. A. M.
    1984 Tourism and Employment in the Gambia. Annals of Tourism Research
    11:249–265.
Geertz, C.
    1963 Peddlers and Princes: Social Development and Economic Change in Two
    Indonesian Towns. Chicago IL: University of Chicago Press.
Gerry, C., and C. Birkbeck
    1981 The Petty Commodity Producer in Third World Cities: Petit-bourgeois or
    "Disguised" Proletarian. *In* The Petite Bourgeoisie: Comparative Studies of the
    Uneasy Stratum, F. Bechhoffer and B. Elliot, eds., pp. 121–154. New York: St.
    Martin's Press.
Griffith, H. D.
    1987 Beach Operations: Their Contributions to Tourism in Barbados. Caribbean
    Finance and Management 3:55–65.
Harris, J. E., and J. G. Nelson
    1993 Monitoring Tourism from a Whole Economy Perspective: A Case from Indone-
    sia. *In* Tourism and Sustainable Development: Monitoring, Planning, Managing,
    J. G. Nelson, R. W. Butler, and G. Wall, eds., pp. 179–200. Waterloo: University
    of Waterloo, Department of Geography.
Hart, K.
    1973 Informal Income Opportunities and Urban Employment in Ghana. Journal
    of Modern African Studies 11:61–89.
Hassall and Associates
    1992 Comprehensive Development Plan for Bali. Denpasar: UNDP and Govern-
    ment of Indonesia.
Henry, S.
    1982 The Working Unemployed: Perspectives on the Informal Economy and Unem-
    ployment. Sociological Review 30:460–477.
Hill, H., and Mubyarto
    1978 Economic Change in Yogyakarta 1970–76. Bulletin of Indonesian Economic
    Studies 14:29–44.
Hudman, L. E.
    1978 Tourist Impacts: The Need for Regional Planning. Annals of Tourism
    Research 5:112–125.
IDRC
    1975 Hawkers and Vendors in Asian Cities. Ottawa: International Development
    Research Center.
ILO
    1972 Employment, Incomes and Equality: A Strategy for Increasing Productive
    Employment in Kenya. Geneva: International Labor Office.
    1985 Informal Sector in Africa. Addis Ababa: Jobs and Skill Programme for Africa.
    Geneva: International Labor Office.
Kermath, B., and R. Thomas
    1992 Spatial Dynamics of Resorts: Sosua, Dominican Republic. Annals of Tourism
    Research 19:173–190.

340   STREET VENDORS

Long, V., and G. Wall
    1995 Small-Scale Tourism Development in Bali. *In* Island Tourism: Management Principles and Practice, M. V. Conlin and T. Baum, eds., pp. 237–257. Chichester: Wiley.
Marsoyo, A.
    1992 Place, Space and Socio-Economic Analysis of Home-Based Enterprises in Yogyakarta, Indonesia. Unpublished Master's Thesis, Asian Institute of Technology, Bangkok.
McGee, T. G.
    1979 The Poverty Syndrome: Making Out in the Southeast Asian City. *In* Casual Work and Poverty in Third World Cities, R. Bromley and C. Gerry, eds., pp. 45–68. Chichester: Wiley.
McGee, T. G., and Y. M. Yeung
    1977 Hawkers in Southeast Asian Cities: Planning for the Bazaar Economy. Ottawa: International Development Research Center.
Michaud, J.
    1991 A Social Anthropology of Tourism in Ladakh, India. Annals of Tourism Research 18:605–621.
Moedjanto, G.
    1986 The Concept of Power in Javanese Culture. Yogyakarta: Gadjah Mada University Press.
Sethuraman, S. V., ed.
    1981a The Informal Sector and the Urban Environment. *In* The Urban Informal Sector in Developing Countries: Employment, Poverty and Environment, S. V. Sethuraman, ed., pp. 171–187. Geneva: International Labor Office.
    1981b The Urban Informal Sector in Developing Countries: Employment, Poverty and Environment. Geneva: International Labor Office.
Thomas, J. J.
    1992 Informal Economic Activity. Ann Arbor MI: University of Michigan Press.
Timothy, D. J., and G. Wall
    1995 Tourist Accommodation in an Asian Historic City. Journal of Tourism Studies 6(2):123–137.
Tokman, V.
    1978 An Exploration into the Nature of Informal–Formal Sector Relations. World Development 6:1065–1075.
Trager, L.
    1987 A Re-examination of the Urban Informal Sector in West Africa. Canadian Journal of African Studies 21:238–255.
Wahnschafft, R.
    1982 Formal and Informal Tourism Sectors: A Case of Pattaya, Thailand. Annals of Tourism Research 9:429–451.
Wall, G.
    1993 Cultural Tourism: How Do We Market It? *In* Universal Tourism Enriching or Degrading Culture, W. Nuryanti, ed., pp. 183–194. Yogyakarta: Gadjah Mada University Press.
    1996 People Outside the Plans. Proceedings: Indonesia–Swiss Forum on Culture and International Tourism. Yogyakarta: Gadjah Mada University.
Yogya Post
    1991 Malioboro, Jalan Yang Tak Pernah Tidur. Yogya Post (November 19):2.

Submitted 5 December 1995
Resubmitted 15 March 1996
Accepted 16 April 1996
Refereed anonymously
Coordinating Editor: Brian Archer

C
International Issues

[18]

 Pergamon

Annals of Tourism Research, Vol. 24, No. 4, pp. 777–795, 1997
© 1997 Elsevier Science Ltd
All rights reserved. Printed in Great Britain
0160-7383/97 $17.00+0.00

PII: S0160-7383(97)00030-3

SUN, SAND, AND HARD CURRENCY
Tourism in Cuba

Pablo Martin de Holan
Nelson Phillips
McGill University, Canada

Abstract: Cuba's decision to focus on tourism as a source of hard currency and economic development makes international competitiveness a critical issue. But what is the basis of international competitiveness in tourism and how can Cuba best develop its tourism industry to meet the twin goals of generating hard currency and economic development? A framework for approaching these questions in the context of underdevelopment and socialist economic planning is presented here. It is argued that the Cuban government's current strategy of expansion and low price, combined with monopoly industry organization, presents high risks for declining returns. **Keywords:** Cuba, strategy, competitiveness, economic development. © 1997 Elsevier Science Ltd

Résumé: Soleil, sable et devises fortes: le tourisme à Cuba. La décision du gouvernement cubain de concentrer ses énergies dans le tourisme comme source de devises et de développement économique fait de la concurrence internationale une question critique. Mais quelles sont les bases de la concurrence internationale dans le tourisme, et comment peut Cuba mieux développer son industrie touristique pour réussir son double objectif de produire des devises et de développer son économie? On présente un cadre théorique pour aborder ces questions dans un contexte de planification économique socialiste dans un pays en voie de développement. On soutient que la stratégie actuelle d'expansion et de bas prix, dans un contexte de monopole, présente un haut niveau de risque pour des rentrées nettes de moins en moins élevées. **Mots-clés:** Cuba, stratégie, compétitivité, développement économique © 1997 Elsevier Science Ltd

> [W]ith her terrible practical sense she could not understand the Colonel's business as he exchanged little fishes for gold coins and then converted the gold coins into little fishes, and so on, with the result that he had to satisfy an exasperating vicious circle (Garcia Marquez 1971:190).

INTRODUCTION

Cuba's experience with tourism has much in common with Colonel Buendia's obsession with little golden fishes: more tourists come to Cuba every year; more hard currency is spent in the country by tourists every year; and, every year, more hard currency must be spent by the Cuban government on infrastructure development and foreign-produced goods and services to accommodate the ever-increasing

Pablo Martin de Holan and **Nelson Phillips** are both in the Faculty of Management at McGill University (Montreal, Quebec, Canada H3A 1G5. Email martin@management. mcgill.ca). A doctoral candidate, the first author's research interests include organizational effectiveness, competitive advantage, and strategic management. The second author has published articles in the *Academy of Management Journal, Organization Science,* and *Organization Studies.* His research interests include organizational collaboration and management in transitional economies.

numbers of tourists. But while the Colonel's golden fishes had the advantage of restoring the peace of spirit that many years of war had taken away, it is unclear whether Cuba's approach to tourism is producing significant returns to Cuba and its people.

In this paper, ideas from strategic management are used to analyze the competitiveness of the rapidly growing Cuban tourism sector and to evaluate the strategy adopted by the Cuban government. This analysis makes a three-fold contribution to the ongoing discussion of economic development in Cuba (*Columbia Journal of World Business* 1995; Suchilicki and Jorge 1995), and, more specifically, of economic development through tourism. First, an analysis of the competitive advantage of the Cuban tourism sector provides a useful framework for understanding the options and possibilities available to the Cuban government in its efforts to maximize hard currency income from tourism. The government has very little hard currency, and even less experience and managerial competence, to invest in developing an internationally competitive tourism sector. This kind of analysis highlights the most important barriers to successful industry development and provides a basis for estimating the probability of success of the various strategies available to the Cuban government in its effort to compete in international markets.

Second, at a more general level, the question of the potential contribution of any country's tourism sector can be answered satisfactorily only if one has a well-developed understanding of the international competitiveness of the industry. Tourism is a highly competitive business where switching costs are relatively low for tour operators and practically nonexistent for the tourists themselves. Therefore, the creation of a sustainable competitive advantage is an essential aspect of the success and profitability of the industry in any country. The approach outlined in this article contributes to the development of a general framework for the analysis of the competitiveness of tourism and for considering the kinds of strategies that may prove effective in different situations.

Third, the general approach developed in this paper provides an example of the usefulness of industry-level analyses of competitiveness in discussions of development options. It is clear from work in this area that countries cannot be good at everything, but rather must develop clusters of industries that are internationally competitive (Porter 1990). Since developing countries have very limited resources, they should choose potentially competitive industries—not single companies or projects scattered throughout their economies—in which to invest their limited time and money. Industry-level analysis is very useful in comparing the relative competitiveness of national industries and in predicting the probability of each succeeding in international markets.

The paper begins with a discussion of the analysis of national competitiveness and national strategies based largely on two important theoretical streams in the field of strategic management: industry dynamics (Porter 1980, 1985) and competitive strategies inferred from the behavior of the social actor (Hafsi and Martin de Holan 1997; Mintzberg 1978; Mintzberg and Waters 1985). This is followed with an outline of the history and current position of the Cuban tourism industry, focusing on its rapid growth in Cuba and on the strategy adopted by the government, then with an analysis of the competitive position of Cuba's tourism, drawing on ideas of competitive advantage and strategic positioning. This leads to a discussion of alternative options available to Cuban government and some of the advantages and disadvantages of these alternatives.

Competitive industries are the foundation of a country's prosperity. Rich countries are rich because they have, over the years, developed industries that are competitive on a global basis and their continuing success ensures the ongoing economic health of the country. No country can be good at everything, and specialization in certain activities that build on key competencies is a hallmark of international competitiveness. Therefore, countries are competitive—and prosperous— insofar as they have successfully specialized in industries that can compete on an ongoing basis in a globalized economy (Porter 1990).

While this view seems intuitively correct at a general level, it does little to explain what determines competitiveness or how countries that do not have competitive industries can develop them. These, however, are two of the most pressing questions for developing nations. In one of the most comprehensive studies of national competitiveness, Porter (1990) argued that three distinct and embedded levels of analysis must be used when considering national competitiveness (Table 1): the firm, the industry, and the nation. Firms are the actors that compete in global markets. Historical studies on why and how firms appear highlight the role of entrepreneurship on the emergence of prosperous and vigorous firms. Public policies that encourage risk taking by entrepreneurs facilitate a process through which opportunities provided by technical know-how and country factor conditions are developed and exploited, creating in the process new opportunities for other entrepreneurs (Brenner 1994).

For their part, firms prosper when they have a competitive advantage over rival firms (i.e., when customers prefer their products to the alternatives). The foundation of any firm's competitive advantage is its strategy, the pattern in a stream of decisions made and actions taken by the firm and its managers (Mintzberg 1978; Mintzberg and

Table 1. Determinants of Competitiveness

Level of Analysis→	Firm	Industry	National Competitiveness
↓	Strategies of Companies Processes Developed by the Firm	Rivalry Substitutes	Factor Conditions Demand Conditions
	Skills Developed by the Firm	Power of Suppliers	Related and Supporting Industries in the Country
		Power of Buyers	
Leads to	Competitive Firms	Dynamic Industries	Prosperity (if many industries)

Waters 1985). The notion of strategy highlights the idea of the *creation* of competitive advantages rather than the passive exploitation of *comparative advantages* that a firm may possess. It is generally believed that competitive advantages based on knowledge (as opposed to, for example, tangible resources) are the most difficult to create and imitate, thus the most likely to generate long-term above average profits for the firm (Nelson and Winter 1982; Peteraf 1993; Prahalad and Hamel 1990). That accumulated knowledge, especially when it has practical applications that can be translated into better product or services or lower costs of operation (Barney 1996:146), can be considered a resource of the firm (Wernerfelt 1984:172). Since resources in a given industry are inelastic and heterogeneously distributed among competing organizations (Barney 1991; Peteraf 1993), organizations that take advantage of the resources they have or build new ones are more likely to enjoy a sustained competitive advantage. This happens when these resources are valuable, rare and difficult to imitate (Barney 1991, 1996:145–163). For example, a hotel or resort in a Caribbean nation may market the beauty of its physical location to attract tourists, a comparative advantage if the location is really the most beautiful, but a hotel or resort with outstanding customer service or exceptionally skilled personnel will be more likely to attract and retain customers. In the latter case, the competitive advantage is the result of a series of organizational processes over which firms, managers, and employees have control. In the former, the competitive advantage, if any, is simply the result of country factor endowments, which are the most difficult to differentiate and to sustain.

But firms are not independent actors. They evolve in industries whose structure limits and constrains the number of opportunities available. Firms, based on their idiosyncratic combination of skills, resources, and competencies, make choices and adopt competitive positions (Porter 1980, 1985:11–26, 1990). Competitive advantage at the firm level is created when the firm's strategy fits with industry-level factors and when this strategy is combined with the implementation of internal processes that enhance the linkages between and among different elements of the firm's value chain (Porter 1985, 1990). At the industry level, five forces shape the ability of firms to achieve extraordinary returns: the power of suppliers, the power of buyers, the threat of new entrants, the availability of substitute products, and the degree of rivalry among existing firms (Porter 1980, 1985:4–10). Of these, rivalry is perhaps the most potent factor in explaining industry-level success: vigorous domestic rivalry sustains a strong and dynamic industry, and pushes firms to innovate and upgrade their competitive advantages. When individual firms enhance their skills and capabilities, they create a powerful incentive for the industry as a whole to do the same or lose out in the race for competitive advantage.

Countries, however, need more than just a handful of separate, competitive firms to prosper. In fact, it is unlikely that single, internationally competitive firms will emerge within a national economy (Porter 1990). Instead, if certain conditions are met, clusters of successful companies in the same industry will emerge, and a strong and dynamic industry will appear in the host country. Four national characteristics appear to support the development of an internationally competitive industry (Porter 1990): the availability of high quality "factors" such as human resources, physical resources, knowledge resources, capital resources, and infrastructure; the existence of a demanding national market; highly developed and competitive related and supporting industries in the home country; and appropriate firm strategy, structure, and rivalry. These four determinants are interrelated in a "diamond" which is influenced by two other variables: chance and government. These two variables can either contribute or hinder the development of competitive advantage and are usually beyond the control of single firms or even entire industries.

These four determinants and two variables work as a system. Sustainable competitive advantage is only created when the four determinants act together. However, having an advantage in all four determinants is not strictly necessary. Nations achieve and maintain success in international competition when they possess advantages in the diamond, creating a unique system that provides overall competitive advantage. But, because different industries require different national characteristics, no single nation can succeed in every industry. However, the diamond may be similar for several industries and a nation can be successful in a cluster of industries, usually linked through vertical or horizontal relationships. In this way, a successful industry helps to create another in a mutually reinforcing process. The industries are usually linked by economic relations (buyer/seller), and they share information, knowledge, and people through informal mechanisms (family ties, ownership, personal relationships, geographic proximity, etc.)

But how are systems—these diamonds—created? Initially, there is often an advantage in only one dimension; that advantage provides impetus for firm and industry development. Once the process is set in motion, competitors come into action, rivalry is created, and advantages in other corners of the diamond appear.

> The ability of an initial seed from whatever source to grow into a competitive industry in the nation will be a function of whether advantages in other determinants are already present or can be created (Porter 1990:160).

In other words, having an advantage in one of the dimensions *can* lead to a competitive industry provided that no significant barriers exist in other dimensions. For Caribbean countries like Cuba, the existence of world-class "sun and sand" provides a basis for competitiveness in tourism, but does not guarantee development or success in the tourism industry. Other factor conditions such as human resources, infrastructure and capital, and the other three determinants that make up the diamond stand as potential barriers to development.

But even countries that have successfully developed competitive industries based on unique configurations of the diamond are at risk over time. As competitive advantages evolve in a global market, national advantage can be lost. When conditions in the national diamond no longer support innovation and change, other competitors gain competitive advantage, displacing the leaders. The most important causes for eroding advantage are the deterioration of factor conditions, local needs falling out of sync with global demand, home buyers losing sophistication, technological change leading to compelling specialized factor disadvantages, the need for new and missing supporting industries, firms losing the flexibility to adjust, and domestic rivalry ebbing. Porter (1990) considers the last to be the most common cause of lost national advantage.

This framework provides a useful approach to the analysis of the current and potential competitiveness of national industries, and thus can be used to evaluate the Cuban tourism industry. In applying the framework, some simplification is possible given the centrally-planned structure of its tourism sector. Most importantly, in evaluating Cuban tourism, the firm and industry levels can be combined, given the monopolistic nature of the Cuban economy. This will become clear during the analysis, but it is important to keep in mind that the application of this framework in other contexts would require more analysis at the firm level.

TOURISM IN CUBA

The Caribbean tourism industry has generated mixed emotions—perhaps most notably a form of resigned ambivalence—among development experts and among the Caribbean countries themselves (de Kadt 1979). While many argue for its potential in developing the economies of poorer countries (Momsen 1985; World Bank 1975), others point to the social, ecological, and cultural problems that tourism can create or exacerbate. Those arguing the positive side point to the increased trade and access to hard currency that tourism brings (Momsen 1985:35). Those arguing the negative side point out that tourism in developing countries, when not carefully controlled, tends to have serious social consequences. It can lead people to work under exploitative conditions, and it creates a situation where residents are tempted to engage in illegal activities including black market trading and prostitution (Hellbom 1977, 1985:61).

In Cuba, in spite of the potential problems, the tourism industry has been identified as one of the few viable alternatives to rescue an economy in the wake of near paralysis (Fitzgerald 1994; Martin de Holan and Phillips 1995a, 1995b; Perez-Lopez 1994; Simon 1995). Recently, its tourism industry has been presented as the most dynamic and successful sector of the economy and has been depicted, both internally and externally, as a model industry in its ability to attract foreign investment and to produce hard currency earnings (CubaHoy 1995b). According to the indicators used by the Cuban government to measure its success (number of tourists, number and volume of foreign investment, and gross revenue generated), its tourism industry has expanded rapidly over the past few years.

This recent focus on tourism is in stark contrast to the previous 30 years of government policy. Tourism, traditionally an important sector of the Cuban economy, suffered a steep intentional decline after the revolution in 1959 with the number of visitors dropping from 350,000 in 1958 to virtually none by 1962, shortly after the American embargo that prevented most US travelers from legally visiting Cuba. Qualitatively, a large number of American tourists were replaced by a small number of more frugal and less demanding visitors from the former Eastern block. The quality of food and accommodation services dropped significantly, with many of the attractions the island had to offer— such as restaurants, casinos, luxury resorts, marinas, and a range of (sometimes illegal) entertainment facilities—dismantled in favor of activities more compatible with the ideology of the new regime. From a strategic management perspective, the core capabilities of the tourism industry were rapidly dissolved.

But this movement away from tourism ended with the fall of the Soviet Union and the resulting collapse of the Cuban economy (Martin de Holan and Phillips 1995a). In a dramatic reversal of its previous policy, the Cuban government identified tourism as a strategic sector of the economy shortly after 1989. Since then, the government has developed two explicit tourism objectives: to systematically increase the revenue generated by the industry and its overall profitability, and to increase the number of tourist arrivals from year to year, reaching 2.5 million visitors by the year 2000, up from 750,000 in 1995 (Martinez Garcia 1994). By late 1995, the government had introduced three measures towards these objectives (Kaplowitz 1995; Suchilicki and Jorge 1975).

First, the Cuban government has developed a number of relationships with international companies to build and manage hotels and other facilities. The need for hard currency investment is part of the reason for this interest in joint ventures, but the government also realizes that the industry lacks the skills required to compete for international tourists. The lack of managerial capabilities needed to successfully deal with tourists has been diagnosed by many observers, including President Fidel Castro himself who declared in a speech to the National Assembly that there was a "lack of competencies in the marketing of tourism", and "we [Cuba] have been terrible in marketing tourism" (*CubaNews* 1995:3). Recognizing the need for managerial skills that are simply not available has led the country to rely heavily on foreign firms. This strategy has proven successful in terms of attracting increasing numbers of tourists, but it remains to be seen if the expected transfer of knowledge and skills occurs in the current Cuban environment.

Second, Cuba is now actively courting foreign investment in all sectors of its economy and has passed a new investment law that is much more liberal than previous arrangements. This change has been driven primarily by practicality. Until recently, foreign investment was regulated by Decree 50, enacted on February 15, 1982, whose purpose was to obtain foreign cooperation in the development of a very limited number of industries in which neither the Cubans nor their socialist partners had expertise. After the fall of the Soviet Union, it quickly became a way to inject large amounts of foreign investment and expertise in an attempt to restart the economy. In addition, a number of other measures were taken to increase foreign activity in Cuba. In 1992, for example, Article 23 of the Constitution

784   TOURISM IN CUBA

was modified to explicitly recognize ownership of joint ventures with foreign partners.

The current framework for foreign investment in Cuba is defined by Law 77, which replaced and expanded Decree 50 on September 5, 1995. According to Article 1.1, the basic purpose of Law 77 (1995) is to encourage foreign investment in all sectors of the economy except health and education:

> [T]his Act has the purpose of promoting and encouraging foreign invest-
> ment in the territory of the Republic of Cuba, in order to carry out profitable
> activities which contribute to the country's economic capacity and sus-
> tainable development, ... and of establishing, for that purpose, the basic
> legal regulations under which this can be realized.

However, the effect of these new "investor friendly" laws has been tempered by the continuing embargo first declared by the US in 1961, and then reinforced by the Toriccelli Law in 1992 and the more recent Helms–Burton law of March 1996, which severely penalizes investors who "traffick" with expropriated property that was once owned by either American companies or American citizens.

Third, a restructuring of the bureaucracy responsible for tourism took place in 1994. The government dismantled INTUR, the mono-lithic institution in charge of all international tourists, creating several holding companies that manage well-defined sectors of activity. The hotel industry, for example, has been divided into market segments, each of which is to be served by one "chain" that controls and manages a variety of hotels, restaurants, and discotheques grouped according to their perceived quality and prestige of the product delivered. Cur-rently, the Gran Caribe hotel chain administers four and five star hotels, prestigious restaurants, and other luxury spots; Horizontes Hotels manages 3- and 2-star hotels; and Islazul takes care of unclassi-fied hotels, usually so below international standards that are reserved to local tourists and extremely frugal international visitors.

This structural arrangement is intended to help the tourism enter-prises gain economies of scale, accelerate learning, and reduce waste-ful competition. Since each one of the chains has a well-defined product–market segment, its managers need not worry about other segments or even other markets. As a result, there is little rivalry among enterprises. Perhaps the most significant ramification of this arrangement is that facilities are assigned to "quality" rating and enterprises gain no advantage from exceeding their "quality" rating. The number of stars associated with a hotel is a goal, not a measure of the actual quality, and is often evaluated taking into account exclus-ively the physical plant of the hotel (e.g., swimming pool, color TV, and air conditioning) rather than the quality of the serviced delivered at the location. Therefore, ratings are a measure of the best case, not necessarily their current level of performance.

The result of the steps taken by the government are not insig-nificant. Despite decades of neglect, tourism is expected to become Cuba's most important source of hard currency in 1995 (Martinez Garcia 1994:6). Since the fall of the Soviet Union, the industry has developed at a rapid pace in terms of the number of visitors, the revenue generated, and the number of joint ventures created. A massive investment plan has been implemented bringing a number of new and refurbished hotels and tourism facilities into operation, and increasing the number of rooms available to foreigners from 5,000 in 1991 to almost 25,000 in 1995 (Simon 1995:29). The revenue generated by the industry has approached $1 billion in 1995, up from $850 million in 1994.

Given the socialist framework of the Cuban economy (that all firms are either wholly-owned by the government or are majority-owned joint ventures with international companies) the firm and industry levels of analysis can be combined in order to examine the international competitiveness of its tourism industry. As already noted, the level of rivalry is very low and much of the rivalry that does occur is politically mediated. This simplifies the analysis greatly by replacing considerations of firm-level strategies with industry-level strategies. The threat of new entrants at an industry level disappears, while the power of suppliers and buyers becomes great, as there is generally only a single source of supply for each good or service.

Firm-/Industry-Level Analysis

The first step in the analysis must be to determine the strategy of the Cuban government. One of the most influential definitions of strategy has been given by Chandler: "[s]trategy is the determination of the basic long term goals and objectives of an enterprise, and the adoption of courses of action and the allocation of resources necessary for carrying out these goals" (1962:13). This definition has been expanded by Andrews (1971:13) and Mintzberg (1978:936). Strategy is the pattern in a stream of decisions and actions in an organization that: (1) determines, shapes and reveals its objectives, purposes, or goals; (2) produces the principal policies and plans for achieving these goals; and (3) defines the activities the organization intends to be in, the kind of economic and noneconomic contribution it intends to make to its shareholders, employees, customers and communities (Andrews 1971:13).

The steps taken by the Cuban government to develop its tourism industry appear to fulfill the definition of strategy for business firms: they involve well-articulated objectives and the plans to achieve them; they involve the allocation of limited and valuable resources; and they can be integrated into a coherent patterns. As such, Cuba's dynamism in the tourism sector can be seen as an explicit, "intended" strategy (Mintzberg and Waters 1985) of the government to create an internationally competitive industry. All the transformations observed in the past five years indicate that the Cuban government is implementing a *price leadership strategy* based on a combination of low price, low cost, and high volume. Even though government officials and, for example, Canadian tour operators euphemistically highlight the "excellent bang for the buck" of Cuba for foreign tourists (Bulletin Voyages 1996), business observers focus on the unidimensionality of the strategy, emphasizing that "Cuba's one competitive advantage over any other island destination in the Caribbean is that Cuba is cheap, cheap, cheap... Cuba costs less than other Caribbean destinations" (Berman 1994:12; Phillips and Martin de Holan 1995; Simon 1995:31). Moreover, comparisons between hotels owned or operated by the same chain show that, all other things being similar, prices are lower for packages to Cuba than competitive Caribbean locations (Berman 1994:13).

But for a low price strategy to be effective (i.e., profitable) cost must be low as well, lower than the price in any case. This acts as a constraint on the industry and limits the *marge de manoeuvre* of the government. As such, the authorities have emphasized cost containment measures based on economies of scale stemming from a large and increasing number of tourists visiting Cuba. The three working assumptions of the Cuban strategy are: it is possible to attract a growing number of tourists every year; costs per visitor will decline (or, at least, remain stable) with increasing numbers of tourists; and the increasing revenue will generate more profits for the Cuban economy. But these assumptions and the long term effectiveness of the Cuban government's tourism strategy can be questioned. First, the assumption that the number of visitors can be more than tripled in the next 5 years is far from assured for two reasons: the current infrastructure (i.e., hotels, roads, and airports) is severely limited in capacity and the total number of tourists traveling to the Caribbean is growing at a much slower rate than the number of visitors to Cuba.

Its general infrastructure is dilapidated after years of little or no maintenance and is likely to stay that way in the foreseeable future due to a combination of severe resource shortages and the advanced state of infrastructure disrepair. In a recent session of the parliament, the Cuban Minister of Finance revealed serious delays in the expansion of the general and tourism infrastructure and acknowledged that in 1995 Cuba only built 40% of the new rooms and hotels it had planned (CubaHoy 1995a). Tripling the number of visitors will require a parallel improvement in general infrastructure development— roads, airports, sidewalks, public transportation, etc.—that is, in practice, off-limits to foreigner investors and that the public sector in Cuba cannot afford to carry out on their own.

Moreover, the number of tourists visiting the region is relatively inelastic. The American embargo prevents Cuba from competing for two lucrative Caribbean markets: cruise ships that could potentially stop over in Havana or Santiago de Cuba and American citizens who made up the bulk of the Cuban tourism industry before the revolution and are today a very significant part of the Caribbean market. The alternative destinations, moreover, have developed distinct reputations and standards of quality that Cuba currently cannot match (Berman 1994). In addition, tourism distribution channels, and especially the ones targeting the low end visitors are controlled by independent companies and wholesalers who select destinations and propose packages according to their own interests and not Cuba's. Here it is worth noting that the growth forecast by the Cuban government can only come at the expense of Cuba's Caribbean neighbors who will, undoubtedly, respond. For example, while the number of visitors to the Caribbean has increased by 19% from 1989 to 1993, similar indicators for Cuba yield 67% for that period. Since the starting point for Cuba was relatively low in absolute and relative numbers (about 326,000 visitors for a market share of <3%), it seems unreasonable to extrapolate that trend. Such an increase will come, at least partially, from other Caribbean countries, which will undoubtedly try to keep their market share. Caribbean destinations have been found to have a high substitution elasticity (Rosenweig 1988). In that vein, aggressive marketing or other economic measures such as the adoption of preferential tourism rates could degenerate into fierce competition for tourists. A price war in the Caribbean will only exacerbate profitability problems, as Cuba strives to compete based on price, while it is unclear they are the true low-cost producer.

By forcefully entering the tourism industry, Cuba has entered a highly competitive industry with powerful buyers, low brand loyalty, low switching costs, and strict international quality standards. The international nature of the industry creates strong competitive pressures at the firm level, whether or not the firm actually competes with other firms in the domestic markets. In other terms, a 3-star hotel in Varadero is implicitly competing with 3-star hotels in other Caribbean countries, even if the government decides not to foster competition among 3-star hotels within Cuba. Moreover, an analysis of the flows of visitors shows that Cuba as a destination is keenly competing against the Dominican Republic for Canadians, Spaniards, and Germans, and against Jamaica for Canadians, Germans, and Italians, nationalities that make the bulk of visitors to Cuba (Simon 1995:32). But while these other destinations have the option of targeting the US market, the embargo prevents Cuba from doing so. Other policy options—such as competitive devaluations—seem more feasible in the Dominican Republic and Jamaica than in Cuba. Of course, the alternative of interregional cooperation or even collusion is a possibility, but in the absence of enforcing mechanisms, countries are vulnerable to unilateral policy changes that could maximize visitors at one location at the expense of the others (Rosenweig 1988). The marginal cost of adding an extra 100,000 tourists is certainly higher for Cuba than it is for its Caribbean neighbors, which have, in addition, more experience in the marketing of tourism. All this challenges the Cuban government's second and third working assumptions: marginal costs may increase not decrease with volume, and increasing revenue may increase leakage.

While Cuba's strategy has been relatively successful to date, it seems likely that it will encounter serious problems in terms of capacity and management skills in the near future. The cost leadership strategy that has been chosen seems to lack the necessary fit between the industry and the skills available in Cuba. Although the tactic of massive joint venture activity has worked well to solve this skill shortage, it creates further problems. If the Cuban tourism sector is examined as an industry, it has one extremely important weakness: it lacks any significant rivalry. The Cuban government has structured the various hotels and other facilities precisely to avoid duplication and competition, which reduces innovation and improvement. The industry does face significant competition from outside, but this is too remote to have a significant impact at the level where improvement is most necessary and the result is a decided lack of dynamism, particularly among wholly-Cuban-owned hotels. Furthermore, this problem is repeated across the Cuban economy. The lack of competition among Cuban-owned monopoly suppliers in the local market gives them far too much power over the tourism sector to provide the necessary innovation and responsiveness that internationally competitive facilities require. The quality of goods and services provided by the Cuban government remains very low and affects the quality of the final tourism product provided by its tourism sector.

National-Level Analysis

At a national level, the first important dimension of competitiveness involves factor conditions. While the Cuban "sun and sand" is clearly of world-class quality, perhaps the most important limitation faced by its tourism industry is the lack of amenities such as restaurants, shopping, and entertainment. Tourists often complain that there is little to do beyond the beach in the two major tourism centers in Havana and Varadero, and that the hotels rarely meet international standards. Perhaps this limitation provides a partial explanation for the low return rate of visitors to Cuba, <10% vs. >40% in Barbados. Moreover, as already noted, human factors are in equally short supply. The ability of Cubans to manage and market a world-class vacation package is severely limited by years of Communist production and, therefore, management and marketing must be purchased internationally. While there are several MBA-type programs being offered to Cuban managers, the need for education and hands-on experience is great. Cuban managers will learn these skills over time, but this process will certainly take many years and the expense in the meantime is considerable.

These infrastructure problems relate to another of the assumptions that underlie the Cuban strategy: the assumption of declining costs. As mentioned before, the success of a low-price/high-volume strategy depends on the ability to become the true *low-cost* producer. Given the nature of the Cuban economic system, the true cost of producing a tourism package is currently impossible to calculate as many inputs are supplied to the tourism industry at world prices despite their production in centrally-planned, and hence uncosted, facilities. In other words, the Cuban produced goods and services supplied to the tourism sector have no determinable hard currency cost, as all the inputs to their production were provided within a centrally-planned system in which values are assigned. The actual cost structure for many goods supplied to the tourism industry by related industries is unknown. But simply based on the very large number of workers involved in the inefficient Cuban production systems, it seems unlikely that they are low cost. The problems of responding to ever greater demands exacerbate this problem, leading one to believe that they actually suffer from negative economies of scale: increasing cost of production as volume increases.

Furthermore, the assumption that the Cuban government's share of hard currency tourism profits will remain constant is also questionable. All tourism activity, especially in developing countries, suffers from some degree of "leakage" where the process of production consumes inputs purchased outside the country in hard currency. Tourism revenue can be assimilated to an export; its contribution to the economy—its multiplier effect—depends on the amount of leakage in the form of savings, imports, and non-respent taxes (Lundberg, Stavenga and Krishnamoorthy 1995:135). Of these, the most important element in the Cuban case, and the one over which the government has the least control, is imports. Large and well-developed tourism destinations have the lowest leakage rates, since they have developed supporting industries which can effectively compete with foreign imports in order to "retain" more hard currency (Bull 1991:48; Simon 1995:29). Conversely, "In a subsistence economy, such as one found on a less-developed island, the new dollar has a negligible multiplier effect. The economy has a high 'import propensity'—most of the money leaves before much of a multiplier develops" (Lundberg, Stavenga and Krishnamoorthy 1995:136). While Cuba is not a "less-developed island", its leakage factor is substantially higher than the Caribbean average of 50% (Simon 1995), perhaps as high as 75%. This is the case for four main reasons: lack of supporting industries capable of producing infrastructure, products, and services needed to care for international tourists; deficient distribution systems; vast inefficiencies of most Cuban firms; and the foreign nature of most international hotels.

Cuba's lack of supporting industries grows out of the COMECON doctrine that whatever a country could not produce could be imported from "sister" nations at preferential rates. Some of what international tourists consider to be the most basic items are not produced in Cuba and have to be imported to insure that the customer is satisfied. The alternative that the Cuban government faces is either to let international hotels import these products and increase the leakage or decide not to import them and face demanding customers who find the whole thing unacceptable. For example, Cuban hotels with large international clientele are under significant pressure to import diet beverages, low-calorie sweeteners and "healthy", low-fat products. The government is left in a position of allowing the imports and losing precious hard currency or denying them and reinforcing the image of Cuba as a low cost, low quality destination that does not meet international standards.

The lack of supporting industries is exacerbated by the fact that Cuban firms are generally unable to produce goods that meet international standards. Many of the goods produced by Cuban firms are perceived, often justly so, as being inferior and not fit for the international tourist. This is especially the case with products such as meat, poultry, and fresh fruits and vegetables, but similar situations can be found in consumer goods and durable goods. One example of this problem was provided by a Canadian tour operator who remembers when he developed the Playa Giron (Bay of Pigs) product (or package) for Canadian tourists: "Obviously, [the destination] was not sellable as it was. We had to import almost everything: from the locks for the doors to the dish-washers for the kitchens, as well as the sports equipment." (Bulletin Voyages 1996:6–9) In general, the distribution system is inadequate and cannot guarantee on-time, on-schedule deliveries, an essential element of a successful tourism industry. Hotels, even the most prestigious ones in Havana, periodically run out of essentials such as certain kinds of drinks, foodstuffs, and items like soap, toilet paper or paper napkins. In the case of foodstuffs, the deficiencies of the distribution system have a direct impact on the quality of the food served at the hotels and restaurants, making it extremely difficult to provide items that are, for example, not too ripe or not too green.

The large and increasing presence of international hotels with foreign partners implies the repatriation of a significant portion of the profits, and all of the management fees in the case of management contracts, as well as increasing pressure to allow firms to import the goods that cannot be obtained locally or that do not meet their standards. During a series of interviews conducted by the first author, this was identified as one of the most contentious points between Cuban firms and their foreign partners. In addition, expensive infrastructure projects, such as airport expansion and telecommunications development, require rapid and massive hard currency investments which further reduce the hard currency contribution (the retained hard currency) provided by the tourism sector to the Cuban economy, at least in the short term. If the number of tourists increases fast enough, the short term leakage could rise to the point where the net contribution to Cuba is close to zero, leaving social and environmental problems as the only remaining impact of the ever growing number of tourists. This point is made clearly by Dwyer and Forsyth, who argued that "It is possible to conceive of circumstances under which foreign investment could be disadvantageous for the host country (for example few domestic tourists, but substantial local investment in the industry...)" (1994:535). In many respects, this can be the case of Cuba today.

Two alternative relationships between total hard currency revenue and retained hard currency revenue are shown in Figure 1. The total hard currency revenue curve is related directly to the number of foreign tourists. While the total hard currency spending per visitor increased fairly rapidly in the early 90s, it has stabilized in the last few years and the curve shown is based on the most recently available data and estimates (Simon 1995). The two alternative curves depend on the assumptions made regarding the relationship between increasing numbers of tourists and hard currency costs. The Cuban government assumes that economies of scale exist that will reduce or stabilize hard currency leakages with increasing numbers of tourists. The first retained hard currency curve reflects this possibility. However, it is possible that in the short term the second curve more accurately reflects the reality of the Cuban situation. More specifically, increasing the number of tourists, in the short term at least, will probably increase costs due to infrastructure and internal supply limitations resulting in a increasing leakage curve and a decrease in

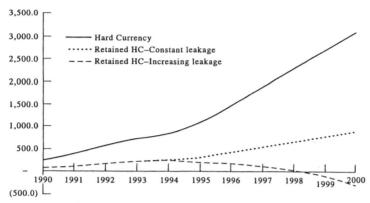

Figure 1. Hard Currency Revenue and Leakage

the hard currency contribution of the tourism sector despite increasing revenues.

Therefore, the odd mix of decayed infrastructure, poorly developed support industries, and limited entertainment limits the government's *marge de manoeuvre* in its efforts to attract tourists. In the short run, this means that Cuba must remain a low-price destination (Berman 1994). However, the wisdom of seeking to massively increase the number of tourists remains in question. In spite of the apparent success in the three most common indicators utilized by the government to highlight the appropriateness of its strategy (number of visitors, amount of foreign investment, and gross revenue from the industry), its profitability, its sustainability and its overall capacity to overcome the structural weaknesses of the economy are questionable.

CONCLUSION

Is Cuba's tourism strategy sustainable? Are there any alternatives? Clearly, its sustainability depends on the accuracy of the assumptions made by Cuban authorities and on the ability of individual firms to create specific skills that will enable them to achieve international standards. Unfortunately, it would appear that Cuban authorities are only taking into account the logic of scale economics. However, in this case, more may not be better.

Perhaps a strategy of developing support industries and addressing the issues that prevent Cuba from extracting more hard currency profits would be a more productive measure. Decreasing leakage by 50% would almost triple the net hard currency contribution to the Cuban economy, create jobs, and build skills that are badly needed to compete in the current international environment. This can be achieved even without increasing the social and environmental problems associated with ever increasing numbers of tourists. But this alternative requires managerial skills and organizational capabilities

Tourism in Developing Countries

that are not readily available in Cuba today (and it is important to be realistic about the time and commitment required). Many governments in the region have attempted to reduce leakage by encouraging local production and the introduction of import quotas, yet in general, these efforts have been unsuccessful because "Caribbean countries tend to be high cost producers and tourists appear to prefer the taste and familiarity of imports from North America" (Momsen 1985:32).

The development of organizational capabilities through competition seems to be essential to the success of such a strategy. This notion, however, runs counter to the ideals of the revolution, since it calls for rivalry, private ownership, decentralization of decision making authority, and grass roots innovation. Porter's (1990) discussion of competitive advantage points to the importance of strong rivalry and internal competition and also to the mediating role of government. The insistence on monopoly production without any participation from the private sector stifles innovation and creativity and ensures that the supporting industries remain uncompetitive and that the international hotels continue to obtain their inputs abroad at a high dollar cost.

Using Porter's diamond as a framework, one can observe that the Cuban government is, *by design*, creating the conditions for an uncompetitive, unprofitable, tourism industry. Cuba enjoys superior factor endowments that could potentially serve as a basis for the creation of a long-lasting competitive advantage. However, the other three corners of the diamond are not as promising. As mentioned above, the conditions that would foster rivalry among firms have not been created. The local market for the tourism industry does not exist. Supporting firms and industries that could help reduce the leakage and increase revenues, do not exist. In short, the Cuban government seems to have chosen a strategy and a structure for its tourism industry which hinders the creation of a competitive industry.

Some alternative strategies are available, but they are only viable insofar as the strict system of central planning which governs the economy and the commitment to enclave tourism are relaxed. First, cost can and should be contained, so more profits are generated even if the revenues remain the same. Second, new sources of income could be developed, so that the amount of money spent by the tourists increases even if the overall number of tourists remains unchanged. Entertainment and activities in general could be developed, taking advantage of the existing infrastructure. Finally, instead of targeting sheer volume, a careful market segmentation could help find customers willing to pay premium prices for Cuba's unparalleled scenic beauty and activities like some of the world's best scuba diving sites, its deserted beaches, open-sea fishing, and its magnificent flora and fauna, among many others (Portela 1995). This option aims to attract a well-defined segment willing to spend more for very specific activities, replacing many low-end tourists by a few high-end ones without losing any profits and while preserving the sites from overcrowding.

On balance, tourism appears to present opportunities and threats to Cuba's economy. If properly managed, tourism could be an effective way to break away from decades of dependence on low-value-added activities and create jobs that could put to use the natural resources, the friendliness of the population, and its high levels of education. But managerial capabilities are scarce in Cuba, and their development is difficult, time consuming, and costly. In the meantime, Cuban authorities may be wasting an opportunity to increase the standard of living of an impoverished population and may be creating a long-lasting reputation of low quality that will be difficult to overcome. Even worse, the emphasis on high-volume tourism increases the social and environmental problems associated with this industry, without many of its benefits. As is often the case, problems with prostitution, black market activities, and crime will continue to increase as the number of tourists increases, as will the problems with traffic, pollution, and overcrowding of the sites (Momsen 1985:28). The challenge for Cuba is straightforward: can it make a low-cost/high-volume strategy work? Can it implement viable alternatives? □ □

REFERENCES

Andrews, K.
  1971 The Concept of Corporate Strategy. Homewood IL: Irwin.
Barney, J.
  1991 Firm Resources and Sustained Competitive Advantage. Journal of Management 17(1):99–120.
  1996 Gaining and Sustaining Competitive Advantage. Reading MA: Addison-Wesley.
Berman, S.
  1994 The Challenge of Cuban Tourism. Cornell Hotel and Restaurant Administration Quarterly 3(5):10–15.
Brenner, R.
  1994 Labyrinths of Prosperity. Ann Arbor MI: University of Michigan Press.
Bull, A.
  1991 The Economics of Travel and Tourism. New York: Wiley.
Bulletin Voyages
  1996 Edition Speciale: Cuba. Bulletin Voyages (Montreal, Quebec) (January).
Chandler, A. D. 1962 Strategy and Structure. Cambridge MA: MIT Press.
Columbia Journal of World Business
  1995 Focus Section: Cuba's Emerging Business Opportunities. Columbia Journal of World Business 30(1).
CubaHoy
  1995a Castro Culpa a los Trabajadores de la Pesima Zafra. CubaHoy (1:94, #3), http://www.netpoint.net/~cubanet.
  1995b Cuba Promete Estabilidad e Incentivos Para Inversion Exterior. CubaHoy (Nov23–24, #3), http://www.netpoint.net/~cubanet.
Dwyer, L., and P. Forsyth
  1994 Foreign Tourism Investment: Motivation and Impact. Annals of Tourism Research 21:512–537.
Fitzgerald, F.
  1994 The Cuban Revolution in Crisis: From Managing Socialism to Managing Survival. New York: Monthly Review Press.
Garcia Marquez, G.
  1971 One Hundred Years of Solitude. New York: Avon Books.
Hafsi, T., and P. Martin de Holan
  1997 National Strategic Management: A Methodological Perspective. In Strategic Management Series, H. Thomas et al, eds., Sussex: Wiley.
Hellbom, A.
  1977 Tourism: A Supranational Instrument for Cultural Imperialism. Transactions of the Finnish Anthropological Society 2:7–12.

794   TOURISM IN CUBA

    1985 The Influence of Tourism on Children and its Consequences for the Con-
         tinuity of Indigenous Cultures. *In* The Impact of Tourism on Regional Devel-
         opment and Cultural Change, E. Gormsen, ed., pp. 60–66. Geographishes
         Institut Der Johannes Gutenberg-Universitat Mainz, Germany.
de Kadt, E., ed.
    1979 Tourism: Passport to Development? Perspectives on the Social and Cultural
         Effects of Tourism in Developing Countries. New York: Oxford University Press.
Kaplowitz, D.
    1995 The Cuba Market: Opportunities and Barriers. Columbia Journal of World
         Business 30(1):6–14.
Lundberg, D., M. Stavenga and M. Krishnamoorthy
    1995 Tourism Economics. New York: Wiley.
Martin de Holan, P., and N. Phillips
    1995a Socialismo o Muerte or the Death of Socialism. Paper presented at the 1995
         Annual Meeting of the Administrative Sciences Association of Canada, Windsor,
         Canada.
    1995b When Cuba Discovered America: An Analysis of Cuba's Transition to a
         Market Economy. Paper Presented at the 1995 Annual Meeting of the Strategic
         Management Society, Mexico City, Mexico.
Martinez Garcia, O.
    1994 Tourism is Changing. Cuba: Foreign Trade (Cuba) (April–June).
Mintzberg, H.
    1978 Patterns in Strategy Formation. Management Science 24:934–948.
Mintzberg, H., and J. A. Waters
    1985 On Strategies, Deliberate and Emergent. Strategic Management Journal
         6:257–272.
Momsen, J.
    1985 Tourism and Development in the Caribbean. *In* The Impact of Tourism
         on Regional Development and Cultural Change, E. Gormsen, ed., pp. 25–36.
         Geographishes Institut Der Johannes Gutenberg-Universitat Mainz, Germany.
Nelson, R., and S. Winter
    1982 An Evolutionary Theory of Economic Change. Cambridge MA: Harvard
         University Press.
Perez-Lopez, J., ed.
    1994 Cuba at Crossroads: Politics and Economics after the Fourth Party. Gaines-
         ville FL: University of Florida Press.
Peteraf, M.
    1993 The Cornerstones of Competitive Advantage: A Resource-Based View.
         Strategic Management Journal 14:179–191.
Phillips, N., and P. Martin de Holan
    1995 Investing in Cuba: A Canadian Perspective. CubaNews 3(3):4–5.
Portela, A.
    1995 Geography: The Keys. CubaNews 3:10.
Porter, M. E. 1980 Competitive Strategy. New York: Free Press.
    1985 Competitive Advantage: Creating and Sustaining Superior Performance. New
         York: Free Press.
    1990 The Competitive Advantage of Nations. New York: Free Press.
Prahalad, C. K., and M. Hamel
    1990 The Core Competence of the Corporation. Harvard Business Review
         68(3):79–91.
Rosenweig, J.
    1988 Elasticities of Substitution in Caribbean Tourism. Journal of Development
         Studies 29:89–100.
Simon, F.
    1995 Tourism Development in Transition Economies. Columbia Journal of World
         Business 30(1):26–39.
Suchilicki, J., and A. Jorge, eds.
    1995 Investing in Cuba, Problems and Prospects. New Brunswick NJ: Transaction
         Books.
Wernerfelt, B.
    1984 A Resource-Based View of the Firm. Strategic Management Journal 5:171–
         180.

MARTIN DE HOLAN AND PHILLIPS   795

World Bank
  1975 Report on the Caribbean Regional Study (Vol. VIa). Tourism. Washington
    DC: World Bank.

Submitted 31 January 1996
Resubmitted 7 November 1996
Accepted 30 January 1997
Refereed anonymously
Coordinating Editor: Georges H. Cazes

[19]

International Tourism and Export Instability

by M. Thea Sinclair and Asrat Tsegaye*

Export diversification has been suggested as a strategy for decreasing the level of export earnings instability which is experienced by many developing countries. In recent years the international tourism sector has made an increasingly important contribution to the economies of many low income countries. This article examines whether diversification into the non-traditional tourism sector has succeeded in decreasing the instability of export earnings. It was found that although tourism has the advantage of high growth rates and is a major source of foreign currency receipts, earnings from international tourism did not bring about a significant decrease in the instability of export earnings of most of the developing and industrialised countries considered. Furthermore, a net increase in the instability of earnings from tourism and merchandise exports occurred in a number of countries, and may be a particular problem in small, open developing economies.

INTRODUCTION

The economic contribution of tourism is attracting increasing recognition given the debt and balance of payments problems of developing countries and the decline in the traditional manufacturing sectors of many industrialised nations. Tourism is argued to be the world's third largest industry after oil and vehicle production, contributing approximately 12 per cent of world GNP [*World Tourism Organisation, 1987*]. The sector has experienced high rates of growth and receipts from international tourism constitute a major component of the current accounts of many countries' balance of payments. Developing countries as diverse as Jamaica, Tunisia and Fiji, for example, obtained 36 per cent, 23 per cent and 16 per cent of their total export receipts in the form of earnings from travel in 1987 [*IMF, 1988*]. In Britain, receipts from tourism are estimated to have contributed approximately £7.6 billion to the balance of payments in 1987, giving Britain fifth place in the world ranking of international tourism earnings, after the US, Italy, Spain and France [*Bluck, 1987*]. Further recognition of the growing importance of tourism in the world economy has resulted from the inclusion of negotiations about tourism in the Uruguay Round of talks on trade liberalisation.

One argument which is sometimes used to support the growth of international tourism is its role in increasing the degree of export diversification. Developing countries are often subject to a high level of export concen-

*University of Kent at Canterbury and University of Zimbabwe respectively. The authors would like to thank Ms A. Clewer, Professor R. Disney, Mr A. Pack, Professor A.P. Thirlwall and an anonymous referee for their comments on an earlier version of this article.

tration, obtaining a large percentage of their export receipts from a small number of primary products. Such specialisation is likely to increase the degree of instability of their export receipts which can, in turn, have adverse effects on their economies. Export instability has, for example, been argued to decrease the rate of domestic savings and productivity of capital [*Guillaumont, 1987*), decrease the country's ability to import the capital goods necessary for development [*Maizels, 1987; Tsegaye, 1987*], lower the level of investment [*Kenen and Voivodas, 1972*], reduce the growth rate of exports [*Glezakos, 1973*] and lower the overall growth rate [*Hitiris, 1985; Lim, 1976; Voivodas, 1974*]. Although some studies have argued that export instability has beneficial effects upon the economy, for example by increasing savings and investment [*Knudsen and Parnes, 1975; Yotopoulos and Nugent, 1976*], or has no clear-cut effects [*MacBean, 1966; Moran, 1983; Behrman, 1987*], it is generally agreed that the instability of export earnings can have considerable adverse effects on some developing countries.

Diversification into non-traditional exports would appear to be an obvious means of decreasing the instability of export earnings. What light does evidence relating to the growth of the non-traditional tourism sector shed on this type of policy? This article will examine whether the growth of tourism receipts in a range of developing and industrialised countries provides support for the commonly held assumption that export diversification reduces the level of instability. The study will first consider the importance of tourism in terms of its contribution to export receipts in a variety of developing and industrialised countries. Since virtually no work on measuring the degree of instability of receipts from tourism has been carried out, the major categories of instability measures will then be used to calculate and compare the degree of instability of tourism receipts with that relating to receipts from more traditional merchandise exports and total exports. The instability of tourism receipts can either offset or amplify the instability of traditional merchandise export receipts. Therefore the main focus of the paper will be concerned with examining the net stabilising or destabilising effects of receipts from international tourism when associated with receipts from more traditional merchandise exports. This will be carried out by calculating the correlation coefficients between the percentage deviations of receipts from tourism and merchandise exports from their estimated time trend and moving log average respectively. The sign, size and significance of the calculated coefficients will indicate whether diversification into tourism is an effective strategy for decreasing the level of export instability. The results obtained for developing and intermediate income countries which have growing tourism sectors are compared with those obtained for industrialised countries, enabling major differences between the two types of countries to be identified.

THE IMPORTANCE OF TOURISM IN A RANGE OF INDUSTRIALISED AND DEVELOPING COUNTRIES

The importance of tourism as a source of foreign currency receipts may be evaluated using a number of different criteria. These include the absolute

INTERNATIONAL TOURISM AND EXPORT INSTABILITY   489

value of receipts, and receipts from tourism as a percentage of total export earnings, and are given in Table 1. The first two columns in the table provide the values of receipts from travel and merchandise exports for a range of developing and industrialised countries. Following the usual practice, IMF data for travel receipts were used as comparable estimates of receipts from tourism. The actual values of tourism receipts differ somewhat from these figures owing to the exclusion from travel receipts of payments which tourists make in advance of journeys [*Archer, 1976*], and to the inclusion of some receipts from visitors who remain within the destination country for less than 24 hours. The latter category is more important for industrialised than for developing countries, highlighting the long identified need for the collection of more reliable tourism statistics [*Gray, 1970*].

As anticipated, the values of both types of receipts by the industrialised countries tend to exceed the values of receipts by the developing countries. However, as column 7 shows, between 1980 and 1985 travel receipts constituted higher percentages of total exports in most of the developing and intermediate income countries in the table, although Austria with 18.5 per cent, and Spain, with 20.6 per cent, have relatively high values within the group of industrialised countries. Some of the calculated percentage shares are very high. Greece, Cyprus and Jamaica, for example, received 19.2 per cent, 24 per cent and 27.5 per cent of their total export earnings from travel in 1980–85, and the percentage shares for most of the developing countries exceeded ten per cent in the same period. The overall picture given in Table 1 is that tourism is a important source of foreign currency receipts in both developing and industrialised countries.

Whereas the percentages for travel receipts by the developing countries tend to be higher during the 1980s than during the years 1960–65, the percentages for the industrialised countries tend to be lower. The percentages for merchandise exports from most of the industrialised and over half of the developing countries are lower during the most recent period than during the early 1960s. Examination of the changes in the percentage shares for both travel and merchandise receipts over the entire period demonstrates a pattern of fluctuations for most of the countries considered, indicating that such receipts may be unstable over time.

The final three columns in the table show receipts from travel, merchandise and total exports as percentages of GDP, and indicate the extent to which instability in export receipts will affect the economy as a whole. The variation in the contribution of travel receipts to GDP is considerably greater for the developing and middle income countries than for the industrialised countries, with the calculated percentages ranging between 0.5 per cent for India and 20.1 per cent for Jamaica. Travel receipts are particularly important in the island economies of Cyprus, Fiji, Jamaica, Malta and Singapore, although the latter's role as a 'stop-over' destination for tourists en route to further destinations makes it somewhat atypical. Among the industrialised countries, travel receipts make the highest contribution to the GDP of Austria, followed by Spain and Ireland. Merchandise and total exports constitute widely

THE JOURNAL OF DEVELOPMENT STUDIES

TABLE 1

RECEIPTS FROM TRAVEL AND MERCHANDISE EXPORTS AND AS PERCENTAGES
OF TOTAL EXPORTS AND GDP (billion SDR)

Country	Travel Receipts	Merchandise Exports	Travel Receipts as a Percentage of Total Exports*				
	1985	1985	1960–1964	1965–1969	1970–1974	1975–1979	1980–1985
	(1)	(2)	(3)	(4)	(5)	(6)	(7)
Developing and Intermediate Income Countries							
Cyprus	0.4	0.4	6.5	6.7	12.5	11.1	24.0
Fiji	0.1	0.2	8.9[a]	17.2	28.4	27.9	26.4
Greece	1.4	4.2	14.8	15.7	19.8	20.2	19.2
India	0.9	9.3	1.9	1.2	1.8	5.8	8.8
Jamaica	0.4	0.6	15.3	22.3	21.8	14.4	27.5
Kenya	0.3	1.0	7.7[a]	10.3	10.7	9.4	13.5
Malta	0.2	0.4	4.7[b]	15.1	17.5	17.9	21.7
Mauritius	0.1	0.4	2.2[b]	3.0	6.5	7.7	8.7
Mexico	2.9	21.3	31.9	36.3	35.0	27.8	13.2
Morocco	0.6	2.1	7.1	14.3	18.0	16.4	15.2
Singapore	1.6	21.2	1.7[a]	2.7	4.8	4.3	6.0
Sri Lanka	0.1	1.3	0.3	0.5	1.6	4.2	7.2
Thailand	1.2	7.0	1.6	5.0	7.8	7.0	11.0
Tunisia	0.6	1.7	3.7	14.2	22.5	24.1	19.5
Turkey	1.1	8.1	1.1	2.0	7.2	8.3	6.7
Industrialised Countries							
Austria	4.4	16.7	19.6	23.2	24.5	23.0	18.5
BLEU	1.6	46.3	3.6	3.5	2.7	2.3	2.1
France	7.9	94.3	7.6	7.0	5.2	5.0	4.8
Ireland	0.5	10.0	17.5	14.5	8.9	6.9	4.9
Italy	8.2	74.7	12.0	11.1	8.3	7.7	8.1
Netherlands	1.5	61.4	4.1	3.6	3.0	2.0	1.9
Spain	8.0	23.2	34.2	40.0	31.5	23.1	20.6
U.K.	7.0	99.2	2.8	2.9	3.5	4.3	3.2
West Germany	5.9	169.2	3.4	2.8	3.0	2.7	2.6

*Average of annual percentages over the period.

a: 1963–64;   b: 1964.

INTERNATIONAL TOURISM AND EXPORT INSTABILITY   491

TABLE 1 (Continued)

Merchandise Exports as a Percentage of Total Exports*					Export Receipts as a Percentage of GDP		
					Travel	Merchandise	Total
1960–1964 (8)	1965–1969 (9)	1970–1974 (10)	1975–1979 (11)	1980–1985 (12)	1985 (13)	1985 (14)	1985 (15)
44.4	45.1	40.1	50.4	38.7	16.4	17.9	57.3
78.7[a]	58.3	48.7	49.6	46.5	12.7	17.9	45.0
50.5	52.3	51.7	52.2	55.2	4.2	12.8	21.2
80.2	82.3	85.3	78.6	70.8	0.5	4.8	6.7
65.0	59.1	63.3	71.1	57.5	20.1	28.1	62.5
60.6[a]	58.6	59.1	65.1	61.7	4.6	17.6	27.8
12.0	22.4	32.1	47.3	46.8	15.2	41.5	82.3
88.2[b]	78.8	74.1	76.0	72.0	5.2	40.5	54.4
58.2	53.3	49.9	54.4	72.3	1.6	12.2	16.8
74.5	74.8	70.8	71.4	71.2	5.1	18.0	26.6
77.8[a]	80.0	70.7	69.4	68.8	9.5	122.7	169.3
88.9	89.1	87.2	86.8	78.1	1.4	22.7	28.3
86.2	66.0	66.8	78.8	71.7	3.1	18.4	26.7
62.7	59.6	57.9	58.2	64.0	6.8	20.7	33.0
75.9	73.0	72.6	72.7	75.7	2.1	15.7	21.6
71.8	67.1	63.9	61.4	55.7	6.8	25.6	44.6
79.2	77.7	74.2	67.8	58.6	2.0	57.2	97.6
72.5	72.6	73.6	69.6	61.3	1.6	18.8	30.2
63.4	66.3	74.3	79.9	81.4	3.0	55.4	66.2
65.7	67.8	69.8	75.4	73.0	2.3	21.1	28.7
74.2	73.7	72.2	71.6	69.5	1.2	49.9	69.1
53.5	47.0	51.6	60.1	61.3	4.9	14.4	23.4
64.6	63.7	61.7	62.4	49.9	1.6	22.4	44.5
83.4	81.2	79.6	79.2	77.3	1.0	27.5	35.7

BLEU = Belgium-Luxembourg Economic Union

Source: International Monetary Fund, *Balance of Payments Yearbook*; 1963 and 1964 data for travel receipts for Fiji were obtained from Ward [1971, Table 5.5: 166]; UN *National Accounts Statistics*.

492   THE JOURNAL OF DEVELOPMENT STUDIES

varying shares of the GDP of all countries, with the export sector of Singapore being of outstanding importance and total exports again making particularly large contributions to the GDPs of the island economies within the group of developing countries. Thus instability in both travel and other export receipts is likely to have considerably greater effects on small, open developing economies than on larger countries such as India, with more closed economies and higher levels of GDP.

THE GROWTH AND INSTABILITY OF RECEIPTS FROM TOURISM, MERCHANDISE AND TOTAL EXPORTS

Past studies have used different measures to calculate the degree of export earnings instability, and the particular measure used has often been selected on an ad hoc basis. The choice of instability measure is, however, important since different measures can produce variations in countries' rankings in terms of their levels of export instability, in addition to differences in the calculated values of the instability measures [Glezakos, 1983; Lawson, 1974; Leith, 1970; Sundrum, 1967]. Therefore in this study the different types of instability measure have been nested into main categories and each of the categories was used to estimate the degree of instability of travel, merchandise and total exports. This approach has the advantage of ensuring that no main category is omitted, and of permitting the results obtained by using the different categories to be compared. The methodology which was used to categorise the different types of instability measure is explained in the appendix and the major categories of instability measure are given in equations 1–4. The instability values for receipts from travel, merchandise and total exports (in real terms) were calculated using equations 1–4. The data sources and units are as given in Table 1. Exports were deflated by the export price index and travel receipts were deflated by the consumer price index [Archer, 1976: 38] except for India, Jamaica, Malta, Mexico, Singapore and Turkey, for which the GDP deflator was used. Instability measures were calculated for the time period 1960–85, which includes the events accompanying the oil price rises of 1973, the commodity price booms of 1972–74 and the price declines of the early 1980s, all of which may have affected the instability of receipts from tourism and merchandise exports.

    The form of time trend which was the best fit to the data for most of the countries was the exponential trend. In those cases where it was a good fit it was used to calculate equations 1 and 2. As Massell [1970] has argued, the use of an exponential trend also has some economic justification in that constant growth rates are often used by policy makers in their planning operations. Summaries of the estimated equations for travel receipts, merchandise exports and total exports are given in Tables A1–A3 in the appendix. The estimated trend coefficients are significant at the 0.05 level and the values of the autocorrelation coefficient, ρ, are statistically insignificant at the 0.05 level for most of the countries in the tables, suggesting an absence of autocorrelation in the residuals. An exponential trend proved a poor fit to the data for the countries not included in the tables, for which instability measures based solely on deviations from a

INTERNATIONAL TOURISM AND EXPORT INSTABILITY   493

moving log average were calculated.

Table 2 provides the rates of growth and the instability values calculated using equations 1–4. One way of ascertaining whether the promotion of tourism is beneficial to an economy is to examine the past growth performance of receipts from tourism. Columns 1, 6 and 11 of the table give the rates of growth of receipts from travel, merchandise and total exports. With the exception of Mexico, the rates of growth of travel receipts by the developing and intermediate income countries are high, ranging between 8.5 per cent for Morocco and 15.6 per cent for Cyprus. Of the industrialised countries, the UK and Austria displayed the highest growth rates, of over six per cent. The growth rates of travel receipts by the developing and middle income countries except Mexico far exceed those of their real merchandise and total export receipts, the opposite being the case for all of the industrialised countries except the UK. This could result, in part, from the fact that the industrialised countries' exports largely consist of manufactured products which tend to have high rates of growth of demand relative to the growth rates for the primary products which usually constitute a higher proportion of the exports of the developing countries. Tourism is, moreover, a relatively new industry in many developing countries and its high growth rates may be related to its low initial level of development. With the exception of the UK, all of the lowest growth rates for merchandise and total exports pertain to the developing countries.

The desire to promote tourism could arise not only from the relatively high rates of growth of travel receipts but from a possible stabilising role of such receipts. The values of the instability measures which were calculated using equations 1–4 are included in the remaining columns of the table. Since the values of the coefficients estimated from the regression of receipts against time changed negligibly as the result of the application of the generalised difference procedure, the instability measures based on equations 1 and 2 were calculated using the re-estimated values of the coefficient where appropriate. The different measures of instability produced some variations in the countries' instability rankings, showing that the choice of measure can be of importance and indicating that the use of only one measure can lead to misleading conclusions.

Examination of the mean instability values calculated using all types of measure clearly demonstrates that the instability of receipts from travel, merchandise and total exports was considerably higher in the developing and intermediate income countries than in the industrialised countries. Jamaica and Turkey always displayed the highest values and the lowest was for Thailand, although the ranking of the other countries varied somewhat in accordance with the measure used. The values of the instability measures for travel receipts were particularly high. For the industrialised countries, the values of the instability measures for travel receipts based on deviations from a fitted trend were highest for Austria, followed by Spain and the Netherlands, while the measures based on deviations from a moving log average were highest for Italy, Spain and the Netherlands. All of the measures produced the lowest level of instability for France, followed by Belgium and Luxembourg (BLEU). The highest instability values for

TABLE 2

MEAN GROWTH RATES (Xg) AND INSTABILITY VALUES FOR TRAVEL RECEIPTS, MERCHANDISE AND TOTAL EXPORTS

	Travel Receipts					Merchandise Exports					Total Exports				
	Xg (1)	I1 (2)	I2 (3)	I3 (4)	I4 (5)	Xg (6)	I1 (7)	I2 (8)	I3 (9)	I4 (10)	Xg (11)	I1 (12)	I2 (13)	I3 (14)	I4 (15)
Developing and Intermediate Income Countries															
Cyprus	15.57	31.42	39.20	23.17	34.62	6.86	8.78	12.85	6.90	10.62	7.55	10.81	14.69	6.36	10.19
Fiji	a	a	a	4.43	5.52	2.15	9.90	12.33	7.01	8.54	4.52	13.43	15.65	6.84	8.14
Greece	10.30	20.79	25.20	10.80	13.25	9.80	9.07	11.08	4.57	5.80	8.99	12.21	15.42	4.93	5.85
India	a	a	a	19.16	27.77	5.23	11.97	14.29	5.31	6.18	5.62	14.36	16.33	5.40	6.34
Jamaica	a	a	a	14.15	18.26	4.61	27.45	30.42	14.11	17.03	5.08	25.75	28.87	12.15	15.31
Mexico	2.75	18.08	23.27	6.54	8.72	8.87	24.86	29.07	7.14	9.03	7.87	14.99	18.21	5.35	6.91
Morocco	8.50	25.33	30.34	5.38	6.04	3.06	10.13	14.58	8.04	10.86	3.26	8.22	11.82	6.15	8.03
Singapore	15.04	23.05	28.45	7.83	10.04	9.66	16.77	19.75	7.82	9.42	9.86	17.62	20.85	5.56	6.67
Thailand	a	a	a	10.91	13.31	8.73	8.62	10.18	5.69	6.76	9.27	6.29	8.40	4.80	5.87
Tunisia	a	a	a	8.15	10.21	4.85	8.05	9.72	5.68	7.24	4.53	9.10	12.36	5.59	7.43
Turkey	a	a	a	13.27	16.03	8.41	22.70	27.51	9.04	11.79	8.46	23.41	28.80	10.52	12.63
Mean	10.43	23.73	29.29	11.25	14.89	6.57	11.79	21.31	9.03	11.47	8.33	17.35	21.27	8.18	10.37
Industrialised Countries															
Austria	6.33	28.14	32.50	3.62	4.38	7.88	5.69	6.91	2.55	3.46	9.07	5.92	7.27	2.20	2.77
BLEU	5.98	5.98	7.34	3.29	4.12	7.24	10.02	13.01	3.23	4.06	8.57	7.93	9.71	3.35	3.98
France	5.84	4.70	5.49	2.89	3.65	7.43	13.31	14.91	2.95	3.67	8.57	10.13	12.22	2.90	3.47
Ireland	a	a	a	4.58	5.08	8.33	3.45	4.00	2.41	2.80	7.04	4.12	4.94	1.96	2.31
Italy	5.87	7.01	9.37	5.56	6.57	7.23	12.97	15.48	2.81	3.43	8.10	15.18	18.16	2.78	3.25
Netherlands	3.50	15.21	20.09	4.72	5.98	6.63	13.78	18.46	2.75	3.34	6.79	18.07	23.98	2.62	3.13
Spain	5.99	19.76	22.31	5.48	6.80	11.63	12.66	15.01	3.34	4.40	10.37	11.83	15.64	3.67	4.43
U.K.	6.37	13.32	17.10	4.49	5.54	4.28	4.50	5.35	2.03	2.68	5.52	4.00	4.94	2.68	3.32
West Germany	5.17	6.27	8.20	4.02	4.74	6.67	8.78	10.81	3.00	4.00	6.93	8.67	10.80	3.03	4.58
Mean	5.63	12.55	15.30	4.29	5.21	7.48	9.46	11.55	2.79	3.54	7.88	9.54	11.96	2.80	3.47

Note: [a] refers to cases where statistically acceptable trend estimates were not obtained.
BLEU = Belgium–Luxembourg Economic Union

merchandise and total exports were for the Netherlands, using equations 1 and 2, and for Spain using equations 3 and 4. All of the measures produced relatively low values for merchandise and total exports by Ireland, Austria and the UK.

Although the instability associated with different categories of exports is of interest, it is the change in instability resulting from variations in the mix of commodities and services exported which is important in indicating whether diversification into a non-traditional sector such as tourism succeeds in reducing export instability. The net effect of the instability of receipts from travel and merchandise exports may be stabilising or destabilising, depending upon whether the algebraic percentage deviations of travel and merchandise export receipts from the trend or moving log average are positively or negatively correlated. A stabilising effect is thus defined as occurring if the instability of tourism receipts partially or totally offsets the instability of receipts from merchandise exports, and a destabilising effect occurs if the instability of tourism receipts amplifies the instability of merchandise export receipts.

Table 3 provides the correlation coefficients between the percentage deviations from travel and merchandise exports receipts. Most of the correlation coefficients are positive, indicating that the overall effect is destabilising. Of the developing and intermediate income countries, the correlation coefficients for the island economies of Cyprus, Fiji and Jamaica and for the Eastern Mediterranean destinations of Greece and Turkey are positive and significant, indicating the potential risk associated with increasing reliance on tourism. The results for Singapore are less clear-cut, the coefficient based on deviations from a trend being positive and significant but that based on deviations from a moving log average being low and insignificant, probably owing to the more developed state of the country's economy, to its role as a 'stop-over' destination for foreign visitors and tourists and to the fact that travel receipts are a smaller share of its total export earnings. With the exception of the large Mexican economy, for which both coefficients are negative and one is significant, the correlation coefficients for the remaining developing countries are low and insignificant, indicating that tourism failed to play a significant role in stabilising export receipts. Thus tourism had either a destabilising or an insignificant effect on the export earnings of the developing and intermediate income countries considered. Among the industrialised countries, the correlation coefficients based on both measures are positive and significant for the UK and Belgium and Luxembourg, as is one of the coefficients for Austria, Italy, the Netherlands and West Germany. The insignificance of the remaining coefficients indicates that, as in the lower income countries, tourism did not significantly stabilise export receipts.

Since the correlation coefficients were calculated between the percentage deviations rather than the absolute values of the deviations, they do not show the extent to which the instability of travel receipts offsets or amplifies the instability of receipts from merchandise exports. The magnitude of the stabilising or destabilising effect is, however, indicated by the values of the mean absolute deviations of each type of receipts from the estimated trend, given in columns 3–4 of the table. It can be seen that the mean deviations of travel receipts for Cyprus and Greece are very high relative to the mean deviations for merchandise exports; the mean deviations of travel receipts exceed 60 per cent of the values for merchandise exports, indicating that the instability of travel receipts played an important role in increasing the overall instability of receipts. The magnitude of the destabilising effect is fairly high for the UK but low for Belgium and Luxembourg. For those countries for which the correlation coefficients are significant for only one of the measures, travel receipts appeared to play a fairly important stabilising role in the case of Mexico and destabilising role in the case of Austria, and were of less importance in the remaining industrialised countries.

CONCLUSIONS

It is clear that international tourism is providing an increasingly important source of export earnings. Although the major share of world receipts from tourism goes to the industrialised countries, the developing countries' share is estimated to be as high as 26 per cent [Lee, 1987: 4–5]. Receipts from tourism often constitute relatively high percentages of national export receipts, particularly in developing countries with established tourism sectors. Tourism is a high growth industry in both industrialised and developing countries and the rates of growth of tourism receipts by many developing countries have exceeded the growth rates for earnings from merchandise exports. It thus appears that international tourism can provide a rapidly growing source of foreign exchange which both industrialised and developing countries are increasingly keen to tap.

Although the promotion of the tourism industry has been supported on the grounds that it provides an additional important source of export receipts and is a feasible means of diversifying a country's economy, diversification into this non-traditional activity has often failed to play its anticipated role of stabilising export earnings. The calculated values of the major categories of instability measures showed receipts from travel to be a relatively unstable source of earnings. The instability values for travel receipts by developing and intermediate income countries exceeded those for merchandise exports for both categories of measure, and the values calculated using deviations from a moving log average gave rise to the same conclusions for the industrialised countries.

Of greater importance is the finding that, rather than offsetting the instability of earnings from more traditional merchandise exports, receipts from travel can amplify net export earnings instability in some developing island economies and in the intermediate income countries of Greece and Turkey. Both categories of instability measure also showed that travel receipts resulted in a net increase in instability in the UK and Belgium and Luxembourg, although this is not likely to be a major problem in industrialised countries where travel receipts are of low importance relative to other merchandise exports and GDP. The conclusion that diversification into tourism generally fails to stabilise export earnings is in line with Love's

TABLE 3
CORRELATIONS BETWEEN PERCENTAGE DEVIATIONS FOR REAL TRAVEL
RECEIPTS AND MERCHANDISE EXPORT RECEIPTS,
AND MEAN ABSOLUTE DEVIATIONS FROM TREND

	Correlations based on Deviations from Estimated Trend	Correlations based on Deviations from Moving Log Average	Mean Absolute Deviations From Trend	
			Travel Receipts	Merchandise Exports
	(1)	(2)	(3)	(4)
Developing and Intermediate Income Countries				
Cyprus	0.412*	0.727*	17.00	23.35
Fiji	a	0.571*	a	a
Greece	0.693*	0.419*	106.10	171.48
India	a	0.090	a	a
Jamaica	a	0.619*	a	a
Mexico	-0.426*	-0.127	244.16	909.20
Morocco	-0.165	-0.102	23.52	124.22
Singapore	0.492*	0.097	66.81	698.97
Thailand	a	-0.193	a	a
Tunisia	a	0.203	a	a
Turkey	a	0.517*	a	a
Industrialised Countries				
Austria	0.671*	-0.188	195.35	336.71
BLEU	0.534*	0.555*	49.60	1280.55
France	0.248	-0.017	163.45	2686.58
Ireland	a	0.333	a	a
Italy	0.033	0.670*	294.44	1701.13
Netherlands	0.632*	0.036	102.06	1640.58
Spain	0.056	0.320	410.52	454.95
U.K.	0.825*	0.482*	265.18	1830.55
West Germany	0.582*	0.084	144.34	4334.62

Notes: [a] refers to cases where statistically acceptable trend estimates were not obtained and * means that the estimated value is statistically significant at 0.05 level.
BLEU = Belgium–Luxembourg Economic Union

498   THE JOURNAL OF DEVELOPMENT STUDIES

[*1983*] finding that diversification into manufactured exports by developing countries failed to generate higher export earnings stability.

The growth of tourism and its associated instability has different policy implications for different types of developing and intermediate income countries. Tourism growth in developing countries with large, relatively closed economies, such as India and Mexico, does not usually pose problems of rising export earnings instability. The increases in instability which occur in some intermediate income countries and small, open developing economies, though potentially more serious, do not imply that diversification into tourism should be rejected as a development strategy, even if this were feasible. For example, the expansion of tourism in intermediate income countries such as Greece and Turkey could help to provide the foreign currency necessary for an import-substitution programme via capital goods imports and the development of the manufacturing sector. This would permit the expansion of the secondary as well as the service sector so that instability should be a decreasing problem over the long run.

The export promotion strategy of tourism development in small island economies usually differs in that the possibility of import substitution and the expansion of the secondary sector is much lower. Thus resources are often transferred from the agricultural sector to tourism without the concomitant growth of manufacturing. The risk associated with switching from dependence on the primary sector to dependence on tourism is therefore considerably greater for small economies in both the short and long run. One possible means of lessening the degree of instability associated with international tourism is via a policy of diversification within the tourism sector itself, by policies such as marketing strategies geared towards obtaining a mix of tourists of different nationalities [*Board, Sinclair and Sutcliffe, 1987*], thereby decreasing the risk of unstable receipts associated with dependence on tourism from a small number of origin countries. Small developing countries could also pursue policies designed to encourage the rural sector to meet the growing needs of the urban and tourist population, so that the growth of tourism receipts is not offset by rising payments for imports. This is particularly important as past studies of tourism development in island economies such as those of the Caribbean and Fiji [*Bryden, 1973; Varley, 1978*] have shown that linkages between the tourism and rural sectors tend to be weak, resulting in a rising propensity to import.

Further work on the net stabilising or destabilising effect of international tourism receipts would be useful and could consist, for example, of the inclusion of equations explaining tourism receipts within econometric models for particular countries. The use of alternative currencies and time periods would provide additional information and might lead to some variations in the results obtained. Such work could provide further information concerning the ways in which diversification into the tourism sector could succeed in offsetting any destabilising effects associated with its growth.

final version received December 1989

REFERENCES

Archer, B.H., 1976, *Demand Forecasting in Tourism*, Bangor Occasional Papers in Economics No.9, University of Wales Press.
Behrman, J.B., 1987, 'Commodity Price Instability and Economic Goal Attainment in Developing Countries', *World Development*, Vol.15, No.5, pp.559–73.
Bluck, D., 1987, Speech given at the World Travel Market Exhibition, Olympia, 2nd December, cited in the *Financial Times*, 3 Dec. 1987.
Board, J., Sinclair, M.T. and C. Sutcliffe, 1987 'A Portfolio Approach to Regional Tourism' *Built Environment*, Vol.13, No.2, pp. 124–37.
Bryden, J.M., 1973, *Tourism and Development. A Case Study of the Commonwealth Caribbean*, Cambridge: Cambridge University Press.
Coppock, J., 1977, *International Trade Instability*, Farnborough: Saxon House.
English Tourist Board, 1986, *Annual Report, 1985/86*, English Tourist Board.
Glezakos, C., 1973, 'Export Instability and Economic Growth: A Statistical Verification', *Economic Development and Cultural Change*, Vol.21, No.4, July, pp.670–78.
Gray, H.P., 1970, *International Travel – International Trade*, Lexington, MA: D.C. Heath,
Guillaumont, P., 1987, 'From Export Instability Effects to International Stabilization Policies', *World Development*, Vol.15, No.5, pp.633–43.
Hitiris, T., 1985, *Export Instability, Level of Development and Rate of Growth: An Empirical Investigation*, Discussion Paper 107, University of York.
International Monetary Fund, 1957–80, *Balance of Payments Yearbook*, Vols.14–31, Washington, DC: IMF.
International Monetary Fund, 1981–88, *Balance of Payments Statistics Yearbook*, Vols.32–37, Washington, DC: IMF.
Kenen, P.B. and Voivodas, C.S., 1972, 'Export Instability and Economic Growth' *Kyklos*, Vol.25, Fasc.4, pp.791–804.
Kingston, J.L., 1973, 'Export Instability in Latin America: The Postwar Statistical Record', *The Journal of Developing Areas*, Vol.7, pp.381–96.
Knapman, B. and S. Schiavo-Campo, 1983, 'Growth and Fluctuations of Fiji's Exports, 1875–1978', *Economic Development and Cultural Change*, Vol.32, No.1, pp.97–119.
Knudsen, O.K. and Parnes, A., 1975 *Trade Instability and Economic Development*, Lexington, MA: D.C. Heath.
Lawson, C.W. 1974 'The Decline in World Export Instability – A Reappraisal' *Oxford Bulletin of Economics and Statistics*, Vol.36, No.1, pp.53–65.
Lee, G., 1987, 'Tourism as a Factor in Development Cooperation', *Tourism Management*, Vol.8, No.1, pp.2–19.
Leith, J.C., 1970, 'The Decline in World Export Instability: A Comment', *Bulletin of the Oxford University Institute of Economics and Statistics*, Vol. 32, No. 3, pp. 267–72.
Lim, D. 1976, 'Export Instability and Economic Growth: A Return to Fundamentals', *Oxford Bulletin of Economics and Statistics*, Vol.38, No.4, Nov., pp.311–22.
Love, J., 1983, 'Concentration, Diversification and Earnings Instability: Some Evidence on Developing Countries' Exports of Manufactures and Primary Products' *World Development*, Vol.11, pp.787–93.
MacBean, A.I., 1966, *Export Instability and Economic Development*, London: Allen & Unwin.
MacBean, A.I. and Nguyen, D.T., 1980, 'Commodity Concentration and Export Earnings Instability: A Mathematical Analysis' *Economic Journal*, Vol.90, June, pp.354–362.
Maizels, A., 1987, 'Commodities in Crisis: An Overview of the Main Issues', *World Development*, Vol.15, No.5, pp.537–49.
Massell, B.F., 1964, 'Export Concentration and Fluctuations in Export Earnings: A Cross-section Analysis' *American Economic Review*, Vol. 54, No.2, March, pp.47–63.
Massell, B.F., 1970, Export Instability and Economic Structure, *American Economic Review*, Vol.60, No.4, pp.618–30.
Michaely, M., 1962, *Concentration in International Trade*, Amsterdam: North-Holland.
Moran, C., 1983, 'Export Fluctuations and Economic Growth: An Empirical Analysis', *Journal of Development Economics*, Vol.12, pp.195–218.

500   THE JOURNAL OF DEVELOPMENT STUDIES

Murray, D., 1978, 'Statistical Measurement of Export Earnings Instability', *The Malayan Economic Review*, Vol.23, No.1, April, pp.87–98.

Naya, S., 1973, 'Fluctuations in Export Earnings and Economic Patterns of Asian Countries' *Economic Development and Cultural Change*, Vol.21, No.4, July, pp.629–41.

Sundrum, R.M., 1967, *The Measurement of Export Instability*, unpublished manuscript.

Tan, G. 1983 'Export Instability, Export Growth and GDP Growth', *Journal of Development Economics*, Vol.12, pp.219–27.

Tsegaye, A., 1987, *Export Instability and Development: A Case Study of Ethiopia*, Ph.D. thesis, University of Kent.

United Nations, 1987, *National Accounts Statistics, 1985*, New York: United Nations.

Varley, R.C.G., 1978, *Tourism in Fiji: Some Economic and Social Problems*, Bangor Occasional Papers in Economics No.12, University of Wales Press.

Voivodas, C.S., 1974, 'The Effect of Foreign Exchange Instability on Growth' *Review of Economics and Statistics*, Vol.LVI, No.3, Aug., pp.410–12.

Ward, M., 1971, *The Role of Investment in the Development of Fiji*, Cambridge: Cambridge University Press.

World Tourism Organization, 1987, *Report of the Secretary-General on the Activities of the Organization*, Madrid: World Tourism Organization.

Yotopoulos, P.J. and J.B. Nugent, 1976, *Economics of Development*, New York: Harper & Row.

APPENDIX

Methodology for Categorising and Measuring the Instability of Export Receipts

The first main category of instability measure is based on deviations from time trends which have been fitted to the data using regression analysis. Many of the studies which have used this category of measure have fitted linear or log-linear time trends to data for export receipts and have made little or no use of econometric criteria for examining whether the estimated trends were appropriate for the countries considered. The time trends which can be appropriate for particular cases range from linear trends to polynomials of the nth degree and, as Tan [*1983*] notes, the fitting of an inappropriate time trend results in bias in the estimated measure of instability. Therefore different forms of time trend were fitted to the data and, in those cases where the value of the Durbin–Watson statistic was low, a generalised difference transformation of the variables was carried out with the aim of correcting for first-order correlation in the residuals. The form of trend which provided the best fit to the data for most of the countries considered was selected as the basis for the calculation of the instability values.

The different measures of instability which have been calculated on the basis of deviations from a fitted trend are of two types. The first is based on the sums of the moduli of the deviations. Studies which have used this type of measure have calculated the mean of the sum of the moduli of the deviations from the trend [*Coppock, 1977; Glezakos, 1973*]. The moduli are sometimes expressed as a fraction of the corresponding trend value [*Kingston, 1973*], so that the calculated value of the instability measure is less sensitive to high values of receipts. The use of the moduli rather than the actual values of the observations prevents positive and negative deviations from offsetting each other. The relevant formula is:

$$I_1 = 100/n \sum_{t=1}^{n} |(X_t - X_t^*)| / X_t^* \tag{1}$$

where X_t is the actual value of receipts in time period t.

n is the number of observations in the time series.

X_t^* is the trend value of receipts estimated from a regression of receipts against time.

The second type of instability measure which is based on deviations from a trend uses the sum of the squared deviations from the trend. This type of measure is more affected by high values of deviations than are measures based on the sums of absolute deviations. Past studies have usually calculated the standard deviation of the deviations from a linear trend [*Kenen and Voivodas, 1972; Knapman and Schiavo-Campo, 1983; Lawson, 1974; Massell, 1964*], or from

INTERNATIONAL TOURISM AND EXPORT INSTABILITY   501

Notes: [a]refers to cases where statistically acceptable trend estimates were not obtained and means that the estimated value is statistically significant at 0.05 level.

     BLEU = Belgium–Luxembourg Economic Union

an exponential trend [*Lawson, 1974; Naya, 1973*], although MacBean and Nguyen [*1980*] used the variance of export earnings around a five-year moving average. The calculated instability values have sometimes been expressed in percentage terms and normalised to take account of differences in scale. Each of the squared deviations from the trend or moving average may be expressed as a fraction of the square of the corresponding trend [*Tsegaye, 1987: 261*]. The formula which was used to calculate the instability of travel, merchandise and total export receipts is given by:

$$I_2 = 100[1/n \sum_{t=1}^{n} \left\{ (X_t - X_t^*)/X_t^* \right\}^2]^{\frac{1}{2}} \tag{2}$$

where all of the variables are defined as above.

     The second major category of instability measure is based on deviations from a moving average of the values of export receipts or from a moving average of the logarithms of export receipts. Instability measures based on the mean of the sum of the moduli of the deviations from a moving average have been estimated by MacBean [*1966*] and Murray [*1978*]. Instability measures based on deviations from a five-year moving log average were calculated for travel, merchandise and total export receipts using the formula:

$$I_3 = 100/(n-4) \sum_{t=3}^{n-2} | (X_t - X_t') | / X_t' \tag{3}$$

where X_t' is the antilog value of a five year centred moving average of the log values of the variables.

     Measures of instability based on the sums of the squared deviations from the moving log average were also quanitified using:

$$I_4 = 100[1/(n-4) \sum_{t=3}^{n-2} \left\{ (X_t - X_t')/X_t' \right\}^2]^{\frac{1}{2}} \tag{4}$$

where all variables are as previously defined.

     All of the above equations express the moduli or the square of the deviations from the trend or moving log average as a fraction, and each instability measure is normalised and given as a percentage. The procedure of expressing the deviations as a share, and normalising and presenting the instability measures in percentage terms, avoids weighting the deviations by the absolute values of export receipts. This generally accepted procedure is sensible since it ensures that the ranking of the calculated instability values is not determined by the absolute values of the different countries' receipts. Thus, for example, it avoids the provision of results which invariably show the industrialised countries as having greater instability values than the developing countries, purely because the values of export earnings of the former are higher in absolute terms. The avoidance of such weighting thus permits the calculated instability measures to demonstrate that instability can be of greater importance, in relative terms, in developing countries with lower absolute values of export earnings.

502   THE JOURNAL OF DEVELOPMENT STUDIES

APPENDIX TABLE A1

TREND ESTIMATES OF REAL TRAVEL RECEIPTS

	a	b	$\bar{R}^2$		ρ	Time Period
Developing and Inter-mediate Income Countries						
Cyprus	1.987	0.145	0.705		0.056	1960-85
	(0.26)	(0.02)			(0.20)	
Greece	4.954	0.098	0.802		0.151	1960-85
	(0.19)	(0.01)			(0.20)	
Mexico	7.328	0.027	0.942		0.106	1960-85
	(0.21)	(0.01)			(0.21)	
Morocco	4.378	0.082	0.856		0.359*	1960-84
	(0.22)	(0.01)			(0.19)	
Singapore	3.647	0.140	0.712		0.256	1963-85
	(0.28)	(0.02)			(0.21)	
Industrialised Countries						
Austria	6.912	0.061	0.934		0.643*	1960-85
	(0.29)	(0.01)			(0.15)	
BLEU	6.077	0.058	0.975		-0.168	1960-85
	(0.04)	(0.00)			(0.23)	
France	7.526	0.057	0.992		0.337	1963-85
	(0.04)	(0.00)			(0.20)	
Italy	7.571	0.057	0.979		0.246	1960-84
	(0.07)	(0.00)			(0.20)	
Netherlands	6.556	0.034	0.965		0.438*	1960-85
	(0.14)	(0.01)			(0.18)	
Spain	7.583	0.058	0.964		0.685*	1960-85
	(0.14)	(0.01)			(0.14)	
U.K.	7.248	0.062	0.975		0.559*	1960-85
	(0.14)	(0.01)			(0.16)	
West Germany	7.424	0.050	0.989		0.250	1960-85
	(0.06)	(0.00)			(0.19)	

Notes: In Tables A1–A3, a is the constant term and b is the regression trend coefficient estimated from the exponential function $X_t = ae^{bt}$ where X is the real value of export receipts and t is time.

R2 $\equiv$ adjusted coefficient of determination;

$\rho \equiv$ first-order autocorrelation coefficient and * means that the estimated value of ρ is statistically significant at the 0.05 level, suggesting the presence of higher order autocorrelation in the residuals which was not removed through a generalised difference transformation of the variables. Figures in brackets are standard errors.

BLEU = Belgium–Luxembourg Economic Union

INTERNATIONAL TOURISM AND EXPORT INSTABILITY   503

APPENDIX TABLE A2

TREND ESTIMATES OF REAL MERCHANDISE EXPORTS

	a	b	R^2	ρ	Time Period
Developing and Inter-mediate Income Countries					
Cyprus	4.431	0.066	0.876	0.047	1960-85
	(0.08)	(0.01)		(0.21)	
Fiji	5.020	0.021	0.911	0.086	1963-85
	(0.11)	(0.01)		(0.22)	
Greece	6.113	0.094	0.965	-0.189	1960-85
	(0.08)	(0.01)		(0.20)	
India	7.681	0.051	0.983	0.473*	1960-83
	(0.12)	(0.01)		(0.18)	
Jamaica	5.467	0.045	0.732	0.096	1960-85
	(0.23)	(0.01)		(0.21)	
Mexico	7.509	0.085	0.935	0.279	1960-85
	(0.28)	(0.02)		(0.20)	
Morocco	6.868	0.030	0.945	0.171	1960-84
	(0.08)	(0.01)		(0.21)	
Singapore	7.258	0.092	0.954	0.067	1963-85
	(0.15)	(0.01)		(0.23)	
Thailand	6.692	0.084	0.967	0.017	1960-85
	(0.07)	(0.00)		(0.20)	
Tunisia	6.370	0.047	0.921	0.178	1960-83
	(0.04)	(0.00)		(0.21)	
Turkey	6.347	0.081	0.817	0.187	1960-83
	(0.22)	(0.01)		(0.21)	
Industrialised Countries					
Austria	7.869	0.076	0.993	-0.117	1960-85
	(0.06)	(0.00)		(0.20)	
BLEU	9.115	0.070	0.991	0.112	1960-85
	(0.12)	(0.01)		(0.20)	
France	9.766	0.072	0.968	0.200	1963-85
	(0.32)	(0.01)		(0.21)	
Ireland	7.043	0.080	0.995	0.230	1960-84
	(0.02)	(0.00)		(0.21)	
Italy	9.556	0.070	0.991	0.160	1960-84
	(0.14)	(0.01)		(0.20)	
Netherlands	9.388	0.064	0.981	0.213	1960-85
	(0.21)	(0.01)		(1.09)	
Spain	7.318	0.110	0.792	-0.056	1960-85
	(0.22)	(0.01)		(0.21)	
U.K.	10.426	0.042	0.998	0.040	1960-85
	(0.05)	(0.00)		(0.20)	
West Germany	10.491	0.065	0.994	-0.113	1960-85
	(0.10)	(0.01)		(0.12)	

BLEU = Belgium–Luxembourg Economic Union

504   THE JOURNAL OF DEVELOPMENT STUDIES

APPENDIX TABLE A3
TREND ESTIMATES OF REAL TOTAL EXPORTS

	a	b	$\bar{R}^2$	ρ	Time Period
Developing and Inter-mediate Income Countries					
Cyprus	5.198 (0.13)	0.073 (0.01)	0.901	0.077 (0.20)	1960-85
Fiji	5.337 (0.13)	0.044 (0.01)	0.914	0.048 (0.23)	1963-85
Greece	6.831 (0.14)	0.086 (0.01)	0.967	-0.045 (0.20)	1960-85
India	7.874 (0.14)	0.055 (0.01)	0.981	0.446* (0.18)	1960-83
Jamaica	5.886 (0.21)	0.050 (0.01)	0.793	0.134 (0.21)	1960-85
Mexico	8.133 (0.16)	0.076 (0.01)	0.974	0.294 (0.20)	1960-85
Morocco	7.163 (0.07)	0.032 (0.00)	0.971	0.177 (0.22)	1960-84
Singapore	7.569 (0.15)	0.094 (0.01)	0.972	0.687* (0.15)	1963-85
Thailand	6.931 (0.05)	0.089 (0.00)	0.977	0.073 (0.20)	1960-85
Tunisia	6.915 (0.08)	0.044 (0.01)	0.969	0.178 (0.21)	1960-83
Turkey	6.641 (0.22)	0.081 (0.02)	0.824	0.315 (0.20)	1960-83
Industrialised Countries					
Austria	8.167 (0.07)	0.087 (0.00)	0.994	0.113 (0.20)	1960-85
BLEU	9.320 (0.10)	0.082 (0.01)	0.993	0.119 (0.20)	1960-85
France	10.025 (0.81)	0.082 (0.01)	0.828	0.312 (0.21)	1963-85
Ireland	7.522 (0.04)	0.068 (0.00)	0.995	0.096 (0.22)	1960-84
Italy	9.648 (0.13)	0.078 (0.01)	0.992	0.482* (0.18)	1960-84
Netherlands	9.633 (0.70)	0.066 (0.01)	0.847	0.341* (0.19)	1960-85
Spain	8.071 (0.14)	0.099 (0.01)	0.982	0.049 (0.20)	1960-85
U.K.	10.788 (0.03)	0.054 (0.00)	0.997	0.126 (0.21)	1960-85
West Germany	10.693 (0.10)	0.067 (0.01)	0.992	-0.123 (0.20)	1960-85

BLEU = Belgium–Luxembourg Economic Union

[20]

JOURNAL OF AFRICAN ECONOMIES, VOLUME 8, NUMBER 2, PP. 209–227

Tourism and Welfare in Sub-Saharan Africa: A Theoretical Analysis

Lein Lein Chen and John Devereux[a]
University of Nevada and [a]Queens College, CUNY

Using the standard theoretical model of trade, we study the welfare effects of tourism for developing countries with particular reference to Sub-Saharan Africa. We show that tourism can reduce welfare for trade regimes dominated by export taxes or import subsidies. In addition, we argue that tourist immiserisation is possible for Sub-Saharan Africa. Finally, we show that direct foreign investment in tourism is, for the most part, beneficial.

1. Introduction

Tourism is an important industry for low income developing countries (LDCs). Indeed, for many LDCs it has replaced agriculture as the largest foreign exchange earner. In particular, the last decade and a half has witnessed a rapid expansion of tourism for Sub-Saharan Africa. However, controversy still surrounds tourism in developing economies. Many of these controversies concern the effects of tourists on the social fabric. We do not address these issues in this paper. There are, however, important economic issues facing the industry. First, there is the fundamental question of whether tourism increases welfare. Policy-makers and tourism researchers in developing economies are often ambivalent on this question. Second, there are still widespread concerns about the role of foreign firms in the industry. So far, trade economists have devoted little attention to these and other questions surrounding tourism (except Copeland, 1991). By contrast, applied researchers have developed a useful body of empirical work on tourism. However, this literature uses partial equilibrium models which are ill suited to answering the questions posed above.[1]

---

[1] For an introduction to this work, see Mathieson and Wall (1982) or Pearse (1989). Much of this research is in journals such as *Annals of Tourism Research*.

In this paper we provide a theoretical analysis of the welfare effects of tourism using the standard general equilibrium model of trade. In addition, we examine the effects of direct foreign investment in tourism. Our goal is to show that trade theory can provide useful guidance for policy-makers and others interested in the economic aspects of tourism. Although our discussion is theoretical, we pay attention to issues that we believe have practical relevance for Sub-Saharan African economies.

The paper is organised as follows. Section 2 presents the model. We then show that the welfare effects of tourism consist of a terms of trade effect and a volume of trade effect. The terms of trade effect is welfare improving in all cases, while the volume of trade effect is ambiguous and depends on the trade regime. We argue that trade regimes are usefully classified into regimes that rely on tariffs and export subsidies, and into regimes that rely on export taxes or import subsidies. The latter trade regime characterises many of the economies of Sub-Saharan Africa. We demonstrate that the volume of trade effects are welfare improving for tariff/export subsidy regimes. It follows from this result that tourism exports will raise welfare for the typical developing economy. For trade regimes with export taxes or import subsidies, as is the case for many Sub-Saharan African economies, the volume of trade effect is negative. This is because tourism exacerbates trade distortions with this regime. The overall effects of tourism for export tax/import subsidy regimes are therefore ambiguous. We argue that tourist immiserisation is a possibility for Sub-Saharan economies.

In Section 3 we turn our attention to the welfare effects of direct foreign investment in tourism. We show that foreign investment does not change the result that tourism increases welfare with trade regimes that use import restrictions or export subsidies, while the effects of tourism are uncertain with export taxes and import subsidies. Finally, we argue that in most cases foreign investment raises the welfare gains associated with tourism.

2. Tourism and Welfare

We study the welfare effects of tourism using the standard competitive model of trade. The economy produces tourism services and N other traded goods under constant returns to scale. There are M factors of production where $M > N + 1$. Throughout, we assume that markets are competitive and that the economy is a price taker. Applied work in this area often models tourism as a differentiated product with a downward sloping demand. We consider this case in Section 3.

Tourism in our model differs from other industries only in the sense that it uses a different mix of factors. This is not to deny that tourism has some unique characteristics. First, it is a service export. Second, it requires the consumer to actually visit the country in question. We omit these and other aspects of tourism from the model because they are not central to the questions that we wish to focus on. Moreover, we make no attempt to model other features, such as unemployment, that must be incorporated into any empirical study of the welfare effects of tourism. Rather, our work is intended to outline some important channels whereby tourism affects welfare.

Given our assumptions, we summarise the behaviour of producers and consumers using the trade expenditure function given in equation (1). This function measures the excess of expenditure over income from production. The first derivative of the trade expenditure function with respect to the *i*th price gives the excess demand function for this good (see Neary and Schweinberger, 1985; Anderson and Neary, 1992).

(1) $$E(p_s, p, U) = e(p_s, p, U) - g(p_s, p).$$

National income is given by the GNP function $g(p_s, p)$ where p_s is the price of tourism services and p is a vector of traded goods prices. Without loss of generality, we take one good in the p vector as our *numéraire*. On the demand side, we assume that the economy consists of a single household. This allows us to model consumer behaviour using the expenditure function $e(p_s, p, U)$ where U is a scalar representing welfare. For the moment, we assume that all factors are domestically owned. We relax this assumption in the next section where we allow for foreign investment.

Equation (2) is the budget constraint for this economy where t is a vector of specific trade taxes and subsidies. The trade tax/subsidy for the *i*th good, t_i, is equal to the difference between the domestic and the world price, $(p_i - p_i^*)$ where a * denotes the world price. Import tariffs and export subsidies are positive elements in the t vector while export taxes and import subsidies are negative elements. Trade theorists, for the most part, have devoted their attentions to trade regimes where these elements are positive. This is not surprising given that export taxes and import subsidies are rare. The exception to this, as shown later, is Sub-Saharan Africa.

212 *Lein Lein Chen and John Devereux*

(2) $$E(p_s, p, U) - tE_p = 0.$$

Initially, we ignore quantitative restrictions. Also, we assume that the government redistributes trade tax revenue in lump sum fashion and that tourism is untaxed.[2] The vector of net trades, m, is given by E_p, a vector of derivatives of the trade expenditure function with respect to prices. Note that exports are a negative element in this vector.

This model gives us a simple yet general framework to study the welfare effects of tourism. Following Copeland (1991), we assume that this industry is created by an increase in the world price of tourism.[3] We adopt this assumption purely for convenience. We could also model tourism growth as due to technological progress, factor accumulation or direct foreign investment, all without changing our conclusions.

Totally differentiating equation (2), we obtain equation (3), which gives the welfare effects of an expansion in tourism. Following the trade literature, we define income changes as $dy = e_u dU$ where e_u is the inverse of the marginal utility of income. e_{py} is a vector of marginal propensities to spend on traded goods. If all goods are normal, then the term multiplying dy in equation (3), the inverse of the tariff multiplier, is positive. More generally, this term is positive from stability considerations. Note that E_s, the compensated excess demand function for tourist services, is the first derivative of the trade expenditure function with respect to the price of tourism.

(3) $$dy(1 - te_{py}) = -E_s dp_s^* + tE_{ps} dp_s^*.$$

The first term on the right-hand side of (3) is the external terms of trade effect of tourism growth. This is equal to the volume of exports multiplied by the change in the world price. Holding trade distortions constant, an expansion of tourism will raise welfare. The second term, where E_{ps} is a vector of cross effects in excess demand, is the tourism produced change in trade distortions. Following Jones (1969), we call this the volume of trade effect. This effect is equal to the change in trade tax revenue. The volume of trade effect is positive if tourism increases the importation of goods subject to import tariffs or the export of goods with export taxes. On the other hand, reductions in trade

---

[2] For evidence that tourists are, in fact, lightly taxed in developing economies see Bird (1992).

[3] More precisely, Copeland assumes that tourism expands because of an increase in world demand which, in turn, drives up the price of tourism services.

for goods with export or import subsidies is welfare improving. The sign of the volume of trade effect depends, first, on the relationship between tourism and other goods in compensated excess demand, that is, on whether tourism and the trade-distorted sectors are net substitutes or complements in excess demand. It also depends on the nature of the trade regime, that is, on the sign of the elements in the *t* vector.

Let us begin with the relationship between tourism and other goods in excess demand. On the demand side, most goods are net substitutes for the broad categories of expenditure considered in this paper. On the supply side, we require stronger assumptions to ensure substitutability. The specific factor model, for example, is one model where substitutability holds in supply. More generally, we know from the resource constraint that substitutability holds, on average, in supply for all models. In what follows, we assume substitutability ($E_{is} > 0$). Given our assumptions, the sign of the volume of trade effect is thus determined by the trade instruments used, that is, by the sign of the elements in the *t* vector.

To gain further insight, we examine two special cases. First, we look at a trade regime that uses import tariffs or export subsidies. This corresponds to the situation for most developing economies. Here, the elements of *t* are positive. From equation (3), tourism increases tariff revenue and reduces export subsidy payments given our assumption of substitutability in excess demand. To obtain the intuition for this result, consider the welfare effects of tourism in the specific factors model with tariffs and export subsidies. Here tourism draws labour from importables and exportables, reducing their outputs and thereby raising government revenue. More generally, we conclude that tourism is welfare improving for trade regimes dominated by import tariffs and export subsidies.[4]

The above result, that tourism raises welfare, need not hold for Sub-Saharan type trade regimes with export taxes and import subsidies. Here, some of the elements of *t* are negative as world prices

---

[4] Of course, tourists consume imports directly. Incorporating this into the model strengthens the finding that tourism is welfare improving for tariff/export subsidy trade regimes. Interestingly, writers in the policy literature often worry about the adverse effects of increased imports from tourists. This is incorrect as for most developing economies imports are to be welcomed since they raise welfare by increasing trade tax revenue. This example underlines the importance of considering tourism in a general equilibrium setting.

214 *Lein Lein Chen and John Devereux*

exceed domestic prices. For simplicity, let us assume that all the elements of *t* are negative. From equation (3), observe that the volume of trade effect reduces welfare for this trade regime. Consider, for example, the effects of tourism in the specific factors model with export taxes. The terms of trade effect of tourism increases welfare. But as tourism draws labour from the export sectors, it worsens trade distortions and lowers trade tax revenue. For this case, the terms of trade and the volume of trade effect work in opposite directions. Consequently, the welfare effects of tourism are ambiguous. From equation (3) note that tourism is most likely to reduce welfare where export taxes are high and the initial volume of tourism exports is low.

Up to now, we have ignored quotas. In many developing economies, and in Sub-Saharan Africa in particular, quantitative restrictions are more important than tariffs. The question naturally arises as to whether our results hold with quantitative restrictions. Details of the quota case are given in the appendix. There, we show that *all* of our results go through if, as we have assumed, substitutability holds in compensated excess demand. But, as explained later, quotas do change how we measure trade regimes.

To conclude this section, we provide some African data to illustrate our earlier arguments.

Table 1 gives data on tourism exports as well as our estimates of export taxes for selected Sub-Saharan economies. The tourism data comes from the World Tourism Organisation. We estimate export taxes by comparing the prices received by producers with those on world markets. This gives us an estimate of the differences between domestic and border prices that takes into account explicit export taxes, multiple exchange rates and the activities of state marketing boards. These estimates are crude. They overstate export taxation in that they omit transport and marketing costs.[5] We measure domestic price as the simple average of the main export goods. More properly, this should be measured as a weighted average of domestic prices. Unfortunately, data on export shares are not available for all countries. The estimates are useful in that they give an indication of the magnitudes involved. Export taxes have long characterised Sub-Saharan Africa. As Table 1 shows, these taxes are high indeed. Domestic prices averaged only

---

[5] Although our estimates of export taxation refer to 1990, data from the World Bank (1994) suggest that not much has changed since then.

Table 1: *Tourism and Export Taxation in Sub-Saharan Africa for 1990*

Country	Tourism Exports as a Percentage of Merchandise Exports	Farm Prices as a Percentage of World Prices
Benin	30	59
Burkina Faso	5	56
Chad	6	55
Ethiopia	9	65
Gambia	42	76
Ghana	11	40
Kenya	45	69
Madagascar	12	30
Mali	14	64
Rwanda	9	51
Senegal	21	64
Sierra Leone	14	63
Tanzania	21	22
Togo	19	53
Uganda	7	23

Sources and Methods: Data on tourism and merchandise exports were obtained from the World Tourism Organisation (1994) and the World Bank's *World Development Report* respectively. Our estimates of the ratio of farm to world prices comes from the World Bank (1992, Table 8.2). To obtain these figures we took a simple average of the ratio of farm to world prices for all reported commodities. In each case, we used data for 1990 or the nearest available year.

about 20% of world prices in Tanzania and Uganda. In addition, African governments use import subsidies through multiple exchange rates, government purchasing agencies etc.

The widespread use of quotas increases the likelihood of immis-erisation. In the applied trade literature, the protection obtained by an industry is calculated by first converting quotas into their tariff equivalents. This estimate is then added to nominal tariffs to obtain overall nominal protection. For the purposes of this paper, this procedure is incorrect. Recall that the effects of the trade regime is determined by the sign of the elements of t. As shown in the appendix, the elements of t are trade taxes/subsidies *on those goods that are not subject to quotas*. In the presence of quotas, only trade taxes or subsidies on other

216 *Lein Lein Chen and John Devereux*

goods matter. Once a good is subject to a binding quota, then the tariff on that good serves solely to redistribute rent domestically and has no allocative effects (see Anderson and Neary, 1992).

This result is important as traditionally Sub-Saharan economies combine import quotas with tariffs on most goods. With quantitative restrictions, it is quite likely that the *t* vectors for many Sub-Saharan economies are dominated by negative elements even if their nominal tariffs are high. This means that we classify an economy with export taxes and high tariffs with quotas on most imports as an export tax regime.

The relative importance of tourism and export taxes varies across African economies. Some countries, e.g., Tanzania, combine large tourist sectors with high export taxes. The probability of immiserisation is greatest, however, when export taxes are high and initial tourism exports are low. Ghana, Madagascar and Uganda fall into this category. To obtain the welfare effects of tourism requires much more work. However, Table 1 points to the possibility of tourist immiserisation for certain economies.

Finally, African economies, reacting to pressure from international organisations, have reduced import restrictions in recent years, often without much change in export taxes. This further increases the likelihood of tourist immiserisation.

Theoretically, the finding that tourism could immiserise is not surprising. After all, the possibility that growth in one industry could potentially reduce welfare is well known (see Johnson, 1967; Bhagwati, 1973). It is not so widely known, however, that export taxes or import subsidies increase the likelihood of such immiserisation.[6] Immiserisation is a possibility for tourism in Sub-Saharan Africa. While the possibility of immiserising growth is widely acknowledged, there seems to be few attempts to identify those industries where it can occur.

3. Tourism Exports, Direct Foreign Investment and Welfare

In this section, we take a closer look at how foreign investment affects the benefits from tourism. Foreign investment is an ever-present

---

[6] In a two sector Heckscher-Ohlin model, Kemp (1968) concluded that an improvement in the external terms of trade increases welfare with a tariff or an export tax. See also Woodland (1982, ch. 9), Lahiri and Ono (1989) and Michael (1992).

feature of this industry in developing economies. In Sub-Saharan Africa, foreign firms or nationals own hotels and tourism facilities. Indeed, for many African economies tourism is best seen as an enclave sector separated from the rest of the economy. This creates controversy in that the benefits of tourism are seen by many Africans as accruing to foreign nationals. Moreover, the argument that foreign investment may reduce the benefits of tourism for the host economy has already received theoretical support from Copeland (1991), albeit for econom- ies with market power. By contrast, we argue that foreign investment increases the benefits of tourism exports to the host economy.

We proceed in two steps. First, we ask if foreign investment changes any of the results of the previous section. We conclude that it does not. Finally, we look at the effects of foreign investment for economies with market power.

3.1 Tourism and Welfare with Direct Foreign Investment

To model direct foreign investment in tourism, we take a long-run perspective in that we assume that there is a perfectly elastic supply of foreign capital to tourism at the world rate of return r^*. We divide the total capital stock in tourism, k, into a fixed endowment owned by domestic nationals, $\bar{k}$, and that owned by non-nationals, k^*. For convenience, we ignore quantitative restrictions.

Equation (4) gives the income equal to expenditure condition for this economy.

(4) $E(p_s,p,U, V) + r^*k^* - tE_p = 0.$

The question of whether foreign capital flows increase the gains from tourism is closely related to the literature on the effects of foreign investment with trade distortions started by Bhagwati (1973) and Brecher and Diaz-Alejandro (1977). This work concentrates on capital flows due to trade policy. Such flows, in general, reduce welfare (Neary, 1988; Neary and Ruane, 1988). Note that in our model tourism growth is identical to an improvement in the external terms of trade. Except for Michael (1992), there is no corresponding literature on capital movements due to changes in the external terms of trade.

We use this model to consider the effects of tourism with capital mobility for a small trade-distorted economy. Copeland (1991), by con- trast, looks at the effects of tourism with foreign ownership of tourism

218 *Lein Lein Chen and John Devereux*

facilities for a large economy without trade taxes. This is considered in the next section. Again, we assume that an increase in the world price creates tourism.

Totally differentiating equation (4) we obtain:

(5) $$dy(1 - te_{py}) = -E_s dp_s{}^* + tE_{ps}dp_s{}^* + tg_{pk}dk.$$

With capital mobility, the volume of trade effect is determined by the capital intensity of the protected sectors, as measured by the vector of generalised Rybcynzski terms, g_{pk}, as well as on the cross effects in excess supply discussed earlier. Intuitively, the third term arises as the inflow of foreign capital to tourism changes the outputs of other industries through general equilibrium effects in supply. Since there is no presumption as to the sign of the elements in g_{pk}, this effect cannot be signed. This is a disturbing result as it seems to imply that the welfare effects of tourism are uncertain for all trade regimes once we allow for direct foreign investment.

Fortunately, this conclusion is too pessimistic. To show this, we need a further tool, the variable factor supply revenue function (henceforth the VFS revenue function) given in equation (6). Neary (1985) introduces this function and explores its properties. The VFS revenue function measures national income less payments to capital. It has the standard properties of a revenue function. In particular, its derivative with respect to an output price is the supply function of the good in question.

(6) $$g(p_s,p,r) = \text{Max } g(p_s,p) - rk.$$

This function gives us an alternative way to present the budget constraint, given by equation (7). We denote the variable factor supply trade expenditure function (henceforth the VFS trade expenditure function) by a ~.

(7) $$\widetilde{E}(p_s,p,r,U) - r\overline{k} - t\widetilde{E}_p = 0.$$

Re-writing (5) using the VFS trade expenditure function, we obtain:

(8) $$dy(1 - te_{py}) = -\widetilde{E}sdp_s{}^* + t\widetilde{E}_{ps}dps^*.$$

Comparing equation (8) with equation (3), which gives the effects of an expansion of tourism without foreign investment, we see that our previous results continue to apply *so long as substitutability or complementarity is defined in terms of the variable factor supply revenue function.*[7] Capital mobility does not alter the fact that goods are, on average, substitutes in excess supply. Therefore, foreign investment does not change our finding that tourism increases welfare with import restrictions or export subsidies while its effects with export taxes or import subsidies are uncertain.[8] Note that this implies that foreign investment in tourism can reduce welfare for economies with export taxes and import subsidies such as is the case in many Sub-Saharan economies.

3.2 The Large Economy Case

So far, we have confined our attention to price-taking economies. Copeland (1991) claims that capital inflows reduce the welfare gains from tourism for an economy with market power in tourism and no trade restrictions. We doubt if there are many African economies with significant market power in tourism. Nonetheless, we take a closer look at his argument because it allows us to clarify the channels through which direct foreign investment in tourism affects welfare.

Following Copeland, we consider the welfare effects of an exogenous increase in tourism demand for a large economy without trade distortions.[9] The foreign demand for tourism services is $E_s^*(p_s,v)$ where v is an exogenous shift factor. Equation (9) is the market clearing condition for tourism. An increase in demand increases the price of tourism.

(9) $E_s^* + E_s = 0.$

The impact of an increase in the foreign demand for tourism on welfare is given by equation (10).

(10) $dy = -E_s dp_s^*.$

---

[7] We have assumed that substitutability always holds. More generally, there is nothing to prevent individual goods that are substitutes in excess demand with fixed factor supplies becoming complements with factor mobility and vice versa.

[8] Michael (1992) concluded that capital flows accompanying changes in the external terms of trade are always beneficial. Our results, by contrast, show that capital inflows can immiserise for trade regimes where export taxes or import subsidies dominate.

[9] Copeland (1991) also shows that an expansion in tourism due to an increase in demand can reduce welfare where there are fixed stocks of foreign-owned factors. This is best seen as a short-run case.

220 *Lein Lein Chen and John Devereux*

Since there are no distortions in this economy, a rise in tourism demand raises welfare. As Copeland (1991) shows, the magnitude of the welfare gains depend on whether foreign investment is allowed or not. Note that the benefits of tourism exports are given by the volume of exports multiplied by the change in world prices. It turns out that the change in the world price is smaller once we allow direct foreign investment in tourism. To see why, note, from the Le Chatelier principle, that foreign investment increases the elasticity of supply of tourism. (We supply a formal demonstration of this in the appendix.) As a result, a given increase in demand produces a smaller rise in the price of tourism. This line of reasoning led Copeland to conclude that foreign investment reduced the gains from tourism.

There is a flaw in Copeland's argument: it is correct only for infinitesimal changes. For discrete changes, foreign investment has ambiguous effects on the welfare gains from tourism. Moreover, foreign investment increases the gains from tourism for price-taking economies. To show how we reach these conclusions, assume that the domestic consumption of tourism services is zero. For this case, the welfare gains from tourism are proportional to the increase in national income due to tourism. The change in income is given by

$$\Delta y = \tilde{g}(p_s^2, p, r) - \tilde{g}(p_s^1, p, r)$$

where p_s^1 is that world price of tourism when exports are zero and p_s^2 is the current price of tourism. Taking a Taylor series approximation to the variable factor supply function at p_s^2 and simplifying, we obtain (11):

(11) $$\Delta y \approx \tilde{g}_s \Delta p_s^* + \tfrac{1}{2}\tilde{g}_{ss}(\Delta p_s^*).$$

For discrete changes, the welfare gains from tourism are thus equal to the volume of exports multiplied by the world price change, considered by Copeland (1991), *plus* the intramarginal gains from tourism, which he ignores. We have seen that foreign investment reduces the magnitude of the first term. On the other hand, foreign investment raises the intramarginal gains from tourism since it increases the price responsiveness of tourism supply, g_{ss}. Copeland ignores this effect. The overall effects of foreign investment on the gains from tourism for a large economy are thus uncertain. Note, however, from (11), that foreign investment must increase the gains from tourism for price-taking economies. This, we suspect, is the relevant case for most

Figure 1: *Capital Mobility and the Welfare Effects of Tourism*

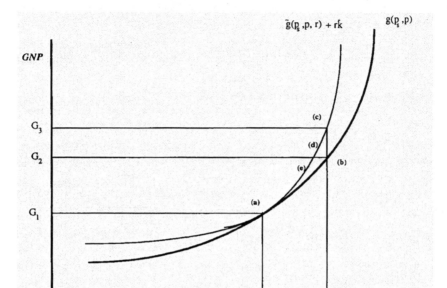

developing economies. We conclude that direct foreign investment increases the benefits of tourism.

We can clarify our discussion with a diagram. Figure 1 shows the relationship between GNP, as given by the revenue function, and the world price of tourism. Recall that the GNP function is convex in prices. We look at the case, considered formally in the appendix, where GNP is the same at p_s^1 with and without direct foreign investment. From the properties of the revenue function, we know that revenue with foreign investment exceeds that without foreign investment except at (a), where, by construction, they are tangent.

Consider a price-taking economy. With foreign investment, an increase in the world price of tourism from p_s^1 to p_s^2 increases GNP to (c). The increase in income is greater than for the case where capital is immobile, given by (b). Foreign investment in tourism is thus welfare improving for small economies holding trade distortions constant.

Consider next the large economy case. We again assume that the

222 *Lein Lein Chen and John Devereux*

world price increases from p_s^1 to p_s^2 without foreign investment. In this case, income increases from (a) to (b). Now let us allow for foreign investment in tourism. We know from our previous discussion that the Copeland case occurs if the economy finds itself at a point such as (e) where the gains from factor mobility are outweighed by the smaller rise in external prices. But this result is not inevitable, as the economy could find itself at a point such as (d) where income has increased more. By concentrating on small changes, Copeland missed this possibility completely.

Moreover, we are skeptical of the policy relevance of Copeland's (1991) arguments. First, we doubt whether many African economies, except perhaps Kenya and South Africa, have market power in tourism. Furthermore, even if foreign investment reduced the benefits of tourism for large economies, it still does not follow that we should discourage foreign investment. After all, the first best response to market power in tourism is to tax tourism exports. With such a tax in place, capital mobility must increase the gains from tourism. Thus, Copeland's (1991) is an argument for taxing tourism exports but not for restricting foreign investment in the industry.

4. Concluding Comments

We began this paper by asking whether tourism exports are welfare improving for developing economies in general and for Sub-Saharan economies in particular. For most developing economies, our theoretical answer to this question is a qualified 'yes' as tourism increases welfare with import restrictions and export subsidies. Moreover, we show that this result holds with quantitative restrictions and foreign investment in tourism. There are, however, circumstances where tourists may reduce welfare that warrant attention for Sub-Saharan Africa. Welfare reduction occurs when tourism worsens the trade distortions associated with export restrictions and import subsidies that dominate the trade regimes of these economies. Thus, it is by no means clear that tourists are a boon to Africa with current trade regimes.

The contribution of tourism to welfare for Sub-Saharan Africa therefore awaits empirical research. Such work will have to incorporate many features of Sub-Saharan economies, such as unemployment, that we ignore in this paper. Our goal is to provide a theoretical discussion of some important channels through which tourism affects welfare. As such, our results should be seen as a first step towards an empirical investigation of tourism. Finally, the reader should note that the result that tourists could in certain circumstances reduce welfare for certain Sub-Saharan economies is not an argument against the tourism industry. Rather, it suggests that the removal of export taxes and import subsidies should be a priority for policy-makers in African economies.

References

Alam, M.S. (1981) 'Welfare Implications of Growth under Quotas', *Economic Letters*, 8: 177–80.

Anderson, J. and J.P. Neary (1992) 'Trade Reform with Quotas, Partial Rent Retention and Tariffs', *Econometrica*, 60: 57–76.

Bhagwati, J. (1973) 'The Theory of Immiserizing Growth: Further Applications', in M. Connolly and A. Swoboda (eds) *International Trade and Money*, Toronto: University of Toronto Press.

Bird, R.M. (1992) 'Taxing Tourism in Developing Economies', *World Development*, 20: 1145–59.

Brecher, R.A. and C.F. Diaz-Alejandro (1977) 'Tariffs Foreign Capital and Immiserizing Growth', *Journal of International Economics*, 7: 317–22.

Copeland, B. (1991) 'Tourism, Welfare and De-industrialization in a Small Open Economy', *Economica*, 58: 515–30.

Falvey, R. (1988) 'Tariffs, Quotas and Piecemeal Policy Reform', *Journal of International Economics*, 25: 177–88.

Fukushima, T. (1981) 'A Dynamic Policy Adjustment Process in a Small Open Economy, and Welfare Effects of Tariff Changes', *Journal of International Economics*, 11: 513–29.

Johnson, H. (1967) 'The Possibility of Income Losses from Increased Efficiency or Factor Accumulation in the Presence of Tariffs', *The Economic Journal*, 151–4.

Jones, R.W. (1969) 'Tariffs and Trade in General Equilibrium', *American Economic Review*, 59: 418–24.

Kemp, M. (1968) 'Some Issues in the Analysis of Trade Gain', *Oxford Economic Papers*, 20: 149–61.

Lahiri, S. and Y. Ono (1989) 'Terms of Trade and Welfare: A General Analysis', *Economic Record*, 65: 27–32.

Mathieson, A. and G. Wall (1982) *Tourism: Economic, Physical, and Social Impacts*, Longman.

Michael, M. (1992) 'International Factor Mobility, Non-traded Goods,

Tariffs and the Terms of Trade', *Canadian Journal of Economics*, 25: 493–9.

Neary, J.P. (1985) 'International Factor Mobility, Minimum Wage Rates and Factor Price Equalization: a Synthesis', *Quarterly Journal of Economics*, 3: 551–70.

Neary, J.P. (1988) 'Tariffs, Quotas and Voluntary Export Restraints With and Without Internationally Mobile Capital', *Canadian Journal of Economics*, 31: 714–35.

Neary J.P. and F. Ruane (1988) 'International Capital Mobility, Shadow Prices and the Cost of Protection', *International Economic Review*, 29: 571–85.

Neary, J.P. and A. Schweinberger (1985) 'Factor Content Functions and the Theory of International Trade', *Review of Economic Studies*, 23: 421–32.

Pearse, D. (1989) *Tourism Development*, Longman.

Woodland, A. (1982) *International Trade and Resource Allocation*, Amsterdam: North Holland.

World Bank (1992) *African Development Indicators*, Washington DC: World Bank.

World Bank (1994) *Adjustment in Africa, Reforms, Results and the Road Ahead*, Washington DC: World Bank.

World Tourism Organisation (1994) *Yearbook of Tourism Statistics*, Madrid: World Tourism Organisation.

Appendix: Tourism and Welfare with Quantitative Restrictions and Direct Foreign Investment

The Quota Case

Let us assume that some goods are subject to trade taxes/subsidies while others face quantitative restrictions. For future reference, recall that the domestic price of each good protected by a quota is endogenous as this good is, at the margin, non-traded. Finally, we assume that quotas are auctioned off competitively and that the proceeds are returned to the private sector in a lump sum fashion.[10]

With quantitative restrictions, the income equal to expenditure condition is given by (1a). Note that p_Q is a vector of domestic prices of goods subject to

[10] Consequently, we ignore cases where there is less than full rent retention. This is considered by Anderson and Neary (1992).

quantitative restrictions and E_Q is a vector of derivatives of the trade expenditure function with respect to these prices. We interpret p and E_p as vectors of prices and net trades of those goods that are free from quantitative restrictions. In practice, of course, most goods subject to trade taxes/subsidies are also subject to quotas. Note that these goods are in the p_Q vector. As mentioned earlier, this has important practical implications. Finally, $(p_Q - p_Q^*)$ is a vector of implicit protection levels or quota premia. We assume that quotas are always binding.

(1a) $E(p_s, p, p_Q, U) - tE_p - (p_Q - p_Q^*)E_Q = 0.$

First, let us consider the case where all trade interventions are by quotas. Totally differentiating equation (1a), and using the assumption that trade taxes/subsidies are zero, we obtain equation (2a) where $\overline{m}$ is a vector of quantitative restrictions. The second term on the right-hand side of this expression is, by assumption, zero since quotas are constant. Consequently, the volume of trade effect vanishes and tourism is welfare improving through the external terms of trade effect.

   This result is an example of Alam's (1981) finding that immiserising growth cannot occur with a quota. Intuitively, welfare must increase in this case because quotas make restricted goods nontraded at the margin so neutralising the volume of trade effect and hence ensuring immiserisation is impossible.

(2a) $dy = - E_s dp_s^* + (p_Q - p_Q^*)d\overline{m}.$

   Equation (3a) gives the welfare effects of tourism for the more general case where quantitative restrictions and trade taxes/subsidies are used.

(3a) $dy(1 - te_{py}) = - E_s dp_s^* + tE_{ps}dp_s^* + tE_{pQ}dp_Q.$

The first term on the right hand side of equation (3a) is the terms of trade effect while the second and third terms give the volume of trade effect. The latter now consists of a direct effect working through substitution in excess demand and an indirect effect working through induced changes in the prices of quota constrained goods. The sign of the indirect effect is determined by the nature of trade interventions, that is, by the sign of the elements in the t vector, and by whether the prices of quota constrained goods increase or fall. Should these prices increase, together with the reliance on tariffs and export subsidies, then the more likely it is that the indirect volume of trade effect is welfare increasing. Recall, however, that the t vector consists of taxes/subsidies on those goods not covered by quotas.

   To solve for changes in the prices of quota constrained goods, we use the fact that net trade in these goods is given by equation (4a).

(4a) $\overline{m} = E_Q.$

Totally differentiating equation (4a), we obtain equation (5a) where E_{QQ} and

226 *Lein Lein Chen and John Devereux*

E_{Qs} are a matrix and a vector respectively of compensated substitution terms in excess demand. Note that our assumptions of substitutability ensure that E_{QQ}^{-1} is negative definite and that E_{Qs} is positive.

(5a) $$dp_Q = - E_{QQ}^{-1}E_{Qs}dp_s^* - E_{QQ}^{-1}e_{Qy}dy.$$

Using equations (3a) and (5a), we obtain equation (6a), which gives the effects of an increase in tourism on welfare where μ is the inverse of the tariff multiplier.[11] Given our assumptions, income increases if the elements in t are positive. Also from equation (5a), observe that tourism also raises the prices of quota constrained goods for this case.

(6a) $$\mu dy = - E_s dp_s^* + tE_{ps}dp_s^* - tE_{pQ}E_{QQ}^{-1}E_{Qs}dp_s^*$$

where

$$\mu = (1 - t(e_{py} - E_{pQ}E_{QQ}^{-1}e_{Qy})) > 0.$$

More generally, it can be verified from equation (6a) that *all* our earlier results go through if, as we have assumed, substitutability holds in compensated excess demand. Thus, in a fundamental sense, adding quantitative restrictions to the model does not change our earlier results.

Direct Foreign Investment and the Elasticity of Supply of Tourism

To determine the effects of foreign investment on $\tilde{g}_{ss}$, we compare two economies, identical in all respects except that foreign investment is allowed for one but not for the other. Initially, we assume that no foreign capital is used in tourism in either economy. This implies that:

(7a) $$\tilde{g}_s(p_s,p,r) = g_s(p_s,p).$$

Totally differentiating equation (7a) with respect to p_s and using the fact that $r = g_k$ where g_k is a vector of derivatives of the revenue function with respect to capital stocks, we obtain equation (8a), which relates the slope of the supply function for tourism without foreign investment, g_{ss}, to that with capital mobility, $\tilde{g}_{ss}$.[12]

(8a) $$\tilde{g}_{ss} = g_{ss} - g_{sk}g_{kk}^{-1}g_{ks}.$$

In equation (8a) g_{sk} is a vector of generalised Rybncznski terms for tourist services with respect to capital. The sign of each element in this vector is deter-

---

[11] Falvey (1988) refers to μ as the marginal propensity to spend evaluated at shadow prices. Fukushima (1981) has shown that it is positive from stability considerations.

[12] This result is due to Neary (1985).

mined by factor intensities. Note that g_{kk}^{-1} is a negative definite matrix and that $g_{sk} = g_{ks}$ from the symmetry of the cross partials of the revenue function. This ensures that the second term on the right-hand side of equation (8a) is positive which, in turn, ensures that supply is more elastic.

[21]

World Development, Vol. 11, No. 2, pp. 141–152, 1983.
Printed in Great Britain.

0305–750X/83/020141–12$03.00/0
© 1983 Pergamon Press Ltd.

Appropriate Policies Towards Multinational Hotel Corporations in Developing Countries

MATTHEW McQUEEN*
University of Reading

Summary. – Despite the prevalence of international hotel chains in the tourism sector of developing countries, little research has been carried out on the structure of the industry, the sources of the competitive advantages of the hotel chains over indigenous hotels, reasons for the alternative forms of involvement of the hotel chains and deriving from this, their potential and actual impact on host countries. This article applies theories developed for the multinational enterprise in the manufacturing sector, to original data and observations on the international hotel industry. Given the state of the art and the limited information on the impact of MNE hotels, the paper is principally concerned with generating potentially useful hypotheses for consideration by host governments and to provide a framework for further research. Certain policy conclusions however, are drawn from the analysis, especially regarding the appropriate form of involvement by the international hotels.

1. INTRODUCTION

International tourism experienced a period of very rapid growth during the period 1960–1973 and even during the subsequent periods of reduced growth of national income in the principal tourist generating countries, it showed a remarkable resiliance. Income elasticities of demand for tourism are high[1] and therefore, in the absence of a prolonged world recession, offer possibilities for growth. One important characteristic of the industry is its dependence on foreign enterprises. In the case of group inclusive tours, the market is largely controlled by tour operators (wholesalers) in the relevant tourist generating countries, while for many developing countries, the successful operation of leisure and business tourism will also largely depend, for the foreseeable future, on a substantial degree of foreign participation both as carriers and in the hotel sector. The degree of success of the international tourism sector both in its growth rate and in its ability to contribute towards the attainment of host country policy objectives, will therefore, to a significant extent, depend upon state policies toward foreign tourist enterprises. The high degree of flexibility of operations between countries of international tour operators and airlines, creates particular difficulties for control by individual developing countries and would probably require regional coordination between host countries. The characteristics of the international hotel industry, however, offer potentially greater possibilities for individual host governments to determine the extent and form of involvement (and therefore the impact) of foreign multinational enterprises (MNEs).

The impact of MNEs normally arises from the amount and type of resources transferred and its degree of control over decisions regarding these and local resources. The impact of MNEs is usually related to host country policy objectives through specific questions, such as the extent to which local value-added (and its distribution between capital and labour), or technological capacity, is affected by the presence of the MNE. This impact in turn depends upon structural variables, such as the form of involvement, the size and the extent of vertical integration of the MNE, as well as home and host country specific factors. This paper therefore proceeds by outlining the structural characteristics of the industry, applies theories[2] of international production to identify the potential competitive advantages of MNEs over indigenous hotel chains and relates this to a small sample of survey data. From this analysis, certain policy conclusions are drawn, particularly regarding the appropriate forms of involvement by international hotel chains and the evolution of host country policy towards MNE hotels.

_____
* I am grateful to Professor John H. Dunning, Department of Economics, University of Reading for information and helpful comment on a draft of this article.

Table 1. *Distribution of transnational corporation-associated hotels abroad by main activity of parent group, 1978*

	Number of transnational corporations	Transnational-associated hotels abroad		In developed market economies		In developing economies	
		Number	%	Number	%	Number	%
Hotel chains associated with airlines	16	277	27.1	113	21.0	164	33.7
Hotel chains independent of airlines	56	687	67.0	384	71.2	303	62.4
Hotel development and management consultants	3	15	1.5	1	0.2	14	2.9
Tour operators and travel agents	6	46	4.5	41	7.6	5	1.0
Total	81	1025	100.0	539	100.0	486	100.0

Source: Survey data.

2. THE STRUCTURAL CHARACTERISTICS OF THE INTERNATIONAL HOTEL INDUSTRY

The international hotel industry is characterized by a sometimes quite complex web of relationships covering arm's-length contracts between individual hotels and a marketing and reservation system, with the hotel listed under the name of the reservation system, through to wholly-owned affiliates of vertically integrated MNEs, with an individual hotel sometimes being associated with more than one international hotel chain under different forms of contractual agreements. The definition of international involvement used in this paper covers any form of transaction by an enterprise outside its national frontiers in which assets, rights or goods are transferred and where there is some continuing *de facto* control over the use of these and complementary indigenous resources. This definition would therefore exclude the simple referral agreement described above, but would include all forms of association where some form of control over the individual hotels was exercised by the MNE, even though there may be no equity involvement. Secondly, the analysis of the international characteristics of the hotel industry is limited to enterprises which had association with two or more foreign hotels at the end of 1978. The data[3] in this sector was collected from trade publications, questionnaires and field studies and covers 81 MNEs from 22 countries. The data in Sections 3 and 4 were obtained from a smaller sample.[4] At that date these 81 MNEs were associated with 1025 foreign hotels and 270,646 rooms and we believe that these account for at least 95% of all the rooms in all foreign associated hotels and that no important MNE with hotel interests is omitted.

Table 1 classifies the international hotel chains into four groups according to the predominant form of MNE association. First there are 16 hotel chains associated with international airlines, of which the United States accounted for six, France two, United Kingdom one and Japan two hotel chains. The international airline-linked hotels accounted for 34% of all MNE-associated hotels in developing countries and had the greatest proportion (59%) of their hotels located in developing countries of the four main groups of MNEs. Most of the major airlines have tour operating and hotel interests and this would therefore appear to provide them with all the benefits and market power associated with vertical integration.

Closer examination, however, shows a limited degree of vertical integration. For example, British Airways (the largest international airline) has important tour operating subsidiaries but only a very small equity participation in hotels in developing countries. Pan American World Airways, which, until 1981 owned Inter-Continental Hotels (now owned by Grant Metropolitan Hotels, UK), has only a very small and indirect interest in tour operations in developing countries. Also, even though in 1978 Inter-Continental Hotels had (along with Holiday Inns) the largest number of MNE-associated hotels located in developing countries, only a minority of these hotels were developed as part of the parent airline company's policy of expansion and for the most part ICH has been operated as an independent profit centre providing an income to partly offset the recurrent financial difficulties of the airline. Similarly, although Trans World Airlines (TWA) own Hilton International (the third largest international hotel chain), the majority of the hotels are located in countries not served by TWA. Thus, of the largest international airlines only Air France would appear to maintain a close integration with its associated hotels in developing countries through the wholly-owned affiliate, Societe des Hôtels Méridien. Secondly, there are the hotel chains not directly associated with airlines (except possibly in some cases through a small minority equity investment, loan capital or referral system) and which are the major group of MNEs. Third are the specialist hotel development and management consultants (as distinct from the other two groups which, in addition to operating hotels, also provide consultancy services) whose involvement has tended to diminish in recent years. The fourth group of MNEs involved in the hotel business are the tour operators, all European-based and largely operating hotels in the developed Mediterranean countries.

Table 2 provides details of the geographical distribution of hotels and hotel rooms by the nationality of the MNEs involved. It is interesting to note that with the exception of the UK and 'other European countries', more than half the foreign associated hotels of the MNEs are located in the developing countries. Also, the geographical distribution of MNE hotels is similar to that for overall foreign direct investment in developing countries, with the United States being comparatively well represented in South-East Asia and Latin America, France in Francophone Africa, Japan in South-East Asia and the United Kingdom in Africa and the Caribbean. The relationship between the distribution of foreign direct investment and the MNE hotels partly reflects common economic, political and cultural determinants and partly the fact that these hotel chains have a competitive advantage in providing accommodation and ancillary facilities for business travel (analysed in Section 3). The importance of this latter factor is emphasized by the rapid growth of MNE-associated hotels in the Middle East.

The relative importance of MNE-associated hotels in host developing countries has been estimated in Table 3. These proportions should, however, be interpreted with care. For example, in the case of Tunisia our survey data shows that in 1978 there were just over 3000 rooms in hotels associated with MNEs. The World Tourism Organization's statistics show that there were just under 3000 rooms in hotels of four-star category and over, and the percentage share is therefore shown as 100%. In fact we know from field study data that a significant proportion of the 3000 MNE-associated rooms are in the three-star category and therefore this column shows the most appropriate percentage share. Conversely it seems probable that in most of the other countries listed, MNEs are only associated with hotels in the four-star category or higher. From this data it would appear likely that at least half or more of the international class hotels in developing countries have some form of foreign control over their operation. Analysis of foreign participation ratios for both developed and developing countries also suggests that the larger the absolute size of the hotel industry in a country, the lower the foreign participation ratio is likely to be. Closer inspection of the data also suggests that the foreign participation ratio is likely to be higher in countries in which hotels are concentrated in cities rather than in resort areas, principally because MNE hotels are more likely to be involved in business rather than leisure tourism.

Multinational corporations become associated with and exercise control over hotels in four possible ways: ownership of the equity, management contracts, franchise arrangements which include supervision by the MNE, and leasing arrangements. The relative importance of these forms of relationship vary over time and between countries. In the period up to the mid 1970s, one-quarter of the MNE associated hotels in the developing countries were owned or part-owned and managed by the hotel chain, with a further 20% associated under leasing arrangements. From 1975 onwards the preferred form of involvement in developing countries has shifted strongly towards management contracts with little or no equity participation. To a limited extent this shift over time in the form of involvement has also occurred in the developed countries but the contrast is still marked. In Europe, MNEs have equity participation in about half of all affiliated hotels while in most developing countries the corresponding proportion is under one-fifth and in the Middle East, less than 5%. Conversely, over 2% of European hotels are associated through management contracts compared to 75% in the Middle East, 72% in Africa, 60% in Asia and 47% in Latin America. In the majority of cases this contrast simply reflects the fact that governments in developing countries often oppose majority equity investments by foreign companies and that capital (either from local private investors, governments or international agencies), is readily available for such projects. Conversely MNEs may regard such investment as risky because they lack adequate knowledge of local laws, social and political conditions (relative to local investors) as well as fears of expropriation. From the point of view of the developing countries, however, these alternative

Table 2. *Distribution by country of origin of transnational corporation-associated hotels and rooms in main host regions, 1978 (percentages)*

| | | | | | | Home countries | | | | | | | | | | | |
| Host regions | United States | | France | | United Kingdom | | Other Europe | | Japan | | Other developed market economies | | Developing countries | | All countries | |
	H	R	H	R	H	R	H	R	H	R	H	R	H	R	H	R
North America	19.1	14.7	0.6	1.7	4.7	7.4	26.1	29.0	26.1	28.3	3.1	6.6	2.7	3.8	13.4	13.0
Europe	26.6	26.2	40.4	45.6	70.5	73.5	56.8	57.4	8.7	11.9	13.9	27.0	2.7	2.9	35.6	35.3
Middle East	8.5	8.0	6.4	6.7	2.0	1.0	–	–	–	–	6.2	9.5	8.1	4.6	6.2	6.0
Africa	5.5	5.3	30.1	26.8	11.4	8.7	5.7	5.5	–	–	12.3	11.3	8.1	6.7	10.5	8.6
Asia	13.4	19.1	–	–	0.7	0.5	–	–	47.8	48.5	1.5	1.9	37.8	50.3	9.3	14.5
Oceania	3.2	2.7	2.6	2.5	–	–	–	–	–	–	47.7	27.9	5.4	3.3	5.6	3.5
Latin America	13.2	13.8	8.3	7.2	1.3	1.0	7.0	7.2	17.4	11.3	3.1	2.1	27.0	17.6	9.9	10.1
Caribbean and W.A.I.	10.6	10.3	11.6	9.5	9.4	8.0	2.3	1.0	–	–	12.3	13.6	8.1	10.8	9.7	9.0
	100.0	100.0	100.0	100.0	100.0	100.0	100.0	100.0	100.0	100.0	100.0	100.0	100.0	100.0	100.0	100.0
Developed market economies	49.5	47.0	41.0	47.3	76.5	81.0	83.0	86.4	43.5	40.0	41.5	48.2	5.4	6.7	52.6	52.5
Developing countries	50.6	53.0	59.0	52.7	23.5	18.2	17.0	13.6	56.5	60.0	58.5	51.8	94.6	93.3	47.4	47.5

Source: Hotel directories and field data.

Note: H = hotels; R = hotel rooms.

Table 3. *Share of MNE-associated hotel rooms in total hotel rooms in selected developing countries by category, 1978*

		% Share of total rooms 4* category and over	3* category and over
	5* category		
Africa			
Cameroon	–	100	56
Kenya	100	40	31
Senegal	100	79	55
Tunisia	100	100	24
Asia and the Pacific			
French Polynesia			
(Tahiti)	100	75	46
Rep. of Korea	89	50	36
New Caledonia	–	100	88
Pakistan	100	78	48
Philippines	74	55	49
Singapore	45	37	35
Middle East			
Egypt	100	63	46
Jordan	100	73	43
Syria	100	84	55

Source: Survey data; and WTO, *Regional Breakdown of World Tourism Statistics 1974–1978* (Madrid: 1980).

forms of involvement by MNEs are important since we would expect them to be associated with different costs and benefits to the host country.

3. THE INVOLVEMENT OF MNE HOTELS IN HOST COUNTRIES: A THEORETICAL FRAMEWORK

In order to formulate policies towards MNE involvement in the hotel sector, it is essential to understand the sources of competitive power of the international hotel chains and the factors determining the preferred form of involvement in the host country.

Industrial organization theory suggests that for enterprises of one nationality to be involved in an industry located in another country, they must possess income-generating assets not available to indigenous firms and of a sufficient magnitude to overcome the inherent advantages which local firms possess in that country (for example, knowledge of local customs, laws and markets). Correspondingly, the potential contribution of MNEs derives from the transfer of these resources to the host country. To evaluate possible sources of the competitive advantages of foreign firms in the hotel industry let us first examine the characteristics of the product supplied by the industry. Essentially it is an 'experience good' (i.e. one whose value to the

consumer cannot be established by visual inspection) rather than a 'search good' (whose attributes can be examined and compared with the advertised claims of the supplier). Second, MNE hotels essentially provide for an internationally mobile clientele who, if acting on their own initiative, might incur substantial transaction costs and risks in identifying and arranging for suitable accommodation in different and probably unfamiliar countries. Our first hypothesis is therefore that the competitive advantages of the MNE hotels is derived from their ability to greatly reduce these transaction costs and risks by producing a 'product' of an appropriate and reliable quality associated with a brand name and which is marketed through an international reservation system.

However, if this were the sole source of the competitive advantage of MNE hotels, then we would predict that the appropriate form of involvement with indigenous hotels would be a referral or franchise agreement, leaving the hotel free to be owned and managed by nationals of the host country. In fact, as we noted in Section 2 (above), expansion in recent years has generally taken the form either of ownership or management contracts, with the latter being the predominant form in developing countries. An important distinguishing feature of foreign involvement through ownership or via a management contract compared to the alternative forms of involvement is that the former enables the MNE to exercise a large degree of *control* over the operation of the hotel. The question then arises as to why the international hotel chains should wish to retain *control* over hotels when standards of quality could be ensured through contracts, reinforced by regular inspection of the hotel, while the quasi-monopoly rents could be extracted in franchise fees.

There are two main reasons why a parent company may wish to exercise control over an associated hotel. One is that the parent enterprise will seek to maximize worldwide profits or growth of the group as a whole and this may not be consistent with the objective of a particular affiliate or associate whose interests are more likely to be directed towards local profits or growth. The second reason lies in the failure of intermediate factor and product markets to function efficiently, forcing the firm to internalize these markets within the organization.

In the case of the international hotel industry, we would predict that a conflict of interests between the MNE and an affiliate is, in most cases, unlikely to be significant enough to warrant global integration. Unlike most exports, international tourism has the peculiar characteristic of being consumed in the exporting and not the importing country. Unless the parent company is in the position of being able to control and direct tourists to specific locations served by the associated hotels, control will not be required to direct intra-group trade in the final product. Vertically integrated tour operators may be in such a position; however, as shown in Table 1, they represent only 1% of all MNE-associated hotels in developing countries. International airline-associated hotels may also be in this position but data on sources of hotel reservations (presented in Section 4) casts doubt on the importance of this factor. Intra-group trade in intermediate products supplied by the central purchasing service of the MNE is another potential reason for central control to be exercised. However, study suggests that in practice this element is of limited importance and in our sample of hotels (see note 4) a relatively small proportion (10–20%) of current purchases and a rather higher proportion (20–60%) of capital goods were obtained through the central purchasing services of the MNE with the higher percentages being recorded for small economies. Furthermore, interviews with hotel managers showed that they had complete autonomy over current purchases and generally a large degree of control over

capital goods purchases, indicating that the MNE was not concerned to direct purchases through the group as a whole. The general reasons given for using the central purchasing unit were the higher cost and lack of availability of local supplies of a suitable quality. The hotel managers interviewed also emphasized that the central purchasing services of the MNE (particularly ones associated with international airlines) were able to search at an international level for supplies and use their bargaining power to obtain supplies of a consistently high quality at very competitive prices. We were unable to test these assertions but they should clearly be considered as part of a calculation of the balance-of-payments effects of international hotel chains.

The market failure which has probably caused the international hotel chains to wish to exercise control over their associated hotels takes two forms. First, although the technology is relatively unsophisticated compared to that of R and D intensive manufactured products of other MNEs, the unique advantage of the international hotel chains fundamentally rests on *knowledge*: knowledge of the market for international travel and knowledge of how to operate a successful hotel chain, both derived from the experience of providing hotel services in the home country of the MNE and in other main tourist generating countries. Knowledge of the market enables the MNE to design a product suitable for the requirements of an international clientele and to differentiate the product from those of its competitors, while catering generally for the upper end of the market. Experience gained from operating in the home market combined with geographical diversification in turn enables the MNE to operate on a superior production function compared to a local hotel in the host country. As with all knowledge, once it has been acquired it can be made available to any newly associated hotel at a much smaller transaction cost than a *de novo* entrant into the hotel industry. Our emphasis on these aspects of knowledge as the sources of the ownership advantages of MNE hotels derives both from the observation of hotel operations and the fact that international hotel chains invest a significant amount of resources in training at the individual hotels, regional centres and at the 'flagship' hotel, and maintain a constant flow of training literature, operations manuals and information on new designs, procedures, techniques and equipment. Admittedly, part of the emphasis on training arises from the size and geographical spread of the hotel chain and the consequent need for additional accounting and control information. However, we would predict that the major return to investment in training is in maintaining the quality of the chain and its distinctive brand image and hence its market share.

Given the central importance of proprietary knowledge, the 'control' route rather than the 'market' route may be explained in terms of what Magee (1977) calls the 'appropriability theory of MNEs'.[5] This theory is derived from the 'appropriability problem' by which we mean the inability of private originators of new ideas to obtain for themselves the social value of the idea. Coase (1960) has pointed out that externalities can be efficiently handled by the market if the legal system clearly establishes property rights.[6] However, legal systems in host countries may not be adequate for the task. We would also argue that in the case of international class hotels, the knowledge is essentially embodied in human capital with enforceable property rights being largely limited to the brand name(s) and trademark of the hotel chain. As we have pointed out, although the knowledge and skills required to successfully operate international class hotels should not be underestimated, the technology is relatively unsophisticated and may, therefore, be copied to a significant extent by competitors. By supplying expertise only through long-term contracts which transfer control over hotel operations to the MNE, by staffing key positions with its own personnel and combining this with a policy of appointing senior management posts only from within the organization (thus 'locking' employees into the organization and reducing the possibility of potential competitors obtaining access to proprietary knowledge through hiring from the MNE), MNE hotels may be able to limit the rate of diffusion of knowledge. (Hilton International, for example, states[7] that it is their unalterable policy to promote from within the organization.) A further defensive strategy is suggested by Magee, namely that MNEs may deliberately increase the size and complexity of the technology (i.e. in our case the size and complexity of the individual hotel) as a barrier to entry. It is in this central aspect of the diffusion of knowledge that we would predict that a conflict of interest may arise between the interests of the international hotel chain and the host country, rather than from conflicts which appear in the manufacturing sector arising from the sourcing policies, restrictive marketing practice and inappropriate technologies of MNEs (although in specific instances these may be important).

A second possible set of reasons why MNEs may wish to exercise control over their affiliated hotel is that, although the technology is not sophisticated, it may, to a significant extent be intangible and thereby difficult to codify completely into instruction manuals. The continued successful operation of a luxury hotel may also require open access to the resources of the group as a whole and not simply the transfer of knowledge by certain key personnel (a synergy effect). As a result of these characteristics of the knowledge created by MNE hotels, its market value to independent hotels will be difficult to quantify and the MNE hotel may therefore experience difficulty in extracting rents through one-period market transactions.

It must be emphasized that these observations should be regarded as generating hypotheses from a first study of the international hotel industry and that they require testing and refinement. However we believe that they are consistent with the structure and operations of the international hotel industry. One further point is that we have been careful to distinguish *ownership* of a hotel from its *control*. It is our understanding of the industry that unlike the resource-based or manufacturing activities of MNEs, these two aspects involve separate sets of decisions, with the ownership of hotels being largely determined by the expected returns from property investment. Some MNE hotels may consider that they have the required skills for such ventures (e.g. Grand Metropolitan Hotels) while others (e.g. Hilton International) may consider that their expertise lies exclusively with hotel operators and leave the ownership of hotels to other local or international investors.

4. SOME ASPECTS OF THE INVOLVEMENT OF MNE-ASSOCIATED HOTELS IN HOST DEVELOPING COUNTRIES

Our data is insufficient to adequately test the hypotheses put forward in Section 3. However we believe that it does shed some light on this under-researched area of study.

It is an axiom of most of the literature on MNEs that to induce them to service a market through overseas production they must possess certain competitive advantages over indigenous producers which more than compensate for the disadvantages of operating in a foreign location. We hypothesized that these advantages took the form of knowledge of markets and knowledge of operating international class hotel chains. As a first step in testing these

Table 4. *Income of hotels classified by selected structural characteristics, 1977*

	Average revenue per hotel room (percentage variation)			
	Rooms* (1)	Food and beverages* (2)	Undistributed expenses[†] (3)	Revenue before fixed charges (4)
1. *Size*				
300–600 rooms compared to 150 rooms or less	+ 19	− 29	− 12	+ 29
2. *Location*				
City compared to resort	0	+ 23	− 14	+ 22
3. *Ownership*				
Chain compared to independent	− 7	+ 66	+ 9	+ 9
4. *Market*				
Holiday tourist compared to other	− 8	− 26	+ 3	− 23
5. *Rating*				
Luxury compared to first class	+ 37	+ 86	+ 37	+ 57

Source: Horwath and Horwath International, *Worldwide Lodging Industry, 1977.*
* Departmental income after deduction of departmental expenses.
† Expenses on administration, marketing, energy, property maintenance and operation.

hypotheses, we sought to determine whether MNE hotels were able to operate with high occupancy rates and/or on a superior production function to locally managed hotels. It is clearly important to standardize the comparison as far as possible and distinguish those effects which reflect the structural characteristics of the hotels such as size, location, market served and class of hotel from those effects which reflect the unique management and operating features of international hotel chains. For example, Table 4 shows that for a sample of 418 hotels average revenue per hotel room was 29% higher for large hotels (whether belonging to chains or independent) compared to small hotels, 57% higher for luxury class hotels compared to first class hotels and 22% higher for hotels located in cities compared to resorts, while hotels catering for leisure tourism recorded average revenue 27% less than other forms of tourism. Thus, in so far as MNE hotels are larger, located in cities catering for business travel and of a luxury class, we would expect them to obtain higher operating profits simply because of these structural characteristics and independent of their multinationality.

In terms of occupancy rates our sample of MNE hotels recorded rates closely grouped around 80% whereas the average for luxury/ first class hotels in South and South-East Asia, Africa and the Middle East,[8] was only a little lower at between 70% to 80%. The general superiority of MNE marketing was also called into question by the fact that in our sample of hotels in developing countries with an established first class hotel sector, only about one-quarter of room reservations came via the MNE reservation system while about 40% of bookings were made either directly by clients or on their behalf by local firms. This suggests that the importance of MNE's marketing and reservation system in attracting guests (a competitive advantage frequently stressed by the MNE hotels) may only be crucial in the initial stage of the development of the international tourism sector and thereafter knowledge of the reputation, efficiency and facilities offered by a hotel become sufficiently general as to reduce the marketing advantage of the MNE.

To test for the relative efficiency of MNE hotel operations compared to local hotels, we examined the gross operating profits (GOP)[9] achieved in hotel operations in relation to sales revenue. In both developed European countries and in developing countries of South and South-East Asia, Africa and the Middle East, our sample of MNE hotels generated profit rates of 33% compared to 25–27% for a sample of 418 MNE-affiliated and non-MNE-affiliated hotels respectively. Value-added as a proportion of gross sales revenue was also higher at 59% compared to 46–51%. Field study reports indicated that this was due to the combined effect of MNE hotels being able to maintain higher house profits (revenue from rooms, food and beverage) as well as operating with lower running costs. It should also be noted that the possibility that MNE-associated hotels may be able to obtain similar occupancy rates to local hotels but with higher room rates is an important qualification to our previous point about the relative importance of the marketing advantage of MNEs.

In terms of the general efficiency and operation of hotels, the field studies indicated important differences between countries with an established international hotel sector such as India, Singapore and Tunisia and lower income countries in Africa with a less well established indigenous hotel sector. For example in one African country, two locally owned and managed international class hotels recorded GOP as a percentage of gross sales revenue of 14 and 15% whereas the two MNE-associated hotels recorded levels of 26 and 28%. Conversely in the case of beach resort hotels in Tunisia, profitability varied considerably but the best financial results were achieved by locally owned and managed hotels rather than MNE-associated hotels (although the least satisfactory results were ·returned by the government-owned and managed hotels).

Our tentative conclusion is that in the initial stages of the development of an international tourism sector, the MNE hotels have a substantial competitive advantage over local hotels but that this competitive advantage is not of long duration. Depending on the initial level of development of the host country and supporting policies from the host government, it appears that knowledge can spread from the original MNE-associated hotels so that over a period of perhaps one or two decades locally owned and managed hotels may become competitive with MNE hotels.

Given the preponderance of the management contract as the most favoured route of MNE involvement in the hotel sector, it is important for host countries to determine whether, and to what extent, the contract permits the transfer of technology to the host country and on what terms. Our research strongly suggests, however, that such control is rarely exercised by host governments and we know of no systematic research on the content and effects of these contracts. Briefly, the period of the management contract is usually between 10 and 15 years and sometimes gives the MNE the right to renew the agreement for a similar period of time on the same terms and conditions. The contractual terms are typically phrased to authorise the MNE to 'supervise direct and control the management and operation of the hotel and render supervise and control the performance of all services and do or cause to be done all things reasonably necessary for the efficient and proper operation of the hotel'. The extent and form of the management fee varies considerably but it is clearly important to determine what specific services are supplied, whether the fee structure creates incentives for the management company

to meet the objectives of the owners, and whether the fee structure leaves a sufficient residual income to meet all other charges on the hotel. Our study indicates that these conditions are not always met. Thus contracts go into considerable detail regarding charges by the associated MNE for such services as technical consultants and specialized experts, the MNE's international communications networks and reservation facilities, advertising and sales promotion, accounting, sales finance and other system experts. The obligations of the MNE, however, are invariably stated in much more general terms, which in case of dispute could be interpreted in different ways. Further safeguards for the MNE are usually provided for in the agreement by various escape clauses such as provision for the agreement to be terminated if the MNE is prevented from or materially restricted in obtaining foreign currency, or in remitting foreign and local currency out of the host country. The agreement may also be terminated by circumstances constituting *force majeure*. Terms of compensation to the MNE are also laid down for these instances and the appropriate laws may be defined as those of the home country of the MNE.

Management free structures vary considerably both between MNEs and between individual hotels depending on a variety of considerations. For example, where a hotel is owned by the government of the host country the principal concern may be the transfer of technology and know-how by the MNE as well as the efficient operation of the hotel. In this case the MNE will negotiate a substantial basic fee or a combination of basic fee plus an incentive fee based on the profits of the hotel. Where the hotel is privately owned and the owners are concerned solely with the profitability of the enterprise, then the fee may be wholly based on profits. Even in this case the strength of the incentive element will depend upon the structure of the fee, whether it is based on room sales, gross operating profit, total revenue, and how the accounting terms are defined. Clearly considerable knowledge and expertise is involved in the negotiation of these contracts and there therefore exists the possibility of a serious imbalance of bargaining ability between the MNE and the government and local hotel owners in the host developing country.

It is difficult to test this proposition by any single criterion since, as we have indicated, the management fee reflects a variety of local and specific considerations regarding the contribution of the MNE. However, it is instructive to note that in our sample of MNE-associated

Table 5. *Effects of variations in the terms of management contracts*

| Hotel | Potential management fees as % gross operating profits | | | | Actual fee paid |
	MNE A	MNE B	MNE C	MNE D	
I	14	22	15	15	18
II	15	24	15	15	23
III	37	40	20	15	42
IV	80	66	38	15	20

Note: Terms of management contracts were:
MNE A = 5% of GOP + 5% of total revenue
MNE B = 20% of GOP + 6% of invoices
MNE C = 10% of GOP + 5% of room sales
MNE D = 15% of GOP

hotels, the management fee varied between 6 and 15% of gross operating profits in developed countries, with an average of 12%; while in the developing countries it averaged 17% of GOP and in some cases reached 23%. Table 5 illustrates the variation in the costs of retaining an MNE management company by applying the fee structures of four MNE hotel management companies to the accounts of four hotels located in developing countries. Clearly the structure of the fees varies considerably between MNEs and this in turn may have important consequences for the efficiency and profitability of the hotel and the distribution of gains between the investors, the management company and the host country. It should also be noted that, with the exception of Hotel IV (which operated at a very low rate of GOP as a percentage of total revenue), the actual fee paid was close to or slightly above the highest of the four possible outcomes.

As we have emphasized throughout the paper, these results are purely illustrative and are not based on a comprehensive sample. Nevertheless it should be appreciated that in addition to the management fee, the MNE will extract further charges for advertising and sales promotion services, computerized reservation facilities, non-routine technical and financial services, and routine visits to the hotel for inspection and consultation. We found no evidence of management contracts giving rise to serious general detrimental effects but we were concerned that hotel owners in the less advanced developing countries may possess only a limited knowledge of the substantial variations in the expertise and contractual terms offered by MNE hotels. This scarcity of private expertise was rarely compensated by host government intervention, as the non-equity forms of foreign involvement appeared to fall between, on the one hand, generally defined controls over foreign direct invest-

ment, and on the other hand, general tourism plans. Part of the reason for this may be in what Green[10] calls 'the myth of uniform terms' (i.e. a standard unalterable contract package) which he considers as dangerous because it leads 'to a fatalistic failure to analyse proposals, to build African capacity for project identification and analysis, and to negotiate effectively and tenaciously' (and not simply limiting negotiation 'to querying clauses in someone else's proposals').

5. POLICY CONSIDERATIONS

It would be inappropriate for this paper to formulate any general policy recommendations. Firstly, host governments must first establish the extent and the form in which tourism in general may contribute towards national economic, social and political objectives. Since these vary considerably between countries, policies towards MNEs may be very different. Second, the impact of MNEs is likely to vary with the form of tourism, the host country's level of economic development, and the structure of resources and infrastructure. Thus the impact of MNE-associated hotels in the larger diversified developing countries is likely to be different from the smaller African and Caribbean countries. Third, even assuming similar policy goals and impacts, appropriate policy instruments may differ between host countries. In some cases this may simply be the result of differences in bargaining power, in other cases governments may not be fully aware of the options open to them, or of the effects of such options on policy objectives; or there may be genuine differences on the choice of correct policy instruments (for example between a market-oriented as compared to a socialist-oriented country).

A further point worth mentioning is that it

is important to distinguish between the impact of MNEs in the tourist sector from the impact of tourism in general and to avoid the temptation to attribute all of the effects of tourism to the multinationality of the enterprises concerned (e.g. the international tourism sector may have a high import content mainly because of the structural characteristics of the host country and the form of tourism promoted, rather than as a consequence of the sourcing policies of the MNEs).

Our analysis of the structural characteristics and form of involvement of MNEs in the international hotel sector of developing countries does, however, suggest certain policy conclusions. Two developments strengthened the position of MNEs in the tourism sector in the 1960s and 1970s. First was the decline in the real cost of air travel which stimulated the rapid growth of leisure travel to countries with little or no tourism infrastructure and expertise.[11] This movement continues today as tourists from the richer nations seek more distant and exotic locations. The second development was the emergence of new business centres throughout the world, stimulating a rapid expansion in business and conference traffic where, as previously analysed, MNEs have particular ownership advantages over indigenous enterprises. The degree of MNE involvement will therefore partly depend upon the planned rate of growth and the form of tourism in relation to the local supply of accommodation and personnel with the required skills. A rapid rate of growth of business tourism in a developing country will, in most cases, require considerable MNE involvement and this need for rapid expansion will reduce the bargaining power of investors within the host country. Conversely, a slower rate of expansion or a higher proportion of leisure tourism, which in some countries may be more easily accommodated by expanding and up-grading local facilities, will increase local bargaining power. It should also be appreciated that there is an interrelationship between the degree of MNE involvement and the form of tourism, in the sense that MNE hotels will exploit those markets in which they possess competitive advantages, namely business and inclusive tour travel, in particular from the home country of the MNE. A strong indigenous hotel sector however will enable diversification in both the form (e.g. special interest tourism) and geographical sourcing of tourism.

It also appears that the ownership advantages of MNE hotels increase the larger the size and complexity of functions of the hotel. Host governments could therefore explore possibilities of reaching the minimum viable size of hotel by grouping hotels around common facilities (such as conference facilities, shops, sports facilities) subject to substantial economies of scale and organizing common marketing facilities and negotiations with foreign tour operators. This would not only increase opportunities for local ownership and management but, by enabling simpler technologies of hotel construction and operation, would increase the possibilities for local purchasing by the hotel sector.

Our analysis also suggests that the ownership advantages of MNE hotels, while possibly substantial in the initial period of the development of the international tourism sector, decrease over time and cannot be sustained in the same way that MNEs in the manufacturing sector can sustain their ownership advantages through research and development. Two conclusions follow from this. First, host governments should view MNE involvement in a dynamic context in which the degree of MNE involvement decreases as indigenous firms gain knowledge and experience of hotel operations. Second, the appropriate form of MNE involvement will also change over time as the resource needs of the host country become more specialized. There are some indications that the market is adapting to these changing conditions with some MNEs being more willing to negotiate contracts other than management contracts, while smaller specialized firms are becoming established to provide technical assistance and marketing services. These developments, by increasing the availability of alternative contractual forms of involvement, will increase the feasible policy instruments available to governments.

6. CONCLUSIONS

The analysis of the growth of the international hotel industry points to the necessity of distinguishing between the ownership of the equity of a hotel and control over its operations which, in the case of developing countries, is invariably exercised through long-term contracts. The competitive advantages of MNE-associated hotels have been found to derive from the characteristics of foreign hotel accommodation as an 'experience good' often purchased in an unfamiliar environment, combined with the knowledge and expertise possessed by the hotel chain which guarantees a certain standard of service and facilities. An important element in maintaining this standard is investment in training (which can be likened to the importance of research and development expenditure by MNEs in certain areas of manufacturing). As the MNE grows in size so its competitive advantage increases, since its human and physical resources can be supplied to newly associated hotels at a lower incremental cost than that incurred by a new entrant into the market.

International hotel chains therefore possess resources which can be significant in developing the international tourism sector of developing countries. It is unlikely that the MNE's will wish to be associated with local hotels through substantial equity participation (either because the MNE's regard themselves as having little expertise in property development or because they regard ownership of hotels in a developing country as a high risk venture, or because expansion would be reduced by the need to borrow large sums of capital) and host countries must therefore in most instances decide on the appropriate form of contract-based involvement by MNEs. Such a choice, however, not only requires a well articulated tourism policy but also adequate policy instruments to monitor, direct and control MNE participation as well as officials with the necessary expertise and experience to put this into practice. Such a combination of conditions is unusual in developing countries and much of the dissatisfaction with the operation of the international hotel chains in developing countries can be ascribed to an absence of these factors rather than a direct conflict of objectives between host governments and the foreign hotel management companies.

Some countries are already pursuing policies which seek to contain or control MNE participation to the extent even of prohibiting management contracts (e.g. India) and normally permitting only franchising and marketing agreements. In Indonesia, Philippines, Taiwan and Thailand there is a distinct trend away from equity involvements and long-term management contracts and towards technical service and marketing agreements. In most cases it is premature to judge the success of these efforts but given our analysis of the ownership advantages of MNE hotels it is important that the quest for independence does not proceed at a rate incompatible with the supply of staff in the middle and upper echelons of management and administration. Hotel schools can only provide some of the necessary expertise and fundamentally the capacity to operate an international class hotel successfully can only come from the experience of working in such a hotel. In this respect the MNE hotels can play an important role by recruiting indigenous personnel and providing managerial and professional training, and it is the responsibility of host governments to ensure that this occurs. This again underlines the importance of governments paying particular attention to the content and terms of contracts concluded between MNEs and local hotel owners. The governments must make clear to both parties what objectives must be met. This in turn again emphasizes that governments should formulate a long-term strategy towards tourism which assesses the resources which the tourism sector will require over several decades and the role of MNEs in supplying these resources.

NOTES

1. The income elasticity of demand for foreign travel has been estimated at between 1.16 and 2.3; see J. R. Artis, 'An econometric analyses of international travel', *IMF Staff Papers*, Vol. 19, No. 3 (1972), pp. 579–614.

2. See especially Part One of J. H. Dunning, *International Production and the Multinational Enterprise* (London: Allen and Unwin, 1981).

3. Part of a research project carried out by Professor John H. Dunning and the author for the UN Centre on Transnational Corporations (UNCTC), published by the UNCTC as *Transnational Corporations in International Tourism* (New York: United Nations, 1982), ST/CTC/18.

4. Interviews at the head offices of the international hotel chains were carried out in Japan, UK, USA, and at MNE associated hotels in Greece, Spain, Kenya, Tunisia, India, Fiji, S. Korea, Singapore and Thailand, and a further 24 MNE hotels answered a detailed questionnaire.

5. S. P. Magee, 'Technology and the appropriability

theory of the multinational corporation', in J. Bhagwati (ed.), *The New International Economic Order* (Cambridge, Mass.: MIT Press, 1977).

6. R. Coase, 'The problem of social cost', *Journal of Law and Economics* (1960).

7. *The Management Path to Profit* (New York: Hilton International, 1978).

8. Trends in the Hotel Business 1978, International Edition (New York: Harris Kerr, Foster and Co., 1979).

9. Gross operating profits are defined as the operating result after deduction of production costs but before deduction of capital costs, depreciation, insurance, and remuneration of the management company.

10. R. H. Green, 'Toward planning tourism in African countries', in E. de Kadt (ed.), *Tourism, Passport to Development?* (Oxford University Press, 1979).

11. For example, in 1967 the Gambia had only two hotels with 52 beds, by 1978 there were 13 hotels with over 2000 beds.

[22]

INTERNATIONAL JOURNAL OF TOURISM RESEARCH
Int. J. Tourism Res. **3**, 179–197 (2001)
DOI: 10.1002/jtr.293

Multinational Hotel Development in Developing Countries: an Exploratory Analysis of Critical Policy Issues†

Salih Kusluvan and Kurtulus Karamustafa*

Erciyes Universitesi, Nevsehir Turizm Isletmeciligi ve Otelcilik Yuksekokulu, 50040 Nevsehir, Turkey

ABSTRACT

Multinational hotel companies, often integrated with tour operators, travel agencies and other businesses in tourist-generating or tourist-receiving countries, play a key role in the development and continuity of an international tourism industry in developing countries. In order to take advantage of benefits and minimise the unwanted adverse effects from multinational hotel involvement, developing countries need the planning, implementation and evaluation of carefully designed policies linked to their particular objectives. This paper reviews the potential benefits and costs of multinational hotel companies and brings together previously scattered critical policy issues in relation to them, while suggesting possible options for developing countries to follow. Seven critical policy areas are identified: establishment of the need for foreign investment; deciding on forms of involvement; deciding on the scale of hotel development; supporting sectoral linkages; supporting indigenous employment/ training; monitoring business practices; and determining foreign investment incentives and regulations. It is argued that policies should be worked out in these areas and co-ordinated in order to achieve a balance between the benefits and costs of multinational hotel involvement in developing countries. Copyright © 2001 John Wiley & Sons, Ltd.

Received 22 November 1999; Revised 3 April 2000; Accepted 11 May 2000

Keywords: multinational hotel companies; developing countries; benefits; costs; policy issues.

INTRODUCTION

In the decades following World War II, international tourism has been a focus of discussion as an instrument for the economic development of developing countries. As Grabum and Jafari (1991) have summarised, the discussion witnessed three stages. First came the studies that did not question the economic benefits of tourism, such as the provision of employment, income and foreign exchange, linkages with other sectors through the multiplier effect, the creation of infrastructure and regional development. Second, a selected wave of studies expressed doubts about the *real* (net) economic contribution of tourism and focused on dependency, leakages, sociocultural adverse effects and environmental hazards. Finally, a balance was struck with perspectives that acknowledged both the opportunities and problems that international tourism may present to developing countries.

Emphasis has now shifted to the management of international tourism, stressing tourism policy objectives, planning, implementation and monitoring of impacts in order to

* Correspondence to: Dr Salih Kusluvan, Erciyes Universitesi Nevsehir Turizm Isletmeciligi ve otekilik Yuksekokulu, 50040 Nevsehir, Turkey.
E-mail: kusluvan@excite.com
† This article is derived from Kusluvan, S. (1994). ''Multinational Enterprises in Tourism: A Case Study of Turkey''. (Strathclyde University, The Scottish Hotel School, Unpublished PhD Thesis. Glasgow).

optimise benefits and reduce any adverse effects that may arise. In this context, this paper tries to answer two questions: 'What are the benefits and disadvantages of multinational hotel involvement in developing countries?'; and 'What are the crucial policy issues for developing countries to address in order to take advantage of the benefits and avoid possible negative impacts?'. Although there are a number of studies on the subject, the advantages and disadvantages of multinational companies' involvement in the accommodation subsector in developing countries as well as real policy issues are dispersed and not presented in an integrated, holistic way (see IUOTO, 1975; Zammit, 1981; UNCTC, 1982, 1990; McQueen, 1983; Ascher, 1985; WTO, 1985; Bull, 1990; Dwyer and Forsyth, 1994; Kusluvan, 1994).

Against the background briefly presented above the objectives of this paper are: (i) to briefly review the potential benefits and costs associated with multinational hotel involvement in developing countries; and (ii) to identify critical policy issues and suggest possible directions for developing countries. In order to achieve these objectives, the methodological approach can be summarised as a systematic review of the relevant literature, which is one of the ways of conducting exploratory research (Churchill, 1996). It should be noted here that exploratory research is used for generating insights, ideas, hypotheses, tentative explanations and identifying areas to study further (Churchill, 1996). Given the objectives and the methodological approach of the study, the outline is as follows: (i) the paper begins with definition of terms and concepts; (ii) it proceeds with a brief review of benefits and costs of multinational hotel involvement in developing countries; and finally (iii) it identifies the seven policy issues and analyses them in order to maximise benefits where possible.

DEFINITION OF TERMS AND CONCEPTS

In considering this subject, it is useful to start with the definition of the terms and concepts considered here: (i) multinational enterprises; and (ii) developing countries.

Multinational enterprise (MNE)

There have been different approaches to the definition of a multinational enterprise. A multinational enterprise can be defined simply as 'an enterprise [which] seeks to extend operational commercial activity beyond the frontiers of its home economy or 'parent' economy' (Bull, 1995, p. 192). This is the threshold definition of a multinational enterprise, and one that is widely accepted in academic circles (Littlejohn, 1985; Casson, 1987; Pitelis and Sugden, 1991; Dunning, 1993).

However, a multinational enterprise was long described as an 'enterprise which owns and controls income-generating assets in more than one country' (Buckley and Casson, 1976, p. 1; Hood and Young, 1979, p. 1). The ownership usually meant majority ownership (more than 50%), hence the control, of enterprises in more than one country. In the United Nations' (UN) definition, the notion of ownership does not appear: 'all enterprises which control assets — factories, mines, sales offices and the like — in two or more countries' (UN, 1973, p. 5). In an attempt to quantify control, the UN argued that firms which either have 10% control of voting stock or 25% of sales or assets in a foreign subsidiary or associate could be regarded as a multinational enterprise. With the rise of non-equity involvement or new forms of international investment (Oman, 1984) across national boundaries, such as franchising, management contracts and leasing, the definition of a multinational enterprise had to be broadened.

In line with the new developments, a multinational enterprise is defined as 'an enterprise which owns or controls value-adding activities in two or more countries. These activities might lead to production of tangible goods or intangible services or some combination of the two' (Dunning, 1989, p. 5). Value addition may involve increasing the quantity of goods, enhancing their quality or improving their distribution, both spatial and temporal (Littlejohn, 1985; Dunning, 1993). Clearly, this definition includes both equity and contractual involvement of firms in more than one country if they are to qualify as multinational enterprises. The only criterion is the *value addition* to the production, quality and distribution of the goods and services for which they receive income. Although MNEs may expand their activities to other industries such as car rental and catering services, three main groups of MNEs in international tourism may be distinguished as hotel companies, airlines and tour operators. In this study, it is only the multinational hotel companies that have relevance.

In the light of what has been said, a multinational hotel company is defined as *an enterprise that owns or controls value-adding activities in the accommodation sector in two or more countries. This involvement in at least two countries can take the form of equity involvement or contractual agreements such as management contracts, franchising, leasing and marketing agreements.* Although there may be different types of multinational accommodation establishments, such as holiday villages, motels, etc., the term 'multinational hotel' or 'multinational associated hotel' is used as a generic term to include all types of multinational-associated accommodation establishments.

Developing countries

The terms 'the Third World', 'underdeveloped countries', 'developing countries', 'periphery', 'poor countries', 'the South' and 'less-developed countries' are mostly used interchangeably for the same group of countries. Indeed, classification of world economies is a very difficult task and a political issue (Weaver, 1998). For the purpose of this study, developing countries refer to *all countries other than high income OECD countries* in World Bank's classification of the world economies (see World Bank, 1998). It is important to note that *high income non-OECD countries* are not considered as developed owing to their relatively low human development indices (see United Nations Development Programme, 1998).

POTENTIAL BENEFITS AND COSTS OF MULTINATIONAL HOTEL INVOLVEMENT IN DEVELOPING COUNTRIES

The question that now needs to be answered is: 'Why do developing countries need multinational hotel companies?'. The answer is simple and the reasons are obvious and lie behind the advantages provided by multi-

national hotel companies in the development of international tourism in those countries. However, the activities of multinational hotel companies may not be all that beneficial. For example, as Figure 1 illustrates, in addition to the advantages of multinational hotel involvement, there are also some costs that may arise from the activities of multinational hotel companies in developing countries.

Potential benefits of multinational hotel involvement

There are seven main benefits that developing countries may obtain from the presence of multinational hotel companies: (i) provision of capital; (ii) transfer of technical and managerial expertise; (iii) provision of market connections; (iv) efficiency; (v) assurance of service quality and security for visitors, and a positive image for destinations; (vi) increased competitiveness and service quality; (vii) demonstration effect for local entrepreneurs.

Provision of financial capital investment. Broadly speaking, developing countries lack financial resources and hotels require investment that needs a large amount of capital (Ascher, 1985). Therefore, with limited financial resources, it may be difficult and risky for a developing country's entrepreneurs to invest in the hotel industry on their own. This is the situation in most of the tourist-receiving developing countries, which explains the importance of financial aid and capital transfers from industrialised countries. In contrast, multinational hotel companies may gain access to international financial institutions, or their prestige may even help them to gain access to a host country's financial institutions and therefore they may not have financial problems in their business activities.

Thus multinational hotel companies may contribute to the financing of a hotel industry, especially in a capital-scarce country. This may range from full ownership to equity participation. In the case of full ownership or equity participation, the supply of financial capital leads to increased investment in the industry and increased tourism resulting from possible price reductions, quality improvement or better marketing (Dwyer and Forsyth, 1994). Nevertheless, considering the strategies of

Int. J. Tourism Res. **3**, 179–197 (2001)

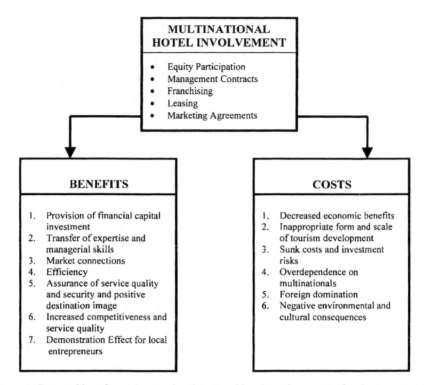

Figure 1. Potential benefits and costs of multinational hotel involvement in developing countries

multinational hotel companies in developing countries in the past, i.e. expansion based largely on management contracts, this is bound to be minimal.

Transfer of expertise and managerial skills. Multinational hotel companies can provide a wide range of technical and managerial expertise both at the pre-opening and operational stage of hotel development. Depending on general and tourism development levels and management know-how, developing countries may unbundle those provisions relating to: (i) the pre-opening stage, i.e. engineering, architecture, interior design, staff training, etc.; and (ii) the operational stage, i.e. preparation of food, drinks, rooms, marketing, reservation systems, accounting, training, etc.

On the other hand multinational hotel companies with their managerial expertise help a host country to improve its international management know-how for the further development of the industry. This can be achieved either by a government policy supporting indigenous employment or unpurposeful trickling down of managerial skills. For example, the opening of both the Hilton in the 1960s and the Sheraton in the 1970s in Istanbul was an opportunity for Turkey to obtain international hotel management know-how. Today in the Turkish resort areas the senior managerial positions of the most successful holiday villages and five-star hotels are occupied by those with Hilton and Sheraton experience (Ermete, 1996). Until recently, before the tourism and hotel educational institutions in the country came into existence, these two international hotel chains were accepted as practical training institutions of the Turkish hotel industry.

      Int. J. Tourism Res. **3**, 179–197 (2001)

Market connections. Multinational hotel companies provide market connections or marketing ties through computerised reservation systems and public relations with the travel trade, i.e. tour operators, travel agents and airlines in tourist-generating countries. The corporate nature of multinational hotel companies, which are sometimes integrated with tour operators, airlines or industrial conglomerates, provides effective world-wide organisation and co-ordination as well as network communications that enable them to direct substantial tourist flows to particular destinations. Overall, the involvement of multinational hotels often results in superior promotional effort owing to the better knowledge of the travel market in the tourist-generating markets (Dwyer and Forsyth, 1994).

Efficiency. Another benefit of multinational hotel companies relates to their efficiency, although this may be a difficult concept to determine in the hotel industry. One way may be to look at the performance, namely net profits or occupancy rates of the same hotel, with and without multinational involvement. This approach fails in that it is very difficult to test it empirically. Another way of evaluating efficiency is to compare performance measures (i.e. occupancy and profit rates, rate of return, consumer satisfaction) of multinational associated hotel companies with indigenous ones of the same class. Given the superior resources and managerial skills, good reputation and better marketing skills, it might be reasonable to hypothesise that multinational hotel companies may be more efficient compared with nationally owned or managed hotels. The validity of this hypothesis, however, depends largely on the type of involvement, the economic environment and market structure in which a multinational hotel company is involved. Therefore, this may be an area for further investigation.

Assurance of service quality and security and positive destination image. One could argue that a host country's tourism enterprises, such as tour operators, hotels and airlines, could together build an image for a destination and not require the services of multinational hotel companies. This may be possible in principle

but seems difficult in practice, because multinational hotel companies — often integrated with tour operators, travel agencies and airlines — have diverse experience and an established image within the international tourism industry. Particularly, at the initial stage of tourism development, multinational hotel companies serve as quality, familiarity and security assuring bodies, because many tourists look for familiarity in unknown, unfamiliar environments. This helps the establishment of an acceptable tourism image for the destination country. As Cohen (1972, p. 166) has observed:

> most tourists seem to need something familiar around them. Something to remind them of home. Whether it is food, newspaper, living quarters or another person from their native country, many of today's tourists are able to enjoy the experience of change and novelty only from a strong base of familiarity which enables them to feel secure enough to enjoy the strangeness of what they experience. They would like to experience the novelty of the macro involvement of a strange place from the security of a familiar micro-environment. And many will not venture abroad except on those well trodden paths equipped with familiar means of transformation, hotels and food.

Also, because holidays are bought 'sight unseen' (Jenkins, 1982a), except for repeat visitors, the knowledge that home-familiar hotels exist in developing countries encourage and reduce 'the information search cost' of potential tourists. In this respect, multinational hotel companies with a good reputation of quality service enhances a destination's positive image.

Increased competitiveness and service quality. The main concern here is that although a developing country has attractions of tourism merit, what it needs is the knowledge of international business know-how and facilities with an acceptable level of services, in order to compete in international tourist markets. As argued by Dieke (1989), international tourism is a highly competitive industry in two respects – price and customer satisfaction. In these respects, a developing country should compete with its rivals in an environment where standards are set by international markets (Jenkins, 1994). In addition, in some cases a developing country may need to compete with a relatively developed country that has expert knowledge of international business activity (e.g. Spain and Turkey). On this basis, it would be very difficult for a particular developing country, in which local entrepreneurs have limited knowledge of international tourism business activity, to compete in international tourist markets. In other words, particularly at the initial stage of tourism development, a developing country's private sector may be embryonic or may have little knowledge of tourism as an industry (Jenkins, 1991). For example, small, independently operated and locally owned accommodation establishments may be at a disadvantage because it may be very difficult for them to compete internationally, particularly when they cannot meet the standard expectations of tourists from developed countries (Williams and Shaw, 1988). Indigenously owned hotels also may not be known by international tourists, which again increases their market disadvantage. In this respect, multinational hotel companies with their expert knowledge of international business activity and an international reputation may help to improve service quality and the competitiveness of that particular developing country in international tourist markets. This argument is also reinforced by Porter's (1998) analysis of 'the competitive advantage of nations', where the competitiveness of the geographical area is influenced directly by both the external business environment and the competence of local enterprises.

Demonstration effect for local entrepreneurs. Multinational hotel companies also may induce the demonstration effect among the indigenous establishments. That is to say, the adoption of multinational hotel companies' design and management techniques by local entrepreneurs, especially the locally owned and operated national hotel chains, may help to improve their competitiveness specifically and the country's tourism industry in general.

Potential costs of multinational hotel involvement

There are both economic and non-economic costs that may arise owing to the presence of multinational associated hotels in developing countries. Six main potential costs of multinational hotel involvement in developing countries can be identified: (i) decreased economic benefits; (ii) inappropriate form and scale of tourism development; (iii) sunk costs and investment risks; (iv) overdependence on multinationals; (v) foreign domination; and (vi) negative environmental and cultural consequences.

Decreased economic benefits. Multinational hotel companies may play a role in decreasing economic benefits to developing countries from international tourism through the repatriation of profits, expatriate labour's income, management and franchising fees and imports. These increase leakages and hence foreign exchange costs. These capital flights decrease foreign exchange earnings that might have accrued in the case of local ownership, management and employment and impact negatively on the balance of payments. Thus they also may inhibit local capital accumulation. Similarly, employment opportunities, especially in managerial positions, for locals may be limited owing to the expatriate labour. However, the decreased economic benefits should be weighted against the revenues earned, which would not have occurred in the absence of multinational company involvement. It can be hypothesised that decreased economic benefits through leakages and expatriate labour employment depend on the general economic development level of a country. For instance, as Dwyer and Forsyth (1994) argue, the additional leakage owing to foreign, as compared with domestic, investment is very small in a developed country such as Australia.

Inappropriate form and scale of tourism development. Multinational hotel companies may affect the scale (size) and type (class) of hotels promoted. The basic issue here is that there may be incompatibility between host governments and international investors with regard to the size and type of hotels to be developed, which affect the general scale of tourist development. The characteristics of mass-tourism tend to favour the development of large scale, integrated, multinational enterprises (Brohman, 1996). The nature of this kind of incompatibility and conflict is discussed further below, under the heading of 'scale of hotel development', which is a critical policy issue itself.

Sunk costs and investment risks. In cases where multinational hotel companies expand on the basis of management contracts and have no capital at stake, they are more flexible in the event of disputes, uncertainties and other social, economic and political factors discouraging tourism both in generating or receiving countries (Ascher, 1985). This means that after such heavy investment in infrastructure and hotels, developing countries may be left with no business and idle capacity when the tourism industry is disrupted by uncontrollable factors, such as terrorist activities in Egypt and continuing violence in Sri Lanka.

Overdependence on multinationals. As defined by Hoogvelt *et al.* (1987), dependency, in its widest and uncritical sense, refers to the degree to which a national economy relies on foreign trade, foreign capital and foreign technology for its survival and growth. Dependency theorists (Matthews, 1978; Britton, 1982a,b; Nash, 1989; Harrison, 1992) examine economic, political and sociocultural relationships between tourist-receiving and tourist-generating countries from the dependency perspectives. As they point out, in these relationships tourist-receiving countries are in a dependent, vulnerable and disadvantageous position because international tourism demand is determined externally, beyond the control of developing countries. As is well documented elsewhere, for instance in the study of Dieke (1989), externalities include the international distribution system, foreign investment expertise, competition and image. Here the externality has two connotations. One externality is related to the various features of the tourism demand, which is seasonal, price and income elastic, and subject to economic, political and social conditions in developed

countries as well as in developing countries (Dieke, 1989). Therefore, it may be either difficult or impossible for a host developing country to influence the tourism demand in a tourist-generating developed country. Another externality refers to control of multinational corporations from developed countries on the tourism demand.

The dependency argument suggests that developing countries will never be able to break away from dependence on multinational hotel companies' skills, expertise and market connections in tourist-generating countries. In the wider context, this dependence is attributed to (i) the fact that developing countries cater primarily for tourism generated in a few developed countries (Jenkins, 1994); (ii) corporate control and direction of tourism demand by tour operators, airlines and hotel chains in tourist-generating countries (Britton, 1982a); and (iii) the use of imported goods, materials and foreign expertise according to the standards and tastes of developed countries. In some countries, e.g. India, this dependency syndrome has been broken by careful and continuous programmes aimed at developing indigenous hotel managers (Jenkins, 1987).

Many researchers suggest that the competitive advantages of multinational hotel companies are transitory (UNCTC, 1982; McQueen, 1983). Obviously, this will depend on the general and tourism development level and appropriate policies pursued by host countries. In the most optimistic scenario, the advantages of multinational hotel companies are unlikely to diminish in two areas: (i) market connections including reservation systems; and (ii) other links with the travel trade, and brand image. There is every reason to believe that these two will dominate the future relationships between host developing countries and multinational hotel companies from developed countries. That is because developing countries 'lack a full understanding of the markets they are reaching out to, their elasticity and what the impact of changes in price and rate might be' (McNulty and Wafer, 1990, p. 294). Therefore, multinational hotel companies are likely to use the information limitation of developing countries (spatial market failure in tourism makes it easier) by emphasising their knowledge of the tourism market, brand image, market power, influential connections and public relations with the travel trade, coupled with financial and managerial resources. Consequently, it can be said that there is a *marketing dependency* on multinational hotel companies together with tour operators, travel agents and airlines. In the medium to long term, the development objective should be to reduce this dependency and create a higher level of interdependency between market agent and receiving countries. For instance, advances in computer technologies and the Internet present opportunities for reducing *marketing dependency* of tourism principals in developing countries (Karamustafa and Kusluvan, 1999). The Internet has given both principals and consumers a new channel of communication and distribution, enabling direct sales/reservations. Tourist product suppliers in developing countries may take advantage of the Internet by encouraging travellers to buy directly through the use of the Internet. However, principals in developing countries will have to surmount some problems (i.e. lack of skilled human resources, technological backwardness, Internet security and weak brand image) before they can take full advantage of the Internet.

Foreign domination. The degree of multinational hotel companies' penetration in developing countries can be an important determinant of the costs of multinational hotel companies' involvement. As Brohman (1996) points out there are three adverse effects of domination by multinational hotel companies, as in the case of Fiji and the Cook islands (Britton, 1982a). First of all, foreign domination 'seriously reduces tourism's potential for generating broadly based growth, as well as the net financial advantages that the industry brings to developing countries' (Brohman, 1996, p. 54). This is because travel agents, tour operators, international transportation and lodging operations are dominantly controlled by vertically integrated multinational corporations. Even in a developed country such as Australia, most of the complaints about foreign ownership of tourism is about the loss of business to national investors (Dwyer and Forsyth, 1994). Secondly, the economic benefits of tourism development would be reduced

and not widely spread to the destination at large, owing to overseas leakages of a substantial portion of the tourism earning thorough profit repatriations, imports, management and franchising fees. Both in cities and holiday resorts multinational hotel companies tend to form enclaves. As Wilkinson (1989, p. 169) argues 'enclave resorts result in minimal economic benefit for the host country because of their dependence on international charter operations, expatriate employees and imported food and other equipment. The overall result is an extremely high leakage rate'.

Finally, high rates of foreign ownership contributes to 'the loss of control over local resources, which may adversely effect the social, economic and ecological well-being of the host communities' (Brohman, 1996, p. 55). Thus foreign domination may increase the resentment of local people towards tourists and foreign involvement. The source of resentment may be the affluence international tourists display while locals suffer chronic poverty or perhaps exclusion of locals from communal resorts or other resources and amenities owned by multinational hotel companies (Tribe, 1995). McNulty and Wafer (1990) report a case from the Côte d'Ivoire (formerly known as Ivory Coast) where a multinational hotel uses a great deal of water in a day whereas nearby villagers have no running water, and condemn 'ghettoism and alienation'. It should be observed of course, that an indigenously owned hotel of similar type and size would use the same amount of water. However, *foreign* ownership and utilisation may focus the feeling of discontent. In addition, given the superior competitive advantages and skills of multinational hotels, foreign domination also may act as a barrier to market entry for potential local companies and force those out of business that are already in operation.

Negative environmental and cultural consequences. Large scale, foreign-owned, enclave-type resorts have been associated with environmental destruction, a declining quality of life, and rising feelings of loss of control and cultural alienation among the local population in the developing countries (Kusluvan, 1994; Broh-

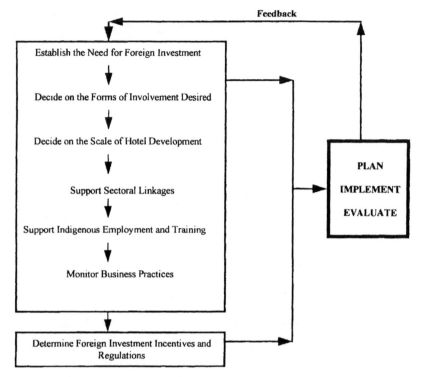

Figure 2. Critical policy issues towards multinational hotel involvement in developing countries

man, 1996). In cultural terms multinational hotels are often accused of transforming the developing world towards 'westernisation' in value systems, beliefs, life-styles and consumption patterns (Solomon, 1979; Kusluvan, 1994).

CRITICAL POLICY ISSUES FOR DEVELOPING COUNTRIES

To reduce the adverse impacts and increase benefits as much as possible, a number of fundamental policy issues with respect to multinational hotel development need to be managed by developing countries. These issues are: the need for foreign investment; forms of involvement; scale of hotel development; sectoral linkages; indigenous employment and training; business practices; and

foreign investment incentives and regulations (Figure 2).

The need for foreign investment

The first policy issue for developing countries is to establish the need for foreign investment in the accommodation subsector of the tourism industry. The need for foreign investment in different developing countries will depend on a number of factors, including political orientation, the level of current foreign investment, general economic and tourism development levels, and the type, scale and stage of tourism development required. In countries with little multinational hotel involvement and international tourism development experience, there is certainly a greater need for multinational hotel involvement. This is because many

Int. J. Tourism Res. **3**, 179–197 (2001)

Tourism in Developing Countries

S. Kusluvan and Kurtulus Karamustafa

Table 1. Percentage of rooms of multinational associated hotels abroad by form and date of involvement (source: UNCTC (1982, p. 26) Reproduced by permission of UNCTC.)

		Equity participation (%)	Leasing (%)	Management contracts (%)	Franchising (%)
Developed countries	Before 1964	41.0	28.1	30.9[a]	
	1965–1974	60.1	10.5	29.5[a]	
	1975 and after	25.7	8.8	65.4[a]	
	All periods	47.8	11.9	23.5	16.8
Developing countries	Before 1964	21.8	45.0	33.2[a]	
	1965–1974	22.2	22.2	56.8[a]	
	1975 and after	6.7	2.7	90.6[a]	
	All periods	17.6	10.3	63.1	9.0
All countries	Before 1960	19.0	38.0	33.8	9.3
	1960–1964	31.7	21.1	47.2	–
	1965–1969	42.2	21.8	29.0	6.9
	1970–1974	38.8	14.9	36.8	10.3
	1975–1978	21.4	10.3	52.2	16.0
	1979 and after	3.3	1.2	87.1	8.3
	All periods	31.4	12.2	44.7	11.7

[a] Management contracts and franchising.

developing countries lack the experience, standards, financial and skilled human capital as well as technical capabilities for building and running an international hotel.

Forms of involvement

There are a variety of ways in which a multinational hotel company may be involved in a developing country. These may be through equity participation (wholly, majority or minority ownership of the investment); management contracts, franchising agreements, leasing, and other technical service agreements, such as a marketing consortium, or a mixture of these (for details, see Housden, 1984). Although developing countries have the

right to legislate the desired form of involvement, it appears that, because of the lack of bargaining power, it is mostly the multinational hotel companies that choose the form of involvement appropriate to their strategies. Empirical investigation shows that multinational hotel companies avoid wholly or majority ownership, and capital participation is observed to be in the form of minority ownership.

As Table 1 shows, management contracts are the preferred form of involvement in developing countries; 63.1% of multinational associated rooms are under management contracts. Franchising agreements make up 9% and leasing agreements another 10.3% of the multinational associated hotel rooms,

Table 2. Forms of international hotel involvement in the Southeast Asia (source: Schlentrich and Ng (1994, p. 411) Hotel development strategies in Southeast Asia: the battle for market & dominance. In: *Tourism: The State of the Art*. Seaton AV, Jenkins CL, Wood RC, Dieke PUC, Bennett MM, MacLellan LR, Smith R (eds). Copyright © John Wiley & Sons, Ltd. Reproduced with permission)

	Before 1985 (%)	Current properties (%)	Planned properties (%)
Wholly owned	9	8	1
Management contract with equity participation	19	20	10
Management contract	44	45	67
Franchise	28	27	22

leaving 17.6% for equity involvement. A more recent study (UNCTC, 1990) surveyed 17 hotel agreements in developing countries and found that only one was under a leasing agreement and one under a franchise agreement, the rest being management contracts.

Similarly Schlentrich and Ng (1994) found the most common form of involvement of international hotel chains in Southeast Asia is the management contract (Table 2).

The appeal of management contracts lies in a number of strategic factors from the point of view of multinational hotel companies. They enable a multinational hotel company to have *de facto* control over day-to-day operations and secure reasonable revenues while avoiding *de jure* ownership and risks (Dunning, 1988). The company also is able to expand and dominate the markets quickly without having to invest substantial 'sunk costs'. They give flexibility and security against the instability of tourism demand and the sociopolitical environment of the host country, i.e. the rise and fall of popularity of destinations. Finally, when there is a conflict between the parties, escape clauses and ambiguities in the management contract enable the less dependent multinational hotel companies to withdraw from the contract (Dave, 1984).

There are several policy issues to be addressed with respect to the type of involvement. First, in order to attract finance and provide future commitment of multinational hotel companies to the project and destination, ownership of the project can be offered. However, this should be weighed against the future profit repatriation of the foreign owner. As noted elsewhere, there are very real economic benefits accruing to the destination when the indigenous ownership and entrepreneurial involvement is at a significant level (Jenkins, 1982a). Provisions should be made to increase local economic participation in order to reduce the possibility of foreign domination. One strategy may be to limit the foreign equity or shares to some extent and encourage joint ventures with local investors requiring a minimum percentage of local and/or control of new investments, as in the case of Mexico and Japan (Bull, 1990). Financial involvement of multinational hotel companies also increases the performance of the project. For

example, the United Nations Centre on Transnational Corporations (UNCTC, 1982) cites an example from the Caribbean that in almost every case where hotel performance had been unsatisfactory, the multinational associated hotel companies had no financial involvement.

Second, developing countries should pay attention to excessive management, franchising and leasing fees. In fact, UNCTC (1982) found that management fees in ten multinational associated hotel companies in developed countries were significantly less than those in developing countries. To increase the effectiveness of management contracts, management fees can be linked to performance, e.g. occupancy or profit rate. In countries, where there is a pool of management resources, the content of the management contract may be influenced by the host government policy through the use of incentives for the training and employment of locals. With the passage of time, management contracts should give way to franchising agreements, or only marketing agreements, as the hotel industry is not technology intensive.

Thirdly, long-term contractual agreements should be avoided because they will affect the achievement orientation of management. Moreover, better deals can be struck in future or expatriate management can be replaced by locals. Renewal of the contracts should remain with the local owner. Finally, it is also important that developing countries obtain references and information regarding the business activities of the company before they enter into any contract. The information may be provided from a national tourist authority, the United Nations Centre on Transnational Corporations, the World Tourism Organisation and other developing countries. There is obviously scope here for an international reference point to provide information and expertise on current contractual arrangements in the hotel sector. Governments and investors in developing countries often lack this important knowledge to assist them in the negotiation process with multinational hotel groups. An improved knowledge base should help prevent too generous arrangements that disadvantage one partner, usually the developing country. Luckily, there now exists a vast amount of literature concerning the nature,

Int. J. Tourism Res. **3**, 179–197 (2001)

Table 3. Trends in the management contract provisions (source: Eyster (1993), Bell (1993) and Sangree and Hathaway (1996))

More equity or loans from the management companies
Increase in basic management fees and increase in operating incentive fees
Decrease in negotiated lengths of initial contract terms, number of renewals and length of renewals
Inclusion of operator performance provisions
Owner input in operational decision making
Contract termination at owner's option without cause, in the event of foreclosure or sale
Easier termination clauses which make it easier for the owner to remove an underperforming operator
An increase in the quality and thoroughness of financial and operational reporting to the demands of the
	owners
Scrutiny on the operators' corporate expenses that can be billed to the property
Inclusion of non-competition covenants in which the operator agrees not to manage or place additional
	properties within a specified geographical area
Guaranteed gross operating profits and/or minimum return (benchmark profit figures management
	companies have to meet)
More control for the owner over his/her property

negotiation and administration of management contracts and franchising agreements as well as recent trends in these areas (see Housden, 1984; Eyster, 1988; UNCTC, 1990), Bell, 1993; Eyster 1993; Sangree and Hathaway, 1996; and these should be consulted.

As Table 3 shows, management contract provisions are shifting in favour of the owner in the developed world and it is likely that the same trend will follow in the developing countries as tourism develops and competition increases among the contractors. In order to evaluate the impact of different forms of multinational hotel involvement, a net benefits ratio, which compares the overall increase generated in national income with the costs in terms of payments to foreign factors of production, can be used (Bull, 1990).

All said, in order to enable hotel owners to negotiate better management contract terms with multinational companies it is preferable to resort to the education of investors and owners rather than government regulations, because too much government interference may be detrimental to foreign investments.

The scale of hotel development

Another policy issue relates to the scale of tourist development in developing countries. It is argued that the scale or size of the hotel development should be such that it should attract international hotel developers. In this context, Jenkins (1982a, p. 236) noted that

'below a unit size operating costs are likely to be unattractive to an (international) investor or management company'. This is because of the economies of scale and the scope that large projects offer to international hotel developers. They either develop and/or manage large business class hotels in big city centres or beach resort hotels in resorts including casino and convention facilities. It is realistic to assume that multinational hotel companies, with preferences that seem to be for large-scale four- and/or five-star hotels, will dictate the size and standards. For instance, UNCTC (1982) found that average room number of multinational associated hotels in developing countries was 264. There are few examples of developing countries that have developed alternatives to large-scale tourism development characterised by multinational hotels with strong ties to international tour and travel operators (Wilkinson, 1989). However, if a destination country wants to develop alternative small-scale, locally owned, managed and integrated tourism in some regions because of the small size of the country and fragile environment or sociocultural concerns, it should carefully evaluate what role, if any, multinational hotel companies can play in that type of development. McNulty and Wafer (1990) give examples of such locally owned and managed small-scale heritage tourism enterprises, which preserves natural and cultural resources and benefits economically local people better than large-scale mass tourism, owned and managed by multinational companies. Similarly, locally owned and small firms have been more successful in generating income, employment and government revenue than larger, internationally owned establishments, resulting in higher multipliers (Milne, 1987; Meyer, 1988). However, this type of tourist development has the problems of achieving scale economies, marketing, low occupancy, low volume, and lack of competitiveness, which determine the commercial viability of the undertaking (Kusluvan, 1994). In some cases, it may be possible to develop a dual structure with large scale, multinational associated hotels along with medium and small scale, locally owned and managed pensions, guest houses and hotels.

These examples reinforce the need for investment incentives to be used selectively. In most developing countries the hotel sector will be differentiated by size and quantity of properties; the Nusa Dua complex in Bali, Indonesia, is mainly deluxe properties with large-scale convention facilities (Jenkins, 1982b). This concentration of foreign investment and management has not prevented the development of smaller, sometimes luxurious hotels in other parts of the island. Investment incentives should be used to support and implement policy decisions.

Sectoral linkages

In an economy, an industry or product line can help development efforts by providing backward (input-supplying) or forward (output-using) linkages through input–output relationships (Hirshman, 1977). Backward linkages lead to new investments and demand for supplying facilities and forward linkages give rise to new investments in output-using facilities (Hirshman, 1977). The hotel sector has a lot of potential for providing intersectoral linkages (especially backward) and acting as a catalyst for agricultural and manufacturing industry. Although the potential is here, the linkage effects of hotels depend on, among other things, the ability of the economy to provide sufficient and desirable inputs and outputs associated with the industry. The policy issue concerning 'the multinational hotel companies and sectoral linkage effect' is

that governments of developing countries should ensure that multinational associated hotels use local goods and services if they are available domestically at comparable prices, quality and delivery date. In practice this policy can be very difficult to implement. For instance, Belisle (1985) examined 60 Jamaican hotels, without distinguishing between multinational and national hotels, and discovered that the 54.2% of the food by value is imported. Unless a government exercises a strict import-licensing system, it can essentially only persuade hotels to consider local suppliers. This argument is taken on the basis that local supplies are of the quality acceptable to tourists and that generally they are available.

There may be many reasons for multinational hotel companies not buying local goods and services. Among the causes of high import content and lack of linkage, Belisle (1983) identified six main factors that influenced multinational hotel companies' links with the local economy, namely: (i) most tourists are conservative in their tastes; (ii) imported food may be cheaper than that produced locally; (iii) hotels will pay more to ensure reliable and high-quality suppliers; (iv) local food may be processed in unhygienic conditions; (v) hotels may be unaware of locally produced food; and (vi) local producers may not know how to contact the hotels. Another reason for the failure of linkages may be the deliberate policies of multinational associated hotels to insist on certain materials marked with company logos and products to be bought from abroad in order to benefit an affiliated company or to maintain customer loyalty. It is noted by UNCTC (1989, p. 26) that:

> in the hotel business that is normally connected with the acquisition of such items as food, beverage, fixtures, inventory, equipment or furniture from certain sources, the requirements may be so specific (and perhaps unnecessarily so) that only a number of (foreign) suppliers can fulfil them.

On the other hand, the sheer volume and variety of demand creates economies of scale that few local suppliers can compete with. Another consideration may be the 'comfort factor' which foreign managers have with established suppliers. It is not an easy network to weaken or dismantle. Obviously, the opportunity to increase intersectoral linkages will depend not only on the diversity of resources but also on the general development level of the country concerned. In other words, the more a country is industrialised and developed, the more it is capable of producing the goods and services required in international tourism, and hence there is a low leakage rate (Cater, 1990). For example, Momsen's work (1986, cited by Shaw and Williams, 1998) on the small Caribbean islands of St Lucia and Montserrat shows an improvement in the linkages between the hotel sector and local agriculture during the period of 1971 to 1983. As that study claimed, in 1971, in St Lucia, 70% of the value of food consumed by tourists was imported, compared with only 58% in 1983. Therefore it is very important for host developing countries to insist on the maximum use of local materials and supplies in the design, construction and operation of hotels. This can be achieved by limiting imports of tourism establishments, charging high tariffs for imported goods that are available, locally or giving incentives for using local goods and services. The macroeconomic implications of such policies should be taken into consideration.

Indigenous employment and training

Of all contributions, the single most important benefit of multinational hotel companies to host developing countries is considered to be in the area of training human resources or so-called 'soft technology' transfer (UNCTC, 1989). However, this should not be taken as a self-evident truth. There is no information about the diffusion of managerial know-how at managerial level in multinational associated hotels in developing countries. On the contrary, research shows that in order to maintain firm specific advantages, key management positions are held by expatriates and only lower-level personnel requiring low skills are trained for reasons of service quality and performance (Ascher, 1985; Dunning, 1988).

At the initial stages of tourist development, expatriate management of multinational associated or national hotels may be justified owing to lack of skilled management personnel and experience in the field. However, policies and ways of implementation should be prepared and sanctioned for increasing the local management pool and reducing the proportion of foreign labour. As Jenkins and Henry (1982: 512) put it:

> the use of foreign expertise is often the only means of jumping the development gap between the indigenously available management and technical skills and the level of experience and competence needed to organise and sustain an international industry. In the short term, the use of foreign nationals in the tourist sector must be regarded as one of the costs of development. In the long term, an integral part of development strategy will be, whenever possible, to replace foreign employees by local people.

In addition to national tourism education and training systems, governments can make use of the considerable expertise and training schemes of multinational hotel companies. For example, training schemes can be negotiated and contracted in the initial dealings with such companies. Alternatively, additional incentives such as tax reductions, accelerated depreciation and training allowances can be used to encourage multinational enterprises for training of local human resources. As most jobs in the hotel industry are low or medium skilled and can be standardised to some extent, the emphasis should be on the training and employment of local people at the managerial level.

In many developing countries work permits are used to control the employment of foreigners. However, without a definite training programme agreed with the multinational company, a succession of foreigners can fill the same position, e.g. one foreign executive chef is replaced by another foreigner. Whenever possible, it is necessary to link a work permit to a training programme aimed at eliminating the need for a foreign employee.

Business practices

Another policy regarding multinational hotel companies considers the business practices that can be detrimental economically to a host developing country. Two such practices, *excessive management or franchising fees* and *deliberate unnecessary imports* have already been mentioned. Transfer pricing is another tool used in accounting that may be disadvantageous for the host country concerned. For example, if a multinational hotel company operates on the basis of a management contract or franchising, the prices of imports it specifies to be bought from certain sources can be inflated (overpriced), so that the affiliated firm abroad can make large profits. Alternatively, if the multinational associated hotel is wholly or majority foreign owned, the imports can be underpriced to decrease tariffs paid or overpriced to reduce total liability for taxes over profits. The latter disguises capital exports as overpayment for imported products. In theory, it is also possible that inclusive tour prices charged can be underpriced to reduce total earnings, hence taxes. The choice often will depend on government tax policies and regulations, import incentives and restrictions, tariff payments and final profitability of each practice. Also, certain business transactions between tour operators in tourist-generating countries and multinational associated hotels in developing countries may reduce foreign exchange flows. The study of UNCTC (1982, p. 79) explains such transactions:

> The organisation providing the tourist services may not, for example, receive foreign exchange directly, but rather a credit with the tour operator in the tourist generating country, upon which it may be able to draw at a future date. An alternative method is for the tour operators to give their customers vouchers which they hand to the local supplier of the tourist service. The latter may then cash the vouchers in the tourist generating country. A third example is where the supplier of the tourist services in the host country is part of a vertically integrated transnational corporation and where payments and receipts between subsidiaries of the enterprise are simple book-keeping transactions recorded at prices designed to promote enterprises' global objective.

These business practices are difficult to monitor and control. As most developing countries decentralise their economies under pressure from international institutions, foreign exchange regulations are being removed. Freedom to operate in the foreign exchange market and to maintain accounts outside national boundaries further complicate monitoring arrangements. Under these circumstances perhaps the best that governments can do is to ensure that financial information is collected from all companies and certainly from those who receive investment incentives. In the tourism industry, governments could become more proactive by encouraging and assisting local investors and suppliers, and wherever possible, use investment incentives as a bargaining measure to achieve development objectives. Finally, bribery should be mentioned as a harmful practice. For example, multinational hotel owners (local ones as well) can offer bribes or donations to political parties or civil servants in return for unlawful concessions such as tax evasion, public contracts, land allocations, etc. As Bull (1990) suggests, direct controls on repatriation of profits or wages could limit the outflows of earnings but this would deter the multinational investors in the case of developing countries.

Against these harmful business practices, several measures can be adopted, such as:

(1) a system of tougher screening of individual investment proposals and guidelines to examine the total value of foreign investment and operation (Bull, 1990);
(2) strict book-keeping requirements for companies and regular inspections;
(3) publication and display of room rates for both groups and individuals;
(4) irregular comparison of prices for imported material among multinational associated and national associated hotels;
(5) adoption of strict legal principles regarding bribery;
(6) limitations on payments that can be made by vouchers or credits between tour operators and hoteliers.

Foreign investment incentives

Once the objectives are firmly established in other policy areas, the final step is to consider the creation of an acceptable and attractive

Table 4. Investment incentives for foreign investors in Turkey (source: Kusluvan (1994) and Ministry of Tourism (1995) Reproduced by permission of S. Kusluvan and Ministry of Tourism.)

General guarantees and privileges	Incentives during the investment phase	Incentives during the operation period
Equality with domestic companies.	Infrastructure provision	Priority in the instalment of telephone and telex facilities
Repatriation of profits, management or royalty fees	Land allocation	Employment of foreign personnel up to 20% of the total workforce
No red tape	Provision of long-term investment credits	Minimum tariff rates are charged for electricity, gas and water bills
Participation in international investment promotion and protection agreements	Exemptions from customs duties	Exemption from property tax
	Exemption from construction tax	Importation of foreign goods and services that are not available in Turkey

investment environment for foreign investors if the benefits of multinational companies' involvement in the hotel sector are to be realised. One of the ways of doing this is through legislation and investment incentives conducive to international investors as well as supportive of other policy issues. Investment incentives can be defined as legislative provisions that are introduced to attract investment funds by offering concessions, usually of a fiscal nature, to enhance the probability of earning a satisfactory return on the capital involved (Jenkins, 1982b). Multinational hotel companies can provide expertise and experience in international tourism; therefore developing countries need to offer some investment incentives to attract foreign investors.

Because of the above-mentioned benefits that multinational hotel companies may provide, together with the lack of expertise and experience in international tourism, developing countries may need to offer some investment incentives to attract foreign investors. These incentives can be general guarantees and privileges, incentives during the investment phase and incentives during the operation phase, as exemplified by the case of Turkey (Table 4).

However, the choice of incentives may vary depending on the competitive position, tourist development level and objectives of each particular developing country. For the effec-

tive management of investment incentives, several strategies can be proposed:

(1) investment incentives should be selective with respect to location, scale (size) and type (class) of hotels, which should be related to any existing tourism development plan;
(2) incentives also should be linked to environment and culture sensitive projects;
(3) provision of land to foreign investors can be on a lease basis rather than ownership;
(4) incentives for foreign investors can be less generous where it is appropriate to encourage domestic investors;
(5) incentive beneficiaries should be monitored so that investment proceeds according to the initial plan;
(6) further reinvestment incentives can be provided to prevent the repatriation of profits and royalties;
(7) A review clause should be put into legislation so that effectiveness of incentives and other repercussions can be evaluated and changes made if necessary.

It always should be noted that any investment incentives are subsidies either to the start-up of business and/or to operating costs. In many countries there has been no analysis made of the relative costs and benefits from using investment incentives. Without this information and subsequent analysis, it is impossible to 'fine tune' investment incentives to make them an effective and flexible development tool. In certain tourism regions, e.g. the Caribbean, investment incentives are used essentially as competitive tools to attract foreign investment into a regionally homogeneous tourism sector (Jenkins, 1982b). Each country bids-up the level of incentives to differentiate not the product (beach tourism) but the location. In such regions where the countries' tourism assets are basically homogeneous, the 'wastes of competition' are easily identified. However, as independent countries operating in a highly substitutable market place, regional harmonisation of investment incentives, often espoused, can be politically impossible to achieve.

As a group, developing countries should notice that homogenisation of investment incentives could be beneficial economically, instead of competing between themselves, which results in further concessions to foreign investors. This can be realised, at least, at the regional level among countries with a similar tourist product and competitive advantage. In the last analysis, it should not be forgotten that investment incentives are only one of the factors that may attract foreign investors. There are other groups of factors that determine the attractions of a particular country for multinational hotel involvement in addition to government policy towards foreign investment:

> First, and most obvious are all the factors determining the volume, kind and rate of growth of tourism, particularly business tourism to a particular country. Second, is the availability of the appropriate infrastructure for tourism, e.g. transport and communication facilities. Third, is the availability and quality of hotel inputs, including hotel staff and essential services which cannot be imported. Fourth, is the general political, economic and social stability of the country and attitudes of the local population to foreign countries (Dunning, 1988, p. 258).

Similarly, as a field study conducted by Dunning and Kundu (1995) has indicated, the most important 'location-specific advantages' perceived by the executives of multinational

hotel companies for developing countries are: the size and growth of markets in the host economy; the general infrastructure of the host country; the host government policy towards direct foreign investment; the political, social and economic stability of host country; and the availability of good quality and low cost inputs.

CONCLUSION

This paper has reviewed the potential benefits and non-benefits that may arise from the involvement of multinational hotel companies in developing countries, and given attention to critical policy issues and alternative courses of actions for governments to ensure that the benefits are maximised. Surely, this kind of analysis assumes a political and economic system where states (governments) intervene, when necessary, in markets to encourage and steer the economic development. No policy issue is dealt with in depth, neither are absolute prescriptions offered for any country. The aim was to emphasise the important policy issues that developing countries need to address in an integrated way if they want to attract and benefit from foreign businesses in the accommodation sector. The appropriate measures in each policy area will vary depending on a number of conditions prevailing in a particular country. In reality, the nature and interest of multinational companies' investment is a very difficult area to analyse. The contractual arrangements between parties are usually private and therefore not available for public scrutiny. For these reasons, there can be no single prescription applicable to the type, extent or administration of policy issues. Such principles should emphasise selectivity, appropriateness and monitoring. What is an appropriate policy can be determined only within the circumstances of each country. That is why case studies from developing countries on the nature of these policies, ways of implementation of each policy, and failures and successes would be helpful.

REFERENCES

Ascher F. 1985. *Tourism: Transnational Corporations and Cultural Identities*. UNESCO: Paris.

Belisle JF. 1983. Tourism and food production in the Caribbean. *Annals of Tourism Research* **10**(3): 497–513.

Belisle JF. 1985. Food production and tourism in Jamaica: obstacles to increasing local food supplies to hotels. *Journal of Developing Areas* **19**(1): 1–20.

Bell CA. 1993. Agreements with chain hotel companies. *The Cornell Hotel and Restaurant Administration Quarterly* **34**(1): 27–33.

Britton SG. 1982a. The political economy of tourism in the third world. *Annals of Tourism Research* **9**(3): 331–358.

Britton SG. 1982b. International tourism and multinational corporations in the Pacific: the case of Fiji. In *The Geography of Multinationals*, Taylor M, Thrift N (eds). Croon-Helm: London; 252–275.

Brohman J. 1996. New directions in tourism for Third World development. *Annals of Tourism Research* **23**(1): 48–70.

Buckley PJ, Casson MC. 1976. *The Future of Multinational Enterprise*. The Macmillan Press: London.

Bull, A. 1990. Australian tourism: effects of foreign investment. *Tourism Management* **11**(4): 325–331.

Bull A. 1995. *The Economics of Travel and Tourism*. Longman: Melbourne.

Casson M. 1987. *The Firm and the Market*. Basil Blackwell: Oxford.

Cater E. 1990. The development of tourism in the least developed countries. In *Marketing in the Tourism Industry the Promotion of Destination Regions*, Goodall B, Ashworth G (eds). Routledge: London; 39–66.

Churchill GA Jr. 1996. *Basic Marketing Research*. The Dryden Press: Forth Worth.

Cohen E. 1972. Towards a sociology of international tourism. *Social Research* **39**: 164–182.

Dave U. 1984. US multinational involvement in the international hotel sector. An analysis. *The Service Industries Journal* **4**(1): 49–63.

Dieke PUC. 1989. Fundamentals of tourism development: a third world perspective. *Hospitality Education and Research Journal* **13**(2): 7–22.

Dunning JH. 1988. *Explaining International Production*. Unwin Hyman: London.

Dunning JH. 1989. Multinational enterprises and the growth of services: some conceptual and theoretical issues. *The Service Industries Journal* **9**(1): 5–39.

Dunning JH. 1993. *Multinational Enterprises and The Global Economy*. Addison-Wesley: Wokingham.

Dunning JH, Kundu SK. 1995. The internationalization of the hotel industry: some new findings from a field. *Management International Review* **35**(2): 101–133.

Dwyer L, Forsyth P. 1994. Foreign tourism invest-

ment: motivation and impact. *Annals of Tourism Research* **21**(3): 512–537.

Ermete T. 1996. We have learnt many things from the foreigners. *Hotel* **4**: 27. (In Turkish.)

Eyster JJ. 1988. *The Negotiation and Administration of Hotel and Restaurant Management Contracts*. Comel University School of Hotel Administration: Ithaca, NY.

Eyster JJ. 1993. The revolution in domestic hotel management contracts. *The Cornell Hotel and Restaurant Administration Quarterly* **34**(1): 16–26.

Graburn NH, Jafari J. 1991. Introduction: tourism and social science. *Annals of Tourism Research* **18**(1): 1–11.

Harrison D. 1992. International tourism and the less developed countries: the background. In *Tourism and the Less Developed Countries*, Harrison D (ed.). Wiley: Chichester; 1–18.

Hirshman A. 1977. A generalised linkage approach to development with special reference to staples. In *Essays on Economic Development and Cultural Change*, Nash M (ed.). The University of Chicago Press: Chicago; 67–98.

Hood N, Young S. 1979. *The Economics of Multinational Enterprise*. Longman: London.

Hoogvelt A, Puxty AG, Stopford JM. 1987. *Multinational Enterprise: an Encyclopaedic Dictionary of Concepts and Terms*. The Macmillan Press: London.

Housden J. 1984. *Franchising and Other Business Relationships in Hotel and Catering Services*. Heinemann: London.

IUOTO. 1975. *The Impact of International Tourism on the Economic Development of Developing Countries*. International Union of Official Travel Organisation: Geneva.

Jenkins CL. 1982a. The effects of scale in tourism projects in developing countries. *Annals of Tourism Research* **9**(2): 229–249.

Jenkins CL. 1982b. The use of investment incentives for tourism in developing countries. *Tourism Management* **3**: 91–97.

Jenkins CL. 1987. Manpower planning in tourism. *Tourism Planning Course in Colombo*. Unpublished Lecture given to WTO/UNDP, Sri Lanka.

Jenkins CL. 1991. Impacts and implications of tourism in development strategies. In *Developing Tourism Destinations Policies and Perspectives*, Lickorish LJ, Jefferson A, Bodlender J, Jenkins CL (eds). Longman: Harlow; 50–118.

Jenkins CL. 1994. Tourism in developing countries: the privatisation issue. In *Tourism: The State of the Art*, Seaton AV, Jenkins CL, Wood RC, Dieke PUC, Bennett MM, MacLellan LR, Smith R (eds). Wiley: Chichester; 1–9.

Jenkins CL, Henry BM. 1982. Government involvement in tourism in developing countries. *Annals of Tourism Research* **9**(3): 499–521.

Karamustafa K, Kusluvan S. 1999. *Tourism in Development: a Situational Analysis of Turkey.* International Center for Research and Studies in Tourism: Aix-En-Provence.

Kusluvan S. 1994. *Multinational enterprises in tourism: a Case study of Turkey.* Unpublished PhD thesis, The Scottish Hotel School, University of Strathclyde: Glasgow.

Littlejohn D. 1985. Towards an economic analysis of trans/multinational hotel companies. *International Journal of Hospitality Management* **4**(4): 157–165.

Matthews HG. 1978. *International Tourism: a Social and Political Analysis.* Schenkmann: Cambridge.

McNulty R, Wafer P. 1990. Transnational corporations and tourism issues. *Tourism Management* **11**(4): 291–295.

McQueen M. 1983. Appropriate policies towards multinational hotel corporations in developing countries. *World Development* **11**(2): 141–152.

Meyer W. 1988. *Beyond the Mask.* Verlag Breitenbach Publishers: Fort Lauderdale.

Milne S. 1987. Differential multipliers. *Annals of Tourism Research* **14**(4): 499–515.

Ministry of Tourism. 1995. *Tourism Investment Opportunities and Procedures in Turkey.* Department for the Guidance of Investments: Ankara.

Momsen JM. 1986. *Linkages between Tourism and Agriculture: Problems for the Smaller Caribbean Economies.* Report No. 45, Department of Geography, University of Newcastle: Newcastle.

Nash D. 1989. Tourism as a form of imperialism. In *Host and Guests: the Anthropology of Tourism,* Smith VL (ed.). University of Pennsylvania Press: Philadelphia; 37–52.

Oman C. 1984. *New Forms of International Investment in Developing Countries.* OECD Publications: Paris.

Pitelis CN, Sugden R. 1991. On the theory of transnational firms. In *The Nature of the Transnational Firm,* Pitelis CN, Sugden R (eds). Routledge: London; 9–15.

Porter ME. 1998. *The Competitive Advantage of Nations.* The Macmillan Press: London.

Sangree DJ, Hathaway PP. 1996. Trends in hotel management contracts. *The Cornell Hotel and Restaurant Administration Quarterly* **36**(5): 26–37.

Schlentrich UA, Ng D. 1994. Hotel development strategies in Southeast Asia: the battle for market dominance. In *Tourism: The State of the Art,* Seaton AV, Jenkins CL, Wood RC, Dieke PUC, Bennett MM, MacLellan LR, Smith R (eds). Wiley: Chichester; 402–414.

Shaw G, Williams AM. 1998. Entrepreneurship, small business culture and tourism development. In *The Geography of the Tourist Industry,* Ioannides D, Debbage KG (eds). Routledge: London; 235–255.

Solomon LD. 1978. *Multinational Corporations and the Emerging World Order.* Kennikat Press: London.

Tribe J. 1995. *The Economics of Leisure and Tourism: Environments, Markets and Impacts.* Butterworth-Heinemann: Oxford.

UN. 1973. *Multinational Corporations in World Development.* United Nations: New York.

UNCTC. 1982. *Transnational Corporations in International Tourism,* United Nations Centre on Transnational Corporations: New York.

UNCTC. 1989. *Transnational Service Corporations and Developing Countries: Impact and Policy Issues.* United Nations Centre on Transnational Corporations: New York.

UNCTC. 1990. *Negotiating International Hotel Chain Management Agreements.* United Nations Centre on Transnational Corporations: New York.

United Nations Development Program (UNDP). 1998. *Human Development Report 1998.* Oxford University Press: New York. [URL: http://www.undp.org]

Weaver DB. 1998. *Ecotourism in the Less Developed World.* CAB International: Wallingford.

Wilkinson P. 1989. Strategies for tourism in island microstates. *Annals of Tourism Research* **16**(2): 153–177.

Williams AM, Shaw G. 1988. Western European tourism in perspective. In *Western European Experiences,* Williams AM, Shaw G (eds). Belhaven Press: London; 12–38.

World Bank. 1998. *World Tables 1997.* The John Hopkins University: Baltimore. [URL: http://www.worldbank.org]

WTO. 1985. *The Role of Transnational Enterprises in the Development of Tourism.* World Tourism Organisation: Madrid.

Zammit A. 1981. Transnationals in developing country tourism. *International Tourism Quarterly* **1**(1): 37–56.

Int. J. Tourism Res. **3**, 179–197 (2001)

D
Scale of Development

[23]

THE EFFECTS OF SCALE
IN ECONOMIC DEVELOPMENT
Tourism in Bali

Eric E. Rodenburg
Department of Anthropology
University of California
Santa Barbara, USA

ABSTRACT

Eric E. Rodenburg, The Effects of Scale in Economic Development: Tourism in Bali. *Annals of Tourism Research* 1980, VII(2):177-196. Planners promote tourism to meet the objectives of economic development. Different scales of enterprise, however, meet the objectives of planners in different ways. Data from Bali, Indonesia, illustrate the differential social and economic effects of three scales of tourism enterprise; large industrial, small industrial and craft tourism. A comparison of these segments of the continuum of tourism enterprises in Bali shows that the objectives of economic planners (increased earnings, foreign exchange, investment, job opportunities, production, entreprenuership, infrastructure, and the minimization of adverse social and cultural effects) are not best met through the promotion of large, industrially scaled enterprises. **Keywords:** *economic development, scale of enterprise, Bali, Indonesia, tourism.*

Eric Rodenburg is a development anthropologist with a special interest in tourism development. In 1980 he will begin a long term investigation of scale dependent social and cultural consequences of tourism development in three communities in Bali, Indonesia.

THE EFFECTS OF SCALE IN ECONOMIC DEVELOPMENT

RESUME

Rodenberg, Eric E., "Les Effets de l'échelle dans le développement: le tourisme au Bali." *Annals of Tourism Research* 1980, VII (2): 177-196. Les planificateurs développent le tourisme pour réaliser les objectifs du développement économique. Néanmoins, les diverses échelles d'entreprise mènent à des façons différentes de réaliser les objectifs des planificateurs. Des données du Bali, Indonésie, illustrent les effets sociaux et économiques différentiels de trois échelles d'entreprises touristiques: grande industrie, petite industrie et tourisme artisanal. Une comparaison de ces segments du continuum des entreprises touristiques au Bali montre que les objectifs des planificateurs économiques (augmentation des profits, devises, investissements, débouchés, production, esprit d'entreprise, infrastructure, minimisation de mauvais effets sociaux et culturels) ne sont pas réalisés le mieux par le développement des entreprises à grande échelle industrielle. **Mots clef**: *développement économique, échelle d'entreprise, Bali, Indonésie, tourisme.*

INTRODUCTION

Is industrialization the best course for economic development? Do industrially scaled enterprises meet the objectives of development more completely than do lesser scales? In particular, does the development of tourism on an industrial scale make any economic or socio-cultural sense?

In this paper an attempt is made to look at the problem of scale and how well different scales of enterprise meet the objectives of developers. Using data on existing and planned tourist accommodations from Bali, Indonesia, this investigation will note the variation among different scales of tourist enterprises and illustrate some of the criteria used by planners in justifying their projects, the variation in tourist situations, and the structure of tourism employment. The conclusions drawn regarding variation among the scales of tourist exploitation will be tempered by the author's knowledge of the situation on Bali, but these conclusions are not restricted to Bali. This analysis is relevant to tourism development wherever similar conditions prevail.

ERIC E. RODENBURG

Table 1

**The growth, 1969-1975, and projected growth, 1976-1982,
of tourism in Bali, Indonesia.**

Year	Tourist Arrivals[1]	Projected Arrivals[2]	Annual Growth (%)[a]
1969	46,765		--
1970	69,251		48.1
1971	80,030		15.6
1972	104,016		30.0
1073	148,734		43.0
1974	166,959		12.3
1975	202,489		21.3
1976		237,196	(17.14)
1977		277,851	(17.14)
1978		325,475	(17.14)
1979		371,261	(17.14)
1980		446,609	(17.14)
1981		523,158	(17.14)
1982		612,827	(17.14)

(a) Of several projections of tourist growth, 17.14% annually seems conservative.

Source: (1) Noronha 1976:3, (2) Bagus and Geriya 1978:1.

The growth of tourism in Bali, over the past ten years, has attracted planners, financiers and industrially organized corporations. They promote industrialization in Bali and other third-world areas, under the guise of "services for tourists." But, service as well as manufacturing can be industrially organized. Herbert Hiller (1977) notes that the tourist industry is just that, an industry. Those who promote large-scale exploitation of the tourist resource and those who promote other heavily capitalized industry hold similar beliefs in the efficiencies and economies of scale, and in the necessity of transforming "backward" societies into modern industrial societies (e.g., Kobrin 1977).

Scale has two meanings here: (1) relative size and capitalization, i.e., physical plant of an enterprise, and its correlate; (2) the relative bureaucratization, i.e., degree of industrial organization. Size and bureaucracy define scales of enterprise which, in the case of hotels and pensions, attract different categories of customers. The values and behaviors of those who manage various scales of tourist enterprises vary consistently and parallel those of their manufacturing cousins, as do relationships between management and employees, among employees, and between employees and clients.

THE EFFECTS OF SCALE IN ECONOMIC DEVELOPMENT

Hiller's reminder of the industrial nature of the tourist industry provides the basis for models of various scales of tourist accommodation, congruent with scales of manufacturing: large industrial, small industrial, and craft tourism. These models represent an underlying continuum which varies consistently on many dimensions. These models are not metaphors. They are the division of a real continuum into types amenable to analysis.

Table 2

Numbers of enterprises and numbers of rooms for three scales of tourist exploitation in Bali.

Scale of Enterprise	Number of Enterprises	Total Rooms
Large Industrial 'international standard hotels'	5 (1)	1431 (2)
Small Industrial 'economy class hotels'	111 (1)	2361 (1)
Craft 'homestays'	195 (2)[a]	1266 (2)[a]

(a) A gross underestimate. This figure represents "homestay" rooms in only four areas: Sanur, Kuta, Denpasar and Ubud. Enterprises in this scale are estimated using 6.5 rooms as the average size (BPRIPB 1977:45).

Source: (1) Noronha 1976:12, (2) BPRIPB 1976:15.

Data from Bali will illustrate this variation and substantiate this typology, for both on the *ground* and in the literature there is a clear distinction among the types. Large industrial tourism corresponds to hotels of "international standard." Small industrial tourism corresponds to "economy class" hotels. Craft tourism corresponds to "homestays" (*losman*, pensions), as well as to independent restaurants and souvenir shops. Tourist accommodations in Bali provide relatively large numbers of rooms in each scale of enterprise.

LARGE INDUSTRIAL TOURISM

Large industrial tourist exploitation is restricted to hotels of "international standard." That standard is defined as "an hotel with not less than 100 rooms equipped with baths, air conditioning, swimming pool,

ERIC E. RODENBURG

and other facilities (restaurant, bar, laundry, shops)'' (Noronha 1976:12). Such a hotel provides everything a tourist could require.

While this definition would appear to be guest-oriented, the contention here is that it is customer-oriented and that customers of this type of enterprise are primarily *retailers* of travel, *not* tourists. This contention is supported by the large percentage (63-80%) of foreign guests of this type on package or group tours (BPRIPB 1976:16; Anonymous 1979:47). These retailers (travel agents, charter operators, hotel booking agents, and travel wholesalers) are concerned not with their own accommodation, but with resale and profit. Large industrial tourism meets their business needs through: ease of communication, information about the existence of the hotel (e.g., through its membership in the Pacific Area Travel Association), opportunity for profit, the ability to make and confirm reservations internationally, and the connections that exist between hotels of this scale and airlines which allow fare discounts. The competitive advantage held by large industrial tourism over other scales, in attracting the business of retailers, is attributable to its economic muscle (advertising, telex, promotion), and its international connections.

Large industrial tourism is a corporate activity. Due to its high entry costs, individual entrepreneurs rarely engage in this scale of tourist exploitation. Such enterprises are built, owned, and managed by corporations--often trans-national--and in Bali always based off-island (Noronha 1976:12). These enterprises require a large amount of foreign exchange for their construction, furnishing and operation. In Bali, 40% of the operating costs of these hotels require payment in foreign exchange (Brown 1978). This high foreign exchange requirement further restricts participation in this scale by individual entrepreneurs.

Nusa Dua - In conjunction with the International Bank for Reconstruction and Development, the Indonesian government has committed itself to the concentration of all new ''international standard'' hotels in Nusa Dua, a tourism estate (which in a manufacturing context would be called an industrial park) on the southern tip of the island of Bali. All data in this article pertaining to the Nusa Dua project were obtained by Donald E. Brown (University of California, Santa Barbara) in interviews with World Bank officials.

To carry out this commitment to the concentration of large hotels, the Indonesian government has forbidden by law the construction of hotels of over 40 rooms outside of Nusa Dua. The Indonesian government has also invested $36.1 million in infrastructure development in the Nusa Dua project. An examination of the justifications and assumptions used by the planners of this project will provide further information on the economics of large industrial tourism.

THE EFFECTS OF SCALE IN ECONOMIC DEVELOPMENT

The original plans for Nusa Dua called for the completion of hotels totalling 2,500 rooms by 1983. As of November 1979 these plans remain basically unchanged although hotel construction has been delayed. The project covers 354 hectares and provides infrastructure investment in water supply, sewage treatment, solid waste disposal, a facilities core, a nursery, roads, telephone and telex connections, and a hotel training school which competes with a well-developed private sector capable of meeting the personnel needs of "international standard" hotels (Noronha 1973:45-57).

Table 3

1973 planned budget for the Nusa Dua Tourist Estate in Bali.
Cost of Project in U.S. dollars.

Item	Cost Per room	Cost of Project ($000's) Local	Foreign	Total
Infrastructure:				
water supply	$2,340	1,403	4,468	5,871
sewage system	671	883	795	1,678
solid waste disposal	139	109	240	347
landscape irrigation	224	229	330	559
landscaping	1,426	3,191	394	3,585
storm water drainage	301	658	94	752
internal roads	478	638	558	1,196
electrical install.	629	364	1,209	1,573
amenity core	927	1,051	1,266	2,317
Bualu-Benoa infrastr.	111	197	80	277
hotel training ctr.	457	534	608	1,142
technical assistance	437	211	882	1,093
project admin.	240	445	155	600
land acquisition	405	1,012		1,012
access road	465	588	574	1,162
Denpasar by-pass	1,367	1,803	1,614	3,416
multi-purpose roads	3,264	4,230	3,930	8,160
telephone and telex	504	385	874	1,259
demonstration farm	40	692	31	100
Sub-total Infrastructure:	$14,440	18,000	18,100	36,100
Superstructure:				
hotel construction	$25,000	37,500	25,000	62,500
Sub-total Superstructure:	$25,000	37,500	25,000	62,500
Grand Total Nusa Dua Tourist Estate:	$39,444	55,500	43,100	98,600

Source: D.E. Brown (1978) from interviews with World Bank officials.

ERIC E. RODENBURG

It can be seen from the breakdown of the infrastructure budget for Nusa Dua that the primary consideration in the planning of Nusa Dua was to attract investors for hotel construction, not to fulfill the needs of tourists nor to fulfill the infrastructure needs of the Balinese. Only \$8.2 million (22.6%) of the planned infrastructure budget of \$36.1 million will be used for multi-purpose roads and is the only item, with the exception of the extension of water and electrical supply lines to two local villages, that can be said to serve both the Balinese and the tourist industry.

The remaining \$28 million in planned infrastructure was expected to require \$14.1 million in foreign exchange. The construction and furnishing of hotels, by private investors, with a total cost of \$62.5 million was expected to require \$25 million in foreign exchange. These figures become more understandable when partitioned into cost per room (production unit). Each room in the Nusa Dua project was planned to have an infrastructure investment of \$14,440, a construction investment of \$25,000, and a total investment of \$39,444. Of this total investment, \$17,240 was required in foreign exchange. An insight into what these costs mean, in the context of the Balinese ecomony, can be gleaned by contrasting them with the average lowest monthly salary received from employment in hotels of "international standard" in Bali, \$42.68, and by contrasting them with the average lowest monthly earnings of peasants in Bali, \$1.52-\$8.33 (various sources cited in Universitas Udayana and Francillon 1975:734).

The cost of this project clashes with the general scale of the Balinese economy and its population of farmers. The reaction of the Balinese to the construction of the Bali Beach Hotel, while primarily couched in terms of its transcendent ugliness and height, was also a reaction to its industrial scale. Design controls and the law now require much more beautiful and harmonious structures at Nusa Dua. Yet, the sheer sale of the Nusa Dua project is, with the exception of the airport, completely without precedent on the island. The Nusa Dua project was not designed to be integrated into the lives of the Balinese, they were expected to integrate themselves into the project. They must adapt to it, not it to them.

In planning the Nusa Dua project, the Indonesian government and the IBRD analyzed the relevant economic and social factors and calculated an economic rate of return fair to all investors. It is clear, however, that in their planning no real thought was given to alternate scales of enterprise, alternate scales which might be more appropriate for Bali.

SMALL INDUSTRIAL TOURISM

Small industrial tourist exploitation refers to "economy class" hotels. The variation within this category reflects its intermediary position between large industrial and craft tourism, the extremes of the continuum. Noronha reports (1976:12) that as of April 1975 there were 116 hotels on Bali - five of

THE EFFECTS OF SCALE IN ECONOMIC DEVELOPMENT

"international standard," five of more than 50 but less than 100 rooms, and 106 small hotels of less than 50 rooms. Of the 2,361 rooms in these 111 establishments (an average of 21 rooms per hotel) only 556 or 23.5% were air conditioned. Other amenities are equally variable. Private baths are common, but shops are distinctly rare, and restaurants and bars may or may not be present.

Table 4

Survey of tourist departures by air.

Scale of Accommodation	Independent	Foreign Group/Package	Total	Domestic	Grand Total
Large industrial	24.0	41.1	65.1	32.1	59.3
Small industrial	18.9	9.3	28.2	58.1	33.4
Craft	5.8	.4	6.2	1.2	5.4
Family/friends	.4	.1	.5	8.6	1.9
Total	49.1 +	50.9 =	100.0	100.0	100.0

Source: Derived from BPRIPB (1976:16 & 53).

In contrast with large industrial tourism, the small industrial type markets its services more directly to guests, not retailers. Fully two-thirds of the foreign guests of this type are independent tourists, and only one-third are on group or package tours. A great part of the group/package component in this type are tourists from the nearby developed countries of Australia and New Zealand. Without the connections and economic resources of the large industrial type, small industrial operators must rely on personal contacts with travel retailers for group and package tour business, even though their services are less expensive.

The entry costs for small industrial tourist enterprises are lower than the entry costs for large industrial tourism. The average investment per room in this scale is only $6,218 (BPRIPB 1977:45,50). Thus *individual* entrepreneurs are able to invest in this scale of enterprise. To a great extent the ownership of these hotels in initially Balinese, but "There has been a gradual shift of ownership. . . out of the hands of the Balinese" (Noronha 1976:12). This can only mean into the hands of other Indonesians and Indonesian corporations. This scale of enterprise relies more on local suppliers and supplies than does the large industrial type, both in construction and in operations. This low foreign exchange requirement helps promote entry into this scale of enterprise by individual entrepreneurs.

ERIC E. RODENBURG

CRAFT TOURISM

Craft tourism includes all "homestays" and small independent restaurants and souvenir shops. This scale of enterprise is homogeneous, tending to be family-owned and operated. What variation exists (presence or absence of electricity, larger-smaller, village-country) is small. The enterprises in this scale of tourist exploitation outnumber those in the other scales combined. In the village of Kuta alone there were, in 1976, 180 "homestays" (with an average of 6.5 rooms), 64 restaurants, and 93 souvenir shops (BPRIPB 1977:45).

This scale of tourist exploitation markets its product directly to guests and has only a minimal (6.5%, Table 4) group/package tour component. Operators of these enterprises attract tourists on the merits of their establishments and inexpensive prices. Restaurants in this scale of enterprise have as their market the entire craft tourist population.

The entry costs for this level of tourism enterprise are small. The average cost per room in a "homestay" is only $1,311 (BPRIPB 1977:45 & 50), within the means of many people. Indeed, the term "homestay" reflects the gradual conversion of private homes to bed and breakfast establishments. As capital is accumulated and the market for their services expands, so too do "homestays." The ownership of this scale of enterprise is almost invariably Balinese, usually local. Because there is *no* foreign exchange requirements in this scale's construction or operation, entry by individuals is relatively easy.

VARIATION IN SCALE

Each of the three scales of tourist exploitation meets the objectives of economic development to differing degrees, providing criteria for judging the most appropriate scale for any situation. The objectives of economic development, in any particular case, are best defined by those promoting that development. M.J. Prajogo, Director General of Tourism, Republic of Indonesia, listed objectives of tourism development (1976) that can be used to judge the appropriate scale of development for Bali; these are 1) increased earnings, 2) increased foreign exchange, 3) increased investment, 4) increased job opportunities, 5) increased production, 6) increased entrepreneurship, 7) increased infrastructure, and 8) the minimization of adverse social and cultural effects. A comparison of data on craft, small industrial, and large industrial tourism, including the assumptions and justifications of the planners of Nusa Dua, will demonstrate how each scale meets these development objectives.

1. Increased Earnings: Tourism brings new money into the Balinese economy and thus generates both direct and indirect employment. There are at least two measures of these increased earnings: salaries and their distribution.

THE EFFECTS OF SCALE IN ECONOMIC DEVELOPMENT

Table 5

**Average monthly salaries of employees
by scale of enterprise (Rps. 410-$1.00).**

Scale of Enterprise	Rupiahs	Dollars
Large industrial (2)	17,500[a]	42.68[a]
Small industrial (1)	14,666	35.77
Craft (1)		
"homestay"	6,588	16.07
restaurant	4,687	11.43
souvenirshop	5,000	12.20
average craft		
salary	5,848	14.26

(a) Average lowest monthly salary.

Source: (1) Derived from BPRIPB 1977:65, (2) Universitas Udayana and
         Francillon 1975:734.

Employee salaries can be seen to vary directly with the scale of the
enterprise in which they work, but the geographic distribution of earnings in
Bali is unbalanced.   All large industrial enterprises are located in the
southern part of the Badung District. Most small industrial and craft level
establishments are also located there, although they can be found
throughout the island. The Nusa Dua project will increase this imbalance
and can be expected to lead to further urban growth in the nearby capital of
Denpasar as people migrate to take advantage of employment opportunities. Large industrial tourism in Nusa Dua can be expected to concentrate rather than disperse earnings and to lead to local population growth.
Craft and small industrial tourism, however, can adapt to local attactions
and succeed economically with smaller numbers of tourists. These lesser
scales represent the best opportunity for providing earnings potential in the
hinterland.

2. Increased Foreign Exchange: International tourism of all scales will provide foreign exchange earnings. Tourism in Bali produces an ever growing
amount of Indonesia's net foreign exchange earnings. From 1969-1973
Bali's foreign exchange earnings increased from $2 million to $9 million.
The great bulk of this growth is attributed to tourism (Universitas Udayana
and Francillon 1975:729). There are two ways to look at foreign exchange
earnings by scale: net earnings and return on foreign exchange invested.

ERIC E. RODENBURG

Table 6

Foreign Exchange Earnings

Scale of Enterprise	Gross Annual Foreign Exchange Earnings	Import Leakages	Net Annual Foreign Exchange Earnings	Total Foreign Exchange Invested	Annual Rate of Return for Foreign Exchange Invested
Large industrial (Nusa Dua projection)	$55,202,371	(35%)[b] 40%	($36,000,000)[b] $33,055,312	$43,100,000	(83.5%)[b] 76.7%
Small industrial	$39,882,637	20%[c]	$31,906,109	$6,218,000[c]	513.1%
Craft	$10,447,668	0%[d]	$10,447,668	-0-[d]	∞

(a) The computation of Gross Annual Foreign Exchange Earnings assumes a 1.7 double occupancy factor, a 75% occupancy rate for the 2500 rooms and an average expenditure per tourist of $46.00 per day in the large industrial scale (Donald Brown, personal communication 1978), $34.28 per tourist per day in the small industrial scale and $8.98 per tourist per day in the craft scale (BPRIPB 1977:74).
(b) These figures are derived from the Nusa Dua planners' assumed foreign exchange earnings of $36 million.
(c) The figure of 20% for Import Leakages in this scale is assumed, in the absence of information, only for the purposes of computation. The figure of $6,218,000 for Total Foreign Exchange Invested assumes the same ratio of cost per room to foreign exchange invested per room as was assumed for the Nusa Dua project excluding infrastructure (2:5:1). Cost per room in this scale was found to be $6,218 (derived from BPRIPB 1977:45 & 50).
(d) In the craft scale there are no Import Leakages. In the craft scale there is no Total Foreign Exchange Invested. Cost per room in this scale was found to be $1,311 (derived from BPRIPB 1977:45 & 51).

Source: D.E. Brown (1978), interviews with World Bank officials and BPRIPB (1977).

Large industrial tourism, represented by assumptions of cost from Nusa Dua, gives greater gross annual foreign exchange earnings than do the same number of rooms in either of the other two scales. Foreign exchange requirements in operating costs, however, result in large import leakages that reduce net annual foreign exchange earnings to only $2-4 million more than those of small industrial tourism (using a conservatively high assumption for small industrial import leakages of 20%). Even craft tourism, with

THE EFFECTS OF SCALE IN ECONOMIC DEVELOPMENT

average daily tourist expenditures only one-fifth as much as is spent by guests of the large industrial type, has net annual foreign exchange earnings of $10 million, fully one-third of that earned by large industrial tourism.

If the rate of return of foreign exchange for foreign exchange invested is calculated, the investment of $43.1 million in the infrastructure and superstructure of Nusa Dua returns 76.7-83.5% annually. Yet, the return on small industrial tourism (using the conservatively high assumption of $6.2 million for foreign exchange invested) is calculated to be 520% annually. The annual rate of return for craft tourism is theoretically infinite as there is practically no foreign exchange requirements in its construction or operating costs. This is, of course, misleading, but it does point to the need for planners to weigh investment strategies against alternatives.

3. Increased Investment: As was seen in Table 3 (1973 Planned Budget of the Nusa Dua Project), large industrial tourist exploitation requires massive capital investment. If the absolute quantity of money was the only criterion used in measuring which scale of enterprise best met the objective of increased investment, large industrial tourism would win.

Table 7

Investment and Employment

Scale of Enterprise	Investment Per Room	Employment Per Room	Investment Per Employee
Large industrial (1)			
Nusa Dua:			
Infrastructure	$14,440	2	$ 7,220
Superstructure	$25,000	2	$12,500
Total	$39,440	2	$19,720
Small industrial (2)	$ 6,218	1.5	$ 4,145
Craft (2)			
"homestay"	$ 1,311	.5	$ 2,789
restaurant	($ 7,261)[a]	(6.4)[a]	$ 1,135
souvenirshop	($ 451)[a]	(1.7)[a]	$ 265

(a) These figures represent investment and employment per enterprise.

Source: (1) D.E. Brown, 1978, interviews with World Bank officials,
         (2) derived from BPRIPB 1977:45-65.

ERIC E. RODENBURG

If investment per room and investment per job are the criteria used to judge the appropriate scale of enterprise, it is clear that both vary directly with the scale. Thus, for the same amount of money more rooms, which means the ability to exploit more tourists, and more jobs can be generated at the small industrial and craft levels. In this sense, the lesser scales of enterprise are more economically desireable.

Capital is not unlimited. Government investment in one sector of the economy implies lack of investment in other sectors (opportunity cost). Massive government investment in the infrastructure of a project such as Nusa Dua means that other projects must be postponed or ignored. Irrigation projects, small-scale manufacturing, the diversification of agriculture and education might be more worthwhile investments in terms of the economic rate of return and in long-term benefits to the people of Bali and Indonesia.

4. Increased Job Opportunities: The common sense notions about the economies of scale would lead one to believe that employment would vary inversely with the scale of enterprise. Employment in Bali shows a contrary result.

Table 8

Job Opportunities

Scale of Enterprise	Employment Per Room	Rooms Per Enterprise	Workers Per Enterprise	Total Rooms	Total Employment
Large industrial	2	286.2	572.4	1431	2862
Small industrial	1.5	21.1	31.7	2361	3542
Craft					
"homestay"	.47[a]	6.5	3.1	1266[b]	595
restaurant	(.37)[c]		6.4		(468)[c]
souvenirshop	(.14)[c]		1.7		(177)[c]
total craft	(.98)[c]				(1240)[c]

(a) Gross underestimate, this figure does not include unpaid family members.
(b) Gross underestimate, this figure includes "homestays" from only four areas.
(c) Assumes a constant ratio of employment per room as found in Kuta (derived from BPRIPB 1977:45-65).

Source: Tables 2 and 7 (BPRIPB 1977:45-65).

THE EFFECTS OF SCALE IN ECONOMIC DEVELOPMENT

Both average employment per enterprise and average employment per room can be seen to vary directly with scale. Common sense notions about the economies of scale do not apply in tourism. Large industrial tourism employs more people per room, and at a greater cost per job, than do the lesser scales. The objective of increased job opportunities, if measured in jobs per room, rather than cost per job, is best met by industrially organized corporations.

5. Increased Production: The increase in production of supplies and materials to meet the demands of tourism is not easily quantifiable. Large industrial tourism puts fewer demands on local supplies, especially food supplies, than do the other scales, the great component of large industrial operating costs that requires foreign exchange is evidence for this.

Brown (personal communication 1979) has pointed out that managers of "international standard" hotels in Bali are objecting to requirements of the Indonesian government that they buy food supplies locally. They reason that by using local supplies they lose their "international" rating. Who would take it from them is unclear. A more reasonable explanation for their resistance, to this requirement, is to be found in their industrially organized kitchens. The mass production of meals from a standard, invariant menu, like the mass production of any product, requires guaranteed supplies of the standard parts. The non-industrially organized agricultural sector in Bali cannot make that guarantee.

In contrast, other scales of tourism in Bali adapt their menus to available supplies. The blackboard rather than the printer becomes the means for communicating that adaptation. This is true internationally.

What is true for food is also true for other supplies. The smaller scale enterprises adapt to what is available. The objective of increased production is best met by small industrial and, especially, craft tourism.

6. Increased Entrepreneurship: In economic development the role of the entrepreneur is crucial. Certainly innovation, experimentation, risk-taking, quick adaptation to changing circumstances and business know-how is necessary for self-propelled economic growth. The lower the entry costs in an enterprise, the greater the number of people who will have the opportunity to become entrepreneurs.

As is expected from their low entry costs, craft level enterprises outnumber all other levels in Bali. Number of entrepreneurs varies inversely with scale. Local ownership means that existing social relations, even if changing, are still important. Local ownership implies that economic success for the entrepreneur results in benefits to the local community. The

ERIC E. RODENBURG

Table 9

Local and Foreign Entrepreneurship

Scale of Enterprise	Number	Local Village	Origin of Owner Greater Bali	Indonesian/ Foreign	Nature of Ownership
Large industrial	5	0 %	0 %	100 %	Corporate
Small industrial	111	33.3%	16.7%	50 %	Corporate/ Individual
Craft					
"homestay"	195[a]	66.7%	28.5%	4.8%	Individual
restaurant	NA[b]	66.7%	33.3%	-0-	Individual
souvenirshop	NA[b]	66.7%	33.3%	-0-	Individual

(a) Gross underestimate, this figure includes "homestays" from only four areas.
(b) The numbers of total craft level restaurants and souvenirshops is not available.

Source: Table 2 (Noronha 1976:12; BPRIPB 1977:45-46).

economic and political power of craft scale entrepreneurs is, however, limited in comparison with those of other scales. Their voice is heard neither internationally, to compete for package tour business, nor locally to push for infrastructure investment to increase the economic potential of their scale and their locality.

7. Increased Infrastructure: The Nusa Dua project is a classic example of investment in infrastructure, the physical framework for development, that does not also benefit the local people. The investment there in water supply, sewage, roads and other facilities is designed as a framework for large industrial development. If the objective of increased infrastructure is to be met, infrastructure investment must serve the needs of the local people as well as the needs of the tourist industry. The concentration of investment in Nusa Dua means that, in Bali, this scale of enterprise does not meet this objective.

THE EFFECTS OF SCALE IN ECONOMIC DEVELOPMENT

Because tourist enterprises of smaller scale are dispersed more widely over the island, especially craft level enterprises, infrastructure investment that benefits enterprises on these lesser scales would also benefit the local populace. Better roads, local water projects, and other small projects would not only help these smaller scale enterprises to compete, they would clearly improve the lives of the local people.

8. The Minimization of Adverse Social and Cultural Effects: The question of scale-dependent social and cultural effects of tourism development in Bali has not yet been addressed. Investigation of this question is scheduled for fieldwork in 1980. But it is obvious that the social and cultural effects of tourist enterprises of various scales cannot be separated from their economic effects.

The primary rationale of the Nusa Dua planners was the minimization of the adverse social and cultural effects of tourism. They wished to concentrate and isolate tourists, like any other industrial effluent, to minimize social and cultural pollution. They *felt* that the adverse effects of their project would be more limited than those tourist enterprises on a smaller scale. The control and correction of whatever adverse effects did result from the Nusa Dua project were, however, seen by the planners to be the responsibility of local Balinese authorities. Curiously, the planners never thought to consult with those authorities in the planning of Nusa Dua (Noronha 1976:9). In 1977 Balinese social scientists rejected the strategy of isolation (Bagus personal communication 1979).

One of the most obvious adverse effects of the southern focus of tourism on Bali is the increasing urbanization of the area and the diversion of irrigated rice lands. Nusa Dua was in part justified to halt the diversion of rice land and was located on waste and non-irrigated land just for that purpose. Over the last 17 years, the area devoted to irrigated rice land in Badung and Gianyar Districts, the two most affected, decreased 8% and 10%, respectively (Noronha 1976:17). Given the time span involved, this decrease cannot be attributed totally to the increase in tourism, rather it is to be attributed to the urbanization that accompanies development. Certainly in Sanur, where all five "international standard" hotels outside of Nusa Dua are located, no irrigated rice land has been directly alienated in their construction (Anonymous 1979:10 & 50). Scales of tourism that promote migration would also promote urbanization, and this urbanization would result in the diversion of irrigated rice land.

ERIC E. RODENBURG

Table 10

Origin of Employees

Scale of Enterprise	Local Village	Greater Bali	Indonesia	Foreign
Large industrial (1)	8.6%	74.4%	15.0%	1.0%
Small industrial (2)	17.5%	69.7%	12.2%	.5%
Craft (2)				
"homestay"	59.5%	40.5%	0 %	0 %
restaurant	68.8%	28.1%	2.1%	0 %
souvenirshop	75.0%	25.0%	0 %	0 %

Source: (1) Research Team of the State University of Udayana (1974:57), and Noronha citing Checchi and Company (1974, 1976:13). (2) BPRIPB (1977:60).

Large industrial tourism promotes migration, as only 8.6% of this scale's employees are native to the location of the enterprise. Migration of employees varies directly with the scale of the enterprise. Migration fosters urbanization with its adverse effects on agricultural land, traditional social relations, social organization, and values.

The kinds of tourists served by each level of enterprise and the interactions they have with Balinese must have important social and cultural effects. What data presently exist on tourist variation in Bali deal with the gross categories *group / package* and *independent*. Simple observation, however, shows that in Bali the amount and degree of interaction varies inversely with the scale of enterprise frequented by a tourist.

The group and package tourist served primarily by large industrial tourism stay a short time on Bali, and average of 4.18 days (Noronha 1976:4). They have minimal interactions with Balinese *not* employed by such enterprises. Their interactions with employees are transient, impersonal and tend to be of superior to menial rather than of guest with host.

Independent tourists, who make up the bulk of the guests of craft level enterprises and the majority of the guests of small industrial tourism, stay longer than do group/package tourists (and average of 5.57 days, although length of stay varies inversely with scale)(Noronha 1976:4), and tend to seek out more normal interactions with Balinese. Especially at the the craft level the independent tourist tends to seek greater understanding and involvement. Tourists at this level have more extensive and intensive interactions with Balinese *not* employed by their homestay. Their interactions with employees tend more toward that of guest with host.

THE EFFECTS OF SCALE IN ECONOMIC DEVELOPMENT

Which of these extremes, the group/package tourist or the independent tourist, is more disruptive of the local culture? It is difficult to say. In Bali it is reported (Budhisantoso 1978), however, that there is no evidence for any breakdown in social organization or families at the craft level ("homestays"). At the large industrial level there is evidence that migration has caused an adjustment in traditional social organization (The Research Team of the State University of Udayana 1977:99).

CONCLUSION

The objectives of development are *not* best met by the development of large industrial tourism. In Bali, craft and small industrial tourism are more appropriate scales to achieve those objectives. Further, the lesser scales of enterprise coincide with the general scale of the Balinese economy and society.

Smaller scale enterprises offer a greater opportunity for profit and control to *local people* than do enterprises on a larger scale. Craft tourism is an indigenous adaptation to the tourist resource and as such is congruent with traditional, social relationships and values. Small industrial tourism, like any indigenous industrial organization (Kobrin 1977:36), accommodates traditional social relationships and values. Large industrial tourism imposes industrial relationships and values, ignoring the traditional.

Different scales of tourism provide different services but compete directly with one another. The competitive advantage held by large industrial tourism, in attracting package and group tourists, is due to its economic muscle and international connections, not to "economies of scale."

Given this analysis, why do multi-national corporations, government planners, and international financial institutions promote industrial scale tourism development? Hiller (1977:118), in his analysis of the tourist industry, reports that:

> The sum of (their) positions is that tourism makes good sense for overseas development because it generates industrially scaled opportunities for metropolitan investments; that local sensibilities encourage backwardness; that there is no argument about the priorities of development and who is to define them. . . It would be naive to assume that the application of industrial values would not reach into the organization of something grown as massive as travel.

Beyond the industrial values and ethnocentrism of the promoters of large industrial tourism, there are serious financial constraints on the promotion of alternative scales of tourist enterprise. International financial in-

ERIC E. RODENBURG

stitutions are unwilling to consider small projects for funding (Noronha, personal communication 1978), and any project must generate sufficient income to repay lending institutions. The overhead costs of funding any project require such institutions to consider only projects of sufficient scale to make their involvement worthwhile. Government planners act within these constraints.

There is a less defensible constraint on the promotion of smaller scales of tourist enterprises, the one intimated by Hiller. There is a lack of imagination and an unthinking commitment to industrialization on the part of development planners. The history of the Nusa Dua project and the assumptions and justifications used by its planners are evidence of this.

What can be done to promote smaller-scale tourism development? Government planners can begin to coordinate investment in infrastructure with the needs of small scale entrepreneurs and the needs of local communities. This would make small industrial and craft enterprises more attractive to both retailers and guests. While protecting tourist attractions, local governments can also allow local entrepreneurs freedom to adapt to the tourism resource. A "hands-off" policy would help maintain local control and minimize massive social disruptions.

Finally, governments could actively promote smaller scale enterprises among travel retailers, dulling the competitive edge held, in this market, by large industrial tourism enterprises.

Tourism can lead to intercultural and interpersonal understanding. It can lead to economic development and the improvement of people's lives. The scale of tourist enterprise used to achieve these possibilities makes a difference. It is necessary to adapt the scale of tourism development to the realities of the local situation. It is not necessary nor is it desireable, to adapt the local situation to the realities of industrialization.□ □

BIBLIOGRAPHY

Anonymous
  1979   An Analysis of Sanur (report of a survey of Sanur, September 1977), translated by Donald Brown, U.C. Santa Barbara, manuscript.
Bagus, I.G.N., and I.W. Geriya
  1979   Social pollution in Kuta, Paper No. III/6. National Seminar on Southeast Asia, Gadjam Mada University, Yogyakarta, Indonesia (May 3-6, 1978).

THE EFFECTS OF SCALE IN ECONOMIC DEVELOPMENT

BPRIPB (Baden Pengembangan Rencana Induk Parawisata Bali)
  1976   Laporan Pendauluan. Survey wisatawan melalui udara di Bali,
  Xerox, Denpasar, Indonesia.

  1977   Penelitian / Survey Social di Desa Kuta. Xerox, Denpasar, Indonesia.

Buhisantoso, S.
  1978   Parawisata dan Penjaruhnya Terhadap Nilai-Nilai Budaya.
  Seminar Pembinaan Kebudayaan dan Pengembangan Keparawisataan,
  translated by Donald Brown, U.C., Santa Barbara, manuscript.

Hiller, Herbert
  1977   Industrialization, tourism, island nations and changing values. *In*
  The Social and Economic Impact of Tourism on Pacific Communities,
  edited by Bryan H. Farrell, pp. 115-121, Santa Cruz, California.

Kobrin, Stephen Jay
  1977   Foreign Direct Investment, Industrialization and Social Change.
  Greenwich, Connecticut: JAI Press.

Noronha, Raymond
  1973   A Report on the Proposed Tourism Project in Bali. Washington,
  D.C.: World Bank.

  1976   Paradise Revisited: Tourism in Bali. Joint UNESCO / IBRD
  Seminar on the social and Cultural Impacts of Tourism, Washington,
  D.C. (8-10 December).

Prajogo, M.J.
  1976   Basic Concepts on the National Development of Tourism. Speech
  given before the Indonesian National Defense Institute (June 12).

Research Team of the State University of Udayana
  1974   Untitled. The Impact of Tourism on the Sociocultural Development of Bali. Bali, Indonesia: Universitas Udayana.

  1977   The Impact of Tourism on Village Community Development.
  Translated into English. Bali, Indonesia: Universitas Udayana.

Universitas Udayana and Gerard Francillon
  1975   Tourism in Bali--Its Economic and Socio-cultural Impact: Three
  Points of View. International Social Science Journal XXVII: 721-757.

Submitted 10 September 1979
Revised version submitted 16 January 1980
Accepted 27 February 1980
Refereed anonymously

[24]

THE EFFECTS OF SCALE IN TOURISM PROJECTS IN DEVELOPING COUNTRIES

C. L. Jenkins
University of Strathclyde
Glasgow, Scotland

ABSTRACT

The paper by Rodenburg (Annals VII:2:177–196) on the effect of scale in tourism development in Bali raises important questions relating to tourism development in Third World countries. One fundamental question is whether large-scale development is inevitable in such countries, or whether there is persuasive evidence to support smaller and craft scale enterprises. This article undertakes a critical review of Rodenburg's analysis and concludes that large scale developments are likely to be inevitable because of external economies of scale and market structures in international tourism, but that the consequences of such developments can be foreseen and therefore mitigated by appropriate pre-project planning.
Keywords: economic development, scale of enterprise, economy of scale, tourism development.

C. L. Jenkins is a Senior Lecturer in Tourism and has a particular interest in the formulation of tourism policies for developing countries.

Annals of Tourism Research, Vol. 9, pp. 229–249, 1982
Printed in the USA. All rights reserved.

0160–7383/82/020229–21803.00/0
© 1982 J. Jafari and Pergamon Press Ltd

THE EFFECTS OF SCALE IN TOURISM PROJECTS

RÉSUMÉ

Les effects de l'échelle sur les projets de tourisme dans les pays en voie de développement. L'étude presentee par Rodenburg (Annals VII:2:177–196) sur les effets du développement du tourisme à Bali soulève des questions importantes quant au développement du tourisme dans les pays du Tiers Monde. Une question principale est: le développement sur une grande échelle est-il inévitable dans de tels pays, ou existe-il des preuves convaincantes pour maintenir les petites entreprises et les pensions? Cet article consiste en une revue critique de l'analyse de Rodenburg et en conclut que les développements sur une grande échelle sont peut-être inévitables à cause des économies d'échelle d'extérieure et à cause des structures du marché du tourisme international, mais qu'on en peut prévoir les résultats et, par conséquent, les attenuer par un procès de planification avant l'approbation des projects. **Mots Clef**: développement économique, l'échelle de l'entreprise, économies d'échelle, développement du tourisme.

INTRODUCTION

The article by Rodenburg raises a number of issues of importance to anyone concerned with the planning of tourism development in Third World countries. Although the article specifically refers to Bali, many of the implications arising from the scale of development have a wider, more general relevance. Given that much of the detailed, non-economic impact of the Nusa Dua project is the subject of current fieldwork, it may be of interest to explore here some of Rodenburg's economic criticisms.

The following comment is structured as a critique of Rodenburg's paper for a number of reasons. First, the tenor of Rodenburg's analysis is related to the impact of tourism development on the host community. He is not unaware, or apparently unsympathetic, to the economic case for tourism per se, but his *primary* concern appears to be with non-economic issues. Although his analysis relates to Bali, Rodenburg can be seen as representing a wider group of tourism writers who have challenged, and continue to challenge, the primacy of *economic* motivation as the main "raison d'etre" for encouraging tourism development in Third World countries. As such, Rodenburg's analysis can be viewed as having a wider *representative* value than his specific comments on Bali would suggest.

Second, although tourism planners involved in development proj-

C. L. JENKINS

ects in the Third World are not unmindful of the social, cultural, and environmental impact of the projects, they tend to accept the economic case for investment in tourism as the prime reason supporting tourism as part of a development strategy. In most, if not all, developing countries, governments tend to support this view. Although there is now available well documented evidence to illustrate the non-economic disadvantages of tourism as a development option, in many countries these options are so limited as to cause— almost instinctively—a lower priority to be given to social and cultural considerations in the investment and development decision. This may not be an acceptable situation to many students of tourism, but in many developing countries it is a statement of fact.

Third, the question of the scale of a proposed development is of critical importance in understanding the two viewpoints outlined above. The Rodenburg analysis argues for a limitation on the scale and type of development in order to conserve and, presumably, enhance the existing socio-economic community norms. That is, any development should be adapted to meet the needs of the *host* community. It might be argued alternatively that any country seeking to establish an *international* tourism sector might have to give precedence to the priorities of the foreign visitor. As such, a dichotomy of views exist on this very important development criterion.

This article does not seek to establish whether economic criteria should prevail over other factors, because ultimately this will depend on political rather than technical considerations, but rather to examine some of the factors which influence the scale and type of tourism developments in Third World countries.

Despite the inherent interest of Rodenburg's article, four general reservations can be raised against his analysis:

In the first place, the analysis is limited to the *domestic* impact of the Nusa Dua project—it does not consider the *external* economies of scale. The statistical evidence presented does not convincingly support his contention that "the objectives of development are not best met by the development of large industrial tourism" but rather implies a fundamental question—can a developing country wanting to encourage an international standard tourism sector *avoid* such large industrial scale developments?

In the second place, the analysis is structured around, and data is presented under, three categories of scale: "large industrial," "small industrial," and "craft tourism." The impression given is that returns to scale are *independent* of each other—"different scales of tourism provide different services which compete directly with one another." This statement is unlikely to stand detailed economic analysis. The probability is that each scale of development will have a

THE EFFECTS OF SCALE IN TOURISM PROJECTS

considerable degree of *interdependence* with the others. It is likely, for example, that a proportion of the per capita earnings (and total demand) of the craft sector will have "trickled down" from the expenditure of tourists buying accomodation in large and small scale hotels.

In the third place, the analysis suggests that on economic and non-economic grounds, the enclave Nusa Dua project is inappropriate. It might be argued that economies of scale together with the distributive system characteristic of the international tourism industry may make such scale and type of development inevitable.

In the fourth place, the plea for government encouragement and support for the small industrial and craft tourism sector ignores some of the external parameters to government intervention in the tourism industry.

Before examining these criticisms in detail it is necessary to consider the framework of international tourism, and to identify those characteristics which affect development, but are exogenous factors to policy formulation in host countries. The following analysis is presented in four sections: (a) an examination of some of the characteristics of tourism demand, (b) the concomitant provision of tourist facilities in the host country, (c) the impact of (a) and (b) on the type and scale of development, and (d) these issues related to Rodenburg's paper.

SOME CHARACTERISTICS OF INTERNATIONAL
TOURISM DEMAND

The Travel Decision

As a tourist destination, Bali—or any tourist-receiving country—is affected by the *mechanics* of the tourist travel decision and the transference of that decision into the tourist distribution system. The most obvious characteristic of this system is that international tourists, by definition, travel to the host country to engage in tourist activity. This feature gives rise to two aspects of demand which are immutable—that for any host country international tourism demand is largely an exogenously determined variable, and that the organization and distribution of that demand is primarily related to the satisfaction of tourists' expectations rather than meeting host country's development priorities. It may be that these two aspects of demand are not necessarily in conflict with host country's expectations, but there is a growing volume of literature which suggests

C. L. JENKINS

that it is an area of concern (de Kadt 1979; Smith 1978; Turner and Ash 1975).

The travel decisions may be separated into three parts:

The Potential Tourist. The potential tourist in the generating country will decide to allocate part of this budget for foreign holiday travel. This decision is itself a complex amalgam of economic and social determinants over which the host country has very little influence, except indirectly through advertising and relative prices. Much of the analysis of demand for international tourism has necessarily been carried out at the macro-level by writers such as Gray (1970), Merigo and Potter (1970), Artus (1972) and, more recently, Schumeister (1979). Although not ignoring the importance of exchange rates and prices in host countries (Gerakis 1965; I.T.Q. 1976), the main determinants of international tourism demand are recognized as being external to the host countries. When an individual (or family) decision has been made to allocate a budget for holiday purposes, most potential tourists consult travel agents for information and advice on possible destinations.

The Travel Retailer. The potential tourist's ultimate choice of destination is likely to be greatly influenced by the information and guidance given by the travel agent. If the potential tourist is seeking to buy an inclusive tour arrangement on a group basis (a growing trend in international tourism demand patterns) then the *availability* of packaged destinations will effectively form a parameter to choice. Under these circumstances, the customer's choice is a function of the travel agent's information and of the travel wholesaler's range of packaged destinations available at the time of purchase. In the United Kingdom, for example, over 80% of foreign holidays are purchased from travel agents. This point-of-sale outlet is a link in the chain of distribution which begins when the tour wholesaler chooses to market a particular destination. With economies of scale having significant effects on tour prices together with the growing number of customers buying inclusive tours, in many generating countries the tour wholesalers have become the "interpreters and coordinators of demand." (Dobbie 1976).

The Tour Wholesaler. The business objectives of tour wholesalers might be represented as being the need to identify and organize travel opportunities to destinations which will be acceptable to customers. This notion of acceptability is of major importance in understanding the type of tourist amenity provided in host countries,

THE EFFECTS OF SCALE IN TOURISM PROJECTS

particularly in developing countries. The tour wholesaler will attempt to ensure that the standard of amenity provided—accommodation, food, recreation facilities, etc.—will cocoon the tourist against the unfamiliar environments. As Cohen (1972:166) has noted "Most tourists seem to need something familiar around them, something to remind them of home, whether it is food, newspapers, living quarters, or another person from their native country. Many of today's tourists are able to enjoy the experience of change and novelty only from a strong base of familiarity, which enables them to feel secure enough to enjoy the strangeness of what they experience. They would like to experience the novelty of the macro-involvement of a strange place from the security of a familiar micro-environment. And many will not venture abroad except on those well-trodden paths equipped with familiar means of transportation, hotels, and food." It is this need to provide *familiarity* an "environmental bubble" which is a central concern in all tour wholesalers' planning. Without *familiarity* there is unlikely to be customer *acceptability* which is necessary to ensure future sales and possible repeat visits.

As most holidays are bought "sight unseen" with the tourist relying heavily on travel retailer/wholesalers' information (and assurance), in one sense the tour wholesaler acts as a *surrogate-guest*. In this role, he interprets the requirements of, and determines, the standards provided for tourists in the host country. The growing trend towards group inclusive travel—particularly to developing countries—intensifies this role as Erbes (1973) and Jenkins (1980) have noted.

TYPE OF TOURIST AMENITY IN HOST COUNTRY

For reasons noted above, the need to provide an *acceptable* tourist amenity in a host country is a *sine qua non* for tourism planners. As Cohen (1972:171) observed, "a tourist infrastructure of facilities based on Western standards has to be created even in the poorest host countries. This tourist infrastructure provides the mass tourist with the protective 'ecological bubble' of his accustomed environment." This notion of acceptability is a powerful influence on tourism planners in host countries, and explains the "invariant menus" offered in international hotels (Rodenburg 1980:190).

The above situation is not unfamiliar to other tourist-receiving developing countries. Dr. A. Mozoomdar, former Director-General of the Indian Tourism Development Corporation noted "if you are going to be in tourism business for attracting tourists positively, for economic purposes, one cannot close one's eyes to the fact that there

C. L. JENKINS

is a considerable section of the potential traffic which wants to go from Inter-Continental to Inter-Continental. One may deplore this, one may not like particular individuals, but I don't have to love every bit ot iron ore that I export" (Mozoomdar 1975). It might be suggested therefore that the type of tourist facility provided by the host country is determined by exogenous considerations, particularly where that country seeks to encourage group tours from developed countries. If this type of development is internationally standardized, an important question in relation to Rodenburg's paper is whether a host country can develop an acceptable standard of facility without inducing an unacceptable *scale* of development.

The reasons for host country government's encouragement for foreign investment in the tourist sector are apparent. Together with the initial capital investment, most foreign companies bring with them the advantages of operational expertise, market contacts, and an international "image." The combination of these factors provides an input to the tourism sector which is unlikely to be available from domestic resources. However limited is the tourist's knowledge of the host country, he relies on the image of the hotel to provide his "ecological bubble." In Doswell's (1979:11) words "the 'brand' of a hotel is its symbolic association in the mind of the buyer."

SCALE OF TOURISM DEVELOPMENTS

Given that large-scale developments should not necessarily correlate with insensitive design or location, the decision relating to scale of development can be examined under five headings.

Infrastructure Cost-efficiency

The cost-efficiency of a specific or alternative level of infra-structure provided at a site is largely determined by engineering economics. It is an important consideration and one which should not be analyzed in isolation from the wider ramifications of the project. As Kaiser and Helber (1976:163) observed "infra-structure elements cannot be designed and developed in a vacuum... infra-structure tends to be the primary area where technical considerations control investment policies." The cost-efficiency of a site proposal will have important implications for the scale of consequent developments.

Operational Efficiency

The basic questions here is the *minimum* unit size which is likely to attract international hotel developers. It is an important param-

THE EFFECTS OF SCALE IN TOURISM PROJECTS

eter for site development because below a unit size, operating costs are likely to be unattractive to an investor or management company. In the interstices of a market it may be possible for a local entrepreneur to provide an upmarket, low volume hotel, but without the back-up resources of a large company, international market penetration would be difficult. It is the international criteria which are relevant for evaluating acceptable standards, because the standards must be acceptable to international tourists. As Doswell (1979:63) stated, "care must be taken to use standard criteria in evaluation of a hotel and not to use criteria determined within the market area alone. For instance, the best existing hotel in a market area does not automatically belong to the upper segment; it may be in the middle segment and be catering for the higher segment only because of the absence of other facilities."

Marketing Impact

The need to meet international standards and to attract foreign tourists is closely related to economies of scale. An indigenous hotel or hotels might sell accomodation to foreign visitors through agency representations or other systems, but it will not have the extensive image development which multi national companies have. Sophis ticated marketing programmes, computerized reservation facilities, and established trade links are powerful advantages. The vertical integration between airlines, tour companies, and hotels have further strengthened the power of the foreign tour generators *vis-a-vis* the host country. As this negotiating power is strengthened, so is the tendency to standardize tourist facilities.

To overcome these problems, small, indigenously-owned hotels will require substantial help. For example, in the case of marketing overseas and staff training, a co-operative solution could be helpful. It should be possible to organize a group of hotels which could combine to sell accommodation overseas through an appointed representative in the main tourist generating countries. Telex links and group bookings could be encouraged through the same outlet. In such situations, a group approach to marketing could reduce the disadvantages of small-scale related to marketing costs. It is likely, however, that in most developing countries such groups would need strong support and encouragement from government or the National Tourist Office, particularly where foreign exchange costs are involved.

Staff training costs could similarly be a shared expense. In a number of developing countries governments and industry have combined to provide excellent training facilities to ensure a supply of

C. L. JENKINS

skilled people for the tourism sector. Countries such as India, Kenya, Hong Kong, and Barbados are examples. The process of developing these special facilities is beyond the scope of this paper, but it will require official intervention and support, and in many countries the only source of this help is the government.

Impact on Host Community

The three factors discussed above are largely exogenously determined. The outcome of the decision on the scale and location of the development will directly affect the host community and region. This impact should be evaluated against the stated objectives for tourism development. In many countries these objectives are either not defined, or are so general as to be inoperative. It therefore becomes necessary to consider objectives at two levels; *general* tourism development objectives, and tourism objectives which are specific to a region or scale of development. One of the common problems in formulating tourism objectives is to overlook the fact that general objectives are only meaningful if they are ranked in terms of priority. For instance, if the Indonesian government sees earnings of foreign exchange as the priority objective for encouraging tourism, other subsidiary priorities such as employment, intersectoral linkages, eradication of regional disparities etc., will be considered, but will not have the same decision-weight as foreign exchange earnings. In some countries, it is this situation which explains the often hideous tourism developments which have occurred. For overall development purposes, national and regional objectives must be identified industry by industry. Using the eight objectives listed by Rodenburg, one could develop an illustrative objectives matrix which would facilitate tourism planning. (Table 1).

Using this simple format it is possible to devise a set of objectives which are relevant to different scales of development in particular regions or locations. This set can then be used as guide-lines for investment incentive legislation. Many countries already gear the level of investment incentives to regional policy. A systematic application of this approach could form the basis for an *integrated* evaluation of economic and social priorities on a regional and sub-regional level. This approach could be used to direct development to meet priority objectives and to ensure that ecologically fragile or culturally sensitive areas could be appraised *before* investment is contemplated. Development strategy would be seen against a set of ranked objectives rather than as an *ad hoc* response to entrepreneurial thrust.

However, although this approach may help to clarify national and

THE EFFECTS OF SCALE IN TOURISM PROJECTS

Table 1
**Tourism Development Objectives by Regional
Location and Scale of Project**

	Large Projects	Small Projects	Craft Projects
P.R.L. Zone	A.B.	C.D.E.[N]	
Specific Objectives Increase:			
1 Foreign Exchange	H	M	L
2 Employment	H	H	H
3 Income	H	H	M
4 Investment	H	M	L
General Objectives Increase:			
5 Infrastructure	L	H	–
6 Production links	M	H	H
7 Entrepreneurship	L	H	H
8 Minimise Adverse Social & Cultural Effects	M	H	H

Ranks   H = High Priority
M = Medium Priority
L = Low Priority
PRL = Preferred Regional Location Zones (e.g., A, B, c[N])

regional tourism development options, it will not avoid the necessity for ultimate value judgement decisions. For example, some decision would have to be made on the relative priorities to be given to Balinese rather than Indonesian considerations. Given that decisions involving governments have a major political dimension, then it is to be expected that a critical element in the decision process will be made on political rather than technical grounds.

Location of Development

In an historical perspective it can be seen that most developed countries have tourism industries which have largely been created by private enterprise, but with some state support. For most developing countries the government or state sector has adopted an entrepreneurial role. This role has been taken because of the deficien-

C. L. JENKINS

cies and underdevelopment in the private sector. Where such deficiencies exist, government often relies on foreign expertise to formulate plans for tourism development, and the large number of national tourism development plans which now exist bear witness to this growth industry. As the study of tourism has advanced so too has our knowledge of the problems that uncontrolled development can bring. One of the areas of concern is that relating to non-economic impact of tourism development on host communities. An important consideration here is whether tourism developments should be integrated into an existing community-based site or developed as an enclave project. There is a range of arguments for and against each type of development, and it would be relevant to discuss briefly the characteristics of each of them.

Enclave Development

There are three basic characteristics of enclave development:

a. The specific infrastructure is not intended to benefit directly the resident-indigenous community. Any "spill-over" effect is purely gratuitious; emphasis is placed on the provision of infrastructure facilities for the tourism development.

b. The site location is physically separate from an existing community or development, with the chosen site intended to generate its own transient tourism "community." The facility will be operated with minimum trading and social links with an existing community.

c. That the facility is most used, if not exclusively used, by foreign tourists. In this circumstance, a level of demands and services will be generated which the indigenous community could not afford to buy, even if it so wanted. In this case *structural enclavism* (i.e., a and b above) is reinforced by *price enclavism*. This latter phenomena develops in most host countries as a natural output from large industrial scale tourism. It is a phenomena found in developed and developing countries, but it is intensified in the latter because of wide disparities in the living standards of residents and visitors.

The social and cultural impact of enclavism has received increasing attention from social scientists, and is of concern to tourism planners. Without an acceptance of tourism and tourists by host communities, even the best planned and managed developments will suffer as a consequence of local apathy or hostility. In some countries, for example, Jamaica, recent problems in the tourism industry have been linked to indigenous unease with tourism and tourists. In Tanzania, enclave tourism has been encouraged by government as a means of limiting the "cultural pollution" from tourism.

In many countries tourism enclaves have developed as a conse-

THE EFFECTS OF SCALE IN TOURISM PROJECTS

quence of market forces rather than as a derivative of formal planning decisions. Foreign developers appraise potential sites and then select the most suitable from *their viewpoint*. Once approval for development is given, the tendency is for a successful project to "suck-in" new investment; the original project acts as a "growth point." Examples of this process can be seen in Montego Bay, Jamaica; Pattaya Beach, Thailand; Penang, Malaysia; and, presumably, Nusa Dua. There are strong social and cultural arguments against this type of development, but the concentration of facilities helps promote a resort image, which in turn can act as a catalyst for wider demand. One would add that the type of image projected might be disagreeable or unacceptable, but unless governments intervene to influence foreign publications, this is likely to be a continuing problem for host countries.

Integrated Development

In this type of development planners will attempt to match the scale of the project to existing community norms. As a general point one would expect to identify a number of common features in an integrated development.

a. The unit scale of facilities would be smaller than in enclave projects. In Bali the small industrial hotels had an average of only 21 rooms. These small units are more easily absorbed by an existing community and into a general infrastructure. Where new infrastructure is required, it spills over to the community within which it is located.

b. Because of the relatively small scale of development, more indigenous capital and management would be attracted to this sector; barriers to entry are lower.

c. Because of lower prices, the type of tourist attracted to these facilities is likely to have different expectations from the tourist staying in international class hotels. It may be (and there is little hard information on this point) that this type of tourist is more easily assimilated into the host community.

If these types of facilities are recognized as causing a lower level of dislocation to the community, then there is a *prima facio* case for advocating this type of project. The encouragement of smaller scale tourism units will have advantages not only to the host community, but will also reduce the financial outlay necessary for very large enclave projects. One reason is that the smaller scale will attract indigenous investors thereby reducing, if not eliminating, the need to import foreign capital. A second reason is that small scale devel-

C. L. JENKINS

opments are often located on existing infrastructure, and perhaps using spare capacity. Where specific infrastructure is built as an extention to an existing provision, it is likely to be less expensive than providing it on a "green-field" site. A further, and important reason, is that any new development is based in the community. What is needed is a policy on the appropriate scales of development for particular regions and locations, and the political will and support necessary to implement such a policy.

d. As this type of facility tends to emerge *from* the indigenous community rather than being imposed *on* the community, tourist acceptance by host community may be a lesser problem.

e. As the facilities are essentially small-scale and related to local economic and social norms, "price enclavism" may not be a feature. In practice this smaller scale of integrated development will usually coexist with large scale development; and indirectly benefit from the external economies which only this scale can bring.

The above comments do not negate the arguments for a very careful appraisal of tourism developments in host countries; a process which requires co-ordination between all levels of planning authorities. Without this co-ordination many of the problems which experience anticipates will be neglected. Too often in developing countries the planning process is very fragmented—one authority being concerned with the impetus for development, with others being expected to manage the impact of the development.

THE NUSA DUA PROJECT

The following comments are related to the eight tourism development objectives stated by Projogo and used by Rodenburg for his analytical framework. In each case the aim is to relate the objectives to the data derived from the Nusa Dua projections.

Increased Earnings

It is not surprising that the enclave Nusa Dua project will intensify the drift of population to urban areas. The effect is not confined only to tourism development on Bali. What is important is whether priority should be given to the *level* of earnings emanating from the project or the regional *location* of these earnings. It is noticeable that the quoted lowest average monthly salary per employee in the large industrial class hotels was approximately 19% greater than that earned in the small industrial category, and three times the average level in the craft tourism sector (Rodenburg, Table 5, p.

THE EFFECTS OF SCALE IN TOURISM PROJECTS

186). It is not stated whether this lowest average salary includes gratuities; if not, then these will considerably enhance the average monthly rate.

In development terms there are positive economic and social arguments for raising the levels of earnings. The large scale, "modern" tourism sector will do this, but this will have implications for the traditional employment sectors, as Todaro (1969) has noted in some selected African countries. It may also have a wider effect of destabilizing prevailing socioeconomic norms. A study of Barbados by Doxey (1971) indicated that very high earnings by those in the tourism sector tended not only to surpass those "middle class" professions such as teachers and lawyers, but stimulated resentment and opposition amongst this group to further tourism development. One would expect any modern sector in a developing country to have a higher per capita level of earnings, and for employees in large units to be higher paid than those in smaller units (excluding the existence of trade union determined rates). An enclave development would have a centrifugal effect on employment location, but this might be regarded as an unavoidable effect of this type of development.

Increased Foreign Exchange

The possibility of foreign exchange earnings to be derived from international tourism is one of the main reasons for government support for the industry (UNCTAD 1971). For a developing country with a balance-of-payments problem, the opportunity to derive foreign exchange from tourism exports, is an opportunity not easily ignored. In relation to the objectives set outlined in Table 1, if earnings of foreign exchange are a national priority, then this will predominate over secondary objectives and regional location decisions.

In relation to Nusa Dua, Rodenburg's figures suggest that the small scale industrial units are relatively efficient earners of foreign exchange. However, it is necessary to try to separate the effects of interdependence on returns to scale. For reasons noted above it is expected that much of the return accruing to the small industrial and craft tourism sector are triggered by the very existence of the large units. It is a very difficult question to answer, but intuitively one feels that interdependence is of importance.

A wider consideration relates to the stage of tourism development in a particular country. It may be that because of its established tourism image, Balinese tourism projects undertaken in the future could move to smaller-scale units *without* reducing their attractiveness to foreign visitors and therefore earnings of foreign exchange. Another country without an established image may initially have to

C. L. JENKINS

rely on large-scale developments to provide an international "ambiance" to attract and reassure foreign tour operators and visitors. It may be tentatively suggested that where foreign exchange earnings are of prime importance and where local limitations inhibit indigenous investment in the sector, large-scale, foreign owned and managed units are probable. This initial characteristic can be modified in later projects once the destination has been established. In one sense, initial large-scale projects might be regarded as a social cost incurred to provide the catalyst for future, more appropriate developments. If there is validity in this viewpoint, then foreign exchange earnings cannot be regarded as being independent to scale, but rather as a function of the total product.

Increased Investment

The figures on Investment and Employment (Rodenburg, Table 7, p. 188) can tell us nothing about the *quality* of jobs created in each scale of development. This aspect is explored below, but it seems erroneous to suggest that "for the same amount of money, more rooms, which means the ability to exploit more tourists, and more jobs can be generated in the small industry and craft levels. In this sense, the lesser scales of enterprise are more economically desirable." (p. 189). Although the figures ostensibly support this reasoning, in practice the situation would be different. More rooms could certainly be built but whether they could be filled is problematical. It will depend to a large extent on the elasticity of substitution in the large industrial market segment whether the 65% of foreign tourists (Rodenburg, Table 4, p. 184) would be prepared to divert to lower levels of accommodation. In a market segment heavily involved with package tours, the position of the foreign tour wholesaler would be a critical factor in determining the outcome.

A further consideration is that if large industrial developments are discouraged, it may severely inhibit the flow of foreign investment to the tourism sector. Some might regard this as a beneficial development, but it is not the usual government viewpoint.

Increased Job Opportunities

As mentioned above, the *quality* of jobs created is of some importance in development strategies. The cost-per-job ratio is a non-qualitative indicator. It is probable that the large industrial scale employers have training facilities which cannot be provided by smaller companies. This training dimension is very important because it not only increases the general skills of a work force but

THE EFFECTS OF SCALE IN TOURISM PROJECTS

should create a skilled labor pool from which those with management potential might be recruited and developed. As Chib (1980) has noted in the context of tourism, it is usually only the very large hotel groups which have the resources, expertise, and career structure to undertake systematic training. Given the usual mobility of labor in the hotel sector, much of this trained labor would eventually move to other sectors.

The question of what type and level of training provided by a company is an area of considerable debate. Much of the training given in hotels is job-related, vocational and has little career orientation. It must also be recognized that much of the employment created in tourism is of a very low-skill, low status level. In the context of the Caribbean, one country's prime minister said that tourism had created "a nation of waiters and bartenders." Whatever the validity of these remarks, most training for tourism in developing countries will be done by large, often multinational companies, supported by some government sponsored vocational training programs.

In the longer term, there is a need to prepare a tourism manpower and training plan. As Jenkins (1980) has noted, tourism education for policymakers might have to take place outside the developing countries. However at the vocational level, steps should be taken to institute training facilities where none exist, for without basic training it is improbable that an eventual management class will emerge. If it is accepted that one of the main aims of development is to indigenize ownership and the management of national assets, then it becomes imperative to give training a high national priority. Some countries, e.g., Kenya, have established (with technical assistance) their own Tourism and Hotel Training College. This College accepts students from regional African countries, and similar developments elsewhere could allow the provision of high quality, relevant and cost-effective training opportunities to be made more widely available. This concept underlies the establishment by the World Tourism Organization (WTO) of a training facility in Mexico.

Increased Production

Rodenburg's comment on the reluctance of managers of international standard hotels to purchase local foodstuffs and supplies, identifies a common situation in many developing countries. Doxey (1971) and later Alleyne (1974) noted this situation in Barbados. This problem not only reduces the linkage effects of tourism, but often exacerbates the leakage of foreign exchange through imports. To a considerable degree this problem is rooted in the centralized purchasing procedures used by most international companies. This system makes the best advantage of economies of bulk-buying, and gives constant control over price and quality. Such a system clearly limits the local manager's ability to buy local supplies even if he wanted to.

A second difficulty is that many local suppliers are not geared to provide, particularly foodstuffs, at the quality and quantity demanded and to an agreed delivery schedule. Without some positive help to local suppliers to gear-up to meet competitive standards, much of the linkage possibility of tourism will remain potential rather than real. The more open the economy, the greater the difficulty in mitigating the importleakage, as an examination of the Caribbean economy will show.

This is another area where positive measures can effect change. Some authority—perhaps government—will have to initiate discussions between buyers and potential suppliers. Once market needs in terms of quantity and quality have been determined, the most effective way of meeting these requirements can be sought. It is unlikely that the process will be rapid or easy, but without some initiative, high leakages will continue to reduce the economic benefits accruing from the tourism sector.

Increased Entrepreneurship

There are very real economic benefits accruing to the local community when indigenous ownership is at a significant level. There are also important social and political implications. Where an industry has a large degree of indigenous ownership and entrepreneurial involvement, this tends to provide a greater degree of stability than when it is foreign-dominated. There is a feeling of permanence and also of local and national interests not being ignored. When ownership of land is involved, foreign ownership can give rise to considerable social and political tensions as de Kadt (1979) noted in the case of the Seychelles. As a tourist industry develops in a country one would expect indigenous capital to be invested in the sector. However, much of the investment will be directed to small or craft projects. As confidence and experience grow, some larger-scale projects might be undertaken.

If local ownership is to be encouraged, the government should structure the investment incentive laws to ensure that local capital, when available, is encouraged into the industry. It could also be possible to "protect" this type of investment opportunity by prohibiting foreign investment in these sectors of the tourism industry.

THE EFFECTS OF SCALE IN TOURISM PROJECTS

Increased Infrastructure

It is difficult to dispute Rodenburg's contention that new tourism infrastructure should benefit the local community as well as tourists. Enclave developments will not meet this premise, and where tourism enclaves provide a level of amenity above that available to the local community, it will tend to create animosity towards tourism and tourists. On these grounds alone there are strong arguments for integrated developments.

It appears to have been the case in Nusa Dua that these arguments were not explored, and that the project was approved and initiated without any discussion with local planning authorities. One of the major anticipated economic benefits derived from tourism projects in host communities is the "spill-over" effect from new infrastructure. It may, in fact, be one of the important effects which help to reconcile local residents to changes induced by tourism. It is clear from Rodenburg's analysis that this was one benefit which did not occur.

The Minimization of Adverse Sociocultural Effects

Although most tourism planners (and governments) subscribe to the view that the adverse effects of tourism development should be minimized, in practice it is one of the most difficult aspects of tourism management. One difficulty is that there is often no channel available to communicate these problems to those charged with their control or mitigation. Small, local concerned groups are often ignored as being "unrepresentative." Another aspect is that in many, if not in all, developing countries, these social and cultural effects have a lower ranking against the economic benefits expected to accrue from the development.

In essence the social and cultural effects are not arguments against tourism as a development strategy, but rather indicate a need to monitor and manage the sector. The system of monitoring should be discussed at the project feasibility stage, for many of the general, non-economic problems noted by Rodenburg are to be found in many host countries. It is clear from his paper that the Nusa Dua project did not benefit from a full coordination between local and tourism planners. This is to be regretted, but, unfortunately, it is not an unusual situation. Without integrated planning, and good coordination between planners, it is difficult to see how these social and cultural problems can be avoided.

C. L. JENKINS

CONCLUSION

Rodenburg's analysis of Nusa Dua provides persuasive evidence in support of his case for more small and craft scale tourism developments. His current fieldwork may well provide further social and cultural reasons to support this view. However, the realities of international tourism suggest that these types of development must co-exist with larger scale projects. It is not reasonable to ignore external economies of scale—"the competitive advantage held by large industrial tourism, in attracting package and group tourists, is due to its economic muscle and international connections, and not to the economies of scale." (P. 194). It is, of course, this economic muscle and the existence of international connections which are the *raison d'etre* for large scale projects.

It may be concluded that developing countries which attract large scale developments have some control over whether they are to be integrated into a community site or placed in an enclave. The main disadvantages of large scale developments, which have been noted by Rodenburg and commented on here, are likely to be mitigated only by very positive actions by the host country government. It is, of course, always possible for most countries to disbar large scale tourism development projects, but it is more likely that they will prefer to co-exist with them.

The nature of this co-existence can be influenced by tourism planners. They must be made aware of the need to identify and evaluate priorities, to ensure that tourism objectives are not frustrated by inadequate preproject planning. There can be no single determinant of the scale of tourism developments in a country, but rather a consideration of an amalgam of complex and often conflicting criterion. Large-scale tourism projects may not be inevitable, but in many developing countries they will be difficult to avoid without positive government intervention in the formulation of tourism objectives. □ □

REFERENCES

Alleyne, F.
    1974   The Expansion of Tourism and its Concomitant Unrealized Potential for
           Agricultural Development in the Barbadian Economy. Unpublished paper,
           presented to the West Indies Agricultural Economics Conference, Barba-
           dos.
Artus, J. R.
    1972   An Econometric Analysis of International Travel. I.M.F. Staff Papers 19
           (November):579—614.

THE EFFECTS OF SCALE IN TOURISM PROJECTS

Chib, S. N.
     1980   Financing Tourism Development: A Recipient's View. International Journal of Tourism Management 1(4):231–237.

Cohen, E.
     1972   Towards a Sociology of International Tourism. Social Research 39(1):164–182.

de Kadt, E., ed.
     1979   Tourism—Passport to Development? Oxford: Oxford University Press.

Dobbie, L.
     1976   Interpreters and Co-ordinators of Tourism Demand. I.T.A. Bulletin No. 3.

Doswell, R. and P. R. Gamble
     1979   Marketing and Planning Hotels and Tourism Projects. London: Barrie & Jenkins.

Doxey, G. V. & Associates
     1971   The Tourist Industry in Barbados—A Socio-Economic Assessment. Ontario: Dusco Graphics, Kitchener Press.

Erbes, R.
     1973   International Tourism and the Economies of Developing Countries. Paris: O.E.C.D.

Gerakis, A.
     1965   The Effect of Exchange Rate Devaluation and Revaluation on Receipts from Tourism. I.M.F. Staff Papers 12(3).

Gray, H. P.
     1970   International Travel—International Trade. Lexington, MA: Heath Lexington.

Jenkins, C. L.
     1980   Tourism Policies in Developing Countries: A Critique. International Journal of Tourism Management 1(1):22–29.
     1980   Education for Tourism Policy-Makers in Developing Countries. International Journal of Tourism Management 1(4):238–242.

Kaiser, C. and L. E. Helber
     1978   Tourism Planning and Development. Boston, MA: C.B.I. Publishing Co.

Merigo, E. and S. Potter
     1970   O.E.C.D. Invisibles in the 1960s. Economic Outlook: Occasional Studies. Paris. O.E.C.D.

Mozoomdar, A.
     1975   Tourism and the Balance of Payments in a Developing Country. Paper presented to the seminar on "The Measurement of Tourism." London: British Tourist Authority.

Rodenburg, E.
     1980   The Effects of Scale on Economic Development: Tourism in Bali. Annals of Tourism Research VII: (2):177–196.

Schulmeister, S.
     1979   Tourism and the Business Cycle. Vienna: Australian Institute for Economic Research.

Smith, V., ed.
     1977   Hosts and Guests: The Anthropology of Tourism. Philadelphia: University of Pennsylvania Press.

Todaro, M. P. and J. R. Harris
     1969   Wages, Industrial Employment and Labor Productivity: The Kenya Experience. East Africa Economic Review 5(1).

C. L. JENKINS

Turner, L. and J. Ash
  1975   The Golden Hordes. London: Constable.
U.N.C.T.A.D.
  1971   Invisibles: Elements of Tourism Policy in Developing Countries. Geneva:
          U.N.C.T.A.D.

Submitted 15 May 1981
Revised version submitted 28 July 1981
Accepted 12 October 1981
Refereed anonymously

[25]

World Development, Vol. 18, No. 1, pp. 109–123, 1990.
Printed in Great Britain.

Flexible Specialization and Small Size:
The Case of Caribbean Tourism

AULIANA POON*
Caribbean Tourism Organization, Christ Church, Barbados

Summary. — If export industrialization was fashionable in the 1960s and 1970s, today flexible specialization is definitely "in." Appealing to the very heart of the developing world — traditional, small-scale and craft production — flexible specialization has become the new passport to development. This article cautions that the prescription of small-scale, flexible specialization (Piore and Sable, 1984) leads to a very dangerous kind of optimism in the developing world. The danger lies in equating flexibility with small size. This is because small size may not be necessary, and certainly is not a sufficient condition, for flexible specialization. The keys to flexible specialization lie elsewhere — in information technology applications, networks, synergies, systems gains, scope economies, production and organizational flexibility — not in small size. This argument is developed with reference to the Caribbean tourist industry. A comparative analysis of Jamaica's Superclub hotel chain and Italy's Benetton textile company is undertaken. This is done with a view to determining the factors in the success of their flexible specialization strategies. Implications for policy are drawn out.

1. INTRODUCTION

Just as the economic miracle of the newly industrialized countries (NICs) in the 1960s and early 1970s generated optimism for export-oriented industrialization, today success stories of traditional sectors in Italy (Benetton) and West Germany (Bosch) rekindle the hopes and prospects for small size and small-scale craft production. "Flexible specialization" is seen to be the underlying principle behind the rise of the "Third Italy," the "Second Denmark," Silicon Valley, and Route 128 circling Boston (Sabel, 1986). This article cautions that the prescription of small-scale, flexible specialization, propounded by Piore and Sabel (1984), can lead to a very dangerous kind of optimism in the developing world. One potential danger lies in equating flexibility and specialization with small size. This can lead to the misguided belief that, just by being small, developing countries can be flexibly specialized, capture niche markets, and move in and out of specialized segments as market demand warrants.

Both the cases of the Italian clothing concern, Benetton, and the Jamaican hotel chain, Superclub, reveal that small size is not a sufficient condition for flexible specialization. The keys to flexible specialization lie in the capacity and intelligence of Benetton and Superclub to reap

synergies, systems gains and *scope economies*; and their possession of *production and organizational flexibility* — characteristics which are not at all unique to small size. The quality and caliber of managerial personnel, the development of network economies, competitive strategies, innovations, and the deployment of new technologies are far more important to the success of flexibly specialized firms than their inherent, static endowments of tradition and small size.

The main objective of this article[1] is to demonstrate to firms and policy makers that they cannot sit back in the hope that their time has come — that just by being small and having traditional sectors they can compete in world markets. Indeed, small size can be a blessing or blight depending upon how it is perceived and exploited. A great deal of effort has to be made in order to ensure the former. This article aims at

*I would like to acknowledge the support of the government of Trinidad and Tobago and the European Economic Community (Lomé III) for their support of my doctoral research, from which this article is derived. I would also like to thank Andrew Barnett, Carlotta Perez, Robin Murray, Wesley Hughes, John Issa, Nick von Tunzelman, and two anonymous referees who commented on an earlier draft of this article. Dr Poon is currently the UNDP/WTO Regional Tourism Consultant, based at the CTO, Barbados.

elucidating some of the variables that firms and policy makers must address in order that small be not only beautiful, but competitive as well. These include: cultivating innovation, social institutions, managerial excellence and entrepreneurial talent; utilizing new information technologies; developing networks, systems and skills; and markets and marketing intelligence.

2. OUTLINE

The article begins by exploring the concepts of small size and flexible specialization. The international development context for flexible specialization, and the specific case of the Caribbean, are examined. The Caribbean tourism economy and the evolution of flexible specialization in Jamaican tourism are considered. Finally, a comparative analysis of the Jamaican Superclub hotel chain and Benetton is undertaken. This is done with a view to determining the conditions for success of their flexible specialization strategies.

3. SMALL SIZE

Two issues are of central concern to the question of small size: size of country and scale of production units. Country size is important to the analysis of the specific case of the Caribbean islands. Plant size or scale of production is important to the analysis of production units engaged in flexible specialization.

There are many criteria upon which one can base a definition of country size: population, geographical area, availability of various natural resources, national income, research intensity, industrial potential, rate of growth, dependency on other countries. There are also a number of ways to define small scale:[2] size of plant, turnover, employment, volume/value of output, size and length of production run, capital outlay.

In this article, no *a priori* measure of small scale will be developed. It will not be arbitrarily specified, for example, that small is equivalent to firms employing 1–50 workers, or hotels with 1–50 rooms. Emphases on the definition and measurement of small size are inappropriate. This is because the key factor in survival and competitiveness is not small size, but the ability to exploit local, regional and international markets. As such, a *case by case* approach will be adopted to explore the issues of small scale and flexible specialization in Superclub (hotels) and Benetton (clothing).

4. FLEXIBLE SPECIALIZATION

Flexible specialization has been taken up as "an idea whose time has come."[3] It owes its intellectual origin to Piore and Sabel, *The Second Industrial Divide* (1984). Piore and Sabel view flexible specialization as a strategy which "veers sharply" from established technological principles (mass production, Taylorism, Fordism) and leads back to those craft methods of production that lost out during the First Industrial Divide (Piore and Sabel, 1984, p. 6). Piore and Sabel posit that the turning point has come for the Second Industrial Divide, where possibilities for prosperity lie in flexible specialization and where mass production must lose out.

Mass production is seen to be characterized by "the use of special purpose (product-specific) machines and of semi-skilled workers to produce standardized goods . . . The more general the goods, the more specialized the machines and the more finely divided the labor that goes into their production" (Piore and Sabel, 1984, pp. 4, 27).

Flexible specialization, by contrast, is seen to consist of a "strategy of permanent innovation: accommodation to ceaseless change, rather than an effort to control it" (Piore and Sabel, 1984, p. 17). Flexible specialization

> is based on flexible (multi-use) equipment; skilled workers; and the creation, through politics, of an industrial community that restricts the forms of competition to those favoring innovation . . . *flexible specialization amounts to a revival of craft forms of production that were emarginated at the first industrial divide* (Piore and Sabel, p. 17) [emphasis added].

A useful classification and comparison of mass production and flexible specialization is provided in the UNDP/UNIDO Cyprus Report (1987). This classification is reproduced in Table 1.

Flexible specialization was not intended as a prescription for developing countries. Piore and Sabel have themselves argued that the key to American industrial competitiveness lies in the development of "a category of business that corresponds to the real requirements of small-scale production, and (in) find(ing) ways of populating that category on a continuing basis" (Piore and Sabel, 1983, p. 421).

The attraction of flexible specialization to the developing world lies in its emphasis on small-scale, traditional, and craft systems (methods) of production. The idea that flexible specialization or craft production is a system whose time has come also goes down very well with developing countries. Indeed, their craft systems have been historically peripheral to the development of mass production in the center economies (see the

FLEXIBLE SPECIALIZATION AND SMALL SIZE   111

Table 1. *Fordism and flexible production compared*

	Fordism	Flexible Production
1. Production concept	Mass production, economies through fixed capital and labor productivity within the production process	Flexible specialization/flexible automation, economies through working capital productivity between production processes and in distribution
2. Technology	Machine purpose built and dedicated, R&D functionally separate and discontinuous	General purpose adaptable machinery, importance of design
3. Products	Limited range of standardized products	Product variety and specialization, "niche" markets
4. Inputs	Materials- and energy-intensive	Materials and energy-saving/information-intensive
5. Work process and skills	Fragmented and standardized tasks, strict division between mental and manual labor. Semi-skilled workers	Open-ended tasks, semi-autonomous groups and decentralized responsibility, closer integration of manual and mental tasks, core of multi-skilled workers linked to sub-contract and semiskilled labor
6. Payment system	Rate for the job, formalized pay bargaining	Payment for person, rising income for skilled core. More informal wage settlement
7. Organization and management	Managerial hierarchies, centralization, multidivisional corporation	Flatter hierarchies, centralized information and planning systems with decentralized production, networks, subcontracting, franchising
8. Markets and customers	Domination of manufacturers over retailers, of producers over users, one-way relations/mass advertising	Domination of retailing, two-way relations between customers and manufacturer, firm rather than product advertising
9. Suppliers	Arm's length stocks held "just in case"	Two-way relations, stocks arrive "just in time"
10. Competitive strategy	Competition through full capacity, utilization and cost-cutting tends to over production, stockpiling and markdowns	Competition through innovation, response to falling markets through diversification, innovation, subcontracting or lay off

Source: UNDP/UNIDO (1987), p. 139.

profuse literature on dependency).[4] In fact, flexible specialization has an almost Marxist appeal, echoing the calls for small-scale, backyard production, basic needs, autarky, appropriate technologies and, more generally, "going back to the roots." It is also noteworthy that Piore and Sabel's model of flexible specialization has recently been prescribed and is in the process of being implemented in the 600,000 person-strong economy of Cyprus (UNDP/UNIDO, 1987).

5. THE INTERNATIONAL CONTEXT OF FLEXIBLE SPECIALIZATION

There are many sources of flexibility. Flexibility can originate from robust designs; from flexible organizational structures (Perez, 1986; Johnson, 1987); from flexible contractual and subcontracting arrangements; from technology-embodied flexible equipment such as computer aided design/manufacture (CAD/CAM), flexible manufacturing systems (FMS), and robotics (Kaplinsky, 1985).

While these individual aspects of flexibility are widely recognized, many analysts increasingly believe that real flexibility can only be had when all aspects of flexibility — organizational, technological, design, work schedules, marketing, sourcing, strategies — become mutually reinforcing. This view is held by Freeman and Perez (1986), for example, as they argue the need for organization, management and institutional change to move *pari passu* with purely technological innovations. Empirical data seem to justify this position. In their study of the Swedish approach to the use of flexible manufacturing systems, Haywood and Bessant (1987, p. 76) conclude that:

> it is clear that in many instances it is not just quantifiable technical factors that have influenced results. In many cases, there have been profound *organizational* changes which have led to improvements in operations [emphasis added].

This extended approach to flexibility is also taken by Womack and Jones in their International Motor Vehicle Program, where the case of Japanese "Kan Ban," "Just in Time" and other methods are seen to be leading the automobile into a new "best practice" of the future (Womack 1987; Jones, 1987). This new best practice, which they also term flexible, is not seen to originate purely from machines, subcontractors, "bottom up" management methods or from marketing strategies. Flexibility is seen to be embedded in the whole socio-institutional and cultural context of the "Japanese way."

Flexibility, then, is not just a matter of having flexible multi-use equipment or utilizing low-wage, small-scale subcontracting firms in developing countries. *Flexibility is a systems concept wherein all aspects of production — from management, design, distribution, and sourcing to strategic thinking — must be flexible.*

6. THE CARIBBEAN CONTEXT

(a) *Small size*

Measured by size of population, Caribbean islands are small. The major islands range from Jamaica with 2.27 million inhabitants to Montserrat with 12,000. The entire English-speaking Caribbean region constitutes 5 million persons. The constraints of small population bases and small domestic markets force Caribbean islands into a path of protracted outward-looking or export-oriented development. This is because the potential for inward-looking growth, through import substituting industrialization (ISI) and autarky, is very limited (Blackman, 1979; Farrell, 1982; St. Cyr, 1982; Poon, 1983).

(b) *Caribbean economic problems*

Caribbean islands are plagued with a number of problems which stem from their history (Best and Levitt, 1975); their dependence on export earnings (Girvan, 1973); poor performance of traditional exports (Lewis, 1977 and 1980); small size (Demas, 1965); a weak and underdeveloped manufacturing sector (Farrell, 1982); and their neglected service sector (Poon, 1987).[5]

During recent times, the lifeblood of Caribbean islands, foreign exchange, has been severely threatened. Their primary export staples continue to receive severe battering on international markets: sugar from high fructose sweeteners, reduced imperial preferences, and reduced demand brought about by a more health-conscious market and the effects of preventive dental care; bauxite from technological and other developments in materials such as steel and plastics; and oil from the difficulties of the Organization of Petroleum Exporting Countries (OPEC) cartel in setting production quotas and stabilizing prices. Their primary, low value-added export staples are also adversely affected by increasing competition from other developing countries, and the recessionary tendencies of developed, market-economy countries in 1973–75 and 1980–81. More recently, the possibility of a "United States of Europe" in 1992 will have tremendous implications for traditional exports from the Caribbean. The ability of Caribbean island economies to generate incomes, employment and foreign exchange from their traditional basket of exports is not very promising.

(c) *Caribbean economic thinking*

The reality of small size, forced export orientation, and poor performance of traditional exports has turned many Caribbean economists away from the traditional dependency/plantation-economy type of analyses. It is argued, for example, that development strategies based on the notion of "self reliance" or concentration of economic activities on producing for the home market will not work (Blackman, 1979; Farrell, 1982; Poon, 1983). There is also a greater focus of the importance of technologies, flexibility, niche markets, and the need to "apply innovations continually and to adapt to changing situations, especially those originating from abroad" (Demas, 1965, p. 8). It has also been argued that small countries should put a premium on "highly efficient information systems, speed of response, flexibility and a capacity for adaptation and innovation" (Farrell, 1982, p. 28).

In a real sense, therefore, flexible specialization is nothing new to Caribbean economic thinking. Indeed, given the small size, the necessity for export orientation and the need to be continuously adapting to changes in the international marketplace, flexible specialization[6] has come to be recognized as a necessary strategy of development. Indeed, the imperative of flexible specialization in Caribbean economies stems both from their small *country* size and their small *firm* size. But will small size be sufficient to render flexibility?

7. TOURISM IN THE CARIBBEAN

The export of tourism services is the single most important source of foreign exchange, incomes and employment for many Caribbean islands. For Antigua and Barbuda, Barbados, Belize, Dominica, Grenada, Jamaica, Montserrat, St. Lucia and St. Vincent, income from tourism in 1980 was equivalent to one-half of the value of commodity and merchandise exports (EIU, 1984, pp. 43–44). This dependence on tourism is likely to increase even further as governments attempt to diversify, widen and strengthen the basket of goods and services which they currently export. Tourism appears to be the obvious, *natural* pivot of growth and diversification. This is largely because of the Caribbean islands' comparative natural "S-advantages" (sun, sand and sea) in tourism.

Caribbean tourism, however, is no different from traditional exports. It also falls victim to the vagaries of international demand patterns. In fact, the Caribbean tourist industry almost identically mirrors the world demand pattern. The postwar boom, the oil crisis of 1973–74 and recession in 1979–80 are clear testimony to this. The Caribbean tourism experience reflects the generally fatalistic view of Caribbean economies: namely, that whatever happens to the world economy will happen to the Caribbean economies.

8. FATALISM OR FLEXIBILITY?

It is conventionally believed that the future of Caribbean tourism depends upon factors which are external to the region. Multinational corporations (MNCs), the strength of the American economy, oil prices and recession are all identified as factors which will decide the fate of

Caribbean tourism. The fact hardly recognized, however, is that participation in the world economy need not be fatalistic or passive. As a matter of fact, the essence of flexibility is the ability to pursue an upwardly mobile growth path despite the hiccups that may pervade the "external" environment. In what follows, an attempt will be made to examine the role that flexible specialization can play in the future survival and competitiveness of Caribbean tourism.

9. EVOLUTION OF FLEXIBLE SPECIALIZATION IN TOURISM

(a) *International tourism*

International Tourism is on the threshold of change. A number of post-war developments (the jet aircraft, promotional fares, charters, cheap oil, Keynesian-inspired economic growth, world peace, prosperity, paid holidays, sun-lust tourists, MNCs, franchising, and vertical and horizontal integration) created mass, standardized and rigidly packaged (MSRP) tourism. There are growing signs that this is changing. One is likely to witness the development of a new tourism — a tourism driven by flexibility, segmentation and diagonal integration (FSDI).[7]

Factors involved in the transformation of MSRP tourism include the diffusion of a system of new information technologies,[8] deregulation, technology competition, changing consumer tastes, incomes and leisure time, and management practices of diagonal integration. Diagonal integration[9] is facilitated by information technologies, and refers to the synergies, systems gains and scope economies that service firms obtain from the provision of a combination (integration) of services rather than producing each separately.

The implication for Caribbean tourism is clear: Caribbean islands have to respond *not* to the MSRP tourism of old, but to the new tourism best practice of flexibility, segmentation and diagonal integration (FSDI).

(b) *Superclub*

Jamaican Superclub hotels have already begun to lead the Caribbean hotel industry into a new best practice — a best practice characterized by flexibility, segmentation and innovation. Superclub hotels were the most innovative of all Caribbean hotels studied. This was clearly evident, for example, in the area of market segmentation. A snapshot analysis of the market charac-

114   WORLD DEVELOPMENT

teristic of Caribbean hotels in 1985 revealed a very narrow and limited market segmentation. Except for the Superclub properties, hotels were segmented along two basic lines — *quality* of service and *size* of property (see Table 2).

Superclub hotels have pioneered the concept of "all-inclusive" vacations, introducing a completely new category of vacations altogether (see Table 2, row 6 under "Jamaica"). The all-inclusive concept has created truly cashless and flexible vacations. Moreover, these flexible and innovative vacations cater to well-targeted segments of the vacation market. They cater, for example, to hedonists, couples, families and people seeking truly authentic Jamaican vacations. It is interesting to note that earlier hotel best practice was based upon the *exact repli-*

cation of *standardized* hotels the world over (Luxenberg, 1985). Today, Superclub has succeeded in providing a new hotel best practice — a hotel chain whose membership is based upon *heterogeneity* and *diversity*.

10. FLEXIBLE SPECIALIZATION: BENETTON[10] AND SUPERCLUB[11] COMPARED

It should be stated at the outset that Benetton and Superclub are involved in different activities — garments and tourism, respectively. Despite this obvious difference, the experience of flexible specialization in Benetton and Superclub can be of great utility in helping to determine some of

Table 2. *Market characteristics of the tourist accommodation sample of Barbados, Jamaica, Tobago and Trinidad**

Market segment	Barbados units	Barbados rms	Jamaica units	Jamaica rms	Tobago units	Tobago rms	Trinidad units	Trinidad rms
1. Small properties† with personalized services	5	70	9	188	3	62	—	—
2. Small exclusive resort properties with high quality service	1	64	1	25	2	77	—	—
3. Very exclusive, first-class, medium-sized‡ properties with exceptional facilities and personalized services	3	466	4	486	—	—	—	—
4. Small-medium resort properties with good quality service and personalized attention	3	467	3	199	2	225	—	—
5. Small, resort self-catering apartments	12	240	—	—	1	77	—	—
6. All-inclusive resort properties with high standards of service	—	—	4	733	—	—	—	—
7. Very large, resort-cum-business properties§	1	306	—	—	—	—	1	442
8. Very large resort apartments	1	300	—	—	—	—	—	—
9. Very large resort properties	—	—	3	1,488	—	—	—	—
10. Business-oriented hotels with moderate to good levels of service	—	—	2	65	—	—	3	338
11. Medium-sized resort-cum-business properties	1	138	—	—	—	—	—	—
12. Small business-oriented properties with above-average levels of service	—	—	1	34	—	—	2	115
Total	27	2,051	27	3,218	8	441	6	895

*This classification is a subjective one. It is based on a combination of published information, (but mainly on) visual impressions, opinions of visitors interviewed as well as personal experience. This level of subjectivity could not be avoided because the properties themselves are not classified (e.g., 4 and 5 star) as they tend to be in the metropole.
†Small = 1–75 rooms,
‡Medium = 76–150 rooms,
§Very large = 300+.

the necessary conditions for successful flexible specialization strategies. This is because the new best practice of flexibility is not unique to specific firms or specific industries, or indeed to manufacturing. Flexibility is an economy-wide paradigm which will leave no sector untouched. The cases of Benetton and Superclub will serve to illustrate this point. The similarities and scope for comparison between these two diverse entities are striking.

(a) *Innovation*

Schumpeter defines innovation as the first commercial transaction involving a *new* good, service, process, system, organization, market, method or raw material (Schumpeter, 1965). By these criteria, Benetton and Superclub were both very innovative. Both were first in the market with their respective inventions. Benetton was the first firm in Italy, and possibly in the world, to introduce the system of franchising in textile and clothing industries. Superclub was the first hotel chain in the world to introduce the concept of all-inclusive vacations. Indeed, Club Med tried to eliminate the use of money on its properties but did not succeed in going all the way. It could not avoid, for example, charging for drinks and cigarettes.[12] Superclub did.

Benetton was also innovative in the modification of knitting machinery, the introduction of post-dyeing methods, knitwear stretching and knitwear automation (Belussi, 1987, pp. 41–42). Innovativeness was also present in Benetton and Superclub marketing and distribution strategies. Benetton sells not only clothing, but also the Benetton style, the shop organization, and marketing strategy. Similarly, Superclub not only markets Jamaica, or sun-lust vacations, but a complete lifestyle[13] — hedonism, family, couples, authenticity ("the *real* thing").

Two attributes of Benetton and Superclub innovation practices are of fundamental importance: first, their capacities for *continuous innovation*, and second, their introduction of *clusters of innovations*. Schumpeter observed that with any invention, there are "swarms of imitators" in the marketplace. Belussi observes the emergence of a second tier of flexibly specialized clothing concerns in Italy (e.g., Stefanel), while in Jamaica, the tourist industry was hit by "all-inclusive mania." With increasing competition, Benetton and Superclub are continuously innovating. Superclub, for example, is continuously seeking out more segmentation possibilities, new concepts and new marketing strategies.[14] Innovation clusters have been equally important. The coupling of innovations mutually reinforced each one. It is conceivable, for example, that if all-inclusive innovation and market segmentation were stand-alone innovations, in stand-alone hotels, they perhaps would not have been as successful as their cluster (system). Similarly, would Benetton have been as successful if it had only introduced post-dyeing methods?

(b) *Entrepreneurship*[15]

Entrepreneurship is another important factor in the success of both firms. Entrepreneurship in both cases was linked to *tradition* and to the *family* — the Issa family in Jamaica and the Benetton family in Italy. The Issas'[16] involvement in tourism goes back to the 1940s, when Abe Issa was one of the first hotel operators in Jamaica. Abe Issa is known as the "father of Jamaican tourism." His nephew, John Issa, now runs the Superclub hotel chain. The Issa family is also involved in a number of other related activities, including retail/distribution, fashion, merchandising and car rentals. The Benetton family — two brothers and one sister — were veterans of the Italian clothing industry (Belussi, 1987, pp. 10–11).

(c) *Information technology (IT)*

Belussi (1987) examined the development of information technologies (ITs) in Benetton's design, warehousing, distribution and organization functions. It was observed that Benetton's utilization of information technologies deepened as expansion and internationalization progressed — moving from a private IT network, to external data networks and links to other private (bank and financial services) networks. Superclub, by contrast, is a young operation, which has only recently begun the process of internationalizing its services. The majority of its hotel properties are in Jamaica; the only Superclub property outside of Jamaica is also Caribbean based. One suspects, however, that the more internationalized the organization becomes, the greater would be the demand for information technologies.[17] It is also noteworthy that the all-inclusive innovation itself has considerably reduced the need for direct information technology applications. ITs within hotels are mainly deployed to link the front office, back office and food and beverage departments. This ensures, for example, that a guest's drink taken at the bar does not go unrecorded. Because no money is

116   WORLD DEVELOPMENT

used in the Superclub hotels, this transaction has been eliminated altogether.

(d) Networks

One of the fundamental attributes of successful specialization is networks — serving to link many discrete activities into a total system of wealth creation. This is an important point because flexibility does not fall from heaven. Flexibility is a manifestation of the wider information techno-economic paradigm[18] which is transforming the entire socioeconomic-institutional system (Perez, 1985; Freeman and Perez, 1986). Moreover, even craft systems that were "emarginated" in the first industrial divide are not simply resurrected or "born again" in their original forms. These craft systems survive and are metamorphosized (survival instinct) even during their hibernation (mass production) period. This metamorphosis has taken the fundamental forms of networks and systems. This network/systems effect, in turn, is due to the overwhelming and pervasive impact of IT — an impact with which mass producers and flexible firms alike must learn to live.

For small firms, networks and systems have become the fundamental survival route. Greater prospects for flexibility can be had by firms which are able to reap scope economies, synergies and systems benefits[19] — be it in the form of cost advantages, marketing muscle, information access, or, ultimately, flexibility.

It should be observed, moreover, that networking does not result in de facto large size: there will always be tradeoffs between economies and diseconomies of scale and scope under different technical, organizational and market conditions. Indeed, information technology, networking, and flexibility in all areas of production transform the relations among inputs and outputs, scale and scope of operations, and the boundaries of the market.

The importance of networks, systems and synergies is evident in both the Benetton and Superclub cases. Benetton, for example, is not just a firm, it is a system of wealth creation with well-networked activities of raw material sourcing (where it enjoys some monopsonistic powers), production, subcontracting, distribution, marketing (franchising) and responding. Similarly, the wealth-creating potential of the Superclub organizational system is far greater than the sum of its discrete units.

(e) Specialization

Both Benetton and Superclub have very well-defined and specialized segments of the market within which they operate. Benetton specializes in the up-market segment of the informal clothing sector for young people. Superclub, on the other hand, specializes on the informal up-market segment of the vacation market. Superclub, for example, caters to "DINKS" (Double-Income, No Kids), "Yuppies" (Young, Upwardly Mobile Professionals), and families.

(f) Marketing and distribution

Benetton and Superclub operate on a very common marketing principle — closeness to the consumers. This principle veers sharply from mass production techniques where large volumes of standardized, low-priced output virtually dictated demand patterns (refer to Table 1, row 8). Benetton, through its network of retail outlets, and Superclub through its direct marketing campaigns, are able to more closely monitor, anticipate and reflect demand patterns. This closeness to the marketplace gives both firms the time advantage[20] and information with which to respond "just in time" to changes in consumer requirements. This closeness to the market is certainly a factor in the high occupancy rates for Superclub (above 90% year-round, compared with Jamaica's national average of 67.9%), and Benetton's relatively low level of unsold stocks and idle capacity.

(g) Politics

The political climate has also been instrumental in providing opportunities and conditions for innovation in both organizations. Benetton's growth was facilitated by the existence of protectionist policy implemented by the industrialized countries to stop (or at least reduce) the competitive pressure of commodities from the NICs, formally concluded in the Multi-Fiber Arrangement of 1974 and 1977. In Jamaica, the volatile political climate provided a good opportunity for rapid development of all-inclusive vacations. First, an unstable political climate made many hotel investments uneconomical, thereby encouraging many multinational operators to abandon their properties or to sell them off to the government. This meant that Superclub and indeed other multinational management companies (e.g., Jack Tar Village) could set up managerial operations without tremendous up-front outlays of capital. Second, all-inclusivity gives the reassurance of safety, despite the politically "unstable" climate. In addition, the severe foreign exchange problems of Jamaica in the mid-1970s ensured government support and encouragement for all-inclusive vacations since they allowed the government to better track foreign exchange expenditures and tax revenues.

(h) *Skilled labor*

Skilled labor is also a feature of the Benetton and Superclub operations. Unlike the mass, standardized tourism best practice which relied on a host of homogeneous, unskilled, low paid labor, all-inclusive vacations rely on *skill-intensity, flexibility* and *innovativeness* in the labor force. It is known, for example, that the authentic "Jamaica Jamaica" hotel employs a very skilled chef who has been exceptionally innovative in the development and use of local ingredients. Superclub employees are not confined to traditionally specified tasks within the hotel. This leads to a greater level of flexibility of the work force. For example, it is not uncommon to find an employee who is a host, tour guide, entertainer, information provider, organizer and sports coach all in one. In the Benetton system, the skills factor is not as clear-cut, as there is such an extreme division of labor between the core superstructure and the peripheral subcontractors. It is noteworthy, however, that whereas worker flexibility is criticized because of the ease with which labor can be dispensed, the flexibility of Benetton and Superclub has led to employment stability. Superclub, for example, has minimized summer/winter hotel occupancy rate variability to 8%, such that employment seasonality is nonexistent. Similarly, Benetton subcontractors supply exclusively to Benetton because stability of demand tends to be guaranteed.

(i) *Flexibility — services vs. manufacturing*

While the flexible response of a typical manufacturing firm would be to download its machines, change production runs, dyes and designs, the flexible response of a typical service firm usually tends to be different. Flexibility of response is not likely to involve downloading hotel beds or the physical conversion of hotels, although this certainly could be a long-term possibility. The main sources of flexibility for service firms lie in organization (e.g., converting whole floors of hotels into first-class service centers), management, marketing (e.g., intro-ducing executive, club class, or super-club class in airline services), distribution (e.g., shifting from recessionary markets to growth-prone ones) and other forms of interactions and interrelationships among guests, hotels, suppliers, and distributors (travel agents, tour operators). What is important, however, is not each of these "stand-alone" aspects, but how they are coupled to create competitive advantages, and hence, capabilities to move with the market. This is important because the very nature of services and their inherent pliability could mean that they are better candidates for flexibility than manufacturing.[21] Moreover, since hotel facilities tend to be rigid, producers who have traditionally catered to mass markets (e.g., the 2,000-room hotels in Spain) could perhaps be less responsive to the flexibility route. This has some implications for many developing countries that are still at the "discovery" or "response" stages of their tourism, and that, moreover, are currently contemplating entry into the institutionalized mass tourism phase.[22]

(j) *Source of flexibility*

The source of flexibility in the Jamaican Superclub holidays is very different from that of Benetton. Superclub does not depend on small-scale subcontractors or flexible, multi-use equipment. Flexibility originates from innovation — in developing the all-inclusive vacation concept, in product differentiation and marketing, and in its network of heterogeneous hotel offerings.[23] Innovativeness is also present in its ability to shift markets, marketing strategies and hotel offerings to suit demand patterns. (This was clearly evident when Superclub launched a marketing offensive in the Canadian market in the early 1980s). Benetton, by contrast, owes its flexibility to a complex of factors, including the deployment of information technologies, the development of networks among producers, retailers and distributors, and the deployment of a host of small-scale flexible suppliers in the traditional clothing sector in Italy.

It can be observed, then, that *there cannot be a unique flexible specialization solution or best practice*. In mass production, large scale and concomitant scale economies were the sole ingredients. By contrast, the best practice for flexible specialization is itself flexible. It is characterized by complexity and diversity. Different firms use different combinations of robust designs, production, product, service, organization, and marketing flexibilities in order to generate flexibility. These combinations may not be capable of being generalized.

(k) *Small size?*

The Caribbean tourist accommodation sector comprises mainly small enterprises. For Barbados, Jamaica, Trinidad and Tobago, 72.5% of all tourist accommodation units (hotels, apartments and guest houses) have at most 50 rooms (see Table 2). Not only are small establishments the most numerous, they also tend to be both locally-owned and managed. Many do not utilize information technologies in their daily management activities and are unable to justify the costs of being linked to computerized reservation systems. Data for technology adoption reveal that 66.2% of Caribbean hotels were at the precomputer stage in 1984; 25% were using stand-alone computers for clerical purposes, and only 8.8% were using computers to integrate their front office, back office and food and beverage departments. A large proportion of the smaller establishments were at the precomputer stage. Size of establishment, quality of management, information access and international connections (be it in the form of a franchise, MNC management, or simply education and training abroad) tended to be important for higher levels of technology adoption.

But how important is small size? The Superclub hotels range between 280–350 rooms. The largest hotels in the Caribbean are about 500 rooms. Superclub hotels, by Caribbean stan-

dards, are certainly not small. Similarly, the Benetton system is not small. However, as a chain of hotels, Superclub is small and Benetton does rely upon a host of small subcontractors in Italy.

Perhaps the best answer to the question of size is the following: could the small Italian clothing subcontractors or the individual hotels of the Superclub chain be as successful without the propulsive cores of the Benetton and Superclub superstructures respectively? This is a very fundamental question. Because, as Belussi argues, Benetton's "flexibility does not necessarily involve small overall size but involves a network system with a propulsive 'core' and an 'adaptable' periphery" (1987, p. 73).

It seems as though the real question is not one of small size but of "loneliness."[24] Herein lies the importance of networks, organizations and institutions that not only insulate small suppliers but also allow them to reap their full competitive potentials. With the growing trend toward internationalization, the increasing diffusion of IT, and the emergence of a new best practice of flexibility, *networks, systems and supporting institutions will become increasingly important* for small firms. There will be no place for the small, stand-alone participants, but the world can become the oyster of small, innovative, flexible and "networked" enterprises.

Small size, therefore, does not automatically imply flexibility. Size is a static concept. It is only when size is dynamized — i.e., embellished with networks, systems, technology, etc. — that small size can be a powerful force with which to reckon in the marketplace.

Table 3. *Size of the Caribbean* hotel sector*

Room size†	Unit frequency	Unit/Total (%)	Room frequency	Rooms/Total (%)
<25	112	51.0	1,737	12.6
26–50	47	19.6	1,659	12.0
51–75	22	9.2	1,394	10.0
76–100	11	5.0	929	6.7
101–200	21	9.0	2,923	21.1
211–300	6	2.5	1,587	11.5
>300	9	3.7	3,581	25.9
Total	239	100.0	13,810	100.0

*Data for Barbados, Jamaica, Trinidad and Tobago.
†The data do not include apartments and villas for Jamaica. If this category were included, the proportion of small establishments would be even larger.
Source: Population data obtained from Tourist Board Listing, 1985.

11. POLICY IMPLICATIONS — CARIBBEAN PERSPECTIVES

(a) *Innovation and entrepreneurship*

This comparative study of Superclub and Benetton demonstrates the importance of entrepreneurship and the need to evolve continuous clusters of innovation. Field interviews with hotel managers in Barbados, Jamaica, and Trinidad and Tobago[25] also confirmed the importance of innovation, entrepreneurship and good quality management in determining their future survival and competitiveness. It seems rather obvious that policies should be directed at finding ways of populating these categories on a continuing basis.

With the tradition of MNC presence in the Caribbean region (35.6% of all hotels are multinational affiliated),[26] however, policies have been overwhelmingly targeted at *ownership*. It is not surprising to find, therefore, that the government and the local private sector together own 75.6% of the total tourist accommodation rooms on all islands, while MNCs own only 15.3%. By contrast, MNCs *manage* 44.5%, government 4.0%, and the local private sector 41.1%. It is clear that, in concentrating on ownership, what governments really bought was national pride and not *control*. This is why future emphasis must be placed upon cultivating a cadre of Caribbeans who could seriously control their own destiny, rather than reducing capital costs for MNCs (as in the case of ownership).

Managerial talent, intelligence and entrepreneurship are key ingredients in the control of one's destiny. Policy geared toward fostering innovation and entrepreneurship seems to be necessary. Such policies should be aimed at the revaluation and cultivation of these attributes within the Caribbean populace. For islands that have inherited a legacy of career aspirations toward bureaucracy, civil service and other "white collar" professions, the need to create and enhance the value of hands-on experience and managerial and entrepreneurial talent is of paramount importance.

(b) *Networks and institutional support*

We have seen the importance of networks for Superclub and Benetton — both of which, by Caribbean standards, are large. We also have seen the impossibility of the Italian subcontractor or Jamaican hotel "going it alone" en route to flexible specialization. But what does this imply for smaller hotels? How will small hotels be able to survive and compete both with the local Superclub hotels and with external predators? Does their small size give them some inherent advantages in the marketplace? This question is of vital importance to the Caribbean tourism economy.

It is in this respect that the UNDP/UNIDO (1987) Cyprus study provides a useful guide to policy for small firms, and more generally, for small countries. The concept of consortia, designed to assist small producers, is an important recommendation of the study. The idea is to establish collaborative ventures (for example in art, design, training, information access, and advertising) which would enable small firms to pool their resources and share some indirect operating costs. This policy of collaborative ventures among small firms seems to be a necessary tool for small tourism establishments in the Caribbean.[27] Networks of shared costs, resources and information will help small hotels to alleviate some of the constraints of small size and enable them to obtain the benefits of scale economies.

(c) *Regional integration*

For Caribbean economies, the concept of collaboration must go beyond small *firms*. It must be extended to the concept of small *countries* as well. In this world of networks, systems, information technologies and flexibility, small countries will find it increasingly difficult to "go it alone." This is increasingly being recognized by the relatively large European countries as they prepare for 1992.

Herein lies a very powerful imperative for Caribbean integration. In the creation of flexible, specialized, island economies, the importance of integration, collaboration and other forms of shared/consortia activities are of vital import. This is necessary in the areas of materials policy,[28] market intelligence, export marketing, investment, technology, training, and policy/strategy coordination. Space does not permit the exploration of all of these issues, but the general point will be illustrated with respect to hotel classification.

One of the problems for Caribbean hotels, particularly small, delinked hotels, is the absence of a system of standards. This puts small hotels, apartments, guest houses and villas at a serious information disadvantage. While smaller establishments may be comparable and even better than large hotels in terms of services, prices and flexibility, there is little way of conveying this information to potential tourists (since the standard 1–5 star classification simply does not apply).[29] There is also need to coordinate this information, not only for a single island, but regionally. In 1985, Barbados began this process of classification and has now successfully developed a classification system. This service could be sold to other islands with the potential that, in time, all hotels, sharing these indirect operating costs and creating an information system, could build advantages in the marketplace. In this way, one island's tourism income is not necessarily at the other's expense. There can be mutual advantages to be had in collaboration, as shown by the University of the West Indies system (integrated campuses in The Bahamas, Barbados, Jamaica, and Trinidad and Tobago). A total wealth-creating and -generating tourism system can be fostered wherein all islands can benefit mutually.

12. CONCLUSION: FLEXIBILITY = SMALL-SCALE, BACKYARD PRODUCTION

One of the first lessons of the Benetton and Superclub experiences is that strategies of flexible specialization are themselves flexible. There is no unique flexible specialization combination. There are a number of ways in which enterprises can create flexibility. In the Italian case, flexibility was based on a model of subcontracting small, traditional firms. In Jamaica, flexibility was achieved through innovation and product differentiation ("niching"). Small size, therefore, is not a *sine qua non* for flexible specialization. What is very clear, however, is that flexible specialization is a systems concept. As such, even where smallness can render flexibility, small size cannot stand alone. It must be embellished with intelligence, support systems, innovation, entrepreneurship, networks, competitive strategies and technology. Policies for the dynamization of small size and for the creation of flexible specialization must address these issues. Regional integration is a central weapon in the survival of small Caribbean tourist economies.

NOTES

1. This article does not intend to provide a systematic critique of the Piore and Sabel thesis (see Williams *et al.*, 1987), or to join the debate on the appropriateness of flexible specialization strategies as a panacea for America's industrial competitiveness (see Jones, 1987; Womack 1987a, 1987b). It will also not focus on the Marxist/labour market/gender implications of flexible specialization (see Fergus Murray, 1983, 1987).

2. Womack (1987b) argues that the flexible specialization literature is handicapped by the lack of operational meaning for most of the terms used — "production organization," "production unit," "technology," "flexible manufacturing."

3. See Williams *et al.* (1987).

4. Seers (1981) provides a useful overview, summary and critique of the dependency tradition.

5. For a brief discussion of these problems, refer to Poon (1987).

6. Note that the issues of flexibility are different when applied to the case of small, open Caribbean economies as opposed to when tendered as a competitive prescription for the large, deficit-ridden, ailing American economy.

7. This is one of the fundamental arguments of the author's doctoral thesis.

8. Components of the system of information technologies (SIT) include computers, computerized reservations systems, electronic funds transfer, videos, video brochures, videotext, interactive videotext, management information systems, airline management and control systems, telephones, digital telephone networks, satellite communications, teleconferencing, mobile communications, electronic safety and energy management systems. The interesting point to note is that it is not a single technology, but this whole system of technologies that are being simultaneously diffused. Moreover, it is not travel agents or hotels or airlines that are using the SIT, but the whole industry. See Poon (1988b).

9. Diagonal integration is a term developed by the author. Refer to Poon (1987c).

10. The data for Benetton are obtained from Belussi's very good case study of Benetton (Belussi, 1987).

11. Data for Superclub are obtained from interviews with managerial personnel and staff of the Superclub organization in 1985. The author was also in residence at one of the properties.

12. For a short report on the early development of Jamaica's all-inclusive vacations, see George Whitfield's open letter to *Travel Weekly*, "Inclusive resorts: Do they spark holiday success?" October 15, 1987; C36.

13. It is observed, for example, that couples meet at *Hedonism 11*, court at *Jamaica Jamaica*, romance and sometimes marry at *Couples* and bring their families to *Boscobel Beach* (Travel Weekly's Special Report on the Caribbean, December 17, 1987).

14. A recent interview (March, 1988) in London with John Issa, Owner/Director of the Superclub hotel chain, indicated that another property, Grand Lido, would open at Bloody Bay, Jamaica. This property was opened in 1989 and caters to super luxury, complete with private yacht.

15. According to Schumpeter, the entrepreneur is the "leader," the "disturber of the peace," who has the "initiative," "authority," "intuition," "foresight" and "psyche" to carry out innovations (Schumpeter, 1965, pp. 74–94).

16. I am grateful to Mr. Basil Buck of the *Daily Gleaner*, Jamaica's daily newspaper, for providing material on the history of the Issa family's involvement in Jamaican tourism.

17. It has been observed that the impact of IT in tourism production systems will be greatest in the area of international marketing, distribution and supplier interrelationships. IT will also have an impact in the international hotel management functions, but will have less impact on the human- and service-intensive areas of service delivery and guest interactions (Poon, 1988).

18. In addition to flexibility, other elements of the techno-economic paradigm include declining costs, and energy-, space- and time-saving (Perez and Freeman, 1986). This new paradigm is seen to be fueled by the microelectronics revolution.

19. For more information on the issues of systems benefits, synergies and scope economies for tourism, see Poon (1987c).

20. It is noted, for example, that Benetton products reach the market about 6–8 weeks before their competitors (Belussi, 1987, p. 65).

21. Indeed Schumpeter, the father of innovation, has stated that it is not the makers of the stage coaches who engineer the railway revolution. By implication, given that the manufacturing sector and automobiles in particular are the epitome of inflexible, Fordist, mass production, there is no reason to expect that flexibility must first originate in manufacturing or automobiles. It has to be at least entertained that services could very well take the lead.

22. This stages approach to tourism development was invented by sociologist E. Cohen (1972, pp. 164–180).

23. Indeed, when it comes to flexibility in the services sector, there is dire need for concepts, measurements and definition. Barras (1986) has made the first attempt to explain the process of innovation diffusion in services.

24. In her study of small electronic companies in Norway, Arnestad (1987) has also found that the problem for small firms is not their inherent small size, but their "loneliness," i.e., whether or not they had network linkages to other firms and markets.

25. Data for the four islands are obtained from interviews with a random selection of the tourist accommodation sector. The sample consists of 68 units representing 60.8% of total rooms.

26. United Nations Center for Transnational Corporations (1982).

27. The following two sections should not be taken to imply that ideas of institutional support and regional networks for small hotels are new to tourism analysis. Tourism experts pointed to these over a decade ago (e.g., de Kadt, 1978). One suspects, however, that with the increasing diffusion of information technologies and the changing, competitive tourism environment, they will become even more important for the survival of small establishments.

28. Common materials policy should be a vital element of regional cooperation in the Caribbean. This is because almost every item that is "locally produced" has an import content. In some cases, a policy of import content should be deliberately pursued where design and quality factors may dictate the use of superior quality materials — some of which may not be available locally. Coordinated regional policy could have advantages in terms of buying power and shared costs and services of information acquisition and market intelligence.

29. By definition, a hotel of international standard must contain at least 100 rooms.

REFERENCES

Arnestad, Maja, "Small firms — great challenges," Summary of a study of small electronics firms in Norway and the basis of a seminar presentation at the Science Policy Research Unit (Brighton: University of Sussex, December 1987).

Barras, Richard, "Towards a theory of innovation in services," *Research Policy*, Vol. 15, No. 3 (1986).

Belussi, Fiorenza, *Benetton: Information Technology in Production and Distribution — A Case Study of the Innovative Potential of Traditional Sectors*, SPRU

Occasional Paper Series, No. 25 (Brighton: Science Policy Research Unit, University of Sussex, 1987).

Best, Lloyd, and Kari Levitt, "The character of the Caribbean economy," in George Beckford (Ed.), *Caribbean Economy: Dependence and Backwardness* (Mona, Jamaica: Institute of Social and Economic Studies, 1975).

Blackman, Courtney N., "The balance of payments crisis in the Caribbean: Which way out?" Paper delivered at an inter-disciplinary seminar sponsored by the Guild of Undergraduates, University of the West Indies (February 5, 1979).

Cohen, Erik, "Towards a sociology of international tourism," *Social Research*, Vol. 39 (1972), pp. 164–182.

De Kadt, Emmanuel (Ed.), *Tourism — Passport to Development* (Oxford: Oxford University Press, 1978).

Demas, William, *The Economics of Development in Small Countries with Special Reference to the Caribbean* (Montreal: McGill University Press, 1965).

Economist Intelligence Unit (EIU), "The Caribbean as a tourist destination," *International Tourism Quarterly*, No. 1, Special Report No. 49 (1984), pp. 37–55.

Farrell, Trevor M. A., "Small size, technology and development strategy," Research Paper Studies, *Caribbean Technology Policy Studies 2* (August 1982).

Freeman, Christopher, and Carlota Perez, "The diffusion of technical innovations and changes in the techno-economic paradigm," Paper presented at the Venice conference on innovation diffusion (Venice: March 17–22, 1986).

Girvan, Norman, "Dependence and development in the old world and the new," *Social and Economic Studies*, Vol. 22, No. 1 (1973).

Haywood, Bill, and John Bessant, "The Swedish approach to the use of flexible manufacturing systems," Occasional Paper No. 3, Innovation Research Group, Business Research Centre (Brighton: Brighton Business School, Brighton Polytechnic, 1987).

Hoffman, Kurt, "Clothing, chips and competitive advantages: The impact of microelectronics on trade and production in the garment industry," *World Development*, Vol. 13, No. 3 (1985), pp. 371–392.

Johnson, Bjorn, "An institutional approach to the small country problem," Paper presented at the IKE Workshop on Technological Change and the Competitiveness of Small Countries (Aalborg, Denmark: August 18–21, 1987).

Jones, Daniel T., "Analytical notes" for the Berkeley Roundtable on the International Economy (BRIE) Workshop on Production, Reorganization and Skills (Berkeley: University of California at Berkeley, September 10–12, 1987).

Kaplinsky, Raphael, "Electronic-based automation technologies and the onset of systemofacture: Implications for Third World industrialization," *World Development*, Vol. 13, No. 3 (1985), pp. 423–439.

Kobayashi, Koji, *Computers and Communications — A Vision of C + C* (Cambridge, MA: The MIT Press, 1986).

Lewis, W. Arthur, "The slowing down of the engine of economic growth," Nobel Prize Lecture, *American Economic Review*, Vol. 70, No. 4 (September 1980).

Lewis, W. Arthur, *The Evolution of the International Economic Order*, the Elliot Janeway Lecture on Historical Economics in Honor of Joseph Schumpeter (Princeton, NJ: Princeton University Press, 1977).

Luxenberg, Stan, *Roadside Empires: How the Chains Franchised America* (New York: Viking, 1985).

Mody, A., and D. Wheeler, "Towards a vanishing middle: Competition in the world garment industry," *World Development*, Vol. 15, No. 10/11 (1987), pp. 1269–1284.

Murray, Fergus, "Flexible specialization in the third Italy," *Capital and Class* (December 1987), pp. 84–95.

Murray, Fergus, "The decentralization of production — the decline of the mass-collective worker?" *Capital and Class*, No. 19 (Spring 1983).

Murray, Robin, "Ownership, control and the market," *New Left Review*, No. 196 (July/August 1987).

Murray, Robin, "Benetton Britain, the new economic order," *Marxism Today*, No. 11 (1985).

Perez, Carlota, "The new technologies: An integrated view," English version of the original Spanish, "Las nuevas technologias: una vision de cobjunto," in C. Ominami (Ed.), *La Tercera Revolucion Industrial: Impactos Internacionales del Actual Viraje Technologico* (Buenos Aires: Grupo Editor Latinamerican, 1986), pp. 44–89.

Perez, Carlota, "Microelectronics, long waves and world structural change: New perspectives of developing countries, *World Development*, Vol. 13, No. 3 (1985), pp. 441–463.

Perez, Carlota, "Structural change and the new technologies," *Futures*, Vol. 15, No. 5 (1983a), pp. 357–375.

Perez, Carlota, "Towards a comprehensive theory of long waves," Paper presented at the IIASA meeting on Long Waves, Depression and Innovation (Siena-Florence: October 26–29, 1983b).

Piore, Michael, "Corporate reform in American manufacturing and the challenge to economic theory," (excerpt). Paper presented to the Berkeley Roundtable on the International Economy (BRIE) Workshop on Production, Reorganization and Skills (Berkeley: University of California at Berkeley, September 10–12, 1987).

Piore, Michael, and Charles Sabel, *The Second Industrial Divide — Possibilities for Prosperity* (New York: Basic Books, 1984).

Piore, Michael, and Charles Sabel, "Italian small business development: Lessons for U.S. industrial policy," in J. Zysman and L. Tyson (Eds.), *American Industry in International Competition — Government Policies and Corporate Strategies* (Ithaca, NY: Cornell University Press, 1983), pp. 391–422.

Poon, Auliana, "Competitive strategies for a new tourism," in C. Cooper (Ed.), *Progress in Tourism, Recreation and Hospitality Management*, Vol. 1 (UK: Belhaven Press, 1989a), pp. 91–103.

Poon, Auliana, "Blueprint for Tourism in Trinidad and Tobago" paper delivered at the Trinidad and Tobago Hotel and Tourism Association Hospitality Festival (November 3, 1989).

Poon, Auliana, "Caribbean Tourism Foreign Direct Investment and the Global Economy — Towards a Regional Action Plan for Services." Paper prepared for the AID/UNCTC Workshop on Services and Development (Trinidad, November 27–December 1, 1989).

Poon, Auliana, "Financing tourism in the Caribbean," Mimeo (Christ Church, Barbados: Caribbean Tourism Organization, 1989b).

Poon, Auliana, "All-inclusive Hotels in the Caribbean

FLEXIBLE SPECIALIZATION AND SMALL SIZE   123

— the case of St. Lucia," Mimeo (Christ Church, Barbados: Caribbean Tourism Organization, 1989c).

Poon, Auliana, "New approaches to tourism," *Caribbean Contact*, Vol. 16, No. 10 (March 1989d), pp. 8–9.

Poon, Auliana, "The future of Caribbean tourism — A matter of innovation," *Tourism Management* (September 1988a), pp. 213–220.

Poon, Auliana, "Information technology and tourism," *Annals of Tourism Research*, Vol. 15, No. 4 (1988b).

Poon, Auliana, "Long term prospects and policies for Caribbean tourism," Consultancy report prepared for the Commonwealth Secretariat to form part of the *Caribbean Perspectives to 2000* study (June 1987a).

Poon, Auliana, "Information technology and innovation in international tourism — implications for Caribbean tourism," Ph.D. dissertation (Brighton: University of Sussex, Science Policy Research Unit, August 1987b).

Poon, Auliana, "Diagonal integration — A new commonsense for tourism and services," Mimeo (Brighton: University of Sussex, SPRU, October 1987c).

Poon, Auliana, "Towards a strategy of export-oriented industrialisation — the case of Trinidad and Tobago," M.Sc. thesis (St. Augustine, Trinidad: University of the West Indies, 1983).

Porter, Michael, "Technology and competitive advantage," *Journal of Business Strategy* (Winter 1985), pp. 60–78.

Rada, Juan F., "Advanced technologies and development: Are conventional ideas about comparative advantage obsolete?" *Trade and Development — An UNCTAD Review*, No. 5 (1984).

Sabel, Charles, "Changing models of economic efficiency and their implications for industrialization in the Third World," in A. Foxley, M. McPherson, and G. O'Donnell (Eds.), *Development, Democracy, and Art of Trespassing: Essays in Honour of Albert O. Hirschman* (Notre Dame, IN: University of Notre Dame Press, 1986), pp. 27–55.

Schumpeter, Joseph A., *The Theory of Economic Development: An Enquiry into Profits, Credit, Interest and the Business Cycle* (Oxford: Oxford University Press, fourth printing, 1965) [originally published 1934].

Seers, Dudley (Ed.), *Dependency Theory: A Critical Assessment* (London: Frances Pinter, 1981).

St. Cyr, Eric B. A., "Towards a long-term economic strategy for Trinidad and Tobago: Some alternative perspectives" (St. Augustine, Trinidad: University of the West Indies, 1982).

Thomas, Clive Y., *Dependence and Transformation* (New York: Monthly Review Press, 1974).

UNDP/UNIDO, *Cyprus Industrial Strategy*, Vol. 1 *Overview and Executive Summary* (New York: United Nations, 1987).

US Congress, *Review of Airline Deregulation and Sunset of the Civil Aeronautics Board (Airline Computer Reservation Systems)*, Hearings before the subcommittee on aviation, 98th Congress, First Session (Washington, DC: US Government Printing Office, July 21–23, 1983).

Williams, K., T. Cutler, J. Williams, and C. Halsam, "The end of mass production," Review article of M. Piore and C. Sabel, *The Second Industrial Divide*, in *Economy and Society*, Vol. 116, No. 3 (1987), pp. 407–440.

Womack, James P., "An automotive strategy for the 21st century," Paper presented to the 35th meeting of the Automotive Parts Manufacturers' Association of Canada (Toronto: April 30, 1987a).

Womack, James P., "Analytical notes" for the Berkeley Roundtable on the International Economy (BRIE) Workshop on Production, Reorganization and Skills (Berkeley: University of California at Berkeley, September 10–12, 1987b).

Zeitlin, J., "The third Italy: Inter-firm co-operation and technological innovation," Paper presented to the South East Development Strategy (SEEDS) meeting (Brighton: March 1987).

Part III
Broader Perspectives

[26]

Annals of Tourism Research, Vol. 20, pp. 535–556, 1993
Printed in the USA. All rights reserved.

TOURISM SPACE IN
DEVELOPING COUNTRIES

Martin Oppermann
Universität Tübingen, Germany

Abstract: This article discusses tourism development theories with respect to their spatio-temporal implications in the Third World. They are all found to be inadequate in explaining the spatial occurrence and temporal development of tourism in developing countries. This is largely due to a lack of differentiation of tourism activity into different sectors. In response, the proposed model of "tourist space in developing countries" acknowledges the influence of the existing social and economic structures in these countries at all stages of tourism development, differentiates the tourism industry into two sectors, and recognizes the spatial segregation and different economic impacts of the sectors. **Keywords:** developing countries, development theory, spatio-temporal development, dual structure, formal/informal sector.

Résumé: L'espace touristique aux pays en voie de développement. L'article examine des théories de développement touristique et leurs implications spatio-temporelles au Tiers-Monde. On trouve qu'aucune des théories ne suffit pour expliquer les circonstances de l'espace et le développement temporel aux pays en voie de développement. Cette insuffisance vient du fait que ces théories ne distinguent pas les différents secteurs de l'activité touristique. Cet article propose donc un modèle qui intègre l'influence des structures sociales et économiques existantes à toutes les phases du développement du tourisme, qui différencie l'industrie touristique en deux secteurs et qui reconnaît la ségrégation spatiale et les effets économiques différents des deux secteurs. **Mots-clés:** pays en voie de développement, théorie du développement, développement spatio-temporel, secteurs formel et informel.

INTRODUCTION

Theoretical aspects of tourism development have seldom been addressed in tourism literature. The majority of tourism research is concerned with case studies of economic, cultural, or social impacts (Mitchell and Smith 1989; Smith 1982). A few studies, however, do discuss aspects of tourism development over time and space (Britton 1982; Butler 1980; Gormsen 1981; Miossec 1976). Most of them can

Martin Oppermann is Research Associate in the Department of Geography, Universität Tübingen (Hölderlinstr. 12, 7400 Tübingen, Germany). His current research focuses on rural and farm tourism in Southern Germany. Other research interests include domestic and international tourist flows, tourism development, and Third World tourism.

be assigned to development theories that have originated outside the specific field of tourism studies. Hence, among the existing theoretical tourism studies one can distinguish those belonging to the diffusionist paradigm (Butler 1980; Christaller 1964; Gormsen 1981; Miossec 1976; Plog 1973; Schlenke and Stewig 1983; Thurot 1973) and those belonging to the world system or dependency paradigm (Britton 1982; Hills and Lundgren 1977; Hoivik and Heiberg 1980; Husbands 1981). Most of these studies are general enough to include developing countries, and some specifically address them. A few theorize the actual spatial distribution of tourism within developing countries, but they usually ignore important aspects, for example, the existence of two different sectors within the tourism industry (Kermath and Thomas 1992; Wahnschafft 1982). This may be partly attributed to the neglect of the intranational travel pattern within the destination areas (Oppermann 1992a).

The aim of this paper is to review and discuss the existing development theories within tourism literature with respect to their implications to the spatio-temporal development of tourism, particularly within developing countries. It distinguishes between studies belonging to the diffusionist and the dependency paradigm. A model of tourist space is then proposed that recognizes the existence of two sectors in the tourism industry in developing countries.

General reviews of tourism development theories and models have been forwarded by Pearce (1987 and 1989a), Din (1990), and Debbage (1988). Pearce discusses development theories exhaustively; however, he does not consider the dichotomy of tourism in developing countries. Din (1990) refers mostly to the varying economic impact of tourism on the different ethnic sectors of the economy. The formal-informal sector notion has been applied to tourism before (Kermath and Thomas 1992; Michaud 1991; Wahnschafft 1982), but these authors focus on resort areas and discuss almost exclusively the influence of government decisions on the development of both sectors. They do not consider the spatial distribution and development of both sectors on national level, which is the aim of this paper.

TOURISM DEVELOPMENT THEORIES

Development Stage Theory

Two of the mainstream theories of the diffusionist paradigm are development stage and diffusion theory (Browett 1979). The main concept underlying the development stage theory is the notion of uni-linear change. Based on an Euro-American point of view, it implies that the less developed countries are in an "earlier phase" of the development process, but will eventually repeat the Euro-American development experience (Browett 1982). The most familiar theory belonging to this perspective is Rostow's (1960) "stages of economic growth." He identifies five successive stages of economic development. Among the evolutionary models in tourism studies a range of tourism development stages are suggested. Thurot (1973) theorizes three phases, Miossec (1976) hypothesizes five, and Butler (1980) proposes six. Gormsen

(1981) identifies six phases of tourism development in the so-called first periphery (resorts of Northern Europe) between 1800 and 1980. Most of these models confine their analyses to increase in tourism volume and change in tourist types. Schlenke and Stewig (1983) associate Rostow's five stages of economic development with the evolution of domestic tourism. They suggest that the participation of the population in domestic tourism is closely related to the industrial development of the whole country. In the stage of a "traditional society" (Rostow's first stage) only the country's elite has enough spare time and finances to afford leisure travel. In the process of economic development, the number of social classes participating in domestic tourism progressively increases. It is not until the final stage of "high mass consumption" that all social classes can afford holiday travel (Schlenke and Stewig 1983).

According to Miossec (1976), the development of tourism starts with a pioneer resort. Multiplication of resorts leads to the establishment of a hierarchy and a functional specialization of resorts. In the last stage, tourism resorts are distributed almost evenly across the country. The connectivity of the resorts with respect to transportation linkages reaches its maximum. Associated with the functional change of the resorts is a change in its clientele. The original visitors leave for more peripheral destinations. Other types of visitors populate the resort. This progression is also mentioned by Christaller (1964), Cohen (1972), Plog (1973), Thurot (1973), and Butler (1980). The originally popular resorts lose attractiveness and the tourists search for different and new places. This implies that the existing hierarchy of resorts within a region or country will disintegrate, because new resorts grow to replace the older ones. While for Butler (1980) the decline phase is one possibility besides rejuvenation, for Plog (1973) eventual decline is inevitable in the development process that proceeds along a continuum of attractiveness from the preponderance of an allocentric to a psychocentric clientele.

Pearce (1989b) notes one deficiency in Miossec's (1976) model. Tourism development typically occurs "within an existing socioeconomic structure where some forms of urban hierarchy and transport network are already found" (Pearce 1989b:18), and not in an "empty space." Another aspect that has been overlooked by Miossec is that tourism development in Third World countries often occurs in the form of isolated resorts, which do not form a highly interconnected hierarchical structure. Thus, the transportation linkages between the resorts remain sparse. The enclavic structure of resorts has been noted by several researchers (Britton 1980; Domrös 1989; Jenkins 1982; Matznetter 1979; Schürmann 1981); however, not all resorts are enclaves. Apart from these enclaves, tourism development takes place within the existing socioeconomic structure of developing countries. This can be seen in the persistent concentration of tourism activity in a few places, very often the economic and political centers of developing countries.

To show the dominance of the capital city in the tourism industry, Mergard (1986) calculated "the importance index of the capital" for 34 developing countries. This index is a ratio of the percentage of tourism accommodation in the capital and the latter's share of the country's population. Except for a few countries in Latin America (Colombia, Jamaica, and Mexico), all other countries had an index of greater than 1. This means that the capital offered, compared to its population, a more than average share of the country's tourist accommodation. India (20.2) and the Philippines (16.8) had the highest index. Notwithstanding, there seems to be a decrease in the capital's dominant position over time (Mergard 1986).

Temporal changes in the importance of transportation types lead to a different degree of concentration (Lundgren 1972). For example, the decreasing number of tourists arriving in Morocco by ship from Europe, coupled with the increasing number of air-travelers, has resulted in a spatial concentration of tourist activities over the last decade (Berriane 1990). A major factor in the concentration of tourist activity appears, therefore, to be the use of air transport for traveling to developing countries. This leads to a low mobility of the tourists within the destination countries. This was the case in Tunisia (Arnold 1972 and 1983; Berriane 1990), Morocco (Berriane 1990), Malaysia (Oppermann 1992b), and the Bahamas (Debbage 1988; Ungefehr 1988).

Diffusion Theory

The main idea of diffusion theory is that at one point of the development process "there will be a spread, a filtering, or a diffusion of growth/development impulses from the most developed to the less developed area" (Browett 1979:65). This "spread," "trickle down," or "filtering" effect will lead eventually to an adjustment of the regional disparities after initial polarization (Alonso 1968; Hirschmann 1958). To effectively eradicate backwardness, it is necessary to establish growth poles. These can either be whole cities or just an economic sector with a high connectivity with other industries and which is thought to have a high multiplier effect (Friedmann 1966; Myrdal 1959; Perroux 1955).

Christaller was among the first who considered tourism to be such a growth pole. "Nowadays, tourism gives the economically underdeveloped regions a chance to develop themselves—for these very regions interest the tourists" (1964:104). Friedmann recommended tourism as a development option for particularly problematic regions that have otherwise little development potential:

> Special problem regions belong to a category of area that, because of the peculiarity of their resources or location, demands a specialized development approach. They will often include regions along national borders, water resource development regions, regions suited to the intensive development of tourism and fisheries, and military zones. . . . Programs for resource development should, in the main, be guided by the evolving demand for specific resources or resource-related services, such as tourism. . . . Thought may be given to the possibility of incorporating within the areas set aside for national forests or national parks all regions of very low economic potential (1966:43, 215).

Thus, tourism was not only considered to have a positive influence on the economy, but it was seen as an "instrument" in the development of peripheral regions. Because tourism consumption occurs at the place of production it has, through its numerous associations with other industries (i.e., agriculture, fishery, forestry, building, handicraft), potential multiplier effects on the local economy. In the earlier years these were considered very high (Clement 1961; Zinder 1969).

To what extent tourism is an agent for diffusion in the process of development remains to be examined. Several studies intimate that tourism is largely concentrated in the capital, economic centers, and the coast. Oppermann (1992b) illustrates in a study on tourism in Malaysia that tourism is least important in peripheral regions, while the economic and political centers of Malaysia have a more than average share in the tourism industry. This distribution appears to be fairly stable as the analysis over one decade suggests. Similar results were found in the Philippines (Bernklau 1991; Thomas 1978), Bali (Dress 1979, Radetzki-Stenner 1989), Tunisia (Arnold 1983; Berriane 1990), Mexico (Müller 1984), Peru (Jurzcek 1985), Morocco (Berriane 1990), and Sri Lanka (Vorlaufer 1980).

The already addressed immobility of international tourists in developing countries leads to a selected development of tourism resorts in the vicinity of existing international airports and, therefore, often close to the capital (Pearce 1987). Only through opening of new international airports can tourist flows be directed towards other regions. Since most pleasure tourists belong to the "sand, sun, and sea" category, such a development is, however, most likely to occur along the coast. If it is a fertile coast, it is liable to belong to the more populated and developed regions of the country. In that case, tourism development will eventually lead to a land use conflict in which agriculture can not compete. If it is a barren coastline or a remote part of the country, tourism will have hardly any backward linkages. All agricultural products and most other necessary material will have to be imported; thus, the multiplier effect is lost from the local economy. A good example for the latter case is Cancun, Mexico. After 15 years of development, almost all of its supplies still come from far away (Spehs 1990).

Low multiplier effects are one of the reasons for the low regional distributive effects of tourism in peripheral regions. Multiplier effects have rarely reached the prognosticated level (Bryden 1973; Bryden and Faber 1971; Müller 1984; Oestreich 1977; Pavaskar 1982), because a considerable percentage of the spending in peripheral regions is drawn away in two ways, namely on a national level towards overseas and on a regional level towards the metropolises (Jurzcek 1985).

Dependency Theory

The dependency paradigm arose out of dissatisfaction with the diffusion paradigm. It maintains that "as a result of dependency, capitalist development in the core continuously creates and perpetuates underdevelopment in the periphery" (Browett 1982:145). It found its way into tourism studies (Britton 1982; Hoivik and Heiberg 1980; Husbands 1981). The central point of the critique of tourism as a development agent was that most development plans and goals were not fulfilled.

The multiplier effects were considerably lower than expected owing to high import rates. The popular assumption that tourism is labor intensive and capital extensive and, therefore, ideal for developing countries has been repeatedly questioned (Diamond 1977; Husbands 1981; Matthews and Richter 1991). Particularly the capital-intensiveness of mass tourism has been established in many places (Möller 1986; Vorlaufer 1988).

Reasons for tourism's failure were seen in its organization and its orientation towards international markets. The necessary high initial investment costs in mass tourism are very often too high for developing countries and, therefore, lead to dependency on foreign capital (Britton 1982; Rodenburg 1980). The leading positions are frequently taken up by foreigners and the destination is marketed by companies in the developed countries.

> The paradox arises therefore, where tourism is being used as a tool for the development of the periphery, but the entire organization and control of the industry reside in the core region. This provides an example of "organizing the dependence on the core" in order to foster development of the periphery (Husbands 1981:42).

The spatial concentration of international tourism in developing countries, combined with the typical standardization of the tourism product in mass tourism, resulted in the establishment of enclavic resorts (Arnold 1972; Britton 1982; Jenkins 1982).

> In physical, commercial and socio-psychological terms, then, tourism in a peripheral economy can be conceptualized as an enclave industry. Tourist arrival points in the periphery are typically the primary urban centers of ex-colonies, now functioning as political and economic centers of independent countries. . . . If on package tours, tourists will be transported from international transport terminals to hotels and resort enclaves. The transport, tour organization and accommodation phases of their itineraries will be confined largely to formal sector tourism companies. Tourists will then travel between resort clusters and return to the primary urban areas for departure (Britton 1982:341)

Thus, according to dependency theory, tourism is an industry like any other, which is used by the developed countries to perpetuate the dependency of the developing countries. Instead of reducing the existing socioeconomic regional disparities within the developing countries, tourism reinforces them through its enclavic structure and its orientation along traditional structures.

Although the arguments of the dependency theory appear to be very convincing, some criticism is appropriate. First, as Din (1990) notes, not all accommodation chains are in the hands of the developed countries, but some of the most important ones in Southeast Asia belong to local companies. Second, the dependency theory analyzes almost exclusively mass tourism and, therefore, only one segment of international tourism in developing countries. Britton (1982) recognizes the existence of a "subsistence sector" besides the formal sector. He argues that the former is largely dependent on the formal sector and that its economic importance is almost negligible. The focus on mass tourism is symptomatic for many tourism studies:

> Attention focuses primarily on the ordinary mass-tourist, whose stereotyped image and behavior-patterns tend to dominate the thinking of contemporary entrepreneurs, planners and critics of tourism (Cohen 1973:89).

Only few studies address the low budget tourists or "drifters" (Cohen 1973; Smith 1990). Some recent studies show that low budget tourists may spend as much money as high budget tourists, due to their longer length of stay and that they are generally better dispersed throughout the destination country (Dankers 1990; Meijers 1989). The diverging spatial patterns of different groups of tourists in developing countries were also disclosed in some studies (Oppermann 1992a; Pearce and Johnston 1986).

The third criticism directed at dependency theory is that by focusing on international tourism alone, domestic tourism (a considerable factor in some developing countries) is neglected. For example, in 1989, domestic tourism contributed 55.9% of all hotel arrivals and 47.8% of all guest-nights in Malaysia (TDC 1990). This does not even include all the nights spent at the residence of friends and relatives that are probably at least as many. In Mexico, domestic tourism is a very important factor in most resorts (Spehs 1990). The tendency of domestic tourism to be better distributed throughout the country is well documented (Pearce 1989b). Fourth, perhaps the most significant limitation of dependency theory is its failure to formulate alternative prescriptions for tourism development into developing countries.

Formal/Informal Sector Concept

The above discussion shows the advantages and deficiencies of development models in tourism studies that refer to the spatio-temporal development of tourism. One aspect is common to all theories, namely the neglect of drifter tourism. Although its existence has been accepted by the disciplines of the diffusionist paradigm, even as a major element in the early phases of tourism development, drifters are generally ignored in tourism research.

The indifference towards drifter tourism leads to the paradox that, although tourists are distinguished into two groups since two decades, namely "institutionalized" and "non-institutionalized" (Cohen 1972), often only one tourist group is analyzed and equated with the whole tourism industry. Nevertheless, the differentiation of tourism into a "formal or upper circuit" and an "informal or lower circuit" sector has profound spatial and economic implications. During the last decade, the notion of "alternative," "integrated," "soft," or "appropriate" tourism has gained widespread attendance (Butler 1990; Singh, Theuns and Go 1989). Alternative tourism, used as a generic term, is generally understood as an alternative to traditional mass tourism (Butler 1990; Cazes 1989; Weaver 1991). This does not imply, however, that alternative tourism is identical with the informal tourism sector or vice versa. The greatest problem in determining the difference between both concepts is that alternative tourism already includes such a wide range of different notions and concepts that it is almost impossible to explicitly define alternative tourism by itself (Butler 1990; Cazes 1989; Cohen 1989).

While some identifying variables may be the same for alternative tourism and the informal tourism sector, others are not. For example, alternative tourism is frequently understood as an elite tourism with a high spending budget (Cazes 1989). This is not part of the informal tourism sector concept. Another difference between both concepts is the spatial component. It appears from many studies on alternative tourism that a tourist resort features either mass tourism or alternative tourism, both being mutually exclusive. While both formal and informal tourism sectors exist, most do not occur in the same tourist resort (Kermath and Thomas 1992; Michaud 1991; Oppermann 1992b).

One problem facing the alternative mass tourism dichotomy and the formal/informal tourism sector dichotomy is the dilemma of positively distinguishing both parts of the spectrum (Butler 1990; Cazes 1989; Cohen 1989; Oppermann 1992b; Wahnschafft 1982). However, within each continuum of extremes, a great number of intermediate forms can be identified (Wahnschafft 1982). Some authors skirt this problem by referring to tendencies or by describing the different types of enterprises rather than quantifying the differences (Michaud 1991; Weaver 1991). This may be the biggest predicament in any further application of the formal/informal sector (and the alternative tourism) concept in tourism.

The formal/informal sector concept has been applied in a few tourism studies (Kermath and Thomas 1992; Michaud 1991; Wahnschafft 1982). Despite the dissimilarity of the various study sites (Pattaya in Thailand; Ladahk in India; Sosúa in Dominican Republic), several analogous notions can be identified. First, all authors state that formal and informal sectors compete with each other. This may be a thesis hard to prove. Is a first class restaurant really vying for the same customers as an informal hawker? How many tourists spending their nights in a luxury hotel would not eat in the same hotel or at least in a restaurant of equal standard? Are not many tourists favoring the habitual type of restaurant over the unfamiliar street vendor simply owing to the tourists' anxiety of the presumed unhygenic condition of food preparation of the latter? For the hawkers themselves, tourist demand provides only for a supplementary income besides their usual local customers. In Southeast-Asian metropolises, which are the major recipients of international tourist flows in these countries, tourist demand may not even contribute 5% of the total turnover of the hawkers.

Second, all authors recognize a government bias towards the formal sector that will eventually lead to an extinction of the informal resort sector. Although a general government bias towards the tax-paying and more "productive" formal sector enterprises is unquestionable, the extinction of the informal sector remains doubtful. This may be the situation in isolated cases where the government tries to radically change the function and type of a whole resort. This may work in small ones. In larger cities (such as the capital) the abolishment of the informal sector is debatable. In Singapore, which strives for a very modern Western outlook, trishaws populate the streets and hawkers are selling home-prepared food in semi-permanent stalls. Kermath and Thomas (1992) suggest that in some type of resorts (in deviation from their proposed model) the informal sector may be purposely retained or supported, because the bustling life of a market place may be the major tourist attraction.

Two aspects, not addressed in the aforementioned studies, are the spatial distribution of both tourism sectors in the whole country and a differentiation of the tourists. Is the dual structure of the tourism industry also applicable to the tourists? The following discussion and model are greatly based on the formal/informal sector concept. In contrast to previous studies, emphasis is placed on the spatial implications of both sectors with respect to the national level.

Formal — Informal Sector Dichotomy

The formal or upper circuit tourism sector in developing countries is characterized by international standard hotels, "Western cuisine" (in countries with a large number of Japanese tourists also "Japanese cuisine"), and air-conditioned buses. The informal or lower circuit is typified by low-budget accommodation in the form of hostels, guesthouses, chalets, inns, etc., as well as "domestic cuisine." Wahnschafft (1982), in his study of formal and informal tourism in Pattaya (Thailand), distinguishes both sectors based on the size of the business. He considers tourism accommodation, restaurants, recreation center, and souvenir-shops as belonging to the formal sector; and hawkers, street vendors, prostitutes, and craftsmen as being part of the informal sector. Michaud (1991) differentiates both sectors by size and organisation of the tourism business. Large hotels and restaurants are part of the formal sector, while small hotels, guesthouses, and hawkers belong to the informal sector. Kermath and Thomas (1992) use the acceptance of credit cards and the provision of regular wages to distinguish both sectors. It appears as if they define all street and beach vendors as belonging to the informal sector and all other establishments as being part of the formal sector. It is not quite clear, however, if guesthouses or chalets exist in Sosua, and if they do, to which sector they belong.

The high initial capital costs needed to start a business in the upper circuit lead to a high foreign participation and dependency, for example, through international hotel chains. Within developing countries, participation is restricted to the upper class, who have the required funds and insights into the needs and wants of international mass tourists (Britton 1982). The upper circuit operation entails high leakages in the form of profit transfers, repatriation of funds from foreigners in managerial positions, large imports of food, and other general items. This does not even include all the imports of furniture and decors when international standard hotels are built.

The lower circuit is exemplified by its low capital requirements. With little resources, chalets and other simple accommodation forms can be built. For a restaurant, it is sufficient to have a few tables and chairs, a roof, and the cheaper food items from domestic suppliers. A foreign-educated cook is not needed. Since the owners of such simple businesses are generally much better integrated into the local economic structure, they would buy their equipment and supplies from local sources and not from the national capital or overseas. Widmer-Münch (1990) observes large differences in the buying behavior of registered and non-registered accommodation facilities in two cities in Morocco. The registered and generally larger hotels bought considerably higher percentages of their required supplies from either somewhere else in the country or overseas sources. The non-registered establishments, on the other hand, bought almost exclusively from local sources. Although it may be far-reaching to equate the non-registered facilities with the lower circuit, non-registration is certainly one characteristic of the informal sector. Different buying behavior of dissimilar types of accommodation was disclosed by Berriane (1978) as well. In five Pacific islands, Milne (1992) notes the lower import propensity of guesthouses as compared to hotels, and subsequently higher income and employment generation of each tourist dollar spent in the former type of accommodation.

Given the higher integration of the informal tourism sector enterprises into the local economic structure, it is capable of producing a higher multiplier effect on the local economy than the formal tourism sector. The informal tourism sector is symbolized by its "open structure" instead of the "enclavic structure" of the formal tourism sector. Both sectors are contrasted with each other with the help of some variables (Table 1). As noted earlier, Table 1 represents the extreme poles of both sectors. It is even plausible that certain informal enterprises do not fulfill all requirements or at least to a different degree.

Table 1. Characteristics of the Two Tourism Sectors

Characteristics	Formal Sector	Informal Sector
Capital	Abundant	Limited
Technology	Capital-intensive	Labor-intensive
Organization	Bureaucratic	Primitive
Ownership	Companies	Individual, Family
Prices	Generally Fixed	Negotiable
Inventories	Large Quantities and/or High Quality	Small Quantities Poor Quality
Fixed costs	Substantial	Negligible
Advertisement	Necessary	Almost None
Credit	Institutional	Non-institutional
Turnover	Large	Small
Profit Margin	Small per Unit and Investment Costs	Large per Unit and Investment Costs
Education	Skilled	Unskilled
Regular Wages	Prevalent	Less Prevalent
Government Aid	Extensive	None or Almost None
Dependence on Foreign Countries	Great, Externally Oriented	Small or None

Source: Oppermann (1992b).

On the other hand, there may be formal enterprises for which certain informal characteristics are appropriate.

The actual balance of the economic impact of both sectors in the tourism industry in developing countries is dependent on several factors: the relative number of tourists in each sector; the leakage rate in both sectors; and the length of stay and per capita expenditure of clientele from both groups. These factors must also be considered and understood.

Spatial Implications

The dual structure of the tourism industry manifests itself in space with the corresponding economic and sociocultural impacts. This aspect has been rarely addressed in previous studies on formal/informal tourism owing to their focus on specific resort sites (Kermath and Thomas 1992; Wahnschafft 1982). Studies on all types of "alternative tourism" have largely remained on the resort case study level as well. However, when the contribution of both sectors is considered on a national level and from a regional development point of view, then the spatial distribution of these sectors is most important. The spatial occurrence and impacts of the upper circuit is limited to a restricted number of resort enclaves often in the vicinity of the capital city and/or international airports. The distribution of the lower circuit is much wider, the leakages are lower and, therefore, the impact on the regional economic structure considerably higher. On a national level, the formal and the informal "tourist spaces" partly overlap each other. Both sectors can be found in the main tourist attractions and the major gateways; however, not all formal tourism sector resorts are frequented by drifters and only a few informal tourism sector resorts are visited by mass tourists. The overlapping of these tourist spaces results in three groups, resorts that feature both sectors; formal tourism sector resorts; and informal tourism sector resorts. This would not be complete, however, without the "Non-touristic space" (Figure 1).

The zone of touristic influence in developing countries is generally confined to a number of locations and the connecting corridors, while the other areas are hardly visited by international tourists. This has been pointed out by Robinson (1957). In a map of Corsica, he differen-

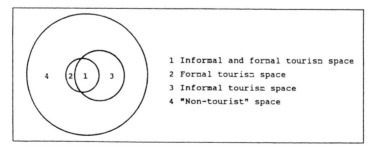

1 Informal and formal tourism space
2 Formal tourism space
3 Informal tourism space
4 "Non-tourist" space

Figure 1. Schematic Model of the "Tourist Space"

tiates between "tourist" and "non-tourist area." Dress (1979) presents in a map of Bali the "spheres of tourists' influence" and implies that all other areas outside are "spheres without tourists' influence."

Figure 1 is naturally only a very simple schematic presentation of the distribution of tourism in developing countries. The actual spatial organization depends among other things on the existing spatial economic and social structures and the location of tourism resources in the individual country. Because the following model of the "tourist space in developing countries," attempts to integrate those structures, they have to be generalized for a hypothetical case. Three distinctive location types of destinations are conceivable: islands, landlocked countries, or countries with access to the sea. Since landlocked countries are a minority among Third World countries, this type will not be considered. The landlocked location appears to be somewhat detrimental with respect to tourism development. Hardly any of these countries has a well-developed tourist industry.

Several tourism studies deal with the specific problems of island destinations (Pearce 1989; Wilkinson 1989). Islands were frequently the case countries for studies on tourism dependency (Britton 1980; Hills and Lundgren 1977). Miossec (1976) uses a hypothetical island destination for his model of tourist development. Thurot (1973) discusses the evolution of tourism in a Caribbean context. No development model makes specific reference to a coastal or landlocked tourist destination. The subsequent model uses a hypothetical non-island destination for the following reasons. First, there are more independent non-island than island countries in the Third World and their sheer areal extent and population size makes them more important. Second, non-island countries are the majority among those developing countries with the highest number of international tourist arrivals (Euromonitor 1988). Third, there may not be such a great difference between both types of destination after all, with respect to the geographical distribution of tourist activity within them. The center-periphery dichotomy of tourism's regional distribution in non-islands countries has to be understood as capital city/coastal areas versus rural/inland areas. In island states, the corresponding dichotomy is main island (with airport) versus outer islands. In the larger island countries, this is supplemented by the capital/coastal areas versus rural/inland areas dichotomy. In the archipelago Indonesia, for example, most tourist activity is concentrated on the two main islands Java and Bali. They feature 61% and 16%, respectively, of the country's hotel accommodation supply. Jakarta alone, however, offers 51% of Java's supply; in Bali, the Badung district with the island's capital Denpasar offers 78% of its tourist beds (DTPT 1987; Zimmermann 1990). Other examples are Dominica with 50% of all accommodation units in the capital Roseau (Weaver 1991), Western Samoa with 86% of all tourist nights in the capital Apia and 92% on the main island (TCSP 1991), Vanuatu with 86% of all tourist nights in Port Vila and 88% on the main island (TCSP 1989), and in the Philippines 70% of all hotel rooms are located in Manila alone (MTP 1987). Access is the critical factor in any tourism development (Pearce 1987; Milne 1991). In developing countries, air access is paramount with respect to international tourism from the main generating countries, which are usually long-haul markets.

> Where, however, overland travel is difficult, the major markets are long-haul ones and the levels of economic development are relatively low, tourism in continental regions, for example in many parts of Africa, may share many of the features characteristic of tourism on islands (Pearce 1987:160).

In few developing countries, land border crossings are more important than airports. Pearce's (1987) analysis of first and second order international tourist flows positively demonstrates that for the majority of developing countries the most important markets are North-America, Europe, Japan, or Australia/New Zealand. Only some developing countries feature a large domestic market that uses accommodation other than the houses of friends/relatives, and only few countries can attract a larger share of short- and medium-haul international travelers from its neighbouring Third World countries. Hence, a Tourist Space model is exemplified on a hypothetical non-island country.

The Tourist Space

Phase 0 (Figure 2) presents some structures in a hypothetical developing country (which can very well be an island country) before the arrival of international pleasure-mass tourism. Some tourism infrastructure in form of tourist accommodation is already in place, but these are chiefly centered in the capital city and other economic centers of the country. They provide accommodation for local business persons or visitors of the government bureaucracy. Some smaller tourism resorts may exist, but they are largely established during colonial times. Examples are the many hill-resorts in almost all Asian countries (Spencer and Thomas 1949; Withington 1961). The local population has also favored recreation areas, but these are primarily close to the place of living and offer rarely tourism infrastructure in the form of hotels. One common characteristic is that they are hardly on the coast.

The existing tourist infrastructure is being used by the first pleasure tourists during Phase 1 (Figure 2). Those "adventurers" adjust to the available supply, bring their own accommodation in form of tents or ask the local population for a place of stay. They have only a very small economic impact on the visited region, but whatever they spend remains in the village or town—little leakage occurs since they use locally owned accommodations and eat the locally produced food. Over time, the increasing demand raises interest, both on the side of the government and on the side of the international tourism industry.

Before the arrival of international mass tourism, which reached most developing countries only after World War II, the basic structure of the subsequent tourism development was already in place. Since most developing countries are located far away from the main origins of international tourism, namely Europe, North-America, and Japan, the tourists rely on planes as their main mode of transportation. Technical innovations in the transportation sector (for example, the intro-

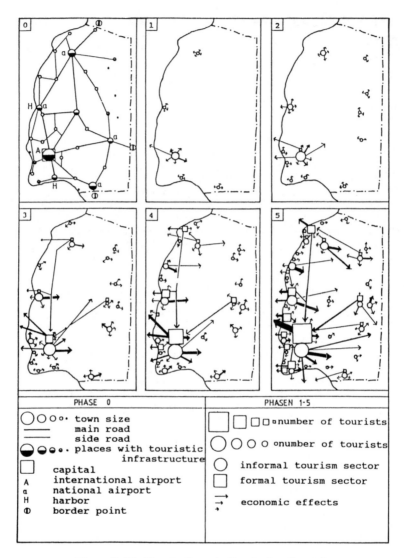

Figure 2. The Tourist Space in Developing Countries

duction of aircraft with intercontinental range) provided for the phe-
nomenal rise in international, intercontinental tourism during the last
few decades. The largest and often only international airport is frequently located close to the capital city or was built there after independence. The "gateway function" along with the largest accommodation
supply resulted in a way in a "doppler effect," meaning the capital
cities of developing countries had from the start all structural and

locational advantages to profit exceedingly from the evolving tourism industry. During the first phase, international tourism is largely concentrated in the capital. Other regions have only minor share in tourism. The regional distributive effects are relatively small.

During Phase 2 (Figure 2), three processes occur: additional supply is provided in the capital; the drifters explore increasingly more of the country, resulting in a greater diffusion of tourism impacts; and the formal tourism sector "discovers" the country and establishes itself in the capital. While new places are "discovered" by the drifters and explorers, these are still destinations with already existing tourism infrastructure. No completely new places are developed. Additional accommodation may be provided in the newly discovered destinations for the increasing number of tourists. The establishment of the formal sector in the capital has more far-reaching consequences. The "higher" requirements of formal tourism necessitate the provision of accommodation with Western comfort and large capacity, as well as furnishing Western food and drinks. Lack of experience with large hotels, Western cuisine, and this type of tourists results in an "import" of experts mainly on managerial level. Very often the hotel will be owned by international companies, or at least the management will be in international hands. Hence, the establishment of the formal tourism sector ensues an increasing leakage of profits towards overseas owing to necessary imports, profit transfers, and payment of foreign labor (Michaud 1991; Pawson, Stanford, Adams and Nurbu 1984). The import propensity or leakage factor depends mostly on the country's economic structure (for example, the level of technology, production of agricultural products, and education level of the local population).

The informal tourism sector experiences a further expansion in Phase 3 (Figure 2). More and more destinations are visited. A few places with no previous tourism infrastructure are integrated into the tourist space of the informal sector. Some of the resorts discovered during the second phase become known. The information circulation on these places (very often through word-of-mouth, but eventually through incorporation into travel guides) arouses the interest of the formal sector, especially the hotel chains and tour operators. Thus, the dual structure of the tourism industry in the capital is transferred to other destinations as well. The newly built tourism infrastructure is not solely financed by foreign capital, but partly by the financial and commercial establishment of the country. These are generally businessmen and/or politicians of the capital city (the national elite) who recognize the potential profits of the tourism industry and invest accordingly (Britton 1982; Wahnschafft 1982). The first investments outside the capital are to test the market, taking risks is not very characteristic in the tourism industry. The destinations into which the formal sector is moving are mostly along the coast and places in the hinterland close to cultural, historical, or physical attractions, if those exist. The capital has gained international exposure and profile and develops slowly into an established destination in the international package-tourism network.

During this phase, the local elite and upper class attempt to emulate the travel behavior of the Western tourists as they usually endeavor to imitate Western trends (Cazes 1989). Since this is a financially well-off population, formal tourism resorts are increasingly visited by them.

While the expenditure of the informal tourism sector still remains mostly within the locality, the expenditures of the formal sector have limited effects in the new destinations outside the capital. A transfer of money towards overseas and the capital occurs in the form of taxes and repatriation of profits and wages (Jurzcek 1985).

The main difference between Phase 3 and Phase 4 lies in the different development of the formal tourism sector space. In Phase 4, the formal sector expands further into destinations that have been already discovered by the informal sector and, contrary to Phase 3, completely new resorts are being drafted on the drawing board (for example, Cancun in Mexico). These are very often spatially separated from any previous tourism infrastructure and often away from any city or village. This type of resort is perhaps the most characteristic expression of tourist enclaves (Britton 1980; Matznetter 1979). They are built along the coast and only in exceptional cases in the interior, for example, close to safari parks in East Africa. Many of these enclaves belong to club-type enterprises. Except for a few locals who find work there, these enclaves have hardly any economic impact on the surrounding region (Berriane 1978; Pawson, Stanford, Adams and Nurbu 1984; Spehs 1990).

A different form of tourist enclaves are ribbon developments outside established tourism destinations along the coast. The original city does not offer enough space for further development and new hotels are built outside the center. The original destination is solely used as a day-trip destination for shopping and its main function is its drawing power as a well-renowned destination. An example for this may be Puerto Vallarta, Mexico (Evans 1979).

A fascinating phenomenon is the different development of travel corridors between tourism destinations. While informal destinations are highly interconnected with respect to tourists traveling among them, formal tourism sector resorts are characterized by their high isolation. They are very often the sole destination from where the tourists only depart for day-trips, which are frequently restricted to the immediate vicinity and rarely to attraction sites further away (Debbage 1988; Oppermann 1992b). Through their acceptance of domestic transportation facilities, the lower-circuit tourists have a much more active intranational travel behavior.

The local population of the developing countries take more and more to Western holiday expectations. Traditional destinations in the hinterland (i.e., hill-resorts) lose part of their attractiveness, while coastal destinations experience above average growth rates. This occurred, for example, in Malaysia over the last decade (TDC 1980, 1990). Big hotel chains and clubs increasingly attempt to address the local market, particularly with special offers during the low season to attain higher occupancy rates. The increasing number of competitors inside the developing country, but also among developing countries forces the big hotels to augment their promotion efforts to capture new customers and markets.

During Phase 5 (Figure 2) still new locations are integrated into the tourist space. Nevertheless, the spatial distribution remains relatively stable. The capital city and the most important other destinations have a dual tourism structure. The informal and formal tourism sectors are to be found there. These places are the first space in the schematic presentation (Figure 1). A few places are solely visited by the formal sector, others only by the informal sector. A large part of the country, the "non-tourist space," remains unvisited by international tourists.

Essentially, several statements can be used to describe the development of the "tourist space" in developing countries. One, the capital city has a dominant role in the industry, especially during the early development phases of international mass tourism, owing to its "pre-touristic" structures. Two, the dominant function of the capital city is magnified when the only or main international airport is located close to it ("gateway effect"). Three, the capital retains the dominant function over a long time. Only in the later years, it loses its relative position, due to the increasing number of resorts in the country. Four, the informal tourism sector has a "discovery function." Five, the formal sector penetrates the established informal resorts. In the later stages, formal tourism sector resorts are also drafted on the drawing board in completely new destinations. Six, not every resort develops through the same stages from discovery through the informal sector, over penetration of the formal sector to a world renown international tourism resort. Seven, the informal sector is characterized through its high integration into the local economic structure that results in a low leakage and, therefore, a high multiplier effect on the local economy. Eight, a high proportion of the formal sector expenditures are lost from the local economy due to high leakages towards the national capital and overseas. Nine, the formal sector is typified in its spatial occurrence as very concentrated, close to international or at least domestic airports, the low absolute number of resorts, and the low connectivity of these resorts with respect to tourist flows among them. Ten, the informal tourism sector is spatially better distributed. Owing to the better acceptance of domestic transportation types, the members of this sector have a higher mobility and informal tourism sector resorts are, therefore, much better connected. Eleven, domestic tourists participate in the formal or informal tourism sector depending on their financial ability. In developing countries, with a larger middle and upper class, the volume of domestic tourism is likely to be larger.

Naturally, as with any generalization, there are exceptions. For example, in Fiji, the main international airport is not located close to the capital, but on the other side of the main island (at Nandi). In the development process, which saw Fiji evolving as one of the main stop-over destinations on route from North America to Australia/New Zealand or vice versa, a lot of accommodation was built around Nandi and along the Coral Coast between Nandi and Suva. The latter remained, however, the calling port for cruise ships. Therefore, the location of the main international airport modified the proposed development process. Otherwise, the propositions 3 to 11 are still relevant. Similar deviations may occur also on other small island or archipelagos and in pilgrimage centers.

CONCLUSIONS

This paper discussed three main development theories and their implications in respect to the spatial distribution of tourism in developing countries. The main deficiency of these theories is their too general view of international tourism in these countries. All focus on the formal tourism sector and neglect the informal sector. In line with Santos' (1979) criticism of the one-sided analysis of the urban economy, one observes that the formal sector of tourism has for too long been analyzed and equated with the whole industry. Reasons for the indifference towards the informal sector are partly to be found in the spatial distribution of both sectors. The formal sector is symbolized by luxury hotels and the spatial pattern of the tourists within the destination countries by organized bus tours. The most extreme case of the formal tourism sector are the "all-inclusive" package tours. Even overnight stays in hotels are registered better than stays in guesthouses or private rooms.

While the neglect of the informal sector by the dependency theory may be understandable (due to its emphasis on the upper circuit), the lack of coverage on this category of activities in the development stage and diffusion theories cannot be readily discerned and is probably due to the prominence of the formal sector. The availability of statistical material on the formal sector is another contributing factor.

A more valid perspective in the conceptualization of the "tourist space" calls for (a) the recognition of the influence of the existing spatial economic and social structures at all stages of tourism development, (b) the differentiation of the tourism industry into a formal and an informal tourism sector, and (c) the cognizance of the spatial segregation and the differing spatial economic impact of both sectors. Although it may prove somewhat difficult to distinguish unambiguously between formal and informal tourism sectors, attempts are needed to gain a better understanding of the spatial impacts of tourism development. □ □

REFERENCES

Alonso, W.
  1968 Urban and Regional Imbalances in Economic Development. Economic Development and Cultural Change 17:1–14.
Arnold, A.
  1972 Der Fremdenverkehr in Tunesien. Entwicklung, Struktur, Funktion und Fremdenverkehrsräume. Würzburger Geographische Arbeiten 37:453–489.
  1983 Fremdenverkehr in Tunesien: Ein Beitrag zur Entwicklungsländer problematik. Geographische Rundschau 35:638–643.
Bernklau, T.
  1991 Tourismus auf den Philippinen. Eine kulturgeographische Untersuchung unter besonderer Berücksichtigung des Binnentourismus. Frankfurt: Peter Lang.
Berriane, M.
  1978 Un type de l'espace touristique marocaine: le littoral méditerranéen. Revue de Géographie du Maroc 29(2):5–28.
  1990 Fremdenverkehr im Maghreb: Tunesien und Marokko im Vergleich. Geographische Rundschau 42(2):94–99.
Britton, S.
  1980 The Spatial Organization of Tourism in a Neo-colonial Economy: A Fiji Case Study. Pacific Viewpoint 21:144–165.

1982 The Political Economy of Tourism in the Third World. Annals of Tourism Research 9:331–358.

Browett, J. G.
1979 Development, the Diffusionist Paradigm and Geography. Progress in Human Geography 4:57–79.
1982 Out of the Dependency Perspectives. Journal of Contemporary Asia 12:145–157.

Bryden, J. M.
1973 Tourism and Development: A Case Study of the Commonwealth Caribbean. Cambridge: Cambridge University Press.

Bryden, J. M., and M. L. Faber
1971 Multiplying the Tourist Multiplier. Social and Economic Studies 20:61–82.

Butler, R. W.
1980 The Concept of a Tourism Area Cycle of Evolution. Implications for the Management of Resources. Canadian Geographer 24:5–12.
1990 Alternative Tourism: Pious Hope or Trojan Horse? Journal of Travel Research 28:40–45.

Cazes, G. H.
1989 Alternative Tourism: Reflections on an Ambiguous Concept. *In* Towards Appropriate Tourism: The Case of Developing Countries, T. V. Singh, et al, eds., pp. 117–126. Frankfurt: Peter Lang.

Christaller, W.
1964 Some Considerations of Tourism Location in Europe: The Peripheral Regions — Underdeveloped Countries — Recreation Areas. Regional Science Association Papers 12:95–103.

Clement, H. G.
1961 The Future of Tourism in the Pacific and Far East. Washington DC: Checci and Coy.

Cohen, E.
1972 Towards a Sociology of International Tourism. Social Research 39:164–182.
1973 Nomads from Affluence: Notes on the Phenomenon of Drifter-Tourism. International Journal of Comparative Sociology 14:89–103.
1989 "Alternative Tourism"—A Critique. *In* Towards Appropriate Tourism: The Case of Developing Countries, T. V. Singh, H. Theuns and F. Go, eds., pp. 117–126. Frankfurt: Peter Lang.

Dankers, W.
1990 Organized and Non-Organized Tourism in Malaysia: An Analysis of the Economic Effects. M.S. thesis, Department of Economics, Tilburg, The Netherlands.

Debbage, K. G.
1988 Activity Spaces in New Environments. Tourist Movements in a Resort Setting in the Bahamas. Ph.D. dissertation, University of Georgia, USA.

Diamond, J.
1977 Tourism's Role in Economic Development: The Case Reexamined. Economic Development and Cultural Change 25:543–553.

Din, K. H.
1990 Bumiputera Entrepreneurship in the Penang-Langkawi Tourist Industry. Ph.D. dissertation, University of Hawaii, USA.

Domrös, M.
1989 Attraktivitätspotential und Organisationsphänomene des Fremdenverkehrs auf den Malediven. Die Erde 120:35–50.

Dress, G.
1979 Der Tourismus als Entwicklungsfaktor in tropischen Überseeländern, dargestellt am Fall der Insel Bali in Indonesien. Frankfurter Wirtschafts- und Sozialgeographische Schriften 30:189–202.

DTPT (Department of Tourism, Post & Telecommunication)
1987 Tourism in Indonesia 1986. Jakarta: DTPT.

Euromonitor
1988 International Marketing Data and Statistics 88/89 (13th ed.). London: Euromonitor.

Evans, N. H.
1979 The Dynamics of Tourism Development in Puerto Vallarta. *In* Tourism —

554   TOURISM IN DEVELOPING COUNTRIES

Passport to Development? E. de Kadt, ed., pp. 305–320. New York: Oxford University Press.
Friedmann, J.
1966 Regional Development Policy: A Case Study of Venezuela. Cambridge: MIT Press.
Gormsen, E.
1981 The Spatio-Temporal Development of International Tourism. Aix-en-Provence: Centre des Hautes Etudes Touristiques.
Hills, T. L., and J. Lundgren
1977 The Impact of Tourism in the Caribbean. Annals of Tourism Research 4: 248–267.
Hirschmann, A. O.
1958 The Strategy of Economic Development. New Haven: Yale University Press.
Hoivik, T., and T. Heiberg
1980 Centre-Periphery Tourism and Self-Reliance. International Social Science Journal 32:69–98.
Husbands, W.
1981 Centres, Peripheries, Tourism and Socio-spatial Development. Ontario Geography 17:37–59.
Jenkins, C. L.
1982 The Effects of Scale in Tourism Projects in Developing Countries. Annals of Tourism Research 9:229–249.
Jurczek, P.
1985 Groß- und kleinräumige Auswirkungen des Ferntourismus auf Peru. Die Erde 115:27–48.
Kermath, B. M., and R. N. Thomas
1992 Spatial Dynamics of Resorts: Sosúa, Dominican Republic. Annals of Tourism Research 29:173–190.
Lundgren, J. O. J.
1972 The Development of the Tourist Travel Systems—A Metropolitan Economic Hegemony par Excellence? Jahrbuch für Fremdenverkehr 20:85–120.
Matthews, H. G., and L. Richter
1991 Political Science and Tourism. Annals of Tourism Research 18:120–135.
Matznetter, J.
1979 Touristische Möglichkeiten der Oberguinealänder am Beispiel der Elfenbeinküste. Frankfurter Wirtschafts- und Sozialgeographische Schriften 30:1–50.
Meijer, W. G.
1989 Rucksacks and Dollars: The Economic Impact of Organized and Non-Organized Tourism in Bolivia. In Towards Appropriate Tourism: The Case of Developing Countries, T. V. Singh, H. Theuns, and F. Go, eds., pp. 227–249. Frankfurt: Peter Lang.
Mergard, C.
1986 Tourismus der Tropen—Eine quantitative Studie zur Entwicklung von 1970 bis 1980. Dissertation, University of Bonn, Germany.
Michaud, J.
1991 A Social Anthropology of Tourism in Ladakh, India. Annals of Tourism Research 18:605–621.
Milne, S.
1992 Tourism and Development in South Pacific Microstates. Annals of Tourism Research 19:191–212.
Miossec, J. M.
1976 Elements pour une theorie de l'espace touristique. Aix-en-Provence: Centre des Hautes Etudes Touristiques.
Mitchell, L., and R. V. Smith
1989 The Geography of Recreation, Tourism, and Sport. In Geography in America, G. L. Gaile and C. J. Willmott, eds., pp. 387–408. Columbus OH: Merrill Publishing.
Möller, H. G.
1986 Tourismus und Regionalentwicklung im Mediterranen Südfrankreich (ohne Korsika). Habilitationsschrift, Universität Hannover, Germany.
MTP (Ministry of Tourism Philippines)
1987 Annual Report 1986. Manila: MTP.

Müller, B.
1984 Fremdenverkehr, Dezentralisierung und regionale Partizipation in Mexiko. Geographische Rundschau 36:20-24.
Myrdal, G.
1959 Ökonomische Theorie und unterentwickelte Regionen. Stuttgart: Gustav Fischer Verlag.
Oestreich, H.
1977 Gambia—Zur sozioökonomischen Problematik des Ferntourismus in einem westafrikanischen Entwicklungsland. Geographische Zeitschrift 65:302-308.
Oppermann, M.
1992a Intranational Tourist Flows in Malaysia. Annals of Tourism Research 19: 482-500.
1992b Tourismus in Malaysia: Eine Analyse der räumlichen Strukturen und intranationalen Touristenströme unter besonderer Berücksichtigung der entwicklungstheoretischen Problematik. Dissertation, Universität Tübingen, Germany.
Pavaskar, M.
1982 Employment Effects of Tourism and the Indian Experience. Journal of Travel Research 21:32-38.
Pawson, I. G., D. D. Stanford, V. A. Adams, and M. Nurbu
1984 Growth of Tourism in Nepal's Everest Region: Impact on the Physical Environment and Structure of Human Settlements. Mountain Research and Development 4:237-246.
Pearce, D. G.
1987 Tourism Today: A Geographical Analysis. Harlow: Longman.
1989a International and Domestic Tourism: Interfaces and Issues. GeoJournal 19: 257-262.
1989b Tourist Development (2nd ed.). Harlow: Longman.
Pearce, D. G., and D. C. Johnston
1986 Travel within Tonga. Journal of Travel Research 24:13-17.
Perroux, F.
1955 Note sur la notion de pole de croissance, translated by I. Livingstone. _In_ Development Economics and Policy. Selected Readings, I. Livingstone, ed. 1979, London: Allen & Unwin.
Plog, S. C.
1973 Why Destination Areas Rise and Fall in Popularity. Cornell Hotel, Restaurant & Administration Quarterly 14:13-16.
Radetzki-Stenner, M.
1989 Internationaler Tourismus und Entwicklungsländer. Die Auswirkungen des Einfach-Tourismus auf eine ländliche Region der indonesischen Insel Bali. Münster: LIT.
Robinson, G. W. S.
1957 Tourists in Corsica. Economic Geography 33:337-348.
Rodenburg, E. E.
1980 The Effects of Scale in Economic Development: Tourism in Bali. Annals of Tourism Research 7:177-196.
Rostow, W. W.
1960 The Stages of Economic Growth. Cambridge: Cambridge University Press.
Santos, M.
1979 The Shared Space. London: Methuen.
Schlenke, U., and R. Stewig
1983 Endogener Tourismus als Gradmesser des Industrialisierungsprozesses in Industrie- und Entwicklungsländern. Erdkunde 37:137-146.
Schürmann, H.
1981 The Effects of International Tourism on the Regional Development of Third World Countries. Applied Geography and Development 18:80-93.
Singh, T. V., H. L. Theuns, and F. M. Go, eds.
1989 Towards Appropriate Tourism: The Case of Developing Countries. Frankfurt: Peter Lang.
Smith, S. L. J.
1982 Reflections on the Development of Geographic Research in Recreation: Hey Buddy, Can You S'Paradigm. Ontario Geography 19:5-28.

556   TOURISM IN DEVELOPING COUNTRIES

Smith, V. L.
    1990 Geographical Implications of "Drifter" Tourism — Boracay, Philippines. Tourism Recreation Research 15:34–42.
Spehs, P.
    1990 Neue staatlich geplante Badeorte in Mexiko. Geographische Rundschau 42: 34–41.
Spencer, J. E., and W. L. Thomas
    1948 The Hill Stations and Summer Resorts of the Orient. Geographical Review 38:637–651.
TCSP (Tourist Council of the South Pacific)
    1989 Vanuatu Visitor Survey 1988. Suva: TCSP.
    1991 Western Samoa Visitor Survey 1990/91. Suva: TCSP.
TDC (Tourist Development Corporation)
    1980 Occupancy Rates by Locality (1979). Kuala Lumpur: TDC.
    1990 Occupancy Rate of Hotels in Malaysia January–December 1989. Kuala Lumpur: TDC.
Thomas, W. L.
    1978 Progressive rather than Centralized Tourism: A Recommendation for Improving International Tourism in the Philippines. Philippines Geographical Journal 22(2):55–82.
Thurot, J. M.
    1973 Le Tourisme Tropical Balneaire: Le model caraibe et ses extensions. Thesis, Centre des Etudes du Tourisme, Aix-en-Provence, France.
Ungefehr, F.
    1988 Tourismus und Offshore-Banking auf den Bahamas. Internationale Dienstleistungen als dominanter Wirtschaftsfaktor in einem kleinen Entwicklungsland. Frankfurt: Peter Lang.
Vorlaufer, K.
    1980 Die räumliche Ordnung der Fremdenverkehrswirtschaft in Sri Lanka. Eine standort-theoretische und empirische Studie zur Entfaltung des Tourismus in der Dritten Welt. Zeitschrift für Wirtschaftsgeographie 24:165–175.
    1984 Ferntourismus und Dritte Welt. Frankfurt: Diesterweg.
    1988 Tourismus und Entwicklung in der Dritten Welt. Materialien zur Fremdenverkehrsgeographie 17:603–636.
Wahnschafft, R.
    1982 Formal and Informal Tourism Sectors. A Case Study in Pattaya, Thailand. Annals of Tourism Research 9:429–451.
Weaver, D. B.
    1991 Alternative to Mass Tourism in Dominica. Annals of Tourism Research 18: 414–432.
Widmer-Münch, R.
    1990 Der Tourismus in Fes und Marrakesch. Strukturen und Prozesse in bipolaren Urbanräumen des islamischen Orients. Basler Beiträge zur Geographie 39.
Wilkinson, P.
    1989 Strategies for Tourism in Island Microstates. Annals of Tourism Research 16: 153–177.
Withington, W. A.
    1961 Upland Resorts and Tourism in Indonesia. Geographical Review 51:418–423.
Zimmermann, G. R.
    1990 Der Tourismus auf Bali in Indonesien. Zur Erklärung der Fremdenverkehrsstruktur in ihrer raum-zeitlichen Entwicklung. *In* Tourismus in der Dritten Welt, Institut für Tourismus, ed., pp. 103–122. Berlin: Institut für Tourismus.
Zinder, H.
    1969 The Future of Tourism in the Eastern Caribbean. Washington DC: Zinder & Associates.

Submitted 2 March 1992
Resubmitted 3 July 1992
Resubmitted 19 August 1992
Accepted 9 September 1992
Refereed anonymously
Coordinating Editor: Kadir H. Din

The Impact of Tourism in Developing Countries on the Health of the Local Host Communities:
The need for more research

Irmgard Bauer

Abstract
Tourism is the fastest growing industry internationally. Popular areas of study are the economic, environmental and sociocultural impacts of tourism in developing countries. Very few studies have been conducted on the impact of tourism on the hosts' health status. Nowadays, the emergence of new infectious diseases or the re-emergence of diseases are causing concern and travel is a major contributor to their spread. The objectives of this study were: to review literature related to the topic as a background for future research; to explore if findings from a field trip to Easter Island/Chile and Peru support the hypotheses derived from the analysis of publications; to recommend a range of research topics based on the outcome of this study; and to propose elements of a possible framework for the assessment of health impacts of tourism. The findings suggest that there are considerable gaps in the current knowledge on tourism's health impacts. Potential indirect and direct health impacts have been identified. Workplace health and safety concerns in relation to local tourism employees have been raised. A wide range of research topics has been suggested based on these findings. Finally, elements of a possible framework for understanding tourism's health impacts and their interrelationships have been identified.

Irmgard Bauer is a lecturer in the School of Nursing Sciences, James Cook University, Australia.

Introduction

Tourism is the fastest growing industry internationally (World Tourism Organization, 1996) with destinations not only in industrialised countries, but also in less developed countries in East Africa, Central America and South East Asia. Developing countries which were previously seen as less likely destinations or were closed to tourism altogether are now considering the marketing of their natural and/or cultural attractions to receive a share of this global industry. Adventure tourism, and cultural tourism take advantage of this development. Each year more exotic places are offered on the tourism market for those who have seen everything else, or prefer destinations 'off the beaten track'. The close contact with locals in isolated areas and their customs seems to be one of the main attractions of developing countries, and this is used extensively in marketing strategies.

At the same time, the scientific study of tourism has developed such that tertiary education institutions worldwide offer degree courses in tourism studies. The perspectives and approaches one can adopt to study the topic are as diverse as tourism itself. Jafari (1990) presented an overview of disciplines and approaches in the study of tourism. The disciplines offered are of considerable diversity but 'health' does not rate a mention in this model of approaches.

Tourism and health

Literature dealing with the combination of tourism and health abundantly covers health aspects of travellers to particular locations, health education, medical aspects of travel preparation, health problems in travellers or in returning tourists, and economic or administrative consequences of tourists' ill health. In short, 'Tourism and Health' usually focuses on the travellers' wellbeing.

However, despite this necessary and applaudable development in protecting travellers from health problems, one needs to consider that there are people on the other end of the journey who may be subjected to a change in their health status as well, due to visiting fellow humans. 'Tourism and Health' rarely includes the hosts in its consideration.

Tourism's potential impact on the health of the local host communities can be direct or indirect. One example of direct impact is the possible trans-mission of diseases from travellers to locals. Nowadays, the emergence of new infectious diseases or the reemergence of diseases thought to be eradicated are causing great concern, and travel is a major contributor to their spread (White, 1977; World Health Organization (WHO), 1996; Wilson, 1994, 1995a). Lea (1988) rightly pointed out that

> tourism has the dual effect of promoting the provision of improved health care in Third World destinations but, in addition, acts as a vehicle to spread some forms of disease (p.70).

Other possible direct health impacts are chronic diseases or disabilities, and accidents causing injuries or deaths of local tourist guides in the course of their employment in tourism. Indirect impacts can be attributed to the social, cultural, environmental and economic impacts which are the usual focus of accounts on tourism impact.

Methodology

Aim of the study

The aim of this study was to ascertain the current knowledge on health impacts of tourism in developing countries, to provide information on gaps in this knowledge as a baseline for future research, to identify research topics which could be investigated by researchers from health, tourism and other disciplines, and to propose elements of a framework for the assessment of health impacts of tourism.

Design of the study

First, a literature review was conducted. Publications related to the topic were identified in the fields of health and tourism. A few sources were located through networking with people working in disciplines pertinent to the subject. The key areas for the search were: travellers' health; tourism and health; tourism in developing countries; economic, environmental, sociocultural impacts of tourism; public health; and tropical medicine. The literature was reviewed to identify any references made in relation to the topic under study to recognise unresearched issues and, if possible, to obtain ideas for an innovative approach of investigation. Only publications in English, German and Spanish were sought and utilised.

Second, a field trip was undertaken to test the findings from the literature analysis against fieldwork in Easter Island/Chile and Peru. First, a range of tourism destinations (including some very popular and others only visited by few individual travellers) were examined with the aim of detecting evidence of positive or negative impacts of tourism on the health of the local population. The emphasis here was on potential environmental impacts; potential health hazards due to running a tourism destination, e.g., construction, equipment, transport; and possible trans-mission of diseases. Second, semi-structured interviews were conducted with health practitioners, tour operators and conservationists to elicit their assessment of tourism's health impacts. Discussions centred around medical aspects, such as changes in disease patterns, introduction of previously non-endemic infectious diseases, and workplace health and safety aspects; tour operators' recol-lection of possible anecdotal evidence of health impacts; and conservationists' views on tourism in environmentally fragile destinations.

Tourism's health impact - A review of the literature

The impact of travel on the health of the hosts: An historical overview

Travel is inseparably linked with human existence. Historical accounts of travel and migrations as the main source of epidemics are numerous (Cossar, 1994; Wilson, 1995a). The Roman Empire was struck by the bubonic plague, spread along the trade routes of the time, leading eventually to the dramatic and largest epidemic of the 'Black Death' in the 14th century. It had started in the Gobi desert in 1320 and reached Europe 30 years later, where it is estimated to have killed one-third to half of the population in some European countries (Wilson, 1995b). Venetian authorities who observed outbreaks after the arrival of ships from the East assumed that travel may have to do with the spread of the plague. The first regulations governing the arrival of ships were introduced in Venice and Rhodos in 1377, detaining ship, passengers, crew and cargo at a distance for 40 days ('quaranta giorni' became quarantine) before being allowed into the harbour (Bruce Chwatt, 1973, cited in Cossar, 1996).

The conquest of the 'New World' is probably the best known event in history which has been linked to the spread of fatal diseases to non-immune peoples. It was clear from the first written accounts of the Spanish invasion of the Americas in the 15th century that the native peoples were not only killed in battle and through hard labour or physical punishment but also succumbed to a great extent to introduced infectious diseases to which they lacked immunity. In some parts of the New World, infections such as smallpox and influenza reduced the native population dramatically. When this lead to an acute shortage in the work force, the ensuing slave trade from West Africa lead to an even greater range of diseases. The arriving ships, for example, not only brought the yellow fever virus but also its vector *Aedes aegypti* (Cossar, 1994).

Similar transmissions occurred in the Pacific region some hundred years later. It is not clear from historic travel logs if early explorers were aware of their potential role in the transmission of diseases. Beaglehole (1934) in his account of the exploration of the Pacific clearly focused on the exploratory aspect of journeys into the area with only one mention of "the visits of European ships destroyed utterly and horribly its primitive freedom from pestilence" (p. 246).

Captain James Cook seems to have been the first to actively attempt the prevention of a

transmission of infectious diseases from crew to native populations by confining any person found to be diseased to the ship while the rest of the crew was permitted to go ashore (Carruthers, 1930). Apart from syphilis, other often deadly diseases such as measles and dysentery were transmitted from Europeans to native people.

Uncertainty about the transmission of diseases did not seem to exist 100 years later when it was purposefully employed as the following excerpt illustrates. In 1860, three captains arrived at Port Resolution on Tanna (Vanuatu) to occupy the island. Alexander (1895) cited Rev. John Paton reporting:

Our watchword is, "Sweep these creatures away and let white men occupy the soil". They then invited a chief by the name of Kapuku on board one of their vessels, promising him a present, and confined him for twenty-four hours without food in the hold among natives ill with measles, and finally sent him ashore without a present to spread the disease. The measles thus introduced spread fearfully, and decimated the population of the island (p. 33).

Epidemics occurring in isolated 'virgin' populations, i.e., populations without immunity to a certain disease, are not confined to the Middle Ages. Forty years ago on Easter Island, Heyerdahl (1958) observed the influenza epidemic which accompanied the arrival of the yearly supply ship from the Chilean mainland:

The conongo was the natives' great terror - the annual influenza epidemic which always accompanied contact with the mainland. It came and went with the regularity of clockwork. After the ship's visit it always raged through the village for a month or two. It got into chests, heads, and stomachs: everyone was ill, and there was always a toll of

human lives before the conongo *passed and left the people in peace for the rest of the year* (p.124).

A mumps epidemic in 1957 on St. Lawrence Island (Alaska) was started by a boy returning from the mainland after undergoing surgery (Philip, Reinhard & Lackman, 1959). Similar outbreaks on other 'virgin' island populations in Alaska occurred in 1965 and 1967-68 (Nelson, 1995). Although it is generally argued that it is unlikely that there are any 'virgin' populations left due to the contacts of people around the world, partial or selective immunity still allows the transmission of diseases by people on the move. Today, business and leisure travel is claimed to be the driving force in the spread of disease and the (re)emergence of infectious diseases (Wilson, 1995a).

Potential indirect impacts of tourism on the health of the host community

The impacts of tourism are a popular topic in the literature, usually covering the economic, environmental and social aspects. However, few discourses are based on research evidence. Cater (1987) attributed this to the difficulty of studying impacts due to their complexity. An additional problem is that social and cultural dimensions are difficult to quantify and, therefore, out of reach of most researchers employing conventional methods. Using the tourism literature as a baseline, one can develop the arguments further and identify ways in which these impacts can affect health in positive or negative ways.

Economic impacts affecting health

Economic benefits are certainly the primary cause for the promotion of tourism in developing countries. The benefits are mainly seen in the gain of (often desperately needed) foreign exchange and the creation of employment. Archer (1986) claimed that "tourism generates a considerable secondary economic activity in a destination country" (p.57) with income percolating to the public sector, business and private households. Consequently, locals' possession of foreign or local currency earned in the tourism industry enables them to purchase more or better food leading to a better health status (although more money may also mean more junk food). It also allows them access to better health facilities if earnings from tourism have been used to improve the services. Hundt (1996) presented Jamaica as an example where tourism development has lead to prosperity and improved health of the population.

tourist areas in Argentina, 96.3% of respondents to a survey claimed that tourism was to blame for increasing costs (Schlüter & Var, 1988), but the results have to be treated cautiously as the study had only a return rate of 23%. There seems to be a paucity of research supporting anecdotal accounts of economic impacts of tourism. Research needs to be conducted into changes of living costs and their effect on locals. For example, D'Sousa (1985) reported from Goa that, in addition to a lack of improved health, local tax payers paid for tourists' free medical care.

A different type of negative economic impact on health was reported by Loval and Feuerstein (1992): "There is said to be a

term problem is water pollution. The following examples are taken from a compilation by Maurer (1992). Frequently, tourism developments in developing countries do not have an appropriate system for sewage and waste management and they use rivers and the sea for disposal. This can pose two problems. First, fish and molluscs eaten by the local population as a source of protein may be unsuitable for consumption due to pollutants deposited in these animals. Second, swimming in polluted water can lead to ear, eye, skin and gastrointestinal infections in even epidemic proportions. Herbicides used on golf courses have been shown to pollute the freshwater supply and impact on health directly or through food obtained from the water. The pollution of waterholes in deserts through the tourists' use of soap and shampoo poses another problem (Maurer, 1992). Redirection and overuse of freshwater for hotels, swimming pools and landscaping purposes in tourism facilities can lead to the local population having less or no clean drinking water which in turn puts them at risk of contracting diseases. Lack of water also impacts on the local agriculture leading to poor crops and a scarcity of food (Maurer, 1992).

> **a potential problem . . . tourism can attract trained health professionals away from the health sector**

However, the same author admitted that "more important is the realisation that the profits of tourism generally are not used to improve the health status of the poor, marginalised natives in host countries" (p. 111). The following example from Peru may illustrate this statement. In 1995, the country received almost half a million tourists (Yunis, 1996). The area around Cusco is certainly one of the main attractions of the country and the majority of foreign tourists include a visit in their itinerary. Tourism generated income, however, does not seem to percolate to everybody in the general population in the area if the nutritional status of children in the Cusco Health District (as investigated by Wolff, Pérez, Gibson, Lopez, Peniston and Wolff, 1985) is taken as one outcome criterion. Tourism development may eventually lead to increasing living costs. In two

drain of trained nurses away from the health sector in some Pacific areas as they seek jobs in tourism" (p. 342). No other reference could be found supporting this claim. Considering the expenses of training health personnel, it is important to know if this is a common trend in developing countries where salaries of health professionals are known to be very low. The problem of locals leaving their traditional activities of fishing or farming for seemingly more lucrative work in the tourism industry has been presented in the literature (Mathieson & Wall, 1982).

Environmental impacts affecting health

Unfortunately, tourism seems to be the culprit for a number of environmental problems that pose health hazards to local communities. A serious long-

There is a need to substantiate examples such as those mentioned above. Very little research evidence supports numerous anecdotal accounts of environmental problems caused, at least partially, by tourism. More specific investigations into pollution and redirection of drinking water need to be carried out. Also, resulting health problems need to be documented carefully to support strategies for improvement.

Garbage generated by tourists poses another public health hazard for host communities as, apart from its unaesthetic appearance, it creates breeding sites for disease-carrying arthropods and rodents. Harrington (1993) reports the pollution of the Amazon through tourists. In 1980, the South American Explorers Club collected approximately 400 kg of unburnable garbage on the Inka trail in Peru (Rachowiecki, 1996). An aspect not yet located in the literature is the possible danger of injuries (cuts, lacerations) caused by garbage. This may be of particular concern if people contract infections but are unable to access or pay for the treatment required.

Clearing for tourism developments or sports facilities (e.g., skiing) causes serious ecological changes and can lead to flooding or landslides destroying crops, homes and lives. Apart from that, mosquitos which are potential vectors for diseases tend to move into cleared areas. When people (locals and tourists) move in to utilise the cleared land, they are at risk of contracting serious diseases such as malaria or yellow fever if the mosquitos are infected. The cutting of firewood along the world's trekking routes adds to the deterioration of forest already damaged due to cutting of wood for domestic purposes as can easily be seen in Nepal (Jefferies, 1984) or Peru. At present, no statistics could be found indicating the exact extent of destruction of forest or bush-land for tourism purposes.

On the other hand, tourism can have positive environmental effects, when generated income is used for environmental planning and education, or for the construction of appropriate sewage systems. Investing in the conservation of natural areas and safe tourist facilities in these areas ultimately benefits the physical and mental well-being of locals and visitors alike. Hellen (1995) argued that research into tourism in the developing world "opens up the prospect that global tourism may itself become a vehicle for investment in

environmental health programs and securing improved health for all" (p. 154). So far, there is a striking paucity of examples supporting this vision.

Socio-cultural impacts affecting health

This third major category of impacts is similarly widely discussed in the literature (Cater, 1987; King, Pizam & Milman, 1993; Mathieson & Wall, 1982; Pearce, 1982, 1994; Rajotte, 1987; Swinglehurst, 1994). Generally, it is stated that tourist-host encounters may lead to better understanding between cultures, remove prejudices and promote cultural pride eventually leading to the preservation or a renaissance of the local art/craft. Despite these positive

arguments, it seems that tourism's impact on society and culture in developing countries is mainly perceived as negative.

It is acknowledged that social and cultural change is a phenomenon attributed to modernisation in general but it seems that the frequent and fast exchange of encounters of people from different backgrounds accelerates this change at a rate not always favourable for the host communities. Obvious health problems accompanying these changes originate in the appearance or increase of prostitution, alcoholism, drug use and violence (Ruiz-de Chávez, Jiménez-Aguado, Márquez-Laposse and Alleyne, 1993). Also, lifestyle and food preferences of visitors seem to be imitated often leading to higher body weight, greater percentage of body fat, and high blood pressure, conditions previously

unknown in these communities. Farrell (1982) named Hawaii and other areas in the Pacific as an example of areas where these changes occurred. Little additional research evidence on unhealthy lifestyles due to the influence of tourism could be located.

Mental health problems are less frequently discussed. Changes in the traditional lifestyle or loss of identity through changes in social and cultural values can put a considerable mental strain on people. Negative implications through changes in social and cultural values (Mathieson & Wall, 1982) include potential mental health problems. Currently, it is unclear how many confirmed diagnoses of mental alterations could be

> The absence of clear research findings relating tourism to changing lifestyles calls attention to an array of research possibilities.

attributed to long-term impacts of tourism.

Physical and mental health problems caused by the forceful removal of peoples to make way for tourism are equally neglected in the literature. Examples of this practice can be found around the globe. A more recent case was reported from Botswana where Kalahari Bushmen appealed to the UN to save them from being evicted from their ancestral lands which were to be used for tourism purposes (Linton, 1996). Forced re-locations of indigenous people in the Peruvian Amazon area are a common method to make space for tourist lodges (Seiler-Baldinger, 1988).

Research into changes of locals' health status is very scarce. Numerous questions arise when evaluating anecdotal evidence on sociocultural impacts. An important issue that needs investigation is if changes to lifestyle, the adoption of unhealthy food preferences, increase in prostitution, alcohol and drug use, and violence can clearly be attributed to tourism, or if they are symptoms of 'development' and modernisation. It is also of interest to ascertain if tourists engage in activities contradicting local rules and taboos, and of what type and frequency these actions are. Additionally, there has to be a closer investigation into the occurrence of people's forceful removal from their home and land for tourism purposes.

Potential direct impacts of tourism on the health of the host community

Health conditions which can affect local people directly and not as secondary implications of other impacts of tourism, are diseases, accidents, and conditions related to employment in tourism.

The potential direct health impacts of tourism are mainly those occurring through the spread of infections by travelling individuals. These infections can be imported from the tourists' country of origin, or they could be contracted while travelling. Table 1 presents the main infection risks for travellers in developing countries as compiled by Warren and Mahmoud (1990, cited in Hellen, 1995). All of those can be transmitted to local individuals.

There are diseases that are easily spread and are common, others require a range of factors and circumstances to be transmitted and are less common. Some diseases may have a minor impact on the individual and/or can be treated easily, others are difficult to treat and/or have serious impacts on the individual. Table 2 presents the ease of spread of a range of diseases which can be transmitted from travellers to hosts and their level of impact on the host individual.

The mode of transmission of some conditions is common knowledge and well researched, the spread of others has not been discussed in the light of tourist-host transmission, possibly because some diseases are less common. Nevertheless, sometimes only one case of infection may be enough to introduce a virulent agent to people without the necessary immunity and lead to a major epidemic. This potential risk warrants the consideration of all possibilities of disease transmission. An additional factor needs to be addressed when discussing the potential spread to people in developing countries, and here particularly indigenous communities. Poor hygiene, unfavourable economic conditions, inadequate housing and nutrition predispose people already to a range of diseases such as tuberculosis, parasitic infections or hepatitis, with individuals often having several acute and chronic conditions at the same time. It is obvious that an additional load of pathogenic agents, especially when the immune system is compromised, can only aggravate health problems.

Field studies on tourism's health impact

One objective of this study was to test if the findings of the analysis of published material applied to real situations in developing countries.

Health problems linked to tourism in Easter Island and Peru

On Easter Island it was found that the (only) campground on the island at Anakena Beach had no fresh water supply, and the sanitary facilities provided, according to the locals, had been locked for a long time. On weekends, hundreds of locals and tourists gather at the beach usually staying the whole day. This was discussed with staff at the hospital who reported a relatively high prevalence of

diarrhoea on the island but had attributed this to vegetables imported from the Chilean mainland. After discussing the lack of sanitary facilities which becomes even more obvious with the added tourists, they agreed that it was worthwhile to investigate this potential health hazard. Staff, however, saw the main problem regarding tourism and health as the transmission of Sexually Transmitted Infections (STIs) from tourists to locals. This anecdotal evidence has not yet been systematically investigated. The issue of the availability of health facilities came up during conversations with locals in the market. It could be concluded that tourism on Easter Island has not improved the locals' health facilities. This may have to do with the fact that tourists generally stay only a short time, either because of the limited facilities on the island or because they are only having a brief stopover on the connection Tahiti - Santiago de Chile. If seriously ill, the people joked, they had "only two options, Santiago [some 3700 km away] or the cemetery".

Health professionals in Peru also maintained that cases of STIs were increasing and tourism was seen as a major contributing factor to this development, but they were unable to substantiate these claims. Toonen *et al.* (1996) conducted a health baseline study in the Camisea area in the Amazonian jungle where the Shell Company is prospecting. The potential risk of the native population to contract STIs was seen as very high because of people coming from outside (here mainly oil workers). The study does not clarify if locals also spoke of tourists, the term 'visitadores' in the study refers to prostitutes.

Other diseases repeatedly named as being spread by people moving around were malaria and leishmaniasis. The important aspect of tourist-host encounters

Table 1: Main Infection Risks for Travellers in Developing Countries.

Risk to Travellers	Disease
high > 1 case per 10 travellers	Diarrhoea Upper respiratory infections
medium < 1 case per 10 travellers	Dengue fever Enteroviral infections Giardiasis Hepatitis A Malaria (without prophylaxis) Salmonellosis STIs

Excerpt from Warren and Mahmoud (1990, cited in Hellen, 1995).

in tribal areas in the jungle could not be examined during this field trip but needs urgent attention. This is so because some villages now seem to contact tour operators suggesting cooperation, and operators sensitive to potential problems need to be provided with information to facilitate their decision making.

Environmental impacts of tourism in trekking areas with problems due to unregulated garbage disposal and the lack of sanitary facilities were suggested in the literature and could be observed in reality. The problem applies to areas with opportunities for short hikes as well as to trails representing major tourist attractions such as routes in the Cordillera Blanca/Huaraz or the Inka Trail near Cusco. The need for urgent action has been recognised in both areas and plans are already under way to implement solutions to the problems. A program is currently being designed to install sanitary facilities along well-used trails. This is of particular importance when the areas represent the main water supply for a large region.

Implications for local tourism employees' health

The neglect of local tourism workers' health in the literature is obvious. The importance of the consideration of this topic became apparent during the field trip. It seems that many tourism

workers in Peru (and other developing countries) earn their living as tourist guides, often in destinations with little tourism infrastructure such as nature based adventure tours. Tourists are given advice about the dangers they may encounter on these trips. But tourists are only exposed to those hazards for a very short time compared to the guides. Their health risks increase through the frequency of exposure due to their job as well as the terrain they are working in.

Adventure tours to the Amazonian jungle are very popular. Like tourists, guides are exposed to health hazards such as snake and other animals' bites, diseases such as malaria or leishmaniasis, and car or boat accidents. Several cases of snake bites and accidents with boats and trucks were named by a tour operator in Cusco.

Probably the highest health risk exists for mountain guides who risk altitude sickness, injury or death in their attempt to lead tourists to spectacular summits. Peak season means a higher income but also a higher health risk. Shlim (1996) reported that in just one storm in the Nepal Himalayas on 10-11 November 1995, 22 foreigners and more than 45 Nepalese guides and porters died in different regions due to heavy snowfall, avalanches and mudslides. It was claimed that up to 30 people

die each year in the Andes including mountain guides (Jake Cosak, personal communication, January 1997). The health of tourism workers, however, can also be in danger in the developed world. More than 50 climbers and guides died within a few weeks in the European Alps in the summer of 1997. Another form of 'occupational health hazard' has been observed on the Argentinian side of the Iguazu Falls where, at a certain point, locals drive tourists in an open boat equipped with a small engine close to the edge of the falls. The engine barely is able to get the boat out of the current and back to shore. A thin rope along the edge clearly is not sufficient to withstand a boat should the engine fail.

Increasingly, developing countries with access to spectacular reefs market their underwater attractions to encourage diving holidays. When the income of a diving guide depends on the number of dives, the minimum surface interval that is required for health reasons may not always be observed, putting them under considerable health risks. A lack of decompression chambers in developing countries, partly due to the failure of enforcing their installation, as Rudkin and Hall (1996) reported from Pacific islands, is of concern not only to the visiting diver but also to the local guide.

In many areas in the developing world, customs prevent people's exposure to physical danger by placing a taboo over a certain area. If such an area happens to become of interest to tourism, the reluctance of locals to go to such places may be overcome by the need to earn money. Two guides together with one tourist died in January 1995 at Mt. Yasur on Tanna/Vanuatu, killed by falling rocks ejected from the volcano. This author has witnessed local guides refusing to accompany visitors to the summit of this volcano.

Health hazards for whitewater rafting guides have been described in the literature. Sisson, Nichols and Hopkins (1983) reported schistosomiasis (blood flukes) infections among US rafting guides on the Omo River/Ethiopia. A year later, Istre, Fontaine, Tarr, and Hopkins (1984) described an outbreak of acute schistosomiasis among rafters on the same river, pointing out that commercial organisations were about to start business. This means that local guides, although partially immune, are exposed to repeated infections. A different potential health problem was identified in porters. For example, on the Inka Trail (with the highest altitude above 4000m.) one can find children carrying backpacks considered too heavy for well nourished healthy adult tourists. This may cause problems in later life such as bone deformation and chronic backpain which can prevent the individual from pursuing regular work.

The examples mentioned give a little insight into this complex area. Unfortunately, no research on this topic could be found. This may be because accidents or other health problems affect individual people, not groups or whole communities, cases are dealt with individually but not linked with other similar events. Because of the absence of data on frequency/occurrence, it is also difficult to make a risk assessment based on assumptions alone. Considering the fact that in developing countries there is rarely any organised support for such workers, health insurance or compensation for themselves or their families, this matter needs urgent attention if tourism is not to be seen as yet another type of exploitation. On the other hand, however, it is to be expected that some local guides can indeed make a living without putting themselves at risk and, subsequently, even lead a much healthier life than before.

The findings of the field work

underline the need for further research. Diseases which had been reported as transmittable through people's movement, were found again in the field. Also, the health problems of local tourism workers proved to be a reality, and research into this area appears to be overdue. Although their numbers may be small compared to the entire population who may be at risk of infectious diseases, the concern over their work safety warrants further investigations. A retrospective and ongoing documentation of illness/death of local tour guides classified into areas of expertise, such as mountain, scuba diving, jungle and so on, should be established and a data bank created with links to neighbouring countries which have similar problems. Also, the health status of guides

and porters should be assessed and monitored. The identification of potential occupational health problems and a documentation of the spread of diseases contracted during employment in tourism to family and community, would assist in strategies to minimise health hazards.

Towards a framework for understanding tourism's health impacts

Anecdotal versus research evidence

This study suggests that, at the moment, there is very little research based evidence on the impact of tourism on locals' health in developing countries. Sources that can be found related to the topic are mainly anecdotal,

Table 2: *Ease of Spread of a Range of Diseases Which can be Transmitted from Travellers to Hosts and Their Level of Impact on the Host Individual.*

Ease of spread	Impact on host individual*	Diseases
high	minor to serious	STIs, gastro-intestinal infections, upper respiratory infections, other viral infections
medium	minor to serious	worm infections (roundworms, tapeworms)
	medium to serious	cholera, malaria, dengue fever, yellow fever, filariasis, leishmaniasis, onchocerciasis, Oropouche fever
	serious	AIDS, other viral infections
low	medium	myiasis
	medium to serious	worm infections (flukes)

* minor: acute illness with usually no complications, no or little temporary incapacitation, complete recovery

    medium: acute or chronic illness affecting an individual's ability to pursue the usual activities, complete recovery, no permanent incapacitation

    serious: acute or chronic illness with high possibility of serious or fatal complications, permanent incapacitation or disfiguration.

e.g., Pryor's (1980) account of residents' attitudes in Rarotonga, Cook Islands, or the many accusations about the role of (Western) tourists as transmitters of STIs and AIDS (Cohen, 1988; Wanjau, 1987). Although there is no doubt that tourism contributes to the spread of diseases, facts are hard to obtain.

Using Doxey's (1975) index of tourist irritation as a framework, one has to assume that anecdotal negative evidence on health impacts may have a lot to do with locals' antagonism toward tourists for whatever reason. Comments, therefore, should be (or should have been) examined from this perspective to allow for a more realistic interpretation. Antagonism may even lead to the perception of transmission of diseases with entirely different aetiology. In this connection, one also needs to consider the well known conflict between national park management and the needs of the locals living within a park or in close proximity. For example, the conservation of flagship species such as the tiger or rhinoceros has to be weighed against the loss of lives of locals caused by those animals (Mishra, 1984). Likewise, loss of livestock and crop destruction have impacts on the population's health status. In the context of this report, it is necessary to identify what events occur within the framework of conservation and which ones can clearly be attributed to tourism.

Numerous gaps have been identified in the current body of knowledge on the impact of tourism on the health of the local population in developing countries and topics for research have been suggested. It has been established that research into potential indirect health impacts has to go beyond the economic, environmental and sociocultural impacts already widely discussed in the literature, and focus specifically on their health implications. Research into potential direct health impacts

should concentrate on epidemiological studies into the transmission of diseases through travellers and on investigations into the workplace health and safety aspects in relation to local tourism employees.

In addition, a wide range of general issues is the focus for basic and applied research providing additional information to achieve a more complete picture of health impacts. Examples are offered here to illustrate the variety of study topics available to researchers from different disciplines. Historians could explore how visitors in the past (invaders, explorers, missionaries) changed the local health status. At present, it seems information on this topic can only be found by chance when studying old documents or travel diaries. Addressing present day concerns, social scientists should establish if there is indeed an association between locals' negative attitudes towards tourism and anecdotal evidence of negative impacts (and then test those claims through epidemiological research). Another focus of interest is an examination of national and regional tourism strategies in developing countries with respect to the consideration of the local public health and specific strategic activities to prevent a deterioration of the health status. Public health interests could lie in: the comparison of the impact of different levels of low, moderate, and high degrees of tourism in small/isolated communities; the investigation of advice given to tourists in their home country or at the destination regarding their impact on local health; an assessment of tourists' knowledge of their potential role as transmitters of diseases; the identification of services offered for tourists' health care and the examination of their utilisation and availability for locals; the documentation of tourists using local health care facilities; or a comparison of the distribution of

health care professionals and health services in touristic and non-touristic areas within one country. Finally, tourism education should be included in research on the topic and curricula in tourism degree courses examined regarding their inclusion of health aspects. These study topics can be researched not only in individual projects focusing on a particular geographic area but allow for comparison between areas with the aim of collaborative efforts in dealing with identified health problems linked to tourism. The addition and consideration of country specific research needs which may be proposed by local health authorities will be of particular importance when deciding on a specific topic for research. An overview of categories of research issues is presented in Figure 1.

The need for research as a basis for tourism planning

The goal of tourism planning is usually said to be economic, sociological, biological and cultural sustainability. Ethical concerns have been raised in connection with tourism development in the 'Third World' (Lea, 1993). The four goals in tourism development:

(1) enhanced visitor satisfaction,

(2) improved economy and business success,

(3) protected resource assets, and

(4) community and area integration
                        (Gunn, 1994)

clearly include participation of and approval by the local population. Any development that does not protect local people and environment could be classified as unethical.

It becomes clear when examining available tourism strategies and plans that tourism planning is an immensely complex activity.

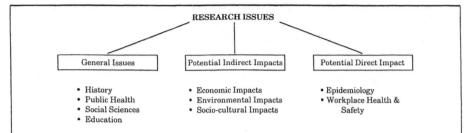

Figure 1: *Categories of research issues into the impacts of tourism in developing countries on the health of the local host communities*

Publications on two areas visited during the field trip have been reviewed with respect to their coverage of issues which may directly or indirectly affect the health of local populations. Aguilar, Hinojosa and Milla (1992) suggested a wide range of strategies and actions to develop tourism in the 'Inka Region', an area extending over the Departments of Cusco, Madre de Dios and Apurímac, but no reference relating to health could be found. The 'Plan for Touristic and Recreation Use of the Huascarán National Park' (Instituto de Montana, 1996) applies to the national park in the Cordillera Blanca/Huaraz which predicted 104,000 conventional tourists and 4,000 adventure tourists (mountain climbers) for the year 1996, and 320,000 conventional tourists and 12,000 adventure tourists for the year 2005 (p. 44). As this plan relates to a national park, it comes as no surprise that considerable emphasis is placed on the environmental impact of tourism (garbage, lack of toilets, water and sewage system). It also recommends that conditions are to be established "for the rural population to participate in tourism in a manner which permits sustainable development" (p.18). Both aspects influence the local health status but health as such is not mentioned explicitly. The plan also suggests that local guides be registered in order to monitor uncontrolled activities in the park. Such a register, if implemented, could be an excellent opportunity to monitor their health status.

Research is the basis to appropriate tourism planning. It is obvious that the lack of research into health issues has prevented their inclusion in tourism strategic plans.

Methodological considerations

The benefit of studying a little investigated area is that there are few conceptual restrictions for the researcher but a great opportunity for creativity and innovative approaches when defining research topics.

Research in some of the areas suggested, clearly poses enormous methodological challenges for the investigator, not least because of the transient character of tourism. Here again creativity is needed in employing a range of different research approaches, going beyond the conventional. Two will be mentioned here. For example, for some of these topics an action research approach based on Critical Social Theory could be adopted. The philosophy behind Critical Social Theory is that empowering people helps them to change their situation, to help themselves. A classic text is Paolo Freire's (1972) *Pedagogy of the Oppressed* on the empowerment through education. In a similar way, communities affected by negative health impacts from tourism could work at overcoming these by adopting the problem solving approach based on empowerment. The core of action research is the employment of a problem solving approach whereby the researcher guides the representatives of a group/community (who also become part of the research team) through the process of change until a satisfactory outcome is achieved.

The usefulness of a Geographical Information System (GIS) for epidemiological purposes is now widely accepted. The inherent geographical element of tourism and the aspect of movement represent factors very suitable for the employment of GIS for research purposes on this topic. Furthermore, its use would allow the combination of epidemiological and tourism variables. At this stage, it could not be established if GIS has ever been used in this form. However, the combination of medicine and geography is not new. Hellen (1995) discussed the use of applied medical geography in, for example, disease hazard mapping, and emphasised the need for a "multidisciplinary approach to safeguarding the health of individuals and ensuring the sustainability of tourism to potentially hazardous areas" (p. 171), albeit from the perspective of travellers' health.

It is quite clear that the range of research questions suggested in this paper indicates that a lot of these need to be approached in a multidisciplinary fashion. This would also provide a unique opportunity to cooperate with local professionals and to train locals as research assistants to enable them to continue research and monitoring on a long-term basis.

Towards a framework for understanding tourism's health impacts

The purpose of research is to generate and test theories. Applied research emphasises its practical applicability to the field of study. Consequently, research undertaken on this hitherto under-investigated topic will contribute to a body of knowledge which may eventually be expressed in a more abstract form as theories and represented as models for easier understanding. The theories, in turn, will have to be tested and refined.

Bushell and Lea (1996) quite rightly pointed out that there is more to 'tourism and health' than traveller illness and suggest a reorientation towards 'traveller and host wellness'. They then continue to present a tourism health model linked to the concept of ecological public health as a framework for research. It defines 'tourism and health' as the interface between (1) tourists, (2) hosts and (3) the natural environment. The model takes into account arguments by Brown (1985) supporting an epidemiology of health in contrast to the traditional epidemiology of diseases. Based on these arguments, the authors also propose a forced field approach considering the perspectives of promoting/preventing wellness/ illness as a guideline for investigations, and request that a new public health framework be integrated in the existing field of 'tourism and health'. Without doubt, this is one possible avenue. However, it can be argued that this model is rather one-sided as

it focuses on health with little evidence of including tourism aspects (apart from the tourists). The model may represent the broad field of tourism and health but it does not depict enough detail to accommodate attributing factors which are mentioned by Bushell and Lea, such as typology of tourists or destination categories. It does not seem refined enough to offer directions for further research incorporating both fields (tourism and health) sufficiently.

A framework can be seen as a system where all components are interdependent and interlinked in a way that variations in one component affect the rest of the system. Based on the results of this study, a framework for understanding tourism's health impacts in developing countries will most likely consist of at least of the following major components: tourists, type of tourism, operators/developers, local population, local authorities, the environment, the level of tourism, and the country's current economic status.

Tourists (as individuals/as groups)

Tourists are probably the most active part in this framework as they are the ones actually moving around and coming into contact with places and people. A range of factors need to be considered as attributes of this constant visitor-host encounter: tourist typology; tourists' health status and educational status; knowledge required for a particular trip; advice given; activities sought and their implications; speed of travel; size and numbers of groups; mode of transport chosen; accommodation (e.g., enclave vs homestay); travel patterns; travel corridors; travel seasons; and the degree of contact with the local population. Some of these factors are deliberately chosen by the individual, others occur unintentionally or have been decided for the tourist.

Type of tourism

A further component is the type of tourism occurring in a particular location, from individual adventure travel to mass tourism. This has an effect on the degree of contact tourists have with locals as well as the potential of introducing diseases or causing other negative impacts, for example, on the environment. Although mass travel implies that large numbers of people travel, the accumulation of large numbers usually only occurs at very popular destinations, and these visitors may not come in contact with locals at all or rarely. The impact of mass tourism on health is likely to be indirect, i.e. through economic, environmental or sociocultural affects discussed in earlier chapters. Adventure tourism is pursued by travelling individuals, alone or in very small groups, but their destinations are usually in more remote and isolated areas where they are also much more likely to come in closer contact with local communities. These interactions most likely prepare the ground for potential direct impacts such as the transmission of diseases.

Tourist activities are another dimension impacting on local destinations. Pearce and Moscardo (1989) developed a tool to investigate the Structure of Tourism Activities for Regions (STAR). A list of attributes allows the classification of activities. Some of those attributes are based on inter-actions between tourists and the environment (and hence important in relation to possible impacts), but no attribute is allocated to a possible interaction with the local population. As this interaction obviously does occur, on a continuum from very little to very close, not only should this dimension be added to the STAR (Structure of Tourism Activities for Regions) instrument, but it is an important factor in the assessment of health impacts of tourism. It may be useful to design a modified STAR tool that allows the creation of profiles of activities and their impact on host communities' health. The dimensions of such a tool would be factors such as impact on the environment, degree of contact with locals, or potential risks to local employees.

Operators/developers

A further important component are those individuals or companies/organisations who develop tourism destinations and provide services and facilities from travel agencies to transport companies and the accommodation industry. Clearly, the primary purpose of those businesses is to make a profit out of the tourism they promote. Ideally, operators should be mediators between tourists and hosts, if only to ensure sustainability of the operations. In reality, however, it seems that the links with the tourists are much closer, tourists and operators are involved in a business transaction with one supplying what the other demands. Operators have a great responsibility when it comes to planning, developing and running tourism products as these rarely occur without impacts on the local populations. Very often, operators decide on activities offered, destinations visited, accommodation constructed and mode of transport provided. They, therefore, do represent a very important element in the health impact framework due to their intermediate position between visitors and hosts.

Local population

Here, we are looking at the more passive, receiving end of the activity 'travel'. The following aspects are of importance: the geographical location; immunity and health status; level of education; previous contact with visitors; dependence on tourism; degree of contact with tourists; attitudes towards tourism; the difference between the cultural

and social values of visitor and host; locals' involvement in tourism planning.

Brown (1985) strongly emphasised that a suitable approach to an epidemiology of health "must take account of complexity, open-endedness, multiple interactions, value choices, social rules and types of personality..." (p. 336). Nothing less should be applied to the local host population.

Local authorities (health/tourism)

So far, little attention has been paid to the role of local health and tourism authorities in the protection of the health of the local population. It is important to recognise the role of these authorities. Although the aims of both authorities may not seem to have much common ground, with one developing and promoting tourism and the principles of business in mind, and the other in charge of the public health status, if they are to achieve sustainable tourism which benefits all parties involved, a close cooperation between both is necessary. This applies particularly to activities such as monitoring the local health status in tourism destinations and implementing strategies of improvement if necessary; investigating health impacts (in

cooperation with other agencies, such as conservation groups); approving of tourism destinations only after a positive outcome of a health impact assessment; or terminating an operation when its impact is detrimental. In this respect, local authorities play a central role in the monitoring of tourists, locals, and operators as well as environmental issues.

Environment

The environment represents an essential resource for tourism. Budowski (1976) proposed three possible relationships between tourism and nature, *conflict*, *coexistence* and *symbiosis*, claiming that the majority of relationships are those of coexistence moving toward conflict. It seems not much has changed 20 years later. Changes in the environment affect humans' health as a short- or long-term consequence. It is, therefore, important that every effort is made to closely observe the environment for changes attributable to tourism to allow for timely action in order to reduce the health risks to locals and tourists.

Economic status

In order to achieve the required monitoring discussed above, not only is a substantial budget

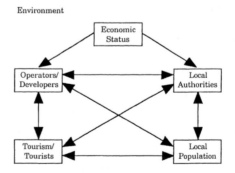

Figure 2: *The elements of a tentative framework for understanding the impacts of tourism in developing countries on the health of the local host communities*

necessary but also professional expertise in fields such as health, tourism, and conservation. The same requirements apply if research is to be conducted into topics suggested throughout this paper. A lesser developed country may well recognise negative impacts of tourism on the health of its people but may be in no position to do anything about it, not least because it is desperately dependent on tourism and foreign currency. Therefore, ways will have to be designed that allow countries with little expertise and economic abilities to still have strategies at hand to minimise a decrease in the local health status attributable to tourism.

These components and their relationships with each other (Figure 2) can be seen as starting points for investigations

A growth of research based knowledge on tourism's health impacts (as well as putting this area on priority lists of funding bodies) will allow the generation of theoretical frameworks in a reasonably near future. Such frameworks are necessary for applying this knowledge to practice, particularly for assessing health impacts. The ultimate goal will be to conduct such an assessment for prospective or current tourism developments in the same way as is already done for economic, environmental or, to a lesser extent, sociocultural impacts as, literally, prevention is better than cure.

Lacking such an assessment framework at the moment, other solutions have to be employed. Short-term solutions may centre around creating an awareness in tourists, locals and operators. In the longer term, other interventions may be necessary. Simmons' (1996) advice was meant for the protection of the environment but is equally applicable to health when he suggests the provision of 'honey-pots' to draw people away from vulnerable spots. In practice, this could mean, rather than searching for isolated tribes in a rainforest, providing tourists with high quality interpretation centres.

The increase in tourism worldwide is likely to continue and the positive aspects of tourism in developing countries are acknowledged. However, it seems that health is being ignored in the process of tourism development, both "in terms of the local people and in the potential impact of travellers on the already scarce health resources" as Rudkin and Hall (1996, p.101) reported from the South Pacific. If visitor-host encounters lead to a decreasing health status of the hosts, action needs to be taken in order to promote people's well-being and, consequently, the sustainability of tourism destinations for the benefit of the visitor *and* the host. Otherwise, the World Tourism Organization's objective"'to accelerate and enlarge the contribution of tourism (international and domestic) to peace, understanding, *health* [my italics], and prosperity throughout the world" (McIntosh, Goeldner & Ritchie, 1995) cannot be met.

Acknowledgement:

The author gratefully acknowledges the supervision of this project by Dr. Alastair Birtles.

References

Aguilar, V., Hinojasa, L., & Milla, C. (1992). Turismo y Desarollo. Posibilidades en la Region Inka [Tourism and Development. Possibilities in the Inka Region]. Cusco: Centro de Estudios Regionales Andinos 'Bartomolé de las Casas'.

Alexander, J. (1895). *The Islands of the Pacific. From the old to the new.* New York: American Tract Society.

Archer, B. (1986). The secondary economic effects of tourism in developing countries. In *Planning for Tourism and Tourism in Developing Countries - Proceedings of Seminars at PTRC 14th Summer Annual Meeting* (pp. 53-63). London: PTRC Education and Research Services.

Beaglehole, J. (1934). *The exploration of the Pacific.* London: A & C Black Ltd.

Brown, V. (1985). Towards an epidemiology of health: A basis for planning community health programs. *Health Policy, 4,* 331-340.

Budowski, G. (1976). Tourism and environmental conservation: Conflict, coexistence, or symbiosis? *Environmental Conservation, 3*(1), 27-31.

Bushell, R., & Lea, J. (1996). *Exploring a new framework for health and tourism development.* Paper presented at the Asia Pacific Tourism Association (APTA) '96 Conference, 14-18 September 1996, Townsville, Australia.

Carruthers, J. (1930). *Captain James Cook, R.N. One Hundred and Fifty Years after.* London: Murray.

Cater, E. (1987). Tourism in the least developed countries. *Annals of Tourism Research, 14*(2), 202-226.

Cohen, E. (1988). Tourism and AIDS in Thailand. *Annals of Tourism Research, 15*(4), 467-486.

Cossar, J. (1994). Influence of travel and disease: An historical perspective. *Journal of Travel Medicine, 1*(1), 36-39.

Cossar, J. (1996). Travellers' health: A medical perspective. In S. Clift & S. Page (Eds.), *Health and the International Tourist* (pp. 23-43). London: Routledge.

Doxey, G. (1975). A causation theory of visitor-resident irritants, methodology, and research inferences. *The Impact of Tourism. Sixth Annual Conference Proceedings of the Travel Research Association.* San Diego: Tourism and Travel Research Association.

D'Sousa, J. (1985). Does tourism mean development? *Contours, 2*(4) 22-23.

Farrell, B. (1982). *Hawaii, the Legend that Sells.* Honolulu: University Press of Hawaii.

Freire, P. (1972). *The pedagogy of the pppressed.* New York: Herder.

Gunn, C. (1994). *Tourism planning. Basics, concepts, cases.* Washington: Taylor & Francis.

Harrington, T. (1993). Tourism damages Amazon region. In S. Place (Ed.), *Tropical rainforests. Latin American nature and society in transition* (pp. 213-216). Wilmington: Scholarly Resources Inc.

Hellen, J. (1995). Tourist health and tourist medicine in the tropics: A case for sustainable development? In B. Iyun, Y. Verhasselt & J. Hellen (Eds.), *The health of nations. Medicine, disease and development in the Third World* (pp. 153-176). Aldershot: Avebury.

Heyerdahl, T. (1958). *Aku-Aku.* London: Allen & Unwin.

Hundt, A. (1996). Impact of tourism development on the economy and health of Third World nations. *Journal of Travel Medicine, 3*(2), 107-112.

Instituto de Montaña (1996). *Plan de Uso Turistico y Recreativo del Parque Nacional Huascarán [Plan for Touristic and Recreational Use of the Huascarán National Park].* Lima.

Istre, G., Fontaine, R., Tarr, J., & Hopkins, R. (1984). Acute schistosomiasis among Americans rafting the Omo River, Ethiopia. *Journal of the American Medical Association, 251*(4), 508-510.

Jafari, J. (1990). Research and scholarship. The basis of tourism education. *The Journal of Tourism Studies, 1*(1), 33-41.

Jefferies, B. (1984). The sherpas of Sagarmatha: The effects of a national park on the local people. In J. McNeely & K. Miller (Eds.), *National parks, conservation, and development. The role of protected areas in sustaining society* (pp. 473-478). Washington: Smithsonias Institution Press.

King, B., Pizam, A., & Milman, A. (1993). Social impacts of tourism: Host perceptions. *Annals of Tourism Research, 20*(4), 650-665.

Lea, J. (1988). *Tourism and development in the Third World.* London: Routledge.

Lea, J. (1993). Tourism development ethics in the Third World. *Annals of Tourism Research, 20*(4), 701-715.

Linton, L. (1996). Bushmen in UN appeal for survival. *Weekend Australian,* 6-7 April, 10.

Loval, H., & Feuerstein, T. (1992). After the carnival: Tourism and community development. *Community Development Journal, 27*(4), 335-352.

Mathieson, A., & Wall, G. (1982). *Tourism: Economic, physical and social impacts.* London: Longman.

Maurer, M. (Ed.). (1992). *Tourismus und Dritte Welt. Ein kritisches Lehrbuch mit Denkanstößen.* Bern: Forschungsinstitut für Freizeit und Tourismus, Universität Bern.

McIntosh, R., Goeldner, C., & Ritchie, J. (1995). *Tourism. Principles, practices, philosophies.* New York: John Wiley & Sons.

Mishra, H. (1984). A delicate balance: Tigers, rhinoceros, tourists and park management vs. the needs of the local people in Royal Chitwan National Park, Nepal. In J. McNeely & K. Miller (Eds.), *National Parks, conservation, and development. The role of protected areas in sustaining society* (pp. 197-205). Washington: Smithsonias Institution Press.

Nelson, K. (1995). Invited commentary on observations on a mumps epidemic in a virgin' population. *American Journal of Epidemiology, 142*(3), 231-232.

Pearce, P. (1982). Tourists and their hosts: Some social and psychological effects of inter-cultural contact. In S. Bochner (Ed.), *Cultures in contact. Studies in cross-cultural interaction.* Oxford: Pergamon Press.

Pearce, P. (1994). Tourism-resident impacts: Examples, explanations and emerging solutions. In W. Theobald (Ed.), *Global tourism. The next decade.* Oxford: Butterworth Heinemann.

Pearce, P., & Moscardo, G. (1989). *STAR: The Structure of Tourist Activities for Regions.* Paper presented at the 20th Annual Conference 'Travel Research: Globalisation The Pacific Rim and Beyond'. The Travel and Tourism Research Association. Honolulu, Hawaii, 11-15 June.

Philip, R., Reinhard, K., & Lackman, D. (1959). Observations on a mumps epidemic in a "virgin" population. *American Journal of Hygiene, 69*, 91-111.

Pryor, P. (1980). An assessment of residents' attitudes and tourism employment in Rarotonga, Cook Islands. In D. Pearce (Ed.), *Tourism in the South Pacific. The contribution of research to development and planning.* Proceedings of UNESCO Tourism Workshop, Rarotonga, 10-13 June 1980 (pp. 69-86).

Rachowiecki, R. (1996). *Peru.* Hawthorn: Lonely Planet.

Rajotte, F. (1987). Safari and beach-resort tourism. In S. Britton &
W. Clarke (Eds.), *Ambiguous alternative. Tourism in small
developing countries* (pp. 78-90). Suva: University of the South
Pacific.

Rudkin, B., & Hall, C. (1996). Off the beaten track. The health
implications of special interest tourism activities in South-East
Asia and the South Pacific. In S. Clift & S. Page (Eds.), *Health
and the international tourist* (pp. 89-107). London: Routledge.

Ruiz-de-Chávez, M., Jiménez-Aguado, R., Márquez-Laposse, M., &
Alleyne, G. (1993). Salud y turismo [Health and tourism].
Salud Publica de Mexico, 36(1), 61-69.

Schlüter, R., & Var, T. (1988). Resident attitudes toward tourism in
Argentina. *Annals of Tourism Research, 15*(3), 442-445.

Seiler-Baldinger, A. (1988). Tourism in the Upper Amazon and its
effects in the indigenous population. *IWGIA Documents,
International Work Group for Indigenous Affairs, Denmark*, no.
61, 177-193.

Shlim, D. (1996). Trekking danger in the world's highest mountains
in Nepal. *Travel Medicine News Share*, 1. Quarter, 5.

Simmons, I. (1996). *Changing the face of the earth: Culture,
environment, history.* Oxford: Blackwell.

Sisson, J., Nichols, C., & Hopkins, R. (1983). Schistosomiasis among
river rafters - Ethiopia. *MMWR Morbidity Mortality Weekly
Report, 32*(44) 585-586.

Swinglehurst, E. (1994). Face to face: The socio-cultural impacts of
tourism. In W. Theobald (Ed.), *Global tourism. The next decade*
(pp. 92-102). Oxford: Butterworth Heinemann.

Toonen, J., Ramirez, G., Llanos, A., Campos, P., Samalvides, F.,
Taype, T., Carbone, F., Figueroa, R., & Hurtado, R. (1996). *A
health baseline study in the Camisea Area, Lower Urubamba,
Peru.* Royal Tropical Institute, Amsterdam; Ministry of Health,
Lima; Instituto Medicina Tropical, Universidad Peruana
Cayetano Heredia, Lima; Vicariato Apostolico de Puerto
Maldonado.

Wanjau, G. (1987). AIDS: A threat to tourism considered. *Contours,
3*(1), 4-6.

White, F. (1977). Imported diseases: An assessment of trends.
Canadian Medical Association Journal, 117(3), 241-245.

Wilson, M. (1994). Disease in evolution. In M. Wilson, R. Levins &
A. Spielman (Eds.), *Disease in evolution. Global changes and
emergence of infectious diseases.* Annuals of the N.Y. Academy
of Sciences. Vol. 740 (pp. 1-12). New York: The N.Y. Academy
of Sciences.

Wilson, M. (1995a). Travel and the emergence of infectious disease.
Emerging Infectious Diseases, 1(2), 39-46.

Wilson, M. (1995b). The power of plague. *Epidemiology, 6*(4), 458-
460.

Wolff, M.C., Pérez, L., Gibson, J., Lopez, L., Peniston, B., & Wolff,
M.M. (1985). Nutritional status of children in the health
district of Cusco, Peru. *American Journal of Clinical Nutrition,
42*(3), 531-541.

World Health Organization (1980). *Environmental sanitation in
European tourism areas.* EURO Reports and Studies 18.
Copenhagen: WHO.

World Health Organization (1996). Infectious diseases kill over 17
million people a year. *Malaria Weekly*, 3 June, 11-16.

World Tourism Organization (1996). *Travel and Tourism Barometer*,
2. Madrid: World Tourism Organization.

Yunis, E. (1996). Peru. *International Tourism Reports*, (2), 41-55.

[28]

The Socio-Economic Costs of Tourism to Developing Countries

Jafar Jafari[*]

Introduction

International tourism represents the largest single trade in the world (estimated receipts of $28 billion, excluding the receipts on international fares, in 1973). Due to its steady growth rate, economic magnitude, and assumed strategic dimensions of its operation, many developing countries believe that tourism is now instrumental in their plans for economic development. Several research organizations have suggested that the potential of tourism as such an instrument is real, and that its realization is within the reach of the developing countries.

Moreover, since the developing countries need to earn foreign currency for their economic development, and since tourism is reported as a relatively 'easy' export to develop for earning scarce foreign exchange, many countries are eager to enter the international tourism trade and expand their markets as fast as possible. Tourism, as a means of economic development and prosperity, has now captured the heart of almost every nation or region in the world. The development of the trade has become an international race among these countries. 'Time is running out. In many countries tourism has become a major industry to feed their national economics and therefore the longer the delay on our part, the greater the chance of our being left in the rear' (1, p. 17).

Therefore, many developing countries, without doing serious feasibility studies of their socio-economic [227] potential and readiness, have responded favorably to the development of the tourism trade. They have given their attention and applied their economic means to the development of tourism, usually at the expense of other economic activities. Furthermore, after these countries have developed their international tourism, and it has become an apparently prosperous economic activity, they have failed to do a cost–benefit analysis of the developed tourist trade.

The time has come to remedy this situation and to do so in a somewhat new and radical fashion with the developing countries in mind. It seems appropriate to extend tourism research from the traditional (promotional) one to an objective exploration and comprehensive research emphasizing a complete picture of the tourism phenomenon. Attention needs to be given to tourism's undesirable and hidden elements by assessing its overall impact on the socio-economic system of the developing countries and to alert them to its derivative ailing influence on their socio-economic development.

The objective of this paper is to point out and discuss some of the less known and relatively ignored negative influences of tourism on the socio-economic development of the developing countries – analyzing both hidden costs of production and broader 'costs' of entering the tourism market. The objective of this paper, by no means, is to work out a balance sheet of tourism's virtues and vices appropriately qualified and weighted. Under present circumstances this would be an overambitious project. Rather, the focus will be on costs – not benefits – of tourism. The benefits derived from tourism have been extensively studied and available at any resource center. It is hoped that this paper will stimulate more research in this neglected area, to either substantiate or refute the points raised below. In either case, the new knowledge gained will serve to better understanding of the tourism phenomenon and its ramifications.

Taking into account the severe limitation in availability of information on the subject, the hypothesis and findings presented below are limited in scope. Various aspects in this study have been seriously impaired [228] by the lack of appropriate tourism data and supporting examples. Although the social and economic costs of engaging in tourism take place simultaneously and interdependently, for the intended purpose of this paper, they are divided into two groups: the economic costs and the social costs. The extent of these costs are, however, in proportion to and in accordance with the size and degree of tourism's economic penetration. Moreover, the following discussion is in reference to the way tourism is really practiced; not to utopian ideal that is 'sold' to the developing countries (2).

Economic Costs of Tourism Development

The tourism industry has been operating and spreading at the national and international levels for many years but comprehensive research stressing both economic costs and benefits of tourism has not yet been undertaken. The past studies have elaborated the benefits derived from tourism while ignoring the elements in the phenomenon which may counteract the development processes in the developing countries. In other words, the economic benefits of tourism, more than any other aspect, has received a great deal of attention, both nationally and internationally. 'The economic role of tourism needs to be emphasized in order to make public authorities, international organizations and business circles tourist-conscious … it is the economic significance that accounts for the interest shown in tourism' (3, p. 4). The arguments for developing the tourism industry and its potentials are oversold on many occasions and thus the tourism picture is 'too brightly and extremely unrealistically painted' (4, pp. 132–134). This emphasis has never been shifted and now it sounds as if benefits are all a country can expect from investment in and development of their tourism markets. This situation has resulted from the absence of an established definition of the purpose of tourism and, frequently, from a lack of objectivity in research that is purely promotional.

In general, the development of the tourism industry is not, as a whole, an ideal or perfect economic investment [229] opportunity for the developing countries. Tourism, like other economic activities and trades, has both positive amd negative consequences. It is only in the light of comparing the positive and negative economic aspects of tourism investment with other economic opportunities that a developing country can evaluate accurately the prospects of developing and expanding the tourism industry.

Frequently, the decision of the developing countries to invest their scarce resources in the development of tourism is taken with no consideration of what the same resources could provide for the country, had they been invested in another industry. In other words, the countries have to investigate the relative economic advantages of investing in tourism when it means sacrificing the development of another industry (for example, agriculture, textiles, handicrafts, etc.). This kind of comparison is commonly known as assessing the 'opportunity costs' of any investment. Moreover, to ensure a steady economic development and prosperity, the developing countries should also consider choosing diverse and flexible economic instruments – not concentrating only on tourism's promises.

In addition to opportunity costs, the negative externalities have to be enumerated and evaluated. All pecuniary and psychic costs imposed on other consumers and producers in the economy by the establishment and expansion of tourism fall into this category of negative externalities.

A. *Offsets to the Foreign Exchange Earnings of Tourism*

Contrary to export of commodities, a country's tourism export takes place when foreign tourists *come* to that country (and their expenditure comprises an export to the host country) and tourism import to the same country takes place when the nationals *leave* the country to visit a foreign destination (and their expenditure comprises an import to their home country).

One of the main reasons for the developing countries' engaging in tourism export is the potential of [230] providing substantial amounts of foreign exchange. However, what is a frequently neglected cost is the amount of foreign exchange that has to be spent to keep the wheels of tourism running – the development, expansion, and promotion of the market. This expenditure by itself reduces the size of *net* foreign exchange earnings. Taking this into account, it is conceivable that an external balance sheet may generate a tourism deficit.

This situation is summarized by economists in terms of the 'conversion factor', the relationship between the total earnings from tourism export to the total expenditure on importing tourism inputs. Thus the industry is profitable, from the foreign exchange earning point of view, when the import content of the tourism market basket is low (5, pp. 85–86).

The importation of tourism inputs depends on the level of economic development of the host countries, the nature of their tourism markets and the demand for their particular tourism product. The volume of import is larger for the poorer countries, especially for those whose market is oriented towards western tourist demands – e.g. well-equipped and air-conditioned tourism facilities. These foreign inputs may include the importatation of various tourism materials, supplies, equipment needed in construction and organization of hotels and restaurants, additional transportation equipment, petroleum, food, beverages, and the like.

To this expenditure of foreign exchange, several other tourism 'leakages' have to be added to show a better picture of the foreign exchange balance sheet of tourism. Some of these are, depending on individual countries, the interest rate paid on the foreign capital borrowed for the purpose of investment in tourism, the profits repatriated by the foreign investors and/or salaries paid to and withdrawn by foreign tourisiers (the skilled and unskilled employees in any branch activities of the tourism industry) and the cost of running overseas and marketing expenses. These all impose further foreign exchange 'leakage' on the country. [231]

B. Productivity Index

The volume of tourism fluctuates with climatic conditions in the tourist destination areas and creates what is known as the tourist season. Thus, the operation and production of the industry as a whole or some of its sectors (noting that tourism generally requires heavy capital investment) has to be reduced during the off-season periods. Since the investment is not fully utilized, this would result in a low productivity index for the investment made in tourism and, therefore, an economic loss to the investors in particular, and to the economy in general, for not having invested their scarce resources in more steadily productive activities (6).

The international tourism trade is also sensitive and responsive to the economic obstacles and fluctuations, general world economy and economies of the tourism exporting and importing countries (4, pp. 143–145). This susceptibility makes the developing countries' choice of investment in tourism more questionable. Moreover, the spending on tourism has to compete with other forms of spendings within its share of the disposable income of potential tourists. 'The tourist industry can be regarded as being, to some extent, volatile, in the sense that short-term changes in economic conditions can have a disproportionate effect on holiday patterns' (7).

Therefore, when prices fluctuate, 'tourists' money is spent where it goes farthest' (8), which is just another way of saying that tourists are very sensitive to prices in various tourism markets. Thus, the impact of economic fluctuations, the devaluation of currency, and the restriction of tourism importing countries on the amount of money to be taken out by their nationals, will be felt in the tourism exporting countries. There are, however, several controversial statements on the impact of economic fluctuation on tourism movement and the extent of tourism susceptibility has not been researched and a definite answer has not been found (9).

The political relations between nations is another factor which influences international tourism movements and thus could endanger the operation of tourism markets. [232] The developing countries may experience a sudden boom in their tourism demand which may be due, for example, to friendly treaties made with other countries. However, the investments are productive as long as the tourists are coming and their coming from the newly friendly countries continues as long as the relations are stable. The political seasons have a broader and more severe impact when the nationals of the tourism importing countries share the political views of their governments. With respect to the present world situation, international relations cannot be predicted, and tourism investments, thus, have to operate in the face of an unstable market demand in the world.

Moreover, tourism is also susceptible to spread of disease (such as cholera), rumour, and internal (national) turmoil.

The tourism industry can be a target in the political arena of the developing countries, where political games or changes are the everyday happenings. A group of anti-government revolutionaries can weaken, paralyze, or overthrow the government of a touristic developing country by randomly murdering some tourists. In a short time, the communication media broadcast the news all over the world – the tourists stop coming, and so does the economy stop functioning. The government's foundation is thus shaken. The fact that many of the tourists are from the developed countries – agents of 'imperialis' – makes tourism an attractive target. The killing of the tourists has built-in messages and implications.

Furthermore, the main products of the tourism industry are services which are 'perishable' (39) and cannot be saved for future sale and consumption. When the tourism facilities are not in full operation, not only the products of the industry are wasted, but also the activities of many industries which supply the various needs of the tourism industry have to be reduced accordingly.

In short, these instabilities in tourism development and operation (climatic seasonality, economic fluctuations, political seasons, and the like) create unemployment, [233] underemployment, and social unrest. These tourism crises can have a disruptive or paralyzing effect on any developing country where the magnitude and dimensions of the industry are significant in the economy, and there are many developing countries in this catagory of tourism involvement: Spain, Mexico, Jamaica, Tunisia, Morocco, to name a few.

C. Tourism Demonstration Effect and Reduction in Savings

When the inhabitants of the developing countries come into contact with superior goods and/ or more extravagant spending patterns, they are subject to what economists call the 'demonstration effect'. This stimulates the observers to emulatation, to feel a certain tension and restlessness, and to increase their propensity to consume (1Q, p. 264). Thus, the money that could have been saved, had they not known about the opportunity, is spent instead on new and fashionable products which frequently are priced beyond their economic constraint.

> We all know that there is a great human urge to 'keep up with the Joneses', to imitate the standard of life we see in our prosperous neighbors. The underdeveloped peoples today constantly have thrown before them the comforts of life in the advanced US: They see our movies and magazines; they meet our tourists; their students bring back the glad tidings. Little wonder, then, that they find themselves spending a high percentage of their incomes in an attempt to enjoy some few of the things we enjoy in abundance. (11, p. 787)

The contacts of the inhabitants with both the arriving international tourists, who are mainly from the more advanced nations (12, p. 35), and the foreign or superior goods made available for tourism consumption would induce the impact of the demonstration effect. In other words, the 'knowledge of or contact with superior consumption patterns extends the imagination and creates new wants. The leading instance of this effect is at present the widespread imitation of American (and European) [234] consumption patterns. The American standard of living enjoys considerable prestige in the world. And it is always easier to adopt superior consumption habits than improved production methods' (10, p. 264).

Therefore, 'the demonstration effect leads directly to increased consumption, or attempts at increasing consumption, rather than investment' and makes an increase in saving 'peculiarly difficult as and when incomes and investment increases' (10, p. 267). The interdependence of consumers' preferences affects the choice between consumption and savings. The reason, for example, that 75 percent of American families save virtually nothing is not because they are too poor to save or because they have no desire to save. It is the demonstration effect – a highly communicable, infectious or contagious disease, best spread among the developing countries by the tourists. 'How can one convince officials [and average consumers in the developing countries] that air conditioning in their offices [and homes] is a waste of valuable foreign-exchange, when Hilton down the road has it in every room' (43)? Therefore, the domestic consumption of superior and foreign goods (a luxurious waste incompatible with economic development) starts to increase. To supply these products the limited sources of capital will be misused in order to meet or please 'the dissatisfaction and impatience which the demonstration effect tends to produce' (10, p. 266). In other words, the domestic (or foreign) profit-seeking investors would spot the market and supply the demanded superior or imported goods. Thus, these prematurely 'modernized' nations feel continually impelled to keep their money income and outlays above what is warranted by their own capacity to produce – and thereby living beyond their means (10, pp. 266–267). This is not too different from the 'conspicuous consumption' concept: the phenomenon of consumers buying goods to show their position or status rather than for the other usefulness of the goods.

Moreover, the direct or indirect contacts with the tourists and their world increases the inhabitants' interest in travelling to the advanced countries – another contagious disease now native to the developing countries. Consequently, their trips to these destinations, which are financed from their savings, cash, and [235] bank deposits increases the 'leakage' in their national economies (tourism import). In addition, upon their return they become westernized, leading to a cultural lag. In other words, the 'marginal man' (an individual caught in the conflict of cultures, an individual who lives in two worlds, yet actually belongs to none) (42) establishes himself in the developing countries. He and his fellow sufferers are dissatisfied with their country because of the inability of their country to respond to their wishes in a modern fashion by providing them with the products demanded and the social atmosphere desired. The marginal man has a strong tendency to strengthen his attachments with the world beyond, the attractive one, the materialistic one, the one which is developed, modernized and 'civilized', by consuming their goods and services and surrounding himself with their products.

The marginal men, housing themselves in the artificial (imported) atmosphere, adopting 'westernized' mannerism and way of life, start to criticize their society for its backwardness and hang-ups and the government for its negligence and incapability to handle and stimulate the economy. This naturally becomes a hot political issue which attracts multiplying listeners and sympathizers.

While some desire for progress is a necessary concomitant of modernization, the kind of acute political friction that is described here would lead to devisive tendencies in the society, difficult social problems, and very probably, political instabiltiy. Therefore, it seems apparent that tourism, among other things, is an agent which prematurely increases the expectation and consumption of superior and/or foreign goods in the host developing countries. The savings of the country which could have been used in basic economic activities needed for economic development are reduced and 'leak' out of the economy. Without the national savings, even an inflow of resources from outside 'cannot lead to any net increase in the rate of investment' (10, p. 271) and the economic development will be postponed.

In short, the 'vicious circle that tends to keep down volume of saving in low income countries is bad enough by [236] itself' (10, p. 266) and the tourism demonstration effect makes the situation worse, thus hindering economic development.

Taking into account the total costs to developing countries of engaging in international tourism, both direct expenditure on import of tourism supplies, good and services and the expenditure of their nationals at the expensive foreign destinations, on one hand, and costs of tourism demonstration effect, on the other hand, it may be that the developing countries are experiencing an overall net loss from tourism. In a static context this suggests a net gain for the *developed* countries from tourism. Such a gain may seem plausible given the parallel dominant position of the rich nations in international trade.

This hypothesis can be illustrated in the following manner: the developed countries have traditionally shown keen interest, leadership, and an open-minded attitude in engaging in and encouraging international tourism. However, the hidden catalyst for this attitude has been one of self-interest. They have long since noted the favorable role that tourism can play in distributing wealth and power among countries in their favor and thus stimulate the international trade by keeping every country in the game. They also have learned that the 'growth of industrialization in the primary producing countries and the colonial territories has severely reduced the demand for their staple industrial products' (5, p. 115).

In a report to the United States Department of Commerce, the Government has been advised to remove any restriction on their nationals travelling abroad. The restriction, the report adds, would not only reduce the size of the U.S. tourism export, but also 'leads to substantially reduced incomes in countries where the United States has long-term economic investment' (13, p. xiv). The Mexicans, for example, see U.S. citizens 'coming to Mexico by plane, staying in hotels, eating food and drinks, touring in a coach, buying souvenirs from a shop, all facilities owned ultimately by American companies. One billion dollars is a lot of money until [237] one starts doing the sums and working out how much sticks to the fingers of Pan Ams, Coca-Colas, Hertzs, Hiltons, and Sear Roebucks of this world' (43).

In another report to the U.S. Government, it has been recognized, 'again at a high level', that the developing countries 'cannot accelerate their development and cannot become better customers for U.S. goods unless they can increase their own export earnings sharply'. Tourism would, it continues, increase the United States 'export and investment' (14).

Therefore, the developed countries have noted that the distribution of chips is only on a temporary basis, and that these are returned to them eventually. As the developing countries' economics grow, enhanced by tourism export earnings, aids, and other external technical and non-technical aids, they will become better customers for the products from the developed countries.

The tourists of developed countries, traveling in the developing countries, tend to 'advertise' and 'market' their products and thus come to be a kind of promotional agent for their countries. They plant the seeds of consumption desire for high quality imported products in the developing countries and among their nationals. Performing this role, the tourism expenditure of the rich nations does not comprise a cost but a prepaid promotional investment that would expand the scope of their international market and demand for the products of their countries.

In short, the *developed* countries' overall earnings from international tourism can be divided into three kinds: the direct earnings from tourism export (foreigners traveling in their markets); the hidden economic earnings induced by the tourism demonstration effect in developing countries which increases the earnings from their foreign investments in those countries and multiplies their volume of exports to them; and they assess a social earning from having their nationals not only take their 'love message' to all corners of the world, but also having them discharge their 'frustrations' (relax, rest and learn) before returning home. The latter point has a built-in implication which may not be grasped at first and should be mentioned. Tourism is likely to renew the nationals' [238] enthusiasm for their own land – cultural shock. The returning tourist cannot help but be happy to be home again, back to the world of civilization, modernization, and prosperity. 'It is a nice place to visit', they would say, 'but I do not want to live there.'

The fundamental question raised here is, of course, whether the overall net balance of international tourism for the *developing* countries could indeed be negative. The points raised surely prevent a denial of the possibility. So far no attempt has been made to quantify such gains and losses, but the crucial point is that the possibility cannot be dismissed out of hand.

D. Additional Damaging Impacts

Tourism has other adverse effects on the economics and the resources of the tourism-exporting developing countries. According to a report prepared on the Hawaiian tourist industry, the tourist demand and expenditures has created inflation in the economy of the island (15). There are other studies or reports which refer to the inflationary effect of tourism. Spain, for example, has been enjoying a price level considerably below that of Europe's for many years. The difference, however, 'has been gradually eroded as the Spanish rate of inflation (6 per cent over the decade) is almost double that of Europe as a whole; while Spanish prices have doubled since 1961, European prices have risen by one-half' (16, p. 22).

It is conceiveable that this inflation is mainly due to Spain's engagement in tourism investment and the lack of planning by the government in response to rising demands. The role of tourism in the Spanish inflation becomes even more apparent when considering that tourism export comprises the predominant proportion of total exports of goods and services of the country (47.4 percent in 1965). Therefore, it can be assumed that the tourism-exporting developing countries will not be spared from inflation.

A description of a broad aspect of tourism spending and respending may suggest how tourism contributes to [239] inflation. If the pattern of international tourism expenditure in the developing countries is considered, it shows that the tourists usually tend to gladly pay for many overvalued goods and services whose prices are, nevertheless, lower than the prices they would have paid had they bought them in their own countries. In the Caribbean, it is noted, the North American ethnos from the great American middle-class 'who had come up through the immigrant ranks and labor, who had made it, partly at least, on the suppression of blacks in America, were willing to indulge in ostentatious spending – to pay whatever was asked to enjoy the experience of having an army of blacks respond to their whim' (17, p. 37). The tourisiers, being aware of this fact, would rather make their goods and services available to those who can best afford to pay the exorbitant prices – the tourists – thereby reducing the supply of the goods and services to the nationals. In addition, the tourism demonstration effect further contributes to this inflationary effect and stabilizes the new prices.

The role of tourism in inflation may be noticed in the tourism markets, especially where the tourist facilities are located and in those quarters or streets in a city that the tourists pass through. The prices in these places are much higher than in the rest of the destination or city. To get a better deal, the providers of the tourism products in the tourist quarters do business with the other areas of the city and thus gradually the prices, citywide and nationwide, are pulled up.

The tourisiers, considering that they are better paid and that some receive tips on top of their salaries, and taking into account that they are in direct contact with the tourists, are usually the forerunners of the tourism demonstration effect among the ordinary residents. Thus, they set off a secondary tourism demonstration effect among the inhabitants and the prices continue to rise.

Another cost to be named is the expenditure on repair and maintenance of the infrastructure. Beside the original investment required to expand the existing [240] infrastructure, it should be clear that a considerable cost would result if expenditures on repair and maintenance of the social overhead facilities, including spending on restoration of the background tourism elements (tourism attractions) as induced by depreciative behavior of tourists, is neglected or underestimated. The deteriorating effect of tourism (broadly referred to as tourism pollution) on the background tourism elements has to be included as another indirect cost. The damages caused on the background tourism elements is not easy or inexpensive to repair or prevent. The developing countries are usually in the habit of not seeing these 'little' and 'unimportant' things, and of letting the deterioration be carried on to a considerable length, which magnifies the indirect costs of the tourism industry. Moreover, this deterioration impact and pollution density can increase to the extent that it actually destroys 'the very essence of what man was looking for in his quest for recreative leisure' – the attractions (18). It is like the Brazilian Indian Tribes where half the population may be killed by diseases brought by those discovering them. 'The act of discovery destroys' (40, p. 195).

The Social 'Costs' of Tourism

The negative social impacts of tourism have been almost totally neglected. The negligence is partly due to the nature of the subject matter. The study of social change is a very sophisticated operation. The elements which cause social change are strangely interwoven, which makes the study of any individual element or phenomenon as a separate unit or system difficult. However, with the recent advances in social science research, especially the use of computers, such study does not seem impossible any more. In this part, below, only some of the more obvious negative social impacts (or social 'costs') of tourism are discussed.

It has always been argued that international tourism is a powerful means of bringing about international understanding and friendship. However, the present [241] practice of tourism does not warrant this utopian claim. Tourists 'learn to appreciate the customs and ways of life in foreign countries only if they are visiting as equals – if they spend and live as the natives; but only to a limited extent if they are observers from the balconies of first-class hotels, with human contacts reduced to brief discussion with waiters, taxidrivers, guides and chambermaids' (5, p. 246). On many occasions, tourists do not really care about the destinations and their socio-cultural attributes anyway. They just want to be away from home:

'Where were you last summer?'
'In Majorca'
'Where's that?'
'I don't know, I flew.' (40, p. 203)

Many tourism markets are now represented by 'tourist ghettos' where 'the visitor meets only other tourists, where there is no community participation, where there is no human relationship between tourist and the local inhabitants'. Tourism in these cases has become 'only a fleeting relationship between the buyer and the seller of a service' (19, p. 15).

A British humorist with more than a grain of truth writes

> In Positano you hear no Italian but only German, in some French parts you cannot get along unless you speak American; and the official language of the Costa Brava is English. I should not be surprised to see a notice in Blanes or Tossa-de-Mar stating: Aqui Se Habla Espanol – Spanish spoken here.
>
> What is the aim of all this traveling? Each nationality has its own different one. The Americans want to take photographs of themselves in: (a) Trafalgar Square with the pigeons, (b) in St. Mark's Square, Venice, with the pigeons, and (c) in front of the Arc de Triomphe, in Paris, without the pigeons. The idea is simply to collect documentary proof that they have been there ... Here in our cosmopolitan England, one is always exposed to the danger of meeting all sorts of [242] peculiar aliens. Not so on one's journey in Europe, if one manages things intelligently. I know many English people who travel in groups, stay in hotels where even the staff is English, eat roast beef and Yorkshire pudding on Sundays and Welsh rarebit and steak and kidney pudding on weekdays, all over Europe. The main aim of the Englishman abroad is to meet people; I mean, of course, nice English people from next door or from the next street. Normally one avoids one's neighbor ('It is best to keep yourself to yourself', 'We leave others alone and want to be left alone', etc., etc.) If you meet your next door neighbor in the High Street or at your front door you pretend not to see him or, at least, nod cooly; but if you meet him in Capri or Granada, you embrace him fondly and stand him a drink or two; and you may even discover that he is quite a nice chap after all and both of you might just as well have stayed at home in Chipping Norton. (20)

The largest newspaper in Spain recently warned Spaniards that their country was threatened by a 'new colonialism', the tourists who are making large parts of the Iberian peninsula into alien communities. 'There are places in some of our tourist centers from which the natives are practically banned', the Madrid newspaper complained. 'In other places, Spanish currency is not accepted' (21).

Clearly, tourism of this kind, the way it is often practiced today, cannot produce the desirable effect supposedly inherent in it: 'an instrument that will enable men to realize the broad ideal of visiting each other in order to know each other, of knowing each other in order to understand each other, of understanding each other in order to become friends, and of becoming friends in order to establish lasting and beautiful peace' (22). Tourism has not even succeeded in bringing people with some commonality together. There is some evidence that black Americans may be even less popular tourists than the whites in the Caribbeans – black Caribbeans destinations. This and other observations do not suggest that tourism is yet a major force for valid integration (43). [243]

In short, tourism may actually create undesirable international situations diametrically opposed to those it was hoped tourism would produce.

A. Social Relationships: Xenophobia

The engagement of a country in tourism export may create or intensify what is known as xenophobia – the undue fear of and contempt for strangers or foreigners. Xenophobia may be generated in many ways.

Local culture, tradition, heritage, and even religion and religious matters and materials are used as 'commodities', processed to produce marketable products for the consumption of the tourists. The local culture is 'deodorized' and 'local' themes and architectures are thought up by the international hotel chains in order to meet the requirements of the tourists' cultural rape (40, p. 194). The creation is then publicized all over the world: 'The Nairobi Hilton is the tallest building in the country', implying 'Lucky Kenya' (43). This 'deodorization' and degradation has a definite meaning: contaminating and polluting the socio-cultural elements and the social fabric of the developing countries – an irreversible pollution – for the enjoyment of the tourists and, of course, for the benefit of the developers.

These heritages which are highly respected by the inhabitants become a constituent part of a *business* named tourism and are 'consumed' by a bunch of *foreigners* or *strangers* called tourists. This would especially irritate the nationals when the tourists search for 'consumption' of the 'commodities' which are strange, unusual, or 'primitive', amusing themselves with the people's way of life. Moreover, the tourists intrude by looking in 'on the private life of another people, a life which is entirely their business, with an eye that, however, friendly it may be, is alien' (23) – to take notes, to take snapshots, and to document what is 'uncivilized'. They show no respect for the tradition and beliefs of the local people, as they visit their sacred temples, churches or mosques in an untraditional manner, entering the sacred places in bathing suit and a can of beer in [244] hand. The government promotes tourism by taking the tourists' side – for example, closing a temple or mosque for worship and treating the holy places as a 'commodity' and, thus, intensifying the hatred. In some other cases, the consumptive or appreciative use of the natural resources by avalanche of tourists during the hunting, fishing, boating, and the like seasons, and the government or tourism authorities doing all in their power to promote and facilitate serving the 'intruders', can also lead to resentment, dislike, or xenophobia.

Many other situations can lead to xenophobia. There is a wide difference in the income level of the tourists and the mass of local residents. The 'travel industry runs the risk of creating an enclave in which affluent foreigners are catered to and use resources which are not available to the mass of the domestic people. The luxury required by a travel industry for its clients may exacerbate any feelings of resentment toward foreigners which local people may already possess. This resentment is particularly probable in countries which have endured periods of colonial rule' (4, p. 158). The 'easy familiarity of many of the tourists makes the nationals wonder if they are not "truly as good or better than the tourists"' (24). Following is another instance which led to the hatred:

It is now the Government of India's declared policy not to extend prohibition to foreign visitors coming to the country. 'In some places, such as Delhi, drinking in public, e.g. hotels and restaurants is prohibited, but overseas visitors can purchase liquor from authorized wine dealers or order it in their hotel rooms. In almost all big cities in India such as Calcutta and Delhi, certain days in the week are observed as 'dry day' when sale of liquor is not permitted on these days. Further, in Delhi and other cities, an additional facility has been provided for foreign visitors. Certain select hotels have been authorized to provide a separate room for the exclusive use of foreign visitors where alcoholic drinks could be served to them and their guests. (25, p. 23) [245]

The idea of saving the best of everything for the tourists' consumption needs further elaboration. The governments of developing countries need the foreign exchange brought in by tourists. They make or enforce several discriminatory regulations in favor of tourists, better treatment of the tourists in public places, e.g. airports, higher standard of sanitation and health services in the tourism facilities, beautification of the places of interest to or on the way of tourists, to name a few. Similarly, the tourisiers in the hotels and restaurants may favor the foreign tourist more than domestic guests; and the farmers and grocers may save their best products for the tourist businesses (26).

The press in Madrid has started to carry stories about the difficulties facing ordinary Spaniards who want to have a holiday of their own. They will be forced to eat their lunch at the (to them) unearthly hour of 12:30 (instead of 2–3 p.m.). Waiters address them in German, English or Dutch. They moan at the way quick-buck showmen are degrading the bull fight by concentrating on all the superficial aspects which appeal to uninitiated foreigners' (43).

In a tourismagnetic area, where tourism is the main source of income to the community, all the economic and non-economic activities become gradually oriented toward the tourist demand which is centered in a short tourism season. The year becomes focused on making preparations for the reappearance of the tourists. Yet, their preparation may be mixed with anxiety and frustration, a period of worry and quiet conversation focused on the fear that the tourist may not return (a decline in tourism comes as abruptly as it rises). Though the residents find the economic gains of tourism advantageous, they regard tourism as unpleasant. The tourism period becomes a bag of mixed blessings: they are happy that the tourists are back again, and the end of the period 'is greeted by manifestation of relief that the tourists are gone' (27, p. 90). The same feeling is shared among other tourismagnetic areas: 'Like in all tourist areas, tourism is both a boon and bane – we welcome tourist income but often resent tourist presence and influence' (28, p. 54). [246]

On some occasions, the resentment may be shared by both the nationals and government: when the former is 'told that he is exchanging one role of servitude for another. He has given up the hoe to put on the busboy jacket' (24, p. 192). This new role is 'trumpeted to the whole world through brochures, advertisements and television commercials' in which they are 'identified in their own lands as waiters, cleaningmaids, bartenders and cab-drivers' (17, p. 37). The latter, government, also realizes that they are throwing everything they have got in a 'building effort simply to produce a crop of waiters, guides, and drink mixers for rich tourists' (29, p. 102). An analysis of jokes about the destinations where tourism has become the major source of economic activity suggest they may be right. A typical one will have a tourist driving through the countryside in the Caribbean, discovering a football match between the locals, which he disrupts by shouting 'waiter!'. All 22 players and the referee are supposed to come running (40, p. 202).

One can only be astonished at how little work has been done on the crucial interaction of tourists and their host societies. It will not be too difficult to find examples of bullish attacks of tourism in the fragile societies of the developing countries.

> For instance, we badly need some good observational studies of the Caribbean industry, where tourists have been important for a number of decades. Many people would argue that it was probably not accidental that the rich tourists haven, Bermuda, should recently have seen the murder of its governor. Incoming tourists, rich arrogant and white, would seem to have become widespread figures of resentment in societies which are racially complex, and where there is growing awareness of the meaninglessness of much political independence when important industries (like tourism) are basically in foreign hands. Local citizens find memories of the old slave and plantation economies

too close to the surface to [247] allow them to accept willingly new subservient roles of bootblacks, waiters and prostitutes. (41)

The tourists themselves suffer a similar reaction – becoming infected by the resentment of the nationals, as well as suffering independent irritations. This may foster disrespect and mistrust towards the host nations and the inhabitants they visit while traveling. For example, the impressions of being gouged and tricked financially induce a xenophobic state of mind in the returning travelers (4, p. 226).

The attitude of the nationals to tourism is also likely to be influenced by the maturity of the industry. There is a distinct 'sequence of phases which raises questions about the contradictions inherent in tourism as an industry and as a source of economic growth' (27, pp. 90–91). At first the benefits from the industry in terms of employment and income injections are the main features that the local residents notice, and, of course, appreciate. It is only later, when the industry is relatively mature, that certain basic questions begin to be asked, reflecting the dawning of disillusionment among the local residents: 'To what extent are tax-free tourist facilities and the tourists bring a drain on community services. ...? Who pays for the subsidy if there is one?' (17, pp. 37–38). Where do the benefits go? 'Does the vast bulk of tourist expenditure find itself outside the local economy? Who, in the final analysis, are the real beneficiaries of the tourism boom?' (27, pp. 90–91). Is it a 'genocide for the natives and untold wealth for the politicians and their rich friends?' (17, pp. 36–38). It may be that the country in general profits but not the inhabitants of the destination area.

> Whether this pattern is typical, whether tourism always builds upon local initiative only to drive the local people out after a certain point in economic development has been reached [after tourism boomed in the area, the local inhabitants were literally driven out]. If the answer to this question [248] is affirmative, perhaps tourism deserves to rank besides industrialization as a perverse and contradictory agent of change. (27, pp. 90–91)

Moreover, similar conclusions are derived when patterns of tourism development and expansion in the developing countries are discussed.

> At first, it was wonderful – the operator [of tourism facilities] was wanted – he made a fine profit during the first years of operation. Now the area has matured and with maturity has come a number of political and psychological problems that he did not bargain for. (24, p. 192)

Thus the attitude of the residents may change over time. An initially warm attitude may be followed up by subsequent disillusionment and a growing resentment. Tourism, especially the way it is practiced today, does not necessarily or invariably enhance the 'promised' integration, international understanding and world citizenship.

B. Social Change: Lack of Integration

The development of a society, which includes the development of many components of the social fabric, culture, tradition, ideology, economy, etc., is a slow process, like that of economic development. Therefore, an injection of foreign ideology and way of life in these 'fragile' societies not only can create an unexpected and premature situation, but also can interrupt a slow process of social development which is unique to each country.

The demonstration effect, noted above, influences the patterns of life, behavior, heritage and ideology of the inhabitants of the host developing countries. The way of life of the tourists is 'superior' to what the residents of developing countries can afford to experience. Therefore, their presence as temporary residents in the developing countries is a *live* presentation of 'modernization' [249] and stimulates new sets of values or ideologies for the inhabitants of the developing nations.

As a result, the tourism demonstration effect can contribute to the birth of an unbalanced and premature imitation of civilization (the marginal man and his world) and modernization in the developing countries and add to the social dualism which plagues them. Many of the host developing countries are still too 'fragile', traditional and 'primitive' to be able to easily comprehend or experience a foreign social injection.

Moreover, the way tourists behave, act, or demonstrate themselves as a group is not anywhere similar or representative of the way of life back home. They do not necessarily adhere to their philosophy of life and mannerism. They lack any seriousness. Their spending pattern is different when they are home as residents. When traveling, they act and spend money like a tourist or vacationeer. The residents of the host developing countries take this manifestation to represent the way of life, norm, modernization and civilization in the developed countries – a way of life that if practiced even in a developed country can paralyze the entire system.

Tourism can destroy many important cultural assets, including many on which its own viability is founded. The tourismagnetic area, for the use of tourists lose the 'value characteristic' of the people and become 'cold complexes with that indefinite international character that represents nothing' (19, p. 15) – a plastic hospitality is born. This situation is aggravated by 'displays of alien affluence in the midst of local poverty'. The cultural heritage becomes a 'commodity', a business, and gradually loses both its character and its inherent value. Everything starts to seem primitive in comparison to what the advanced nations are experiencing, and thus has to be changed or forgotten.

Paradoxically this kind of 'imperialism' at the cultural level is seldom recognized, let alone resisted, by the developing nations. They tend to accept foreign values without even realizing it. This was the theme of one of President Sukarno's exhortations to the young. [250]

> And you, young men and young women, you who are certainly against economic imperialism and oppose economic imperialism, you who oppose political imperialism – why is it that amongst you many do not oppose cultural imperialism ...? (31)

Tourism is often credited for its role in enhancing the process of acculturation. Acculturation is defined as the process by which members of one society divest themselves of some of their own cultural elements and take on elements from a foreign culture. However, the important thing that has to be pointed out is that the acculturation between the tourists from the developed countries and localities in the developing countries is not on the give-and-take basis. It is only the inhabitants of the developing countries who have shown a great receptiveness to the acculturation: accepting the values of the Western World while discarding their own – a one way acculturation, to the inevitable disadvantage of the inhabitants.

Specific situations of interference with the maturing process of socio-economic development shed further light on the subject. It has to be remembered, however, that the social impact of tourism and the demonstration effect are interwoven and influence the situation interdependently.

Tourism affects various aspects of life and social organization. The degree of social differentiation increases with economic growth and non-occupational class identification begins to develop (27, p. 85). When the cultural heritage becomes a tourist 'commodity', some of the inhabitants start to identify themselves with 'the new consumer way of life, whereas the rest (of the inhabitants) appear to be receding into an ever more private cultural world, leaving only the outward forms of their life for touristic consumption' (27, p. 87). 'Alienation' has been used by several social scientists to refer to the consequences of similar commercialization. Its 'cultural shocking' potential for the traditional inhabitants of the developing countries inevitably accentuate the social dualism and distinctions. [251]

Since the tourisiers are usually those who have most of the contacts with the tourists, they may be the forerunners in accepting or imitating foreign values. This is particularly facilitated because the tourisiers may be better paid than workers in many other occupations: they 'exhibit feelings of superiority towards their less fortunate fellow citizens' and this creates a situation of 'financial dislocations and resentment'. A tourist gives, e.g., a $1.00 tip to a bell-boy who carries his bags to his room while the bell-boy's father, who may be working on a farm, might earn a total of $1.00 or $1.50 per day (32, p. 40).

This situation is bound to aggravate social difficulties in the host countries. A psychologist reported that tourism has increased the incidence of ulcers, and shifted the divorce rate upwards in the island of Hawaii. The divorce rate on the island of Hawaii, where tourism is the number one trade and comprises the major source of out of state earnings also increased 180 percent between 1963 and 1970 compared with a 52 percent increase for the entire State of Hawaii. Farmers' wives in Hawaii make twice as much as their husbands. 'The husbands frequently become suspicious of their wives' improved grooming and dress and accuse them of interest in other men. Presumably such accusations and stresses in the new way of life cause ulcers in the women' (33, p. 145).

In summary, 'the harmless individual tourist is transformed by commercial logic into the "mass tourist" , whose impact is often compared with the cultural devastation left in the wake of the great barbarian migrations of Gauls and Goths, Huns and Mongols' (41). The tourism trade can bring many things that the developing countries have not bargained for: cultural disintegration, cultural lag, and social distance, topping their other problems.

Balance Sheet of Tourism

A. *Socio-Economic Development in Isolation*

To reduce the influence of the demonstration effect and to minimize the costs of tourism for socio-economic [252] development, the contacts between the developed and developing countries may have to be narrowed and tourist arrivals in these countries prohibited. The radical isolation of two important countries from the rest of the world played an important part in their rapid socio-economic development, Japan and the USSR.

It is well known that Japan, in the early courses of her industrialization, imitated the Western World in everything except consumption patterns. She had kept herself in a state of isolation for centuries, and it was comparatively easy for her to maintain this isolation in regard to consumption patterns. There is no doubt that this was part of the secret of her success in domestic capital formation.

The other instance of radical isolation is Soviet Russia's iron curtain (which of course is not merely a result of the present tension but was well established before World War II). While it certainly has other reasons for its existence, I am inclined to attach significance also to its economic function; that is, to the possible 'materialist interpretation' of the iron curtain. Anyway, it illustrates the possibility that isolation may help to solve the economic problem of capital formation, in a world of great discrepancies in national living standards, by severing contact and communication among nations. Without communication, the discrepancies, however great, may become of little or no consequence and the 'demonstration effect' may lose at least some of its potency. (10, p. 269)

Russia now appreciates the economic gains derived from foreign tourists. However, efforts are made to minimize any possible tourism demonstration effect: the choices of international travelers are limited, with most choices being made by the Russian authorities, tourism facilities for lavish life and entertainment [253] are very limited or non-existent, the movements of tourists are strictly controlled, tipping is forbidden, etc., which all in all suggest methods of and need for minimizing the tourism demonstration effect.

This situation in Russia has remained the same even after President Nixon's trip to Moscow. The political 'thaw' in effect between Washington and Moscow 'does not mean that Russia has become a wide-open place where Western tourists are free to "play it by ear" – to strike out on their own and go wherever they want and mingle freely with whomever they please. Nothing could be further from the truth. If anything, the Kremlin has become more suspicious and wary of the interchange of ideas and opinions between Westerners and Russians' (34, p. 59). The sheer volume of tourism has exposed most Eastern European countries to what the Communist Party call 'a Western policy of peaceful interference that puts emphasis on undermining socialism from within' (35).

A third example of radical isolation further illustrates the hypothesis: cutting off tourist contacts with a rapidly growing country, China, to reduce the impact of agents enhancing the demonstration effect.

The question may be asked if it is entirely because of the undesirable impacts of the demonstration effect that Russia, China, and a few other nations have reduced or eliminated all sort of contacts with the outside world, especially with the developed countries. But it can certainly be one important reason.

B.   Uncertainty

In the preceding pages some – by no means all – of the situations and influences of tourism affecting the socio-economic development of the developing countries have been sketched. Tourism seems as beneficial in some respects, as many tourism studies show, as its socio-economic costs are damaging in others. Can these conditions and negative impacts be overcome?

There has been a 'halo bias' surrounding the study of tourism, concentrating on one aspect of tourism [254] (socio-economic benefits) to the exclusion of others (socio-economic costs). Research on the negative aspects of tourism has been excluded in various tourism works, apparently assuming that 'these social [and economic] costs are probably unduly exaggerated' (36) or optimistically indicating that 'with adequate foresight and planning ... the worst of such ills can be avoided and the benefits of tourism further increased' (30). Several studies have deliberately or otherwise concealed or discarded any discussion of the undesirable and uneconomical impacts of tourism, while the entire works are devoted to the economic 'benefits', resulting in an overpainted picture of the tourism industry and encouraging the developing countries to blindly invest or overinvest their scarce resources in tourism, without sufficiently examining other channels of economic activity and economic development (37).

It is difficult to understand how tourism, 'a surprisingly large-scale phenomenon, representing one of the largest peacetime movements of people [215 million *international* tourists, excluding domestic tourism, in 1973], goods, services, and money [$28 billion receipts from *international* tourism, 1973] in human history', has escaped the serious attention of the social and economic researchers (27, p. 81). Tourism, unlike other economic activities and social phenomena, has not been analytically researched and profoundly evaluated. The positive and negative aspects of tourism need neither blind acceptance nor blind resistance. It is also difficult to comprehend why the ever increasing crop of economists specializing in the field of economic development have largely neglected studying the possible benefits of tourism to the developing countries and, at the same time, neglecting the possible threat of tourism to the economic development strategies of those developing countries *already* engaged or drowned in the tourism trade. A possible answer to this question, it is suggested, is that the 'economists, historically oriented to manufacturing activities, try to ignore it; [and] sociologists are still not quite sure that anything to do with "fun" is quite worthy of serious analysis' (40, p. 181).

Therefore, tourism seems to be an innocent trade for the developing countries, but its impact is diverse, [255] far-reaching and long-term (43). The way tourism is understood today, it seems to be so complex that it is hard to ask the right question, much less to come up with the right answer. One of the disturbing dimensions the tourism industry faces today, as seems to be the case in some other fields, is its dearth of knowledge. It is not what is known about tourism, but rather what is not known about it that must be of primary concern. There is a definite need to improve not only the tourism 'know-how', but also the tourism 'know-why'. The latter, which has been unquestionably neglected, disputes any unscientific and unreasonable assumption or hypothesis that is made in the foundation and implications of the tourism trade (38).

Here, it is not meant to suggest that, due to the very many elements or uncertainty in the nature and implications of tourism, the developing countries have to remove tourism from the face of their nations. For one thing, as it is evident from this paper, a comprehensive balance sheet of tourism has not yet been researched and developed. The costs and benefits of tourism to the developing countries may be an open question. Moreover, it may be argued that the result of the tourism balance sheet is different from country to country.

There seems to be no going back for the developing countries which are already deeply involved in tourism and have invested their scarce resources in this industry. To some of the developing countries, it may make sense at this point of involvement in the tourism industry to conjecturally accept the benefits assumed to derive from their investment in tourism. However, attempts have to be made to sensitize the developing countries to the tourism problems and suggest and encourage them to adopt protective measures. Particular attention must be given to the problem of living with the negative impacts of tourism and energies must be directed toward reducing the adverse effects of tourism on their economic development.

To conclude, it is extremely important that this rapidly expanding industry in the developing countries be purged of its negative feedbacks. Tourism's value in enhancing their economic development will continue to [256] depend upon whether or not it can be 'tamed' with sufficient intelligence, or contain the damaging influences, to enhance the positive effects and to design and formulate strategies for shaping, accelerating or decelerating developmental phases of all the components of the tourism industry. This is the problem.

To achieve this, tourism has to receive more attention from the social scientists and researchers from various disciplines – encouraging a cross fertilization of minds. It has to become, due to its nature, an inter-disciplinary field of study: a pathological approach addressing itself to various problems of tourism as a whole, many of which are yet to be identified.

Notes

1. *Indian Hotelier and Caterer*, 'Editorial: Realities Must Be Faced', October 1971.
2. This paper is a revised chapter of the author's M.S. Thesis, *Role of Tourism on Socio-economic Transformation of Developing Countries*, submitted to the faculty of the Graduate School of Cornell University, 1973, 262 pages. Other chapters are on 'Emergence of International Tourism', 'Economic Magnitude of International Tourism', 'The Components and Nature of the Tourism Phenomenon', 'Impact of Tourism on Socio-economic Development', 'Planning Tourism Development and Growth', and 'Summary and Conclusions'. The chapter on the 'Impact of Tourism on Socio-economic Development' discusses some of the possible benefits that can be derived from tourism. The author wishes to thank Prof. Willard Bailey (Sociology, University of Wisconsin-Stout) and Prof. James Eggert (Economics, University of Wisconsin-Stout) for reading this article and making valuable suggestions. [257]
3. K. Krapf, *Tourism as a Factor in Economic Development: Role and Importance of International Tourism*, United Nations Conference on International Travel and Tourism, Item 10 (a) of the Provisional Agenda, UNECOSOC, Conf. 47/15, July 12, 1963.
4. Peter H. Gray, *International Travel – International Trade*, Heath Lexington Books, Lexington, Mass., 1970.
5. L.J. Lickorish and A.G. Kershaw, *The Travel Trade*, Practical Press Limited, London, 1958.
6. Several attempts to mitigate seasonal problems by price variation and by staggering school and industrial holidays has met only with some success.
7. John Hamilton, Robert Cleverden, and Quentin Clough, *International Tourism, Quarterly Economic Review*, Special, No. 7, The Economist Intelligence Unit, London, 1970, p. 25.
8. Andreas S. Gerakis, 'Economic Man: The Tourist', *Finance and Development*, Vol III, No. 1, March 1968, pp. 41–48.
9. However, according to the *U.S. News & World Report*, the devaluation of the American dollar in 1972 which cheapened it by 12 percent, on the average, in relation to European currencies, 'is not expected to deter U.S. tourists from going overseas'. A spot check of advance bookings on transatlantic airlines, it continues, even 'indicate an increase of 8 to 10 percent over last year's tourist travel' (*U.S. News & World Report*, 'Leisure Boom: Biggest Ever and Still Growing', April 17, 1972, p. 45). *The St. Paul Sunday Pioneer Press* also reports that 'neither tight money at home nor threat of war nor cholera outbreak could keep the American tourist in the USA in the summer of 1970' (Leisure section, September 27, 1970, p. 9). But this categorical statement is not made in direct relation to the tourism industry in the developing countries.

10. Rangnar Nurkse, 'Some International Aspects of the Problem of Economic Development', *The Economics of Underdevelopment*, edited by Agarvala and Singh, Oxford University Press, fourth print, 1970.

11. Paul A. Samuelson, *Economics, An Introductory Analysis*, McGraw-Hill Book Co., New York, 1961 ed.

12. David H. Davis, 'Potentials of Tourism in Developing Countries', *Finance and Development*, Vol. V, No. 4, December 1968, pp. 34–39.

13. *The Future of Tourism in the Pacific and Far East* (written by Harry G. Clement), Checchi and Company, [258] under contract with the U.S. Department of Commerce and co-sponsored by the Pacific Area Travel Association, Government Printing Office, Washington, D.C., 1961.

14. Action Committee of the National Export Expansion Council (U.S.A.), *Trade and Investment in Developing Countries*, February 15, 1967, revised April 3, 1967.

15. *The Visitor Industry and Hawaii's Economy: A Cost–Benefit Analysis*, prepared for State of Hawaii Department of Planning and Economic Development, Mathematica, Princeton, N.J., February 20, 1970.

16. 'National Report No. 2: Spain', *International Tourism Quarterly*, No. 2, 1971.

17. Norwell Harrigan, Organization of American States, *First Special Inter-American Travel Congress*, Seminar 'To Secure Lasting Tourism', OEA/Ser. K/III. 2, Turismo 5, 22 June 1972.

18. Horace Sutton, 'The Erosion of Eden: Is Tourism Creating Its Own Pollution?' *Saturday Review*, June 6, 1970, pp. 58–61 and 71–72.

19. Ricardo Anzola-Betancourt, 'An Architectural Approach to Tourism in the Caribbean', *First Special Inter-American Travel Congress*, op. cit., pp. 13–23.

20. George Mikes, *How to Be Inimitable, Coming of Age in England*, André Deutsch Limited, 1960, pp. 25–27.

21. William S. Beller, 'Tourism in an Ecological Light', *First Special Inter-American Travel Congress*, op. cit., p. 107.

22. *Focus on Mexico*, Vol. VI, No. 10, October 1970, p. 2.

23. V.S. Pritchett, *The Offensive Traveller*, Alfred A. Knopf, Inc., N.Y., 1964, p. 4.

24. Eric Green, cited by Donald E. Lunberg, *The Tourist Business*, Institutions/Volume Feeding Management Magazine, Chicago, 1972, p. 192.

25. Hardy's Encyclopedia, *Hotels des India & Nepal, A Traveller's Guide*, New Delhi, Hardy & Ally (India), 1966, p. 23.

26. The governments encouraging foreign tourism investment by discriminatory laws and regulations, very common in the developing countries (*Economic Review*, op. cit., 1970 ed., p. 44) creates a kind of xenophobia among local tourism investors, who feel more entitled to make money on their tourist facilities than the foreigners, in particular. [259]

27. David J. Greenwood, 'Tourism as an Agent of Change: a Spanish Basque Case', *Ethnology*, Vol. XI, No. 1, January 1972, pp. 80–91.

28. Neville Linton, 'Caribbean Tourism – the Need for a Model', *First Special Inter-American Travel Congress*, op. cit., pp. 47–57.

29. *Proceedings of First Annual Conference*, The Travel Research Assoc., August 16–19, 1970.

30. World Bank, *Annual Report*, 1970, 1971 Reports, p. 28. As an example, an International Bank for Reconstruction and Development (World Bank) mission to Morocco resulted in the publication of a book entitled the *Economic Development of Morocco* (John Hopkins Press, Baltimore, 1966). As it turned out, the report concentrated on economic feasibility of different sectors of Moroccan economy. The development and expansion of tourism, among other industries, was favorably recommended. However, the task of the mission was not only 'to assess the development potential of the economy', but also to take 'into account factors which impose a limitation on growth, the resources base, and the economic and social infrastructure' (p. vii). The socio-economic cost of tourism was totally left out. The Bank has done similar studies on some other developing countries' economic development, has recommended the development of tourism in these countries and has provided loans for the development of their tourism industry.

31. Cited in *Economic Development, the Cultural Context*, Thomas R. DeGregori and Oriol Pi-Sunyer, John Wiley & Sons, Inc. N.Y., 1969, p. 7.

32. Robert McIntosh, *Tourism: Principles, Practices, Philosophies*, GRID, Inc., Columbus, Ohio, 1972.
33. Frances Cottington, cited by Lundberg, op. cit.
34. 'If You're Going Abroad', *US News & World Report*, February 12, 1973.
35. William D. Patterson and Somerset R. Waters, *The Big Picture*, 1972–1973, Annual Report, ASTA Travel News, New York, p. 49.
36. *Tourism in New Zealand*, Publication No. 4 of the Central Research Unit of the N.Z. Institute of Economic Research (Inc.), 1969, p. 50.
37. As an example, Mr. Peter Gray in his book entitled *International Travel – International Trade*, op. cit., pinpoints a deliberate or unqualified work done on the [260] economic impact of tourism on the Pacific and Far East Area (The Checchi Report, *The Future of Tourism in Pacific and Far East*, op. cit), produced for the United States Department of Commerce. As Mr. Gray notes, the purpose of the undertaking was, and he quotes the report, 'Promoted by a desire to assist the countries in the Pacific and Far East region ... in building up the basis for a prosperous tourist business as an element in their economic development'. The work, he explains, makes a 'fundamental error' in calculating the multiplier effect which is a basis, directly or indirectly, for all the recommendations given in the report. He warns the developing countries against the exaggerated findings of the Checchi Report, in his words, that 'Any work using the values of the multipliers generated in the Checchi Report as the basis for an estimate of the value of travel exports to a nation will obtain grossly exaggerated measures of the benefits to be derived from an expansion of tourist capacity'. He also notes that the estimates are 'widely used' in many works done on tourism (Gray, op. cit., pp. 148–151).
38. Jafar Jafari, 'The Components and Nature of Tourism – the Tourism Market Basket of Goods and Services' , *Annals of Tourism Research*, Vol. I, No. 3, January 1974, p. 87.
39. The products of the tourism industry are made up of many different kinds of goods and services, provided for the tourists' consumption: provision of transport services, accommodation, entertainment, food service, and the like. Though the diversity of the gross tourism products falls within a vast scope of economic activities, they all share one characteristic in common: none of the services can be stored. Most of the products in normal sense, such as a radio or refrigerator, can be produced and stored, awaiting future sale. If they are not sold today, the opportunity may come tomorrow. However, this is not true with the tourism products (mainly services). There is a sense of immediacy about the tourism products. Unlike the goods in normal sense they have to be 'consumed' when they are 'produced'. The act of consumption and production is often linked. The space and facilities provided in a guestroom, for instance, has to be rented (sold) every night. If the room goes unrented for one night, the opportunity is gone and the 'time related' product is wasted. Thus, other products of the industry are 'perishable' in this sense. Jafar Jafari, 'The Components [261] and Nature of Tourism – the Tourism Market Basket of Goods and Services', *Annals of Tourism Research*, Vol. I, No. 3, January 1974, pp. 83–85.
40. Louis Turner, 'Tourism and Social Sciences – from Blackpool to Benidorm and Bali' , *Annals of Tourism Research*, Vol. I, No. 6, pp. 180–206.
41. Louis Turner and John Ash, 'The Golden Hordes' , *New Society* (UK), April 19, 1973.
42. James W. Vander Zanden, *American Minority Relations*, The Ronald Press Company, N.Y., 1963, p. 280.
43. Louis Turner, *Multinational Companies and the Developing World* (forthcoming), Allen Lane/ Penguin, London; Hill and Wang, New York, 1974. [262]

*Jafar Jafari, Dept. of Habitational Resources-Tourism, University of Wisconsin-Stout.

Please note folios in square brackets throughout text represent original page numbers.

PERGAMON

Tourism Management 21 (2000) 613–633

**TOURISM
MANAGEMENT**

www.elsevier.com/locate/tourman

Limits to community participation in the tourism development process in developing countries

Cevat Tosun*

School of Tourism and Hotel Management, Bilkert University, 06533 Bilkert, Ankara, Turkey

Received 18 February 1999; accepted 20 August 1999

Abstract

This study deals with a normative concept of participatory development approach, which originates in the developed world. In particular, it analyses and explains the limitations to the participatory tourism development approach in the context of developing countries. It was found that there are operational, structural and cultural limits to community participation in the TDP in many developing countries although they do not equally exist in every tourist destination. Moreover, while these limits tend to exhibit higher intensity and greater persistence in the developing world than in the developed world, they appear to be a reflection of prevailing socio-political, economic and cultural structure in many developing countries. On the other hand, it was also found that although these limitations may vary over time according to types, scale and levels of tourism development, the market served, and cultural attributes of local communities, forms and scale of tourism developed are beyond the control of local communities. It concludes that formulating and implementing the participatory tourism development approach requires a total change in socio-political, legal, administrative and economic structure of many developing countries, for which hard political choices and logical decisions based on cumbersome social, economic and environmental trade-offs are sine qua non alongside deliberate help, collaboration and co-operation of major international donor agencies, NGOs, international tour operators and multinational companies. © 2000 Elsevier Science Ltd. All rights reserved.

Keywords: Community participation; Tourism development; Limits; Developing countries

1. Introduction

Community participation in the tourism development process (TDP) has emerged and been refined in the context of developed countries. It has also been popularised by advocates writing on developed countries. These scholars have made substantial contributions to studies of the participatory tourism development approach by advocating it under the prevailing conditions in the developed world (Blank, 1989; Gunn, 1988; Haywood, 1988; Keogh, 1990; Murphy, 1985; Reed, 1997; Simmons, 1994). However, practicality of participatory tourism development approach in developing countries seems not to be considered in detail. On the other hand, it is claimed that '[d]eveloping countries may avoid many of the problems that have plagued past tourism ... by involving diverse social groups from the popular sectors of local communities in decision making' (Brohman, 1996,

p. 568) without examining socio-cultural, economic and political conditions of tourist destinations although it is these conditions that determine whether the community participation in the TDP will work or not. As Todaro (1994, pp. 36–37) asserts in the context of developing countries:

> ... it is often not the correctness of economic policies alone that determines the outcome of national approaches to critical development problems. The political structure and the vested interests and allegiances of ruling elites ... will typically determine what strategies are possible and where the main roadblocks to effective economic and social change may lie. ...

Moreover, he contends that the pattern of power and wealth distribution among various groups in most developing countries is itself the reflection of their economic, social and political histories and it is likely to vary from one nation to the next. Nonetheless, developing nations are ruled by a small group of well-organised powerful elites to a larger extent than developed countries are.

* Fax: 00-90-312-266-4607.
E-mail address cevattosun@hotmail.com (C. Tosun).

0261-5177/00/$ - see front matter © 2000 Elsevier Science Ltd. All rights reserved.
PII: S 0 2 6 1 - 5 1 7 7 (0 0) 0 0 0 0 9 - 1

614   C. Tosun / Tourism Management 21 (2000) 613–633

This study suggests that although community participation in the TDP is highly desirable, there seems to be formidable operational, structural and cultural limitations to this tourism development approach in many developing countries. As Din (1997, p. 78) has recognised, the notion of community participation in the TDP 'may not be readily applicable to Third World destinations where public scrutiny is lacking owing to a universal ignorance of the planning procedure, especially with regards to the role of the review process'. It should be noted that community involvement in the TDP can be 'viewed from at least two perspectives: in the decision-making process and in the benefits of tourism development' (Timothy, 1999, p. 372). It is the main aim of this article to examine these limitations to public participation in the decision-making process of tourism development in developing countries though public participation in the benefits of tourism is not totally ignored. Moreover, although desirability and practicality of the participatory tourism development approach appear to be interrelated, this study will primarily focus on barriers to practicality of applying the community participation. Following a review of definitions of community participation the article progresses to consider these limitations to community participation in the decision-making process of tourism development.

It is argued that 'Third World' tourism has been set up by agreements between foreign image-makers/investors and local elites. There has been no participation by, and consultation of, the people of the host country in shaping the phenomenon' (Linton, 1987, p. 96). In this regard, the reader is reminded here that there is insufficient written material on particularly limitations to the participatory tourism development approach in developing nations. This is not surprising since 'there are few examples from the Old South of where this (community participation in the TDP) has successfully occurred ...' (Harrison, 1994, p. 717). As Timothy (1999, p. 383) argues in the context of Indonesia, 'The education of local residents and the involvement of locals in the economic benefits of tourism are happening in theory ... and to a lesser extent in practice. However, residents and other stakeholders participation in decision-making has not been recognised as important in planning documents, nor has it been addressed in practice ..., except in a few isolated cases'. Although McIntyre, Hetherington and Inskeep (1993) have given the cases of Zambia and Mexico as examples of community involvement in tourism development, these cases also represent manipulative participation, passive participation or pseudo participation. That is to say, there seems to be no evidence which shows that participatory tourism development practices have gone beyond community consultation or manipulative participation in the developing world. After examining several participatory tourism development practices in developing nations, Mowforth and Munt (1998, p. 240) have

stated that 'the push for local participation comes from a position of power, the first world: It is easier to promote the principles of local participation on paper, from a distance, than to practice them'. Several cases regarding participatory tourism development practices in developing countries, which they have analysed are examples of, in their words, 'manipulative participation or passive participation according to Pretty's typology' (Mowforth & Munt, 1998, p. 242). The World Tourism Organisation (WTO) (1994) has given 25 case studies of tourism planning in the developing world. Only one of them, the Sri Lanka tourism plan, considered community consultation (indirect participation or degree of tokenism) via tourism committees composed of local interest groups and local agents of central government. However, it has not been operationalised and remained as a proposal.

Nevertheless, it may be said that it is impossible to discuss every relevant issue regarding participatory tourism development approach based upon merely the literature on developing countries. Consequently, some of the perceived problems of the participatory tourism development approach in the developing world are examined and argued based upon the related arguments for the developed world by carefully taking into account socio-political, economic and cultural structure of developing countries. This should not be surprising since some of the limitations to the participatory development approach do apply internationally (especially when one considers peripheral regional development in developed countries). However, effects of these problems on operation of the participatory development approach vary from developed nations to developing nations. It is likely that these limitations make community participation in the TDP less probable in developing countries that do not have the basis of the pre-industrial phase experienced last century in Western Europe and North America, where now better economic, legislative and political structure are in operation, than in developing countries.

2. Community participation in the development process

It is argued that 'the notion of community participation is deeply ideological in that it reflects beliefs derived from social and political theories about how societies should be organised' (Midgley, 1986, p. 4) and how development should take place. However, to Sewell and Coppock (1977), its emergence as a new catchword is rooted in the failures of these theories. They have argued that involvement of the public in a development process has two main considerations. The first is philosophical and the second is pragmatic. The former is related to political theories of democracy that people have the right to be informed and consulted and convey their views on matters which affect them to decision-makers. In modern

C. Tosun / Tourism Management 21 (2000) 613–633 615

democratic government, elected representatives have, however, failed to represent grassroots and at least significant segments of communities have feelings of alienation towards governmental decision-making. Pragmatic considerations are chiefly related to the failure of plans and the decision-making process which could not determine public preferences correctly. Therefore, planners and politicians had subsequently difficulties in obtaining public support; either at the ballot box or after implementation.

Moreover, proponents of community participation have contended that community participation as an element of development has been considered, promoted and woven into the development process in different ways since the 1950s and early 1960s under different terms and names (de Kadt, 1982; Gow & Vansant, 1983). That is to say; the concept of community participation has been a component of the political dynamics of the post-industrial era, which mirrored in part a longer term movement toward a new public administration. In other words, the interest of the citizen in participating in government decision-making and the demand for direct participation in the development process have emerged due to the needs of government itself, as a response to community action (Smith, 1981), and as a result of the absence of the affluence and security of the period following World War II.

The overall result is that since the 1970s in many ways, community participation has become an umbrella term for a supposedly new genre of development intervention. Not surprisingly, to propose a development strategy that is not participatory is now almost reactionary. More importantly, major aspects of development intervention, research, planning, implementation and control, have been reoriented so as to make them more participatory. 'Where the targets of a plan are not fully realised, this is often attributed as much to inadequate public involvement as to a lack of labour or capital' (Department of Economic and Social Affairs, 1970, p. 31).

In the course of researching community participation in the development process, it seems quite natural to ask for a definition of the concept of community participation. As de Vaus (1996, p. 48) argues, 'concepts do not have real or set meanings can lead to conceptual anarchy, a problem with no entirely satisfactory solution. The most practical action is to clarify how a concept has been defined and to keep this definition clearly in mind when drawing conclusions and comparing the findings with those of other researchers'. Following this recommendation it seems to be useful to examine definitions of community participation.

2.1. Definitions of community participation in the development process

Community participation implies a desire to avoid using traditional bureaucratic paternalism, according to which agencies believe that they are close to the ideas of members of the community, and they know best what is good for people in the community (Skelcher, 1993). By way of definition, community participation refers to a form of voluntary action in which individuals confront opportunities and responsibilities of citizenship. The opportunities for such participation include joining in the process of self-governance, responding to authoritative decisions that impact on one's life, and working co-operatively with others on issues of mutual concern (Til, 1984). Hence, to some extent, it is an educational and empowering process in which people, in partnership with those able to assist them, identify problems and needs and increasingly assume responsibility themselves to plan, manage, control and assess the collective actions that are proved necessary (Askew, 1989). 'In this sense community participation, as an ideal type, involves a shift of power, from those who have had major decision-making roles to those who traditionally have not had such a role' (Willis, 1995, p. 212). That is to say, community participation is a tool to readjust the balance of power and reassert local community views against those of the developers or the local authority, or to redefine professionalism, which may determine the conditions of successful participation and prevent manipulation of a community in the participation process.

In other words, community participation is to design 'development in such a way that intended beneficiaries are encouraged to take matters into their own hands, to participate in their own development through mobilising their own resources, defining their own needs, and making their own decisions about how to meet them' (Stone, 1989, p. 207). This may imply that community participation as a development strategy is based on community resources, needs and decisions. Hence, community is the main actor in the development process. On the other hand, the concept of community participation is seen as a powerful tool to educate the community in rights, laws and political good sense (Low, 1991 quoting Tocqueville, n.d.). Moreover, it is stated that 'since the leadership of society would inevitably be in the hands of an elite, it was necessary to ensure that its members were educated in the broadest sense and deeply valued individual liberty and democracy. The individual would, therefore, learn the politics of democracy by participating in local institutions and associations' (Low, 1991, p. 86, quoting Mill, 1973). 'We do not learn to read or write, to ride or swim, by merely being told how to do it but by doing it, so it is only by practicing popular government on a limited scale, that people will ever learn how to exercise it on a large scale' (Low, 1991, p. 86, quoting Mill, 1973, p. 186). On the basis of Low's argument, it may be proposed that active and direct participation of local people in local affairs is an indispensable tool for public education. Without using this instrument, democracy and individual liberty may not be sustainable.

The conceptual argument regarding community participation seems to have focused on political dimension and ignored the economic and financial considerations which are often the primary drivers at the local level. This may be owing to the fact that it is the political structure or system that determines pre-conditions for participation in the development process. For example, ' … high levels of literacy and mass communications have not produced democracy in Singapore, Malaysia, or the many oil-rich states of the Gulf' (Diamond, Linz & Lipzet, 1995, p. 23). However, the role of an advanced level of economic development, which produced greater economic security and more wide-spread education, is important to reduce socioeconomic inequality and mitigate feelings of relative deprivation and injustice in the lower class. Thus, it facilitates and encourages participation of local community in their affairs. 'Economic development also tends to alter the relationship between state and society, to increase the number and variety of independent organisations that check the state and broaden political participation, and to reduce corruption, nepotism, and state control over jobs and opportunities to accumulate wealth' (Lipset, 1981, p. 51). Therefore, this study will also examine economic factors such as lack of financial and human resources that discourage community participation in the TDP.

As the above definitional arguments suggest that the concept of community participation in the development process is multi-dimensional and includes representation from many disciplines. Hence, it may not be possible to encapsulate the concept within one single and definite term. It has been implied that it may take very different forms, ranging between citizen power to manipulation or it can vary from minimal forms involving information exchange (surveys, handouts, questionnaires, and the like) to full forms of community control (Arnstein, 1971; Willis, 1995). Indeed, it is a tricky concept, not easy either to define or to accomplish and, like democracy, it creates socially desirable expectations which cannot be met easily in the real world. It may be easy for policy makers to see it as an evolving concept and popular to accept in theory, but troublesome to execute in practice and putting the idea into operation is not precisely comprehended, particularly in developing countries.

2.2. Community participation in the tourism development process

The infrastructures of community participation are the legacies of western ideology; the influence of community development programs in developing countries; western social work and community radicalism; and the United Nations' (UN) participatory development programs, which, indeed, provided a source of inclination for community participation as a modern concept in housing, transportation, education, health, etc. Naturally, accumulation of participatory experiences in social, political and economic life have become the modern sources of inclination for community participation in the tourism development process. However, students of tourism seem not to have benefited from these participatory experiences in those sectors of economy as there are very few references in the tourism literature to these sectoral studies. They have not yet explained what community participation in the TDP or community-based tourism development approach means.

It has been stated that the people who enjoy or suffer the main impacts of tourism are those who live in the communities in tourist destination areas; thus communities at the tourist destination must participate in planning decisions regarding tourism development (Lea, 1988; Murphy, 1985). It is also argued that 'communities are the destination of most travelers … it is in communities that tourism happens. Because of this, tourism industry development and management must be brought effectively to bear in communities' (Blank, 1989, p. 4). It is noted that the outcome of numerous tourism impact and resident attitude studies in host communities 'has been a call for increased public participation and, in particular, a more community-oriented approach to tourism planning' (Keogh, 1990, p. 450). In this context, it is debated that a destination community is an important component of the tourism product and 'the industry uses the community as a resource, sell it as a product, and in the process affects the lives of everyone' (Murphy, 1985, p. 165). Hence, community participation in the TDP is needed for 'a reasonable degree of consensus' that is essential for long-term success of the tourist destination (Ritchie, 1988, p. 199); 'strong community support' that is important for successful tourism development (Getz, 1983, p. 87); 'desired guest–host relationships' (Haywood, 1988, p. 117); and for increasing the quality of tourism's benefits to national development (Lea, 1988).

In parallel to these statements, Inskeep (1991) pointed out that host communities must have a voice in shaping their future community as their right and has called for the maximum involvement of the local community to maximise socio-economic benefits of tourism for the community. George Washington University International Institute of Tourism Studies (1991, p. 9) has stated that, as its assembly report of 'Policy Issues for the 1990s, '[r]esident responsive tourism is the watchword for tomorrow: community demands for active participation in the setting of the tourism agenda and its priorities for tourism development and management cannot be ignored'. Murphy (1985) has argued that community-oriented tourism development requires to find a way of creating more workable partnerships between the tourism industry and local communities and develop facilities both for host and guest. Mathieson and Wall (1982, p. 181) have

C. Tosun / Tourism Management 21 (2000) 613–633 617

noted that 'the public now demand that their concerns be incorporated into the decisions-making process ... there has been little public involvement in tourism planning. This explains the neglect of this topic in the literature on tourism'.

Prentice (1993, p. 218) has stated that 'community involvement in tourism development have become an ideology of tourism planning'. It is argued that 'a community-based approach to tourism development is a prerequisite to sustainability' (Woodley, 1993, p. 137). Willams and Gill (1994, p. 184) have claimed that 'community involvement in establishing desirable conditions is perhaps the single most important element of growth management' in tourist destinations. Ryan and Montgomery (1994, p. 369) have noted that ' ... communities need only to be educated about the benefits of tourism, and that their involvement in good visitor management techniques will actually solve problems'.

Simmons (1994, p. 99) has argued that involvement of a community in the tourism development process is vital 'if any region wishes to deliver tourism experiences which ensure both visitor satisfaction and ongoing benefits for the residents of destination areas'. Hall (1994) has claimed that ' ... satisfying local needs it may also be possible to satisfy the needs of the tourist', which is one of the key components of the notion of community participation. Brohman (1996) has advocated community participation in the tourism development process as a tool to solve major problems of tourism in developing nations. He has contended that community participation in the TDP will achieve more equal distribution of the benefits, discourage undemocratic decision-making and will meet the needs of local community in better way.

The above theoretical arguments for participatory tourism development approach seem to be good news. If applied, most of the problems of tourism development may be avoided. Perhaps, thus it is difficult to challenge them. However, these arguments have left enough room to pose some interesting and, perhaps, difficult questions about the approach's validity and practicality. For example, who is the local community or who should participate and who should not participate in the TDP? How will the participatory tourism development approach be initiated? Who will initiate it? Why will they do so? How will participation by local people in the TDP ensure a better distribution of benefits of tourism? Can local people protect or defend their interests? Will any form of community participation contribute to tourists' satisfaction? What should be the form and mode of participation? Is every form of participation effective under every circumstance? Who will decide on the form and level of participation? Is the participatory tourism development approach feasible in terms of politics and finance? How will the level of development in a community, and scale and type of tourism development affect community participation in the TDP?

The intention of the author in posing the above questions is to imply that there are limits to community participation in the decision-making process of tourism development in the context of developing countries, rather than providing immediate answers to them. However, it is not claimed that these limits do not exist at any level or to any extent in the developed world. Some of these limits to participatory tourism development approach may be observed especially in rural regions of, or peripheral regional economic development, in advanced economies as well.

As argued, it is very difficult to define community participation, but it appears to be essential to clarify it for the purpose of this article since mere reference to conceptual arguments in the previous section of this study does not indicate what exactly it implies or means in the context of this article. Hence, it should be noted that community participation here refers to Arnstein's (1971, pp. 70–71) degrees of citizen power (partnership, delegated power and citizen control) and Pretty's (1995) interactive participation and self-mobilisation. That is to say, this study will focus on community participation in the decision-making process though public involvement in the benefits of tourism development is not ignored.

Before progressing further, it seems to be useful to consider the meaning and scope of the term 'developing countries' as this article will examine limits to community participation in the TDP in the context of developing countries

2.3. Definition of the terms of developing countries

There is an ongoing debate on meaning and usefulness of the terms 'the Third World', 'First World' and 'Second World' among some of the world system theorists (Harrison, 1988). Moreover, the terms 'the Third World', 'underdeveloped countries', 'developing countries', 'poor countries', 'the South' and 'less developed countries' (LDC's) are mostly used interchangeably. But it is not an easy task to define precisely what is meant by these terms (McQeen, 1977). Although 'they are all attempts at grouping a large number of countries into one category, often knowing that the reality is quite different. In essence, they all include the same countries with a few deviations depending on who is conducting the classification' (Oppermann & Chon, 1997, p. 4).

On the other hand, it is argued that the changes in Eastern Europe diminished those features that differentiated it from 'the Third World'. 'The emphasis on civil society, new economic and political institutions, even on national identities, is reminiscent of the 'new nations' of the 1950s and 1960s and, arguably, the nations of Eastern Europe are only now emerging from a period of colonialism' (Harrison, 1992, p. 1). That is to say, 'Times have changed. With the Second World no longer an actor on the geopolitical stage, it is now simply illogical to posit

618   *C. Tosun / Tourism Management 21 (2000) 613–633*

the existence of a Third World' (Harrison, 1994, p. 707). In fact, 'as well as in terminology, the disappearance of the Second World entails the disappearance of the Third World' (Harrison, 1992, p. 1).

Consequently, we are increasingly dealing with 'a heterogeneous yet hierarchical and inegalitarian structure of capitalist states, each with increasingly polarized internal class divisions' (Cliffe & Seldon, 1991, p. 9). 'When discussing issues of development, it is no longer possible to regard Albania, Romania and Bulgaria, for example, as obviously different from Egypt, Zambia or Pakistan. The whiff of convergence is in the air' (Harrison, 1992, p. 1; 1994). Now, it has become more obvious that developing countries are so heterogeneous, economically, culturally and in virtually every other way, that they exhibit no single defining feature. Although Buchanan (1971, p. 20 quoting New Left Review, 1963, p. 4) describes 'the Third World is a universe of radical scarcity ... , [where] 'the inadequacy of means of livelihood is the first and distinguishing truth of this area', it seems to be very difficult to give a comprehensive definition of the terms of the Third World/developing countries to everybody's satisfaction.

Although it may not be acceptable to everybody, in this article reference will be made to developing countries/developing nations, rather than to the 'Third World', which is no longer deemed appropriate, for reason already given, for the purpose of this article. However, mere reference to developing nations does not indicate which countries should be placed in that category. In the context of this article, at the risk of overgeneralisation, developing countries collectively refers to Asian, Latin American and the former second world countries to distinguish them from the economically advanced 'capitalist democratic' countries. In other words, developing nations/countries here refer to countries not regarded by the World Bank as High Income Economies, as well as about a dozen oil-rich states and a few island economies with relatively high GNP per capita (see Harrison, 1992, p. 2). Clearly, in this heterogeneous collection of nation states some countries are closer to 'development' than others. Thus, depending upon level of development in each country the limits to participatory tourism development approach exhibit different intensity and persistence in each developing country.

2.4. Limitations to community participation in the TDP

As analysis of studies on participatory tourism development approaches suggests that its proponents have popularised it in the context of developed countries and made considerable contribution to theoretical foundation of this proactive tourism development approach. However, limitations to participatory tourism development approach have hardly been debated by scholars of tourism. The literature of developmental studies in general has revealed that there seems to be an agreement amongst the scholars that in spite of an insistence on community participation in the development process, it has been observed that the performance of participatory development strategy is not encouraging and authentic participation (Arnstein's citizen power or Petty's self mobilization and interactive participation) seldom occurs. Though an agreement on the limited success of community participation has emerged, there seems to be no consensus on what are the reasons for it.

By keeping in mind the structure of international tourism, limitations to community participation in the TDP in developing countries may be analysed under three main headings; limitations at the operational level; structural limitations; and cultural limitations. It should be noted that such areas of limitations are not mutually exclusive. Although there is no special reason beyond this classification, it is supposed that it will facilitate understanding of limits to community participation in the TDP, at least at a theoretical level.

2.5. Limitations at the operational level

Implementation of participatory development approaches in developing countries is likely to meet obstacles usually associated with the operational procedures of the task. Some of these obstacles include the centralisation of public administration of tourism development, lack of co-ordination between involved parties and lack of information made available to the local people of the tourist destination.

- *Centralization of public administration of Tourism*: Formulation and implementation of any kind of community participation approach requires decentralisation of the political, administrative and financial powers of central government to local government at least to some extent. However, as UN (1981, p. 15) noted, in many developing countries planning is a highly centralised activity. The planning organisation has been established at national level and is under the direct management of national chief political executive.

  The effect of this is to restrict the influence of community-level groups on the planning process, and implementing plans. Under these circumstances, centralisation has stifled popular participation in planning. It has increased the vertical distance between planners and the broad mass of the population.

It may be added that the UN's comment is not for a specific sector of an economy. It seems to be valid for tourism as well; since governments in developing countries have seen tourism as a relatively easy, effective and cheap instrument to achieve export-led industrialisation

C. Tosun / Tourism Management 21 (2000) 613–633 619

as a core principle of free market economy recommended by international donor agencies (Tosun, 1998c). That is why, developing countries recognised that tourism is too important to leave to the market, and governmental posts at the cabinet level were created to develop, monitor and administer tourism policy (Poirier, 1997). That is to say, planning and management of tourism has been centralised in a way that can contribute to achieving pre-determined governments' objectives. Hence, it is not easy to persuade governments in developing countries to delegate its various powers to regional or local authorities. For example, since the late 1950s and early 1960s decentralization has been advocated and tried in practice, but the overall results were not always satisfactory (Tosun & Jenkins, 1996). Moreover, many developing countries such as India, Mexico, Thailand and Turkey have a strong central government that has practiced administrative tutelage on local government. This tutelage practice of the central government has precluded an emergence of responsive, effective and autonomous institutions at the local level (see Das Gupta, 1995; Jones, 1990; Koker, 1995). Ultimately, this has ushered in non-participation or pseudo-participation of local people in their own affairs including tourism development. This implies that the public administration system in many developing countries seems to be too bureaucratic to respond to public needs effectively and efficiently.

On the other hand, it is argued that 'there is a lack of political will to implement participation because of the implications for the distribution of power and resources' (Desai, 1995, p. 40). By winning elections and being in power for certain time intervals, politicians and their appointees seem to have claimed that they are entitled to take all necessary decisions in the name of those who elected them without further participation requirements during their terms of office. Moreover, by reference to totalitarian regimes in the developing world, it has been argued that the state is not only disinterested in development, but also "[r]igorously suppress the effort of progressive elements to bring about meaningful changes' (Midgley, 1987, p. 11). That is to say, in developing countries politicians seem to be far from the realisation of development ideals, particularly the participatory development strategy (Benicourt, 1982). Ultimately, this may create lack of co-ordination and co-operation amongst agencies, which can hinder community participation in the tourism development process. Moreover, politicians and their appointees have seen grassroots movements as nothing more than residents' egotism, narrow personal and local interests.

The above argument suggests that unwillingness of politicians and their appointees at central level, and highly centralised public administration system appear to hinder emergence and operationalisation of participatory tourism development approach in many developing countries. As developing world politicians are motivated/forced to satisfy international agencies and organised business class, it seems to be difficult to gain support of the politicians for participatory tourism development approach which may pose questions about current style and scale of tourism development in the developing countries unless a growth of patronal NIMBY (not in my backyard) takes place.

● *Lack of co-ordination*: 'The lack of co-ordination and cohesion within the highly fragmented tourism industry is a well-known problem' to tourism professionals (Jamal & Getz, 1995, p. 186). It is obvious that ' ... No one business or government establishment can operate in isolation' (Gunn, 1988, p. 272). Thus, development of co-ordination mechanisms among the formal bodies, between the public and the private sector, and among private enterprises is essential for the highly fragmented tourism industry (Inskeep, 1991).

However, 'too often in developing countries the planning process is very fragmented one authority being concerned with the impetus for development, while others are expected to manage the impact of the development' (Jenkins, 1982, p. 241). In many tourist destinations in developing countries such as Turkey (Tosun, 1998c), Thailand (Elliott, 1983), Kenya (Dieke, 1991) and Bali (Jenkins, 1982), this may be a missing ingredient of the tourism development process. In this regard, it is argued that tourism projects did not benefit from a full co-ordination between local and tourism planners (Jenkins, 1982) owing to the fact that there is a traditional powerful bureaucracy which dominates legislative and operational processes. Any approaches which are in conflict with this unnecessary traditional bureaucracy are not acceptable to the powerful bureaucrats. Particularly, this traditional bureaucracy is an obstacle to establishing co-ordination and co-operation between and among the various bodies. Moreover, there is also 'bureaucratic jealousys' among official authorities. For example, the Ministry of Tourism may not tolerate any bureaucratic department trespassing on what it regards as its territory. Ultimately, this may create a lack of co-ordination amongst agencies (Tosun, 1998a). Clearly, under such bureaucratic structure operating a co-ordinated strategy may demand ministers to reduce their range of responsibilities, and thus their role to offer patronage to their clients; both of which are not acceptable for them. Moreover, 'Third World politicians can also be very opportunist, offering sops where political gain is likely to accrue, and yielding where political pressure is greatest. Such serving incrementalism can be very damaging to co-ordinated policy-making' (Jones, 1990, p. 264). It is to be regretted, but, unfortunately, lack of co-ordination appears to be a usual situation in the TDP in many developing countries, if not all.

620　　　　　　　　　　　　　　*C. Tosun / Tourism Management 21 (2000) 613–633*

Tourism is an amalgam of many different components that constitute a whole product. What happens in other sectors has important implications for the tourism product. Therefore, lack of co-ordination and co-operation between departments of government can be very damaging to not only the quality of the tourism product, but also to the effectiveness of participatory tourism development approach. On the other hand, lack of definition in roles of agencies, overlap in responsibilities of government departments and little accountability between them make the most needed co-ordination for participatory tourism development approach less possible. In brief, a participatory tourism development strategy will invite more actors to play roles in the tourism development process, and thus increase the need for interaction amongst agencies. Any lack of co-ordination may frustrate potential opportunities for the community to involve itself in tourism development.

- *Lack of Information*: In most developing countries, tourism data are insufficient, even that collected may not have been disseminated to the citizens in ways that are comprehensible to them. Most residents are not well-informed regarding tourism development; therefore, low public involvement should be expected. Thus, the general public is in need of information which may allow it to participate in the TDP in a more informed manner. For example, Tosun and Jenkins (1996) argued in relation to Turkey that The Ministry of Tourism and the bodies responsible for authorisation of tourism investment and incentives are not accessible for the majority of indigenous people in local tourist destinations. They are accessible for the rich and educated elites. In this sense, there is a big communication gap between communities and decision-makers. This lack of communication does not only increase the knowledge gap between local communities and decision-makers but also accelerates isolation of the local community from the tourism development process. Consequently, the knowledge gaps between centralised authorities and local communities make it difficult for a host community to participate in the tourism development process.

On the other hand, decision-makers may not have up-dated information about socio-economic structures of local communities in tourist destinations due to the fact that gathering such data requires continuous research that is not possible in the absence of financial resources and expertise. The implication of the above argument may be that greater awareness and interest among members of local communities could be achieved if meaningful and comprehensible information contained in reports and plans is disseminated. Thus, for the purpose of achieving better tourism development through community participation, information about the structure of local communities and data regarding local, national and international tourism should be collected in a comprehensible manner and disseminated to local communities and institutions.

2.6. Structural limitations to community participation in the TDP

Emergence and implementation of a participatory tourism development approach seem to be problematic due to the prevailing structural constraints in many developing countries. These are usually associated with institutional, power structures, legislative, and economic systems. Some of these structural limitations will be examined below.

- *Attitudes of professionals*: The role of technocrats (professionals) in shaping tourism policies in developing countries cannot be ignored. Some professionals claim that planning and development efforts are 'value-free' or politically neutral exercises. Hence, the participation of a community in the development process can only serve to politicise it and deviate it from its professional base. Although some professionals are sensitive to the need for some forms of participation, they may consider a 'present-oriented' mentality makes it impossible for them to projects beyond current needs and problems (UN, 1981).

The main tension between technocracy and participation stems from the confidence of the technocrat that his/her professional qualifications find the 'One Right Answer' to development problems (Wolfe, 1972). The technical service officers, who formulated draft plans, are usually confident of the quality of their work. That is to say, the possibility of other and better alternatives being suggested by amateurs is seen as unrealistic. It is understandable and reasonable for professional groups not to allow lay people to become involved in the decisions-making process. It may also cost the professional groups time and money.

It is not easy to persuade professionals, most of who do not have close contact with local people and lack a tourism background, to accept participatory tourism development as a viable approach in many developing countries. In this context, emergence and acceptance of participatory tourism development may depend largely on the existence of powerful non-governmental organisations (NGOs) aiming at defending participatory development as a democratic right of host communities in tourist destinations. Establishment and efficiency of NGOs may require support by central government who is not always willing to share its powers with such organizations (see Mathur, 1995). The question of how to persuade tourism professionals to accept participatory tourism development remains an unknown under the current complex socio-economic and political structures in

C. Tosun / Tourism Management 21 (2000) 613–633 621

developing countries. But, it seems obvious that without a positive attitude by professionals towards participatory tourism development, the emergence of such an approach may not be possible, unless specifically written into the project terms of references.

- *Lack of expertise*: It is contended that although community participation seems to be highly desirable, few developing countries have sufficient experience in this area. Lack of qualified personal and the working attitudes of professionals who have been trained in traditional planning techniques which do not involve community participation, and who have little idea of how to incorporate it in their planning (Desai, 1995). This is particularly true for the tourism industry in developing countries since tourism has recently been recognised as a professional area in these developing countries. That is to say, owing to its relatively short history in the economies of these countries, as Inskeep (1988) has stated, the services of tourism planners for projects in both the public and private sectors are currently in demand in developing countries that still lack expertise in tourism planning even though they may have qualified urban and regional planners.

Developed countries have responded to the need for tourism planning by adopting suitable educational and research programs on tourism planning. Many developing countries have already failed to do so. Adopting appropriate educational and research programs developed in and for developed countries seems to be difficult due to the fact that they require expertise and financial resources. For example, it is reported that 'planning lags behind change, as it often does in Turkey, and change brings the destruction of much of the country's rich historical heritage' (The Economist, 1996, p. 3). In the absence of expertise, tourism development has been seen as tourism growth and tourism development plans refer to improving infrastructures, increasing bed capacity and other components of tourist superstructure. In the broader context of sectoral development planning, these activities in relation to tourism growth is not effective planning and do not reflect concerns of contemporary approaches to tourism development. As a result, myopic tourism development approaches have emerged in many developing countries.

However, although some developing countries have achieved accumulation of qualified human capital in tourism via sending students to developed countries (e.g. Turkey, India and Malaysia), and sharing the experiences of international donor agencies and international consultants (e.g. Turkey, Sri-Lanka, Egypt, India, Indonesia, etc.), personal experience of the author suggests that these countries appear not to have benefited from these human resources educated abroad because of widespread favoritism, nepotism and personality clashes.

Moreover, in the absence of equal opportunity for personal promotion, these Western-educated experts tend to seek job opportunities in Western countries or in private sector.

On the other hand, Tosun and Jenkins (1998) argued that in most developing countries tourism development planning often proceeds in an ad hoc way. Substantive tourism planning is usually donor-assistance driven. The planning team is based on foreign expertise (being paid for by foreign donors) with some counterpart training. The steering committee to oversee the planning exercise, is usually more concerned with outputs rather than objectives. In these circumstances, notions of sustainability and community participation are icons to current development jargon rather than realistic implementable parameters.

The above argument reveals that the lack of expertise in field of tourism is a significant barrier to practicing a participatory tourism development approach in the developing world. Community participation as a multi-dimensional phenomenon does not only require tourism planners, but also sociologists, economists, social-psychologists and political scientists with some prior knowledge of tourism. In the absence of these experts, it appears to be difficult to formulate and implement participatory tourism development approach. Moreover, it suggests that the prevailing human resources management system does not encourage the limited numbers of Western-educated experts to use their expertise for developing tourism in a better way via the participatory development approach.

- *Elite domination*: In some developing countries there is very little democratic experience or semi-democratic experience or no prospect of an opening to freedom. In some other developing nations although there is a formal structure of constitutional, multiparty democracy, these democratic institutions and regulations are not shared with the majority. That is to say, in these countries democracy is limited to business elites and state elites (e.g. Thailand, Brazil, South Korea, Chile, etc.) (Diamond et al., 1995). 'Even a democratic state in the developing world is almost indistinguishable in crucial aspects from its authoritarian counterpart' (Sangmpam, 1992, p. 402). Elites have a fear that the propertyless and uneducated masses could use their numerical strength to take care of their interests through political power or coercion. Therefore, they do not want to share fruits of democracy with the hitherto excluded who constitute the majority in many developing countries.

It is this elitist approach to the democratisation process and development that have ushered in clientelism in many developing countries 'where the ruling party's access to immense state resources, and the clientelistic tradition that gave the political class wide scope in distributing state resources ... ' (Diamond et al., 1995, p. 32). That is to say, there is a haphazard resources allocation system by the state authorities and preferential access to state decision-making bodies that is extremely important for being successful in business in the developing world. Of course, 'political patronage is not unknown in the North (consider the notorious 'pork barrel' system in the United States) but it is widespread throughout the developing world, where it takes the form of 'clientelism' (John, 1990, p. 269). It is not surprising that patron–client relations have also affected tourism development in many developing nations. For example, there were rumours of corruption and gossip about the partnership between the bourgeoisie, the upper echelons of the party, and the favoured businessmen regarding too generous incentives given to the tourism industry in many developing countries (Clancy, 1999; Tosun, 1999). For instance, in Turkey one of the biggest daily newspapers reported that misuse of incentives given to the tourism industry appeared in different forms. In this regard, it was claimed that 'there were cases where incentives were given on the bases of inner party courtesy or intimacy of friendship and relationship rather than entrepreneur capability' (Tosun, 1998b, p. 602, quoting Kusluvan, 1994).

Given the elitist approach to democratic rule and regulation in the developing world, it tends to become a rule rather than an exception to favour the interest of the dominant class at the expense of the vast majority who has been historically excluded from political and modern economic activities. As a result, felt needs of local indigenous communities in some tourist destinations of the developing world have been ignored so as to serve dominant business interests. For example, in the case of Varna, Bulgaria in the early 1990s while residents of the town suffered cuts in electricity supply, the hotels were unaffected (Harrison, 1994).

With special reference to Santa Cruz, Mexico, it is argued that local residents anticipated many problems owing to irresponsible tourism development. For instance, shops could not maintain adequate stocks to meet needs of the increased number of people. Public transportation capacity was not sufficient; buses had irregular schedules and taxis were usually full. Residents complained that a visit to the public health clinic took an entire day, as there were insufficient facilities and staff for the demand. They sought out private doctors in the town of Pochutla, an hour's bus ride away (Long, 1991). Moreover, it is stated that local people have already lost their beaches. For example the Club Med resort did not allow non-guests to enter any part of its facility. ' ... as soon as the resort was in operation, they (local people) would no longer be able to use the beaches ... . They saw Santa Cruz Bay as the future playground for foreigners' (Long, 1991, p. 210). Additionally, it is also reported that 'the original residents of Santa Cruz were suddenly faced with social stratification .... The new upper and middle class

community members openly referred to the indigenous people of Santa Cruz as ugly and stupid ....' (Long, 1991, p. 211). Wider evidence in this regard suggests that while the local people do not have acceptable houses, schools of national standard, proper irrigation systems and modern agricultural equipment, luxury hotels and leisure facilities for tourists have received a major share from public funds as incentives to comfort the Western mass tourist by creating a protective ecological bubble of his accustomed environment.

On the other hand, foreign domination of the developing world tourism industry resulted in the loss of control over resources which may increase any adverse impacts of tourism development. Members of local communities usually find themselves caught up in a 'globally integrated system of resources over which they cannot exercise control' (Brohman, 1996, p. 55). Decision-makers at central level and elitist bodies who are exogenous to communities in tourist destinations target to control local communities and their resources upon which they depend. Decisions affecting their daily life, future and many local matters are normally made without considering these local people, rather they are made 'according to the narrow interests of those that control the tourism industry' (Brohman, 1996, p. 55). The struggle between elites and local people to control resources has been ignored by local and central governments. Since more and more regions are developed for mass tourism, adoption of political economic policies that effect a balance between local ownership and external ownership of resources and control over those resources as well as between tourism and other sectors of the economy becomes a crucial need. Thus if communities in tourist destinations are not empowered in a real sense, involvement may be restricted to elites in the community, which often results in their interests being considered rather than the interests of the community. In other words, domain of elites in participatory decision-making may enhance their own status and legalise what they are doing at the expense of excluded communities.

Consequently, the stimulus towards community participation provides little more than a symbolic sham intended to defuse discontent. From this point of view, many important decisions occur out of the community eye, emerging as non-decisions. Therefore, it is not surprising that tourism development in many tourist destinations in developing countries is not driven by the community, but driven by local elites in conjunction with international tour operators as a reflection of Britton's (1982) 'three-tiered hierarchy' of the industry. Under the given structure of the international tourism system it is difficult for developing countries to develop a proactive tourism development approach by which to decrease or eradicate the influences of external actors on tourism development. That is to say, a participatory tourism development approach may not function to contribute to

C. Tosun / Tourism Management 21 (2000) 613–633 623

a better tourism development under the current power structure of developing countries where the majority of populations live in poverty which limits and excludes them from local and national affairs unless deliberate measures are urgently taken to empower indigenous local communities via special educational programs, financial and fiscal instruments, and political decentralisation. However, it should be kept in mind that utilising these instruments/strategies to empower local communities requires hard political choices, a confident decision-making process and the collaboration of international tour operators and donor agencies.

- *Lack of appropriate legal system*: Participatory tourism development strategies may bring unorganised groups into the policy-making process. Creating opportunities for those who are poorly organised may not negate the influence of the interest groups already active in tourist development. Thus, a legal structure which can defend community interests and ensure a community's participatory right in tourism development may be needed. However, legal structures in many developing countries do not encourage local people to participate in their local affairs; rather the legislative structure puts a distance between grass-roots and formal authorities, and it is difficult to understand how it is operated from a lay person's point of view. In this context, it is argued with special references to India that participatory attempts are not effective and efficient owing to the lack of enabling environment. The legal structure is not encouraging to educate communities about their rights and how they can establish organisations to promote their interests. Moreover, such organisations must get government approval, for which a level of literacy, that the poor clearly lack, is essential (Mathur, 1995).

There is evidence that 'For the sake of expediency and in the interests of short-term profits local environmental laws are frequently flouted. Such an example is the recent construction of the Ramada Hotel Varca in southern Goa, India, which violated both the maximum height and minimum distance from the sea criteria' (Cater, 1991, p. 12). In some developing countries such as Turkey and Mexico local indigenous communities' right to use public places such as beaches and sea is violated by tourism operators (see Long, 1991; Tosun, 1998a). In the context of developing countries, it is contended that the state has not usually been the expression of societies. It acts in accordance with a mercantilist model. Laws favour a small group of elites and discriminates against the interests of the powerless majority, which has token legality. The system does not only 'concentrate the nation's wealth in a small minority but it also concedes to that minority the right to that wealth' (Llosa, 1995, p. 291). Of course, the inappropriate legal system that works against participatory development varies from one

country to another one. For example, legal structure are often in place in ex-colonies but they just are not implemented by existing local government. This may confirm de Kadt's (1979) assertion that the ability of local authorities to impose laws and regulation are limited and directed by important interest groups outside the community in the developing world.

The above argument implies that although participatory rights are needed as legal protection, they may not themselves guarantee authentic community participation in the TDP because of other structural limitations prevailing in many developing countries. As Leftwich (1995, p. 436) stated, ' … if the politics do not give rise to the kind of state which can generate, sustain and protect an effective and independent capacity for governance, then there will be no positive developmental consequences'. That is to say, efficient and effective participatory tourism development approach requires high level of supporting institutions, both within and outside the state. Unless the institutions enforce rule and regulation to be obeyed, it is meaningless to establish legal framework.

- *Lack of trained human resources*: 'Most economists would probably agree that it is the human resources of a nation, not its capital or its natural resources, that ultimately determine the character and pace of its economic and social development' (Todaro, 1994, p. 363). That is to say, ' … human beings are the active agents who accumulate capital, exploit natural resources, build social, economic and political organisations, and carry forward national development' (Harbison, 1973, p. 3). However, lack of qualified human resources in the tourism sector in many local destinations in the developing world has stimulated an influx of employees from other parts of country to work in tourism. The few attractive jobs requiring high skills are occupied by foreigners (e.g. the law relating to the tourism industry allows companies to employ up to 20 percentage foreigners in Turkey) and well-educated people from high income groups. The low status, unskilled jobs associated with low wages and hard working conditions have been left for members of destination communities who were working on farms or for those unskilled people who moved from less developed parts of the country in order to work in the construction of the tourism industry, and then have become cheap labour input. This has not only limited the participation of local people in tourism, it has also created a cultural backlash between local people and the seasonal workers and increased the burden on public services (Inskeep & Kallenberger, 1992; Long, 1991; Tosun & Jenkins, 1996).

'Clearly, a country which is unable to develop the skills and knowledge of its people and to utilise them effectively in the national economy will be unable to develop

624 *C. Tosun / Tourism Management 21 (2000) 613–633*

anything else' (Harbison, 1973, p. 3). That is to say, '[w]ithout a trained local work force, the industry can only function by importing staff, in which case the principle of ensuring local benefits from tourism is thwarted' (Woodley, 1993, p. 143). Thus, for active participation of local people in tourism, training is an essential element, which must be outfitted to the needs of the community. In this regard, it is contended that training must occur at the local level, otherwise residents would not be interested in participating (Woodley, 1993). Additionally, the personal experience of the author suggests that low literacy rates in developing countries may necessitate the replacement of traditional training manuals and written materials to be effective. However, formulation and implementation of training programs will require expertise and financial resources. These are often scarce, expensive, and thus not attainable in the developing world.

- *Relatively high cost of community participation*: Community participation requires considerable time, money and skills to organise and sustain participation (Paul, 1987). That is to say, 'it is more time consuming and may lead to conflicting objectives amongst the local aims' (WTO, 1994, p. 10) since it may raise expectations in the community, which may not be easy to meet. On the other hand, as Murphy (1985) noted, effective management of tourism industry requires day-to-day and season-to-season operational decisions. It may not be possible to ask community to participate in these day-to-day decisions. Therefore, this time consuming and complex process of participatory development strategy may lead to delay in decision-making, which may burden the developers with high loan interest (Fogg, 1981). This may also disappoint those who expect quick return from investment.

Moreover, public bodies may not want to spend their limited financial resources on organising community participation whose benefit appears to be relatively long term. Private sector may avoid practicing participatory tourism development strategy since it involves contradictory investment criteria. To overcome these problems may be the real test for this kind of development approach. Thus, most state agencies may resist the kinds of reforms which demand them always to follow and elaborate costly procedures intended to increase community involvement (Ethridge, 1982). On the other hand, it may not be accepted by local authorities since their representatives' role may be questioned through moves towards citizens' empowerment in addition to being expensive in terms of resource implication.

The above argument suggests that a participatory tourism development approach is likely to require relatively more bureaucratic formalities that demand more money, organisational skills, time and effort. As the financial and qualified human resources are scarce in many developing countries, these scarce resources will be likely directed to physical investments, rather than costly administrative procedures, particularly at the beginning of tourism development. As a result, it may be said that because participatory tourism development increases demands on scarce resources in developing countries, this is another limitation on participatory tourism development.

- *Lack of financial resources*: The introduction of tourism within communities usually requires funds to be allocated to develop a tourist infrastructure of facilities (Reed, 1997). These facilities often are based on Western standards even in the poorest host countries (Cohen, 1972). However, financial resources needed for tourism investment are very scarce and in most cases, not readily available in developing countries (see Pearce, 1991; Long, 1991; Tosun, 1998b). This shortcoming has appeared as a major limitation to the implementation of participatory tourism development in developing countries and even in relatively undeveloped regions of developed countries. In this context, it is stated that ownership and investment is one of the most important variables that determine control over the tourism industry. In many relatively less developed communities financing for tourism is not sufficient at local level, and thus must come from outside interests. When financial resources originate from non-local interests, the loss of control which emerges from outside investment is not easy to overcome. In spite of efforts to encourage community participation, if residents do not own the tourism infrastructure, control over growth and style of development is difficult to achieve (Woodley, 1993).

For example, it is reported that the opportunities created by tourism development were vast but their importance was not understood fully by indigenous people in Mexico. Whereas, the in-immigrants entrepreneurs who were attracted by the tourism development understood the types of business in demand at the development site. 'When the project was first announced there were opportunities for small-scale business investment, but many local leaders doubted its viability or success, thus missing those opportunities' (Long, 1991, p. 212). The Mexican case does not only reflect the lack of financial resources that has prevented the local community participating in the tourism development process as entrepreneurs, it also mirrors existing of cultural barriers to participation of local community. The case of Urgup, Turkey appears to be similar to the Mexican case. It is stated that 'the local people do not have enough capital to establish proper hotels and shops to serve tourists. The capital must come from non-local sources. Thus, it is very difficult for the local people to play a leading role as entrepreneurs in the tourism industry' (Tosun, 1998b, p. 601).

As the above comments imply, resources at the local level are not enough to finance the present scale of

C. Tosun / Tourism Management 21 (2000) 613–633 625

tourism development particularly at the local level in many developing countries, which is one of the structural barriers to community participation in the tourism development process. As popularly argued in the tourism literature, tourism is an industry developed for and by foreigners in developing countries due to the fact that developing countries lack financial and qualified human resources to invest in and manage tourism particularly on a large scale. Severe macro-economic problems prevailing in these countries made them accept tourism as a part of an export-led development strategy without considering the nature of international tourism that has dependency as its central feature. This argument may suggest that tourism growth in developing countries is beyond the control of these countries. Therefore, implementation of a participatory tourism development approach as a pro-active development strategy is largely at the mercy of foreigners such as international tour operators and multinational companies.

2.7. Cultural limitations

There seem to be some cultural factors such as limited capacity of poor people to handle development effectively, and apathy and low level of awareness in the local community, that function as obstacles to emergence and operationalisation of participatory tourism development approach.

- *Limited capacity of poor people*: Grass-roots have limited capacity to handle the things which directly affect their dignity (Oakley & Marsden, 1984; UN, 1981). 'Depending on their motives, power holders can hire poor people to co-opt them, to placate them or to utilise the have-nots' specials skills and insights' (Arnstein, 1971, p. 74). Moreover, as it is pointed out, the vast majority of the people in the developing world have difficulty meeting basic and felt needs, which limits them to get closely involved in issues of community concern. Satisfaction of the people's needs are at the mercy of government administrators. The lack of effective grass-root organisations that can be instrumental in determining and improving the collective interests of the poor intensifies this dependence. 'In the absence of corrective measures, popular participation in administration, under these circumstances, is likely to be manipulative in nature' (UN, 1982, p. 22)

The UN seems to have touched on a significant point which exists in tourist destinations of many developing countries. Host communities usually and widely have difficulty in accessing services of a welfare state (see Long, 1991; Tosun, 1998b). Many governments in developing nations have focused on serving organised groups such as civil servants and employed workers in the modern sectors of the economy. People in rural areas living on farming have not been given enough opportunities to use basic welfare services such as hospitals and schools. Logically, and according to Maslow's need hierarchy, they are motivated to meet their basic needs and felt-needs by ignoring wider socio-political issues which indeed prevent them from satisfying their needs in more efficient ways.

The above argument suggests that the biggest challenge for the poor in many local tourist destinations in the developing world appears to be mere survival, which occupies all the time and consumes their energy. Hence, participating in the TDP which demands time and energy may be a luxury that the host communities cannot afford. Furthermore, when tourism development has taken place in local destinations of developing countries, central and local governments may have invested large amounts of public resources in tourism to create tourist infrastructure based on Western standards to attract maximum numbers of foreign tourists while host communities live on the poverty limit. That is to say, socio-economic and political issues have been handled in isolation from local communities in tourist destinations. Consequently, host communities have not been given an opportunity to develop their capacity. Under these conditions implementation of participatory tourism development approach is likely to be ineffective and token in nature.

- *Apathy and Low Level of awareness in the local community*: The perception of a low level of interest in and awareness about socio-cultural, economic and political issues amongst the grassroots is generally accepted. There seems to be several reasons for this argument. Firstly, for years, indeed centuries in some cases, the grass-roots has been excluded from the affairs which have affected their dignity, that have rendered them apathetic about taking a hand in matters beyond their immediate family domain. Apathy among the poor stops them effectively demanding that the institutions which serve them accommodate their needs. The output is that 'their plight worsens and their capacity for effective action is further weakened. A vicious cycle of poverty reinforces a vicious cycle of bureaucratic dysfunction' (Miller & Rein, 1975, p. 7).

Secondly, 'Citizens tend to participate only when strongly motivated to do so, and most of the time they are not motivated' (Rosener, 1982, p. 344). This may arise from the belief that their idea will not be considered, which does not motivate them to express an interest. And indeed, many poor people often act with a fear of making objections which could be used against them at a later date. In this regard, Brohman (1996) has contended that the current style of tourism development has increased alienation amongst local populations. It may be further argued that it is this kind of alienation which may force local people to be apathetic which causes low levels of

626   *C. Tosun / Tourism Management 21 (2000) 613–633*

awareness about potential and current costs and the possible benefits of tourism development. Ultimately, alienation of local people may have stopped them from having sufficient knowledge about the nature of tourism development in their locality.

To Simmons (1994) and Tosun (1998b), the potential poor knowledge of tourism amongst local people make considerable efforts necessary to persuade the general public to participate in the tourism development process. That is to say, 'there is evidence of a need for greater public awareness about tourism, its benefits and its costs, how the industry is structured, about its current contribution to a community's welfare, and about how tourism might evolve' (Simmons, 1994, p. 105). Moreover, McIntyre, Hetherington and Inskeep (1993, p. 28) argue that though the community usually try to gain benefits from tourism, they may not have 'a realistic understanding of what they are doing in achieving this development and what are the impacts of tourism'. Jamal and Getz (1995) also note that lack of awareness is one of the factors which acts as barriers to effective communication at community level tourism development. Additionally, in many tourist destinations a lack of indigenous tourism planners has resulted in planners from a different cultural background being brought in to lead the process. This may create communication barriers and low credibility arising from the cultural differences. On the other hand, sometimes, there are language differences between planners and residents, which also create barriers to effective participation.

In brief, the above argument may suggest that apathy and low level of awareness in host communities in developing countries exist as one of the main limitations to a participatory tourism development approach. To tackle this problem is a difficult task that requires considerable time and money.

As evidence suggests, political instability, patron-client relationship, low level of literacy, unfair and unequal distribution of income, severe macro-economic problems, lack of services of welfare state, lack of democratic institutions, lack of democratic understanding among state elites, unwillingness of elite to share fruits of development with majority of society in the developing world have ushered in these limitations to community participation in the TDP at higher intensity and greater persistence than in the developed world.

3. Conclusion

This article has investigated and discussed the limits to community participation in the TDP in the context of developing countries. Clearly, the described limitations may not be only specific to participatory tourism development strategy. Some of them may also be seen as common problems of development and participatory de-

velopment in general in many developing countries. Hence, it should be accepted that these limitations may be an extension of the prevailing social, political and economic structure in developing countries, which have prevented them from achieving a higher level of development. That is to say, '[t]o the extent that problems in any sector, such as tourism, reflect the existing socio-economic situation ...' (de Kadt, 1979, p. 45). In this respect, eradication of these barriers to participatory tourism development approach largely depends upon mitigating common problems of developing countries. Thus, it may be naive to suppose that participatory tourism development approach will change existing structure of a local tourism industry in a developing country without changing dominant socio-economic and political structure of that locality. On the other hand, it should be accepted that community participation as citizen power is not a simple matter but it involves different ideological beliefs, political forces, administrative arrangements, re-distribution of wealth and power, and varying perceptions of what is possible, which seem to be unacceptable for the prevailing ruling class in many developing countries. Hence, community participation in the development process cannot become much of a reality unless specific and deliberate strategies at local, national and international levels are developed to tackle with the outlined limitations. Obviously, there is no single blueprint and a set of fixed rules to operationalise participatory tourism development approach. Any intervention must be adapted to the specific environment in which it is to be implemented. In this context, the following recommended policy suggestions should be seen as broad guidelines to lessen excessive and aggressive bureaucratisation, centralisation and depersonalisation of government-administered tourism development, and empower the poor in a gradual manner.

That is to say, several broad conclusions can be drawn from the overall discussion, which may function as policy implications for participatory tourism development approach in the developing world and as well as a summary of this study. First, as noted, community involvement in tourism can be considered from at least two viewpoints: in the decision-making process and in the benefits of tourism development. However, community participation in the TDP in many developing countries has been recognised as helping local people get more economic benefits via employing them as workers or encouraging them to operate a small scale business, rather than creating opportunities for local people to have a say in the decision-making process of tourism development. Several studies have already revealed that without creating opportunities for local people to take part in the decision-making process it would be very difficult for local communities to get adequate benefits from tourism development (see Clancy, 1999; Long, 1991; Tosun, 1998b; Timothy, 1999). On the other hand, although

C Tosun / Tourism Management 21 (2000) 613–633 627

local people at the initial stage of tourism development (Butler's, 1980, exploration stage) own and operate small scale guest-houses, economy class hotels or souvenir shops, and work as workers in the tourism industry in many developing countries (Long, 1991; Tosun, 1998b, Pearce, 1989 quoting Haider, 1985 and Rodrnburg, 1980) after Noronba's (1976) discovery, and local response and initiative stages it becomes gradually more difficult for these indigenous people to operate a tourism-related business and work in the sector since tourism development becomes institutionalised (Butler's development stage). This attracts capital owners to open large scale businesses. In other words, in a gradual manner local control over tourism development is lost as local tourist destinations attract more Plog's (1973) allocentrics and Cohen's (1972) institutionalised tourists. Due to the emergence of a strong competition under the imperfect market conditions, these locally owned small businesses in the tourism industry cannot survive and are closed. That is to say, as local tourist destinations move towards development stage from exploration stage in Butler's tourist area cycle of evolution model, local people may lose control over local tourism development. In brief, relatively larger capital flows to local tourist destinations tend to threaten local control over local tourism development, rather than strengthening local people to participate in the benefits and decision-making process of tourism development in a better way. This may reflect the assertion that 'the technical, economic and commercial characteristics of modern tourist travel favour the development of integrated enterprises, further reducing the possibility of local participation' (Pearce, 1989, p. 94).

The above argument about the relationship between tourist area cycle of evolution and local people participation in the TDP may imply that the opportunities for communities to participate in the TDP may vary over time with the type and scale of tourism developed, thresholds of entry, and the markets served. In this regard, it is suggested that deliberate measurements must be taken at the 'exploration stage' of tourist destinations to empower local people to keep control over tourism development before local destinations become more popular and attractive for large capital owners.

Second, one may argue that these limitations in debate may not be equally valid for ecotourism and alternative tourism in the developing world. In other words, it may be claimed that sustainable or alternative tourism including ecotourism can create better opportunities for achieving development and public participation in the TDP (see Brohman, 1996; Smith & Eadington, 1992). Although this seems to be true to some extent, there are several reasons which constrain its validity. First, it is ironic, but perhaps not unreasonable, to postulate that 'the high profile of ecotourism or alternative tourism is directly dependent upon the existence of well-developed mass-tourism sectors, which account for most of the

participants' (Weaver, 1998, p. 205). Second, it is argued that only the educated and often moneyed elite is accepted within privileged fraternities of alternative tourists whose travel patterns are largely driven by ego enhancement and status building (Butler, 1990). That is to say, as a deliberate sector, these alternative tourism activities constitute only a very small-scale portion of the tourism sector owing to the fact that 'much of Third World tourism today is not small-scale, ecologically oriented or even broadly participatory' (Clancy, 1995, p. 5). For example, it is argued that specialised alternative tourist accommodation accounts for only a small minority of available rooms. If it is quantified strictly in terms of primary-purpose visits and especially the provision of specialised accommodation, alternative tourism is negligible since these appear to account for only a very small minority of the tourism sector. Clearly, the benefits of alternative forms of tourism such as the direct revenue and employment generating capacity are limited by the dominance of popular, casual, passive and diversionary ecotourists, whose expenditures within the protected areas or in adjacent communities tend to be minimal. Park entry fees and possibly some local food and souvenir purchases are amongst the few associated direct outlays, although alternative tourists themselves may only account for a small proportion of such expenditures when assessed against total park visitation. Furthermore, 'park entry fees are usually nominal and accrue to the government rather than local communities' (Weaver, 1998, p. 209). Third, as de Kadt (1992) contended, the compulsory call for community control via alternative tourism often neglects the tendency of the local elite to adopt the organs of participation for its own benefit or the possibility that these communities will become dependent on outside experts owing to their lack of prior experience in tourism planning. On the other hand, the local communities may actually want to develop a more intensive mode of tourism. This may become a problem for those experts who do not accept the legitimacy of mass tourism. 'If these experts attempt to impose an AT (alternative tourism) model or to re-educate the local people so that they change their preferences, the entire issue of local decision-making control and community-based tourism is called into question' (Weaver, 1998, p. 15).

Fourth, highly centralised public administration system and planning activities are a common problem of many developing countries, which work against participatory tourism development approach. As a result, the structure of local governments in many developing countries has been shaped by the state, reflecting bureaucratic and fiscal concerns of the central governments, and has not been a source of democratic citizen participation in local public spaces (see Gow & Vansant, 1983; Koker, 1995). Obviously, moving towards a more participatory tourism development policy requires decentralisation of public administration system including tourism planning activities. In this context, political and administrative decentralisation should be supported in parallel to the conception that local bodies know local problems and feelings, and so what is suitable, better than the central authorities possibly can. That is to say, meaningful participation necessitates a systematic local autonomy, through which communities bring to light the possibilities of exercising choice and thereby becoming capable of handling their own development. Hence, local governments should be re-organised to defend, protect and reflect concerns and interests of local people in their administrative territories. Additional financial resources should be made available for local governments to use particularly for community development projects and organisation of participatory activities. In other words, there must be an explicit and adequate financial commitment to the community involvement in the TDP. In this regard, goodwill is not enough.

On the other hand, public officers and private sector lack of experience in participatory development activities, and their experience in tourism is negligible in many local tourist destinations in the developing world. The lack of expertise and competence in tourism-related matters may influence the effectiveness and efficiency of participatory tourism development approach. Moreover, re-organisation and empowerment of local governments may move patron–client relations to provincial level. 'Traditional local elites are likely to be most intransigent in their traditional, local settings. If power is passed to them, the repression of the weaker and disadvantaged castes and classes is likely to worsen' (Mathur, 1995, p. 158). In this vein, a cautionary approach is needed. New measures should ensure the equality of treatment of all residents and should avoid creating other problems or shaping the form of prevailing problems rather than solving them. By taking into account specific local circumstances appropriate policies and institutional framework can be formulated to avoid this type of problem. Moreover, within the proposed decentralised public administration structure, special education and training programs should be designed to enable local indigenous people to become involved in the tourism development process as entrepreneurs and employees. As part of this educational and training program, free consultancy services should be made available to tourism-related and other small business in local tourist destinations. While entrepreneurial skills and professional qualifications of local people could be developed through the education and training programs, tourism entrepreneurs could be induced to employ local people by fiscal and monetary policies. Moreover, local tourism development workers may be hired to work with local people to develop tourism products and market the local value added aspects of the area to tour operators, travel agents and individual tourists.

Fifth, socio-political, cultural and economic structure of developing countries have 'overpoliticised the state', that has ushered in patron–client relationship between politicians and elite business interests. This socio-political and cultural pathology push for particularistic preferences rather than universal norms in the allocation of scare resources of many developing countries. Tourism as a high priority sector in the export-led growth strategy of the developing world has been shaped and directed by this clientelistic approach, that operates at the expense of the majority at local, regional and national level. Consequently, the noted structure of developing countries has not only isolated local people from their affairs including tourism development, but it also undermined the principles of sustainable development such as improving the basic needs of a given community, reduction of inequality and eradication of absolute poverty so as to lead people to gain self-esteem and to feel free from the three evils of want, ignorance and squalor without compromising the ability of future generations to meet their own need. It is suggested that 'if the forces making for inequality are left free rein in their society and if policies aimed at the eradication of poverty are not vigorously pursued' (de Kadt, 1979, p. 45), it will be very difficult to implement a participatory tourism development approach whose aim is to enable hitherto excluded to have a say in their affairs and benefit from fruits of development based upon equal opportunity right.

The overall discussion regarding to the limits of community participation in the TDP reveals that implementation of participatory tourism development approach requires a total change in socio-political, legal and economic structure of developing countries. These changes should stimulate developing nations to move towards establishing a 'democratic state' which ultimately works against clientelism and favouritism, and empower grassroots to participate in their affairs. Once the democratic state is established, it makes it easier to utilise financial, fiscal, and educational instruments to enable local people to involve in the TDP. However, although a democratic state facilitates implementation of participatory development approach, and thus is highly desirable, 'it has been politics and the state rather than governance or democracy that explains the differences between successful and unsuccessful development records' (Leftwich, 1995, p. 437). Hence, a 'developmental state', which refers to 'a state whose political and bureaucratic elite has the genuine developmental determination and autonomous capacity to define, pursue and implement developmental goals' (Leftwich, 1995, p. 437), is also sine quo non for the success of participatory development approach. This suggests that genuine community participation also requires a change in attitudes and behaviour of decision-makers to deal with hitherto excluded, which may lead to new patterns of distributing power and controlling resources. Without such a state no developing nation is likely to achieve participatory development since 'democratic market-friendly strategies will sooner or

C. Tosun / Tourism Management 21 (2000) 613–633 629

later break up on the rocks of their own internally generated economic inequalities and escalating political strife, especially in 'premature' democracy' (Leftwich, 1995, p. 438).

Sixth, evidence in other sectors of the economy suggests that Non-Governmental Organisations (NGOs) have increasingly played an important role in the development projects some of which have employed community participation as an instrument in developing countries (Desai, 1995; Mathur, 1995; Paul, 1987). 'The tradition of the oppressed teaches us that the 'state of emergency' in which we live is not the exception but the rule' (Walter Benjamin n.d. cited in Taussig, 1989, p. 64) in developing nations. Hence, mobilisation of local communities by external organisations seems to be an essential condition when there is lack of confidence and fear in the community leaders and communities themselves (Desai, 1995). This appears to be true for many indigenous local communities in many local tourist destinations in developing countries since any reaction of poor people about type, scale, direction and distribution of benefit of tourism development may be seen as a threat for mass tourism development from which the indigenous people have alleged benefits. Moreover, such reaction of local communities may be viewed by dominant groups as revolutionary ideological movements. This possibility of misunderstanding may frustrate local people to express their opinions about local tourism development matters.

'As agents of development for the poor, NGOs ... are closer to the people and therefore understand them better' (Mathur, 1995, p. 158). Under the noted socio-political, cultural and economic pathology of many developing countries, NGOs seems to be a good institutional tool to empower indigenous host communities via various educational, organisational, financial, socio-cultural, psychological and political means to move towards a more participatory tourism development approach. NGOs may have two main functions in this context: service delivery and policy advocacy (see Desai, 1995). Service delivery means to provide technical, legal, educational and training services to indigenous host communities for involving in the TDP. Policy advocacy means to bring about social, economic and political changes by influencing attitudes, policy and practice, seeking to reform state approach to tourism development and lobbying directly for the policy changes.

NGOs may assist indigenous host communities, community-based organisations particularly to access other institutions such as municipalities, banks, technical training schools, fiscal and financial incentives provided by governments for tourism, etc. On the other hand, 'it is increasingly recognised that NGOs do a better job than governments not only in promoting participation but also in converting aid money into development that lasts. They are becoming an important resource in the implementation of donor-aided participatory approaches'

(Mathur, 1995, p. 158). When lack of financial resources especially at local level is considered, the role of NGOs becomes obvious to find additional financial resources for initiating and maintaining participatory tourism development approach. As a result, they can give ordinary local people a greater stake and more influence in the success of the local tourism industry through a better organised local tourism industry.

However, NGOs are obliged to operate in a 'crowded' institutional environment and they are influenced by external relationships with multiple actors such as local and central governments, donor and other (often competing) NGOs, community organisations and beneficiaries (Desai, 1995). It is suggested that the interaction between governments and NGOs does not proceeds in a totally trouble-free manner. Many NGOs see poverty and inequality as resulting from governmental policies and actions. Their participatory approach, especially their emphasis on empowerment, thus tends to be viewed by dominant groups as subversive or revolutionary ideology (Mathur, 1995). Hence, the particular political conditions and bureaucratic procedures of governments authorities control many opportunities of NGOs activity, and set very specific parameters to the extent to which communities and NGOs participate in the TDP. Consequently, this may reduce the role of NGOs in participatory tourism development approach.

Seventh, chronic macro-economic problems of many developing countries, the structure of international tourism system such as domination of Transnational Tourism Corporations, dependency on a few international tour operators and tourist generating countries, and intense competition between identical tourist destinations in terms of price, rather than product differentiation and quality put developing countries in a position where they cannot afford to reject or oppose decisions of international tour operators and other related dominant actors due to the real possibility of losing substantial economic benefits from international tourism for which they have already made massive and irreversible fixed investment. Under these market conditions macro-economic imperatives, and the noted socio-political pathology it appears to be very difficult, if not impossible, for many developing countries to develop and implement a pro-active tourism development approach such as 'participatory tourism development' whose main principles and objectives versus interests of these dominant international and national actors at least in the short term.

It becomes clear that developing countries need deliberate help from and collaboration and co-operation of a wide range of international donor-agencies, international NGOs, international tour operators and Transnational Companies in order to move towards a more participatory tourism development practices which requires re-structuring the public administration system, and re-distribution of power and wealth, for which hard

630   C. Tosun / Tourism Management 21 (2000) 613–633

political choices and logical decisions based on cumbersome social, economic and environmental trade-off are sine qua non. That is to say, without the collaboration and the willingness of western governments, international donor agencies and multinational companies to share their accumulated experiences it is unlikely that a participatory tourism development approach will emerge and be implemented in developing countries. In this context, future research should focus particularly on how developing countries can collaborate with these external actors to encourage community participation through which tourism can be developed in a more sustainable manner. In this regard, it can be debated that while many developing countries encounter growing mass poverty, economic, financial and political instability, and environmental degradation, the developed world may not live in isolated enclaves of prosperity as this appears to be unacceptable on humanitarian grounds and the long-term well-being of developed countries is linked to economic progress, preservation of the environment and peace and stability in the developing world.

Seventh, it should be accepted that community participation in the TDP is in part determined by cultural attributes of local communities. In this context, it is contended that although community participation in decision-making for tourism in the sense of Western paradigms seems to rarely occur in developing countries, it may not be right to claim that local people involvement does not happen at all. Public participation in the TDP can take place in many forms, 'which may be a result of a melange of place-specific conditions, such as the cultural attributes of the community and its decision-making traditions that are already in place' (Timothy, 1999, p. 388). For example, as Sofield (1996) demonstrated in his study of Solomons, Island culture requires consultation with communities. If that consultation does not take place, rights have been affronted with the result that violence can occur. As it is clearly reported in the Solomon Islands case, ignorance of local culture which requires proper consultation with local people by foreign investor escalated a conflict. The dispute between the local people (the customary land owners) and the foreign investor has not only created a conflict, but it also brought about a serious diplomatic rift between two sovereign states (Solomon Islands and Australia). The 'final result was the complete dismantling of the resort and repossession of the island by the local community' (Sofield, 1996, p. 183).

However, such a strong participatory culture does not exist equally in all host communities. Thus, it should not be generalised for all developing societies, and expectations from this strategy should not be exaggerated. As it is asserted 'the cultural remoteness of host communities to tourism-related businesses in developing countries appears to be an important limitation to local participation in the tourism development process' (Tosun, 1998b,

p. 607). 'Unlike the ideal-typical case as depicted in evolutionary models in tourism literature, the extent of local entrepreneurial involvement is usually very limited, owing to the fact that the local indigenous groups are rarely adequately preadapted to the business culture in tourism' (Din, 1988, p. 563). But, without a financial commitment by local communities, community participation as a strategy might be ineffective. It should be noted that removing the cultural barriers to participatory tourism development approach requires long educational process and flexibility rather than once-over rigid development efforts. That is to say, participatory capacity cannot be built like a road or dam; it must be developed. Rigid schedules are inappropriate and can lead to initiatives or pressures that impede long-term progress. Hence, flexibility is an essential ingredient of any form of participatory development approach; it is part of the requirement of realism in the context of the participatory development approach.

Ninth, as implied, in many developing countries tourism development planning is a foreign-inspired process (Tosun & Jenkins, 1998a–c). Governments of developing countries have received advice from foreign experts who recommended large-scale tourism development (Pearce, 1989). In this foreign-inspired tourism development process, local participation as a call for community empowerment that has been invoked in many UN agency reports has not been recognised. 'This leaves the interest of the indigenous group perpetually marginalised from the development process' (Din, 1997, p. 79). In this regard, this article suggests that more attempts should be made to comprehend why there is a lack of local participation and how this can be removed. One solution may be that the role of technical advisors be re-examined to make sure that tourism planning team will pay sufficient attention to the interest of indigenous people when giving advice to authorities in destination areas of developing countries. That is to say, tourism experts and researchers must direct more attention towards ensuring a greater degree of indigenous participation and begin looking at the development process from the viewpoint of local host communities. Only then the interest of local people can be incorporated in the TDP.

Finally, it should be noted that the political economy of tourism suggests that tourism development itself is a reflection of political economy of the industry and broader historical, economic and political relations among regions, countries, and classes. In many developing countries, particularly within the hotel industry, ownership and control is confined mainly to foreign chains and large-scale national business. This ensures that only multi-national companies and large-scale national capital reap most of benefits associated with the industry. As Briton's (1982) studies with special references to small Pacific Island destinations reveal, the multi-national companies control much of transport, accommodation, and packaged tourism products. Under such dependency situation, local groups — namely elite classes — also obtain some benefits, while subordinated classes receive the smallest portion. This may suggest that direct participation by local people in management and operation of tourism facilities is also negligible.

This article has been written as an attempt to open up much needed discussion on participatory tourism development approaches in developing countries. In this context, it suggests that future research should investigate pre-conditions for participatory tourism development approach and develop strategies to operationalise this pro-active tourism development approach with special references to a specific local or national tourist destination alongside investigating the role of external actors in promoting participatory tourism development approach in the developing world.

Acknowledgements

The author wishes to thank the anonymous reviewers for their helpful comments.

References

Arnstein, R. S. (1971). Eight rungs on the ladder of citizen participation. In S. E. Cahn, & A. B. Passett, *Citizen participation· Effecting community change* (pp. 69–91). New York: Praeger Publishers.

Askew, I. (1989). Organising community participation in family planning projects in South-Asia. *Studies in Family Planning*, 20(4), 185–202.

Benicourt, J. (1982). Popular participation in development in Africa. *Assignment Children*, 59/60, 57–77.

Blank, U. (1989). *The community tourism industry imperative: The necessity, the opportunities, its potential.* Venture Publishing: State College.

Britton, S. G. (1982). The political economy of tourism in the Third World. *Annals of Tourism Research, 9*(3), 331–358.

Brohman, J. (1996). New directions in tourism for third world development. *Annals of Tourism Research, 23*(1), 48–70.

Buchanan, R. (1971). Profiles of the Third World and The Third World-and Beyond. In B. A. Mountjoy, *Developing the underdeveloped countries* (pp. 17–51). Bristol: MacMillan.

Butler, R. W. (1980). The concept of a tourist area cycle of evolution: Implications for management of resources. *Canadian Geographer*, XXIV, 1, pp. 5–12.

Butler, R W. (1990). Alternative tourism: Pious hope or Trojan Horse? *Journal of Travel Research*, 28, 40–45.

Cater, E. (1991). *Sustainable tourism in the third world: Problems and prospects.* Reading: Department of Geography, University of Reading.

Clancy, M. J. (1999). Tourism and development: Evidence from Mexico. *Annals of Tourism Research, 26*(1), 1–20.

Cliffe, L., & Seldon, D. (1991). Africa in a new world order. *Review of African Political Economy, 50*, 3–11.

Cohen, E. (1972). Towards a sociology of international tourism. *Social Research, 39*, 164–182.

Das Gupta, J. (1995). India: Democratic becoming and developmental transition. In L. Diamond, J. J. Linz, & S. M. S. Lipset, *Politics in developing countries* (pp. 263–322). London: Lynne Rienner Publishers, Inc.

de Kadt, E. (1979). Social planning for tourism in the developing countries. *Annals of Tourism Research, 6*(1), 36–48.

de Kadt, E. (1982). Community participation for health: The case of Latin America. *World Development, 10*(7), 573–584.

de Kadt, E. (1992). Making the alternative sustainable: lessons from development for tourism. In V. L. Smith, & W. Eadington, *Tourism alternatives. Potentials and problems in the development of tourism* (pp. 47–75). Philadelphia: University of Pennsylvania Press.

de Vaus, D. A. (1996). *Surveys in social research* (4th Ed.). London: Allen and Unwin.

Department of Economic and Social Affairs. (1970). Rural community development and planning: Promise and reality. *International Social Development Review, 2*, 28–33.

Desia, V. (1995). *Community participation and slum housing. A study of Bombay.* New Delhi: Sage Publications.

Diamond, L., Linz, J. J., & Lipset, S. M. (1995). Introduction: What makes for Democracy?. In L. Diamond, J. J. Linz, & S. M. S. Lipset, *Politics in developing countries* (pp. 1–66). London: Lynne Rienner Publishers, Inc.

Dieke, P. U. C. (1991). Policies for tourism development in Kenya. *Annals of Tourism Research, 18*, 269–294.

Din, K. H. (1988). Reports: Social cultural impacts of tourism. *Annals of Tourism Research, 15*(4), 563–566.

Din, K. H. (1997). Indigenization of tourism development: Some constraints and possibilities. In M. Oppermann, *Pacific rim tourism* (pp. 76–82). New York: CAB International.

Elliott, J. (1983). Politics, power, and tourism in Thailand. *Annals of Tourism Research, 10*, 377–393.

Ethridge, M. E. (1982). The policy impact of citizen participation procedures — a comparative state study. *American Politics Quarterly, 10*(4), 489–509.

Fogg, A. (1981). Public participation in Australia. *Town Planning Review, 52*(3), 259–266.

Getz, D. (1983). Tourism, Community Organisation and the Social Multiplier. *Leisure, Tourism and Social Change, Congress Proceedings of the International Geographical Union Commission of the Geography of Tourism and Leisure*, Vol. 2, (pp. 85–99).

Gow, D. G., & Vansant, J. (1983). Beyond the rhetoric of rural development participation: How can it be done? *World Development, 11*, 427–46.

Gunn, C. A. (1988). *Tourism planning* (2nd ed.). New York: Taylor and Francis.

Hall, C. M. (1994). *Tourism and politics Policy, power and place.* Chichester: Wiley.

Harbison, F. H. (1973). *Human resources as the wealth of nations.* New York: Oxford University Press.

Harrison, D. (1988). *The sociology of modernization and development.* London: Unwin Hyman.

Harrison, D. (1992). International Tourism and the Less Developed Countries: The Background. In D. Harrison, *International Tourism and the less Developed Countries* (pp. 1–19). London: Belhaven Press.

Harrison, D. (1994). Learning from the old south by the new south? The case of tourism. *Third World Quarterly, 15*(4), 707–721.

Haywood, K. M. (1988). Responsible and responsive tourism planning in the community. *Tourism Management, 9*(2), 105–118.

Inskeep, E. (1988). Tourism planning. *Journal of the American Planning Association, 54*(3), 360–371.

Inskeep, E. (1991). *Tourism planning, an integrated and sustainable development approach.* New York: Van Nostrand Reinhold.

Inskeep, E., & Kallenberger, M. (1992). *An integrated approach to resort development.* Madrid: World Tourism Organisation.

International Institute of Tourism Studies (1991). *Global assessment of tourism policy.* Washington: The George Washington University.

Jamal, B. T., & Getz, D. (1995). Collaboration theory and community tourism planning. *Annals of Tourism Research, 22*(1), 186–204.

Jenkins, C. L. (1982). The Effects of Scale in Tourism Projects in Developing Countries. *Annals of Tourism Research, 9*(2), 229–250.

Jones, H. (1990). *Social welfare in third world development.* London: MacMillan.

Keogh, B. (1990). Public participation in community tourism planning. *Annals of Tourism Research, 17*, 449–465.

Koker, L. (1995). Local politics and democracy in Turkey: An appraisal. *The Annals of the American Academy of Political and Social Science, 540*, 51–62.

Lea, J. (1988). *Tourism and development in the third world.* London: Routledge.

Leftwich, A. (1995). Governance, Democracy and Development in the Third World. In S. Corbridge, *Development studies* (pp. 427–437). London: Edward Arnold.

Linton, N. (1987). Trends in tourism and development: A third world perspective. *Tourism Management*, 96–97.

Lipset, S. M. (1981). Economic development and democracy: The political man: The social bases of politics. (pp. 27–63). Baltimore: John Hopkins University Press.

Llosa, M. V. (1995). Foreword to 'The Other Path: The Invisible Revolution in the Third World' by Hernando de Soto. In S. Corbridge, *Development studies* (pp. 288–295). London: Edward Arnold.

Long, V. H. (1991). Government-industry-community interaction in tourism development in Mexico. In M. T. Sinclair, & M. J. Stabler, *The tourism industry: An international analysis* (pp. 205–222). Wallingford: CAB International.

Low, N. (1991). Planning, politics and the state: Political foundations of planning thoughts. London: Unwin Hyman.

Mathieson, A., & Wall, G. (1982). *Tourism. Economic, physical and social impacts.* Essex: Longman Group Ltd.

Mathur, H. M. (1995). The role of social actors in promoting participatory development at local level: A view from India. In H. Schneider, & M. H. Libercier, *Participatory development from advocacy to action* (pp. 153–169). Paris: OECD Publication.

McIntyre, G., Hetherington, A., & Inskeep, E. (1993). Sustainable tourism development guide for local planner. Madrid: World Tourism Organisation.

McQeen, M. (1977). *Britain, the EEC and the developing world.* Heinemann London: Educational Books.

Midgley, J. (1986). Introduction: Social development, the state and participation. In J. Midgley, A. Hall, M. Hardiman, & D. Narine, *Community participation, social development and the state* (pp. 1–11). New York: Methuen and Co.

Midgley, J. (1987). Popular participation, statism and development. *Journal of Social Development in Africa, 2*(1), 5–15.

Miller, S. M., & Rein, M. (1975). Community participation: Past and future. In D. Jones, & M. Mayo, *Community work two* (pp. 3–23). London: Routledge and Kegan Paul.

Mowforth, M., & Munt, I. (1998). *Tourism and sustainability: New tourism in the third world.* London: Routledge

Murphy, P. E. (1985). *Tourism a community approach.* New York: Methuen.

Noronba, R. (1976), *Review of the sociological literature on tourism.* New York: World Bank.

Oakley, P., & Marsden, D. (1984). *Approaches to participation in rural development.* Geneva: International Labour Office.

Oppermann, M., & Chon, K. S. (1997). *Tourism in developing countries.* London: International Thomson Business Press.

Paul, S. (1987). *Community participation in development projects: The world bank Experience.* World Bank Discussion Papers, No. 6. Washington, DC: The World Bank.

Pearce, D. G. (1989). *Tourist development.* Essex: Longman.

Pearce, D. G. (1991). Challenge and change in East European tourism: A Yugoslav example. In M. T. Sinclair, & M. J. Stabler, *The tourism industry An international analysis* (pp. 223–240). Wallingford: CAB International.

Plog, S. C. (1973) Why destination areas rise and fall in popularity. *Cornell Hotel and Restaurant Administration Quarterly*, November, pp. 13–16. Cohen, E. (1972), 'Towards a sociology of international tourism', *Social Research*, 39, pp. 164–182.

Poirier, R. A. (1997). Political risk analysis and tourism. *Annals of Tourism Research, 24*(3), 675–686.

Prentice, R. (1993). Community-driven tourism planning and residents' preferences. *Tourism Management, 14*(3), 218–227.

Pretty, J. (1995). The many interpretations of participation. *Focus, 16*, 4–5.

Reed, M. (1997). Power relations and community-based tourism planning. *Annals of Tourism Research, 24*(3), 566–591.

Ritchie, J. R. B. (1988). Consensus policy formulation in tourism: Measuring resident views via survey research. *Tourism Management, 9*(3), 199–212.

Rosener, J. B. (1982). Making bureaucrats responsive: A study of the impact of citizen participation and staff recommendations on regulatory decision making. *Public Administration Review, 42*(4), 339–345.

Ryan, C., & Montgomery, D. (1994). The attitudes of Bakewell residents to tourism and issues in community responsive tourism. *Tourism Management, 15*(5), 358–369.

Sangmpam, S. N. (1992). The overpoliticized state and democratization. *Comparative Politics*, 401–417.

Sewell, W. R. D., & Coppock, J. T. (1977). A perspective on public participation in planning. In W. R. D. Swell, & J. T. Coppock, *Public participation in planning* (pp. 2–14). London: John Wiley and Sons.

Simmons, D. G. (1994). Community participation in tourism planning. *Tourism Management, 15* (2), 98–108.

Skelcher, C. (1993). Involvement and enpowerment in local public services. *Public Money and Management, 13*(3), 13–19.

Smith, L. (1981). A model for the development of public participation in local authority decision - making. In D. Jones, & L. Smith, *Deprivation, participation, and community action* (pp. 1–36). London: Routledge.

Smith, V. L. & Eadington, W. R. (1992). *Tourism alternatives potentials and problems in the Development of Tourism.* Philadelphia: University of Pennsylvania Press.

Sofield, T. (1996). Anuha island resort, Solomon Islands: A case study of failure. In R. Butler, & T. Hinch, *Tourism and indigenous peoples* (pp. 176–202). London: International Thomson Press.

Stone, L. (1989). Cultural cross-roads of community participation in development: A case from Nepal. *Human Organisation, 48*(3), 206–213.

Taussig, M. (1989). Terror as Usual. *Social Text*, 3–20.

The Economist (1996). A Survey of Turkey. 8th June, 1996.

Til, V. J. (1984). Citizen participation in the future. *Policy Studies Review, 3* (2), 311–322.

Timothy, D. (1999). Participatory planning: A view of tourism in Indonesia. *Annals of Tourism Research, 26*(2), 371–391.

Todaro, M. P. (1994). *Economics for a development world.* New York: Longman.

Tosun, C. (1998a). Challenges of sustainable tourism development in the developing world: The case of Turkey. In D. Hall, & L. O'Hanlon, Conference Proceedings: Rural tourism management: Sustainable options (pp. 539–561). International Conference 9–12th September, The Leisure and Tourism Management Department of The Scottish Agricultural College (SAC)Ayr/Scotland.

Tosun, C. (1998b). Roots of unsustainable tourism development at the local level: The case of Urgup in Turkey. *Tourism Management, 19*(6), 595–610.

Tosun, C. (1998c). Deficits in approaches to tourism development planning in developing countries: The case of Turkey. In Conference Proceedings: International Travel and Tourism: Policy, Law and Management, (pp. 238–248). 19–21 April 1998. Newcastle upon Tyne: University of Northumbria.

Tosun, C. (1999). An analysis of contribution of international inbound tourism to the Turkish economy. *Tourism Economics, 5*(3), 217–251.

Tosun, C., & Jenkins, C. L. (1996). Regional planning approaches to tourism development: The case of Turkey. *Tourism Management, 17*(7), 519–531.

Tosun, C., & Jenkins, C. L. (1998). The evolution of tourism planning in third world countries: A critique. *Progress in Tourism and Hospitality Research, 4*(2), 101–114.

United Nations (1981). *Popular participation as a strategy for promoting community-level action and national development.* Department of International Economic and Social Affairs. New York: United Nations.

Weaver, D. B. (1998). *Ecotourism in the less developed world.* London: Cab International.

Williams, P. W., & Gill, A. (1994). Tourism carrying capacity management. Issues. In W. F. Theobald, *Global tourism* (pp. 174–187). Oxford: Butterworth-Heinemann Ltd.

Willis, K. (1995). Imposed structures and contested meanings — politics of public participation. *Australian Journal of Social Issues, 30*(2), 211–227.

Wolfe, M. (1982). Participation in economic development: A conceptual framework. *Assignment Children, 59/60,* 79–109.

Woodley, A. (1993). Tourism and sustainable development: The community perspective. In J. G. Nelson, R. Butler, & G. Wall, *Tourism and sustainable development monitoring, planning, managing* (pp. 135–146). Waterloo: Heritage Resources Centre, University of Waterloo.

World Tourism Organisation (WTO) (1994). *National and regional tourism planning. A world tourism organization (WTO) publication.* London: Routledge.

Cevat Tosun is a visiting Professor at Bilkert University, Turkey. He obtained his M. Phil. and Ph.D. degrees from University of Strathclyde, UK. His research interests are aspects of community involvement in tourism development in developing countries, sustainable tourism development in developing countries, tourism policy and planning in developing countries.

[30]

 **Pergamon**

www.elsevier.com/locate/atoures

Annals of Tourism Research, Vol. 31, No. 2, pp. 428–446, 2004
© 2004 Elsevier Ltd. All rights reserved.
Printed in Great Britain
0160-7383/$30.00

doi:10.1016/j.annals.2004.01.001

THE DEMONSTRATION
EFFECT REVISITED

David Fisher
Lincoln University, New Zealand

Abstract: The demonstration effect is a concept that has been intuitively accepted by many observers as a natural consequence of tourism. But, it is a vague concept, the results of which are hard to isolate from other factors. This paper argues that it can be broken down into four forms: exact imitation, deliberately inexact imitation, accidental inexact imitation, and social learning. Each of these forms occur as a result of the decision-making process that takes place after the potential imitator has come into contact with the demonstrator. By understanding how decisions are made to imitate, it should be possible to distinguish tourism from other agents of change. **Keywords:** demonstration effect, imitation, cultural change. © 2004 Elsevier Ltd. All rights reserved.

Résumé: Un réexamen de l'effet de démonstration. L'effet de démonstration est une notion qui a été accepté intuitivement par beaucoup d'observateurs comme une conséquence naturelle du tourisme. Mais c'est une notion vague dont les résultats sont difficiles à isoler d'autres facteurs. Cet article soutient que la notion peut se décomposer en quatre formes : imitation exacte, imitation délibérément inexacte, imitation inexacte accidentelle et apprentissage social. Chaque forme se produit comme résultat du processus de prise de décision qui a lieu après que l'imitateur éventuel est entré en contact avec le démonstrateur. Si on comprend comment les gens prennent la décision d'imiter, il devrait être possible de distinguer le tourisme des autres agents de changement. **Mots-clés:** effet de démonstration, imitation, changement culture. © 2004 Elsevier Ltd. All rights reserved.

INTRODUCTION

The demonstration effect is a concept that is advanced regularly in tourism literature. It is an idea that seems intuitively correct, but with little empirical evidence. This is because it is difficult to distinguish between the effects of tourists' behavior on local people and other influences such as advertising, television, films, and the like. This paper will argue that the processes of demonstration and imitation have not been sufficiently well defined. Different forms of demonstration will be suggested together with mechanisms for the transfer of information from one group of people to another. These will provide for a better understanding of the processes involved and offer the opportunity for the collection of empirical data.

David Fisher is Lecturer in Tourism in the Environment, Society and Design Division of Lincoln University (PO Box 84, Canterbury, New Zealand. Email <Fisherd@lincoln.ac.nz>). He has research interests in heritage tourism, Pacific islands, and impacts on host populations. His PhD focused on cross-cultural conceptualizations of heritage tourism in Fiji and he is currently working on the multiple meanings of heritage on New Zealand's West Coast.

The concept of the demonstration effect was introduced into tourism research at an early stage. Those who belonged to what Jafari (1989) referred to as the "cautionary" school of tourism studies, were concerned about the social consequences of tourism, especially in developing countries. They argued that local inhabitants copy the behavioral patterns of tourists (de Kadt 1979; Turner and Ash 1975). Metalka is more specific in suggesting that patterns of behavior are transferred from advanced cultures to "more economically primitive cultures" (1986:30). Mathieson and Wall suggest that the demonstration effect can be defined as hosts trying to copy the "behaviors and spending patterns" of tourists (1982:142). This echoes de Kadt who states, "[t]he effect is most easily and frequently seen in the local patterns of consumption which change to imitate those of tourists" (1979:65). Turner and Ash (1975) claim that status is achieved in Dominica by the consumption of imported alcoholic drinks rather than the locally produced versions. De Kadt (1979) also reports the adoption of imported tastes in the Seychelles. The implication of this, apart from the cultural change that it induces, is a lessening of some of the economic benefits that are claimed for tourism development. If tourists consume imported goods, then an imitative change in the consumption patterns of local people will increase the overall propensity to import (Harris and Howard 1996).

While the demonstration effect is usually perceived as being negative it can also have positive outcomes, but these have not received as much attention. Jafari (1989) obliquely considers an increase in the hosts' pride in their own culture. Van den Berghe (1995) goes further in suggesting that tourist interest in native Mexicans has increased Hispanic Mexicans' appreciation of this ethnic group.

Despite Smith's claim that the demonstration effect "is now seldom mentioned" (1993:630), it is still a term used uncritically in recent texts (Böröcz 1996; Bull 1995; Burns 1999; Lockhart 1997; Nash 1996; Saleem 1996; Shaw and Williams 1994; Vellas and Becherel 1995). Nevertheless, it has been criticized for a variety of reasons. Bryden argues,

> [t]he demonstration effect is...a vague and unsatisfactory concept. It does not, by itself, explain who is demonstrating what to whom and why, or to what extent and at what pace such "demonstration" is occurring (1973:96).

English complains, "no-one has yet attempted to verify the statistical significance of the demonstration effect" (1986:49). McElroy and de Albuquerque state, "despite the critical preoccupation in the literature" of the demonstration effect, there is no agreed definition of it and it has come to mean "almost any negative spillover casually associated with tourist activity" (1986:31).

In one of the few attempts to test the hypothesis McElroy and de Albuquerque, in their study on the Caribbean, conclude that "non-tourist influences are more important predictors of ... consumption behavior" (1986:33). As other authors have noted, tourism is only one aspect of change (Berno 1995; Crick 1989; English 1986; MacNaught

1982; Smith 1993). Local people will also see examples of foreign life-styles and consumption in advertisements, magazines, on television, and in films. Tourism cannot be considered the sole cause of cultural change.

Some writers (Harrison 1992; Henning Brown 1984; MacNaught 1982) argue that there is also something overtly patronizing about the implicit assumption that the cultures of host societies are so weak that they need protecting from contact with tourists, because they may want to copy the tourists' behavior. A number of other assumptions are made by those who blame tourism for the demonstration effect. First, they appear to assume that tourist behavior is being copied blindly. There may be other factors that are involved. Economic domination may result in the marketing and sale of Western goods, which force out the sale of local alternatives. Second, assumptions may be made about the behavior of local people who are apparently copying tourists. Harrison (1992) shows that women who wear jeans in Swaziland run the risk of being thought to be engaging in immoral behavior, when, in fact, jean wearing is a statement against a male authority. Third, change as a result of tourism is a negative conse-quence, but as Crick (1989) points out, all cultures are in a continual process of change so why should change as a result of tourism be con-sidered destructive. Fourth, host populations are passive, but "sub-ordinated or marginal groups select and invent from materials transmitted to them by a dominant or metropolitan culture" (Pratt 1992:6), a process ethnographers term "transculturation". Mowforth and Munt suggest this process "may result in change towards the wishes of the dominant culture" (1998:109) but the extent to which this cultural adaptation is a "blind" demonstration effect rather than a negotiated change needs to be investigated more fully. Casteñada (1996), for example, considers that the negotiation can be multi-directional. This could be particularly true in the case of a tourism destination such as Fiji, where tourists of different cultures meet hosts who also display a range of cultures.

DEMONSTRATING AND IMITATING

The difficulty with the demonstration effect involves understanding how, why, and when it occurs. This paper is intended to provide a more detailed theoretical interpretation, because doing so may pro-vide a more useful set of definitions, allowing for better testing of the concept and isolating it from other factors involved in cultural change. The origins of the concept are presented, followed by refine-ments introduced in evolutionary biology, and their applicability to tourism.

While the demonstration effect is generally defined as behavior that members of the host population copy from tourists, it must be noted that tourists may also copy the behavior patterns of the host com-munity. In either case, however, for it to exist three basic propositions are suggested. First, the behavior of tourists and hosts is initially dif-ferent; second, behavioral patterns are transferred from one group to the other; and third, the imitators maintain the demonstrated behavior. Thus, the approach taken is based on decision-making by both the host and guest populations, as something not acted upon is not considered to show the demonstration effect. As a result, an understanding of *why* the effect occurs rather than just *what* occurs is developed. Of course, a tourist behavior may result in a reaction that is not being demonstrated, but this is relevant to broader impact studies on host–guest interactions, rather than the demonstration effect.

Because the demonstration effect suggests that behavior patterns are transferred from one group to another, theories of copying and decision-making processes from different disciplines are analyzed. These ideas are then adapted for use when tourism is the medium of exchange.

Economic Origins of the Demonstration Effect

It seems likely that the concept of a demonstration effect was borrowed from economics. McElroy and de Albuquerque (1986) claim that the term was formulated by Nurkse (1953) though Nurkse himself credits Duesenberry (1952). However, as a concept within economics, the idea goes as far back as Adam Smith (1776/1991) and David Hume (1739/1978). As 18th century Britain moved from a feudal to a capitalist society, it became acceptable to imitate one's "betters" (Xenos 1989). This resulted in what Smith described as "envy" and Hume called "esteem". A fundamental change in consumption patterns occurred with the rise of the middle classes from one where an individual's position dictated lifestyle (and hence consumption) to one where lifestyle dictated position (Xenos 1989). In other words, people came to copy the consumption patterns of those higher up the social scale in order to improve their social status.

Once social status can be *achieved*, rather than just inherited, people may have an increased propensity to exhibit the trappings of wealth and power. Goods become a signifier of status and the only barrier to obtaining these goods is one's level of wealth (Ewer 1988). Duesenberry (1952) refined this to argue that the significance of the purchase was only within the context of the subculture of the purchaser (and in the process probably coined the phrase "the demonstration effect"). He questioned why there are different propensities to consume among people with the same incomes in the same societies. His major finding was that real consumption tended towards the average of the subgroup to which the consumer belonged. If average consumption were varied among different groups within a society, then the propensity to consume would vary among people with the same incomes but within different groups. The study of a northern English mining community by Dennis, Henriques and Slaughter (1956) is cited to illustrate this point, where social censure and mild ridicule discouraged conspicuous personal consumption. Thus,

> household consumption was kept down to the standard of the lower
> paid. The surplus earnings were skimmed off in convivial entertainment

of their mates, in betting, and in subscriptions to many charitable and
social activities. It was a high-consumption-low-saving economy (Douglas
and Isherwood 1979:123).

However, even within economic literature, there is little empirical evidence to be found in support of the demonstration effect (Hirsch
1976). Some of the development economics literature mentions it
(for example, Meier 1984), following Nurkse (1953), but again it is a
concept that is accepted because it seems to have an intuitive correct-
ness. Herrick and Kindleberger define it as

> imitative behavior, following exposure to hitherto-unknown or -unap-
> preciated modes of consumption or methods of production frequently
> applied to consumption or production patterns seen as economically
> inappropriate in the context into which they are transplanted
> (1983:510).

It is argued that high-income earners in poor countries copy the consumption patterns in the West, which results in a low propensity to
save. However, as Hagen points out, "[t]he theoretical foundation for
the demonstration-effect thesis is rather shaky" (1962:41). There is no
evidence that there were high levels of savings in pre-contact times.
Hagen does not dispute the possibility that there may be a shift in the
sort of goods that are consumed by the elite but, by implication, he
does restrict this change to the elite.

Behavioral Demonstrations

Proponents of the demonstration effect that results from tourism,
go beyond purely economic behavior. Tourism has also been accused
of affecting social behavior. Members of the host population, particularly those in the younger age group, may imitate what tourists do.
This has the effect of challenging traditional value systems (King
1993; Kousis 1989; Saldanha 2002). Again, however, it is difficult to
separate the effects of tourism from other forms of acculturation.
Changing values are also a consequence of urbanization and industrialization. The implication of the arguments put forward by the proponents of an active tourism demonstration effect is that it is more
powerful than other forms of globalization, such as television. This is
because the nature of the contact is face-to-face. However, television
broadcasts into MacCannell's (1976) "back-stage", newspapers and
magazines are read there, and relatives from overseas talk there.
While tourists may be seen by local people on a regular basis, they are
less likely to be invited into private homes than other examples of
Western, affluent lifestyles.

On a more general level of consumer behavior, some work has
been carried out in economics. Studies have attempted to uncover
mechanisms by which consumers make choices. If the conventional
economic assumption of perfect knowledge is relaxed, then people
have to make choices in an environment of uncertainty. The theory of
informational cascades (Bikhchandani, Hirshleifer and Welch 1992;

Hirshleifer 1995) deals with this by suggesting that people imitate others because they assume that others have more information. However, this imitation is restricted to "localized conformity", because "people in different places don't observe each other's behavior" (Hirshleifer 1995:188). People learn by observing others even if what they "learn" is not in their best interest (Becker 1991; Choi 1993; Hirshleifer 1995). This is the demonstration effect under a different name, with more sophisticated variations. Again echoing Adam Smith and David Hume, the hypothesis is that people are more likely to imitate those of higher prestige, believed to be better informed, even though they are of the same cultural group. This is necessary because "only through the acquisition of a complex and culturally specific conceptual framework can sense data be understood" (Hodgson 1992:254). In other words, people can only properly understand the behavior of others if they are culturally similar.

Even so, there are times when, for no obvious reason, one product becomes fashionable. Thompson (1979) explains the phenomenon in terms of catastrophe theory, while expounding his own "rubbish theory" of how some things go in and out of fashion. Very often the originally inexplicable choice of one product over another becomes self-reinforcing and thus understandable in the long run. Once one product gains dominance over another, people buy it because it is the dominant product (Arthur 1988). People buy it because people buy it.

The demonstration effect, as a concept, has also been developed by evolutionary biologists. In many ways copying behavior by organisms has received a more detailed definition than in the social sciences (Blackmore 1999; Dawkins 1991). The biological definitions offer the possibility of greater understanding in the social sciences because the act of copying is broken down into three forms. These are accurate imitation; inaccurate imitation, which results in different actions from that of the original; and social learning, which is a result of individuals having to learn to carry out an action rather than blindly imitating another organism.

One addition must be made to these biological distinctions when relating them to human activity. Inexact imitation can take two forms: accidental and deliberate. Accidental inexact imitation occurs when a failed attempt is made to imitate exactly. In this case, the imitator may be aware or unaware of the failure to imitate exactly. Deliberate inexact imitation occurs when it is not possible to imitate exactly. An example of this could be an attempt to copy a recipe without being able to obtain all the correct ingredients. The cook may use black pepper rather than cayenne. Deliberate inexact copying can become adaptation and social learning if there is a degree of experimentation involved.

Tourism and the Demonstration Effect

These ideas raise a number of questions in the context of tourism. Therefore, an analysis of the demonstration effect in tourism must consider whether local people are imitating tourists' consumption and behavior patterns (correctly or incorrectly) or whether local people are observing different behavior patterns and adapting them to local conditions and culture. Other questions that need asking in relation to tourism are whether tourism has to reach a certain level before the demonstration effect comes into being; whether it requires a certain type of tourist or a host population that has reached a particular level of development; whether it will be observed in all levels of the host society or just within certain groups initially and how this would filter into other groups; and whether a need or desire to change exists.

Some differentiation between patterns of consumption and patterns of behavior is also necessary. For example, it would seem likely that a member of the host population changing the brand of beer they consume after observing what tourists buy is less significant than someone deciding to consume beer instead of a culturally more specific beverage such as palm wine or kava. This, in turn, would be less significant than someone from a group that rejects all intoxicants (for example, a Muslim villager) deciding to consume beer as a result of tourist behavior. The first scenario would be a change in brand loyalty, the second would be a case of substituting one good for another, and the third would be substituting one set of moral beliefs for another resulting in a different basis by which goods are chosen. Finally, allowance must be made for technical advance. The desire to obtain a particular good may be a result of wanting to complete an existing task more easily. A metal axe is more functional than a stone one. A gun is better than a spear. An aqualung is better than a snorkel. Using a new tool, which has been taken from another culture, allows for the technological advancement of the borrowing culture.

Tourists and Tourism

The concepts of demonstration are relevant to both the tourist and the host culture. First, the choice of destination for a tourist is not taken in isolation but as a result of marketing and/or recommendation. It would be very rare for a tourist to select a destination without knowing anything about it beforehand (or at least thinking that they know something about it). However, potential tourists can only know what they are told. This links with Barthes' (1973) concerns about descriptions in travel guides, and the power that guidebooks have in directing the "gaze" of tourists, who copy the instructions given to them by others. This will also occur while touring. Word of mouth and the observations of other tourists can influence the activities and behavior patterns of tourists (Fisher 2000). The second, as Smith (1993) argues, is that the demonstration effect works in two directions: tourists demonstrate to their friends and acquaintances where they have been by the souvenirs they return with. Different types of tourists are likely to want different types of souvenirs, including photographs (Fairweather, Swaffield and Simmons 1998), as well as different sorts of experience.

DAVID FISHER   435

For hosts there are two sorts of choices to make: as consumers and as producers. In the former, according to the informational cascade hypothesis, decisions are made based on knowledge or the supposed superior knowledge of someone else. Thus, if tourists are seen as having superior knowledge, then their patterns of consumption will be followed. If not, then local consumption will not change. However, if a misunderstanding of tourist behavior occurs, the resulting change in local consumption patterns will not resemble those of the tourists. In this scenario, tourists have caused change but it is not obviously that of the demonstration effect. The host as producer of the tourism product will make choices about which goods and services are supplied to the market and the way in which they are supplied based on what is demonstrated by tourists. The level and amount of change made will be dependent on the host society.

Another mechanism for the demonstration effect could be as a result of the elite copying the consumption patterns of the West and later the local population copying the elite. In this scenario it may appear that local people are copying tourists when, in fact, they are not. This would combine the theories of the developmental economists with those of Bikhchandani, Hirshleifer, and Welch (1992) and Hirshleifer (1995). It would, however assume that the hierarchical nature of the society in question is fragile. Someone of lower social standing would have to feel that they are culturally allowed to exhibit greater wealth than their "betters". As Blackmore points out, "(w)e are more likely to be persuaded by someone we perceive as similar to ourselves" (1999:163). Therefore, following Polanyi (1977), a comprehension of social institutions is necessary in order to understand economic activity within a society (Dalton 1971).

Dissecting the Demonstration Effect

In order to be able to test for the demonstration effect, it is necessary to know what is being tested. Following Blackmore (1999) and Dawkins (1991), what is needed initially is to decide which of the four forms of the demonstration effect is occurring. Are the behaviors that are a result of copying an exact imitation, an accidental inexact imitation, a deliberate inexact imitation or an aspect of social learning?

To distinguish among these, it is necessary to understand the decision-making processes that are taking place. The fundamental concept behind the demonstration effect is that people learn by experimentation and by copying others. The individual as scientist was an idea first postulated by psychologist George Kelly then incorporated into psychological and behavioral economics (Earl 1990). Kelly suggested that in order to make a decision an individual uses a previously developed procedure to evaluate the known facts relevant to the decision required. However, a novel situation requires the development of a new procedure. The individual subconsciously puts forward a hypothesis and tests it. If the test proves successful, the hypothesis becomes a new procedure, which is used in similar situations. If the test proves unsuccessful another hypothesis is developed.

The starting point is that people strategically deal with this awareness that they lack knowledge (Elster 1984). Thus, in this framework, the individual acts proactively rather than reactively as orthodox economics suggests, and action or behavior is a result of a desire to achieve a particular goal (or retain a particular situation).

Pearce, Moscado and Ross (1996) examined the response of communities to tourism using social representation theory. They suggested that attitudes are broken down into three component parts: the cognitive (that is, obtaining the necessary information), the evaluation of this information, and the resulting behavior or action. In addition to individual attitude creation are the influences of cultures, subcultures, and groups. However, while this is true of hosts, it is equally applicable to the guests, especially if van den Berghe's (1995) idea that tourists become part of a "super-ethny" is accepted.

As a result, people learn to behave in given situations based on: Modes of behavior that have been passed on from previous generations (cultural behavior), how they have personally behaved in the past (learnt behavior), the results that they have observed in other people's behavior (observed behavior), and the meanings that they ascribe to particular objects, institutions, and patterns of behavior (meaning). For an individual, the weighting given to each of these forms of learning will depend, to some extent, on the structure of the society in which they live. Douglas (1982) calls this "cultural bias".

The Cultural Circle

The cultural circle (Figure 1) is based on von Cranach's (1992) model linking actions with social representations, and Pearce, Moscardo and Ross's (1996) adaptations of Dann's model linking individual and social representations. In this diagram, the links between individual and cultural behavior, and individual and cultural experience, are illustrated. An individual's behavior is dependent on the values and processes that have been learned in the past from group cultural attachments and from personal experiences. To use the terminology of the behavioral economists, learned behavior dictates future choices in action irrespective of whether it was individually learnt or whether it came from cultural and social instruction.

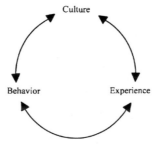

Figure 1. Cultural Circle

However, behavior is iterative. If an individual behaves in a particular way, s/he will learn or gain experience from the action taken, and if the action takes place within the individual's social group, other people will observe the consequences of the action of the individual. However, few cultures are closed systems. Ideas and different methods of achieving goals can come from external sources.

The cultural circle should not be taken as including all members of the population all the time. Within every group there are likely to be subgroups. Young people may influence one another in ways that older people do not, or people of one ethnic group within the host population may influence others within that group differently to those of another group. Similarly, tourists influence one another. This can occur directly, through observation and instruction, or indirectly, through cultural links or informational cascades. Tourists are likely to take note of people they believe are better informed and/or whom they believe are of a similar culture or class. Tourists can be influenced by their "betters" in the Smith and Hume sense, and by their peers with whom they feel they have more in common.

Knowledge Acquisition

Knowledge acquisition is a continuing process (Scholl 1992). It is motivated by curiosity and experimentation (Choi 1993; Earl 1990). However, an individual's knowledge is limited and decisions are made with an understanding of this fact (Simon 1959/1988). It is also "biased toward consistency with the (cognitive) self-image, toward enhancement of (affective) self-esteem and toward support for (conative) self-commitments or identities" (Scholl 1992:38). In other words, when a new idea presents itself, an individual will consider whether to incorporate that idea into his/her body of knowledge and whether to act upon it after making a decision on the consequences of that action. The consequences will include both the immediate results and the reaction of the community to behaving in such a way and the individual's own self-image. Community reactions are, in turn, going to be affected by the social rules within the society. Entrepreneurial spirit, for example, could be warmly applauded in many Western, individualistic cultures, but severely discouraged in societies that are more communally based.

Figure 2 shows the links between social and individual learning for both tourists and the host population. It also illustrates the decision-making process that occurs when a member of the host group imitates the tourist or a member of the tourist group imitates the host (a demonstration effect can occur in both directions). The actual decision-making process goes through five stages: observation, analysis, comparison, evaluation, and finally the decision itself. At each of these stages, an error may occur in the decision-maker's understanding, or a choice may be made to deviate from the behavior of that which is being demonstrated. It is here that the four forms of the demonstration effect can be seen to occur.

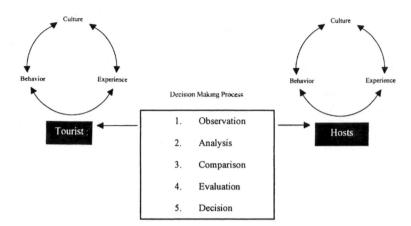

Figure 2. Decision Making Process

Observation. The observer sees the behavior that is being demonstrated. This stage must occur if the demonstration effect is to take
place. However, what is observed may not be a complete observation.
It may be that the observer does not see the context in which the
action takes place or only sees part of the action. If an inaccurate
observation takes place, then an exact imitation cannot occur. However, this does not mean that imitation does not occur, only that it is
an accidental inexact imitation or a stimulus for social learning.

Analysis. Once the activity has been noted, the observer will carry
out some form of analysis which will decide whether what is being
seen is relevant to his or her life. This analysis will be dependent on
two variables, but in either case the results will be the same. Is what is
being observed understood by the observer? At one extreme is perfect understanding and at the other is total incomprehension. The
former will lead to the next stage, comparison, if the observer
believes that what has been noted has relevance to his/her life. The
latter is likely to result in a decision being made not to copy, though
it is possible that a belief in the superiority of the demonstrator can
result in the observer attempting to copy because of a belief that it
must be a good idea. If this were to happen, then it is likely that an
accidental inexact copy will take place. It is also possible that the
analysis will result in misunderstanding. Again, if this were to occur,
then an inexact copy or some form of social learning is likely to
result.

Comparison. If there is some level of understanding, a comparison is
made by the observer with what s/he does in similar circumstances at
present. The result of the comparison will yield four possible alternatives: "We do this better than what I'm observing; we don't do this
and there are no advantages to doing it; we do this but not as well as
what I'm observing; and, we don't do this but there are advantages to

doing it." If the observer feels that s/he already does the action better or sees no point in carrying out the action, then a decision will be
made not to imitate. An evaluation will not take place. However, if the
remaining two scenarios are believed, then the next stage is
approached.

Evaluation. The purpose of the evaluation stage is for the viewer to
decide whether it is possible to copy the observation in some form. A
positive assessment will result in the action being copied. A negative
reaction can be the result of a number of different forces. The most
obvious evaluation is the physical ability to carry out the action. There
may also be economic and social factors. It is possible that the
observer is able and willing to carry out the action, but the social consequences will be negative. In this case, a decision not to imitate will
be the result of not wishing to limit other, unrelated, actions. However, a negative evaluation could result in social learning or deliberate
inexact copying taking place. In other words, the observer may adapt
what is being done to make it economically or socially feasible, or
may attempt to achieve the same ends by developing a different set of
procedures to achieve them. For example, it may be considered a sign
of sophistication to be seen drinking bottled water, but the consumer
may not be able to afford it. Economic factors prevent the imitation.
However, obtaining a bottled water bottle and filling it with tap water
may result in the appearance of sophistication when the imitator is
seen using it. Alternatively, a member of the host population may see
tourists scuba diving, an activity well outside his/her financial means.
An example of social learning demonstration will occur if the
observer then obtains a job with a dive company in the expectation
that s/he will then be taught to dive without having to pay the fees.
Of course, it may be that the evaluation is inaccurate. An incorrect
negative evaluation is not very likely to result in the individual carrying out the action until someone else from the same community does
it. An incorrect positive evaluation is likely to result in the activity
being discontinued as soon as the error is realized.

Decision. The decision that is finally made is likely to be the result of
a number of constraints. For pure imitation to occur, an individual
will have to observe correctly and analyze what is occurring, consider
that the action is better than what s/he does at present, and give the
consequences a positive evaluation. For the copied action to continue, the imitator will not need to re-evaluate the procedure; it must
be possible to maintain it; and it must not be superseded by other
actions. However, by successfully copying one example of tourist
behavior, it may become psychologically easier to copy other aspects
of their behavior. Similarly, if, by copying, negative social consequences occur, the individual may be less willing to try to copy tourists again.

Accidental inexact copying may occur because the initial observation is not complete or the analysis is inaccurate. In both cases, the
decision-making process will continue through the comparison and
evaluation stages, but the decision will be based on an incorrect perception of what the tourist is actually doing. Any resultant action is

likely to be different from that of the tourist, but a result of the demonstration effect, nevertheless.

Deliberate inexact copying will occur at the evaluation stage. The
action will have been correctly observed, analyzed, and compared;
however, for some reason, the observer will feel that it is advantageous to change, in some way, what the tourist did. If the earlier
stages have been misinterpreted, then there is the possibility that perceived deliberate inexact copying would occur as far as the copier is
concerned. However, an omnipotent observer is likely to consider the
action to be the result of inexact copying being altered. It is also possible for social learning to correct the misinterpretation in which case
the action could be interpreted as exact copying.

Finally, social learning will occur when then exact results of actions
observed in tourists are desired, but without the understanding of
how to achieve the goal (a result of poor analysis or observation).
Alternatively, social learning will also occur if the evaluation dictates
that an exact copy of the behavior is not possible, yet that similar
goals can be achieved by altering, in some way, the processes that the
tourist goes through to achieve the particular end. In both these
cases, the final result of the demonstration effect is likely to be different from the way the tourist behaves.

In addition, it may be that the individual decides to copy only in
certain circumstances. This can occur, for example, if kith and kin do
not observe the action, or if tourists are observing the action. The
imitation can also be delayed. A re-evaluation at a later date may
result in the demonstration being copied when originally it was not.
This time delay may be a result of how the cultural group will react to
behaving in a way similar to that of tourists.

Tourism and Other Demonstrations

Tourism is not the only factor causing local people to change their
behavior and consumption patterns. Local people also watch television, listen to the radio, read newspapers, and are influenced by
advertising. In addition, in many places they are also influenced by
friends and relatives who live in other countries and by any visits they
have made to other countries as tourists or workers.

Figure 3 links by arrows other factors influencing tourists and hosts.
A double arrow indicates that the influence can occur in both directions. With each factor the individual tourist or local person will gain
information (make an observation) and go through the decision-making process. It is possible that an observation in one place reinforces
the same elsewhere. A decision is then made on what is considered
the most reliable source of information.

By breaking down the demonstration effect into different parts, it is
easier to understand the processes taking place. A researcher may
question local respondents about their behavior and discover the reasons behind the decisions made. This would also help to differentiate
between those decisions resulting from the tourism demonstration
effect and those from other acculturating factors. The researcher

DAVID FISHER   441

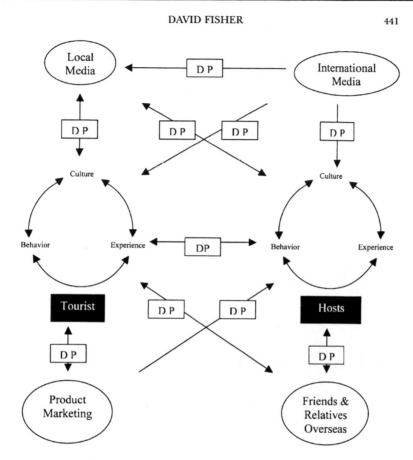

D P = Decision Making Process

Figure 3. The Tourism Demonstration and other Factors of Influence

must learn what is being observed before any causal interpretation is made. However, it should be noted that an observation of one particular action may reinforce previous observations made in other contexts. This helps give the potential imitator a belief that the analysis is likely to be correct.

CONCLUSION

Currently the level of analysis of the tourism generated demonstration effect has been poor, because there has been no real understanding of how it can occur. It has been difficult to explain the processes taking place for an imitation to occur and to isolate tourism demonstrations from those of other influences. There has been an intuitive belief that some members of the host population will copy the behavior or purchasing patterns of tourists in certain circumstances, but hard evidence of this has been difficult to find.

For the demonstration effect to be successfully evaluated it is necessary to understand how individuals behave as a result of contact with tourists, why they choose to behave so, and how their peer group and society will respond to any changes in behavior. Individuals make choices based on their current knowledge and what they anticipate will result from them. The particular choice may be related to a very simple experiment: "they are drinking that; I wonder if it tastes better than what I drink". On the other hand, there may be more complex decisions related to how other people will view the individual if a particular action is chosen. Similarly, the results of imitating tourists may not be immediately identifiable as examples of the demonstration effect. By analyzing the form of demonstration effect, it should be possible to gain a better understanding of how, or if, tourists influence local people.

In addition it is also important to understand why, in certain situations, the demonstration effect does not occur. This knowledge is key to understanding why particular demonstration effects occur and which activities are a result of non-exact copying. It may be that one particular form of imitation will be evident in some societies but not in others. This will only be explained by analyzing the decision-making processes that individuals go through, in conjunction with the kind of society they live in. A member of a hierarchical society is not likely to copy tourists in the same way as someone from a more competitive social background. Decisions are likely to be affected by the reactions to them of others from within the same community. Individuals make decisions in the context of the groups within which they exist. If tourists influence members of the host population, then it is highly likely that other residents also influence them. The converse is not true, though. If an individual is influenced by other members of the society in which s/he lives, it cannot be assumed that tourists also influence that individual. It is possible, however, that indirect influence occurs through informational cascades. Someone may copy the behavior of another individual in the same society who has earlier been influenced by tourists.

Nevertheless, tourism may act as a catalyst for more culturally specific forms of decision-making to take place. A particular good, for example, may be imported for tourists. This action results in the good becoming available to local people, who choose to buy it according to their own decision-making paradigms. In addition, the cultural distance between societies must also be acknowledged. The demonstration effect will be more noticeable when it occurs between very different societies. However, if the distance is too great, then the low level of understanding of what members of another culture are doing could prevent the demonstration from taking place. Finally, and probably most importantly, by understanding why people choose to change their behavior and spending patterns, it will be possible to separate the changes of behavior as a result of tourism from those that occur from other activities. Until this is satisfactorily achieved, the demonstration effect can be no more than a hypothesis. ∎

REFERENCES

Arthur, B.
    1988   Self-reinforcing Mechanisms in Economics. *In* The Economy as an Evolving Complex System, P. Anderson, K. Arrow and D. Pines, eds., pp. 9–31. Redwood City: Addison-Wesley.
Barthes, R.
    1973   Mythologies. London: Paladin Grafton.
Becker, G.
    1991   A Note on Restaurant Pricing and Other Examples of Social Influences on Price. Journal of Political Economy 99:1109–1116.
Berno, T.
    1995 The Socio-cultural and Psychological Effects of Tourism on Indigenous Cultures. Ph.D. Dissertation in psychology. University of Canterbury, Christchurch, New Zealand.
Bikhchandani, S., D. Hirshleifer, and I. Welch
    1992   A Theory of Fads, Fashion, Custom and Cultural Change as Informational Cascades. Journal of Political Economy 100:993–1026.
Blackmore, S.
    1999   The Meme Machine. Oxford: Oxford University Press.
Böröcz, J.
    1996   Leisure Migration: A Sociological Study on Tourism. Oxford: Pergamon.
Bryden, J.
    1973   Tourism and Development: A Case Study of the Commonwealth Caribbean. Cambridge: Cambridge University Press.
Bull, A.
    1995   The Economics of Travel and Tourism. (2nd ed.). Melbourne, Australia: Pitman.
Burns, P.
    1999   An Introduction to Tourism and Anthropology. London: Routledge.
Castañeda, Q.
    1996   In the Museum of Maya Culture. Minneapolis: University of Minnesota Press.
Choi, Y.
    1993   Paradigms and Conventions: Uncertainty, Decision Making and Entrepreneurship. Ann Arbor: University of Michigan Press.
Crick, M.
    1989   Representations of International Tourism in the Social Sciences: Sun, Sex, Sights, Savings and Servility. Annual Review of Anthropology 18: 307–344.
de Kadt, E., ed.
    1979   Tourism: Passport to Development?. New York: Oxford University Press.
Dalton, G.
    1971   Economic Anthropology and Development: Essays on Tribal and Peasant Economies. New York: Basic Books.
Dawkins, R.
    1991   The Blind Watchmaker. Harmondsworth: Penguin.
Dennis, N., F. Henriques, and C. Slaughter
    1956   Coal is our Life. London: Eyre & Spottiswoode.
Douglas, M.
    1982   In an Active Voice. London: Routledge.
Douglas, M., and B. Isherwood
    1979   The World of Goods: Towards an Anthropology of Consumption. London: Allen Lane.

444   DEMONSTRATION EFFECT

Duesenberry, J.
   1952   Income Saving and the Theory of Consumer Behavior. Cambridge:
      Harvard University Press.
Earl, P.
   1990   Economics and Psychology: A Survey. The Economic Journal 100:
      718–755.
Elster, J.
   1984   Ulysses and the Sirens. Studies in Rationality and Irrationality.
      Cambridge: Cambridge University Press.
English, E.
   1986   The Great Escape? An Examination of North-South Tourism. Ottawa:
      North-South Institute.
Ewer, S.
   1988   All Consuming Images: The Politics of Style in Contemporary Culture.
      New York: Basic Books.
Fairweather, J., S. Swaffield, and D. Simmons
   1998 Understanding Visitors' Experiences in Kaikoura Using Photographs of
      Landscape and Q Method. Kaikoura Case Study Report No. 5, Lincoln Uni-
      versity, New Zealand.
Fisher, D.
   2000 The Socio-Economic Consequences of Tourism in Levuka, Fiji. PhD. Dis-
      sertation in tourism development. Lincoln University, New Zealand.
Hagen, E.
   1962   On the Theory of Social Change: How Economic Growth Begins.
      Homewood: The Dorsey Press.
Harris, R. and J. Howard, eds.
   1996   Dictionary of Travel, Tourism and Hospitality. Elsternwick: Hospitality
      Press.
Harrison, D.
   1992   International Tourism and the Less Developed Countries: The Back-
      ground. *In* Tourism and the Less Developed Countries, D. Harrison, ed., pp.
      1–18. New York: Halsted.
Henning Brown, C.
   1984   Tourism and Ethnic Competition in a Ritual Form: The Firewalkers of
      Fiji. Oceania 54:223–244.
Herrick, B., and C. Kindleberger
   1983   Economic Development. (4th ed.). New York: McGraw-Hill.
Hirsch, F.
   1976   Social Limits to Growth. Cambridge: Harvard University Press.
Hirshleifer, D.
   1995   The Blind Leading the Blind: Social Influence, Fads and Informational
      Cascades. *In* The New Economics of Human Behavior, M. Tommasi and K.
      Ierulli, eds., pp. 188–215. Cambridge: Cambridge University Press.
Hodgson, G.
   1992   Rationality and the Influence of Institution. *In* Real-Life Economics:
      Understanding Wealth Creation, P. Ekins and M. Max-Neef, eds., pp. 40–48.
      London: Routledge.
Hume, D.
   1739/1978   A Treatise of Human Nature. Oxford: Clarendon Press.
Jafari, J.
   1989   Sociocultural Dimensions of Tourism. An English Language Literature
      Review. *In* Tourism as a Factor of Change: A Sociocultural Study, J. Bystrza-
      nowski, ed., pp. 17–60. Vienna: European Coordination Centre for Research
      and Documentation in Social Sciences.
King, V.
   1993   Tourism and Culture in Malaysia. *In* Tourism in South-East Asia,
      M. Hitchcock, V. King and M. Parnwell, eds., pp. 99–116. London: Routle-
      dge.
Kousis, M.
   1989   Tourism and the Family in a Rural Cretan Community. Annals of Tour-
      ism Research 16:318–332.

Lockhart, D.
  1997 Islands and Tourism: An Overview. *In* Island Tourism: Trends and Prospects, D. Lockhart, G. Douglas and D. Drakakis-Smith, eds., pp. 3–20. London: Pinter.
MacCannell, D.
  1976 The Tourist: A New Theory of the Leisure Class. New York: Schocken Books.
MacNaught, T.
  1982 Mass Tourism and the Dilemmas of Modernization in Pacific Island Communities. Annals of Tourism Research 9:359–381.
Mathieson, A., and G. Wall
  1982 Tourism: Economic, Physical, and Social Impacts. London: Longman.
McElroy, J., and K. de Alburquerque
  1986 The Tourism Demonstration Effect in the Caribbean. Journal of Travel Research 25:31–34.
Meier, G., ed.
  1984 Leading Issues in Economic Development. (4th ed.). New York: Oxford University Press.
Metalka, C., ed.
  1986 The Dictionary of Tourism. (2nd ed.). Albany: Delmar Industries.
Mowforth, M., and I. Munt
  1998 Tourism and Sustainability: New Tourism in the Third World. London: Routledge.
Nash, D.
  1996 Anthropology of Tourism. Oxford: Pergamon.
Nurkse, R.
  1953 Problems of Capital Formation in Underdeveloped Countries. Oxford: Basil Blackwell.
Pearce, P., G. Moscardo, and G. Ross
  1996 Tourism Community Relationship. Oxford: Pergamon.
Polanyi, K.
  1977 The Livelihood of Man. New York: Academic Press.
Pratt, M.
  1992 Imperial Eyes: Travel Writing and Transculturation. Routledge: London.
Saldanha, A.
  2002 Identity, Spatiality and Post-colonial Resistance: Geographies of the Tourism Critique in Goa. Current Issues in Tourism 5:94–111.
Saleem, N.
  1996 A Strategy for Sustainable Tourism in Sri Lanka. *In* Sustainable Tourism in Islands & Small States: Case Studies, L. Briguglio, R. Butler, D. Harrison and W. Leal Filho, eds., pp. 50–62. London: Pinter.
Scholl, W.
  1992 The Social Production of Knowledge. *In* Social Representations and the Social Basis of Knowledge, M. von Cranach, W. Doise and G. Mugny, eds., pp. 37–42. Lewiston: Hogrefe & Huber.
Shaw, G., and A. Williams
  1994 Critical Issues in Tourism: A Geographical Perspective. Oxford: Blackwell.
Simon, H.
  1959/1988 Theories of Decision-making in Economic and Behavioral Sciences. Reprinted in Behavioural Economics. Vol. 1., P. Earl, ed., pp. 77–108. Aldershot: Gower Publishers.
Smith, A.
  1776/1991 The Wealth of Nations. London: Everyman's Library.
Smith, V.
  1993 Demonstration Effect. *In* VNR's Encyclopedia of Hospitality and Tourism, M. Khan, M. Olsen and T. Var, eds., pp. 629–635. New York: Van Nostrand Reinhold.
Thompson, M.
  1979 Rubbish Theory. Oxford: Oxford University Press.

446   DEMONSTRATION EFFECT

Turner, L., and J. Ash
    1975   The Golden Hordes: International Tourism and the Pleasure Periphery.
           London: Constable.
van den Berghe, P.
    1995   Marketing Mayas: Ethnic tourism Promotion in Mexico. Annals of Tour-
           ism Research 22:568–588.
Vellas, F., and L. Becherel
    1995   International Tourism. New York: St Martin's Press.
von Cranach, M.
    1992   The Multi-level Organisation of Knowledge and Action: An Integration
           of Complexity. *In* Social Representations and the Social Basis of Knowledge,
           M. von Cranach, W. Doise and G. Mugny, eds., pp. 10–22. Lewiston: Hogrefe
           & Huber.
Xenos, N.
    1989   Scarcity and Modernity. London: Routledge.

*Submitted 7 August 2001. Resubmitted 30 April 2003. Accepted 29 October 2003. Final
version 21 November 2003. Refereed anonymously.* **Coordinating Editor: Valene L. Smith**

[31]

International Tourism and Cultural Change in Southeast Asia

Robert E. Wood
University of Massachusetts—Boston

I. Introduction

International tourism is one of the most rapidly expanding links between the advanced capitalist nations and the underdeveloped world. During the 1960s, international tourism emerged as the largest single item in world trade,[1] although increases in oil prices in the 1970s have pushed it back to second place. Annual growth rates are rapid: tourist arrivals in Southeast Asia increased by 13.1% between 1974 and 1975.[2] Hong Kong, Malaysia, Singapore, Taiwan, and Thailand all now receive over 1 million tourists annually.

Tables 1 and 2 document the general expansion of tourism over a 25-year period and the increasing importance of Asian and Pacific destinations. Table 2 shows a fourfold increase in the numbers of international tourists visiting Asia and Australasia between 1965 and 1975 and a doubling of the region's share of the world market. During this decade the region's tourist receipts increased from $484 million to $4.5 billion. Table 3 presents data on the rapid growth of tourism for specific Southeast Asian nonsocialist destinations.[3]

The rapid growth of international tourism is likely to have important cultural implications everywhere, but this seems particularly so in Southeast Asia, where societies are deeply divided culturally and where tourism

---

[1] Michael Peters, *International Tourism* (London: Hutchinson Publishing Group, Ltd., 1969), p. 4.

[2] Robin Dannhorn, "Asia's Tourism Catalyst," *Far Eastern Economic Review* 95, no. 3 (January 21, 1977): 36–37.

[3] To date, socialist Asia has only a minimal tourist industry, and its "tourism of the revolution" is of a fundamentally different nature than tourism in the rest of Asia. Accordingly, socialist countries will not be included in this analysis, nor will be pre-liberation Indochina. However, I am including Taiwan and South Korea because they are part of the Southeast Asian regional tourist market and are often linked to other Southeast Asian destinations in the itineraries of organized tours. Furthermore, they share many common attributes of underdevelopment and tend to get lost if they are lumped with Japan in a separate East Asia category. For tourism of the revolution, see the chapter, "Tourists of the Revolution," in Hans Magnus Enzenberger, *The Consciousness Industry* (New York: Seabury Press, 1974).

Economic Development and Cultural Change

has taken up culture as a major marketable attraction. Virtually all returning travelers to Asia have been struck by the changes tourism has wrought, but very few studies of its cultural consequences exist. A "sociology of tourism" is gradually emerging, but most of the empirical studies have been carried out in Greece, Turkey, Spain, and Portugal, and most remain unpublished.[4] In this paper I want to explore the complex relationship between international tourism and culture, particularly in Southeast Asia.

I will begin by suggesting that, by and large, existing studies and commentaries on the cultural consequences of international tourism pose the issue in unfruitful ways. There are three major aspects to this. First, there is an overreliance on normative categories informed by Western ethnocentrism and romanticism. This is related to a second problem: the use of an oversimplified conception of the cultural contexts which international tourism enters. Third, the existing literature tends to adopt a misleading conception of how tourism affects culture. The first part of

TABLE 1

WORLD INTERNATIONAL TOURIST ARRIVALS
AND RECEIPTS, 1950–75

Year	Tourist Arrivals (Millions)	Tourist Receipts (US$ Billions)
1950	25.3	2.1
1960	71.2	6.8
1965	115.5	11.0
1970	168.	17.9
1975	213.0	31.9

SOURCE.—World Tourism Organization, *Economic Review of World Tourism, 1976* (Madrid: World Tourism Organization, 1976).

TABLE 2

ASIA-AUSTRALASIA REGIONAL SHARE OF WORLD INTERNATIONAL TOURISM, 1950–75

	1950	1960	1965	1970	1975
Tourist arrivals:					
Millions	.2	.9	2.0	5.4	8.0
% of world total	.9	1.2	1.7	3.2	3.8
Tourist receipts:					
$ millions	35.7	229.6	484.0	1,200.0	4,500.0
% of world total	1.7	3.3	4.1	6.7	14.0

SOURCES.—International Union of Official Travel Organizations, *Economic Review of World Tourism*, 1968 and 1972 eds. (Geneva: International Union of Official Travel Organizations, 1968, 1972); World Tourism Organization, *Economic Review of World Tourism, 1976* (Madrid: World Tourism Organization, 1976); Michael Peters, *International Tourism* (London: Hutchinson Publishing Group, Ltd., 1969).

[4] A very useful survey of the literature on the social and cultural dimensions of tourism by Raymond Noronha will soon be published by the World Bank.

Robert E. Wood

TABLE 3

FOREIGN VISITORS TO SOUTHEAST ASIA, 1960, 1970, AND 1976

Destination	1960	1970	1976
Hong Kong......	163,661	927,256	1,559,977
Indonesia........	6,335	129,319	430,000
South Korea.....	5,930*	173,335	834,239
Malaysia........	26,865†	76,374	1,224,815
Philippines......	50,657	144,071	615,159
Singapore.......	90,128	521,654	1,320,625
Taiwan.........	20,796	...	1,000,000
Thailand........	81,340	628,671	1,098,442

SOURCES.—International Union of Official Travel Organizations, *International Travel Statistics, 1960, 1970* (Geneva: International Union of Official Travel Organizations, 1960, 1970); World Tourism Organization, *World Travel Statistics, 1976* (Madrid: World Tourism Organization, 1976), and *Economic Review of World Tourism, 1976* (Madrid: World Tourism Organization, 1976); William Glenn, "Taiwan: Temporary Wives Too," *Far Eastern Economic Review 95*, no. 3 (January 21, 1977): 70.
  * Arrivals by air only.
  † 1963 data.

this paper, accordingly, will analyze these problems and suggest an alternative framework for analyzing tourism and culture in Southeast Asia.

In the second part of this paper, I pose three aspects of the relationship between tourism and culture which seem particularly important and worthy of further exploration. These involve the expanded cultural role of the state, the unique articulation with culture which tourism as an industry in Southeast Asia involves, and the way in which tourism constitutes a new cultural institution in its own right.

II. Conceptual Problems

Serious attention to the cultural consequences of international tourism is relatively new. In December 1976, Unesco and the World Bank sponsored a joint Seminar on the Social and Cultural Impacts of Tourism, which adopted a set of policy recommendations on the subject.[5] The section of these recommendations on culture, however, focuses primarily on how the local culture should be presented to tourists and on how tourists can be trained to be better mannered. On the whole, concern with the cultural consequences of international tourism receives lip service at best. At its 1977 convention in Hong Kong, the Pacific Area Travel Association, which includes 50 governments as well as large tourist businesses, implicitly negated the Unesco resolutions by choosing the slogan, "The consumer—the only person who matters." In a similar vein, the Twenty-first United Nations General Assembly designated 1967 "International Tourist Year" with a unanimous resolution asserting that "tourism is a

[5] See Joint Unesco/IBRD Seminar on the Social and Cultural Impacts of Tourism, *Policy Recommendations*, mimeographed (Washington, D.C., December 10, 1976).

Economic Development and Cultural Change

basic and most desirable human activity deserving the praise and encouragement of all peoples and governments."[6]

Recently, however, more critical voices have been raised. An interesting example is a two-part article by Jacques Bugnicourt in the UN publication, *Development Forum*, that takes a highly critical stance toward tourism's cultural effects.[7] Bugnicourt accuses tourism of demeaning and distorting culture: it encourages the imitation of foreigners and the downgrading of local inhabitants in relation to foreign tourists; it incites the pillage of artwork and other historical artifacts; it leads to the degeneration of classical and popular dancing, the profanation and vulgarization of places of worship, and the perversion of religious ceremonies; and it creates a sense of inferiority and a cultural demoralization which "fans the flames of anti-development" through the acquisition of undesirable cultural traits. This is strong language for a generally cautious UN publication, for it represents an attack on a large and powerful international industry.

Bugnicourt's critique is interesting not only for its critical stance in a field where tourism's cultural effects are often assumed to be unproblematic but also for the way it reflects several limitations of most of the literature on the subject. Perhaps the most obvious one is proof: Bugnicourt offers very little evidence to back up his assertions, and a review of the literature leaves one with an awareness of how little these questions have been researched. The conceptual limitations are equally important, however, and it is on these that I want to focus in this section.

Normative Categories

Bugnicourt's approach typifies the literature on the cultural consequences of tourism in its overreliance on normative categories: it is asked whether cultures are spoiled, broken down, demeaned, preserved, strengthened. These questions betray a Western ethnocentrism and romanticism in their desire to "preserve" cultures. It is simply assumed that to preserve cultural forms is better than to change them. Even in less polemical works, such as the useful collection of essays recently published as *Hosts and Guests: The Anthropology of Tourism*,[8] the recurring use of these normative categories continually constrains the analysis. When the editor sums up the collective thrust of the essays by commenting that "it appears that the existent forms of tourism tend overall to be more negative than positive in impact, but this is not irremediable," we see what a straitjacket these normative categories have become.[9] Frantz Fanon's reminder of the in-

---

[6] Quoted in A. J. Burkart and S. Medlik, *Tourism: Past, Present and Future* (London: William Heinemann, 1974), p. 57.

[7] Jacques Bugnicourt, "Tourism with No Return!" *Development Forum* 5, no. 5 (June–July 1977): 1–2, and "The Other Face," ibid., no. 6 (August–September 1977): 8.

[8] Valene L. Smith, ed., *Hosts and Guests: The Anthropology of Tourism* (Philadelphia: University of Pennsylvania Press, 1977).

[9] Ibid., p. 14.

Robert E. Wood

exorable and potentially liberating movement of culture is forgotten:

> Culture has never the translucidity of custom; it abhors all simplification. In its essence it is opposed to custom, for custom is always the deterioration of culture.
>
> The struggle [for national sovereignty] itself in its development and in its internal progression sends culture along different paths and traces out entirely new ones for it. The struggle for freedom does not give back to the national culture its former value and shapes; this struggle which aims at a fundamentally different set of relations between men cannot leave intact either the form or the content of the people's culture.[10]

I am not arguing here for a value-free social science but for one which takes this long-term struggle for freedom seriously. Overreliance on ethnocentric normative categories has tended to shut off analyses of actual cultural change in underdeveloped countries. We need to go beyond evaluations based on Western romantic ideals of cultural preservation to analyze the precise components of cultural change and to relate these to the emergence of new social formations and to new potentialities for social transformation. On an a priori basis, it is possible to argue quite inconsistent positions, for example, that the demeaning of culture will lead to a nation of "flunkeys"[11] or, alternatively, to political radicalization.[12] We need to go beyond labeling to an analysis of the concrete cultural meanings of the changes tourism sets in motion. As we shall see, however important the preservation/dissolution question may be, the significance of international tourism for culture extends far beyond this.

Inadequate Conception of Culture

Recourse to these simple normative categories is facilitated by an oversimplified view of what culture is and how tourism can affect it. The way questions are posed often suggests a billiard ball model, in which a moving object (tourism) acts upon an inert one (culture), at best through the intermediary of a third object (culture brokers). The assumption is that culture is unitary, passive, and inert. Such an approach to culture in Southeast Asia misses the dynamic context tourism enters and the variety of active responses to tourism which shape its cultural meaning. To understand the relationship between tourism and culture, we need to recognize culture as internally differentiated, active, and changing.

It is striking how much of the writing on the cultural effects of tourism treats culture as a unified reality set against the alien intrusion of tourism. In part, this is a unit-of-analysis question: the tendency to study small-scale locales rather than larger social units. It also, however, reflects a kind of anthropological populism which minimizes internal cultural divi-

[10] Frantz Fanon, *The Wretched of the Earth* (New York: Grove Press, 1966), pp. 180, 197.
[11] Bugnicourt, p. 8.
[12] Louis Turner, *Multinational Companies and the Third World* (New York: Hill & Wang, 1973), p. 227.

Economic Development and Cultural Change

sions. Tourism in Southeast Asia operates in cultural contexts which are characterized by a variety of competing claims: (1) internal divisions within traditional cultures (e.g., the *abangan, prijaji,* and *santri* strains within Javanese culture); (2) horizontal cultural pluralism, including that created by the colonial introduction of substantial Chinese minorities in such countries as Malaysia and Indonesia; (3) the claims of a new syncretic national culture; and (4) the image of international Western culture. This cultural differentiation is particularly interesting to the extent that it relates to class and other forms of social conflict. Rather than looking for international tourism's impact on some undifferentiated notion of culture, we need to ask how tourism becomes a factor in these oppositions and helps shape the outcomes of conflict.

In Indonesia, for example, we should look at (1) how tourism may affect the internal balance of Javanese and other complex cultures; (2) how the uneven spread of tourism and varying responses to it may affect the relations between different cultural and racial groups within Indonesian society; (3) how tourism may foster or undermine the Indonesian state's claim of a distinctive national identity; and (4) how tourism promotes acculturation to foreign cultural values. Questions such as these, I submit, promise more interesting answers than the simple normative ones discussed in the previous section.

In analyzing these questions, it is important to remember that Southeast Asian cultures are not inert; most have been deeply transformed by colonialism and their integration into the capitalist world economy. This creates methodological problems in evaluating the specific consequences of tourism, since it is often very difficult to isolate its effects. Tourism as an institution and economic policy is part of an externally oriented approach to development which includes reliance on foreign aid and investment, imported technology, and many other links with the advanced capitalist countries. The cultural effects of tourism are often therefore "overdetermined." Indeed, tourists are often shocked to discover the cultural artifacts which have preceded them—tape decks blaring rock music in Philippine buses and "Six Million Dollar Man" T-shirts in the longhouses of Borneo.

We must also recognize that cultures are not passive, and we must become more sensitive to the cultural strategies people develop to limit, channel, and incorporate the effects of international tourism. The best and most detailed study of this generally neglected phenomenon is an unpublished Ph.D. dissertation by Philip McKean, based on research in Bali. McKean criticizes the lack of attention to such strategies in the literature: "There is, in short, little analysis of any mechanisms available to indigenous populations so that they might resist change, and retain and revitalize their social fabric and customs. What attempts are there to conserve culture within the changed conditions wrought by the tourist industry? If this question has not been asked by anthropologists, it has

566

Robert E. Wood

most certainly been overlooked by other writers who typically turn up their noses in disdain at tourists and their effect on the host area."[13]

McKean argues that the Balinese have been quite successful in devising ways both to insulate and to strengthen cultural traditions. For example, dance performances for tourists are altered in subtle ways which change their religious meaning so as to avoid profaning these normally sacred events, and proceeds are channeled into voluntary cultural associations. McKean asserts: "In short, and perhaps most dramatically stated, the traditions of Bali will prosper in direct proportion to the success of the tourist industry. Far from destroying, ruining, or 'spoiling' the culture of Bali, I am arguing here that the advent and increase of tourists is likely to fortify and foster the arts: dance, music, architecture, carving, and painting."[14]

McKean's analysis is vitiated by a lack of attention to class differentiation among the Balinese, but his study is one of the few which emphasizes active cultural responses to tourism. One of the things which his data show is that there are many levels of response and that these represent new arenas of conflict. Planning and licensing are two arenas where conflicts show up particularly clearly between the central government and the regional government, between cultural preservation associations and business interests, etc.

These active cultural strategies can be expected to shape tourism itself in varying degrees. Young has gone even further to argue that the structural characteristics of a society determine the type of tourism which will develop. Looking at 29 Caribbean islands, Young hypothesizes that "the tourist institutions in the more rigid or 'plantation' types of societies will develop along similarly rigid lines and that in the more flexible, democratic or socially progressive islands, the industry will be a widespread phenomenon."[15] While the types of tourism she comes up with (comprehensive, luxury, and plantation) seem vaguely delimited and overlapping, her article is important for its general thrust.

Interpersonal Interaction
Studies of the cultural impact of tourism have had a natural tendency to focus on the direct interaction between tourists and local people and to assume that it is out of this interaction that the process of cultural change emerges. Studies in Southeast Asia, for example, have examined the effects of tourists participating in the elaborate funeral ceremonies of the Toraja in Sulawesi and the types of interaction with locals on bus tours

[13] Philip F. McKean, "Cultural Involution: Tourists, Balinese, and the Process of Modernization in an Anthropological Perspective" (Ph.D. diss., Brown University, 1973), p. 9.
[14] Ibid., p. 1.
[15] Ruth C. Young, "The Structural Context of the Caribbean Tourist Industry: A Comparative Study," *Economic Development and Cultural Change* 25, no. 4 (July 1977): 657–72, esp. p. 658.

Economic Development and Cultural Change

in Singapore.[16] Elsewhere, studies have shown how public forms of sociability among Eskimos have disappeared in the face of tourist photography,[17] how ceremonies of collective solidarity among the Basque have lost their traditional meaning as they have become tourist attractions,[18] and how interaction with tourists promotes national stereotyping.[19]

This practice of focusing on face-to-face interaction in specific situations might seem at first particularly appropriate for Southeast Asia, where tourism is highly concentrated geographically. Most international tourists go to the same few places. On the assumption that the existence of accommodations meeting Western standards is an indicator of the spread of tourism, table 4 presents the number of cities and towns with hotels listed in the 1976/77 edition of *Fodor's* guidebooks to the Southeast Asian region. Only 90 locations are listed for the entire region, and over one-third of these are in the Philippines.[20] Only 20 cities or towns offer more than five tourist-standard hotels. Similarly, the *Hotel and Travel Index*, used by travel agents in booking hotel reservations, lists only 104 locations for the entire region.[21]

TABLE 4

NUMBER OF LOCATIONS WITH HOTELS LISTED IN FODOR'S GUIDES, BY COUNTRY AND NUMBER OF HOTEL LISTINGS

	NUMBER OF HOTEL LISTINGS			
COUNTRY	1	2–5	Over 5	Total
Brunei	...	1	...	1
Hong Kong	...	...	1	1
Indonesia	4	9	2	15
South Korea	...	...	2	2
Macao	...	...	1	1
Malaysia	8	10	2	20
Philippines	4	19	9	32
Singapore	...	...	1	1
Taiwan	5	4	1	10
Thailand	4	2	1	7
Total	25	45	20	90

SOURCES.—*Fodor's Southeast Asia 1976/77* (New York: David McKay Co., 1976), and *Fodor's Japan and South Korea 1977* (New York: David McKay Co., 1977).

[16] Eric Crystal, "Tourism in Toraja," in Smith; Riaz Hassan, "International Tourism and Intercultural Communication: The Case of Japanese Tourists in Singapore," *Southeast Asian Journal of Social Science* 3, no. 2 (1975): 25–37.

[17] Valene Smith, "Eskimo Tourism: Micro-Models and Marginal Men," in Smith (n. 8 above).

[18] Davydd J. Greenwood, "Culture by the Pound: An Anthropological Perspective on Tourism as Cultural Commoditization," in Smith.

[19] Oriol Pi-Sunyer, "Through Native Eyes: Tourists and Tourism in a Catalan Maritime Community," in Smith.

[20] It should be noted, however, that *Fodor's* appears to attempt to be more complete where Western-style accommodations are the exception. Its Korean listings are particularly incomplete, and the guide notes that "it is definitely possible to find adequate accommodation in any important artistic, scenic, recreational or resort area in Korea now" (*Fodor's Japan and S. Korea* [New York: David McKay Co., 1977], p. 502).

[21] *Hotel and Travel Index* (New York: Ziff-Davis Publishing Co., Autumn 1976).

Robert E. Wood

This geographic concentration stems from a number of factors. One is the nature of organized tours, which generally attempt to cover "the Orient" rather than explore a single country in depth. This leaves time only for a few days in each country, and the natural temptation is to cover the same internationally recognized attractions. The 1975 surveys reported to the World Tourism Organization show that the average lengths of stay for Southeast Asian countries range between 4 and 8 days.[22]

Despite the geographical concentration of Southeast Asian tourism, it is probably incorrect to assume that the most important cultural consequences of tourism arise directly out of interaction with tourists. It has been observed by various writers that the most disruptive forms of tourism are the types which involve the least direct interaction with locals—what has been called "bubble tourism."[23] The growth of a tourism industry not only introduces new groups from outside the society but also transforms the relationships between members of the society itself. It is the participation of people in an altered social and cultural system resulting from tourism which is most important for cultural change. The cultural consequences of tourism extend far beyond the immediate locales where interaction with tourists takes place.

III. Three Arenas of Change
Expanded Cultural Role of the State
The expanded cultural role of the state which results from the growth of tourism is one of the significant ways tourism promotes cultural change. This expanded role results both from the way tourism involves new forms of integration into the world economy and from the particular importance of cultural attractions in Southeast Asian tourism.

Tourism represents a new relationship with both the national and world economy and, because of this, nearly always involves a greatly expanded role of the state. At the minimum, the state must cooperate with tourist development, for example, in visa policy, foreign exchange requirements, and import regulations. But usually the state plays an active role in opening up new areas to mass tourism, because either government expenditures or resources from international agencies are required for the provision of infrastructure (roads, airport, electricity, etc.) and often for tourist facilities themselves.

The new role of the state is often particularly striking, because the tourist appeal of many areas stems precisely from their relative isolation until recent times. There seems to be a kind of centrifugal tendency of Southeast Asian tourist development, leading to the incorporation of selected outlying, relatively isolated peoples rather than a generalized dispersion of facilities. This means that when a new area is incorporated

[22] World Tourism Organization, *World Travel Statistics 1975* (Geneva: World Tourism Organization, 1975).
[23] See Nelson Graburn, "Tourism: The Sacred Journey," in Smith, p. 31.

Economic Development and Cultural Change

tourism increases very rapidly. Airport arrivals in Bali jumped from 46,765 in 1969 to 202,489 in 1975.[24] In South Sulawesi, Indonesia, international tourists increased from 2,317 in 1973 to 15,850 in 1975.[25]

Examples of relatively isolated cultural groups in Southeast Asia being partly integrated economically through tourism include the hill tribes in northern Thailand; the Toraja in central Sulawesi, Indonesia; the Igorots in central Luzon, Philippines; and the Ibans and Kayans near Kuching and along the Rajang River in East Malaysia. An additional dynamic leads to the singling out of the most isolated and traditional groups within these populations. For example, in Bali, the original Balinese (Bali Aga) villages of Tenganan and Trungan are now common tourist stops.

Tourists to Southeast Asia thus are often drawn to those areas which have been bypassed by other modes of economic integration, and hence they often become a symbol of the loss of autonomy and local control which economic integration and an expanded state presence tend to involve. Noronha has discussed this in terms of a three-phase process of "institutionalization" and has argued that local resentment toward tourism is really directed more toward outside interests (the state, entrepreneurs from other regions, immigrant labor) than toward tourists themselves.[26]

The expansion of government presence necessarily involves new forms of cultural intervention in such areas as education and law, but the state's interest in promoting cultural tourism results in other forms of cultural intervention as well. One which is particularly interesting is the role of the state as the self-appointed arbiter of the culture which is to be preserved and presented to tourists. Several case studies have discussed this phenomenon in areas outside of Asia. Nunez reports that in the Mexican village of Cajititlan the state assigned three rural police to suppress cultural forms which were considered unappealing from the tourist point of view.[27] The tourists were mostly wealthy Mexicans (who were mistaken, however, by many villagers for Americans), and it is interesting to observe that the reforms involved some customs which might have been much more intriguing to international tourists than to middle-class Mexicans: horse racing, livestock in the street, and traditional forms of male dress. In Greece, the central government has stepped in to preserve traditional architectural styles, often bringing itself into conflict with local interests.

The state's perceived self-interest in presenting a particular view of

[24] Raymond Noronha, "Paradise Reviewed: Tourism in Bali," mimeographed (paper prepared for Joint Unesco/IBRD Seminar on the Social and Cultural Impacts of Tourism, December 1976), p. 4.

[25] David Jenkins, "Westerners Are Ugly," *Far Eastern Economic Review* 95, no. 3 (January 21, 1977): 75.

[26] See Raymond Noronha, "Social and Cultural Dimensions of Tourism: A Review of the Literature in English" (draft of a working paper, May 1977).

[27] Theron A. Nunez, "Tourism, Tradition, and Acculturation: *Weekendismo* in a Mexican Village," *Ethnology* 2, no. 3 (July 1963): 349–50.

Robert E. Wood

the national culture may conflict with the tendency of cultural tourism to spread to the most isolated—and hence least "modern"—peoples. Tourist interest in the Masai has long been a dilemma for East African governments concerned with combating the stereotypes of "primitive" Africa. It is likely that the authorities in East Malaysia have a similar ambivalence about the heads still dangling from the rafters of many Iban longhouses.

In addition to being an arbiter of living culture, the state also organizes cultural reproductions. The national museums which all Southeast Asian countries support make a cultural statement directed both to international tourists and to their own citizens. The swarms of local schoolchildren being shepherded through them testify to the authorities' belief that they contain something to be learned about the national culture. (I know of no analyses of their contents or implicit messages, however.)

In Southeast Asia, the museum idea has been extended to artificial reproductions of traditional houses, craftsmen's ateliers, and often whole villages or minisocieties spread out over many acres. This type of cultural production, located near the capital city and attempting to provide an overview of the national culture, now exists in Indonesia, Korea, the Philippines, and Thailand. In the case of Indonesia, Anderson has described how Mini-Indonesia, a pet project of President Suharto's wife, became a major object of political controversy over what conception of Indonesian culture was to be presented to international tourists and to Indonesians. It required the forceful intervention of President Suharto to override the widespread public opposition.[28]

Such projects provide an interesting example of the link between international and domestic tourism. They would probably not be built except for the development of international tourism, but the majority of their visitors are in fact nationals. They testify to the fact that urbanization and class differentiation exist to such an extent that members of the national upper and middle classes can find it enjoyable—and apparently preferable—to seek out an artificial and sanitized experience of how the majority of their own fellow citizens live, rather than journeying an equal distance in another direction to see the real thing.

Part of marketing cultural experiences to tourists involves interpreting them. Most Southeast Asian governments license official guides and in some areas insist that cultural troupes performing for tourists be approved by a government agency. Government tourist boards spend millions of dollars annually to attract tourists, partly by presenting a picture of the local culture. Singapore's Tourist Promotion Board, for example, spent $6 million in 1974 for the 1.4 million visitors who came.[29] Most advertising of this sort is done abroad, but it may have an indirect effect on local cultural awareness through the expectations tourists bring. In addition,

[28] Benedict Anderson, "Notes on Contemporary Indonesian Political Communication," *Indonesia* 16 (October 1973): 39–80.
[29] "Recognizing the Need for Cohesive Policies," *Far Eastern Economic Review* 87, no. 11 (March 14, 1975): 4.

Economic Development and Cultural Change

in some countries (particularly in the Caribbean), governments have undertaken campaigns directed at their own citizens, encouraging a more friendly attitude toward tourists.[30]

This interpretive role of the state merges into such spin-off industries as travel agents, tourist guides, publishers of guidebooks, etc., which grow up to help tourists make some sense of what they see and to channel their perceptions—and spending—in particular directions. McKean found that government tourist publications and privately published guidebooks for tourists constituted the main reading materials used in preparation by Balinese guides.[31] In Tonga, when a government-sponsored survey of tourists revealed their complaint that local people did not know enough of their own culture and history, the government published a pamphlet for local distribution to rectify the problem.[32] These examples suggest that the interpretations generated by the state and by the tourism industry may filter down to the human objects of tourism as well.

A good deal of cultural misinformation gets passed on to tourists in this process. In Indonesia, for example, guides and guidebooks routinely inform tourists that the struggles in the dramas and dances they see represent a Manichaean struggle between good and evil, whereas in fact one of their most fascinating themes is the ambiguity of moral categories and the relativity of human values. Anderson has observed that other changes in Indonesian life are tending to redefine the *wayang* in this direction;[33] the Western-oriented cultural interpretation produced for tourism probably contributes to this tendency. Tourism's power to redefine cultural meaning increases to the extent that it becomes, as McKean puts it, "the patron of a particular aspect of the culture."[34]

Government interest in promoting tourism may skew research into local cultures. One anthropologist has suggested to me that it is much easier to get permits in Southeast Asia for archaeological digs than for cultural anthropological research, partly because the governments hope to turn up more tangible tourist attractions.

Unique Cultural Characteristics of Tourism Industry

The unique nature of international tourism is partly captured by its paradoxical designation by economists as an "export" industry. Its crucial characteristic distinguishing it from other exports is, of course, the fact that the sale of goods and services to foreigners takes place

[30] E.g., several years ago the Bahamas instituted a "Friendliness through Understanding" program to encourage courtesy toward tourists, with Sidney Poitier reading letters from disgruntled tourists over the radio. See Donald E. Lundberg, *The Tourist Business* (Chicago: Institutions/Volume Feeding Management Magazine, 1972).

[31] McKean, p. 170.

[32] Charles F. Urbanowicz, "Tourism in Tonga: Troubled Times," in Smith (n. 8 above).

[33] Benedict Anderson, *Mythology and the Tolerance of the Javanese*, Modern Indonesia Project monograph series, no. 37 (Ithaca, N.Y.: Cornell University, 1965).

[34] McKean, p. 285.

Robert E. Wood

within the country itself. When it is the experience of the local culture which is being sold, the unique quality of international tourism becomes even more evident.

Tourists go to Southeast Asia, as elsewhere, with a variety of motivations. The literature on the sociology of tourism makes a crude distinction between "sunlust" and "wanderlust" motivations, although there have been several attempts at more discriminating typologies.[35] Sunlust tourists want relaxation (mainly on beaches) and sports, whereas wanderlust tourists are in search of cultural and other exotic experiences. To date, Southeast Asia has been too far away from the centers of demand to compete for the pure sunlust market, which is very price competitive. The tremendous growth of Japanese tourism is changing this, however, and one study predicts that by the end of the century sunlust tourism in Southeast Asia will generate revenues twice that of wanderlust tourism.[36] The rapid growth resorts like Pattaya, Thailand, and Penang, Malaysia, testify to the importance of sunlust tourism, although by and large they depend on tourists who are drawn to Southeast Asia primarily on the basis of wanderlust motivations.

Guidebooks for Southeast Asia and the itineraries of organized tours reflect a strong cultural focus, and the predominant form of tourism in Southeast Asia can be characterized as cultural tourism, in the sense that the dominant tourist motivation is to experience the local cultures. The issue is complicated by the large amount of regional travel within Southeast Asia, however. The definition of "tourist" used by international organizations is extremely broad, almost synonymous with foreign visitors. Table 5 shows that regional tourists constitute a substantial proportion

TABLE 5

REGIONAL TOURISM: TOTAL NUMBER OF SOUTHEAST
ASIAN VISITORS AND PROPORTION OF
TOTAL VISITORS, 1975

Destination	Southeast Asian Visitors (*N*)	Proportion of Total Visitors (%)
Malaysia............	668,129	56
Singapore..........	556,565	42
Thailand............	378,461	32
Hong Kong.........	331,217	25
Philippines..........	45,523	9
South Korea.........	52,570	8

SOURCE.—World Tourism Organization, *World Travel Statistics, 1975* (Madrid: World Tourism Organization, 1975).

[35] See H. Peter Gray, *International Travel: International Trade* (Lexington, Mass.: Lexington Books, D. C. Heath & Co., 1970), and "Toward an Economic Analysis of Tourism Policy," *Social and Economic Studies* 23, no. 3 (September 1974): 386–97; Valene L. Smith, "Introduction," in Smith.

[36] Gray, *International Travel*, pp. A.

Economic Development and Cultural Change

of the total for Malaysia, Singapore, Thailand, and Hong Kong. In Singapore, Malaysians and Indonesians are the two largest groups of international visitors; in Malaysia, Thais and Singaporeans. Malaysians are the largest single group in Thailand. In Hong Kong, Southeast Asian visitors collectively lag behind only the Japanese. It is unwise simply to assume that these regional visitors are just like Western tourists.[37] Undoubtedly, they follow to some extent the footsteps of the cultural tourists from the rich countries, but we know little about how much. Certainly, their economic impact is less significant; in Malaysia, for example, U.S. visitors accounted for less than 6% of visitor arrivals but over 58% of tourist receipts, while regional visitors, accounting for 56% of visitor arrivals, provided less than 10% of tourist receipts.[38] If the majority of regional tourists are, as I suspect, petty traders, persons visiting relatives, and shoppers taking advantage of duty-free ports, the official statistics substantially overstate the number of people properly considered cultural tourists.

Much more than sunlust tourism, cultural tourism raises the interesting question of the way cultural forms vary in their "fit" with international tourism. This may offer a partial explanation of the particular geographic spread of cultural tourism, as well as tourism's selective articulation with specific cultural institutions. For example, the following comparison of Javanese and Balinese culture by Hildred Geertz suggests some contrasts which may be touristically relevant:

> In contrast to Java, where the practice of the arts, while more subtle and profound, is today largely confined to court circles and to a few professional dramatic and orchestral troupes, aesthetic expression in Bali is an activity pursued by large numbers of persons from all segments of society. . . . Art for both cultures has perhaps greater significance than elsewhere in the archipelago, possessing a central and dynamic religious meaningfulness. In Java this significance is philosophical and mystical, concerned with the achievement of psychological and moral inner stasis, while in Bali external ritual display and more direct aesthetic pleasure are involved.[39]

The exuberant Balinese dances are a prime attraction for tourists in Bali, but efforts to make Javanese dance and theater accessible to tourists have been less successful. In Jogjakarta, the Agastya Institute and Nitour (the government tour agency) sponsor shortened, 2-hour versions of the usually nightlong puppet theater, but even these are too long for the majority of tourists, who leave before the performance is over. Moreover, the Javanese cultural forms displayed to tourists involve almost exclusively the *prijaji*, or court, culture; *abangan* (peasant animist) and *santri* (orthodox Moslem) cultural forms remain outside the tourist orbit.

[37] This assumption seems to be made in an article on regional tourism, "Tourism: The New Spenders," *Asiaweek* 3, no. 7 (February 18, 1977): 26–30.

[38] World Tourism Organization (n. 22 above).

[39] Hildred Geertz, *Indonesian Cultures and Communities* (New Haven, Conn.: HRAF Press, 1963), p. 31.

Robert E. Wood

For most tourists to experience the culture of a foreign society, it must be produced and marketed in some way. The transformation of culture into a commodity for sale is a fundamental process cited in a number of tourism studies. There are two major ways in which cultural experiences are marketed to tourists. One may be called "tours of living culture." These consist of guided groups which venture out to see cultural forms in their natural settings: religious shrines, markets, ceremonies, etc. In Bali, tour organizations even offer tours to such events as cremations, weddings, tooth-filing ceremonies, and priestly ordinations. These events are not staged for tourists, but the presence of tourists may alter them in subtle ways. In addition, the guides may discretely intervene to make them conform to tourist expectations. For example, an essay by Bali's most famous guide, Nyoman Oka, describes his intervention to make a cremation ceremony more photogenic for his client:

> We were the first to arrive and the last to leave, because he wanted to take pictures of the towers burning. . . . At last I saw some people topple the small tower to burn it in a lying position. A picture of this would be nothing. When I saw they were going to do the same thing to the taller tower, I approached the host, whom I happened to know, and explained to him who my guest was and what he was doing in Bali. I asked him to leave the tower standing when they were going to burn it, and he obliged. My guest got a very beautiful picture of the burning cremation tower for which he was very thankful. I have made for Bali an ardent admirer and propagandist.[40]

In the same essay, Nyoman Oka, addressing his remarks to would-be guides, advises them to obscure from the tourist's view the growing tendency for temples and compounds to ask for donations, so as to preserve Bali's hospitable image: "Now you find a donation in more and more places is expected. You have to expect this today, so be prepared. The foreigner need not know this. If you can avoid it, you should, to keep the image of Balinese being friendly and hospitable. You should pay the donation yourself, without the tourist noticing it."[41] Cultural experiences are also marketed to tourists through staged productions. These include dance and theater performances, ceremonies, craftsmen working, chefs cooking, etc. As the remarks of Nyoman Oka above indicate, the distinction between "natural" and "staged" attractions is not always a sharp one. In fact, one result of cultural tourism may be the "staging" of daily life, to the extent that forms of dress, architecture, etc., are deliberately preserved for the sake of tourism.

It seems inevitable that these two ways of marketing cultural experiences impose new cultural meanings on both everyday life and the cultural forms which are staged. For one thing, it seems likely that tourism increases cultural self-consciousness. A Unesco-sponsored study of Bali observes that

[40] Quoted in McKean (n. 13 above), p. 178.
[41] Ibid., p. 179.

575

Economic Development and Cultural Change

> a sincere desire appears among the caretakers of the temples and other holy places to learn about their ins and outs, their history, the names of the host deities, their services and cults, etc., in order to be able to give satisfactory answers to the tourists whenever they ask questions.
>
> A strong desire also appears in the population for an awareness of Hinduism and to learn about the religion, not only for their own benefit, but also because they are often confronted with tourists who ask questions relating to problems of the Hindu-Balinese religion.[42]

It does not seem possible to predict on an a priori basis what the cultural consequences of this increased self-consciousness will be. Too much of the literature tries to answer normative questions—is the culture being spoiled, demeaned, etc.—rather than exploring what it is in the lives of the people and the structures of their communities which really changes.

The expanded cultural role of the state discussed in the previous section is sometimes countered by the resurgence of local identities which tourism may encourage. The economic importance of cultural tourism may provide new leverage against the claims of the central government. In Bali, for example, cultural tourism has provided a base for a new regional assertiveness about the place of the Balinese language and culture within the schools. In Sulawesi, the Toraja have translated the tourist importance of their religion into new power in the regional legislative council and official recognition by the Ministry of Religion.

While tourists are drawn to cultural attractions, the heart of the tourist industry is always the hotel sector providing food and accommodation. In Southeast Asia much more than in Europe, the hotel sector is sharply bifurcated between cheap, traditional style facilities and expensive, "international standard" hotels. Every government in non-socialist Southeast Asia has opted for capital-intensive, international standard hotels as the basis of its tourist industry. This is a political choice, entailing the subsidy of the hotel sector by the state, which has a number of cultural ramifications. A strong case could be made for developing a type of tourism based on modernizing and expanding the traditional accommodation systems of the region, for example, the *losmen* in Indonesia. The tremendous increase of young Western travelers living cheaply—known as "W.T.'s" (world travelers) among themselves and as "hippies" among unsympathetic Western observers and local government officials—has fostered such an expansion in a number of areas. Virtually no studies of this phenomenon exist, however, and most Western observers and Southeast Asian governments see these young travelers as a greater cultural threat than other tourists.[43] Immigration offices in Malay-

[42] Universitas Udayana and Gerard Francillon, "Tourism in Bali—Its Economic and Socio-cultural Impact: Three Points of View," *International Social Science Journal* 27, no. 4 (1975): 742–43.

[43] For reports reflecting this hostility toward "hippies" and blaming them for the negative cultural consequences of tourism, see Willard A. Hanna, "Bali in the Seventies. Part I: Cultural Tourism," American Universities Field Staff Reports, *Southeast Asia Series* 20, no. 2 (January 1972): 1–7; and Universitas Udayana and G. Francillon, pp. 721–52.

Robert E. Wood

sia prominently display signs defining "hippies" and threatening immediate and irrevocable expulsion of persons so designated.

In addition to fearing the alleged cultural influence of hippies, officials commonly assert that hippies do not spend enough money to make tourism profitable—in fact, the Malaysian definition pretty much reduces the issue to whether one pays to sleep in licensed hotels. Given the extremely high import content of the luxury hotels, however, the net foreign exchange gains of luxury tourism are often quite small.[44] In contrast, virtually all foreign exchange brought in by W.T. tourism goes for goods and services locally produced. Therefore, W.T. tourism involves a very different structure of entrepreneurial opportunity than mass luxury tourism, with very different class and cultural implications. I know of no studies which have undertaken such comparisons, but an analysis of the villages of Sanur and Kuta in Bali would be an instructive example. In Sanur the beach is lined with huge hotels, many with foreign names—Intercontinental, Hyatt, Machetti, etc.—which have drastically disrupted the balance of Balinese community and nature and which are almost all owned by outsiders. In Kuta, on the other hand, W.T. tourism has spawned the growth of several hundred (250 by one count in 1975) "homestays," where five to 15 rooms have been added on to and integrated into existing family compounds set amid the coconut palm groves back from the beach. Kuta indeed has been transformed by this process, not to everyone's liking, but the entrepreneurial response has been overwhelmingly local and dispersed. A similar comparison might be made in Jogjakarta, where most luxury tourists stay in the luxury hotels outside of the main part of the city, while in the city center small *losmen* and hotels catering to W.T.'s have mushroomed. (In this case, however, local Chinese seem to have been the main investors.)

Tourism generates a wide range of associated occupations, altering stratification systems in many ways. Prostitution is a particularly important spin-off business in a number of Southeast Asian cities, and it is striking how the prestigious *Asia Guide* goes into considerable detail on procuring prostitutes in most Asian capitals. Japanese "sex tours" to Southeast Asia have become a source of conflict both in the region and in Japan itself.[45] Perhaps of the greatest significance for cultural change is the corps of young men in virtually every Southeast Asian country ready to "practice their English"—that is, to bask in the glory of contacts with tourists and make money by providing them with an array of services. Often dressed in the latest Western fashions, they seem prime candidates for playing the role of "culture brokers" discussed in the literature.[46] By

[44] See Robert E. Wood, "Tourism and Underdevelopment in Southeast Asia," *Journal of Contemporary Asia* 9, no. 3 (1979): 274–87.

[45] Susumu Awanohara, "Protesting the Sexual Imperialists," *Far Eastern Economic Review* 87, no. 11 (March 14, 1975): 5–6.

[46] See Noronha, "Social and Cultural Dimensions" (n. 26 above) for a review of the different types of culture brokers cited in the literature.

Economic Development and Cultural Change

getting very sizable kickbacks from the places where they take tourists, some of these are able to accumulate substantial sums of money—although their conspicuous consumption often works against this.

Cohen, in a study of young Arab men and young tourist women in an Israeli resort town, found that tourism acted as a kind of safety valve for the structural constraints faced by Arab youths. Foreign female tourists were believed to offer possible solutions to their sexual and occupational frustrations: companionship, with the possibility of sexual relations, and aid for emigration.[47] My experience in Jogjakarta suggests that tourists play a similar role for a substantial number of young, male Indonesian "guides" who hang around the hotels and eating places of W.T.'s. Their unofficial leader was a young man who had married a Swiss tourist, returned to Switzerland with her to accumulate capital (in the form of Swiss watches), and then came back to Jogjakarta to buy batik paintings for resale in Europe.

Tourism as a Cultural Institution

Tourism in Southeast Asia no longer can be seen simply as an intrusion from the outside: tourism itself is now a local cultural institution. In this section I want to explore two aspects of tourism as a cultural institution: its projection of an image of modernity and its function as a form of elite international integration.

MacCannell has suggested that tourists' experience with "nonmodernity" establishes "in consciousness the definition and boundary of modernity by rendering concrete and immediate that which modernity is not."[48] It seems likely that the reverse is also true, and herein lies one of the important political and cultural implications of tourism: Since modernity is an undisputed goal in the underdeveloped world, the particular definition that tourism gives to it acquires a strategic importance.[49]

Tourism's image of modernity is most obviously conveyed through the luxurious hotels which stand in such stark contrast to the poverty around them. They are, as Conrad Hilton has characterized his own, "little Americas," and they constitute a powerful cultural statement. The

---

[47] Erik Cohen, "Arab Boys and Tourist Girls in a Mixed Jewish-Arab Community," *International Journal of Comparative Sociology* 12, no. 4 (December 1971): 217–32.

[48] Dean MacCannell, *The Tourist: A New Theory of the Leisure Class* (New York: Schocken Books, 1976), p. 9.

[49] The political dimension of tourism has naturally been most recognized in those countries self-consciously trying to build a different kind of society from the capitalist West. In Tanzania, e.g., a university student-youth group of the political party published an analysis of tourism asserting the incompatibility of tourism with Tanzanian socialism. Arguing that "the ways and values we import through tourism are in no way compatible with our aspiration to build a rural based ujamaa society," they insisted that tourism be evaluated in terms of its implications for socialist goals. Their position sparked a lively debate in the English-language newspaper, the *Standard*. The debate is reprinted in I. G. Shivji, ed., *Tourism and Socialist Development* (Dar es Salaam: Tanzania Publishing House, 1973).

Robert E. Wood

Bali Beach Hotel has provided since its inception free tours for Balinese who want to see this symbol of development—which is ironic, for the Indonesian government has since banned the construction of more hotels like it, so inappropriate is its design. Luxury hotels often host elite weddings, celebrations, and meetings, and, hence, international tourism may support in many places a style of life which the local elite could not finance on its own.

Tourists themselves are part of the cultural statement which tourism makes, although Noronha's review of the literature suggests that locally resident culture brokers are crucial for its transmission. Virtually all studies of modern mass tourism emphasize the extremely limited direct interaction with local people it entails. Boorstin, for example, writes that "the traveler used to go about the world to encounter the natives. A function of travel agencies is to prevent this encounter. They are always devising efficient new ways of insulating the tourist from the travel world." Cohen similarly argues that the institutionalization of tourism has meant that "what were previously formal barriers *between* different countries become informal barriers *within* countries."[50] Even in the absence of real interaction, tourists are the objects of many inquisitive eyes. For many people, tourists are as close as they will come to the "modern" world.

Lengyel argues that

> tourism, unfortunately, is a rather poor culture carrier. The typical tourist is perceived by the host communities as both richer (more leisured, more free-spending, possibly better accommodated and certainly more relaxed) and poorer (less knowledgeable, less active, less articulate and less individualistic) than he is at home.
>
> But in the case of Bali, cultural movement has been markedly one way. . . . Balinese creativity is better known abroad than foreign creativity is known in Bali. No symphony orchestras, drama or ballet companies from overseas perform in Bali. Imported films are of the crudest variety and the poor selection and rarity even of foreign books, records or tapes is striking. . . . Who can predict what influence exposure to the more refined aspects of foreign cultures may have on Balinese sensibilities?[51]

The cultural content of different forms of tourism deserves study. Here again, however, it is important not to let normative questions shut off analysis. Lengyel cites motor scooters as one of the (apparently unrefined) imports of the West. The possibility of lucrative rentals to W.T.'s has enabled significant numbers of Balinese to purchase motor cycles. Is this incipient class differentiation at work? What are the consequences of the geographical mobility they offer? To what other economic, social, and cultural purposes have motorcycles been put? It is these questions which

[50] Daniel J. Boorstin, *The Image: A Guide to Pseudo-Events in America* (New York: Atheneum Press, 1972), pp. 91–92; Erik Cohen, "Toward a Sociology of International Tourism," *Social Research* 39, no. 1 (Spring 1972): 174.

[51] Peter Lengyel, "A Rejoinder," *International Social Science Journal* 27, no. 4 (1975): 756–57.

Economic Development and Cultural Change

need to be raised, rather than laments about their noisy disruption of
Balinese tranquility.

Tourism not only projects an image of modernity; it also represents
a new mode of leisure for the dominant classes. The degree to which the
modern institution of tourism is discontinuous with traditional forms of
travel and recreation is variable, but cultural tourism is probably without
much precedent. Data presented by McKean show that of 40,057 tourists
staying at international standard hotels in Bali in 1969 almost one-third
(12,894) were Indonesians.[52] Studies of tourist spending in Singapore indicate that the biggest spenders, ahead of Australians, New Zealanders, and
Japanese, are Indonesians.[53] These figures suggest that tourism may constitute a significant mode of cultural integration of the dominant classes
of underdeveloped societies into the capitalist world system.

IV. Conclusion

International tourism is growing too rapidly, and with too few adequate
studies, to draw many hard and fast conclusions about its relationship to
cultural change. Most fundamentally, international tourism is a fact to
be examined rather than lamented. We must go beyond the ethnocentric
normative categories which have constrained analyses of the cultural consequences of international tourism and utilize a more sophisticated conception of culture and cultural change.

I have suggested three areas particularly worthy of study. First, we
should look carefully at how the development of tourism leads to an expanded cultural role of the state. At the same time, however, we should
pay attention to how tourism may simultaneously provide new leverage
for cultural claims *against* the state. Tourism, in other words, may constitute a new terrain of political struggle over cultural issues facing Southeast Asian societies. Second, a number of unique characteristics of tourism
as an industry warrant special attention, particularly those stemming from
the predominance of cultural tourism. Tourism is a unique "export."
Third, we need to grasp the significance of the fact that tourism has become a new cultural institution within Southeast Asian societies themselves.

International tourism is part of an externally oriented, dependent
strategy of development. Debate will continue to flourish over whether it
represents the most judicious use of limited resources.[54] Virtually all non-
socialist Southeast Asian governments have opted for this strategy, how-

[52] McKean (n. 13 above), p. 29.
[53] Janet Wookey, "The Orient—with Plumbing," *Far Eastern Economic Review*
97, no. 32 (August 12, 1977): 59.
[54] For a critique of tourism as a development strategy for Caribbean countries,
see John M. Bryden, *Tourism and Development: A Case Study of the Commonwealth
Caribbean* (Cambridge: Cambridge University Press, 1973).

Robert E. Wood

ever, and there is every reason to assume that international tourism will continue to grow at a rapid pace. As it expands, we need to locate its contribution to the forces of stagnation and change in the region and to grasp its unique and complex articulation with the cultural oppositions which characterize Southeast Asian societies.

Tourism Economics, 2004, 10 (1), 45–61

Are tourists willing to pay for aesthetic quality? An empirical assessment from Krabi Province, Thailand

MICHELLE CATHERINE BADDELEY

Director of Studies and College Lecturer (Economics), Gonville and Caius College and Faculty of Economics and Politics, University of Cambridge, Cambridge CB2 1TA, UK. Tel: +44 1223 332497. Fax: +44 1223 332456. E-mail: mb150@cam.ac.uk.

This paper assesses the relationships between the viability of the tourism industry and willingness to pay for aesthetic aspects of environmental quality. Incentives to provide high-quality tourism are limited given asymmetric information, adverse selection and positive search costs, with implications both for the sustainability of the tourism industry and for environmental sustainability more broadly defined. An econometric model is estimated in which willingness to pay is captured using resort rents and related to aesthetic quality, after controlling for service levels. A negative relationship is found. Some policy issues are assessed, focusing on the implications for tourism as an engine for sustainable development.

Keywords: sustainability; development; aesthetic quality; search costs; reputation; adverse selection

In developing countries, the pressures of tourism demand from industrialized countries have been magnified in recent years with the development of a highly successful mass tourism industry that focuses increasingly on promoting new 'unspoilt' destinations. Rising incomes in industrialized countries and intensive advertising campaigns have led to a substantial increase in tourism-demand pressures from the developed countries. This has been compounded by growth in tourism demand from consumers within South East Asia, accompanying the rapid economic growth in the Asian Tiger economies as well as Japan, at least until the financial crises of 1997.

Will these changes affect the viability of the tourism industry in developing countries? And are the changes likely to help or hinder the process of economic development in the South East Asian region? Assessing the economic impacts of this growth in tourism is a difficult task because tourism delivers a complex set of direct and indirect benefits and costs to developing economies. Where economic resources and opportunities are particularly scarce, tourism can provide much-needed employment, income and foreign exchange. Tourism can provide resources for the erection of infrastructure (such as roads, sewerage

The author would like to acknowledge the help of Natapon and Sophia Buranakul of the Network for Environmentally and Socially Sustainable Tourism – Thailand (NESSThai), who played an invaluable role in the collection of the survey data.

plans, power generators, etc) necessary to promote broad-based economic development. In these ways, at least in theory, tourism can be a key factor in promoting sustainable long-term development in peripheral regions. This may be particularly beneficial as tourism often taps into resources that have only marginal value in other economic uses.

On the other hand, the additional inflow of tourists represents a substantial pressure on the limited facilities available in developing countries, and the capacity of developing economies to mediate large increases in tourist flows is limited by their dependent position in the world economy. Less developed countries may be forced by necessity, despite reservations about long-term consequences, to encourage tourism because it provides a valuable source of foreign exchange. With the pressures of increasing globalization, the ability of developing countries to moderate commercial and economic pressures easily for environmentally insensitive tourism developments is likely to be compromised without effective regional, national and international policy coordination. If, however, the development of tourism will in itself encourage the careful management and preservation of resources, particularly environmental resources, then the benefits of tourism developments may well outweigh the costs.

There are inevitable trade-offs between the goals of improving standards of living and moderating the environmental consequences of tourist activity. Holden (2000) emphasizes that tourism requires inputs from natural as well as human resources, but addressing the broader environmental impacts of tourist activity involves inevitable value judgements that reflect anthropocentric views and changing attitudes. Furthermore, the definition of the environment is uncertain: there are social, cultural, economic and political aspects to the environment, as well as physical and ecological dimensions. Tourism, even if it is a relatively benign form of economic activity, has a range of complex environmental impacts, including ecological change, noise/water and aesthetic pollution and behavioural impacts. All of these impacts have negative implications for physical and cultural environments. Holden (2000) argues that, because the tourism system is like a spider's web of sub-systems (including transport, destination and retailing sub-systems) the ability to analyse these numerous interactions effectively is limited. Assessing the compatibility of environmental sustainability in the tourism system and a successful tourism industry is complex, especially as there are so many facets – ecological, social, economic and cultural – to environmental sustainability (Murphy, 1983). González and León (2001) argue that complex interactions between tourism and environmental quality mean that the survival of tourism is dependent on environmental preservation. Environmental impacts are complex and wide-ranging and operate on a global and resort-based scale as well as on a local scale – and when limits on carrying capacity are ignored there can be significant implications for environmental preservation.

Given the complexity of these issues, this paper concentrates on just one aspect: tourists' willingness to pay for aesthetic quality. Assessing this aspect of environmental impact is limited because there are so many environmental effects that are unseen, at least in the short term. The linkages between the sustainability of the tourism industry and aesthetic quality are clearer and can be explained in the context of the product life cycle models of Butler (1980) and Haywood (1986), among others. The aesthetic quality of resort areas deteriorates in tandem with the various stages of the tourist product life cycle, with implications not only for the environment but also for the economic viability of the tourist industry. Russo (2001) highlights the problems surrounding the vicious circle of tourist development. In an unregulated market, a decline in the attractiveness of a tourist area is an almost inevitable consequence of the area's initial attractiveness. Russo argues that, in preventing these vicious-circle effects, issues of quality and accessibility must be addressed.

In assessing this, some theoretical issues related to free-riding behaviour, short-termism and asymmetric information are explored. Analyses of atomistic human behaviour, as seen in classical microeconomic analysis, will be misleading when it comes to the assessment of tourism demand; and when it comes to assessing tourists' willingness to pay for environmental quality, the limits on rational, maximizing behaviour should be recognized. If tourists consume irresponsibly, it may be because they want to free-ride on the responsible behaviour of others but, equally, their behaviour may reflect problems of asymmetric information and adverse selection.

Following on from the theoretical discussion, the empirical section assesses some evidence about tourists' willingness to pay for aesthetic environmental quality based on survey results from Krabi Province, Thailand. An econometric model of tourism demand, as captured by resort rents, is estimated with tourism demand regressed against a range of variables associated with the quality of the tourism product. The paper concludes with a brief assessment of policy implications.

Theoretical issues: incentives for environmentally responsible tourism

Deteriorating environmental quality in tourist areas will not only compromise broad-based sustainable development; it will also limit the economic viability of the tourism industry. Tourism life cycle theories analyse the evolution of tourism areas as a process of almost inevitable rise and decline, with tourists' preferences shifting in the long term away from older resorts as their environmental quality deteriorates. If the market mechanism ensures that tourism operators who operate in a relatively unspoilt environment are rewarded with higher rents and profits, then there may be an incentive for tourism operators to preserve the environment. This will promote the economic viability of the local tourism industry while simultaneously slowing environmental decay. If the provision of a high-quality environment is not rewarded financially by higher rents and profits, however, the consequent environmental damage may threaten even the short-term to medium-term viability of the local tourism industry.

Quite apart from the complex issues associated with the relationship between tourism and sustainable development,[1] the short-term viability of an environmentally sound tourism operation depends on consumers' willingness to pay for environmental quality. It is not clear, however, that the price mechanism will operate effectively to maintain the viability of the tourism industry in a world of market failure. Market forces will properly moderate resource exploitation if there are no negative externalities, if tourism operators adopt a long time horizon and if all agents are perfectly informed. If any of these conditions is violated, then the classical microeconomic model focusing on the demand for tourism services from rational, self-interested utility maximizers becomes redundant.[2] In the following sub-sections, the economic constraints on environmentally responsible tourism are examined.

Environmental externalities and free-riding behaviour

One constraint on environmentally responsible tourist consumption as applied to communal resources will emerge as a result of free-riding behaviour: when consumers seek the benefits of others' environmentally responsible behaviour (such as a clean beach) without necessarily being prepared to make concessions themselves. This is a classic tragedy of the commons problem (as described by Hardin, 1968). No one person has an incentive to take responsibility for maintaining a common resource; everyone will have an incentive to use the resource before it disappears. A Prisoner's Dilemma emerges, in which individually rational behaviour is inconsistent with the maximization of social welfare. In a static world there may be two solutions: taxation or allocation of property rights. With taxation, one of the key problems lies in measuring the socially optimal level of tourist activity in order to calculate the appropriate tax consistent with Pareto optimality. Another solution lies in property rights. According to Coase's theorem, when property rights are fully allocated (and assuming costless transactions and perfect information), the trade of these rights will ensure the achievement of Pareto optimality, regardless of the initial allocation of the property rights. The problem with this approach, however, lies in the logistical hurdles that would emerge in deciding how property rights to environmental resources could be allocated. In addition, it is unlikely that transaction costs in the trade of environmental property rights would be zero and the legal costs involved in monitoring and regulating the trade in property rights might be substantial. While a property rights solution to the externalities problem may lead a tourist enterprise to the economically efficient point, it is not necessarily true that it will lead the enterprise to an ecologically sustainable point.

Even if such solutions were possible and a Pareto efficient outcome were achieved, in a world of myopic tourists and hotel managers the economically efficient solution would not necessarily be compatible with an ecologically sustainable solution. This introduces the problems surrounding the dynamic consequences of environmentally irresponsible behaviour and these are discussed in the next section.

The inter-temporal dimension: problems of discounting

In the above analysis, environmental externalities are presented in the context of static economic efficiency. But the effects of externalities are not necessarily felt only within one time period. It is also important to examine the differences between economically efficient outcomes in a static context and long-term ecological sustainability in a dynamic context.

In the examination of inter-temporal consequences, it is also important to separate the concepts of physical and natural capital. If a resort operator is assessing the net present value (NPV) of physical investments, for example a decision to build a hotel, substantial costs are incurred up-front and benefits in terms of revenues accrue in the future. In using natural capital the opposite happens: the benefits associated with high environmental quality are realized immediately and the costs of environmental degradation may be spread over many time periods. Even if the economic value of natural capital could be measured, distortions would emerge if the same discount rates were used for natural as for physical capital. Assuming positive discount rates, environmental costs incurred over a long time horizon are discounted away. So, for natural capital, the benefits of exploiting the natural environment are distorted upwards and costs are distorted downwards relative to physical capital. This will reinforce the dominance of the consumption preferences of the present generations over those of future generations.

The practical implication of these insights is that, if businesses operate with short time horizons then there is an incentive to build and/or finance resorts in one area and to abandon these resorts as their environmental quality deteriorates and tourism demand wanes. Business concerns about the long-term viability of tourism are likely to be limited, particularly if tourism developers do not have a stake in the long-term prospects of a geographical area. For tourism ventures funded by multinational and even national companies, it is relatively easy to move operations to other areas once the environmental quality of a resort has deteriorated (Parnwell, 1992). So these companies will have less incentive to worry about long-term consequences as long as short-term profits are ensured, unless multinational corporations respond to pressures from environmentally concerned consumers.

Asymmetric information

A further complication that emerges for market solutions lies in the problems associated with asymmetric information. In particular, there is the pre-contractual problem of adverse selection,[3] which occurs when buyers do not have information about the differential quality of products in the market. Akerlof's (1970) Lemons Principle of adverse selection shows that, in markets for goods of heterogeneous quality, buyers will pay a price reflecting the average quality of the goods. This means that there is no incentive for sellers to supply high-quality products and so average price and average quality will deteriorate, the end result being that the market will disappear. While it is possible that buyers would be prepared to incur search costs to identify high-quality goods, Diamond (1971) shows that in a world of adverse selection the perfectly competitive result will hold only when search costs are zero (see also Stiglitz, 1989; Salop, 1977).

Shapiro (1983) extends this idea to show that sellers will have an incentive to reduce quality and cut costs before buyers catch on. One way out of this problem is via signalling and screening (Stiglitz, 1975). High-quality producers need to signal reputation so that buyers know when they are buying high-quality products and sellers are rewarded for the extra costs incurred in investing in the production of high-quality goods, enabling the sale of high-quality items at a premium above cost.

These ideas can be applied to the tourism industry. For example, Keane (1997) shows that reputational effects, which occur when quality is discovered only after a commodity has been bought, may be limited in the tourism industry. If tourists are driven by experiential motivations and prefer new and unusual destinations for their holidays, reputational effects will be limited. Similarly, Goeldner *et al* (2000) argue that, while perceptions are important, misleading advertising may affect judgments of quality, particularly if resorts are unlikely to attract repeat clientele. Thus high prices as a signal of environmental quality have the potential to play an important positive role in sustaining the tourism industry. In addition, the premium component in high prices also allows tourism operators to concentrate on minimizing the deterioration in quality via environmental innovation. This is important because the investments required for resorts to meet high environmental standards involve substantial additional fixed costs in terms of equipment and additional variable expenditure in terms of processing costs (for example for each unit of sewerage and water). In other words, if responsible operators can extract a premium then they have an incentive to incur extra costs in providing a high-quality product whilst simultaneously signalling quality. The extent to which environmentally responsible hotel managers can extract a premium will also depend on the elasticity of demand of the responsible tourists. If the demand from responsible tourists is relatively inelastic, for example because there are fewer substitute resorts for responsible consumers than for less discriminating tourists, then responsible operators will be able to extract a high premium. As new responsible operators enter the market however, premiums will be eroded with the increasing elasticity of demand from responsible tourists faced by individual hotels. The key issues to address, therefore, are whether or not consumers are willing to pay a premium for environmentally certified resorts and what sort of premium they are prepared to pay. If the premium is low or non-existent, then there will be no profit incentive in the short term to provide environmentally sound resorts.

Tourism and the economy in Thailand

In this section, some of these ideas about the relationship between environmental externalities, asymmetric information and short-termism in tourist decision making are analysed empirically and applied in a case study of the tourism industry in Krabi Province, Thailand.

In July 2001 the Thai Ministry for Finance highlighted tourism as its priority industry in its Economic Stimulus Package (NESDB, 2001). Slowing GDP growth following the financial crisis was being restrained only by a booming tourism industry. Following an intensive promotional campaign, tourism experienced an 8.3% year-on-year growth in an otherwise sluggish economy (Business Monitor International, 2001). International tourist arrivals in Thailand increased from 7.8 million in 1998 to 9.6 million in 2000, an increase in annual volume of 23.1% (data from the Thailand Tourism Authority's Website, 2001). Of these tourists, 4.4 million (45%) were from developed countries.

The increase appeared to have positive overall effects on incomes and development, as measured by the World Bank's Human Development Indicator (HDI). Figures 1 and 2 capture the relationship between tourism receipts as

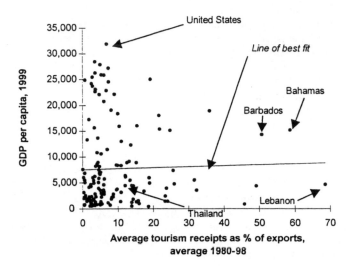

Figure 1. Average tourism receipts as a percentage of exports versus GDP per capita.

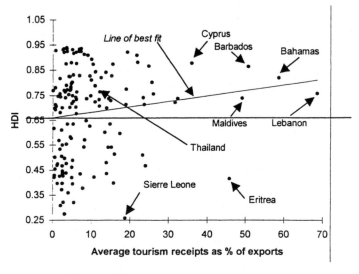

Figure 2. Human Development Index versus average tourism receipts as a percentage of exports.

a proportion of exports versus the HDI and versus GDP per capita (UNDP, 2001).[4] These data suggest that on balance growth in tourism and improvements in broad measures of development and income have gone hand-in-hand.[5] For Thailand, tourism receipts appear to have had a particularly strong positive correlation, above the international average. The broader implications of this increased demand for the macro-economy include positive employment effects at both regional and national levels.[6]

This tourism may reflect an efficient use of scarce resources to the extent that the key regions for tourism in Thailand are the impoverished Northern upland regions and poor Southern coastal regions; in both areas small-scale primary industries were the dominant form of production and unused resources of land and labour were available that could be harnessed by the tourism industry. But what are the broader implications for environmental quality? In recent years, and following the 1997 financial crisis, tourism has been under some pressure to develop at an unsustainable pace (Kontogeorgopoulos, 2000). Furthermore, in his study of Ko Samui, another recently fashionable Thai resort, Parnwell (1992) observed that local participation in tourist developments was initially high but later expansion involved more and more outsiders. Only 20% of Ko Samui islanders were employed by the tourism industry in 1989. Parnwell argues that the consequent development of tourism was unsympathetic to the local biophysical and socio-cultural environment and to the long-term viability of the tourism industry. If local operators are heavily involved in the development of tourism, they may have to focus on satisfying their basic needs in the short term. They are not able to take a longer-term view about their own industry, let alone about the desirability of sustaining the environmental resources they are forced by necessity to exploit. Parnwell (1992) notes that, as infrastructure started to build-up in Ko Samui, more affluent tourists started to join the back-packers and the pressures increased for up-market accommodation and recreation facilities. A boom developed that was uncontrolled and largely unanticipated. Much of the construction activity took place without planning controls, ignoring the already limited building restrictions. Coral reef and marine life came under considerable pressure from boats dropping anchor, scuba diving and souvenir hunting, and from the flow of untreated effluent from the resorts (the resorts had limited sewerage treatment and waste-disposal facilities). The coastal landscape changed dramatically, leading to irreversible changes in the natural environment. Parnwell argues that there is scarce evidence that local communities benefited from these developments, particularly as conservation plans were introduced at such a late stage.

In terms of new tourist developments, there is still the potential to encourage responsible growth in the industry, particularly if recent changes in consumer taste associated with the increasing emphasis on 'green' tourism can be harnessed in the form of an 'environmental premium' on resort rents. One way to assess this issue is to look at what is happening in the new fashionable resorts, and specifically, in this paper, at what is happening in Krabi Province, Thailand. An empirical assessment of tourists' willingness to pay for the aesthetic aspects of environmental quality in Krabi Province is presented in the following section.

Empirical analysis of the determinants of resort rents

As explained above, the aim of this analysis is to assess whether or not tourists value the aesthetic aspects of environmental quality. Empirical evidence on the extent to which tourists are aware of the environmental aspects of their consumption decisions is examined in the destination choice literature. This has revealed contradictory results about tourists' willingness to pay for a high-quality environment. Crase and Jackson (2000) describe quantitative evidence from a tourist–native model that shows how the presence of informed and uninformed consumers creates market fragilities. In contrast, González and León (2001) analyse evidence from a postal questionnaire which indicates that, despite complex feedback effects between environmental quality and demand for tourism in Gran Canaria, hotels did adopt environmental innovations when these required low investment and increased profits.

Holden (2000) observes that a new class of environmentally aware tourists has evolved in the past couple of decades: tourists who are more flexible, independent and quality-conscious than the old-style mass-market tourists. Hillery *et al* (2001) assess the evidence about tourists' awareness of environmental impacts. They observe that old studies revealed a lack of environmental awareness among tourists in assessing the more subtle impacts of their visits to natural areas, except in relation to the most obvious activities, such as littering. Some of the more recent evidence on these issues is more heartening, however, and the analysis by Hillery *et al* of tourists' perceptions of ten sites in Central Australia indicates that 56% of the respondents in their survey were aware of relevant environmental threats. This may reflect the fact that public awareness of environmental issues has grown rapidly over the past twenty years. In a similar vein, for tourists from the UK, Huybers and Bennett (2000) found that survey evidence collected using choice modelling techniques indicated that potential tourists were willing to pay to visit destinations with higher levels of environmental quality, but their definition of environmental quality focused very much on superficial, aesthetic aspects assessed on a subjective basis.

For this analysis, a survey of local tourism operators in Krabi Province was conducted using face-to-face interviews. Data were collected on room rents and other variables for 80 types of room in 18 hotels across the four key tourist resorts of Krabi province, for the tourist seasons 1999–2000. This follows González and León's (2001) approach in their postal questionnaire: they argue that the focus on physical units rather than organizations is justified because environmental management is not homogeneous across production units. The room rents data were collected by asking hotel operators, in face-to-face interviews, the average prices that their customers were paying. Assuming that the hotel operators are profit maximizers and are therefore balancing the marginal revenues from renting a room against the marginal costs of providing that room, these data measure the point of equilibrium at which demand and supply meet and so reflect a combination of supply and demand factors. The supply-side factors are controlled by using a range of variables designed to capture service levels, as discussed below.

Given the limitations on data available regarding more complex aspects of environmental quality, this survey focused on the aesthetic aspects of the environmental experience in assessing whether or not tourists were prepared to pay a premium for superficial aspects of environmental quality. To assess the extent of willingness to pay, each hotel room type in a sample of 80 was assigned an aesthetic environmental quality ranking by scaling the immediate area according to three facets of the environmental experience: proximity to the resort centre (5 = more than 15-minute walk from the centre; 1 = in the centre), proximity to roads (5 = vehicular access prohibited; 1= in a network of roads) and proximity to unimpeded views (5 = no buildings visible; 1= surrounded by other buildings). These three variables were included to capture noise pollution, traffic congestion and aesthetic pollution, respectively. [7]

In only a very limited sense can this method be said fully to capture the environmental consequences of tourism. By assessing the role of environmental quality in determining room rents, however, we can draw some inferences about any environmental discipline imposed on resort operators by pressures from environmentally aware tourist consumers.

Obviously, room rents are very much determined by levels of service, so to control for such factors that might affect tourists' willingness to pay, and consistent with the characteristics approach (see, for example, Papatheodorou, 2000), other variables were included to capture the characteristics of the tourism products being consumed in Krabi province. These included the class of hotel, the number of employees per room (labour intensity), the use of seasonal versus skilled labour, and the provision of air-conditioning, en-suite facilities, suite accommodation and other facilities. In addition, a tourist origin variable was incorporated to capture international demand pressures. Assuming that tourists from outside Asia are prepared to pay higher rents, this origin variable can give a very approximate measure of developed-country demand pressures. In order to provide estimates of the elasticity of room rents with respect to environmental quality and labour intensity, these variables were incorporated in natural log form.

Seasonal dummies were incorporated to capture the difference between low and high season rents and the difference in rents between the four resorts. Resort-area dummies were included to capture differences in rents across the main resorts of Krabi province: Krabi Town, Ao Nang Bay, Phi Phi Island and Railay. The nature of the resorts is quite different: Krabi Town is a more down-market, urban area that caters for a large number of back-packers in budget accommodation. Phi Phi Island was experiencing a boom, probably helped in part by the publicity surrounding the book *The Beach* and the film based on it. Ao Nang is on the mainland, in a busy area but with the compensation of proximity to a good beach. Railay is a relatively quiet area, with a number of holiday houses. It is not particularly well provided for in terms of restaurants and bars, but it is peaceful and benefits from its proximity to the nearby up-market Dusit Rayavadee Resort. In ensuring a representative sample, hotels representing each stage in the resort cycle were included, from the deteriorating hotels in Krabi town, to the hotels in the overcrowded centres of the Phi Phi Island, to the developed areas of Ao Nang Bay resort and to the less developed areas of Railay.

To summarize, in assessing whether the price mechanism operated to reward tourist operators who sustained environmental quality, the following model of resort room rents was constructed:[8]

$$\ln R_i = \alpha + \beta_1 \ln Q_i + \beta_2 \ln LI_i + \delta_1 O_i + \delta_2 LS + \delta_3 C_I + \delta_4 A_I + \delta_5 E_I + \delta_6 S_i + \delta_7 X_i$$

$$+ \delta_8 HS_i + \Sigma \delta_r \text{Area}_{ri} + \varepsilon_i$$

R is room rent, Q is environmental quality variable and LI is labour intensity (rooms per employee). The dummy variables were: O, origin of tourists; LS, use of seasonal labour force; C, class of room; A, air-conditioning; E, ensuite facilities; S, suite accommodation; and X, other extra facilities. HS is the high season dummy; and 'Area' is the vector of dummy variables used to capture variations in room rents in Phi Phi, Ao Nang or Railay relative to Krabi Town (the reference category). ε_i is the stochastic error term.

Given the likelihood of measurement error and sample selection bias, Instrumental Variable (IV) techniques were used. Various diagnostic tests were conducted to gauge the reliability of the estimation techniques: these included the Breusch–Godfrey LM Test for serial correlation in the error term, Ramsey's RESET test for model misspecification, Jarque-Bera's test for non-normality in the error term, and an LM test for heteroscedasticity.

The results from the regressions and associated tests are outlined in the Appendix. The diagnostic tests confirmed that the stochastic error term was well behaved and the IV regression results are outlined in Table A1. All variables were significant at a 5% significance level, apart from the seasonal labour variable and the en-suite variable. These variables were deleted in the constrained regression, but only after F, LM and LR variable deletion tests had been conducted to confirm the reliability of the t-tests (the power of which may be compromised by multicollinearity). These variable deletion test results are recorded in Table A2 and confirm the results of the t-tests.

Results and discussion

The empirical analysis indicates that all the variables are positively correlated with room rents – with the exception of the environmental quality variable, which is negatively correlated with room rents.

The one encouraging finding from the empirical analysis is the significance of the labour intensity variable: rents are higher for rooms with a high degree of labour intensity. This suggests that the development of tourism will have positive effects on employment as the tourism industry develops. It should be noted, however, that these findings tell us little about the appropriateness of wages paid, labour productivity and the problems of underemployment and disguised unemployment, which often characterize service industries, particularly in less developed countries. The results do suggest that tourists are prepared to pay for higher levels of service.

In terms of macroeconomic consequences, particularly those associated with globalization, the tourist origin variable is significantly positive, which indicates that, all things being equal, resort room rents are higher for resorts with mainly non-Asian tourists. Thus there may be a danger that demand pressures from developed countries will contribute to inflationary pressures in the tourist centres. This will affect the purchasing power of local workers and, if higher prices are not accompanied by commensurately higher incomes, the local community will suffer and living standards will fall. The pressures of demand from developed-country tourists will undoubtedly compromise efforts to protect the biophysical environment.[9] If these demand pressures focus on developed-country consumption patterns, there are also implications for local socio-cultural sustainability.

The negative relationship between rents paid and environmental quality conflicts with the findings of Huybers and Bennett (2000), Sinclair and Stabler (1997), Sinclair *et al* (1990), Clewer (1992) and Anstine (2002). This discrepancy in empirical findings may be explained by the fact that hedonic pricing research has tended to focus on the value placed on environmental characteristics in *developed* countries. In parallel with arguments about the export of industrial pollution to developing countries, it is possible that tourists from developed countries are not particularly concerned by environmental consequences that they will not have to live with (or revisit), and so they will be less prepared to pay higher prices for environmental quality.

But how can the *negative* relationship be explained? Two explanations are possible: either tourists do not value environmental quality or they value it but do not have enough information to judge environmental attributes properly before they go on holiday.

To assess the first possibility: perhaps tourists prefer to be close to plentiful amenities and facilities and these are more likely to be provided close to roads and other facilities. Therefore, tourists are more willing to pay for convenience and are not so concerned about aesthetic environmental quality as long as they are close to a good beach, for example. The effects will be exacerbated because less obvious aspects of environmental quality are likely to be compromised in congested areas. The more pristine remote areas are likely to suffer from drawbacks such as limited sewerage facilities and limited clean water supplies.

To assess the second possibility: if the bulk of overseas tourists have booked their holiday after looking at Internet sites and/or printed brochures, and if these information sources present information and photographs selectively, tourists will not have an accurate impression of the environmental quality of their *specific* hotel or bungalow resort before they arrive. Tourists may be willing to pay for relatively pristine environments, but may not have the information to satisfy their demand when they book their holiday, particularly if their selected resort/ hotel is in a distant, unfamiliar country.

So how much do tourists really know when they book a holiday? Information sources are improving markedly as more and more Internet sites are introduced. Best and Pujari (2001) present evidence which shows that modern technology in the form of the Internet has allowed large numbers of people to access information from local tourist sites, thus reducing the extent of asymmetric information. Best and Pujari found that Barbados tourism sites attracted on average 462 visits per day.

As for the more traditional high-street retail outlets, the information they circulate about Krabi Province was assessed by examining the full range of travel brochures available. It seems clear that few operators provide reliable detailed information.

All the brochures had a similar range of generic photographs (usually one or two of the general area alongside pictures of rooms). Only one gave concrete information about how far a particular hotel was from the locations photographed.

All focused on facilities and services. Some were dominated by photographs of private beaches for the top-class resorts, beaches that are not accessible for non-residents of the resort in which they are located.

As for more detailed environmental information, one brochure had a 'reality check' section, but even in this case the environmental information was quite limited. The same brochure published its information in collaboration with a well known travel guide, perhaps in an attempt to signal reliability. Another brochure did highlight environmental aspects, but it concentrated on 'natural beauty' and the lack of commercialization rather than providing detailed information about environmentally responsible management practices.

From the examination of the travel brochures it seems likely that it would be difficult for tourists booking with any of the mainstream travel groups properly to judge the environmental aspects of their holiday decisions.

Conclusions and policy implications

Overall, the evidence presented above suggests that, once tourists have selected a resort, they are not necessarily paying a premium for higher levels of aesthetic environmental quality: the statistical findings suggest that tourists do not pay a premium for reductions in aesthetic pollution, congestion or noise pollution. The implication is that the economic incentives for hotel managers to focus on environmental quality are limited. This may lead to the evolution of unsustainable tourism developments that move quickly from brief boom periods into a vicious circle of environmental degradation and economic decline. Such vicious circles will have particularly profound implications if they develop in areas with few economic alternatives.

Therefore, it is important that effective policies are formulated to encourage environmental responsibility in the management of tourist resorts. This could be achieved via a command-and-control approach of strictly regulating the construction of new resorts, but problems of local corruption and excessive bureaucracy may limit the efficacy of such strategies. If the problem is emerging because tourists are making their choices on the basis of limited information, then, as Deng *et al* (2002) suggest, the solution may lie in developing evaluation and rating systems to allow environmentally responsible operators to signal reputation. González and León (2001) also suggest that eco-labels would encourage the adoption of environmental innovations.

Even if the long-term viability of tourism is safe-guarded by local interests or the adoption of environmental standards, this does not necessarily mean that environmental sustainability is guaranteed: tourism developments may have far-reaching and undesirable socio-economic, cultural and environmental effects which will not directly affect the desirability of a resort. The environmental impacts of tourism extend beyond the superficial characteristics that will attract a continuing stream of tourists. Tourists can also adversely affect less obvious environmental factors, not to mention the effects on wealth distribution and other socio-economic aspects. The theoretical and empirical evidence presented in this paper suggests that responsible tourists do not pay for higher aesthetic environmental quality, but they will pay for high levels of service and convenience. If the short-term profit motivations of tourism operators do not promote the economic viability of aesthetically pleasing resorts, it seems even more unlikely that market mechanisms will ensure the economic viability of broad-based environmental sustainability.

If resort managers are propelled mainly by profit motives, operate with a short time horizon, do not have a long-term stake in a region, and/or do not anticipate the effects of a deteriorating environment on the long-term viability of their business, prospects look dim. As far as the global tourism industry is concerned, it is in the industry's best interests to minimize environmental degradation if the long-term viability of the world stock of tourism resources is to be secured.

Endnotes

1. For a detailed assessment of the associations between tourism and sustainable development see Tisdell, 2001.

2. For a detailed assessment of the basic determinants of tourism demand see Sinclair and Stabler, 1997.

3. Adverse selection is a similar but distinct problem to moral hazard, which is 'reneging' behaviour that emerges as a result of post-contractual monitoring constraints. In this analysis, we focus on adverse selection because the bulk of the tourists visit resorts only once.

4. This correlation is included just to give a broad picture of the impact of tourism on a measure that extends beyond GDP per capita. Data sources: HDI and GDP per capita – UNDP's *World Development Report 2001*; tourism receipts – World Trade Organization. It must be noted that the HDI has a number of limitations in terms of capturing a large number of aspects of the development process.

5. Two simple regressions of GDP per capita and HDI per capita on tourism receipts suggested an elasticity of GDP per capita with respect to tourism receipts of 0.142 ($t = 1.79$, probability value = 8%) and an elasticity of HDI with respect to tourism receipts of 0.045 ($t = 2.12$, probability value = 4%). Therefore, both relationships are significant at 10%. This very simplistic analysis of the macroeconomic issues is provided just to give a picture of the broad correlations between the variables. This paper concentrates on the microeconomic issues; a comprehensive macroeconomic analysis of the issues will be pursued in future research. The outliers identified in the figures above suggest that political, social and other factors are likely to be extremely important in any proper statistical analysis of the macroeconomic issues.

6. The survey conducted for this analysis indicates that, in Krabi Province, a number of the employees are seasonal migrant workers from North Eastern Thailand who are employed in rice farming outside the tourist season.

7. Assessing environmental quality without access to measurable objective factors is problematic given the limits on the quantification of environmental information. While traditional indicators used in Environmental Impact Assessments (EIAs) have focused on the separate categories of economic, social and biophysical environmental factors, there will be considerable overlaps of these aspects and weighting/assessing the three categories independently is problematic. Also, indicators may send conflicting signals (Bossel, 1999; Sors, 2001). It may be difficult to rank objectively or select the individual criteria. Sors suggests that aggregate sustainability indicators such as the Index of Sustainable Economic Welfare (ISEW), the Environmental Pressure Index (EPI) and the Genuine Progress Indicator (GPI) give a more general picture of broad-based environmental impacts. However, there can be no completely objective criterion for assigning appropriate weights to the various components of these indicators. While the Barometer of Sustainability (BS) may go some way towards resolving these problems, subjectivism inevitably creeps in. For the BS, the fact that human well-being and eco-system well-being are considered of equal importance involves a large element of subjectivism. Some may think that human well-being should have a greater weight; others may think that *homo sapiens* is only one species and therefore assigning human and eco-system well-being an equal weight involves an implicit overestimation of human priorities. Even approaches such as the Ecological Footprint (EP) methodology involve assuming that all space is equal in quality and importance. But is it

appropriate to assume that all people should be entitled to equal environmental space? Different people/organizations create different externalities, positive and negative, in terms of their economic and social activities. Should a brothel have the same entitlement to land as a university? Also, all space is not equal in usefulness to people: many people would probably value an acre in Sydney more highly than 100 acres in the Simpson Desert. For all the measures mentioned, measurement problems are compounded in less developed countries because collecting, harmonizing and regionally disaggregating data will be difficult tasks. This all suggests that adopting a more disaggregated and partial approach to environmental assessment is a necessary compromise in a less than ideal world.

8. It should be noted that this environmental quality variable captures only the most superficial aspects of the environment. Consequences of tourism activity, such as damage to local ecosystems from boats, souvenir-hunting, sewage and effluent discharges, etc, factors that are hard to measure from a superficial assessment, are not captured by this variable. However, the variable does capture how tourists respond to superficial factors and thus may reveal some useful preliminary findings about the pressures of tourism.

9. This is true not only for Thailand but also globally. See Gossling (2000) for an analysis of the energy-use implications arising from the movement of tourists from industrialized countries.

References

Akerlof, G. (1970), 'The market for lemons: quality uncertainty and the market mechanism', *Quarterly Journal of Economics*, Vol LXXXIV, pp 488–500.

Andsager, J.L., and Drzewiecka, J.A. (2002), 'Desirability of differences in destinations', *Annals of Tourism Research*, Vol 29, No 2, pp 401–421.

Anstine, J. (2002), 'Consumers' willingness to pay for recycled content in plastic kitchen bags: a hedonic price approach', *Applied Economics Letters*, Vol 7, No 1, pp 35–39.

Best, S., and Pujari, D. (2001), 'Internet marketing effectiveness: an exploratory examination in tourism industry', Working Paper No 0023, University of Bradford Management Centre Working Paper Series, March.

Bossel, H. (1999), *Indicators for Sustainable Development: Theory, Method, Applications*, International Institute for Sustainable Development, Winnipeg.

Business Monitor International (2001), *Thailand Quarterly Forecast Report – June*, Business Monitor International, London.

Butler, R.W. (1980), 'The concept of a tourist area cycle of evolution: implications for management of resources', *Canadian Geographer*, Vol 24, No 11, pp 5–12.

Clewer, A. (1992), 'Price competitiveness and inclusive tour holidays in European cities', in Johnson, P., and Thomas, B., eds, *Choice and Demand in Tourism*, Mansell, London.

Crase, L., and Jackson, J. (2000), 'Assessing the effects of information asymmetry in tourism destinations', *Tourism Economics*, Vol 6, No 4, pp 321–334.

Deng, J., King, B., and Bauer, T. (2002), 'Evaluating natural attractions for tourism', *Annals of Tourism Research*, Vol 29, No 2, pp 422–438.

Diamond, P.A. (1971), 'A model of price adjustment', *Journal of Economic Theory*, Vol 3, pp 156–168.

Goeldner, C. R., Ritchie, J. R. B., and McIntosh, R. W., eds (2000), *Tourism Principles, Practices, Philosophies*, 8th edition, John Wiley & Sons, New York.

González, M., and León, C.J. (2001), 'The adoption of environmental innovations in the hotel industry of Grand Canaria', *Tourism Economics*, Vol 7, No 2, pp 177–190.

Gossling, S. (2000), 'Sustainable tourism development in developing countries: some aspects of energy use', *Journal of Sustainable Tourism*, Vol 8, No 5, pp 410–425.

Hardin, G. (1968), 'The tragedy of the commons', *Science*, pp 1243–1247.

Haywood, M. (1986), 'Economic business cycles and the tourism lifecycle concept', in Ioannides, D., and Debbage, K.G., eds, *The Economic Geography of the Tourism Industry: A Supply-Side Analysis*, Routledge, London.

Hillery, M., Nancarrow, B., Griffin, G., and Syme, G. (2001), 'Tourist perception of environmental impact', *Annals of Tourism Research*, Vol 28, No 4, pp 853–867.

Holden, A. (2000), *Environment and Tourism*, Routledge, London.

Huybers, T., and Bennett, J. (2000), 'Impact of the environment of holiday destination choices of prospective UK tourists: implications for Tropical North Queensland', *Tourism Economics*, Vol 6, No 1, pp 21–46.

Keane, M. (1997), 'Quality and pricing in tourism destinations', *Annals of Tourism Research*, Vol 24, No 1, pp 117–130.

Kontogeorgopoulos, N. (2000), 'Sustainable tourism or sustainable development? Financial crisis, ecotourism and the "Amazing Thailand" campaign', *Current Issues in Tourism*, Vol 2, No 4, pp 316–322.

Lancaster, K.J. (1966), 'A new approach to consumer theory', *Journal of Political Economy*, Vol 84, 1966, pp 132–157.

Murphy, P. (1983), 'Perceptions and attitudes of decision making groups in tourism areas', *Journal of Travel Research*, Vol 21, No 3, pp 8–12.

NESDB (2001), *Strategy Plan Framework: Toward Quality and Sustainability of Thailand Economic Development*, National Economic and Social Development Board Ministry of Finance, Bangkok, July.

Papatheodorou, A. (2000), 'Why people travel to different places', *Annals of Tourism Research*, Vol 28, No 1, pp 164–179.

Parnwell, M.J.G. (1992), 'Environmental issues and tourism in Thailand', in Hitchcock, M., King, V.T., and Parnwell, M., eds, *Tourism in South-East Asia: Theory & Practice*, Routledge, London.

Rosen, S. (1974), 'Hedonic prices and implicit markets: production differentiation in pure competition', *Journal of Political Economy*, Vol 82, No 1, pp 34–55.

Russo, A.P. (2001), 'The "vicious circle" of tourism development in heritage cities', *Annals of Tourism Research*, Vol 29, No 1, pp 165–182.

Salop, S. (1977) 'The noisy monopolist: imperfect information, price dispersions and price discrimination', *Review of Economic Studies*, Vol 44, pp 393–406.

Shapiro, C. (1983), 'Premiums of high quality products as returns to reputations', *Quarterly Journal of Economics*, Vol 98, No 4, pp 659–680.

Sinclair, M. T., and Stabler, M. (1997), *The Economics of Tourism*, Routledge, London.

Sinclair, M.T., Clewer, A., and Pack, A. (1990), 'Hedonic prices and the marketing of package holidays', in Ashworth, G., and Goodall, B., eds, *Marketing Tourism Places*, Routledge, London.

Sors, J.C. (2001), *Measuring Progress Towards Sustainable Development in Venice: A Comparative Assessment of Methods & Approaches*, Fondazione Eni Enrico Mattei, Milan.

Stiglitz, J. E. (1989), 'Imperfect information in the product market', in Schmalensee, R., and Willing, R.D., eds, *Handbook of Industrial Organisation*, Elsevier, Amsterdam.

Stiglitz, J.E. (1975), 'The theory of "screening", education and the distribution of income', *American Economic Review*, Vol 65, No 3, pp 283–300.

Tisdell, C. (2001), *Tourism, Economics, the Environment and Development: Analysis and Policy*, Edward Elgar, Cheltenham.

UNDP (2001), *World Development Report 2001*, Oxford University Press, Oxford.

Appendix

Table A1. Regression results.

Dependent variable:	Natural log of rents charged per room per night
Reference Category:	Krabi Town

	Unconstrained regression			Constrained regression		
	Parameter estimate	t-test of $H_0: \beta_k = 0$	p value[10]	Parameter estimate	t-test of $H_0: \beta_k = 0$	p value
Labour intensity	0.32	3.7**	0.00	0.30	3.8**	0.00
Environmental quality	-0.36	-2.3*	0.02	-0.35	-2.3*	0.03
Control dummy variables						
Tourists' origin	0.15	2.2*	0.03	0.15	2.2*	0.03
Use of seasonal labour	0.10	1.2	0.24	...	...	...
Level of service:						
Hotel class	0.50	7.1**	0.00	0.48	7.7**	0.00
Air-conditioning	0.69	10.0**	0.00	0.68	10.3**	0.00
En-suite facilities	0.01	0.14	0.89	...	...	...
Suite	0.56	4.8**	0.00	0.58	5.2**	0.00
Other facilities	0.17	2.4*	0.02	0.16	2.3*	0.02
Season	0.33	5.6**	0.00	0.34	5.8**	0.00
Phi Phi Island	1.13	3.9**	0.00	1.20	4.6**	0.00
Ao Nang Bay	0.46	2.7**	0.01	0.53	3.7**	0.00
Railay	1.18	4.7**	0.00	1.23	5.7**	0.00
Constant	5.13	34.1**	0.00	5.12	34.6**	0.00
R^2 (adjusted)	0.94			0.94		
F-test of explanatory power	$F(13,66) = 94.7^*$	$(p = 0.00)$		$F(11,68) = 112.6^{**}$	$(p = 0.00)$	
Diagnostic tests						
Breusch–Godfrey LM test	$\chi^2(1) = 0.33$	$(p = 0.57)$		$\chi^2(1) = 0.32$	$(p = 0.57)$	
Ramsey's RESET test	$\chi^2(1) = 0.94$	$(p = 0.33)$		$\chi^2(1) = 0.23$	$(p = 0.63)$	
Jarque–Bera's test	$\chi^2(2) = 0.64$	$(p = 0.73)$		$\chi^2(2) = 0.85$	$(p = 0.65)$	
LM test for heteroscedasticity	$\chi^2(1) = 0.91$	$(p = 0.34)$		$\chi^2(1) = 0.04$	$(p = 0.85)$	

* significant at 5%; ** significant at 1%
Note: p values are probability values; that is, they give exact significance levels and measure the likelihood of committing a Type I error if H_0 is rejected.

Table A2. Variable deletion tests.

Tests of $H_0: \delta_5 = \delta_6 = 0$; that is, that the en-suite and seasonal labour variables are not significant.

	Test statistic	p value
Lagrange Multiplier test	$\chi^2(1) = 1.83$	0.401
Likelihood Ratio test	$\chi^2(1) = 1.85$	0.397
F-test	$F(2,66) = 0.771$	0.467

[33]

PERGAMON

Tourism Management 23 (2002) 161–174

TOURISM MANAGEMENT

www.elsevier.com/locate/tourman

Developing countries and tourism ecolabels

Vinod Sasidharan[a,*], Ercan Sirakaya[b], Deborah Kerstetter[a]

[a] *Department of Recreation, Parks and Tourism, San Diego State University, 5500 Campanile Drive, San Diego, CA 92192-4531, USA*
[b] *Department of Recreation, Park and Tourism, Texas A&M University, USA*

Received 9 June 2000; accepted 2 January 2001

Abstract

The provision of ecolabels to environmentally sensitive tourism enterprises is currently being practiced in developed nations in an attempt to protect the natural capital through improvements in existing environmental standards within the industry. The tourism industry in developing countries could soon follow suit by championing the utilization of internationally recognized ecolabeling schemes as a strategy for environmental management, and for setting the course for the environmentally compatible development of the industry. The achievement and promotion of internationally recognized environmental awards would be instrumental to the tourism enterprises of developing countries in marketing their services to high spending, environmentally conscious western tourists. This paper provides a conceptual analysis of the feasibility of adopting ecolabeling schemes for certifying tourism enterprises in developing countries. Key issues and potential barriers that could hinder the ecolabeling process in developing countries are discussed and testable propositions are developed to guide future research for evaluating the effectiveness of tourism ecolabels in developing countries. © 2002 Elsevier Science Ltd. All rights reserved.

Keywords: Tourism ecolabels; Ecolabeling schemes; Ecolabeling process; Developing countries; Environmental impacts; Tourism enterprises; Environmentally compatible tourism

1. Introduction

Ecolabeling schemes, environmental certifications and awards, and environmental quality assurance and evaluation systems are currently being utilized as instrumental tools by the tourism industry in developed nations for protecting the natural environment on which the industry depends (Morgan, 1999), and for setting the course for the environmentally compatible development of the tourism industry. The forward thrust towards certification of tourism enterprises emerged as a result of Agenda 21, approved by 182 countries during the 1992 United Nations Earth Summit (or Rio Summit), which emphasized the need for businesses to comply with environmental regulations and policies to mitigate global environmental problems. While some developing nations are becoming increasingly interested in the adoption of tourism ecolabeling initiatives, there is growing concern that the small-scale, tourism enterprises of developing countries would be ill-equipped to

conform to the environmental standards and criteria circumscribed by international ecolabeling schemes originating in developed nations. Oftentimes referred to as the North–South divide, certification standards prescribed by international ecolabeling schemes may be used as protectionist strategies to preserve the business interests of developed countries and their tourism enterprises, thereby exacerbating the North–South divide (Honey & Rome, 2000a). Considering these circumstances, it is important to understand how less well-resourced, developing countries may react to the tourism ecolabeling phenomena which is gaining wide recognition within developed nations. This paper provides a conceptual analysis of the ecolabeling process while examining the feasibility of adopting ecolabeling schemes for certifying tourism enterprises in developing countries. It develops a series of propositions pertaining to: (1) impact assessment phase of the ecolabeling process, (2) criteria development phase of the ecolabeling process, (3) stakeholder involvement in ecolabeling schemes, (4) representation of developing countries in ecolabeling schemes, and (5) potential of ecolabels to educate tourists. The discourse presented in this paper is intended to generate greater awareness regarding the

*Corresponding author. Tel.: +1-619-594-5110; fax: +1-619-594-3320.
E-mail address: vxs18@psu.edu (V Sasidharan).

162   *V. Sasidharan et al. / Tourism Management 23 (2002) 161–174*

concealed hurdles relating to the practicability of tourism ecolabeling schemes for developing countries. Additionally, the developed propositions are expected to guide future research for examining the feasibility and effectiveness of ecolabeling schemes in developing countries.

According to Middleton and Hawkins (1998, p. 240), the tourism industry uses ecolabels (from now on this term will be used interchangeably to mean ecoseals or environmental awards) as "trademarks or logos" to communicate the environmental credentials of a company, with the hopes that customers develop positive attitudes toward their product or service. In the market place, this type of strategy can give companies a differential advantage over their competitors. The use of ecolabels (e.g., Blue Flag, Seaside Award, Green

Table 1
Ecolabeling schemes in the tourism industry[a]

Ecolabeling scheme	Type of awarding agency	Focus area
International		
Audubon Cooperative Sanctuary System	NGO	All
Audubon Cooperative Signature Program	NGO	All
Ecofriendly Hotels Worldwide	Private	Facilities (accommodation)
Ecotel	Private	Facilities (accommodation)
Green Globe	Industry Association	All
Regional		
Blue Flag (Europe)	NGO	Facilities (marinas)
		Location (beaches)
Committed to Green (Europe)	Industry Association	Location (golf courses)
European Charter for Sustainable Tourism in Protected Areas (Europe)	NGO	Location (protected areas)
Kleinwalser Valley Environmental Award (Germany and Austria)	Public Authority	Facilities (accommodation)
PATA Green Leaf (Asia Pacific)	Industry Association	All
Tyrolean Environmental Seal of Quality (Austria and Italy)	Public Authority	Facilities (accommodation and catering)
National		
Austrian Ecolabel for Tourism (Austria)	Public Authority	(accommodation and catering)
David Bellamy Award (United Kingdom)	Private Industry Association	Facilities (holiday parks, campsites)
Environmental Squirrel (Germany)	Industry Association	Facilities (accommodation, catering and gas stations)
Gîtes Panda (France)	NGO Industry Association	Facilities (accommodation in parks)
Green Key (Denmark)	NGO Industry Association	Facilities (accommodation)
Green Leaf (Thailand)	Industry Association Public Authority	Facilities (accommodation)
Green Suitcase (Germany)	NGO	Facilities, services and location (accommodation, destinations and tour operators)
NASC (Ireland)	Public Authority	Location (destinations)
National Ecotourism Accreditation Program (Australia)	Industry Association	Facilities, services and location (accommodation, natural attractions and tour operators)
Seaside Award (United Kingdom)	NGO	Location (beaches)
We Are an Environmentally-Friendly Operation (Germany)	Industry Association	Facilities (accommodation and catering)
Sub-national		
Distintivo Ecoturistico (Spain, Alcudia)	Public Authority	Facilities (accommodation)
Ecotur (Spain, Balearic Islands)	Public Authority	Facilities and location (accommodation and destinations)
Green Tourism Business Scheme (United Kingdom, Scotland)	Public Authority	Facilities (accommodation)
ÖKO Grischun (Switzerland, Grabunden)	NGO	Facilities (accommodation and farm food)
ÖKO Tourismuspreis (now merged with national scheme)	Public Authority	Facilities (accommodation)
Scottish Golf Course Wildlife Initiative (United Kingdom, Scotland)	NGO Industry Association Public Authority	Location (golf courses)

[a] Source: Adopted from UNEP (1998, pp. 8–9).

V. Sasidharan et al. / Tourism Management 23 (2002) 161–174

Globe, Blue Angel, Green Leaf, Green Suitcase, etc.) issued by respected accreditation schemes are usually intended to (1) curb tourism's negative environmental impacts on the natural resource base of destination areas by encouraging tourism enterprises to attain high environmental standards (UNEP, 1998), (2) educate tourists regarding the impacts of their tourism-related actions and decisions, thereby prompting them to act in favor of 'environmentally benign' tourism enterprises through their purchasing decisions (UNEP, 1998), and (3) develop standards for environmentally friendly tourism products and services (Mihalic, 2000). Tourism enterprises that earn ecolabels promote their environmental achievements in their marketing campaigns through pamphlets, flyers, brochures, press releases, notice boards, and display of award logos (and flags), both within and off-premises (Morgan, 1999).

Tourism ecolabeling schemes, promoted by both private and public sectors, are currently most prevalent among developed nations at four geopolitical levels— international, regional, national, and sub-national (see Table 1; UNEP, 1998, pp. 8–9). The tourism industry of developing countries may benefit by following suit by championing the utilization of internationally recognized ecolabeling schemes (Mihalic, 2000). The adoption of tourism ecolabels would dovetail with policies relating to natural resource management, environmental conservation and protection, and pollution control while conforming to the concept of environmentally friendly tourism development (Hashimoto, 1999). The ecolabeling concept would be highly appealing to the tourism enterprises of developing countries owing to increasing governmental pressure on the tourism industry to improve environmental performance by adopting effective and tangible environmental management techniques (Zhang, Chong, & Ap, 1999). Furthermore, achievement and promotion of internationally recognized environmental awards would be instrumental to the tourism enterprises of developing countries in marketing their services (UNEP, 1998; Mihalic, 2000) to high spending, environmentally conscious western tourists who are no longer satisfied with the traditional 'sun, sea and sand' type of vacation but engage in holidays that are personally rewarding and environmentally friendly.

2. Tourism development in developing countries and the need for ecolabels

Besides generating foreign exchange earnings and investments, tourism has stimulated economic diversification and job creation in many communities around the globe. Owing to its economically lucrative nature and irrepressible role in nourishing vital economic capillaries, tourism is ostensibly promoted and marketed on a global scale by private and public sectors of the tourist-generating countries as well as host countries. Contrary to these positive impacts, tourism development has, inadvertently, played a precursory role in creating considerable sociocultural and environmental problems at tourist destinations, especially in developing nations. Increased land prices and inflation, high leakage of economic benefits, cultural degradation and acculturation, introduction of exotic species to local flora and fauna, damage to cultural heritage sites, destruction of coral reefs in the Caribbean, disturbance of breeding birds in the Antarctic, pollution through waste and sewage disposal in popular tourist destinations (Erize, 1987; Holder, 1988; Wilkinson, 1989; Brierton, 1991; Cater, 1993; Healy, 1994; Place, 1995; Sirakaya, 1997a; Hall & McArthur, 1998) are just a few examples of tourism's potential for destruction. The detrimental impacts of tourism development in developing countries have been well documented and discussed in the past (De Kadt, 1979, p. 65; Britton, 1982; Mathieson & Wall, 1982; Holder, 1988; Butler, 1990; Sirakaya, 1997a; Akama, 1999; Shackley, 1999; Sindiga, 1999; Sindiga & Kanunah, 1999; Zhang et al., 1999). The incremental inflow of mass tourists from developed countries has further exacerbated the scale, magnitude and intensity of problems (Wheeller, 1997) associated with tourism development in developing countries. Recognizing the natural environment as a vital tourism resource, public and private sectors of the tourism industry are increasingly adopting and implementing environmentally compatible development measures in order to curtail the negative environmental impacts associated with tourism development. Key elements of environmentally sensitive tourism development, in general, include tapping the 'elite', higher spending niche segments of the travel market for low-impact special activity tours, restricting and regulating new development, preserving and protecting areas of outstanding natural beauty and biological diversity and rehabilitating older resorts and destinations (Lockhart, 1997).

Indisputably, tourism development in developing countries has the potential to produce negative environmental impacts, thereby altering the ecological resources of host destinations (Baker, 1997; Obua & Harding, 1997). In light of the quintessential need to maintain the delicate balance between tourism development and the environment in these regions through appropriate planning and management of tourism resources, recommendations for regulating tourism's negative impacts by 'ecolabeling' tourism products are being put forth by concerned parties (Middleton & Hawkins, 1998; UNEP, 1998). In the midst of growing controversy regarding the appropriate interpretation of environmentally compatible (or sustainable) development, the equally ambiguous 'ecolabeling' (environmental labeling) approach proposed by several private and public sector agencies is being identified as a strategic tool for officially approving and marketing environmentally benign products (Jensen, Christiansen, & Elkington, 1998) while ensuring actions towards a more sustainable future. Within the context of travel and tourism, regulatory authorities and other interested parties seek to promote the design, production, marketing and use of tourism products which have a reduced environmental impact (during their entire life cycle), and furnish tourism consumers with 'better' information on the environmental impacts of tourism products (Middleton & Hawkins, 1998).

Particularly, the 'ecolabeling' approach may be applied to tourism enterprises (businesses or companies) such as hotels/resorts/marinas, travel agencies, tour-operators, ground and water transportation services, and airlines and may also be extended to certify the environmental soundness of tourist destinations and the natural resources at these destinations (UNEP, 1998; Mihalic, 2000). While tourism enterprises of developing countries are predominantly comprised of privately owned, large, internationally franchised chains on one hand, and small-scale entrepreneurial businesses on the other, tourism resources in these countries are largely controlled and operated by the public sector (Zhang et al., 1999). Considering the former, the adoption of tourism ecolabeling schemes in developing countries for the purpose of ensuring environmentally sound management and development of environmentally sensitive tourism would be fraught with impasses (Wildavsky, 1996). Certification efforts of these ecolabeling schemes would be beleaguered by issues such as conflicts of interest among stakeholders (Hemmelskamp & Brockmann, 1997), distrust in scientific accuracy of assessments (Salzhauer, 1991), and industry pressure for relaxation of certification criteria (West, 1995).

3. Ecolabeling schemes for the tourism industry

The unplanned and unanticipated growth of the tourism industry in developing countries catalyzed by burgeoning numbers of tourists to these areas has consequently resulted in the degradation, depletion and, in some cases, total destruction of essential economy-supporting natural resources (Shackley, 1996; Baker, 1997; Obua & Harding, 1997). Tourism industry stakeholders may consider the adoption of 'ecolabeling' schemes as a viable option to curb tourism's direct negative (environmental) impacts on the natural resource base of host destinations (UNEP, 1998). Third-party public and private sector tourism industry stakeholders may potentially award 'ecolabels' or 'seals of approvals' to tourism enterprises judged to have fewer impacts on the environment than other similar

enterprises. These ecolabels would provide tourists in originating countries (mostly developed) with information regarding the environmental performance of tourism enterprises, thereby enabling them to make informed choices while purchasing products and services from tour-operators, travel agencies, resorts/hotels, and/or other tourism service providers for their vacations (Rhodes & Brown, 1997; Sirakaya, 1997b; Weissman, 1997; Sirakaya & McLellan, 1998; Sirakaya & Uysal, 1998; Sirakaya, Sasidharan, & Sönmez, 1999). Most importantly, such ecolabels would prompt tourists to seek out environmentally friendly tourism enterprises for their holiday needs. In response to the increasing demand among tourists for environmentally benign tourism, tourism enterprises would be pressured to monitor their industrial practices and improve their environmental standards, thereby supplying tourists with products and services having reduced environmental impacts (West, 1995). In practice, a tourism enterprise seeking an ecolabel or ecoseal is required to meet specified standards and preset criteria identified by the third-party environmental accreditation scheme offering the label (Mihalic, 2000). The following discussion furnishes the reader with a step-by-step description of the tourism ecolabeling process.

3.1. The tourism ecolabeling process

According to Davis (1997, p. 138), the procedures followed by third-party ecolabeling programs may be broadly classified into six central steps. Within the tourism context, ecolabels would be awarded to qualifying tourism enterprises by third-party ecolabeling programs through a systematic process encapsulating these six steps (see Fig. 1):

Step 1: Tourism sector selection. This step necessitates strong involvement from a panel representing an array of tourism stakeholders, including tourism planners and government officials, private tourism enterprises and associations, environmentally oriented non-governmental organizations, local citizens' groups, tourists, and staff members of the ecolabeling organization. Stakeholders would select a particular category from a non-exhaustive list of tourism sectors—tour-operators, travel agencies, resorts/hotels, and/or other tourism service providers.

Step 2: Environmental impact evaluation. In this phase of the ecolabeling process, all possible environmental impacts of the tourism sector selected in Step 1, e.g., tour-operators, would be documented using the life-cycle assessment (LCA) or "cradle-to-grave" environmental accounting methodology (Grodsky, 1993; Wildavsky, 1996; Hemmelskamp & Brockmann, 1997; Rhodes & Brown, 1997; Jensen et al., 1998). Ideally, this would include environmental impacts such as air and water pollution, noise pollution, solid waste, changes in

Tourism Ecolabeling Process[3]

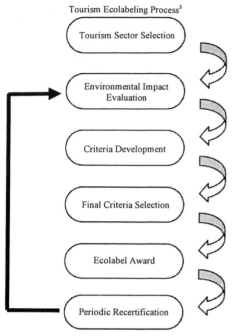

ªSource: Adapted from Davis (1997, p. 138)

Fig. 1. Tourism ecolabeling process.

the composition of flora and fauna, soil erosion, geophysical changes, utilization of raw materials, and energy consumption. Next, the most critical environmental impacts produced by the tourism sector are identified.

Step 3: Criteria development. A preliminary index of criteria for reducing the environmental impacts associated with the tourism sector, identified in Step 2 are peer-reviewed by the panel of tourism stakeholders involved in Step 1.

Step 4: Final criteria selection. Based upon a consensus of the stakeholder peer-reviewers, a final index of limited multiple-attribute criteria (Grodsky, 1993) for environmental impacts associated with the tourism sector is determined by the ecolabeling agency.

Step 5: Ecolabel award. A tourism enterprise applying for an 'ecoseal' or 'ecolabel' would be awarded the same by the ecolabeling agency only if the business either surpasses or at least meets the final criteria of environmental impacts (Grodsky, 1993) associated with its sector (e.g., tour operators) of the tourism industry. If the tourism enterprise meets the final criteria set forth by

the ecolabeling agency, it would then pay a licensing fee to the ecolabeling agency (Kusz, 1997; Shimp & Rattray, 1997) for the use of its eco-certification, symbol, logo or flag in its marketing and promotional efforts as well as day-to-day operations.

Step 6: Periodic recertification. The index of environmental impact criteria are re-evaluated, usually every three years (Shimp & Rattray, 1997), to determine whether the existing criteria match technological and innovative advancements in the tourism industry pertaining to the amelioration of environmental impacts. If new reinforced criteria (for inducing additional environmental improvements) are adopted by the ecolabeling agency, previously certified tourism enterprises would be required to apply for recertification by the ecolabeling agency.

Scientifically, ecolabeling schemes for the tourism industry would assess the environmental impacts of tourism enterprises through their entire life cycle.[1] Owing to the multi-resource dependence of the tourism industry, life-cycle assessments would not be effective in identifying the entire scale, magnitude, and range of environmental impacts generated by tourism enterprises. Moreover, most of these impacts are far-reaching and impossible to measure using the life-cycle assessment technique. Ecolabeling agencies would have to be well acquainted with the gamut of impacts (including their scale and magnitude) produced by various sectors of the tourism industry before performing the impact analysis and improvement analysis phases of life-cycle assessment.

4. Natural resource impacts of tourism development in developing countries

Tourism development depends upon diverse arrays of overlaying resource characteristics relating to the biophysical environment (climatic conditions, topographic features, ecosystems and habitats), unlike other industries that are single resource-based (Wilkinson, 1994; Burton, 1995). The scarcity of natural resources faced by most developing countries (Zhang et al., 1999) increases the susceptibility and vulnerability of these resources to tourism development activities in host

---

[1] By definition, the life-cycle analysis technique used to assess the environmental impacts of the tourism enterprise would include: (1) life cycle inventory—the identification and quantification of energy consumption, raw materials used and the wastes discharged into the environment by the enterprise during the course of providing tourism-related services, (2) environmental impact analysis—the computation of the cumulative environmental impacts produced by the inputs and outputs over the life of the enterprise (Salzhauer, 1991; Grodsky, 1993), and (3) improvement analysis—the utilization of information gathered through the previous steps to reduce the environmental impacts of tourism enterprises during their respective life-cycles (Salzhauer, 1991).

166   *V. Sasidharan et al. / Tourism Management 23 (2002) 161–174*

destinations. Owing to tourism's complex multi-faceted nature and multi-resource dependence, tourism development in such regions inadvertently instills far-reaching impacts on their natural environment, biotas and ecosystems (Freestone, 1991; Mitchell & Barborak, 1991; Smith, 1992; Maragos, 1993; Nunn, 1994; Gilman, 1997).

Tourism development in developing countries is manifested in three core forms—nature-based (or eco-) tourism, coastal (or beach) tourism, and heritage (or cultural) tourism (Lumsdon & Swift, 1998). Tourism in these countries is promoted primarily on the appeal of their natural resources and landscape (Fennell & Eagles, 1990). Moreover, tourism in developing countries is oftentimes built around sensitive ecosystems (Butler, 1990). Natural resource problems associated with tourism development include—degradation of ecosystems (including flora and fauna) in national parks, forests, preserves and wetlands (Sindiga, 1999; Sindiga & Kanunah, 1999; Kousis, 2000); animal harassment by tourist vehicles (Sindiga & Kanunah, 1999); intensive water extraction and effluent solid waste disposal (Sindiga & Kanunah, 1999; Kousis, 2000), depletion of grazing lands and water resources (Ap & Crompton, 1998; Akama, 1999); loss of vegetation coverage, soil erosion and increasing mineral soil exposure, and tree damage and root exposure (Obua & Harding, 1997); habitat fragmentation and degradation, introduction of exotic (non-native) species, and commercialization of wildlife leading to the decline and extinction of wildlife species (Baker, 1997); and noise, fresh water, land and air pollution (Shackley, 1996; Kousis, 2000).

Coastal ecosystem types particularly prone to severe impacts as a result of tourism-related activities include: shorelines (Dobias & Bunpapong, 1990); offshore waters, estuaries, coral reefs, sea-grass beds, sandy beaches (Clark, 1990; GFANC, 1997; Hinrichsen, 1998); mangrove forests (Wright, Urish, & Runge, 1991; GFANC, 1997; Hinrichsen, 1998); riparian habitats and near-coastal wetlands (GFANC, 1997; Hinrichsen, 1998); and salt marshes and coastal dunes (GFANC, 1997). The natural resources of coastal regions are susceptible to tourism's detrimental impacts due to their unique characteristics: frailty of biotas (Nunn, 1994), biomes and ecosystems, and strong interface and interrelationships between terrestrial and marine environments (Wilkinson, 1994, p. 41), combined with increasing population density (Farrell, 1986; Yapp, 1986; WCC, 1993; Hinrichsen, 1998) and inadequate legislative framework, administrative infrastructure and management capabilities (Hickman & Cocklin, 1992; Wilkinson, 1994; Wescott, 1998).

Evidently, tourism development in developing countries has the potential to destroy the very unique natural resources and biophysical environment required for the sustainability of the industry, including the ecosystems that serve as habitats for human populace and large numbers of flora, fauna and aquatic species. The inherently unique character of the host destinations of developing countries and the distinctiveness of the tourism industry nourished by the uncommon characteristics of these areas have played a complementary role in producing endemic environmental impacts (Wong, 1993). While some of these impacts (e.g., the total amount of energy consumed and the quantity of solid waste generated) are quantifiable and easy to calculate, assessments of other impacts (e.g., the micro- and macro-level effects of emissions on air and water quality, public health, natural ecosystems, or on the global climate) are often tedious and impossible to ascertain (Salzhauer, 1991). Thus, the prospect of determining the environmental impacts of a tourism enterprise during the course of its entire life cycle remains bleak and ill conceived. Furthermore, tourism ecolabel awards are often based on a circumscribed collection of measurable criteria and do not address all measurable environmental indicators (Williams & Morgan, 1995). The lack of appropriate scientific techniques to analyze the whole spectrum of environmental impacts associated with a tourism enterprise would pose serious obstacles for ecolabeling agencies during the vital phases of their programs. Besides the obvious setbacks of impact analysis within the life-cycle assessment stage of ecolabeling, several logistical factors have the potential to dog ecolabeling schemes, as described in the following section.

5. Practicability issues relating to tourism ecolabeling in developing countries

The introduction of ecolabeling schemes focusing on tourism in developing countries would provide an opportunity for potential tourists to review the environmental sensitivity of tourism-related services and products before making their final travel (purchasing) decisions, while prompting tourism industry sectors to meet prescribed environmental standards that would minimize their impacts on natural resources. However, a close analysis of the feasibility of utilizing ecolabels for certifying tourism enterprises in developing countries brings to surface a number of unworkable issues pertaining to the entire concept, ranging from the conflicting roles played by stakeholders in the ecolabeling process to the inaccurate methodology used for developing evaluation criteria. Based on Sasidharan and Font's (2001) review of the potential pitfalls of ecolabeling programs, the proceeding discussion presents a conceptual analysis of the ecolabeling process for developing countries. Additionally, key issues and potential obstacles that could severely encumber the ecolabeling process in developing countries are

V. Sasidharan et al. / Tourism Management 23 (2002) 161–174 167

introduced as untested hypotheses. These hypotheses are proposed with the intention of facilitating and guiding future research for evaluating the effectiveness of ecolabels, in general, and with particular emphasis on the feasibility of adopting ecolabeling schemes for certifying tourism enterprises in developing countries.

5.1. Impact assessment criteria: business interests versus environmental protection

Owing to the lack of a universally accepted scientific methodology for the assessment of environmental impacts (West, 1995; Wildavsky, 1996) produced by a tourism enterprise throughout its entire life cycle, the identification of indicators and criteria for the environmental impact assessment phase of the ecolabeling process is oftentimes based on the discretion of the ecolabeling agency (Salzhauer, 1991; Dudley, Elliott, & Stolton, 1997). The unavailability of tailor-made databases for documenting life-cycle inventories of various sectors of the tourism industry and low levels of cooperation from tourism enterprises towards disclosure of operations-related information would adversely effect the scientific accuracy of the inventory and impact analysis phases of life-cycle assessments for tourism enterprises. This would lead to the identification of environmental impacts which are easily addressable, thereby furnishing unreliable improvement analyses (Salzhauer, 1991) for business enterprises within the tourism industry.

The identification of environmental impacts and development of evaluation criteria for tourism enterprises would be highly influenced by the preferences of parties with vested interests in the tourism industry. The domination of the private-sector tourism lobby in ecolabeling programs would shape the impact assessment criteria as a product created through compromises between environmental protection and profit-oriented agenda of tourism businesses (West, 1995; Dudley et al., 1997; Kusz, 1997), rather than serving as a tool for assessing the environmental standards of a tourism enterprise (Kusz, 1997). For example, under ISO 14001, an environmental management system standard against which a tourism business is certified, a company would be able to meet International Standards Organization (ISO) requirements and gain certification, even if it is in legal dispute or in conflict with environmentalists and local communities of the tourism destination (Honey & Rome, 2000a). Hence, impacts that pose undesirable economic consequences to tourism enterprises would be addressed to a greater extent compared to scientifically important and complex ones such as impacts on species composition, biodiversity, migration, etc. For instance, one of the essential criteria for receiving certification from Blue Flag, an international program for certifying beaches and marinas, is that no industrial pollution or

sewage-related discharges may adversely impact the beach area of the tourism destination (Honey & Rome, 2000a). While the environmental impacts of a tourism enterprise on the beach area may be prioritized by an ecolabeling agency primarily due to its ecological, aesthetic and economic undesirability, the non-localized, detrimental effects of the tourism enterprise on the general ecosystem of the area and surrounding coastal waters do not receive adequate attention and are often downplayed. Thus, the local-level , site-specific orientation and interests of tourism businesses would concentrate the focus of ecolabeling programs on site-specific environmental impacts, rather than macro-level impacts (such as global climate change). Socio-cultural impacts such as erosion of cultural identity, over-development of cultural landscapes and heritage sites, and changing attitudes of local communities are likely to be downplayed, and even overlooked, by ecolabeling programs due to the methodological complications associated with measuring these impacts and resolving them. The effectiveness of tourism ecolabeling schemes would depend on the adoption of scientifically reliable life-cycle assessment techniques that identify both environmental as well as socio-cultural impacts associated with tourism enterprises. Based on this review, the first proposition may be offered as follows:

Proposition 1. *Impact assessment criteria will emerge as a compromised product, and not necessarily as an altruistic means for evaluating a tourism enterprise's overall environmental performance.*

5.2. Ecolabeling decisions: domination by the privileged

The board members of ecolabeling agencies and stakeholders from the tourism industry involved in the ecolabeling process may be comprised of representatives from both public and private sector of the tourism industry. The involvement of a wide range of tourism industry stakeholders, representing diverse interests (e.g., environmental conservation, community involvement and development, economic revitalization, etc.) may generate potential conflicts of interest during the process of making ecolabeling decisions. These conflicts would result in procedural difficulties while addressing issues pertaining to tourism sector category selection and criteria finalization. While the majority of the tourism industry stakeholders, representing the large-scale enterprises of the private sector, involved in the ecolabeling process (Grodsky, 1993) would work towards the development of environmental standards that best suit their business interests, the fear of failing to meet the set standards would discourage most small-scale enterprises originating in the developing countries from participating in the initiation phase of ecolabeling programs (Kusz, 1997). For example, local industry representation and participation in global tourism

168   *V. Sasıdharan et al. / Tourism Management 23 (2002) 161–174*

ecolabeling programs such as Green Globe 21, ECO-TEL or Blue Flag is extremely negligible or non-existent in tourism destinations in Africa (Honey & Rome, 2000a). Thus, ecolabeling decisions would reflect the judgement(s) of the group or groups with the sufficient time and resources (personnel and financial) to participate in the ecolabeling process (West, 1995). Certification programs such as Green Globe 21 are developed, financed and staffed by tourism industry trade associations and other major players, such as hotel chains, within the tourism industry who comprise the majority of stakeholders involved in the design and implementation of ecolabeling schemes (Honey & Rome, 2000a). Most tourism ecolabeling schemes are prone to be plagued by the problem of greater involvement from large-scale enterprises of the private-sector coupled with underrepresentation from small-scale businesses (Grodsky, 1993) and other groups, such as government personnel, citizens groups and tourists, who would be deterred from attending resource (time, money and personnel) intensive working sessions during crucial phases of ecolabeling programs (West, 1995). Consequently, the final decisions made during various phases of the ecolabeling process would seldom represent a justifiable consensus among tourism industry stakeholders. For example, the three-tiered certification approach, endorsed by The International Ecotourism Society (TIES), Rainforest Alliance, and Australia's Nature and Ecotourism Accreditation Program (NEAP), which separately certifies ecotourism, sustainable tourism and mass tourism enterprises is not accepted by others involved in certification programs (Honey & Rome, 2000a). Ecotourism experts and environmentalists in Central America and Sri Lanka believe that there should be only one tier in a certification program, covering the entire range from conventional to ecotourism businesses, rather than three certification tiers. In order to claim and establish business credibility, it would be necessary for ecolabeling programs to maintain an independent and neutral status while avoiding certification biases arising from discrepancies in the composition of representatives (e.g., more large-scale enterprise representatives than others) (West, 1995).

The inadequacy of time, money and personnel resources would also affect the extent to which stakeholders are involved during the environmental impact identification phase of ecolabeling programs. Owing to the limited amount of resources available to most stakeholders to conduct the same, once again large-scale enterprises of the private-sector would play the lead role in recommending and funding environmental scientists, researchers and specialists, with expertise in environmental and natural resource issues, for analyzing environmental impacts associated with tourism sectors. In the case of ISO 14001, a private circle

of tourism industry representatives were responsible for establishing international environmental standards, without accounting for participation in environmental decision-making from governmental and non-governmental entities from developing countries (Honey & Rome, 2000a). Thus, only a selected few, with the personnel and financial sponsorship from affluent, large-scale enterprises, would be responsible for conducting and interpreting environmental impact analyses, thereby incapacitating other stakeholders from participating in the same. Small-scale tourism enterprises and other underprivileged, resource-deficient parties or stakeholders involved in the ecolabeling process would have little involvement when it comes to making decisions regarding allowable thresholds of environmental damages/impacts for tourism sectors, in terms of scale and magnitude. Ecolabeling schemes should recognize the environmental preferences and priorities of these underprivileged stakeholders as well as tourists and other users of the natural resource during the entire course of the certification process (Morgan, 1999). Based on this review, the second proposition may be offered as follows:

Proposition 2. *Ecolabeling decisions will reflect the judgments of the group with adequate time and resources (personnel and financial) to participate in the ecolabeling process.*

5.3. Certification criteria: re-establishment of standards

Privately owned, small-scale tour-operators, travel agents, lodges, hotels, etc. (Friel, 1999) constitute the major portion of the tourism industry in developing countries. The majority of these small-scale enterprises and agencies would be incapable of meeting the strict criteria and standards developed by ecolabeling schemes, usually owing to the lack of financial capacity to operate environmentally friendly tourism services. The high costs of operating eco-sensitive tourism projects in developing countries are often affordable only to large-scale companies and multinational enterprises. The financial inadequacy and incapability of the small-scale tourism enterprises in these countries to meet the stringent standards and criteria set by ecolabeling schemes as well as their inability to absorb the sharp initiation and compliance monitoring costs associated with the ecolabeling process (Grodsky, 1993) would discourage them from participating in tourism ecolabeling programs. According to a study by the Pacific Institute, the financial costs for attaining certification from ISO 14001 (a program which promotes improved environmental performance) are usually high (ranging from $500 to $15,000) and affordable only to the largest hotels and this prohibitive cost may restrict market access for small and medium enterprises and firms in developing countries (Honey & Rome,

V. Sasidharan et al. / Tourism Management 23 (2002) 161–174 169

2000a). Tourism enterprises that manage to meet the criteria set forth by ecolabeling schemes may potentially reconsider their continued affiliation with ecolabeling programs due to the high certification and licensing fees to be paid to the ecolabeling agency for awarding and issuing ecolabels to tourism enterprises, the possibility of future non-recertification due to unsatisfactory standards and practices that fail to meet new, re-established criteria, and the surmounting costs associated with periodic recertification (usually after one to three years) (Salzhauer, 1991; Shimp & Rattray, 1997). Additionally, the prevalence of conflicts between profit-oriented private sector stakeholders and pro-environmental stakeholders with antibusiness agendas (Salzhauer, 1991) would lead to escalating industry disinterest in ecolabeling programs. Responding to the concern of environmental interests being marginalized from the ecolabeling process and the inhibitory effect of stringent criteria and standards on tourism industry stakeholder involvement, environmental interest stakeholders may have to ease their set standards and reestablish new criteria for acceptable levels of environmental impacts. Eventually, ecolabeling programs would be pressured into lowering their certification standards (West, 1995) for offsetting both the increasing non-involvement of tourism industry stakeholders in ecolabeling schemes, particularly among small-scale enterprises (Kusz, 1997) and the consequent insufficiency of sponsors for funding ecolabeling initiatives. The lowering of certification criteria and standards would increase industry participation in ecolabeling schemes while extending the mileage of such programs.

Tourism ecolabeling programs present the hidden risk of impeding innovative initiatives within the industry toward ameliorating the negative environmental impacts associated with tourism development. Since the ecolabel awarded to tourism enterprises would be the same, regardless of whether they meet the highest standards of environmental sensitivity or the minimal standards identified in the evaluation criteria (Shimp & Rattray, 1997), most ecolabeled enterprises would have little interest in committing themselves to future efforts for identifying better, innovative ways to reduce detrimental resource impacts (Wildavsky, 1996). Additionally, environmental certification programs will hold businesses such as eco-lodges that are already maintaining superior environmental standards to much higher standards than their competitors who do not adhere to environmentally-sensitive business practices (Honey & Rome, 2000a). Most small-scale tourism enterprises of developing countries would be precluded from future recertification by ecolabeling programs owing to their financial insufficiency to meet the prohibitive expenses associated with the adoption of innovative measures for complying with stricter re-established criteria and standards in the future, while maintaining adequate

profit margins (Salzhauer, 1991). Based on this review, the third proposition may be offered as follows:

Proposition 3. *Non-involvement from small enterprise stakeholders in tourism ecolabeling schemes and the consequent insufficiency of sponsors for funding ecolabeling programs will result in the lowering of certification standards for increasing industry participation and for increasing the mileage of such programs.*

5.4. Ecolabels: market exclusion through eco-protectionism

Ecolabeling schemes and programs for manufactured goods have predominantly originated in developed countries e.g., United States, Canada, Germany, Austria, Sweden, France, Japan, Australia, (Lal, 1996; Eiderströem, 1997; Hemmelskamp & Brockmann, 1997; Kusz, 1997; Parris, 1998). Similarly, most tourism ecolabeling schemes have their origins and/or funding sources located in developed nations. Tourism ecolabeling schemes initiated by developing countries are oftentimes supported, through management and funding, by similar programs based in developed countries. For example, the Caribbean Alliance for Sustainable Tourism (CAST), a non-profit subsidiary company of the Caribbean Hotel Association responsible for hotel certification, works in joint-partnership with Green Globe 21, a for-profit agency based in the United Kingdom (Honey & Rome, 2000b). Costa Rica's Certification for Sustainable Tourism (CST), an accommodation certification agency which works closely with Blue Flag (owned and operated by the Foundation for Environmental Education in Europe or FEEE), is operated by the Costa Rican Tourism Institute and INCAE, a business school connected with the United States' Harvard University (Honey & Rome, 2000b). Similarly, the ISO 14001: Sri Lanka Pilot Project, a certification program for beach resorts in Sri Lanka, is financed by USAID (Honey & Rome, 2000b), an independent United States federal government agency that conducts foreign assistance and humanitarian aid to advance the political and economic interests of the United States. The environmental standards and criteria set forth by tourism ecolabeling schemes would largely downplay the local industry perspectives of developing countries, and would be mainly geared toward business interests of developed countries (West, 1995; Lal, 1996). Furthermore, the conflicting economic, political, social, and environmental agendas (and priorities) of developed and developing countries would hinder attempts to set up tourism ecolabeling initiatives that are mutually acceptable to both parties. Stringent certification standards for industry practices, leaning towards the politicized criteria identified by developed countries, imposed by ecolabeling schemes within the profit-oriented tourism development policies of the developing

170   *V. Sasidharan et al. / Tourism Management 23 (2002) 161–174*

countries would be logistically unattainable to most local tourism enterprises of developing countries (West, 1995).

Ecolabeling programs in developing countries run the risk of being influenced by both the business protectionist strategies of large-scale tourism enterprises such as resorts, hotel chains, tour-operators and travel agencies as well as the environmental orientation of tourists mostly from western, developed countries. Large-scale tourism enterprises owned and operated by companies originating in developed nations could use their eco-certification as a strategy, i.e., eco-proctectionism, for inveigling 'environmentally conscious' western tourists, thereby offsetting competition for such tourists from non-ecolabeled local tourism enterprises of developing countries (Lal, 1996; Wildavsky, 1996). Thus, ecolabeled foreign business enterprises would acquire a sizeable amount of the 'environmentally conscious tourist' market share by vilifying non-ecolabeled local businesses based on their environmental incompatibility while promoting themselves as being eco-sensitive. The business profitability threat posed to non-ecolabeled, local enterprises through market exclusion and loss of the 'environmentally conscious tourist' market share and subsequent decline would potentially lead to the ostracism of foreign ecolabeling schemes by local businesses and governments of developing countries. This would be followed by the establishment of locally owned and controlled tourism ecolabeling programs to counteract the efforts of foreign schemes. For example, in Costa Rica, four different ecolabeling programs namely, CST, New Key, Green Globe, and ECOTEL, have all rated and certified accommodations and hotels based on their environmental standards (Honey & Rome, 2000a). The presence of a plethora of ecolabels, environmental certifications, and awarding bodies would impede the tourists' ability to clearly understand the environmental sensitivity of tourism enterprises. Consequently, tourists will base their judgements and decisions on the amount of facts and data, disclosed by environmental certification agencies, regarding the environmental performance and associated impacts of ecolabeled tourism enterprises. Based on this review, the fourth proposition may be offered as follows:

Proposition 4. *The certification criteria set forth by tourism ecolabeling schemes will be based upon local interests in developed countries and will not take developing countries and their local industry perspectives into account.*

5.5. Information disclosure: incomprehensive and confusing

Information furnished through tourism ecolabels is meant to assist tourists in identifying and selecting environmentally friendly products and services offered by tourism enterprises by shedding light on key environmental performance indicators pertaining to the operational characteristics of these enterprises (Lynch, 1997). Since the criteria developed for measuring and evaluating tourism enterprises' environmental sensitivity would emerge as a product of negotiations and compromise between industry stakeholders and environmental proponents, the information furnished by tourism ecolabels would provide a deliberately abridged account of the environmental impacts associated with tourism enterprises. Thus, tourism ecolabels would not enlighten tourists with altruistic descriptions of the entire gamut of environmental impacts produced by a particular tourism enterprise. Moreover, several aspects of the environment are subjectively judged and categorized as suitable or unsuitable by ecolabeling agencies, while disregarding the diverse preferences (and priorities) of users of the natural resource as well as the varying uses of the resource (Morgan, 1999). The subjectively filtered, technically constructed and circumlocutory narrative (Wildavsky, 1996; Davis, 1997) offered by tourism ecolabeling schemes may deprive potential tourists of an unbiased, comprehensive environmental sensitivity assessment, thereby misinforming them regarding environmentally relevant issues (Shimp & Rattray, 1997). For instance, Green Globe 21 allows tourism enterprises and destinations that become members to use its logo from the time they are officially committed to becoming certified (Honey & Rome, 2000a, p. 21). ECOTEL offers lodging facilities with a different logo for each of five areas—(1) solid waste management, (2) energy efficiency, (3) water conservation, (4) employee environmental education and community, and (5) environmental legislation compliance and native land preservation involvement—and each logo is a product of a three-level scoring system, 'allowing members to display a combination of logos as they progress to different levels in each of the five areas' (Honey & Rome, 2000a, p. 22). The Costa Rican CST ranks its certified tourism enterprises by scoring them on a scale of one to five for their performance in four different areas (Honey & Rome, 2000a, p. 22). The wide array of value-laden technical jargons (e.g., recycled, pollution-free, sustainable, etc.) used by various tourism ecolabeling programs and the contradictory information disseminated by such schemes would impede tourists from making objective judgements regarding the legitimacy of tourism enterprises' environmental sensitivity claims (Wildavsky, 1996) in addition to exacerbating their confusion. The proliferation of ecolabels and awarding bodies in the absence of a non-aligned, neutral, widely accepted agency for monitoring, controlling and regulating the efforts of tourism ecolabeling schemes in developing countries would raise suspicion and distrust among tourists towards the credibility of ecolabels (House & Herring, 1995;

Morgan, 1999). Further, tourists would become increasingly indifferent to the environmental claims raised by ecolabeled tourism enterprises and eco-certification programs.

Owing to the primary focus of tourism ecolabels on the environmental performance of tourism enterprises, socio-cultural impacts produced by tourism enterprises that could potentially damage the social fabric, cultural identity, traditional lifestyles and quality of life of host destinations and indigenous populations of developing countries are likely to be downplayed by ecolabels. For instance, the Eco-Management and Audit Scheme (EMAS), a certification scheme regulated by the European Union requires certification seeking businesses to furnish an initial environmental impact assessment in addition to information on environmental improvements in the companies' annual reports (Honey & Rome, 2000a). Such certification schemes lack mandates for the disclosure of data on business-related impacts having social and cultural consequences. Ecolabeled tourism enterprises would utilize their (environmental) market distinction to project themselves as forerunners of environmentally compatible business practices while actively espousing the cause of environmental compliance to overshadow the socio-cultural impacts produced as a direct result of their operations and services. Since most tourists remain unaware regarding the existence of tourism ecolabels and certification programs and far fewer understand the meaning of the same, tourism industry stakeholders would have to undertake the preeminent task of educating tourists with respect to the need, utility, purpose, goals and scope of tourism ecolabels (Morris, Hastak & Mazis, 1995; Eisen, 1997) alongside efforts towards creating or adopting tourism ecolabeling programs. Based on this review, the fifth proposition may be offered as follows:

Proposition 5. *Tourism ecolabeling schemes will provide potential tourists with only a subjective and filtered narrative of the environmental impacts produced by a particular tourism enterprise, thereby misinforming and depriving them of a validated, in-depth environmental impact analysis.*

6. Conclusion

Utilization of tourism ecolabels would be highly compatible with the environmentally compatible tourism initiatives of developing countries (Jensen et al., 1998). The potential of ecolabels to maintain and even enhance the physical environment by educating potential tourists regarding the environmental attributes of tourism enterprises and fostering environmentally sensitive business operations among such enterprises would make the concept particularly appealing to developing

countries (see Table 2). The principal objective of the discussion presented in this paper is to generate awareness regarding the problems associated with the adoption of ecolabeling programs by developing countries. As highlighted by the propositions presented in the previous section of this paper, several hidden barriers relating to the applicability and workability of tourism ecolabeling schemes for developing countries become evident upon analyzing the ecolabeling process. Ecolabeling issues faced by developing nations would vary depending on the environmental resources of individual countries as well as their characteristic socio-cultural, economic, and political climates. Although this paper vacillates from offering specific, cookie-cutter courses of action for dealing with ecolabeling problems confronted by developing countries, it is important for developing nations to give due consideration to these issues in the design and operation of tourism ecolabeling schemes. In spite of the fact that ecolabeling agencies continue to advocate the environmental benefits of their schemes, to date no conclusive evidence exists to support their assertive claims that ecolabels improve the environment (Weissman, 1997). Further, social science research suggests that environmental education of consumers and increasing environmental awareness does not stimulate environmentally responsible purchasing behavior (Hemmelskamp & Brockmann, 1997). Similarly, despite the environment-oriented educative potential of tourism ecolabels, potential tourists may not respond favorably to ecolabels and the enterprises that market their eco-sensitive tourism services and products (House & Herring, 1995; Morgan, 1999).

Tourists may respond positively to ecolabeling schemes established by groups already well known and respected for efforts in protecting the natural environment in developing countries (Salzhauer, 1991). However, the high costs incurred by tourism enterprises in the process of acquiring ecolabels (Shimp & Rattray, 1997) and the costs associated with running an environmentally sensitive operation coupled with the business objective of increasing profit margins would lead ecolabeled enterprises to increase the prices of their tourism services and products offered to tourists. The additional costs for the tourists, entailed with the 'purchase' of ecolabeled services (Hemmelskamp & Brockmann, 1997) may dissuade them from making 'high-priced' purchasing decisions in favor of eco-labeled tourism enterprises. Non-ecolabeled tourism enterprises would ultimately benefit from the growing sensitivity of tourists towards the high prices of eco-labeled services.

Most importantly, the great degree of scientific uncertainty and unreliability pertaining to the environmental impact analyses performed by tourism ecolabeling agencies would have an adverse effect on the levels of participation of stakeholders in ecolabeling programs.

172 *V. Sasidharan et al. / Tourism Management 23 (2002) 161–174*

Table 2
Benefits of tourism ecolabels

Benefactor	Benefits
Tourism industry	Curbs tourism's negative environmental impacts by encouraging tourism enterprises to attain high environmental standards
	Exerts pressure on the tourism industry to improve environmental performance by adopting effective and tangible environmental management techniques
	Improves industry practices by fostering environmentally sensitive business operations
	Assists the tourism industry in developing standards for environmentally sensitive tourism services and products
	Conforms to the concept of environmentally compatible tourism alongside of natural resource management, environmental conservation and protection, and pollution control policies
	Strategic tool for officially approving and promoting the design, production, marketing and use of environmentally benign services and products having a reduced environmental impact
	Disseminates externally validated information on the environmental impacts of tourism products and services among tourism consumers
	Can be extended to certify the environmental soundness of tourist destinations and the natural resources at these destinations
Tourism enterprises	Communicates the environmental credentials of companies
	Gives companies differential advantage over their competitors (gainful market position) as a result of fewer impacts on the environment than other similar enterprises
	Promotes the environmental achievements of companies via marketing campaigns (pamphlets, flyers, brochures, press releases, notice boards, and display of award logos and flags), both within and off-premises
	Serves as an incentive for companies to maintain and improve environmental performance standards, thereby reducing environmental impacts
	Assists companies in marketing their environmentally friendly services and/or products to high spending, environmentally conscious tourists
	Tourists develop positive attitudes toward the companies' products and/or services
Tourists	Educates tourists in originating countries regarding the impacts of their tourism-related actions and decisions
	Furnishes tourists with 'better' information on the environmental impacts of tourism enterprises
	Prompts tourists to act in favor of environmentally sensitive tourism enterprises through their purchasing decisions
	Enables tourists to make informed choices while selecting tourism enterprises for their vacations

Further, conflicts of interest among stakeholders involved in the ecolabeling process and the predominance of profit-oriented tourism industry interests would affect the environmental focus and agenda of ecolabeling schemes in the long run. Additionally, the resource insufficiency of small-scale tourism enterprises of developing countries to make heavy investments in technology required for environmental protection while maintaining adequate profit margins would preclude such enterprises from meeting the prohibitive standards and criteria prescribed by ecolabeling schemes. Thus, ecolabels would facilitate the emergence of large, multi-national tourism enterprises as 'environmental market leaders', thereby providing them with a marketing edge over small-scale enterprises of developing countries. Overall, tourism ecolabels would serve as a protectionist strategy for large-scale enterprises in their efforts toward capturing the tourism market share, irrespective of their environmental impact potential. Rather than contributing to environmentally sensitive tourism development and protection of natural resources of developing countries from the detrimental environmental impacts of tourism, ecolabels are likely to function as nothing more than marketing gimmicks for large-scale enterprises of the growing tourism industry.

References

Akama, J. S. (1999). Marginalization of the Maasai in Kenya. *Annals of Tourism Research, 26,* 716–718.

Ap, J., & Crompton, J. L. (1998). Developing and testing a tourism impact scale. *Journal of Travel Research, 37,* 120–130.

Baker, J. E. (1997). Trophy hunting as a sustainable use of wildlife resources in Southern and Eastern Africa. *Journal of Sustainable Tourism, 5,* 304–321.

Brierton, U. A. (1991). Tourism and the environment. *Contours, 5,* 18–19.

Britton, S. G. (1982). The political economy of tourism in the Third World. *Annals of Tourism Research, 9,* 331–358.

Burton, R. (1995). *Travel geography* (2nd ed.). Singapore: Longman Singapore Publishers Pte. Ltd.

Butler, R. (1990). Alternative tourism: Pious hope or Trojan horse? *Journal of Travel Research, 28,* 40–45.

Cater, E. (1993). Ecotourism in the Third World: Problems for sustainable tourism development. *Tourism Management, 14,* 85–90.

Clark, J. R. (1990). Carrying capacity: Defining the limits to coastal tourism. In M. L. Miller, & J. Auyong (Eds.), *Proceedings of the 1990 congress on coastal and marine tourism* (pp. 117–131). Newport, OR: National Coastal Resources Research and Development Institute.

Davis, G. (1997). How green the label? *Forum for Applied Research and Public Policy, 12,* 137–140.

De Kadt, E. (Ed.). (1979). *Tourism: Passport to development?* New York: Oxford University Press.

Dobias, R. J., & Bunpapong, S. (1990). Turn of the tide: Making tourism work for marine park conservation. In M. L. Miller, &

J. Auyong (Eds.), *Proceedings of the 1990 congress on coastal and marine tourism* (pp. 175–179). Newport, OR: National Coastal Resources Research and Development Institute.

Dudley, N., Elliott, C., & Stolton, S. (1997). A framework for environmental labeling. *Environment*, 39, 16–20; 42–45.

Eiderströem, E. (1997). Ecolabeling: Swedish style. *Forum for Applied Research and Public Policy*, 12, 141–144.

Eisen, M. (1997). Ecolabeled products find home at depot. *Forum for Applied Research and Public Policy*, 12, 124–127.

Erize, F. (1987). The impact of tourism on the Antarctic environment. *Environment International*, 13, 133–136.

Farrell, B. H. (1986). Cooperative tourism and the coastal zone. *Coastal Zone Management Journal*, 14, 113–146.

Fennell, D. A., & Eagles, P. F. J. (1990). Ecotourism in Costa Rica: A conceptual framework. *Journal of Park and Recreation Administration*, 8, 23–34.

Freestone, D. (1991). Problems of coastal zone management in Antigua and Barbuda. In G. Cambers, & O. T. Magoon (Eds.), *Coastlines of the Caribbean* (pp. 61–69). New York: American Society of Civil Engineers.

Friel, M. (1999). Marketing practice in small tourism and hospitality firms. *International Journal of Tourism Research*, 1, 97–109.

German Federal Agency for Nature Conservation (GFANC) (Ed.). (1997). *Biodiversity and tourism: Conflicts on the world's seacoasts*. New York: Springer.

Gilman, E. L. (1997). Community based and multiple purpose protected areas: A model to select and manage protected areas with lessons from the Pacific Islands. *Coastal Management*, 25, 59–91.

Grodsky, J. (1993). Certified green. The law and future of environmental labeling. *The Yale Journal on Regulation*, 10, 147–227.

Hall, C. M., & McArthur, S. (1998). *Integrated heritage management*. London: Stationary Office.

Hashimoto, A. (1999). Comparative evolutionary trends in environmental policy: Reflections on tourism development. *International Journal of Tourism Research*, 1, 195–216.

Healy, R. G. (1994). The 'common pool' problem in tourism landscapes. *Annals of Tourism Research*, 21, 596–611.

Hemmelskamp, J., & Brockmann, K. (1997). Environmental labels—The German 'Blue Angel'. *Futures*, 29, 67–76.

Hickman, T., & Cocklin, C. (1992). Attitudes toward recreation and tourism development in the coastal zone: A New Zealand study. *Coastal Management*, 20, 269–289.

Hinrichsen, D. (1998). *Coastal waters of the world: Trends, threats, and strategies*. Washington, DC: Island Press.

Holder, J. S. (1988). Pattern and impact of tourism on the environment of the Caribbean. *Tourism Management*, 9, 119–127.

Honey, M., & Rome, A. (2000a). *Ecotourism and sustainable tourism certification: Where are we today?* Draft report, prepared for the ecotourism and sustainable certification workshop, November 17–19, Mohonk Mountain House, New Paltz, New York.

Honey, M., & Rome, A. (2000b). *Ecotourism and sustainable tourism certification: Case studies*. Draft report, prepared for the ecotourism and sustainable certification workshop, November 17–19, Mohonk Mountain House, New Paltz, New York.

House, M. A., & Herring, M. (1995). *Aesthetic pollution public perception survey*. Report to Water Research Center, Flood Hazard Research Center, Middlesex University, Middlesex.

Jensen, A., Christiansen, K., & Elkington, J. (1998). *Life cycle assessment: A guide to approaches, experiences and information sources. Environmental issues series no.* 6. Copenhagen: European Environment Agency.

Kousis, M. (2000). Tourism and the environment: A social movement perspective. *Annals of Tourism Research*, 27, 468–489.

Kusz, J. (1997). Ecolabel investments: Whats behind label? *Forum for Applied Research and Public Policy*, 12, 133–136.

Lal, R. (1996). Eco-labels—an instrument to hasslefree marketing. *Colourage*, 43, 15–18.

Lockhart, D. G. (1997). Islands and tourism: An overview. In D. G. Lockhart, & D. Drakakis-Smith (Eds.), *Island tourism: Trends and prospects* (pp. 3–20). London: Pinter (Cassell imprint).

Lumsdon, L. M., & Swift, J. S. (1998). Ecotourism at a crossroads: The case of Costa Rica. *Journal of Sustainable Tourism*, 16, 155–172.

Lynch, J. (1997). Environmental labels: A new policy strategy. *Forum for Applied Research and Public Policy*, 12, 121–123.

Maragos, J. E. (1993). Impact of coastal construction on coral reefs in the U.S.-affiliated Pacific Islands. *Coastal Management*, 21, 235–269.

Mathieson, A., & Wall, G. (1982). *Tourism: Economic, physical and social impacts*. Harlow: Longman.

Middleton, V. T., & Hawkins, R. (1998). *Sustainable tourism: A marketing perspective*. Oxford: Butterworth-Heinemann (Reed Elsevier plc group).

Mihalic, T. (2000). Environmental management of a tourist destination: A factor of tourism competitiveness. *Tourism Management*, 21, 65–78.

Mitchell, B. A., & Barborak, J. R. (1991). Developing coastal park systems in the tropics: Planning in the Turks and Caicos Islands. *Coastal Management*, 19, 113–134.

Morgan, R. (1999). A novel, user-based rating system for tourism beaches. *Tourism Management*, 20, 393–410.

Morris, L. A., Hastak, M., & Mazis, M. B. (1995). Consumer comprehension of environmental advertising and labeling claims. *Journal of Consumer Affairs*, 29, 328–350.

Nunn, P. D. (1994). *Oceanic islands*. Oxford: Blackwell.

Obua, J., & Harding, D. M. (1997). Environmental impact of ecotourism in Kibale National Park, Uganda. *Journal of Sustainable Tourism*, 5, 213–223.

Parris, T. (1998). Seals of approval: Environmental labeling on the net. *Environment*, 40, 3–4.

Place, S. E. (1995). Ecotourism for sustainable development: Oxymoron or plausible strategy? *GeoJournal*, 35, 161–174.

Rhodes, S., & Brown, L. (1997). Consumers look for the ecolabel. *Forum for Applied Research and Public Policy*, 12, 109–115.

Salzhauer, A. (1991). Obstacles and opportunities for a consumer ecolabel. *Environment*, 33, 10–15; 33–37.

Sasidharan, V., & Font, X. (2001). Pitfalls of ecolabeling. In X. Font, & R. Buckley (Eds.), *Tourism ecolabeling: Certification and promotion of sustainable management*. Wallingford: CAB International, pp. 105–118.

Shackley, M. (1996). Community impact of the camel safari industry in Jaisalmar, Rajasthan. *Tourism Management*, 17, 213–218.

Shackley, M. (1999). Tourism development and environmental protection in Southern Sinai. *Tourism Management*, 20, 543–548.

Shimp, R., & Rattray, T. (1997). Ecoseals: Little more than a pretty package. *Forum for Applied Research and Public Policy*, 12, 128–132.

Sindiga, I. (1999). Alternative tourism and sustainable development in Kenya. *Journal of Sustainable Tourism*, 7, 108–127.

Sindiga, I., & Kanunah, M. (1999). Unplanned tourism development in sub-Saharan Africa with special reference to Kenya. *Journal of Tourism Studies*, 10, 25–39.

Sirakaya, E. (1997a). Attitudinal compliance with ecotourism guidelines. *Annals of Tourism Research*, 24, 919–950.

Sirakaya, E. (1997b). Assessment of factors affecting conformance behavior of ecotour operators with industry guidelines. *Tourism Analysis*, 2, 17–36.

Sirakaya, E., & McLellan, R. W. (1998). Modeling tour operations voluntary compliance with ecotourism principles: A behavioral approach. *Journal of Travel Research*, 36, 42–55.

174 *V. Sasidharan et al. / Tourism Management 23 (2002) 161–174*

Sirakaya, E., Sasidharan, V., & Sönmez, S. (1999). Redefining ecotourism: The need for a supply-side view. *Journal of Travel Research, 38,* 168–172.

Sirakaya, E., & Uysal, M. (1998). Can sanctions and rewards explain conformance behavior of tour operator's with ecotourism guidelines? *Journal of Sustainable Tourism, 5,* 322–332.

Smith, R. A. (1992). Conflicting trends of beach resort development: A Malaysian case. *Coastal Management, 20,* 167–187.

United Nations Environment Programme (UNEP). (1998). *Ecolabels in the tourism industry.* United Nations Publication, UNEP, Industry and Environment, 39–43 quai André Citroën, 75739 Paris Cedex 15, France.

Weissman, A. (1997). Greener marketplace means cleaner world. *Forum for Applied Research and Public Policy, 12,* 116–120.

Wescott, G. (1998). Reforming coastal management to improve community participation and integration in Victoria, Australia. *Coastal Management, 26,* 3–15.

West, K. (1995). Ecolabels: The industrialization of environmental standards. *The Ecologist, 25,* 16–20.

Wheeller, B. (1997). Tourisms troubled times: Responsible tourism is not the answer. In L. France (Ed.), *The Earthscan reader in sustainable tourism* (pp. 61–67). London: Earthscan Publications Ltd.

Wildavsky, B. (1996). Sticker shock. *National Journal, 28,* 532–535.

Wilkinson, P. F. (1989). Strategies for tourism in island microstates. *Annals of Tourism Research, 16,* 153–177.

Wilkinson, P. F. (1994). Tourism and small island states: Problems of resource analysis, management and development. In A. V. Seaton, C. L. Jenkins, R C. Wood, P. U. C. Dieke, M. M. Bennett, L. R. MacLellan, & R. Smith (Eds.), *Tourism: The state of the art* (pp. 41–51). Chichester, UK: Wiley.

Williams, A. T., & Morgan, R. (1995). Beach awards and rating systems. *Shore and Beach, 63,* 29–33.

Wong, P. (Ed.). (1993). *Tourism vs. environment: The case for coastal areas.* Boston: Kluwer Academic Publishers.

World Coast Conference (WCC). (1993). *Preparing to meet the coastal challenges of the 21st century.* Conference report of the Intergovernmental Panel on Climate Change, April 1994.

Wright, R. M., Urish, D. W., & Runge, I. (1991). The hydrology of a Caribbean mangrove island. In G. Cambers, & O. T. Magoon (Eds.), *Coastlines of the Caribbean* (pp. 170–184). New York: American Society of Civil Engineers.

Yapp, G. A. (1986). Aspects of population, recreation, and management of the Australian coastal zone. *Coastal Zone Management Journal, 14,* 47–66.

Zhang, H. Q., Chong, K., & Ap, J. (1999). An analysis of tourism policy development in modern China. *Tourism Management, 20,* 471–485

[34]

Annals of Tourism Research, Vol. 20, pp. 701–715, 1993
Printed in the USA. All rights reserved.

TOURISM DEVELOPMENT ETHICS IN THE THIRD WORLD

John P. Lea
University of Sydney, Australia

Abstract: The origins of ethical concern about tourism development in the Third World are traced in both the sociology of development and environmental ethics literature. New secular and religious writings single out the traveler and the tourism industry as objects of ethical concern. This paper presents a preliminary overview of the growing "responsible tourism" and travel ethics literature and explores the significance of anti-tourism activity in the Indian State of Goa. In conclusion, a three-part grouping into Third World development ethics, tourism industry ethics, and personal travel ethics categories is suggested. **Keywords:** travel ethics, responsible tourism, environmental ethics, Third World tourism, sex tourism, Goa.

Résumé: Une éthique du développement du tourisme au Tiers-Monde. Dans cet article, on remonte la filière du souci éthique au sujet du tourisme au Tiers-Monde dans la littérature de la sociologie du développement et dans la littérature de l'éthique environnementale. De nouveaux écrits d'ordre religieux et profane identifient le voyageur et l'industrie touristique comme des sujets d'intérêt éthique. On présente une vue d'ensemble de la croissance d'une littérature du "tourisme responsable" et de l'éthique du voyage. On étudie la signification de l'activité anti-touristique dans l'état indien de Goa. Pour conclure, on propose un groupement de ces questions en trois catégories: l'éthique du développement au Tiers-Monde, l'éthique de l'industrie touristique et l'éthique des voyages individuels. **Mots-clés:** éthique du voyage, tourisme responsable, éthique environnementale, tourisme au Tiers-Monde, sexe et tourisme, Goa.

INTRODUCTION

> When issues are defined ethically—phrased, that is, in terms of right and wrong—it is hard to remain indifferent. People seldom compromise their ethical convictions . . . (Nash, 1989:166).

There is growing awareness that a new subset of tourism studies has emerged that redefines and extends concerns about tourist behavior and the operation of the international tourism industry. Notions of

John Lea is director of the I.B. Fell Research Centre, Faculty of Architecture, University of Sydney (NSW 2006, Australia) where he teaches in urban and regional planning. His publications include books and papers on tourism and development, tourism policy in Africa, and northern Australian and Pacific Island development.

morality, ethics, and codes of conduct have been debated in the sociology of development literature in the past (Goulet 1973, 1974, 1975), but the emphasis then was primarily on behavior as it affected other humans. Today, this is coupled with a new ethic that places the environment at center stage. Of particular significance is the fact that much of the push to explore questions pertaining to tourism and to effect changes in some government policies and commercial practices is coming from sources in the developing world. To what extent does this questioning of tourism's *bona fides* really represent the concerns of ordinary people in developing countries? The Christian-inspired origins of some of the anti-tourism (this term denotes opposition towards certain "irresponsible" aspects of behavior and practice) protest literature may have stereotyped the debate as a diatribe in some quarters, or even as a new kind of missionary activity, leading industry apologists to play down the ethical issues involved.

As yet, there has been little critical analysis of the growing tourism consciousness and anti-tourism literature. Its origins are quite varied, with some of it being an extension of the 1960s *dependencia* movement and the language of liberation, others have women's development studies origins, and still more have identifiable religious connections. Works stemming from each of these three backgrounds, for example, can be found for Sri Lanka in the contributions of Goonatilake (1978), Samarasuriya (1982), and Mendis (1981), respectively. The picture is also complicated by the existence of special issues foci in some distinct regions, with one of the most obvious being the increasing sexual exploitation of women and children in certain Asian tourism destinations. Similarly, few researchers (e.g., Botterill 1991; Gonsalves 1991) have investigated critically the growing presence of interest groups concerned with aspects of the tourism industry's impact on society and the environment. It would also be wrong to limit the debate to destination-based concerns alone in view of increasing evidence that a new climate of corporate responsibility has reached some parts of the international tourism industry, as evidenced in a succession of recent articles in vocational journals (Enghagen 1991a, 1991b; Hegarty 1990; and Whitney 1990). Concerns expressed here are social as well as environmental and in some cases have been codified into new industry guidelines (Australian Tourism Industry Association 1990).

Although not pointedly anti-tourism in its focus, there is also the recent addition of an environmental ethics literature, which now claims a global audience (Attfield 1983, Nash 1989, Rolston 1988). The industry will come under increasing scrutiny by environmentalists for obvious reasons. But the negative side of some developments is ameliorated by the growing popularity of ecotourism and the potential of the industry to conserve flora, fauna, and landscape that otherwise might be destroyed. Of immediate relevance to tourism planners and developers, however, is the fact that the rapid growth of the industry and its scale of development in the Third World (in urban and rural locations) has stirred up direct forms of activism in both origin and destination countries with the potential to change some industry practices.

This paper explores various facets of the new morality. The discussion begins with a brief historical perspective on the present debate from both human and environmental perspectives. This is followed by a short review of the tourism ethics literature and by a look at organized and radical responses in Asia to threats posed by sections of the industry, using the example of Goa. The discussion concludes with a preliminary assessment of the significance of the new focus on tourism ethics and some comments on the present role and future development of the protest movement.

TOURISM DEVELOPMENT ETHICS IN THE THIRD WORLD

Evolution of Tourism Ethics

Contemporary ideas about the human and environmental impacts of international tourism have their origins in the writings of development theorists and ecologists in the 25 years following the Second World War. The two streams of literature appear to have had little to do with each other until the late 1980s and the importance of tourism was understandably of minor consequence when compared to the huge infrastructure building projects that accompanied post-war reconstruction. The scope of the development debate itself did not widen to include ethics as a central question until the 1970s when the growth of tourism became the economic mainstay of many small countries in the developing world. There is insufficient space here to trace the development ethics debate in any detail from its early origins but it is important, at the risk of oversimplification, to recall the introduction of some influential ideas.

Denis Goulet's (1973) famous book, *The Cruel Choice: A New Concept in the Theory of Development*, is credited today with transforming notions about development. Its importance was not only to bring ethical concerns to the forefront in development studies but to present them from the perspective of a Third World scholar. He drew his inspiration from the Frenchman Louis Joseph Lebret (Malley 1968) whom he called the "pioneer of development ethics" and whose work was not well-known to English-speaking audiences. He also introduced to that same audience the power and relevance of the "language of liberation," as the writings of Fanon (1967), Freire (1970), and others came to be known. His definition of ethics was simple: "Since the time of early Greek philosophers, the term "ethics" has meant for Westerners the reflective study of what is good or bad in that part of human conduct for which men have some responsibility. . . . (Goulet 1973:334). [It is also] "those conditions of knowledge and will men require in order to exercise a genuine choice of ends or means" (Goulet 1973:331–332).

Development was defined in the broadest possible sense to include political, cultural, economic, and social goals applying both as an end product and as a process. Sustainability was not identified in a sophisticated way (as, for example, is found in Commonwealth of Australia 1991b), but a whole chapter was devoted to "World Resources and Priority Needs." For Goulet " . . . survival, health, and creativity require that major human efforts be devoted to protecting the 'dynamic stability' and the regenerative powers of the world's ecological systems"

(Goulet, 1973:273). But what of the emerging presence of tourism? There are some clear and early warnings in the liberation literature about a pattern of development which has become commonplace today.

Twenty years ago, the Tanzanian economist Issa Shivji (1973:ix) drew attention to Fanon's (1967:123) description of a settler town in a colonized country as being an equally accurate description of the new tourist hotels:

> The settler's town is a strongly built town, all made of stone and steel. It is a brightly-lit town with streets covered in asphalt, and the garbage-cans swallow all the leavings . . . The settler's feet are never visible, except perhaps in the sea; but there you never get close enough to see them. . . . The settler's town is a well-fed town, an easy going town: its belly is always full of good things. The settler's town is a town of white people, of foreigners (1967:123).

Shivji did not go on to quote the next passage of Fanon's book, which is even of more direct relevance:

> The national bourgeoisie will be greatly helped on its way toward decadence by the Western bourgeoisies, who come to it as tourists avid for the exotic, for big-game hunting and casinos. The national bourgeoisie organises centres for rest and relaxation, and pleasure resorts to meet the wishes of the Western bourgeoisie. Such activity is given in the name of tourism, and for the occasion will be built up as a national industry. . . . It is worthwhile having a look at what happened in Latin America. The casinos of Havana and of Mexico, the beaches of Rio, the little Brazilian and Mexican girls, the half-bred 13-year-olds, the ports of Acapulco and Copacabana — all these are the stigma of this deprivation of the middle class . . . . [which because it is bereft of ideas] will have nothing better to do than to take on the role for Western enterprise, and it will in practice set up its country as the brothel of Europe (cited in Crick 1989:323).

Apart from the neo-Marxist dialectic, there is little difference here from the parallel descriptions found today about many places on the international tourism circuit. There is, then, clear documentation accumulated over more than two decades that suggests that the nature and scale of some forms of tourism in parts of the Third World is leading to an unacceptable destruction of social structure and cultural values. The effects are not uniform and range from the fabled resilience of Balinese culture to the shock of mass tourism (Picard 1990) to much more vulnerable examples in some African countries (Crush and Wellings 1983; Lea 1981, 1988).

It is rather surprising, given the importance of ethics in both the development studies and environmental literature, that so little space is devoted in contemporary reviews of tourism studies to modern writing originating from this background (exceptions are found in Crick 1989 and Botterill 1991). Even the introduction to the Special Issue of *Annals* on "Tourism Social Science" (Graburn and Jafari 1991) makes only passing reference to its existence and has little to say about organized and indigenous anti-tourism activism.

This wide-ranging discussion has deliberately set out to cut across a number of disciplines and to indulge in some academic poaching, following Geertz's assertion that " . . . an adequate understanding of the new countries of the 'Third World' demands that one pursue scientific quarry across any fenced-off academic fields into which it may wander" (1963:xviii). In this spirit, the focus now shifts to the question of environmental ethics where the separate significance of tourism development is less clear cut. This is not an appropriate place to trace the origins of radical environmentalism in any detail, but there is plenty of evidence to be found in a large literature that the movement is having major effects on some forms of development in the Third World. These encompass well-publicized examples, such as worldwide reaction to the ruin of rain forests in Papua New Guinea and Brazil to concern about the encroachment by indigenous farmers onto animal habitats in Africa. Tourism occupies an ambiguous position in its development effects, possessing both conservation and destructive characteristics.

The significance of environmental ethics in this discussion lies far more in the way in which a succession of seminal publications has revolutionized and expanded popular thinking about the place of nature in modern life than with any direct link to tourism. The industry is caught up in the debate because of its sheer scale of operation and its obvious connections with those parts of the world most would wish to conserve. The claims now being made by those at the frontier of this intellectual transformation are far-reaching indeed. In his major book on the rights of nature, Roderick Nash asserts:

> The emergence of this idea that the human-nature relationship should be treated as a moral issue conditioned or restrained by ethics is one of the most extraordinary developments in recent intellectual history. Some believe it holds the potential for fundamental and far-reaching change in both thought and behavior comparable to that which the ideal of human rights and justice held at the time of the democratic revolutions in the seventeenth and eighteenth centuries (1989:4).

He traces the evolution of ethical thought from an early period in human history when self-interest was paramount, via steps when the family, tribe, and region were important, to a present occupation with nations, races, humans, and animals. In the future will come the rights of plants, life, rocks, ecosystems, the planet and the universe. Major milestones along the way (for Western civilization) are seen in the Magna Carta, the American Declaration of Independence, the abolition of slavery, emancipation of women, civil rights for Black Americans, and the Endangered Species Acts of the 1970s. Similar changes are found in many Western countries and are beginning to include the rights of nature:

> Ideas like these, to be sure, are on the far frontier of moral theory. From the perspective of intellectual history, environmental ethics is revolutionary; it is arguably the most dramatic expansion of morality in the course of human thought (Nash 1989:7).

For Aboriginal and Islander Australians, indigenous North Americans, and other peoples in what is sometimes called the Fourth World, some of these ideas are not particularly revolutionary at all. To them the modern awakening in the United States, Europe, and Oceania to the importance of ecology and the land simply reaffirms their central beliefs. Nash (1989:55) credits much of this modern awareness to the American ecologist Aldo Leopold who wrote that "all ethics rest upon a single premise: that the individual is a member of a community of interdependent parts" (1949:203). This biocentric morality Leopold termed the "Land Ethic." If a written Aboriginal history similar to the Hindu and Buddhist epic works was available in North America, Australia, and other countries with ancient indigenous peoples, it could have popularized such notions long ago.

By the 1960s, environmental awareness had spread to a "greening of religion" in Western countries and attempts to overcome the Judaeo-Christian preoccupation with people as masters rather than members of the natural world. The historian White (1967) is seen as starting a debate culminating in an ecotheology that recognizes a sort of spiritual democracy of God's creation (Nash 1989:6). Eastern religions, of course, do not support anthropocentricism of the Christian kind and assume the oneness of the natural world. Other special considerations, especially regarding tourism in Islamic countries, are discussed in detail by Din (1989), who notes that negative attitudes to some of the industry's social impacts in the Islamic world does not stop Muslim tourists from participating in forbidden activities elsewhere. It is also ironic that changes seen in popular attitudes towards the environment in Western industrialized countries today might be placing a higher premium on nature at home than on human welfare elsewhere.

There are several implications arising from this changing focus in popular opinion for all those important development activities that generate multiple social and physical impacts in the Third World. For international tourism, these include increasing attention by major aid donors, non-governmental organizations, and community groups to some aspects of tourism behavior. The industry itself is commonly recognized " . . . as a capitalistically organized activity driven by the inherent and defining social dynamics of that system . . . " (Britton 1991:451). Although these dynamics are regularly changing, from mass consumption to more individual modes (Urry 1990), there is plenty of evidence to show that leisure and tourism have become increasingly commodified. Control still rests overwhelmingly with the metropolitan countries where most tourists come from and it is here, logically, that attempts must also be made to halt or modify certain industry practices. Thus, the pattern of tourist activism and concern that has its origins in some of the developing countries most severely impacted by the negative effects of the industry, is starting to take hold in the main capital accumulation centers of the Western World and Japan (Botterill 1991).

Notions of changing ethical responsibility for the shape of tourism developments is starting to surface in major national studies in the tourist generating countries. The recent reports of Australia's Ecologically Sustainable Development Working Groups (Commonwealth of

Australia 1991a, 1991b), for example, make specific reference to this need: "An ecologically sustainable tourism industry ought not to contribute towards unsustainable activities in other countries" (Commonwealth of Australia 1991a:221). The extent to which such responsibility can actually be assessed depends on several factors, including the way in which the tourist developments themselves are evaluated and the scope of their impacts are measured in the countries concerned.

Travel Ethics

The last 20 years has seen a transformation in the extent and quality of advice available to international tourists visiting developing countries. It would be hard to imagine, for example, a more extreme contrast to the advocates of today's responsible travel scene than the one described in Dalton's (1973) guidebook on Indonesia (cited in Connell forthcoming), where the traveler is advised that "going to Bali is like stepping on a giant tab of LSD. The people there are high all year round on that good ol' time religion, festivals constantly." At Kuta "score grass on beach itself, ask around among the freaks." Drink "tuak" (palm wine) with old men stroking their fighting cocks and, at Denpasar, "Good whore village 1k in back of Adi Yasa's over rice paddies, 500 rp. short time, see twinkling lights in distance. Take flashlight." Indeed, Balinese culture has proved to be remarkably resistant to the onslaught of mass tourism and may represent an interesting exception to the experience of many other developing countries. The extent to which culture and tourism have become reconciled in the island has become the subject of a celebrated debate and focus of major research over 20 years (Hanna 1972; McKean 1973; Picard 1984, 1990).

Besides the evolution of much more comprehensive and far less controversial guide books (Dalton's 1990 edition on Bali alone is 428 pages), there is now a growing literature on responsible travel. Starting with the well-known 12-point "Code of Ethics for Tourists" developed by the Christian Conference of Asia in the early 1980s, there are also special codes for activities like ocean cruising (North American Co-ordinating Centre for Responsible Tourism, San Anselmo, California), and book-length manuals and advisories of all kinds. A fine dividing line exists between preaching to would-be travelers and the promotion of understanding and this is reflected in the literature. The Bangkok-based Ecumenical Coalition on Third World Tourism (ECTWT), for example, is the direct or indirect source of many publications characterized by a distinct missionary zeal (Amoa 1985; Gonsalves 1987; Gonsalves and Holden 1985; Holden 1984; Holden, Horlemann and Pfafflin 1985; R. O'Grady 1981; A. O'Grady 1990). In the more recent material, the declared purpose is "to raise awareness by providing information; to stimulate thinking and discussion and to encourage individuals and groups to become involved in working for more authentic human encounter" (O'Grady 1990).

Contributions with a more secular flavor are found in pamphlets and book-length guides to "responsible travel" (Community Aid Abroad 1990; Graham 1991). These sensible and rather unexceptional advisories subscribe to the three chief principles of responsible travel, which are to understand the culture that you are visiting; to respect and be sensitive to the people who are hosting your visit; and to tread softly on the environment of your hosts. There is a noticeable convergence here between the social consciousness of the aid organizations and the environmental concerns of ecotourism.

New responsible travel developments in Australia, for example, include the One World Travel Tour Development Unit of Community Aid Abroad (based in Adelaide), which aims to provide responsible travel alternatives to those offered by standard commercial holidays and the magazine *Tread Lightly*, which offers such appropriate adventures for sale as cycling through China and tracking Timber Wolves in the wilderness of Minnesota! One company specializing in adventures for women bravely displays a picture of a hot air balloon over Alice Springs (the site of Australia's worst balloon accident in the recent past).

Although the underlying presence of ethical concern is obvious in all the responsible travel literature, it is not as clear whether local people in the developing world faced with the impacts of mass tourism are at all convinced that the new ideas will be adopted in time to reverse present trends. The example of popular resistance to unbridled tourism development in Goa is a good example of grass roots organization to fight for the retention of a way of life and amenity which has clearly been adversely affected.

Organized Activism Against Tourism in Goa

The former Portuguese colony of Goa, situated on India's south west coast, became part of India in 1961 after 451 years of colonial rule. It has a population of some 1.2 million and its colorful past and mix of cultures has helped it to attract almost a million domestic and international tourists annually (Jagrut Goencaranchi Fauz 1991). In the post-hippie era, modern marketing has portrayed Goa as a place of beaches and churches, with its culture, exotic food, and Eastern ambience as the main attractions (*Sydney Morning Herald* 1991). By 1990, 69 hotels had been developed along the 107 km of Goan coastline (*Times of India* 1990). Three years earlier, a militant group of Goan youths, workers, students, professionals, and individuals, calling themselves the Jagrut Goencaranchi Fauz (JGF), published a five-part declaration against the rapid and unwelcome overdevelopment of Goa by five-star resorts.

> The JGF will mobilise the people of Goa in the cities and villages to fight for: (1) a total ban on any new five-star hotels, (2) a freeze on the expansion of the existing five-star hotels, (3) the withdrawal of the declaration of tourism as an industry by the Government of Goa, (4) a strict code of conduct to be observed by hoteliers with regard to their advertising Goa in a manner that is detrimental to Goan culture and women, and (5) the Government's non-collusion with hoteliers by organizing and sponsoring infrastructures required for five-star tourism. JGF warns the Government that if these demands are not met immediately, the JGF will paralyse the functioning of the Government and its tourism programmes (Srisang 1987:9).

This signaled the beginning of an active campaign that was to result in disruption to the State's tourism development program, the gaining of widespread international publicity, and successful legal action against developers who were breaking local environmental legislation. The protest activity was the culmination of community unrest in Goa, which had its origins back in the 1960s at the height of the "hippie invasion" of India. The advent of young Westerners and their casual attitudes to sex and drugs had a severe impact on the predominantly Roman Catholic Christian Goan community, as is vividly described by Mehta.

> Calingute Beach was also used as a shortcut by little Indian Christian schoolgirls, led by novitiates hiding behind cowls and veils, to get to the convent on the other side of the beach for their daily catechism lessons. Imagine the shock of the tiny demoiselles, under the basilisk gaze of their stern duennas, when they came upon the following scene of merriment: hundreds of naked bodies, of every hue and national origin, coupling in the sand. In the middle of the alfresco sensuality cavorted monkeys, pinching a thigh there, the nape of a neck there (1980:92–93).

It was not long before the mixture of high rates of domestic tourism from India itself and the suitability of the coastline for developers of international luxury beach resorts brought with it a wide range of additional negative effects of both social and physical kinds. The JGF waged a war of opposition to arriving Western tourists, handing out stern warnings at the airport. The opening words of the letter addressed to German Condor tourists in 1989 are representative:

> So, you come yet once again, CONDOR, the large hungry Vulture, that you are, a vicious bird of prey! . . . DO NOT come to Goa. Our limited resources cannot be sacrificed to meet your lustful luxury demands. Our people, for example, thirst for drinking water while the same is provided by the hotels, for you to SWIM in (English translation of part of a letter in German, handed out by JGF at Dabolim Airport of Goa, on 3 November 1989).

There then followed a series of court challenges by anti-tourism activists that have received considerable coverage in the Indian press. In 1988, the JGF had appealed to a judge of the Bombay High Court with jurisdiction in Goa to halt alleged illegal construction of hotels in contravention of building bylaws (particularly regarding environmental clearances required for construction close to the 500 metre "forbidden zone" above high water mark) (letter from S. Carvalho, Convenor of JGF, to Justice C. Dharmadhikari, dated 3 October 1988). The Court found in favor of JGF. Later, in 1990, the Goa Foundation (an environmental lobby group) filed a Writ seeking a stay on construction of one five-star hotel because of similar violations of environmental and town planning laws. This resulted in demolition notices being issued to eight beachside hotels by the Indian Ministry of Environment and Forests (MEF).

It was a short-lived victory and the Indian government reversed its earlier decision in June 1990 and relaxed the limit of the no-construction zone from 500 to 200 metres from the high waterline. This was reported to have caused jubilation in the hotel industry, with every likelihood that the State government would seek further relaxation to 90 metres. Worse still, the monitoring committee that had been set up by MEF to ensure that environmental safeguards were complied with by the beach hotels was dissolved. The Committee had imposed a 3–5 year moratorium on further hotel development in Goa and the door was opened for unbridled construction to meet Goa's "planned potential" of 2.5 million tourists annually by the turn of the century (*Times of India* 1990).

Events swung back in favor of the Foundation in late 1990 after further court action against the offending five-star hotel was upheld (*Deccan Herald* 1990). In a still later report, it appears that new Central Government controls have enabled MEF to re-establish objections to illegal hotel construction, and demolition was about to begin at various resorts. The State Town and Country Planning Department was later reported to have banned the building of any more hotels in the North Goa belt (*Contours* 1991a:25).

The Goan experience is one of the few well-documented examples of organized anti-tourism activity in the Third World and articles by Goanese activists are reaching a wide audience (de Rosa 1990). They demonstrate an awareness of the power exercised by environmental groups in the West and a preparedness to adopt their well-proven protest strategies. The ethical considerations involved have shifted from an early focus on social concerns to include important questions of physical amenity, demonstrated in complaints about water and energy supplies and the destruction of community amenities like the beach zone.

CONCLUSIONS

It is possible to make some preliminary generalizations about the place of ethical concern portrayed in the tourism literature. Collectively, this material can be grouped into three broad categories: one, development ethics in the Third World, in general, of which the tourism industry is becoming an increasingly significant component; two, tourism impacts of both social and physical kinds that can be identified at an industry level; and three, the consideration of tourism ethics where the focus moves to the individual behavior of travelers. This simple categorization is based on only a partial review of the growing literature and requires testing and elaboration. If nothing else, it demonstrates that any attempt to group ethical responses and reactions to tourism must contend with the same kinds of difficulties in definition that have always been a characteristic of the industry itself.

As discussed, development ethics is a well-established field within the sociology of development literature and has expanded in recent times to include environmental concerns of many kinds. International tourism is viewed here as a major component of world trade between rich and poor countries and its effects (both positive and negative) must be seen in the overall context of the condition of development of the country concerned. In other words, the industry cannot be satisfactorily studied or understood in isolation of this reality.

There are other aspects of tourism found at an industry level that are sufficiently important or controversial to be singled out for ethical attention. Among the more obvious factors are questions relating to levels of local ownership and control, the use of local resources, the extent to which local amenities are alienated, and marketing strategies. There is also growing evidence that parts of the industry are becoming increasingly concerned about their ethical responsibilities in matters of this kind and are seeking to modify some existing practices. The most easy to identify of these concerns relate to the environment. They were the subject of a special conference organized by the *Observer* (London) in January 1990, which resulted in the suggestion of 10 guidelines (covering issues as diverse as sewage disposal, to the use of local produce and the printing of brochures on recycled paper) to assist tourism company practice (de Rosa 1990).

At the individual level of the traveler, the extent of ethical concern in both origin and destination countries can be derived from the huge growth in responsible tourism opportunities for all groups of potential tourists. This is not thought to be a temporary phenomenon and is expanding the range of individually planned holidays available in many countries. In the mass market, the more obvious problems experienced in tourist-host interaction are probably lessened when separation occurs in resort enclaves. Such isolation has been identified as beneficial to the preservation of local culture in Indonesia (Noronha 1979), but is not a feasible solution in many instances and in any case is characterized by the alienation of some of the most attractive visitor locations from local use.

There are considerable difficulties facing small groups of Third World tourism activists attempting to build a movement strong enough to react effectively to the challenges presented by these issues in their countries. Calls have been made to establish international treaties to limit tourism in certain cases, supported by effective boycotts (de Rosa 1990). In some countries, the obstacles to achieving this will be hard to overcome, but in others (where reasonable institutional controls over development exist), the position may be brighter. Most popular coalitions of activists come up against difficulties in sustaining effective action because of failures to address differences among the groups involved. Ethical solidarity in particular appeals to those with higher incomes and levels of education and can exclude the people most likely to suffer from inappropriate tourism developments (de Rosa 1990, citing Freudenberg 1984). It might be argued, for example, that groups such as those described in Goa are not particularly representative of the community at large, having a membership drawn mainly from people with educated and professional backgrounds.

Opportunities for local activists to change government direction in tourism development policy are strictly limited in most of the developing world, unless the groups concerned are able to exert considerable pressure on the industry itself. This may be achieved by cooperative action with similar-minded groups in the tourist generating countries. Some success in this regard has been achieved in Germany with the passing of new laws to allow the prosecution (at home) of German nationals who are accused of crimes committed abroad against non-German children under the age of 14 (Ingham 1991). On a wider plane, there exists the possibility of organized networking on a global scale among activists from rich and poor countries representing both ends of the tourism spectrum. The actual mechanics of global networking can be hard to unravel, as Botterill describes when Goan activists were asked by the British group, Tourism Concern, to assist with the setting up of an alternative tourism project. The Goan group ultimately declined the offer because " . . . it would mean sanctioning the current working arrangements within the industry that confine the control over the tourism product to a set of negotiations between interested parties and to the exclusion of local communities . . . " (Botterill 1991:208).

The First Network Meeting of Tourism Activists (at a global scale) was held in Cyprus in September 1991. It was convened by ECTWT and the Third World European Ecumenical Network (TEN) to take stock of progress in the past decade and to define "modes of relatedness" between groups in the future (*Contours* 1991b:4). Resolutions were passed to operate as a global network and to establish closer cooperation with human rights and environmental organizations. Interestingly, a new and negative definition of international tourism was coined at the meeting:

> Tourism is essentially the commercialization of the human needs to travel, for the sake of money and profit on the part of the tourism promoters and at the expense of other people, their culture and environment (*Contours* 1991b:14).

Although this viewpoint is much too extreme to win universal support, it is certain that tourism ethics in general and environmental ethics in particular will become an important subdiscipline within tourism studies in the near future. A far more sophisticated understanding of its place and potential in development will be necessary. As Crick (1989: 338) observes "We need to know the local perceptions and understandings of tourism, we need to know the local perceptions of change and continuity, and we need to recognise that any culture is likely to have contradictory things to say about both" (1989:338). □ □

REFERENCES

Amoa, B. D.
  1985 Tourism in Africa. Nairobi: All Africa Conference of Churches.
Attfield, R.
  1983 The Ethics of Environmental Concern. Oxford: Basil Blackwell.
Australian Tourist Industry Association
  1990 Environmental Guidelines for Tourist Developments. Sydney: ATIA.
Botterill, T. D.
  1991 A New Social Movement: Tourism Concern: The First Two Years. Leisure
    Studies 10:203–217.
Britton, S.
  1991 Tourism, Capital and Place: Towards a Critical Geography of Tourism.
    Environment and Planning D: Society and Space 9:451–478.

Commonwealth of Australia
  1991a Ecologically Sustainable Development Working Groups; Final Report — Executive Summaries. Canberra: Australian Government Publishing Service.
  1991b Ecologically Sustainable Development Working Groups; Final Report — Tourism. Canberra: Australian Government Publishing Service.
Community Aid Abroad
  1990 Travel Wise and be Welcome: A Guide to Responsible Travel in the 90s. Melbourne: Community Aid Abroad.
Connell, J.
  Forthcoming Bali Revisited: Death, Rejuvenation and the Tourist Cycle. Environment and Planning D: Society and Space.
Contours
  1991a Administration and Hotel Lobby on Collision Course in Goa. Contours 5(2): 24–25.
Contours
  1991b Highlights from the Executive. Contours 5(4):14.
Crick, M.
  1989 Representations of International Tourism in the Social Sciences: Sun, Sex, Sights, Savings and Servility. Annual Review of Anthropology 18:307–344.
Crush, J. S., and P. A. Wellings
  1983 The Southern African Pleasure Periphery, 1966–1983. Journal of Modern African Studies 21:673–698.
Dalton, B.
  1973 Indonesia. Moon: Sydney.
de Rosa, G. P.
  1990 The Debate on International Tourist Boycotts and the Use of International Law to Protect the Indian Environment from Luxury Tourism and its Infrastructurally Related Activities. Special Paper No. 12. Panaji Goa: Goan Policy Research Unit.
Din, K. H.
  1989 Islam and Tourism: Patterns, Issues and Options. Annals of Tourism Research 16:542–563.
Enghagen, L. K.
  1991a Ethics in Hospitality Education: A Survey. Hospitality Research Journal 14: 113–118.
  1991b Teaching Ethics in Hospitality and Tourism Education. Hospitality Research Journal 14:467–475.
Fanon, F.
  1967 The Wretched of the Earth. Harmondsworth: Penguin.
Freudenberg, N.
  1984 Not in Our Backyards! Community Action for Health and the Environment. New York: Monthly Review Press.
Geertz, C.
  1963 Agricultural Involution: The Processes of Ecological Change in Indonesia. Berkeley: University of California Press.
Gonsalves, P. S.
  1987 Alternative Tourism: An Operations Manual for Third World Groups. Bangalore: Equations.
  1991 Alternative Tourism: A Third World Perspective. Lokayan Bulletin 9(2):23–28.
Gonsalves, P. S., and P. Holden
  1985 Alternative Tourism: A Resource Book. Bangkok: Ecumenical Coalition on Third World Tourism.
Goonatilake, S.
  1978 Tourism in Sri Lanka: The Mapping of International Inequalities and their Internal Structural Effects. Center for Developing Area Studies, McGill University, Canada.
Goulet, D.
  1973 The Cruel Choice: A New Concept in the Theory of Development. New York: Atheneum.
  1974 A New Moral Order: Studies in Development Ethics and Liberation Theology. New York: Orbis Books.

1975 On the Ethics of Development Planning: Some General principles and Special Application to Value Conflicts in Technology. School of Architecture and Urban Planning, University of California at Los Angeles, USA.

Graburn, N. H. H., and J. Jafari
1991 Introduction. Annals of Tourism Research 18:3–11.

Graham, S.
1991 Handle with Care: A Guide to Responsible Travel in Developing Countries. Chicago: Noble Press.

Hanna, W. A.
1972 Bali in the Seventies. Part 1: Cultural Tourism. American Universities Field Staff Reports. South East Asia Series 20/2:1–7.

Hegarty, J. A.
1990 Ethics in Hospitality Education. International Journal of Hospitality Management 9:106–109.

Holden, P., ed.
1984 Alternative Tourism. Bangkok: ECTWT.

Holden, P., J. Horlemann, and G. F. Pfafflin, eds.
1985 Tourism Prostitution Development: Documentation. Bangkok: ECTWT.

Ingham, R.
1991 Germany Moves to Rein in its Sex Tourists. Contours 5(4):15.

Jagrut Goencaranchi Fauz
1991 Tourism and Prostitution: Its Implications for Goa Today. Contours 5(2):15–16.

Lea, J. P.
1981 Changing Approaches Towards Tourism in Africa: Planning and Research Perspectives. Journal of Contemporary African Studies 1:19–40.
1988 Tourism and Development in the Third World. London: Routledge.

Leopold, A.
1949 A Sand County Almanac and Sketches Here and There. New York: Oxford University Press.

Malley, F.
1968 Le Pere Lebret, L'Economie au Service des Hommes. Paris: Les Editions du Cerf.

McKean, P. F.
1973 Cultural Involution: Tourists, Balinese, and the Process of Modernization in an Anthropological Perspective. Ph.D. dissertation, Brown University, USA.

Mehta, G.
1980 Karma Cola. London: Jonathan Cape.

Mendis, E. D. L.
1981 The Economic, Social and Cultural Impact of Tourism on Sri Lanka. Colombo: Christian Workers' Fellowship.

Nash, R. F.
1989 The Rights of Nature: A History of Environmental Ethics. Madison: University of Wisconsin Press.

Noronha, R.
1979 Paradise Reviewed: Tourism in Bali. In Tourism. Passport to Development? Perspectives on the Social and Cultural Effects of Tourism in Developing Countries, E. de Kadt, ed., pp. 177–204.

O'Grady, A.
1990 The Challenge of Tourism: Learning Resources for Study and Action. Bangkok: Ecumenical Coalition on Third World Tourism.

O'Grady, R.
1981 Third World Stopover: The Tourism Debate. Geneva: World Council of Churches.

Picard, M.
1984 "Tourisme Culturel" et "culture touristique": Rite et divertissement dans les arts du spectacle a Bali. Ph.D. dissertation, École des Hautes Etudes en Sciences Sociales, France.
1990 Kebalian Orang Bali: Tourism and the Uses of "Balinese Culture" in New Order Indonesia. Rima 24:1–38.

Rolston, H.
1988 Environmental Ethics. Philadelphia: Temple University Press.

Samarasuriya, S.
  1982 Who Needs Tourism? Employment for Women in the Holiday-industry of
    Sudugama, Sri Lanka. Colombo and Leiden: Research Project Women and
    Development.
Shivji, I., ed.
  1973 Tourism and Socialist Development. Dar es Salaam: Tanzania Publishing
    House.
Simpson, L.
  1991 Sydney Morning Herald (December 12).
Srisang, K.
  1987 A Goan Army Against Five-Star Tourism. Contours 3(3):9–13.
Sura's Tourist Guide to Goa.
  1991 Sura's Tourist Guide to Goa. Madras: Sura College of Competition.
Sydney Morning Herald
  1991 A Day in the Life of Bogmala Beach. Sydney Morning Herald (December
    19).
Times of India
  1990 Times of India (June 26).
Urry, J.
  1990 The Tourist Gaze: Leisure and Travel in Contemporary Societies. London:
    Sage.
White, L.
  1967 The Historical Roots of Our Ecological Crisis. Science 155:1203–1207.
Whitney, D. L.
  1990 Ethics in the Hospitality Industry with a Focus on Hotel Managers. Interna-
    tional Journal of Hospitality Management 9:59–68.

Submitted 24 March 1992
Resubmitted 14 September 1992
Accepted 30 October 1992
Refereed anonymously
Coordinating Editor: Kadir H. Din

Name Index